The Earth and Its Peoples

A Global History

BRIEF EDITION   FIFTH EDITION

The Earth and Its Peoples

A Global History

Richard W. Bulliet
Columbia University

Pamela Kyle Crossley
Dartmouth College

Daniel R. Headrick
Roosevelt University

Steven W. Hirsch
Tufts University

Lyman L. Johnson
University of North Carolina–Charlotte

David Northrup
Boston College

WADSWORTH
CENGAGE Learning

Australia • Brazil • Japan • Korea • Mexico • Singapore • Spain • United Kingdom • United States

The Earth and Its Peoples: A Global History, Brief Edition Fifth Edition
Bulliet, Crossley, Headrick, Hirsch, Johnson, Northrup

Senior Publisher: Suzanne Jeans

Senior Sponsoring Editor: Nancy Blaine

Senior Development Editor: Tonya Lobato

Assistant Editor: Lauren Floyd

Editorial Assistant: Emma Goehring

Senior Media Editor: Lisa Ciccolo

Senior Marketing Manager: Katherine Bates

Marketing Coordinator: Lorreen Pelletier

Marketing Communications Manager: Caitlin Green

Senior Content Project Manager: Carol Newman

Senior Art Director: Cate Rickard Barr

Senior Print Buyer: Judy Inouye

Senior Rights Acquisition Specialist (text): Katie Huha

Senior Rights Acquisition Specialist (photos): Jennifer Meyer Dare

Production Service: Lachina Publishing Services

Text Designer: Janet Theurer/Theurer Briggs Design

Cover Designer: Dutton & Sherman Design

Cover Image: Women Riding the First Bicycles in Shanghai, 1900. Leonard de Selva/Corbis Art

Compositor: Lachina Publishing Services

For product information and technology assistance, contact us at
Cengage Learning Customer & Sales Support, 1-800-354-9706

For permission to use material from this text or product,
submit all requests online at **www.cengage.com/permissions**.
Further permissions questions can be emailed to
permissionrequest@cengage.com.

Library of Congress Control Number: 2010932862

Student Edition:
ISBN-13: 978-0-495-91310-8
ISBN-10: 0-495-91310-3

Wadsworth
20 Channel Center Street
Boston, MA 02210
USA

Cengage Learning is a leading provider of customized learning solutions with office locations around the globe, including Singapore, the United Kingdom, Australia, Mexico, Brazil and Japan. Locate your local office at **international.cengage.com/region**.

Cengage Learning products are represented in Canada by Nelson Education, Ltd.

For your course and learning solutions, visit **www.cengage.com**.

Purchase any of our products at your local college store or at our preferred online store **www.cengagebrain.com**.

Printed in Canada
1 2 3 4 5 6 7 14 13 12 11 10

BRIEF CONTENTS

CONTENTS

PART TWO

The Formation of New Cultural Communities, from 1200 B.C.E.   84

GREECE AND IRAN, 1500 B.C.E–500 C.E.   86

INDIA AND SOUTHEAST ASIA, 1500 B.C.E.–1025 C.E.   111

AN AGE OF EMPIRES: ROME AND HAN CHINA, 753 B.C.E.–330 C.E.   134

PART FOUR

Interregional Patterns of Culture and Contact, 1200–1550   284

PART FIVE

The Globe Encompassed, 1500–1800   382

TRANSFORMATIONS IN EUROPE, 1500–1750   384

THE AMERICAS, THE ATLANTIC, AND AFRICA, 1530–1770   408

SOUTHWEST ASIA AND THE INDIAN OCEAN, 1500–1750   433

PART SEVEN

Global Diversity and Dominance, 1850–1949   572

MAPS

FEATURES

ENVIRONMENT & TECHNOLOGY

ISSUES IN WORLD HISTORY

DIVERSITY & DOMINANCE

MATERIAL CULTURE

When a textbook reaches its fifth edition, the authors feel justified in assessing their work a success. The first edition contained a basic concept. The second used the myriad valuable comments made by teachers and reviewers to make major adjustments in the presentation of that concept. The third and fourth editions incorporated a further round of comments and suggestions aimed at filling lacunae and improving the flow of the exposition. At the same time, pedagogical aids were steadily improved to make the text more accessible to both students and teachers.

Our overall goal in *The Earth and Its Peoples* remains unchanged: to produce a textbook that not only speaks for the past, but speaks to today's students and today's instructors. Students and instructors alike should take away from this text a broad vision of human societies beginning as sparse and disconnected communities reacting creatively to local circumstances; experiencing ever more intensive stages of contact, interpenetration, and cultural expansion and amalgamation; and arriving at a twenty-first-century world situation in which people increasingly visualize a single global community.

Process, not progress, is the keynote of this book: a steady process of change over time, at first differently experienced in various regions, but eventually interconnecting peoples and traditions from all parts of the globe. Students should come away from this book with a sense that the problems and promises of their world are rooted in a past in which people of every sort, in every part of the world, confronted problems of a similar character and coped with them as best they could. We believe our efforts will help students see where their world has come from and learn thereby something useful for their own lives.

Central Themes and Goals of the Text

We have subtitled *The Earth and Its Peoples* "A Global History" because the book explores the common challenges and experiences that unite the human past. Although the dispersal of early humans around the world resulted in many different economic, social, political, and cultural systems, all societies displayed analogous patterns in meeting their needs and exploiting their environments. Our challenge was to select the particular data and episodes that would best illuminate these global patterns of human experience.

To meet this challenge, we adopted two themes to serve as the spinal cord of our history: "Technology and Environment" and "Diversity and Dominance." The first theme represents the commonplace material bases of all human societies at all times. It grants no special favor to any cultural group even as it embraces subjects of the broadest topical, chronological, and geographical range. The second theme expresses the reality that every human society has constructed or inherited structures of domination. We examine practices and institutions of many sorts: military, economic, social, political, religious, and cultural, as well as those based on kinship, gender, and literacy. Simultaneously we recognize that alternative ways of life and visions of societal organization continually manifest themselves both within and in dialogue with every structure of domination.

With respect to the first theme, it is vital for students to understand that technology, in the broad sense of experience-based knowledge of the physical world, underlies all human activity. Writing is a technology, but so is oral transmission from generation to generation of lore about medicinal or poisonous plants. The magnetic compass is a navigational technology, but so is a Polynesian mariner's hard-won knowledge of winds, currents, and tides that made possible the settlement of the Pacific islands.

All technological development has come about in interaction with environments, both physical and human, and has, in turn, affected those environments. The story of how humanity has changed the face of the globe is an integral part of this central theme. Yet technology and the environment do not explain or underlie all important episodes of human experience. The theme of "Diversity and Dominance" informs all our discussions of politics, culture, and society. Thus, when narrating the histories of empires, we describe a range of human experiences within and beyond the imperial frontiers without assuming that the imperial institutions are a more suitable topic for discussion than the economic and social organization of pastoral nomads or the lives of peasant women. When religion and culture occupy our narrative, we focus not only on the dominant tradition but also on the diversity of alternative beliefs and practices.

Changes in the Brief Fifth Edition

We have once again transformed the visual layout of *The Earth and Its Peoples* to keep up with the preferences of today's students. The fifth edition features a bold new two-column design that is more modern and magazine-like in appearance, a reading layout that students have told us they prefer. In addition, every map in the text has been redesigned to be more dynamic and visually engaging. Finally, we have added four more new topics for the feature Material Culture, a student favorite: four-wheeled vehicles, salt, bells, and lamps and candles.

Several changes have been made to the organization of the text to make the narrative more logical and accessible. In **Part Two: The Formation of New Cultural Communities,** we have added a new **Chapter 5: India and Southeast Asia** with material formerly scattered in several places as well as new material from the full edition. Likewise, **Chapter 7: Peoples and Civilizations of the Americas** now contains material on the Olmec and Chavín civilizations, formerly in found Chapter 2. By bringing together the sections on India and Southeast Asia and on the Americas, respectively, we emphasize the continuity of these civilizations.

In **Chapter 15: The Maritime Revolution,** we have brought forward the material on the Columbian Exchange from Chapter 17, on the grounds that the exchange of plants, animals, and diseases began almost immediately after the first maritime contacts between the Eastern and Western Hemispheres.

Finally, we have rewritten **Chapter 29: The Cold War and Decolonization,** bringing the narrative up to 1991 and including new information on the collapse of the Soviet Union. And **Chapter 30: Challenges of the New Century** has been rewritten to reflect long-range trends such as the emergence of China as a great power, new patterns of global migration, the changing environment of the earth, and the nascent global culture and its consequences.

Suggested reading lists have been revised and are available on the textbook website, accessible through cengagebrain.com.

Organization

The brief edition of *The Earth and Its Peoples,* fifth edition, retains the eight broad chronological divisions of previous editions to define its conceptual scheme of global historical development.

In **Part One: The Emergence of Human Communities, to 1500** B.C.E., we examine important patterns of human communal organization. Small, dispersed human communities living by foraging spread to most parts of the world over tens of thousands of years. They responded to enormously diverse environmental conditions, at different times and in different ways discovering how to cultivate plants and utilize the products of domestic animals. On the basis of these new modes of sustenance, populations grew, permanent towns appeared, and political and religious authority, based on collection and control of agricultural surpluses, spread over extensive areas.

Part Two: The Formation of New Cultural Communities, from 1200 B.C.E. introduces the concept of a "cultural community," in the sense of a coherent pattern of activities and symbols pertaining to a specific human community. While all human communities develop distinctive cultures, including those discussed in Part One, historical development in this stage of global history prolonged and magnified the impact of some cultures more than others. In the geographically contiguous African-Eurasian landmass, the cultures that proved to have the most enduring influence traced their roots to the second and first millennia B.C.E.

Part Three: Growth and Interaction of Cultural Communities, 600–1200 deals with early episodes of technological, social, and cultural exchange and interaction on a continental scale both within and beyond the framework of imperial expansion. These are so different from earlier interactions arising from more limited conquests or extensions of political boundaries that they constitute a distinct era in world history, an era that set the world on the path of increasing global interaction and interdependence that it has been following ever since.

In **Part Four: Interregional Patterns of Culture and Contact, 1200–1550,** we take a look at the world during three centuries that saw both intensified cultural and commercial contact and increasingly confident self-definition of cultural communities in Europe, Asia, and Africa. The Mongol conquest of a vast empire extending from the Pacific Ocean to eastern Europe greatly stimulated trade and interaction. In the West, strengthened European kingdoms began maritime expansion in the Atlantic, forging direct ties with sub-Saharan Africa and laying the base for expanded global contacts after 1500.

Part Five: The Globe Encompassed, 1500–1800 treats a period dominated by the global effects of European expansion and continued economic growth. European ships took over, expanded, and extended the maritime trade of the Indian Ocean, coastal Africa, and the Asian rim of the Pacific Ocean. This maritime commercial enterprise had its counterpart in European colonial empires in the Americas and a new Atlantic trading system. The contrasting capacities and fortunes of traditional land empires and new maritime empires, along with the exchange of domestic plants and animals between the hemispheres, underline the technological and environmental dimensions of this first era of complete global interaction.

In **Part Six: Revolutions Reshape the World, 1750–1870,** the word *revolution* is used in several senses: in the political sense of governmental overthrow, as in France and the Americas; in the metaphorical sense of radical transformative change, as in the Industrial Revolution; and in the broadest sense of a perception of a profound change in circumstances and world-view. Technology and environment lie at the core of these developments. With the rapid ascendancy of the Western belief that science and technology could overcome all challenges, technology became not only an instrument of transformation but also an instrument of domination, to the point of threatening the integrity and autonomy of cultural traditions in nonindustrial lands.

Part Seven: Global Diversity and Dominance, 1850–1949 examines the development of a world arena in which people conceived of events on a global scale. Imperialism, world war, international economic connections, and world-encompassing ideological tendencies, like nationalism and socialism, present the picture of a globe becoming increasingly interconnected. European dominance took on a worldwide dimension, seeming at times to threaten the diversity of human cultural experience with permanent subordination to European values and philosophies, while at other times triggering strong political or cultural resistance. The accelerating pace of technological change deepened other sorts of cleavages as well.

For **Part Eight: Perils and Promises of a Global Community, 1945 to the Present,** we decided to divide the last half of the twentieth century into two time periods: 1945 to 1991, and 1991 to the present. Nevertheless, there is a good deal of continuity from chapter to chapter. The challenges of the Cold War, postcolonial nation building, and post–Cold War frictions between different powers and cultures dominate the period and involve global economic, technological, and political forces that become increasingly important factors in all aspects of human life. Technology takes center stage in this part, both because of its integral role in the growth of a global community and because its many benefits in improving the quality of life seem clouded by real and potential negative impacts on the environment.

The brief edition is produced in two formats: A complete edition covers the entire chronology from prehistory to the present, and a two-volume edition can be used for the two-semester survey. Volume I covers the period from prehistory to 1550, and Volume II covers 1500 to the present. There is a brief introduction to Volume II that orients students to the general political and social climate of the world before and up to 1500.

Features and Pedagogical Aids

As with previous editions, the fifth edition offers a number of valuable features and pedagogical aids designed to pique student interest in specific world history topics and help them process and retain key information.

In the fifth edition, as already mentioned, we have included more chapter essays on Material Culture, a feature that calls particular attention to the many ways in which objects and processes of everyday life can help us understand human history on a broad scale. Thus essays like "Wine and Beer in the Ancient World" and "Cotton Clothing" are not only interesting in and of themselves but also suggestive of how today's world historians find meaning in the ordinary dimensions of human life.

The Environment and Technology feature, which has been a valuable resource in all prior editions of *The Earth and Its Peoples*, serves to illuminate the major theme of the text by demonstrating the shared material bases of all human societies across time.

Historical essays for each of the eight parts called Issues in World History were added in the previous edition and were specifically designed to alert students to broad and recurring conceptual issues that are of great interest to contemporary historians; this feature has proved to be an instructor and student favorite.

Finally, Diversity and Dominance, also core to the theme of the text, is the primary source feature that brings a myriad of real historical voices to life in a common struggle for power and autonomy.

Pedagogical aids include the following:

Chapter Opening Focus Questions These questions are keyed to every major subdivision of the chapter through a system of color-coding and serve to help students focus on the core chapter concepts. The unique color-coded system helps students keep track of where they are in the text and easily identify which focus question corresponds to each section of the chapter. The color-coding carries through to the end of each chapter, where the focus questions for each section are answered and summarized.

Section Reviews Short bullet-point reviews appear at the end of each major section in every chapter and remind students of key information.

New Chapter Conclusions Every chapter now ends with a comparative conclusion that will help students synthesize chapter material and understand how it fits into the larger picture.

Key Terms with Definitions Students can handily find definitions for bolded key terms right on the page of the text where the term first appears.

New Icons Throughout each chapter, icons direct students to corresponding online tools, including interactive maps and primary sources.

Chapter Reviews Keyed to the chapter opening focus questions through a system of color-coding, the Chapter Reviews summarize the most important concepts addressed in the chapter, making studying more efficient and effective.

Pronunciation Guide Phonetic spellings for unfamiliar names and terms have been integrated into the text.

Supplements

A wide array of supplements accompanies this text to assist students with different learning needs and to help instructors master today's various classroom challenges.

Instructor Resources

PowerLecture CD-ROM with ExamView® and JoinIn® This dual-platform, all-in-one multimedia resource includes the Instructor's Resource Manual; Test Bank (content developed by Kathleen Addison of California State University, Northridge, and includes key term identification and multiple-choice, short answer, and essay questions); Microsoft® PowerPoint® slides of both lecture outlines and images and maps from the text that can be used as offered or customized by importing personal lecture slides or other material; and JoinIn® PowerPoint® slides with clicker content. Also included is ExamView, an easy-to-use assessment and tutorial system that allows instructors to create, deliver, and customize tests in minutes. Instructors can build tests with as many as 250 questions using up to 12 question types, and using ExamView's complete word-processing capabilities, they can enter an unlimited number of new questions or edit existing ones.

HistoryFinder This searchable online database allows instructors to quickly and easily download thousands of assets, including art, photographs, maps, primary sources, and audio/video clips. Each asset downloads directly into a Microsoft® PowerPoint® slide, allowing instructors to easily create exciting PowerPoint presentations for their classrooms.

eInstructor's Resource Manual Prepared by Sheila Phipps of Appalachian State University. This manual has many features, including instructional objectives, chapter outlines, lecture suggestions, suggested debate and research topics, cooperative learning activities, and suggested online resources. It is available on the instructor's companion website.

WebTutor™ Toolbox on Blackboard® and WebCT® This simplified WebTutor product links directly to the valuable study and assessment tools on the companion website, which includes learning objectives, a glossary, flashcards, crossword puzzles, Internet exercises, interactive quizzing, and web links. Additionally, the WebTutor Toolbox includes the test bank content.

History CourseMate *The Earth and Its Peoples* includes History CourseMate, a complement to your textbook. History CourseMate includes:

- An interactive eBook
- Interactive teaching and learning tools including:
  - Quizzes
  - Flashcards
  - Videos
  - Primary sources
  - Interactive maps
  - and more
- Engagement Tracker, a first-of-its-kind tool that monitors student engagement in the course

Go to login.cengage.com to access these resources, and look for this icon , which denotes a resource available within CourseMate.

Student Resources

The Earth and Its Peoples Website This book-specific website for students features a wide assortment of resources to help them master the textbook subject matter. The website includes a glossary, flashcards, crossword puzzles, learning objectives, interactive quizzing, essay questions, MP3 chapter summaries, an audio pronunciation guide, web links, and more.

Cengagebrain.com This online store saves students time and money by giving them a choice in formats and savings. It is a single destination for more than 10,000 new textbooks, eTextbooks, eChapters, study tools, and audio supplements. Students have the freedom to purchase a-la-carte exactly what they need when they need it. They can save 50 percent on the electronic textbook and can pay as little as $1.99 for an individual eChapter.

Wadsworth World History Resource Center Wadsworth's World History Resource Center gives students access to a "virtual reader" with hundreds of primary sources, including speeches, letters, legal documents and transcripts, poems, maps, simulations, timelines, and additional images that bring history to life, along with interactive assignable exercises. A map feature including Google Earth™ coordinates and exercises will aid in student comprehension of geography and use of maps. Students can compare the traditional textbook map with an aerial view of the location today. It's an ideal resource for study, review, and research. In addition to this map feature, the resource center provides blank maps for student review and testing.

Rand McNally Historical Atlas of the World, 2e This valuable resource features over 70 maps that portray the rich panoply of the world's history from preliterate times to the present. They show how cultures and civilizations were linked and how they interacted. By presenting the dynamics of expansion, cooperation, and conflict, the maps make it clear that history is not static; rather, it is about change and movement across time. This atlas includes maps that display the world from the beginning of civilization; the political development of all major areas of the world; expanded coverage of Africa, Latin America, and the Middle East; the current Islamic world; and the world population change in 1900 and 2000.

Writing for College History, 1e Prepared by Robert M. Frakes, Clarion University. This brief handbook for survey courses in American history, Western civilization/European history, and world civilization guides students through the various types of writing assignments they encounter in a history class. Providing examples of student writing and candid assessments of student work, this text focuses on the rules and conventions of writing for the college history course.

The History Handbook, 1e Prepared by Carol Berkin of Baruch College, City University of New York, and Betty Anderson of Boston University. This book teaches students both basic and history-specific study skills such as how to take notes, get the most out of lectures and readings, read primary sources, research historical topics, and correctly cite sources. Substantially less expensive than comparable skill-building texts, *The History Handbook* also offers tips for Internet research and evaluating online sources. Additionally, students can purchase and download the *eAudio* version of *The History Handbook* or any of its eighteen individual units at www.cengagebrain.com to listen to on the go.

Doing History: Research and Writing in the Digital Age, 1e Prepared by Michael J. Galgano, J. Chris Arndt, and Raymond M. Hyser of James Madison University. Whether starting down the path as a history major or simply looking for a straightforward and systematic guide to writing a successful paper, students will find this text an indispensable handbook to historical research. Its "soup to nuts" approach to researching and writing about history addresses every step of the process, from locating sources and gathering information to writing clearly and making proper use of various citation styles to avoid plagiarism. Students will also learn how to make the most of every tool available—especially the technology that helps them conduct the process efficiently and effectively.

The Modern Researcher, 6e Prepared by Jacques Barzun and Henry F. Graff of Columbia University. This classic introduction to the techniques of research and the art of expression is used widely in history courses, but it is also appropriate for writing and research methods courses in other departments. Barzun and Graff thoroughly cover every aspect of research, from the selection of a topic through the gathering, analysis, writing, revision, and publication of findings, presenting the process not as a set of rules but through actual cases that put the subtleties of research in a useful context. Part One covers the principles and methods of research; Part Two covers writing, speaking, and getting one's work published.

Reader Program Cengage Learning publishes a number of readers, some containing exclusively primary sources, others a combination of primary and secondary sources, and some designed to guide students through the process of historical inquiry. A complete list of readers is available at Cengage.com/history.

Custom Options Because no one knows students like their teacher, Cengage Learning offers custom solutions for this course—whether it's making a small modification to *The Earth and Its Peoples* to match the syllabus or combining multiple sources to create something truly unique. Instructors can pick and choose chapters, include their own material, and add additional map exercises along with the Rand McNally Atlas to create a text that fits the way they teach. They can ensure that students get the most out of their textbook dollar by giving them exactly what they need. A Cengage Learning representative can help teachers explore custom solutions for this course.

Acknowledgments

We are grateful to the following colleagues who took the time to provide their feedback to help us prepare the fifth edition of *The Earth and Its Peoples:*

Daniel Albert, Salem State College
Steven Berg, Schoolcraft College
Kathryn E. Holland Braund, Auburn University
Ras Michael Brown, Southern Illinois University

Stephen Chappell, James Madison University
Mariana L. R. Dantas, Ohio University
Eric Goldner, California State University, Northridge
Yuxin Ma, University of Louisville
Paul Moore, Tennessee Temple University
Mark R. Munzinger, Radford University
Charles H. Parker, Saint Louis University
Scott Reese, Northern Arizona University
Michael J. Seth, James Madison University
Gregory S. Taylor, Chowan University
Ann Tschetter, University of Nebraska, Lincoln

We also want to extend our thanks to Lynda Schaffer for her early conceptual contributions and to the history departments of Shippensburg University, the United States Air Force Academy, and the State University of New York at New Paltz for arranging reviewer conferences that provided crucial feedback for our revisions.

Our debt to the staff of Cengage Learning remains undiminished in the fifth edition. Nancy Blaine, Senior Sponsoring Editor, has offered us firm but sympathetic guidance throughout the revision process. The authors are grateful for the wonderful work of Tonya Lobato, Senior Development Editor; Carol Newman, Senior Content Project Manager; Nicole Lee Petel, Project Manager; and Catherine Schnurr, Senior Image Research Manager.

Finally, we thank the many students whose questions and concerns, expressed directly or through their instructors, shaped much of this revision. We continue to welcome all our readers' suggestions, queries, and criticisms. Please contact us at our respective institutions.

Richard W. Bulliet Professor of Middle Eastern History at Columbia University, Richard W. Bulliet received his Ph.D. from Harvard University. He has written scholarly works on a number of topics: the social history of medieval Iran (*The Patricians of Nishapur*), the historical competition between pack camels and wheeled transport (*The Camel and the Wheel*), the process of conversion to Islam (*Conversion to Islam in the Medieval Period*), and the overall course of Islamic social history (*Islam: The View from the Edge*). His most recent books include a global history of human-animal relations (*Hunters, Herders, and Hamburgers*) and an affirmation of the historical kinship of Islam and Christianity (*The Case for Islamo-Christian Civilization*). He is the editor of the *Columbia History of the Twentieth Century*. He has published four novels, coedited *The Encyclopedia of the Modern Middle East,* and hosted an educational television series on the Middle East. He was awarded a fellowship by the John Simon Guggenheim Memorial Foundation.

Pamela Kyle Crossley Pamela Kyle Crossley received her Ph.D. in Modern Chinese History from Yale University. She is currently the Robert and Barbara Black Professor of History at Dartmouth College. Her books include *The Wobbling Pivot: An Interpretive History of China Since 1800; What Is Global History?; A Translucent Mirror: History and Identity in Qing Imperial Ideology; The Manchus; Orphan Warriors: Three Manchu Generations and the End of the Qing World;* and (with Lynn Hollen Lees and John W. Servos) *Global Society: The World Since 1900.*

Daniel R. Headrick Daniel R. Headrick received his Ph.D. in History from Princeton University. Professor of History and Social Science at Roosevelt University in Chicago, he is the author of several books on the history of technology, imperialism, and international relations, including *The Tools of Empire: Technology and European Imperialism in the Nineteenth Century; The Tentacles of Progress: Technology Transfer in the Age of Imperialism; The Invisible Weapon: Telecommunications and International Politics; When Information Came of Age: Technologies of Knowledge in the Age of Reason and Revolution, 1700–1850; Technology: A World History;* and *Power over Peoples: Technology, Environments, and Western Imperialism, 1400 to the Present.* His articles have appeared in the *Journal of World History,* the *Journal of Modern History,* and other journals. He has been awarded fellowships by the National Endowment for the Humanities, the John Simon Guggenheim Memorial Foundation, and the Alfred P. Sloan Foundation.

Steven W. Hirsch Steven W. Hirsch holds a Ph.D. in Classics from Stanford University and is currently Associate Professor of Classics and History at Tufts University. He has received grants from the National Endowment for the Humanities and the Massachusetts Foundation for Humanities and Public Policy. His research and publications include *The Friendship of the Barbarians: Xenophon and the Persian Empire,* as well as articles and reviews in the *Classical Journal,* the *American Journal of Philology,* and the *Journal of Interdisciplinary History.* He is currently working on a comparative study of ancient Mediterranean and Chinese civilizations.

Lyman L. Johnson Professor of History at the University of North Carolina at Charlotte, Lyman L. Johnson earned his Ph.D. in Latin American History from the University of Connecticut. A two-time Senior Fulbright-Hays Lecturer, he also has received fellowships from the Tinker Foundation, the Social Science Research Council, the National Endowment for the Humanities, and the American Philosophical Society. His recent books include *Workshop of Revolution: Plebeian Buenos Aires 1776–1810* (forthcoming Duke University Press); *Aftershocks: Earthquakes and*

Popular Politics in Latin America (edited with Jürgen Buchenau); *Death, Dismemberment, and Memory; The Faces of Honor* (edited with Sonya Lipsett-Rivera); and *Colonial Latin America* (with Mark A. Burkholder). He has also published in journals, including the *Hispanic American Historical Review,* the *Journal of Latin American Studies,* the *International Review of Social History,* and *Desarrollo Económico.* He has served as president of the Conference on Latin American History.

David Northrup Professor of History at Boston College, David Northrup earned his Ph.D. in African and European History from the University of California at Los Angeles. He earlier taught in Nigeria with the Peace Corps and at Tuskegee Institute. Research supported by the Fulbright-Hays Commission, the National Endowment for the Humanities, and the Social Science Research Council led to publications concerning precolonial Nigeria; the Congo (1865–1940); the Atlantic slave trade; and Asian, African, and Pacific islander indentured labor in the nineteenth century. His most recent writing has concerned Atlantic history, and his latest book is the second edition of *Africa's Discovery of Europe, 1450–1850.* In 2004 and 2005 he was president of the World History Association.

NOTE ON SPELLING AND USAGE

Where necessary for clarity, dates are followed by the letters C.E. or B.C.E. The abbreviation C.E. stands for "Common Era" and is equivalent to A.D. (*anno Domini,* Latin for "in the year of the Lord"). The abbreviation B.C.E. stands for "before the Common Era" and means the same as B.C. ("before Christ"). In keeping with our goal of approaching world history without special concentration on one culture or another, we chose these neutral abbreviations as appropriate to our enterprise. Because many readers will be more familiar with English than with metric measurements, however, units of measure are generally given in the English system, with metric equivalents following in parentheses.

In general, Chinese has been romanized according to the *pinyin* method. Exceptions include proper names well established in English (e.g., *Canton, Chiang Kai-shek*) and a few English words borrowed from Chinese (e.g., *kowtow*). Spellings of Arabic, Ottoman Turkish, Persian, Mongolian, Manchu, Japanese, and Korean names and terms avoid special diacritical marks for letters that are pronounced only slightly differently in English. An apostrophe is used to indicate when two Chinese syllables are pronounced separately (e.g., *Chang'an*).

For words transliterated from languages that use the Arabic script—Arabic, Ottoman Turkish, Persian, Urdu—the apostrophe indicating separately pronounced syllables may represent either of two special consonants, the *hamza* or the *ain*. Because most English-speakers do not hear the distinction between these two, they have not been distinguished in transliteration and are not indicated when they occur at the beginning or end of a word. As with Chinese, some words and commonly used place-names from these languages are given familiar English spellings (e.g., *Quran* instead of *Qur'an, Cairo* instead of *al-Qahira*). Arabic romanization has normally been used for terms relating to Islam, even where the context justifies slightly different Turkish or Persian forms, again for ease of comprehension.

Before 1492 the inhabitants of the Western Hemisphere had no single name for themselves. They had neither a racial consciousness nor a racial identity. Identity was derived from kin groups, language, cultural practices, and political structures. There was no sense that physical similarities created a shared identity. America's original inhabitants had racial consciousness and racial identity imposed on them by conquest and the occupation of their lands by Europeans after 1492. All of the collective terms for these first American peoples are tainted by this history. *Indians, Native Americans, Amerindians, First Peoples,* and *Indigenous Peoples* are among the terms in common usage. In this book the names of individual cultures and states are used wherever possible. *Amerindian* and other terms that suggest transcultural identity and experience are used most commonly for the period after 1492.

There is an ongoing debate about how best to render Amerindian words in English. It has been common for authors writing in English to follow Mexican usage for Nahuatl and Yucatec Maya words and place-names. In this style, for example, the capital of the Aztec state is spelled *Tenochtitlán,* and the important late Maya city-state is spelled *Chichén Itzá.* Although these forms are still common even in the specialist literature, we have chosen to follow the scholarship that sees these accents as unnecessary. The exceptions are modern place-names, such as *Mérida* and *Yucatán,* which are accented. A similar problem exists for the spelling of Quechua and Ay-mara words from the Andean region of South America. Although there is significant disagreement among scholars, we follow the emerging consensus and use the spellings *khipu* (not *quipu*), *Tiwanaku* (not *Tiahuanaco*), and *Wari* (not *Huari*). However, we keep *Inca* (not *Inka*) and *Cuzco* (not *Cusco*), since these spellings are expected by most of our potential readers and we hope to avoid confusion.

The Earth and Its Peoples

A Global History

Part One

The Emergence of Human Communities, to 1500 B.C.E.

© Cengage Learning

	8000 B.C.E.	7000 B.C.E.	6000 B.C.E.	5000 B.C.E.
AMERICAS		• **7000** Incipient plant domestication in Peru		• **5000** Maize, beans, and squash domestication in Mesoamerica
EUROPE	Spread of Indo-European languages		• **6000** Farming in southern Europe	
AFRICA	• **8000** Farming in eastern Sahara			• **5500** Farming in Egypt
MIDDLE EAST	• **8000** Domestication of plants and animals in Fertile Crescent			• **5000** Irrigation in Mesopotamia
ASIA AND OCEANIA			• **6500** Rice cultivation in China	• **5000** Farming in India

Human beings evolved over several million years from primates in Africa. Able to walk upright and possessing large brains, hands with opposable thumbs, and the capacity for speech, early humans used teamwork and created tools to survive in diverse environments. They spread relatively quickly to almost every habitable area of the world, hunting and gathering wild plant products. Around 10,000 years ago some groups began to cultivate plants, domesticate animals, and make pottery vessels for storage. This led to permanent settlements—at first small villages but eventually larger towns as well.

The earliest complex societies arose in the great river valleys of Iraq, Egypt, Pakistan, and northern China. In these arid regions agriculture depended on river water, and centers of political power arose to organize the labor required to dig and maintain irrigation channels. Kings and priests dominated these early societies from the urban centers, helped by administrators, scribes, soldiers, merchants, craftsmen, and others with specialized skills. Surplus food grown in the countryside by a dependent peasantry sustained the activities of these groups.

Certain centers came to dominate broader expanses of territory, seeking access to raw materials, especially metals. This change also stimulated long-distance trade and diplomatic relations between major powers. Artisans made weapons, tools, and ritual objects from bronze. Culture and technology spread to neighboring regions, such as southern China, Nubia, Syria-Palestine, Anatolia, and the Aegean.

In the Western Hemisphere, different geographical circumstances called forth distinctive patterns of technological and cultural response in the early civilizations in southern Mexico and the Andean region of South America.

4000 B.C.E.	3000 B.C.E.	2000 B.C.E.	1000 B.C.E.
• **4000** Quinoa and potato domestication in Peru	• **3000** Farming in central Mexico	• **2000** Farming in Peru	• **1200** Rise of Olmec civilization in Mesoamerica • **900** Rise of Chavín civilization in Peru
• **4000** Megaliths	**3000–1100** Aegean civilization		• **1000** Iron metallurgy
	• **3100** Unification of Egypt	2575–2134 Old Kingdom Egypt **2040–1640** Middle Kingdom Egypt • **2000** Rise of Kush in Nubia **1532–1070** New Kingdom Egypt	• **800** Rise of Nubian Kingdom at Napata
	• **3100** Mesopotamian civilization Advent of horses in western Asia **2000** • • **2350** Akkadian kingdom	• **1750** Hammurabi's law code **1700–1200** Hittites dominant in Anatolia	• **911** Rise of Neo-Assyrian Empire
	Bronze metallurgy in China **2000** • **2600–1900** Indus Valley civilization	**1600–1027** Shang kingdom in China	**1027–221** Zhou kingdom in China

From the Origins of Agriculture to the First River-Valley Civilizations

© Cengage Learning

CHAPTER PREVIEW

Before Civilization
How did plant and animal domestication set the scene for the emergence of civilization?

Mesopotamia
How did Mesopotamian civilization emerge?

Egypt
What role did the environment and religion play in Egyptian civilization?

Conclusion

MATERIAL CULTURE: Lamps and Candles

 Visit the CourseMate website at **www.cengagebrain.com** for additional study tools and review materials for this chapter.

Some 5,000 years ago in Mesopotamia (present-day Iraq), people living in Sumer, the world's first urban civilization, cherished the story of Gilgamesh, superhero king of the city of Uruk. The goddess of creation, it recounted, fashioned the wild man Enkidu (EN-kee-doo):

> There was virtue in him of the god of war, of Ninurta himself. His body was rough, he had long hair like a woman's; it waved like the hair of Nisaba, the goddess of corn. His body was covered with matted hair like Samuqan's, the god of cattle. He was innocent of mankind; he knew nothing of the cultivated land. Enkidu ate grass in the hills with the gazelle and jostled with the wild beasts at the water-holes; he had joy of the water with the herds of wild game.

When Gilgamesh learns of Enkidu from a hunter, he sends a temple prostitute to tame him. After her seduction causes the wild beasts to shun him, she says:

> Come with me. I will take you to strong-walled Uruk (OO-rook), to the blessed temple of Ishtar and of Anu, of love and of heaven ... there all the people are dressed in their gorgeous robes, every day is holiday, the young men and the girls are wonderful to see. How sweet they smell! ... O Enkidu, you who live life, I will show you Gilgamesh.[1]

The prostitute clothes Enkidu and teaches him to eat cooked food, drink beer, and bathe and oil his body. Her words and actions signal the principal traits of civilized life in Sumer, just as the comparisons of the wild Enkidu to various divinities show Sumer's dependence on grain and livestock.

It has long been said that the first civilizations arose in Mesopotamia and Egypt sometime before 3000 B.C.E. However, since people tend to judge everything by their own viewpoint, it is not safe to accept this assertion without questioning. The Sumerians equated civilization with their own way of life, but other peoples did the same, and lifestyles varied. This, along with the ambiguity of the term *civilization,* makes it difficult to say where civilization began.

Scholars agree that settled agricultural life and certain political, social, economic, and technological traits are indicators of **civilization**, if not of every

civilization. These traits include (1) cities as administrative centers, (2) a political system based on defined territory rather than kinship, (3) many people engaged in specialized, non-food-producing activities, (4) status distinctions based largely on accumulation of wealth, (5) monumental building, (6) a system for keeping permanent records, (7) long-distance trade, and (8) sophisticated interest in science and art.

The earliest societies exhibiting these traits appeared in the floodplains of great rivers: the Tigris (TIE-gris) and Euphrates (you-FRAY-teez) in Iraq, the Indus in Pakistan, the Yellow (Huang He (hwang huh)) in China, and the Nile in Egypt (see Map 1.1). Periodic flooding fertilized the land with silt and provided water for agriculture but also threatened lives and property. To control the floods, the peoples living near the rivers created new technologies and forms of political and social organization.

In this chapter, we describe the origins of domestication among the scattered groups of foragers living at the end of the last Ice Age (a long period when glaciers covered much of North America, Europe, and Asia) and the slow development of farming and herding societies. We then trace the rise of complex societies in Mesopotamia and Egypt from approximately 3500 to 1500 B.C.E. (China, developing slightly later, is discussed in Chapter 2. The Indus Valley civilization will be discussed in Chapter 5.) This story roughly coincides with the origins of writing, allowing us to document aspects of human life not revealed by archaeological evidence alone.

Before Civilization

How did plant and animal domestication set the scene for the emergence of civilization?

Though much remains to be learned, scientists have uncovered a great deal of evidence about life in the earliest periods of human history. Perhaps the most impressive findings are artistic. Evidence of human

civilization An ambiguous term often used to denote more complex societies but sometimes used by anthropologists to describe any group of people sharing a set of cultural traits.

creativity first came to light in 1940 near Lascaux in southwestern France with the discovery of a vast underground cavern. The cavern walls were covered with paintings of animals, including many that had been extinct for thousands of years. Similar cave paintings have been found in Spain and elsewhere in southern France.

To even the most skeptical person, these artistic troves reveal rich imaginations and sophisticated skills, qualities also apparent in the stone tools and in the evidence of complex social relations uncovered from prehistoric sites. The production of such artworks and tools over wide areas and long periods of time demonstrates that skills and ideas were not simply individual expressions but were deliberately passed along within societies. These learned patterns of action and expression constitute **culture**. Culture includes material objects, such as dwellings, clothing, tools, and crafts, along with nonmaterial values, beliefs, and languages. Although it is true that some animals also learn new ways, their activities are determined primarily by inherited instincts. Only human communities trace profound cultural developments over time. The development, transmission, and transformation of cultural practices and events are the subject of **history**.

Stone toolmaking, the first recognizable cultural activity, first appeared around 2 million years ago. The **Stone Age**, which lasted from then until around 4,000 years ago, can be a misleading label. Stone tools abound at archaeological sites, but not all tools were of stone. They were made as well of bone, skin, and wood, materials that survive poorly. In addition, this period encompasses many cultures and subperiods. Among the major subdivisions, the **Paleolithic** (pay-lee-oh-LITH-ik) (Old Stone Age) lasted until 10,000 years ago, about 3,000 years after the end of the last Ice Age. The **Neolithic** (nee-oh-LITH-ik) (New Stone Age), which is associated with the origins of agriculture, followed.

Food Gathering and Stone Technology

Fossilized animal bones bearing the marks of butchering tools testify to the scavenging and hunting activities of Stone Age peoples, but anthropologists do not believe that early humans lived primarily on meat. Modern **foragers** (hunting and food-gathering peoples) in the Kalahari Desert of southern Africa and the Ituri Forest of Central Africa derive the bulk of their day-to-day nourishment from wild vegetable foods, eating meat primarily at feasts. Stone Age peoples probably did the same, even though the tools and equipment for gathering and processing vegetable foods have left few archaeological traces.

Like modern foragers, ancient humans would have used skins and baskets woven from plant fibers for collecting fruits, berries, and wild seeds, and they would have dug up edible roots with wooden sticks. Archaeologists suspect that the doughnut-shaped stones often found at Stone Age sites served as weights to make wooden digging sticks more effective.

Cooking makes both meat and vegetables tastier and easier to digest, something early humans may have discovered inadvertently after wildfires. Humans may have begun setting fires deliberately 1 million to 1.5 million years ago, but proof of cooking does not appear until some 12,500 years ago, when clay cooking pots came into use in East Asia.

Studies of present-day foragers also indicate that Ice Age women probably did most of the gathering and cooking, which they could do while caring for small children. Women past childbearing age would have been the most knowledgeable and productive food gatherers. Men, with stronger arms and shoulders, would have been better suited for hunting, particularly

---

culture Socially transmitted patterns of action and expression. *Material culture* refers to physical objects, such as dwellings, clothing, tools, and crafts. Culture also includes arts, beliefs, knowledge, and technology.

history The study of past events and changes in the development, transmission, and transformation of cultural practices.

Stone Age The historical period characterized by the production of tools from stone and other nonmetallic substances. It was followed in some places by the Bronze Age and more generally by the Iron Age.

Paleolithic The period of the Stone Age associated with the evolution of humans. It predates the Neolithic period.

Neolithic The period of the Stone Age associated with the ancient Agricultural Revolutions. It follows the Paleolithic period.

foragers People who support themselves by hunting wild animals and gathering wild edible plants and insects.

Chronology

	Mesopotamia	Egypt
3500 B.C.E.		
3000 B.C.E.	**3000–2350** B.C.E. Early Dynastic (Sumerian)	**3100–2575** B.C.E. Early Dynastic
2500 B.C.E.	**2350–2230** B.C.E. Akkadian (Semitic)	**2575–2134** B.C.E. Old Kingdom **2134–2040** B.C.E. First Intermediate Period
2000 B.C.E.	**2112–2004** B.C.E Third Dynasty of Ur (Sumerian) **1900–1600** B.C.E. Old Babylonian (Semitic)	**2040–1640** B.C.E. Middle Kingdom
1500 B.C.E.	**1500–1150** B.C.E. Kassite	**1640–1532** B.C.E Second Intermediate Period **1532–1070** B.C.E. New Kingdom

for hunting large animals. Some early cave art suggests male hunting activities.The same studies, along with archaeological evidence from Ice Age campsites, indicate that early foragers lived in groups that were big enough to defend themselves from predators and divide responsibility for food collection and preparation, but small enough not to exhaust the food resources within walking distance. Even bands of around fifty men, women, and children would have moved regularly to follow migrating animals or collect seasonally ripening plants in different places.

In regions that had severe climates or that lacked natural shelters like caves, people built huts of branches, stones, bones, skins, and leaves as seasonal camps. Animal skins served as clothing, with the earliest evidence of woven cloth appearing about 26,000 years ago. Groups living in the African grasslands and other game-rich areas probably spent only three to five hours a day securing food, clothing, and shelter. This would have left a great deal of time for artistic endeavors, toolmaking, and social life.

The foundations of what later ages called science, art, and religion also date to the Stone Age. Gatherers learned which local plants were edible and when

they ripened, as well as which natural substances were effective for medicine, consciousness altering, dyeing, and other purposes. Hunters learned the habits of game animals. People experimented with techniques of using plant and animal materials for clothing, twine, and construction. Knowledge of the environment included identifying which minerals made good paints and which stones made good tools. All of these aspects of culture were passed orally from generation to generation.

Early music and dance have left no traces, but visual artwork has survived abundantly. Cave paintings appear as early as 32,000 years ago in Europe and North Africa and somewhat later in other parts of the world. Because many feature food animals like wild oxen, reindeer, and horses, some scholars believe that the art recorded hunting scenes or played a magical and religious role in hunting. A newly discovered cave at Vallon Pont-d'Arc (vah-LOH pon-DAHRK) in southern France, however, features rhinoceros, panthers, bears, owls, and a hyena, which probably were not hunted for food. Other drawings include people dressed in animal skins and smeared with paint and stencils of human hands. Some scholars suspect that other marks in cave paintings and on bones may represent efforts at counting or writing. Some cave art suggests that Stone Age people had well-developed religions, but without written texts, it is hard to know what they believed. Some graves from about 100,000 years ago contain stone implements, food, clothing, and red-ochre powder, indicating that early people revered their leaders enough to honor them in death and may have believed in an afterlife.

The Agricultural Revolutions

Around 10,000 years ago, some human groups began to meet their food needs by raising domesticated plants and animals. Gradually over the next millennium, most people became food producers, although hunting and gathering continued in some places.

The term *Neolithic Revolution*, commonly given to the changeover from food gathering to food producing, can be misleading. *Neolithic* means "new stone," but the new tool designs that accompanied the beginnings of agriculture were not the most important feature of this changeover. Nor was the "revolution" a single event. The changeover occurred at different times in different parts of the world. The term **Agricultural Revolutions** is more precise because it emphasizes the central role of food production and signals that the changeover occurred several times. The adoption of agriculture often included the domestication of animals for food.

Food gathering gave way to food production over hundreds of generations. The process may have begun when forager bands, returning year after year to the same seasonal camps, scattered seeds and cleared away weeds to encourage the growth of foods they liked. Such semicultivation could have supplemented food gathering without necessitating permanent settlement. Families choosing to concentrate their energies on food production, however, would have had to settle permanently near their fields.

Specialized stone tools first alerted archaeologists to new food-producing practices: polished or ground stone heads to work the soil, sharp stone chips embedded in bone or wooden handles to cut grasses, and stone mortars to pulverize grain. Early farmers used fire to clear fields of shrubs and trees and discovered that ashes were a natural fertilizer. After the burn-off, farmers used blades and axes to keep the land clear.

Selection of the highest-yielding strains of wild plants led to the development of domesticated varieties over time. As the principal gatherers of wild plant foods, women probably played a major role in this transition to plant cultivation, but the task of clearing fields probably fell to the men.

In the Middle East, the region with the earliest evidence of agriculture, human selection had transformed certain wild grasses into higher-yielding domesticated grains, now known as emmer wheat and barley, by 8000 B.C.E. Farmers there also discovered that alternating the cultivation of grains and pulses (plants yielding edible seeds such as lentils and peas) helped maintain fertility.

While plants domesticated in the Middle East spread to adjacent lands, agriculture also arose independently in many parts of the world. Exchanges of crops and techniques occurred between regions, but societies that had already settled into farming life borrowed new plants, animals, and farming techniques more readily than foraging groups that were often on the move.

The eastern Sahara, which went through a wet period after 8000 B.C.E., preserves the oldest traces of food production in northern Africa. As in the Middle East, emmer wheat and barley became the principal crops and sheep, goats, and cattle the main domestic animals. When drier conditions set in around 5000 B.C.E., many Saharan farmers moved to the Nile Valley. The river's edge was swampy, but annual flooding provided water for crops farther from the riverbanks.

In Greece, wheat and barley cultivation began as early as 6000 B.C.E. Shortly after 4000 B.C.E., farming developed in the light-soiled plains of central Europe and along the Danube River. As forests receded over the next millennium because of climate changes and human clearing, agriculture spread to other parts of Europe.

Agricultural Revolutions (ancient) The change from food gathering to food production that occurred between ca. 8000 and 2000 B.C.E. Also known as the Neolithic Revolution.

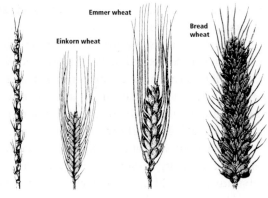

Emmer wheat

Einkorn wheat

Bread wheat

Wild wheat   **Later domesticated varieties**

Domestication of Wheat   Through selection of the largest seeds of this wild grass, early farmers in the Middle East were able to develop varieties with larger edible kernels. Bread wheat was grown in the Nile Valley by 5000 B.C.E.   From Iris Barn, *Discovering Archaeology* (London: Stonehenge, in association with the American Museum of Natural History, 1981)

Early farmers in Europe and elsewhere practiced shifting cultivation, also known as swidden agriculture. After a few growing seasons, farmers left the fields fallow (abandoned to natural vegetation) and cleared new fields nearby. Between 4000 and 3000 B.C.E., for example, communities of forty to sixty people in the Danube Valley supported themselves on about 500 acres (200 hectares) of farmland, cultivating a third or less each year while leaving the rest fallow to regain its fertility. From around 2600 B.C.E., people in central Europe began using ox-drawn wooden plows instead of hoes to till heavier and richer soils.

Although the lands around the Mediterranean seem to have shared a complex of crops and farming techniques, geographical conditions blocked the spread of wheat and barley elsewhere. Rainfall patterns south of the Sahara favored instead locally domesticated grains—sorghums, millets, and (in Ethiopia) teff. Middle Eastern grains did not grow at all in the humidity of equatorial West Africa; there, yams became an early domestic crop.

Domestic rice originated in southern China, the northern half of Southeast Asia, or northern India, possibly as early as 10,000 B.C.E. but more likely closer to 5000 B.C.E. The warm, wet climate of southern China particularly favored rice. Along with rice, Indian farmers were cultivating hyacinth beans and green and black grams (types of legumes) by about 2000 B.C.E.

In the Americas a decline of game animals in the Tehuacán (teh-wah-KAHN) Valley of Mexico after 8000 B.C.E. increased people's dependence on wild plants. Agriculture based on maize (mayz) (corn) developed there about 3000 B.C.E. and gradually spread. At about the same time, the inhabitants of Peru developed a food production pattern based on potatoes and quinoa (kee-NOH-uh), a protein-rich seed grain. People in the more tropical parts of Mesoamerica cultivated tomatoes, peppers, squash, and potatoes. In South America's tropical forests, the root crop manioc became the staple food after 1500 B.C.E. Manioc and maize then spread to the Caribbean islands.

The domestication of animals expanded rapidly during these same millennia. The first domestic animal, the dog, may have helped hunters well before the Neolithic period and may also have served as a food source. Neolithic period domestic animals initially provided meat but eventually supplied milk, wool, and energy as well.

Refuse dumped outside Middle Eastern villages shows a gradual decline in the number of wild gazelle bones after 7000 B.C.E. This probably reflects the depletion of wild game through overhunting by local farmers. Meat eating, however, did not decline. Sheep and goat bones gradually replaced gazelle bones. Possibly wild sheep and goats learned to graze around agricultural villages to take advantage of the suppression of predators by humans. The tamer animals may gradually have accepted human control and thus became a ready supply of food. The bones of tame animals initially differ so little from those of their wild ancestors that the early stages of domestication are hard to date. However, selective breeding for characteristics like a wooly coat and high milk production eventually yielded distinct breeds of domestic sheep and goats.

Elsewhere, other wild species evolved domestic forms during the centuries before 3000 B.C.E.: cattle in northern Africa and/or the Middle East, donkeys in northern Africa, water buffalo in China, humped-back Zebu (ZEE-boo) cattle in India, horses and two-humped camels in Central Asia, one-humped camels in Arabia, chickens in Southeast Asia, and pigs in several places. Like domestic plant species, varieties of domesticated animals spread from one region to another. The Zebu cattle originally domesticated in India, for example, became important in sub-Saharan Africa about 2,000 years ago.

Zebu cattle and water buffalo became sufficiently tame to be yoked to plows many centuries after domestic stocks first appeared, but once this change occurred, they became essential to the agricultural cycle of grain farmers. In addition, animal droppings provided valuable fertilizer. Wool and milk production also occurred a long time after initial domestication.

In the Americas, domestic llamas provided meat, transport, and wool, while guinea pigs and turkeys provided meat. Dogs assisted hunters and also provided meat. Scholars believe that these were the only domesticated American species. However, despite the geographical isolation of the Americas, domestic chickens first appeared before the coming of the Europeans, presumably by way of Pacific Ocean seafarers.

Pastoralism, a way of life dependent on large herds of grazing livestock, came to predominate in arid regions. As the Sahara approached its maximum dryness around 2500 B.C.E., pastoralists replaced farmers who migrated southward (see Chapter 8). Moving herds to new pastures and watering places throughout the year made pastoralists almost as mobile as foragers and discouraged substantial dwellings and the accumulation of bulky possessions. Like modern pastoralists, early cattle keepers probably relied more heavily on milk than on meat, since killing animals diminished the size of their herds. During wet seasons, they may also have engaged in semicultivation or bartered meat and skins for plant foods from nearby farming communities.

Why did the Agricultural Revolutions occur? Some theories assume that growing crops had obvious advantages. Grain, for example, provided both a dietary staple and the makings of beer. Beer drinking appears frequently in ancient Middle Eastern art and can be dated to as early as 3500 B.C.E. Most researchers today, however, believe that climate change and growing population density drove people to abandon foraging in favor of pastoralism and agriculture. So great was the global warming that ended the last Ice Age that geologists have given the era since about 11,000 B.C.E. a new name: the **Holocene** (HAWL-oh-seen). Scientists have also found evidence that temperate lands

were exceptionally warm between 6000 and 2000 B.C.E., when people in many parts of the world adopted agriculture. The precise nature of the climatic crisis probably varied. In the Middle East, shortages of wild food caused by dryness or overhunting may have stimulated food production. Elsewhere, a warmer, wetter climate could have turned grasslands into forest and thereby reduced supplies of game and wild grains.

In many drier parts of the world, where wild food remained abundant, agriculture did not arise. The inhabitants of Australia relied exclusively on foraging until recent centuries, as did some peoples on other continents. Amerindians in the arid grasslands from Alaska to the Gulf of Mexico hunted bison, and salmon fishing sustained groups in the Pacific Northwest. Ample supplies of fish, shellfish, and aquatic animals permitted food gatherers east of the Mississippi River to become increasingly sedentary. In the equatorial rain forest and in the southern part of Africa, conditions also favored retention of older ways.

Whatever the causes, the gradual adoption of food production transformed most parts of the world. A hundred thousand years ago, world population, mostly living in the temperate and tropical regions of Africa and Eurasia, did not exceed 2 million. The population may have fallen still lower during the last glacial epoch, between 32,000 and 13,000 years ago. Agriculture supported a gradual population increase, perhaps to 10 million by 5000 B.C.E., and then a mushrooming to between 50 million and 100 million by 1000 B.C.E.[2]

Life in Neolithic Communities

Evidence that an ecological crisis may have triggered the transition to food production has prompted reexamination of the assumption that farmers enjoyed a better life than foragers. Early farmers probably had to work much harder and for much longer periods than food gatherers. Long days spent clearing and cultivating the land yielded meager harvests. Guarding herds from predators, guiding them

Holocene The geological era since the end of the Great Ice Age about 13,000 years ago.

to fresh pastures, and tending to their needs imposed similar burdens.

There were other problems as well. Although early farmers commanded a more reliable food supply, their diet contained less variety and nutrition than that of foragers. Skeletons show that Neolithic farmers were shorter on average than earlier foragers. Death from contagious diseases ravaged farming settlements, which were contaminated by human waste, infested by disease-bearing vermin and insects, and inhabited by domestic animals—especially pigs and cattle—whose diseases could infect people.

However, a dependable supply of food that could be stored between harvests to see people through nonproductive seasons, droughts, and other calamities proved decisive in the long run. Over several millennia, farmers came to outnumber nonfarmers, permanent settlements generated cultural changes, and specialized crafts appeared in fledgling towns.

Some researchers envision violent struggles between farmers and foragers. Others see a more peaceful transition. Violence may well have accompanied land clearance that constrained the foragers' food supplies. And farmers probably fought for control of the best land. In most cases, however, farmers seem to have displaced foragers by gradual infiltration rather than by conquest.

The archaeologist Colin Renfrew maintains that, over a few centuries, farming populations in Europe could have increased by a factor of fifty to one hundred just on the basis of the dependability of their food supply. In his view, as population densities rose, individuals with fields farthest away from their native village formed new settlements, thus contributing to a steady, nonviolent expansion of agriculture consistent with the archaeological record. An expansion by only 12 to 19 miles (20 to 30 kilometers) in a generation could have brought farming to every corner of Europe between 6500 and 3500 B.C.E.[3] Yet it probably happened gradually enough to minimize sharp conflicts with foragers, who would simply have stayed clear of the agricultural frontier or gradually adopted agriculture themselves. Studies that map genetic changes in the population also suggest a gradual spread of agricultural people across Europe from southeast to northwest.[4]

As they did in forager bands, kinship and marriage bound farming communities together. Nuclear family size (parents and their children) may not have increased, but kinship relations traced back over more generations brought distant cousins into a common kin network. This network encouraged the holding of land by large kinship units known as lineages (LIN-ee-ij) or clans.

Because each person has two parents, four grandparents, eight great-grandparents, and so on, each individual has a bewildering number of ancestors. Some societies trace descent equally through both parents, but most give greater importance to descent through either the mother (matrilineal [mat-ruh-LIN-ee-uhl] societies) or the father (patrilineal [pat-ruh-LIN-ee-uhl] societies). Some scholars believe that descent through women and perhaps rule by women prevailed in early times. The traditions of Kikuyu (ki-KOO-yoo) farmers on Mount Kenya in East Africa, for example, relate that women ruled until the Kikuyu men conspired to get all the women pregnant at once and then overthrew them while they were unable to fight back. No specific evidence can prove or disprove legends such as this, but it is important not to confuse tracing descent through women (matrilineality) with rule by women (matriarchy [MAY-tree-ahr-key]).

Religiously, kinship led to reverence for departed ancestors. Old persons often received elaborate burials. A plastered skull from Jericho (JER-ih-koe) in the Jordan Valley of modern Israel may be evidence of early ancestor reverence or worship at the dawn of agriculture.

The religions of foragers tended to center on sacred groves, springs, and wild animals. In contrast, the rituals of farmers often centered on the Earth Mother, a deity believed to be the source of new life, and divinities representing fire, wind, and rain. Pastoralists tended to worship the all-powerful (and usually male) sky-god.

Assemblages of **megaliths** (meaning "big stones") seem to relate to religious beliefs. One complex built in the Egyptian desert before 5000 B.C.E. includes stone burial chambers, a calendar circle, and pairs of upright stones that frame the rising sun on the

---

megaliths Structures and complexes of very large stones constructed for ceremonial and religious purposes in Neolithic times.

summer solstice. Stonehenge, a famous megalithic site in England constructed about 2000 B.C.E., marked the position of the sun and other celestial bodies at key points in the year. In Central Asia, the Americas, and other parts of the world, giant earth burial mounds may have served similar ritual and symbolic functions.

In some parts of the world, a few Neolithic villages grew into towns, which served as centers of trade and specialized crafts. Two towns in the Middle East, Jericho on the west bank of the Jordan River and Çatal Hüyük (cha-TAHL hoo-YOOK) in central Anatolia (modern Turkey), have been extensively excavated (Map 1.1 shows their location). Jericho revealed an

elaborate early agricultural settlement. The round mud-brick dwellings characteristic of Jericho around 8000 B.C.E. may have imitated the shape of the tents of foragers who once had camped near Jericho's natural spring. A millennium later, rectangular rooms with finely plastered walls and floors and wide doorways opened onto central courtyards. Surrounding the 10-acre (4-hectare) settlement, a massive stone wall protected against attacks.

The ruins of Çatal Hüyük, an even larger Neolithic town, date to between 7000 and 5000 B.C.E. and cover 32 acres (13 hectares). Its residents lived in plastered mud-brick rooms with elaborate decorations, but Çatal Hüyük had no wall. Instead, the outer

Map 1.1   River-Valley Civilizations, 3500–1500 B.C.E. The earliest complex societies arose in the floodplains of large rivers: in the fourth millennium B.C.E. in the valley of the Tigris and Euphrates Rivers in Mesopotamia and the Nile River in Egypt, in the third millennium B.C.E. in the valley of the Indus River in Pakistan, and in the second millennium B.C.E. in the valley of the Yellow River in China.   © Cengage Learning

 Interactive Map

walls of its houses formed a continuous barrier without doors or large windows. Residents entered their houses by climbing down ladders through a hole in the roof. Long-distance trade at Çatal Hüyük featured obsidian, a hard volcanic rock that artisans chipped, ground, and polished into tools, weapons, mirrors, and ornaments. Other residents made fine pottery, wove baskets and woolen cloth, made stone and shell beads, and worked leather and wood. House sizes varied, but nothing indicates that Çatal Hüyük had a dominant class or a centralized political structure.

Representational art at Çatal Hüyük makes it clear that hunting retained a powerful hold on people's minds. Wall paintings of hunting scenes closely resemble earlier cave paintings. Many depict men and women adorned with leopard skins. Men were buried with weapons rather than with farm tools, and bones from rubbish heaps prove that wild game featured prominently in people's diet.

Yet Çatal Hüyük's economy rested on agriculture. The surrounding fields produced barley and emmer wheat, as well as legumes (LEG-yooms) and other vegetables. Pigs were kept along with goats and sheep. Nevertheless, foragers' foods, such as acorns and wild grains, had not yet disappeared.

Çatal Hüyük had one religious shrine for every two houses. At least forty rooms contained shrines with depictions of horned wild bulls, female breasts, goddesses, leopards, and handprints. Rituals involved burning dishes of grain, legumes, and meat but not sacrificing live animals. Statues of plump female deities far outnumber statues of male deities, suggesting that the inhabitants venerated a goddess as their principal deity. The large number of females who were buried elaborately in shrine rooms may have been priestesses of this cult. The site's principal excavator maintains that although male priests existed, "it seems extremely likely that the cult of the goddess was administered mainly by women."[5]

Metalworking became a specialized occupation in the late Neolithic period. At Çatal Hüyük, objects of copper and lead, which occur naturally in fairly pure form, date to about 6400 B.C.E. Silver and gold also appear at early dates in various parts of the world. Because of their rarity and their softness, these metals did not replace stone tools and weapons. The discovery of decorative and ceremonial objects of metal in

SECTION REVIEW

- Paleolithic peoples lived mainly by foraging and hunting; women probably did most of the foraging, and men most of the hunting.
- Stone tools, cave paintings, and evidence of food-gathering techniques suggest that Stone Age peoples laid the foundations of science, art, and religion.
- During the Neolithic period, environmental factors prompted an agricultural revolution through which peoples across the globe shifted from foraging and hunting to settled farming.
- In addition to cultivating crops suited to their environments, Neolithic farmers domesticated animals.
- Neolithic communities tended to cohere around extended kinship ties and religious veneration of ancestors.
- In some parts of the world, Neolithic villages grew into towns in which farm produce supported residents engaged in specialized crafts.

graves indicates that they became symbols of status and power.

Towns, specialized crafts, and religious shrines forced the farmers to produce extra food for non-farmers like priests and artisans. The building of permanent houses, walls, and towers, not to mention megalithic monuments, also called for added labor. Stonehenge, for example, took some 30,000 person-hours to build. Whether these tasks were performed freely or coerced is unknown.

Mesopotamia

How did Mesopotamian civilization emerge?

Mesopotamia means "land between the rivers" in Greek, reflecting the importance of the Euphrates and Tigris Rivers to the way of life in this region. Because of the unpredictable spring floods of these rivers, the peoples of ancient Mesopotamia saw themselves at the mercy of gods who embodied the forces of nature. The

Babylon The largest and most important city in Mesopotamia. It achieved particular eminence as the capital of the Amorite king Hammurabi in the eighteenth century B.C.E. and the Neo-Babylonian king Nebuchadnezzar in the sixth century B.C.E.

Babylonian Creation Myth (**Babylon** was the most important city in southern Mesopotamia in the second and first millennia B.C.E.) climaxes in a cosmic battle between Marduk, the chief god of Babylon, and Tiamat (TIE-ah-mat), a female figure who personifies the salt sea. Marduk cuts up Tiamat and from her body fashions the earth and sky. He then creates the divisions of time, the celestial bodies, rivers, and weather phenomena. From the blood of a defeated rebel god, he creates human beings. Myths of this sort explained to the ancient inhabitants of Mesopotamia the environment in which they were living.

Settled Agriculture in an Unstable Landscape

The plain alongside and between the Tigris and Euphrates Rivers, which originate in the mountains of eastern Anatolia (modern Turkey) and empty into the Persian Gulf, has gained fertility from the silt deposited by river floods over many millennia. Today the plain is mostly in Iraq; it gives way to mountains in the north and east: an arc extending from northern Syria through southeastern Anatolia to the Zagros (ZAG-ruhs) Mountains that separate the plain from the Iranian Plateau. To the west and southwest lie the Syrian and Arabian Deserts, to the southeast the Persian Gulf. Floods in this plain, caused by snow melting in the northern mountains, can be sudden and violent. They come inconveniently in the spring when crops, planted in winter to avoid the torrid summer temperatures, are ripening. Floods can also cause the rivers to change course, abruptly cutting off fields and towns from water and river communication.

Although the first domestication of plants and animals around 8000 B.C.E. occurred nearby, in the "Fertile Crescent" region of northern Syria and southeastern Anatolia, agriculture did not reach Mesopotamia until approximately 5000 B.C.E. "Dry" (unirrigated) farming requires at least 8 inches (20 centimeters) of rain a year. The hot, arid climate of southern Mesopotamia calls for irrigation, the artificial provision of water to crops. Initially, people probably channeled water from smaller streams flowing from the Zagros Mountains. But shortly after 3000 B.C.E. they learned to construct canals from the Tigris and Euphrates to supply water as needed and carry it to more distant fields.

Ox-drawn plows, developed by around 4000 B.C.E., cut a furrow in the earth into which carefully measured amounts of seed dropped from an attached funnel. Farmers favored barley as a cereal crop because it could tolerate the Mesopotamian climate and withstand the toxic effects of salt drawn to the earth's surface by evaporation. Fields stood fallow (unplanted) every other year to replenish the nutrients in the soil. Date palms provided food, fiber, and wood; garden plots produced vegetables; and reeds growing along the rivers and in the marshy southern delta yielded raw material for mats, baskets, huts, and boats. Fish was a dietary staple. Herds of sheep and goats, which grazed on fallow land or the nearby desert, provided wool, milk, and meat. Donkeys, originally domesticated in northeast Africa, joined cattle as beasts of burden in the third millennium B.C.E., as did camels from Arabia and horses from the mountains in the second millennium B.C.E.

The written record begins with the **Sumerians** and marks the division, by some definitions, between prehistory and history. Archaeological evidence places the Sumerians in southern Mesopotamia at least by 5000 B.C.E. and perhaps even earlier. They created the framework of civilization in Mesopotamia during a long period of dominance in the third millennium B.C.E. Other peoples lived in Mesopotamia as well. As early as 2900 B.C.E., personal names recorded in inscriptions from the more northerly cities reveal a non-Sumerian **Semitic** (suh-MIT-ik) language. (*Semitic* refers to a family of languages spoken in parts of western Asia and northern Africa. They include the Aramaic [ar-uh-MAY-ik] and Phoenician [fe-NEE-shuhn] of the ancient world and the Hebrew and Arabic of today.) Possibly the descendants of nomads from the

---

Sumerians The people who dominated southern Mesopotamia through the end of the third millennium B.C.E. They were responsible for the creation of many fundamental elements of Mesopotamian culture—such as irrigation technology, cuneiform writing, and religious conceptions—later adopted by their Semitic successors.

Semitic Family of related languages long spoken across parts of western Asia and northern Africa. In antiquity these languages included Hebrew, Aramaic, and Phoenician. The most widespread modern members of the Semitic family are Arabic and Hebrew.

desert west of Mesopotamia, these Semites seem to have lived in peace with the Sumerians, adopting their culture and sometimes achieving positions of wealth and power.

By 2000 B.C.E., the Semitic peoples had become politically dominant. From this time on, Akkadian (uh-KAY-dee-uhn), a Semitic language, took precedence over Sumerian, although the Sumerian cultural legacy survived in translation. The Sumerian-Akkadian dictionaries compiled at the time to facilitate translations from Sumerian allow us today to read the language, which has no known relatives. The characteristics and adventures of the Semitic gods also indicate cultural borrowing. This cultural synthesis parallels a biological merging of Sumerians and Semites through intermarriage. Though other ethnic groups, including Kassites (KAS-ite) from the eastern mountains and Elamites (EE-luh-mite) and Persians from farther south in Iran, played roles in Mesopotamian history, the Sumerian/Semitic cultural heritage remained fundamentally unaltered until the arrival of Greeks in the late fourth century B.C.E.

Cities, Kings, and Trade

Mesopotamian farmers usually lived in villages. A group of families, totaling a few hundred persons perhaps, could protect one another, work together at key times in the agricultural cycle, and share tools, barns, and threshing floors. Village society also provided companionship and a pool of potential marriage partners.

Occasionally, as a particularly successful village grew, small satellite villages developed nearby and eventually merged with the main village to form an urban center. Many early Mesopotamian city dwellers went out each day to labor in nearby fields. Other city dwellers, however, depended for food on the surplus food production of the villagers. Some specialized in crafts—for example, pottery, artwork, and weapons, tools, and other objects forged out of metal. Others served the gods or carried out administrative duties. Mesopotamian cities controlled the agricultural land and collected crop surpluses from villages in their vicinity. In return, the city provided rural districts with military protection against bandits and raiders and a market where villagers could acquire manufactured goods produced by urban specialists.

The term **city-state** refers to a self-governing urban center and the agricultural territories it controlled. Stretches of uncultivated land, either desert or swamp, served as buffers between the many small city-states of early Mesopotamia. Nevertheless, disputes over land, water rights, and movable property often sparked hostilities between neighboring cities and the building of protective walls of sun-dried bricks. At other times, cities cooperated, sharing water and allowing traders safe passage through their territories.

Mesopotamians opened new land to agriculture by building and maintaining irrigation networks. Canals brought water from river to field; drainage ditches carried the water back to the river before evaporation could draw harmful salt and minerals to the surface. Weirs (partial dams) raised the water level of the river so that water could flow by gravity into the canals. Dikes along the riverbanks protected against floods. The silt carried by floods clogged the canals, which required frequent dredging. In some places, levers with counterweights lifted buckets of irrigation water out of a river or canal.

Successful operation of such sophisticated irrigation systems depended on leaders compelling or persuading large numbers of people to work together. Other projects called for similar cooperation: harvesting, sheep shearing, building of fortifications and large public buildings, and warfare. Two centers of power, the temple and the palace of the king, have left written records, but details of governmental life remain scanty, as are the hints at some sort of citizens' assembly that may have evolved from traditional village councils.

One or more temples, centrally located, housed each city-state's deity or deities and their associated cults (sets of religious rituals). Temples owned agricultural lands and stored the gifts that worshipers donated. The central location of the temple buildings confirms the importance of cults. Head priests, who

---

city-state A small independent state consisting of an urban center and the surrounding agricultural territory. A characteristic political form in early Mesopotamia, archaic and classical Greece, Phoenicia, and early Italy.

controlled each shrine and managed its wealth, played prominent political and economic roles.

In the third millennium B.C.E., Sumerian documents show the emergence of a *lugal* (LOO-guhl) or "big man"—what we would call a king. An increase in warfare as ever-larger communities quarreled over land, water, and raw materials may have prompted this development, but details are lacking. According to one theory, communities chose certain men to lead their armies in time of war, and these individuals found ways to prolong their authority in peacetime and assume judicial and ritual functions. Although the lugal's position was not hereditary, it often passed from a father to a capable son.

The location of the temple in the city's heart and the less prominent siting of the king's palace symbolize the later emergence of royalty. The king's power grew at the expense of the priesthood, however, because the army backed him. Although the priests and temples retained influence because of their wealth and religious mystique, they gradually became dependent on the palace. Some Mesopotamian kings claimed divinity, but this concept did not take root. Normally the king portrayed himself as the deity's earthly representative.

By the late third millennium B.C.E., kings assumed responsibility for the upkeep and building of temples and the proper performance of ritual. Other royal responsibilities included maintaining city walls and defenses, extending and repairing irrigation channels, guarding property rights, warding off foreign attacks, and establishing justice.

The *Epic of Gilgamesh* referred to at the beginning of this chapter shows both the ambition of the kings and their value to the community. Gilgamesh, who is probably based on a historical king of Uruk, stirs resentment by demanding sexual favors from new brides, but the community relies on his immense strength, wisdom, and courage. In quest of everlasting glory, Gilgamesh walls the city magnificently, stamping his name on every brick. His journey to the

Primary Source: The Epic of Gilgamesh Find out how Gilgamesh's friend Enkidu propels him on a quest for immortality, and whether or not that quest is successful.

faraway Cedar Mountains reflects the king's role in accessing valuable resources.

A few city-states became powerful enough to dominate their neighbors. Sargon (SAHR-gone), ruler of Akkad (AH-kahd) around 2350 B.C.E., pioneered in uniting many cities under one king and capital. His title, King of Sumer and Akkad, symbolized this claim to universal dominion. Sargon and the four family members who succeeded him over 120 years secured their power in several ways. They razed the walls of conquered cities and installed governors backed by garrisons of Akkadian troops. They gave soldiers land to ensure their loyalty. Being of Semitic stock, they adapted the cuneiform (kyoo-NEE-uh-form) system of writing used for Sumerian (discussed later in the chapter) to express their own language. Their administration featured a uniform system of weights and measures and standardized formats for official documents. These measures facilitated assessment and collection of taxes, recruitment of soldiers, and organization of labor projects.

For reasons that remain obscure, the Akkadian state fell around 2230 B.C.E. The Sumerian language and culture revived in the cities of the southern plain under the Third Dynasty of Ur (2112–2004 B.C.E.), a five-king dynasty that maintained itself for a century through campaigns of conquest and prudent marriage alliances. The Akkadian state had controlled more territory, but tighter government control based on a rapidly expanding bureaucracy and obsessive recordkeeping now secured Ur's dominance. Messengers and well-maintained road stations speeded up communications; and an official calendar, standardized weights and measures, and uniform writing practices improved the central administration. To protect against nomadic Semitic Amorites (AM-uh-rites) from the northwest, the kings erected a wall 125 miles (200 kilometers) long. Eventually, however, nomad incursions combined with an Elamite attack from the southeast toppled the Third Dynasty of Ur.

The Amorites founded a new city at Babylon, not far from Akkad. Toward the end of a long reign, **Hammurabi** (HAM-uh-rah-bee) (r. 1792–1750 B.C.E.) initiated a series of aggressive military campaigns, and Babylon became the capital of what historians have named the "Old Babylonian" state, which eventually stretched beyond Sumer and Akkad into the north and northwest, from 1900 to 1600 B.C.E. Hammurabi's famous Law Code, inscribed on a polished black stone pillar, provided judges with a lengthy set of examples illustrating the principles to be used in deciding cases. Some examples called for severe physical punishments to compensate for crimes. These Amorite notions of justice differed from the monetary penalties prescribed in earlier codes from Ur.

Conquest gave some Mesopotamian city-states access to vital resources. Trade offered an alternative, and long-distance commerce flourished in most periods. Evidence of seagoing vessels appears as early as the fifth millennium B.C.E. Wood, metals, and stone came from foreign lands in exchange for wool, cloth, barley, and vegetable oil. Cedar forests in Lebanon and Syria yielded wood, Anatolia produced silver, Egypt gold, and the eastern Mediterranean and Oman (on the Arabian peninsula) copper. Tin, which in alloy with copper made bronze, came from Afghanistan (in South-Central Asia), and chlorite, a greenish, easily carved stone, from the Iranian plateau. Jewelers and stone-carvers used black diorite from the Persian Gulf,

blue lapis lazuli (LAP-is LAZ-uh-lee) from Afghanistan, and reddish carnelian (kahr-NEEL-yuhn) from Pakistan.

Most merchants worked for the palace or the temple in the third millennium B.C.E. Only these institutions commanded the financial resources and organizational skills needed for acquiring, transporting, and protecting valuable commodities. Merchants exchanged surpluses from the royal or temple farmlands for raw materials and luxury goods. In the second millennium B.C.E., independent merchants and merchant guilds gained increasing influence.

Sources do not reveal whether the most important commercial transactions took place in the area just inside the city gates or in the vicinity of the docks. Wherever they occurred, coined money played no role. Coins—stamped metal pieces of state-guaranteed value—first appeared in the sixth century B.C.E. and did not reach Mesopotamia until several centuries later. For most of Mesopotamian history, items that could not be bartered—traded for one another—had their value calculated in relation to fixed weights of precious metal, primarily silver, or measures of grain.

Mesopotamian Society

Urbanized civilizations foster social division, that is, obvious variation in the status and privileges of different groups according to wealth, social function, and legal and political rights. Urbanization, specialization of function, centralization of power, and the use of written records enabled certain groups to amass unprecedented wealth. Temple leaders and the kings controlled large agricultural estates, and the palace administration collected taxes from subjects. How elite individuals acquired large private landholdings is unknown, since land was rarely put up for sale. In some cases, however, debtors lost their land to creditors, or soldiers and priests received land in return for their services.

The Law Code of Hammurabi in the eighteenth century B.C.E. reflects social divisions that may also

Law Code of Hammurabi The 282 laws inscribed in cuneiform writing on this diorite stone reflect the divinely sanctioned authority of the Babylonian ruler Hammurabi (r. 1792–1750 B.C.E.). The frieze at the top of the stone depicts the king in an attitude of adoration before the seated sun-god Shamash. Almost a thousand years earlier a king of the Sumerian city of Ur is mentioned in an inscription as rendering decisions "according to the just laws of Shamash." Réunion des Musées Nationaux/Art Resource, NY

Hammurabi Amorite ruler of Babylon (r. 1792–1750 B.C.E.). He conquered many city-states in southern and northern Mesopotamia and is best known for a code of laws, inscribed on a black stone pillar, illustrating the principles to be used in legal cases.

have been valid for other places and times, despite inevitable fluctuations. It identifies three classes: (1) the free landowning class: royalty, high-ranking officials, warriors, priests, merchants, and some artisans and shopkeepers; (2) the class of dependent farmers and artisans, whose legal attachment to royal, temple, or private estates made them the primary rural work force; and (3) the class of slaves, primarily employed in domestic service.

Penalties prescribed in the Law Code depended on the class of the offender. The lower orders received the most severe punishments. Slaves, many of them prisoners of war from the mountains, and insolvent debtors played a lesser economic role than they would in the later societies of Greece and Rome (see Chapters 4 and 6). Identified by a distinctive hairstyle rather than chains or brands, they would have a barber shave off the telltale mark if they were lucky enough to regain their freedom. Because commodities such as food and oil were distributed to all people in proportion to their age, gender, and task, documents do not always distinguish between slaves or dependent workers and free laborers. In the Old Babylonian period, the class of people who were not dependent on the temple or palace grew, the amount of land and other property in private hands increased, and free laborers became more common.

The daily lives of ordinary Mesopotamians, especially those in villages or on large estates, left few archaeological or literary traces. Peasants built with mud brick and reeds, which quickly disintegrate, and they had few metal possessions. Being illiterate, they left no written record of their lives. It is especially difficult to discover much about the experiences of women. Males dominated the position of **scribe**—an administrator or scholar charged by the temple or palace with reading and writing tasks—and, for the most part, their writings reflect elite male activities. Archaeology only partially fills this gap.

Anthropologists theorize that women lost social standing and freedom with the spread of agriculture.

In hunting and gathering societies, they believe, women's foraging provided most of the community's food. But in Mesopotamia, food production depended on the heavy physical labor of plowing, harvesting, and digging irrigation channels, jobs usually performed by men. Since food surpluses made larger families possible, bearing and raising children became the primary occupation of many women, leaving them little time to acquire the specialized skills of a scribe or artisan.

Women could own property, maintain control of their dowry, and even engage in trade, but men monopolized political life. Some women worked outside the household in textile factories and breweries or as prostitutes, tavern keepers, bakers, or fortunetellers. Home tasks for nonelite women probably included helping with farming, growing vegetables, cooking, cleaning, fetching water, tending the household fire, and weaving baskets and textiles.

The standing of women seems to have declined further in the second millennium B.C.E., perhaps because of the rise of an urbanized middle class and an increase in private wealth. Husbands gained authority in the household and benefited from marriage and divorce laws. A man normally took just one wife, but he could obtain a second if the first gave him no children. In later Mesopotamian history, kings and rich men had several wives. Marriage alliances arranged between families made women instruments for preserving and enhancing family wealth. Alternatively, a family might decide to avoid a daughter's marriage, with the resulting loss of a dowry, by dedicating her to temple service as "god's bride." Constraints on women's lives, such as remaining at home and wearing veils in public, may date back to the second millennium B.C.E. (see Chapter 9).

Gods, Priests, and Temples

The Sumerian gods embodied the forces of nature: Anu the sky, Enlil the air, Enki the water, Utu the sun, and Nanna the moon. The goddess Inanna governed

Primary Source: The State Regulates Health Care: Hammurabi's Code and Surgeons Get a glimpse of the various rewards and perilous punishments for surgeons who either succeed or fail at their job in 1800 B.C.E.

scribe In the governments of many ancient societies, a professional position reserved for men who had undergone the lengthy training required to be able to read and write using cuneiforms, hieroglyphics, or other early, cumbersome writing systems.

Mesopotamian Cylinder Seal   Seals indicated the identity of an individual and were impressed into wet clay or wax to "sign" legal documents or mark ownership of an object. This seal, produced in the period of the Akkadian Empire, depicts Ea (second from right), the god of the underground waters, symbolized by the stream with fish emanating from his shoulders; Ishtar, whose attributes of fertility and war are indicated by the date cluster in her hand and the pointed weapons showing above her wings; and the sun-god Shamash, cutting his way out of the mountains with a jagged knife, an evocation of sunrise.   Courtesy of the Trustees of the British Museum

sexual attraction and violence. When the Semitic peoples became dominant, they equated their deities with those of the Sumerians. The Sumerian gods Nanna and Utu, for example, became the Semitic Sin and Shamash, and the goddess Inanna became Ishtar. The Semitic gods took over the myths and many of the rituals of their Sumerian predecessors.

People imagined their gods as anthropomorphic (an-thruh-po-MORE-fik), that is, like humans in form and conduct. The gods had bodies and senses, sought nourishment from sacrifice, enjoyed the worship and obedience of humanity, and experienced the human emotions of lust, love, hate, anger, and envy. Religious beliefs instilled fear of the gods, who could alter the landscape, and a desire to appease them.

Public, state-organized religion stands out in the archaeological record. Cities built temples and showed devotion to the divinity or divinities who protected the community. All the peoples of Sumer regarded Nippur (see Map 1.1) as a religious center because of its temple to the air-god Enlil. As with other temples, they considered it the god's residence and believed the cult statue in its interior shrine embodied his life force. Priests attended this divine image, trying to anticipate and meet its every need

in a daily cycle of waking, bathing, dressing, feeding, moving around, entertaining, soothing, and revering. These rituals reflected the message of the Babylonian Creation Myth that humankind existed only to serve the gods. Several thousand priests may have staffed a large temple like that of the god Marduk at Babylon.

Priests passed their office and sacred lore to their sons, and their families lived on rations of food from the deity's estates. The amount an individual received depended on his rank within a complicated hierarchy of status and specialized function. The high priest performed the central acts in the great rituals. Certain priests pleasured the gods with music, others exorcised evil spirits, and still others interpreted dreams and divined the future by examining the organs of sacrificed animals, reading patterns in rising incense smoke, or casting dice.

A high wall surrounded the temple precinct, which contained the shrine of the chief deity; open plazas; chapels for lesser gods; housing, dining facilities, and offices for priests and other temple staff; and buildings for crafts, storage, and other services. The compound focused on the **ziggurat** (ZIG-uh-rat), a multistory, mud-brick, pyramid-shaped tower approached by ramps and stairs. Scholars are still debating the ziggurat's function and symbolic meaning.

Scholars similarly debate whether common people had much access to temple buildings and how religious practices and beliefs affected their everyday lives. Individuals placed votive statues in the sanctuaries in the belief that these miniature replicas of themselves could continually seek the deity's favor. The survival of many **amulets** (small charms meant to protect the bearer from evil) and representations of a host of demons suggests widespread belief in magic—the use of special words and rituals to manipulate the forces of nature. For example, people believed that a demon caused headaches and could be driven out of the ailing body. Lamashtu, the demon who caused miscarriages, could be frightened off if a pregnant woman wore an amulet with the likeness of the hideous but beneficent demon Pazuzu. A god or goddess might also be persuaded to reveal the future in return for a gift or sacrifice.

Elite and common folk came together in great festivals such as the twelve-day New Year's festival held each spring in Babylon as the new grain was beginning to sprout in the fields. In the early days of the festival, in conjunction with rituals of purification and invocations of Marduk, a priest read to the god's image the text of the Babylonian Creation Epic. Many subsequent activities in the temple courtyard and streets reenacted the events of the myth. Following their belief that time moved in a circular path through a cycle of birth, growth, maturity, and death, people hoped through this ritual to persuade the gods to grant a renewal of time and life at winter's end.

Technology and Science

The term *technology* comes from the Greek word *techne*, meaning "craft" or "specialized knowledge." It normally refers to the tools and processes by which humans manipulate the physical world. However, many scholars also use it more broadly for any specialized knowledge used to transform the natural environment and human society. Ancient Mesopotamian irrigation techniques that expanded agricultural production fit the first definition, priestly belief in their ability to enhance prosperity through prayers and rituals the second.

Writing, which first appeared in Mesopotamia before 3300 B.C.E., partakes more of the second

definition than of the first. The earliest inscribed tablets, found in the chief temple at Uruk, date from a time when the temple was the community's most important economic institution. The most plausible current theory maintains that writing originated from a system of tokens used to keep track of property—sheep, cattle, wagon wheels—as wealth accumulated and the volume and complexity of commerce strained people's memories. The shape and number of tokens inserted in clay "envelopes" (balls of clay) indicated the contents of a shipment or storeroom, and pictures of the tokens incised on the outside of the envelope reminded the reader of what was inside.

Eventually people realized that the incised pictures, the first written symbols, provided an adequate record of the transaction and made the tokens inside the envelope redundant. Each early symbol represented a thing, but it could also stand for the sound of the word for that thing when that sound was a syllable of a longer word. For example, the symbols *shu* for "hand" and *mu* for "water" could be combined to form *shumu,* the word for "name."

The usual method of writing involved pressing the point of a sharpened reed into a moist clay tablet. Because the reed made wedge-shaped impressions, the early pictures, which were more or less realistic, evolved into stylized combinations of strokes and wedges, a system known as **cuneiform** (Latin for "wedge-shaped") writing. Mastering cuneiform, which in any particular period involved several hundred signs, compared to the twenty-five or so in an alphabetic system, required years of practice. In the "tablet-house" attached to a temple or palace,

---

ziggurat A massive pyramidal stepped tower made of mud bricks. It is associated with religious complexes in ancient Mesopotamian cities, but its function is unknown.

amulet Small charm meant to protect the bearer from evil. Found frequently in archaeological excavations in Mesopotamia and Egypt, amulets reflect the religious practices of the common people.

cuneiform a system of writing in which wedge-shaped symbols represented words or syllables. It originated in Mesopotamia and was used initially for Sumerian and Akkadian but later was adapted to represent other languages of western Asia. Because so many symbols had to be learned, literacy was confined to a relatively small group of administrators and scribes.

students learned writing and mathematics under a stern headmaster and endured bullying by older student tutors called "big brothers." The prestige and regular employment that went with their position may have made scribes reluctant to simplify the cuneiform system. Although in the Old Babylonian period the growth of private commerce brought an increase in the number of people who could read and write, literacy remained a rare accomplishment.

Developed originally for the Sumerian language, cuneiform—a system of writing rather than a language—later served to express the Akkadian language of the Mesopotamian Semites as well as other languages of western Asia, such as Hittite, Elamite, and Persian. The remains of the ancient city of Ebla (EH-bluh) in northern Syria illustrate the Mesopotamian influence on other parts of western Asia. Ebla's buildings and artifacts follow Mesopotamian models, and thousands of tablets inscribed with cuneiform symbols bear messages in both Sumerian and the local Semitic dialect. The high point of Ebla's wealth and power occurred from 2400 to 2250 B.C.E., roughly contemporary with the Akkadian Empire. Ebla then controlled extensive territory and derived wealth from agriculture, manufacture of woolen cloth, and trade with Mesopotamia and the Mediterranean coast.

Economic concerns predominate in the earliest Sumerian documents, but cuneiform came to have wide-ranging uses beyond the recordkeeping that apparently inspired its invention. Legal acts that had formerly been validated by the recitation of oral formulas and performance of symbolic acts came to be accompanied by written documents marked with the seals of the participants. Cuneiform similarly served political, literary, religious, and scientific purposes.

Other technologies met the challenges of the physical environment. Irrigation, the basis of Mesopotamian agriculture, required the construction and maintenance of canals, weirs, and dikes. Cattle drew carts and sledges in some locations. In the south, where numerous water channels cut up the landscape, boats and barges predominated. In northern Mesopotamia, donkeys served as pack animals for overland caravans in the centuries before the advent of the camel around 1200 B.C.E.

To improve on stone tools, the Mesopotamians imported ores containing copper, tin, and arsenic. From these they made bronze, a form of copper alloyed with either tin or arsenic. Craftsmen poured molten bronze into molds shaped like weapons or tools. The cooled metal took a sharper edge than stone, was less likely to break, and was more easily repaired. Yet stone implements remained in use among poor people who could not afford bronze.

Clay, Mesopotamia's most abundant resource, went into the making of mud bricks. Whether dried in the sun or baked in an oven for greater durability, these constituted the main building material. Construction of city walls, temples, and palaces required practical knowledge of architecture and engineering. For example, the reed mats that Mesopotamian builders laid between the mud-brick layers of ziggurats served the same stabilizing purpose as girders in modern high-rise construction. The abundance of good clay also made pottery the most common material for dishes, storage vessels, and oil lamps (see Material Culture: Lamps and Candles). By 4000 B.C.E., potters had begun to use a revolving platform called a potter's wheel. Spun by hands or feet, the potter's wheel made possible rapid manufacture in precise and complex shapes.

Military technology changed as armies evolved from the early militias called up for short periods to the well-trained and well-paid full-time soldiers of the late third and second millennia B.C.E. In the early second millennium B.C.E., horses appeared in western Asia, and the horse-drawn chariot, a technically complicated device, came into vogue. Infantry found themselves at the mercy of swift chariots carrying a driver and an archer who could easily overtake them. Using increasingly effective siege machinery, Mesopotamian soldiers learned to climb over, undermine, or knock down the walls protecting the cities of their enemies.

Mesopotamians used a base-60 number system (the origin of the seconds and minutes we use today), in which numbers were expressed as fractions or multiples of 60 (in contrast to our base-10 system). Such advances in mathematics along with careful observation of the skies made the Mesopotamians sophisticated practitioners of astronomy. Mesopotamian priests compiled lists of omens or unusual sightings on earth and in the heavens, together with a record of the events that coincided with them. They consulted these texts at critical times, for they believed that the

Material Culture

Lamps and Candles

It is hard to imagine today how dark the world was after the sun went down throughout most of human history. The glow of a fire did not extend far. Nor were torches easy to make or long-lasting. A stick wrapped with oil-soaked cloth at one end does make an effective torch, but humans were in need of light long before they figured out how to make cloth. As for flammable oil, vegetable oils extracted from the seeds of olive or palm trees, or from plants like flax, lettuce, and corn, became abundant only with the spread of plant domestication in the Neolithic period. Prior to that, animal fat or tallow could be used, though it had the disadvantage of smelling like meat.

The Neolithic revolutions made available not only vegetable oils but also pottery, and later metal, vessels that could be used as lamps. A fireproof vessel would be filled with oil, and a wick would be placed so that one end was immersed in the oil and the other open to the air. The oil would saturate the wick, and a flame touched to the wick would vaporize a small amount of oil and ignite the resultant gas. A poor wick might sputter, smoke, or go out. The pith or inner porous core of plants of the rush family could be used as wicks in rushlamps, or the oil-soaked pith stiffened by part of the outer skin of the rush could be stood upright and lit like slender candles in rushlights.

Aside from the pith of rushes, wicks were usually made of string or a sliver of wood. Since a wick of greater diameter produces a larger flame, braiding was used to make a thicker string. Of all natural fibers, cotton makes the best wicks because of its absorbency. Different varieties of cotton were native to India and pre-Columbian America, but cotton became a major crop in the Middle East only in the early Islamic period of the eighth century C.E.. Christian Europe knew cotton only as an expensive import until the twelfth century, when a cotton industry was founded in northern Italy. Access to superior wicks contributed to an increase in European candle use.

Waxes differ from oils in being solid at room temperature. Molding wax around a wick produces a candle. Beeswax provided an ideal material for odorless candles and was in use for lighting as early as ancient Egyptian times. However, beeswax was scarce and expensive. Some premodern trade routes, such as those going south to the Middle East

Erich Lessing/Art Resource, NY

Ancient Lamp Vessel This 2,500-year-old oil lamp from Megiddo in Israel has grooves for two wicks. It is made of bronze, a valuable metal. Pottery lamps were much cheaper and show up abundantly in ancient archaeological sites.

along the rivers of Russia, featured beeswax as a major product. Beeswax candles came to play a prominent and often symbolic role in Christian, Jewish, and Buddhist religious rituals. Mosques, on the other hand, were traditionally lit by oil lamps.

Though whaling was practiced in certain coastal regions in prehistoric times, the extraction of whale oil on an industrial scale began in the sixteenth century and grew rapidly over the next three hundred years. Oil extracted from the whale's fat, or blubber, was widely used for lamps. Of even greater value was a wax called spermaceti that was made from an oily substance in the heads of sperm whales. A large whale might yield three tons of spermaceti. It burned without odor in candles and became the standard for candle making until the discovery of paraffin, a wax made from petroleum, in 1830. Paraffin generally replaced spermaceti as the preferred wax for candles.

The small flames of oil lamps and candles did not produce much illumination. Candela is the name of a unit of light intensity that became increasingly precise over the course of the nineteenth and twentieth centuries. It is intended to represent the light produced by a single candle, though many technical specifications, such as the color of the light, make it only an approximation. An even rougher approximation equates 120 candelas with the illumination provided by a 100-watt light bulb. This last approximation suggests how little light a single lamp or candle could provide in premodern times for reading, sewing, or doing any kind of fine work after sundown.

QUESTIONS FOR ANALYSIS

1. How would the provision of artificial light affect patterns of life with the change of seasons?
2. What human activities, such as storytelling, might have been enhanced by a lack of light?
3. How did gradual adoption of gaslight (1792) and the electric light bulb (1879) change people's lives?

recurrence of such phenomena could provide clues to future developments. The underlying premise was that the elements of the material universe, from the microcosmic to the macrocosmic, were interconnected in mysterious but undeniable ways.

Egypt

What role did the environment and religion play in Egyptian civilization?

No place exhibits the impact of the natural environment on the history and culture of a society better than ancient Egypt. Though located at the intersection of Asia and Africa, Egypt was less a crossroads than an isolated land protected by surrounding barriers of desert and a harborless, marshy seacoast. Whereas Mesopotamia was open to migration or invasion and was dependent on imported resources, Egypt's natural isolation and material self-sufficiency fostered a unique culture that for long periods had relatively little to do with other civilizations.

The Land of Egypt: "Gift of the Nile"

The world's longest river, the Nile flows northward from Lake Victoria and draws water from several large tributaries in the highlands of tropical Africa. Carving a narrow valley between a chain of hills on either side, it terminates at the Mediterranean Sea (see Map 1.2). Though bordered mostly

Map 1.2   Ancient Egypt The Nile River, flowing south to north, carved out of the surrounding desert a narrow green valley that became heavily settled in antiquity.
© Cengage Learning

Interactive Map

Model of Egyptian River Boat, ca. 1985 B.C.E.
This model was buried in the tomb of a Middle Kingdom official, Meketre, who is shown in the cabin being
entertained by musicians. The captain stands in front
of the cabin, the helmsman on the left steers the boat
with the rudder, while the lookout on the right lets out a
weighted line to determine the river's depth. The vessel is
being rowed downstream (northward); the white post in
the middle would support a mast and sail when traveling
upstream.   Image copyright © The Metropolitan Museum of
Art/Art Resource, NY

History in Focus *Examine the image, paying particular
attention to what the figures are doing. What aspects of
ancient Egyptian culture and worldview does this model
represent? Find the answer online.*

by desert, the banks of the river support lush vegetation. About 100 miles (160 kilometers) from the Mediterranean, the river divides into channels to form a
triangular delta. Most of Egypt's population lives on
the twisting, green ribbon of land along the river or in
the Nile Delta. Bleak deserts of mountains, rocks, and
dunes occupy the remaining 90 percent of the country.
The ancient Egyptians distinguished between the low-
lying, life-sustaining "Black Land" with its dark soil
and the elevated, deadly "Red Land" of the desert. The
fifth-century B.C.E. Greek traveler Herodotus (he-RA-
duh-tuhs) called Egypt the "gift of the Nile."

Travel and communication centered on the river,
with the most important cities located upstream away
from the Mediterranean. Because the river flows from
south to north, the Egyptians called the southern
part of the country "Upper Egypt" and the northern
delta "Lower Egypt." The First Cataract of the Nile,
the northernmost of a series of impassable rocks and
rapids below Aswan (AS-wahn) (about 500 miles [800
kilometers] south of the Mediterranean), formed
Egypt's southern boundary in most periods, but Egyptian control sometimes extended farther south into
what was called "Kush" (later Nubia, today part of
southern Egypt and northern Sudan). The Egyptians

also settled certain large oases west of the river, green
and habitable "islands" in the midst of the desert.

The hot, sunny climate favored agriculture.
Though rain rarely falls south of the delta, the river
provided water to irrigation channels that carried
water out into the valley and increased the area suitable for planting. In one large depression west of the
Nile, drainage techniques reduced the size of Lake
Faiyum (fie-YOOM) and allowed land to be reclaimed
for agriculture. Each September, the river overflowed
its banks, spreading water into the bordering valley.
Unlike the Mesopotamians, the Egyptians needed no
dams or weirs to raise the level of the river and divert
water into channels. Moreover, the Nile, unlike the
Tigris and Euphrates, flooded at the best time for
grain agriculture. When the flood receded and its
waters drained back into the river, the land had a fertile new layer of mineral-rich silt, and farmers could
easily plant their crops in the moist soil. The Egyptians' many creation myths commonly featured the
emergence of a life-supporting mound of earth from
a primeval swamp.

The level of the flood's crest determined the
abundance of the following harvest. Too little water
left fertile land unirrigated and hence uncultivable,
plunging the country into famine. The ebb and flow
of successful and failed regimes seems linked to the
cycle of floods. Nevertheless, remarkable stability

Primary Source: Hymn for the Nile Discover the
degree to which the Nile River is viewed as godlike
and the perceived power it has over the survival of the
people of Egypt.

characterized most eras, and Egyptians viewed the universe as an orderly and beneficent place.

Egypt had other resources besides the Nile. Papyrus reeds growing in marshes yielded fibers that made good sails, ropes, and a kind of paper. The wild animals and birds and the abundant river fish attracted hunters and fishermen. Building stone could be quarried and floated downstream from southern Egypt. And the state organized armed expeditions and forced labor to exploit nearby resources such as the copper and turquoise deposits in the Sinai desert to the east and gold from Nubia to the south.

The farming villages that appeared in Egypt as early as 5500 B.C.E. relied on domesticated plant and animal species that had emerged several millennia earlier in western Asia. Egypt's emergence as a focal point of civilization, however, stemmed at least partially from a gradual change in climate from the fifth to the third millennium B.C.E. Before that time, the Sahara, today the world's largest desert, had a relatively mild and wet climate. Its lakes and grasslands supported a variety of plant and animal species as well as populations of hunter-gatherers (see Chapter 8). As the climate changed and the Sahara began to dry up, displaced groups migrated into the then marshy Nile Valley, where they developed a sedentary way of life.

Divine Kingship

The increasing population called for greater complexity in political organization, including a form of local kingship. Later generations of Egyptians saw the unification of such smaller units into a single state by Menes (MEH-neez), a ruler from the south, as a pivotal event. Scholars question whether this event, dated to around 3100 B.C.E., took place at the hands of a historical or a mythical figure, but many authorities equate Menes with Narmer, a historical ruler who is shown on a decorated slate palette exulting over defeated enemies. Later kings of Egypt bore the title "Ruler of the Two Lands"—Upper and Lower Egypt—and wore two crowns symbolizing the unification of the country. Unlike Mesopotamia, therefore, Egypt discovered unity early in its history.

Following the practice of Manetho, an Egyptian priest from the fourth century B.C.E., historians divide Egyptian history into thirty dynasties (sequences of kings from the same family). The rise and fall of dynasties often reflect the dominance of one or another part of the country. Scholars also divide Egyptian history into "Old," "Middle," and "New Kingdoms," each a period of centralized political power and brilliant cultural achievement. "Intermediate Periods" signal political fragmentation and cultural decline. Although experts debate the specific dates, the chronology reflects current opinion.

The Egyptian state centered on the king, often known by the New Kingdom term **pharaoh**, from an Egyptian phrase meaning "palace." From the Old Kingdom on, if not earlier, Egyptians considered the king a god on earth, the incarnation of Horus and the son of the sun-god Re (ray). In this role he maintained **ma'at** (muh-AHT), the divinely authorized order of the universe. As a link between the people and the gods, his benevolent rule ensured the welfare and prosperity of the country. The Egyptians' conception of a divine king, the source of law and justice, may explain the apparent absence in Egypt of an impersonal code of law comparable to Hammurabi's Code in Mesopotamia.

So much depended on the kings that their deaths evoked elaborate efforts to ensure the well-being of their spirits on their journey to rejoin the gods. Carrying out funerary rites, constructing royal tombs, and sustaining the kings' spirits in the afterlife by perpetual offerings in adjoining funerary chapels demanded massive resources. Flat-topped, rectangular tombs made of mud brick sufficed for the earliest rulers, but around 2630 B.C.E., Djoser (JO-sur), a Third Dynasty king, ordered the construction of a stepped **pyramid**—a series of stone platforms laid one on top of the other—at Saqqara (suh-KAHR-uh), near Memphis.

pharaoh The central figure in the ancient Egyptian state. Believed to be an earthly manifestation of the gods, he used his absolute power to maintain the safety and prosperity of Egypt.

ma'at Egyptian term for the concept of divinely created and maintained order in the universe. Reflecting the ancient Egyptians' belief in an essentially beneficent world, the divine ruler was the earthly guarantor of this order.

pyramid A large, triangular stone monument, used in Egypt and Nubia as a burial place for the king. The largest pyramids, erected during the Old Kingdom near Memphis with stone tools and compulsory labor, reflect the Egyptian belief that the proper and spectacular burial of the divine ruler would guarantee the continued prosperity of the land.

Pyramids of Menkaure, Khafre, and Khufu at Giza, ca. 2500 B.C.E. With a width of 755 feet (230 meters) and a height of 480 feet (146 meters), the Great Pyramid of Khufu is the largest stone structure ever built. The construction of these massive edifices depended on relatively simple techniques of stonecutting, transport (the stones were floated downriver on boats and rolled to the site on sledges), and lifting (the stones were dragged up the face of the pyramid on mud-brick ramps). However, the surveying and engineering skills required to level the platform, lay out the measurements, and securely position the blocks were very sophisticated and have withstood the test of time.

Michele Burgess/SuperStock

History in Focus *These pyramids were built at the very beginning of Egyptian civilization. Why has no one ever built a larger stone structure since then? Find the answer online.*

Rulers of the Fourth Dynasty filled in the steps of Djoser's tomb to create the smooth-sided, limestone pyramids that most often symbolize ancient Egypt. Between 2550 and 2490 B.C.E., the pharaohs Khufu **(KOO-foo)** and Khefren **(KEF-ren)** erected huge pyramids at Giza, several miles north of Saqqara, the largest stone structures ever built. Khufu's pyramid originally reached a height of 480 feet (146 meters).

Egyptians accomplished this construction with stone tools (bronze was still expensive and rare) and no machinery other than simple levers, pulleys, and rollers. Calculations of the human muscle power needed to build a pyramid within a ruler's lifetime indicate that large numbers of people must have been pressed into service for part of each year, probably during the flood season, when no agricultural work could be done. The Egyptian masses probably considered this demand for labor a kind of religious service that would help ensure prosperity. Most of Egypt's surplus resources went into constructing these artificial mountains of stone. The age of the great pyramids

lasted about a century, though construction of pyramids on a smaller scale continued.

Administration and Communication

Ruling dynasties usually placed their capitals in the area of their original power base. **Memphis**, near today's Cairo at the apex of the Nile Delta, held this central position during the Old Kingdom; but **Thebes**, far to the south, often supplanted it during the Middle and New Kingdoms (see Map 1.2). A complex bureaucracy kept detailed records of the country's resources. At the village, district, and central government levels, bureaucrats kept track of land, labor, products, and people, extracting as taxes as much as 50 percent of the annual revenues of the country. This income supported the palace, bureaucracy,

Memphis The capital of Old Kingdom Egypt, near the head of the Nile Delta. Early rulers were interred in the nearby pyramids.
Thebes Capital city of Egypt and home of the ruling dynasties during the Middle and New Kingdoms. Amon, patron deity of Thebes, became one of the chief gods of Egypt. Monarchs were buried across the river in the Valley of the Kings.

and army, paid for building and maintaining temples, and made possible great monuments celebrating the king's grandeur. The government maintained a monopoly over key sectors of the economy and controlled long-distance trade. The urban middle-class traders who increasingly managed the commerce of Mesopotamia had no parallel in Egypt.

A writing system had been developed before the Early Dynastic period, and literacy was the hallmark of the administrative class. **Hieroglyphics** (high-ruh-GLIF-iks), the earliest form of this system, featured picture symbols standing for words, syllables, or individual sounds. We can read ancient Egyptian writing today only because of the discovery in the early nineteenth century C.E. of the Rosetta stone, an inscription from the second century B.C.E. that gave hieroglyphic and Greek versions of the same text.

Hieroglyphic writing was used on monuments and ornamental inscriptions for a long time. By 2500 B.C.E., however, administrators and copyists had developed a cursive script, in which the original pictorial nature of the symbol was less apparent, for their everyday needs. They wrote with ink on a writing material called **papyrus** (puh-PIE-ruhs), made from the stems of the papyrus reed that grew in the Nile marshes. Papyrus makers laid out the stems in a vertical and horizontal grid pattern, moistened them, and then pounded them with a soft mallet until they adhered into a sheet of writing material. A uniquely Egyptian product, papyrus served scribes throughout the ancient world and was exported in large quantities. The word *paper* comes from Greek and Roman words for papyrus.

Apart from administrative recordkeeping, Egyptian literary compositions included tales of adventure and magic, love poetry, religious hymns, and instruction manuals on technical subjects. Scribes in workshops attached to the temples made copies of traditional texts.

Strong monarchs appointed and promoted officials on the basis of merit and accomplishment, giving them grants of land cultivated by dependent peasants. Low-level officials worked in villages and district capitals; high-ranking officials served in the royal capital. During the Old Kingdom, the tombs of officials lay near the monumental tomb of the king so they could serve him in death as they had in life.

Egyptian history exhibits a recurring tension between the centralizing power of the monarchy and the decentralizing tendencies of the bureaucracy. The shift of officials' tombs from the vicinity of the royal tomb to the home districts where they spent much of their time and exercised power more or less independently signaled the breakdown of centralized power in the late Old Kingdom and First Intermediate Period. Inheritance of administrative posts similarly indicated a decline in centralized power. The early monarchs of the Middle Kingdom restored centralized power by reducing the power and prerogatives of the old elite and creating a new middle class of administrators.

The common observation that Egypt was a land of villages without real cities stems from its capitals being primarily extensions of the palace and central administration. Compared to Mesopotamia, a far larger percentage of the Egyptian population lived in farming villages, and Egypt's wealth derived to a higher degree from cultivating the land. The towns and cities that did exist unfortunately lie buried beneath modern urban sites, since Egypt has too little land in its cultivable region to afford abandonment of a large area.

 Primary Source: Advice to Ambitious Young Egyptians: Rise Above the Masses, Become a Scribe! This interesting piece of propaganda serves to convince potential scribes that the job of scribe is the best of all possible occupations.

hieroglyphics A system of writing in which pictorial symbols represented sounds, syllables, or concepts. It was used for official and monumental inscriptions in ancient Egypt. Because of the long period of study required to master this system, literacy in hieroglyphics was confined to a relatively small group of scribes and administrators. Cursive symbol-forms were developed for rapid composition on other media, such as papyrus.

papyrus A reed that grows along the banks of the Nile River in Egypt. From it was produced a paper-like writing medium used by the Egyptians and many other peoples in the ancient Mediterranean and Middle East.

Egypt largely stuck to itself during the Old and Middle Kingdoms, all foreigners being technically regarded as enemies. When necessary, local militia units backed up a small standing army of professional soldiers. Nomadic groups in the eastern and western deserts and Libyans to the northwest posed a nuisance more than a real danger. The king maintained limited contact with other advanced civilizations in the region, and Egypt's interests abroad focused on maintaining access to resources rather than on acquiring territory. Trade with the coast of the Levant (luh-VANT) (modern Israel, Lebanon, and Syria) brought in cedar wood in return for grain, papyrus, and gold.

Egypt's strongest interests involved goods from the south. Nubia contained gold mines (in Chapter 2 we examine the rise in Nubia of a civilization influenced by Egypt but also vital, original, and long lasting), and the southern course of the Nile offered access to sub-Saharan Africa. In the Old Kingdom, Egyptian noblemen living at Aswan on the southern border led donkey caravans south in search of gold, incense, and products from tropical Africa such as ivory, ebony, and exotic animals. Forts along the border protected Egypt from attack. In the early second millennium B.C.E., Egyptian forces invaded Nubia and extended the Egyptian border as far as the Third Cataract of the Nile, taking possession of the gold fields.

The People of Egypt

The estimated million to a million and a half inhabitants of Egypt included various physical types, ranging from dark-skinned people related to the populations of sub-Saharan Africa to lighter-skinned people akin to the populations of North Africa and western Asia who spoke Berber and Semitic languages, respectively. Though Egypt experienced no migrations or invasions on a scale common in Mesopotamian history, settlers periodically trickled into the Nile Valley and mixed with the local people.

Egypt had less pronounced social divisions than Mesopotamia, where a formal class structure emerged. The king and high-ranking officials enjoyed status, wealth, and power. Below them came lower-level officials, local leaders, priests and other professionals, artisans, and well-to-do farmers. Peasants, at the bottom, constituted the vast majority of the population.

Peasants lived in rural villages and devoted themselves to the seasonally changing tasks of agriculture: plowing, sowing, tending emerging shoots, reaping, threshing, and storing. They maintained irrigation channels, basins, and dikes. Fish and meat from domesticated animals—cattle, sheep, goats, and poultry—supplemented a diet based on wheat or barley, beer, and vegetables. Villages probably shared implements, work animals, and storage facilities and helped one another at peak times in the agricultural cycle and in building projects. Festivals to the local gods and other public celebrations occasionally brought feasting and ceremonies into their lives; labor conscripted for pyramid construction and other state projects brought hardship. If the burden of taxation or compulsory service proved too great, flight into the desert usually offered the only escape.

This account of village life depends on guesswork and bits and pieces of archaeological and literary evidence. Tomb paintings of the elite sometimes depict the lives of common folk. The artists employed conventions to indicate status: obesity for the rich and comfortable, baldness and deformity for the working classes. Egyptian poets frequently employed metaphors of farming and hunting, and papyrus documents preserved in the hot, dry sands tell of property transactions and legal disputes among ordinary people.

Slavery existed on a limited scale and was of little economic significance. Prisoners of war, condemned criminals, and debtors could be found on country estates or in the households of the king and wealthy families. But humane treatment softened the burden of slavery, as did the possibility of being freed.

Scarceness of sources also clouds the experiences of women. What is known about the lives of elite women derives from the possibly distorted impressions of male artists and scribes. Tomb paintings, rendered with dignity and affection, show women of the royal family and elite classes accompanying their husbands and engaging in domestic activities. Subordination to men is evident. The convention of depicting men with a dark red and women with a yellow flesh tone implies that elite women stayed indoors, away from the searing sun. In the beautiful love poetry of the New Kingdom, lovers address each other in terms of apparent equality and express emotions akin to our own ideal of romantic love. Whether this poetry represents the attitudes prevalent in other periods or among nonelite groups remains unknown.

Legal documents show that Egyptian women could own property, inherit from their parents, and will their property to whomever they wished. Marriage, usually monogamous, arose from a couple's decision to establish a household together rather than through legal or religious ceremony. Either party could dissolve the relationship, and the woman retained rights over her dowry in case of divorce. At certain times, queens and queen-mothers played significant behind-the-scenes roles in the politics of the royal court, and priestesses sometimes supervised the cults of female deities. In general, the limited evidence suggests that women in ancient Egypt enjoyed greater respect and more legal rights and social freedom than women in Mesopotamia and other ancient societies.

Belief and Knowledge

Egyptian religion evoked the landscape of the Nile Valley and the vision of cosmic order that this environment fostered. The sun rose every day into a clear and cloudless sky, and the river flooded on schedule every year, ensuring a bounteous harvest. Recurrent cycles and periodic renewal seemed a part of the natural world. Egyptians imagined the sky to be a great ocean surrounding the inhabited world. The sun-god Re traversed its waters in a boat by day, then returned through the Underworld at night, fighting off the attacks of demonic serpents so that he could be born anew each morning. In one especially popular story, Osiris (oh-SIGH-ris), a god who once ruled the land of Egypt, dies at the hand of his jealous brother Seth, who scatters his dismembered remains. Isis, Osiris's sister and wife, finds and reassembles the pieces, while Horus, his son, takes revenge on Seth. Restored to life and installed as king of the Underworld, Osiris represented hope for a new life in a world beyond this one.

The king, represented as Horus and as the son of Re, fit into the pattern of the dead returning to life and the sun-god renewing life. As Egypt's chief priest, he intervened with the gods on behalf of his land and people. When a particular town became the capital

of a ruling dynasty, the chief god of that town gained prominence throughout the land. Thus did Ptah (puh-TAH) of Memphis, Re of Heliopolis (he-lee-OP-uh-lis), and Amon (AH-muhn) of Thebes become gods of all Egypt, serving to unify the country and strengthen the monarchy.

Egyptian rulers zealously built new temples, refurbished old ones, and made lavish gifts to the gods, at the same time overseeing construction of their own tombs. Thus, much of the country's wealth went for religious purposes in the ceaseless effort to win the gods' favor, maintain the continuity of divine kingship, and ensure the renewal of life-giving forces.

Some deities normally appear with animal heads; others always take human form. Few myths about the origins and adventures of the gods have survived, but there must have been a rich oral tradition. Many towns had temples in which locally prominent deities were thought to reside. Such local deities could be viewed as manifestations of the great gods, and gods could merge to form hybrids, such as Amon-Re. Ordinary believers were excluded from cult activities in the inner reaches of the temples, where priests served the daily needs of the deity by attending to his or her statue. Food offered to the image was later distributed to temple staff. As in Mesopotamia, some temples possessed extensive landholdings worked by dependent peasants, and the priests who administered the deity's wealth played an influential role locally and sometimes throughout the land.

During great festivals, the priests paraded a boat-shaped litter carrying the shrouded statue and cult items of the deity around the town. This brought large numbers of people into contact with the deity in an outpouring of devotion and celebration. Little is known about the day-to-day beliefs and practices of the common people, however. At home, family members revered and made small offerings to Bes, the

Primary Source: The Egyptian Book of the Dead's Declaration of Innocence Read the number of potential sins that would likely tarnish a journeying spirit and prevent entrance into the realm of the blessed.

grotesque god of marriage and domestic happiness, to local deities, and to the family's ancestors. They relied on amulets and depictions of demonic figures to ward off evil forces. In later times, Greeks and Romans commented on the Egyptian devotion to magic.

Egyptians believed in the afterlife and prepared extensively for a safe passage and a comfortable existence once they arrived. Hazards abounded on the soul's journey after death. The Egyptian Book of the Dead, present in many excavated tombs, contained rituals and spells to protect the journeying spirit. The weighing of the deceased's heart (believed to be the source of personality, intellect, and emotion) in the presence of the judges of the Underworld presented the ultimate challenge—the one that determined whether the deceased had led a good life and deserved to reach the blessed destination.

The Egyptians' obsession with the afterlife caused concerns about the physical condition of the dead body and led them to perfect techniques of mummification for preserving it. The idea probably derived from the slow decomposition of bodies buried in hot, dry sand on the edge of the desert, an early practice. The elite classes spent the most on mummification. Specialists removed vital organs for preservation and storage in stone jars laid out around the corpse and filled the body cavities with various packing materials. After immersing the cadaver for long periods in dehydrating and preserving chemicals, they wrapped it in linen. They then placed the **mummy** in one or more decorated wooden caskets within a tomb.

Building tombs at the edge of the desert left the lowlands free for farming. Pictures and samples of food and objects from everyday life accompanied the mummy to provide whatever he or she might need in the next life. Much of what is now known about ancient Egyptian life comes from examining utilitarian and luxury household objects found in tombs. Small figurines called shawabtis (shuh-WAB-tees) represented the servants whom the deceased might need or the laborers he might send as substitutes if asked to provide compulsory labor. The elite classes ordered chapels attached to their tombs and left endowments to subsidize the daily attendance of a priest and offerings of foodstuffs to sustain their spirits for eternity.

The form of the tomb also reflected wealth and status. Simple pit graves or small mud-brick chambers sufficed for the common people. Members of the privileged classes built larger tombs and covered the walls with pictures and inscriptions. Kings erected pyramids and other grand edifices, employing trickery to hide the sealed chamber containing the body and treasures, as well as curses and other magical precautions to deter tomb robbers. Rarely did they succeed, however. Archaeologists have seldom discovered an undisturbed royal tomb.

The ancient Egyptians explored many areas of knowledge and developed advantageous technologies. They learned about chemistry through developing the mummification process, which also provided opportunities to learn about human anatomy. Egyptian doctors served in royal courts throughout western Asia because of their relatively advanced medical knowledge and techniques.

The endless cycle of flooding and irrigation spurred the development of mathematics to determine the dimensions of fields and calculate the quantity of agricultural produce owed to the state. Through careful observation of the stars, Egyptians constructed the most accurate calendar in the world. They knew that when the star Sirius appeared on the horizon shortly before sunrise, the Nile flood surge was imminent.

For pyramids, temple complexes, and other monumental building projects, vast quantities of earth had to be moved and the construction site made level. Large stones had to be quarried, dragged on rollers, floated downstream on barges, lifted into place along ramps of packed earth, carved to the exact size needed, and then made smooth. Long underground passageways connected mortuary temples by the river

mummy A body preserved by chemical processes or special natural circumstances, often in the belief that the deceased will need it again in the afterlife. In ancient Egypt the bodies of people who could afford mummification underwent a complex process of removing organs, filling body cavities, dehydrating the corpse, and then wrapping the body with linen bandages and enclosing it in a wooden sarcophagus.

SECTION REVIEW

- In the benign environment of the Nile Valley, a unified Egypt emerged from a collection of small kingdoms.

- The ruler was the divine pharaoh responsible for maintaining cosmic order.

- The state was administered from royal capitals and through a bureaucracy in which scribes kept detailed records in hieroglyphic script.

- Less urban than Mesopotamia, Egypt primarily concerned itself with maintaining the flow of important resources.

- Social division in Egypt was less pronounced than in Mesopotamia: slavery was limited, and women enjoyed greater freedoms than elsewhere in the ancient world.

- Egyptian religion reflected the predictability of the environment and centered on the afterlife, the inspiration for many of Egypt's important technologies.

with tombs near the desert's edge. More practically, several Egyptian kings dredged a canal more than 50 miles (80 kilometers) long to connect the Nile Valley to the Red Sea and expedite the transport of goods.

Besides river barges for transporting building stones, the Nile carried lightweight ships equipped with sails and oars. These sometimes ventured into the Mediterranean and Red Seas. Canals and flooded basins limited the use of carts and sledges, but archaeologists have discovered an 8-mile (13-kilometer) road made of slabs of sandstone and limestone connecting a rock quarry with Faiyum Lake. The oldest known paved road in the world, it dates to the second half of the third millennium B.C.E.

Conclusion

It is surely no accident that the first civilizations to develop high levels of political centralization, urbanization, and technology were situated in river valleys where rainfall was insufficient for reliable agriculture. Mesopotamian and Egyptian rulers channeled significant human resources into the construction and maintenance of canals, dams, and dikes. This effort required the formation of political centers that could organize the necessary labor force.

In both Egypt and Mesopotamia, kingship emerged as the dominant political form. The Egyptian king's divine origins and symbolic association with the forces of renewal made him central to the welfare of the entire country and gave him a religious monopoly superseding the authority of the temples and priests. Egyptian monarchs lavished much of the country's wealth on their tombs, believing that a proper burial would ensure the continuity of kingship and the attendant blessings that it brought to the land and people. Mesopotamian rulers, who were not normally regarded as divine, built new cities, towering walls, splendid palaces, and religious edifices as lasting testaments to their power.

The unpredictable floods in the Tigris-Euphrates Basin were a constant source of alarm for the people of Mesopotamia. In contrast, the predictable, opportune, and gradual Nile floods were eagerly anticipated events in Egypt. The relationship with nature stamped the worldview of both peoples. Mesopotamians tried to appease their harsh deities so as to survive in a dangerous world. Egyptians largely trusted in and nurtured the supernatural powers they believed guaranteed orderliness and prosperity. The Egyptians also believed that, although the journey to the next world was beset with hazards, the righteous spirit that overcame them could look forward to a blessed existence. In contrast, terrifying visions of the afterlife torment Gilgamesh, the Mesopotamian hero king: disembodied spirits stumbling around in the darkness of the Underworld for all eternity, eating dust and clay and slaving for the heartless gods of that realm.

Although the populations of Egypt and Mesopotamia were ethnically diverse, both regions experienced a remarkable degree of cultural continuity. New immigrants assimilated to the dominant language, belief system, and lifestyles of the civilization. Mesopotamian women's apparent loss of freedom and legal privilege in the second millennium B.C.E. may have been related to the higher degree of urbanization and class stratification in this society. In contrast, Egyptian pictorial documents, love poems, and legal records indicate respect and greater equality for women in the valley of the Nile.

CHAPTER REVIEW

Download the MP3 audio file of the
Chapter Review to listen to on the go.

How did plant and animal domestication set the scene for the emergence of civilization? (page 5)

Domestic plants and animals made it possible for sizeable populations to live even in regions that offered little support for foraging groups. As farming became the main source of food, settlement in villages became a normal way of life. In time, this led to complex political structures and the division of labor characteristic of civilized life.

How did Mesopotamian civilization emerge? (page 13)

The first Mesopotamian people to keep written records were the Sumerians. Some Sumerian towns grew into city-states composed of an urban center that ruled surrounding agricultural land. Priests originally dominated these states, but they gave way to kings who assumed religious, administrative, legal, and military responsibilities. Sharp social divisions were reflected in the class-based penalties of the Law Code of Hammurabi. Mesopotamian gods embodied the uncertain forces of the environment. The people strove to appease them through state-organized rites focused on temples maintained by priests. Mesopotamian cultures pioneered cuneiform writing, canal irrigation, bronze casting, and monumental architecture.

What role did the environment and religion play in Egyptian civilization? (page 23)

Protected by deserts and coastal marshes and nurtured by the predictable flooding of the Nile River, Egyptian civilization was relatively self-sufficient and secure. As the Sahara Desert dried and the population in the Nile Valley increased, political organization became more complex, eventually unifying into a single kingdom under a divine king, the pharaoh. Less urban and socially stratified than Mesopotamian society, Egypt relied on peasant farmers with few slaves and a comparatively free female population. Egyptian religion embodied the orderly and benign qualities of the Nile and involved a complex vision of the afterlife. Much wealth went for religious purposes: preparing for the afterlife and glorifying the pharaoh. To this end the Egyptians constructed monumental tombs and temples and applied their knowledge of chemistry and anatomy to mummification.

Key Terms

civilization (p. 5)

culture (p. 6)

history (p. 6)

Stone Age (p. 6)

Paleolithic (p. 6)

Neolithic (p. 6)

foragers (p. 6)

Agricultural Revolutions (p. 8)

Holocene (p. 10)

megalith (p. 11)

Babylon (p. 13)

Sumerians (p. 14)

Semitic (p. 14)

city-state (p. 15)

Hammurabi (p. 17)

scribe (p. 18)

ziggurat (p. 20)

amulet (p. 20)

cuneiform (p. 20)

pharaoh (p. 25)

ma'at (p. 25)

pyramid (p. 25)

Memphis (p. 26)

Thebes (p. 26)

hieroglyphics (p. 27)

papyrus (p. 27)

mummy (p. 30)

Web Resources

Pronunciation Guide

Interactive Maps

- MAP 1.1 River-Valley Civilizations, 3500–1500 B.C.E.
- MAP 1.2 Ancient Egypt

Primary Sources

- The Epic of Gilgamesh
- The State Regulates Health Care: Hammurabi's Code and Surgeons
- Hymn for the Nile
- Advice to Ambitious Young Egyptians: Rise Above the Masses, Become a Scribe!
- The Egyptian Book of the Dead's Declaration of Innocence

Answers to the History in Focus Questions

See photos on page 24, "Model of Egyptian River Boat, ca. 1985 B.C.E." and page 26 "Pyramids of Menkaure, Khafre, and Khufu at Giza, ca. 2500 B.C.E."

Visit the CourseMate website at www.cengagebrain.com for additional study tools and review materials for this chapter.

New Civilizations in the Eastern Hemisphere

© Cengage Learning

CHAPTER PREVIEW

Early China, 2000–221 B.C.E.
How did early Chinese rulers use religion to justify and strengthen their power?

Nubia, 3100 B.C.E.–350 C.E.
How did the technological and cultural influences of Egypt affect the formation of Nubia?

The Origins of Indo-European Languages, 4500–1800 B.C.E.
How did most Europeans come to speak Indo-European languages?

Celtic Europe, 1000–50 B.C.E.
What is known about the Celts, and how did their religious beliefs help to shape their society?

Conclusion

DIVERSITY AND DOMINANCE: Human Nature and Good Government in the *Analects* of Confucius and the Legalist Writings of Han Fei

Visit the CourseMate website at **www.cengagebrain.com** for additional study tools and review materials for this chapter.

Around 2200 B.C.E. an Egyptian official named Harkhuf (HAHR-koof), who lived at Aswan (AS-wahn) on the southern boundary of Egypt, set out on his fourth trek to a place called Yam, far to the south in the land that later came to be called Nubia. He brought gifts from the Egyptian pharaoh for the ruler of Yam, and he returned home with three hundred donkeyloads of incense, ebony, ivory, and other exotic products. Despite the diplomatic fiction of exchanging gifts, we should probably consider Harkhuf a trader; and the prize of this trip was so special that the eight-year-old boy pharaoh Pepi II could not contain his excitement. He wrote:

> Come north to the residence at once! Hurry and bring with you this pygmy whom you brought from the land of the horizon-dwellers live, hale, and healthy, for the dances of the god, to gladden the heart, to delight the heart of king Neferkare [Pepi] who lives forever! When he goes down with you into the ship, get worthy men to be around him on deck, lest he fall into the water! When he lies down at night, get worthy men to lie around him in his tent. Inspect ten times at night! My majesty desires to see this pygmy more than the gifts of the mine-land and of Punt![1]

Some scholars identify Yam with Kerma, later the capital of the kingdom of Nubia, on the upper Nile in modern Sudan. For Egyptians, Nubia was a wild and dangerous place—though pygmies came from farther south. But it was developing a more complex political organization that fostered trade with Egypt and tropical regions farther south.

The civilizations we saw in Chapter 1 (as well as the first civilizations in South Asia, East Asia, and the Americas that we will see in later chapters) originated in river valleys surrounded by dry lands where farming was difficult or impossible without irrigation. Peasants dissatisfied with their situation had nowhere else to go and were therefore forced to pay rent, taxes, and tithes and provide free labor when the leaders of the society demanded it.

On rain-watered lands, however—that is, in areas that received at least 8 inches (20 centimeters) of rain a year during the growing season—the situation was very different. If Neolithic farmers did not form complex societies with cities and governments until much later, it was not because they did not think to, but because, with ample land available, those dissatisfied with their fields or their neighbors could find new arable land elsewhere. It was therefore difficult for some members of a community to demand labor or a share of the crops of others in exchange for political protection or religious services. Not until the population grew enough to occupy most of the arable land could the most powerful members of society turn their weaker neighbors into civilized peasants. Only then did civilization spread to areas in contact with the original civilizations, where a growing population began to fully occupy the arable land.

Some of the complex societies examined in this chapter developed in river valleys; others did not. Whereas the Egyptian and Mesopotamian civilizations discussed in the last chapter were originally largely self-sufficient, the civilizations discussed in this chapter and the next were partially shaped by networks of long-distance trade.

In the second millennium B.C.E. a civilization based on irrigation agriculture arose along the valley of the Yellow River and its tributaries in northern China. In the same epoch, in Nubia (southern Egypt and northern Sudan), the first complex society in tropical Africa continued to develop from the roots observed earlier by Harkhuf. Earlier, the first millennium B.C.E. witnessed the spread of Celtic peoples across much of continental Europe. These societies had no contact with one another and represent a variety of responses to environmental and historical circumstances. However, as we shall see, they have certain features in common and collectively point to a distinct stage in the development of human societies.

Early China, 2000–221 B.C.E.

How did early Chinese rulers use religion to justify and strengthen their power?

On the eastern edge of the great Eurasian landmass, Neolithic cultures developed as early as 8000 B.C.E., and a more complex civilization evolved in the second millennium B.C.E. Under the Shang and Zhou monarchs, many of the institutions and values of classical Chinese civilization emerged and spread south and west. As elsewhere, the rise of cities, specialization of labor, bureaucratic government, writing, and other advanced technologies depended on intensive agriculture along a great river system—the Yellow River (Huang He [hwong HUH]) and its tributaries. Although archaeological finds indicate some movement of goods and ideas from western to eastern Asia, developments in China were largely independent of the complex societies in the Middle East and the Indus Valley.

Geography and Resources

With mountains and deserts to the west and north making overland travel difficult and slow (see Map 2.1), the great river systems of eastern China—the Yellow and the Yangzi (yang-zuh) Rivers and their tributaries—provide the main axes of east-west movement. In the eastern river valleys dense populations practiced intensive agriculture; on the steppe lands of Mongolia, the deserts and oases of Xinjiang (shin-jyahng), and the high plateau of Tibet, sparser populations lived largely

Map 2.1   China in the Shang and Zhou Periods, 1750–221 B.C.E. The Shang dynasty arose in the second millennium B.C.E. in the floodplain of the Yellow River. Whereas southern China benefits from the monsoon rains, northern China depends on irrigation. As population increased, the Han Chinese migrated from their eastern homeland to other parts of China, carrying with them their technologies and cultural practices. Other ethnic groups predominated in more outlying regions, and the nomadic peoples of the northwest constantly challenged Chinese authority.   © Cengage Learning

Interactive Map

Chronology

	China	Nubia	Celtic Europe
	8000–2000 B.C.E. Neolithic cultures	**4500 B.C.E.** Early agriculture in Nubia	
2500 B.C.E.			
		2200 B.C.E. Harkhuf's expeditions to Yam	
2000 B.C.E.	**2000 B.C.E.** Bronze metallurgy **1750–1027 B.C.E.** Shang dynasty	**1750 B.C.E.** Rise of kingdom of Kush based on Kerma	
1500 B.C.E		**1500 B.C.E.** Egyptian conquest of Nubia	
1000 B.C.E	**1027–221 B.C.E.** Zhou dynasty	**1000 B.C.E.** Decline of Egyptian control in Nubia **750 B.C.E.** Rise of kingdom based on Napata **712–660 B.C.E.** Nubian kings rule Egypt	**1000 B.C.E.** Origin of Celtic culture in central Europe
500 B.C.E.	**551–479 B.C.E.** Confucius		**500 B.C.E.** Celtic elites trade for Mediterranean goods **500–300 B.C.E.** Migrations across Europe
		300 B.C.E.–350 C.E. Kingdom of Meroë	

by herding. Within the eastern agricultural zone, the north and the south have strikingly different environments. The monsoons that affect South and Southeast Asia also drench southern China with heavy rainfall in the summer, the most beneficial time for agriculture. Rainfall is more erratic and sparse in northern China. As in Mesopotamia, where civilizations developed in relatively unfriendly environments, China's early history unfolded in the demanding environment of the northern plains. By the third century C.E., however, the gradual flow of population toward the warmer southern lands caused the political and intellectual center to move south.

Since prehistoric times, winds blowing from Central Asia had deposited a yellowish-brown dust called **loess** (less) on the North China Plain, creating an abundance of potentially productive land (this dust suspended in the water gives the Yellow River its distinctive hue and name). The thick soil was extremely fertile and soft enough to be worked with wooden digging sticks. However, in some areas forests had to be cleared; more importantly, recurrent floods on the Yellow River necessitated earthen dikes and overflow channels. In this landscape, agriculture demanded the coordinated efforts of large groups of people. To cope with the periodic droughts, catch basins (reservoirs) were dug to store river water and rainfall. As the population grew, people built retaining walls to partition the hillsides into tiers of flat arable terraces.

loess A fine, light silt deposited by wind and water. It constitutes the fertile soil of the Yellow River Valley in northern China. Because loess soil is not compacted, it can be worked with a simple digging stick, but it leaves the region vulnerable to devastating floods.

The staple crops were millet, a grain indigenous to China, and wheat, originally from the Middle East. Rice required a warmer climate and prospered in the south. The cultivation of rice in the Yangzi River Valley and the south required a great outlay of labor. Rice paddies—the fields where rice is grown—must be absolutely flat and surrounded by irrigation channels to bring or drain water according to precise schedules. Seedlings sprout in a nursery and are transplanted one by one to the paddy, which is then flooded. Flooding eliminates weeds and rival plants and supports microscopic organisms that keep the soil fertile. When the crop is ripe, the paddy is drained, the rice stalks are harvested with a sickle, and the edible kernels are separated out. The reward for this effort is a harvest that can feed more people per cultivated acre than any other grain, which explains why the south eventually became more populous than the north.

Archaeological evidence shows that the Neolithic populations grew millet, raised pigs and chickens, and used stone tools. They made pottery on a wheel and fired it in high-temperature kilns. They also pioneered silk production, first raising silkworms on mulberry trees, then unraveling their cocoon filament to spin into thread. Lacking stone, they built walls by hammering soil inside temporary wooden frames until it became hard as cement. By 2000 B.C.E. they had begun casting bronze (roughly a thousand years after the Middle East Bronze Age).

Legends say that the ancient dynasty of the Xia ruled the core region of the Yellow River Valley. Some archaeologists identify the Xia with the Neolithic Longshan cultural complex in the centuries before and after 2000 B.C.E. However, history proper begins with the rise of the Shang clans, which coincides with the earliest Chinese written records.

The Shang Period, 1750–1027 B.C.E.

The **Shang** (shahng) originated in the part of the Yellow River Valley that lies in the present-day province of Henan (heh-nahn). After 1750 B.C.E. they extended their control north into Mongolia, west as far as Gansu (gahn-soo), and south to the Yangzi River Valley. The warrior aristocracy that dominated Shang society reveled in warfare, hunting (for recreation and to fine-tune battle skills), exchanging gifts, and feasting. The king ruled the core area of the Shang state directly. Aristocrats served as generals, ambassadors, and supervisors of public projects. Other members of the royal family and high-ranking nobility governed outlying provinces. The most distant regions were governed by native rulers who swore allegiance to the Shang king.

The king was often on the road, traveling to the courts of his subordinates to reinforce their loyalty. Frequent military campaigns, often against the nomadic peoples who occupied the steppe and desert regions to the north and west, occupied the warrior elite and yielded considerable plunder. Prisoners of war taken in these campaigns served as slaves in the Shang capital.

The Shang kingdom had several capitals. The last and most important was near modern Anyang (ahn-yahng) (see Map 2.1). Shang cities were centers of political control and religion. Surrounded by massive walls of pounded earth, they contained palaces, administrative buildings, storehouses, royal tombs, shrines of gods and ancestors, and housing for aristocrats. Commoners lived in agricultural villages outside these centers. Urban street grids aligned with the north star and gates opening to the cardinal directions demonstrate an ongoing Chinese concern with feng shui (fung shway), the spatial orientation of buildings according to a sense of cosmic order.

Writing was the key to effective administration. Pictograms (pictures representing objects and concepts) and phonetic symbols representing the sounds of syllables were combined to form a complex system of hundreds of signs. Only a small educated elite had the time to master this system. Despite substantial changes through the ages, the fundamental principles of the Chinese system still endure. As a result, people speaking languages that sound quite different, such as Mandarin and Cantonese, can read and understand the same text.

Shang ideology glorified the king as the intermediary between the people and Heaven. Shang

---

Shang The dominant people in the earliest Chinese dynasty for which we have written records (ca. 1750–1027 B.C.E.). Ancestor worship, divination by means of oracle bones, and the use of bronze vessels for ritual purposes were major elements of Shang culture.

Women Beating Chimes
This scene, from a bronze vessel of the
Zhou era, illustrates the important role of music in
festivals, religious rituals, and court ceremonials. During the politically fragmented later (Eastern) Zhou era, many small
states marked their independence by having their own musical scales and distinctive arrangements of orchestral instruments.   Drawn from a bronze vessel in the Sichuan Museum, China

religion also revered and made sacrifices to male ancestors, who were believed to be intensely interested in the fortunes of their descendants. Burials of kings also entailed sacrifices, not only of animals but also of humans, including noble officials of the court, women, servants, soldiers, and prisoners of war. Before taking any action, the Shang rulers used divination to determine the will of Heaven.

Bronze weapons and ritual vessels symbolized authority and nobility. Shang tombs contain many such objects. The relatively modest tomb of one queen yielded 450 bronze articles (ritual vessels, bells, weapons, and mirrors)—remarkable because copper and tin, the principal ingredients of bronze, were not plentiful in northern China. (Also found in the same tomb were numerous objects of jade, bone, ivory, and stone, seven thousand cowrie shells, sixteen sacrificed men, women, and children, and six dogs!)

Finding and mining deposits of copper and tin, transporting the refined metal to the capital, and crafting these beautifully wrought weapons and vessels constituted a major Shang enterprise. Bronzesmiths working in foundries outside the main cities also made chariot fittings and musical instruments. Stylized depictions of real and imaginary animals were a favorite decorative theme.

Far-reaching networks of trade brought jade, ivory, and mother of pearl (a hard, shiny substance from the interior of mollusk shells) used for jewelry, carved figurines, and decorative inlays to the Shang. Some evidence suggests that Shang China may have exchanged goods and ideas with distant Mesopotamia. The horse-drawn chariot, which the Shang adopted from the nomads of the northwest, became a formidable instrument of war.

The Zhou Period, 1027–221 B.C.E.

Shang domination of central and northern China lasted more than six centuries. In the eleventh century B.C.E. the last Shang king was defeated by Wu, the ruler of **Zhou** (joe), a dependent state in the Wei (way) River Valley. The Zhou line of kings (ca. 1027–221 B.C.E.) was the longest-lasting and most revered of all dynasties in Chinese history. Just as the Semitic peoples in Mesopotamia had adopted and adapted the Sumerian legacy (see Chapter 1), the Zhou preserved the essentials of Shang culture and added new elements of ideology and technology.

To justify their seizure of power to the restive remnants of the Shang clans, the early Zhou monarchs styled themselves "Son of Heaven." Their rule

Zhou The people and dynasty that took over the dominant position in north China from the Shang and created the concept of the Mandate of Heaven to justify their rule. The Zhou era, particularly the vigorous early period (1027–771 B.C.E.), was remembered in Chinese tradition as a time of prosperity and benevolent rule. In the later Zhou period (771–221 B.C.E.), centralized control broke down, and warfare among many small states became frequent.

Warring States Period Bronze Figurine The figurine of a youth, made of bronze, was produced in the Warring States Period, but the jade birds perched atop the staffs were originally carved in the Shang era. The youth has braided hair and is wearing boots and an elaborately decorated robe. The chain may indicate that these were live birds rather than images. Museum of Fine Arts, Boston, Maria Antoinette Evans Fund. Photograph © 2008 Museum of Fine Arts, Boston 31.976

was called the **Mandate of Heaven**. According to the new theory advanced by their propagandists, the ruler had been chosen by the supreme deity, known as "Heaven," and would retain his backing as long as he served as a wise, principled, and energetic guardian of his people. Prosperity and stability proved divine favor, but royal misbehavior, a fault attributed to the last Shang ruler, could forfeit Heaven's mandate. Corruption, violence, and insurrection were signs of divine displeasure.

The Zhou kings continued some of the Shang rituals, but there was a marked decline in the practice of divination and in extravagant sacrifices and burials. The priestly power of the ruling class, the only ones who had been able to make contact with the spirits of ancestors during the Shang period, faded away. The resulting separation of religion and government made way for the development of important philosophical and mystical systems. The bronze vessels that had been sacred implements in the Shang period now became family treasures.

The early period of Zhou rule, the eleventh through ninth centuries B.C.E., is sometimes called the Western Zhou era because of the location of the capitals in the western part of the kingdom. These centuries saw the development of a sophisticated administrative apparatus. The Zhou built a series of capital cities with pounded-earth foundations and walls. The major buildings all faced south, in keeping with the feng shui principles of harmonious relationship with the terrain, the forces of wind, water, and sunlight, and the invisible energy perceived to be flowing through the natural world. All government officials, including the king, were supposed to be models of morality, fairness, and concern for the welfare of the people.

Like the Shang, the Zhou regime was decentralized. Members and allies of the royal family ruled more than a hundred largely autonomous territories. Elaborate court ceremonials, embellished by music and dance, impressed on observers the glory of Zhou rule and reinforced the bonds of obligation between rulers and ruled.

Around 800 B.C.E. Zhou power began to wane. Ambitious local rulers operated ever more independently and waged war on one another, while nomadic peoples attacked the northwest frontiers (see Map 2.1). In 771 B.C.E. members of the Zhou lineage relocated to a new, more secure, eastern capital near Luoyang (LWOE-yahng), initiating the five-hundred-year Eastern Zhou era. There they continued to hold the royal title and receive at least nominal homage from local rulers, the real power brokers of the age. Historians conventionally divide this period of political fragmentation, shifting centers of power, and fierce competition among numerous small states into the "Spring and Autumn Period," from 771 to 481 B.C.E., after a collection of chronicles that give annual entries for those

Mandate of Heaven Chinese religious and political ideology developed by the Zhou, according to which it was the prerogative of Heaven, the chief deity, to grant power to the ruler of China and to take away that power if the ruler failed to conduct himself justly and in the best interests of his subjects.

two seasons, and the "Warring States Period," from 480 to the unification of China in 221 B.C.E.

Numerous competing kingdoms meant numerous capital cities, some of which became quite large. To the north, long walls of pounded earth were constructed, the ancestors of the Great Wall of China, to protect the kingdoms from each other and from nomads. Chinese armies adopted the nomad practice of putting fighters on horseback. The northwest nomads were probably also the source of the iron-working skills that led to iron replacing bronze as the primary metal for tools and weapons around 600 B.C.E. Bureaucracies in many states expanded their functions, composing law codes, collecting taxes directly, imposing monetary standards, and managing large-scale public works projects. Eventually this activity led to a philosophy called **Legalism**, which argued that maintaining the wealth and power of the state justified authoritarian political control. Legalists maintained that human nature is essentially wicked and that people behave properly only if compelled by strict laws and harsh punishments. They believed that every aspect of human society ought to be controlled and personal freedom sacrificed for the good of the state.

Confucianism, Daoism, and Chinese Society

Bureaucratic government superseded aristocratic rule in some of the major Zhou states. To maintain their influence, aristocrats sought a new role as advisers to the rulers. Kongzi (551–479 B.C.E.)—known in the West by the Latin form of his name, **Confucius**—lived through the political flux and social change of this anxious time. Coming from one of the smaller states, he had not been particularly successful in obtaining administrative posts. However, his doctrine of duty and public service, initially aimed at fellow aristocrats, was to become a central influence in Chinese thought.

Many elements in Confucius's teaching had roots in earlier Chinese belief, including folk religion and the rites of the Zhou royal family, such as the veneration of ancestors and elders and worship of the deity Heaven. Confucius drew a parallel between the family and the state. Just as the family is a hierarchy, with the father at its top, sons next, then wives and daughters in order of age, so too the state is a hierarchy, with the ruler at the top, the public officials as the sons, and the common people as the women.

Confucius took a traditional term for the feelings between family members (*ren*) and expanded it into a universal ideal of benevolence toward all humanity, which he believed was the foundation of moral government. Government exists, he said, to serve the people, and the administrator or ruler gains respect and authority by displaying fairness and integrity. Confucian teachings emphasized benevolence, avoidance of violence, justice, rationalism, loyalty, and dignity.

Though Confucius had little influence in his own time, his later follower Mencius (Mengzi, 371–289 B.C.E.), who opposed despotism and argued against the authoritarian ideology of the Legalists, made the master's teachings much better known (see Diversity and Dominance: Human Nature and Good Government in the *Analects* of Confucius and the Legalist Writings of Han Fei). Confucianism eventually became the dominant political philosophy and the core of the educational system for government officials (see Chapter 6).

The Warring States Period also saw the rise of the school of thought known as **Daoism** (DOW-izm). According to tradition, Laozi (low-zuh), the originator of Daoism (believed to have lived in the sixth century B.C.E., though some scholars doubt his existence), sought to stop the warfare of the age by urging humanity to follow the *Dao*, or "path." Daoists

---

Legalism In China, a political philosophy that emphasized the unruliness of human nature and justified state coercion and control. The ruling class invoked it to validate the authoritarian nature of the regime and its profligate expenditure of subjects' lives and labor. It was later superseded by a more benevolent Confucian doctrine of governmental moderation.

Confucius Western name for the Chinese philosopher Kongzi (551–479 B.C.E.). His doctrine of duty and public service had a great influence on subsequent Chinese thought and served as a code of conduct for government officials.

Daoism Chinese school of thought, originating in the Warring States Period with Laozi (604–531 B.C.E.). Daoism offered an alternative to the Confucian emphasis on hierarchy and duty. Daoists believe that the world is always changing and is devoid of absolute morality or meaning. They accept the world as they find it, avoid futile struggles, and deviate as little as possible from the Dao, or "path" of nature.

Diversity & Dominance

Human Nature and Good Government
in the *Analects* of Confucius and the Legalist Writings of Han Fei

Although monarchy (the rule of one man) was the standard form of government in ancient China and was rarely challenged, political theorists and philosophers thought a great deal about the qualities of the ideal ruler, his relationship to his subjects, and the means by which he controlled them. These considerations about how to govern people were inevitably molded by fundamental assumptions about the nature of human beings. In the Warring States Period, as the major states struggled desperately with one another for survival and expansion, such discussions took on a special urgency, and the Confucians and Legalists came to represent two powerful, and largely contradictory, points of view.

The Analects *are a collection of sayings of Confucius, probably compiled and written down several generations after he lived, though some elements may have been added even later. They cover a wide range of matters, including ethics, government, education, music, and rituals. Taken as a whole, they are a guide to living an honorable, virtuous, useful, and satisfying life. While subject to reinterpretation according to the circumstances of the times, Confucian principles have had a great influence on Chinese values and behavior ever since.*

Han Fei (280–233 B.C.E.), who was, ironically, at one time the student of a Confucian teacher, became a Legalist writer and political adviser to the ruler of the ambitious state of Qin. Eventually he lost out in a power struggle at court and was forced to kill himself.

The following selections illuminate the profound disagreements between Confucians and Legalists over the essential nature of human beings and how the ruler should conduct himself in order to most effectively govern his subjects and protect his kingdom.

Confucius

4:5 Confucius said: "Riches and honors are what all men desire. But if they cannot be attained in accordance with the *dao* [the way] they should not be kept. Poverty and low status are what all men hate. But if they cannot be avoided while staying in accordance with the *dao*, you should not avoid them. If a Superior Man departs from *ren* [humaneness], how can he be worthy of that name? A Superior Man never leaves *ren* for even the time of a single meal. In moments of haste he acts according to it. In times of difficulty or confusion he acts according to it."

16:8 Confucius said: "The Superior Man stands in awe of three things: (1) He is in awe of the decree of Heaven. (2) He is in awe of great men. (3) He is in awe of the words of the sages. The inferior man does not know the decree of Heaven; takes great men lightly and laughs at the words of the sages."

4:14 Confucius said: "I don't worry about not having a good position; I worry about the means I use to gain position. I don't worry about being unknown; I seek to be known in the right way."

7:15 Confucius said: "I can live with coarse rice to eat, water for drink and my arm as a pillow and still be happy. Wealth and honors that one possesses in the midst of injustice are like floating clouds."

13:6 Confucius said: "When you have gotten your own life straightened out, things will go well without your giving orders. But if your own life isn't straightened out, even if you give orders, no one will follow them."

12:2 Zhonggong asked about the meaning of ren. The Master said: "Go out of your home as if you were receiving an important guest. Employ the people as if you were assisting at a great ceremony. What you don't want done to yourself, don't do to others. Live in your town without stirring up resentments, and live in your household without stirring up resentments."

1:5 Confucius said: "If you would govern a state of a thousand chariots (a small-to-middle-size state), you must pay strict attention to business, be true to your word, be economical in expenditure and love the people. You should use them according to the seasons."

2:3 Confucius said: "If you govern the people legalistically and control them by punishment, they will avoid crime, but have no personal sense of shame. If you govern them by means of virtue and control them with propriety, they will gain their own sense of shame, and thus correct themselves."

12:7 Zigong asked about government. The Master said, "Enough food, enough weapons and the confidence of the people." Zigong said, "Suppose you had no alternative but to give up one of these three, which one would be let go of first?" The Master said, "Weapons." Zigong said, "What if you had to give up one of the remaining two, which one would it be?" The Master said, "Food. From ancient times, death has come to all men, but a people without confidence in its rulers will not stand."

12:19 Ji Kang Zi asked Confucius about government saying: "Suppose I were to kill the unjust, in order to advance the just. Would that be all right?"

Confucius replied: "In doing government, what is the need of killing? If you desire good, the people will be good. The nature of the Superior Man is like the wind, the nature of the inferior man is like the grass. When the wind blows over the grass, it always bends."

2:19 The Duke of Ai asked: "How can I make the people follow me?" Confucius replied: "Advance the upright and set aside the crooked, and the people will follow you. Advance the crooked and set aside the upright, and the people will not follow you."

2:20 Ji Kang Zi asked: "How can I make the people reverent and loyal, so they will work positively for me?" Confucius said, "Approach them with dignity, and they will be reverent. Be filial and compassionate and they will be loyal. Promote the able and teach the incompetent, and they will work positively for you."

Han Fei

Past and present have different customs; new and old adopt different measures. To try to use the ways of a generous and lenient government to rule the people of a critical age is like trying to drive a runaway horse without using reins or whips. This is the misfortune that ignorance invites. . . .

Humaneness [ren] may make one shed tears and be reluctant to apply penalties, but law makes it clear that such penalties must be applied. The ancient kings allowed law to be supreme and did not give in to their tearful longings. Hence it is obvious that humaneness cannot be used to achieve order in the state. . . .

The best rewards are those that are generous and predictable, so that the people may profit by them. The best penalties are those that are severe and inescapable, so that the people will fear them. The best laws are those that are uniform and inflexible, so that the people can understand them. . . .

Hardly ten men of true integrity and good faith can be found today, and yet the offices of the state number in the hundreds. . . . Therefore the way of the enlightened ruler is to unify the laws instead of seeking for wise men, to lay down firm policies instead of longing for men of good faith. . . .

When a sage rules the state, he does not depend on people's doing good of themselves; he sees to it that they are not allowed to do what is bad. If he depends on people's doing good of themselves, then within his borders he can count fewer than ten instances of success. But if he sees to it that they are not allowed to do what is bad, then the whole state can be brought to a uniform level of order. Those who rule must employ measures that will be effective with the majority and discard those that will be effective with only a few. Therefore they devote themselves not to virtue but to law. . . .

When the Confucians of the present time counsel rulers, they do not praise those measures that will bring order today, but talk only of the achievements of the men who brought order in the past. . . . No ruler with proper standards will tolerate them. Therefore the enlightened ruler works with facts and discards useless theories. He does not talk about deeds of humaneness and rightness, and he does not listen to the words of scholars. . . .

Nowadays, those who do not understand how to govern invariably say, "You must win the hearts of the people!" . . . The reason you cannot rely on the wisdom of the people is that they have the minds of little children. If the child's head is not shaved, its sores will spread; and if its boil is not lanced, it will become sicker than ever . . . for it does not understand that the little pain it suffers now will bring great benefit later. . . .

Now, the ruler presses the people to till the land and open up new pastures so as to increase their means of livelihood, and yet they consider him harsh; he draws up a penal code and makes the punishments more severe in order to put a stop to evil, and yet the people consider him stern. . . . He makes certain that everyone within his borders understands warfare and sees to it that there are no private exemptions from military service; he unites the strength of the state and fights fiercely in order to take its enemies captive, and yet the people consider him violent. . . . [These] types of undertaking all ensure order and safety to the state, and yet the people do not have sense enough to rejoice in them.

QUESTIONS FOR ANALYSIS

1. What do Confucius and Han Fei believe about the nature of human beings? Are they intrinsically good and well-behaved, or bad and prone to misbehave?
2. What are the qualities of an ideal ruler for Confucius and Han Fei?
3. By what means can the ruler influence his subjects in Confucian thought? How should the ruler compel obedience in the people in Legalist thought?
4. What do Confucians and Legalists think about the value of the past as a model for the present?
5. Why might Confucius's passionate concern for ethical behavior on the part of officials and rulers arise at a time when the size and power of governments were growing?

Source: Confucius excerpts from *The Analects of Confucius*, translated by A. Charles Muller at http://www.acmuller.net/con-dao/analects.html. Copyright © Charles Muller 2010. Reprinted by permission of the author. Han Fei selections from *Sources of Chinese Tradition*, vol. 1, 2nd ed., by Wm. Theodore de Bary and Irene Bloom. Copyright © 2000 Columbia University Press. Reprinted with permission of the publisher.

accepted the world as they found it, adhering to the "path" of nature and avoiding useless struggles. They avoided violence if at all possible and took the minimal action necessary for a task; rather than fight the current of a stream, a wise man allows the onrushing waters to pass around him. This passivity arose from the Daoist's sense that the world was always changing and lacked any absolute morality or meaning. In the end, Daoists believed, all that matters is the individual's fundamental understanding of the "path."

The original Daoist philosophy was greatly expanded in subsequent centuries to incorporate popular beliefs, magic, and mysticism. Daoism represented an important stream of thought throughout Chinese history. By idealizing individuals who find their own "path" to right conduct, it offered an alternative to the Confucian emphasis on hierarchy and duty and to the Legalists' approval of force.

Social organization also changed in this period. The kinship structures of the Shang and early Zhou periods, based on the clan (a relatively large group of related families), gave way to the three-generation family of grandparents, parents, and children as the fundamental social unit. A related development was the emergence of the concept of private property. Land was considered to belong to the men of the family and was divided equally among the sons when the father died.

Little is known about the conditions of life for women in early China. Some scholars believe that women may have acted as shamans, entering into trances to communicate with supernatural forces, making requests on behalf of their communities, and receiving predictions of the future. By the time written records begin to illuminate our knowledge of women's experiences, however, they show women in a subordinate position in the strongly patriarchal family.

Confucian thought codified this male-female hierarchy. Only men could conduct rituals and make offerings to the ancestors, though women could help

SECTION REVIEW

- Neolithic farming communities grew in the Yellow and Yangzi River Valleys and adapted to the very different environments of each.

- The Shang dynasty emerged in the Yellow River Valley and grew to encompass parts of the Yangzi River Valley.

- Shang technologies included pictographic writing, bronze work, and artifacts related to royal divination, male ancestor worship, and the power of the warrior aristocracy.

- The first king of the Zhou dynasty defeated the Shang, claiming the Mandate of Heaven as justification for this victory.

- Like the Shang, the Zhou state was decentralized, and it devolved into a collection of independent and hostile states.

- Legalism became the major political philosophy, but Confucianism and Daoism also emerged and established most of the basic principles of Chinese culture.

maintain the household's ancestral shrines. Fathers held authority over the women and children, arranged marriages for their offspring, and could sell the labor of family members. A man was limited to one wife but was permitted additional sexual partners, who had the lower status of concubines. The elite classes used marriage to create political alliances, and it was common for the groom's family to offer a substantial "bride-gift," a proof of the wealth and standing of his family, to the family of the prospective bride. A man whose wife died had a duty to remarry in order to produce male heirs to keep alive the cult of the ancestors.

These differences in male and female activities were explained by the concept of **yin** and **yang**, the complementary nature of female and male roles in the natural order. The male principle (yang) was equated with the sun—active, bright, and shining; the female principle (yin) corresponded to the moon—passive, shaded, and reflective. Female gentleness balanced male toughness, female endurance and need for completion balanced male action and initiative, and

 Primary Source: The Book of Documents Read along as a new king receives advice and warnings about the careful path he must tread to keep his kingdom safe from ruin.

yin/yang In Chinese belief, complementary factors that help to maintain the equilibrium of the world. Yin is associated with feminine, dark, and passive qualities; yang with masculine, light, and active qualities.

female supportiveness balanced male leadership. In its earliest form, the theory considered yin and yang as equal and alternately dominant, like night and day, creating balance in the world. However, as a result of the changing role of women in the Zhou period and the pervasive influence of Confucian ideology, the male principle came to be seen as superior to the female.

Nubia, 3100 B.C.E.–350 C.E.

How did the technological and cultural influences of Egypt affect the formation of Nubia?

Since the first century the name *Nubia* has been applied to a 1,000-mile (1,600-kilometer) stretch of the Nile Valley lying between Aswan and Khartoum (kahr-TOOM) and straddling the southern part of the modern nation of Egypt and the northern part of Sudan (see Map 1.2). The ancient Egyptians called it Tasety, meaning "Land of the Bow," after the favorite weapon of its warriors. Nubia is the only trade corridor and continuously inhabited stretch of territory connecting sub-Saharan Africa (the lands south of the Sahara Desert) with North Africa. It was richly endowed with natural resources such as gold, copper, and semiprecious stones.

Egypt's quest for Nubian gold helps explain the early rise of a civilization with a complex political organization, social stratification, metallurgy, monumental building, and writing. However, most scholars today have moved away from the traditional view that Nubian civilization derived from Egypt and emphasize the mutually beneficial interactions between the two lands and the growing evidence that Nubian culture drew on influences from sub-Saharan Africa.

Early Cultures and Egyptian Domination, 2300–100 B.C.E

The central geographical feature of Nubia, as of Egypt, is the Nile River. The Nubian segment of the Nile River flows through a landscape of rocky desert, grassland, and fertile plain. In a torrid climate with minimal rainfall, agriculture depended on river irrigation. Six cataracts, barriers formed by large boulders and rapids, obstructed boat traffic. Boats operating between the cataracts and caravans skirting the river made travel possible.

In the fifth millennium B.C.E. bands of people in northern Nubia made the transition from seminomadic hunting and gathering to a settled life based on grain agriculture and cattle herding. The majority of the population came to live in agricultural villages alongside the river. Even before 3000 B.C.E. Egyptian craftsmen were working in ivory and ebony that must have come from tropical Africa by way of Nubia.

As we saw with the journey of Harkhuf at the beginning of this chapter, Nubia enters the Egyptian historical record around 2200 B.C.E. in accounts of trade missions. At that time Aswan, just north of the First Cataract, was the southern limit of Egyptian control. Egyptian noblemen stationed there led donkey caravans south in search of gold, incense, ebony, ivory, slaves, and exotic animals. This was dangerous work, requiring delicate negotiations with local Nubian chiefs to secure protection, but it brought substantial rewards to those who succeeded.

During the Middle Kingdom (ca. 2040–1640 B.C.E.), Egypt adopted a more aggressive stance toward Nubia. Egyptian rulers sought to control the gold mines in the desert east of the Nile and to cut out the Nubian middlemen who drove up the cost of luxury goods from the tropics. A string of mud-brick forts on islands and riverbanks south of the Second Cataract were built to protect Egypt's southern frontier and regulate the flow of commerce. These Egyptian garrisons were sufficiently intimidating that relations with the indigenous population of northern Nubia, while intermittent, were generally peaceful.

Farther south, where the Nile makes a great U-shaped turn in a fertile plain (see Map 1.2), a more complex political entity evolved from the chiefdoms of the third millennium B.C.E. The Egyptians gave the name **Kush** to the kingdom whose capital was located

Kush An Egyptian name for Nubia, the region alongside the Nile River south of Egypt, where an indigenous kingdom with its own distinctive institutions and cultural traditions arose in the early second millennium B.C.E. It was deeply influenced by Egyptian culture and at times under the control of Egypt, which coveted its rich deposits of gold and luxury products from sub-Saharan Africa carried up the Nile corridor.

Gebel Barkal This model of Gebel Barkal, the "Holy Mountain" of Nubia, made of sandstone and with traces of the original paint, was deposited in the Temple of Amon at Gebel Barkal by a Nubian king. The original door is missing, as well as the seated figurine inside, possibly an image of Amon. Resting on a band representing a swamp with papyrus reeds, the doorway is flanked on either side by relief images of a winged goddess and a king wearing a short kilt.   Museum of Fine Arts, Boston. Harvard University, Boston Museum of Fine Arts Expedition, Maria Antoinette Evans Fund. Photograph © Museum of Fine Arts, Boston 21.3234

at Kerma, one of the earliest urbanized centers in tropical Africa. Beginning around 1750 B.C.E. the kings of Kush marshaled a labor force to build monumental walls and structures of mud brick. Royal burials containing dozens and even hundreds of sacrificed servants and wives, along with sumptuous objects, testify to the wealth and power of the rulers of Kush and suggest a belief in some sort of afterlife in which attendants and possessions would be useful. Kushite craftsmen showed skill in metalworking, whether for weapons or jewelry, and their pottery surpassed anything produced in Egypt.

During the expansionist New Kingdom (ca. 1532–1070 B.C.E.) the Egyptians penetrated more deeply into Nubia (see Chapter 3). They destroyed Kush and its capital and extended their frontier to the Fourth Cataract. A high-ranking Egyptian official called "Overseer of Southern Lands" or "King's Son of Kush" ruled Nubia from a new administrative center at Napata (nah-PAH-tuh), near Gebel Barkal (JEB-uhl BAHR-kahl), the "Holy Mountain," believed to be the home of a local god. Egypt exploited the gold mines of Nubia to help buttress its commerce with other lands. Fatalities were high among native workers in the brutal desert climate, and the army had to ward off attacks from desert nomads.

Five hundred years of Egyptian domination in Nubia left many traces. The Egyptian government imposed Egyptian culture on the native population. Children from elite families who were brought to the Egyptian royal court to guarantee the good behavior of their fathers absorbed Egyptian language, culture,

 History in Focus *In what ways do the carvings on this object reflect Egyptian influences? What is distinctively Nubian about it? Find the answer online.*

and religion, which they later carried home with them. Other Nubians served the Egyptians as archers. The manufactured goods that they brought back to Nubia have been found in their graves. The Nubians built Egyptian-style towns and erected stone temples to Egyptian gods, particularly Amon. The frequent depiction of Amon with the head of a ram may reflect a blending of the chief Egyptian god with a Nubian ram deity.

The Kingdom of Meroë, 800 B.C.E.–350 C.E.

Egypt's weakness after 1200 B.C.E. led to the collapse of its authority in Nubia. In the eighth century B.C.E. a powerful new native kingdom emerged in southern Nubia. Its history can be divided into two parts. During the early

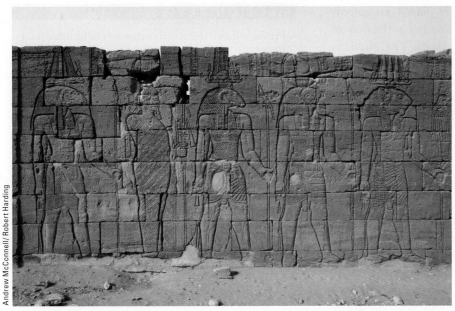

Andrew McConnell/ Robert Harding

Temple of the Lion-Headed God Apedemaq at Naqa in Nubia, First Century C.E.
The carved reliefs on this temple wall depict King Natakamani in the company of gods Horus and Apedemak. The architectural form and artistic style are Egyptian, but the gods are part-Nubian, part-Egyptian. The costume of the monarch also reflects the trend in the Meroitic era to draw upon sub-Saharan examples.

period, between the eighth and fourth centuries B.C.E., Napata, the former Egyptian headquarters, was the primary center. During the later period, from the fourth century B.C.E. to the fourth century C.E., the center was farther south, at **Meroë** (MER-oh-ee), near the Sixth Cataract.

For half a century, from around 712 to 660 B.C.E., the kings of Nubia ruled all of Egypt as the Twenty-fifth Dynasty. They conducted themselves in the age-old manner of Egyptian rulers, using Egyptian titles, costumes, and burial customs. However, they kept their Nubian names and were depicted with physical features suggesting peoples of sub-Saharan Africa. Building on a monumental scale for the first time in centuries and reinvigorating Egyptian art, architecture, and religion, they inaugurated an artistic and cultural renaissance. The Nubian kings resided at Memphis, the Old Kingdom capital, while Thebes, the New Kingdom capital, was the residence of a celibate female member of the king's family who was titled "God's Wife of Amon."

The Nubian dynasty made a disastrous mistake in 701 B.C.E. when it offered help to local rulers in Syria-Palestine who were struggling against the Assyrian Empire. The Assyrians retaliated by invading Egypt and driving the Nubian monarchs back to their southern domain by 660 B.C.E. Napata again became the chief royal residence and religious center of the kingdom. However, Egyptian cultural influences remained strong. Court documents continued to be written in Egyptian hieroglyphs, and the mummified remains of the rulers were buried in modestly sized sandstone pyramids along with hundreds of shawabti (shuh-WAB-tee) figurines.

By the end of the fourth century B.C.E. the center of gravity had shifted south to Meroë, perhaps because Meroë was better situated for agriculture and trade, the economic mainstays of the Nubian kingdom. As a result, sub-Saharan cultural patterns gradually replaced Egyptian ones. Egyptian hieroglyphs gave way to a new set of symbols, still essentially undeciphered, for writing the Meroitic language. People continued to worship Amon as well as Isis, an Egyptian goddess connected to fertility and sexuality, but those deities had to share the stage with Nubian deities like the lion-god Apedemak. Meroitic art combined Egyptian, Greco-Roman, and indigenous traditions.

Meroë Capital of a flourishing kingdom in southern Nubia from the fourth century B.C.E. to the fourth century C.E. In this period Nubian culture shows more independence from Egypt and the influence of sub-Saharan Africa.

Women of the royal family played an important role in Meroitic politics, another reflection of the influence of sub-Saharan Africa. The Nubians employed a matrilineal system in which the king was succeeded by the son of his sister. Nubian queens sometimes ruled by themselves and sometimes in partnership with their husbands. Greek, Roman, and biblical sources refer to a queen of Nubia named Candace. Since these sources relate to different times, Candace was probably a title rather than a proper name. At least seven queens ruled between 284 B.C.E. and 115 C.E. They are depicted in scenes reserved for male rulers in Egyptian imagery, smiting enemies in battle and being suckled by the mother-goddess Isis. Roman sources marvel at the fierce resistance put up by a one-eyed warrior-queen.

Meroë was a huge city for its time, more than a square mile in area, and it overlooked fertile grasslands and dominated converging trade routes. Great reservoirs were dug to catch precious rainfall. The city was a major center for iron smelting (after 1000 B.C.E. iron had replaced bronze as the primary metal for tools and weapons). The Temple of Amon was approached by an avenue of stone rams, and the enclosed "Royal City" was filled with palaces, temples, and administrative buildings. In 2002 archaeologists using a magnetometer to detect structures buried in the sand discovered a large palace, which they plan to excavate.

Meroë collapsed in the early fourth century C.E. It may have been overrun by nomads from the western desert who had become more mobile because of the arrival of the camel in North Africa. However, Meroë had already been weakened when profitable commerce with the Roman Empire was diverted to the Red Sea and to the rising kingdom of Aksum (AHK-soom) in present-day Ethiopia (see Chapter 6).

The Origins of Indo-European Languages, 4500–1800 B.C.E.

How did most Europeans come to speak Indo-European languages?

Before about 3000 B.C.E., Europe was populated in part by hunter-gatherers and in part by Neolithic farmers. The lower Danube Valley was the most populated part

SECTION REVIEW

- Fertile and rich in natural resources, Nubia became an important source of raw materials for Egypt.

- Egyptian cultural influence moved deeper into Nubia as the Middle and New Kingdoms extended Egyptian authority farther south.

- The rich Nubian kingdom of Kush fell to the New Kingdom, but after five hundred years a Nubian dynasty rose and took control of Egypt itself for a short time.

- After the fall of this dynasty, Meroë assumed control of southern Nubia, which was dominated by sub-Saharan cultural practices.

- Royal women played important roles throughout Meroë's history.

- Meroë was a large and powerful city in its prime, but it was already weak by the time it fell, perhaps to nomadic invaders.

of Europe, with many large farming villages. These people, ancestors of present-day Europeans, spoke languages that have long since disappeared.

Meanwhile, on the steppes of southern Russia north of the Black Sea and the Capsian Sea, there were no farmers; instead, some of the people who lived there hunted and gathered, while others herded sheep, goats, and cattle in the river valleys. Among the herders were people who spoke a language that linguists have reconstructed and named Proto-Indo-European. Between 4800 and 4600 B.C.E., these people domesticated the horse. Because they could herd far more animals on horseback than on foot, they became the wealthiest people in the region. Around 3500–3100 B.C.E., when they invented wagons with solid wheels that could be pulled by teams of oxen, they were able to leave the river valleys and spread out over the grasslands year-round, carrying tents, equipment, and water for weeks at a time.

With these innovations and their large herds, nomadic herdsmen were able to migrate long distances. Some made their way to Iran and eventually to India, while others migrated westward to central and western Europe. (It is because of the affinities between the oldest written language of India, Sanskrit, and the oldest written languages of Europe, Greek and Latin, that linguists call them Indo-European languages.)

Others moved into the lower Danube Valley after 3100 B.C.E. and from there spread out over the rest of Europe. With their horseback-riding skills and their impressive wealth in livestock, they attracted followers among the indigenous peoples or defeated those who resisted. As they divided into migrating groups, their original mother-tongue changed into several daughter languages, the ancestors of Greek, Latin, Romance languages, and Germanic languages. The language group that settled in the westernmost part of Europe, along the Atlantic coast and the British Isles, became known as the Celts.

Celtic Europe, 1000–50 B.C.E.

What is known about the Celts, and how did their religious beliefs help to shape their society?

The southern peninsulas of Europe—present-day Spain, Italy, and Greece—share in the relatively mild climate of all the Mediterranean lands and are separated from "continental" Europe to the north by high mountains (the Pyrenees and Alps). Consequently, the history of southern Europe in antiquity is primarily connected to that of the Middle East, at least until the Roman conquests north of the Alps (see Chapters 3, 4, and 6).

Continental Europe (including the modern nations of France, Germany, Switzerland, Austria, the Czech Republic, Slovakia, Hungary, Poland, and Romania) was more forested but was well suited to agriculture and herding. It contained broad plains with good soil and had a temperate climate with cold winters, warm summers, and ample rainfall. Large, navigable rivers (the Rhone, Rhine, and Danube) facilitated travel and the exploitation of natural resources like timber and metals.

Humans had lived in this part of Europe for many thousands of years, but their lack of a writing system limits our knowledge of the earliest inhabitants. Around 500 B.C.E. Celtic peoples spread across a substantial portion of Europe and, by coming into contact with the literate societies of the Mediterranean, entered the historical record. Information about the early **Celts** (kelts) comes from the archaeological record, Greek and Roman authors, and the

Celtic oral traditions of Wales and Ireland that were written down during the European Middle Ages.

The Spread of the Celts

The term *Celtic* refers to a branch of the Indo-European family of languages found throughout Europe and in western and southern Asia. Scholars link the Celtic language group to archaeological remains first appearing in parts of present-day Germany, Austria, and the Czech Republic after 1000 B.C.E. Many early Celts lived in or near hill-forts—lofty natural locations made more defensible by earthwork fortifications. By 500 B.C.E. Celtic elites were trading with Mediterranean societies for craft goods and wine. This contact may have stimulated the new styles of Celtic manufacture and art that appeared at this time.

These new cultural features coincided with Celtic migrations to many parts of Europe. The motives behind these population movements, their precise timing, and the manner in which they were carried out are not well understood. Celts occupied nearly all of France and much of Britain and Ireland, and they merged with indigenous peoples to create the Celtiberian culture of northern Spain. Other Celtic groups overran northern Italy in the fifth century B.C.E., raided into central Greece, and settled in central Anatolia (modern Turkey). By 300 B.C.E. Celtic peoples were spread across Europe north of the Alps, from present-day Hungary to Spain and Ireland.

Although these widely diffused Celtic groups shared language and culture, there was no Celtic "state." Instead they were divided into hundreds of small, loosely organized chiefdoms. Traditional depictions of Celtic society come largely from the observations of Greek and Roman writers. However, current scholarship focuses on the differences as much as the similarities among Celtic peoples. It is unlikely that the ancient Celts ever identified themselves as

Celts Peoples sharing a common language and culture that originated in central Europe in the first half of the first millennium B.C.E. After 500 B.C.E., they spread as far as Anatolia in the east and Spain and the British Isles in the west. They were later overtaken by Roman conquest and Germanic invasions. Their descendants survive on the western fringe of Europe (Brittany, Wales, Scotland, and Ireland).

belonging to anything akin to our modern conception of "Celtic civilization."

The Greeks and Romans remarked particularly on the appearance of male Celts—their burly size, long red hair (which they often made stiff and upright by applying a cement-like solution of lime), shaggy mustaches, and loud, deep voices. Trousers (usually an indication of horse-riding peoples) and twisted gold neck collars were similarly distinctive, but not as unusual as the terrifying warriors who fought naked and collected the skulls of defeated enemies. The surviving accounts describe the Celts as wildly fond of war, courageous, childishly impulsive and emotional, and fond of boasting and exaggeration, yet quick-witted and eager to learn.

Celtic Society

The Roman general Julius Caesar, who conquered Gaul (present-day France) between 58 and 51 B.C.E., penned the greatest source of information about Celtic society. Many Celtic groups in Gaul had once been ruled by kings, but by about 60 B.C.E. they periodically chose public officials, perhaps under Greek and Roman influence. Their society was divided into an elite class of warriors, professional groups of priests and bards (singers of poems about glorious deeds), and commoners. The warriors owned land and flocks of cattle and sheep and monopolized both wealth and power. The common people labored on their land. The Celts built houses (usually round in Britain, rectangular in France) out of wattle and daub—a wooden framework filled in with clay and straw—with thatched straw roofs. Several such houses belonging to related families might be surrounded by a wooden fence for protection.

The warriors of Welsh and Irish legend reflect a stage of political and social development less complex than that of the Celts in Gaul. They raided one another's flocks, reveled in drunken feasts, and engaged in contests of strength and wit. At banquets warriors would fight to the death just to claim the choicest cut of the meat, the "hero's portion."

Druids, the Celtic priests in Gaul and Britain, formed a well-organized fraternity that performed religious, judicial, and educational functions. Trainees spent years memorizing prayers, secret rituals, legal precedents, and other traditions. The priesthood was the one Celtic institution that crossed tribal lines. The Druids sometimes headed off warfare between feuding groups and served as judges in cases involving Celts from different groups. In the first century C.E. the Roman government attempted to stamp out the Druids, probably because of concern that they might

The Gundestrup Cauldron This silver vessel was found in a peat bog in Denmark, but it must have come from elsewhere. It is usually dated to the second or first century B.C.E. On the inside left are Celtic warriors on horse and on foot, with lozenge-shaped shields and long battle-horns. On the inside right is a horned deity, possibly Cernunnos.   The National Museum of Denmark

Druids The class of religious experts who conducted rituals and preserved sacred lore among some ancient Celtic peoples. They provided education and mediated disputes between kinship groups.

serve as a rallying point for Celtic opposition to Roman rule, and also because of their involvement in human sacrifices.

The Celts supported large populations by tilling the heavy but fertile soils of continental Europe, and their metallurgical skills probably surpassed those of the Mediterranean peoples. Celts living on the Atlantic shore of France built sturdy oceangoing boats, and they developed extensive trade networks along Europe's large, navigable rivers. One lucrative commodity was tin, which Celtic traders from southwest England brought to Greek buyers in southern France. By the first century B.C.E. some hill-forts were evolving into urban centers.

Women's lives were focused on child rearing, food production, and some crafts. Their situation was superior to that of women in the Middle East and in the Greek and Roman Mediterranean. Greek and Roman sources depict Celtic women as strong and proud. Welsh and Irish tales portray self-assured women who sit at banquets with their husbands, engage in witty conversation, and provide ingenious solutions to vexing problems. Marriage was a partnership to which both parties contributed property, and each party had the right to inherit the estate if the other died. Celtic women also had greater freedom in their sexual relations than did their southern counterparts.

Tombs of elite women have yielded rich collections of clothing, jewelry, and furniture for use in the next world. Daughters of the elite were married to leading members of other tribes to create alliances. When the Romans invaded Celtic Britain in the first century C.E., they sometimes were opposed by Celtic tribes headed by queens, although some experts see this as an abnormal circumstance created by the Roman invasion itself.

Belief and Knowledge

Historians know the names of more than four hundred Celtic gods and goddesses, mostly associated with particular localities or kinship groups. More widely revered deities included Lug (loog), the god of light, crafts, and inventions; the horse-goddess Epona (eh-POh-nuh); and the horned god Cernunnos (KURN-you-nuhs). "The Mothers," three goddesses depicted together holding symbols of abundance, probably played a part in a fertility cult. Halloween and May

SECTION REVIEW

- From central and eastern Europe, Celtic peoples spread across the continent.
- These peoples shared language and culture but no single state.
- Although Celtic societies varied in complexity, they all shared the institution of the Druid priesthood, practiced agriculture, and developed sophisticated technologies.
- Celtic women enjoyed relatively high status, and some even led warriors against Roman invaders.
- Celtic religion involved a vast array of deities and some sort of afterlife.
- Celtic culture declined under Roman rule, and the Germanic migrations pushed it to the western margin of Europe.

Day preserve the ancient Celtic holidays of Samhain (SAH-win) and Beltaine (BEHL-tayn), respectively, which took place at key moments in the agricultural cycle.

The early Celts did not build temples, but instead worshiped wherever they felt the presence of divinity—at springs, groves, and hilltops. At the sources of the Seine and Marne Rivers in France, archaeologists have found huge caches of Celtic wooden statues thrown into the water by worshipers.

Wagons filled with extensive grave goods show up in elite burials, suggesting a belief in some sort of afterlife. In Irish and Welsh legends, heroes and gods pass back and forth between the natural and supernatural worlds much more readily than in the mythology of other cultures, and magical occurrences are commonplace. Celtic priests set forth a doctrine of reincarnation—the rebirth of the soul in a new body.

The evolution of Celtic society in Spain, southern Britain, France, and parts of central Europe slowed after the Roman conquests from the second century B.C.E. to the first century C.E. The peoples in these lands largely assimilated Roman ways (see Chapter 6). From the third century C.E. on, Germanic invaders from the east diminished the Celts still further. Only on the western fringes of the European continent—in Brittany (northwest France), Wales, Scotland, and Ireland—did Celtic peoples maintain their language, art, and culture into modern times.

Conclusion

The civilizations of early China, Nubia, and Celtic Europe emerged in very different ecological contexts in widely separated parts of the globe. The patterns of organization, technology, behavior, and belief that they developed were, in large part, responses to the challenges and opportunities of those environments.

In the North China Plain, as in the river-valley civilizations of Mesopotamia and Egypt, the presence of great, flood-prone rivers and the lack of dependable rainfall led to the formation of powerful institutions capable of organizing large numbers of people to dig and maintain irrigation channels and build dikes. An authoritarian central government has been a recurring feature of Chinese history, beginning with the Shang monarchy and warrior elite.

In Nubia, the initial impetus for the formation of a strong state was the need for protection from desert nomads and from the Egyptian rulers who coveted Nubian gold and other resources. Control of these resources and of the trade route between sub-Saharan Africa and the north, as well as the agricultural surplus to feed administrators and specialists in the urban centers, made the rulers of Kush, Napata, and Meroë wealthy and formidable.

The Celtic peoples of continental Europe never developed a strong state. They occupied fertile lands with adequate rainfall for agriculture, grazing territory for flocks, and timber for fuel and construction. Kinship groups dominated by warrior elites and controlling compact territories were the usual form of organization.

CHAPTER REVIEW

 Download the MP3 audio file of the Chapter Review to listen to on the go.

How did early Chinese rulers use religion to justify and strengthen their power? (page 35)

Throughout history, elites have used religion to bolster their position. The Shang rulers of China were indispensable intermediaries between their kingdom and powerful and protective ancestors and gods. Bronze vessels were used to make offerings to ancestral spirits, and royal and elite families were buried in elaborate tombs that were intended to serve the occupant in the afterlife. Their Zhou successors developed the concept of the ruler as divine Son of Heaven who ruled in accord with the Mandate of Heaven.

How did the technological and cultural influences of Egypt affect the formation of Nubia? (page 45)

The civilization that developed in Nubia was powerfully influenced by its interactions with the more complex and technologically advanced neighboring society in Egypt. Nubia was engaged in trade with Egypt for most of its history, and Egyptians often sought to control and dominate the gold trade. In the New Kingdom period, the Egyptian government imposed Egyptian culture, language, and religion on the native population, and Nubian architecture came to be based on Egyptian models. In the eighth century B.C.E. the kingdom of Meroë emerged and Nubia controlled all of Egypt for half a century. While they kept their Nubian names, the rulers imitated the style of Egyptian rulers and kept many Egyptian traditions. By the fourth century, power shifted south to Meroë and sub-Saharan African cultural influences replaced Egyptian ones.

How did most Europeans come to speak Indo-European languages? (page 48)

Most of the languages of Europe, Iran, and India originated with nomadic herdsmen who domesticated horses and invented ox-drawn wagons. Those who migrated to Europe after 3100 B.C.E. induced the indigenous inhabitants to adopt their languages, including the ancestor of the language of the Celts.

What is known about the Celts, and how did their religious beliefs help to shape their society? (page 49)

The Celtic elites of central Europe initially traded for luxury goods with the Mediterranean, and when they began to expand into lands to the west and south after 500 B.C.E. they came into even closer contact with Mediterranean peoples. Eventually many Celtic groups were incorporated into the Roman Empire. Druids, the Celtic priests in Gaul and Britain, performed religious and other functions. Rather than constructing temples, the Celts worshiped hundreds of gods and goddesses in natural surroundings, where they felt the presence of divinity. By the first century C.E., the Romans had conquered parts of Europe and assimilated many Celts to their ways.

Key Terms

loess *(p. 37)*

Shang *(p. 38)*

Zhou *(p. 39)*

Mandate of Heaven *(p. 40)*

Legalism *(p. 41)*

Confucius *(p. 41)*

Daoism *(p. 41)*

yin/yang *(p. 44)*

Kush *(p. 45)*

Meroë *(p. 47)*

Celts *(p. 49)*

Druids *(p. 50)*

Web Resources

Pronunciation Guide

Interactive Map

- MAP 2.1 China in the Shang and Zhou Periods, 1750–221 B.C.E.

Primary Source

- The Book of Documents

Answer to the History in Focus Question

See photo on page 46, "Gebel Barkal."

 CourseMate Visit the CourseMate website at www.cengagebrain.com for additional study tools and review materials for this chapter.

The Mediterranean and Middle East

© Cengage Learning

CHAPTER PREVIEW

The Cosmopolitan Middle East, 1700–1100 B.C.E.
How did a cosmopolitan civilization develop in the Middle East during the Late Bronze Age, and what forms did it take?

The Aegean World, 2000–1100 B.C.E.
What civilizations emerged in the Aegean world, and what relationship did they have to the older civilizations to the east?

The Assyrian Empire, 911–612 B.C.E.
How did the Assyrian Empire rise to power and eventually dominate most of the ancient Middle East?

Israel, 2000–500 B.C.E.
How did the civilization of Israel develop, following both familiar cultural patterns and a unique course of its own?

Phoenicia and the Mediterranean, 1200–500 B.C.E.
How did the Phoenicians rise to commercial dominance over much of the Mediterranean world?

Failure and Transformation, 750–550 B.C.E.
What factors prompted the transformation of the ancient Middle East between 750 and 550 B.C.E.?

Conclusion

ENVIRONMENT AND TECHNOLOGY: Ancient Textiles and Dyes

Visit the CourseMate website at **www.cengagebrain.com** for additional study tools and review materials for this chapter.

Ancient stories—even those that are not historically accurate—provide valuable insights into how people thought about their origins and identity. One story concerned the city of Carthage (KAHR-thuhj) in present-day Tunisia, which for centuries dominated the commerce of the western Mediterranean. Tradition held that Dido, a member of the royal family of the Phoenician city-state of Tyre (tire) in southern Lebanon, fled with her supporters to the western Mediterranean after her brother, the king of Tyre, murdered her husband. On the North African coast the refugees made friendly contact with local people, who agreed to give them as much land as a cow's hide could cover. By cleverly cutting the hide into narrow strips, they were able to mark out a substantial piece of territory for Kart Khadasht, the "New City" (called Carthago by their Roman enemies). Later, faithful to the memory of her dead husband, Dido committed suicide rather than marry a local chieftain.

This story highlights the spread of cultural patterns from older centers to new regions in the Mediterranean lands and western Asia. Just as Egyptian cultural influences helped transform Nubian society, influences from the older centers in Mesopotamia and Egypt penetrated throughout western Asia and the Mediterranean. Far-flung trade, diplomatic contacts, military conquests, and the relocation of large numbers of people spread knowledge, beliefs, practices, and technologies.

By the end of the second millennium B.C.E. many of the societies of the region had entered the **Iron Age**. Iron offered advantages over bronze. It was a single metal rather than an alloy and thus was simpler to obtain, and iron ore was plentiful. Once the technology of iron making had been mastered—high-temperature heating to turn the ore into a soft "bloom" followed by pounding to remove impurities and quenching for hardness—iron tools were found to have sharper and longer-lasting edges than bronze tools.

The Hittites of iron-rich Anatolia had learned to make iron implements by 1500 B.C.E. but did not share their knowledge. Some scholars believe that, in the disrupted period after 1200 B.C.E., blacksmiths from the Hittite core area migrated and spread the technology. Others speculate that metalworkers who could not obtain copper and tin turned to dumps of slag (the byproduct of bronze production) containing iron residue and found that they could create useful objects from it.

The first part of this chapter picks up the story of Mesopotamia and Egypt in the Late Bronze Age, the second millennium B.C.E.: their complex relations with neighboring peoples, the development of a prosperous, "cosmopolitan" network of states in the Middle East, and the destruction and decline that set in around 1200 B.C.E. We also look at how the Minoan and Mycenaean civilizations of the Aegean Sea adopted the technologies and cultural patterns of the older Middle Eastern centers and prospered through long-distance trading.

Turning to the Early Iron Age, from 1000 to 500 B.C.E., the focus will be on three societies: the Assyrians of northern Mesopotamia; the Israelites; and the Phoenicians of Lebanon, Syria, and their Carthaginian colonies in the western Mediterranean.

The Cosmopolitan Middle East, 1700–1100 B.C.E.

How did a cosmopolitan civilization develop in the Middle East during the Late Bronze Age, and what forms did it take?

Although outside invaders overwhelmed Mesopotamia and Egypt in the seventeenth century B.C.E. (see Chapter 1), the outsiders were eventually either ejected or assimilated, and conditions of stability and prosperity returned. Between 1500 and 1200 B.C.E. large territorial states dominated the Middle East (see Map 3.1). Smaller city-states, kingdoms, and kinship groups fell under their control as they competed for access to commodities and trade routes.

Historians have called the Late Bronze Age a "cosmopolitan" era, meaning a time of widely shared cultures and lifestyles. Diplomatic relations and

Iron Age Historians' term for the period during which iron was the primary metal for tools and weapons. The advent of iron technology began at different times in different parts of the world.

commercial contacts between states fostered flows of goods and ideas, and elite groups shared similar values and high living standards. The peasants who constituted the majority of the population may have seen some improvement in their standard of living, but they reaped far fewer benefits from the increasing contacts and trade.

Western Asia

By 1500 B.C.E. Mesopotamia was divided into two distinct political zones: Babylonia in the south and Assyria in the north (see Map 3.1). The city of Babylon had first gained ascendancy under the dynasty of Hammurabi in the eighteenth and seventeenth centuries B.C.E., but Kassite (KAS-ite) peoples from the Zagros (ZAH-groes) Mountains to the east had seized power by 1500 B.C.E. Though

Kassite names derive from their native, non-Semitic language, the Kassites otherwise embraced Babylonian language and culture and intermarried with the native population. For 350 years, the Kassite lords of Babylonia defended their core area and traded for raw materials, but they did not pursue territorial conquest.

The Assyrians of the north proved more ambitious. As early as the twentieth century B.C.E. the city of Ashur (AH-shoor), the leading urban center on the northern Tigris, anchored a busy trade route across the northern Mesopotamian plain and onto the Anatolian Plateau. Assyrian merchants established settlements outside the walls of important Anatolian cities. They imported textiles and tin, used to make bronze, in exchange for Anatolian silver. In the eighteenth century B.C.E. an Assyrian dynasty briefly controlled

Map 3.1 The Middle East in the Second Millennium B.C.E. Although warfare was not uncommon, treaties, diplomatic missions, and correspondence in Akkadian cuneiform fostered cooperative relationships between states. All were tied together by extensive networks of exchange centering on the trade in metals. Peripheral regions, such as Nubia and the Aegean Sea, were drawn into the web of commerce. © Cengage Learning

Interactive Map

Chronology

	Western Asia	Egypt	Syria-Palestine	Mediterranean
2000 B.C.E.	**2000 B.C.E.** Horses in use	**2040–1640 B.C.E.** Middle Kingdom		**2000 B.C.E.** Rise of Minoan civilization; early Greeks arrive
			1800 B.C.E. Abraham migrates to Canaan	
	1700–1200 B.C.E. Hittites dominate Anatolia	**1640–1532 B.C.E.** Hyksos in northern Egypt		
		1532 B.C.E. New Kingdom begins		**1600 B.C.E.** Rise of Mycenaean civilization
1500 B.C.E.	**1500 B.C.E.** Hittites pioneer iron	**1490 B.C.E.** Hatshepsut's Punt expedition	**1500 B.C.E.** "Alphabetic" script at Ugarit	
	1500 B.C.E. Kassites in Mesopotamia			**1450 B.C.E.** Destruction of Minoan palaces in Crete
		1290–1224 B.C.E. Ramesses the Great	**1250–1200 B.C.E.** Israelites in Canaan	**1200–1150 B.C.E.** Destruction of Mycenaean centers in Greece
	1200 B.C.E. Hittite kingdom ends	**1200–1150 B.C.E.** Sea Peoples attack Egypt	**1150 B.C.E.** Philistines settle Israel's coast	
1000 B.C.E.		**1070 B.C.E.** New Kingdom ends	**1000 B.C.E.** Jerusalem made Israelite capital	
	911 B.C.E. Neo-Assyrian Empire	**750 B.C.E.** Kush controls Egypt	**969 B.C.E.** Hiram of Tyre comes to power	**814 B.C.E.** Foundation of Carthage
	744–727 B.C.E. Tiglathpileser	**671 B.C.E.** Assyrians conquer Egypt	**721 B.C.E.** Assyrian conquest of northern kingdom	
	668–627 B.C.E. Ashurbanipal			
600 B.C.E.	**612 B.C.E.** Fall of Assyria			
			587 B.C.E. Capture of Jerusalem	**550–330 B.C.E.** Rivalry of Carthaginians and Greeks in western Mediterranean
			515 B.C.E. Deportees from Babylon return to Jerusalem	

the upper Euphrates River near the present-day Syria-Iraq border. The trade routes connecting Mesopotamia to Anatolia and the Syria-Palestine coast were key to the power of this "Old Assyrian" kingdom. After 1400 B.C.E. a resurgent "Middle Assyrian" kingdom again engaged in campaigns of conquest and economic expansion.

Other ambitious states developed around the Mesopotamian heartland, including Elam in southwest Iran. Most formidable were the **Hittites** (HIT-ites), who

Hittites A people from central Anatolia who established an empire in Anatolia and Syria in the Late Bronze Age. With wealth from the trade in metals and military power based on chariot forces, the Hittites vied with New Kingdom Egypt for control of Syria-Palestine before falling to unidentified attackers ca. 1200 B.C.E.

The Mortuary Temple of Queen Hatshepsut at Deir el-Bahri, Egypt, ca. 1460 B.C.E. This beautiful complex of terraces, ramps, and colonnades featured relief sculptures and texts commemorating the famous expedition to Punt.

 History In Focus *What does the structure and placement of the building in the landscape tell you about the role Hatshepsut played in the Egypt of her day? Find the answer online.*

became the foremost power in Anatolia from around 1700 to 1200 B.C.E. From their capital at Hattusha (haht-tush-SHAH), near present-day Ankara (ANG-kur-ruh) in central Turkey, they deployed the fearsome new technology of horse-drawn war chariots. Iron was the Hittites' specialty, and Anatolia's rich deposits of copper, silver, and iron played a major role in Hittite commerce.

During the second millennium B.C.E. Mesopotamian political and cultural concepts spread across much of western Asia. Akkadian (uh-KAY-dee-uhn) became the language of diplomacy and correspondence between governments. The Elamites (EE-luh-mites) and Hittites, among others, adapted the cuneiform system to write their own languages. In the Syrian coastal city of Ugarit (OO-guh-reet) thirty cuneiform symbols were used to write consonant sounds, an early example of the alphabetic principle and a considerable advance over the hundreds of signs required in conventional cuneiform writing.

New Kingdom Egypt

After flourishing for nearly four hundred years (see Chapter 1), the Egyptian Middle Kingdom lost strength in the seventeenth century B.C.E. Egypt entered a period of political fragmentation and economic decline. Around 1640 B.C.E. it came under foreign rule for the first time, at the hands of the Hyksos (HICK-soes), or "Princes of Foreign Lands."

Historians are uncertain who the Hyksos were. Semitic peoples had been migrating from the Levant (present-day Syria, Lebanon, Jordan, Israel, and the Palestinian territories) into the eastern Nile Delta for centuries. In the chaotic conditions of this time, other peoples may have joined them, establishing control first in the delta and then in the middle of the country. The Hyksos had war chariots and composite bows made of wood and horn for greater range, which gave them an advantage over the Egyptians. The Hyksos intermarried with Egyptians and assimilated to native ways. They spoke Egyptian and maintained

Egyptian institutions and culture. Nevertheless, unlike in Mesopotamia, the Egyptians continued to regard the Hyksos as "foreigners."

As with the formation of the Middle Kingdom five hundred years earlier, the reunification of Egypt under a native dynasty was accomplished by princes from Thebes. After three decades of warfare, Kamose (KAH-mose) and Ahmose (AH-mose) expelled the Hyksos from Egypt and inaugurated the New Kingdom, which lasted from about 1532 to 1070 B.C.E.

New Kingdom Egypt saw a shift from traditional Egyptian isolationism to aggressive expansionism northward into the Levant and southward into Nubia. Timber, gold, and copper in taxes and tribute (payments from conquered territories) were the prizes of this expansion. The occupied lands also provided a buffer against foreign attack. In Nubia, Egypt imposed direct control and pressed the native population to adopt Egyptian language and culture (see Chapter 2). In the Levant, the Egyptians stationed garrisons at strategically placed forts and supported local rulers willing to collaborate.

The New Kingdom was a period of innovation. Egyptian soldiers, administrators, diplomats, and merchants traveled widely and learned about exotic fruits and vegetables, as well as new technologies, such as new musical instruments and improved potter's wheels and weaver's looms.

At least one woman held the throne of New Kingdom Egypt. When Pharaoh Tuthmosis (tuth-MOE-sis) II died, his queen, **Hatshepsut** (hat-SHEP-soot), served as regent for her young stepson and soon claimed the royal title for herself (r. 1473–1458 B.C.E.). In inscriptions she often used the male pronoun to refer to herself, and drawings and sculptures show her wearing the long beard of the ruler of Egypt.

Around 1490 B.C.E. Hatshepsut sent a naval expedition down the Red Sea to Punt (poont), an exotic land that historians believe may have been near the coast of eastern Sudan or Eritrea. Hatshepsut was in quest of myrrh (murr), a reddish-brown resin that the Egyptians burned in religious rites and used in medicines and cosmetics. She hoped to bypass the middlemen who drove up the price exorbitantly and establish direct trade between Punt and Egypt. When the expedition returned with myrrh and various sub-Saharan luxuries—ebony and other rare woods, ivory,

live monkeys, panther skins—Hatshepsut celebrated the achievement in words and pictures on the walls of a mortuary temple she built for herself. She may have used the success of this expedition to bolster her claim to the throne. After her death, in a reaction that reflected some official opposition to a woman ruler, her image was defaced and her name blotted out wherever it appeared.

Another ruler who departed from traditional ways ascended the throne as Amenhotep (ah-muhn-HOE-tep) IV. He soon began to refer to himself as **Akhenaten** (ah-ken-AHT-n) (r. 1353–1335 B.C.E.), meaning "beneficial to the Aten (AHT-n)" (the disk of the sun). He thus publicized his belief in Aten as the supreme deity. He closed the temples of other gods, challenging the age-old supremacy of the chief god Amon (AH-muhn) and the power and influence of Amon's priests.

Some scholars maintain that Akhenaten pioneered monotheism—the belief in one exclusive god. Akhenaten's goal, however, was more likely a reassertion of the king's superiority over the priests and a renewal of belief in the king's divinity. Worship of Aten was confined to the royal family: the people of Egypt were pressed to revere the divine ruler.

Akhenaten built a new capital at modern-day Amarna (ah-MAHR-nuh), halfway between Memphis and Thebes (see Map 3.1). He relocated thousands of Egyptians to construct the site and serve the ruling elite. His artists created a new style that broke with the conventions of earlier art: the king, his wife Nefertiti (nef-uhr-TEE-tee), and their daughters were depicted in fluid, natural poses with strangely elongated heads and limbs and swelling abdomens.

Hatshepsut Queen of Egypt (r. 1473–1458 B.C.E.). She dispatched a naval expedition down the Red Sea to Punt (possibly northeast Sudan or Eritria), the faraway source of myrrh. There is evidence of opposition to a woman as ruler, and after her death her name and image were frequently defaced.

Akhenaten Egyptian pharaoh (r. 1353–1335 B.C.E.). He built a new capital at Amarna, fostered a new style of naturalistic art, and created a religious revolution by imposing worship of the sun-disk. The Amarna letters, largely from his reign, preserve official correspondence with subjects and neighbors.

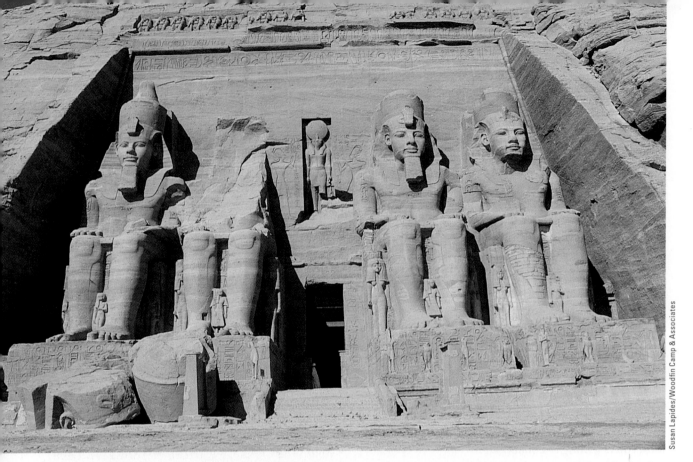

Colossal Statues of Ramesses II at Abu Simbel Strategically placed at a bend in the Nile River so as to face the southern frontier, this monument was an advertisement of Egyptian power. A temple was carved into the cliff behind the gigantic statues of the pharaoh. In a modern marvel of engineering, the monument was moved to higher ground in 1960 C.E. to protect it from rising waters when a dam was constructed.

Government officials, priests, and others whose privileges and wealth were linked to the traditional system strongly resented these reforms. After Akhenaten's death the temples were reopened, Amon was reinstated as chief god, the capital returned to Thebes, and the priests regained their influence. The boy-king Tutankhamun (tuht-uhnk-AH-muhn) (r. 1333–1323 B.C.E.), one of the immediate successors of Akhenaten and famous solely because his tomb had not been pillaged by tomb robbers when it was found, reveals both in his name (meaning "beautiful in life is Amon") and in his insignificant reign the ultimate failure of Akhenaten's revolution.

In 1323 B.C.E. the general Haremhab seized the throne and established a new dynasty, the Ramessides (RAM-ih-side). The rulers of this line renewed the policy of conquest and expansion that Akhenaten had neglected. **Ramesses** (RAM-ih-seez) **II**—sometimes called Ramesses the Great—ruled for sixty-six years (r. 1290–1224 B.C.E.) and dominated his age. Living into his nineties, he may have fathered more than a hundred children. Since 1990 archaeologists have been excavating a network of more than a hundred corridors and chambers carved deep into a hillside in the Valley of the Kings where many sons of Ramesses were buried.

Commerce and Communication Early in his reign Ramesses II fought a major battle against the Hittites at Kadesh in northern Syria (1285 B.C.E.). Although Egyptian propaganda boasted of a great victory, the lack of territorial gains suggests that it was essentially a draw. In subsequent years Egyptian and Hittite diplomats negotiated a

> **Ramesses II** A long-lived ruler of New Kingdom Egypt (r. 1290–1224 B.C.E.). He reached an accommodation with the Hittites of Anatolia after a standoff in battle at Kadesh in Syria. He built on a grand scale throughout Egypt.

SECTION REVIEW

- The Late Bronze Age saw the rise of a cosmopolitan culture in the ancient Middle East.

- Mesopotamia was divided between Babylonia and the increasingly powerful Assyrians.

- In Anatolia, the technologically advanced Hittites became the major political force, and both they and other outlying peoples absorbed Mesopotamian cultural and political concepts.

- After a century of foreign domination, the New Kingdom in Egypt ushered in a period of expansion abroad and innovation at home.

- During the Late Bronze Age, long-distance trade in metals expanded, and the arrival of the horse made possible larger states and empires.

treaty, which was strengthened by Ramesses's marriage to a Hittite princess. At issue was control of Syria-Palestine. The inland cities of Syria-Palestine—such as Mari (MAR-ree) on the upper Euphrates and Alalakh (UH-luh-luhk) in western Syria—were hubs of international trade. The coastal towns—particularly Ugarit and the Phoenician towns of the Lebanese seaboard—served as transshipment points for trade to and from the lands ringing the Mediterranean Sea.

Commerce in metals energized the long-distance trade. We have seen the Assyrian traffic in silver from Anatolia and the Egyptian passion for Nubian gold (see Chapter 2). Copper came from Anatolia and Cyprus, tin from Afghanistan and possibly the British Isles. Both commodities traveled long distances and passed through many hands before reaching their final destinations.

New modes of transportation expedited communications and commerce across great distances and inhospitable landscapes. Horses arrived in western Asia around 2000 B.C.E. First used by nomads in Central Asia, they were brought into Mesopotamia through the Zagros Mountains and reached Egypt by 1600 B.C.E. The speed of the horse contributed to the creation of large states and empires. Soldiers and government agents could cover great distances quickly, and swift, maneuverable horse-drawn chariots became the premier instrument of war.

Sometime after 1500 B.C.E. in western Asia, but not for another thousand years in Egypt, people began to make common use of camels, though the animal was domesticated much earlier in southern Arabia. Their strength made them ideal pack animals, and their ability to go without water made travel across barren terrain possible.

The Aegean World, 2000–1100 B.C.E.

What civilizations emerged in the Aegean world, and what relationship did they have to the older civilizations to the east?

In this era of far-flung trade and communication, the emergence of the Minoan (mih-NO-uhn) civilization on the island of Crete and the Mycenaean (my-suh-NEE-uhn) civilization of Greece demonstrates the fertilizing influence of older centers on outlying lands and peoples. The landscape of southern Greece and the Aegean islands is rocky and arid, with small plains lying between ranges of hills. The limited arable land was suitable for grains, grapevines, and olive trees. Flocks of sheep and goats grazed the slopes. Sharply indented coastlines, natural harbors, and small islands within sight of one another made the sea the fastest and least costly mode of travel. Lacking metals and timber, Aegean peoples had to import these commodities from abroad. As a result, the rise, success, and eventual fall of the Minoan and Mycenaean societies were closely tied to their relations with other peoples in the region.

Minoan Crete

The **Minoan** civilization that had come into being on the island of Crete by 2000 B.C.E. (see Map 3.1) featured centralized government, monumental building, bronze metallurgy, writing, and recordkeeping. Archaeologists named this civilization after the legendary King Minos, who was said to have ruled a vast naval empire, including southern Greece, and to have kept the monstrous

---

Minoan Prosperous civilization on the Aegean island of Crete in the second millennium B.C.E. The Minoans engaged in far-flung commerce around the Mediterranean and exerted powerful cultural influences on the early Greeks.

Minotaur (MIN-uh-tor) (half-man, half-bull) beneath his palace in a mazelike labyrinth built by the ingenious inventor Daedalus (DED-ih-luhs).

The ethnicity of the Minoans is uncertain, and their writing has not been deciphered. But their sprawling palace complexes at Cnossus (NOSS-suhs), Phaistos (FIE-stuhs), and Mallia (mahl-YAH) and the distribution of Cretan pottery and other artifacts around the Mediterranean and Middle East testify to widespread trading connections. Egyptian, Syrian, and Mesopotamian influences can be seen in the design of the Minoan palaces, but the absence of identifiable representations of Cretan rulers contrasts sharply with the grandiose depictions of kings in the Middle East and suggests a different conception of authority. Also noteworthy are the absence of fortifications at the palace sites and the presence of high-quality indoor plumbing.

Statuettes of women with elaborate headdresses and serpents coiling around their limbs may represent fertility goddesses. Colorful frescoes (paintings done on a moist plaster surface) on palace walls portray groups of women in frilly, layered skirts engaged in conversation or watching rituals or entertainment, as well as young acrobats vaulting over the horns of an onrushing bull, either for sport or as a religious activity. Servants carrying jars and fishermen throwing nets and hooks from their boats suggest a joyful attitude toward work, but this may say more about elite ideals than about the reality of daily toil. Stylized vase paintings depicting plants with swaying leaves and playful octopuses with undulating tentacles reflect a delight in nature's beauty.

All the Cretan palaces except Cnossus, along with the houses of the elite and peasants in the countryside, were deliberately destroyed around 1450 B.C.E. Because Mycenaean Greeks took over at Cnossus, most historians regard them as the likely culprits.

Mycenaean Greece

Most historians believe that speakers of an Indo-European language ancestral to Greek migrated into the Greek peninsula around 2000 B.C.E. Through intermarriage, blending of languages, and melding of cultural practices, the indigenous population and the newcomers created the first Greek culture. For centuries this society remained simple and static. Farmers and shepherds lived in Stone Age conditions, wringing a bare living from the land. Then, sometime around 1600 B.C.E., life changed relatively suddenly.

More than a century ago a German businessman, Heinrich Schliemann (SHLEE-muhn), set out to prove that the *Iliad* and the *Odyssey* were true. These epics attributed to the poet Homer, who probably lived shortly before 700 B.C.E., spoke of Agamemnon (ag-uh-MEM-non), the king of **Mycenae** (my-SEE-nee) in southern Greece. In 1876 Schliemann stunned the scholarly world by discovering at Mycenae a circle of graves at the base of deep, rectangular shafts. These **shaft graves** contained the bodies of men, women, and children and were filled with gold jewelry and ornaments, weapons, and utensils. Clearly, some people in this society had acquired wealth, authority, and the capacity to mobilize human labor. Subsequent excavation uncovered a large palace complex, massive walls, more shaft graves, and other evidence of a rich and technologically advanced civilization that lasted from around 1600 to 1150 B.C.E.

The sudden appearance of Mycenaean culture in mainland Greece is puzzling. There is no archaeological evidence of Cretan political control of the mainland, but Crete exerted an undeniable cultural influence. The Mycenaeans borrowed the Minoan ideas of the palace, centralized economy, and administrative bureaucracy, as well as the Minoan writing system. They adopted Minoan styles and techniques of architecture, pottery making, and fresco and vase painting. But how did they suddenly accumulate power and wealth? Most historians look to the profits from trade and piracy and perhaps also to the pay and booty brought back by mercenaries (soldiers who served for pay in foreign lands).

Mycenae Site of a fortified palace complex in southern Greece that controlled a Late Bronze Age kingdom. In Homer's epic poems, Mycenae was the base of King Agamemnon, who commanded the Greeks besieging Troy. Contemporary archaeologists call the complex Greek society of the second millennium B.C.E. "Mycenaean."

shaft graves A term used for the burial sites of elite members of Mycenaean Greek society in the mid-second millennium B.C.E. At the bottom of deep shafts lined with stone slabs, the bodies were laid out along with gold and bronze jewelry, implements, weapons, and masks.

Gate of Mycenae This gate topped with a relief sculpture of lions, symbols of the city of Mycenae, protected the entrance to the city. The massive stones show the dangers and insecurity of life in Greece in the second millennium B.C.E.

Art Kowalsky/Alamy

Excavations at other centers have revealed that Mycenae exemplifies the common pattern: a citadel built on a hilltop and surrounded by high, thick fortifications made of stones so large that later Greeks believed that the legendary giant, one-eyed Cyclopes (SIGH-kloe-pees), had lifted them into place. The fortified enclosure provided refuge for the community in time of danger and contained the palace and administrative complex. The large central hall with an open hearth and columned porch was surrounded by courtyards, living quarters for the royal family and their retainers, and offices, storerooms, and workshops. Brightly painted scenes of war, the hunt, and daily life, as well as natural motifs, covered the palace walls.

Over four thousand baked clay tablets written in a script called **Linear B** provide additional information. Like its predecessor, the undeciphered Minoan script called Linear A, Linear B uses pictorial signs to represent syllables, but the language is an early form of Greek. The palace bureaucracy kept track of people, animals, and objects in exhaustive detail. The tablets list everything from the number of chariot wheels in palace storerooms and the rations paid to textile workers to the gifts dedicated to various gods and the ships stationed along the coasts. The government organized and coordinated grain production and controlled the wool industry. Scribes kept track of flocks in the field, the sheared wool and its allocation to spinners and weavers, and the production, storage, and distribution of textiles. However, individual people—even kings—receive no mention, leaving us largely in the dark about the political and legal systems, social structures, gender relations, and religious beliefs, not to mention particular historical events.

In Homer's *Iliad*, Agamemnon, the king of Mycenae, leads a great expedition of Greeks from different regions against the city of Troy in northwest Anatolia. In addition, the Mycenaean centers reflect a remarkable similarity in buildings, tombs, utensils, tools, clothing, and works of art. Some scholars argue that political unity must have lain behind this cultural uniformity. The *Iliad*, however, revolves around the difficulties Agamemnon has in asserting control over other leaders. Moreover, the archaeological remains and the Linear B tablets suggest that Mycenae, Pylos (PIE-lohs), and other centers wielded power independently.

The seafaring skills of the Minoans and Mycenaeans encouraged long-distance trade. Commercial vessels depended primarily on sails, and their crews navigated during daylight hours to keep the land in sight and then went ashore at night to eat and sleep.

Linear B A set of syllabic symbols, derived from the writing system of Minoan Crete, used in the Mycenaean palaces of the Late Bronze Age to write an early form of Greek. It was used primarily for palace records, and the surviving Linear B tablets provide substantial information about the economic organization of Mycenaean society and tantalizing clues about political, social, and religious institutions.

The ships' shallow keels enabled the crews to pull them up onto the beach.

Cretan and Greek pottery and crafted goods are found not only around the Aegean but also in other parts of the Mediterranean and Middle East, sometimes in enough quantity and variety to suggest settlements of Aegean peoples. The oldest artifacts are Minoan, but eventually Greek wares predominated. This indicates that Cretan merchants pioneered trade routes and then admitted Mycenaean traders, who eventually supplanted them in the fifteenth century B.C.E.

The many Aegean pots found throughout the region must once have contained such products as wine and olive oil. Weapons and other crafted goods may also have been exported, along with slaves and mercenary soldiers. As for imports, amber from northern Europe and ivory carved in Syria have been discovered at Aegean sites, and the large population of southwest Greece probably relied on imported grain. Above all, the Aegean lands needed metals, both the gold prized by rulers and the copper and tin needed to make bronze. Sunken ships carrying copper ingots, probably from Cyprus, have been found at the bottom of the Mediterranean (see Map 3.1). As in early China, metal goods belonged mostly to the elite and may have been symbols of their superior status. Homer's description of bronze tripods piled up in the storerooms of heroes brings to mind the bronze vessels buried in Shang tombs (see Chapter 2).

Mycenaeans were tough, warlike, and acquisitive. They traded with those who were strong and took from those who were weak. This may have provoked conflict with the Hittite kings of Anatolia in the fourteenth and thirteenth centuries B.C.E. Documents found in the archives at Hattusha, the Hittite capital, refer to the king and land of Ahhijawa (uh-key-YAW-wuh), most likely a Hittite rendering of Achaeans (uh-KEY-uhns), the term used most frequently by Homer for the Greeks. The documents indicate that relations were sometimes friendly, sometimes strained, and that the people of Ahhijawa were aggressive and tried to take advantage of Hittite preoccupation or weakness. The *Iliad*, Homer's tale of the Achaeans' ten-year siege and eventual destruction of Troy, a city on the fringes of Hittite territory that controlled the sea route between the Mediterranean and Black Seas, should be seen against this backdrop. Archaeology has confirmed a destruction at Troy around 1200 B.C.E.

The Fall of Late Bronze Age Civilizations

For reasons that remain obscure, large numbers of people were on the move around 1200 B.C.E. As migrants swarmed into one region, they displaced other peoples, who then joined the tide of refugees. This process culminated in the destruction of many of the old Middle Eastern and Mediterranean centers. Around 1200 B.C.E. unidentified invaders destroyed Hattusha and the Hittite kingdom. Moving south into Syria, the tide of destruction swept away the great coastal city of Ugarit. Around 1220 B.C.E., Merneptah (mehr-NEH-ptuh), the son and successor of Ramesses II, repulsed an assault on the Nile Delta by people he described as "Libyans and Northerners coming from all lands." About thirty years later Ramesses III checked a major invasion of southern Syria-Palestine by "Sea Peoples," who became known as Philistines (FIH-luh-steens) (the origin of the name *Palestine*, sometimes used for this region). Although he claimed a great victory, the Philistines occupied the coast, and Egypt soon withdrew. The Egyptians also lost their foothold in Nubia, opening the way for the emergence of the native kingdom centered in Napata (see Chapter 2).

Among the invaders listed in the Egyptian inscriptions are the Ekwesh (ECK-wesh), who could be Achaeans—that is, Greeks. Whether or not the Mycenaeans participated in these or other invasions, their own centers collapsed in the first half of the twelfth century B.C.E. The rulers apparently saw trouble coming; at some sites they undertook more extensive fortifications and measures to ensure water supplies. But their efforts were in vain. Nearly all the palaces were destroyed. The Linear B tablets survive only because they were baked hard in the resulting fires.

Curiously, archaeology reveals no trace of foreign invaders. Yet it is unlikely to be coincidental that Mycenaean civilization collapsed at roughly the same time as the fall of other regional civilizations. The position of the Mycenaean ruling class may have depended on imports of vital commodities and profits from trade, and they may have suffered from the destruction of trading partners and disruption of routes. Competition for limited resources may have led to internal unrest and, ultimately, political collapse.

SECTION REVIEW

- Influenced by contact with older cultures, Minoan Crete was the first European civilization to develop a complex government and advanced technologies.

- The Minoans participated in extensive long-distance trade, which prompted a blending of foreign and indigenous cultural forms and practices.

- Minoan civilization was deliberately destroyed, perhaps by Mycenaean Greeks.

- In Greece, Mycenaean civilization rose suddenly and developed common patterns of settlement, organization, and technology.

- The Mycenaeans participated in long-distance trade and piracy activities, which likely became the basis of later heroic legends.

- Large migrations precipitated the collapse of many Late Bronze Age civilizations, including the Mycenaean, after which Greece entered a Dark Age.

The destruction of the palaces ended the domination of the ruling class. The administrative apparatus revealed in the Linear B tablets disappeared, and writing passed out of use along with the palace officials who had utilized it. Archaeological studies indicate the depopulation of some regions of Greece and a flow of people to other regions that escaped destruction. The Greek language persisted, and a thousand years later people were still worshiping gods mentioned in the Linear B tablets. People also continued to make the vessels and implements that they were familiar with, although there was a marked decline in artistic and technical skill in the now impoverished society. Mycenaean cultural uniformity gave way to regional variations in shapes, styles, and techniques, reflecting the increased isolation of different Greek areas. The peoples of the region entered a centuries-long "Dark Age" of poverty, isolation, and loss of knowledge.

The Assyrian Empire, 911–612 B.C.E.

How did the Assyrian Empire rise to power and eventually dominate most of the ancient Middle East?

New centers emerged in the centuries after 1000 B.C.E. The chief force for change was the powerful and aggressive **Neo-Assyrian Empire** (911–612 B.C.E.). Although historians sometimes apply the term *empire* to earlier regional powers, the Assyrians of this era were the first to rule over far-flung lands and diverse peoples.

The Assyrian homeland in northern Mesopotamia differs substantially from the flat expanse of Sumer and Akkad to the south. It is hillier, has a more temperate and rainier climate, and is exposed to raiders from the mountains to the east and north and the arid plain to the west. Peasant farmers, accustomed to defending themselves against marauders, provided the foot-soldiers for the ceaseless campaigns of the Neo-Assyrian Empire: westward across the steppe and desert as far as the Mediterranean, north into mountainous Urartu (ur-RAHR-too) (modern Armenia), east across the Zagros range onto the Iranian Plateau, and south along the Tigris River to Babylonia.

These campaigns followed important trade routes and provided immediate booty and the prospect of tribute and taxes. They also secured access to iron and silver and brought the Assyrians control of international commerce. As noted earlier, Assyria had a long tradition of commercial and political interests in Syria and Anatolia. However, what started out as an aggressive program of self-defense and reassertion of old claims soon became more ambitious. Driven by pride, greed, and religious conviction, the Assyrians defeated the great kingdoms of the day—Elam (southwest Iran), Urartu, Babylon, and Egypt. Larger in extent than its predecessors, the Assyrian Empire was founded on the principle of enriching the imperial center at the expense of the subjugated periphery.

The king was literally and symbolically the center of the Assyrian universe. The land belonged to him, and all the people, even the highest-ranking officials, were his servants. Assyrians believed that the gods chose the king as their earthly representative. Normally the king chose a son as successor, and his choice

Neo-Assyrian Empire An empire extending from western Iran to Syria-Palestine, conquered by the Assyrians of northern Mesopotamia between the tenth and seventh centuries B.C.E. They used force and terror and exploited the wealth and labor of their subjects. They also preserved and continued the cultural and scientific developments of Mesopotamian civilization.

Section of Balawat Gates Bronze bands with images of military campaigns and court life were affixed to the cedar-wood gates of a palace built by the Assyrian king Shalmaneser III (r. 858–824 B.C.E.).

British Museum/Michael Holford

was confirmed by divine oracles and the Assyrian elite. In the revered ancient city of Ashur the high priest anointed the new king by sprinkling his head with oil and gave him the insignia of kingship: a crown and scepter. The kings were buried in Ashur.

Every day messengers and spies brought the king information from every corner of the empire. He made decisions, appointed officials, and heard complaints. He dictated his correspondence to an army of scribes and received and entertained foreign envoys and high-ranking government figures. As the country's military leader, the king was responsible for planning campaigns, and he often was away from the capital commanding operations in the field.

Among other responsibilities, the king supervised the state religion, devoting much time to public and private rituals and to temple maintenance. He consulted the gods through elaborate rituals, and all state actions were carried out in the name of Ashur, the chief god. Military victories gave proof of Ashur's superiority over the gods of the conquered peoples.

Relentless government propaganda secured popular support for military campaigns that mostly benefited the king and the nobility. Royal inscriptions posted throughout the empire catalogued military victories, extolled the king, and promised ruthless punishments for those who resisted. Relief sculptures depicting hunts, battles, sieges, executions, and deportations covered the walls of the royal palaces at Kalhu (KAL-oo) and Nineveh (NIN-uh-vuh). The king loomed over most scenes, larger than anyone else, muscular and fierce, with the appearance of a god. Visitors to the Assyrian court were undoubtedly awed—and intimidated.

Conquest and Control

Superior military organization and technology made the Assyrians' unprecedented conquests possible. At first, armies consisted of soldiers who served in return for grants of land and peasants and slaves contributed by large landowners. Later, King Tiglathpileser (TIG-lath-pih-LEE-zuhr) (r. 744–727 B.C.E.) maintained a core of professional soldiers made up of Assyrians and the most warlike subject peoples. At its peak the Assyrian state could mobilize half a million troops, including lightly armed bowmen and

Primary Source: An Assyrian Emperor's Résumé: Ferocious Conquests a Specialty Destruction, devastation, and severed heads: find out what happens when the Assyrian emperor is slighted.

slingers, armored spearmen, cavalry equipped with bows or spears, and four-man chariots.

Iron weapons and cavalry gave the Assyrians their edge. However, Assyrian engineers also developed ways of attacking fortified towns. They tunneled under the walls, built movable towers for their archers, and applied battering rams to weak points. Some of the best-fortified cities of the Middle East—Babylon, Thebes in Egypt, Tyre in Phoenicia, and Susa in Elam—yielded to these tactics. Couriers and signal fires provided long-distance communication, while a network of spies gathered intelligence.

Terror tactics discouraged resistance and rebellion. Civilians were thrown into fires, prisoners were skinned alive, and the severed heads of defeated rulers were hung on city walls, all of which was well publicized. **Mass deportation**—the forcible uprooting and resettling of entire communities—broke the spirit of rebellious peoples. Sumer, Babylon, Urartu, Egypt, and the Hittites had done this before, but the Neo-Assyrian monarchs used deportation on an unprecedented scale. Surviving documents record the relocation of over one million people, and historians estimate that the true figure exceeds four million. Deportation also shifted human resources from the periphery to the center, where the deportees worked on royal and noble estates, opened new lands for agriculture, and built palaces and cities. Deportees who were craftsmen and soldiers could be assigned to the Assyrian army.

Faced with an array of peoples with different languages, customs, religions, and political organization, the Assyrians never found a single, enduring method of governing. Control tended to be tight and effective at the center and in lands closest to the core area, and less so farther away. The Assyrian kings waged many campaigns to reimpose control on territories subdued in previous wars.

Assyrian provincial officials oversaw the payment of tribute and taxes, maintained law and order, raised troops, undertook public works, and provisioned armies and administrators passing through their territory. Provincial governors were subject to frequent inspections by royal overseers. The elite class was bound to the monarch by oaths of obedience, fear of punishment, and the expectation of land grants or shares of booty and taxes. Skilled

professionals—priests, diviners, scribes, doctors, and artisans—were similarly bound.

The Assyrians ruthlessly exploited the wealth and resources of their subjects to fund their military campaigns and administration. Wealth from the periphery flowed to the center, where the king and nobility grew rich. Proud kings expanded the ancestral capital and religious center at Ashur and built magnificent new royal cities encircled by high walls and containing ornate palaces and temples. Dur Sharrukin (DOOR SHAH-roo-keen), the "Fortress of Sargon," was completed in a mere ten years, thanks to a massive labor force composed of prisoners of war and Assyrian citizens who owed periodic service to the state.

Yet the Assyrian Empire was not simply parasitic. There is some evidence of royal investment in provincial infrastructure. The cities and merchant classes thrived on expanded long-distance commerce, and some subject populations were surprisingly loyal to their Assyrian rulers.

Assyrian Society and Culture

In the core area people belonged to the same three classes that had existed in Hammurabi's Babylon a millennium before (see Chapter 1): (1) free, landowning citizens, (2) farmers and artisans attached to the estates of the king or other rich landholders, and (3) slaves. Slaves—debtors and prisoners of war—had legal rights and, if sufficiently talented, could rise to positions of influence.

The government normally did not distinguish between native Assyrians and the increasingly large number of immigrants and deportees residing in the Assyrian homeland. All were referred to as "human beings," entitled to the same legal protections and liable for the same labor and military service. Over time the inflow of outsiders changed the ethnic makeup of the core area.

The vast majority of subjects worked on the land. The agricultural surpluses they produced allowed

mass deportation The forcible removal and relocation of large numbers of people or entire populations. The mass deportations practiced by the Assyrian and Persian Empires were meant as a terrifying warning of the consequences of rebellion. They also brought labor to the imperial center.

SECTION REVIEW

- One of the most important civilizations to emerge after the upheavals of the Late Bronze Age was the Neo-Assyrian Empire.

- Led by all-powerful kings, the Assyrians waged campaigns of aggressive expansion.

- The Assyrians' military success rested on superior organization and technology, such as iron weapons, cavalry, and the ability to attack fortifications.

- The Assyrians controlled subject peoples through terror tactics and mass deportations.

- The Assyrian state exploited subject territories, transporting wealth from the periphery to the center of the empire.

- The Assyrians built upon the social structures and technologies of earlier Mesopotamian civilizations and left important records of Mesopotamian life.

substantial numbers of people—the standing army, government officials, religious experts, merchants, and artisans—to engage in specialized activities.

Most trade took place at the local level, with individual artisans and small workshops producing pottery, tools, and clothing. The state fostered long-distance trade, since imported luxury goods—metals, fine textiles, dyes, gems, and ivory—pleased the elite and brought in substantial customs revenues. Silver was the basic medium of exchange, weighed out for each transaction in a time before the invention of coinage.

Building on earlier Mesopotamian traditions, Assyrian scholars recorded lists of plant and animal names, geographic terms, and astronomical occurrences, and they made original contributions in mathematics and astronomy. Exorcists sought to expel the demons they believed caused disease, but more rational physicians experimented with medicines and surgical treatments.

Some Assyrian temples may have had libraries. At Nineveh the palace of **Ashurbanipal** (ah-shur-BAH-nee-pahl) (r. 668–627 B.C.E.), one of the last Assyrian kings, yielded more than twenty-five thousand tablets or fragments of tablets, including official documents as well as literary and scientific texts. Some were originals that had been brought to the capital; others were copies made at the king's request. Ashurbanipal avidly collected the literary and scientific heritage of

Mesopotamia, and the "House of Knowledge" referred to in some of the documents may have been an academy of learned men in the imperial center. Much of what we know about Mesopotamian art, literature, and science and earlier Mesopotamian history comes from discoveries at Assyrian sites.

Israel, 2000–500 B.C.E.

How did the civilization of Israel develop, following both familiar cultural patterns and a unique course of its own?

On the western edge of the Assyrian Empire lived a people who were destined to play an important role in world history. The history of ancient Israel is marked by two interconnected dramas that played out from around 2000 to 500 B.C.E. First, a loose collection of nomadic kinship groups engaged in herding and caravan traffic became a sedentary, agricultural people, developed complex political and social institutions, and became integrated into the commercial and diplomatic networks of the Middle East. Second, these people transformed the austere cult of a desert god into the concept of a single, all-powerful, and all-knowing deity, in the process creating the ethical and intellectual traditions that underlie the beliefs and values of Judaism, Christianity, and Islam.

The land at the heart of this story has borne various names—Canaan, Israel, Syria-Palestine—as have the people—Hebrews, Israelites, Jews. For the sake of consistency, the people are referred to here as Israelites, the land they occupied in antiquity as **Israel**.

Being at a crossroads between Syria, Egypt, Arabia, and Mesopotamia has given Israel an importance in history out of all proportion to its size. Its

Ashurbanipal The seventh century B.C.E. Assyrian ruler who assembled a large collection of writings drawn from the ancient literary, religious, and scientific traditions of Mesopotamia. The many tablets unearthed by archaeologists constitute one of the most important sources of present-day knowledge of the long literary tradition of Mesopotamia.

Israel In antiquity, the land between the eastern shore of the Mediterranean and the Jordan River, occupied by the Israelites from the early second millennium B.C.E.

natural resources are few. The Negev Desert and the vast wasteland of the Sinai (SIE-nie) lay to the south. The Mediterranean coastal plain was occupied throughout much of this period by Philistines, who were of uncertain ethnic origin. The center of Israel featured rock-strewn hills. Galilee to the north, with its sea of the same name, was a relatively fertile land of grassy hills and small plains from which the narrow ribbon of the Jordan River flowed down into the Dead Sea, so named because its high salt content is toxic to life.

Origins, Exodus, and Settlement

The fundamental source of information about ancient Israel is the collection of writings preserved in the **Hebrew Bible** (called the Old Testament by Christians). The Hebrew Bible brings together several collections of materials that originated with different groups, employed distinctive vocabularies, and gave particular interpretations of past events. Traditions about the Israelites' early days were long transmitted orally. Not until the tenth century B.C.E. were they written down in a script borrowed from the Phoenicians. The text that we have today dates from the fifth century B.C.E., with a few later additions, and reflects the point of view of the priests who controlled the Temple in Jerusalem. Historians disagree about how accurately this document represents Israelite history. In the absence of other written sources, however, it provides a foundation to be used critically and modified in light of archaeological discoveries.

The Hebrew language of the Bible reflects the speech of the Israelites until about 500 B.C.E. It is a Semitic language, most closely related to Phoenician and Aramaic (which later supplanted Hebrew in Israel), more distantly related to Arabic and the Akkadian language of the Assyrians. This linguistic affinity probably parallels the Israelites' ethnic relationship to the neighboring peoples.

The early history of Israel embodies a familiar story of nomadic pastoralists who occupied marginal land between the arid desert and settled agricultural areas. Early on, these nomads raided the farms and villages of settled peoples, but eventually they settled down to an agricultural way of life and later developed a unified state.

The Hebrew Bible focuses on the family of Abraham. Born in the city of Ur in southern Mesopotamia, Abraham rejected the idol worship of his homeland and migrated with his family and livestock across the Syrian Desert. Eventually he arrived in the land of Israel, which, according to the biblical account, had been promised to him and his descendants as part of a "covenant," or pact, with the Israelite god, Yahweh.

These "recollections" of the journey of Abraham (who, if he was a real person, probably lived in the twentieth century B.C.E.) may compress the experiences of generations of pastoralists who migrated from the grazing lands between the upper reaches of the Tigris and Euphrates Rivers to the Mediterranean coastal plain. Following the usual pattern in the region, Abraham, his family, and his companions camped by a permanent water source in the dry season and then drove herds of sheep, cattle, and donkeys to traditional grazing areas during the rest of the year. The animals provided them with milk, cheese, meat, and cloth.

The early Israelites and the settled peoples of the region were suspicious of one another. This friction between nomadic herders and settled farmers, as well as the Israelites' view of their ancestors as having been nomads, comes through in the story of the innocent shepherd Abel, who was killed by his farmer brother Cain.

Abraham's son Isaac and then his grandson Jacob became the leaders of this wandering group of herders. In the next generation the squabbling sons of Jacob's several wives sold their brother Joseph as a slave to passing merchants heading for Egypt. The Bible relates that through luck and ability Joseph became a high official at Pharaoh's court. Thus he was able to help his people when drought struck and

 Primary Source: Moses Descends Mount Sinai with the Ten Commandments Discover what happens when God speaks to Moses.

Hebrew Bible A collection of sacred books containing diverse materials concerning the origins, experiences, beliefs, and practices of the Israelites. Most of the extant text was compiled by members of the priestly class in the fifth century B.C.E. and reflects the concerns and views of this group.

forced the Israelites to migrate to Egypt. The sophisticated Egyptians feared and looked down on these rough herders and eventually reduced the Israelites to slaves, putting them to work on the building projects of the pharaoh.

Several points need to be made about this version of events. First, the biblical account glosses over the period from 1700 to 1500 B.C.E., when Egypt was dominated by the Hyksos. Since the Hyksos are thought to have been Semitic groups that infiltrated the Nile Delta from the northeast, the Israelite migration to Egypt and later enslavement could have been connected to the Hyksos' rise and fall. Second, although the surviving Egyptian sources do not refer to Israelite slaves, they do complain about *Apiru* (uh-PEE-roo), a derogatory term applied to caravan drivers, outcasts, bandits, and other marginal groups. The word seems to designate a class of people rather than a particular ethnic group, but some scholars believe there may be a connection between the similar-sounding terms *Apiru* and *Hebrew*. Third, the period of alleged Israelite slavery coincided with the era of ambitious building programs launched by several New Kingdom pharaohs.

The Bible further relates that Moses, an Israelite with connections to the Egyptian royal family, led the Israelites out of captivity. The narrative of their departure, the Exodus, is overlaid with folktale motifs, including the ten plagues that Yahweh inflicted on Egypt to persuade the pharaoh to release the Israelites and the miraculous parting of the Red Sea that enabled the refugees to escape. It is possible that oral tradition may have preserved memories of a real emigration from Egypt followed by years of wandering in the wilderness of Sinai.

During their reported forty years in the desert, the Israelites became devoted to a stern and warlike god. According to the Hebrew Bible, Yahweh made a covenant with the Israelites: they would be his "Chosen People" if they promised to worship him exclusively. This pact was confirmed by tablets that Moses brought down from the top of Mount Sinai. Written on the tablets were the Ten Commandments, which set out the basic tenets of Jewish belief and practice. The Commandments prohibited murder, adultery, theft, lying, and envy and demanded respect for parents and rest from work on the Sabbath, the seventh day of the week.

Joshua, Moses's successor, is named as leading the Israelites from the east side of the Jordan River into the land of Canaan (KAY-nuhn) (modern Israel and the Palestinian territories). They attacked and destroyed Jericho (JEI-rih-koe) and other Canaanite (KAY-nuh-nite) cities. Archaeological evidence confirms the destruction of some Canaanite towns between 1250 and 1200 B.C.E., though not precisely the towns mentioned in the biblical account. Shortly thereafter, lowland sites were resettled and new sites were established in the hills, thanks to the development of cisterns carved into rock to hold rainwater and the construction of terraces for farming. The material culture of the new settlers was cruder but continued Canaanite patterns.

Most scholars doubt that Canaan was conquered by a unified Israelite army. In a time of widespread disruption, movements of peoples, and decline and destruction of cities throughout this region, it is more likely that Israelite migrants took advantage of the disorder and were joined by other loosely organized groups and even refugees from the Canaanite cities.

In a pattern common throughout history, the new coalition of peoples invented a common ancestry. The "Children of Israel," as they called themselves, were divided into twelve tribes supposedly descended from the sons of Jacob and Joseph. Each tribe installed itself in a different part of the country. Its chief was primarily responsible for mediating disputes and safeguarding the group. Charismatic figures called "Judges" famed for their bravery or diplomacy enjoyed a special standing that transcended tribal boundaries. The tribes also shared a shrine in the hill country at Shiloh (SHIE-loe), which housed the Ark of the Covenant, a sacred chest containing the tablets that Yahweh had given Moses.

Rise of the Monarchy

The time of troubles that struck the eastern Mediterranean around 1200 B.C.E. brought the Philistines to the coastal plain, where they fought frequently with the Israelites in the hills. The long-haired strongman Samson, who toppled a Philistine temple, and the shepherd boy David, whose slingshot felled the towering Philistine warrior Goliath, became biblical heroes. A religious leader named Samuel recognized the need for a stronger central authority to lead the Israelites

Artist's Rendering of Solomon's Jerusalem Strategically located in the middle of lands occupied by the Israelite tribes and on a high plateau overlooking the central hills and the Judaean desert, Jerusalem was captured around 1000 B.C.E. by King David, who made it his capital (the City of David is at left, the citadel and palace complex at center). The next king, Solomon, built the First Temple to serve as the center of worship of the Israelite god, Yahweh. Solomon's Temple (at upper right) was destroyed during the Neo-Babylonian sack of the city in 587 B.C.E. The modest structure soon built to take its place was replaced by the magnificent Second Temple, erected by King Herod in the last decades of the first century B.C.E. and destroyed by the Romans in 70 C.E.

against the Philistine city-states, and he anointed Saul as the first king of Israel around 1020 B.C.E. When Saul perished in battle, the throne passed to David (r. ca. 1000–960 B.C.E.), who oversaw Israel's transition from a tribal confederacy to a unified monarchy. He strengthened royal authority by making the captured hill city of Jerusalem, which lay outside tribal boundaries, his capital. Soon after, David brought the Ark to Jerusalem, making the city the religious as well as the political center of the kingdom.

The reign of David's son Solomon (r. ca. 960–920 B.C.E.) marked the high point of the Israelite monarchy. Alliances and trade linked Israel with near and distant lands. Solomon and Hiram, the king of Phoenician Tyre, together commissioned a fleet that sailed into the Red Sea and brought back gold, ivory, jewels, sandalwood, and exotic animals. The story of the visit to Solomon by the queen of Sheba, who brought gold, precious stones, and spices, may be mythical, but it reflects the reality of trade with Saba (SUH-buh) in south Arabia (present-day Yemen) or the Horn of

Africa (present-day Somalia). Such wealth supported a lavish court life, a sizeable bureaucracy, and an intimidating chariot army that made Israel a regional power. Solomon undertook an ambitious building program employing slaves and the compulsory labor of citizens. To strengthen the link between religious and secular authority, he built the **First Temple** in Jerusalem.

The Temple priests became a powerful and wealthy class, receiving a share of the annual harvest

---

First Temple A monumental sanctuary built in Jerusalem by King Solomon in the tenth century B.C.E. to be the religious center for the Israelite god Yahweh. The Temple priesthood conducted sacrifices, received a tithe or percentage of agricultural revenues, and became economically and politically powerful. The First Temple was destroyed by the Babylonians in 587 B.C.E. and was rebuilt on a modest scale in the late sixth century B.C.E. It was replaced by King Herod's Second Temple in the late first century B.C.E. and destroyed by the Romans in 70 C.E.

in return for making animal sacrifices to Yahweh. The expansion of Jerusalem, new commercial opportunities, and the increasing prestige of the Temple hierarchy contributed to a growing gap between urban and rural, rich and poor. Fiery prophets, claiming revelation from Yahweh, accused the monarchs and aristocracy of corruption, impiety, and neglect of the poor.

The Israelites lived in extended families, several generations residing together under the authority of the eldest male. Arranged marriages were an important economic as well as social institution. To prove his financial worthiness, the groom gave a substantial gift to the father of the bride. Her entire family participated in the ceremonial weighing of silver or gold. The wife's dowry often included a slave girl who attended her for life.

Male heirs were of paramount importance, and firstborn sons received a double share of the inheritance. If a couple had no son, they could adopt one, or the husband could have a child by the wife's slave attendant. If a man died childless, his brother was expected to marry his widow and father an heir.

Women provided the family with important goods and services but could not inherit property or initiate divorce. An unfaithful woman could be put to death. Working-class women shared in farming and herding chores in addition to caring for the house and children. Some urban women worked outside the home as cooks, bakers, perfumers, wet nurses (a recent mother hired to suckle another person's child), prostitutes, and singers of laments at funerals. A few women reached positions of influence, such as Deborah the Judge, who led troops in battle against the Canaanites. Women known collectively as "wise women" appear to have composed sacred texts in poetry and prose. This reality has been obscured, in part by the male bias of the Hebrew Bible, in part because the status of women declined as Israelite society became more urbanized.

Fragmentation and Dispersal

After Solomon's death around 920 B.C.E., resentment over royal demands and the neglect of tribal rights split the monarchy into two kingdoms: Israel in the north, with its capital at Samaria (suh-MAH-ree-yuh), and Judah (JOO-duh) in the southern territory around Jerusalem. The two were sometimes at war, sometimes allied.

This period saw the final formulation of **monotheism**, the absolute belief in Yahweh as the one and only god. Nevertheless, religious leaders still had to contend with cults professing polytheism (the belief in multiple gods). The rituals of the Canaanite storm-god Baal (BAHL) and the fertility goddess Astarte (uh-STAHR-tee) attracted many Israelites. Prophets condemned the adoption of foreign rituals and threatened that Yahweh would punish Israel severely.

The small states of Syria and the two Israelite kingdoms laid aside their rivalries to mount a joint resistance to the Neo-Assyrian Empire, but to no avail. In 721 B.C.E. the Assyrians destroyed the northern kingdom of Israel and deported much of its population to the east. New settlers were brought in from Syria, Babylon, and Iran, changing the area's ethnic, cultural, and religious character. The kingdom of Judah survived for more than a century, sometimes rebelling, sometimes paying tribute to the Assyrians or the Neo-Babylonian kings (626–539 B.C.E.) that succeeded them.

When the Neo-Babylonian monarch Nebuchadnezzar (NAB-oo-kuhd-nez-uhr) captured Jerusalem in 587 B.C.E., he destroyed the Temple and deported to Babylon the royal family, the aristocracy, and many skilled workers. The deportees prospered so well in their new home "by the waters of Babylon" that half a century later most of their descendants refused the offer of the Persian monarch Cyrus (see Chapter 4) to return to their homeland. This was the origin of the **Diaspora** (die-ASS-peh-rah)—a Greek word meaning "dispersion" or "scattering." This dispersion outside the homeland of many Jews—as we may now call these people, since an independent Israel no

monotheism Belief in the existence of a single divine entity. Some scholars cite the devotion of the Egyptian pharaoh Akhenaten to Aten (sun-disk) and his suppression of traditional gods as the earliest instance. The Israelite worship of Yahweh developed into an exclusive belief in one god, and this concept passed into Christianity and Islam.

Diaspora A Greek word meaning "dispersal," used to describe the communities of a given ethnic group living outside their homeland. Jews, for example, spread from Israel to western Asia and Mediterranean lands in antiquity and today can be found throughout the world.

- As the Hebrew Bible suggests, the Israelites began as nomadic pastoralists who, after a period of enslavement, settled permanently in Canaan.

- Pressure from hostile Philistines forced the Israelites to adopt a more complex government.

- The resulting monarchy unified the Israelites into the kingdom of Israel, which reached its height under Solomon.

- During the monarchy, the temple priests became a powerful class, and Israelite society became more urban and economically divided.

- Patrilineal extended families became the basic social unit, and the status of women steadily declined.

- After the breakup of Israel, Jewish monotheism reached its final form, successive conquests created the Diaspora, and a distinct Jewish identity emerged.

longer existed—continues to this day. To maintain their religion and culture, the Diaspora communities developed institutions like the synagogue (Greek for "bringing together"), a communal meeting place that served religious, educational, and social functions.

The Babylonian Jews that did make the long trek back to Judah met with a cold reception from the local population. Persevering, they rebuilt the Temple in modest form and drafted the Deuteronomic (doo-tuhr-uh-NAHM-ik) Code of law and conduct (*deuteronomic* is Greek for "second set of laws"). The fifth century B.C.E. also saw the compilation of much of the Hebrew Bible in roughly its present form.

Exile and loss of political autonomy sharpened Jewish identity. Jews lived by a rigid set of rules. Dietary restrictions forbade the eating of pork and shellfish and mandated that meat and dairy products not be consumed together. Ritual baths were used to achieve spiritual purity, and women were required to take ritual baths after menstruation. The Jews venerated the Sabbath (Saturday, the seventh day of the week) by refraining from work and from fighting, following the example of Yahweh, who, according to the Bible, rested on the seventh day after creating the world. These strictures and others, including a ban on marrying non-Jews, tended to isolate the Jews from other peoples, but they also fostered a powerful sense of community.

Phoenicia and the Mediterranean, 1200–500 B.C.E.

How did the Phoenicians rise to commercial dominance over much of the Mediterranean world?

The people who occupied the coast of Lebanon developed their own **Phoenician** (fuh-NEE-shun) civilization. Ancient writers generally used this Greek word instead of "Can'ani"—Canaanites—the word they used for themselves.

The Phoenician City-States

Many Canaanite settlements were destroyed during the violent upheavals and mass migrations around 1200 B.C.E. discussed earlier. Aramaeans (ah-ruh-MAY-uhns)—nomadic pastoralists like the early Israelites—migrated into the interior portions of Syria while Israelites and Philistines gained dominance farther south.

By 1100 B.C.E. Canaanite territory had shrunk to a narrow strip of Lebanon between the mountains and the sea. New political forms and seaborne commerce provided the keys to Canaanite survival. Sometime after 1000 B.C.E. the Canaanites encountered the Greeks, who referred to them as *Phoinikes*, or Phoenicians. The term may mean "red men" and refer to the color of their skin, or it may refer to the precious purple dye they extracted from the murex snail (see Environment and Technology: Ancient Textiles and Dyes).

Rivers and rocky spurs sliced the Lebanese coastal plain into a series of small city-states, notably Byblos (BIB-loss), Sidon (SIE-duhn), and Tyre. Exchange of raw materials (cedar and pine, metals, incense, papyrus), foodstuffs (wine, spices, salted fish), and crafted luxury goods (textiles, carved ivory, glass) brought wealth and influence to the Phoenician city-states.

Phoenicians Semitic-speaking Canaanites living on the coast of Lebanon and Syria in the first millennium B.C.E. From major cities such as Tyre and Sidon, Phoenician merchants and sailors explored the Mediterranean, engaged in widespread commerce, and founded Carthage and other colonies in the western Mediterranean.

Ancient Textiles and Dyes

Throughout human history the production of textiles—cloth for clothing, blankets, carpets, and coverings of various sorts—required an expenditure of human labor second only to the work necessary to provide food. Nevertheless, textile production in antiquity has left few archaeological traces. The plant fibers and animal hair used for cloth quickly decompose except in rare circumstances. Some textile remains have been found in the hot, dry conditions of Egypt, the cool, arid Andes of South America, and the peat bogs of northern Europe. But most of our knowledge of ancient textiles depends on the discovery of equipment used in textile production—such as spindles, loom weights, and dyeing vats—and on pictorial representations and descriptions in texts.

Cloth production usually has been the work of women for a simple but important reason. Responsibility for child rearing limits women's ability to participate in other activities but does not consume all their time and energy. In many societies textile production has been complementary to child-rearing activities, for it can be done in the home, is relatively safe, does not require great concentration, and can be interrupted without consequence. The growing and harvesting of plants such as cotton or flax (from which linen is made) and the shearing of wool from sheep and, in the Andes, llamas are outdoor activities, but the subsequent stages of production can be carried out inside the home. The basic methods of textile production did not change much from early antiquity until the late eighteenth century C.E., when the fabrication of textiles was transferred to mills and mass production began.

When textile production has been considered "women's work," most of the output has been for household consumption. However, women weavers in Peru developed new raw materials, new techniques, and new decorative motifs around three thousand years ago. They began to use the wool of llamas and alpacas in addition to cotton. Three women worked side by side and passed the weft from hand to hand to produce a fabric of greater width. Women weavers also introduced embroidery and decorated garments with new religious motifs, such as the jaguar-god. Their high-quality textiles were given as tribute to the elite and were used to trade for luxury goods.

More typically, men dominated commercial production. In ancient Phoenicia, fine textiles with bright, permanent colors became a major export product. Most prized was the red-purple known as Tyrian purple because Tyre was the major source. Persian and Hellenistic kings wore robes dyed this color, and a white toga with a purple border was the sign of a Roman senator.

The production of Tyrian purple was an exceedingly laborious process. The spiny dye-murex snail lives on the sandy Mediterranean bottom at depths ranging from 30 to 500 feet (10 to 150 meters). Nine thousand snails were needed to produce 1 gram (0.035 ounce) of dye. The dye was made from a colorless liquid in the snail's hypobranchial gland. The gland sacs were removed, crushed, soaked with salt, and exposed to sunlight and air for some days; then they were subject to controlled boiling and heating.

Huge mounds of broken shells on the Phoenician coast are testimony to the ancient industry. The snail may have been rendered nearly extinct at many locations, and some scholars speculate that Phoenician colonization in the Mediterranean was motivated in part by the search for new sources of snails.

Ancient Peruvian Textiles The weaving of Chavín was famous for its color and symbolic imagery. Artisans both wove designs into the fabric and used paint or dyes to decorate plain fabric. This early Chavín painted fabric was used in a burial. Notice how the face suggests a jaguar and the headdress includes the image of a serpent.   Private collection.

Expansion to the Mediterranean

Before 1000 B.C.E. Byblos was the most important Phoenician city-state. The English word *bible* comes from the Greek *biblion*, meaning "book written on papyrus from Byblos." The Greeks recognized the Phoenicians as the inventors of the alphabet, which used about two dozen symbols, each of which represented a consonant or long vowel. (The Greeks added symbols for short vowel sounds—see Chapter 4.) Little Phoenician writing survives, probably because scribes used perishable papyrus. As a result, little is known about the internal affairs of the Phoenician cities beyond the names of some kings.

After 1000 B.C.E. Tyre surpassed Byblos. Located on an offshore island, Tyre was practically impregnable. It had two harbors—one facing north, the other south—that were connected by a canal. The city boasted a large marketplace, a magnificent palace

complex with treasury and archives, and temples to the gods Melqart (MEL-kahrt) and Astarte. Some of its thirty thousand or more inhabitants lived in suburbs on the mainland. Its one weakness was its dependence on the mainland for food and fresh water.

In the century following Tyre turned its attention westward, establishing colonies on Cyprus, a copper-rich island 100 miles (161 kilometers) from the coast (see Map 3.2). In the ninth century B.C.E., the Phoenicians of Lebanon began to explore and colonize parts of the western Mediterranean, including the coasts of North Africa and Spain, and the islands of Sicily and Sardinia. The Phoenicians were primarily interested in access to valuable raw materials and trading opportunities.

By 700 B.C.E., when Homer mentions Phoenician seafarers in the Aegean Sea, a string of settlements in the western Mediterranean formed a "Phoenician

Map 3.2　Colonization of the Mediterranean　In the ninth century B.C.E., the Phoenecians of Lebanon began to explore and colonize parts of the western Mediterranean, including the coast of North Africa, southern and eastern Spain, and the islands of Sicily and Sardinia. The Phoenecians were primarily interested in access to valuable raw materials and trading opportunities.
© Cengage Learning

Interactive Map

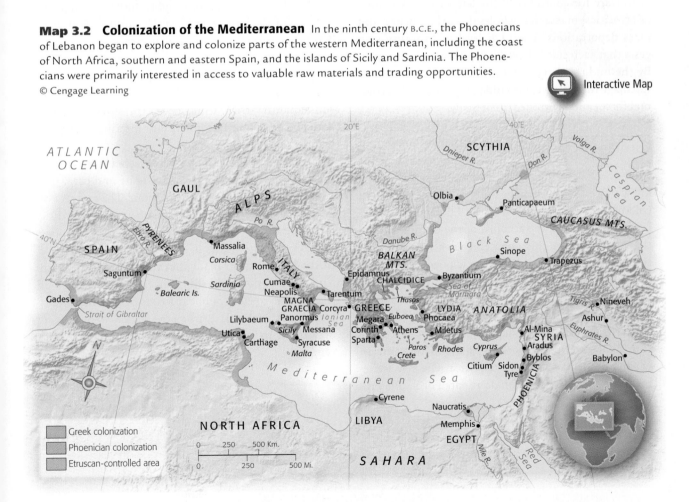

- Greek colonization
- Phoenician colonization
- Etruscan-controlled area

triangle": the North African coast from western Libya to Morocco; the south and southeast coast of Spain, including Gades (GAH-days) (modern Cadiz [kuh-DEEZ]) on the Strait of Gibraltar; and the islands of Sardinia, Sicily, and Malta off the coast of Italy (see Map 3.2). The colonists situated many of these new settlements on promontories or offshore islands in imitation of Tyre.

Overseas settlement provided new sources of trade goods and new trading partners as well as an outlet for excess population. Tyre tried to stave off the Assyrian kings by paying tribute, but in 701 B.C.E. it finally fell to an Assyrian army. Sidon then became the leading city in Phoenicia.

Phoenician activities in the west often involved conflict with the Greeks, who were also expanding trade and establishing colonies. This rivalry centered on Sicily. Phoenicians occupied the western end of the island, Greeks its eastern and central parts. Centuries of warfare for control of Sicily left written accounts of atrocities, massacres, wholesale enslavements, and mass deportations. The high level of brutality suggests that each side believed its survival to be at stake. By the mid-third century B.C.E., the Tyrian colony of Carthage in Tunisia commanded the Phoenician colonial forces and controlled all of Sicily.

Carthage's Commercial Empire

Thanks to Greek and Roman reports about their wars, historians know more about **Carthage** and the other Phoenician colonies than they do about the Phoenician homeland. For example, the account of the origins of Carthage that began this chapter comes from Roman sources (most famously Virgil's epic poem *The Aeneid*) but is probably based on a Carthaginian original. Archaeological excavation has roughly confirmed the city's traditional foundation date of 814 B.C.E. Situated just outside the present-day city of Tunis, Carthage controlled the middle portion of the Mediterranean where Europe comes closest to Africa. The new settlement grew rapidly and soon dominated other Phoenician colonies in the west.

Occupying a narrow promontory, Carthage stretched between Byrsa (BURR-suh), the original hilltop citadel of the community, and a double harbor.

The inner harbor could accommodate 220 warships. A watchtower allowed surveillance of the surrounding area, and high walls made it impossible to see in from the outside. The outer commercial harbor was filled with docks for merchant ships and shipyards. In case of attack, a huge iron chain could close off the harbor.

Government offices ringed a large central square where magistrates heard legal cases outdoors. The inner city was a maze of narrow, winding streets, multistory apartment buildings, and sacred enclosures. Farther out lay a sprawling suburban district where the wealthy built spacious villas amid fields and vegetable gardens. This entire urban complex was enclosed by a wall 22 miles (35 kilometers) in length. At the most critical point—the 2.5-mile-wide (4-kilometer-wide) isthmus connecting the promontory to the mainland—the wall was over 40 feet (13 meters) high and 30 feet (10 meters) thick and had high watchtowers.

With a population of roughly 400,000, Carthage was one of the largest cities in the world by 500 B.C.E. The population was ethnically diverse, including people of Phoenician stock, indigenous peoples likely to have been the ancestors of modern-day Berbers, and immigrants from other Mediterranean lands and sub-Saharan Africa. Contrary to the story of Dido's reluctance to remarry, Phoenicians intermarried quite readily with other peoples.

Each year two "judges" were elected from upper-class families to serve as heads of state and carry out administrative and judicial functions. The real seat of power was the Senate, where members of the leading merchant families, who sat for life, formulated policy and directed the affairs of the state. An inner circle of thirty or so senators made the crucial decisions. From time to time the leadership convened an Assembly of the citizens to elect public officials or vote on important issues, particularly when the leaders were divided or wanted to stir up popular enthusiasm for some venture.

Carthage City located in present-day Tunisia, founded by Phoenicians ca. 800 B.C.E. It became a major commercial center and naval power in the western Mediterranean until defeated by Rome in the third century B.C.E.

There is little evidence at Carthage of the kind of social and political unrest that later plagued Greece and Rome (see Chapters 4 and 6). This perception may be due in part to the limited information in existing sources about internal affairs at Carthage. However, a merchant aristocracy (unlike an aristocracy of birth) was not a closed circle, and a climate of economic and social mobility allowed newly successful families and individuals to push their way into the circle of politically influential citizens. The ruling class also made sure that everyone benefited from the riches of empire.

Carthaginian power rested on its navy, which dominated the western Mediterranean for centuries. Phoenician towns provided a chain of friendly ports. The Carthaginian fleet consisted of fast, maneuverable galleys—oared warships. A galley had a sturdy, pointed ram in front that could pierce the hull of an enemy vessel below the water line, while marines (soldiers aboard a ship) fired weapons. Innovations in the placement of benches and oars made room for 30, 50, and eventually as many as 170 rowers.

Carthaginian foreign policy reflected Carthage's economic interests. Protecting the sea-lanes, gaining access to raw materials, and fostering trade mattered most to the dominant merchant class. Foreign merchants were free to sail to Carthage to market their goods, but if they tried to operate on their own, they risked having their ships sunk by the Carthaginian navy. Treaties between Carthage and other states included formal recognition of this maritime commercial monopoly.

The archaeological record provides few clues about the commodities traded. Commerce may have included perishable goods—foodstuffs, textiles, animal skins, slaves—and raw metals such as silver, lead, iron, and tin, whose Carthaginian origin would not be evident. We know that Carthaginian ships carried goods manufactured elsewhere and that products brought to Carthage by foreign traders were re-exported.

There is also evidence for trade with sub-Saharan Africa. Hanno (HA-noe), a Carthaginian captain of the fifth century B.C.E., claimed to have sailed through the Strait of Gibraltar into the Atlantic Ocean and to have explored the West African coast (see Map 3.2). His report includes vivid descriptions of ferocious savages, drums in the night, and rivers of fire. Scholars

SECTION REVIEW

- After the Late Bronze Age migrations, the Phoenician city-states rose on the coast of Lebanon.
- Under pressure from the east, the Phoenicians steadily expanded westward through the Mediterranean, establishing colonies that often clashed with those of the Greeks.
- This expansion resulted in a powerful maritime commercial network, through which goods and technologies spread throughout the Mediterranean world.
- Carthage became the leading Phoenician city and the major power of the western Mediterranean.
- Carthaginian seafarers traveled into the Atlantic, exploring the coasts of Africa and Europe.
- Carthage ruled most of its commercial empire indirectly, did not emphasize warfare, and practiced child sacrifice.

have had difficulty matching Hanno's topographic descriptions and distances to the geography of West Africa, and some regard his account as outright fiction. Others believe that he misstated distances and exaggerated dangers to keep others from following his route. Other Carthaginians explored the Atlantic coast of Spain and France and secured control of an important source of tin in the "Tin Islands," probably Cornwall in southwestern England.

War and Religion

Carthage did not directly rule a large amount of territory. A belt of fertile land in northeastern Tunisia, owned by Carthaginians but worked by native peasants and imported slaves, provided a secure food supply. Beyond this core area the Carthaginians ruled most of their "empire" indirectly and allowed other Phoenician communities in the western Mediterranean to remain independent. These communities looked to Carthage for military protection and followed its lead in foreign policy. Only Sardinia and southern Spain came under the control of a Carthaginian governor and garrison, presumably to safeguard their resources.

Trade may explain the unusual fact that citizens were not required to serve in the army: they were of more value as traders and sailors. Since the indigenous North African population was not politically or militarily well organized, Carthage had little to fear from

The Tophet of Carthage Here, from the seventh to second centuries B.C.E., the cremated bodies of sacrificed children were buried. Archaeological excavation has confirmed the claim in ancient sources that the Carthaginians sacrificed children to their gods at times of crisis. Stone markers, decorated with magical signs and symbols of divinities as well as family names, were placed over ceramic urns containing the ashes and charred bones of one or more infants or, occasionally, older children.

JTB Photo/Photolibrary

enemies close to home. When Carthage was drawn into wars with the Greeks and Romans from the sixth through third centuries B.C.E., it relied on mercenaries from the most warlike peoples in its dominions or from neighboring areas—Numidians from North Africa, Iberians from Spain, Gauls from France, and various Italian peoples. These well-paid mercenaries served under the command of Carthaginian officers.

Another sign that war was not the primary business of the state was the separation of military command from civilian government. Generals were chosen by the Senate and kept in office for as long as they were needed. In contrast, the kings of Assyria and the other major states of the ancient Middle East normally led military campaigns.

Like the deities of Mesopotamia (see Chapter 1), the Carthaginian gods—chiefly Baal Hammon (BAHL ha-MOHN), a male storm-god, and Tanit (TAH-nit), a female fertility-goddess—were powerful and capricious entities. Roman sources report that members of the Carthaginian elite would sacrifice their own male children to appease the gods in times of crisis.

Excavations at Carthage and elsewhere have turned up tophets (TOE-fets)—walled enclosures with thousands of small, sealed urns containing the burned bones of children. Although some scholars argue that these were infants born prematurely or taken by childhood illnesses, most maintain that the western Phoenicians practiced child sacrifice on a more or less regular basis. Originally practiced by the upper classes, child sacrifice seems to have become more common and to have involved broader elements of the population after 400 B.C.E.

Plutarch (PLOO-tark), a Greek who lived around 100 C.E., long after the demise of Carthage, wrote the following on the basis of earlier sources:

> The Carthaginians are a hard and gloomy people, submissive to their rulers and harsh to their subjects, running to extremes of cowardice in times of fear and of cruelty in times of anger; they keep obstinately to their decisions, are austere, and care little for amusement or the graces of life.[1]

We should not take the hostile opinions of Greek and Roman sources at face value. Still, it is clear that the Carthaginians were perceived as different and that cultural barriers, leading to misunderstanding and prejudice, played a significant role in ongoing conflicts. The struggle between Carthage and Rome for control of the western Mediterranean was especially protracted and bloody (see Chapter 6).

Failure and Transformation, 750–550 B.C.E.

What factors prompted the transformation of the ancient Middle East between 750 and 550 B.C.E.?

The extension of Assyrian power over the entire Middle East had enormous consequences for all the peoples of this region and caused the stories of Mesopotamia, Israel, and Phoenicia to converge. In 721 B.C.E. the Assyrians destroyed the northern kingdom of Israel, and for over a century the southern kingdom of Judah was exposed to relentless pressure. Assyrian threats spurred the Phoenicians to colonize and exploit the western Mediterranean. Even Egypt, for so long impregnable behind its desert barriers, fell to Assyrian invaders in the mid-seventh century B.C.E. Thebes, its ancient capital, never recovered.

Closer to the Assyrian homeland, the southern plains of Sumer and Akkad, the birthplace of Mesopotamian civilization, were reduced to a protectorate, while Babylon was alternately razed and rebuilt by Assyrian kings. Urartu and Elam, Assyria's great power rivals, were destroyed. By 650 B.C.E. Assyria stood unchallenged in western Asia. But the arms race with Urartu, war expenditures, and ever-lengthening borders sapped Assyrian resources. Brutality and exploitation aroused the hatred of conquered peoples. At the same time, changes in the ethnic composition of the army and the population of the homeland reduced popular support for the Assyrian state.

Two new political entities spearheaded resistance to Assyria. First, Babylonia had been revived by the Neo-Babylonian, or Chaldaean (chal-DEE-uhn), dynasty (the Chaldaeans had infiltrated southern Mesopotamia around 1000 B.C.E.). Second, the Medes (MEEDS), an Iranian people, were extending

their kingdom in the Zagros Mountains and Iranian Plateau in the seventh century B.C.E. The two powers launched a series of attacks on the Assyrian homeland that destroyed its chief cities by 612 B.C.E.

The rapidity of the Assyrian fall is stunning. The destruction systematically carried out by the victors led to the depopulation of northern Mesopotamia. Two centuries later, when a corps of Greek mercenaries passed by mounds that concealed the ruins of the Assyrian capitals, the Athenian chronicler Xenophon (ZEN-uh-fahn) had no inkling that their empire had ever existed.

Conclusion

Beside the already ancient river-valley kingdoms, the period from 2000 to 500 B.C.E. saw two kinds of societies emerge in the Middle East and the Mediterranean world. One kind was a great and powerful empire, that of the Assyrians, which used advanced military tactics and weapons, and sheer brutality, to conquer and exploit a large area with many diverse peoples. The other was small kingdoms like Israel and Minoan Crete or even city-states like those of Phoenicia and Carthage that lived from trade rather than tribute. Small states and societies were always vulnerable to attack by larger, more powerful neighbors, and sometimes they succumbed, like Israel and the Phoenician cities. Yet just as often, they survived or reappeared. And sometimes, as we shall see in the next chapter, they turned the tables on their bigger adversaries.

CHAPTER REVIEW

 Download the MP3 audio file of the Chapter Review to listen to on the go.

How did a cosmopolitan civilization develop in the Middle East during the Late Bronze Age, and what forms did it take? (page 55)

Historians refer to the Late Bronze Age in the Middle East as a "cosmopolitan" era because it was a time of shared cultures and lifestyles. The patterns of culture that originated in the river-valley civilizations of Egypt and Mesopotamia persisted into this era. Peoples such as the Amorites, Kassites, and Chaldaeans, who migrated into the Tigris-Euphrates plain, were largely assimilated into the Sumerian-Semitic cultural tradition, adopting its language, religious beliefs, political and social institutions, and forms of artistic expression. Similarly, the Hyksos, who migrated into the Nile Delta and controlled much of Egypt for a time, adopted the ancient ways of Egypt. When the founders of the New Kingdom finally ended Hyksos domination, they reinstituted the united monarchy and the religious and cultural traditions of earlier eras.

What civilizations emerged in the Aegean world, and what relationship did they have to the older civilizations to the east? (page 61)

The Late Bronze Age expansion of commerce and communication stimulated the emergence of new civilizations, including the Minoan and Mycenaean peoples in the Aegean Sea. These new civilizations often borrowed heavily from the technologies and cultural practices of Mesopotamia and Egypt, creating dynamic syntheses of imported and indigenous elements. Cretan art and architecture display the wide range of cultural influences from the Minoans' extensive trading contacts, as well as the unique forms of Minoan civilization. The Mycenaean Greeks built their own civilization under the influence of Minoan Crete, and their palaces served as centers for crafts, trade, and administrative recordkeeping. Trade brought the Mycenaeans, like the Minoans, into steady contact with older eastern civilizations.

How did the Assyrian Empire rise to power and eventually dominate most of the ancient Middle East? (page 65)

Ultimately, the very interdependence of the societies of the Middle East and eastern Mediterranean made them vulnerable to the destructions and disorder of the decades around 1200 B.C.E. The entire region slipped into a "Dark Age" of isolation, stagnation, and decline that lasted several centuries. The early centuries after 1000 B.C.E. saw a resurgence of political organization and international commerce, as well as the spread of technologies and ideas. The Neo-Assyrian Empire, the great power of the time, represented a continuation of the Mesopotamian tradition, though the center of empire moved to the north. The king wielded supreme authority in all areas, and state propaganda presented him as all-powerful and victorious. The Assyrians won control of their empire through superior organization and military technology and maintained it through terror and mass deportation of subject peoples. Assyrian social structure mirrored that of earlier Mesopotamian cultures, with most people working the land. Assyrian scholarship built on earlier traditions, and Ashurbanipal's library collected the literary and scientific heritage of Mesopotamia.

How did the civilization of Israel develop, following both familiar cultural patterns and a unique course of its own? (page 68)

Our main textual source of information about the Israelites, the Hebrew Bible, must be reconciled with archaeological findings. It recounts that the Israelites began as nomadic pastoralists who wandered from Mesopotamia to the Mediterranean coastal plain and then to Egypt, where they suffered enslavement. During the Exodus, Yahweh and the Israelites entered into the covenant. The Israelites then settled permanently in Canaan, where they coalesced into a political federation, the "Children of Israel." Conflict with the Philistines forced them to adopt a more complex political structure. The resulting monarchy reached its height under Solomon, during whose reign the Temple priests rose to prominence and Israelite society grew more urban and economically stratified. After Solomon's death the kingdom divided into Samaria and Judah, and the monotheism that Judaism would bequeath to the world reached its final form. While the long, slow evolution of the Israelites from a society of nomadic pastoralists to an agriculturally based monarchy followed a common pattern in ancient western Asia, the religious and ethical concepts that they formulated were unique and have had a powerful impact on world history.

How did the Phoenicians rise to commercial dominance over much of the Mediterranean world? (page 73)

After the upheavals of the Late Bronze Age, the Phoenician city-states along the coast of Lebanon flourished. Under pressure from the Neo-Assyrian Empire, the Phoenicians, with Tyre in the lead, began spreading westward into the Mediterranean. Overseas expansion increased trade and often brought Phoenician colonists into conflict with the Greeks. In addition to pursuing international trade, the Phoenicians developed an alphabetic writing system that many other cultures borrowed and adapted to their languages. Carthage became the most important city outside the Phoenician homeland. Ruled by leading merchant families, it extended its commercial empire throughout the western Mediterranean, maintaining power through naval superiority.

What factors prompted the transformation of the ancient Middle East between 750 and 550 B.C.E.? (page 79)

The far-reaching expansion and subsequent rapid fall of the Assyrian Empire was the most important factor in the transformation of the ancient Middle East. The Assyrians destroyed many older states and, directly or indirectly, displaced large numbers of people. Their brutality, as well as the population shifts that resulted from their mass deportations, undercut support for their state. The Chaldaeans and Medes led resistance to Assyrian rule, and the empire swiftly collapsed.

Key Terms

Iron Age *(p. 55)*	mass deportation *(p. 67)*
Hittites *(p. 57)*	Ashurbanipal *(p. 68)*
Hatshepsut *(p. 59)*	Israel *(p. 68)*
Akhenaten *(p. 59)*	Hebrew Bible *(p. 69)*
Ramesses II *(p. 60)*	First Temple *(p. 71)*
Minoan *(p. 61)*	monotheism *(p. 72)*
Mycenae *(p. 62)*	Diaspora *(p. 72)*
shaft graves *(p. 62)*	Phoenicians *(p. 73)*
Linear B *(p. 63)*	Carthage *(p. 76)*
Neo-Assyrian Empire *(p. 65)*	

Web Resources

Pronunciation Guide

Interactive Maps
- MAP 3.1 The Middle East in the Second Millennium B.C.E.
- MAP 3.2 Colonization of the Mediterranean

Visit the CourseMate website at www.cengagebrain.com for additional study tools and review materials for this chapter.

Primary Sources
- An Assyrian Emperor's Résumé: Ferocious Conquests a Specialty
- Moses Descends Mount Sinai with the Ten Commandments

Answer to the History in Focus Question
See photo on page 58, "The Mortuary Temple of Queen Hatshepsut at Deir el-Bahri, Egypt, ca. 1460 B.C.E."

Animal Domestication

Because the earliest domestication of plants and animals took place long before the existence of written records, we cannot be sure how and when humans first learned to plant crops and make use of tamed animals. Historians usually link the two processes as part of a Neolithic Revolution, but they were not necessarily connected.

The domestication of plants is much better understood than the domestication of animals. Foraging bands of humans primarily lived on wild seeds, fruits, and tubers. Eventually some humans tried planting seeds and tubers, favoring varieties that they particularly liked, and a variety that may have been rare in the wild became more common. When such a variety suited human needs, usually by having more food value or being easier to grow or process, people stopped collecting the wild types and relied on farming and further developing their new domestic type.

In the case of animals, the basis of selection to suit human needs is less apparent. Experts looking at ancient bones and images interpret changes in hair color, horn shape, and other visible features as indicators of domestication. But these visible changes did not generally serve human purposes. It is usually assumed that animals were domesticated for their meat, but even this is questionable. Dogs, which may have become domestic tens of thousands of years before any other species, were not eaten in most cultures, and cats, which became domestic much later, were eaten even less often. As for the uses most commonly associated with domestic animals, some of the most important, such as milking cows, shearing sheep, and harnessing oxen and horses to pull plows and vehicles, first appeared hundreds and even thousands of years after domestication.

Cattle, sheep, and goats became domestic around ten thousand years ago in the Middle East and North Africa. Coincidentally, wheat and barley were being domesticated at roughly the same time in the same general area. This is the main reason historians generally conclude that plant and animal domestication are closely related. Yet other major meat animals, such as chickens, which originated as jungle fowl in Southeast Asia, and pigs, which probably became domestic separately in several parts of North Africa, Europe, and Asia, have no agreed-upon association with early plant domestication. Nor is plant domestication connected with the horses and camels that became domestic in western Asia and the donkeys that became domestic in the Sahara region around six thousand years ago. Moreover, though the wild forebears of these species were probably eaten, the domestic forms were usually not used for meat.

In the Middle East humans may have originally kept wild sheep, goats, and cattle for food, though wild cattle were large and dangerous and must have been hard to control. It is questionable whether, in the earliest stages, keeping these animals captive for food would have been more productive than hunting. It is even more questionable whether the humans who kept animals for this purpose had any reason to anticipate that life in captivity would cause them to become domestic.

Human motivations for domesticating animals can be better assessed after a consideration of the physical changes involved in going from wild to domestic. Genetically transmitted tameness, defined as the ability to live with and accept handling by humans, lies at the core of the domestication process. In separate experiments with wild rats and foxes in the twentieth century, scientists found that wild individuals with strong fight-or-flight tendencies reproduce poorly in captivity, whereas individuals with the lowest adrenaline levels have the most offspring in captivity. In the wild, the same low level of excitability would have made these individuals vulnerable to predators and kept their reproduction rate down. However, early humans probably preferred the animals that seemed the tamest and destroyed those that were most wild. In the rat and fox experiments, after twenty generations or so, the surviving animals were born with much smaller adrenal glands and greatly reduced fight-or-flight reactions. Since adrenaline production normally increases in the transition to adulthood, many of the low-adrenaline animals also retained juvenile characteristics, such as floppy ears and pushed-in snouts, both indicators of domestication.

Historians disagree about whether animal domestication was a deliberate process or the unanticipated outcome of keeping animals for other purposes. Some assume that domestication was an understood and reproducible process. Others argue that, since a twenty-generation time span for wild cattle and other large quadrupeds would have amounted to several human lifetimes, it is unlikely that the people who ended up with domestic cows had any recollection of how the process started. This would also rule out the possibility that people who had unwittingly domesticated one species would have attempted to repeat the process with other species, since they did not know what they and their ancestors had done to produce genetically transmitted tameness.

Historians who assume that domestication was an understood and reproducible process tend to conclude that humans domesticated every species that could be domesticated. This is unlikely. Twentieth-century efforts to domesticate bison, eland, and elk have not fully succeeded, but they have generally not been maintained for as long as twenty generations. Rats and foxes have more rapid reproduction rates, and the experiments with them succeeded.

Animal domestication is probably best studied on a case-by-case basis as an unintended result of other processes. In some instances, sacrifice probably played a key role. Religious traditions of animal sacrifice rarely utilize, and sometimes prohibit, the ritual killing of wild animals. It is reasonable to suppose that the practice of capturing wild animals and holding them for sacrifice eventually led to the appearance of genetically transmitted tameness as an unplanned result.

Horses and camels were domesticated relatively late, and most likely not for meat consumption. The societies within which these animals first appeared as domestic species already had domestic sheep, goats, and cattle for meat, and they used oxen to carry loads and pull plows and carts. Horses, camels, and later reindeer may represent successful experiments with substituting one draft animal for another, with genetically transmitted tameness an unexpected consequence of separating animals trained for riding or pulling carts from their wilder kin.

Once human societies had developed the full range of uses of domestic animals—meat, eggs, milk, fiber, labor, transport—the likelihood of domesticating more species diminished. In the absence of concrete knowledge of how domestication had occurred, it was usually easier for people to move domestic livestock to new locations than to attempt to develop new domestic species. Domestic animals accompanied human groups wherever they ventured, and this practice triggered enormous environmental changes as domestic animals, and their human keepers, competed with wild species for food and living space.

Part Two

The Formation of New Cultural Communities, from 1200 B.C.E.

© Cengage Learning

	1000 B.C.E.	800 B.C.E.	600 B.C.E.
AMERICAS	1200–400 Olmec civilization in Mesoamerica		
		900–250 Chavín civilization in Peru	Gold metallurgy in Chavín 500 •
EUROPE	• 1000 Iron metallurgy	800–500 Archaic period in Greece	Celts spread across Europe 500 • Roman Republic 507 • 477–404 Athenian Empire and democracy
AFRICA	Rise of Nubian kingdom at Napata 800 •	• 814 Carthage founded 712–660 Nubian domination of Egypt	Hanno of Carthage explores West African coast 465 •
MIDDLE EAST	• 1000 David establishes Jerusalem as capital of Israel 911–612 Neo-Assyrian Empire	Babylonian conquest of Jerusalem 587 •	522–486 Darius I rules Persian Empire
ASIA AND OCEANIA	• 1000 Aryans settle Ganges Plain 1027–221 Zhou kingdom in China	Iron metallurgy in China 600 •	563–483 Life of the Buddha 551–479 Life of Confucius

From 1000 B.C.E. to 600 C.E. important changes in the ways of life established in the river-valley civilizations in the two previous millennia occurred, and the scale of human institutions and activities increased. On the shores of the Mediterranean and in Iran, India, and Southeast Asia, new centers arose in lands watered by rainfall and worked by a free peasantry. These societies developed new patterns of political and social organization and economic activity, and they moved in new intellectual, artistic, and spiritual directions.

The rulers of the empires of this era constructed extensive networks of roads and promoted urbanization. These measures brought more rapid communication, trade over greater distances, and the broad diffusion of religious ideas, artistic styles, and technologies. Large cultural zones unified by common traditions emerged—Iranian, Hellenistic, Roman, Hindu, and Chinese—and exercised substantial influence on subsequent ages.

The expansion of agriculture and trade and improvements in technology led to population increases, the spread of cities, and the growth of a comfortable middle class. In many places iron replaced bronze as the preferred metal for weapons, tools, and utensils, and metals were available to more people than in the preceding age. People using iron tools cleared extensive forests around the Mediterranean, in India, and in eastern China. Iron weapons gave an advantage to the armies of Greece, Rome, and imperial China.

New systems of writing, more easily and rapidly learned, moved the preservation and transmission of knowledge out of the control of specialists and gave birth to new ways of thinking, new genres of literature, and new types of scientific endeavor.

In the Western Hemisphere, the development of urban, agricultural civilizations in the Andes, the Yucatán lowlands, and the central plateau of Mexico, first noted among the Olmec of Mesoamerica and the Chavín culture of Peru, climaxed in the Maya, Aztec, and Andean cultures. The cultural exchanges and interactions that mark this era in Eurasia and Africa have counterparts in the Western Hemisphere.

400 B.C.E. — **200 B.C.E.** — **B.C.E. C.E.** — **200 C.E.**

- **399** Trial and death of Socrates
- **290** Rome takes control of Italy
- **264–201** Rome defeats Carthage
- **200–30** Rome absorbs Hellenistic eastern Mediterranean
- **31 B.C.E.–14 C.E.** Augustus establishes Principate
- **45–58** Paul spreads Christianity
- **212** Caracalla grants Roman citizenship to all free males
- **324** Constantinople founded

400 B.C.E.–300 C.E. Kingdom of Meroë in Nubia
- **323–30** Ptolemies rule Hellenistic kingdom in Egypt
- **30** Rome conquers Egypt

- **334–323** Alexander of Macedonia conquers western Asia
- **301–64** Seleucid kingdom in western Asia
- **30** Crucifixion of Jesus
- **66–73** Jewish Revolt crushed by Rome

- **324–184** Maurya Empire in India
- **221** Qin emperor unites eastern China
- **206 B.C.E.–220 C.E.** Han Empire in China
- **ca. 50** Funan establishes first empire in Southeast Asia
- **320–550** Gupta Empire in India

© Cengage Learning

CHAPTER PREVIEW

Ancient Iran
How did the Persian Empire rise from its Iranian homeland and spread to encompass diverse cultures?

The Rise of the Greeks
How did Greek civilization evolve and spread beyond its original territories?

The Struggle of Persia and Greece
How did the Persian Wars lead into the Hellenistic Age that followed?

The Hellenistic Synthesis
How did a cultural synthesis develop during the Hellenistic Age?

Conclusion

MATERIAL CULTURE: Wine and Beer in the Ancient World

86

Visit the CourseMate website at **www.cengagebrain.com** for additional study tools and review materials for this chapter.

The Greek historian Herodotus (heh-ROD-uh-tuss) (ca. 485–425 B.C.E.) relates that the Persian king Darius (duh-RIE-us) I, whose empire stretched from eastern Europe to northwest India, questioned some Greek and Indian sages. Under what circumstances, he asked the Greeks, would they eat their deceased fathers' bodies? The Greeks, who practiced cremation, recoiled in revulsion. Darius then asked the Indians whether they would ever burn the bodies of their dead parents. This similarly repelled them because they practiced ritual eating of the bodies of the dead. Herodotus argues from this that every group of people regards its own practices as "natural" and superior. This story reminds us that ancient sources such as Herodotus's writings are sometimes accurate, as Herodotus is about Greek funerary customs, and sometimes wildly inaccurate, as are his views on Indian rituals.

The story also reminds us that the Persian Empire and the Hellenistic Greek kingdoms that succeeded it brought together peoples and cultural systems from Europe, Africa, and Asia that previously had had little direct contact with one another. This cross-cultural interaction both alarmed and stimulated the peoples involved, in some instances giving rise to new cultural syntheses.

This chapter recounts the experiences of the Persians and Greeks in the first millennium B.C.E. Historians traditionally consider the rivalry of Greeks and Persians the first act of an age-long drama: the clash of East and West, of fundamentally different ways of life destined to collide. Ironically, Greeks and Persians had more in common than they realized. They spoke related languages belonging to the Indo-European family, and they inherited similar cultural traits, forms of social organization, and religious outlooks from their shared past.

Ancient Iran

How did the Persian Empire rise from its Iranian homeland and spread to encompass diverse cultures?

Iran, the "land of the Aryans," links western Asia and southern and Central Asia. In the sixth century B.C.E., the Persians of southwest Iran created the largest empire the world had yet seen. Heirs to the Assyrian and Babylonian imperial tradition, they introduced distinctly Iranian elements and developed new forms of political and economic organization.

Scant written evidence from within the Persian Empire forces us to rely on works by Greeks—ignorant outsiders at best, usually hostile, and interested primarily in events affecting themselves. This leaves us largely uninformed about developments in the central and eastern portions of the Persian Empire, though archaeology and close analysis of the few writings from within the empire can supplement and help correct the Greek perspective.

Geography and Resources

The Zagros Mountains bound Iran on the west, the Caucasus (KAW-kuh-suhs) Mountains and Caspian Sea on the northwest and north, and the mountains of Afghanistan (ancient Arachosia) and the desert of Baluchistan (buh-loo-chi-STAN) (ancient Gedrosia) on the east and southeast. The southern limit is a barren seacoast on the Persian Gulf and Indian Ocean. The northeast lies open to attacks or population movements from Central Asia.

Winter precipitation in the mountains feeds streams that either flow away from the central plateau into rivers that drain into seas or flow into the plateau and terminate in salt lakes and deserts. Husbanding water is the key to survival in Iran's arid interior. Lacking a great river like the Nile, Indus, or Tigris-Euphrates, ancient Iran had a sparse population, most numerous in the moister north and west and decreasing toward the arid south and east. The Great Salt Desert, covering much of eastern Iran and Baluchistan, did not support life. Mountain barriers separated scattered settlements on the southern coastal plains from the interior plateau.

Wheat and barley grown during the comparatively wet winter season were the most common crops. However, by 800 B.C.E., Iranian farmers had worked out techniques for digging underground irrigation channels that prevented evaporation and used gravity to deliver water from the subsurface water table in the foothills of the mountains to fields in otherwise uncultivable desert. Constructing these channels and the vertical shafts that gave access to them demanded labor cooperation, but since each village had its own channel, the large-scale, government-sponsored irrigation projects typical of Mesopotamia were probably not required. This favored the rise of local aristocracies capable of defending their lands.

The mountains yielded copper, tin, iron, gold, and silver, all exploited on a limited scale in antiquity, as well as wood for fuel, construction, and crafts, the hillsides being more heavily wooded than they are now. Export goods consisted largely of metals and products from farther east carried across Iran by traders.

The Rise of the Persian Empire

The term *Iranian* as used for premodern history describes a group or peoples speaking related languages and sharing certain cultural characteristics. They lived in a broad swath of territory between the Zagros Mountains and Central Asia, with some groups as far east as northwest China. One group, the Medes (Mada in Iranian),* gained political dominance in northwestern Iran in the late second millennium B.C.E., influenced in part by the ancient centers in Mesopotamia and Urartu (modern Armenia and northeast Turkey). The Medes played a major role in destroying the Assyrian Empire in the late seventh century B.C.E. and extended their control westward across Assyria into Anatolia (modern Turkey). They also projected power southeastward into the land of the Elamites, which was increasingly identified with an immigrant Iranian people known as the Persians (Parsa).

The Persian rulers, called Achaemenids (a-KEY-muh-nids) because of an ancestor named Achaemenes, cemented relations with the Median court through marriage. **Cyrus** (Kurush), the son of a Persian chieftain and a Median princess, united the Persian tribes and overthrew the Median monarch around 550 B.C.E. The differences between these two peoples being slight—notably in dialect and costume—Cyrus placed both Medes and Persians in positions of responsibility and retained the framework of Median rule. The Greeks could not readily tell the two apart and may not have recorded their history accurately.

Patriarchal family organization among the Medes and Persians, like that of the Greeks, Romans, and most other Indo-European peoples, gave the male head of the household authority over family members. The warrior class dominated the other two social and occupational classes, the priests and peasants. Noble warriors, the king the most illustrious among them, owned land and took pleasure in hunting, fighting, and feasting. The priests, or magi (*magush*), supervised sacrifices and other rituals. Village-based farmers and shepherds made up the third class.

Over the course of two decades, Cyrus (r. 550–530 B.C.E.) redrew the map of western Asia. In 546 B.C.E., he won a cavalry battle outside Sardis, the capital of Lydia in western Anatolia, reportedly because the smell of his camels caused a panic among his opponents' horses. All Anatolia, including the Greek city-states on the western coast, came under Persian control. In 539 B.C.E., he swept into southern Mesopotamia, where the Neo-Babylonian dynasty had ruled since the collapse of Assyrian power (see Chapter 3). Disaffected elements within Babylon surrendered the city to Cyrus. Cyrus respected the Babylonian priesthood and had his son crowned king in accordance with local tradition.

Cyrus died in 530 B.C.E. while campaigning against nomadic Iranians in the northeast. His son Cambyses (kam-BIE-sees) (Kambujiya, r. 530–522 B.C.E.) set his sights on Egypt. Defeating the Egyptians in bloody battle, the Persians sent exploratory expeditions south to Nubia and west to Libya. Greek sources depict Cambyses as a cruel and impious madman, but contemporary Egyptian documents reflect a practical outlook. Like his father, he cultivated local priests and notables and respected their traditions.

---

* Familiar Greek names of Iranian groups and individuals are followed by the original Iranian names in parentheses.

Cyrus (600–530 B.C.E.) Founder of the Achaemenid Persian Empire. Between 550 and 530 B.C.E. he conquered Media, Lydia, and Babylon. Revered in the traditions of both Iran and the subject peoples, he employed Persians and Medes in his administration and respected the institutions and beliefs of subject peoples.

Chronology

	Greece and the Hellenistic World	Persian Empire
1500 B.C.E.	1150–800 B.C.E. Greece's "Dark Age"	
1000 B.C.E.		ca. 1000 B.C.E. Persians settle in southwest Iran
800 B.C.E.	ca. 800 B.C.E. Greek seafaring resumes	
600 B.C.E.		550–530 B.C.E Reign of Cyrus
500 B.C.E.		480–470 B.C.E. Xerxes invades Greece
400 B.C.E.	431–404 B.C.E. Peloponnesian War	
300 B.C.E.		334–323 B.C.E. Alexander the Great defeats Persia
100 B.C.E.	30 B.C.E. Rome annexes Egypt	

When Cambyses died in 522 B.C.E., **Darius I** (Darayavaush) seized the throne, crushing challengers with skill, energy, and ruthlessness. The Medes now played lesser roles; most important posts went to leading Persian nobles. Darius (r. 522–486 B.C.E.) extended Persian control eastward to the Indus Valley and westward into Europe, bridging the Danube River and chasing the nomadic Scythians (SITH-ee-uhns) north of the Black Sea. In maritime matters, Darius dispatched a fleet to explore the route from the Indus Delta to the Red Sea and completed a canal linking the Red Sea with the Nile.

Imperial Organization and Ideology

Each of the empire's twenty provinces, stretching from eastern Europe to Pakistan, was placed under a Persian **satrap** (SAY-trap), or governor, usually a relative or connection by marriage. The satrap's court mirrored the royal court on a smaller scale. Governorships frequently became hereditary, so that satraps' families lived in the province governed by their head, acquired knowledge about local conditions, and formed connections with the local elite. The farther a province was from the empire's center, the more autonomy the satrap had, since slow communications made contact with the royal center difficult.

Darius prescribed how much precious metal each province owed annually; the satrap collected and sent it. Some went for necessary expenditures, but most was hoarded. This increasingly took precious metal out of circulation, forcing up the price of gold and silver and making it hard for provinces to meet their quotas. Evidence from Babylonia shows increasing taxes and official corruption and a corresponding economic decline by the fourth century B.C.E.

Royal roads, well maintained and patrolled, connected outlying provinces to the imperial center. Way stations sheltered important travelers and couriers. Garrisons controlled movements at strategic points: mountain passes, river crossings, and important urban centers. The ancient Elamite capital of Susa, in southwest Iran, served as the imperial administrative center. Greeks and others went there with requests and messages for the king. It took at least three months to make the journey to Susa. For Greek ambassadors, the time spent traveling, waiting for an audience, and returning home could take a year or more.

The king lived and traveled with numerous wives and children. Information about the royal women comes from foreign sources and is thus suspect. The Book of Esther in the Hebrew Bible tells how King Ahasuerus (uh-HAZZ-yoo-ear-uhs) (Xerxes [ZERK-sees] to the Greeks) picked the Jewish woman Esther as a wife, putting her in a position to save the Jewish

Darius I (ca. 558–486 B.C.E.) Third ruler of the Persian Empire (r. 522–486 B.C.E.). He crushed the widespread initial resistance to his rule and gave all major government posts to Persians rather than to Medes. He established a system of provinces and tribute, began construction of Persepolis, and expanded Persian control in the east (Pakistan) and west (northern Greece).
satrap The governor of a province in the Achaemenid Persian Empire, often a relative of the king. He was responsible for protection of the province and for forwarding tribute to the central administration. Satraps in outlying provinces enjoyed considerable autonomy.

Courtesy of the Oriental Institute of the University of Chicago

View of the East Front of the Apadana (Audience Hall) at Persepolis, ca. 500 B.C.E. To the right lies the Gateway of Xerxes. Persepolis, in the Persian homeland, was built by Darius I and his son Xerxes, and it was used for ceremonies of special importance to the Persian king and people—coronations, royal weddings, funerals, and the New Year's festival. The stone foundations, walls, and stairways of Persepolis are filled with sculpted images of members of the court and embassies bringing gifts, offering a vision of the grandeur and harmony of the Persian Empire.

people from a plot to massacre them. Greek sources depict royal women as pawns in power struggles and as intriguers, poisoning rival wives and plotting their sons' paths to the throne.

The king's entourage also included (1) sons of Persian aristocrats, who were educated at court and also served as hostages for their parents' loyalty; (2) noblemen who attended the king when not on other assignments; (3) administrative officers; (4) the royal bodyguard; and (5) courtiers and slaves. Long gone were the simple days when the king hunted and caroused with his warrior companions. Inspired by Mesopotamian conceptions of monarchy, the Persian king became an aloof figure of majesty and splendor: "The Great King, King of Kings, King in Persia, King of countries." He referred to everyone, even the Persian nobility, as "my slaves," and anyone who approached him had to bow down before him.

The king owned vast tracts of land throughout the empire, some of which he gave to his supporters. Donations called "bow land," "horse land," and "chariot land" in Babylonian documents obliged the recipient to provide military service. The *paradayadam* (meaning "walled enclosure"—the term has come into English as *paradise*), consisting of gardens or orchards belonging to the king or high nobility, symbolized the prosperity of the king and his servants.

Tradition remembered Darius as issuing the "laws of the King," appointing royal judges throughout the empire, and encouraging the codification of the laws of subject peoples. As master of a decentralized empire, he allowed each people its own traditions and ordinances.

Sometimes the kings returned to **Persepolis** (Parsa), a ceremonial capital in the Persian homeland

Persepolis A complex of palaces, reception halls, and treasury buildings erected by the Persian kings Darius I and Xerxes in the Persian homeland. It is believed that the New Year's festival was celebrated here, as well as the coronations, weddings, and funerals of the Persian kings, who were buried in cliff-tombs nearby.

in southwest Iran that had been founded by Darius and completed by his son Xerxes (Ahasueras). The palaces, audience halls, treasury buildings, and barracks built on an artificial platform extending from a mountainside took inspiration from Mesopotamia, where the Assyrian kings had created fortress-cities to advertise their power.

Texts found in Persepolis and inscribed in Elamite cuneiform on baked clay tablets show government officials distributing food and other goods to workers of various nationalities, some of them prisoners of war working on construction projects, irrigation networks, or royal estates. Women received less than men of equivalent status, but pregnant women and new mothers received more. Skilled workers of either sex received more than the unskilled.

The relief sculptures on the foundations, walls, and stairwells at Persepolis feature representatives of the peoples of the empire—recognizable by distinctive hairstyles, beards, dress, hats, and footwear—bringing gifts to the king. These images did not depict a real ceremony but rather advertised the vast extent, abundant resources, and cooperative spirit of the empire. One scene shows erect subjects effortlessly shouldering a giant platform bearing Darius's throne. Similar scenes from the Assyrian Empire show the subjects staggering under the weight. Persepolis probably served as a setting for New Year's festivals, coronations, marriages, and funerals. Tombs cut into the cliffs at nearby Naqsh-i Rustam (NUHK-shee ROOS-tuhm) sheltered the remains of Darius and his successors.

Several dozen inscriptions cut into cliff faces provide perspectives on the imperial ideology. At Naqsh-i Rustam, for example, Darius claims:

> Ahuramazda (ah-HOOR-uh-MAZZ-duh) [the chief Persian deity], when he saw this earth in commotion, thereafter bestowed it upon me, made me king. . . . By the favor of Ahuramazda I put it down in its place. . . . I am of such a sort that I am a friend to right, I am not a friend to wrong. It is not my desire that the weak man should have wrong done to him by the mighty; nor is that my desire, that the mighty man should have wrong done to him by the weak.[1]

Since the religion of **Zoroastrianism** (zo-ro-ASS-tree-uh-niz-um) recognized Ahuramazda as god, it seems certain that Darius and his successors were Zoroastrians. Questions surround the origins of this religion. Worshipers believe that Zarathustra (Zoroaster in Greek) wrote hymns called Gathas, the dialect and physical setting of which indicate an origin in northern Afghanistan. Scholarly guesses place Zarathustra's life sometime between 1700 and 500 B.C.E. According to Zarathustra, Ahuramazda, "the wise lord," created the world. Angra Mainyu (ANG-ruh MINE-yoo), "the hostile spirit," and a host of demons threaten it. In this dualist universe, the struggle between good and evil plays out over 12,000 years. At the end of time, good will prevail, and the world will return to the pure state of creation. In the meantime, humanity participates in this cosmic struggle, and individuals reap rewards or torments in the afterlife according to their actions.

The Persians also drew on pre-Zoroastrian moral and metaphysical concepts. Alive to the beauties of nature, they venerated water, which they kept pure, and fire, which burned continuously at altars. Bodily purity, a matter of intense concern, ceased with death. Zoroastrians exposed corpses to carrion-eating birds and the elements to avoid sullying the earth through burial or fire through cremation. Some earlier gods, such as Mithra, a sun-deity and defender of oaths and compacts, retained divine status despite Zarathustra's focus on one god. The Persians honored promises and

Primary Source: Gathas Listen in as Zarathustra ponders the fate of the righteous and the liars.

Zoroastrianism A religion originating in ancient Iran with the prophet Zoroaster. It centered on a single benevolent deity—Ahuramazda—who engaged in a twelve-thousand-year struggle with demonic forces before prevailing and restoring a pristine world. Emphasizing truth-telling, purity, and reverence for nature, the religion demanded that humans choose sides in the struggle between good and evil. Those whose good conduct indicated their support for Ahuramazda would be rewarded in the afterlife. Others would be punished. The religion of the Achaemenid Persians, Zoroastrianism may have spread within their realms and influenced Judaism, Christianity, and other faiths.

telling the truth. Darius's inscriptions castigate evildoers as followers of "the Lie."

Zoroastrianism preached belief in one supreme deity, maintained high ethical standards, and promised salvation. Expanding with the advance of the Persian Empire, it may have influenced Judaism and thus, indirectly, Christianity. God and the Devil, Heaven and Hell, reward and punishment, the Messiah and the end of time: all appear in this belief system. Yet the Islamic conquest of Iran in the seventh century C.E. (see Chapter 9) triggered the faith's decline. Only tiny communities survive in Iran now. Larger communities, called Parsees, live in South Asia.

The Rise of the Greeks

How did Greek civilization evolve and spread beyond its original territories?

The cultural features that emerged in resource-poor Greece in the first millennium B.C.E. depended on access to foreign markets and sources of raw materials. Greek merchants and mercenaries brought home not only raw materials and crafted goods but also ideas. Population pressure, poverty, war, and political crises prompted Greeks to venture throughout the Mediterranean and western Asia, carrying with them their language and culture and exerting influence on other societies. Greek identity and interest in

geography, ethnography, and history grew from experience with non-Greek practices and beliefs, as well as from a two-century-long rivalry with the Persian Empire.

Geography and Resources

Bounded by the Atlantic, the Alps, the Syrian Desert, and the Sahara, the lands of the Mediterranean climatic zone share seasonal weather patterns and many plants and animals. In summer, a stalled weather front near the entrance of the Mediterranean holds up storms from the Atlantic and allows winds from the Sahara to flow over the region. In winter, the front dissolves, and ocean storms roll in, bringing waves, wind, and cold. Such similarities facilitated migration within the zone, since people did not have to change familiar practices and occupations.

Greek civilization arose on the Greek mainland, the Aegean islands, and Anatolia's western coast. As we saw in Chapter 3, small plains between low mountain ranges characterize southern Greece, a land with no navigable rivers. The islands dotting the Aegean, inhabited from early times, made sailing from Greece to Ionia (western Anatolia) comparatively easy. From about 1000 B.C.E., Greeks began to settle Ionia, where rivers with broad, fertile plains made for a comfortable life. These coastal Greeks maintained closer contact with Greeks across the Aegean than with the peoples of Anatolia's rugged interior. The sea served as a connector, not a barrier.

Mainland farmers depended on rainfall to water their crops. In the south, limited land, thin topsoil, and sparse rainfall supported only small populations. Farmers planted the plains with barley, which is hardier than wheat, and the edges of the plains with olive trees. Grapevines grew on the terraced lower slopes of the foothills. Sheep and goats grazed the hillsides. Northern Greece, with more rainfall and broader plains, supported herds of cattle and horses. Resources included abundant building stone and fine marble, but few metal deposits or forests.

The difficulty and expense of overland transport, the availability of good anchorages, and the need to import metals, timber, and grain drew the Greeks to the sea. They obtained timber from the northern Aegean, gold and iron from Anatolia, copper from Cyprus, tin from the western Mediterranean, and grain from the Black Sea, Egypt, and Sicily. Though never comfortable with "the wine-dark sea," as Homer called it, the Greeks relied on it, their small, frail ships hugging the coastline or island hopping where possible.

The Emergence of the Polis

After the destruction of the Mycenaean palace-states (see Chapter 3), Greece lapsed into a "Dark Age" (ca. 1150–800 B.C.E.), a time of depopulation, poverty, and backwardness that has left few archaeological traces. Decline of trade and lack of access to resources lay behind the poverty of the Dark Age. Within Greece, regional distinctiveness in pottery and crafts indicates declining interconnections.

By reestablishing contact between the Aegean and the Middle East, Phoenician traders (see Chapter 3) gave Greek civilization a push that inaugurated the Archaic period of Greek history (ca. 800–480 B.C.E.). Greek seafarers reappeared in Mediterranean waters looking for raw materials, trade opportunities, and fertile farmland.

Lifelike human and animal figures and imaginative mythical beasts on painted Greek pottery signal new ideas from the east, as does the adoption of an alphabetic writing system of Phoenician inspiration. Cuneiform or hieroglyphics, systems in which several hundred symbols stood for syllables rather than letters, took years of training and remained the preserve of an elite scribal class. By contrast, the alphabetic symbols made literacy easier to acquire.

First used for economic purposes or for preserving oral poetry, the Greek alphabet facilitated new forms of literature, law codes, religious dedications, and epitaphs. Yet Greek culture continued to center on storytelling, rituals, and performances. Theatrical drama, philosophical dialogues, and political and courtroom oratory demonstrate the dynamic interaction of speaking and writing.

Population grew rapidly during the Archaic period. Cemeteries around Athens show a five- to sevenfold increase during the eighth century B.C.E. Herding gave way to intensive farming on the previously uncultivated margins of the plains. Increasing population and prosperity stimulated the importation of food and raw materials, a merging of villages into urban centers, and specialization of labor. Freed from farming by rising surpluses, some people developed skills in crafts, commerce, and religion.

The Greek **polis** (POE-lis), or city-state, ranging in size from a few thousand souls to several hundred thousand in the case of Athens, consisted of an urban center and the surrounding countryside. Typically, a fortified hilltop, the *acropolis* ("top of the city"), offered refuge in emergencies. The town spread around its base. In the open area around government buildings and markets, called an *agora* ("gathering place"), citizens debated the decisions of leaders and organized for war. Walls surrounded the urban center, but population growth prompted construction beyond them. Food came from surrounding farms, though many who lived within the walls worked nearby fields. Unlike the dependent rural workers of Mesopotamia, Greek farmers enjoyed full citizenship.

Frequent city-state conflicts led, by the early seventh century B.C.E., to a kind of warfare based on **hoplites**—heavily armored infantrymen who fought in close formation. Protected by helmet, breastplate, and leg guards, each hoplite brandished a thrusting spear while guarding his left side and the right side of the hoplite beside him with a round shield, keeping a sword in reserve. Victory depended on maintaining one's battle line while breaking open the enemy's. The losers suffered most of their casualties while fleeing.

Private citizens, mostly farmers called up for brief periods rather than professional soldiers, served as hoplites. Courage to stand one's ground counted for more than strength for bearing weapons and armor. When an army approached, the farmers of the polis under attack mustered to defend their land and

polis The Greek term for a city-state, an urban center and the agricultural territory under its control. It was the characteristic form of political organization in southern and central Greece in the Archaic and Classical periods. Of the hundreds of city-states in the Mediterranean and Black Sea regions settled by Greeks, some were oligarchic, others democratic, depending on the powers delegated to the Council and the Assembly.

hoplite A heavily armored Greek infantryman of the Archaic and Classical periods who fought in the close-packed phalanx formation. Hoplite armies—militias composed of middle- and upper-class citizens supplying their own equipment—were for centuries superior to all other military forces.

buildings. The clash of hoplite lines resulted in quick decisions. Battles rarely lasted more than a few hours, with the survivors promptly returning home to their farms.

As population growth strained the agricultural resources of the small plains, many city-states sent excess population abroad to establish independent colonies. Sometimes people were chosen by lot to be colonists and forbidden to return on pain of death. At other times people in search of adventure or an escape from poverty volunteered. Colonists sought the approval of the god Apollo at his sanctuary at Delphi and then departed by sea carrying a fire from the communal hearth of the mother city, a symbol of the kinship and religious ties that would connect the two communities. The "founder," a prominent member of the mother city, chose a hill or other natural refuge, assigned parcels of land, and drafted laws. Sometimes colonists intermarried with local inhabitants; alternatively, they drove them away or reduced them to semiservility.

From the mid-eighth through the mid-sixth centuries B.C.E., colonists spread Greek culture to the northern Aegean area, the Libyan coast of North Africa, and around the Black Sea, with southern Italy and Sicily becoming heavily Greek. Establishing new homes, farms, and communities posed many challenges, but the similarity in climate and ecology helped the Greek settlers transplant their way of life.

Greeks called themselves *Hellenes* (HELL-leans) (the Romans later used *Graeci*) to distinguish themselves from *barbaroi* (literally "non-Greek speakers," whence the English word *barbarian*). Interaction with new peoples and exposure to their cultures made the Greeks aware of their unity of language, religion, and lifestyle. It also introduced them to new ideas and technologies. Developments in the colonial world traveled back to the Greek homeland: urban planning, forms of political organization, and new intellectual currents.

Coinage, invented in the early sixth century B.C.E. in Lydia (western Anatolia), spread throughout the Greek world and beyond. Scarcity, durability, divisibility, and ease of use made silver, gold, and copper appropriate for minting into metal pieces of state-guaranteed weight and purity. (Societies in other parts of the world used items with similar qualities,

including beads, hard-shelled beans, and cowrie shells.) Coinage made weighing quantities of metal obsolete and fostered quicker trading transactions, better recordkeeping, and easier wealth storage. Trade grew, as did the total wealth of communities, but different weight standards used by different states often confused exchanges of currencies.

Colonization relieved pressures within the Archaic Greek world but did not eliminate political instability. At some point, councils representing the noble families superseded the Dark Age kings depicted in Homer's *Iliad* and *Odyssey*. This aristocracy derived wealth and power from landownership. The peasants who farmed these lands kept only a portion of their harvest. Debt slaves, people who lost their freedom when they could not repay money or seed borrowed from the lord, also worked the land. Free peasants owned small farms and joined urban-based craftsmen and merchants as part of a "middle class."

Tyrants—individuals who seized power in violation of normal political institutions—gained control of many city-states in the mid-seventh and sixth centuries B.C.E. Often disgruntled aristocrats with middle-class backing, such tyrants appealed to hoplite soldiers, whose numbers increased with growing prosperity and lower prices for weaponry. The tyrants granted these supporters political rights.

Some tyrants passed their positions on to sons, but communities eventually expelled the tyrant families and opted for oligarchy (OLL-ih-gahr-key), in which a group of the wealthiest men held power, or **democracy**, in which all free adult males shared power. The absence of a professional military class made this broadening of the political system possible.

---

tyrant The term the Greeks used to describe someone who seized and held power in violation of the normal procedures and traditions of the community. Tyrants appeared in many Greek city-states in the seventh and sixth centuries B.C.E., often taking advantage of the disaffection of the emerging middle class and, by weakening the old elite, unwittingly contributing to the evolution of democracy.

democracy A system of government in which all "citizens" (however defined) have equal political and legal rights, privileges, and protections, as in the Greek city-state of Athens in the fifth and fourth centuries B.C.E.

Vase Painting Depicting a Sacrifice to the God Apollo, ca. 440 B.C.E. For the Greeks, who believed in a multitude of gods who looked and behaved like humans, the central act of worship was the sacrifice, the ritualized offering of a gift. Sacrifice created a relationship between the human worshiper and the deity and raised expectations that the god would bestow favors in return. Here we see a number of male devotees, wearing their finest clothing and garlands in their hair, near a sacred outdoor altar and statue of Apollo. The god is shown at the far right, standing on a pedestal and holding his characteristic bow and laurel branch. The first worshiper offers the god bones wrapped in fat. All of the worshipers will feast on the meat carried by the boy. Bildarchiv Preussischer Kultburbesitz/Art Resource, NY

Even before they invaded the Greek peninsula at the end of the third millennium B.C.E., the Greeks worshiped several sky-gods, such as Zeus, who sent storms and lightning, and Poseidon, who controlled the sea and earthquakes. Homer's *Iliad* and *Odyssey*, which schoolboys memorized and performers recited, gave personalities to these deities. He portrayed them as anthropomorphic (an-thruh-puh-MORE-fik), or humanlike in appearance (though taller, more beautiful, and more powerful, with a supernatural radiance), with humanlike emotions of love, anger, and jealousy. More than anything else, immortality distinguished gods from humans.

State religious ceremonies conferred civic identity. **Sacrifice**, the central ritual, took place at altars in front of temples where the gods were thought to reside. Gifts as humble as a small cake or a cup of wine poured on the ground accompanied prayers for favor and protection. In grander sacrifices, people would kill one or more animals, smear the altar with its blood, and burn parts of its body so that the aroma would ascend to the gods.

Oracles situated at sacred sites responded to human pleas for information, advice, or prediction. At Delphi in central Greece, the most honored site, the god Apollo spoke through his priestess, the Pythia (PITH-ee-uh). The male priests who administered the sanctuary interpreted her obscure utterances. Our dependence on literary texts that express the values of an educated urban elite limits our knowledge of fertility cults, which were usually based on female deities and appealed to the agricultural majority of the population.

sacrifice A gift given to a deity, often with the aim of creating a relationship, gaining favor, and obligating the god to provide some benefit to the sacrificer, sometimes in order to sustain the deity and thereby guarantee the continuing vitality of the natural world. The object devoted to the deity could be as simple as a cup of wine poured on the ground, a live animal slain on the altar, or, in the most extreme case, the ritual killing of a human being.

New Intellectual Currents

Prosperity, new technologies, and social and political development led to innovations in intellectual and artistic outlook, including a growing emphasis on the individual. In early Greek communities, the family enveloped the individual, and land belonged collectively to the family, including ancestors and descendants. Ripped from this communal network and forced to resettle elsewhere, colonists became models of individualism, as did the tyrant who seized power for himself alone. The concept of humanism—a valuing of the uniqueness, talents, and rights of the individual—remains a central tenet of Western civilization.

In the new lyric poetry, short verses deal with personal subjects drawn from the poet's experience. Archilochus (ahr-KIL-uh-kuhs), a soldier and poet living in the first half of the seventh century B.C.E., wrote:

> Some barbarian is waving my shield, since I was obliged to leave that perfectly good piece of equipment behind under a bush. But I got away, so what does it matter? Let the shield go; I can buy another one equally good.[2]

Here Archilochus pokes fun at the heroic ideal that scorned soldiers who ran from the enemy. In challenging traditional values and expressing personal feelings, lyric poets pointed toward the modern Western conception of poetry.

In religion, thinkers now known as pre-Socratic philosophers called into question Homer's representations of the gods. Xenophanes (zeh-NOFF-eh-nees), living in the sixth century B.C.E., protested:

> But if cattle and horses or lions had hands, or were able to draw with their hands and do the works that men can do, horses would draw the forms of the gods like horses, and cattle like cattle, and they would make their bodies such as they each had themselves.[3]

The term *pre-Socratic* refers to philosophers before Plato, a student of Socrates, who in the later fifth century B.C.E. shifted the focus of philosophy to ethical questions. They rejected traditional explanations of the origins and nature of the world and sought more rational answers: How was the world created? What is it made of? Why does it change? Some postulated that earth, air, fire, and water, the primal elements, combine or dissolve to form the substances found in nature. One taught that microscopic atoms (from a Greek word meaning "indivisible") move through the void of space, colliding randomly and combining in various ways to form the natural world. This intuition coincidentally resembles modern atomic theory. Most pre-Socratics came from Ionia and southern Italy, where Greeks lived close to non-Greeks. Encountering peoples with different ideas may have stimulated some of their thoughts.

Also in Ionia in the sixth century B.C.E., men later referred to as logographers ("writers of prose accounts") gathered information on ethnography (the physical characteristics and cultural practices of a people), Mediterranean geography, the foundation of cities, and the origins of famous families. They called their accumulation of information *historia*, "investigation/research." **Herodotus** (ca. 485–425 B.C.E.), from Halicarnassus in southwest Anatolia, published his *Histories*. Its early parts contain geographic and ethnographic reports, legends, folktales, and marvels. Later parts focus on the Persian-Greek wars of the previous generation. He opens his work as follows:

> I, Herodotus of Halicarnassus, am here setting forth my history, that time may not draw the color from what man has brought into being, nor those great and wonderful deeds, manifested by both Greeks and barbarians, fail of their report, and, together with all this, the reason why they fought one another.[4]

His search for causes reveals the thinking of a true historian. Thus did *historia* begin to narrow and acquire the modern meaning of *history*, with Herodotus gaining the nickname *Father of History*.

Primary Source: A Lyric Poem Laments an Absent Lover Read an ancient expression of heartache.

Herodotus (ca. 485–425 B.C.E.) Heir to the technique of historia—"investigation"—developed by Greeks in the late Archaic period. He came from a Greek community in Anatolia and traveled extensively collecting information in western Asia and the Mediterranean lands. He traced the antecedents of and chronicled the Persian Wars between the Greek city-states and the Persian Empire, thus originating the Western tradition of historical writing.

The Acropolis at Athens This steep, defensible plateau jutting out from the Attic Plain served as a Mycenaean fortress in the second millennium B.C.E. The site of Athens has been continuously occupied since that time. In the mid-sixth century B.C.E. the tyrant Pisistratus built a temple to Athena, the patron goddess of the community. It was destroyed by the Persians when they invaded Greece in 480 B.C.E. In the 440s, Pericles instituted a building program using funds from the naval empire that Athens headed. These construction projects, including a new temple to Athena—the Parthenon—brought glory to the city and popularity to Pericles and to the new democracy that he championed.

Robert Harding World Imagery

History in Focus *Why did the Athenians build their temple on top of a hill rather than in the city below? What does this tell you about their views on the relationship between gods and humans? Find the answer online.*

Athens and Sparta

Athens and Sparta, the pre-eminent city-states of the late Archaic and Classical periods, differed in character despite environmental and cultural similarities. The Spartans' ancestors migrated into the Peloponnese (PELL-eh-puh-neze), the southernmost part of Greece, around 1000 B.C.E. Their community resembled others until the seventh century B.C.E., when the population increases and shortage of farmland that affected all communities prompted them to react differently. Instead of sending out colonies, the Spartans invaded the fertile plain of Messenia to the west. The resulting takeover, aided perhaps by hoplite tactics, saw the Messenians reduced to the status of helots (HELL-uts), the most abused and exploited population on the Greek mainland.

The Spartan state quickly turned into a military camp, always prepared for a helot uprising. The state divided Messenia and Laconia, the Spartan homeland, into several thousand lots, each assigned to a Spartan citizen. Helots worked the land and turned over part of their harvest to their Spartan masters. Freed from farming, the Spartans devoted their lives to military affairs.

The Spartan army outclassed all others because it did not rely on militias summoned only during crises. The Spartans paid a price, however. Taken from their families and put into barracks at age seven, boys underwent a severe regimen of discipline, beatings, and deprivation. The demands of the state consumed a Spartan male's whole life.

The economic, political, and cultural revival of the Archaic Greek world passed Sparta by: no poets or artists, no precious metals or coinage, no commerce or other activities that could introduce inequality. The fifth-century B.C.E. historian Thucydides (thoo-SID-ih-dees), a native of Athens, remarked that in his day Sparta looked like a large village and that no future observer of the site would be able to guess its power.

Other Greeks admired Spartan courage, commitment, and martial skills but abhorred their arrogance, ignorance, and cruelty. The Spartan Council of Elders and two kings, who commanded in battle, practiced a cautious and isolationist foreign policy. Reluctant to venture far for fear of a helot uprising, they worked for peace through the Peloponnesian League, a system of alliances with their neighbors.

Athens, by comparison, possessed an unusually large and populous territory: the fertile plains of Attica with their groves of olive trees. By the fifth century B.C.E., Athens numbered approximately 300,000 people. Villages and a few larger towns dotted the peninsula where the urban center stood beside the sheer-sided Acropolis some 5 miles (8 kilometers) from the sea.

In 594 B.C.E., to avoid civil war, the Athenians conferred lawgiving powers on Solon, an aristocrat with ties to the merchant community. He divided the citizens into four classes based on the yield of their farms. The top three classes could hold state offices. The lowest class, with little or no property, held no offices but could participate in meetings of the Assembly. Although a far cry from democracy, this linkage between rights, privileges, and wealth broke the power of a dominant cluster of aristocratic families and favored social and political mobility. By abolishing debt slavery, Solon also guaranteed the freedom of Athenian citizens.

Despite Solon's efforts, in 546 B.C.E. an aristocrat named Pisistratus (pie-SIS-truh-tuhs) seized power. Most Athenians still lived in villages, identified primarily with their district, and accepted the leadership of landlords who lived in sturdy manor houses. So the tyrant Pisistratus turned to the urban population as opposed to the villagers loyal to the landlords. He undertook building projects, including a Temple of Athena on the Acropolis, and instituted or expanded popular urban festivals: the City Dionysia (die-ul-NIZ-eeuh), later famous for dramatic performances, and the Panathenaea (pan-ath-uh-NEE-uh), a religious procession combined with athletic and poetic competitions.

With Spartan assistance, the Athenians expelled Pisistratus's sons, who had inherited his position. In the 460s and 450s B.C.E., **Pericles** (PER-eh-kleez) led a democratic movement to transfer all power to popular organs of government: the Assembly, the Council of 500, and the People's Courts. Henceforward, Athenians of moderate or slender means could hold office and participate in politics. Selected by lot for even the highest positions, officials now received pay for their services so they could afford to leave their other occupations. Some key offices—managing public money, commanding military forces—were filled by elections that took into account the candidates' abilities.

The Assembly of all citizens held open debates several times a month; anyone could speak to the

SECTION REVIEW

- Geographical and environmental barriers turned Greeks to the sea.

- Under Phoenician influence, the Greeks built a new civilization centered on the polis.

- Overseas colonization extended Greek culture, but it did not relieve political instability.

- State religious ceremonies solidified civic identity.

- New forms of intellectual inquiry and artistic production emerged.

- Evolving along divergent paths, Athens and Sparta became the preeminent city-states.

issues of the day. Members of the Council of 500 took turns presiding and representing the Athenian state. Through effective political organizing, Pericles dominated Athenian politics from 461 B.C.E. until his death in 429 B.C.E.

Athens's economic position paralleled its political evolution. From the time of Pisistratus, Athenian pottery becomes increasingly prominent at archaeological sites around the Mediterranean. These pots often contained olive oil, Athens's chief export, but elegant painted vases were themselves luxury commodities. Trade-related increases in the size and prosperity of the middle class help explain the growth of Athenian democracy.

The Struggle of Persia and Greece

How did the Persian Wars lead into the Hellenistic Age that followed?

The Persian-Greek wars dominated Greek life in the fifth and fourth centuries B.C.E. Persians probably

Pericles (ca. 495–429 B.C.E.) Aristocratic leader who guided the Athenian state through the transformation to full participatory democracy for all male citizens, supervised construction of the Acropolis, and pursued a policy of imperial expansion that led to the Peloponnesian War. He formulated a strategy of attrition but died from the plague early in the war.

considered developments farther east more important. Nevertheless, in the end, the encounters profoundly affected the history of the eastern Mediterranean and western Asia.

Early Encounters

Cyrus's conquest of Lydia in 546 B.C.E. led to the subjugation of the Ionian Greek cities. Some groups and individuals collaborated with the Persian government, but in 499 B.C.E. Greeks and other subject peoples on the western frontier staged the Ionian Revolt. The Persians needed five years and massive infusions of troops and resources to stamp out the insurrection.

This failed revolt led to the **Persian Wars**: two Persian attacks on Greece in the early fifth century B.C.E. In 490 B.C.E., Darius dispatched a naval fleet to punish Eretria (er-EH-tree-uh) and Athens, two mainland Greek states allied with the Ionian rebels. Disloyal citizens betrayed Eretria to the Persians, who marched the survivors off to exile. In this, as in many other things, the Persians copied their Assyrian predecessors, although they did not boast of mass deportations. Athens would probably have suffered a similar fate if its hoplites had not defeated the lighter-armed Persian troops in a sharp engagement at Marathon, 26 miles (42 kilometers) from Athens.

Xerxes (Khshayarsha, r. 486–465 B.C.E.) succeeded his father in 486 B.C.E. and soon turned his attention to the troublesome Greeks. In 480 B.C.E., he gathered a huge invasion force, including contingents from all over the Persian Empire and a large fleet. Crossing the Hellespont (the narrow strait separating Europe and Asia) and traversing Thrace, the Persian throng descended into central and southern Greece. Xerxes sent messengers ahead demanding of the city-states "earth and water"—tokens of submission.

Many city-states complied. But in southern Greece the Spartans formed an alliance that historians call the Hellenic League. At the pass of Thermopylae (thuhr-MOP-uh-lee) in central Greece, three hundred Spartans and their king fought to the last man to buy time for their fellows to escape. The Persians sacked Athens, but the outnumbered Athenians lured the Persian navy into narrow waters at nearby Salamis (SAH-lah-miss), where, despite their numbers, they could not maneuver. The Persians lost their advantage, and the Athenians administered

a devastating defeat. A rout of the Persian a[...] Plataea the following spring relieved the immed[...] threat.

Athens's stubborn refusal to submit and the effectiveness of the Athenian navy earned the city great respect. Naval strategies dominated the next phase of the war, which was designed to liberate Greek states still under Persian control. This gave Athens priority over land-based, isolationist Sparta. The Delian League, formed in 477 B.C.E., brought the Greek states together. In less than twenty years, League forces led by Athenian generals swept the Persians from the eastern Mediterranean and freed all Greek communities except those in distant Cyprus.

The Height of Athenian Power

Scholars date the Classical period of Greek history (480–323 B.C.E.) to this defense of the Greek homeland. Ironically, Athens exploited its crucial role in these events to become an imperial power. Some Greek allies contributed money instead of troops, and the Athenians used the money to strengthen their navy. They treated other members of the Delian League as subjects and demanded annual contributions. States attempting to leave the League were brought back by force, stripped of their defenses, and subordinated to Athens.

Athenian naval technology transformed Greek warfare and brought power and wealth to Athens itself. Unlike commercial sailing ships, which over time had developed a stabler and more capacious round-bodied design, military vessels relied on large numbers of rowers. Having little deck room or storage space, these ships hugged the coastline and put ashore nightly to replenish food supplies and let the crew sleep. Fifty-oared ships had dominated naval warfare

Persian Wars Conflicts between Greek city-states and the Persian Empire, ranging from the Ionian Revolt (499–494 B.C.E.) through Darius's punitive expedition that failed at Marathon (490 B.C.E.) and the defeat of Xerxes' massive invasion of Greece by the Spartan-led Hellenic League (480–479 B.C.E.). This first major setback for Persian arms launched the Greeks into their period of greatest cultural productivity. Herodotus chronicled these events in the first "history" in the Western tradition.

Replica of Ancient Greek Trireme Greek warships had a metal-tipped ram in front to pierce the hulls of enemy vessels and a pair of steering rudders in the rear. Though equipped with masts and sails, in battle these warships were propelled by 170 rowers. This modern, full-sized replica, manned by international volunteer crews, is helping scholars to determine attainable speeds and maneuvering techniques.

Paul Lipke/Trireme Trust USA

until the late sixth century B.C.E., when sleek, fast **triremes** (TRY-reems) powered by 170 rowers brought an end to crude engagements in which warriors cleared the enemy's decks with spears and arrows before boarding and fighting hand to hand. Approximately 115 by 18 feet (35 by 6 meters) in size, the trireme positioned rowers on three levels with oars of different lengths to avoid interference. The fragile vessels could achieve up to 7 knots in short bursts. Athenian crews, by constant practice, became the best in the eastern Mediterranean. They disabled enemy vessels by sheering off their oars, smashing their hulls below the water line with an iron-tipped prow, or forcing collisions by running around them in ever-tighter circles.

The primacy of the fleet contributed to a democratic system in which each male citizen had, at least in principle, an equal voice. The middle or upper class produced hoplites, who bought their own armor and weapons. Rowers came from the lower classes, but they insisted on full rights as protectors of the community.

Athenian maritime power reached farther than any citizen militia. Victors in Greek wars seldom occupied enemy lands permanently (the exception being Sparta's takeover of Messenia). Booty with minor adjustments to boundary lines sufficed. But Athens could exert continual domination and readily did so to promote its commerce. Athens's port, Piraeus

(pih-RAY-uhs), became the most important commercial center in the eastern Mediterranean.

Annual dues from subject states subsidized the increasingly expensive Athenian democracy and paid the construction costs of the Parthenon, a majestic temple to Athena on the Acropolis. The Athenian leader Pericles gained extraordinary popularity by hiring many Athenians to construct and decorate this and other monuments. When political enemies protested Pericles' use of Delian League funds for construction, he replied: "They [Athens's subjects] do not give us a single horse, nor a soldier, nor a ship. All they supply is money. . . . It is no more than fair that after Athens has been equipped with all she needs to carry on the war, she should apply the surplus to public works, which, once completed, will bring her glory for all time."[5]

The proceeds of empire indirectly subsidized the festivals at which the dramatic tragedies of Aeschylus, Sophocles, and Euripides and the comedies of Aristophanes (ar-uh-STOFF-uh-neze) were performed.

---

trireme Greek and Phoenician warship of the fifth and fourth centuries B.C.E. It was sleek and light, powered by 170 oars arranged in three vertical tiers. Manned by skilled sailors, it was capable of short bursts of speed and complex maneuvers.

The brightest and most creative artists and thinkers flocked to Athens. Traveling teachers called Sophists ("wise men") provided instruction in logic and public speaking to fee-paying pupils. The new discipline of rhetoric—the crafting of attractive and persuasive arguments—gave those with training and quick wits a great advantage in politics and the courts. Greeks became connoisseurs of oratory, eagerly listening for each innovation yet so aware of the power of words that *sophist* came to mean one who uses cleverness to manipulate reality.

These intellectual currents came together in 399 B.C.E. when the philosopher **Socrates** (ca. 470–399 B.C.E.) went on trial charged with corrupting the youth of Athens and not believing in the city's gods. A sculptor by trade, Socrates spent his time conversing with young men who enjoyed hearing him deflate the pretensions of those who thought themselves wise. He wryly commented that he knew one more thing than everyone else: that he knew nothing.

At his trial, Socrates easily disposed of the actual charges: he was a deeply religious man, and the families of the young men he associated with supported him. He argued that the real basis of the prosecution was twofold: (1) blame for attempts by several of his aristocratic students to overthrow the Athenian democracy and (2) blame for the controversial teachings of the Sophists, which many believed undermined morality and religious tradition. In Athenian trials, juries of hundreds of citizens decided guilt and punishment, often spurred by emotion more than legal principles. Convicted by a close vote, Socrates maintained his innocence and said he should be rewarded for his services instead. This led the jury to condemn him to death by drinking hemlock. Socrates' disciples considered him a martyr, and smart young men like Plato withdrew from public life and dedicated themselves to philosophical pursuits.

Socrates himself wrote nothing, preferring to converse with people he met in the street. His disciple Plato (ca. 428–347 B.C.E.) may represent the first truly literate generation. He learned from books and habitually wrote down his thoughts. On the outskirts of Athens, Plato founded the Academy, a school where young men could pursue higher education. Yet even Plato reflected the oral culture of his upbringing by writing dialogues—an oral form—in which his protagonist, Socrates, uses the "Socratic method" of question and answer to reach a deeper understanding of values like justice, excellence, and wisdom. Plato refused to write down the most advanced teachings of the Academy. Higher reality, he believed, appeared only in pale reflection in the sensible world and could be grasped only by "initiates" who had completed the earlier stages.

Inequality in Classical Greece

The Athenian democracy that historically underlies modern traditions of democracy included only a small percentage of Attica's population: true citizens—free adult males of pure Athenian ancestry. Excluding women, children, slaves, and foreigners, this group amounted to 30,000 or 40,000 people out of approximately 300,000. Equally exclusive practices probably existed in less well-known Greek democracies.

Slaves, mostly foreigners, constituted perhaps one-third of the population of Attica in the fifth and fourth centuries B.C.E. The average Athenian family owned one or more. Slaves ran the shop or worked the farm while the master attended meetings of the Assembly or served on a board overseeing the day-to-day activities of the state. As "living pieces of property," slaves did any work, submitted to any sexual acts, and suffered any punishments their owners ordained, though some communities prohibited arbitrarily killing slaves. Overall, Greece saw few of the extremes of cruelty and abuse inflicted on slaves in other places and times.

Farms being small, most slaves performed domestic service rather than field labor, often working with the master or mistress on the same tasks. Daily contact fostered relationships between owners and slaves that made it hard for owners to act inhumanely. Still, Greek thinkers justified slavery by arguing that *barbaroi* (non-Greeks) lacked the capacity to reason and

Socrates Athenian philosopher (ca. 470–399 B.C.E.) who shifted the emphasis of philosophical investigation from questions of natural science to ethics and human behavior. He attracted young disciples from elite families but made enemies by revealing the ignorance and pretensions of others, culminating in his trial and execution by the Athenian state.

thus were better off under Greek owners. The stigma attached to slavery was so great that most Athenians refused to work as wage laborers because following an employer's orders resembled being his slave.

The position of women varied. Spartan women, who were expected to bear and raise strong children, exercised regularly and enjoyed a level of public visibility and outspokenness that shocked other Greeks. At the opposite extreme, Athenians confined and oppressed women. Ironically, the exploitation of women in Athens reflects the high degree of freedom that Athenian men enjoyed in the democratic state.

Inequality marked Athenian marriages. A man of thirty—reasonably educated, a war veteran, and experienced in business and politics—commonly married, after negotiating with her parents, a teenage girl with no formal education and minimal training in weaving, cooking, and household management. Coming into the home of a husband she hardly knew, the wife had no political rights and limited legal protection. Given the differences in age, social experience, and authority, the relationship between husband and wife resembled that of father and daughter. The function of marriage was to produce children, preferably male. The ancients were sufficiently ashamed of infanticide—the killing through exposure of unwanted children—to say little about it. But it is likely that more girls than boys were abandoned.

The husband spent his day outdoors attending to work or political responsibilities; he dined with male friends at night (see Material Culture: Wine and Beer in the Ancient World). The wife stayed home to cook, clean, raise the children, and supervise the servants. The closest relationship in the family was likely to be between the wife and her slave attendant, a woman of roughly the same age. The servant could be sent on errands. The wife stayed home, except to attend funerals and certain festivals or make discreet visits to female relatives. Greek men claimed that confinement to the home stifled female promiscuity and prevented illegitimate births that could threaten family property and erode regulation of citizenship rights. Athenian law allowed a husband to kill an adulterer caught in the act with his wife.

Without documents written by women, we cannot tell how Athenian women felt about their situation. Women's festivals, such as the Thesmophoria (thes-moe-FOE-ree-uh), provided a rare opportunity for women to get out. During this three-day festival, the women of Athens lived together and managed their own affairs in a great encampment, carrying out mysterious rituals meant to enhance the fertility of the land. Bold and self-assertive women appeared on the Athenian stage: the defiant Antigone (an-TIG-uh-nee) of Sophocles' play, who buried her brother despite the king's prohibition; and the wives in Aristophanes' comedy Lysistrata (lis-us-STRAH-tuh), who withheld sex from their husbands until the men ended a war. Although imagined by men and probably reflecting a fear of strong women, these characters must partly reflect the playwrights' mothers, sisters, and wives.

To find their intellectual and emotional "equal," men often looked to other men. Bisexuality arose as much from the social structure as from biological inclinations. An older man commonly admired, pursued, and mentored a youth, thus making bisexuality part of the youth's education and initiation into the adult male community. Though commonplace among the intellectual groups that loom large in the written sources, the frequency of bisexuality and the confinement of women among the Athenian masses remain uncertain.

Failure of the City-State and Triumph of the Macedonians

Athens's rise to empire led in 431 B.C.E. to the outbreak of the **Peloponnesian War**, a struggle for survival between Athenian and Spartan alliances that encompassed most of the Greek world. To insulate themselves from attack by land, in midcentury the Athenians had built three long walls connecting the city with the port of Piraeus and the adjacent shoreline. As long as Athens controlled the sea-lanes and could provision itself, a land-based siege could not starve it into submission.

Peloponnesian War A protracted (431–404 B.C.E.) and costly conflict between the Athenian and Spartan alliance systems that convulsed most of the Greek world. The war was largely a consequence of Athenian imperialism. Possession of a naval empire allowed Athens to fight a war of attrition. Ultimately Sparta prevailed because of Athenian errors and Persian financial support.

Material Culture

Wine and Beer in the Ancient World

The most prized beverages of ancient peoples were wine and beer. Sediments found in jars excavated at a site in northwest Iran prove that techniques for the manufacture of wine were known as early as the sixth millennium B.C.E. Beer dates back at least as far as the fourth millennium B.C.E. Archaeological excavations have brought to light the equipment used in preparing, transporting, serving, and imbibing these beverages.

In Egypt and Mesopotamia, beer, which was made from wheat or barley by a rather elaborate process, was the staple drink of both the elite and the common people. Women prepared beer for the family in their homes, and breweries produced large quantities for sale. Because the production process left some chaff floating on the surface of the liquid, various means were employed to filter out this unwelcome byproduct. Sculptures on Mesopotamian stone reliefs and seals show a number of drinkers drawing on straws immersed in a single large bowl. Archaeologists have found examples of the perforated metal cones that fit over the submerged ends of the straws and filtered the liquid beer drawn through them. It is likely that the sharing of beer from a common vessel by several people had social implications, creating a bond of friendship among the participants. Archaeologists have also found individual beer "mugs" resembling a modern watering can: closed bowls with a perforated spout to filter the chaff and a semicircular channel carrying the liquid into the drinker's mouth.

In Greece, Rome, and other Mediterranean lands, where the climate was suitable for cultivating grape vines, wine was the preferred beverage. Vines were prepared in February and periodically pinched and pruned. The full-grown grapes were picked in September, then crushed (with a winepress or by people trampling on them) to produce a liquid that was sealed in casks for fermentation. The new vintage was sampled the following February. Exuberant religious festivals marked the key moments in the cycle. Initially expensive and therefore confined to the wealthy and for religious ceremonies, in later antiquity wine became available to a wider spectrum of people. Unlike beer, which requires refrigeration, wine can be stored for a long time in sealed containers and thus could be transported and traded across the ancient Mediterranean lands, continental Europe, and western Asia. The usual containers for wine were long, conical pottery jars, which the Greeks called amphoras.

The Greeks normally mixed wine with water, and they developed an elaborate array of vessels, made of pottery, metal, and glass, to facilitate mixing, serving, and drinking the precious liquid. Kraters were large mixing bowls into which the wine and water were poured. The hydria was used to carry water, and a heater could be used to warm the water when that was desired. Another special vessel could be used to chill the wine by immersion in cold water. Ladles (long-handled spoons) and elegantly narrow vessels with spouts were used to pour the concoction into the drinkers' cups. The most popular shapes for individual drinking vessels were a shallow bowl with two handles, called a kylix, and the

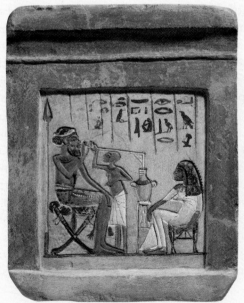

Royal Guard Drinking Beer Through a Straw Early forms of beer were nutritious foods but contained unappetizing residue from the fermentation process. Straws up to 40 centimeters in length had one end closed but with tiny perforations to filter the liquid. Common people used straws of clay or reed, but the elite might use silver or gold. As with fermented drinks in some parts of Africa today, beer drinking was often a social occasion with more than one person sipping from a large beer container at the same time. Bildarchiv Preussischer Kulturbesitz/Art Resource, NY kantharos, a large, deep, two-handled cup. Another popular implement in Greece and western Asia was the rhyton, a horn-shaped vessel that tapered into the head and forepaws of an animal with a small hole at the base. The drinker would fill the horn, holding his thumb over the hole until he was ready to drink or pour, then move his thumb and release a thin stream of wine that appeared to be coming out of the animal's mouth.

The drinking equipment belonging to wealthy Greeks was often decorated with representations of the god of wine, Dionysus, holding a kantharos and surrounded by a dense tangle of vines and grape clusters. His entourage included the half-human, half-horse centaurs and the maenads, literally "crazy women." These were female worshipers who drank wine and engaged in frenzied dancing until they achieved an ecstatic state and sensed the presence of the god.

Greeks, Romans, and other Mediterranean peoples used wine for more conventional religious ceremonies, pouring libations on the ground or on the altar as an offering to the gods. It was also used on occasion for medical purposes, as a disinfectant and painkiller, or as an ingredient in various medicines. Above all, wine was featured at the banquets and drinking parties that forged and deepened social bonds. In the Greek world, the symposion (meaning "drinking together") was held after the meal. Someone, usually the host, presided over the affair, making the crucial decision about the proportion of water to wine, suggesting topics of conversation, and trying to keep some semblance of order. There might be entertainment in the form of musicians, dancers, and acrobats.

In Shang China, magnificent bronze vessels whose surfaces were covered with abstract designs and representations of otherworldly animals were fashioned for use in elaborate ceremonies at ancestral shrines. The vessels contained offerings of wine and food for the spirits of the family's ancestors, who were imagined to still need sustenance in the afterlife. The treasured bronze vessels were often buried with their owners so that they could continue to employ them after death. In later periods, as the ancestral sacrifices became less important, beautiful bronze vessels, as well as their ceramic counterparts, became part of the equipment at the banquets of the well-to-do.

At the start of the war, Pericles broke precedent by refusing to engage the Spartan-led armies that invaded Attica each year. He knew that the enemy hoplites must soon return to their farms. Thus, instead of culminating in a short, decisive battle, the Peloponnesian War dragged on for nearly three decades, with great loss of life and resources. It sapped the morale of all Greece and ended only with the defeat of Athens in a naval battle in 404 B.C.E. The Persian Empire had bankrolled the construction of ships by the Spartan alliance, so Sparta was able to take the conflict into Athens's own element, the sea.

The victorious Spartans, who had entered the war championing "the freedom of the Greeks," took over Athens's overseas empire until their increasingly high-handed behavior aroused the opposition of other city-states. Indeed, the fourth century B.C.E. was a time of nearly continuous skirmishing among Greek states. The independent polis that lent glory to Greek culture also fostered rivalries and fears among neighbors.

The Persians recouped old losses. By the King's Peace of 387 B.C.E., encompassing most of the war-weary Greek states, all of western Asia, including the Ionian Greek communities, went to Persia. The Persian king guaranteed a status quo that kept the Greeks divided and weak until rebellions in Egypt, Cyprus, and Phoenicia, combined with trouble from some western satraps, diverted his attention from thoughts of another Greek invasion.

Meanwhile, in northern Greece Philip II (r. 359–336 B.C.E.) was transforming his previously backward kingdom of Macedonia into a premier military power. (Although southern Greeks long doubted the "Greekness" of the rough and rowdy Macedonians, modern scholarship considers their language and culture Greek at base, though influenced by non-Greek neighbors.) Philip improved the traditional hoplite formation. He increased its striking power and mobility by equipping his soldiers with longer thrusting spears and lighter armor. Using horses bred on Macedonia's

- Greek rebellion against Persian dominion provoked the Persian Wars.
- During successive Persian invasions, Athens and Sparta led Greek resistance.
- Victory left Athens a naval power with imperial aspirations, and its wealth nourished the great cultural achievements of the Classical period.
- Athenian democracy rested upon several forms of inequality, including the subjugation of women and slaves.
- Spartan/Athenian rivalry sparked the Peloponnesian War, which destroyed Athens and weakened all the city-states.
- Macedonia then became the dominant power in Greece, conquering the city-states and, under Alexander the Great, the Persian Empire.

broad grassy plains, he experimented with coordinating infantry and cavalry. Finally, his engineers developed new siege weapons, including the first catapults—machines using the power of twisted cords that, when relaxed, hurled arrows or stones great distances.

In 338 B.C.E., Philip defeated a southern coalition and established the Confederacy of Corinth to control the Greek city-states. Appointed military commander of all the Greeks, he planned a campaign against Persia and established a bridgehead on the Asiatic side of the Hellespont. These plans may have reflected the advice of Greek thinkers who urged an anti-Persian crusade to unify their quarrelsome countrymen.

An assassin cut short Philip's ambitions in 336 B.C.E. **Alexander** (356–323 B.C.E.), his son, crossed into Asia in 334 B.C.E., vowing revenge for Xerxes' invasion a century and half earlier. He defeated the Persians in three pitched battles—against the western satraps at the Granicus River in northwest Anatolia and against King Darius III (r. 336–330 B.C.E.) himself at Issus in southeast Anatolia and at Gaugamela (GAW-guh-mee-luh), north of Babylon.

Alexander the Great, as he came to be called, maintained the Persian administrative system but replaced Persian officials with Macedonians and Greeks. To control strategic points, he settled wounded and aged ex-soldiers in a series of Greek-style cities, beginning with Alexandria in Egypt. After his victory at Gaugamela (331 B.C.E.), he experimented with leaving cooperative Persian officials in place, also admitting some Persians and other Iranians into his army and court circle. Adopting elements of Persian dress and court ceremonials, he married several Iranian women who had royal or aristocratic connections and pressed his leading comrades to do the same.

In opting for unexpected policies that the Macedonian nobility fiercely resented, Alexander probably acted from both pragmatic and idealistic motives. His Asian campaign began with visions of glory, booty, and revenge. But the farther east he traveled, the more he saw himself as the legitimate successor of the Persian king (a claim facilitated by the death of Darius III). Alexander may have recognized that he had responsibilities to all the peoples who fell under his control and that controlling so vast an empire would require the cooperation of local leaders. In this, he followed the example of the Achaemenids.

The Hellenistic Synthesis

How did a cultural synthesis develop during the Hellenistic Age?

Historians call the epoch following Alexander's conquests the **Hellenistic Age** (323–30 B.C.E.) because large parts of northeastern Africa and western Asia became "Hellenized"—that is, influenced by Greek culture. Greeks migrated in large numbers from their overcrowded homeland to serve as a privileged class of soldiers and administrators on the new frontiers, where they replicated the lifestyle of the city-state. This

Alexander (356–323 B.C.E.) King of Macedonia in northern Greece. Between 334 and 323 B.C.E. he conquered the Persian Empire, reached the Indus Valley, founded many Greek-style cities, and spread Greek culture across the Middle East. Later known as Alexander the Great.

Hellenistic Age Historians' term for the era, usually dated 323–30 B.C.E., in which Greek culture spread across western Asia and northeastern Africa after the conquests of Alexander the Great. The period ended with the fall of the last major Hellenistic kingdom to Rome, but Greek cultural influence persisted until the seventh century C.E.

Map 4.1 Hellenistic Civilization After the death of Alexander the Great in 323 B.C.E., his vast empire split apart into a number of large and small political entities. A Macedonian dynasty was established on each continent: the Antigonids ruled the Macedonian homeland and tried to extend their control over southern Greece; the Ptolemies ruled Egypt; and the Seleucids inherited most of Alexander's conquests in Asia, but lost control of the eastern portions to the Parthians in the second century B.C.E. This period saw Greeks emigrating in large numbers from their overcrowded homeland to serve as a privileged class of soldiers and administrators in the new territories, where they replicated the lifestyle of the city-state.   © Cengage Learning

Interactive Map

era of large kingdoms containing ethnically mixed populations, great cities, powerful rulers, pervasive bureaucracies, and vast disparities in wealth differed profoundly from the Archaic and Classical ages with their small, homogeneous, independent city-states. The Hellenistic world more closely resembled our own in its long-distance trade and communications, new institutions like libraries and universities, new kinds of scholarship and science, and sophisticated tastes in art and literature.

When he died suddenly in 323 B.C.E. at the age of thirty-two, Alexander had no plans for the succession. A half-century of chaos followed as the most ambitious and ruthless of his generals struggled to

succeed him. When the dust cleared, they had broken the empire into three major kingdoms, each ruled by a Macedonian dynasty: the Seleucid (sih-LOO-sid), Ptolemaic (tawl-uh-MAY-ik), and Antigonid (an-TIG-uh-nid) kingdoms (see Map 4.1). The Antigonids ruled the Macedonian homeland and tried with varying success to extend their control over southern Greece; the Ptolemies ruled Egypt; and the Seleucids inherited the majority of Alexander's conquests in Asia. A rough balance of power prevented any of the three from gaining the upper hand and enabled smaller states to survive by playing off the great powers.

The Seleucids, who ruled the bulk of Alexander's empire, faced the greatest challenges. The Indus Valley and Afghanistan soon split off, and over the course of the third and second centuries B.C.E., Iran fell to the Parthians (see Chapter 8). Thereafter Mesopotamia, Syria, and parts of Anatolia constituted the Seleucid core; the kings ruled from Antioch in Syria. Like the Persians before them, they governed many different ethnic groups organized under various political and social forms. In the farming villages, where most of the population resided, the Seleucids maintained an administration modeled on the Persian system. They also continued Alexander's policy of founding Greek-style cities to serve as administrative centers and attract colonists from Greece. The Seleucids desperately needed Greek soldiers, engineers, and administrators.

In Europe, the Antigonid dynasty ruled the Macedonian homeland and parts of northern Greece. Compact and ethnically homogeneous, the Antigonid kingdom experienced little of the hostility that the Seleucid and Ptolemaic rulers faced. Macedonian garrisons gave the Antigonids a toehold in central and southern Greece, and the shadow of Macedonian intervention always threatened the south. The southern states responded by joining confederations, such as the Achaean (uh-KEY-uhn) League in the Peloponnese, in which the member states maintained local autonomy but pooled resources and military power.

Athens and Sparta stood apart from these confederations. Never abandoning their myth of invincibility, the Spartans made a number of heroic but futile stands against Macedonian armies. Athens, now cherished for the artistic and literary accomplishments of the fifth century B.C.E., pursued a policy of neutrality. The city became a large museum, filled with the relics and memories of a glorious past, as well as a university town that attracted the children of the well-to-do from all over the Mediterranean and western Asia.

Egypt under the Ptolemies

The dynasty of the **Ptolemies** (TAWL-uh-meze) ruled Egypt and sometimes laid claim to Palestine. Since most Egyptians belonged to one ethnic group and lived in villages alongside the Nile, the Ptolemies took over much of the administrative structure of the pharaohs. The Ptolemies ruled from **Alexandria**. Memphis and Thebes, the capitals of ancient Egypt, had been located upriver. Alexandria, situated near the mouth of the westernmost branch of the Nile, linked Egypt with the Mediterranean world. In the language of the Ptolemaic bureaucracy, Alexandria was technically "beside Egypt" rather than in it, as if to emphasize the gulf between rulers and subjects and the fact that it was not on the Nile River.

Like the Seleucids, the Ptolemies encouraged Greek immigration. In return for collaboration in the military or civil administration, the immigrants received land and a privileged position in the new society. But the Ptolemies did not plant Greek-style cities throughout the Egyptian countryside and made no effort to force the Greek language or customs on the Egyptian population. So separate was the ruling class from the subject population that only the last Ptolemy, Queen Cleopatra (r. 51–30 B.C.E.), bothered to learn the Egyptian language. The advent of new masters brought few changes to the Egyptian peasants. Vast revenues poured into the royal treasury from rents (the king owned most of the land), taxes, and royal monopolies on olive oil, salt, papyrus, and other key commodities. Nevertheless, from the early second century B.C.E., native insurrections in the countryside, though quickly stamped out by government forces and Greek and Hellenized settlers, indicate growing resentment of Greek exploitation and arrogance.

Alexandria, the greatest Hellenistic city with a population of nearly half a million, had at its heart the royal compound, containing the palace and administrative buildings. The magnificent Mausoleum of

Ptolemies The Macedonian dynasty descended from one of Alexander the Great's officers that ruled Egypt for three centuries (323–30 B.C.E.). From their magnificent capital at Alexandria on the Mediterranean coast, the Ptolemies largely took over the system created by Egyptian pharaohs to extract the wealth of the land, rewarding Greeks and Hellenized non-Greeks serving in the military and administration.

Alexandria City on the Mediterranean coast of Egypt founded by Alexander. It became the capital of the Hellenistic kingdom of the Ptolemies. It contained the famous Library and the Museum—a center for leading scientific and literary figures. Its merchants engaged in trade with areas bordering the Mediterranean and the Indian Ocean.

- The death of Alexander the Great and the breakup of his empire inaugurated the Hellenistic Age.

- Large kingdoms were ruled by Macedonian dynasties in which Greek culture was fused with local traditions.

- Most Greek city-states retained autonomy through alliances, but Sparta and Athens stood apart and lost power.

- Egypt under the Ptolemies was the most successful Hellenistic state, and its capital Alexandria became the greatest Hellenistic city.

Alexander enshrined Alexander's body, which the first Ptolemy had stolen during its return to Macedonia for burial. He had hoped that the luster of the great conqueror, who was declared to be a god, would give him legitimacy as a ruler.

The famed Library of Alexandria had several hundred thousand volumes. The Museum, or "House of the Muses" (divinities who presided over the arts and sciences), supported the work of the greatest poets, philosophers, doctors, and scientists. A great lighthouse—a multistory tower with a fiery beacon visible at a distance of 30 miles (48 kilometers)—guided seafarers to two harbors serving the commerce of the Mediterranean, the Red Sea, and the Indian Ocean.

Alexandrian Greeks enjoyed citizenship in a polis, complete with Assembly, Council, and officials overseeing local affairs. They took advantage of Greek-style amenities and institutions: public baths and shaded arcades, theaters featuring revivals of ancient plays, and concert halls for musical performances and demonstrations of oratory. Young men of the privileged elite took classes at gymnasiums where athletics and fitness combined with music and literature in the curriculum. Jews had their own civic corporation, officials, and courts and predominated in two of the five main residential districts. The sights, sounds, and smells of Syria, Anatolia, and the Egyptian countryside lent distinctiveness to other quarters.

Hellenistic Societies

In all the Hellenistic states, ambitious members of the indigenous populations learned the Greek language and adopted elements of the Greek lifestyle, because doing so helped them become part of a privileged and wealthy ruling class. Language and customs more than physical traits made a person a Greek. The Hellenistic Age saw a spontaneous synthesis of Greek and indigenous ways. Egyptians migrated to Alexandria, and Greeks and Egyptians intermarried in the villages. Greeks living amid the monuments and descendants of the ancient civilizations of Egypt and western Asia learned the mathematical and astronomical wisdom of Mesopotamia, the mortuary rituals of Egypt, and the attractions of foreign religions. With little official planning or blessing and stemming for the most part from the day-to-day experiences of ordinary people, a great multicultural experiment unfolded as Greek and Middle Eastern cultural traits clashed and merged.

Conclusion

Greece and Iran represent two ways in which societies with shared Indo-European linguistic and religious roots adapted to different geographical environments and indigenous cultures. Although scholars can easily trace resemblances among gods, customs, and philosophical outlooks in these areas, the peoples themselves had no sense of kinship with one another. Only briefly, under Alexander the Great, did they come into direct contact in meaningful ways, and the resulting Hellenistic culture touched all three regions.

While some technologies, such as coinage, took hold in all areas and trade flourished, both overland and across the Mediterranean Sea, local circumstances dictated political and social formations. The ancient cultural centers of Egypt and Mesopotamia influenced the Greeks and the Persians.

In comparing the histories of these regions, the question arises of the degree to which different states and societies follow similar paths because of shared heritages, as opposed to responding similarly but independently to analogous challenges. We will explore this subject in the next chapter through a comparison of Rome and China under the Han dynasty.

CHAPTER REVIEW

 Download the MP3 audio file of the Chapter Review to listen to on the go.

How did the Persian Empire rise from its Iranian homeland and spread to encompass diverse cultures? (page 87)

The Medes, who were the first Iranians to build a complex political order, helped destroy the Assyrian Empire. Cyrus then united the Persians and overthrew the Medes, prompting the two similar cultures to blend. Expansion into Mesopotamia, Syria, and Anatolia connected the Persian Empire with older cultural and commercial networks. Under Darius I, the empire reached its fullest extent and basic governmental structure: provinces governed by satraps, tribute money funneled to the center, and a decentralized legal system. An extensive road and post system connected the imperial center with the periphery.

How did Greek civilization evolve and spread beyond its original territories? (page 92)

A rugged geography inhibiting overland travel turned the Greeks to the sea. The focus of this Greek civilization was the polis, whose citizens participated in government and defended it as hoplites. Population pressures spurred overseas colonization, which spread Greek culture throughout the Mediterranean world. This period saw the emergence of new forms of literary and intellectual endeavor, such as history and philosophical inquiry.

How did the Persian Wars lead into the Hellenistic Age that followed? (page 98)

Athens, Sparta, and their allies repulsed Persian invasions on land and at sea. Victory left Athens a naval power with an overseas empire and sufficient wealth from tribute and trade to finance temples on the Acropolis and other cultural achievements in drama and philosophy. Rivalry between Sparta and Athens exploded into the Peloponnesian War, which shattered Athens and weakened the other city-states. Exploiting this weakness, Persia recovered old losses but encountered Macedonian expansion and ultimate defeat by Alexander the Great.

How did a cultural synthesis develop during the Hellenistic Age? (page 105)

The death of Alexander the Great ushered in the Hellenistic Age. From his empire his generals carved kingdoms for themselves, founding Macedonian dynasties that presided over an international Greek culture. The Seleucids ruled the largest kingdom, founding Greek-style cities but ruling in the Persian manner. Both they and the Ptolemies encouraged Greek immigration, but in Egypt Greeks remained a class apart and had little to do with native Egyptians. The Antigonids ruled Macedonia, but the southern and central Greek cities resisted them through alliances. Sparta and Athens remained apart, both losing power in the region. Alexandria became the major Hellenistic city, a showcase of the cultural synthesis that marked the age.

Key Terms

Cyrus *(p. 88)*

Darius I *(p. 89)*

satrap *(p. 89)*

Persepolis *(p. 90)*

Zoroastrianism *(p. 91)*

polis *(p. 93)*

hoplite *(p. 93)*

tyrant *(p. 94)*

democracy *(p. 94)*

sacrifice *(p. 95)*

Herodotus *(p. 96)*

Pericles *(p. 98)*

Persian Wars *(p. 99)*

trireme *(p. 100)*

Socrates *(p. 101)*

Peloponnesian War *(p. 102)*

Alexander *(p. 105)*

Hellenistic Age *(p. 105)*

Ptolemies *(p. 107)*

Alexandria *(p. 107)*

Web Resources

Pronunciation Guide

Interactive Map
• MAP 4.1 Hellenistic Civilization

CourseMate Visit the CourseMate website at www.cengagebrain.com for additional study tools and review materials for this chapter.

Primary Sources
• Gathas
• A Lyric Poem Laments an AbsentLover

Answer to the History in Focus Question
See photo on page 97, "The Acropolis at Athens."

India and Southeast Asia

© Cengage Learning

CHAPTER PREVIEW

The Indus Valley Civilization
What does material evidence tell us about the Indus Valley civilization and the most likely reason for its collapse?

Foundations of Indian Civilization
What historical forces led to the development of complex social groupings in ancient India?

Indian Imperial Expansion and Collapse
In the face of powerful forces that tended to keep India fragmented, how did the Mauryan Empire of the fourth to second centuries B.C.E. and the Gupta Empire of the fourth to sixth centuries C.E. succeed in unifying much of India?

Southeast Asia, 50–1025 C.E.
How did the geography of Southeast Asia contribute to its commerce and to the influence of Hinduism and Buddhism?

Conclusion

ENVIRONMENT AND TECHNOLOGY: Indian Mathematics

Visit the CourseMate website at **www.cengagebrain.com** for additional study tools and review materials for this chapter.

In the Bhagavad-Gita (BUH-guh-vahd GEE-tuh), the most renowned Indian sacred text, the legendary warrior Arjuna (AHR-joo-nuh) rides out in his chariot to the open space between two armies preparing for battle. Torn between his social duty to fight for his family's claim to the throne and his conscience, which balks at the prospect of killing relatives, friends, and former teachers in the enemy camp, Arjuna slumps down in his chariot and refuses to fight. But his driver, the god Krishna (KRISH-nuh) in disguise, persuades him, in a carefully structured dialogue, both of the necessity to fulfill his duty as a warrior and of the proper frame of mind for performing these acts. In the climactic moment of the dialogue Krishna endows Arjuna with a "divine eye" and permits him to see the true appearance of God:

> It was a multiform, wondrous vision,
> with countless mouths and eyes
> and celestial ornaments,
>
> Everywhere was boundless divinity
> containing all astonishing things,
> wearing divine garlands and garments,
> anointed with divine perfume.
>
> If the light of a thousand suns
> were to rise in the sky at once,
> it would be like the light
> of that great spirit.
>
> Arjuna saw all the universe
> in its many ways and parts,
> standing as one in the body
> of the god of gods.[1]

In all of world literature, this is one of the most compelling attempts to depict the nature of deity. Graphic images emphasize the vastness, diversity, and multiplicity of the god, but in the end we learn that Krishna is the organizing principle behind all creation, that behind diversity and multiplicity lies a higher unity.

1. From Bhagavad-Gita, translated by Barbara Stoler Miller, translation copyright © 1986 by Barbara Stoler Miller. Used by permission of Bantam Books, a division of Random House, Inc.

This is an apt metaphor for Indian civilization. The enormous variety of the Indian landscape is mirrored in the patchwork of ethnic and linguistic groups that occupy it, the political fragmentation that has marked most of Indian history, the elaborate hierarchy of social groups into which the Indian population is divided, and the thousands of deities who are worshiped at innumerable holy places that dot the subcontinent. Yet, in the end, one can speak of an Indian civilization united by shared views and values.

This chapter surveys the history of South and Southeast Asia from approximately 1500 B.C.E. to 1025 C.E., highlighting the evolution of defining features of Indian civilization. Considerable attention is given to Indian religious conceptions, due both to religion's profound role in shaping Indian society and the sources of information available to historians. For reasons that will be explained below, writing came late to India, and ancient Indians did not develop a historical consciousness like other peoples of antiquity and took little interest in recording specific historical events.

The Indus Valley Civilization

What does material evidence tell us about the Indus Valley civilization and the most likely reason for its collapse?

Civilization developed almost as early in South Asia as in Mesopotamia and Egypt. Just as each Middle Eastern civilization centered on a great river valley, so civilization in the Indian subcontinent originated on the fertile floodplain of the Indus River, where settled farming created the agricultural surplus essential to urbanized society.

Natural Environment A plain of more than 1 million acres (400,000 hectares) stretches between the mountains of western Pakistan and the Thar Desert to the east in Sind, the central portion of the Indus Valley (see Map 5.1). Silt carried downstream and deposited on the land by the Indus River over many centuries has elevated the riverbed and its banks above the level of the plain. Twice a year, the river overflows and inundates surrounding land as far as 10 miles (16 kilometers) distant. Snow-

Chronology

	India	Southeast Asia
2500 B.C.E.	**2600 B.C.E.** Beginnings of Indus Valley civilization	
2000 B.C.E.	**1900 B.C.E.** End of Indus Valley civilization	
1500 B.C.E.	**ca. 1500 B.C.E.** Indo-Europeans in northwest India	**ca. 1600 B.C.E.** Beginnings of migrations from mainland Southeast Asia to islands in the Indian and Pacific Oceans
1000 B.C.E.	**ca. 1000 B.C.E.** Indo-Europeans settle the Ganges Plain	
500 B.C.E.	**ca. 500 B.C.E.** Beginning of Buddhism and Jainism	
300 B.C.E.	**300 B.C.E.** Tamil kingdoms	
	324 B.C.E. Maurya Empire founded	
1 C.E.		**ca. 50–560 C.E.** Funan dominates southern Indochina and the Isthmus of Kra
300 C.E.	**320 C.E.** Gupta Empire begins	
500 C.E.		**ca. 500 C.E.** Trade route develops through the Straits of Malacca
600 C.E.	**606–647 C.E.** Reign of Harsha Vardhana	**683 C.E.** Rise of Srivijaya in Sumatra
700 C.E.		**770–825 C.E.** Construction of Borobodur in Java
1000 C.E.		**1025 C.E.** Decline of Srivijaya

melt from the Pamir (pah-MEER) and Himalaya Mountains feeds the flood in March and April. In August, the monsoons bring rains from the southwest that feed a second flood. Though extremely dry for the rest of the year, Sind's floods make two crops a year possible. In ancient times, the Hakra (HAK-ruh) River (sometimes referred to as the Saraswati), which has since dried up, ran parallel to the Indus about 25 miles (40 kilometers) to the east and supplied water to a second cultivable area.

Adjacent regions shared distinctive cultural traits with this core area. In Punjab (literally "five waters"), to the northeast, five rivers converge to feed the main stream of the Indus. Closer to the northern mountains, the Punjab receives more rainfall but less floodwater than Sind. Culturally similar settlements extend from the Punjab as far east as Delhi (DEL-ee) in northwest India. Settlement also extended through the Indus delta in southern Sind down into India's hook-shaped Kathiawar (kah-tee-h-WAHR) Peninsula, an area of alluvial plains and coastal marshes. The Indus Valley civilization, as scholars labeled this area of cultural homogeneity when they first discovered it eighty years ago, covered an area roughly equivalent to modern France.

Material Culture

Although archaeologists have located several hundred communities that flourished from approximately 2600 to 1900 B.C.E., the remains of two urban sites, known by the modern names **Harappa** and **Mohenjo-Daro** (moe-hen-joe-DAHR-oh), best typify the Indus Valley civilization. Unfortunately, the high water table at these sites makes excavation of the earliest levels of settlement nearly impossible.

Scholars once believed that the people who created this civilization spoke Dravidian (druh-VID-ee-uhn) languages related to those spoken today in

Harappa Site of one of the great cities of the Indus Valley civilization of the third millennium B.C.E. It was located on the northwest frontier of the zone of cultivation (in modern Pakistan) and may have been a center for the acquisition of raw materials, such as metals and precious stones, from Afghanistan and Iran.

Mohenjo-Daro Largest of the cities of the Indus Valley civilization. It was centrally located in the extensive floodplain of the Indus River in contemporary Pakistan. Little is known about the political institutions of Indus Valley communities, but the large scale of construction at Mohenjo-Daro, the orderly grid of streets, and the standardization of building materials are evidence of central planning.

southern India. Invaders from the northwest speaking Indo-European languages, they thought, conquered these people around 1500 B.C.E., causing some of them to migrate to the southeast. Skeletal evidence, however, indicates that the population of the Indus Valley has remained stable from ancient times to the present. Settled agriculture in this region seems to date back to at least 5000 B.C.E.

The writing system of the Indus Valley people contained more than four hundred signs to represent syllables and words. Archaeologists have recovered thousands of inscribed seal stones and copper tablets. The inscriptions are so brief, however, that no one has yet deciphered them, though some scholars believe they represent an early Dravidian language.

Harappa, 3.5 miles (5.6 kilometers) in circumference, may have housed a population of 35,000, and Mohenjo-Daro several times that. These cities show marked similarities in planning and construction: high, thick, encircling walls of brick; streets laid out in a rectangular grid; and covered drainpipes to carry away waste. The consistent width of streets and length of city blocks, and the uniformity of the mud bricks used in construction, suggest a strong central authority, located possibly in the citadel—an elevated, enclosed compound containing large buildings. Scholars think the well-ventilated structures near the citadel stored grain for local use and for export. The presence of barracks may point to some regimentation of skilled artisans.

Though it is presumed that these urban centers controlled the surrounding farmlands, different centers may have served different functions, which might account for their locations. Mohenjo-Daro seems to dominate the great floodplain of the Indus. Harappa, which is nearly 500 miles (800 kilometers) to the north, sits in the zone where farmlands give way to pasturelands. No settlements have been found west of Harappa, which may have served as a gateway for copper, tin, precious stones, and other resources coming from the northwest. Coastal towns to the south engaged in seaborne trade with Sumer and lands around the Persian Gulf, as well as in fishing and gathering highly prized seashells. Although published accounts of the Indus Valley civilization tend to treat Mohenjo-Daro and Harappa, the most extensively excavated sites, as the norm, most people surely

Man from Mohenjo-Daro, ca. 2600–1900 B.C.E. This statue of a seated man wearing a cloak and headband was carved from a soft stone called steatite. It is often called the "Priest-King" because some scholars believe it may represent someone with religious and secular authority, but the true identity and status of this person are unknown. Scala/Art Resource, NY

 History in Focus *Besides the cloak and headband, do you see any other clues to this person's status? What does his facial expression tell you? Find the answer online.*

lived in smaller settlements, which exhibit the same artifacts and the same standardization of styles and shapes as the large cities.

Metal appears more frequently in Indus Valley sites than in Mesopotamia or Egypt. Tools and other useful objects outweigh in importance the decorative objects—jewelry and the like—so often found in those other regions. Whereas metal goods were largely the possessions of elite groups in the Middle East, in the Indus Valley they belonged to a broad cross-section of the population.

Technologically, the Indus Valley people showed skill in irrigation, used the potter's wheel, and fired

- As in Mesopotamia and Egypt, and roughly in the same time period, the wide, fertile Indus Valley supported a large urban civilization.

- Cities like Harappa and Mohenjo-Daro and their artifacts display uniformity of planning and construction and standardization of styles and shapes.

- The Indus Valley civilization developed sophisticated technologies, including a still-undeciphered writing system.

- Cities exchanged goods with each other and maintained extensive trade contacts with other ancient civilizations.

- The Indus Valley civilization collapsed when the cities were abandoned, most likely because of "systems failure."

bricks in kilns for use in the foundations of large public buildings (sun-dried bricks exposed to floodwaters would have dissolved quickly). Smiths worked with various metals—gold, silver, copper, and tin. The varying ratios of tin to copper in their bronze objects suggest awareness of the hardness of different mixtures. They used less tin, a relatively scarce metal, in objects that did not require maximum hardness, like knives, and more tin in things like axes that had to be harder.

Archaeological finds point to widespread trading contacts. Mountain passes through the northwest granted access to the valuable resources of eastern Iran and Afghanistan, as well as to ore deposits in western India. These resources included metals (such as copper and tin), precious stones (lapis lazuli, jade, and turquoise), building stone, and timber. Rivers provided thoroughfares for transporting goods within the zone of Indus Valley culture.

Inhabitants of the Indus Valley and of Mesopotamia obtained raw materials from some of the same sources. The discovery of Indus Valley seal stones in the Tigris-Euphrates Valley indicates that merchants from the former region may have acted as middlemen in long-distance trade, obtaining raw materials from the northwest and shipping them to the Persian Gulf.

We know little about the political, social, economic, and religious structures of Indus Valley society. Efforts to link artifacts and images to cultural features characteristic of later periods of Indian history, including sociopolitical institutions (a system of hereditary occupational groups, the predominant role of priests), architectural forms (bathing tanks like those later found in Hindu temples, private interior courtyards in houses), and religious beliefs and practices (depictions of gods and sacred animals on the seal stones, a cult of the mother-goddess), remain speculative. Further knowledge on these matters awaits additional archaeological finds and deciphering of the Indus Valley script.

Transformation of the Indus Valley Civilization

The Indus Valley cities were abandoned sometime after 1900 B.C.E. Archaeologists once thought that invaders destroyed them, but they now believe this civilization suffered "systems failure"—a breakdown of the fragile interrelationship of political, social, and economic systems that sustained order and prosperity. The precipitating cause may have been one or more natural disasters, such as an earthquake or massive flooding. Gradual ecological changes may also have played a role as the Hakra river system dried up and salinization (an increase in the amount of plant-inhibiting salt in the soil) and erosion increased.

Towns left dry by a change of riverbed, seaports removed from the coast by silt deposited in deltas, and regions suffering loss of fertile soil would have necessitated the relocation of populations and a change in the livelihood of those who remained. The causes, patterns, and pace of change probably varied, with urbanization persisting longer in some regions than in others. The urban centers eventually succumbed, however, and village-based farming and herding took their place. As the interaction between regions lessened, regional variation replaced the standardization of technology and style of the previous era.

Historians can do little more than speculate about the causes behind the changes and the experiences of the people who lived in the Indus Valley around 1900 B.C.E. Two tendencies bear remembering, however. In most cases like this, the majority of the population adjusts to the new circumstances. But members of the political and social elite, who depend on urban centers and complex political and economic structures, lose the source of their authority and merge with the population as a whole.

Foundations of Indian Civilization

What historical forces led to the development of complex social groupings in ancient India?

India is called a *subcontinent* because it is a large—roughly 2,000 miles (3,200 kilometers) in both length and breadth—and physically isolated landmass within the continent of Asia. The Himalayas (him-uh-LAY-uhs), the world's highest mountains, form a barrier to the north; the Indian Ocean bounds it on the east, south, and west (see Map 5.1). The one frontier easily accessible to invaders and migrating peoples lies to the northwest. But people using this corridor must cross over the mountain barrier of the Hindu Kush in Afghanistan and the Thar (tahr) Desert east of the Indus River.

The Indian Subcontinent

This region divides into three topographical zones. The mountainous northern zone takes in the heavily forested foothills and high meadows on the edge of the Hindu Kush and Himalaya ranges. Next come the great basins of the Indus and Ganges Rivers. Originating in the Himalayas, these rivers flood annually, leaving layers of silt that over time have created large fertile plains. The Vindhya range and the Deccan (de-KAN), an arid, rocky plateau reminiscent of the American Southwest, separate northern India from the third zone, the peninsula proper. The Malabar Coast in the west, the Coromandel Coast in the east with its web of rivers descending from the Deccan, the flatlands of Tamil Nadu on the southern tip of the peninsula, and the island of Sri Lanka often have followed paths of political and cultural development separate from those of northern India.

The mountainous northern rim shelters the subcontinent from cold Arctic winds and gives it a subtropical climate. The **monsoon** (seasonal wind) comes annually when the Indian Ocean lags behind the Asian landmass in heating and cooling with the changing seasons. The temperature difference between water and land acts like a bellows, producing a great wind over the ocean. The southwest monsoon begins in June off the coast of East Africa, picks up moisture from the Indian Ocean, and delivers heavy precipitation to the Ganges Basin and the rain-forest belt on India's western coast. The moist, flat Ganges Delta (modern Bengal) favors rice production. Elsewhere, wheat, barley, and millet predominate. Indus Valley farmers, in contrast, see little precipitation and therefore rely on extensive irrigation.

Indian Ocean mariners learned to ride the monsoon winds across open waters from northeast to southwest in January and to make the return voyage in July. Ships ventured across the Arabian Sea to the Persian Gulf, the southern coast of Arabia, and East Africa, and east across the Bay of Bengal to Indochina and Indonesia (see Chapter 8).

The Vedic Age, 1500–500 B.C.E.

Many features of later Indian civilization surely date back to the Indus Valley civilization of the third and early second millennia B.C.E. Since the writing from that period remains undeciphered, the earliest textual knowledge about Indian roots comes from the period 1500 to 500 B.C.E., called the "Vedic Age" after religious texts known as the **Vedas**. While most historians believe that Indo-European speaking nomads migrated into northwest India at the beginning of the period, others argue for a much earlier Indo-European presence in this region deriving from the spread of agriculture (see Chapter 2).

After the collapse of the Indus Valley civilization, the central authority presumed to have organized large-scale irrigation disappeared. The region became home to bands of Vedic-speaking cattle herders who

---

monsoon Seasonal winds in the Indian Ocean caused by the differences in temperature between the rapidly heating and cooling landmasses of Africa and Asia and the slowly changing ocean waters. These strong and predictable winds have long been ridden across the open sea by sailors, and the large amounts of rainfall that they deposit on parts of India, Southeast Asia, and China allow for the cultivation of several crops a year.

Vedas Early Indian sacred "knowledge"—the literal meaning of the term—long preserved and communicated orally by Brahmin priests and eventually written down. These religious texts, including the thousand poetic hymns to various deities contained in the Rig Veda, are our main source of information about the Vedic period (ca. 1500–500 B.C.E.).

Map 5.1 Ancient India Mountains and ocean largely separate the Indian subcontinent from the rest of Asia. Migrations and invasions usually came through the Khyber Pass in the northwest. Peoples speaking Indo-European languages migrated into the broad valleys of the Indus and Ganges Rivers in the north. Dravidian-speaking peoples remained the dominant population in the south. The diversity of the Indian landscape, the multiplicity of ethnic groups, and the primary identification of people with their class and caste lie behind the division into many small states that has characterized much of Indian political history. © Cengage Learning

Interactive Map

also engaged in farming. As with other Indo-European peoples—Celts, Greeks, Iranians, Romans—patriarchal traditions made the father dominant in the family just as the king ruled the group as a whole. Warriors boasted of their martial skill and courage, relished combat, feasted on beef, and filled their leisure time with chariot racing and gambling.

After 1000 B.C.E., some groups pushed eastward into the Ganges Plain. Iron tools—harder than bronze and able to hold a sharper edge—allowed settlers to fell trees and work the newly cleared land with ox-drawn plows. The fertile plain, watered by the annual monsoon, sustained two or three crops a year. As in Greece at roughly the same time, the use of iron tools must have led to a population increase.

Stories about this era, written down much later but preserved by oral recitation, speak of rivalry and warfare between two peoples: the Aryas, speakers of Vedic Sanskrit and practitioners of the sacrificial religion prescribed in the Vedas, and the Dasas, indigenous speakers of Dravidian languages, whose religion, it is pointedly noted in the Vedas, did not involve sacrifice to or worship of the Vedic gods. Some scholars argue that the real process by which Arya groups became dominant in the north involved the absorption of some Dasas into Arya populations and a merging of elites from both groups. For the most part, however, Aryas pushed the Dasas south into central and southern India, where their descendants still live. Indo-European languages descended from those of the Aryas predominate in northern India today, while Dravidian languages prevail in the south.

The cultural and religious differences between the Aryas and the indigenous peoples contributed to sharp social divisions. A system of *varnas*, literally "colors" but usually translated as "castes," indicated something akin to classes. Individuals belonged by birth to one of four varnas: *Brahmins*, the group comprising priests and scholars; *Kshatriyas* (kshuh-TREE-yuhs), warriors and the king; *Vaishyas* (VIESH-yuhs), all other Aryas; and *Shudras* (SHOOD-ras), non-Aryas who were servants and slaves of the other three varnas. The designation *Shudra* originally may have signified Dasa. Indeed, the term *dasa* came to mean "slave." Eventually a fifth group emerged: the Untouchables. Excluded from the caste system and shunned by the other castes, they worked in demeaning or polluting trades such as tanning, which involved touching dead animals, and sweeping away ashes after cremations.

According to one creation myth, a primordial man named Purusha allowed himself to be sacrificed. From his mouth sprang the varna of Brahmin priests. From his arms came the Kshatriya warriors; from his thighs the Vaishya merchants, artisans, and peasants; and from his feet the Shudra workers.

Within the broad varna divisions, the population further divided into numerous smaller groups, called *jatis*, or castes. Each jati had its proper occupation, duties, and rituals. Members of a given jati lived and married within the group and ate only with fellow jati members. Elaborate rules governed interactions between groups. Members of higher-status groups feared pollution from contacting lower-caste individuals and had to undergo rituals of purification to remove any taint.

The caste system became connected to a belief in reincarnation. Brahmin priests taught that every living creature had an immortal essence: the *atman*, or "self." Separated from the body at death, the atman returned in the body of an insect, an animal, or a human depending on the **karma**, or deeds, of the atman in its previous incarnations. People of exemplary goodness returned in a higher caste. Those who misbehaved fell to a lower caste or even a lower life form. The underlying message ran: You are where you deserve to be, and the only way to improve your lot in the next incarnation is to accept your current station and its attendant duties.

Many of the Vedic deities, mostly male, were associated with the heavens. Indra, like Zeus a god of war and master of the thunderbolt, commanded the greatest devotion and represented the chieftains who led their warriors into battle. Agni, the fire-god, consumed the sacrifice and bridged the spheres of gods and humans. Vedic religion centered on sacrifice, the dedication to a god of a valued possession, often a living creature. The offerings invigorated the gods and thereby sustained their creative powers and promoted stability in the world.

Brahmin priests alone knew the rituals and prayers. The Rig Veda, a collection of more than a thousand poetic hymns to various deities, and the Brahmanas, detailed prose descriptions and explanations of ritual procedures, all in the Sanskrit language of the Arya upper classes, passed orally from one generation of priests to the next. The Brahmins may have opposed the introduction of writing. This would explain why this technology did not spread in India until the Gupta period (320–550 C.E.). The priests' "knowledge" (the term *veda* means just that) earned them rewards for officiating at sacrifices and gave them social and political power as the intermediaries between gods and humans.

---

varna/jati Two categories of social identity of great importance in Indian history. *Varna* are the four major social divisions: the *Brahmin* priest class, the *Kshatriya* warrior/administrator class, the *Vaishya* merchant/farmer class, and the *Shudra* laborer class. Within the system *varna* are many jati, regional groups of people who have a common occupational sphere, and who marry, eat, and generally interact with other members of their group.

karma In Indian tradition, the residue of deeds performed in past and present lives that adheres to a "spirit" and determines what form it will assume in its next life cycle. The doctrines of karma and reincarnation were used by the elite in ancient India to encourage people to accept their social position and do their duty.

Primary Source: The Rig Veda Read how Indra, "the thunder-wielder," slew Vritra, "firstborn of dragons," and how Purusha created the universe through an act of ritual sacrifice.

As elsewhere in the ancient world, the lives of Indian women left few traces. Limited evidence indicates that in the Vedic period women studied sacred lore, composed religious hymns, and participated in sacrifices. They could own property and usually did not marry until their middle or late teens. A number of strong and resourceful women appear in the Mahabharata epic (explained below). In the Ramayana epic, on the other hand, we see the familiar motif of the hero Rama rescuing his wife Sita after she has been abducted.

The internal divisions of Indian society, the complex hierarchy of groups, and the claims of some to superior virtue and purity provided each individual with a clear identity and role and offered the benefits of group solidarity and support. Sometimes groups even upgraded their status within the system, which was not entirely static and provided mechanisms for releasing social tensions. Many of these features persisted into modern times.

Challenges to the Old Order: Jainism and Buddhism

After 700 B.C.E., reactions against Brahmin power and privilege emerged. People who objected to the rigid social hierarchy could always retreat to the forest that covered much of ancient India. Never far away, these wild places symbolized freedom from societal constraints. Individuals who wandered in the forest sometimes attracted followers. Questioning priestly power and the necessity of sacrifices, they offered alternate paths to salvation: individual pursuit of insight into the nature of the self and the universe through physical and mental discipline (*yoga*), which included dietary restrictions and meditation. They taught that by distancing oneself from desire for the things of this world, one could achieve *moksha*, or liberation, "a deep, dreamless sleep" that released one from endless reincarnations through union with the divine force of the universe. The Upanishads, which continue the explanations of ritual begun in the Brahmanas, also reflect this questioning of Vedic ritualism.

Jainism (JINE-iz-uhm) and Buddhism challenged not only Vedic ritualism but also the authority of the Vedic priests themselves. Jainism took its name from the teacher Mahavira (540–468 B.C.E.), known to his followers as Jina, "the Conqueror." Mahavira respected

the life force so much that he commanded strict nonviolence. Jains wore masks to avoid inadvertently inhaling small insects and brushed off the seat before sitting down. Some practiced extreme asceticism by practicing nudity and eventually starving themselves to death. Less zealous Jains engaged in commerce in cities, since agricultural work inevitably involved killing.

Buddhism, a far more successful movement, stemmed from the life of Siddhartha Gautama (563–483 B.C.E.), known as the **Buddha**, "the Enlightened One," about whom myriad legends have arisen. From a Kshatriya family in what is now Nepal, he enjoyed the princely lifestyle that was his birthright until he experienced a change of heart and gave up family and privilege to become a wandering ascetic. After six years, he decided that asceticism was no more likely to produce spiritual insight than his earlier luxurious life, so he opted for a "Middle Path." Sitting under a tree in a deer park near Benares on the Ganges River, he gained a sudden and profound insight, which he set forth as "Four Noble Truths": (1) life is suffering, (2) suffering arises from desire, (3) the solution to suffering lies in curbing desire, and (4) desire can be curbed if a person follows the "Eightfold Path" of right views, aspirations, speech, conduct, livelihood, effort, mindfulness, and meditation. Rising up, the Buddha preached his First Sermon, a central text of Buddhism, and set into motion the "Wheel of the Law." He soon attracted followers, some of whom took vows of celibacy, nonviolence, and poverty.

At first, Buddhism centered on the individual. It denied the usefulness of the gods to a person seeking enlightenment. What mattered was living moderately to minimize desire and suffering, and searching for

moksha The Hindu concept of the spirit's "liberation" from the endless cycle of rebirths. There are various avenues—such as physical discipline, meditation, and acts of devotion to the gods—by which the spirit can distance itself from desire for the things of this world and be merged with the divine force that animates the universe.

Buddha (563–483 B.C.E.) An Indian prince named Siddhartha Gautama, who renounced his wealth and social position. After becoming "enlightened" (the meaning of *Buddha*) he enunciated the principles of Buddhism. This doctrine evolved and spread throughout India and to Southeast, East, and Central Asia.

Carved Stone Gateway Leading to the Great Stupa at Sanchi Pilgrims traveled long distances to visit stupas, mounds containing relics of the Buddha. The complex at Sanchi, in central India, was begun by Ashoka in the third century B.C.E., though the gates probably date to the first century C.E. This relief shows a royal procession bringing the remains of the Buddha to the city of Kushina-gara.

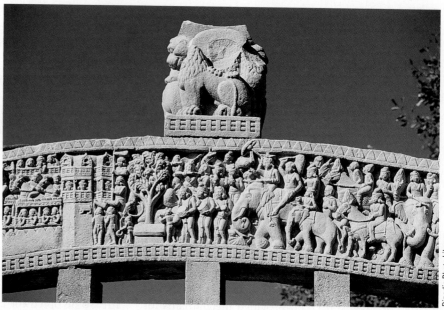

Dinodia Photo Library

spiritual truth through self-discipline and meditation. One should seek *nirvana*, literally "snuffing out the flame," a release from the cycle of reincarnations and enjoyment of perpetual tranquility. Whereas the Upanishadic tradition emphasized the eternal survival of the atman, the "self" or nonmaterial essence of the individual, Buddhism regarded the individual as a composite of features such as breath and wind, but without a soul.

At his death, Buddha left no final instructions, urging his disciples to "be their own lamp." His followers spread his philosophy throughout India and into Central, Southeast, and East Asia. Its wide appeal subverted its individualistic and atheistic underpinnings. Buddhist monasteries with hierarchies of monks and nuns came into being. Worshipers erected *stupas* (large earthen mounds symbolizing the universe) over relics of the cremated founder and other holy men and walked around them in a clockwise direction. Believers began to worship the Buddha himself as a god. Many Buddhists also revered *bodhisattvas* (boe-dih-SUT-vuhs), men and women who had achieved enlightenment and were on the threshold of

nirvana but chose rebirth into mortal bodies to help others along the path to salvation.

Early representations show the Buddha only indirectly, through symbols such as his footprints, begging bowl, or the tree under which he achieved enlightenment, as if to emphasize his achievement of a state of nonexistence. From the second century C.E., however, statues of the Buddha and bodhisattvas proliferated, sculpted in styles that showed the influence of the Greek settlements established in Bactria (northern Afghanistan) by Alexander the Great. A schism emerged within Buddhism. Devotees of **Mahayana** (mah-huh-YAH-nuh) ("Great Vehicle") **Buddhism** embraced the popular new features. Practitioners of **Theravada** (there-eh-VAH-duh) ("Teachings of the Elders") **Buddhism** followed most of the original teachings of the founder.

 Primary Source: Setting in Motion the Wheels of Law Siddartha's first sermon contains the core teaching of Buddhism: to escape, by following the Middle Path, the suffering caused by desire.

Mahayana Buddhism "Great Vehicle" branch of Buddhism followed in China, Japan, and Central Asia. The focus is on reverence for Buddha and for bodhisattvas, enlightened persons who have postponed nirvana to help others attain enlightenment.

Theravada Buddhism "Way of the Elders" branch of Buddhism followed in Sri Lanka and much of Southeast Asia. Theravada remains close to the original principles set forth by the Buddha; it downplays the importance of gods and emphasizes austerity and the individual's search for enlightenment.

The Rise of Hinduism

Challenged by the new religious movements, Vedic religion evolved by the fourth century C.E. into **Hinduism**, the dominant religion in South Asia today. (The term *Hinduism* originated with Islamic invaders in the eleventh century C.E. as a label for the diverse practices they encountered: "what the Indians do.") Though based on the Vedic religion of northern India, Hinduism incorporated Dravidian cultural elements from the south, such as intense devotion to a deity and the prominence of goddesses.

Brahmin priests survived the transition with their social status and influence intact, but sacrifice lost its central place. Opportunities for individual worshipers to have direct contact with deities increased. Hinduism emphasized the worshiper's personal devotion to a particular deity, usually Vishnu or Shiva, or Devi ("the Goddess"). The goddess is of Dravidian origin, and her incorporation into the cult shows how Arya and indigenous cultures fused to form Hindu civilization. Vishnu, who has a clear Aryan pedigree, remains more popular in northern India, and Shiva is dominant in the south. These deities appear in many guises, bear various cult names, and give rise to a complex symbolism of stories, companion animals, birds, and objects.

Vishnu, the preserver, benevolently helps his devotees in time of need. Hindus believe that whenever demonic forces threaten the cosmic order, an *avatara*, or incarnation of Vishnu, appears on earth. His avatars include the legendary hero Rama, the cowherd god Krishna, and the Buddha (a clear attempt to co-opt the rival religion's founder). Shiva, who lives in ascetic isolation on Mount Kailasa in the Himalayas, represents a cyclical process of creation and destruction that is symbolized in statues showing him dancing. Devi can manifest herself as a full-bodied mother goddess representing fertility and procreation, as Shiva's loving wife, Parvati, or as the frightening deity who, under the name Kali or Durga, lets loose violence and destruction.

The multiplicity of gods (330 million according to one tradition), sects, and local practices within Hinduism reflects the ethnic, linguistic, and cultural diversity of India. Yet within this variety, there is unity. A worshiper's devotion to one god or goddess does not entail denial of the other main deities or the host of lesser divinities and spirits. Ultimately, all are manifestations of a single divine force pervading the universe. This underlying unity appears in the way various manifestations of Devi represent different female potentials, in composite statues—half Shiva, half Vishnu—signifying complementary aspects of one cosmic principle.

Hindus may approach god and obtain divine favor through special knowledge of sacred truths, mental and physical discipline, or extraordinary devotion to the deity. Worship centers on temples, which range from humble shrines to richly decorated stone edifices built under royal patronage. Statues beckon the deity to take up temporary residence within the image and be available to eager worshipers. *Puja*, or service to the deity, can include bathing, clothing, or feeding the statue. Glimpsing the divine image conveys potent blessings.

Sacred places where a worshiper can directly sense and benefit from divine power dot the Indian subcontinent. Mystery and sanctity surround certain mountains, caves, trees, plants, and rocks. *Tirthayatra*, the term for a pilgrimage site, means "journey to a river crossing," illustrating the association of Hindu sacred

Hinduism A general term for a wide variety of beliefs and ritual practices that have developed in the Indian subcontinent since antiquity. Hinduism has roots in ancient Vedic, Buddhist, and south Indian religious concepts and practices. It spread along the trade routes to Southeast Asia.

Meenakshi Temple, Madurai, India
Some 15,000 pilgrims a day visit the large Hindu temple of Meenakshi (the fish-eyed goddess) in the ancient holy city of Madurai in India's southeastern province of Tamil Nadu. The temple complex dates from at least 1000 C.E., although the elaborately painted statues of these gopuram (gate towers) have been rebuilt and restored many times. The largest gopura rises 150 feet (46 meters) above the ground.

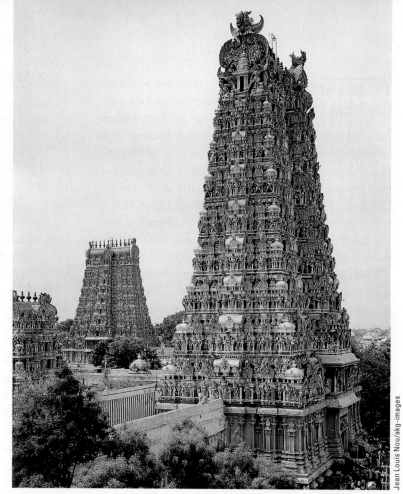

Jean Louis Nou/akg-images

places with flowing water. The Ganges River is especially sacred. Millions of worshipers travel each year to bathe and receive the restorative and purifying power of its waters. Pilgrimage to shrines fosters contact and exchange of ideas among people from different parts of India, helping to create a broad Hindu identity and the concept of India as a single civilization.

Religious duties depend on social standing and gender as well as stage of life. Young men from the three highest classes (Brahmin, Kshatriya, and Vaishya) undergo ritual rebirth through the ceremony of the sacred thread, marking attainment of manhood and readiness to receive religious knowledge. The life cycle then passes through four stages: (1) student of the sacred texts, (2) married householder with children and material goods, (3) forest dweller meditating on the meaning of existence after the birth of his grandchildren, and (4) wandering ascetic awaiting death. The person living such a life fulfills first his duties to society and then his duties to himself, leaving him disconnected from the world and prepared for moksha (liberation).

Hinduism responded to the needs of people for personal deities with whom they could establish direct connections. The austerity of early Buddhism, its denial of the importance of gods, and its demand that individuals find their own path to enlightenment may have required too much of ordinary people.

What eventually made Mahayana Buddhism popular—gods, saints, and myths—also made it more easily absorbed into the social and cultural fabric of Hinduism.

Indian Imperial Expansion and Collapse

In the face of powerful forces that tended to keep India fragmented, how did the Mauryan Empire of the fourth to second centuries B.C.E. and the Gupta Empire of the fourth to sixth centuries C.E. succeed in unifying much of India?

Political unity has rarely lasted in India. The varied terrain—mountains, foothills, plains, forests, steppes, deserts—favors different forms of organization and economic activity. Peoples occupying topographically diverse zones may also differ in language and cultural practices. Caste and family have generated the strongest feeling of personal identity, allegiance to a higher political authority being a secondary concern. Nevertheless, two empires arose in the Ganges Plain: the Mauryan Empire of the fourth to second centuries B.C.E. and the Gupta Empire of the fourth to sixth centuries C.E.

The Mauryan Empire, 324–184 B.C.E.

Among the many kinship groups and independent states that dotted the north Indian landscape, the kingdom of Magadha, in the modern Indian state of Bihar, began to play an influential role around 600 B.C.E. thanks to wealth based on agriculture, iron mines, and strategic location astride the trade routes of the eastern Ganges Basin. In the late fourth century B.C.E., Chandragupta Maurya (MORE-yuh), a man of Vaishya or Shudra origins, took control of Magadha and founded the **Mauryan Empire**. Greek tradition claimed that Alexander the Great met an Indian native named "Sandracottus," an apparent corruption of "Chandragupta," when his armies reached the Punjab (northern Pakistan) in 326 B.C.E., implying that he might have served as a role model for the new ruler.

Greek rule in the Punjab collapsed after Alexander's death, allowing Chandragupta (r. 324–301 B.C.E.) and his successors Bindusara (r. 301–269 B.C.E.) and Ashoka (r. 269–232 B.C.E.) to extend Mauryan control over the entire subcontinent except for its southern tip.

Tradition holds that Kautilya, a crafty elderly Brahmin, guided Chandragupta and wrote a treatise on government, the *Arthashastra*. Although recent studies have shown that the existing form of the Arthashastra dates only to the third century C.E., its core may well go back to Kautilya. This pragmatic guide to political success advocates the so-called *mandata* (circle) theory of foreign policy: "My enemy's enemy is my friend." It also lists schemes for enforcing and increasing tax collection and prescribes the use of spies to keep watch on one's subjects.

A quarter of all agricultural output went in taxes to support the Mauryan government. Relatives and associates of the king governed districts based on ethnic boundaries. The imperial army—with infantry, cavalry, chariot, and elephant divisions—secured central authority, which also controlled mining,

shipbuilding, and arms making. Standard coinage fostered support for the government and promoted trade.

The Mauryan kings ruled from Pataliputra (modern Patna), where five tributaries join the Ganges. Descriptions by foreign visitors testify to the international connections of the Indian monarchs. Surrounded by a timber wall and moat, the city extended along the river for 8 miles (13 kilometers). Six governing committees oversaw manufacturing, trade, sales, taxes, the welfare of foreigners, and the registration of births and deaths.

Ashoka, Chandragupta's grandson, began his reign by extending the boundaries of the empire. After killing, wounding, or deporting thousands of people during his conquest of Kalinga (modern Orissa, a coastal region southeast of Magadha), remorse overcame him and he converted to Buddhism, thereafter preaching nonviolence, morality, moderation, and religious tolerance in both government and private life.

Ashoka publicized this program through edicts inscribed on great rocks and polished sandstone, the earliest decipherable Indian texts:

> For . . . many hundreds of years the sacrificial slaughter of animals, violence toward creatures, unfilial conduct toward kinsmen, improper conduct toward Brahmins and ascetics [have increased]. Now with the practice of morality by King [Ashoka], the sound of war drums has become the call to morality. . . . You [government officials] are appointed to rule over thousands of human beings in the expectation that you will win the affection of all men. All men are my children. Just as I desire that my children will fare well and be happy in this world and the next, I desire the same for all men. . . . King [Ashoka] . . . desires that there should be the growth of the essential spirit of morality or holiness among all sects. . . .

Mauryan Empire The first state to unify most of the Indian subcontinent. It was founded by Chandragupta Maurya in 324 B.C.E. and survived until 184 B.C.E. From its capital at Pataliputra in the Ganges Valley it grew wealthy from taxes on agriculture, iron mining, and control of trade routes.

Ashoka Third ruler of the Mauryan Empire in India (r. 269–232 B.C.E.). He converted to Buddhism and broadcast his precepts on inscribed stones and pillars, the earliest surviving Indian writing.

There should not be glorification of one's own sect and denunciation of the sect of others for little or no reason. For all the sects are worthy of reverence for one reason or another.[2]

Despite his commitment to employ peaceful means whenever possible, Ashoka reminded potential transgressors that "the king, remorseful as he is, has the strength to punish the wrongdoers who do not repent."

Commerce and Culture in an Era of Political Fragmentation

The Mauryan Empire prospered for a time after Ashoka's death in 232 B.C.E. Then, weakened by dynastic disputes, it collapsed under attacks from the northwest in 184 B.C.E. Five hundred years passed before another state succeeded in extending control over northern India. Despite the political fragmentation, however, economic, cultural, and intellectual development continued. The roads and towns of the Mauryans fostered commerce within the subcontinent, while land and sea routes linked India to China, Southeast Asia, Central Asia, the Middle East, East Africa, and the lands of the Mediterranean. Guilds of merchants and artisans regulated the lives of their members and had an important voice in local affairs. They patronized culture and endowed religious sects, particularly Buddhism and Jainism, with temples and monuments.

During the last centuries B.C.E. and the first centuries C.E., the greatest Indian epics, the Ramayana and the Mahabharata, based on centuries-old oral predecessors, achieved their final form. They place the events they describe in the distant past, but their proud kings, beautiful queens, family wars, heroic conduct, and chivalric values seem to reflect the late Vedic period, when Aryan warrior societies moved onto the Ganges Plain.

The Ramayana relates the exploits of Rama, a heroic prince who came to be considered an incarnation of Vishnu. When the chief of the demons kidnaps his wife, Sita, he destroys the demons with the help of his brother and a troop of monkeys. The vast **Mahabharata**—eight times the length of the *Iliad* and *Odyssey* combined—tells how two sets of cousins, the Pandavas and Kauravas, quarreled over succession to the throne and fought a cataclysmic battle at Kurukshetra. The battle is so destructive on both sides that

Yudhishthira, the eldest of the Pandava brothers and their leader, accepts the fruits of victory only reluctantly because the battle losses were so great.

The **Bhagavad-Gita** is a self-contained (and perhaps originally separate) episode set in the battle. The hero Arjuna shrinks from fighting his kinsmen until his charioteer, the god Krishna, tutors him on the necessity of fulfilling his duty as a warrior. Death means nothing in a universe of endless reincarnation. The Bhagavad-Gita resolves the tension in Indian civilization between duty to society and duty to one's soul. Dutiful action taken without regard for personal benefit serves society and may earn release from the cycle of rebirths.

Science and technology flourished in this era as well. Indian doctors applied herbal remedies and served in the courts of western and southern Asia. In linguistics, Panini (late fourth century B.C.E.) undertook a detailed analysis of Sanskrit word forms and grammar. This led to the standardization of Sanskrit, which arrested its natural development and turned it into a formal, literary language. Prakrits—popular dialects—emerged to become the ancestors of the modern languages of northern and central India.

Historians of southern India consider the period from the third century B.C.E. to the third century C.E., dominated by three often feuding **Tamil kingdoms**—the Cholas, Pandyas, and Cheras—a "classical" period for Tamil art and literature. Patronized by the Pandya kings and guided by an academy of five hundred authors, Tamil writers composed grammatical treatises, collections of ethical proverbs, epics, and short poems about love, war, wealth, and the beauty of nature while performers excelled in music, dance, and drama.

Mahabharata A vast epic chronicling the events leading up to a cataclysmic battle between related kinship groups in early India. It includes the Bhagavad-Gita, the most important work of Indian sacred literature.

Bhagavad-Gita The most important work of Indian sacred literature, a dialogue between the great warrior Arjuna and the god Krishna on duty and the fate of the spirit.

Tamil kingdoms The kingdoms of southern India, inhabited primarily by speakers of Dravidian languages, which developed in partial isolation, and somewhat differently, from the Aryan north. They produced epics, poetry, and performance arts. Elements of Tamil religious beliefs were merged into the Hindu synthesis.

Indian Mathematics

The so-called Arabic numerals used in most parts of the world today were developed in India. The Indian system of place-value notation was far more efficient than the unwieldy numerical systems of Egyptians, Greeks, and Romans, and the invention of zero was a profound intellectual achievement. This system is used even more widely than the alphabet derived from the Phoenicians (see Chapter 4) and is, in one sense, the only truly global language.

In its fully developed form the Indian method of arithmetic notation employed a base-10 system. It had separate columns for ones, tens, hundreds, and so forth, as well as a zero sign to indicate the absence of units in a given column. This system makes possible the economical expression of even very large numbers. And it allows for the performance of calculations not possible in a system like the numerals of the Romans, where any real calculation had to be done mentally or on a counting board.

A series of early Indian inscriptions using the numerals from 1 to 9 are deeds of property given to religious institutions by kings or other wealthy individuals. They were incised in the Sanskrit language on copper plates. The earliest known example has a date equivalent to 595 C.E. A sign for zero is attested by the eighth century, but textual evidence leads to the inference that a place-value system and the zero concept were already known in the fifth century.

This Indian system spread to the Middle East, Southeast Asia, and East Asia by the seventh century. Other peoples quickly recognized its capabilities and adopted it, sometimes using indigenous symbols. Europe received the new technology somewhat later. Gerbert of Aurillac, a French Christian monk, spent time in Spain between 967 and 970, where he was exposed to the mathematics of the Arabs. A great scholar and teacher who eventually became Pope Sylvester II (r. 999–1003), he spread word of the "Arabic" system in the Christian West.

Knowledge of the Indian system of mathematical notation eventually spread throughout Europe, partly through the use of a mechanical calculating device—an improved version of the Roman counting board, with counters inscribed with variants of the Indian numeral forms. Because the counters could be turned sideways or upside down, at first there was considerable variation in the forms. But by the twelfth century they had become standardized into forms close to those in use today. As the capabilities of the place-value system for calculations became clear, the counting board fell into disuse. This led to the adoption of the zero sign—not necessary on the counting board, where a column could be left empty—by the twelfth century. Leonardo Fibonacci, a thirteenth-century C.E. Italian who learned algebra in Muslim North Africa and employed the Arabic numeral system in his mathematical treatise, gave additional impetus to the movement to discard the traditional system of Roman numerals.

Why was this marvelous system of mathematical notation invented in ancient India? The answer may lie in the way its range and versatility correspond to elements of Indian cosmology. The Indians conceived of immense spans of time—trillions of years (far exceeding current scientific estimates of the age of the universe as approximately 14 billion years)—during which innumerable universes like our own were created, existed for a finite time, then were destroyed. In one popular creation myth, Vishnu is slumbering on the coils of a giant serpent at the bottom of the ocean, and worlds are being created and destroyed as he exhales and inhales. In Indian thought our world, like others, has existed for a series of epochs lasting more than 4 million years, yet the period of its existence is but a brief and insignificant moment in the vast sweep of time. The Indians developed a number system that allowed them to express concepts of this magnitude.

Copper Plate with Indian Numerals This property deed from western India shows an early form of the symbol system for numbers that spread to the Middle East and Europe and today is used all over the world.   Facsimile by Georges Ifrah. Reproduced by permission of Georges Ifrah.

The Gupta Empire, 320–550 C.E.

Like its Mauryan predecessor, the **Gupta Empire** grew from the kingdom of Magadha and had its capital at Pataliputra. Its founder called himself Chandra Gupta (r. 320–335 C.E.), borrowing the name of the Mauryan founder. Though they never controlled as much land as the Mauryans, the Gupta monarchs took the title "Great King of Kings."

Trade, agriculture, and iron mining brought prosperity to the Guptas as they had to the Mauryans, and the kings followed similar methods of taxation and administration. In addition to a 25 percent tax on agriculture, users of the irrigation network paid fees, and some commodities were subject to special taxes. The state maintained monopolies over mining and salt production, exploited state-owned farmlands, and required subjects to work a specified number of days on maintaining roads, wells, and irrigation works.

The Gupta administration and intelligence network were smaller and less pervasive than those of the Mauryans. A powerful army maintained tight control of the empire's core, but provincial governors had a freer hand, which they sometimes used to exploit the populace. Governorships often passed from father to son within high-ranking military or administrative families. The most distant areas, controlled by kinship groups or subordinate kings, made annual donations of tribute. Garrisons stationed at frontier points kept trade routes open and ensured the collection of customs duties.

A constant round of solemn rituals, dramatic ceremonies, and cultural events in Pataliputra demonstrated to visitors from remote areas the benefits of belonging to the empire. Modern historians call such a regime a **theater-state**. Ruler and subjects in the Gupta theater-state had an economic relationship. The former accumulated luxury goods and profits from trade and redistributed them to dependents through gifts and other means. Subordinate

princes gained prestige by emulating the center and maintained close ties through visits, gifts, and marriages with the Gupta family. Gupta patronage also supported the Indian mathematicians, who invented the concept of zero and developed the so-called Arabic numerals and place-value notation (see Environment and Technology: Indian Mathematics).

The moist climate of the Ganges Plain does not favor the preservation of buildings and artifacts, so archaeology has little to say about the Gupta era. However, a Chinese Buddhist monk named Faxian (fah-shee-en), who made a pilgrimage to the homeland of his faith around 400 C.E., penned a description of the Gupta kingdom:

> The cities and towns of this country are the greatest of all in the Middle Kingdom. The inhabitants are rich and prosperous, and vie with one another in the practice of benevolence and righteousness. . . . The heads of the Vaishya families in them establish in the cities houses for dispensing charity and medicines. All the poor and destitute in the country, orphans, widowers, and childless men, maimed people and cripples, and all who are diseased, go to those houses, and are provided with every kind of help.[3]

At this time, the civil disabilities of women, which had always existed as custom, hardened into law with the emergence of law books like *The Laws of Manu*. Indian women lost the right to own or inherit property, and girls married at increasingly early ages, sometimes at six or seven. The husband could thus ensure his wife's virginity, and, by bringing her up in his own household, he could train her to suit his purposes. As in Confucian China, a woman owed obedience to her father, then her husband, and finally her sons (see Chapter 2). In certain parts of India, a practice called *sati* (suh-TEE) required a widow to cremate

Primary Source: The Laws of Manu See how the principle of Dharma justifies the traditional roles of men and women, and of priests, warriors, merchants, and servants in Hindu society.

Gupta Empire A powerful Indian state based, like its Mauryan predecessor, on a capital at Pataliputra in the Ganges Valley. It controlled most of the Indian subcontinent through a combination of military force and its prestige as a center of sophisticated culture.

theater-state Historians' term for a state that acquires prestige and power by developing attractive cultural forms and staging elaborate public ceremonies (as well as redistributing valuable resources) to attract and bind subjects to the center. The Gupta Empire is an example of such a state.

herself on her husband's funeral pyre. Widows who refused to follow this custom could not remarry and suffered social rejection.

Entry into a Jainist or Buddhist religious community offered some women an escape from male control. Women from powerful families and courtesans trained in poetry and music, as well as sexual technique, sometimes enjoyed high social standing and gave money for Buddhist stupas and other shrines.

The Gupta monarchs sought sanctity through reviving Vedic practices. The influence of Brahmin priests gained renewed prominence. Yet the kings also patronized Buddhist and Jain endeavors. Buddhist monasteries with hundreds, even thousands, of monks and nuns flourished in the cities. Northern India drew Buddhist pilgrims from Southeast and East Asia to the birthplace of their faith.

The classic form of the Hindu temple, evolved during the Gupta era, symbolizes the sacred mountain or palace where the gods reside. Sitting atop a raised platform surmounted by high towers, it mirrored the order of the universe. From an exterior courtyard, worshipers approached the central shrine containing the statue of the deity. In rich temples, painted or sculpted gods and mythical events covered the walls. Frescoes and statues also adorned cave temples carved into cliffs.

The vibrant commerce of the period of fragmentation continued under the Guptas. Coins served as the medium of exchange, and artisan guilds influenced the economic, political, and religious life of towns. The Guptas sought control of the ports on the Arabian Sea but saw trade with the weakening Roman Empire decline. Trade with Southeast and East Asia increased, however. Merchants from eastern and southern India voyaged to the Malay (muh-LAY) Peninsula and the islands of Indonesia to exchange cotton cloth, ivory, metalwork, and exotic animals for Chinese silk or Indonesian spices. The overland Silk Road from China brought further trade but was vulnerable to disruption by Central Asian nomads (see Chapter 6).

The Gupta Empire collapsed around 550 C.E. under the pressure of nomadic invaders from the northwest. In the early seventh century, Harsha Vardhana (r. 606–647 C.E.), the ruler of the region around Delhi, briefly restored imperial power. An account of his reign by a courtier named Bana shows him to be a

SECTION REVIEW

- Chandragupta Maurya took control of the kingdom of Magadha and established the Mauryan Empire.

- The collapse of Greek rule in the Punjab enabled Chandragupta and his successors to expand the empire.

- The empire reached its fullest extent under Ashoka, after whose death the empire disintegrated.

- Economic and cultural activity continued during an era of fragmentation; to the south, Tamil culture entered its classical period.

- Also centered in Magadha, the Gupta Empire was less centralized than the Mauryan, but it thrived on the same economies.

- The Guptas revived Vedic practices and presided over both the legal hardening of gender discrimination and the expansion of overseas trade.

fervent Buddhist, poet, patron of artists, and dynamic warrior. After Harsha's death, northern India reverted to political fragmentation and remained divided until the Muslim invasions of the eleventh and twelfth centuries (see Chapter 12).

Southeast Asia, 50–1025 C.E.

How did the geography of Southeast Asia contribute to its commerce and to the influence of Hinduism and Buddhism?

Southeast Asia consists of three geographical zones: the Indochina mainland, the Malay Peninsula, and thousands of islands extending on an east-west axis far out into the Pacific Ocean (see Map 5.2). Encompassing a vast area of land and water, this region is now occupied by the countries of Myanmar (myahn-MAH) (Burma), Thailand, Laos, Cambodia, Vietnam, Malaysia, Singapore, Indonesia, Brunei (broo-NIE), and the Philippines. Poised between the ancient centers of China and India, Southeast Asia has been influenced by the cultures of both civilizations. The region first rose to prominence and prosperity because of its intermediate role in the trade exchanges between southern and eastern Asia.

The strategic importance of Southeast Asia is enhanced by the region's natural resources. This is a geologically active zone; the islands are the tops of a chain of volcanoes. Lying along the equator, Southeast Asia has a tropical climate. The temperature hovers around 80 degrees Fahrenheit (30 degrees Celsius), and the monsoon winds provide dependable rainfall throughout the year. Thanks to several growing cycles each year, the region is capable of supporting a large human population. The most fertile agricultural lands lie along the floodplains of the largest silt-bearing rivers or contain rich volcanic soil deposited by ancient eruptions.

Early Civilization

Rain forest covers much of Southeast Asia. As early as 2000 B.C.E. people in this region were clearing land for farming by cutting and burning the vegetation. The cleared land was farmed for several growing seasons. When the soil was exhausted, the farmers abandoned the patch, allowing the forest to reclaim it, while they cleared and cultivated other nearby fields in similar fashion. Rice was the staple food—labor-intensive, but able to support a large population. A number of plant and animal species spread from Southeast Asia to other regions, including rice, soybeans, sugar cane, yams, bananas, coconuts, chickens, and pigs.

The Malay peoples who became the dominant population in this region were the product of several waves of migration from southern China beginning around 3000 B.C.E. Some indigenous peoples merged with the Malay newcomers; others retreated to remote mountain and forest zones. Subsequently, rising population and disputes within communities prompted streams of people to leave the Southeast Asian mainland for the islands. By the first millennium B.C.E. Southeast Asians had developed impressive navigational skills. They knew how to ride the monsoon winds and interpret the patterns of swells, winds, clouds, and bird and sea life. Over a period of several thousand years groups of Malay peoples in large, double outrigger canoes spread out across the Pacific and Indian Oceans—half the circumference of the earth—to settle thousands of islands.

The inhabitants of Southeast Asia clustered along riverbanks or in fertile volcanic plains. Their fields and villages were never far from the rain forest, with its wild animals and numerous plant species. Forest trees provided fruit, wood, and spices. The shallow waters surrounding the islands teemed with fish. This region was also an early center of metallurgy. Metalsmiths heated copper and tin ore to the right temperature for producing and shaping bronze implements by using hollow bamboo tubes to funnel oxygen to the furnace.

Northern Indochina, by its geographic proximity, was vulnerable to Chinese pressure and cultural influences, and it was under Chinese political control for a thousand years (111 B.C.E.–939 C.E.). Farther south, larger states emerged in the early centuries C.E. in response to two powerful forces: commerce and Hindu-Buddhist culture. Southeast Asia was situated along the trade routes that merchants used to carry Chinese silk westward to India and the Mediterranean. The movements of nomadic peoples had disrupted the old land route across Central Asia. But in India demand for silk was increasing—both for domestic use and for transshipment to satisfy the fast-growing luxury market in the Roman Empire. Gradually merchants extended this exchange network to include goods from Southeast Asia, such as aromatic woods, resins, and cinnamon, pepper, cloves, nutmeg, and other spices. By serving this trade network and controlling key points, Southeast Asian centers rose to prominence.

The other force leading to the rise of larger political entities was the influence of Hindu-Buddhist culture imported from India. Commerce brought Indian merchants and sailors into the ports of Southeast Asia. As Buddhism spread, Southeast Asia became a way station for Indian missionaries and East Asian pilgrims going to and coming from the birthplace of their faith. Shrewd Malay rulers looked to Indian traditions as a rich source of ideas and prestige. They borrowed Sanskrit terms such as *maharaja* (mah-huh-RAH-juh) (great king), utilized Indian models of bureaucracy, ceremonial practices, and forms of artistic representation, and employed priests, administrators, and scribes skilled in Sanskrit writing to expedite government business Their special connection to powerful gods and higher knowledge raised them above their rivals.

The Southeast Asian kingdoms, however, were not just passive recipients of Indian culture. They took what was useful to them and synthesized it with indigenous beliefs, values, and institutions—for example, local concepts of chiefship, ancestor worship, and

Map 5.2 **Southeast Asia** Southeast Asia's position between the ancient centers of civilization in India and China had a major impact on its history. In the first millennium C.E. a series of powerful and wealthy states arose in the region by gaining control of major trade routes: first Funan, based in southern Vietnam, Cambodia, and the Malay Peninsula, then Srivijaya on the island of Sumatra, then smaller states on the island of Java. Shifting trade routes led to the demise of one and the rise of others. © Cengage Learning

forms of oaths. Moreover, they trained their own people in the new ways, so that the bureaucracy contained both foreign experts and native disciples. The whole process amounted to a cultural dialogue between India and Southeast Asia, in which both were active participants.

The first major Southeast Asian center, called "**Funan**" (FOO-nahn) by Chinese visitors, flourished between the first and sixth centuries C.E., (see Map 5.2). Its capital was at the modern site of Oc-Eo in southern Vietnam. Funan occupied the delta of the Mekong (MAY-kawng) River, a "rice bowl" capable of supporting a large population. The rulers mobilized large numbers of laborers to dig irrigation channels and prevent destructive floods. By extending its control over most of southern Indochina and the Malay Peninsula, Funan was able to dominate the trade route from India to China. The route began in the ports of northeast India, crossed the Bay of Bengal, continued by land over the Isthmus of Kra on the

Malay Peninsula, then across the South China Sea (see Map 5.2). Indian merchants found that offloading their goods from ships and carrying them across the narrow strip of land was safer than making the 1,000-mile (1,600-kilometer) voyage around the Malay Peninsula—a dangerous trip marked by treacherous currents, rocky shoals, and pirates. Once the portage across the isthmus was finished, the merchants needed food and lodging while waiting for the monsoon winds to shift so they could make the last leg of the voyage to China by sea. Funan stockpiled food and provided security for those engaged in this trade—in return for customs duties and other fees.

Funan An early complex society in Southeast Asia between the first and sixth centuries C.E. It was centered in the rich rice-growing region of southern Vietnam, and it controlled the passage of trade across the Malaysian isthmus.

Chinese observers have left reports of the prosperity and sophistication of Funan, emphasizing the presence of walled cities, palaces, archives, systems of taxation, and state-organized agriculture. Nevertheless, Funan declined in the sixth century. The most likely explanation is that international trade routes changed and Funan no longer held a strategic position.

The Srivijayan Kingdom

By the sixth century a new, all-sea route had developed. Merchants and travelers from south India and Sri Lanka sailed through the Strait of Malacca (between the west side of the Malay Peninsula and the northeast coast of the island of Sumatra) and into the South China Sea. This route presented both human and navigational hazards, but it significantly shortened the journey.

A new center of power, **Srivijaya** (sree-vih-JUH-yuh)—Sanskrit for "Great Conquest"—dominated the new southerly route by 683 C.E.. The capital of the Srivijayan kingdom was at modern-day Palembang in southeastern Sumatra, 50 miles (80 kilometers) up the broad and navigable Musi River, with a good natural harbor. The kingdom was well situated to control the southern part of the Malay Peninsula, Sumatra, parts of Java and Borneo, and the Malacca (muh-LAH-kuh) and Sunda straits—vital passageways for shipping (see Map 5.2).

The Srivijayan capital gained ascendancy over its rivals and assumed control of the international trade route by fusing four distinct ecological zones into an interdependent network. The core area was the productive agricultural plain along the Musi River. The king and his clerks, judges, and tax collectors controlled this zone directly. Control was less direct over the second zone, the upland regions of Sumatra's interior, with its commercially valuable forest products. Local rulers there were bound to the center by oaths of loyalty, elaborate court ceremonies, and the sharing of profits from trade. The third zone consisted of river ports that had been Srivijaya's main rivals. They were conquered and controlled thanks to an alliance between Srivijaya and neighboring sea nomads, pirates who served as a Srivijayan navy in return for a steady income.

The fourth zone was a fertile "rice bowl" on the central plain of the nearby island of Java—a region

SECTION REVIEW

- Climate and resources enabled Southeast Asia to support large human populations.
- Located on the trade and pilgrimage routes between China and India, Southeast Asia came under strong Hindu and Buddhist influence.
- Shrewd rulers used Indian knowledge and personnel to enhance their power and prestige.
- Funan rose to prominence between the first and sixth centuries C.E. by controlling the trade route across the Malay Peninsula.
- The Srivijayan kingdom flourished between the seventh and eleventh centuries C.E. and dominated the new international trade route through the Straits of Malacca.

so productive, because of its volcanic soil, that it houses and feeds the majority of the population of present-day Indonesia. Srivijayan monarchs maintained alliances, cemented by intermarriage, with several ruling dynasties in this region, and the Srivijayan kings claimed descent from the main Javanese dynasty. These arrangements gave Srivijaya access to large quantities of foodstuffs that people living in the capital and merchants and sailors visiting the various ports needed.

The kings of Srivijaya who constructed and maintained this complex network of social, political, and economic relationships were men of energy and skill. Although their authority depended in part on force, it owed more to diplomatic and even theatrical talents. Like the Gupta monarchy, Srivijaya was a theater-state, securing its preeminence and binding dependents by its sheer splendor and its ability to attract labor, talent, and luxury products. The court was the scene of ceremonies designed to dazzle observers and reinforce an image of wealth, power, and sanctity. Subordinate rulers took oaths of loyalty carrying

Srivijaya A state based on the Indonesian island of Sumatra, between the seventh and eleventh centuries C.E. It amassed wealth and power by a combination of selective adaptation of Indian technologies and concepts, control of the lucrative trade routes between India and China, and skillful showmanship and diplomacy in holding together a disparate realm of inland and coastal territories.

Aerial View of the Buddhist Monument at Borobodur, Java The great monument of volcanic stone was more than 300 feet (90 meters) in length and over 100 feet (30 meters) high. Pilgrims made a 3-mile-long (nearly 5-kilometer-long) winding ascent through ten levels intended to represent the ideal Buddhist journey from ignorance to enlightenment. Numerous sculptured reliefs depicting Buddhist legends provide glimpses of daily life in early Java.

Luca Tettoni/Robert Harding World Imagery

dire threats of punishment for violations, and in their home locales they imitated the splendid ceremonials of the capital.

The Srivijayan king, drawing upon Buddhist conceptions, presented himself as a bodhisattva, one who had achieved enlightenment and utilized his precious insights for the betterment of his subjects. The king was believed to have magical powers, controlling powerful forces of fertility associated with the rivers in flood and mediating between the spiritually potent realms of the mountains and the sea. He was also said to be so wealthy that he deposited bricks of gold in the river estuary to appease the local gods, and a hillside near town was covered with silver and gold images of the Buddha. The gold originated in East or West Africa and came to Southeast Asia through trade with the Muslim world (see Chapter 8).

The kings built and patronized Buddhist monasteries and schools. In central Java local dynasties allied with Srivijaya built magnificent temple complexes to advertise their glory. The most famous of these, **Borobodur** (booh-roe-boe-DOOR), built between 770 and 825 C.E., was the largest human construction in the Southern Hemisphere.

The kings of Srivijaya carried out this marvelous balancing act for centuries. But the system was vulnerable to shifts in the pattern of international trade. Some such change must have contributed to the decline of Srivijaya in the eleventh century, even though the immediate cause was a destructive raid on the capital by forces of the Chola kingdom of southeast India in 1025 C.E.

After the decline of Srivijaya, leadership passed to new, vigorous kingdoms on the eastern end of Java, and the maritime realm of Southeast Asia remained prosperous and connected to international trade networks. Through the ages Europeans remained dimly aware of this region as a source of spices and other luxury items. Some four centuries after the decline of Srivijaya, an Italian navigator serving under the flag of Spain—Christopher Columbus—sailed westward across the Atlantic Ocean, seeking to establish a direct route to the fabled "Indies" from which the spices came.

Borobodur A massive stone monument on the Indonesian island of Java, erected by the Sailendra kings around 800 C.E. The winding ascent through ten levels, decorated with rich relief carving, is a Buddhist allegory for the progressive stages of enlightenment.

Conclusion

This chapter traces the emergence of complex societies in India and Southeast Asia between the second millennium B.C.E. and the first millennium C.E. Because of migrations, trade, and the spread of belief systems, an Indian style of civilization spread throughout the subcontinent and adjoining regions and eventually made its way to Southeast Asia. In this period were laid cultural foundations that in large measure still endure.

The development and spread of belief systems—Vedism, Buddhism, Jainism, and Hinduism—have a central place in this chapter because nearly all the sources are religious. Ancient Indians did not develop a historical consciousness like their Israelite, Greek, and Chinese contemporaries because they held a strikingly different view of time. The distinctive Indian conception—of vast epochs in which universes are created and destroyed again and again and the essential spirit of living creatures is reincarnated repeatedly—made the particulars of any brief moment seem relatively unimportant.

Political and social division has been the norm throughout much of the history of India, a consequence of the diversity of the subcontinent and the complex mix of ethnic and linguistic groups inhabiting it. The elaborate structure of classes and castes was a response to this diversity. Strong central governments, such as those of the Mauryan and Gupta kings, rose to dominance by gaining control of resources and important trade routes and developing effective military and administrative institutions. However, the periods of fragmentation and multiple centers of power were as dynamic as the periods of unity.

Many distinctive social and intellectual features of Indian civilization—the class and caste system, models of kingship and statecraft, and Vedic, Jainist, and Buddhist belief systems—originated in the north, where descendants of Indo-European immigrants predominated. Hinduism embraced elements drawn from the Dravidian cultures of the south as well as from Buddhism. The capacity of the Hindu tradition to assimilate a wide range of popular beliefs facilitated the spread of a common Indian civilization across the subcontinent, although there was considerable variation from one region to another.

Southeast Asia, as a crossroads of trade, received influences from China and India. Commerce brought migrants and merchants from both regions to Southeast Asia. As Buddhism spread, Southeast Asia became a way station for Indian missionaries and Chinese pilgrims. Malay rulers looked to Indian traditions as a rich source of ideas and prestige, and used Indian models of bureaucracy, ceremonial practices, and forms of artistic representation. Thus the Southeast Asian kingdoms synthesized foreign cultural influences with indigenous beliefs, values, and institutions.

CHAPTER REVIEW

 Download the MP3 audio file of the Chapter Review to listen to on the go.

What does material evidence tell us about the Indus Valley civilization and the most likely reason for its collapse? (page 112)

The cities of Harappa and Mohenjo-Daro provide evidence of early civilization in the fertile Indus Valley. Both display a striking uniformity of planning and construction, including high brick walls and a rectangular grid of streets. Excavated artifacts exhibit standard shapes and styles, with some evidence indicating trade with resource-rich regions to the north and Mesopotamia to the west. Unfortunately, the writing system of this civilization remains undeciphered. The abandonment of the cities signaled the end of this civilization. The probable cause was "systems failure" resulting from ecological changes in the river valley and along the coast.

What historical forces led to the development of complex social groupings in ancient India? (page 116)

Arya kinship groups moving into northwest India after 1500 B.C.E. established a religiously sanctioned class (varna) system of priests, warriors, landowners and merchants, and peasants and laborers. With further subdivisions into castes (jati), this system ordered the relations among ethnically, linguistically, and culturally diverse populations. Various forms of resistance to the secular and religious domination of the Brahmins arose, including the more egalitarian Buddhist and Jainist belief systems. Traditionalists responded to this through Hinduism, which provided people with a number of ways to make personal connections with the gods.

In the face of powerful forces that tended to keep India fragmented, how did the Mauryan Empire of the fourth to second centuries B.C.E. and the Gupta Empire of the fourth to sixth centuries C.E. succeed in unifying much of India? (page 122)

Despite geographical obstacles, religious diversity, and social orientation toward the caste system, the Mauryan (fourth to second centuries B.C.E.) and Gupta (fourth to sixth centuries C.E.) rulers brought most of the subcontinent under their control. Both dynasties exploited the agricultural productivity of the Ganges Plain, monopolized mining and weapons production, built standing armies, and developed complex bureaucracies and networks of spies. These centralizing factors encouraged urban growth, long-distance trade, and new forms of art and literature.

How did the geography of Southeast Asia contribute to its commerce and to the influence of Hinduism and Buddhism? (page 127)

Southeast Asia, a region rich in resources with a tropical climate favorable for agriculture, generated a lively trade, both locally and with South and East Asia. South Asian sailors, merchants, and pilgrims brought Hinduism and Buddhism to the region. Kingdoms in southern Indochina, the Malay Peninsula, and Java found their ideas appealing. Malay rulers blended Indian religions with local traditions to produce a distinctive civilization.

Key Terms

Harappa *(p. 113)*

Mohenjo-Daro *(p. 113)*

monsoon *(p. 116)*

Vedas *(p. 116)*

varnas/jati *(p. 118)*

karma *(p. 118)*

moksha *(p. 119)*

Buddha *(p. 119)*

Mahayana Buddhism *(p. 120)*

Theravada Buddhism *(p. 120)*

Hinduism *(p. 121)*

Mauryan Empire *(p. 123)*

Ashoka *(p. 123)*

Mahabharata *(p. 124)*

Bhagavad-Gita *(p. 124)*

Tamil kingdoms *(p. 124)*

Gupta Empire *(p. 126)*

theater-state *(p. 126)*

Funan *(p. 129)*

Srivijaya *(p. 130)*

Borobodur *(p. 131)*

Web Resources

Pronunciation Guide

Interactive Maps

- MAP 5.1 Ancient India
- MAP 5.2 Southeast Asia

Primary Sources

- The Rig Veda
- Setting in Motion the Wheels of Law
- The Laws of Manu

Answer to the History in Focus Question

See photo on page 114, "Man from Mohenjo-Daro, ca. 2600–1900 B.C.E."

Visit the CourseMate website at www.cengagebrain.com for additional study tools and review materials for this chapter.

An Age of Empires: Rome and Han China

© Cengage Learning

Visit the CourseMate website at **www.cengagebrain.com** for additional study tools and review materials for this chapter.

134

According to Chinese sources, in the year 166 C.E., a group of travelers identifying themselves as delegates from Andun, the king of distant Da Qin, arrived at the court of the Chinese emperor Huan, one of the Han rulers. Andun was Marcus Aurelius Antoninus, the emperor of Rome.

These first known "Romans" to reach China probably hailed from one of Rome's eastern provinces, perhaps Egypt or Syria, and may have stretched the truth in claiming to be representatives of the Roman emperor. The Chinese officials had had no direct contact with the Roman Empire, however, and so the travelers, probably merchants hoping to trade for highly prized Chinese silk, easily got away with the imposture.

Direct or regular contact between the empires never developed, but the episode reveals that in the early centuries C.E. Rome and China dimly recognized each other's existence across the far-flung trading networks that spanned the Eastern Hemisphere. Both states, moreover, emerged from the last centuries B.C.E. and the first centuries C.E. as a new kind of empire, both qualitatively and quantitatively.

Since neither empire influenced the other, what caused them to arise and flourish at the same time? Some stress supposedly common factors, such as climate change or challenges from Central Asian nomads, but no theory has won the general support of scholars. The Roman Empire encompassed the lands surrounding the Mediterranean Sea and substantial portions of inland Europe and the Middle East. The Han Empire, named for China's ruling family, stretched from the Pacific Ocean to the oases of Central Asia. The largest empires the world had yet seen, they nevertheless managed to centralize control, achieve unprecedented stability and longevity, and assert dominance over the many cultures and peoples within their borders.

Rome's Creation of a Mediterranean Empire, 753 B.C.E.–330 C.E.

How did Rome create and maintain its vast Mediterranean empire?

The boot-shaped Italian peninsula, with the large island of Sicily, constitutes a bridge almost linking Europe and Africa (see Map 6.1). Rome too lay at a crossroads, being situated at the midpoint of the peninsula, about 15 miles (24 kilometers) from its western coast, where a north-south road intersected an east-west river route. The Tiber River on one side and a double ring of seven hills on the other afforded natural protection to the site.

The Apennine Mountains form Italy's spine, separating the eastern and western coastal plains, and the arc of the Alps shields it on the north. Navigable rivers and passes through the Apennines, and even through the snowcapped Alps, eased travel by merchants and armies. The Mediterranean climate afforded a long growing season and favorable conditions for a wide variety of crops. Hillside forests, today largely gone, provided timber for construction and fuel. Iron and other metals came from the region of Etruria in the northwest.

Although hills account for 75 percent of Italy's land area, the coastal plains and river valleys provide arable land, with fertile volcanic soil capable of supporting a much larger population than Greece. As it expanded within Italy, the Roman state tapped these human resources.

A Republic of Farmers

According to legend, Romulus, cast adrift on the Tiber River as a baby and nursed by a she-wolf, founded Rome in 753 B.C.E. Archaeological research, however, has revealed occupation on the Palatine Hill, one of the city's seven hills, dating to 1000 B.C.E. Several hilltop communities merged shortly before 600 B.C.E., forming an urban nucleus made possible by the draining of a swamp on the site of the future Roman Forum (civic center).

The Latin speech and cultural patterns of the inhabitants of the site resembled those of most of the other peoples of the peninsula. However, tradition remembered Etruscan immigrants arriving in the seventh century B.C.E. and being taken in; Rome came to pride itself on offering hospitality to exiles and outcasts.

Agriculture anchored the economy of early Rome, and land constituted wealth. Landownership brought social status and political privilege while buttressing fundamental values. Most early Romans cultivated their own small plots of land, but a few families managed to acquire large tracts of land. The heads of these wealthy families served in the Senate, a "Council of

Map 6.1 The Roman Empire The Roman Empire came to encompass all the lands surrounding the Mediterranean Sea, as well as parts of continental Europe. When the emperor Augustus died in 14 C.E., he left instructions to his successors not to expand beyond the limits he had set, but his successor Claudius invaded southern Britain in the mid-first century and the soldier-emperor Trajan added Romania early in the second century. Deserts and seas provided solid natural boundaries, but the long and vulnerable river border in central and eastern Europe would eventually prove expensive to defend and vulnerable to invasion by Germanic and Central Asian peoples. © Cengage Learning

Interactive Map

Legend:
- Roman Empire by death of Augustus, 14 C.E.
- Territory added by death of Hadrian, 138 C.E.
- Territory gained and lost, with dates held
- Parthian Empire, ca. 200 C.E.
- ★ Major battle

ATLANTIC OCEAN

North Sea

CALEDONIA (85–105 C.E.)
Hadrian's Wall 122 C.E.
Eburacum (York)
BRITAIN
Camulodunum (Colchester)
Londinium (London)

Baltic Sea

GERMANIA (4–9 C.E.)
LOWER GERMANY
Colonia Claudia Agrippinensis (Cologne)
Moguntiacum (Mainz)
UPPER GERMANY
BELGICA
GAUL
Lutetia Parisiorum (Paris)
LUGDUNENSIS
Lugdunum (Lyons)
AQUITANIA
NARBONENSIS
Nemausus (Nîmes)
Narbo
Massilia (Marseilles)
Alesia 52 B.C.E.
Rhine R.
Rhône R.

Elbe R.
Vistula R.
Vindobona (Vienna)
Aquincum (Budapest)
RAETIA
NORICUM
PANNONIA
ALPS
CISALPINE GAUL
Mediolanum (Milan)
ETRURIA
Arretium
ITALY
Rome
Ostia
Pompeii
Mt. Vesuvius
Po R.

Danube R.

DACIA (107–272 C.E.)
Singidunum (Belgrade)
DALMATIA
MOESIA
Adriatic Sea
Brundisium
MACEDONIA
Thessalonica
EPIRUS
Actium 31 B.C.E.
Corinth
ACHAEA
Athens

BOSPORAN KINGDOM
Dnieper R.
Don R.
Volga R.

Black Sea

THRACE
Byzantium
BITHYNIA AND PONTUS
Pergamum
GALATIA
ASIA
PAMPHYLIA
Ephesus
ANATOLIA
CAPPADOCIA
LYCIA
CILICIA
Tarsus
Rhodes
Crete
Cyprus

Caspian Sea
Aral Sea

CAUCASUS MTS.

ARMENIA (114–117 C.E.)
ASSYRIA (116–117 C.E.)
MESOPOTAMIA (115–117 C.E.)
Tigris R.
Euphrates R.
Palmyra
SYRIA
Antioch
Damascus
Nisa

PARTHIA
Ecbatana
Ctesiphon
Seleucia
Babylon
Susa
Persepolis
Persian Gulf

ARABIAN DESERT

JUDAEA
Jerusalem
Petra
ARABIA
Red Sea

Mediterranean Sea

SPAIN
LUSITANIA
Emerita Augusta (Mérida)
Corduba (Córdoba)
BAETICA
TARRACONENSIS
Tarraco
Saguntum
Ebro R.
Burdigala (Bordeaux)
Balearic Is.
Corsica
Sardinia
Sicily
Syracuse
Malta
Carthage
AFRICA PROCONSULARIS
Leptis Magna
NUMIDIA
NORTH AFRICA
MAURETANIA
SAHARA

CYRENAICA
Cyrene

EGYPT
Alexandria
Nile R.
Bahriya Oasis

0 200 400 Km.
0 200 400 Mi.

Chronology

	Rome	China
	1000 B.C.E. First settlement on site of Rome	
	507 B.C.E. Establishment of the Republic	
500 B.C.E.		**480–221 B.C.E.** Warring States Period
300 B.C.E.	**264–202 B.C.E.** Wars against Carthage guarantee Roman control of western Mediterranean	
		221 B.C.E. Qin emperor unites eastern China
		206 B.C.E. Han dynasty succeeds Qin
200 B.C.E.	**200–146 B.C.E.** Wars against Hellenistic kingdoms lead to control of eastern Mediterranean	
100 B.C.E.		**187–40 B.C.E.** Emperor Wu expands the Han Empire
	88–31 B.C.E. Civil wars and failure of the Republic	
	31 B.C.E.–14 C.E. Augustus establishes the Principate	
50 C.E.		**23 C.E.** Han capital transferred from Chang'an to Luoyang
200 C.E.		
	235–284 C.E. Third-century crisis	**220 C.E.** Fall of Han Empire
300 C.E.	**324 C.E.** Constantine moves capital to Constantinople	

Elders" that dominated the politics of the Roman state. Their families constituted the senatorial class. Tradition maintains that seven kings ruled Rome between 753 and 507 B.C.E., Romulus being the first and the tyrannical Tarquinius Superbus the last. In 507 B.C.E., members of the senatorial class, led by Brutus "the Liberator," deposed Tarquinius Superbus and instituted a *res publica*, a "public possession," or republic.

Far from being a democracy, the **Roman Republic**, which lasted from 507 to 31 B.C.E., vested power in several assemblies. Male citizens could attend their sessions, but the votes of the wealthy counted for more than the votes of the poor. The hierarchy of state officials, elected for one year, culminated in two consuls, who presided over the Senate and other assemblies and commanded the army on campaigns.

Technically an advisory council, first to the kings and later to the annually changing Republican officials, the **Roman Senate** increasingly made policy and governed. Senators nominated their sons for public offices and filled senatorial vacancies with former officials. This self-perpetuating body, whose members served for life, brought together wealth, influence, and political and military experience.

Roman families consisted of several generations as well as domestic slaves. The oldest living male, the *paterfamilias*, exercised absolute authority over every family member. This *auctoritas*, enjoyed by important male members of the society as a whole, enabled a man to inspire and demand obedience from his inferiors.

Complex ties of obligation, such as the **patron/ client relationship**, bound together individuals and families. *Clients* sought the help and protection of *patrons*, men of wealth and influence. A senator might

Roman Republic The period from 507 to 31 B.C.E., during which Rome was largely governed by the aristocratic Roman Senate.

Roman Senate A council whose members were the heads of wealthy, landowning families. Originally an advisory body to the early kings, in the era of the Roman Republic the Senate effectively governed the Roman state and the growing empire. Under Senate leadership, Rome conquered an empire of unprecedented extent in the lands surrounding the Mediterranean Sea. In the first century B.C.E. quarrels among powerful and ambitious senators and failure to address social and economic problems led to civil wars and the emergence of the rule of the emperors.

patron/client relationship In ancient Rome, a fundamental social relationship in which the patron—a wealthy and powerful individual—provided legal and economic protection and assistance to clients, men of lesser status and means, and in return the clients supported the political careers and economic interests of their patron.

have dozens or even hundreds of clients to whom he provided legal advice and representation, physical protection, and monetary loans in tough times. In turn, the client followed his patron out to battle, supported him in the political arena, worked on his land, and even contributed to his daughter's dowry. Throngs of clients awaited their patrons in the morning and accompanied them to the Forum for the day's business. Especially large retinues brought great prestige. Middle-class clients of the aristocracy might be patrons to poorer men. Rome thus accepted and institutionalized inequality and made of it a system of mutual benefits and obligations.

Roman women played no public role and hence appear infrequently in sources. Nearly all information pertains to those in the upper classes. In early Rome, a woman never ceased to be a child in the eyes of the law. She started out under the absolute authority of her paterfamilias. When she married, she came under the jurisdiction of the paterfamilias of her husband's family. Unable to own property or represent herself in legal proceedings, she had to depend on a male guardian to advocate her interests.

Despite the limitations, Roman women seem less constrained than their Greek counterparts (see Chapter 4). Over time, they gained greater personal protection and economic freedom. Some took advantage of a form of marriage that left a woman under the jurisdiction of her father and independent after his death. Many stories involve strong women who greatly influenced their husbands or sons and thereby helped shape Roman history. Roman poets expressed love for women who appeared educated and outspoken, and the careers of the early emperors abound with tales of self-assured and assertive queen-mothers and consorts.

Like other Italian peoples, Romans believed in invisible, shapeless forces known as *numina*. Vesta, the living, pulsating energy of fire, dwelled in the hearth. Janus guarded the door. The Penates watched over food stored in the cupboard. Other deities resided in hills, caves, grottoes, and springs. Small offerings of cakes and liquids supplicated the favor of these spirits. Certain gods operated in larger spheres—for example, Jupiter, the god of the sky, and Mars, initially a god of agriculture as well as war.

The Romans strove to maintain the *pax deorum* ("peace of the gods"), a covenant between the gods and the Roman state. Boards of priests drawn from the aristocracy performed sacrifices and other rituals to win the gods' favor. In return, the Roman state counted on the gods for success in its undertakings. When the Romans encountered the Greeks of southern Italy, they equated their major deities with gods from the Greek pantheon, such as Zeus (Jupiter) and Ares (Mars), and took over the myths attached to them.

Expansion in Italy and the Mediterranean

The fledgling Roman Republic of 500 B.C.E. did not stand out among the city-states of Latium, a region of central Italy. Three and a half centuries later, Rome commanded a huge empire encompassing virtually all the Mediterranean lands. Expansion began slowly but picked up momentum, peaking in the third and second centuries B.C.E.

Some scholars ascribe Rome's success to the greed and aggressiveness of a people fond of war. Others observe that the structure of the Roman state encouraged

Statue of a Roman Carrying Busts of His Ancestors, First Century B.C.E. Roman society was extremely conscious of status, and the status of an elite Roman family was determined in large part by the public achievements of ancestors and living members. A visitor to a Roman home found portraits of distinguished ancestors in the entry hall, along with labels listing the offices they held. Portrait heads were carried in funeral processions. Alinari/Art Resource, NY recourse to war, because the two consuls had only one year in office in which to gain military glory. The Romans invariably claimed they were only defending themselves. Possibly fear drove the Romans to expand their territory: each new conquest became vulnerable, necessitating ever more buffers against attack.

Ongoing friction between the pastoral hill peoples of the Apennines, who depended on herding, and the farmers of the coastal plains sparked Rome's conquest of Italy. In the fifth century B.C.E., Rome achieved leadership within a league of central Italian cities organized for defense against the hill peoples. In the fourth century B.C.E., the Romans occasionally defended the wealthy and sophisticated cities of Campania, the region on the Bay of Naples possessing the richest farmland in the peninsula. By 290 B.C.E., after three wars with the peoples of Samnium in central Italy, the Romans had extended their "protection" over nearly the entire peninsula.

The Romans consolidated their hold over Italy by granting the political, legal, and economic privileges of citizenship to conquered populations. In this, they contrasted with the Greeks, who did not share citizenship with outsiders (see Chapter 4). The Romans co-opted the most influential elements within the conquered communities and made Rome's interests their interests. Rome also demanded that its Italian subjects provide soldiers; this seemingly inexhaustible reservoir of manpower bolstered military success. Rome could endure higher casualties than the enemy and prevail by sheer numbers.

Between 264 and 202 B.C.E., Rome fought two protracted wars against the Carthaginians, those energetic descendants of the Phoenicians who had settled in Tunisia and dominated the commerce of the western Mediterranean (see Chapter 3). The Roman state emerged as the master of the western Mediterranean and acquired its first overseas provinces in Sicily, Sardinia, and Spain (see Map 6.1). Between 200 and 146 B.C.E., a series of wars pitted the Roman state against the major Hellenistic kingdoms in the eastern Mediterranean. Reluctant to occupy such distant territories, the Romans withdrew their troops. But when the settlements they imposed failed to take root, a frustrated Roman government took over direct administration of these turbulent lands. The conquest of the Celtic peoples of Gaul (modern France; see Chapter

2) by Rome's most brilliant general, Gaius Julius Caesar, between 59 and 51 B.C.E. led to the first territorial acquisitions in Europe's heartland.

The Romans resisted extending to distant provinces the governing system and privileges of citizenship they employed in Italy. Indigenous elite groups willing to collaborate with Rome enjoyed considerable autonomy, including responsibility for local administration and tax collection. Every year a senator, usually someone who had held high office, served as governor in each province. Accompanied by a surprisingly small retinue of friends and relations who served as advisers and deputies, the governor defended the province against outside attack and internal disruption, oversaw the collection of taxes, and judged legal cases.

Over time, this system proved inadequate. Officials chosen through political connections often lacked competence, and the one-year period of service gave them little time to gain experience. A few governors extorted huge sums of money from the provincial populace. Rome still depended on the institutions and attitudes of a city-state to govern an ever-growing empire.

The Failure of the Republic

The frequent wars and territorial expansion of the third and second centuries B.C.E. set off changes in the Italian landscape. Peasant farmers spent long periods of time away from home on military service, while most of the wealth generated by conquest and empire ended up helping the upper classes purchase Italian land. Investors easily acquired the property of absent soldier-farmers by purchase, deception, or intimidation. The small self-sufficient farms of the Italian countryside, whose peasant owners provided the backbone of the Roman legions (units of 6,000 soldiers), gave way to *latifundia*, literally "broad estates," or ranches.

The new owners had ample space to graze herds of cattle or grow grapes for wine in the place of less profitable wheat. Thus, much of Italy, especially in the cities, became dependent on expensive imported grain. Meanwhile, cheap slave labor provided by war prisoners made it hard for peasants who had lost their farms to find work in the countryside (see Diversity and Dominance: The Treatment of Slaves in Rome and China). They moved to Rome and other cities, but found no work

Diversity & Dominance

The Treatment of Slaves in Rome and China

Although slaves were found in most ancient societies, Rome was one of the few in which slave labor became the indispensable foundation of the economy. In the course of the frequent wars of the second century B.C.E., large numbers of prisoners were carried into slavery. The prices of such slaves were low, and landowners and manufacturers found they could compel slaves to work longer and harder than hired laborers. Periodically, the harsh working and living conditions resulted in slave revolts.

The following excerpt, from one of several surviving manuals on agriculture, gives advice about controlling and efficiently exploiting slaves.

When the head of a household arrives at his estate, after he has prayed to the family god, he must go round his farm on a tour of inspection on the very same day, if that is possible, if not, then on the next day. When he has found out how his farm has been cultivated and which jobs have been done and which have not been done, then on the next day after that he must call in his manager and ask him which are the jobs that have been done and which remain, and whether they were done on time, and whether what still has to be done can be done, and how much wine and grain and anything else has been produced. When he has found this out, he must make a calculation of the labor and the time taken. If the work doesn't seem to him to be sufficient, and the manager starts to say how hard he tried, but the slaves weren't any good, and the weather was awful, and the slaves ran away, and he was required to carry out some public works, then when he has finished mentioning these and all sorts of other excuses, you must draw his attention to your calculation of the labor employed and time taken. If he claims that it rained all the time, there are all sorts of jobs that can be done in rainy weather—washing wine-jars, coating them with pitch, cleaning the house, storing grain, shifting muck, digging a manure pit, cleaning seed, mending ropes or making new ones; the slaves ought to have been mending their patchwork cloaks and their hoods.

On festival days they would have been able to clean out old ditches, work on the public highway, prune back brambles, dig up the garden, clear a meadow, tie up bundles of sticks, remove thorns, grind barley and get on with cleaning. If he claims that the slaves have been ill, they needn't have been given such large rations. When you have found out about all these things to your satisfaction, make sure that all the work that remains to be done will be carried out. . . . The head of the household [on his tour of inspection] should examine his herds and arrange a sale; he should sell the oil if the price makes it worthwhile, and any wine and grain that is surplus to needs; he should sell any old oxen, cattle or sheep that are not up to standard, wool and hides, an old cart or old tools, an old slave, a sick slave—anything else that is surplus to requirements. The head of a household ought to sell, and not to buy. (Cato the Elder, *Concerning Agriculture*, bk. 2, second century B.C.E.)

Cato, the Roman author of that excerpt, was notorious for his stern manner and hard-edged traditionalism, and while he does not represent the approach of all Roman masters—in reality, the treatment of slaves varied widely—he expresses a point of view that Roman society found acceptable.

Slavery was far less prominent in ancient China. During the Warring States Period, dependent peasants as well as slaves worked the large holdings of the landowning aristocracy. The Qin government sought to abolish slavery, but the institution persisted into the Han period, although it involved only a small fraction of the population and was not a central component of the economy. The relatives of criminals could be seized and enslaved, and poor families sometimes sold unwanted children into slavery. In China, slaves, whether they belonged to the state or to individuals, generally performed domestic tasks, as can be seen in the following text.

Wang Ziyuan of Shu Commandery went to the Jian River on business, and went up to the home of the widow Yang Hui, who had a male slave named Bianliao. Wang Ziyuan requested him to go and buy some wine. Picking up a big stick, Bianliao climbed to the top of the grave mound and said: "When my master bought me, Bianliao, he only contracted for me to care for the grave and did not contract for me to buy wine for some other gentleman."

Wang Ziyuan was furious and said to the widow: "Wouldn't you prefer to sell this slave?"

Yang Hui said: "The slave's father offered him to people, but no one wanted him." Wang Ziyuan immediately settled on the sale contract.

The slave again said: "Enter in the contract everything you wish to order me to do. I, Bianliao, will not do anything not in the contract."

Wang Ziyuan said: "Agreed."

The text of the contract said:

Third year of Shenjiao, the first month, the fifteenth day, the gentleman Wang Ziyuan, of Zizhong, purchases from the lady Yang Hui of Anzhi village in Zhengdu, the bearded male slave, Bianliao, of her husband's household. The fixed sale [price] is 15,000 [cash]. The slave shall obey orders about all kinds of work and may not argue.

He shall rise at dawn and do an early sweeping. After eating he shall wash up. Ordinarily he should pound the grain mortar, tie up broom straws, carve bowls and bore wells, scoop out ditches, tie up fallen fences, hoe the garden, trim up paths and dike up plots of land, cut big flails, bend bamboos to make rakes, and scrape and fix the well pulley. In going and coming he may not ride horseback or in the cart, [nor may he] sit crosslegged or make a hubbub. When he gets out of bed he shall shake his head [to wake up], fish, cut forage, plait reeds and card hemp, draw water for gruel, and help in making zumo [drink]. He shall weave shoes and make [other] coarse things. . . .

In the second month at the vernal equinox he shall bank the dikes and repair the boundary walls [of the fields]; prune the mulberry trees, skin the palm trees, plant melons to make gourd [utensils], select eggplant [seeds for planting], and transplant onion sets; burn plant remains to generate the fields, pile up refuse and break up lumps [in the soil]. At midday he shall dry out things in the sun. At cockcrow he shall rise and pound grain in the mortar, exercise and curry the horses, the donkeys, and likewise the mules. . . . [The list of tasks continues for two-and-a-half pages.]

He shall be industrious and quick-working, and he may not idle and loaf. When the slave is old and his strength spent, he shall plant marsh grass and weave mats. When his work is over and he wishes to rest he should pound a picul [of grain]. Late at night when there is no work he shall wash clothes really white. If he has private savings they shall be the master's gift, or from

guests. The slave may not have evil secrets; affairs should be open and reported. If the slave does not heed instructions, he shall be whipped a hundred strokes.

The reading of the text of the contract came to an end. The slave was speechless and his lips were tied. Wildly he beat his head on the ground, and beat himself with his hands; from his eyes the tears streamed down, and the drivel from his nose hung a foot long.

He said: "If it is to be exactly as master Wang says, I would rather return soon along the yellow-soil road, with the grave worms boring through my head. Had I known before I would have bought the wine for master Wang, I would not have dared to do that wrong." (Wang Bao, first century B.C.E.)

This story was meant to be humorous and no doubt exaggerates the amount of work that could be demanded from a slave, but it shows that Chinese slaves could be forced to work hard and engaged in many of the same menial tasks as their Roman counterparts. It is hard to imagine a Roman slave daring to refuse a request and arguing publicly with a nobleman without being severely punished. It also appears that slaves in China were legally protected by contracts that specified and limited what could be demanded of them.

QUESTIONS FOR ANALYSIS

1. Why might slavery have been less important in Han China than in the Roman Empire? Why would the treatment of slaves have been less harsh in China than in Rome?

2. In what ways were slaves treated like other forms of property, such as animals and tools? In what ways was a slave's "humanity" taken into account?

3. What are some of the passive-resistance tactics that slaves resorted to, and what did they achieve by these actions?

Source: First selection from Thomas Wiedemann, *Greek and Roman Slavery* (Baltimore: Johns Hopkins University Press, 1981), 183–184. © 1981 by Johns Hopkins University Press. Reproduced by permission of Taylor & Francis Books UK. Second selection from C. Martin Wilbur, *Slavery in China During the Former Han Dynasty, 206 B.C.–A.D. 25* (New York: Russell & Russell, 1967). Reprinted with permission of Scribner, a division of Simon & Schuster, Inc. from *Slavery in China During the Former Han Dynasty* by Clarence Martin Wilbur (Russell & Russell, New York, 1967).

there either and ended up living in poverty. The grow-ing urban masses, idle and prone to riot, would play a major role in the political struggles of the late Republic.

The decline of peasant farmers in Italy produced a shortage of men who owned the minimum amount of property required for military service. During a war that the Romans fought in North Africa at the end of the second century B.C.E., Gaius Marius—a "new man" as the Romans labeled politically active individuals from outside the traditional ruling class—achieved political prominence by enlisting in the legions poor propertyless men to whom he promised farms upon retirement from military service. These grateful troops helped Marius get elected to an unprecedented (and illegal) six consulships.

Between 88 and 31 B.C.E., several ambitious indi-viduals—Sulla, Pompey, Julius Caesar, Mark Antony, and Octavian—commanded armies that were more loyal to them than to the state. Their use of Roman troops to increase their personal power led to civil wars between military factions. The generals who seized Rome on several occasions executed their polit-ical opponents and exercised dictatorial control.

Julius Caesar's grandnephew and heir, Octavian (63 B.C.E.–14 C.E.), eliminated all rivals by 31 B.C.E. and set about refashioning the Roman system of govern-ment while retaining the offices, honors, and social prerogatives of the senatorial class. A dictator in fact, he never called himself king or emperor, claiming merely to be *princeps*, "first among equals"; hence the term **Roman Principate** for the period following the Roman Republic. **Augustus**, a title Octavian received from the Senate, implied prosperity and piety and became the name by which he is known to posterity. Augustus's ruthlessness, patience, and intuitive grasp of psychology enabled him to manipulate each group in society. When he died in 14 C.E., after forty-five years of carefully veiled rule, scarcely anyone could remember the Republic. During his reign, the empire expanded into Egypt and parts of the Middle East and central Europe, leaving only the southern half of Brit-ain and modern Romania to be added later.

 Primary Source: A Man of Unlimited Ambition: Julius Caesar Read about the plots and intrigues of the Roman court.

Peter Rockwell, Rome

Scene from Trajan's Column, Rome, ca. 113 C.E. The Roman emperor Trajan erected a marble column 125 feet (38 meters) in height to commemorate his triumphant campaign in Dacia (modern Romania). The relief carving, which snakes around the column for 656 feet (200 meters), illustrates numerous episodes of the conquest and provided a detailed pictorial record of the equipment and practices of the Roman army in the field. This panel depicts soldiers building a fort.

Roman Principate A term used to characterize Roman government in the first three centuries C.E., based on the ambiguous title *princeps* ("first citi-zen") adopted by Augustus to conceal his military dictatorship.

Augustus (63 B.C.E.–14 C.E.) Honorific name of Octa-vian, founder of the Roman Principate, the military dictatorship that replaced the failing rule of the Roman Senate. After defeating all rivals, between 31 B.C.E. and 14 C.E. he laid the groundwork for several centuries of stability and prosperity in the Roman Empire.

Roman Aqueduct near Tarragona The growth of towns and cities challenged Roman officials to provide an adequate supply of water. Aqueducts channeled water from a source, sometimes many miles away, to an urban complex using only the force of gravity. To bring water from high ground into the city, Roman engineers designed long, continuous rows of arches that maintained a steady downhill slope. Scholars can sometimes estimate the population of an ancient city by calculating the amount of water that was available to it.

So popular was Augustus that four members of his family succeeded to the position of "emperor" (as we call it) despite serious personal and political shortcomings. After the mid-first century C.E., other families obtained the post. In theory, the Senate affirmed the early emperors; in reality, the armies chose them. By the second century C.E., the so-called Good Emperors instituted a new mechanism of succession: each designated as his successor a mature man of proven ability whom he adopted as his son and with whom he shared offices and privileges.

Augustus had allied himself with the ***equites***, the class of well-to-do Italian merchants and landowners second in wealth and social status only to the senatorial class. These competent and self-assured individuals became the core of a new civil service. At last Rome had an administrative bureaucracy capable of managing a large empire with considerable honesty, consistency, and efficiency.

An Urban Empire

Calling the Roman Empire of the first three centuries C.E. an "urban" empire does not mean that most people lived in cities and towns. Perhaps 80 percent of the empire's 50 to 60 million people lived in agricultural villages or on isolated farms. The network of towns and cities served as administrative centers, however, with corresponding benefits for the urban populace.

Numerous towns had several thousand inhabitants. A handful of major cities—Alexandria in Egypt, Antioch in Syria, and Carthage—had populations of several hundred thousand. Rome itself had approximately a million residents. The largest cities put huge strains on the government's technical ability to provide food and water and remove sewage.

At Rome, the upper classes lived in elegant hillside townhouses. The house centered around an *atrium*, a rectangular courtyard with an open skylight to let in light and rainwater for drinking and washing. A dining room for dinner and drinking parties, an interior garden, a kitchen, and perhaps a private bath surrounded the atrium with bedrooms on an upper level. Pebble mosaics on the floors and frescoes of mythological

equites In ancient Italy, prosperous landowners second in wealth and status to the senatorial aristocracy. The Roman emperors allied with this group to counterbalance the influence of the old aristocracy and used the *equites* to staff the imperial civil service.

Roman Shop Selling Food and Drink The bustling town of Pompeii on the Bay of Naples was buried in ash by the eruption of Mt. Vesuvius in 79 C.E. Archaeologists have unearthed the streets, stores, and houses of this typical Roman town. Shops such as this sold hot food and drink served from clay vessels set into the counter. Shelves and niches behind the counter contained other items. In the background can be seen a well-paved street and a public fountain where the inhabitants could fetch water.

Courtesy, Leo C Curran

scenes or outdoor vistas on the walls and ceilings gave a sense of openness in the absence of windows. Many aristocrats owned a number of villas in the countryside as retreats from the pressures of city life.

The poor inhabited crowded slums in the lowlying parts of the city. Damp, dark, and smelly, with few furnishings, their wooden tenements suffered from frequent fires. Fortunately, Romans could spend the day outdoors for much of the year.

Other cities and towns, including the ramshackle settlements that sprang up beside frontier forts, mirrored the capital city in political organization, physical layout, and appearance. A town council and two annually elected officials drawn from prosperous members of the community maintained law and order and collected both urban and rural taxes. In return for the privilege of running local affairs and in appreciation of the state's protection of their wealth and position, this "municipal aristocracy" served Rome loyally. In striving to imitate Roman senators, they lavishly endowed their cities and towns, which had little revenue of their own, with attractive elements of Roman urban life: a forum, government buildings, temples, gardens, baths, theaters, amphitheaters, and games and public entertainments of all sorts. These amenities made the situation of the urban poor superior to that of the rural poor. Poor people in a city could pass time at the baths, seek refuge from the elements under the colonnades, and attend the games.

Hard work and drudgery marked life in the countryside, relieved only by occasional festive days and the everyday pleasures of sex, family, and social exchange. Rural people had to fend for themselves in dealing with bandits, wild animals, and other hazards. People outside urban centers had little direct contact with the government beyond an occasional run-in with bullying soldiers and the dreaded arrival of the tax collector.

The concentration of ownership reversed temporarily during the civil wars that ended the Republic; it resumed under the emperors. But the end of new conquests reduced the number of slaves and forced landowners to find new labor. Landlords turned to tenant farmers, whom they allowed to live on and cultivate plots of land in return for a portion of their crop. The landowners themselves still lived in cities and hired foremen to manage their estates. Thus, wealth based on rural productivity became concentrated in the cities.

Some urban dwellers became rich from manufacture and trade. The *pax romana* ("Roman peace"),

pax romana Literally, "Roman peace," it connoted the stability and prosperity that Roman rule brought to the lands of the Roman Empire in the first two centuries C.E. The movement of people and trade goods along Roman roads and safe seas allowed for the spread of cultural practices, technologies, and religious ideas.

the safety and stability guaranteed by Roman might, favored commerce. Meat and vegetables usually could be exchanged only locally because transportation was costly and many products spoiled quickly. The city of Rome, however, depended on grain shipments from Sicily and Egypt to feed its huge population. Special naval squadrons performed this task.

Some exporters dealt in glass, metalwork, delicate pottery, and other fine manufactures. The centers of production, first located in Italy, moved into the provinces as knowledge of the necessary skills spread. Roman armies on the frontiers provided a large market, and their presence promoted the prosperity of border provinces. Other merchants traded in luxury items from beyond the empire's boundaries, especially Chinese silks, Indian spices, and Arabian incense. The tax revenues of rich provinces like Gaul (France) and Egypt flowed to Rome to support the emperor and the central government, and to the frontier provinces to subsidize the armies.

Romanization, the spread of the Latin language and Roman way of life, proved an enduring consequence of empire among the diverse peoples in the western provinces. Hellenism dominated the eastern Mediterranean (see Chapter 4). Portuguese, Spanish, French, Italian, and Romanian evolved from the Latin language, proving that the language of the conquerors spread among the common people as well as the elite. However, in frontier areas along the Rhine and Danube Rivers, where Roman control was tenuous and migrations by Germanic peoples were changing the ethnic balance by the third century C.E., Latin made only limited headway.

The Roman government did not force Romanization. The inhabitants of the provinces themselves chose Latin and adopted cultural practices like wearing the *toga* (the traditional cloak worn by Roman male citizens). Making this choice brought advantages, as do learning English and wearing a suit and tie today in some developing nations. Latin facilitated dealings with the administration and helped merchants get contracts to supply the military. Many also must have been drawn by the aura of success surrounding the language and culture of a people who had created so vast an empire.

As towns sprang up and acquired the Roman urban amenities, they attracted ambitious members of the indigenous populations. The empire gradually and reluctantly extended Roman citizenship, with its attendant privileges, legal protections, and certain tax exemptions, to people living outside Italy. Completing a twenty-six-year term of service in the native military units that backed up the Roman legions earned soldiers citizenship that could pass to their descendants. Emperors granted citizenship to individuals or entire communities as rewards for service. Then in 212 C.E. the emperor Caracalla granted citizenship to all free, adult, male inhabitants of the empire.

The gradual extension of citizenship mirrored the empire's transformation from an Italian dominion over the Mediterranean lands into a commonwealth of peoples. As early as the first century C.E., some of the leading literary and intellectual figures came from the provinces. By the second century, even the emperors hailed from Spain, Gaul, and North Africa.

The Rise of Christianity

The Jewish homeland of Judaea (see Chapter 3), roughly equivalent to present-day Israel, came under direct Roman rule in 6 C.E. Over the next half-century, the insensitivity of the Roman governors to the Jewish belief in one god increased tensions with the inhabitants. Various kinds of opposition to Roman rule sprang up. Many Jews anticipated the arrival of the Messiah, the "Anointed One," presumed to be a military leader who would liberate the Jewish people and drive the Romans out.

It is in this context that we must see the career of **Jesus**, a young carpenter from the Galilee region in northern Israel. In place of what he considered

---

Romanization The process by which the Latin language and Roman culture became dominant in the western provinces of the Roman Empire. The Roman government did not actively seek to Romanize the subject peoples, but indigenous peoples in the provinces often chose to Romanize because of the political and economic advantages that it brought, as well as the allure of Roman success.

Jesus (ca. 5 B.C.E.–34 C.E.) A Jew from Galilee in northern Israel who sought to reform Jewish beliefs and practices. He was executed as a revolutionary by the Romans. Hailed as the Messiah and son of God by his followers, he became the central figure in Christianity, a belief system that developed in the centuries after his death.

excessive concern with money and power among Jewish leaders and perfunctory religious observance by mainstream Jews, Jesus prescribed a return to the personal faith and spirituality of an earlier age. He eventually attracted the attention of the Jewish authorities in Jerusalem, who regarded popular reformers as potential troublemakers. They turned him over to the Roman governor, Pontius Pilate. Jesus was imprisoned, condemned, and executed by crucifixion, a punishment usually reserved for common criminals. His followers, the Apostles, subsequently sought to spread his teachings and their belief that he had been resurrected (returned from death to life) among their fellow Jews.

Paul, a Jew from the Greek city of Tarsus in southern Anatolia, converted to the new creed and between 45 and 58 C.E. devoted himself to spreading the word. Traveling throughout Syria-Palestine, Anatolia, and Greece, he found most Jews unwilling to accept his claim that Jesus was the Messiah and had ushered in a new age. Frustrated, Paul redirected his efforts toward non-Jews (sometimes called "gentiles") who were also experiencing a spiritual hunger. He set up a string of Christian (from the Greek term *christos*, meaning "anointed one," given to Jesus by his followers) communities in the eastern Mediterranean.

Paul's career exemplifies the cosmopolitan nature of the Roman Empire in this era. Speaking both Greek and Aramaic, he moved comfortably between the Greco-Roman and Jewish worlds. He used Roman roads, depended on the peace guaranteed by Roman arms, called on his Roman citizenship to protect him from local authorities, and moved from city to city in his quest for converts.

In 66 C.E., tensions in Roman Judaea erupted in a revolt that lasted until 73. The Jerusalem-based Christian community, which focused on converting Jews, fell victim to the Roman reconquest. This cleared the field for Paul's non-Jewish converts, and Christianity began to diverge more and more from its Jewish roots. The sect grew slowly but steadily. Many early converts came from disenfranchised groups: women, slaves, and the urban poor. They hoped to receive the respect not accorded them in the larger society and to obtain positions of responsibility when the early Christian communities elected their leaders. However, as the religious movement grew and prospered, it developed a hierarchy of priests and bishops and engaged in bitter disputes over theological doctrine (see Chapter 10).

As monotheists forbidden to worship other gods, early Christians met persecution from Roman officials, who often took their refusal to worship the emperor as a sign of disloyalty. Nevertheless, despite mob attacks and occasional government attempts at suppression (or perhaps because of them), the Christian movement continued to attract converts. By the late third century C.E., adherents to Christianity were a sizeable minority within the empire and included many educated and prosperous people holding local and imperial posts.

During the Greek Classical period, a number of "mystery" cults had gained popularity by claiming to provide secret information about the nature of life and death and promising a blessed afterlife to their adherents. In the Hellenistic and Roman periods, belief systems making similar promises arose in the eastern Mediterranean and spread throughout the Greco-Roman lands, responding to a spiritual and intellectual hunger not satisfied by paganism. These included the cults of the mother-goddess Cybele in Anatolia, the Egyptian goddess Isis, and the Iranian sun-god Mithra. As we shall see, the ultimate victory of Christianity over these rivals arose from historical circumstances as much as from spiritual appeal.

Technology and Transformation

The ease and safety of travel brought by Roman arms and engineering helped the early Christians spread their faith. Surviving remnants of roads, fortification walls, aqueducts, and buildings testify to the Romans' engineering expertise. Some of the best engineers served with the army, building bridges, siege works, and siege weapons. In peacetime,

Paul (ca. 5–65 C.E.) A Jew from the Greek city of Tarsus in Anatolia, he initially persecuted the followers of Jesus but became a Christian after receiving a revelation on the road to Syrian Damascus. Taking advantage of his Hellenized background and Roman citizenship, he traveled throughout Syria-Palestine, Anatolia, and Greece, preaching the new religion and establishing churches. Finding his greatest success among pagans ("gentiles"), he began the process by which Christianity separated from Judaism.

soldiers often worked on construction projects. **Aqueducts**—long elevated or underground conduits—used gravity to carry water from a source to an urban center. The Romans pioneered the use of arches, which allowed the even distribution of great weights without thick supporting walls. The invention of concrete—a mixture of lime powder, sand, and water that could be poured into molds—enabled the construction of vast vaulted and domed interior spaces, in contrast to the rectilinear post-and-lintel designs employed by the Greeks and Egyptians.

Defending borders that stretched for thousands of miles posed a great administrative challenge. In a document released after his death, Augustus advised against expanding the empire because the costs of administration and defense would exceed any increase in revenues. His successors' reorganization and redeployment of the Roman army reflect the shift from an offensive to a defensive strategy. Mountains, deserts, and seas protected the empire at most points. But the lengthy Rhine/Danube frontier in Germany and central Europe was vulnerable and thus was guarded by forts whose relatively small garrisons were not always up to the task of repelling raiders. On more desolate frontiers in Britain and North Africa, the Romans built long walls to keep out the peoples who lived beyond.

Most of Rome's neighbors lacked sufficient technology and military organization to pose a serious threat. The one exception lay on the eastern frontier, where the Parthian kingdom controlled the lands that are today Iran and Iraq. Rome and Parthia fought exhaustingly for centuries, with neither side gaining significant territory.

The Roman state prospered for two and a half centuries after Augustus stabilized the political situation and instituted a program of reforms. In the third century C.E., cracks in the edifice became visible. Historians call the period from 235 to 284 C.E. the **third-century crisis**, a time when political, military, and economic problems nearly destroyed the empire. A frequent change of rulers marked the crisis, as twenty or more men claimed the office of emperor during this period. Most reigned for only a few months or years before being overthrown by a rival or killed by their own troops. Germanic peoples on the Rhine/Danube frontier took advantage of the disorders to raid

deep into the empire. For the first time in centuries, Roman cities built protective walls. Some regions, feeling a lack of imperial protection, turned to anyone who promised to put their interests first.

Political and military emergencies devastated the empire's economy. Buying the loyalty of the army and paying to defend the increasingly permeable frontiers drained the treasury. The resultant demands for more tax revenues from the provinces, as well as the interruption of commerce by fighting, eroded urban prosperity. Shortsighted emperors, desperate for cash, secretly reduced the amount of precious metal in Roman coins and pocketed the excess. But the public quickly caught on, and the devalued coinage became less and less acceptable in the marketplace. Indeed, the empire reverted to a barter economy, which curtailed large-scale and long-distance commerce even more.

The municipal aristocracy, once the empire's most vital and public-spirited class, suffered heavily. As town councilors, its members had to make up any shortfall in taxes owed to the state. As the decline in trade eroded their wealth, which often derived from manufacture and commerce, many evaded their civic duties and even went into hiding.

Population shifted out of the cities and into the countryside. Many people sought employment and protection from raiders and government officials on the estates of wealthy and powerful country landowners. Just when things looked bleakest, one man pulled the empire back from the brink. Diocletian, like several other emperors, hailed from one of the eastern European provinces most vulnerable to invasion. Of humble origins, he rose through the ranks of the army

---

aqueduct A conduit, either elevated or underground, that used gravity to carry water from a source to a location—usually a city—that needed it. The Romans built many aqueducts in a period of substantial urbanization.

third-century crisis Historians' term for the political, military, and economic turmoil that beset the Roman Empire during much of the third century C.E.: frequent changes of ruler, civil wars, barbarian invasions, decline of urban centers, and near-destruction of long-distance commerce and the monetary economy. After 284 C.E. Diocletian restored order by making fundamental changes.

and gained power in 284. He was so successful that he ruled for over twenty years and died in bed.

To halt inflation (the process by which prices rise as the value of money declines), Diocletian issued an edict specifying the maximum prices for various commodities and services. To ensure an adequate labor supply in vital services, he froze people in their professions and made them train their sons to succeed them. This unprecedented regulation of prices and vocations had unforeseen consequences. A "black market" arose among buyers and sellers who chose to ignore the price controls. More broadly, many imperial citizens began to see the government as an oppressive entity that no longer deserved their loyalty.

When Diocletian resigned in 305, the old divisiveness reemerged as various claimants battled for the throne. By 324, a general named **Constantine** (r. 306–337) had reunited the empire under his sole rule. In 312, Constantine won a key battle at the Milvian Bridge over the Tiber River near Rome. He later claimed that before this battle, he had seen in the sky a cross (the sign of the Christian God) superimposed on the sun. Believing that the Christian God had helped him achieve the victory, Constantine converted to Christianity. Throughout his reign, he supported the Christian church, although he tolerated other beliefs as well. Historians disagree about whether Constantine's conversion resulted from spiritual motives or from a pragmatic desire to unify the empire under a single religion. Regardless of the reason, large numbers of people now converted because they saw that Christians had advantages over non-Christians in seeking offices and favors.

Constantine also transferred the capital in 324 from Rome to Byzantium, an ancient Greek city on the Bosporus (BAHS-puhr-uhs) strait connecting the Mediterranean and the Black Sea. Renamed Constantinople (cahn-stan-tih-NO-pul) ("City of Constantine"), it represented a concentration of attention on the threatened imperial borders in eastern Europe (see Map 6.1). The cities and middle classes of the eastern provinces had better withstood the third-century crisis than those in the west. In addition, more educated people and more Christians lived in the east (see Chapter 10).

Some see the conversion of Constantine and the transfer of the imperial capital as events marking the

SECTION REVIEW

- From a collection of farming communities, Rome evolved into a republic dominated by wealthy landowning families who controlled the Senate.
- Through a series of wars, the Republic grew into an overseas empire.
- Political crises destroyed the Republic, and under Augustus and his successors, Rome expanded as a prosperous urban empire.
- Christianity emerged from tensions between Jewish and Roman culture and spread through the preaching of Paul of Tarsus.
- The third-century crisis nearly destroyed the empire until Diocletian's reforms stabilized the state briefly.
- Constantine reunited the empire, granted tolerance to Christianity, and moved the capital to Byzantium.

end of Roman history. But many of the important changes that culminated during Constantine's reign had their roots in the previous two centuries, and the Roman Empire as a whole survived for at least another century. Moreover, the eastern, or Byzantine, portion of it (discussed in Chapter 10) survived Constantine by more than a thousand years. Nevertheless, the Roman Empire of the fourth century differed fundamentally from what had existed before, a fact that justifies seeing Constantine's reign as the beginning of a new epoch in the West.

The Origins of Imperial China, 221 B.C.E.–220 C.E.

How did imperial China evolve from its beginnings into the Han state?

A fragmentation seemingly dictated by geography characterized the early history of China (see Chapter 2). The Shang (ca. 1750–1027 B.C.E.) and Zhou (1027–221 B.C.E.) wielded authority over a relatively compact zone in northeastern China. The last few centuries of

Constantine (285–337 C.E.) Roman emperor (r. 306–337). After reuniting the Roman Empire, he moved the capital to Constantinople and made Christianity a favored religion.

nominal Zhou rule—the Warring States Period—saw rivalry among a group of small states, a situation reminiscent of the contemporary Greek city-states (see Chapter 4). As in Greece, competition and conflict fostered many elements of a national culture.

In the second half of the third century B.C.E. the Qin (chin) state in the Wei (way) Valley conquered its rivals and created China's first empire (221–206 B.C.E.). But it barely survived the death of its founder, Shi Huangdi. Power passed to a new dynasty, the Han,

which ruled China from 206 B.C.E. to 220 C.E. (see Map 6.2). The imperial tradition of political and cultural unity thus begun lasted into the twentieth century and still has meaning for China today.

Resources and Population

An imperial state controlling lands of great diversity in topography, climate, plant and animal life, and human population faced greater obstacles to long-distance communications and a uniform way of

Interactive Map

Map 6.2 Han China The Qin and Han rulers of northeast China extended their control over all of eastern China and extensive territories to the west. A series of walls in the north and northwest, built to check the incursions of nomadic peoples from the steppes, were joined together to form the ancestor of the present-day Great Wall of China. An extensive network of roads connecting towns, cities, and frontier forts promoted rapid communication and facilitated trade. The Silk Road carried China's most treasured product to Central, South, and West Asia and the Mediterranean lands.
© Cengage Learning

life than did the Roman Empire. Rome's territories were roughly similar in climate and agriculture, and Rome benefited from an internal sea—the Mediterranean—that facilitated rapid and inexpensive transport. What resources, technologies, institutions, and values made the Chinese empire possible? Agriculture produced the wealth and taxes that supported the institutions of imperial China. The main tax, a percentage of the annual harvest, funded government activities ranging from the luxurious lifestyle of the royal court to the military garrisons on the frontiers. The imperial capitals, first Chang'an (chahng-ahn) and later Luoyang (LWOE-yahng), housed large populations that had to be fed. As intensive agriculture spread in the Yangzi River Valley, the need to transport southern crops to the north spurred the construction of canals to connect the Yangzi with the Yellow River. The government also stored surplus grain during prosperous times for sale at reasonable prices during shortages.

To assess its labor resources, the government periodically conducted a census. Results survive for the years 2 C.E. and 140 C.E. The earlier survey indicates approximately 12 million households and 60 million people; the later, not quite 10 million households and 49 million people. Then as now, the vast majority of the population lived in the eastern river-valley regions that supported intensive agriculture. The early demographic center in the Yellow River Valley and North China Plain had begun to shift south to the Yangzi River Valley by early Han times.

In the intervals between seasonal agricultural tasks, able-bodied men donated one month of labor to public building projects—palaces, temples, fortifications, and roads—or to transporting goods, excavating and maintaining canals, cultivating imperial estates, or mining. The state also required two years of military service. On the frontiers, conscripted young Chinese men built walls and forts, kept an eye on barbarian neighbors, fought when necessary, and grew crops to support themselves. Registers of land and households enabled imperial officials to keep track of money and services due. Like the Romans, the Chinese governments depended on a large population of free peasants to contribute taxes and services to the state.

Throughout the Han dynasty, the Han Chinese gradually expanded into the territory of other ethnic groups. Population growth in the core regions and a shortage of good land spurred the pioneers onward. Sometimes the government organized new settlements—at strategic sites, for example, and on the frontiers. Neighboring kingdoms also invited Chinese settlers so they could exploit their skills and learn their technologies.

Han people preferred regions suitable to the agriculture they had practiced in the eastern river valleys. On the northern frontier, they pushed back nomadic populations. They also expanded into the tropical forests of southern China and settled in the western oases. Places not suitable for their preferred kind of agriculture, particularly the steppe and deserts, did not attract them.

Hierarchy, Obedience, and Belief

The Han Chinese brought with them their social organization, values, language, and other cultural practices. The Chinese family, the basic social unit, included not only the living generations but also the ancestors. The Chinese believed their ancestors maintained an ongoing interest in the fortunes of the family and therefore consulted, appeased, and venerated their ancestors to maintain their favor. Viewed as a living, self-renewing organism, the family required sons to perpetuate itself and ensure the immortality offered by the ancestor cult.

The doctrine of Confucius (Kongzi), which had its origins in the sixth century B.C.E. (see Chapter 2), became a fundamental source of values in the imperial period. Confucianism considered hierarchy a natural social phenomenon and assigned tasks and rules of conduct to each person. Absolute authority rested with the father, who presided over the rituals that linked living family members to the ancestors. People saw themselves as having responsibilities within the domestic hierarchy according to gender, age, and family relationship rather than as individual agents. The same concepts operated in society as a whole. Peasants, soldiers, administrators, and rulers all contributed distinctively to the welfare of society. Confucianism optimistically maintained that education, imitation of role models, and self-improvement could guide people to the right path. Because the state mirrored the family, the basic family values of loyalty, obedience to authority, respect for elders and ancestors, and concern for honor and appropriate conduct carried over into relations between individuals and the state.

Contemporary written sources say little about the experiences of women. Confucian ethics stressed the impropriety of women participating in public life. Traditional wisdom about the appropriate female conduct appears in a story of the mother of the Confucian philosopher Mencius (Mengzi):

> A woman's duties are to cook the five grains, heat the wine, look after her parents-in-law, make clothes, and that is all! . . . [She] has no ambition to manage affairs outside the house. . . . She must follow the "three submissions." When she is young, she must submit to her parents. After her marriage, she must submit to her husband. When she is widowed, she must submit to her son.[1]

This ideal, perpetuated by males of the upper classes who composed most of the surviving texts, placed women under considerable pressure to conform. Women of the lower classes, less affected by Confucian ways of thinking, may have been less constrained than their more "privileged" counterparts.

After her parents arranged her marriage, a young bride went to live with her husband's family, who saw her as a stranger until she proved herself. Ability and force of personality (as well as the capacity to produce sons) could make a difference, but dissension between the wife and her mother-in-law and sisters-in-law grew out of their competition for influence with husbands, sons, and brothers and for a larger share of the economic resources held in common by the family.

Like the early Romans, the Chinese believed that divinity resided within nature rather than outside and above it. They worshiped and tried to appease the forces of nature. The state maintained shrines to the lords of rain and winds, as well as to certain great rivers and high mountains. Gathering at mounds or altars dedicated to local earth spirits, people sacrificed sheep and pigs and beat drums to promote fertility. Unusual natural phenomena like eclipses or heavy rains prompted them to tie a red cord around the sacred spot, symbolically restraining the deity. A belief that supernatural forces, bringing good and evil fortune, flowed through the landscape led experts in *feng shui*, "earth divination," to determine the most favorable location and orientation for buildings and graves. The faithful adapted their lives to the complex rhythms of nature.

Some people sought to cheat death by taking life-enhancing drugs or building ostentatious tombs, flanked by towers or covered by mounds of earth, and filling them with what they believed they would need for a blessed afterlife. The objects in these tombs provide a wealth of knowledge about Han society.

The First Chinese Empire

As mentioned, in the second half of the third century B.C.E., the state of the **Qin** suddenly burst forth and took over the other "warring states" one by one. By 221 B.C.E., the first emperor had united the northern plain and the Yangzi River Valley under one rule, marking the creation of China and the inauguration of the imperial age. The name *China* may derive from *Qin*.

The Qin ruler, entitled **Shi Huangdi** ("First Emperor"), and his adviser Li Si were able and ruthless men who exploited the exhaustion resulting from centuries of interstate rivalry. The Qin homeland in the valley of the Wei, a tributary of the Yellow River, provided a large pool of sturdy peasants to serve in the army but was less urbanized and commercialized than the kingdoms farther east. Mobilizing manpower for irrigation and flood control works had

Primary Source: Lessons for Women Get a taste of what life was like for women of the Han state.

Qin A people and state in the Wei Valley of eastern China that conquered rival states and created the first Chinese empire (221–206 B.C.E.). The Qin ruler, Shi Huangdi, standardized many features of Chinese society and ruthlessly marshaled subjects for military and construction projects, engendering hostility that led to the fall of his dynasty shortly after his death. The Qin framework was largely taken over by the succeeding Han Empire.

Shi Huangdi Founder of the short-lived Qin dynasty and creator of the first Chinese Empire (r. 221–210 B.C.E.). He is remembered for his ruthless conquests of rival states, standardization of practices, and forcible organization of labor for military and engineering tasks. His tomb, with its army of life-size terracotta soldiers, has been partially excavated.

Terracotta Soldiers from the Tomb of Shi Huangdi, "First Emperor" of China Thousands of these life-size, baked-clay figures, each with distinctive features, have been unearthed. This buried model army reflects the power and totalitarian rule of the Qin Empire.

History in Focus *What does this image suggest about the political situation in which Shi Huangdi came to imperial power? Find the answer online.*

strengthened the authority of the Qin king at the expense of the nobles and taught his administrators organizational skills.

Shi Huangdi and Li Si created a totalitarian structure that subordinated the individual to the needs of the state. They cracked down on Confucianism, regarding its demands for benevolent and nonviolent conduct from rulers as a check on the absolute power they sought. They favored instead a philosophy known as Legalism (see Chapter 2). Its major proponent, Li Si himself, considered the will of the ruler supreme. Discipline and obedience maintained through the rigid application of rewards and punishments defined the lives of his subjects.

The new regime sought to eliminate the landowning aristocracy of the conquered states and the system supporting their wealth and power. It abolished primogeniture—the eldest son's inheritance of a family's lands—because it allowed a few individuals to accumulate vast estates. Estates now had to be broken up and passed on to several heirs.

Slaves and peasant serfs, who owed the landlord a substantial portion of their harvest, worked the

lands of the aristocracy. The Qin abolished slavery and established a free peasantry who owed taxes and labor, as well as military service, to the state.

During the Warring States Period, the small states had emphasized their independence through differing symbolic practices. For example, each state had its own forms of music, with different scales, systems of notation, and instruments. The Qin imposed standard weights, measures, and coinage, a uniform law code, a common system of writing, and even regulations governing the axle length of carts so as to standardize road and street widths.

Thousands of miles of roads, comparable in scale to the roads of the Roman Empire, connected the parts of the empire and helped move Qin armies quickly. The Qin also built canals to connect the northern and southern river systems. The 20-mile-long (32.2-kilometer-long) Magic Canal, which ingeniously linked two rivers that flowed in opposite directions with strong currents, is still in use. The frontier walls of the old states were gradually combined into a continuous barricade, the precursor of the Great Wall, to protect cultivated lands from raids by northern nomads. But

Shi Huangdi's financial exploitation and demands for forced labor led, after his death in 210 B.C.E., to rebellions that ended the dynasty.

The Long Reign of the Han

When the dust cleared, Liu Bang, possibly a peasant by background, established a new dynasty, the **Han** (206 B.C.E.–220 C.E.). Rejecting the excesses and mistakes of the Qin, he restored the institutions of a venerable past. Yet the Han administration retained much of the structure and Legalist ideology put in place by the Qin, though with less fanatical zeal. A form of Confucianism revised to address the circumstances of a large, centralized political entity tempered the Legalist methods. This Confucianism emphasized the benevolence of government and the appropriateness of particular rituals and behaviors in a manifestly hierarchical society. The Han administration became the standard for later ages, and the Chinese people today refer to themselves ethnically as Han.

After eighty years of imperial consolidation, Emperor Wu (r. 140–87 B.C.E.) launched a period of military expansion, south into Fujian, Guangdong, and present-day North Vietnam and north into Manchuria and present-day North Korea. Han armies went west, to inner Mongolia and Xinjiang (SHIN-jyahng), to secure the lucrative Silk Road (see Chapter 8). However, controlling the newly acquired territories proved expensive, so Wu's successors curtailed further expansion.

The Han Empire endured, with a brief interruption, for more than four hundred years. **Chang'an**, in the Wei Valley, an ancient seat of power from which the Zhou and Qin dynasties had emerged, served as the capital from 202 B.C.E. to 8 C.E.—the period of the Early, or Western, Han. From 23 to 220 C.E., the Later, or Eastern, Han established its base in the more centrally located Luoyang.

A wall of pounded earth and brick 15 miles (24 kilometers) in circumference surrounded Chang'an, which had a population of 246,000 in 2 C.E. Contemporaries described it as a bustling place, filled with courtiers, officials, soldiers, merchants, craftsmen, and foreign visitors. Broad thoroughfares running north and south intersected others running east and west. High walls protected and restricted access to the imperial palaces, administrative offices, barracks, and storehouses. Temples and marketplaces were scattered about the civic center. Chang'an became a model of urban planning, its main features being imitated throughout the Han Empire.

Living in multistory houses, wearing fine silks, and traveling about the capital in ornate horse-drawn carriages, well-to-do officials and merchants devoted their leisure time to art and literature, occult religious practices, elegant banquets, and various entertainments: music and dance, juggling and acrobatics, dog and horse races, cock and tiger fights. Common people inhabited a sprawling warren of alleys, living in dwellings packed "as closely as the teeth of a comb," as one poet put it.

As in the Zhou monarchy (see Chapter 2), people thought that the emperor, the "Son of Heaven," enjoyed the Mandate of Heaven, standing at the center of government and society like a father wielding authority in a family and linking the living generations with the ancestors. The emperor brought the support of powerful imperial ancestors and guaranteed the harmonious interaction of Heaven and earth. More than his Roman counterpart, he was regarded as a divinity on earth. His word was law. Failure to govern well, however, could lose him the backing of Heaven. Given their belief that events in Heaven, the natural world, and human society corresponded, his subjects might regard floods, droughts, and earthquakes as both the consequences and symptoms of ethical failure and mismanagement. Successful revolutions thus proved to many that Heaven had withdrawn its support from an unworthy ruler.

Secluded within the palace compound, surrounded by his many wives and children, servants, courtiers, and officials, the emperor presided over an unceasing round of pomp and ritual emphasizing

---

Han A term used to designate the ethnic Chinese people who originated in the Yellow River Valley and spread throughout regions of China suitable for agriculture, as well as the dynasty of emperors who ruled from 206 B.C.E. to 220 C.E.

Chang'an City in the Wei Valley in eastern China. It became the capital of the Qin and early Han Empires. Its main features were imitated in the cities and towns that sprang up throughout the Han Empire.

the worship of Heaven and imperial ancestors, as well as the practical business of government. When the emperor died, his chief widow chose his heir from the male members of the ruling clan, thus making the royal compound a hive of intrigue.

A prime minister, a civil service director, and nine ministers charged with military, economic, legal, and religious responsibilities ran the central government. As in imperial Rome, the Han depended on local officials for the day-to-day administration of the vast empire. Local people collected taxes and dispatched revenues to the central government, oversaw conscription for the army and labor projects, provided local protection, and settled disputes. The remote central government rarely impinged on the lives of most citizens, who normally contacted only local officials. Who, then, were these local officials?

The Han period saw the rise of a class that scholars call the **gentry**. To weaken the rural aristocrats, the Qin and Han emperors allied themselves with the class next in wealth below them. These moderately prosperous landowners, usually men with education and valued expertise, resembled the Roman *equites* favored by Augustus and his successors. The local officials who came from this class became a privileged and respected group within Chinese society and made the government more efficient and responsive.

The new gentry class, with imperial support, adopted a version of Confucianism that provided a system for training officials to be intellectually capable and morally worthy of their roles and set forth a code of conduct for measuring their performance. Chinese tradition speaks of an imperial university, located outside Chang'an and said to have thirty thousand students, as well as provincial centers of learning. From these centers, students entered government service, receiving distinctive emblems and privileges, including preferential legal treatment and exemption from military service, as they advanced in rank. In theory, young men from any class could rise in the state hierarchy. In practice, sons of the gentry had an advantage because they received better training in the Confucian classics. Gradually, the gentry became a new aristocracy of sorts, banding together in cliques and family alliances that worked to advance the careers of group members.

Daoism, which originated in the Warring States Period (see Chapter 2), took deeper root among the common people in the Han period. With its emphasis on the *Dao,* or "path," of nature, its valuing of harmony with the cycles and patterns of the natural world, and its search for enlightenment through solitary contemplation and physical and mental discipline rather than education, Daoism called into question age-old beliefs and values and rejected the hierarchy, rules, and rituals of Confucianism. It urged passive acceptance of the disorder of the world, denial of ambition, contentment with simple pleasures, and trust in one's own instincts.

Technology and Trade

Chinese tradition, which seems to recognize the importance of technology for the success and spread of Chinese civilization, credits the legendary first five emperors with the introduction of major new technologies.

The advent of bronze tools around 1500 B.C.E. helped open land for agriculture on the North China Plain. A millennium later, iron arrived, and the Qin took full advantage of this technology. Chinese metalworkers used more advanced techniques than metalworkers elsewhere in the world. Whereas Roman blacksmiths produced wrought-iron tools and weapons by hammering heated iron, the Chinese mastered the technique of liquefying iron and pouring it into molds. The resulting cast-iron and steel tools and weapons had a higher carbon content and were harder and more durable.

In the succeeding centuries, crossbows and cavalry helped the Chinese military to beat off the attacks of nomads. The watermill, which harnessed the power of running water to turn a grindstone, appeared in China long before it did in Europe. Horse collar and breast strap harnessing that did not constrict the animal's neck allowed horses in China to pull heavier loads than European horses could.

gentry In China, the class of prosperous families, next in wealth below the rural aristocrats, from which the emperors drew their administrative personnel. Respected for their education and expertise, these officials became a privileged group and made the government more efficient and responsive than in the past.

Han-Era (First Century B.C.E.) Stone Rubbing of a Horse-Drawn Carriage The "trace harness," a strap running across the horse's chest, was a Chinese invention that allowed horses to pull far heavier loads than were possible with the constricting throat harness used in Europe. In the Han period, officials, professionals, and soldiers who served the regime enjoyed a lifestyle made pleasant by fine clothing, comfortable transportation, servants, and delightful pastimes, but at the same time they were guided by a Confucian emphasis on duty, honesty, and appropriate behavior. From Wu family shrine, Jiaxiang, Shantung. From *Chin-shih-so* [Jinshisuo]

The Han rulers continued the Qin road-building program. Besides using the roads to move troops and supplies, the government created a network of official couriers using horses, boats, and even footpaths, with food and shelter provided at relay stations. Canal construction also continued, and river navigation improved.

The population growth and increasing trade that resulted gave rise to local market centers. Some of these became county seats from which imperial officials operated. Estimates of the proportion of the population living in Han towns and cities range from 10 percent, a number roughly comparable to Europe, to 30 percent.

Silk dominated China's export trade. Silk cocoons are secreted onto the leaves of mulberry trees by silkworms. The Chinese understood this and kept it a closely guarded secret, which gave them a monopoly on the manufacture of silk. Carried through the Central Asian oases to the Middle East, India, and the Mediterranean, and passing through the hands of middlemen who added their own fees to the price, this beautiful textile may have increased in value a hundred-fold by the end of its journey. Controlling the Silk Road and its profits justified periodic military campaigns into Central Asia and the installation there of garrisons and Chinese colonies.

The Decline of the Han Empire

For the Han, as for the Romans, maintaining frontier security, particularly in the north and northwest, posed a serious challenge. In the end, non-Chinese peoples raiding across the frontier or moving into imperial territory proved a major factor in bringing the empire down.

The different ways of life of farmers, who usually accepted Han rule, and herders, who preferred their own kings, gave rise to insulting stereotypes on both sides. The settled Chinese thought of nomads as "barbarians"—rough, uncivilized people—a viewpoint much like that of the Romans, who looked down on the Germanic peoples on their frontiers.

Often, the closeness of herding and farming populations led to commercial exchange. The nomads sought agricultural products and crafted goods, while the settled peoples bought horses and other herd animals and animal products. Sometimes, however, nomad raiders seized what they wanted from farming

Gold Belt Buckle, Xiongnu, Second Century B.C.E.
The Xiongnu, herders in the lands north of China, shared the artistic conventions of nomadic peoples across the steppes of Eurasia, such as this fluid, twisting representation of the animals on which they depended for their livelihood. Shi Huangdi's military incursions into their pasturelands in the late third century B.C.E. catalyzed the formation of the Xiongnu Confederacy, whose horse-riding warriors challenged the Chinese for centuries.   Image copyright © The Metropolitan Museum of Art/Art Resource, NY

settlements. Tough and warlike because of their way of life, mounted nomads struck swiftly and as swiftly disappeared.

Although nomadic groups tended to be small and inclined to fight one another, circumstances and a charismatic leader could bring them together from time to time. In the Han period, the **Xiongnu** (SHE-OONG-noo), a great confederacy of Turkic peoples, threatened the empire, though they were usually contained on the frontier by cavalry forces created to match the nomads' mobility. This strategy made access to good horses and pastureland a state priority. Other strategies included maintaining garrisons and colonies of soldier-farmers on the frontier, settling compliant nomads within the borders to serve as a buffer, bribing nomad chiefs to promote disunity, and paying protection money. The "tributary system," in which nomad rulers accepted Chinese supremacy and exchanged tribute payments for marriages to Chinese princesses, receptions at court, and imperial gifts worth more than the tribute, often worked well.

Yet military vigilance burdened Han finances and made the economic troubles of later Han times worse. Despite measures to suppress the aristocracy and turn land over to a free peasantry, by the end of the first century B.C.E. nobles and successful merchants again acquired control of huge estates, and many peasants sought their protection against the exactions of the imperial government. This trend spread over the next two centuries. As strongmen largely independent of imperial control emerged, the central government lost tax revenues and manpower. Military conscription broke down, forcing the government to hire more and more foreign soldiers and officers. These served for pay, but their loyalty was weak.

The Han regime fell in 220 C.E. for several reasons: factional intrigues within the ruling clan, official corruption and inefficiency, uprisings of desperate and hungry peasants, the spread of banditry, unsuccessful reform movements, attacks by nomads, and the ambitions of rural warlords. China entered a period of political fragmentation and economic and cultural regression that lasted until the rise of the Sui (sway) and Tang (tahng) dynasties in the late sixth and early seventh centuries C.E., a story that we take up in Chapter 11.

Xiongnu A confederation of nomadic peoples living beyond the northwest frontier of ancient China. Chinese rulers tried a variety of defenses and stratagems to ward off these "barbarians," as they called them, and finally succeeded in dispersing the Xiongnu in the first century C.E.

- Imperial China rested on a foundation of agriculture, and periodic censuses ensured a ready supply of labor for public works.

- The extended family was the basic social unit, and Confucianism provided the value system.

- The Qin established the first empire, in which all individuality was subordinate to the state.

- Under the Han dynasty, the empire grew, the Confucian scholar-official rose to prominence, and Daoism gained more popularity with the common people.

- The Qin and Han periods saw technological advancement, steady urbanization, and expansion of the silk trade.

- The burden of defense against nomadic invaders weakened the empire, which collapsed because of several factors, ushering in a period of fragmentation.

Conclusion

Agriculture was the fundamental economic activity and source of government revenues in both Roman and Chinese civilizations. Both empires depended initially on free peasantry—sturdy farmers who could be pressed into military service or other forms of compulsory labor. Conflicts over who owned the land and how it was to be used caused political and social turmoil in both places. Roman and Chinese autocratic rulers secured their positions by breaking the power of old aristocratic families, seizing their excess land, and giving it to small farmers and to themselves. Later, when wealthy noblemen again gained control of vast estates worked by dependent tenant farmers, the authority of the state eroded.

From ethnically homogeneous cores, both empires spread into territories with diverse ecosystems, populations, and ways of life. The cultural unity that resulted has persisted, at least in part, to the present day. Military conquest paved the way, but Italian and Han settlers, outstripping the resources of their core areas, moved into new regions, bringing along their languages, beliefs, customs, and technologies. Conquered peoples were also attracted to the culture and success of the ruler nation. To administer far-flung territories and large populations, both empires

delegated considerable autonomy to local officials. Administrators were drawn from educated and capable members of a prosperous middle class.

Roads built to expedite the movement of troops became the highways of commerce and culture. Urban networks provided local administrative bases, furthering commerce and radiating imperial culture to the countryside. While a large majority of the population lived in the country, city-dwellers enjoyed most of the advantages of empire. Rome and Chang'an provided models for outlying cities. Travelers could find in outlying regions the same types and styles of buildings and public spaces that they knew from the capital.

Similar problems of defense—long borders located far from the capital and aggressive neighbors—prompted both empires to build walls and chains of forts to protect against incursions. Frontier defense was so costly that it eventually eroded both empires' prosperity. As governments demanded more taxes and services from the civilian population, they lost the loyalty of the people, many of whom sought protection on the estates of powerful landowners. The Roman and Han governments eventually came to rely on soldiers hired from the same "barbarian" peoples confronting them on the frontiers. As the empires became weaker, the borders were overrun and the central governments collapsed. Ironically, the triumphant immigrant groups respected the imperial culture so deeply that they strove to maintain it once they were in power.

Though the empires failed in similar fashion, the long-term consequences differed. In China the imperial model revived in subsequent eras, but the lands of the Roman Empire never reunified. One reason is that the two cultures had different attitudes toward the individual and the state. In China individuals were deeply embedded in families with precisely defined hierarchies, unquestioning obedience, and solemn rituals of deference to elders and ancestors. Respect for authority was deep-seated. Confucianism, which sanctified family hierarchy and provided a code of conduct for public officials, preceded the imperial system. This cultural base could adapt with little change to diverse political circumstances. The Roman family also respected hierarchy and obedience, but it was not the organizational model of the Roman state.

Confucianism had no Roman equivalent to orient society when the state collapsed.

Moreover, opportunities for economic and social mobility were greater in the Roman Empire than in ancient China. Whereas the merchant class in China was frequently disparaged and constrained by the government, the absence of government interference in the Roman Empire resulted in greater economic mobility and a thriving and influential middle class in the towns and cities. The Roman army also differed from the Chinese, the former being composed of professional soldiers who increasingly gained privileges and took part in political conflict, and the latter relying on draftees who served for two years and remained on the margins of power struggles.

Although Roman emperors tried to create an ideology to bolster their position, Republican traditions and ambiguities about the imperial role stemming from the time of Augustus presented obstacles. Thus Roman rulers were likely to be chosen by the army or by the Senate. The dynastic principle never took root, and the cult of the emperor had little spiritual content. In contrast, the Chinese believed that the emperor was the divine Son of Heaven and drew authority from the power of the royal ancestors.

Finally, Christianity's insistence on monotheism negated the Roman emperor's pretensions to divinity, which had evolved from Hellenistic polytheism. The spread of Christianity during the Late Roman Empire and the decline of the western half of the empire in the fifth century C.E. (see Chapter 10) constituted an irreversible break with the past. By contrast, Buddhism, which came to China in the early centuries C.E. and flourished in the post-Han era (see Chapter 11), was more easily reconciled with traditional Chinese values and beliefs.

CHAPTER REVIEW

 Download the MP3 audio file of the Chapter Review to listen to on the go.

How did Rome create and maintain its vast Mediterranean empire? (page 135)

The Romans were successful empire-builders because of their superior military organization and training, and a series of very capable generals. They co-opted the ruling elites and brought peace and prosperity to the peoples of the lands they annexed. Yet Rome's military success led to social and economic disruption and acute political struggles. Out of this crisis emerged the Principate, which persevered for several centuries. The emperors developed more effective administrative techniques, and local elites embraced Roman culture.

How did imperial China evolve from its beginnings into the Han state? (page 148)

In China, the "First Emperor" established the Qin Empire with key elements for unification already in place. The preceding Shang and Zhou states, though not empires, had controlled the North China Plain and developed the concept of the Mandate of Heaven, a claim to divine backing for the ruler as the Son of Heaven. Furthermore, the Legalist political philosophy justified authoritarian measures. But the harshness of the new order generated resistance that soon brought down the Qin, and its Han successors built a durable imperial regime on a moderated version of Qin structures that incorporated Confucian principles.

Key Terms

Roman Republic *(p. 137)*	Paul *(p. 146)*
Roman Senate *(p. 137)*	aqueduct *(p. 147)*
patron/client relationship *(p. 137)*	third-century crisis *(p. 147)*
	Constantine *(p. 148)*
Roman Principate *(p. 142)*	Qin *(p. 151)*
Augustus *(p. 142)*	Shi Huangdi *(p. 151)*
equites *(p. 143)*	Han *(p. 153)*
pax romana *(p. 144)*	Chang'an *(p. 153)*
Romanization *(p. 145)*	gentry *(p. 154)*
Jesus *(p. 145)*	Xiongnu *(p. 156)*

Web Resources

Pronunciation Guide

Interactive Maps

- MAP 5.1 The Roman Empire
- MAP 5.2 Han China

 Visit the CourseMate website at www.cengagebrain.com for additional study tools and review materials for this chapter.

Primary Sources

- A Man of Unlimited Ambition: Julius Caesar
- Lessons for Women

Answer to the History in Focus Question

See photo on page 152, "Terracotta Soldiers from the Tomb of Shi Huangdi, 'First Emperor' of China."

Peoples and Civilizations of the Americas

© Cengage Learning

CHAPTER PREVIEW

 Visit the CourseMate website at **www.cengagebrain.com** for additional study tools and review materials for this chapter.

160

Humans reached the Western Hemisphere through a series of migrations from Asia. Some scholars believe that the first migrations occurred as early as 35,000 to 25,000 B.C.E., but most accept a later date of 20,000 to 13,000 B.C.E. Although some limited contacts with other cultures—for example, with Polynesians—may have occurred later, the peoples in the Western Hemisphere were virtually isolated from the rest of the world for at least 15,000 years. Thus, while technological innovations passed back and forth among the civilizations of Asia, Africa, and Europe, the peoples of the Americas faced the challenges of the natural environment on their own.

As people spread throughout the hemisphere, they encountered environments that ranged from polar extremes to tropical rain forests to towering mountain ranges. Mesoamerica (Mexico and northern Central America) and the mountainous Andean region of South America proved conducive to the emergence of complex societies. Well before 1000 B.C.E., plant domestication, technological innovation, and a limited trade led to greater social stratification and the beginnings of urbanization in both regions. Cultural elites used their increasing political and religious authority to organize great numbers of laborers for projects such as large-scale irrigation and drainage works, cleared forests, and hillside terracing, thus providing the economic platform for the construction of urban centers.

The Amerindian[1] hereditary elites organized their societies to meet these challenges, even as their ambitions ignited new conflicts. No single set of political institutions or technologies worked in every environment, and American cultures varied widely. Productive and diversified agriculture and cities that rivaled the Chinese and Roman capitals in size and beauty developed in Mesoamerica and the Andean region of South America. In the rest of the hemisphere, indigenous peoples maintained a wide variety of settlement patterns, political forms, and cultural traditions based on combinations of hunting and agriculture.

First Civilizations of the Americas: The Olmec and Chavín, 1200–250 B.C.E.

What role did nature and the environment play in the early civilizations of the Americas?

By 1000 B.C.E. the major urban centers of Mesoamerica and the Andes, dominated by monumental structures devoted to religions and the elite, had begun to project their political and cultural power over broad territories: they had become civilizations. The cultural legacies of the two most important of these early civilizations, the Olmec of Mesoamerica and the Chavín of the Andes, would persist for more than a thousand years.

The Mesoamerican Olmec, 1200–400 B.C.E.

Mesoamerica is extremely active geologically, experiencing both earthquakes and volcanic eruptions. Mountain ranges break the region into microenvironments, including the temperate climates of the Valley of Mexico and the Guatemalan highlands, the tropical forests of the Peten and Gulf of Mexico coast, the rain forest of the southern Yucatán and Belize, and the drier scrub forest of the northern Yucatán (see Map 7.1).

Within these ecological niches, craftsmen made use of a wide variety of indigenous plants, as well as minerals like obsidian, quartz, and jade. But no animals were domesticated. Eventually, contacts across these environmental boundaries led to trade and cultural exchange. Enhanced trade, increasing agricultural productivity, and rising population led, in turn, to urbanization and the appearance of powerful political and religious elites. Yet even though all Mesoamerican civilizations shared fundamental elements of material culture, technology, religious belief and ritual, political organization, art, architecture, and sports, the region was never unified politically.

The most influential early Mesoamerican civilization was the Olmec, flourishing between 1200 and 400 B.C.E. (see Map 7.1). The center of Olmec civilization was located near the tropical Atlantic coast of what are now the Mexican states of Veracruz and Tabasco. Olmec cultural influence reached as far as

Map 7.1 Olmec and Chavín Civilizations The regions of Mesoamerica and the Andean highlands of South America have hosted impressive civilizations since early times. The civilizations of the Olmec and Chavín were the originating civilizations of these two regions, providing the foundations of architecture, city planning, and religion. © Cengage Learning

Interactive Map

Major Olmec sites, ca. 1200–300 B.C.E.

▲ Olmec-influenced site

Chavín cultural zone, ca. 1200–200 B.C.E.

■ Chavín-influenced site

the Pacific coast of Central America and the Central Plateau of Mexico.

The earliest settlements in the region depended on rich plant diversity and fishing, but by 3500 B.C.E. the staples of the Mesoamerican diet—maize, beans, and squash—had been domesticated. Manioc, a calorie-rich root crop, was also grown in the floodplains of the region. The ability of farmers to produce dependable surpluses of these products permitted the first stages of craft specialization and social stratification. As religious and political elites emerged, they used their prestige and authority to organize the population to dig irrigation and drainage canals, develop raised fields in wetlands that could be farmed more

intensively, and construct the large-scale religious and civic buildings that became the cultural signature of Olmec civilization.

San Lorenzo and some smaller centers nearby formed the cultural core of the early **Olmec** civilization (1200–900 B.C.E.). La Venta (la-BEN-tah), which

---

Olmec The first Mesoamerican civilization. Between ca. 1200 and 400 B.C.E., the Olmec people of central Mexico created a vibrant civilization that included intensive agriculture, wide-ranging trade, ceremonial centers, and monumental construction. The Olmec had great cultural influence on later Mesoamerican societies.

Chronology

	Mesoamerica	Northern Peoples	Andes
3500 B.C.E.	3500 B.C.E. Early agriculture		3500 B.C.E. Early agriculture
			2600 B.C.E. Rise of Caral
1200 B.C.E.	1200–900 B.C.E. Rise of Olmec civilization centered on San Lorenzo		
900 B.C.E.	900–600 B.C.E. La Venta, the dominant Olmec center		900–250 B.C.E. Chavín civilization
500 B.C.E.			500 B.C.E. Early metallurgy
100 B.C.E.	100 B.C.E. Teotihuacan founded		
100 C.E.		100–400 Hopewell culture in Ohio River Valley	
200			200–700 Moche culture of Peruvian coast
	250 Maya early classic period begins		
500			500–1000 Tiwanaku and Wari control Peruvian highlands
700		700 Anasazi and Mississippian cultures begin	
800	CA. 750 Teotihuacan destroyed 800–900 Maya centers abandoned, end of classic period		
900	968 Toltec capital of Tula founded		
1000		1050–1250 Cahokia reaches peak power	
1100	1156 Tula destroyed	1150 Collapse of Anasazi centers begins	
1200		1200 Anasazi culture declines	1200 Chimú begins military expansion
1300	1325 Aztec capital Tenochtitlan founded		
1400			1438 Inca expansion begins 1465 Inca conquer Chimú
1500		1500 Mississippian culture declines	1500–1525 Inca conquer Ecuador
	1502 Moctezuma II crowned Aztec ruler		

developed at about the same time, became the most important Olmec center after 900 B.C.E. when San Lorenzo was abandoned or destroyed. Très Zapotes (TRACE zah-POE-tess) was the last dominant center, rising to prominence after La Venta collapsed or was destroyed around 600 B.C.E. (see Map 7.1). Relationships among these centers are unclear. Scholars have found little evidence to suggest that they were either rival city-states or dependent units of a centralized political authority. It appears that each center developed independently to exploit and exchange specialized products like salt, cacao (chocolate beans), potters' clay, and limestone. Each major Olmec center was eventually abandoned, its monuments defaced and buried and its buildings destroyed. Archaeologists interpret these events differently;

some see them as evidence of internal upheavals or military defeat by neighboring peoples, and others suggest that they were associated with the death of a ruler.

Large artificial platforms and mounds of packed earth dominated Olmec urban centers and framed the collective ritual and political activities that brought the rural population to the cities at special times in the year. Some of the platforms also served as foundations for elite residences. The Olmec laid out their cities in alignment with the paths of certain stars, reflecting concern for astronomical events. Since these centers had small permanent populations, the scale of construction suggests that the Olmec elite could command the labor of thousands of men and women from the surrounding area for low-skill tasks like moving dirt and stone. Skilled artisans who lived in or near the urban core decorated the buildings with carvings and sculptures. They also produced the exquisite carved jade figurines, necklaces, and ceremonial knives and axes that distinguish Olmec culture. Archaeological evidence points to merchants trading with distant peoples for obsidian, jade, and pottery.

It seems likely that the rise of major urban centers coincided with the appearance of a form of kingship that combined religious and secular roles. Finely crafted objects decorated the households of the elite and distinguished their dress from that of the commoners, who lived in dispersed small structures constructed of sticks and mud. Colossal carved stone heads, some as large as 11 feet (3.4 meters) high, seem to reflect the authority of the

rulers and their families. Since each head is unique and suggestive of an individual personality, most archaeologists believe they were carved to memorialize individual rulers. This theory is reinforced by the location of the heads close to the major urban centers, especially San Lorenzo. These remarkable stone sculptures are the best-known monuments of Olmec culture.

The organization of collective labor by the Olmec elites benefited the commoners by increasing food production and making it more diverse and reliable. Ceramic products such as utilitarian pots and small figurines as well as small stone carvings associated with religious belief have been found in commoner households. This suggests that at least some advantages gained from urbanization and growing elite power were shared broadly in the society.

The Olmec elite used elaborate religious rituals to control this complex society. Thousands of commoners were drawn from the countryside to attend awe-inspiring ceremonies at the centers. The elevated platforms and mounds with carved stone veneers served as potent backdrops for these rituals. Rulers

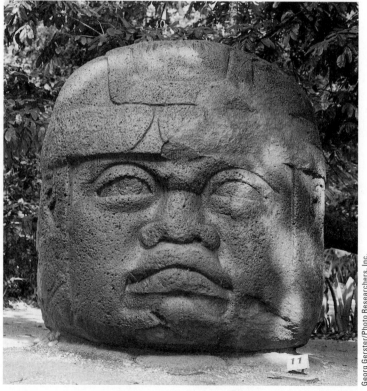

Olmec Head Giant heads sculpted from basalt are a widely recognized legacy of Olmec culture. Sixteen heads have been found, the largest approximately 11 feet (3.4 meters) tall. Experts in Olmec archaeology believe the heads are portraits of individual rulers, warriors, or ballplayers.

Georg Gerster/Photo Researchers, Inc.

and their close kin associated themselves with the gods through bloodletting and human sacrifice, evidence of which is found in all the urban centers. The Olmec were polytheistic, and most of their deities had dual (male and female) natures. Human and animal characteristics were also blended. Surviving representations of jaguars, crocodiles, snakes, and sharks suggest that these powerful animals provided the most enduring images used in Olmec religious representation. Humans transforming themselves into these animals constitute a common decorative motif. Rulers were especially associated with the jaguar.

Practical advice about the periodic rains essential to agricultural life came from a class of shamans and healers. They directed the planning of urban centers to reflect astronomical observations and were responsible for developing a form of writing that may have influenced later innovations among the Maya. From their close observation of the stars, they produced a calendar that was used to organize ritual life and agriculture. The Olmec were also the likely originators of a ritual ball game that became an enduring part of Mesoamerican ceremonial life.

The discovery of Olmec products and images, such as jade carvings decorated with the jaguar-god, as far away as central Mexico provides evidence that the Olmec exercised cultural influence over a wide area even though they never created an empire. This influence would endure for centuries.

Early South American Civilization: Chavín, 900–250 B.C.E.

Geography played an important role in the development of human society in the Andes. The region's diverse environment—a mountainous core, arid coastal plain, and dense interior jungles—challenged human populations, encouraging the development of specialized regional production as well as complex social institutions and cultural values that facilitated interregional exchanges and shared labor responsibilities. These adaptations to environmental challenge became enduring features of Andean civilization.

The earliest urban centers in the Andean region were villages of a few hundred people built along the coastal plain or in the foothills near the coast. The abundance of fish and mollusks along the coast

of Peru provided a dependable supply of food that helped make the development of early cities possible. The coastal populations traded these products along with decorative shells for maize, other foods, and textiles produced in the foothills. The two regions also exchanged ceremonial practices, religious motifs, and aesthetic ideas. Recent discoveries demonstrate that as early as 2600 B.C.E. the vast site called Caral had developed many of the characteristics now viewed as the hallmarks of later Andean civilization, including ceremonial plazas, pyramids, elevated platforms and mounds, and extensive irrigation works. The scale of the public works in Caral suggests a population of thousands and a political structure capable of organizing the production and distribution of maritime and agricultural products over a broad area.

Chavín, one of the most impressive of South America's early urban civilizations (see Map 7.1), inherited many of the cultural and economic characteristics of Caral. Its capital, Chavín de Huantar (cha-BEAN day WAHN-tar), was located at 10,300 feet (3,139 meters) in the eastern range of the Andes north of the modern city of Lima. Between 900 and 250 B.C.E., a period roughly coinciding with Olmec civilization in Mesoamerica, Chavín dominated a densely populated region that included large areas of the Peruvian coastal plain and Andean foothills. Chavín de Huantar's location at the intersection of trade routes connecting the coast with populous mountain valleys and the tropical lowlands on the eastern flank of the Andes allowed the city's rulers to control trade among these distinct ecological zones and gain an important economic advantage over regional rivals.

Chavín's dominance as a ceremonial and commercial center depended on earlier developments in agriculture and trade, including the introduction of maize cultivation from Mesoamerica. Maize increased the food supplies of the coast and interior foothills,

Chavín The first major urban civilization in South America (900–250 B.C.E.). Its capital, Chavín de Huántar, was located high in the Andes Mountains of Peru. Chavín became politically and economically dominant in a densely populated region that included two distinct ecological zones, the Peruvian coastal plain and the Andean foothills.

allowing greater levels of urbanization. As Chavín grew, its trade linked the coastal economy with the producers of quinoa (a local grain), potatoes, and llamas in the high mountain valleys and, to a lesser extent, with Amazonian producers of coca and fruits.

Reciprocal labor obligations that permitted the construction and maintenance of roads, bridges, temples, palaces, and large irrigation and drainage projects, as well as textile production, developed as well. In later times groups of related families who held land communally and claimed descent from a common ancestor organized these labor obligations. Group members thought of each other as brothers and sisters and were obligated to aid each other, providing a model for the organization of labor and the distribution of goods at every level of Andean society.

Llamas, the only domesticated beasts of burden in the Americas, played an important role in the integration of the Andean region. They were first domesticated in the mountainous interior of Peru and were crucial to Chavín's development. Llamas provided meat and wool and helped transport goods. A single driver could control ten to thirty animals, each carrying up to 70 pounds (32 kilograms); a human porter could carry only about 50 pounds (22.5 kilograms). The increased use of llamas to move goods from one ecological zone to another promoted specialization of production and increased trade.

The enormous scale of the capital and the dispersal of Chavín's pottery styles, religious motifs, and architectural forms over a wide area suggest that Chavín imposed some form of political integration and trade dependency on its neighbors that may have relied in part on military force. However, most modern scholars believe that, as in the case of the Olmec civilization, Chavín's influence depended more on the development of an attractive and convincing religious belief system and related rituals. Chavín's most potent religious symbol, a jaguar deity, was dispersed over a broad area, and archaeological evidence suggests that Chavín de Huantar served as a pilgrimage site.

The architectural signature of Chavín was a large complex of multilevel platforms made of packed earth or rubble and faced with cut stone or adobe (sun-dried brick made of clay and straw). Small buildings used for ritual purposes or as elite residences were built on these platforms. Nearly all the buildings were decorated with relief carvings of serpents, condors,

jaguars, or humans. The largest building at Chavín de Huantar measured 250 feet (76 meters) on each side and rose to a height of 50 feet (15 meters). About one-third of its interior is hollow, containing narrow galleries and small rooms that may have housed the remains of royal ancestors.

American metallurgy was first developed in the Andean region. The later introduction of metallurgy in Mesoamerica, like the appearance of maize agriculture in the Andes, suggests sustained contacts between the two regions. Archaeological investigations of Chavín de Huantar and smaller centers have revealed remarkable three-dimensional silver, gold, and gold alloy ornaments that represent a clear advance over earlier technologies. Bronze and iron, however, were unknown.

Improvements in both the manufacture and the decoration of textiles are also associated with the rise of Chavín. The quality of these products, which were probably used only by the elite or in religious rituals, added to the reputation and prestige of the culture and aided in the projection of its power and influence. The most common decorative motif in sculpture, pottery, and textiles was a jaguar-man similar in conception to the Olmec symbol. In both civilizations and in many other cultures in the Americas, this powerful predator provided an enduring image of religious authority and a vehicle through which the gods could act in the world of men and women.

Class distinctions also appear to have increased in Chavín. Priests directed religious life, and there is evidence that both local chiefs and a more powerful chief or king dominated Chavín's politics. Excavations of graves reveal that superior-quality textiles as well as gold crowns, breastplates, and jewelry distinguished rulers from commoners.

There is no convincing evidence, like defaced buildings or broken images, that the eclipse of Chavín (unlike the Olmec centers) was associated with conquest or rebellion. However, recent investigations

---

llama A hoofed animal indigenous to the Andes Mountains. It was the only domesticated beast of burden in the Americas before the arrival of Europeans. The use of llamas to transport goods made possible specialized production and trade among people living in different ecological zones and fostered the integration of these zones by Chavín and later Andean states.

SECTION REVIEW

- From farming communities of Mesoamerica emerged the urban civilization of the Olmec.

- Olmec cities were centers of specialized crafts, long-distance trade, royal authority, and mass religious observance.

- Shamans and healers directed urban planning, issued practical advice, and devised many of the technologies and rituals inherited by later civilizations of the region.

- In the ecologically diverse Andes, a wide range of settled communities developed, from which emerged the Chavín civilization.

- Chavín de Huantar dominated a large territory as a ceremonial and commercial center, and its rulers organized extensive construction projects.

- The Chavín people used domesticated llamas, developed important technologies, and devised a unifying religious system, all of which influenced later Andean civilizations.

have suggested that increased warfare throughout the region around 200 B.C.E. disrupted Chavín's trade and undermined the authority of the governing elite. Regardless of what caused the collapse of this powerful culture, the technologies, material culture,

statecraft, architecture, and urban planning associated with Chavín influenced the Andean region for centuries.

Classic-Era Culture and Society in Mesoamerica, 200–900

What were the most important shared characteristics of Mesoamerican cultures in the classic period?

Between 200 and 900, the peoples of Mesoamerica created a civilization based on similarities in material culture, religious beliefs and practices, and social structures, despite differences in language and the absence of regional political integration. Building on the achievements of the Olmec and others, the peoples then living in Mesoamerica developed new political institutions, made great strides in astronomy and mathematics, and improved agricultural productivity.

Archaeologists call this mix of achievements the classic period. Population grew, a greater variety of products were traded over longer distances, social hierarchies became more complex, and great cities

Chrysler Museum of Art/Justin Kerr

The Mesoamerican Ball Game From Guatemala to Arizona, archaeologists have found evidence of an ancient ball game played with a solid rubber ball on slope-sided courts shaped like a capital T. Among the Maya the game was associated with a creation myth and thus had deep religious meaning. There is evidence that some players were sacrificed. In this scene from a ceramic jar, players wearing elaborate ritual clothing—which includes heavy, protective pads around the chest and waist—play with a ball much larger than the ball actually used in such games. Some representations show balls drawn to suggest a human head.

Map 7.2 Major Mesoamerican Civilizations, 1000 B.C.E.–1519 C.E. The Maya civilization, with its many rival cities, covered the highlands of Guatemala and the Yucatán Peninsula. From their island capital of Tenochtitlan, the Aztecs militarily and commercially dominated southern Mexico. Aztec achievements were built on the legacy of earlier civilizations such as the Olmec and Maya.
© Cengage Learning

Interactive Map

served as governing and religious centers. Impressive platforms and pyramids were devoted to religious functions. Large urban populations, divided into classes, served hereditary political and religious elites who also controlled the nearby towns and countryside.

The agricultural foundation of Mesoamerican civilization had been developed centuries earlier. The major agricultural technologies—irrigation, wetland drainage, and hillside terracing—preceded the cities built after 200 C.E. by more than a thousand years. What made the achievements of the classic era possible was the extended reach and power of religious and political leaders. The impressive architecture and great size of Teotihuacan (teh-o-tee-WAH-kahn) and the great Maya cities such as Tikal illustrate both Mesoamerican aesthetic achievements and the development of powerful political institutions.

Teotihuacan

At the height of its power, from 450 to 600 C.E., **Teotihuacan** (100 B.C.E.–750 C.E.), located about 30 miles (48 kilometers) northeast of modern Mexico City (see Map 7.2), housed between 125,000 and 200,000 inhabitants. The largest city in the Americas, it outshone all but a few contemporary European and Asian cities.

The religious architecture of Teotihuacan included enormous pyramids dedicated to the sun and moon and more than twenty smaller temples devoted to other gods, all of which flanked a central avenue. The god Quetzalcoatl (kate-zahl CO-ah-tal), the feathered serpent, was considered the originator of agriculture and the arts. Like the Olmec, the people of Teotihuacan practiced human sacrifice as a sacred duty toward the gods and as a necessity for the well-being of human society. The excavation of the temple of Quetzalcoatl uncovered scores of sacrificial victims.

Teotihuacan's urban population had grown rapidly from the forced relocation of villagers following

Teotihuacan A powerful city-state in central Mexico (100 B.C.E.–750 C.E.). Its population was about 150,000 at its peak in 600.

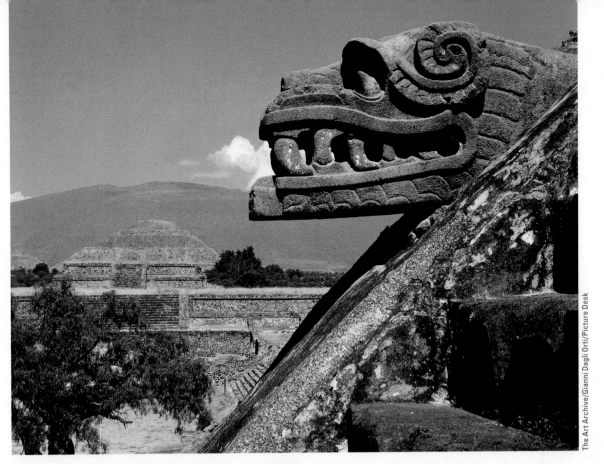

The Art Archive/Gianni Dagli Orti/Picture Desk

The Pyramid of the Sun The Pyramid of the Sun is the largest pyramid in Teotihuacan. The smaller Temple of Quetzacoatl displays the serpent images associated with this culture god common to most Mesoamerican civilizations.

volcanic eruptions. Nevertheless, more than two-thirds of the city's residents continued to farm, walking from their city homes to the fields. The elite used the city's growing labor resources to expand agriculture by draining swamps, building irrigation works, and cutting terraces into hillsides. They also expanded **chinampas** (chee-NAM-pahs), misleadingly called "floating gardens." These narrow artificial islands, anchored by trees and created by heaping lake muck and waste material on beds of reeds, were crucial in sustaining the growing population because the sub-surface irrigation resisted frost and thus permitted year-round agriculture.

The housing of commoners changed as the population grew. Apartment-like stone buildings housed, among other people, the craftsmen who produced goods for export. Teotihuacan pottery has turned up throughout central Mexico and even in the Maya region of Guatemala. More than 2 percent of the urban population crafted similarly widespread obsidian tools and weapons.

The city's role as a religious center signified divine approval of the increasingly prosperous elite. Members of this elite controlled the state bureaucracy, tax collection, and commerce. Their diet and style of dress reflected their prestige, and they lived in separate aristocratic compounds. Temple and palace murals confirm the central position and great prestige of the priestly class. Pilgrims came to Teotihuacan from far away, and some became permanent residents.

Unlike other classic-period societies, the people of Teotihuacan did not have a single ruler. The deeds of the rulers do not feature in public art, nor were rulers represented by statues as in other Mesoamerican civilizations. Thus historians debate the role of the military at Teotihuacan. Unlike later postclassic civilizations, Teotihuacan was not an imperial state controlled by a military elite, and the absence of walls or

chinampas Raised fields constructed along lakeshores in Mesoamerica to increase agricultural yields.

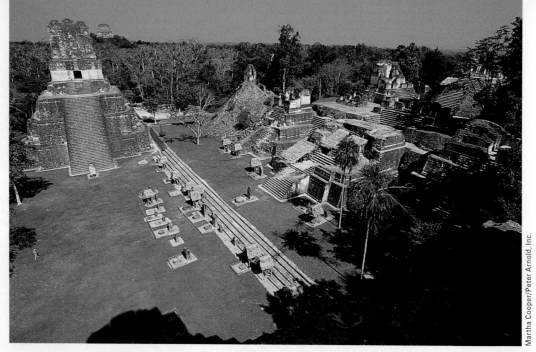

Martha Cooper/Peter Arnold, Inc.

The Great Plaza at Tikal Still visible in the ruins of Tikal, in modern Guatemala, are the impressive architectural and artistic achievements of the classic-era Maya. Maya centers provided a dramatic setting for the rituals that dominated public life. Construction of Tikal began before 150 B.C.E.; the city was abandoned about 900 C.E. A ball court and residences for the elite were part of the Great Plaza.

other defensive structures before 500 suggests relative peace. However, archaeology points to a powerful military protecting long-distance trade and compelling peasants to hand over their surplus production. Representations of soldiers in typical Teotihuacan dress in the Maya region of Guatemala may indicate that the military were used to expand trade.

The forces that brought about the end of Teotihuacan about 750 remain a mystery, but evidence of weakness appears as early as 500, when the urban population declined to about 40,000 and the city began to build defensive walls. Fortifications and pictorial evidence from murals suggest that the city's final decades were violent. Indications of conflict within the ruling elite and of mismanagement of resources have challenged earlier theories of conquest by a rival city nearby or by nomadic peoples from the north. Class conflict and the breakdown of public order may explain the destruction of the most important temples in the city center, the defacing of religious images, and the burning of elite palaces. The eclipse of Teotihuacan reverberated throughout Mexico and into Central America.

The Maya

Contemporary with Teotihuacan, the **Maya** developed a civilization in the region that today includes Guatemala, Honduras, Belize, and southern Mexico (see Map 7.2). The

History in Focus *Examine the image "The Great Plaza at Tikal." Try to imagine the scale of these religious structures, and keep in mind that the mass of common people stood below on the flat ground. What do you think they would see during the frequent public rituals? What do you think they would not see? What does that suggest to you about the nature of Maya ritual and its role in public life? Find the answer online.*

difficulties of a tropical climate and fragile soils make the cultural and architectural achievements of the Maya all the more remarkable. Although they shared a single culture, they never unified politically. Instead, rival kingdoms led by hereditary rulers competed for dominance.

Today, Maya farmers cut down small trees and brush and burn the dead vegetation to fertilize the land. This swidden agriculture produces high yields for a few years, but it exhausts the soil's nutrients, eventually forcing a move to fresh land. The high population levels of the Maya classic period (250–900 C.E.) required more intensive forms of agriculture.

Maya Mesoamerican civilization concentrated in Mexico's Yucatán Peninsula and in Guatemala and Honduras but never unified into a single empire. Major contributions were in mathematics, astronomy, and development of the calendar.

Maya living near the major urban centers achieved high yields by draining swamps and building elevated fields. They used irrigation in areas with long dry seasons and built terraced hillsides in the cooler highlands. Nearly every household planted a garden to provide condiments and fruits. The Maya also practiced forest management, favoring the growth of useful trees and shrubs and promoting the conservation of deer and other animals hunted for food.

During the classic period, city-states proliferated, the most powerful controlling groups of smaller dependent cities. Religious temples and rituals linked the power of kings to the gods. Unlike earlier sites, these cities had dense central precincts dominated by buildings that were commonly aligned with the movements of the sun and Venus. High pyramids and elaborately decorated palaces, often built on high ground or constructed mounds, surrounded open plazas, an awesome prospect for the masses drawn in for religious and political rituals.

Bas-reliefs and bright paint covered nearly all public buildings. Common motifs included religious allegories, the genealogies of rulers, and important historical events. Carved altars and stone monoliths arose near major temples. Masses of men and women aided only by levers and stone tools cut and carried construction materials and lifted them into place.

The Maya cosmos consisted of three layers connected along a vertical axis that traced the course of the sun. The earthly arena of human existence came between the heavens, conceptualized as a sky-monster, and a dark underworld. A sacred tree rose through the layers, its roots in the underworld and its branches in the heavens. The temple precincts of Maya cities physically represented this cosmology: the pyramids as sacred mountains reaching to the heavens, their doorways as portals to the underworld.

Rulers and other members of the elite decorated their bodies with paint and tattoos and wore elaborate costumes of textiles, animal skins, and feathers to project both secular power and divine sanction. Kings communicated directly with the supernatural residents of the other worlds and with deified royal ancestors through bloodletting rituals and hallucinogenic trances. Scenes of rulers drawing blood from lips, ears, and penises are common in frescoes and on painted pottery.

Warfare in particular was infused with religious meaning and elaborate rituals. Scenes of battle and the torture and sacrifice of captives appear frequently. Days of fasting, sacred ritual, and purification rites preceded battle. The king, his kinsmen, and other ranking nobles fought personally, with the goal of taking captives. Elite captives nearly always became sacrificial victims; commoners usually became slaves.

Few women directly ruled Maya kingdoms, though women from ruling lineages did play important political and religious roles. The consorts of male rulers participated in bloodletting rituals and in other public ceremonies. Their noble blood helped legitimate their husbands' rule. Though generally patrilineal (tracing descent in the male line), some male rulers traced their lineages from both the male and the female lines. Some rulers emphasized the female line if it held higher status. As for women of the lower classes, scholars believe that they played a central role in religious ritual, household economy, gardening, and weaving.

Building on Olmec precedents, the Maya developed the calendar, mathematics, and writing. The complexity of their calendric system, with each day marked by three separate dating systems, reflects their interest in time and the cosmos. Like other Mesoamerican peoples, the Maya had a calendar that tracked the ritual cycle (260 days divided into 13 months of 20 days) as well as a solar calendar (365 days divided into 18 months of 20 days, plus 5 "unfavorable days" at the end of the year). The concurrence of these two calendars every 52 years was considered especially ominous. Alone among Mesoamerican peoples, the Maya also maintained a continuous "long count" calendar, which began at a fixed date in the past that scholars have identified as 3114 B.C.E., a date probably associated with creation.

The Maya system of mathematics, which underlay the calendar, incorporated the concept of the zero and place value, but it had limited notational signs. Maya writing used hieroglyphs that signified whole words or concepts as well as phonetic cues or syllables. Aspects of public life, religious belief, and the biographies of rulers and their ancestors were recorded in deerskin and bark-paper books, on pottery, and on the stone columns and monumental buildings of the urban centers.

- Between 200 and 900 C.E., Mesoamerican peoples built civilizations with characteristics derived from Olmec culture.

- Their achievements were made possible by the increased power of political and religious leaders.

- Both Teotihuacan and the Maya city-states were supported by intensive agriculture and contained monumental religious architecture.

- Teotihuacan grew into a powerful economic and religious center without a single ruler or powerful military elite.

- The Maya city-states were ruled by kings and elites that practiced ritualized warfare.

- Maya women appear to have enjoyed high status, and both civilizations adopted practices and technologies from their Olmec predecessors.

Abandonment or destruction befell many of the major urban centers between 800 and 900, although a small number survived for centuries. In some areas, decades of urban population decline and increased warfare preceded the collapse. Some experts maintain that the destruction of Teotihuacan after 650 disrupted trade, thus undermining the legitimacy of Maya rulers who used trade goods in rituals. Others suggest that population pressure led to environmental degradation and declining agricultural productivity. This, in turn, might have caused social conflict and warfare as desperate elites sought additional agricultural land through conquest.

The Postclassic Period in Mesoamerica, 900–1500

What role did warfare play in the postclassic period of Mesoamerica?

The collapse of Teotihuacan and many of the major Maya centers occurred over more than a century and a half, making the division between classic and postclassic periods somewhat arbitrary. In fact, some important classic-period civilizations survived unscathed, and essential cultural characteristics in religious belief and practice, architecture, urban planning, and social organization carried over to the postclassic period.

Nevertheless, important differences exist. The population of Mesoamerica apparently expanded

Maya Scribe Maya scribes used a complex writing system to record religious concepts and memorialize the actions of their kings. An artisan painted this picture of a scribe on a ceramic plate.

© Justin Kerr

during the postclassic period, causing an intensification of agricultural practices and increased warfare. The governing elites of the major postclassic states—the Toltecs and the Aztecs—increased the size of their armies and developed political institutions that facilitated control of large territories gained through conquest.

The Toltecs

Scholars speculate that the **Toltecs** (TOLL-teks) originated as a satellite population protecting the northern frontier of Teotihuacan from nomad raids. After migrating south, they created an important postclassic civilization on the legacy of Teotihuacan. Memories of their military achievements and the violent imagery of their political and religious rituals dominated the Mesoamerican imagination in the late postclassic period. In the fourteenth century, the Aztecs and their contemporaries erroneously believed that the Toltecs created nearly all of Mesoamerica's cultural monuments. One Aztec source declared:

> In truth [the Toltecs] invented all the precious and marvelous things.... All that now exists was their discovery.... And these Toltecs were very wise; they were thinkers, for they originated the year count, the day count. All their discoveries formed the book for interpreting dreams.... And so wise were they [that] they understood the stars which were in the heavens.[2]

Actually, the most important Toltec innovations came in politics and war. The Toltecs created the first conquest state as they extended their political influence from north of modern Mexico City to Central America. Established about 968, Tula (TOO-la), the Toltec capital, followed the grand style (see Map 7.2), with public architecture that featured colonnaded patios and numerous temples. Though smaller than Teotihuacan, Tula dominated central Mexico. Nearly all its public buildings and temples carried scenes of human sacrifice, and representations of warriors on public buildings reflect an increasingly warlike and violent world-view.

Two chieftains or kings apparently ruled the Toltec state together, a system that may eventually have sapped Toltec power and opened Tula to destruction. Sometime after 1000, a struggle between elite groups from rival religious cults undermined the state. According to later Aztec legends, Topiltzin (tow-PEELT-zeen)—one of the two rulers and a priest of the cult of Quetzalcoatl—and his followers bitterly accepted exile in the east. One text relates the following:

> Thereupon he [Topiltzin] looked toward Tula, and then wept.... And when he had done these things ... he went to reach the seacoast. Then he fashioned a raft of serpents. When he had arranged the raft, he placed himself as if it were his boat. Then he set off across the sea.[3]

Toltec decline set in after 1150. By 1175 internal conflict and northern invaders had wreaked destruction upon Tula, triggering a centuries-long process of cultural and political assimilation to produce a new political order based on the Toltec heritage. The Aztecs became the most important of these late postclassic peoples.

The Aztecs

The Mexica (meh-SHE-ca), more commonly known as the **Aztecs**, pushed into central Mexico from the north after Tula's fall. As their power grew through political alliances and military conquest, they created a regional power called the Aztec Empire. When they arrived, the Mexica were organized as an **altepetl** (al-TEH-pe-tel), an ethnic state led by a tlatoani (tlah-toh-AHN-ee) or ruler. A group of **calpolli** (cal-POH-yee), each with up to a hundred families, served as the foundation of the altepetl, controlling land allocation, tax collection, and local religious life.

Adapting to the political and social practices that they found among the urbanized agriculturalists of the Valley of Mexico, the Mexica first worked as serfs and mercenaries for more powerful neighbors. Once

---

Toltecs Powerful postclassic empire in central Mexico (900–1156) that influenced much of Mesoamerica. Aztecs claimed ties to this earlier civilization.

Aztecs Also known as Mexica, the Aztecs created a powerful empire in central Mexico (1325–1521). They forced defeated peoples to provide goods and labor.

altepetl An ethnic state in ancient Mesoamerica, the common political building block of that region.

calpolli A group of up to a hundred families that served as a social building block of an altepetl in ancient Mesoamerica.

they gained strength around 1325, they relocated to some small islands near the shore of Lake Texcoco, where they founded their twin capitals, **Tenochtitlan** (teh-noch-TIT-lan) and Tlatelolco (tla-TEH-lol-co) (together the foundation for modern Mexico City).

The increased economic independence and political security gained by seizing control of farmland along the lakeshore eased the introduction of a monarchical system similar to that of more powerful neighboring states. Power increasingly flowed to hereditary aristocrats and monarchs, though the latter did not wield absolute power. A council of powerful aristocrats selected new rulers from males of the ruling lineage. The ruler demonstrated his divine mandate by making new conquests and renegotiating tribute payments from dependencies. War acquired religious meaning, providing the ruler with legitimacy and increasing the prestige of successful warriors.

One Spaniard who witnessed the conquest of the Aztec Empire remembered his first meeting with the Aztec ruler Moctezuma (mock-teh-ZU-ma) II (r. 1502–1520): "Many great lords walked before the great Montezuma [Moctezuma II], sweeping the ground on which he was to tread and laying down cloaks so that his feet should not touch the earth. Not one of these chieftains dared look him in the face."[4] Although warfare increased male privilege, women held substantial power and influence. Following the birth of a boy, his umbilical cord was buried on the battlefield and he was given implements to signal his occupation or his role as a warrior. In the case of a girl, her umbilical cord was buried near the hearth and she was given weaving implements and female clothing. Death rituals also marked gender identities as distinct but complementary. Women dominated the household and the markets and served as teachers and priestesses. They also founded lineages, including the royal line.

As kinship-based clans lost influence, social divisions sharpened. Conquest allowed the warrior elite to seize land and peasant labor as spoils of war. The elite owned extensive estates cultivated by slaves and landless commoners. The lower classes received some benefits from imperial expansion but lost most of their influence over decisions. Hereditary nobles monopolized the highest social ranks, although some commoners gained status through success on

the battlefield or by entering the priesthood. Calpolli members fought together as military units.

Small dwellings and a limited diet of staples marked the life of commoners. Nobles enjoyed more luxuries: well-built two-story houses, rich dress and jewelry, meat, and expensive imports like chocolate brought from Maya country to the south. Polygamy was a noble privilege.

The Aztec state fed an urban population of approximately 150,000 by efficiently organizing the clans and additional laborers sent by defeated peoples to expand agricultural land. Land reclamation centered on a dike more than 5 miles (9 kilometers) long by 23 feet (7 meters) wide that separated the freshwater and saltwater parts of Lake Texcoco. The dike, whose construction consumed 4 million person-days, supported greater irrigation and more chinampas, which contributed maize, fruits, and vegetables to the Tenochtitlan markets. A **tribute system** imposed on conquered peoples helped relieve the capital's population pressure. Nearby political dependencies supplied one-quarter of Tenochtitlan's maize, beans, and other crops. The Aztecs also demanded cotton cloth, military equipment, luxury goods like jade and feathers, and sacrificial victims.

A specialized class of merchants controlled long-distance trade. Lacking draft animals and wheeled vehicles, they mostly traded lightweight and valuable products like gold, jewels, feathered garments, cacao, and animal skins. Merchants also provided political and military intelligence. Operating beyond the reach of Aztec military power, merchant expeditions carried arms and often used them. Although some merchants became wealthy and powerful, none could enter the ranks of the high nobility.

Tenochtitlan Capital of the Aztec Empire, located on an island in Lake Texcoco. Its population was about 150,000 on the eve of Spanish conquest. Mexico City was constructed on its ruins.

tribute system A system in which defeated peoples were forced to pay a tax in the form of goods and labor. This forced transfer of food, cloth, and other goods subsidized the development of large cities. An important component of the Aztec and Inca economies.

- Postclassic civilizations carried on the basic forms of religious belief and ritual, architecture, city planning, and social organization of their predecessors.

- Mesoamerican populations increased, causing intensified agriculture and warfare.

- The Toltecs built upon Teotihuacan's legacy, achieving notable innovations in politics and war.

- Adopting Toltec practices, the Aztecs built an urban, imperial state ruled by kings and aristocrats who practiced ritualized warfare.

- Clan ties gave way to class-based distinctions reinforced by ceremony, and a tribute system evolved to support urban populations.

- Merchants controlled long-distance trade, and religious ritual involving human sacrifice dominated public life.

Mesoamerican commerce took place without money or credit, but cacao, quills filled with gold, and cotton cloth provided standard units of value in barter transactions. Aztec expansion integrated producers and consumers in the central Mexican economy so that the markets of Tenochtitlan and Tlatelolco offered goods from as far away as Central America and what is now the southwestern border of the United States. Hernán Cortés (1485–1547), the Spanish adventurer who conquered the Aztecs, admired the abundance of the Aztec marketplace:

> One square in particular is twice as big as that of Salamanca and completely surrounded by arcades where there are daily more than sixty thousand folk buying and selling. . . . There is nothing to be found in all the land which is not sold in these markets, for over and above what I have mentioned there are so many and such various things that on account of their very number . . . I cannot detail them.[5]

The combined population of Tenochtitlan and Tlatelolco and the cities and hamlets of the surrounding lakeshore totaled approximately 500,000 by 1500. In the island capital, canals and streets intersected at right angles. Three causeways connected the city to the lakeshore.

Religious rituals dominated public life. The Aztecs worshiped numerous gods, most of them having both male and female natures. As the Aztec state grew in power and wealth, the cult of Huitzilopochtli (wheat-zeel-oh-POSHT-lee), the southern hummingbird, grew in importance. Although originally associated with war, Huitzilopochtli eventually symbolized the sun, which was worshiped as a divinity throughout Mesoamerica. To bring the sun's warmth to the world, Huitzilopochtli required a daily diet of human hearts. Twin temples devoted to Huitzilopochtli and Tlaloc, the rain-god—the two symbolizing war and agriculture as the bases of the Aztec system—dominated Tenochtitlan.

Sacrificial victims—preferably war captives but also criminals, slaves, and people provided as tribute—transformed the Mesoamerican tradition of human sacrifice by increasing its scale. Thousands of lives were taken every year. Some scholars have emphasized the politically intimidating nature of this rising tide, noting that sacrifices took place before large crowds that included leaders from enemy and subject states, as well as the masses of Aztec society.

Northern Peoples

In what ways did Mesoamerica influence the cultural centers in North America?

Mesoamerica's classic period ended around 900 C.E. By then, settled life and complex social and political structures based on improved agriculture and population growth had appeared in the southwestern desert of today's United States and in eastern river valleys. Along the Ohio River, Amerindian peoples living in large villages with monumental earthworks practiced hunting and gathering and harvested locally domesticated seed crops.

Cultivating maize introduced from Mesoamerica required large-scale irrigation projects in the southwestern desert and the eastern river valleys. However, the two regions evolved different political traditions. The Anasazi (ah-nah-SAH-zee) and their neighbors in the southwest maintained a relatively egalitarian social structure and a political organization based on kinship and age. The mound builders of the east had hereditary chiefs who wielded both secular and religious authority over the political center and subordinate small towns.

Mesa Verde Cliff Dwelling Located in southern Colorado, the Anasazi cliff dwellings of the Mesa Verde region hosted a population of about 7,000 in 1250 C.E. The construction of housing complexes and religious buildings in the area's large caves was prompted by increased warfare in the region.

Southwestern Desert Cultures

Immigrants from Mexico brought irrigation agriculture to Arizona around 300 B.C.E. With two harvests per year, population grew and villages appeared. The Hohokam of the Salt and Gila River Valleys show strong Mexican influence, with platform mounds and ball courts similar to those of Mesoamerica. Hohokam pottery, clay figurines, cast copper bells, and turquoise mosaics also reflect Mexican influence. By 1000 C.E., the Hohokam had constructed an elaborate irrigation system that included one canal more than 18 miles (30 kilometers) in length. Hohokam agricultural and ceramic technology gradually spread, but it was the Anasazi to the north who left the most vivid legacy.

Archaeologists use **Anasazi**, a Navajo word meaning "ancient ones," to identify a number of dispersed desert cultures in the Four Corners region of Arizona, New Mexico, Colorado, and Utah. Between 500 and 750 C.E. the early Anasazi lived in large villages and grew maize, beans, and squash. Their cultural life centered on underground buildings called kivas, which they may have used for weaving cotton and making pottery with geometric patterns. After 900, they began to construct large multistory residential and ritual centers.

Chaco Canyon sheltered one of the largest communities: eight large towns in the canyon itself and four more on surrounding mesas, suggesting a regional population of approximately 15,000. Each town contained hundreds of rooms arranged in tiers around a central plaza. At Pueblo Bonito, the largest town, a four-story block of residences and storage spaces contained more than 650 rooms. Pueblo Bonito had thirty-eight kivas, including a great kiva more than 65 feet (19 meters) in diameter. Social life and craft activities took place in small, open plazas or common rooms. Hunting, trade, and irrigation work often drew men away from the village. Besides preparing food and caring for children, women shared

Anasazi Important culture of what is now the southwest United States (700–1200). Centered on Chaco Canyon in New Mexico and Mesa Verde in Colorado, the Anasazi culture built multistory residences and worshiped in subterranean buildings called kivas.

in agricultural tasks and many crafts. Among modern Pueblos, the cultural descendants of the Anasazi, houses and furnishings belong to women formed into extended families with their mothers and sisters.

Late in Chaco's development, traders provided turquoise to Toltec-period peoples in northern Mexico in exchange for shell jewelry, copper bells, macaws, and trumpets. More important signs of Mesoamerican influence, such as pyramid-shaped mounds, ball courts, and class distinctions signaled by burials or residences, do not appear at Chaco. It appears more likely that the Chaco Canyon culture developed from earlier societies in the region.

Drought probably forced the abandonment of Chaco Canyon in the twelfth century. Nevertheless, the Anasazi continued in the Four Corners region for more than a century. Anasazi settlements on the Colorado Plateau and in Arizona used large natural caves high above valley floors. Such hard-to-reach locations suggest increased warfare, probably provoked by population pressure on limited arable land. The Pueblo peoples of the Rio Grande Valley and Arizona still live in multistory villages and worship in kivas.

Mound Builders: The Hopewell and Mississippian Cultures

From around 100 C.E. the Hopewell culture spread through the Ohio River Valley. Hopewell people constructed large villages characterized by monumental earthworks. Once established, Hopewell influence spread west to Illinois, Michigan, and Wisconsin, east to New York and Ontario, and south to Alabama, Louisiana, Mississippi, and even Florida. For sustenance the Hopewell people depended on hunting and gathering and a limited agriculture based on domesticated seed crops. Hopewell is an early example of a North American **chiefdom**—a territory with a population as large as 10,000 ruled by a hereditary leader with both religious and secular responsibilities. Chiefs organized periodic rituals of feasting and gift giving that established bonds among diverse kinship groups and guaranteed access to specialized crops and craft goods. They also managed long-distance trade that provided luxury goods and additional food supplies.

The largest Hopewell towns in the Ohio River Valley served as ceremonial and political centers and had several thousand inhabitants. Large mounds housing elite burials and serving as platforms for temples and the chief's residence dominated these centers. Elite burial vaults containing valuable goods like river pearls and copper jewelry sometimes entomb women and retainers apparently sacrificed to accompany a dead chief into the afterlife. The abandonment of major Hopewell sites around 400 C.E. has no clear environmental or political explanation.

Hopewell technology and mound building were linked to the development of Mississippian culture (700–1500 C.E.). Maize, beans, and squash suggest an indirect link to Mesoamerica. The urbanized Mississippian chiefdoms resulted from the accumulated effects of small increases in agricultural productivity, the adoption of the bow and arrow, and the expansion of trade networks. The largest towns shared a common urban plan based on a central plaza surrounded by large platform mounds. There, people bartered essential commodities, such as flint used for weapons and tools.

SECTION REVIEW

- In parts of North America, agricultural improvements and population growth stimulated the development of complex societies.

- In Chaco Canyon, the Anasazi practiced irrigated agriculture and produced architecture that suggests an egalitarian society.

- Some Chaco Canyon settlements exerted broad territorial influence until changing conditions forced relocation to less accessible sites.

- The Hopewell peoples built large villages with monumental earthworks and organized themselves into hierarchical chiefdoms.

- The Mississippian culture built on these patterns, with great sites such as Cahokia revealing stratified societies.

chiefdom Form of political organization with rule by a hereditary leader who held power over a collection of villages and towns. Less powerful than kingdoms and empires, chiefdoms were based on gift giving and commercial links.

The Mississippian culture culminated in the urban site of Cahokia, located near East St. Louis, Illinois. North America's largest mound, a terraced structure 100 feet (30 meters) high and 1,037 by 790 feet (316 by 241 meters) at the base, stands at its center, an area of elite housing and temples ringed by areas where commoners lived. At its height in about 1200, Cahokia had a population of some 30,000—as large as the great Maya city of Tikal.

Cahokia controlled surrounding agricultural lands and a number of secondary towns ruled by subchiefs. One tomb containing more than fifty young women and retainers sacrificed to accompany a ruler after death suggests the exalted position of Cahokia's chiefs. Nothing links the decline and eventual abandonment of Cahokia (1250) to military defeat or civil war, although climate changes and population pressures may have undermined its vitality. Smaller Mississippian centers flourished in the southeastern United States until the arrival of Europeans.

Andean Civilizations, 200–1500

How did the Amerindian peoples of the Andean area adapt to their environment and produce socially complex and politically advanced societies?

Much of the Andean region's mountainous zone seems too high for agriculture and human habitation, and the arid plain of its Pacific coastland poses difficult challenges to cultivation. To the east of the Andes Mountains, the hot, humid Amazon headwaters also discouraged the organization of complex societies. Yet the Amerindian peoples of the region developed some of the most socially complex and politically advanced societies of the Western Hemisphere (see Map 7.3).

Cultural Response to Environmental Challenge

People living in the high mountain valleys and on the dry coastal plain overcame their environmental challenges through effective organization of labor using a record-keeping system more limited than those of Mesoamerica. A system of knotted colored cords, **khipus** (KEY-pooz), helped administrators record population counts and tribute obligations. Large-scale drainage

Map 7.3   Andean Civilizations, 200 B.C.E.–1532 C.E.
In response to environmental challenges posed by an arid coastal plain and high interior mountain ranges, Andean peoples made complex social and technological adaptations. Irrigation systems, the domestication of the llama, metallurgy, and shared labor obligations helped provide a firm economic foundation for powerful, centralized states. In 1532 the Inca Empire's vast territory stretched from modern Chile in the south to Colombia in the north.
© Cengage Learning

Interactive Map

and irrigation works and the terracing of hillsides to control erosion and provide additional farmland increased agricultural production. People worked collectively on road building, urban construction, and even textile production.

khipus   System of knotted colored cords used by preliterate Andean peoples to transmit information.

The clan, or **ayllu** (aye-YOU), provided the foundation for Andean achievement. Members of an ayllu claiming descent from a common ancestor, though not necessarily related in fact, held land communally. Ayllu members thought of each other as brothers and sisters with obligations to help each other in tasks beyond the ability of a single household.

When territorial states ruled by hereditary aristocracies and kings developed after 1000 B.C.E., these obligations grew in scale. The **mit'a** (MEET-ah) system required ayllu members to work the fields and care for the herds of llamas and alpacas owned by religious establishments, the royal court, and the aristocracy. Each allyu met a yearly quota of workers for specific tasks. Mit'a laborers built and maintained roads, bridges, temples, palaces, and large irrigation and drainage projects. They produced textiles and goods essential to ritual life, such as coca and beer made from maize.

Jobs divided along gender lines, but the work of men and women was interdependent. Men hunted and served as soldiers and administrators, while women had responsibilities in textile production, agriculture, and the home. One early Spanish commentator remarked:

> [Women] did not just perform domestic tasks, but also [labored] in the fields, in the cultivation of their lands, in building houses, and carrying burdens.... And more than once I heard that while women were carrying these burdens, they would feel labor pains, and giving birth, they would go to a place where there was water and wash the baby and themselves. Putting the baby on top of the load they were carrying, they would then continue walking as before they gave birth.[6]

The unique environmental challenges of the Andean region led to distinctive highland and coastal cultures. Here, more than in Mesoamerica, geography influenced regional cultural integration and state formation. Because the region's mountain ranges created a multitude of small ecological areas with specialized resources, each community sought to control a variety of environments to gain access to essential goods. Coastal regions produced maize, fish, and cotton, and mountain valleys contributed quinoa, potatoes, and other tubers. Higher elevations contributed the wool and meat of llamas and alpacas. The Amazonian region provided coca and fruits. Colonists sent

to exploit these ecological niches remained linked to their original region and ayllu by marriage and ritual. Historians commonly refer to this system of controlled exchange across ecological boundaries as vertical integration, or verticality.

Moche and Chimú

Around 200 C.E., some four centuries after the collapse of Chavín, the **Moche** (MO-che) achieved dominance of the north coastal region of Peru. They did not establish a centralized state, but they did deploy military forces, and major urban centers like Cerro Blanco (see Map 7.3) established hegemony over smaller towns and villages.

The Moche cultivated maize, quinoa, beans, manioc, and sweet potatoes with the aid of massive irrigation works. At higher elevations, they produced coca, which was used ritually. Complex networks of canals and aqueducts connecting fields with water sources as far away as 75 miles (121 kilometers) depended on mit'a labor imposed on Moche commoners and subject peoples. Large herds of llamas transported goods across difficult terrain. Their wool, along with cotton, provided raw material for textile production, and their meat was an important dietary element.

Murals and decorated ceramics show Moche society to be stratified and theocratic. Labor organization helped to promote class divisions. Wealth and power, along with political control, lay with the priests and military leaders, a situation reinforced by military conquest of neighboring regions. The elite lived above the commoners on large platforms at Moche ceremonial centers. Their rich clothing, including tall headdresses, confirmed their divine status and set them further apart from commoners. Gold and gold alloy jewelry signified social position: gold plates suspended from the noses concealed the lower portion of the faces, and large gold plugs decorated the ears.

ayllu Andean lineage group or kin-based community.
mit'a Andean labor system based on shared obligations to help kinsmen and work on behalf of the ruler and religious organizations.
Moche Civilization of north coast of Peru (200–700 C.E.). An important Andean civilization that built extensive irrigation networks as well as impressive urban centers dominated by brick temples.

One tomb of a warrior-priest buried from the Lambeyeque Valley contained a treasure that included gold, silver, and copper jewelry, textiles, feather ornaments, and shells. Two women and three men accompanied him in death. Each retainer had one foot amputated to ensure continued subservience and dependence in the afterlife (see Diversity and Dominance: Burials as Historic Texts).

Commoners lived by subsistence farming and labored for their ayllu and the elite. Agriculture, the care of llama herds, and the household economy involved both men and women. Commoners lived in one-room buildings clustered in the outlying areas of cities and in surrounding agricultural zones.

Moche textiles, ceramics, and metallurgy give evidence of numerous skilled artisans. As in Chavín, women played a major role in textile production; even elite women devoted time to weaving. Moche craftsmen produced highly individualized portrait vases, ceramics decorated with line drawings representing myths and rituals, and vessels depicting explicit sexual acts. Their metalwork included gold and silver objects devoted to religious and decorative functions or to elite adornment, as well as heavy copper and copper alloy tools for agricultural and military purposes.

The archaeological record shows that the rapid decline of the major centers coincided with a succession of natural disasters in the sixth century and the rise of a new military power in the Andean highlands. When an earthquake altered the course of the Moche River, major flooding caused serious damage, and a thirty-year period of drought expanded the area of coastal sand dunes, which then blew over cultivated fields, overwhelming the irrigation system. As the land dried, periodic heavy rains caused erosion, which further damaged the economy. Religious and political leaders whose privileges stemmed from a claimed ability to control natural forces through rituals lost credibility. Despite massive efforts to maintain irrigation and the construction of new urban centers in less vulnerable valleys to the north, Moche civilization never recovered. In the eighth century, a new military power, the **Wari** (WAH-ree), put pressure on trade routes linking the coastal region with the highlands and thus contributed to the disappearance of the Moche.

At the end of the Moche period, the **Chimú** (chee-MOO) developed a more powerful coastal civilization centered on Chan Chan, a capital built around 800 C.E. near the earlier Moche cultural center. Chimú expanded aggressively after 1200 and at the apex of its power controlled 625 miles (1,000 kilometers) of the Peruvian coast.

Within Chan Chan was a series of walled compounds, each one containing a burial pyramid. Scholars believe that each Chimú ruler built his own walled compound in Chan Chan and was buried there beneath a pyramid. Sacrifices and rich grave goods accompanied each royal burial. As with the Moche, Chimú's rulers separated themselves from the masses and demonstrated divine favor by consuming rare and beautiful textiles, ceramics, and precious metals. The Chimú dynasty may have practiced split inheritance, the goods and lands of the deceased ruler going to secondary heirs or for religious sacrifices. The heir who inherited the throne therefore had to construct his own residence compound and undertake new conquests to fund his household. After the Inca conquered the northern coast in 1465, they borrowed from the rituals and court customs of Chimú.

Tiwanaku and Wari

After 500 C.E., two powerful civilizations developed in the Andean highlands. At nearly 13,000 feet (3,962 meters) on the high, treeless plain near Lake Titicaca in modern Bolivia stand the ruins of **Tiwanaku** (tee-wah-NA-coo) (see Map 7.3). Initial occupation may have occurred as early as 400 B.C.E., but significant urbanization began only after 200 C.E. Modern excavations provide the outline of vast drainage projects that reclaimed nearly 200,000 acres (8,000 hectares) of rich lakeside marshes for agriculture. This system of raised fields and ditches permitted intensive cultivation similar to that achieved through chinampas in Mesoamerica. Fish and llamas added protein to a diet largely dependent on potatoes and grains. Llamas

Wari Andean civilization culturally linked to Tiwanaku, perhaps beginning as a colony of Tiwanaku.
Chimú Powerful Peruvian civilization based on conquest. Located in the region earlier dominated by Moche. Conquered by Inca in 1465.
Tiwanaku Name of capital city and empire centered on the region near Lake Titicaca in modern Bolivia (500–1000 C.E.).

Burials as Historic Texts

Efforts to reveal the history of the Americas before the arrival of Europeans depend on the work of archaeologists. The burials of rulers and other members of elites can be viewed as historical texts that describe how textiles, precious metals, beautifully decorated ceramics, and other commodities were used to reinforce the political and cultural power of ruling lineages. In public, members of the elite were always surrounded by the most desirable goods and rarest products as well as by elaborate rituals and ceremonies. The effect was to create an aura of godlike power. The material elements of political and cultural power were also integrated into the experience of death and burial as members of the elite were sent into the afterlife.

The first photograph is of an excavated Moche tomb in Sipán, Peru. The Moche (200 C.E.–ca. 700 C.E.), one of the most important of the pre-Inca civilizations of the Andean region, were masters of metallurgy, ceramics, and textiles. The excavations at Sipán revealed a "warrior-priest" buried with an amazing array of gold ornaments, jewels, textiles, and ceramics. Also buried with him were five human sacrifices: two women, perhaps wives or concubines, two male servants, and a warrior. Three of these victims—the warrior, one woman, and a male servant—are each missing a foot, as if to guarantee their continued faithfulness to the deceased ruler in the afterlife.

The second photograph shows the excavation of a classic-era (250 C.E.–ca. 900 C.E.) Maya burial at Río Azul in Guatemala. After death this elite male was laid out on a carved wooden platform and cotton mattress and his body painted with decorations. Mourners covered his body in rich textiles and surrounded him with valuable goods. These included a necklace of individual stones carved in the shape of heads, perhaps a symbol of his prowess in battle, and high-quality ceramics, some filled with foods consumed by the elite like cacao. The careful preparation of the burial chamber had required the work of numerous artisans and laborers, as was the case in the burial of the Moche warrior-priest. In death, as in life, these early American civilizations acknowledged the high status, political power, and religious authority of their elites.

QUESTIONS FOR ANALYSIS

1. If these burials are texts, what are stories?
2. Are there any visible differences in the two burials?
3. What questions might historians ask of these burials that cannot be answered?
4. Can modern burials be read as texts in similar ways to these ancient burials?

Heinze Plenge/National Geographic Stock

George Mobley/National Geographic Stock

Burials Reveal Ancient Civilizations *(Left)* Around 300 C.E. this Moche warrior-priest was buried amid rich tribute at Sipán in Peru. Also buried were the bodies of retainers or kinsmen probably sacrificed to accompany this powerful man. The body lies with the head on the right and the feet on the left. *(Right)* Similarly, the burial of a member of the Maya elite at Río Azul in northern Guatemala indicates the care taken to surround the powerful with fine ceramics, jewelry, and other valuable goods.

also serviced long-distance trade that brought in maize, coca, tropical fruits, and medicinal plants.

Tiwanaku's construction featured high-quality stone masonry. An organized work force—probably thousands of laborers over a period of years—moved large stones and quarried blocks many miles to construct a terraced pyramid, walled enclosures, and a reservoir. With copper alloy tools their only metallic resource, Tiwanaku's artisans cut stone so precisely that little mortar was needed to fit the blocks. They also produced gigantic human statuary; the largest example, a stern figure with a military bearing, was cut from a single stone 24 feet (7 meters) high.

Evidence of daily life is scarce, but Tiwanaku clearly had a stratified society ruled by a hereditary elite. Most women and men devoted their time to agriculture and the care of llamas, though construction and pottery required specialized artisans. Tiwanaku ceramics found in distant places suggest a specialized merchant class as well.

Many scholars portray Tiwanaku as the capital of a vast empire, a precursor to the later Inca state. The elite certainly controlled a large, disciplined labor force in the surrounding region, and conquests and the establishment of colonies provided the highland capital with products from ecologically distinct zones. Tiwanaku influence also extended eastward to the Amazon rain forest and southward to the coastal oases of the Atacama Desert in Chile. But archaeological evidence suggests that, in comparison with contemporary Teotihuacan in central Mexico, Tiwanaku had a relatively small full-time population of around 30,000 and served as a ceremonial and political center for a large regional population more than as a metropolis.

The contemporary site of Wari, about 450 miles (751 kilometers) to the northwest, had cultural and technological links to Tiwanaku, but the exact relationship remains unclear. Each had a unique cultural signature. Wari exceeded Tiwanaku in size, measuring nearly 4 square miles (10 square kilometers). A massive wall surrounded the city center, which included a large temple and numerous multifamily housing blocks. Housing for commoners sprawled across a suburban zone. Unlike most other urban centers in the Andes, Wari had no central planning.

The small scale of its monumental architecture and the near absence of cut stone masonry in public and private buildings distinguish Wari from Tiwanaku.

Wari ceramic style also differs, the difference enabling experts to trace Wari's expansion, at a time of increasing warfare throughout the Andes, to the coastal area earlier controlled by the Moche and to the northern highlands. Wari roads maintained communications with remote fortified dependencies. Perhaps as a consequence of military conflict, both Tiwanaku and Wari declined to insignificance by about 1000 C.E.

The Inca   In little more than one hundred years, the **Inca** developed a vast imperial state, which they called "Land of Four Corners." By 1525, this empire had a population of more than 6 million inhabitants and stretched from the Maule River in Chile to northern Ecuador and from the Pacific coast across the Andes to the upper Amazon and, in the south, into Argentina (see Map 7.3). In the early fifteenth century, the Inca competed for power locally in the southern highlands, an area of limited significance after the collapse of Wari. Centered in the valley of Cuzco, the Inca were initially organized as a chiefdom based on reciprocal gift giving and the redistribution of food and textiles. In the 1430s strong leaders consolidated political authority and undertook a campaign of military expansion.

The Inca state incorporated traditional Andean social customs and economic practices. Tiwanaku had used colonists to provide resources from ecologically distinct zones. The Inca built on this practice by using their large, professional military to conquer distant territories and by increasing the scale of forced exchanges.

Like earlier highland civilizations, the Inca were pastoralists, their prosperity and military strength depending on vast herds of llamas and alpacas. Both men and women cared for these herds—the women weaving woolen cloth, the men driving animals in long-distance trade. This pastoral background led the Inca to believe that the gods and their ruler shared the obligations of the shepherd to his flock, an idea reminiscent of the Old Testament image conveyed by the lines "The Lord is my Shepherd."

Cuzco, the imperial capital, and the provincial cities, the royal court, the imperial armies, and the

Inca Largest and most powerful Andean empire. Controlled the Pacific coast of South America from Ecuador to Chile from its capital of Cuzco.

state's religious cults all rested on the efforts of mit'a laborers. The mit'a system also provided the bare necessities for the old, weak, and ill of Inca society. Each ayllu contributed approximately one-seventh of its adult male population to meet these collective obligations. These draft laborers served as soldiers, construction workers, craftsmen, and runners to carry messages along post roads. They also drained swamps, terraced mountainsides, filled in valley floors, built and maintained irrigation works, and built storage facilities and roads. Inca laborers constructed 13,000 miles (20,930 kilometers) of road, which facilitated military troop movements, administration, and trade.

Imperial administration incorporated existing political structures and established elite groups. The hereditary chiefs of ayllus carried out administrative and judicial functions. As the Inca expanded, they generally left local rulers in place. Rebellion was possible, but the Inca controlled this risk by taking hostages and building military garrisons. Rulers of defeated regions sent their heirs to live at the Inca court in Cuzco, and representations of important local gods were brought to Cuzco to join the imperial pantheon.

Conquests magnified the authority of the Inca ruler and led to the creation of an imperial bureaucracy drawn from his kinsmen. The royal family claimed descent from the sun, the primary Inca god. Members of the royal family lived in palaces maintained by armies of servants. Political and religious rituals dominated the lives of the ruler and his family and helped legitimize their authority. Because extending imperial boundaries by warfare constituted an imperial duty, each new ruler began his reign with conquest.

At the height of Inca power in 1530, Cuzco had a population of fewer than 30,000, a fifth that of Tenochtitlan at the same time. Nevertheless, Cuzco contains impressive buildings constructed of carefully cut stones fitted together without mortar. Laid out in the shape of a giant puma (a mountain lion), the city's center contained the palaces each ruler built on ascending the throne, as well as the major temples. The Temple of the Sun had an interior lined with sheets of gold and a patio decorated with golden representations of llamas and maize. The ruler made every effort to awe and intimidate visitors and residents with a nearly continuous series of rituals, feasts, and sacrifices. Sacrifices of textiles, animals,

SECTION REVIEW

- Andean peoples overcame the challenges of their environment through superior organization.
- The Moche used these technologies to maintain a decentralized, socially stratified state.
- The Chimú built a centralized monarchy based on split inheritance and conquest.
- Tiwanaku and Wari exploited highland resources; the latter city was larger but had no central planning.
- The Inca extended traditional Andean practices to build the largest empire in the region.
- The Inca developed no new technologies but increased agricultural yield to support ever-growing populations.

and other goods sent as tribute dominated the city's calendar. The destruction of these valuable commodities and a small number of human sacrifices conveyed an impression of splendor and sumptuous abundance that appeared to validate the ruler's descent from the sun.

We know that astronomical observation occupied the priestly class, as in Mesoamerica, but the Inca calendar is unknown. Nonoral communication involved the khipus borrowed from earlier Andean civilizations. Inca weaving and metallurgy, building on earlier regional developments, excelled that of Mesoamerica. Inca craftsmen produced tools and weapons of copper and bronze along with decorative objects of gold and silver. Inca women produced textiles of extraordinary beauty from cotton and llama and alpaca wool.

The Inca did not introduce new technologies, but they increased economic output and added to the region's prosperity. Ruling large populations in environmentally distinct regions allowed the Inca to multiply exchanges between ecological niches. But imperial economic and political expansion reduced equality and diminished local autonomy. The imperial elite lived in richly decorated palaces in Cuzco and other urban centers, increasingly cut off from common people. The royal court held members of the provincial nobility at arm's length, and commoners faced execution if they looked directly at the ruler's face.

After only a century of regional dominance, the Inca Empire faced a crisis in 1526. The death of the Inca ruler Huayna Capac at the conclusion of the conquest of Ecuador initiated a bloody struggle for the throne. Powerful factions coalesced around two sons whose rivalry compelled both the military and the Inca elite to choose sides. The resulting civil war weakened imperial institutions and ignited the resentments of conquered peoples spread over more than 3,000 miles (4,830 kilometers) of mountainous terrain. On the eve of the arrival of Europeans, this violent conflict undermined the institutions and economy of Andean civilization.

Conclusion

The Aztec and Inca Empires culminate long historical developments in Mesoamerica and the Andes. Each empire was created militarily and depended as much on strong armies as on wise rulers or economic productivity. Both adopted and adapted political institutions, economic forms and technologies, and religious practices from their predecessors. Their rulers legitimized their authority by serving as intermediaries with the gods, and major cities were religious political centers with dominating religious architecture. Both regions depended on mobilizing ever-larger work forces to meet growing needs rather than on technological innovation.

Elementary markets developed in Mesoamerica to distribute specialized regional production, although the forced payment of goods as tribute helped sustain cities like Tenochtitlan and Cuzco. In the Andes reciprocal labor obligations and managed exchange relationships were used to allocate goods. The Aztecs forced defeated peoples to provide food, textiles, and even sacrificial victims, but they left local hereditary elites in place. The Inca, in contrast, created a centralized imperial administrative structure managed by a trained bureaucracy and used reciprocal labor obligations to produce and distribute goods.

Agricultural technology centering on maize, beans, and squash diffused from Mesoamerica to influence the major cultures of North America. In the southwestern desert of the United States, the Anasazi and other peoples utilized irrigated agriculture, a technology crucial also to Mesoamerican and Andean cultures.

As the Western Hemisphere's long isolation drew to a close in the late fifteenth century, both Aztec and Inca Empires were challenged by powerful neighbors or internal revolts. Similar challenges had contributed to the earlier decline of great civilizations in both regions. In previous cases, a long period of adjustment and development of new institutions followed the collapse of powers such as the Toltecs in Mesoamerica and Tiwanaku in the Andes. The arrival of Europeans was to change this pattern.

CHAPTER REVIEW

 Download the MP3 audio file of the Chapter Review to listen to on the go.

What role did nature and the environment play in the early civilizations of the Americas? (page 161)

The people of the Americas lived in virtual isolation from the rest of the world for at least 15,000 years. During this period, they learned to adapt to their natural environment on their own. The Olmec organized their population to dig irrigation and drainage canals and to cultivate the land. Chavín agriculture depended on the introduction of maize cultivation as well as trade with other regions. Llamas were used to transport goods along newly constructed roads and bridges. Artificial platforms and mounds of packed earth dominated both civilizations' urban centers. Olmec shamans planned urban centers to be aligned with the stars.

What were the most important shared characteristics of Mesoamerican cultures in the classic period? (page 167)

Mesoamerican civilization was based largely on a relationship with the gods and the environment. At Teotihuacan, people worshiped many gods and constructed pyramids devoted to the sun, the moon, and Quetzalcoatl. Human sacrifice was deemed essential to the well-being of society. Maya city-states also featured impressive temples, often built on high ground and reflecting the Maya cosmos.

As both political leaders and priests, rulers participated in bloodletting rituals and hallucinogenic trances. The people of Teotihuacan brought marginal lands into production and expanded the use of chinampas. The Maya contended with a tropical climate and fragile soils. People living near cities manipulated their environment by draining swamps and building elevated fields.

What role did warfare play in the postclassic period of Mesoamerica? (page 172)

The Toltecs were known for their military achievements. Images of war and violence appear on nearly all their public buildings and temples. The Mexica created a regional power called the Aztec Empire. Aztec rulers demonstrated their divine mandates by undertaking military conquests. Their chief deity was Huitzilopochtli, who was originally associated with war and came to be identified as the sun. The Aztecs offered up human sacrifices to the gods, usually consisting of war captives, criminals, and slaves.

In what ways did Mesoamerica influence the cultural centers in North America? (page 175)

Cultural centers in the southwest United States exhibit strong Mexican influence. Hohokam sites have platform mounds and ball courts, as well as pottery, clay figurines, and turquoise mosaics. To the north lived the Anasazi, who left the most vivid legacy of desert culture. One of the largest communities of the Anasazi was located in Chaco Canyon. Though Chaco trade goods show up in Toltec-period sites in northern Mexico, the Chaco culture seems to have developed independently. Beginning around 100 C.E., the Hopewell culture spread through the Ohio River Valley. Hopewell earthen mounds housed elite burials and served as platforms for temples and homes for chiefs. Similar mound building occurred in the Mississippian culture. Evidence of a Mesoamerican influence on either culture is rare.

How did the Amerindian peoples of the Andean area adapt to their environment and produce socially complex and politically advanced societies? (page 178)

Both the Andes Mountains and the bordering coastal plain posed great environmental challenges. The Amerindian response was effective organization of human labor for digging irrigation works, terracing hillsides, and building roads. Andean societies functioned through clans called ayllus that provided labor and goods to their hereditary chiefs. They also exchanged goods across ecological boundaries. Each community's production suited its ecological niche: coastal regions produced maize, fish, and cotton; mountain valleys contributed quinoa and potatoes; higher elevations contributed the wool and meat of animals; and the Amazonian region provided coca and fruits. The institutions of the ayllu and the state managed exchanges that fostered integration and growth.

Key Terms

Olmec (p. 162)	tribute system (p. 174)
Chavín (p. 165)	Anasazi (p. 176)
llama (p. 166)	chiefdom (p. 177)
Teotihuacan (p. 168)	khipus (p. 178)
Chinampas (p. 169)	ayllu (p. 179)
Maya (p. 170)	mit'a (p. 179)
Toltecs (p. 173)	Moche (p. 179)
Aztecs (p. 173)	Wari (p. 180)
altepetl (p. 173)	Chimú (p. 180)
calpolli (p. 173)	Tiwanaku (p. 180)
Tenochtitlan (p. 174)	Inca (p. 182)

Web Resources

Interactive Maps

- MAP 7.1 Olmec and Chavín Civilizations
- MAP 7.2 Major Mesoamerican Civilizations, 1000 B.C.E.–1519 C.E.
- MAP 7.3 Andean Civilizations, 200 B.C.E.–1532 C.E.

Answer to the History in Focus Question

See photo on page 170, "The Great Plaza at Tikal."

Visit the CourseMate website at www.cengagebrain.com for additional study tools and review materials for this chapter.

Networks of Communication and Exchange

© Cengage Learning

CHAPTER PREVIEW

The Silk Road
What factors contributed to the growth of trade along the Silk Road?

The Sasanid Empire and the Silk Road, 224–600
How did the Sasanid Empire evolve under the influence of east-west trade?

The Indian Ocean Maritime System
How did geography affect Indian Ocean trade routes?

Routes Across the Sahara
Why did trade begin across the Sahara Desert?

Sub-Saharan Africa
What accounts for the substantial degree of cultural unity in Africa south of the Sahara?

The Spread of Ideas
Why do some goods and ideas travel more easily than others?

Conclusion

DIVERSITY & DOMINANCE:
Travel Accounts of Africa and India

 Visit the CourseMate website at **www.cengagebrain.com** for additional study tools and review materials for this chapter.

nspired by the tradition of the Silk Road, a Chinese poet named Po Zhuyi (boh joo-yee) nostalgically wrote:

> Iranian whirling girl, Iranian whirling girl—
> Her heart answers to the strings,
> Her hands answer to the drums.
> At the sound of the strings and drums, she raises her arms,
> Like whirling snowflakes tossed about, she turns in her twirling dance.
> Iranian whirling girl,
> You came from Sogdiana (sog-dee-A-nuh).
> In vain did you labor to come east more than ten thousand tricents.
> For in the central plains there were already some who could do the Iranian whirl,
> And in a contest of wonderful abilities, you would not be their equal.[1]

The western part of Central Asia, the region around Samarkand (SAM-mar-kand) and Bukhara (boo-CAR-ruh) known in the eighth century C.E. as Sogdiana, was 2,500 miles (4,000 kilometers) from the Chinese capital of Chang'an (chahng-ahn). The route between these points was called in modern times the **Silk Road**, after one of the major products that were traded. Caravans took more than four months to trek across the mostly unsettled deserts, mountains, and grasslands, carrying with them agricultural goods, manufactured products, and ideas. Musicians and dancing girls traveled, too—as did camel pullers, merchants, monks, and pilgrims. The Silk Road was a means of connecting peoples and parts of the world as well as a social system.

With every expansion of territory, the growing wealth of temples, kings, and emperors enticed traders to venture ever farther afield for precious goods. For the most part, the customers were wealthy elites. But the new products, agricultural and industrial processes, and foreign ideas and customs these long-distance traders brought with them sometimes affected an entire society.

1. From *The Columbia Anthology of Traditional Chinese Literature*, edited and translated by Victor H. Mair. Copyright © 1994 Columbia University Press. Reprinted with permission of the publisher.

Travelers and traders seldom owned much land or wielded political power. Socially isolated (sometimes by law) and secretive because any talk about markets, products, routes, and travel conditions could help their competitors, they nevertheless contributed more to drawing the world together than did all but a few kings and emperors.

This chapter examines the social systems and historical impact of exchange networks that developed between 300 B.C.E. and 600 C.E. in Europe, Asia, and Africa. The Silk Road and the Indian Ocean Maritime System illustrate long-distance trade in this era. At the same time that shorter trade routes developed across the Sahara, the Bantu-speaking peoples within sub-Saharan Africa began a folk migration throughout Africa, carrying with them technologies, language, and ideas. A third pattern of cultural contact and exchange is illustrated by the spread of Buddhism in Asia and Christianity in Africa and Asia; Chapter 6 discussed the spread of Christian missionary activity in the Roman Empire.

The Silk Road

What factors contributed to the growth of trade along the Silk Road?

Archaeology and linguistic studies show that the peoples of Central Asia engaged in long-distance movement and exchange from at least 1500 B.C.E. In Roman times Europeans became captivated by the idea of a trade route linking the lands of the Mediterranean with China by way of Mesopotamia, Iran, and Central Asia. This Silk Road experienced several periods of heavy use (see Map 8.1), the first beginning around 100 B.C.E.

Origins and Operations

The Seleucid kings who succeeded to the eastern parts of Alexander the Great's empire in the third century B.C.E. focused their energies on Mesopotamia and Syria. This allowed an Iranian nomadic leader to establish an independent kingdom in northeastern Iran. The

Silk Road Caravan routes connecting China and the Middle East across Central Asia and Iran.

Interactive Map

Map 8.1 Asian Trade and Communication Routes The overland Silk Road was vulnerable to political disruption, but it was much shorter than the maritime route from the South China Sea to the Red Sea, and ships were more expensive than pack animals. Moreover, China's political centers were in the north. © Cengage Learning

Chronology

	Silk Road	Indian Ocean Trade	Saharan Trade
500 B.C.E.	247 B.C.E. Parthian rule begins in Iran 128 B.C.E. General Zhang Jian reaches Ferghana 100 B.C.E.–300 C.E. Kushans rule northern Afghanistan and Sogdiana		500 B.C.E. –CA. 1000 C.E. Bantu migrations CA. 200 B.C.E. Camel nomads in southern Sahara 46 B.C.E. First mention of camels in northern Sahara
1 C.E. 300 C.E.	1st century C.E. First evidence of the stirrup CA. 400 Buddhist pilgrim Faxian travels Silk Road	1st century C.E. Indonesian migration to Madagascar	CA. 300 Beginning of camel nomadism in northern Sahara
		CA. 900 Arab and Persian merchants in Canton	

Parthians, a people originally from east of the Caspian Sea, had become a major force by 247 B.C.E. They left few written sources, and recurring wars with Greeks and Romans to the west prevented travelers from the Mediterranean region from gaining firm knowledge of their kingdom. It seems likely, however, that they helped foster the Silk Road by being located on the threshold of Central Asia and sharing customs with steppe nomads farther to the east. In 128 B.C.E. a Chinese general named Zhang Jian (jahng jee-en) made his first exploratory journey across the deserts and mountains of Inner Asia on behalf of Emperor Wu of the Han dynasty. After crossing the broad and desolate Tarim Basin north of Tibet, he reached the fertile valley of Ferghana (fer-GAH-nuh) and for the first time encountered westward-flowing rivers. There he found horse breeders whose animals far outclassed any horses he had seen. Later Chinese historians looked on General Zhang, who ultimately led eighteen expeditions, as the originator of overland trade with the western lands, and they credited him with personally introducing a whole garden of new plants and trees to China.

Long-distance travel suited the people of the steppes more than the Chinese. The populations of Ferghana and neighboring regions included many nomads who followed their herds. Their migrations had little to do with trade, but they provided pack animals and controlled transit across their lands. The trading demands that brought the Silk Road into being were Chinese eagerness for western products, especially horses, and, on the western end, the organized Parthian state, which had captured

Iranian Musicians from Silk Road This three-color glazed pottery figurine, 23 inches (58.4 centimeters) high, comes from a northern Chinese tomb of the Tang era (sixth to ninth centuries C.E.). The musicians playing Iranian instruments confirm the migration of Iranian culture across the Silk Road. At the same time, dishes decorated by the Chinese three-color glaze technique were in vogue in northern Iran. The National Museum of Chinese History

Parthians Iranian ruling dynasty between ca. 247 B.C.E. and 224 C.E.

Lee Boltin/The Bridgeman Art Library

Scythian Breastplate This superbly crafted gold ornament from the fourth century B.C.E. features animal combat in the lower tier, flower motifs in the center, and scenes from Scythian pastoral life in the upper. Two men prepare a fleece garment in the middle of the upper tier while on either side young animals are suckling and a ewe is being milked. Note the contrast between the simplicity of nomadic life and the luxury represented by the gold ornament itself.

SECTION REVIEW

- The rise of the Parthian kingdom helped foster the Silk Road to meet Middle Eastern and European demand for Chinese silk.

- General Zhang led expeditions that established the route from China through Central Asia.

- Central Asian nomads facilitated the movement of goods through their lands.

- Central Asian cities grew as a result of Silk Road trade.

- In addition to silk, agricultural products traveled both ways along the Silk Road.

the flourishing markets of Mesopotamia from the Seleucids.

By 100 B.C.E., Greeks, and later the Romans, could buy Chinese silk from Parthian traders in Mesopotamian border entrepôts. Yet caravans also bought and sold goods along the way in prosperous Central Asian cities like Samarkand and Bukhara. These cities grew and flourished, often under the rule of local princes.

General Zhang definitely seems to have brought two plants to China: alfalfa and wine grapes. The former provided the best fodder for horses. In addition, Chinese farmers adopted pistachios, walnuts, pomegranates, sesame, coriander, spinach, and other new crops. Chinese artisans and physicians made good use of other trade products, such as jasmine oil, oak galls (used in tanning animal hides, dyeing, and making ink), sal ammoniac (for medicines), copper oxides, zinc, and precious stones.

In addition to silk, traders going west from China carried new fruits such as peaches and apricots, which the Romans mistakenly attributed to other eastern lands, calling them Persian plums and Armenian plums, respectively. They also carried cinnamon, ginger, and other spices that could not be grown in the West.

Nomadism in Central and Inner Asia

The Silk Road could not have functioned without pastoral nomads to provide animals, animal handlers, and protection. Descriptions of steppe nomads known as Scythians appear in the history of the Greek writer Herodotus in the sixth century B.C.E., who portrays them as superb riders, herdsmen, and hunters living in the steppes north of the Black and Caspian Seas. The Scythians moved regularly and efficiently with flocks and herds of enormous size to prevent overgrazing. They were also fearsome horse archers. Their homes, which were made of felt spread over a lightweight framework, were transported on four-wheeled wagons drawn by oxen. This custom continued for another two thousand years in the grasslands and deserts extending eastward to the borders of China.

Nomads were familiar with agriculture and willing to use products grown by farmers, but their ideal was self-sufficiency. Since their wanderings with their herds normally took them far from any farming region, self-sufficiency dictated foods they could provide for themselves—primarily meat and milk—and clothing made from felt, leather, and furs. Women oversaw the breeding and birthing of livestock and the preparation of furs.

Sasanid Silver Plate with Gold Decoration The Sasanid aristocracy, based in the countryside, invested part of its wealth in silver plates and vessels. This image of a Sasanid king hunting on horseback also reflects a favorite aristocratic pastime. Erich Lessing/Art Resource, NY

Nomads were most dependent on settled regions for the bronze or iron used in bridles, stirrups, cart fittings, and weapons. They acquired metal implements in trade and reworked them to suit their purposes. Scythians in the Ukraine worked extensively with iron as early as the fourth century B.C.E., and Turkish-speaking peoples had large ironworks in western Mongolia in the 600s C.E. Steppe nomads situated near settled areas also traded wool, leather, and horses for wood, silk, vegetables, and grain.

The Sasanid Empire and the Silk Road, 224–600

How did the Sasanid Empire evolve under the influence of east-west trade?

The rise of the **Sasanid Empire** in Iran brought a continuation of the rivalry between Rome and the Parthians along the Euphrates frontier and an intensification of trade along the Silk Road; but otherwise this empire differed greatly from its Parthian predecessor. Ardashir, a descendant of an ancestor named Sasan, defeated the Parthians around 224 and became sole ruler of Iran two years later. Unlike the Parthians,

who originated as nomads in northeastern Iran, the Sasanids came from the southwest, the same region that earlier gave rise to the Achaemenids (see Chapter 4).

In contrast to the sparse material remains of the Parthian period, Sasanid silver work and silk fabrics testify to the sumptuous and sedentary lifestyle of the warrior elite. Cities in Iran were small walled communities that served more as military strongpoints protecting long-distance trade than as centers of population and production.

The Silk Road now brought many new crops to Mesopotamia. Sasanid farmers pioneered in planting cotton, sugar cane, rice, citrus trees, eggplants, and other crops adopted from India and China. Although the acreage devoted to new crops increased slowly, these products became important consumption and trade items in later centuries.

Religions and the Sasanid Empire

The Sasanids established their Zoroastrian faith (see Chapter 4) as a state religion similar to Christianity in the Byzantine Empire (see Chapter 6). The proclamation of Christianity and Zoroastrianism as official faiths marked the fresh emergence of religion as an instrument of politics both within and between the empires. This politicization of religion greatly affected the culture of the Silk Road.

Both Zoroastrianism and Christianity practiced intolerance. A late-third-century inscription in Iran boasts of the persecutions of Christians, Jews, and Buddhists carried out by the Zoroastrian high priest. Yet sizeable Christian and Jewish communities

Sasanid Empire Iranian empire, established ca. 224, with a capital in Ctesiphon, Mesopotamia. The Sasanid emperors established Zoroastrianism as the state religion. Islamic Arab armies overthrew the empire ca. 640.

remained, especially in Mesopotamia. Similarly, from the fourth century onward, councils of Christian bishops declared many theological beliefs heretical—so unacceptable that they were un-Christian.

Christians became pawns in the political rivalry with the Byzantines and were sometimes persecuted, sometimes patronized, by the Sasanid kings. In 431 a council of bishops called by the Byzantine emperor declared the Nestorian Christians heretics for overemphasizing the humanness of Christ. The Nestorians believed that a human nature and a divine nature coexisted in Jesus and that Mary was not the mother of God, as many other Christians maintained, but the mother of the human Jesus. After the bishops' ruling, the Nestorians sought refuge under the Sasanid shah and engaged in missionary activities along the Silk Road.

A parallel episode within Zoroastrianism transpired in the third century. A preacher named Mani founded a new religion in Mesopotamia: Manichaeism. He preached a dualist faith—a struggle between Good and Evil—theologically derived from Zoroastrianism. Although at first Mani enjoyed the favor of the shah, he and many of his followers were martyred in 276. His religion survived and spread widely, particularly along the Silk Road. Nestorian missionaries thus competed with Manichaean missionaries for converts in Central Asia.

The Impact of the Silk Road

As trade became a more important part of Central Asian life, Iranian-speaking peoples increasingly settled in trading cities and surrounding farm villages. By the sixth century C.E., nomads originally from the Altai Mountains farther east had spread across the steppes and become the dominant pastoral group. These peoples spoke Turkic languages unrelated to the Iranian tongues. The nomads continued to live in the round, portable felt huts called yurts that can still occasionally be seen in Central Asia, but prosperous individuals, both Turks and Iranians, built stately homes decorated with brightly colored wall paintings. The paintings show people wearing Chinese silks and Iranian brocades and riding on richly outfitted horses and camels. They also indicate an avid interest in Buddhism (see below), which competed with Nestorian Christianity, Manichaeism, and Zoroastrianism in a lively and inquiring intellectual milieu.

SECTION REVIEW

- Originating in southern Iran, the Sasanids overthrew the Parthians and continued their predecessors' rivalry with Rome.

- Sasanid farmers pioneered the cultivation of Silk Road crops.

- Sasanid kings made Zoroastrianism the state religion, and other religions, particularly Christianity, experienced both toleration and persecution.

- Silk Road trade encouraged movements of peoples in Iran and Central Asia, as well as the exchange of religious ideas and military technology.

Missionary influences exemplify the impact of foreign customs and beliefs on the peoples along the Silk Road. Military technology affords an example of the opposite phenomenon, steppe customs radiating into foreign lands. Chariot warfare and the use of mounted bowmen originated in Central Asia and spread eastward and westward through military campaigns and folk migrations that began in the second millennium B.C.E. and recurred throughout the period of the Silk Road.

Evidence of the **stirrup**, one of the most important inventions, comes first from the Kushan people who ruled northern Afghanistan in approximately the first century C.E. At first a solid bar, then a loop of leather to support the rider's big toe, and finally a device of leather and metal or wood supporting the instep, the stirrup gave riders far greater stability in the saddle—which itself was in all likelihood an earlier Central Asian invention. Using stirrups, a mounted warrior could supplement his bow and arrow with a long lance and charge his enemy at a gallop without fear that the impact of his attack would push him off his mount. Far to the west, the stirrup made possible the armored knights who dominated the battlefields of Europe (see Chapter 10), and it contributed to the superiority of the Tang cavalry in China (see Chapter 11).

stirrup Device for securing a horseman's feet, enabling him to wield weapons more effectively. First evidence of the use of stirrups was among the Kushan people of northern Afghanistan in approximately the first century C.E.

Indian Ocean Sailing Vessel Ships like this one, in a rock carving on the Buddhist temple of Borobodur in Java, probably carried colonists from Indonesia to Madagascar.

The Indian Ocean Maritime System

How did geography affect Indian Ocean trade routes?

A multilingual, multiethnic society of seafarers established the **Indian Ocean Maritime System**, a trade network across the Indian Ocean and the South China Sea. These people left few records and seldom played a visible part in the rise and fall of kingdoms and empires, but they forged increasingly strong economic and social ties between the coastal lands of East Africa, southern Arabia, the Persian Gulf, India, Southeast Asia, and southern China.

This trade took place in three distinct regions: (1) In the South China Sea, Chinese and Malays (including Indonesians) dominated trade. (2) From the east coast of India to the islands of Southeast Asia, Indians and Malays were the main traders. (3) From the west coast of India to the Persian Gulf and the east coast of Africa, merchants and sailors were predominantly Persians and Arabs. However, Chinese and Malay sailors could and did voyage to East Africa, and by 900 C.E. Arab and Persian traders reached Canton in southern China.

From the time of Herodotus in the fifth century B.C.E., Greek writers regaled their readers with stories of marvelous voyages down the Red Sea into the Indian Ocean and around Africa from the west. Most often, they attributed such trips to the Phoenicians, the most fearless of Mediterranean seafarers. Occasionally a Greek appears. One such was Hippalus, a Greek ship's pilot who was said to have discovered the seasonal monsoon winds that facilitate sailing across the Indian Ocean (see Diversity and Dominance: Travel Accounts of Africa and India).

Of course, the regular seasonal alternation of steady winds could not have remained unnoticed for thousands of years, waiting for an alert Greek to happen along. The great voyages and discoveries made before written records became common should surely be attributed to the peoples who lived around the Indian Ocean rather than to interlopers from the Mediterranean Sea. The story of Hippalus resembles the Chinese story of General Zhang Jian, whose role in opening trade with Central Asia overshadows the anonymous contributions made by the indigenous peoples. The Chinese may indeed have learned from

Indian Ocean Maritime System In premodern times, a network of seaports, trade routes, and maritime culture linking countries on the rim of the Indian Ocean from Africa to Indonesia.

Diversity & Dominance

Travel Accounts of Africa and India

The most revealing description of ancient trade in the Indian Ocean and of the diversity and economic forces shaping the Indian Ocean trading system, "The Periplus of the Erythraean Sea," a sailing itinerary (periplus in Greek), was composed in the first century C.E. by an unknown Greco-Egyptian merchant. It highlights the diversity of peoples and products from the Red Sea to the Bay of Bengal. Historians believe that the descriptions of market towns were based on firsthand experience. The following passages deal with East Africa and the coastal lands of the Indian subcontinent (see Map 8.1).

Of the designated ports on the Erythraean Sea [Indian Ocean], and the market-towns around it, the first is the Egyptian port of Mussel Harbor. To those sailing down from that place, on the right hand . . . there is Berenice. The harbors of both are at the boundary of Egypt. . . .

On the right-hand coast next below Berenice is the country of the Berbers. Along the shore are the Fish-Eaters, living in scattered caves in the narrow valleys. Further inland are the Berbers, and beyond them the Wild-flesh-Eaters and Calf-Eaters, each tribe governed by its chief; and behind them, further inland, in the country towards the west, there lies a city called Meroe.

Below the Calf-Eaters there is a little market-town on the shore . . . called Ptolemais of the Hunts, from which the hunters started for the interior under the dynasty of the Ptolemies. . . . But the place has no harbor and is reached only by small boats. . . .

Beyond this place, the coast trending toward the south, there is the Market and Cape of Spices, an abrupt promontory, at the very end of the Berber coast toward the east. . . . A sign of an approaching storm . . . is that the deep water becomes more turbid and changes its color. When this happens they all run to a large promontory called Tabae, which offers safe shelter. . . .

Beyond Tabae [lies] . . . another market-town called Opone. . . . [I]n it the greatest quantity of cinnamon is produced . . . and slaves of the better sort, which are brought to Egypt in increasing numbers. . . .

[Ships also come] from the places across this sea, from . . . Barygaza, bringing to these . . . market-towns the products of their own places; wheat, rice, clarified butter, sesame oil, cotton cloth . . . and honey from the reed called sacchari [sugar cane]. Some make the voyage especially to these market-towns, and others exchange their cargoes while sailing along the coast. This country is not subject to a King, but each market-town is ruled by its separate chief.

Beyond Opone, the shore trending more toward the south . . . this coast [the Somali region of Azania, or East Africa] is destitute of harbors . . . until the Pyralax islands [Zanzibar]. . . . [A] little to the south of south-west . . . is the island Menuthias [Madagascar], about three hundred stadia from the mainland, low and wooded, in which there are rivers and many kinds of birds and the mountain-tortoise. There are no wild beasts except the crocodiles; but there they do not attack men. In this place there are sewed boats, and canoes hollowed from single logs. . . .

Two days' sail beyond, there lies the very last market-town of the continent of Azania, which is called Rhapta [Dar es-Salaam]; which has its name from the sewed boats (rhapton ploiarion) . . . ; in which there is ivory in great quantity, and tortoise-shell. Along this coast live men of piratical habits, very great in stature, and under separate chiefs for each place. . . .

And these markets of Azania are the very last of the continent that stretches down on the right hand from Berenice; for beyond these places the unexplored ocean curves around toward the west, and running along by the regions to the south of Aethiopia and Libya and Africa, it mingles with the western sea. . . .

Now the whole country of India has very many rivers, and very great ebb and flow of the tides. . . . But about Barygaza [Broach] it is much greater, so that the bottom is suddenly seen, and now parts of the dry land are sea, and now it is dry where ships were sailing just before; and the rivers, under the inrush of the flood tide, when the whole force of the sea is directed against them, are driven upwards more strongly against their natural current. . . .

The country inland from Barygaza is inhabited by numerous tribes. . . . Above these is the very warlike nation of the Bactrians, who are under their own king. And Alexander, setting out from these parts, penetrated to the Ganges. . . . [T]o the present day ancient drachmae are current in Barygaza, coming from this country, bearing inscriptions in Greek letters, and the devices of those who reigned after Alexander. . . .

Inland from this place and to the east, is the city called Ozene [Ujjain]. . . . [F]rom this place are brought down all things needed for the welfare of the country about Barygaza, and many things for our trade: agate and carnelian, Indian muslins. . . .

There are imported into this market-town, wine, Italian preferred, also Laodicean and Arabian; copper, tin, and lead; coral and topaz; thin clothing and inferior sorts of all kinds . . . gold and silver coin, on which there is a profit when exchanged for the money of the country. . . . And for the King there are brought into those places very costly vessels of silver, singing boys, beautiful maidens for the harem, fine wines, thin clothing of the finest weaves, and the choicest ointments. There are exported from these places [spices], ivory, agate and carnelian . . . cotton cloth of all kinds, silk cloth. . . .

Beyond Barygaza the adjoining coast extends in a straight line from north to south. . . . The inland country back from the coast toward the east comprises many desert regions and great mountains; and all kinds of wild beasts—leopards, tigers, elephants, enormous serpents, hyenas, and baboons of many sorts; and many populous nations, as far as the Ganges. . . .

This whole voyage as above described . . . they used to make in small vessels, sailing close around the shores of the gulfs; and Hippalus was the pilot who by observing the location of the ports and the conditions of the sea, first discovered how to lay his course straight across the ocean. . . .

About the following region, the course trending toward the east, lying out at sea toward the west is the island Palaesimundu, called by the ancients Taprobane [Sri Lanka]. . . . It produces pearls, transparent stones, muslins, and tortoiseshell. . . .

Beyond this, the course trending toward the north, there are many barbarous tribes, among whom are the Cirrhadae, a race of men with flattened noses, very savage; another tribe, the Bargysi; and the Horse-faces and the Long-faces, who are said to be cannibals.

After these, the course turns toward the east again, and sailing with the ocean to the right and the shore remaining beyond to the left, Ganges comes into view. . . . And just opposite this river there is an island in the ocean, the last part of the inhabited world toward the east, under the rising sun itself; it is called Chryse; and it has the best tortoise-shell of all the places on the Erythraean Sea.

After this region under the very north, the sea outside ending in a land called This, there is a very great inland city called Thinae, from which raw silk and silk yarn and silk cloth are brought on foot. . . . But the land of This is not easy of access; few men come from there, and seldom.

The Chinese traveler Xuanzang (600–664) journeyed across Inner Asia to India, making pilgrimage to Buddhist holy places and searching for Sanskrit scriptures to take back to China with him. His descriptions of the places he visited reflect his interests. The following passages come from his description of India.

Towns and Buildings

The towns and villages have inner gates; the walls are wide and high; the streets and lanes are tortuous, and the roads winding. The thoroughfares are dirty and the stalls arranged on both sides of the road with appropriate signs. Butchers, fishers, dancers, executioners, and scavengers, and so on, have their abodes without the city. In coming and going these persons are bound to keep on the left side of the road till they arrive at their homes. Their houses are surrounded by low walls, and form the suburbs. The earth being soft and muddy, the walls of the town are mostly built of brick or tiles. The towers on the walls are constructed of wood or bamboo; the houses have balconies and belvederes, which are made of wood, with a coating of lime or mortar, and covered with tiles. The different buildings have the same form as those in China: rushes, or dry branches, or tiles, or boards are used for covering them. The walls are covered with lime and mud, mixed with cow's dung for purity. At different seasons they scatter flowers about. Such are some of their different customs.

Dress and Appearance

Their clothing is not cut or fashioned; they mostly affect fresh-white garments; they esteem little those of mixed color or ornamented. The men wind their garments round their middle, then gather them under the armpits, and let them fall down across the body, hanging to the right. The robes of the women fall down to the ground; they completely cover their shoulders.

They wear a little knot of hair on their crowns, and let the rest of their hair fall loose. Some of the men cut off their moustaches, and have other odd customs. . . . In North India, where the air is cold, they wear short and close-fitting garments. . . . The dress and ornaments worn by the nonbelievers are varied and mixed. Some wear peacocks' feathers; some wear as ornaments necklaces made of skull bones; some have no clothing, but go naked; some wear leaf or bark garments; some pull out their hair and cut off their moustaches; others have bushy whiskers and their hair braided on the top of their heads. The costume is not uniform, and the color, whether red or white, not constant.

QUESTIONS FOR ANALYSIS

1. How do the differing interests of a trader and a religious pilgrim show up in what they report?
2. How do these narratives show the influence of the countries the authors are coming from?
3. Given the different viewpoints of travelers, what is the value of travel accounts as sources for history?

Source: Samuel Beal, *Buddhist Records of the Western World*, translated from the Chinese of Hiuen Tsiang (A.D. 629) (London: Trubner and Company, 1884; reprint Delhi: Oriental Books Reprint Corporation, 1969), 73–76.

General Zhang and the Greeks from Hippalus, but other people played important roles anonymously.

Indian Ocean voyages differed in several ways from Mediterranean voyages. Mediterranean sailors of the time of Alexander used square sails and long banks of oars to maneuver among the sea's many islands and small harbors. In contrast, Indian Ocean vessels relied on roughly triangular lateen sails in running before the wind on long ocean stretches. Whereas Mediterranean shipbuilders nailed their vessels together, the planks of Indian Ocean ships were pierced, tied together with palm fiber, and caulked with bitumen. Mediterranean sailors rarely ventured out of sight of land. Indian Ocean sailors, thanks to the monsoon winds, could cover long reaches entirely at sea.

These technological differences prove that the world of the Indian Ocean developed differently than the world of the Mediterranean Sea, where the Phoenicians and Greeks established colonies that maintained contact with their home cities (see Chapters 3 and 4). The traders of the Indian Ocean, where distances were greater and contacts less frequent, seldom retained political ties with their homelands. The colonies they established were sometimes socially distinctive but rarely independent of the local political powers.

Origins of Contact

By 2000 B.C.E. Sumerian records indicate regular trade between Mesopotamia, the islands of the Persian Gulf, Oman, and the Indus Valley. However, this early trading contact broke off, and later Mesopotamian trade references mention East Africa more often than India.

A similarly early chapter in Indian Ocean history concerns migrations from Southeast Asia to Madagascar, the world's fourth largest island, situated off the southeastern coast of Africa. About two thousand years ago, people from one of the many Indonesian islands of Southeast Asia established themselves in that forested, mountainous land 6,000 miles (9,500 kilometers) from home. They could not possibly have carried enough supplies for a direct voyage across the Indian Ocean, so their route must have touched the coasts of India and southern Arabia. No physical remains of their journeys have been discovered, however.

Apparently, the sailing canoes of these people plied the seas along the increasingly familiar route for several hundred years. Settlers farmed the new land and entered into relations with Africans who found their way across the 250-mile-wide (400-kilometer-wide) Mozambique (moe-zam-BEEK) Channel around the fifth century C.E. Descendants of the seafarers preserved the language of their homeland and some of its culture, such as the cultivation of bananas, yams, and other native Southeast Asian plants. These food crops spread to mainland Africa. But the memory of their distant origins gradually faded, not to be recovered until modern times, when scholars established the linguistic link between the two lands.

The Impact of Indian Ocean Trade

The demand for products from the coastal lands inspired mariners to persist in their long ocean voyages. Africa produced exotic animals, wood, and ivory. Since ivory also came from India, Mesopotamia, and North Africa, the extent of

African ivory exports cannot be determined. The high-lands of northern Somalia and southern Arabia grew the scrubby trees whose aromatic resins were valued as frankincense and myrrh. Pearls abounded in the Persian Gulf, and evidence of ancient copper mines has been found in Oman in southeastern Arabia. India shipped spices and manufactured goods, and more spices came from Southeast Asia, along with manufactured items, particularly pottery, obtained in trade with China. In sum, the Indian Ocean trading region had a great variety of highly valued products. Given the long distances and the comparative lack of islands, however, the volume of trade there was undoubtedly much lower than in the Mediterranean Sea.

The culture of the Indian Ocean ports was often isolated from the hinterlands, particularly in the west. The coasts of the Arabian peninsula, the African side of the Red Sea, southern Iran, and northern India (today's Pakistan) were mostly barren desert. Ports in all these areas tended to be small, and many suffered from meager supplies of fresh water. Farther south in India, the monsoon provided ample water, but steep mountains cut off the coastal plain from the interior of the country. Thus few ports between Zanzibar and Sri Lanka had substantial inland populations within easy reach. The head of the Persian Gulf was one exception: ship-borne trade was possible from the port of Apologus (the precursor of modern Basra) as far north as Babylon.

By contrast, eastern India, the Malay Peninsula, and Indonesia afforded more hospitable and densely populated shores with easier access to inland populations. Though the fishers, sailors, and traders of the western Indian Ocean system supplied a long series of kingdoms and empires, none of these consumer societies became primarily maritime in orientation, as the Greeks and Phoenicians did in the Mediterranean. In contrast, seaborne trade and influence seem to have been important even to the earliest states of Southeast Asia (see Chapter 5).

In coastal areas throughout the Indian Ocean system, small groups of seafarers sometimes had a significant social impact despite their lack of political power. Women seldom accompanied the men on long sea voyages, so sailors and merchants often married local women in port cities. The families thus established were bilingual and bicultural. As in many

SECTION REVIEW

- The Indian Ocean Maritime System grew from the voyages of a collection of diverse seafaring traders.
- Unlike the Mediterranean, the Indian Ocean developed no network of colonies with home ties.
- The system originated in early Mesopotamian trade routes and the migrations of Southeast Asian peoples to Madagascar.
- Trade in a broad range of goods flourished in ports where distinct cultures evolved.

other situations in world history, women played a crucial though not well-documented role as mediators between cultures. Not only did they raise their children to be more cosmopolitan than children from inland regions, but they also introduced the men to customs and attitudes that they carried with them when they returned to sea. As a consequence, the designation of specific seafarers as Persian, Arab, Indian, or Malay often conceals mixed heritages and a rich cultural diversity.

Routes Across the Sahara

Why did trade begin across the Sahara Desert?

The windswept Sahara, a desert stretching from the Red Sea to the Atlantic Ocean and broken only by the Nile River, isolates sub-Saharan Africa from the Mediterranean world (see Map 8.2). The current dryness of the Sahara dates only to about 2500 B.C.E. The period of drying out that preceded that date lasted twenty-five centuries and encompassed several cultural changes. During that time, travel between a slowly shrinking number of grassy areas was comparatively easy. However, by 300 B.C.E., scarcity of water was restricting travel to a few difficult routes initially known only to desert nomads. Trade over **trans-Saharan caravan routes**, at first only a trickle, eventually expanded into a significant stream.

trans-Saharan caravan routes Trading network linking North Africa with sub-Saharan Africa across the Sahara.

Cattle Herders in Saharan Rock Art These paintings represent the most artistically accomplished type of Saharan art. Herding societies of modern times living in the Sahel region south of the Sahara strongly resemble the society depicted here.

Courtesy, Mrs. Irene Lhote. Photo: Henri Lhote

History in Focus *Examine the paintings. What clues does the depiction of people, animals, and objects give us about early Saharan society and culture? Find the answer online.*

Early Saharan Cultures

Sprawling sand dunes, sandy plains, and vast expanses of exposed rock make up most of the great desert. Stark and rugged mountain and highland areas separate its northern and southern portions. The cliffs and caves of these highlands, the last spots where water and grassland could be found as the climate changed, preserve rock paintings and engravings that constitute the primary evidence for early Saharan history.

Though dating is difficult, what appear to be the earliest images, left by hunters in much wetter times, include elephants, giraffes, rhinoceros, crocodiles, and other animals that have long been extinct in the region. Overlaps in the artwork indicate that the hunting societies were gradually joined by new cultures based on cattle breeding and well adapted to the sparse grazing that remained. Domestic cattle may have originated in western Asia or in North Africa. They certainly reached the Sahara before it became completely dry. The beautiful paintings of cattle and scenes of daily life seen in the Saharan rock art depict pastoral societies that bear little similarity to any

in western Asia. The people seem physically akin to today's West Africans, and the customs depicted, such as dancing and wearing masks, as well as the breeds of cattle, particularly those with piebald coloring (splotches of black and white), strongly suggest later societies to the south of the Sahara. These factors support the hypothesis that some southern cultural patterns originated in the Sahara.

Overlaps in artwork also show that horse herders succeeded the cattle herders. The rock art changes dramatically in style, from the superb realism of the cattle pictures to sketchier images that are often strongly geometric. Moreover, the horses are frequently shown drawing light chariots. According to the most common theory, intrepid charioteers from the Mediterranean shore drove their flimsy vehicles across the desert and established societies in the few remaining grassy areas of the central Saharan highlands. Some scholars suggest possible chariot routes that refugees from the collapse of the Mycenaean and Minoan civilizations of Greece and Crete (see Chapter 3) might have followed deep into the desert around the twelfth century B.C.E. However, no archaeological evidence of actual chariot use in the Sahara has been discovered, and it is difficult to imagine large numbers of refugees from the politically chaotic Mediterranean region driving chariots into a waterless, trackless desert in search of a new homeland

Interactive Map

Map 8.2 **Africa and the Trans-Saharan Trade Routes** The Sahara and the surrounding oceans isolated most of Africa from foreign contact before 1000 C.E. The Nile Valley, a few trading points on the east coast, and limited transdesert trade provided exceptions to this rule, but the dominant forms of sub-Saharan African culture originated far to the west, north of the Gulf of Guinea.

© Cengage Learning

somewhere to the south. As with the cattle herders, therefore, the identity of the Saharan horse breeders and the source of their passion for drawing chariots remain a mystery. Only with the coming of the camel is it possible to make firm connections with the Saharan nomads of today through the depiction of objects and geometric patterns still used by the veiled, blue-robed Tuareg (TWAH-reg) people of the highlands in southern Algeria, Niger, and Mali.

Some historians maintain that the Romans inaugurated an important trans-Saharan trade, but they lack firm archaeological evidence. More plausibly, Saharan trade relates to the spread of camel domestication. Supporting evidence comes from rock art, where overlaps of images imply that camel riders in desert costume constitute the latest Saharan population. The camel-oriented images are decidedly the crudest to be found in the region.

The first mention of camels in North Africa comes in a Latin text of 46 B.C.E. Since the native camels of Africa probably died out before the era of domestication, the domestic animals likely reached the Sahara from Arabia by way of Egypt in the first millennium B.C.E. They could have been adopted by peoples farther and farther to the west, from one central Saharan highland to the next, only much later spreading northward and coming to the attention of the Romans. Camel herding made it easier for people to move away from the Saharan highlands and roam the deep desert.

Trade Across the Sahara

Linkage between two different trading systems, one in the south, the other in the north, developed slowly. Southern traders concentrated on supplying salt from large deposits in the southern desert to the peoples of sub-Saharan Africa. Traders from the equatorial forest zone brought forest products, such as kola nuts (a condiment and source of caffeine) and edible palm oil, to trading centers near the desert's southern fringe. Each group received the products they needed in their homelands from the other, or from the farming peoples of the **Sahel** (SAH-hel)—literally "the coast" in Arabic, the southern borderlands of the Sahara (see Map 8.2). Middlemen who were native to the Sahel played an important role in this trade, but precise historical details are lacking.

SECTION REVIEW

- Early Saharan cultures included hunting societies and, in isolated areas, groups of cattle breeders.
- Later, horse and camel herders joined these groups.
- Camel-riding nomads most likely pioneered the trans-Saharan trade routes, linking North African and sub-Saharan trade networks.

In the north, Roman colonists supplied Italy with agricultural products, primarily wheat and olives. Surviving mosaic pavements depicting scenes from daily life show that people living on the farms and in the towns of the interior consumed Roman manufactured goods and shared Roman styles. This northern pattern began to change only in the third century C.E. with the decline of the Roman Empire, the abandonment of many Roman farms, the growth of nomadism, and a lessening of trade across the Mediterranean.

Sub-Saharan Africa

What accounts for the substantial degree of cultural unity in Africa south of the Sahara?

The Indian Ocean network and later trade across the Sahara provided **sub-Saharan Africa**, the portion of Africa south of the Sahara, with a few external contacts. The most important African network of cultural exchange from 500 B.C.E. to 1000 C.E., however, arose within the region and took the form of folk migration. These migrations and exchanges put in place enduring characteristics of African culture.

A Challenging Geography

Many geographic obstacles impede access to and movement within sub-Saharan Africa (see Map 8.2). The Sahara, the Atlantic and Indian Oceans, and the Red Sea form the boundaries of the region. With the exception of the Nile, a ribbon of green

Sahel Belt south of the Sahara; literally "the coast" in Arabic.
sub-Saharan Africa Portion of the African continent lying south of the Sahara.

traversing the Sahara from south to north, the major river systems empty into oceans: the Senegal, Niger, and Zaire (zah-EER) Rivers empty into the Atlantic, and the Zambezi River empties into the Mozambique Channel of the Indian Ocean. Rapids limit the use of these rivers for navigation.

Stretching over 50 degrees of latitude, sub-Saharan Africa encompasses dramatically different environments. A 4,000-mile (6,500-kilometer) trek from the southern edge of the Sahara to the Cape of Good Hope would take a traveler from the flat, semiarid plains of the Sahel region to tropical **savanna** covered by long grasses and scattered forest, and then to **tropical rain forest** on the lower Niger and in the Zaire Basin. The rain forest gives way to another broad expanse of savanna, followed by more steppe and desert, and finally by a region of temperate highlands at the southern extremity, located as far south of the equator as Greece and Sicily are to its north. East-west travel is comparatively easy in the steppe and savanna regions—a caravan from Senegal to the Red Sea would have traversed a distance comparable to that of the Silk Road—but difficult in the equatorial rain-forest belt and across the mountains and deep rift valleys that abut the rain forest to the east and separate East from West Africa.

The Development of Cultural Unity

Cultural heritages shared by the educated elites within each region of the world—heritages that some anthropologists call **"great traditions"**—typically include a written language, common legal and belief systems, ethical codes, and other intellectual attitudes. They loom large in written records as traditions that rise above the diversity of local customs and beliefs commonly distinguished as **"small traditions."**

By the year 1 C.E. sub-Saharan Africa had become a distinct cultural region, though one not shaped by imperial conquest or characterized by a shared elite culture, a "great tradition." The cultural unity of sub-Saharan Africa rested on similar characteristics shared to varying degrees by many popular cultures, or "small traditions." These had developed during the region's long period of isolation from the rest of the world and had been refined, renewed, and interwoven by repeated episodes of migration and social interaction. Historians know little about this complex prehistory. Thus, to a greater degree than in other regions, they call on anthropological descriptions, oral history, and comparatively late records of various "small traditions" to reconstruct the broad outlines of cultural formation.

Sub-Saharan Africa's cultural unity is less immediately apparent than its diversity. By one estimate, Africa is home to two thousand distinct languages, many corresponding to social and belief systems endowed with distinctive rituals and cosmologies. There are likewise numerous food production systems, ranging from hunting and gathering—very differently carried out by the Mbuti (m-BOO-tee) Pygmies of the equatorial rain forest and the Khoisan (KOI-sahn) peoples of the southwestern deserts—to the cultivation of bananas, yams, and other root crops in forest clearings and of sorghum and other grains in the savanna lands. Pastoral societies, particularly those depending on cattle, display somewhat less diversity across the Sahel and savanna belt from Senegal to Kenya.

Sub-Saharan Africa covered a larger and more diverse area than any other cultural region in the first millennium C.E. and had a lower overall population density. Thus societies and polities had ample room to form and reform, and a substantial amount of space separated different groups. The contacts that did occur did not last long enough to produce rigid cultural uniformity.

In addition, for centuries external conquerors could not penetrate the region's natural barriers and impose a uniform culture. The Egyptians occupied

---

savanna Tropical or subtropical grassland, either treeless or with occasional clumps of trees. Most extensive in sub-Saharan Africa but also present in South America.

tropical rain forest High-precipitation forest zones of the Americas, Africa, and Asia lying between the Tropic of Cancer and the Tropic of Capricorn.

"great traditions" Anthropologists' term for a literate, well-institutionalized complex of religious and social beliefs and practices adhered to by diverse societies over a broad geographical area.

"small traditions" Anthropologists' term for a localized, usually nonliterate, set of customs and beliefs adhered to by a single society, often in conjunction with a "great tradition."

Nubia, and some traces of Egyptian influence appear in Saharan rock art farther west, but the Nile cataracts and the vast swampland in the Nile's upper reaches blocked movement farther south. The Romans sent expeditions against pastoral peoples living in the Libyan Sahara but could not incorporate them into the Roman world.

African Cultural Characteristics

European travelers who got to know the sub-Saharan region well in the nineteenth and twentieth centuries observed broad commonalities underlying African life and culture. In agriculture, the common technique was cultivation by hoe and digging stick. Musically, different groups of Africans played many instruments, especially types of drums, but common features, particularly in rhythm, gave African music as a whole a distinctive character. Music played an important role in social rituals, as did dancing and wearing masks, which often showed great artistry in their design.

African kingdoms varied, but kingship displayed common features, most notably the ritual isolation of the king himself. Fixed social categories—age groupings, kinship divisions, distinct gender roles and relations, and occupational groupings—also show resemblances from one region to another, even in societies too small to organize themselves into kingdoms. Though not hierarchical, these categories played a role similar to the divisions between noble, commoner, and slave prevalent where kings ruled. Such indications of underlying cultural unity have led modern observers to identify a common African quality throughout most of the region, even though most sub-Saharan Africans themselves did not perceive it. An eminent Belgian anthropologist, Jacques Maquet, has called this quality "Africanity."

Some historians hypothesize that this cultural unity emanated from the peoples who once occupied the southern Sahara. In Paleolithic times, periods of dryness alternated with periods of wetness as the Ice Age that locked up much of the world's fresh water in glaciers and icecaps came and went. When European glaciers receded with the waning of the Ice Age, a storm belt brought increased wetness to the Saharan region. Rushing rivers scoured deep canyons. Now filled with fine sand, those canyons are easily visible on flights over the southern parts of the desert. As the glaciers receded farther, the storm belt moved northward to Europe, and dryness set in after 5000 B.C.E. As a consequence, runs the hypothesis, the region's population migrated southward, becoming increasingly concentrated in the Sahel, which may have been the initial incubation center for Pan-African cultural patterns.

Increasing dryness and the resulting difficulty in supporting the population would have driven some people out of this core into more sparsely settled lands to the east, west, and south. In a parallel development farther to the east, migration away from the growing aridity of the desert seems to have contributed to the settling of the Nile Valley and the emergence of the Old Kingdom of Egypt (see Chapter 1).

The Advent of Iron and the Bantu

Archaeology confirms that agriculture had become common between the equator and the Sahara by the early second millennium B.C.E. It then spread southward, displacing hunting and gathering as a way of life. Moreover, botanical evidence indicates that banana trees, probably introduced to southeastern Africa from Southeast Asia, made their way north and west, retracing in the opposite direction the presumed migration routes of the first agriculturists.

Archaeology has also uncovered traces of copper mining in the Sahara from the early first millennium B.C.E. Copper appears in the Niger Valley somewhat later and in the Central African copper belt after 400 C.E. Most important of all, iron smelting began in northern sub-Saharan Africa in the early first millennium C.E. and spread southward from there.

Many historians believe that the secret of smelting iron, which requires very high temperatures, was discovered only once, by the Hittites of Anatolia (modern Turkey) around 1500 B.C.E. (see Chapter 3). If that is the case, it is hard to explain how iron smelting reached sub-Saharan Africa. The earliest evidence of ironworking from the kingdom of Meroë, situated on the upper Nile and in cultural contact with Egypt, is no earlier than the evidence from West Africa (northern Nigeria). Even less plausible than the Nile Valley as a route of technological diffusion is the idea of a spread southward from Phoenician settlements in

SECTION REVIEW

- An environmentally diverse region, sub-Saharan Africa includes many barriers to travel and communication.
- Sub-Saharan Africa achieved a cultural unity of similar "small traditions."
- Shared characteristics include agricultural methods, approaches to music, forms of kingship, and fixed social categories.
- The likely mechanism of this unity was the Bantu migrations, which were also responsible for the spread of iron smelting throughout sub-Saharan Africa.

North Africa, since archaeological evidence has failed to substantiate the vague Greek and Latin accounts of Phoenician excursions to the south. A more plausible scenario focuses on Africans' discovering for themselves how to smelt iron. Some historians suggest that they might have done so while firing pottery in kilns. No firm evidence exists to prove or disprove this theory.

Linguistic analysis provides the strongest evidence of extensive contacts among sub-Saharan Africans in the first millennium C.E.—and offers suggestions about the spread of iron. More than three hundred languages spoken south of the equator belong to the branch of the Niger-Congo family known as **Bantu**, after the word meaning "people" in most of the languages.

The distribution of the Bantu languages both north and south of the equator is consistent with a divergence beginning in the first millennium B.C.E. By comparing core words common to most of the languages, linguists have drawn some conclusions about the original Bantu-speakers, whom they call "proto-Bantu." These people engaged in fishing, using canoes, nets, lines, and hooks. They lived in permanent villages on the edge of the rain forest, where they grew yams and grains and harvested wild palm nuts from which they pressed oil. They possessed domesticated goats, dogs, and perhaps other animals. They made pottery and cloth. Linguists surmise that the proto-Bantu homeland was near the modern boundary of Nigeria and Cameroon.

Because the presumed home of the proto-Bantu lies near the known sites of early iron smelting, migration by Bantu-speakers seems a likely mechanism for the southward spread of iron. The migrants probably used iron axes and hoes to hack out forest clearings and plant crops. According to this scenario, their actions would have established an economic basis for new societies capable of sustaining much denser populations than could earlier societies dependent on hunting and gathering alone. Thus the period from 500 B.C.E. to 1000 C.E. saw a massive transfer of Bantu traditions and practices southward, eastward, and westward and their transformation, through intermingling with preexisting societies, into Pan-African traditions and practices.

The Spread of Ideas

Why do some goods and ideas travel more easily than others?

Ideas, like social customs, religious attitudes, and artistic styles, can spread along trade routes and through folk migrations. In both cases, documenting the dissemination of ideas, particularly in preliterate societies, poses a difficult historical problem.

Ideas and Material Evidence

Historians know about some ideas only through the survival of written sources. Other ideas do not depend on writing but are inherent in material objects studied by archaeologists and anthropologists. Customs surrounding the eating of pork are a case in point. Scholars disagree about whether pigs became domestic in only one place, from which the practice of pig keeping spread elsewhere, or whether several peoples hit on the same idea at different times and in different places.

Southeast Asia was an important early center of pig domestication. Anthropological studies tell us that the eating of pork became highly ritualized in this area and that it was sometimes allowed only on ceremonial occasions. On the other side of the Indian Ocean, wild swine were common in the Nile swamps of ancient Egypt. There, too, pigs took on a sacred role,

Bantu Collective name of a large group of sub-Saharan African languages and of the peoples speaking these languages.

being associated with the evil god Set, and eating them was prohibited. The biblical prohibition on the Israelites' eating pork, echoed later by the Muslims, probably came from Egypt in the second millennium B.C.E.

In a third locale in eastern Iran, an archaeological site dating from the third millennium B.C.E. provides evidence of another religious taboo relating to pork. Although the area around the site was swampy and home to many wild pigs, not a single pig bone has been found. Yet small pig figurines seem to have been used as symbolic religious offerings, and the later Iranian religion associates the boar with an important god.

What accounts for the apparent connection between domestic pigs and religion in these far-flung areas? There is no way of knowing. It has been hypothesized that pigs were first domesticated in Southeast Asia by people who had no herd animals—sheep, goats, cattle, or horses—and who relied on fish for most of their animal protein. The pig therefore became a special animal to them. The practice of pig raising, along with religious beliefs and rituals associated with the consumption of pork, could conceivably have spread from Southeast Asia along the maritime routes of the Indian Ocean, eventually reaching Iran and Egypt. But no evidence survives to support this hypothesis. In this case, therefore, material evidence can only hint at the spread of religious ideas, leaving the door open for other explanations.

A more certain example of objects' indicating the spread of an idea is the practice of hammering a carved die onto a piece of precious metal and using the resulting coin as a medium of exchange. From its origin in the Lydian kingdom in Anatolia in the first millennium B.C.E. (see Chapter 4), the idea of trading by means of struck coinage spread rapidly to Europe, North Africa, and India. Was the low-value copper coinage of China, made by pouring molten metal into a mold, also inspired by this practice from far away? It may have been, but it might also derive from indigenous Chinese metalworking.

 Primary Source: Setting in Motion the Wheel of the Law Find out which two extremes the Buddha advised his followers to avoid.

The Spread of Buddhism

While material objects associated with religious beliefs and rituals are important indicators of the spread of spiritual ideas, written sources deal with the spread of today's major religions. Buddhism grew to become, with Christianity and Islam (see Chapter 9), one of the most popular and widespread religions in the world. In all three cases, the religious ideas spread without dependency on a single ethnic or kinship group.

King Ashoka, the Mauryan ruler of India, and Kanishka, the greatest king of the Kushans of northern Afghanistan, promoted Buddhism between the third century B.C.E. and the second century C.E. However, monks, missionaries, and pilgrims who crisscrossed India, followed the Silk Road, or took ships on the Indian Ocean brought the Buddha's teachings to Southeast Asia, China, Korea, and ultimately Japan (see Map 8.1).

One such traveler was the Chinese pilgrim Faxian (fah-shee-en) (died between 418 and 423 C.E.), who left a written account of his travels. Faxian began his trip in the company of a Chinese envoy to an unspecified ruler or people in Central Asia. After traveling from one Buddhist site to another across Afghanistan and India, he reached Sri Lanka, a Buddhist land, where he lived for two years. He then embarked for China on a merchant ship with two hundred men aboard. A storm drove the ship to Java, which he chose not to describe since it was Hindu rather than Buddhist. After five months ashore, Faxian finally reached China on another ship.

Less reliable accounts make reference to missionaries traveling to Syria, Egypt, and Macedonia, as well as to Southeast Asia. One of Ashoka's sons allegedly led a band of missionaries to Sri Lanka. Later, his sister brought a company of nuns there, along with a branch of the sacred Bo tree under which the Buddha had received enlightenment. At the same time, there are reports of other monks traveling to Burma, Thailand, and Sumatra. Ashoka's missionaries may also have reached Tibet by way of trade routes across the Himalayas.

The different lands that received the story and teachings of the Buddha preserved or adapted them in different ways. Theravada Buddhism, "Teachings of the Elder," was centered in Sri Lanka. Holding closely to the Buddha's earliest teachings, it maintained

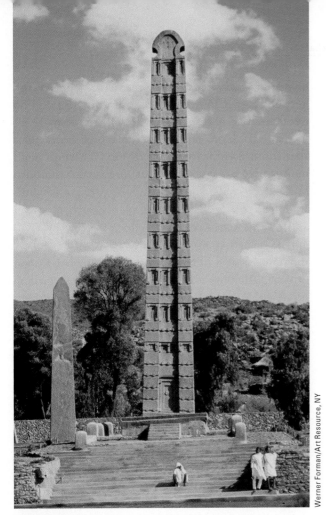

Werner Forman/Art Resource, NY

Stele of Aksum This 70-foot (21-meter) stone is the tallest remnant of a field of stelae, or standing stones, marking the tombs of Aksumite kings. The carvings of doors, windows, and beam ends imitate common features of Aksumite architecture, suggesting that each stele symbolized a multistory royal palace. The largest stelae date from the fourth century C.E.

that the goal of religion, available only to monks, is *nirvana*, the total absence of suffering and the end of the cycle of rebirth (see Chapter 5). This teaching contrasted with Mahayana, or "Great Vehicle" Buddhism, which stressed the goal of becoming a *bodhisattva*, a person who attains nirvana but chooses to remain in human company to help and guide others.

The Spread of Christianity

The post-Roman development of Christianity in Europe is discussed in Chapter 10. The Christian faith enjoyed an earlier spread in Asia and Africa before its confrontation with Islam (described in Chapter 9). Jerusalem in Palestine, Antioch in Syria, and Alexandria in Egypt became centers of Christian authority

soon after the crucifixion, but the spread of Christianity to Armenia and Ethiopia illustrates the connections between religion, trade, and imperial politics.

Situated in eastern Anatolia (modern Turkey), **Armenia** served recurrently as a battleground between Iranian states to the south and east and Mediterranean states to the west. Each imperial power wanted to control this region so close to the frontier where Silk Road traders met their Mediterranean counterparts. In Parthian times, Armenia's kings favored Zoroastrianism. The invention of an Armenian alphabet in the early fifth century opened the way to a wider spread of Christianity. The Iranians did not give up domination easily, but within a century the Armenian Apostolic Church had become the center of Armenian cultural life.

Far to the south Christians similarly sought to outflank Iran. The Christian emperors in Constantinople (see Chapter 6) sent missionaries along the Red Sea trade route to seek converts in Yemen and **Ethiopia** In the fourth century C.E. a Syrian philosopher traveling with two young relatives sailed to India. On the way back the ship docked at a Red Sea port occupied by Ethiopians from the prosperous kingdom of Aksum. Being then at odds with the Romans, the Ethiopians killed everyone on board except the two boys, Aedisius—who later narrated this story—and Frumentius. Impressed by their learning, the king made the former his cupbearer and the latter his treasurer and secretary.

When the king died, his wife urged Frumentius to govern Aksum on her behalf and that of her infant son, Ezana. As regent, Frumentius sought out Roman Christians among the merchants who visited the country and helped them establish Christian communities. When he became king, Ezana, who may have become a Christian, permitted Aedisius and Frumentius to return to Syria. The patriarch of Alexandria, on learning about the progress of Christianity in Aksum, elevated Frumentius to the rank of bishop, though he had not previously been a clergyman, and sent him back to Ethiopia as the first leader of its church.

Armenia One of the earliest Christian kingdoms, situated in eastern Anatolia and the western Caucasus and occupied by speakers of the Armenian language.
Ethiopia East African highland nation lying east of the Nile River.

SECTION REVIEW

- Material evidence can offer hints about the spread of ideas.

- Material and documentary evidence show the spread of Buddhism from India along the land and sea trade routes to elsewhere in Asia.

- Lands in which Buddhism took hold adapted its teachings in different ways, a process that resulted in the split between Mahayana and Theravada.

- Christianity spread through a combination of trade and imperial politics, with significant Christian societies emerging in Armenia and Ethiopia.

The spread of Christianity into Nubia, the land south of Egypt along the Nile River, proceeded from Ethiopia rather than Egypt. Politically and economically, Ethiopia became a power at the western end of the Indian Ocean trading system, occasionally even extending its influence across the Red Sea and asserting itself in Yemen (see Map 8.2).

Conclusion

The growing networks of transportation and trade that developed in the third century B.C.E. linked societies and cultures throughout the Eastern Hemisphere.

Merchants and pilgrims were the first to pioneer connections across long distances and often forbidding terrains, such as across Central Asia, the Himalayas, or the Sahara Desert. Due to the cost of travel, merchants could only carry items of great value and small bulk, such as silk and precious metals. But they also brought animals, such as camels, that could withstand the trip. Seeds of useful plants, such as cotton and fruits, were also spread by traders. New technologies, such as stirrups for horseback riders, made their way across Eurasia, while iron-making spread throughout Africa.

Along with physical objects came ideas. Missionaries spread religions far from their origins. Zoroastrians from Iran and Christians from the Middle East penetrated into Central Asia. Shipping across the Indian Ocean helped Hinduism spread to Southeast Asia. Most successful was Buddhism, which spread from India to Southeast Asia, Tibet, China, and Japan. Languages and other cultural forms also migrated with people; the diffusion of Bantu languages into East and Central Africa is a case in point. In short, in the last centuries before the Common Era, travel and commerce was increasingly bringing together the various parts of Eurasia and Africa and the once-separate cultures and civilizations.

CHAPTER REVIEW

 Download the MP3 audio file of the Chapter Review to listen to on the go.

What factors contributed to the growth of trade along the Silk Road? (page 187)

Occasional contacts across the heart of Asia undoubtedly occurred for many centuries before the Silk Road regularized communication. Cooperative relations between caravan traders and pastoral nomads in the Central Asian grasslands were the key to this regularization. The fact that the Parthian rulers of Iran were themselves of nomadic origin played an important role. In later centuries, trans-Asian trade fared best when pastoral peoples dominated either China or Iran or both.

How did the Sasanid Empire evolve under the influence of east-west trade? (page 191)

Originating in southwest Iran, the Sasanids overthrew the Parthians and took on their predecessors' conflicts with Rome. Benefiting from Silk Road trade, Sasanid farmers introduced the cultivation of many new crops from India and China. Sasanid kings supported Zoroastrianism as the state religion, continuing a larger trend toward the politicization of religion. Other religions often suffered persecution, but the Sasanid king welcomed Nestorian Christians fleeing official persecution in Byzantium. Nestorians traveled the Silk Road as missionaries, but they were only one of many religious groups that used the route to spread their ideas. Silk Road trade prompted many Iranians to move into cities and drew the Turks into the steppes north of Iran. In addition to goods and ideas, military technology moved along the Silk Road, particularly the stirrup, which revolutionized mounted warfare.

How did geography affect Indian Ocean trade routes? (page 193)

Maritime trade in general is strongly affected by such things as wind patterns, the presence of islands, and good seaports. The monsoon system in particular determined the seasons of trade across the Indian Ocean. In addition, coastal areas that had ample water supplies and easy communications with inland markets and population centers developed different relations with sea traders than did regions where coastal deserts were cut off from the interior by mountains.

Why did trade begin across the Sahara Desert? (page 197)

The beginnings of trade across the barren wastes of the Sahara bear comparison with the Silk Road and Indian Ocean trade. Political and economic contacts between pastoral nomads who supply caravan animals played an important role, but trade was also influenced by the location of markets on both the northern and southern sides, as well as the connections those markets had with suppliers and consumers farther away from the desert.

What accounts for the substantial degree of cultural unity in Africa south of the Sahara? (page 200)

The Sahara changed over time from a verdant state to one of exceptional dryness. This change forced cattle-herding peoples who lived in the areas that were drying up to move southward. This movement, in turn, contributed to the widespread migrations of Bantu-speaking peoples. Their shared linguistic and cultural characteristics led to a high degree of cultural similarity despite the fact that the various migrating groups settled in places that were not so close together as to encourage complex political development stretching over large parts of the continent.

Why do some goods and ideas travel more easily than others? (page 203)

The Bantu migrations contrast with contacts made along trade routes in terms of the sorts of cultural characteristics that enjoy wide geographic spread. Migrating in groups, the Bantu were able to maintain their social structures and rituals along with their techniques of agriculture and metal using. Along overland and seaborne trade routes where the number of travelers was comparatively small, on the other hand, the social practices of the merchants had less influence than the goods they carried, which were often highly prized. To be sure, religious missionaries often traveled by caravan or ship, but the doctrines they preached seldom fully replaced earlier religions.

Key Terms

Silk Road *(p. 187)*

Parthians *(p. 189)*

Sasanid Empire *(p. 191)*

stirrup *(p. 192)*

Indian Ocean Maritime System *(p. 193)*

trans-Saharan caravan routes *(p. 197)*

Sahel *(p. 200)*

sub-Saharan Africa *(p. 200)*

savanna *(p. 201)*

tropical rain forest *(p. 201)*

"great traditions" *(p. 201)*

"small traditions" *(p. 201)*

Bantu *(p. 203)*

Armenia *(p. 205)*

Ethiopia *(p. 205)*

Web Resources

Pronunciation Guide

Interactive Maps

- MAP 8.1 Asian Trade and Communication Routes
- MAP 8.2 Africa and the Trans-Saharan Trade Routes

Primary Source

- Setting in Motion the Wheel of the Law

Answer to the History in Focus Question

See photo on page 198, "Cattle Herders in Saharan Rock Art."

Visit the CourseMate website at www.cengagebrain.com for additional study tools and review materials for this chapter.

Oral Societies and the Consequences of Literacy

The availability of written documents is one of the key factors historians use to divide human prehistory from history. When we can read what the people of the past thought and said about their lives, we can begin to understand their cultures, institutions, values, and beliefs in ways that are not possible based only on the material remains unearthed by archaeologists.

There are profound differences between nonliterate and literate societies. However, literacy and nonliteracy are not absolute alternatives. Personal literacy ranges from illiteracy through many shades of partial literacy (the ability to write one's name or to read simple texts with difficulty) to the fluent ability to read that is possessed by anyone reading this textbook. And there are degrees of societal literacy, ranging from nonliteracy through so-called craft literacy—in which a small specialized elite uses writing for limited purposes, such as administrative recordkeeping—and a spectrum of conditions in which more and more people use writing for more and more purposes, up to the near-universal literacy and the use of writing for innumerable purposes that is the norm in the developed world in our times.

The vast majority of human beings of the last five to six thousand years living in societies that possessed the technology of writing were not themselves literate. If most people in a society rely on the spoken word and memory, that culture is essentially "oral" even if some members know how to write. The differences between oral and literate cultures are immense, affecting not only the kinds of knowledge that are valued and the forms in which information is preserved, but also the very use of language, the categories for conceptualizing the world, and ultimately the hard-wiring of the individual human brain (now recognized by neuroscientists to be strongly influenced by individual experience and mental activity).

Ancient Greece of the Archaic and Classical periods (ca. 800–323 B.C.E.) offers a particularly instructive case study because we can observe the process by which writing was introduced into an oral society as well as the far-reaching consequences. The Greeks of the Dark Age and early Archaic period lived in a purely oral society; all knowledge was preserved in human memory and passed on by telling it to others. The Iliad and the Odyssey (ca. 700 B.C.E.), Homer's epic poems, reflect this state of affairs. Scholars recognize that the creator of these poems was an oral poet, almost certainly not literate, who had heard and memorized the poems of predecessors and retold them his own way. The poems are treasuries of information that this society regarded as useful—events of the past; the conduct expected of warriors, kings, noblewomen, and servants; how to perform a sacrifice, build a raft, put on armor, and entertain guests; and much more.

Embedding this information in a story and using the colorful language, fixed phrases, and predictable rhythm of poetry made it easier for poet and audience to remember vast amounts of material. The early Greek poets, drawing on their strong memories, skill with words, and talent for dramatic performance, developed highly specialized techniques to assist them in memorizing and presenting their tales. They played a vital role in the preservation and transmission of information and thus enjoyed a relatively high social standing and comfortable standard of living. Analogous groups can be found in many other oral cultures of the past, including the bards of medieval Celtic lands, Norse skalds, west African griots, and the tribal historians of Native American peoples.

Nevertheless, human memory, however cleverly trained and well practiced, can only do so much. Oral societies must be extremely selective about what information to preserve in the limited storage medium of human memory, and they are slow to give up old information to make way for new.

Sometime in the eighth century B.C.E. the Greeks borrowed the system of writing used by the

Phoenicians of Lebanon and, in adapting it to their language, created the first purely alphabetic writing, employing several dozen symbols to express the sounds of speech. The Greek alphabet, although relatively simple to learn as compared to the large and cumbersome sets of symbols in such craft-literacy systems as cuneiform, hieroglyphics, or Linear B, was probably known at first only to a small number of people and used for restricted purposes. Scholars believe that it may have taken three or four centuries for knowledge of reading and writing to spread to large numbers of Greeks and for the written word to became the primary storage medium for the accumulated knowledge of Greek civilization. Throughout that time Greece was still primarily an oral society, even though some Greeks, mostly highly educated members of the upper classes, were beginning to write down poems, scientific speculations, stories about the past, philosophic musings, and the laws of their communities.

It is no accident that some of the most important intellectual and artistic achievements of the Greeks, including early science, history, drama, and rhetoric, developed in the period when oral and literate ways existed side-by-side. Scholars have persuasively argued that writing, by opening up a virtually limitless capacity to store information, released the human mind from the hard discipline of memorization and ended the need to be so painfully selective about what was preserved. This made previously unimaginable innovation and experimentation possible. We can observe changes in the Greek language as it developed a vocabulary full of abstract nouns, accompanied by increasing complex sentence structure now that the reader had time to go back over the text.

Nevertheless, all the developments associated with literacy were shaped by the deeply rooted oral habits of Greek culture. It is often said that Plato (ca. 429–347 B.C.E.) and his contemporaries of the later Classical period may have been the first generation of Greeks who learned much of what they knew from books. Even so, Plato was a disciple of the philosopher Socrates, who wrote nothing, and Plato employed the oral form of the dialogue, a dramatized sequence of questions and answers, to convey his ideas in written form.

The transition from orality to literacy met stiff resistance in some quarters. Groups whose position in the oral culture was based on the special knowledge only they possessed—members of the elite who judged disputes, priests who knew the time-honored formulas and rituals for appeasing the gods, oral poets who preserved and performed the stories of a heroic past—resented the consequences of literacy. They did what they could to inflame the common people's suspicions of the impiety of literate men who sought scientific explanations for phenomena, such as lightning and eclipses, that had traditionally been attributed to the will and action of the gods. They attacked the so-called Sophists, or "wise men," who charged fees to teach what they claimed were the skills necessary for success, accusing them of subverting traditional morals and corrupting the young.

Other societies, ancient and modern, offer parallel examples of these processes. Oral "specialists" in antiquity, including the Brahmin priests of India and the Celtic Druids, preserved in memory valuable religious information about how to win the favor of the gods. These groups jealously guarded their knowledge because it was the basis of their livelihood and social standing. Determined to select and maintain control over those who received this knowledge, they resisted committing it to writing even after that technology was available. The ways in which oral authorities feel threatened by writing and resist it can be seen in the following quotation from a twentieth-century C.E. "griot," an oral rememberer and teller of the past in Mali in West Africa:

> We griots are depositories of the knowledge of the past.... Other peoples use writing to record the past, but this invention has killed the faculty of memory among them. They do not feel the past anymore, for writing lacks the warmth of the human voice. With them everybody thinks he knows, whereas Learning should be a secret.... What paltry learning is that which is congealed in dumb books! ... For generations we have passed on the history of kings from father to son. The narrative was passed on to me without alteration, for I received it free from all untruth.[2]

This point of view is hard for us to grasp, living as we do in an intensely literate society in which the written word is often felt to be more authoritative and objective than the spoken word. It is important, in striving to understand societies of the past, not to superimpose our assumptions on them and to appreciate the complex interplay of oral and literate patterns in many of them.

Part Three

Growth and Interaction of Cultural Communities, 600–1200

© Cengage Learning

	300 B.C.E.	B.C.E. C.E.	300 C.E.
AMERICAS	• **300** Migrants from Mesoamerica bring irrigation farming to Arizona • **100** Teotihuacan founded		**250–900** Classic period of Maya civilization **200–700** Moche culture in coastal Peru
EUROPE	• **146** Rome destroys Carthage, begins direct control of territories ouside Europe		Council of Nicaea **325** • Fall of Roman Empire in West **476** • Reign of Roman emperor Diocletian **284–305**
AFRICA	**500 B.C.E.–1000 C.E.** Bantu migrations	• **ca. 100** Bananas and yams reach Africa from Southeast Asia	• **ca. 330** First Christian bishop in Ethiopia
MIDDLE EAST	**248 B.C.E–226 C.E** Kingdom of Parthia in Iran • **300** Petra flourishes as caravan city in Jordan		• **276** Prophet Mani martyred **226–650** Sasanid Empire in Iraq and Iran
ASIA AND OCEANIA	• **128** Chinese general Zhang Jian explores Silk Road **206 B.C.E–220 C.E** Han Empire in China	• **ca. 100** Stirrup developed in Afghanistan	**200–400** Rice introduced to Japan from Korea

In 300 B.C.E., societies had only limited contacts beyond their frontiers. By 1200 C.E., this situation had changed. Traders, migrating peoples, and missionaries brought peoples together. Products and technologies moved along long-distance trade networks: the Silk Road across Asia, Saharan caravan routes, and sea-lanes connecting the Indian Ocean coastlands.

Migrating Bantu peoples from West Africa spread iron and new farming techniques through much of sub-Saharan Africa and helped foster a distinctive African culture. Conquering Arabs from the Arabian peninsula, inspired by the Prophet Muhammad, established Muslim rule from Spain to India, laying the foundation of a new culture.

In Asia, missionaries and pilgrims helped Buddhism spread from India to Sri Lanka, Tibet, Southeast Asia, and East Asia. The new faith interacted with older philosophies and religions to produce distinctive cultural patterns. Simultaneously, the Tang Empire in China disseminated Chinese culture and technologies throughout Inner and East Asia.

In Europe, monks and missionaries spread Christian beliefs that became enmeshed with new political and social structures: a struggle between royal and church authority in western Europe; a union of religious and imperial authority in the Byzantine east; and a similar but distinctive society in Kievan Russia. The Crusades reconnected western Europe with the lands of the east.

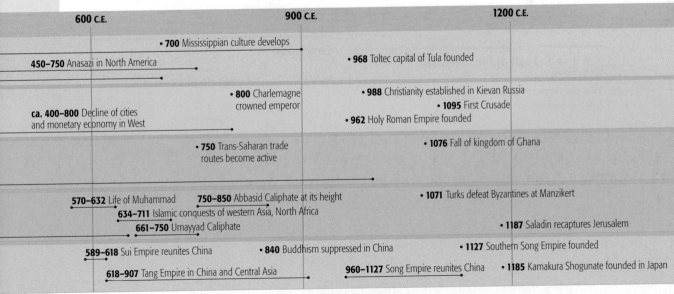

600 C.E. | **900 C.E.** | **1200 C.E.**

- **700** Mississippian culture develops
- **450–750** Anasazi in North America
- **968** Toltec capital of Tula founded
- **800** Charlemagne crowned emperor
- **988** Christianity established in Kievan Russia
- **1095** First Crusade
- **ca. 400–800** Decline of cities and monetary economy in West
- **962** Holy Roman Empire founded
- **750** Trans-Saharan trade routes become active
- **1076** Fall of kingdom of Ghana
- **570–632** Life of Muhammad
- **750–850** Abbasid Caliphate at its height
- **1071** Turks defeat Byzantines at Manzikert
- **634–711** Islamic conquests of western Asia, North Africa
- **661–750** Umayyad Caliphate
- **1187** Saladin recaptures Jerusalem
- **589–618** Sui Empire reunites China
- **840** Buddhism suppressed in China
- **1127** Southern Song Empire founded
- **618–907** Tang Empire in China and Central Asia
- **960–1127** Song Empire reunites China
- **1185** Kamakura Shogunate founded in Japan

The Rise of Islam

© Cengage Learning

CHAPTER PREVIEW

The Origins of Islam

How did the traditions and religious views of pre-Islamic peoples become integrated into the culture shaped by Islam?

The Rise and Fall of the Caliphate, 632–1258

Was the Baghdad caliphate really the high point of Muslim civilization?

Islamic Civilization

How did regional diversity affect the development of Islamic civilization?

Conclusion

MATERIAL CULTURE: Head Coverings

 Visit the CourseMate website at **www.cengagebrain.com** for additional study tools and review materials for this chapter.

Knowledge of papermaking, which spread from China to the Middle East after Arab conquests in the seventh century C.E. established an Islamic caliphate stretching from Spain to Central Asia, provided a medium that was superior to papyrus and parchment and well suited to a variety of purposes. Maps, miniature paintings, and, of course, books became increasingly common and inexpensive. With cheaper books came bookstores, and one of the most informative manuscripts of the period of the Islamic caliphate is a *Fihrist*, or descriptive catalog, of the books sold at one bookstore in Baghdad.

Abu al-Faraj Muhammad al-Nadim, a man with good connections at the caliph's court, compiled the catalog, though his father probably founded the bookstore. Its latest entry dates to ca. 990, al-Nadim's death date. Superbly educated, al-Nadim wrote such well-informed comments on books and authors that

his catalog presents a detailed survey of the intellectual world of Baghdad.

The first of the *Fihrist*'s ten books deals with Arabic language and sacred scriptures: the Quran, the Torah, and the Gospel. The second covers Arabic grammar, and the third writings from people connected with the caliph's court: historians, government officials, singers, jesters, and the ruler's boon companions. *Al-Nadim* means "book companion," so it is assumed that he knew this milieu well. After dealing with Arabic poetry, Muslim sects, and Islamic law in Books 3 through 6, he comes to Greek philosophy, science, and medicine in Book 7.

Most things we would find today in a bookstore are relegated to the final three chapters. Book 8 divides into three sections, the first being "Story Tellers and Stories." Here he lists a Persian book called *A Thousand Stories*, which in translation became *The Arabian Nights*. Al-Nadim's version no longer survives. The collection we have today comes from a manuscript written five hundred years later.

Then come books about "Exorcists, Jugglers, and Magicians," followed by "Miscellaneous Subjects and Fables." These include books on "Freckles, Twitching, Moles, and Shoulders," "Horsemanship, Bearing of Arms, the Implements of War," "Veterinary Surgery,"

History in Focus *Pay special attention to the placement of the figures in relation to each other in this image. What does this suggest about social distinctions within the world of Islamic scholarship? Find the answer online.*

Scholarly Life in Medieval Islam Books being scarce and expensive, teachers dictated to their students, as shown on the right. Notice that the student is writing on a single sheet of paper while the scholar in the center holds an entire book. On the left, an author presents his work to a wealthy patron.

Bibliothèque nationale de France

"Birds of Prey, Sport with Them and Medical Care of Them," "Interpretation of Dreams," "Perfume," "Cooked Food," "Poisons," and "Amulets and Charms."

Non-Muslim sects and foreign lands—India, Indochina, and China—fill Book 9, leaving Book 10 for a few final notes on philosophers not mentioned previously.

All together, the thousands of titles and authors commented on by al-Nadim provide both a panorama of what interested book buyers in tenth-century Baghdad and a saddening picture of how profound the loss of knowledge has been since that glorious era.

The Origins of Islam

How did the traditions and religious views of pre-Islamic peoples become integrated into the culture shaped by Islam?

The Arabs of 600 C.E. lived exclusively in the Arabian peninsula and on the desert fringes of Syria, Jordan, and Iraq. Along their Euphrates frontier, the Sasanids subsidized nomadic Arab chieftains to protect their empire from invasion. The Byzantines did the same with Arabs on their Jordanian frontier. Arab pastoralists farther to the south remained isolated and independent, seldom engaging the attention of the shahs and emperors. It was in these interior Arabian lands that the religion of Islam took form.

The Arabian Peninsula Before Muhammad

Throughout history people living on the Arabian peninsula have subsisted more as farmers than as pastoral nomads. Farming villages have supported the comparatively dense population of Yemen, where abundant rainfall waters the highlands during the spring monsoon, and small inlets along the southern coast have favored fishing and trading communities. But the enormous sea of sand known as the "Empty Quarter" isolated many southern regions from the Arabian interior. In the seventh century, most people in southern Arabia knew more about Africa, India, and the Persian Gulf than about the forbidding interior and the scattered camel- and sheep-herding nomads who lived there.

Caravan trading provided a rare link among peoples. Nomads derived income from providing camels, guides, and safe passage to merchants bringing the primary product of the south, the aromatic resins frankincense and myrrh, to northern customers. Return caravans brought manufactured products from Mesopotamia and Syria.

Nomad dominance of the caravan trade received a boost from the invention of militarily efficient camel saddles. This invention contributed to the rise of Arab-dominated caravan cities and to Arab pastoralists becoming the primary suppliers of animal power throughout the region. By 600 C.E., wheeled vehicles—mostly ox carts and horse-drawn chariots—had all but disappeared from the Middle East, replaced by pack camels and donkeys.

Arabs who accompanied the caravans became familiar with the cultures and lifestyles of the Sasanid and Byzantine Empires, and many of those who pastured their herds on the imperial frontiers adopted one form or another of Christianity. Even in the interior deserts, Semitic polytheism, with its worship of natural forces and celestial bodies, began to encounter more sophisticated religions.

Mecca, a late-blooming caravan city, occupies a barren mountain valley halfway between Yemen and Syria and somewhat inland from the Red Sea coast. A nomadic kin group known as the Quraysh (koo-RYYSH) settled in Mecca in the fifth century and assumed control of trade. Mecca rapidly achieved a measure of prosperity, partly because it was too far from Byzantine Syria, Sasanid Iraq, and Ethiopian-controlled Yemen for them to attack it.

A cubical shrine with idols inside called the Ka'ba (KAH-buh), a holy well called Zamzam, and a sacred precinct surrounding the two wherein killing was prohibited contributed to the emergence of Mecca as a pilgrimage site. Some Meccans associated the shrine with stories known to Jews and Christians. They regarded Abraham (Ibrahim in Arabic) as the builder of the Ka'ba, and they identified a site outside Mecca as the location where God asked Abraham to sacrifice his son. The son was not Isaac (Ishaq in Arabic), the son of Sarah, but Ishmael (Isma'il in Arabic), the

Mecca City in Arabia; birthplace of Muhammad; location of the Ka'ba, the holiest shrine in Islam.

Chronology

	The Arab Lands	Iran and Central Asia
600	570–632 Life of the Prophet Muhammad 634 Conquests of Iraq and Syria commence 639–642 Conquest of Egypt by Arabs 656–661 Ali caliph; first civil war 661–750 Umayyad Caliphate rules from Damascus	
700	711 Berbers and Arabs invade Spain from North Africa 750 Beginning of Abbasid Caliphate 755 Umayyad state established in Spain	711 Arabs capture Sind in India
800	776–809 Caliphate of Harun al-Rashid 835–892 Abbasid capital moved from Baghdad to Samarra	
900	909 Fatimids seize North Africa, found Shi'ite caliphate 929 Abd al-Rahman III declares himself caliph in Cordoba 945 Shi'ite Buyids take control in Baghdad 969 Fatimids conquer Egypt	875 Independent Samanid state founded in Bukhara 945 Buyids from northern Iran take control of Abbasid Caliphate
1000	1055 Seljuk Turks take control in Baghdad 1099 First Crusade captures Jerusalem	1036 Beginning of Turkish Seljuk rule in Khurasan
1100	1171 Fall of Fatimid Egypt 1187 Saladin recaptures Jerusalem	
1220	1250 Mamluks control Egypt 1258 Mongols sack Baghdad and end Abbasid Caliphate 1260 Mamluks defeat Mongols at Ain Jalut	

son of Hagar, cited in the Bible as the forefather of the Arabs.

Muhammad in Mecca

Born in Mecca in 570, **Muhammad** grew up an orphan in the house of his uncle. He engaged in trade and married a Quraysh widow named Khadija (kah-DEE-juh), whose caravan interests he superintended. Their son died in childhood, but several daughters survived. Around 610 Muhammad began meditating at night in the mountainous terrain around Mecca. During one night vigil, known to later tradition as the "Night of Power and Excellence," a being whom Muhammad later understood to be the angel Gabriel (Jibra'il in Arabic) spoke to him:

Proclaim! In the name of your Lord who created. Created man from a clot of congealed blood. Proclaim! And your Lord is the Most Bountiful. He who has taught by the pen. Taught man that which he knew not.[1]

For three years Muhammad shared this and subsequent revelations only with close friends and family members. This period culminated in his conviction that he was hearing the words of God (Allah [AH-luh] in Arabic). Khadija, his uncle's son Ali, his friend Abu Bakr (ah-boo BAK-uhr), and others close to him

Muhammad (570–632 C.E.) Arab prophet; founder of religion of Islam.

shared this conviction. The revelations continued until Muhammad's death in 632.

Like most people of the time, including Christians and Jews, the Arabs believed in unseen spirits: gods, demonic *shaitans*, and desert spirits called *jinns* who were thought to possess seers and poets. Therefore, when Muhammad recited his rhymed revelations in public, many people believed he was inspired by an unseen spirit, even if it was not, as Muhammad asserted, the one true god.

Muhammad's earliest revelations called on people to witness that one god had created the universe and everything in it, including themselves. At the end of time, their souls would be judged, their sins balanced against their good deeds. The blameless would go to paradise; the sinful would taste hellfire:

> By the night as it conceals the light;
> By the day as it appears in glory;
> By the mystery of the creation of male and female;
> Verily, the ends ye strive for are diverse.
> So he who gives in charity and fears God,
> And in all sincerity testifies to the best,
> We will indeed make smooth for him the path to Bliss.
> But he who is a greedy miser and thinks himself self-sufficient,
> And gives the lie to the best,
> We will indeed make smooth for him the path to misery.[2]

The revelation called all people to submit to God and accept Muhammad as the last of his messengers. Doing so made one a **Muslim**, meaning one who makes "submission," **Islam**, to the will of God.

Because earlier messengers mentioned in the revelations included Noah, Moses, and Jesus, Muhammad's hearers connected his message with Judaism and Christianity, religions they were already familiar with. Yet his revelations charged the Jews and Christians with being negligent in preserving God's revealed word. Thus, even though they identified Abraham/Ibrahim, whom Muslims consider the first Muslim, as the builder of the Ka'ba, which superseded Jerusalem as the focus of Muslim prayer in 624, Muhammad's followers considered his revelation more perfect than the Bible because it had not gone through an editing process.

Some scholars maintain that Muhammad appealed especially to people distressed over wealth replacing kinship as the most important aspect of social relations and over neglect of orphans and other powerless people. Most Muslims, however, put less emphasis on a social message than on the power and beauty of Muhammad's recitations.

Formation of the Umma

Mecca's leaders feared that accepting Muhammad as the sole agent of the one true God would threaten their power and prosperity. They pressured his kin to disavow him and persecuted the weakest of his followers. Stymied by this hostility, Muhammad and his followers fled Mecca in 622 to take up residence in the agricultural community of **Medina** 215 miles (346 kilometers) to the north. This hijra (HIJ-ruh) marks the beginning of the Muslim calendar.

Prior to the hijra, Medinan representatives had met with Muhammad and agreed to accept and protect him and his followers because they saw him as an inspired leader who could calm their perpetual feuding. Together, the Meccan migrants and major groups in Medina bound themselves into a single **umma** (UM-muh), a community defined by acceptance of Islam and of Muhammad as the "Messenger of God," his most common title. Partly because three Jewish kin groups chose to retain their own faith, the direction of prayer was changed from Jerusalem toward the Ka'ba in Mecca, now thought of as the "House of God."

Having left their Meccan kin groups, the immigrants in Medina felt vulnerable. During the last decade of his life, Muhammad took active

Muslim An adherent of the Islamic religion; a person who "submits" (in Arabic, *Islam* means "submission") to the will of God.

Islam Religion expounded by the Prophet Muhammad (570–632 C.E.) on the basis of his reception of divine revelations, which were collected after his death into the Quran. In the tradition of Judaism and Christianity, and sharing much of their lore, Islam calls on all people to recognize one creator god—Allah—who rewards or punishes believers after death according to how they led their lives.

Medina City in western Arabia to which the Prophet Muhammad and his followers emigrated in 622 to escape persecution in Mecca.

umma The community of all Muslims. A major innovation against the background of seventh-century Arabia, where traditionally kinship rather than faith had determined membership in a community.

responsibility for his umma. Fresh revelations provided a framework for regulating social and legal affairs and stirred the Muslims to fight against the still-unbelieving city of Mecca. At various points during the war, Muhammad charged the Jewish kin groups, whom he had initially hoped would recognize him as God's messenger, with disloyalty, and he finally expelled or eliminated them. The sporadic war, largely conducted by raiding and negotiating with desert nomads, sapped Mecca's strength and convinced many Meccans that God favored Muhammad. In 630 Mecca surrendered, and Muhammad and his followers made the pilgrimage to the Ka'ba unhindered.

Muhammad stayed in Medina, which had grown into a bustling city-state. Delegations came to him from all over Arabia and returned home with believers who could teach them about Islam and collect their alms. Muhammad's mission to bring God's message to humanity had brought him unchallenged control of a state that was coming to dominate the Arabian peninsula.

In 632, after a brief illness, Muhammad died. Within twenty-four hours a group of Medinan leaders, along with three of Muhammad's close friends, determined that Abu Bakr, one of the earliest believers and the father of Muhammad's favorite wife A'isha (AH-ee-shah), should succeed him. They called him the *khalifa* (kah-LEE-fuh), or "successor," the English version of which is *caliph*. But calling Abu Bakr a successor did not clarify his powers. Everyone knew that neither Abu Bakr nor anyone else could receive revelations, and they likewise knew that Muhammad's revelations made no provision for succession or for any government purpose beyond maintaining the umma.

Abu Bakr continued and confirmed Muhammad's religious practices, notably the so-called Five Pillars of Islam: (1) avowal that there is only one god and Muhammad is his messenger, (2) prayer five times a day, (3) fasting during the lunar month of Ramadan, (4) paying alms, and (5) making the pilgrimage to Mecca at least once during one's lifetime. He also reestablished and expanded Muslim authority over Arabia's communities, some of which had abandoned their allegiance to Medina or followed various would-be prophets. Muslim armies fought hard to confirm the authority of the newborn **caliphate**. In the process, some fighting spilled over into non-Arab areas in Iraq.

Reportedly, Abu Bakr ordered the men who had written down Muhammad's revelations to collect them in a book. Hitherto written haphazardly on pieces of leather or bone, these now became a single document gathered into chapters. Muslims believe the **Quran** (kuh-RAHN), or the Recitation, acquired its final form around the year 650. They see it not as the words of Muhammad but as the unalterable word of God. Theologically, it compares not so much to the Bible, a book written by many hands over many centuries, as to the person of Jesus Christ, whom Christians consider an earthly manifestation of God.

Though united in accepting God's will, the umma soon disagreed over the succession to the caliphate. When rebels assassinated the third caliph, Uthman (ooth-MAHN), in 656, and the assassins nominated Ali, Muhammad's first cousin and the husband of his daughter Fatima, to succeed him, civil war broke out. Ali had been passed over three times previously, even though many people considered him to be the Prophet's natural heir. Those who believed Ali was the Prophet's heir came to be known as **Shi'ites**, after the Arabic term *Shi'at Ali* ("Party of Ali").

When Ali accepted the nomination to be caliph, two of Muhammad's close companions and his favorite wife A'isha challenged him. Ali defeated them in the Battle of the Camel (656), so called because the fighting raged around the camel on which A'isha was seated in an enclosed woman's saddle.

After the battle, the governor of Syria, Mu'awiya (moo-AH-we-yuh), a kinsman of the slain Uthman

Primary Source: The Constitution of Medina: Muslims and Jews at the Dawn of Islam Learn about the contract Muhammad sets forth between the Muslims and Jews of his time.

caliphate Office established in succession to the Prophet Muhammad, to rule the Islamic empire; also the name of that empire.

Quran Book composed of divine revelations made to the Prophet Muhammad between ca. 610 and his death in 632; the sacred text of the religion of Islam.

Shi'ites Muslims belonging to the branch of Islam that believes that God vests leadership of the community in a descendant of Muhammad's son-in-law Ali. Shi'ism is the state religion of Iran.

SECTION REVIEW

- Islam emerged among the nomadic pastoralists and caravan traders of the Arabian peninsula.

- Mecca grew as a caravan city and pilgrimage site identified with Jewish and Christian stories.

- Muhammad experienced revelations that called people to submit to God's will.

- Facing hostility in Mecca, Muhammad and his followers fled to Medina, where they formed the umma.

- As caliph succeeding Muhammad, Abu Bakr confirmed the Five Pillars of Islam and ordered the composition of the Quran.

- Civil war within the umma resulted in the Sunni/Shi'ite division and the foundation of the Umayyad Caliphate.

from the Umayya clan of the Quraysh, renewed the challenge. Inconclusive battle gave way to arbitration. The arbitrators decided that Uthman, whom his assassins considered corrupt, had not deserved death and that Ali had erred in accepting the caliphate. Ali rejected these findings, but before fighting could resume, one of his own supporters killed him for agreeing to the arbitration. Mu'awiya offered Ali's son Hasan a dignified retirement and thus emerged as caliph in 661.

Mu'awiya chose his own son, Yazid, to succeed him, thereby instituting the **Umayyad** (oo-MY-ad) **Caliphate**. When Hasan's brother Husayn revolted in 680 to reestablish the right of Ali's family to rule, Yazid ordered Husayn and his family killed. Sympathy for Husayn's martyrdom helped transform Shi'ism from a political movement into a religious sect.

Several variations in Shi'ite belief developed, but Shi'ites all agree that Ali was the rightful successor to Muhammad and that God's choice as Imam, leader of the Muslim community, has always been one or another of Ali's descendants. They see the caliphal office as more secular than religious. Because the Shi'ites seldom held power, their religious feelings came to focus on outpourings of sympathy for Husayn and other martyrs and on messianic dreams that one of their Imams would someday triumph.

Those Muslims who supported the first three caliphs gradually came to be called "People of Tradition and Community"—in Arabic, *Ahl al-Sunna wa'l-Jama'a*, **Sunnis** for short. Sunnis consider the caliphs

to be Imams. As for Ali's followers who had abhorred his acceptance of arbitration, they evolved into small and rebellious Kharijite sects (from *kharaja*, meaning "to secede or rebel") claiming righteousness for themselves alone. These three divisions of Islam, the last now quite minor, still survive.

The Rise and Fall of the Caliphate, 632–1258

Was the Baghdad caliphate really the high point of Muslim civilization?

The Islamic caliphate built on the conquests the Arabs carried out after Muhammad's death gave birth to a dynamic and creative religious society. By the late 800s, however, one piece after another of this huge realm broke away. Yet the idea of a caliphate, however unrealistic, remains today a touchstone of Sunni belief in the unity of the umma.

Sunni Islam never gave a single person the power to define true belief, expel heretics, and discipline clergy. Thus, unlike Christian popes and patriarchs, the caliphs had little basis for reestablishing their universal authority once they lost political and military power.

The Islamic Conquests, 634–711

Arab conquests outside Arabia began under the second caliph, Umar (r. 634–644). Arab armies wrenched Syria (636) and Egypt (639–642) away from the Byzantine Empire and defeated the last Sasanid shah, Yazdigird III (r. 632–651). After a decade-long lull, expansion began again. Tunisia fell and became the governing center from which was organized, in 711, the conquest of Spain by an Arab-led army mostly composed of Berbers from North Africa. In the same year, Sind—the southern

Umayyad Caliphate First hereditary dynasty of Muslim caliphs (661 to 750). From their capital at Damascus, the Umayyads ruled an empire that extended from Spain to India. Overthrown by the Abbasid Caliphate.

Sunnis Muslims belonging to the branch of Islam that believes that the community should select its own leadership. The majority religion in most Islamic countries.

Indus Valley in today's Pakistan—succumbed to invaders from Iraq. The Muslim dominion remained roughly stable in size for three centuries until conquest began anew in the eleventh century. India and Anatolia experienced invasions; sub-Saharan Africa and other regions saw Islam expand peacefully by trade and conversion.

Muhammad's close companions, men of political and economic sophistication inspired by his charisma, guided the conquests. The social structure and hardy nature of Arab society lent itself to flexible military operations; and the authority of Medina, reconfirmed during the caliphate of Abu Bakr, ensured obedience.

The decision made during Umar's caliphate to prohibit Arabs from assuming ownership of conquered territory proved important. Umar tied army service, with its regular pay and windfalls of booty, to residence in military camps—two in Iraq (Kufa and Basra), one in Egypt (Fustat), and one in Tunisia (Qairawan). East of Iraq, Arabs settled around small garrison towns at strategic locations and in one large garrison at Marv in present-day Turkmenistan. This policy kept the armies together and ready for action and preserved normal life in the countryside, where some three-fourths of the population lived. Only a tiny proportion of the Syrian, Egyptian, Iranian, and Iraqi populations understood the Arabic language.

The million or so Arabs who participated in the conquests over several generations constituted a small, self-isolated ruling minority living on the taxes paid by a vastly larger non-Arab, non-Muslim subject population. The Arabs had little material incentive to encourage conversion, and there is no evidence of coherent missionary efforts to spread Islam during the conquest period.

The Umayyad and Early Abbasid Caliphates, 661–850

The Umayyad caliphs presided over an Arab realm rather than a religious empire. Ruling from Damascus, their armies consisted almost entirely of Muslim Arabs. Sasanid and Byzantine administrative practices continued in force. Only gradually did the caliphs replace non-Muslim secretaries and tax officials with Muslims and introduce Arabic as the language of government. Distinctively Muslim silver and gold coins introduced early in the eighth century symbolized the new order. Henceforward, silver dirhams and gold dinars bearing Arabic religious phrases circulated in monetary exchanges from Morocco to the frontiers of China.

The Umayyad dynasty fell in 750 after a decade of growing unrest. Converts to Islam numbered no more than 10 percent of the indigenous population, but they were still important because of the comparatively small number of Arab warriors. These converts resented Arab social domination. In addition, non-Syrian Arabs envied the Syrian domination of caliphal affairs, and pious Muslims looked askance at the secular and even irreligious behavior of the caliphs. Finally, Shi'ites and Kharijites attacked the Umayyad family's legitimacy as rulers, launching a number of rebellions.

In 747 a rebellion began in Khurasan (kor-uh-SAHN) in what is today northeastern Iran, and overthrew the last Umayyad caliph three years later, though one family member escaped to Spain to found an Umayyad principality there in 755. Many Shi'ites supported the rebellion, thinking they were fighting for the family of Ali. As it turned out, the family of Abbas, one of Muhammad's uncles, controlled the secret organization that coordinated the revolt. Upon victory they established the **Abbasid** (ah-BASS-id) **Caliphate**. Some of the Abbasid caliphs who ruled after 750 befriended their relatives in Ali's family, and one even flirted with transferring the caliphate to them. The Abbasid family, however, held on to the caliphate until 1258, when Mongol invaders killed the last of them in Baghdad (see Chapter 11).

Initially, the Abbasid dynasty made a fine show of leadership and piety. Theology and religious law became preoccupations at court and among a growing community of scholars devoted to interpreting the Quran, collecting the sayings of the Prophet, and compiling Arabic grammar. (In recent years, some Western scholars have maintained that the Quran,

---

Abbasid Caliphate Descendants of the Prophet Muhammad's uncle, al-Abbas, the Abbasids overthrew the Umayyad Caliphate and ruled an Islamic empire from their capital in Baghdad (founded 762) from 750 to 1258.

the sayings of the Prophet, and the biography of the Prophet were all composed around this time to provide a legendary base for the regime. This reinterpretation of Islamic origins has not been generally accepted either in the scholarly community or among Muslims.) Some caliphs sponsored ambitious projects to translate great works of Greek, Persian, and Indian thought into Arabic.

With its roots among the semi-Persianized Arabs of Khurasan, the new dynasty gradually adopted the ceremonies and customs of the Sasanid shahs. Government grew increasingly complex in Baghdad, the newly built capital city on the Tigris River. As more non-Arabs converted to Islam, the ruling elite became more cosmopolitan. Greek, Iranian, Central Asian, and African cultural currents met in the capital and gave rise to an abundance of literary works, a process facilitated by the introduction of papermaking from China. Arab poets neglected the traditional odes extolling life in the desert and wrote instead wine songs (despite Islam's prohibition of alcohol) or poems in praise of their patrons.

The translation of Aristotle into Arabic, the founding of the main currents of theology and law, and the splendor of the Abbasid court—reflected in stories of *The Arabian Nights* set in the time of the caliph Harun al-Rashid (hah-ROON al-rah-SHEED) (r. 776–809)—in some respects warrant calling the early Abbasid period a "golden age." Yet the refinement of Baghdad culture only slowly made its way into the provinces. Egypt remained predominantly Christian and Coptic-speaking in the early Abbasid period. Iran never adopted Arabic as a spoken tongue. Most of Berber-speaking North Africa rebelled and freed itself of direct caliphal rule after 740.

Gradual conversion to Islam among the conquered population accelerated in the second quarter of the ninth century. Social discrimination against non-Arab converts gradually faded, and the Arabs themselves—at least those living in cosmopolitan urban settings—lost their previously strong attachment to kinship and ethnic identity.

Political Fragmentation, 850–1050

Abbasid decline became evident in the second half of the ninth century as conversion to Islam accelerated (see Map 9.1). No government

ruling so vast an empire could hold power easily. Caravans traveled only 20 miles (32 kilometers) a day, and the couriers of the caliphal post system usually did not exceed 100 miles (160 kilometers) a day. News of frontier revolts took weeks to reach Baghdad. Military responses might take months.

During the first two Islamic centuries, revolts against Muslim rule had been a concern. The Muslim umma had therefore clung together, despite the long distances. But with the growing conversion of the population to Islam, fears that Islamic dominion might be overthrown faded. Once they became the overwhelming majority, Muslims realized that a highly centralized empire did not necessarily serve the interests of all the people.

By the middle of the ninth century, revolts targeting Arab or Muslim domination gave way to movements within the Islamic community concentrating on seizure of territory and formation of principalities. None of the states carved out of the Abbasid Caliphate after that time repudiated or even threatened Islam. They did, however, cut the flow of tax revenues to Baghdad, thereby increasing local prosperity. Increasingly starved for funds by breakaway provinces and by an unexplained fall in revenues from Iraq itself, the caliphate experienced a crisis in the late ninth century. Distrusting generals and troops from outlying areas, the caliphs purchased Turkic slaves, **mamluks** (MAM-luke), from Central Asia and established them as a standing army. Well trained and hardy, the Turks proved an effective but expensive military force. When the government could not pay them, the mamluks took it on themselves to seat and unseat caliphs, a process made easier by the construction of a new capital at Samarra, north of Baghdad on the Tigris River.

The Turks dominated Samarra without interference from an unruly Baghdad populace that regarded them as rude and highhanded. However, the money and effort that went into the huge city, which was occupied only from 835 to 892, further sapped the

mamluks Under the Islamic system of military slavery, Turkic military slaves who formed an important part of the armed forces of the Abbasid Caliphate of the ninth and tenth centuries. Mamluks eventually founded their own state, ruling Egypt and Syria (1250–1517).

Map 9.1 **Rise and Fall of the Abbasid Caliphate** Though Abbasid rulers occupied the caliphal seat in Iraq from 750 to 1258, when Mongol armies destroyed Baghdad, real political power waned sharply and steadily after 850. The rival caliphates of the Fatimids (909–1171) and Spanish Umayyads (929–976) were comparatively short-lived.   © Cengage Learning

Interactive Map

caliphs' financial strength and deflected labor from more productive pursuits.

In 945, after several attempts to find a strongman to save it, the Abbasid Caliphate fell under the control of rude mountain warriors from Daylam in northern Iran. Led by the Shi'ite Buyid (BOO-yid) family, they conquered western Iran as well as Iraq. Each Buyid commander ruled his own principality. After two centuries of glory, the sun began to set on Baghdad. The Abbasid caliph remained, but the Buyid princes controlled him. Being Shi'ites, the Buyids had no special reverence for the Sunni caliph. The Shi'ite teachings they followed held that the twelfth and last Imam had disappeared around 873 and would return as a messiah only at the end of time. Thus they had no Shi'ite Imam to defer to and retained the caliph only to help control their predominantly Sunni subjects.

Dynamic growth in outlying provinces paralleled the caliphate's gradual loss of temporal power. In the east in 875, the dynasty of the Samanids

(sah-MAN-id), one of several Iranian families to achieve independence, established a glittering court in Bukhara, a major city on the Silk Road (see Map 9.1). Samanid princes patronized literature and learning, but the language they favored was Persian written in Arabic letters. For the first time, a non-Arabic literature rose to challenge the eminence of Arabic within the Islamic world.

In the west, the Berber revolts against Arab rule led to the appearance after 740 of the city-states of Sijilmasa (sih-jil-MAS-suh) and Tahert (TAH-hert) on the northern fringe of the Sahara. The Kharijite beliefs of these states' rulers interfered with their east-west overland trade and led them to develop the first regular trade across the Sahara desert. Once traders looked to the desert, they discovered that Berber speakers in the southern Sahara were already carrying salt from the desert into the Sahel region. The northern traders discovered that they could trade salt for gold by providing the southern nomads, who

Tomb of the Samanids in Bukhara This early-tenth-century structure has the basic layout of a Zoroastrian fire temple: a dome on top of a cube. However, geometric ornamentation in baked brick marks it as an early masterpiece of Islamic architecture. The Samanid family achieved independence as rulers of northeastern Iran and western Central Asia in the tenth century.

Bridgeman-Giraudon/Art Resource, NY

controlled the salt sources but had little use for gold, with more useful products, such as copper and manufactured goods. Sijilmasa and Tahert became wealthy cities, the former minting gold coins that circulated as far away as Egypt and Syria.

The earliest known sub-Saharan beneficiary of the new exchange system was the kingdom of **Ghana** (GAH-nuh). It first appears in an Arabic text of the late eighth century as the "land of gold." Few details survive about the early years of this realm, which was established by the Soninke (soh-NIN-kay) people and covered parts of Mali, Mauritania, and Senegal, but it prospered until 1076, when it was conquered by nomads from the desert. It was one of the first lands outside the orbit of the caliphate to experience a gradual and peaceful conversion to Islam.

The North African city-states lost their independence after the Fatimid (FAT-uh-mid) dynasty, whose members claimed (perhaps falsely) to be Shi'ite Imams descended from Ali, established itself in Tunisia in 909. After consolidating their hold on northwest Africa, the Fatimids culminated their rise to power by conquering Egypt in 969. Claiming the title

of caliph in a direct challenge to the Abbasids, the Fatimid rulers governed from a palace complex outside the old conquest-era garrison city of Fustat (fuss-THAT). They named the complex Cairo. For the first time Egypt became a major cultural, intellectual, and political center of Islam. The abundance of Fatimid gold coinage, now channeled to Egypt from West Africa, made the Fatimids an economic power in the Mediterranean.

Cut off from the rest of the Islamic world by the Strait of Gibraltar and, from 740 onward, by independent city-states in Morocco and Algeria, Umayyad Spain developed a distinctive Islamic culture blending Roman, Germanic, and Jewish traditions with those of the Arabs and Berbers. Historians disagree on how rapidly and completely the Spanish population converted to Islam. If we assume a process similar to that in the eastern regions, it seems likely that the most rapid surge in Islamization occurred in the middle of the tenth century.

As in the east, governing cities symbolized the Islamic presence in al-Andalus, as the Muslims called

 Primary Source: The Book of Routes and Realms Find out about the ruler who became king when he was eighty-five years old.

Ghana First known kingdom in sub-Saharan West Africa between the sixth and thirteenth centuries C.E. Also the modern West African country once known as the Gold Coast.

Model of a Water-Lifting Device The artist's effort to render a three-dimensional construction in two dimensions shows a talent for schematic drawing.

their Iberian territories. Cordoba, Seville, Toledo, and other cities grew substantially, becoming much larger and richer than contemporary cities in neighboring France. Converts to Islam and their descendants, unconverted Arabic-speaking Christians, and Jews joined with the comparatively few descendants of Arab settlers to create new architectural and literary styles. In the countryside, where the Berbers preferred to settle, a fusion of preexisting agricultural technologies with new crops, notably citrus fruits, and irrigation techniques from the east gave Spain the most diverse and sophisticated agricultural economy in Europe.

The rulers of al-Andalus took the title *caliph* only in 929, when Abd al-Rahman (AHB-d al-ruh-MAHN) III (r. 912–961) did so in response to a similar declaration by the newly established (909) Fatimid ruler in Tunisia. By the century's end, however, this caliphate encountered challenges from breakaway movements that eventually splintered al-Andalus into a number of small states. Political decay did not impede cultural growth. Some of the greatest writers and thinkers in Jewish history worked in Muslim Spain in the eleventh and twelfth centuries, sometimes

writing in Arabic, sometimes in Hebrew. Judah Halevi (1075–1141) composed exquisite poetry and explored questions of religious philosophy. Maimonides (1135–1204) made a major compilation of Judaic law and expounded on Aristotelian philosophy. At the same time, Islamic thought in Spain attained its loftiest peaks in Ibn Hazm's (994–1064) treatises on love and other subjects, the Aristotelian philosophical writings of Ibn Rushd (IB-uhn RUSHED) (1126–1198, known in Latin as Averroës [uh-VERR-oh-eez]) and Ibn Tufayl (IB-uhn too-FILE) (d. 1185), and the mystic speculations of Ibn al-Arabi (IB-uhn ahl-AH-rah-bee) (1165–1240). Christians, too, shared in the intellectual and cultural dynamism of al-Andalus. Translations from Arabic to Latin made during this period had a profound effect on the later intellectual development of western Europe (see Chapter 10).

The Samanids, Fatimids, and Spanish Umayyads, three of many regional principalities, represent the political diversity and awakening of local awareness that coincided with Abbasid decline. Yet drawing and redrawing political boundaries did not result in the rigid division of the Islamic world into kingdoms.

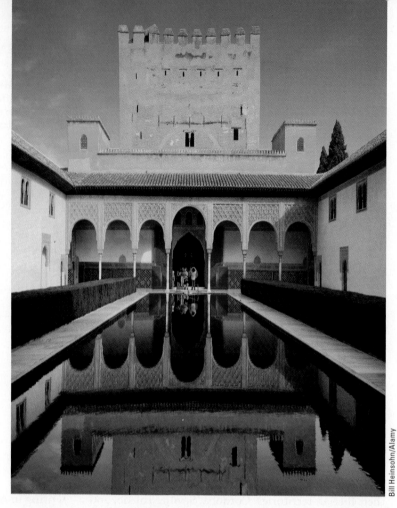

The Alhambra of Granada A palace built in the mid-fourteenth century by the kings of Granada, the Alhambra is considered the purest example of Hispano-Moorish architecture. Carefully restored, it is now a UNESCO World Heritage Site.

Bill Heinsohn/Alamy

Religious and cultural developments, particularly the rise in cities of a social group of religious scholars known as the **ulama** (oo-leh-MAH)—Arabic for "people with (religious) knowledge"—worked against any permanent division of the Islamic umma.

Assault from Within and Without, 1050–1258

The role played by Turkish mamluks in the decline of Abbasid power established an enduring stereotype of the Turk as a ferocious, unsophisticated warrior. This image gained strength in the 1030s when the Seljuk (sel-JOOK) family established a Turkish Muslim state based on nomadic power. Taking the Arabic title *Sultan*, meaning "power," and the revived Persian title *Shahan-shah*, or King of Kings, the Seljuk ruler Tughril (TUUG-ruhl) Beg created a kingdom that stretched from northern Afghanistan to Baghdad, which he occupied in 1055. After a century under the thumb of the Shi'ite Buyids, the Abbasid caliph breathed easier under the slightly lighter thumb of the Sunni Turks. The Seljuks pressed on into Syria and Anatolia, administering a lethal blow to Byzantine power at the Battle of Manzikert (MANZ-ih-kuhrt) in 1071. The Byzantine army fell back on Constantinople, leaving Anatolia open to Turkish occupation.

Under Turkish rule, cities shrank as pastoralists overran their agricultural hinterlands. Irrigation works suffered from lack of maintenance in the unsettled countryside, and tax revenues fell. Quarreling twelfth-century princes fought over cities, but few Turks participated in urban cultural and religious life. The gulf between a religiously based urban society and the culture and personnel of the government deepened. When factional riots broke out between Sunnis and Shi'ites, or between rival schools of Sunni law, rulers generally remained aloof, even as destruction and loss of life mounted.

By the early twelfth century, unrepaired damage from floods, fires, and civil disorder had reduced old Baghdad on the west side of the Tigris to ruins. The withering of Baghdad reflected a broader environmental problem: the collapse of the canal system on which agriculture in the Tigris and Euphrates Valley depended. For millennia a center of world

ulama Muslim religious scholars. From the ninth century onward, the primary interpreters of Islamic law and the social core of Muslim urban societies.

civilization, Mesopotamia underwent substantial population loss and never again regained its geographical importance.

The Turks alone cannot be blamed for the demographic and economic misfortunes of Iran and Iraq. Too-robust urbanization and an apparent chilling of the climate after 1000 had strained food resources. The growing practice of paying soldiers and courtiers with land grants led to absentee landlords using agents to collect taxes. These agents gouged villagers and took little interest in improving production, thus intensifying the agricultural crisis.

Internecine feuding was preoccupying the Seljuk family when the first Christian crusaders reached the Holy Land and captured Jerusalem in 1099 (see Chapter 10). Though charged with the stuff of romance, the Crusades had little lasting impact on the Islamic lands. The four crusader principalities of Edessa, Antioch, Tripoli, and Jerusalem simply became pawns in the shifting pattern of politics already in place. Newly arrived knights eagerly attacked the Muslim enemy, whom they called "Saracens" (SAR-uh-suhn), but veteran crusaders recognized that practicing diplomacy and seeking partners of convenience among rival Muslim princes offered a sounder strategy.

The Muslims finally unified to face the European enemy in the mid-twelfth century. Nur al-Din ibn Zangi (NOOR al-DEEN ib-uhn ZAN-gee) established a strong state based in Damascus and sent an army to terminate the Fatimid Caliphate in Egypt. A nephew of the Kurdish commander of that expedition, Salah-al-Din, known in the West as Saladin, took advantage of Nur al-Din's timely death to seize power and unify Egypt and Syria. The Fatimid dynasty fell in 1171. In 1187 Saladin recaptured Jerusalem from the Europeans.

Saladin's descendants fought off subsequent Crusades. After one such battle, however, in 1250, Turkish mamluk troops seized control of the government in Cairo, ending Saladin's dynasty. In 1260 these mamluks rode east to confront a new invading force. At the Battle of Ain Jalut (ine jah-LOOT) (Spring of Goliath) in Syria, they met and defeated an army of Mongols from Central Asia (see Chapter 12), thus stemming an invasion that had begun several decades before and legitimizing their claim to dominion over Egypt and Syria.

SECTION REVIEW

- By 711, Arab armies had conquered an empire ranging from Sind in the east to Spain in the west.

- The Umayyad caliphs ruled an ethnic empire; they governed from Damascus using Sasanid and Byzantine administrative methods.

- The Umayyads fell to rebels who established the Abbasid Caliphate at Baghdad, while surviving Umayyads fled to Spain.

- Influenced by Persian culture, the Abbasids presided over significant spiritual, intellectual, and artistic activity.

- Abbasid decline led to fragmentation of the caliphate into independent states, but the Islamic umma remained intact.

- Political divisions continued as successor states to the former caliphate fell, replaced by Seljuk Turk, Crusader, mamluk, and Mongol states.

During the ensuing Mamluk period a succession of slave-soldier sultans ruled Egypt and Syria until 1517. Fear of new Mongol attacks receded after 1300, but by then the new ruling system had become fixed. Young Turkish or Circassian slaves, the latter from the eastern end of the Black Sea, were imported from non-Muslim lands, raised in training barracks, and converted to Islam. Owing loyalty to the mamluk officers who purchased them, they formed a military class that was socially disconnected from the Arabic-speaking native population.

The Mongol invasions, especially their destruction of the Abbasid Caliphate in Baghdad in 1258, shocked the world of Islam. The mamluk sultan enthroned a relative of the last Baghdad caliph in Cairo, but the Egyptian Abbasids were mere puppets serving mamluk interests. From Iraq eastward, non-Muslim rule lasted for much of the thirteenth century. Although the Mongols left few ethnic or linguistic traces in these lands, their initial destruction of cities and slaughter of civilian populations, their diversion of Silk Road trade from Baghdad to more northerly routes ending at Black Sea ports, and their casual disregard, even after conversion to Islam, for Muslim religious life and urban culture hastened currents of change already under way.

Islamic Civilization

How did regional diversity affect the development of Islamic civilization?

Though increasingly unsettled in its political dimension and subject to economic disruptions caused by war, the ever-expanding Islamic world underwent a fruitful evolution in law, social structure, and religious expression. Religious conversion and urbanization reinforced each other to create a distinct Islamic civilization. The immense geographical and human diversity of the Muslim lands allowed many "small traditions" to coexist with the developing "great tradition" of Islam.

Law and Dogma

The Shari'a, the law of Islam, provides the foundation of Islamic civilization. Yet aside from certain Quranic verses conveying specific divine ordinances—most pertaining to personal and family matters—Islam had no legal system in the time of Muhammad. Arab custom and the Prophet's own authority offered the only guidance. After Muhammad died, the umma tried to follow his example. This became harder and harder to do, however, as those who knew Muhammad best passed away and many Arabs found themselves living in far-off lands. Non-Arab converts to Islam, who at first tried to follow Arab customs they had little familiarity with, had an even harder time.

Islam slowly developed laws to govern social and religious life. The full sense of Islamic civilization, however, goes well beyond the basic Five Pillars mentioned earlier. Some Muslim thinkers felt that the reasoned consideration of a mature man offered the best resolution of issues not covered by Quranic revelation. Others argued for the sunna, or tradition, of the Prophet as the best guide. To understand that sunna they collected and studied thousands of reports, called **hadith** (hah-DEETH), purporting to convey the precise words or deeds of Muhammad. It became customary to precede each hadith with a chain of oral authorities leading back to the person who had direct acquaintance with the Prophet.

Many hadith dealt with ritual matters, such as how to wash before prayer. Others provided answers to legal questions not covered by Quranic revelation or suggested principles for deciding such matters. By the eleventh century most legal thinkers had accepted the idea that Muhammad's personal behavior provided the best role model and that the hadith constituted the most authoritative basis for law after the Quran itself.

Yet the hadith posed a problem because the tens of thousands of anecdotes included both genuine and invented reports, the latter sometimes politically motivated, as well as stories derived from non-Muslim religious traditions. Only a specialist could hope to separate a sound from a weak tradition. As the hadith grew in importance, so did the branch of learning devoted to their analysis. Scholars discarded thousands for having faulty chains of authority. The most reliable they collected into books that gradually achieved authoritative status. Sunnis placed six books in this category; Shi'ites, four.

As it gradually evolved, the Shari'a embodied a vision of an umma in which all subscribed to the same moral values and political and ethnic distinctions lost importance. Every Muslim ruler was expected to abide by and enforce the religious law. In practice, this expectation often lost out in the hurly-burly of political life. But the Shari'a proved an important basis for an urban lifestyle that varied surprisingly little from Morocco to India.

Converts and Cities

Conversion to Islam, more the outcome of people's learning about the new rulers' religion than an escape from the tax on non-Muslims, as some scholars have suggested, helped spur urbanization. Conversion did not require extensive knowledge of the faith. To become a Muslim, a person simply stated, in the presence of a Muslim: "There is no God but God, and Muhammad is the Messenger of God."

Few converts spoke Arabic, and fewer could read the Quran. Many converts knew no more of the Quran than the verses they memorized for daily prayers. Muhammad had established no priesthood to define and spread the faith. Thus new converts, whether Arab or non-Arab, faced the problem of finding out

hadith A tradition relating the words or deeds of the Prophet Muhammad; next to the Quran, the most important basis for Islamic law.

for themselves what Islam was about and how they should act as Muslims. This meant spending time with Muslims, learning their language, and imitating their practices.

In many areas, conversion involved migrating to an Arab governing center. The alternative, converting to Islam but remaining in one's home community, was difficult because religion had become the main component of social identity in Byzantine and Sasanid times. Converts to Islam thus encountered discrimination if they stayed in their Christian, Jewish, or Zoroastrian communities. Migration both averted discrimination and took advantage of the economic opportunities opened up by tax revenues flowing into the Arab governing centers.

The Arab military settlements of Kufa and Basra in Iraq blossomed into cities and became important centers for Muslim cultural activities. As conversion rapidly spread in the mid-ninth century, urbanization accelerated in other regions, most visibly in Iran, where most cities previously had been quite small. Nishapur in the northeast grew from fewer than 10,000 pre-Islamic inhabitants to between 100,000 and 200,000 by the year 1000. Other Iranian cities experienced similar growth. In Iraq, Baghdad and Mosul joined Kufa and Basra as major cities. In Syria, Aleppo and Damascus flourished under Muslim rule. Fustat in Egypt developed into Cairo, one of the largest and greatest Islamic cities. The primarily Christian patriarchal cities of Jerusalem, Antioch, and Alexandria, not being Muslim governing centers, shrank and stagnated.

Conversion-related migration meant that cities became heavily Muslim before the countryside did. This reinforced the urban orientation deriving from the fact that Muhammad and his first followers came from the commercial city of Mecca. Mosques in large cities served both as ritual centers and as places for learning and social activities.

Islam colored all aspects of urban social life. Initially the new Muslims imitated Arab dress and customs and emulated people they regarded as particularly pious. In the absence of a central religious authority, local variations developed in the way people practiced Islam and in the hadith they attributed to the Prophet. This gave the rapidly growing religion the flexibility to accommodate many different social situations.

By the tenth century, urban growth was affecting the countryside by expanding the consumer market. Citrus fruits, rice, and sugar cane, introduced by the Sasanids, increased in acreage and spread to new areas. Cotton became a major crop in Iran and elsewhere and stimulated textile production. Irrigation works expanded. Abundant coinage facilitated a flourishing intercity and long-distance trade that provided regular links between isolated districts and integrated the pastoral nomads, who provided pack animals, into the region's economy. Trade encouraged the manufacture of cloth, metal goods, and pottery.

Science and technology also flourished. Building on Hellenistic traditions and their own observations and experience, Muslim doctors and astronomers developed skills and theories far in advance of their European counterparts. Working in Egypt in the eleventh century, the mathematician and physicist Ibn al-Haytham (IB-uhn al-HY-tham) wrote more than a hundred works. Among other things, he determined that the Milky Way lies far beyond earth's atmosphere, proved that light travels from a seen object to the eye and not the reverse, and explained why the sun and moon appear larger on the horizon than overhead.

Women and Islam

Women seldom traveled. Those living in rural areas worked in the fields and tended animals. Urban women, particularly members of the elite, lived in seclusion and did not leave their homes without covering themselves (see Material Culture: Head Coverings). Seclusion of women and veiling in public already existed in Byzantine and Sasanid times. Through interpretation of specific verses from the Quran, these practices now became fixtures of Muslim social life. Although women sometimes became literate and studied with relatives, they did so away from the gaze of unrelated men, and while they played influential roles within the family, public roles were generally barred. Only slave women could perform before unrelated men as musicians and dancers. A man could have sexual relations with as many slave concubines as he pleased, in addition to marrying as many as four wives.

Muslim women fared better legally under Islamic law than did Christian and Jewish women under their

Material Culture

Head Coverings

Covering the head is one of the most universal of human cultural characteristics. It is also one of the most common ways of signaling social status. Examples can be drawn from every part of the world, from earliest times down to the modern era. In premodern Chinese society the color and design of a man's cap indicated his rank as clearly as the insignia on military head coverings does today. In most European societies in the seventeenth and eighteenth centuries, men and frequently women of the higher social orders wore wigs, a practice that still survives in the costume of British judges. Head coverings were particularly important for royalty. From ancient Egypt, where the earliest Pharaonic crowns symbolized the union of the northern and southern parts of the Nile Valley, down to the twentieth century and the jewel-studded crown of the shah of Iran, each land developed its own distinctive royal headdress. This also held true for Native American societies in pre-Columbian times and for African and Polynesian societies. In some societies, such as Sasanid Iran and the Ottoman Empire in what is today Turkey, each ruler's crown or turban had a distinctive design that signaled his rule.

Head coverings have also played significant roles in religion. In orthodox Judaism, for example, men wear hats or skullcaps, and married women wear wigs, as signs of acceptance of God's laws. In Islam, head coverings for women, borrowed from pre-Islamic practice in the Middle East, have become politically controversial in recent years; but prior to the twentieth century it was considered equally improper for a Muslim man to go bareheaded.

Wearing no hat at all was usually a characteristic of slaves or of the poorest elements in society. But it could also signify a deliberate desire to be regarded as humble. Sumerian priests, Buddhist monks and nuns, and certain Sufis in the Muslim world shaved their heads clean. In Europe, early Christian monks and priests shaved the crown of their heads in the Roman Catholic tradition. This form of tonsure competed with and eventually superseded an Irish Catholic practice of shaving the front of the head. Yet head shaving did not always signify humility. Japanese samurai, or warriors, also shaved the front of their heads.

Head coverings for women, as well as wigs and hairdressing styles, sometimes show greater diversity than those for men. This has been particularly true in societies where women of high status mix with men on public occasions. A magnificent wig, hat, or coiffure under these circumstances might speak as much for the social rank of the woman's husband as for her own.

Given this long history of distinctive head coverings, the abandonment of both men's and women's hats in the second half of the twentieth century marked a major turning point in the history of symbolism. Around the world, the hat-making industry has greatly contracted. Whether one visits China, Egypt, India, France, or Brazil, one finds it difficult to determine the rank or status of most people by looking at what they have on their heads. Heads of government typically pose for group photographs with no hats on at all. Aside from conservative religious groups, the head coverings that remain most often indicate occupations: military, police, construction, athletics, and so on.

The reasons for this change are unclear. The spread of democracy and decline of aristocracy may have contributed to it, but hats have become equally uncommon in dictatorships. A more likely cause is the worldwide role of news photographs, movies, and other pictorial media. The media developed in Europe and the United States tend to take Western customs as normal and exoticize non-Western styles as "native costumes." People everywhere have thus felt pressure to switch to Western styles, including bareheadedness, to fit into the image of the modern world.

François Guenet/Art Resource, NY

Christ Before Caiphas
Though distinctive hair and hat customs were a hallmark of the Christian churches, Jesus stands out for his untrimmed hair and lack of a head cover, except for a crown of thorns.

Institute Amatiler d'Art Hispanic. © Patrimonio Nacional, Madrid

Women Playing Chess in Muslim Spain As shown in this thirteenth-century miniature, women in their own quarters, without men present, wore whatever clothes and jewels they liked. Notice the henna decorating the hands of the woman in the middle. The woman on the left, probably a slave, plays an oud.

respective religious codes. Because Islamic law guaranteed daughters a share in inheritance equal to half that of a son, the majority of women inherited some amount of money or real estate. This remained their private property to keep or sell. Muslim law put the financial burden of supporting a family exclusively on the husband, who could not legally compel his wife to help out.

Women could also remarry if their husbands divorced them, and they received a cash payment upon divorce. Although a man could divorce his wife without stating a cause, a woman could initiate divorce under specified conditions. Women could also practice birth control. They could testify in court, although their testimony counted as half that of a man. They could also go on pilgrimage. Nevertheless, a misogynistic tone sometimes appears in Islamic writings. One saying attributed to the Prophet observed: "I was raised up to heaven and saw that most of its denizens were poor people; I was raised into the hellfire and saw that most of its denizens were women."[3]

In the absence of writings by women about women from this period, the status of women must be deduced from the writings of men. Two episodes involving the Prophet's wife A'isha, the daughter of Abu Bakr, provide examples of how Muslim men appraised women in society. Only eighteen when Muhammad died, A'isha lived for another fifty years. Early reports stress her status as Muhammad's favorite, the only virgin he married and the only wife to see the angel Gabriel. These reports emanate from A'isha herself, who was an abundant source of hadith. As a fourteen-year-old she had become separated from a caravan and rejoined it only after traveling through the night with a man who found her alone in the desert. Gossips accused her of being untrue to the Prophet, but a revelation from God proved her innocence. The second event was her participation in the Battle of the Camel, fought to derail Ali's caliphate. These two episodes came to epitomize what Muslim men feared most about women: sexual infidelity and meddling in politics. Even though the earliest literature dealing with A'isha stresses her position as Muhammad's favorite, his first wife, Khadija, and his daughter, Ali's wife Fatima, eventually surpassed A'isha as ideal women. Both appear as model wives and mothers with no suspicion of sexual irregularity or political manipulation.

As the seclusion of women became commonplace in urban Muslim society, some writers extolled homosexual relationships, partly because a male lover could appear in public or go on a journey. Although Islam deplored homosexuality, one ruler wrote a book advising his son to follow moderation in all things and thus share his affections equally between men and women. Another ruler and his slave-boy became models of perfect love in the verses of mystic poets.

Islam allowed slavery but forbade Muslims from enslaving other Muslims or so-called People of the Book—Jews, Christians, and Zoroastrians, who revered holy books respected by the Muslims. Being enslaved as a prisoner of war constituted an exception. Later centuries saw a constant flow of slaves into Islamic territory from Africa and Central Asia. A hereditary slave society, however, did not develop. Usually slaves converted to Islam, and many masters then freed them as an act of piety. The offspring of slave women and Muslim men were born free.

The Recentering of Islam

Early Islam centered on the caliphate, the political expression of the unity of the umma. No formal organization or hierarchy, however, directed the process of conversion. Thus there emerged a multitude of local Islamic communities so disconnected from each other that numerous competing interpretations of the developing religion arose. Inevitably, the centrality of the caliphate diminished (see Map 9.1). The appearance of rival caliphates in Tunisia and Cordoba accentuated the problem of decentralization. The rise of the ulama as community leaders did not prevent growing fragmentation because the ulama themselves divided into contentious factions. During the twelfth century factionalism began to abate, and new socioreligious institutions emerged to provide the umma with a different sort of religious center. These new developments stemmed in part from an exodus of religious scholars from Iran in response to economic and political disintegration during the late eleventh and twelfth centuries. The flow of Iranians to the

Arab lands and to newly conquered territories in India and Anatolia increased after the Mongol invasion. Fully versed in Arabic as well as their native Persian, immigrant scholars were warmly received. They brought with them a view of religion developed in Iran's urban centers. A type of religious college, the *madrasa* (MAH-dras-uh), gained sudden popularity outside Iran, where madrasas had been known since the tenth century. Scores of madrasas, many founded by local rulers, appeared throughout the Islamic world.

Iranians also contributed to the growth of mystic groups known as *Sufi* brotherhoods in the twelfth and thirteenth centuries. The doctrines and rituals of certain Sufis spread from city to city, giving rise to the first geographically extensive Islamic religious organizations. Sufi doctrines varied, but a quest for a sense of union with God through rituals and training was a common denominator. Sufism had begun in early Islamic times and had doubtless benefited from the ideas and beliefs of people from religions with mystic traditions who converted to Islam.

The early Sufis had been saintly individuals given to ecstatic and poetic utterances and wonderworking. They attracted disciples but did not try to organize them. The growth of brotherhoods, a less ecstatic form of Sufism, set a tone for society in general. It soon became common for most Muslim men, particularly in the cities, to belong to at least one brotherhood.

A sense of the social climate the Sufi brotherhoods fostered can be gained from a twelfth-century manual:

> Every limb has its own special ethics. . . . The ethics of the tongue. The tongue should always be busy in reciting God's names (*dbikr*) and in saying good things of the brethren, praying for them, and giving them counsel. . . . The ethics of hearing. One should not listen to indecencies and slander. . . . The ethics of sight. One should lower one's eyes in order not to see forbidden things.[4]

Special dispensations allowed people who merely wanted to emulate the Sufis and enjoy their company to follow less demanding rules:

> It is allowed by way of dispensation to possess an estate or to rely on a regular income. The Sufis' rule in this matter is that one should not use all of it for himself, but should dedicate this to public

SECTION REVIEW

- The foundation of Islamic civilization is the Shari'a, which is derived from the Quran and hadith.

- Urbanization and religious conversion reinforced each other and prompted the expansion of agriculture, trade, science, and technology.

- Women in general enjoyed relatively high status under Islamic law, though urban women tended to live in seclusion.

- Islamic attitudes toward homosexuality were ambivalent, and slavery was an accepted and continuous practice.

- Iranian scholars centered Islam on the madrasa and contributed to the rise of Sufism.

charities and should take from it only enough for one year for himself and his family. . . .

There is a dispensation allowing one to watch all kinds of amusement. This is, however, limited by the rule: What you are forbidden from doing, you are also forbidden from watching.[5]

Some Sufi brotherhoods spread in the countryside. Local shrines and pilgrimages to the tombs of Muhammad's descendants and saintly Sufis became popular. The end of the Abbasid Caliphate enhanced the religious centrality of Mecca, which eventually became an important center of madrasa education, and gave renewed importance to the annual pilgrimage.

Conclusion

Islam began as a religious movement that united the peoples of Arabia. So powerful was its message, however, that it inspired Arabian warriors to spread out from Arabia to neighboring countries, which rapidly succumbed to the new conquerors. For many years, in the lands that Arabians had conquered they kept themselves separate from their subjects, imposing taxes and laws but tolerating the practice of Judaism and Christianity. The appeal of Islam and the practical advantages offered to Muslims in the Arab Empire were so strong that many of the subject peoples converted to Islam and joined the umma. In the process, Islam was influenced by the cultural traditions of the newly converted, especially Iranian, Egyptian, and Spanish Muslims. Even as the Abbasid Caliphate became weaker from the ninth century onward, the number of Muslims grew and the religion of Islam gained new converts far from the original centers of Islamic life in Arabia and the Middle East. Muslim states arose in West Africa, in Southeast Asia and Indonesia, and in Central Asia. The Arabic language, an important aspect of Islam because it is the language of the Quran, replaced the common languages of the Middle East and North Africa, but it did not spread to Iran or beyond, nor to sub-Saharan Africa. As Islam distanced itself from its original identification with Arabians, it became a universal world religion.

CHAPTER REVIEW

 Download the MP3 audio file of the Chapter Review to listen to on the go.

How did the traditions and religious views of pre-Islamic peoples become integrated into the culture shaped by Islam? (page 214)

During Muhammad's lifetime, virtually all Muslims were Arabs from central or southern Arabia. Their cultural traditions underlie many verses of the Quran. But the conquests brought many other peoples under the rule of the caliphate. Non-Arabs who converted to Islam, as well as Arabs from previously Christian groups in Syria and Iraq, brought with them some of the traditions and religious views of their former faith communities. Bits of this cultural heritage sometimes became incorporated into the body of lore accepted as the sayings of Muhammad. Other materials, notably in science and philosophy, were translated in book form into Arabic. And still more seeped into the rich store of legend and customary knowledge in different parts of the caliphate.

Was the Baghdad caliphate really the high point of Muslim civilization? (page 218)

A division of the caliphate into smaller political units accompanied this growth in ethnic diversity. The glittering cosmopolitan Baghdad of the early Abbasid Caliphate lost its luster as the conversion of non-Arabs to Islam increased and other cities from Spain to Pakistan evolved into regional Muslim centers. Despite Baghdad's reputation, these later centers, looked at collectively, contributed more to the distinctiveness of medieval Islamic culture than did Baghdad.

How did regional diversity affect the development of Islamic civilization? (page 226)

Spain, Egypt, and Iran were three regions that flourished as Baghdad declined. Each developed a particular intellectual, religious, and artistic character within the overall unity of Islam. Politically as well, regional variation was important. The coming of the Turks and Mongols left North Africa and Spain mostly untouched, the Crusades were of negligible importance for Iran, and the confrontation of the Muslims of Spain with the Christians to their north meant little to the Egyptians. Yet all of these events contributed to the shaping of medieval Islamic civilization as a whole.

Key Terms

Mecca *(p. 214)*

Muhammad *(p. 215)*

Muslim *(p. 216)*

Islam *(p. 216)*

Medina *(p. 216)*

umma *(p. 216)*

caliphate *(p. 217)*

Quran *(p. 217)*

Shi'ites *(p. 217)*

Umayyad Caliphate *(p. 218)*

Sunnis *(p. 218)*

Abbasid Caliphate *(p. 219)*

mamluks *(p. 220)*

Ghana *(p. 222)*

ulama *(p. 224)*

hadith *(p. 226)*

Web Resources

Pronunciation Guide

Interactive Map

- MAP 9.1 Rise and Fall of the Abbasid Caliphate

Primary Sources

- The Constitution of Medina: Muslims and Jews at the Dawn of Islam
- The Quran: Muslim Devotion to God
- The Book of Routes and Realms

Answer to the History in Focus Question

See photo on page 213, "Scholarly Life in Medieval Islam."

 CourseMate Visit the CourseMate website at www.cengagebrain.com for additional study tools and review materials for this chapter.

Christian Europe Emerges

© Cengage Learning

Visit the CourseMate website at **www.cengagebrain.com** for additional study tools and review materials for this chapter.

n 800, **Charlemagne** (SHAHR-leh-mane) (from Latin *Carolus magnus*, "Charles the Great") became the first man in western Europe to bear the title *emperor* in over three hundred years. Rome's decline and Charlemagne's rise marked a shift of focus for Europe—away from the Mediterranean and toward the north and west. German custom and Christian piety transformed the Roman heritage to create a new civilization. Irish monks preaching in Latin became intellectual leaders in Germanic lands, while the memory of Greek and Roman philosophy faded. Urban life continued the decline begun in the later days of the Roman Empire. Historians originally called this era "**medieval**," literally "middle age," because it comes between the era of Greco-Roman civilization and the intellectual, artistic, and economic changes of the Renaissance in the fourteenth century. In fact, many aspects of medieval culture were as rich and creative as those that came earlier and later.

Charlemagne was not the only ruler in Europe to claim the imperial title. Another emperor held sway in the Greek-speaking east, where Rome's political and legal heritage continued in the Eastern Roman or **Byzantine Empire**. While western Europeans lived amid the ruins of empire, the Byzantines maintained and reinterpreted Roman traditions. The authority of the Byzantine emperors blended with the influence of the Christian church in a cultural synthesis that helped shape the emerging kingdom of **Kievan Russia**. Byzantium's centuries-long conflict with Islam helped spur the crusading passion that overtook western Europe in the eleventh century.

The comparison between western and eastern Europe appears paradoxical. Byzantium inherited a robust and self-confident late Roman society and economy, while western Europe could not achieve political unity and suffered severe economic decline. Yet by 1200 western Europe was showing renewed vitality and flexing its military muscles, while Byzantium was showing signs of decline and military weakness. As we explore these different historical paths, we must remember that the emergence of Christian Europe included both developments.

The Byzantine Empire, 600–1200

How did the Byzantine Empire maintain Roman imperial traditions in the east?

The Byzantine emperors established Christianity as their official religion (see Chapter 6). They also represented a continuation of Roman imperial rule and tradition. Whereas only provincial forms of Roman law survived in the west, Byzantium inherited imperial law intact. Combining the imperial role with political oversight of the Christian church, the emperors made a comfortable transition into the role of all-powerful Christian monarchs. The Byzantine drama, however, played on a steadily shrinking stage. Territorial losses and almost constant military pressure from north and south deprived the empire of long periods of peace.

Church and State

In 324, in the nineteenth year of his reign, the emperor Constantine (r. 306–337) led a procession marking the expanded limits of his new capital: the millennium-old Greek city of Byzantium, located on a long, narrow inlet at the entrance to the Bosporus strait. In the forum of the new Constantinople (cahn-stan-tih-NO-pul), he erected a 120-foot-tall (36-meter) column topped with a statue of Apollo, and he retained the old Roman title *pontifex maximus* (PAHN-tih-fex

Charlemagne (742–814) King of the Franks (r. 768–814); emperor (r. 800–814). Through a series of military conquests he established the Carolingian Empire, which encompassed all of Gaul and parts of Germany and Italy. Though illiterate himself, he sponsored a brief intellectual revival.

medieval Literally "middle age," a term that historians of Europe use for the period ca. 500 to ca. 1500, signifying its intermediate point between Greco-Roman antiquity and the Renaissance.

Byzantine Empire Historians' name for the eastern portion of the Roman Empire from the fourth century onward, taken from "Byzantion," an early name for Constantinople, the Byzantine capital city.

Kievan Russia State established at Kiev in Ukraine ca. 879 by Scandinavian adventurers asserting authority over a mostly Slavic farming population.

Chronology

	Western Europe	Eastern Europe
600		**634–650** Muslims conquer Byzantine provinces of Syria, Egypt, and Tunisia
	711 Muslim conquest of Spain **732** Charles Martel stops Muslim advance into France at the Battle of Tours	
800	**800** Coronation of Charlemagne **843** Treaty of Verdun divides Carolingian Empire among Charlemagne's grandsons **910** Monastery of Cluny founded **962** Beginning of Holy Roman Empire	**882** Varangians take control of Kiev **980** Vladimir becomes grand prince of Kievan Russia
1000	**1054** Formal schism between Latin and Orthodox Churches **1066** Normans under William the Conqueror invade England **1076–1078** Climax of investiture controversy **1095** Pope Urban II preaches First Crusade	
1200		**1081–1118** Alexius Comnenus rules Byzantine Empire, calls for western military aid against Muslims **1204** Western knights sack Constantinople in Fourth Crusade

MAX-ih-muhs) (chief priest). Nevertheless, he leaned toward Christianity—historians disagree on when he embraced it fully—and he and his mother studded both his capital and the Christian centers of Jerusalem and Rome with important churches.

Constantine appointed the patriarch of Constantinople and involved himself in doctrinal disputes over which beliefs constituted heresy. In 325 he called hundreds of bishops to a council at the city of Nicaea (nye-SEE-uh) (modern Iznik in northwestern Turkey) to resolve disputes over religious doctrine. The bishops rejected the views of a priest from Alexandria named Arius, who maintained that Jesus was of lesser importance than God the Father. The Arian doctrine enjoyed greatest popularity among the Germanic peoples then migrating along the Danube frontier and into the western Roman lands. An Arian bishop named Ulfilas (ca. 311–383), himself belonging to the Germanic people known as Goths, translated the Bible into Gothic, reportedly using an alphabet of his own devising. This set the Arians apart from Christians who relied on scriptures written in Latin or Greek. Following the Arian controversy, disputes

over theology and quarrels among the patriarchs of Constantinople, Alexandria, and Antioch continued to tear at the Byzantine Empire. Literature of the period shows widespread concern for religious affairs, which deeply permeated society. A fourth-century bishop reported: "Everything is full of those who are speaking of unintelligible things.... I wish to know the price of bread; one answers, 'The Father is greater than the Son.' I inquire whether my bath is ready; one says, 'The Son has been made out of nothing.'"[1]Early Christians had established communities in many cities (see Map 10.1 on page 237). The most prominent were in Jerusalem, Antioch, Alexandria, and Rome, and their bishops became recognized as patriarchs, or paramount leaders. Other important theologians, like St. Augustine (354–430), the bishop of Hippo in North Africa, were not patriarchs. Constantine made Constantinople a fifth patriarchate (PAY-tree-ar-kayt). The patriarchs appointed bishops throughout their regions, and each bishop consecrated priests within his area of jurisdiction, called a diocese or see. Church rules set by the patriarch or by councils of bishops guided priests in serving ordinary believers.

Priests commemorated Christ's sacrifice on the cross in the consumption of wine and a wafer of bread in the Mass, or church service. Church leaders differed on the precise form of other rituals and on which should be considered sacred mysteries, or sacraments. Before baptism became standardized as a ritual for newborns, for example, it was sometimes postponed until late in life so that the person could benefit from the forgiveness of sin that it conveyed.

One area of disagreement within the church hierarchy centered on Jesus's relationship to God the Father and to the Holy Spirit. The bishops gathered for the Council of Nicaea agreed that, contrary to the Arian view, the three formed a divine Trinity in which three aspects or manifestations of God somehow came together. But they did not all understand the Trinity in the same way. They also disagreed on whether Mary was the mother of God or the mother of a human named Jesus. Some Christians thought that images of God or Jesus or Mary, called icons, were proper objects to pray before because they stimulated pious thoughts; others, known as iconoclasts, or image-breakers, condemned the practice as too much like praying to pagan statues.

For some four centuries after 300, disagreements like these led to charges and countercharges of heresy. A heresy was a belief or practice so unacceptable as to be un-Christian. The most severe disagreements arose in North Africa and the lands of the eastern Mediterranean and resulted in **schism** (SKIZ-uhm) or formal theological break. Monophysite (muh-NAH-fi-site) (Greek for "one nature") doctrine, for example, emphasized the divinity of Jesus Christ and minimized his human characteristics. Finding abhorrent the idea that Christ suffered like an ordinary human on the cross, some Monophysites maintained that another man had been substituted for him. Versions of Monophysitism persist to this day in Egyptian, Ethiopian, and Armenian churches.

Christianity progressed most rapidly in urban centers. Though the country folk (Latin *pagani*, whence the word *pagan* used as a negative label for polytheists) long retained customs deriving from worship of the old gods, the emperor Julian (r. 361–363) tried in vain to restore the old polytheism as the state cult. When a blind Christian addressed Julian by the pejorative term "apostate" (renegade from Christianity)—historians commonly call him Julian the Apostate—the emperor said, "You are blind, and your God will not cure you." To this the Christian

Byzantine Church from a Twelfth-Century Manuscript The upper portion shows the church façade and domes. The lower portion shows the interior with a mosaic of Christ enthroned at the altar end.   Bibliothèque nationale de France

 History in Focus *Examine the figures carefully; notice how they appear and the space they occupy. What does this image suggest about the major goals of Byzantine religious artists? Find the answer online.*

schism A formal split within a religious community.

replied, "I thank God for my blindness, since it prevents me from beholding your impiety."[2] In 392 the emperor Theodosius banned all pagan ceremonies. The following year he terminated the eleven-hundred-year-old tradition of the Olympic Games, which had originated as religious rites but had become increasingly professionalized in Roman times.

Having a single ruler endowed with supreme legal and religious authority prevented the breakup of the Eastern Empire into petty principalities, but a series of territorial losses sapped the empire's strength. A strong emperor might temporarily recover lost ground, as Justinian (r. 527–565) did in seizing Tunisia

from Germanic Vandal rulers and reasserting Byzantine control along the east coast of Italy, but military pressures seldom abated. A new Iranian empire ruled by the Sasanid family (see Chapter 8) threatened from the east in the fourth century. Various enemies, including the Germanic Goths and the nomadic Huns of Central Asia, threatened from the north at different periods. Bribes, diplomacy, and occasional military victories usually persuaded the Goths and Huns to settle peacefully or move on and attack western Europe. War with the Sasanids, however, flared up repeatedly for almost three hundred years. Finally, a new enemy appeared from the Arabian peninsula:

Map 10.1   The Spread of Christianity By the early eighth century, Christian areas around the southern Mediterranean from northern Syria to northern Spain, accounting for most of the Christian population, had fallen under Muslim rule; the slow process of conversion to Islam had begun. This accentuated the importance of the patriarchs of Constantinople, the popes in Rome, and the later converting regions of northern and eastern Europe.   © Cengage Learning

 Interactive Map

followers of the Arab prophet Muhammad (see Chapter 9). Between 634 and 650, Arab armies destroyed the Sasanid Empire and captured Byzantine Egypt, Syria, and Tunisia. By the end of the twelfth century, at least two-thirds of the Christians in these former Byzantine territories had adopted the Muslim faith.

The loss of such populous and prosperous provinces shook the empire and reduced its power. Although the empire had largely recovered and reorganized militarily by the tenth century, it never regained the lost lands and eventually succumbed to Muslim conquest in 1453. The later Byzantine emperors faced new enemies in the north and south. Following the wave of Germanic migrations, Slavic and Turkic peoples appeared on the northern frontiers as part of centuries-long population migrations in Eurasian steppe lands. Other Turks led by the Seljuk family became the primary foe in the south.

At the same time, relations with the popes and princes of western Europe steadily worsened. In the mid-ninth century the patriarchs of Constantinople had challenged the territorial jurisdiction of the popes of Rome and some of the practices of the Latin Church. These arguments worsened over time and in 1054 culminated in a formal schism between the Latin Church and the Orthodox Church—a break that has been only partially mended.

Society and Urban Life

Imperial authority and urban prosperity in the eastern provinces of the old Roman Empire initially sheltered Byzantium from the economic reverses and population losses western Europe suffered from the third century on. However, the territorial losses to Arab invaders coming on the heels of a devastating sixth-century epidemic of bubonic plague, known as "the plague of Justinian," gave Byzantium a taste of decline. Popular narratives of saints' lives show a transition from stories about educated saints hailing from cities to stories about saints who originated as peasants. In many areas, barter replaced money transactions; some cities declined in population and wealth; and the traditional class of local urban notables nearly disappeared.

As the urban elite shrank, high-ranking aristocrats at the imperial court and rural landowners gained importance. Power organized by family began to rival power from class-based officeholding. By the end of the eleventh century, a family-based military aristocracy had emerged. Of Byzantine emperor Alexius Comnenus (uh-LEX-see-uhs kom-NAY-nuhs) (r. 1081–1118) it was said: "He considered himself not a ruler, but a lord, conceiving and calling the empire his own house."[3]

The situation of women changed, too. Although earlier Roman family life was centered on a legally all-powerful father, women enjoyed comparative freedom in public. After the seventh century women increasingly found themselves confined to the home. Some sources indicate that when they went out, they concealed their faces behind veils. Paradoxically, however, from 1028 to 1056 women ruled the Byzantine Empire alongside their husbands. The apparent increase in the seclusion of women resembles simultaneous developments in neighboring Islamic countries, but a firm linkage between them has yet to be found.

Economically, the Byzantine emperors continued the Late Roman inclination to set prices, organize grain shipments to the capital, and monopolize luxury goods like Tyrian purple cloth. Such government intervention may have slowed technological development and economic innovation. In the countryside, Byzantine farmers continued to use slow oxcarts and light scratch plows, which were efficient for many, but not all, soil types, long after farmers in western Europe had begun to adopt more efficient techniques.

Because Byzantium's Roman inheritance remained so much more intact than western Europe's, few people recognized the slow deterioration. Gradually, however, pilgrims and visitors from the west saw the reality beyond the awe-inspiring, incense-filled domes of cathedrals and beneath the glitter and silken garments of the royal court. An eleventh-century French visitor wrote:

> The city itself [Constantinople] is squalid and fetid and in many places harmed by permanent darkness, for the wealthy overshadow the streets with buildings and leave these dirty, dark places to the poor and to travelers; there murders and robberies and other crimes which love the darkness are committed. Moreover, since people live lawlessly in this city, which has . . . almost as many thieves as poor men, a criminal knows neither fear nor shame, because crime is not punished by law and never entirely comes to light. In

every respect she exceeds moderation; for, just as she surpasses other cities in wealth, so too, does she surpass them in vice.[4]

A Byzantine contemporary, Anna Comnena, the brilliant daughter of Emperor Alexius Comnenus, expressed the view from the other side. She scornfully described a prominent churchman and philosopher who happened to be from Italy: "Italos . . . was unable with his barbaric, stupid temperament to grasp the profound truths of philosophy; even in the act of learning he utterly rejected the teacher's guiding hand, and full of temerity and barbaric folly, [believed] even before study that he excelled all others."[5]

Cultural Achievements

Justinian's collection of Roman laws endured far longer than his restoration of Byzantine rule in Italy and North Africa. At his command a team of seventeen legal scholars made a systematic compilation, in Latin, of a thousand years of Roman legal tradition. The *Corpus Juris Civilis* (*Body of Civil Law*), as it has been called since the sixteenth century, consisted of four sections: a general introduction and survey, a digest for lawyers and judges containing specific laws and quotations from well-known commentaries, a collection of imperial decrees since the time of the emperor Hadrian (r. 117–138), and another collection of recent decrees not previously collected. In the eleventh century a legal scholar named Irnerius (ca. 1055–ca. 1130) revived the study of this code (see below) at the University of Bologna (boe-LOAN-yuh) in Italy, and it subsequently became the basis of most modern European legal systems.

Constantinople's cathedral, the Hagia Sophia (AH-yah SOH-fee-uh) ("Sacred Wisdom"), also dates in its present form to the reign of Justinian and his influential wife, the empress Theodora. Its great dome became a hallmark of Byzantine architecture. Artistic creativity appeared in the design and ornamentation of other churches and monasteries as well. Byzantine religious art, featuring stiff but arresting images of holy figures against gold backgrounds, strongly influenced painting in western Europe down to the thirteenth century, and Byzantine musical traditions strongly affected the chanting employed in medieval Latin churches.

Other important Byzantine achievements date to the empire's long period of political decline. In the

SECTION REVIEW

- With Christianity as the state religion, the Byzantine Empire continued Roman imperial and legal traditions in the east.

- The empire faced political threats from the Arabs, crusaders, Slavs, and Turks and religious challenges from Islam and the Western Church.

- Plagues and invasions caused significant cultural and political shifts.

- Emperors continued Late Roman economic policies, and even Constantinople declined as a result.

- Byzantine civilization included notable achievements in art, architecture, music, and missionary work among the Slavs.

ninth century, two brothers named Cyril and Methodius embarked on a highly successful mission to the Slavs of Moravia (part of the modern Czech Republic). Like the Gothic bishop Ulfilas in the fourth century, they preached in the local language, and their followers perfected a writing system, called Cyrillic (sih-RIL-ik), that came to be used by Slavic Christians adhering to the Orthodox—that is, Byzantine—rite. Their careers also mark the beginning of a competition between the Greek and Latin forms of Christianity for the allegiance of the Slavs. The use today of the Cyrillic alphabet among the Russians and other Slavic peoples of Orthodox Christian faith, and of the Roman alphabet among the Poles, Czechs, and Croatians, testifies to this competition.

Early Medieval Europe, 600–1000

How did the culture of early medieval Europe develop in the absence of imperial rule?

The disappearance of the imperial legal framework that had persisted to the final days of the Western Roman Empire (see Chapter 6) and the rise of various kings, nobles, and chieftains changed the legal and political landscape of western Europe. In region after region, the family-based traditions of the Germanic peoples, which often fit local conditions better than previous practices, supplanted the edicts of the Roman emperors (see Map 10.2).

Map 10.2 Germanic Kingdoms Though German kings asserted authority over most of western Europe, German-speaking peoples were most numerous east of the Rhine River. In most other areas, Celtic languages such as Breton or languages derived from Latin predominated. Though the absolute number of Germanic settlers seems to have been fairly limited, the Germanic Anglo-Saxon tongue increasingly supplanted the Celtic Welsh and Scottish in Britain.
© Cengage Learning

Interactive Map

Fear and physical insecurity led communities to seek the protection of local strongmen. In places where looters and pillagers might appear at any moment, a local lord with a castle in which peasants could take refuge counted for more than a distant king. Dependency of weak people on strong people became a hallmark of the post-Roman period in western Europe.

The Time of Insecurity

By 530 the Western Roman Empire had fragmented into a handful of dissimilar kingdoms under Germanic rulers. The Franks held much of Gaul, the Visigoths ruled in Spain, and the Ostrogoths ruled in Italy and present-day Austria and Hungary. By 600 the Lombards had replaced the Ostrogoths in northern Italy, and the Byzantine Empire had regained footholds in the south and around Ravenna along the east coast. The city of Rome lost most of its population and its political importance but retained prominence as the seat of the bishop of Rome. Local noble families competed for control of this position, which over several centuries acquired the title *pope* along with supreme power in the Latin-speaking church.

The educated few, most of them Christian priests and monks, spoke and wrote a simplified form of Latin, but the uneducated masses who had lived under Roman rule spoke Romance dialects that eventually became modern Portuguese, Spanish, French, Italian, and Romanian. In the north and east of the Rhine River, where Roman culture had scarcely penetrated, people spoke Germanic and related Scandinavian languages. East of the Elbe River, Slavic speakers formed a third major group. Whatever sense of unity Europe may have experienced under Roman rule gave way to strongly localized identities.

In 711 a frontier raiding party of Muslim Arabs and Berbers crossed the Strait of Gibraltar and defeated the Visigoths in Spain (see Chapter 9). After pushing the remaining Christian chieftains into the northern mountains, the Muslims moved on to France. They occupied much of the southern coast

Boatbuilding Scene from the Bayeux Tapestry Eleventh-century shipwrights prepare vessels for William of Normandy's invasion of England in 1066.

and penetrated as far north as Tours, less than 150 miles (240 kilometers) from the English Channel, before the Frankish leader Charles Martel, Charlemagne's grandfather, stopped their most advanced raiding party in 732 at the Battle of Tours.

Military effectiveness was key to the rise of the Carolingian (kah-roe-LIN-gee-uhn) family (from Latin *Carolus*, "Charles"), first as protectors of the Frankish kings, then as kings themselves under Charlemagne's father Pépin (r. 751–768), and finally with Charlemagne as emperors. Charlemagne's Carolingian Empire encompassed all of Gaul and parts of Germany and Italy. When Charlemagne's son Louis the Pious died, the Germanic tradition of splitting property among sons led to the Treaty of Verdun (843), which divided the empire into three parts. French-speaking in the west (France) and middle (Burgundy), and German-speaking in the east (Germany), the three regions never reunited (see Map 10.2). Nevertheless, the Carolingian economic system

 Primary Source: The Life of Charlemagne: The Emperor Himself Would you know Charlemagne if you saw him? Check out this description of the great man's appearance and habits.

based on landed wealth and a brief intellectual revival sponsored personally by Charlemagne—himself illiterate—provided a common heritage.

In 793, Viking sea raiders from Scandinavia attacked and plundered an English coastal monastery, the first of hundreds of similar raids. Local sources from France, the British Isles, and Muslim Spain reflect widespread dread of Viking warriors descending from multi-oared, dragon-prowed boats to pillage monasteries, villages, and towns. Versatile Vikings could both brave the stormy North Atlantic and maneuver up rivers. By the ninth century raiders from Denmark and Norway were harrying the British and French coasts while Varangians (va-RAN-gee-anz) (Swedes) pursued raiding and trading interests along the rivers of eastern Europe and Russia. In the 800s and 900s Viking captains organized the settlement of Iceland and Greenland, and, around the year 1000, they reached the northern tip of Newfoundland, which they called Vinland ("the land of grapevines").

Vikings long settled on lands they had seized in Normandy (in northwestern France) organized the most important and ambitious expeditions in terms of numbers of men and horses and long-lasting impact. William the Conqueror, the duke of Normandy, invaded England in 1066 and brought Anglo-Saxon domination of the island to an end. Other Normans (from "north men") attacked Muslim Sicily in the 1060s and, after thirty years of fighting, permanently severed it from the Muslim world.

A Self-Sufficient Economy

Archaeology and monastic records reveal a profound economic transformation that accompanied the Germanic political order. The new rulers cared little for the Romans' urban-based culture, which accordingly shrank in importance. Change was more rapid in some regions than others, but most cities lost population, or even became villages. Roman roads fell into disuse and disrepair. Small thatched houses sprang up beside abandoned villas, and marble public buildings became dilapidated. Paying for purchases in coin gave way to bartering goods and services. Trade across the Mediterranean largely dried up before the Arab conquests, but occasional shipments from North Africa and Syria continued to reach western ports.

Roman centralization had channeled the wealth and production of the empire to the capital, which in turn radiated Roman cultural styles and tastes to the provinces. As the new Germanic territorial lords found the riches of their own culture more appealing than those of Rome, local self-sufficiency became more important. The decline of literacy and other aspects of Roman life made room for the growth of Celtic and Germanic cultural traditions.

The northern diet featured beer, lard or butter, and bread made of barley, rye, or wheat, all supplemented by pork from herds of swine fed on forest acorns and beechnuts, and by game from the same forests. Nobles ate better than peasants, but even the peasant diet was reasonably balanced. The Roman diet based on wheat, wine, and olive oil persisted in the south. The average western European of the ninth century was probably better nourished than his or her descendants three hundred years later, when population increased and the nobles monopolized the resources of the forests.

In both north and south, self-sufficient farming estates known as **manors** became centers of agricultural production. Fearful farmers in the most vulnerable regions gave their lands to large landowners in return for political and physical protection. The warfare and instability of the post-Roman centuries made

unprotected country houses especially vulnerable to pillaging. Isolated by poor communications and lack of organized government, landowners depended on their own resources for survival. Many became warriors, maintained a force of armed men, or swore allegiance to landowners who had such a force.

A well-appointed manor possessed fields, gardens, grazing lands, fishponds, a mill, a church, workshops for making farm and household implements, and a village where the farmers dependent on the lord of the manor lived. Protection ranged from a ditch and wooden stockade to a stone wall surrounding a fortified keep (a stone building).

Manor life reflected personal status. Nobles and their families exercised almost unlimited power over their **serfs**—agricultural workers who belonged to the manor, tilled its fields, and owed other dues and obligations. Serfs could not leave the manor where they were born and attach themselves to another lord. Most peasants in England, France, and western Germany were unfree serfs in the tenth and eleventh centuries. In Bordeaux (bore-DOE), Saxony, and a few other regions, free peasantry survived based on the egalitarian social structure of the Germanic peoples during their period of migration. Outright slavery, the mainstay of the Roman economy (see Chapter 6), diminished as more and more peasants became serfs in return for a lord's protection. At the same time, taking prisoners to serve as slaves became less important as an object of warfare.

Early Medieval Society

Reversion to a self-sufficient economy limited the freedom and potential for personal achievement of most people, but an emerging class of nobles reaped great benefits. During the Germanic migrations and later among the Vikings of Scandinavia, men regularly answered the call to arms issued by war chiefs, to whom they swore allegiance. All

---

manor In medieval Europe, a large, self-sufficient landholding consisting of the lord's residence (manor house), outbuildings, peasant village, and surrounding land.

serf In medieval Europe, an agricultural laborer legally bound to a lord's property and obligated to perform set services for the lord.

Armored Knights in Battle This painting from around 1135 shows the armament of knights at the time of the Crusades. Chain mail, a helmet, and a shield carried on the left side protect the rider. The lance carried underarm and the sword are the primary weapons. Notice that riders about to make contact with lances have their legs straight and braced in the stirrups. Pierpont Morgan Library/Art Resource, NY

Starting in the sixteenth century, it became common to refer to medieval Europe as a "feudal society" in which kings and lords gave land to "vassals" in return for sworn military support. By analyzing original records, more recent historians have discovered this to be an oversimplification. Relations between landholders and serfs and between lords and vassals differed too much from one place to another, and from one time to another, to fit together in anything resembling a system.

The German foes of the Roman legions had equipped themselves with helmets, shields, and swords, spears, or throwing axes. Most fought on foot. Horsemen, using stirrups first invented by Central Asian pastoralists around the first century C.E., were able to stand in the saddle and absorb the impact when their lances struck the enemy at full gallop. This type of warfare required grain-fed horses that were larger and heavier than the small, grass-fed animals of the Central Asian nomads. Thus agricultural Europe rather than the Eurasian steppelands produced the charges of armored knights that came to dominate the battlefield.

By the eleventh century, knights had come to dominate the battlefield. They wore an open-faced helmet and a long linen shirt, or hauberk (HAW-berk), studded with small metal disks (see Environment and Technology: Iron Production). A century later, knightly equipment commonly included a visored helmet that covered the head and neck and a hauberk of chain mail.

warriors shared in the booty gained from raiding. As settlement enhanced the importance of agricultural tasks, laying down the plow and picking up the sword at the chieftain's call became harder.

Those who continued to join the war parties included a growing number of horsemen. Mounted warriors became the central force of the Carolingian army. At first, fighting from horseback did not make a person either a nobleman or a landowner. By the tenth century, however, nearly constant warfare to protect land rights or support the claims of a lord brought about a gradual transformation in the status of the mounted warrior. At different rates in different areas, landholding became almost inseparable from military service.

Iron Production

Despite the collapse of the Roman economy, iron-working expanded throughout Europe. The iron swords of the Germans outperformed traditional Roman weapons, which became obsolete. The spreading use of armor also increased the demand for iron. Archaeologists have found extensive evidence of iron smelting well beyond the frontiers of the Roman Empire. Helg Island in a lake near Stockholm, Sweden, had a large walled settlement that relied entirely on iron trading. Discoveries of a Buddha from India and a christening spoon from Egypt, both datable to the sixth century C.E., indicate the range of these trade contacts. At Zelechovice in the Czech Republic remains of fifty "slag-pit" furnaces have been dated to the ninth century.

Most iron smelting was done on a small scale. Ore containing iron oxide was shoveled onto a charcoal fire in an open-air hearth pit. The carbon in the charcoal combined with the oxygen in the ore to form carbon dioxide gas. This left behind a soft glowing lump of iron called a "bloom." This bloom was then pounded on a stone to remove the remaining impurities, like sand and clay, before being turned over to the blacksmith for fabricating into swords or armor.

During the post-Roman centuries, smelters learned to build walls around the hearth pits and then to put domes and chimneys on them. The resulting "slag-pit" furnaces produced greater amounts of iron. They also consumed great amounts of wood. Twelve pounds of charcoal, made from about 25 pounds of wood, were needed to produce 1 pound of bloom iron, and about 3 pounds of useless slag. Though bellows were developed to force oxygen into the fire, temperatures in slag-pit furnaces never became high enough to produce molten metal.

Iron Smelting Two bellows blowing alternately provide a constant stream of air to the furnace. The man on the right pounds the bloom into bars or plates that a blacksmith will reheat and shape.

The British Library Board, Sloane 3983, f. 50

Noblewoman Directing Construction of a Church This picture of Berthe, wife of Girat de Rouissillion, acting as mistress of the works comes from a tenth-century manuscript that shows a scene from the ninth century. Wheelbarrows rarely appear in medieval building scenes.

More armor for knight and horse meant a greater financial outlay. Since land was the basis of wealth, a knight needed financial support from land revenues. Accordingly, kings began to reward armed service with grants of land from their own property. Lesser nobles with extensive properties built their own military retinues the same way. A grant of land in return for a pledge to provide military service was often called a **fief**. At first, kings granted fiefs to their noble followers, known as **vassals**, on a temporary basis. By the tenth century, most fiefs could be inherited as long as the specified military service continued to be provided. Kings and lords commanded the service of their vassals for only part of the year. Vassals could hold land from several different lords and owe loyalty to each one. Moreover, the allegiance that a vassal owed to one lord could entail military service to that lord's master in time of need.

A typical medieval realm—actual practices varied widely—consisted of lands directly owned by a king or a count and administered by royal officers. The king's or count's major vassals held and administered other lands, often the greater portion, in return for military service. These vassals, in turn, granted land to their own vassals. The lord of a manor rather than the king provided governance and justice locally. Members of the clergy, along with the extensive agricultural lands owned by monasteries and convents, fell under the jurisdiction of the church, which further limited the reach and authority of the monarch.

Noblewomen became enmeshed in this tangle of obligations as heiresses and as candidates for marriage. A man who married the widow or daughter of a lord with no sons could gain control of that lord's property. Marriage alliances affected entire kingdoms. Noble daughters and sons had little say in marriage matters; issues of land, power, and military service took precedence.

Nevertheless, a noblewoman could own land or administer her husband's estates when he was away at war. Nonnoble women usually worked alongside their menfolk, performing agricultural tasks such as

fief In medieval Europe, land granted in return for a sworn oath to provide specified military service.
vassal In medieval Europe, a sworn supporter of a king or lord committed to rendering specified military service to that king or lord.

raking and stacking hay, shearing sheep, and picking vegetables. As artisans, women spun, wove, and sewed clothing. The Bayeux (bay-YUH) Tapestry, a piece of embroidery 230 feet (70 meters) long and 20 inches (51 centimeters) wide depicting William the Conqueror's invasion of England in 1066, was designed and executed entirely by women, though historians do not agree on who those women were.

The Western Church

What role did the Western Church play in the politics and culture of Europe?

Just as eastern European Christians followed the religious guidance of the patriarch of Constantinople, so did the pope wield authority over church affairs in western Europe. And while Orthodox missionaries spread Christianity among the Slavs, Catholic missionaries added territory to Christendom in the British Isles and the lands of the Germans.

In the west, when Roman nobles lost control of the **papacy**—the office of the pope—after the tenth century, it became a more powerful international office. Councils of bishops—which normally set rules called canons to regulate the priests and laypeople under their jurisdiction—became increasingly responsive to papal direction.

Nevertheless, regional disagreements over church regulations, shortages of educated clergy, difficult communications, and political disorder posed formidable obstacles to unifying church standards and practices. Clerics in some parts of western Europe were still issuing prohibitions against the worship of rivers, trees, and mountains as late as the eleventh century. Church problems included lingering polytheism, lax enforcement of prohibitions against priests marrying, nepotism (giving preferment to close kin), and simony (selling ecclesiastical appointments, often to laymen). The persistence of the papacy in asserting its legal jurisdiction over clergy, combating polytheism and heretical beliefs, and calling on secular rulers to recognize the pope's authority constituted a rare force for unity and order in a time of disunity and chaos.

Politics and the Church

The pope needed allies. Charlemagne's father Pepin was a strong supporter of the papacy. The relationship between kings and popes was tense, however, since both considered themselves ultimate authorities. In 962 the pope crowned the first "Holy Roman Emperor" (Charlemagne never held this full title). This designation of a secular political authority as the guardian of collective Christian interests proved more apparent than real. Essentially a loose confederation of German princes who named one of their own as emperor, the **Holy Roman Empire** had little influence west of the Rhine River.

Although the pope crowned the early Holy Roman Emperors, this did not signify political superiority. The law of the church (known as canon law because each law was called a canon) gave the pope exclusive legal jurisdiction over clergy and church property wherever located. But bishops who held land as vassals owed military support or other services and dues to kings and princes. The secular rulers demanded the power to appoint those bishops because that was the only way to guarantee fulfillment of their duties as vassals. The popes disagreed.

---

papacy The central administration of the Roman Catholic Church, of which the pope is the head.
Holy Roman Empire Loose federation of mostly German states and principalities, headed by an emperor elected by the princes. It lasted from 962 to 1806.

In the eleventh century, this conflict over the control of ecclesiastical appointments came to a head. Hildebrand (HILL-de-brand), an Italian monk, capped a career of reorganizing church finances when the cardinals (a group of senior bishops) meeting in Rome selected him to be Pope Gregory VII in 1073. His personal notion of the papacy (preserved among his letters) represented an extreme position, stating among other claims, that

§ The pope can be judged by no one;
§ The Roman church has never erred and never will err till the end of time;
§ The pope alone can depose and restore bishops;
§ He alone can call general councils and authorize canon law;
§ He can depose emperors;
§ He can absolve subjects from their allegiance;
§ All princes should kiss his feet.[6]

Such claims antagonized lords and monarchs, who had become accustomed to *investing*—that is, conferring a ring and a staff as symbols of authority on bishops and abbots in their domains. Historians apply the term **investiture controversy** to the medieval struggle between the church and the lay lords to control ecclesiastical appointments; the term also refers to the broader conflict of popes versus monarchs. When Holy Roman Emperor Henry IV defied Gregory's reforms, Gregory excommunicated him in 1076, thereby cutting him off from church rituals. Stung by the resulting decline in his influence, Henry stood barefoot in the snow for three days outside a castle in northern Italy waiting for Gregory, a guest there, to receive him. Henry's formal act of penance induced Gregory to forgive him and restore him to the church; but the reconciliation, an apparent victory for the pope, proved hollow. In 1078 Gregory deposed Henry but then had to flee from Rome to Salerno, where he died two years later.

A compromise was reached in 1122 at Worms, a town in Germany. In the Concordat of Worms, Emperor Henry V renounced his right to choose bishops and abbots or bestow spiritual symbols upon them. In return, Pope Calixtus II permitted the emperor to invest papally appointed bishops and abbots with any lay rights or obligations before their spiritual consecration. Such compromises did not fully solve the problem, but they reduced tensions between the two sides.

Assertions of royal authority triggered other conflicts as well. Though barely twenty when he became king of England in 1154, Henry II, a great-grandson of William the Conqueror, acted to strengthen the power of the Crown and weaken the nobility. He appointed traveling justices to enforce his laws and made juries, a holdover from traditional Germanic law, into powerful legal instruments. He also established the principle that criminal acts violated the "king's peace" and should be tried and punished in accordance with charges brought by the Crown instead of in response to charges brought by victims.

Henry had a harder time controlling the church. His closest friend and chancellor, or chief administrator, Thomas à Becket (ca. 1118–1170), lived the grand life of a courtier. In 1162 Henry persuaded Becket to become a priest and assume the position of archbishop of Canterbury, the highest church office in England. Becket agreed but cautioned that from then on he would act solely in the interest of the church. When Henry sought to try clerics accused of crimes in royal instead of ecclesiastical courts, Archbishop Thomas, now leading an austere and pious life, resisted. In 1170 four of Henry's knights, knowing that the king desired Becket's death, murdered the archbishop in Canterbury Cathedral. Their crime backfired, and an outpouring of sympathy caused Canterbury to become a major pilgrimage center. In 1173 the pope declared the martyred Becket a saint. Henry allowed himself to be publicly whipped twice in penance for the crime, his authority badly damaged.

Henry II's conflict with Thomas à Becket, like the Concordat of Worms, yielded no clear victor. The problem of competing legal traditions made political life in western Europe more complicated than in Byzantium. So-called feudal law, rooted in Germanic custom, gave supreme power to the king. Canon law, based on Roman precedent, visualized a single church

---

investiture controversy Dispute between the popes and the Holy Roman Emperors over who held ultimate authority over bishops in imperial lands.

with jurisdiction over all of western Christendom. In the eleventh century Roman civil law, contained in the *Corpus Juris Civilis*, added a third tradition.

Monasticism

Monasticism featured prominently in the religious life of almost all Christian lands. The origins of group monasticism lay in the eastern lands of the Roman Empire. Pre-Christian practices such as celibacy, continual devotion to prayer, and living apart from society (alone or in small groups) came together in Christian form in Egypt.

Monasticism in western Europe, however, normally involved groups of monks or nuns living together in organized communities. The person most responsible for introducing this practice to the Latin west was Benedict of Nursia (ca. 480–547) in Italy. Benedict began his pious career as a hermit in a cave but eventually organized several monasteries, each headed by an abbot. In the seventh century monasteries based on his model spread far beyond Italy. The Rule of Benedict, written to govern the monks' behavior, envisions a balance between devotion and work, along with obligations of celibacy, poverty, and obedience to the abbot. Those who lived by this or other monastic rules became *regular clergy*, in contrast to *secular clergy*, priests who lived in society instead of in seclusion. The Rule of Benedict was the starting point for most forms of western European monastic life and remains in force today in Benedictine monasteries.

Though monks and nuns (women who lived by monastic rules in convents) constituted a small percentage of the total population, their secluded way of life reinforced the separation of religious affairs from ordinary politics and economics. Monasteries followed Jesus's axiom to "render unto Caesar what is Caesar's and unto God what is God's" better than the many town-based bishops who behaved like lords.

Monasteries preserved literacy and learning in the early medieval period, although some rulers, like Charlemagne, encouraged scholarship at court. Regular clergy saw copying manuscripts and even writing books as a religious calling, thereby preserving many Roman works that would otherwise have disappeared. The survival of Greek works depended more on Byzantine and Muslim scribes in the east.

Monasteries could plant Christianity in new lands, as Irish monks did in parts of Germany, service the needs of travelers, organize agricultural production on their lands, and raise abandoned infants. Convents provided refuge for widows and other women who lacked male protection or desired a spiritual life. Yet oversight was a problem. A bishop might have authority over an abbot or abbess (head of a convent), but he could not exercise constant vigilance over what went on behind monastery walls.

Primary Source: The Rule of Saint Benedict: Work and Pray Learn what Benedict considered the enemy of the soul.

monasticism Living in a religious community apart from secular society and adhering to a rule stipulating chastity, obedience, and poverty. It was a prominent element of medieval Christianity and Buddhism. Monasteries were the primary centers of learning and literacy in early medieval Europe.

A reform movement focused on monastic discipline took shape in the Benedictine abbey of Cluny (KLOO-nee) in eastern France. William the Pious, the first duke of Aquitaine, founded Cluny in 910 and freed it of lay authority. A century later the local bishop conferred similar freedom. Cluny's abbots pursued a vigorous campaign, eventually allying with reforming popes like Gregory VII to improve monastic discipline and administration. A magnificent new abbey church—with later additions, the largest in the world—symbolized Cluny's preeminence.

At the peak of Cluny's influence, nearly a thousand Benedictine abbeys and priories (lower-level monastic houses) in various countries accepted the authority of its abbot. The Benedictine Rule made each monastery independent; but the Cluniac reformers stipulated that every abbot and prior (head of a priory) be appointed by the abbot of Cluny and have personal experience of the religious life of Cluny. Monastic reform gained new impetus in the second half of the twelfth century with the rapid rise of the Cistercian order, which emphasized a life of asceticism and poverty.

Kievan Russia, 900–1200

What was the significance of the adoption of Orthodox Christianity by Kievan Russia?

Though Latin and Orthodox Christendom later followed different paths, which would flourish more was not apparent in 900. Many Slavs living in the north eventually accepted the Catholicism of Rome as taught by German missionaries. The Serbs and other southern Slavs took their faith from Constantinople.

The conversion of Kievan Russia, farther to the east, shows how economics, politics, and religious life were closely intertwined. The choice of Orthodoxy over Catholicism had important consequences for later European history.

The Rise of the Kievan Empire

The territory between the Black and Caspian Seas in the south and the Baltic and White Seas in the north divides into a series of east-west zones. Frozen tundra in the far north gives way to a cold forest zone, then to a more temperate forest, then to a mix of forest and steppe grasslands, and finally to grassland only. Several navigable rivers, including the Volga, the Dnieper (d-NYEP-er), and the Don, run from north to south across these zones.

Early historical sources reflect repeated linguistic and territorial changes, seemingly under pressure from population migrations. Most of the Germanic peoples, along with some Iranian and west Slavic peoples, migrated into eastern Europe from Ukraine and Russia in Roman times. The peoples who remained behind spoke eastern Slavic languages, except in the far north and south: Finns and related peoples lived in the former region, Turkic-speakers in the latter.

Forest dwellers, farmers, and steppe nomads complemented each other economically. Nomads traded animals for the farmers' grain; and honey, wax, and furs from the forest became important exchange items. Traders could travel east and west by steppe caravan (see Chapter 8), or they could use boats on the rivers to move north and south.

Hoards containing thousands of Byzantine and Islamic coins buried in Poland and on islands in the Baltic Sea where fairs were held attest to the trading activity of Varangians (Swedish Vikings) who sailed across the Baltic and down Russia's rivers. They exchanged forest products and slaves for manufactured goods and coins, which they may have used as jewelry rather than as money, at markets controlled by the Khazar Turks, whose powerful kingdom centered around the mouth of the Volga River.

Historians debate the early meaning of the word *Rus* (from which *Russia* is derived), but at some point it came to refer to Slavic-speaking peoples ruled by Varangians. Unlike western European lords, the Varangian princes and their *druzhina* (military retainers) lived in cities, while the Slavs farmed. The princes occupied themselves with trade and fending off enemies. The Rus of the city of Kiev (KEE-yev), which was taken over by Varangians in 882, controlled trade on the Dnieper River and dealt more with Byzantium than with the Muslim world because the Dnieper flows into the Black Sea. The Rus of Novgorod (NOHV-goh-rod) played the same role on the Volga. The semilegendary account of the Kievan Rus conversion to Christianity must be seen against this background.

Erich Lessing/Art Resource, NY

Baptism of Vladimir I In 988 Vladimir I, the ruler of Kiev, opted to convert to the Greek Orthodox form of Christianity. This portrayal of the event in a Greek manuscript may be largely invented, but it is probably realistic in showing the full immersion of the king in the baptismal font.

In 980 Vladimir (VLAD-ih-mir) I, a ruler of Novgorod who had fallen from power, returned to Kiev with a band of Varangians and made himself the grand prince of Kievan Russia (see Map 10.3). Though his grandmother Olga had been a Christian, Vladimir built a temple on Kiev's heights and placed there the statues of the six gods his Slavic subjects worshiped. The earliest Russian chronicle reports that Vladimir and his advisers decided against Islam as the official religion because of its ban on alcohol, rejected Judaism (the religion to which the Khazars had converted) because they thought that a truly powerful god would not have let the ancient Jewish kingdom be destroyed, and even spoke with German emissaries advocating Latin Christianity. Why Vladimir chose Orthodox Christianity over the Latin version is not precisely known. The magnificence of Constantinople seems to have been a consideration. After visiting Byzantine churches, his agents reported: "We knew not whether we were in heaven or on earth, for on earth there is no such splendor of [sic] such beauty, and we are at a loss how to describe it. We know only that God dwells there among men, and their service is finer than the ceremonies of other nations."[7]

After choosing a reluctant bride from the Byzantine imperial family, Vladimir converted to Orthodox Christianity, probably in 988, and opened his lands to Orthodox clerics and missionaries. The patriarch of Constantinople appointed a metropolitan (chief bishop) at Kiev to govern ecclesiastical affairs. Churches arose in Kiev, one of them on the ruins of Vladimir's earlier hilltop temple. Writing was introduced, using the Cyrillic alphabet devised earlier for the western Slavs. This extension of Orthodox Christendom northward provided a barrier against the eastward expansion of Latin Christianity. Kiev became firmly oriented toward trade with Byzantium and turned its back on the Muslim world, though the Volga trade continued through Novgorod.

Struggles within the ruling family and with other enemies, most notably the steppe peoples of the south, marked the later political history of Kievan Russia. But down to the time of the Mongols in the thirteenth century (see Chapter 11), the state remained and served as an instrument for the Christianization of the eastern Slavs.

Society and Culture

In Kievan Russia political power derived from trade rather than from landholding, so the manorial agricultural system of western Europe never developed. Farmers practiced shifting cultivation of their own lands. They would burn a section of forest, then lightly scratch the ash-strewn surface with a plow. When fertility waned, they would move to another section of forest. Poor land and a short growing season in the most northerly latitudes made food scarce. Living on their own estates, the druzhina evolved from infantry into cavalry and focused their efforts more on horse breeding than on agriculture.

Large cities like Kiev and Novgorod may have reached 30,000 or 50,000 people—roughly the size of contemporary London or Paris, but far smaller than Constantinople or major Muslim metropolises like Baghdad and Nishapur. Many cities amounted to little more than fortified trading posts. Yet they served as centers for the development of crafts, some, such as glassmaking, based on skills imported from Byzantium. Artisans enjoyed higher status in society than peasant farmers. Construction relied on wood from

Map 10.3 Kievan Russia and the Byzantine Empire in the Eleventh Century
By the mid-eleventh century, the princes of Kievan Russia had brought all the eastern Slavs under their rule. The loss of Egypt, Syria, and Tunisia to Arab invaders in the seventh to eighth century had turned Byzantium from a far-flung empire into a fairly compact state. From then on the Byzantine rulers looked to the Balkans and Kievan Russia as the primary arena for extending their political and religious influence.   © Cengage Learning

Interactive Map

the forests, although Christianity brought the building of stone cathedrals and churches on the Byzantine model.

Christianity penetrated the general population slowly. Several polytheist uprisings occurred in the eleventh century, particularly in times of famine. Passive resistance led some groups to reject Christian burial and persist in cremating the dead and keeping the bones of the deceased in urns. Women continued to use polytheist designs on their clothing and

bracelets, and as late as the twelfth century they were still turning to polytheist priests for charms to cure sick children. Traditional Slavic marriage practices involving casual and polygamous relations particularly scandalized the clergy.

Christianity eventually triumphed, and its success led to increasing church engagement in political and economic affairs. In the twelfth century, Christian clergy became involved in government administration, some of them collecting fees and taxes related to trade. Direct and indirect revenue from trade provided the rulers with the money they needed to pay their soldiers. The rule of law also spread as Kievan Russia experienced its peak of culture and prosperity in the century before the Mongol invasion of 1237.

Western Europe Revives, 1000–1200

How did Mediterranean trade help revive western Europe?

Between 1000 and 1200 western Europe slowly emerged from nearly seven centuries of subsistence economy. Population and agricultural production climbed, and a growing food surplus found its way to town markets, speeding the return of a money-based economy and providing support for larger numbers of craftspeople, construction workers, and traders.

Historians have attributed western Europe's revival to population growth spurred by new technologies and to the appearance in Italy and Flanders, on the coast of the North Sea, of self-governing cities devoted primarily to seaborne trade. For monarchs, the changes facilitated improvements in central administration, greater control over vassals, and consolidation of realms on the way to becoming stronger kingdoms.

The Role of Technology

A lack of concrete evidence confirming the spread of technological innovations frustrates efforts to relate revival to technological change. Nevertheless, most historians agree that technology played a significant role in the near doubling of the population of western Europe between 1000 and 1200. The population of England seems to have risen from 1.1 million in 1086 to 1.9 million in 1200, and the population of the territory of modern France seems to have risen from 5.2 million to 9.2 million over the same period.

The history of plows and draft harnesses illustrates the difficulty of drawing historical conclusions from scattered evidence. Farmers in southern Europe and Byzantium continued to use the Roman plow, which scratched shallow grooves into loose, dry Mediterranean soils. But a new plow cut deep into the soil with a knifelike blade, while a curved board mounted behind the blade lifted the cut layer and turned it over, making it possible to farm the heavy, wet clays of the northern river valleys. This required more energy, which meant harnessing several teams of oxen or horses.

Horses plowed faster than oxen but were more demanding. Iron horseshoes, which were widely adopted in this period, helped protect their hooves, but like the plow itself, they added to the farmer's expenses. Roman horse harnesses put such pressure on the animal's throat that a horse pulling a heavy load risked strangulation. A mystery surrounds the adoption of more efficient designs. The **horse collar**, which moves the point of traction from the animal's throat to its shoulders, first appeared around 800 in a miniature painting, and it is shown clearly as a harness for plow horses in the Bayeux Tapestry, embroidered after 1066. The simpler breast-strap harness, appearing around 500, was not as suitable for the heaviest work but was preferred in southern Europe.

horse collar Harnessing method that increased the efficiency of horses by shifting the point of traction from the animal's neck to the shoulders; its adoption favors the spread of horse-drawn plows and vehicles.

In both cases, linguists have traced key technical terms to Chinese or Turko-Mongol words and have argued for an eastern origin. Yet third-century Roman farmers in Tunisia and Libya used both types of harness to hitch horses and camels to plows and carts. This technology, which is still employed in Tunisia, appears clearly on Roman bas-reliefs and lamps; but there is no more evidence of its movement northward into Europe than there is of similar harnessing moving across Asia. Thus the question of where efficient harnessing came from and whether it began in 500 or in 800 or was known even earlier but not extensively used, cannot be easily resolved.

Hinging on this problem is the question of when and why landowners in northern Europe began to use teams of horses to pull plows through soils that were too heavy for teams of oxen. Horses increased productivity by reducing the time needed for plowing, but they cost more to feed and equip. Thus, it is difficult to say that one technology was always better. Agricultural surpluses did grow and better plowing did play a role in this growth, but areas that continued to use oxen and even old-style plows shared in the general population growth of the period.

Cities and the Rebirth of Trade

Independent cities governed and defended by communes appeared first in Italy and Flanders and then elsewhere. Communes were groups of leading citizens who banded together to defend their cities and demand the privilege of self-government from their lay or ecclesiastical lord. Lords who granted such privileges benefited from the commune's economic dynamism. Lacking extensive farmlands, these cities enacted laws to encourage manufacturing and trade. Cities in Italy that had shrunk within walls built by the Romans now pressed against those walls, forcing the construction of new ones. Pisa, for example, built a new wall in 1000 and expanded it in 1156.

Islands at the northern end of the Adriatic Sea had been largely uninhabited in Roman times. Now settlers organized themselves into the city of Venice. In the eleventh century it became the dominant sea power in the Adriatic, competing with Pisa and Genoa, on the western side of Italy, for leadership in

SECTION REVIEW

- Between 1000 and 1200, western Europe experienced economic and political revivals.
- Populations grew throughout Europe, stimulated in part by new agricultural methods and technologies.
- Independent cities emerged and grew into trade and manufacturing centers.
- Long-distance trade, dominated by Italian cities, resumed throughout the Mediterranean area.
- Flemish cities dominated the fishing and wool trades of the North Sea region.
- Extensive coinage signaled the return of a money-based economy.

trade with Muslim ports. One merchant's list mentions trade in some three thousand "spices" (including dyestuffs, textile fibers, and raw materials), some of them products of Muslim lands and some coming via the Silk Road or the Indian Ocean trading system (see Chapter 8). Among them were eleven types of alum (for dyeing), eleven types of wax, eight types of cotton, four types of indigo, five types of ginger, four types of paper, and fifteen types of sugar. By the time of the Crusades (see below), European commerce depended heavily on Italian ships.

Ghent, Bruges (broozh), and Ypres (EEP-r) in Flanders rivaled the Italian cities in prosperity and trade. Granted privileges by the counts of Flanders, these cities dominated the fishing and wool industries of the North Sea region. Around 1200 raw wool from England began to be woven into cloth for a very large market.

Coinage also signaled the upturn in economic activity. In the ninth and tenth centuries most gold coins had come from Muslim lands and the Byzantine Empire. Worth too much for most trading purposes, they seldom reached Germany, France, and England. The widely imitated Carolingian silver penny sufficed. With economic revival in the twelfth century came the minting of silver coins in Scandinavia, Poland, and other outlying regions. In the following century the Italian cities followed with a new and abundant gold coinage.

Courtesy, Master and Fellows of Trinity College, Cambridge, Ms. R17.I.f.260 (detail)

Vertical Two-Beam Loom These women weavers set up their loom out of doors. The vertical strands are the warp threads around which the weft is interwoven. The pole across the bottom of the loom holds the warp threads taut. The kneeling weaver holds a beater to compact the weft at the loom's bottom. In Europe, horizontal looms were more common and paved the way for the mechanization of weaving.

The Crusades, 1095–1204

What were the origins and impact of the Crusades?

Revival coincided with and contributed to the **Crusades**, a series of religiously inspired Christian military campaigns against Muslims in the eastern Mediterranean. Four great expeditions between 1095 and 1204 (see Chapter 9), the last redirected against Constantinople, which the Catholic knights looted, constituted the region's largest military undertakings since the fall of Rome. As a result of the Crusades, noble courts and burgeoning cities in western Europe consumed more goods from the east and later adopted ideas, artistic styles, and industrial processes from the lands of Islam.

The Roots of the Crusades

Several social and economic currents of the eleventh century contributed to the Crusades. First, church reformers seeking to soften warlike habits popularized the Truce of God, a movement to limit

Crusades (1095–1204) Armed pilgrimages to the Holy Land by Christians determined to recover Jerusalem from Muslim rule. The Crusades brought an end to western Europe's centuries of intellectual and cultural isolation.

fighting between Christian lords by specifying times of truce, such as during Lent (the forty days before Easter) and on Sundays. Many knights welcomed a religiously approved alternative to fighting other Christians. Second, ambitious rulers, like the Norman chieftains who invaded Sicily, were looking for new lands to conquer. Nobles, particularly younger sons in areas where the oldest son inherited everything, were hungry for land and titles. Third, Italian merchants wanted trading posts in Muslim territory. Without the rivalry between popes and kings and without the desire of the church to demonstrate its political authority, the Crusades might never have occurred.

Several factors focused attention on the Holy Land, which had been under Muslim rule for four centuries. **Pilgrimages** played an important role in European religious life. In western Europe, pilgrims traveled under royal protection. Some were actually thieves, beggars, and peddlers, but genuinely pious pilgrims thronged to visit old churches and sacred relics. Rome and Constantinople were favored destinations, but the most intrepid went on to Jerusalem and Antioch to fulfill a vow or atone for a sin.

Pilgrims who crossed northern Spain to pray at the shrine of Santiago de Compostela learned of exploits of Christian kings fighting the Muslims to the south. The Umayyad Caliphate in al-Andalus had broken up in the eleventh century, leaving its smaller successor states prey to Christian attacks from the north (see Chapter 9). The word *crusade*, taken from Latin *crux* for "cross," was first used in Spain. Pilgrims returning from Palestine urged both churchmen and nobles to consider the Muslims a proper target for Christian arms. Muslim rulers generally tolerated and protected Christian pilgrims, but after 1071, when the Seljuks defeated the Byzantines at Manzikert (see Chapter 9), security along the pilgrimage route through Anatolia, already none too good, deteriorated further.

Despite the theological differences between the Orthodox and Catholic churches, the Byzantine emperor Alexius Comnenus asked the pope and western European rulers for help against the Muslims. Pope Urban II responded at the Council of Clermont in 1095. He addressed a huge crowd of people gathered in a field and called on them, as Christians, to stop fighting one another and go to the Holy Land to fight Muslims.

"God wills it!" exclaimed voices in the crowd. People cut cloth into crosses and sewed them on their shirts to symbolize their willingness to march on Jerusalem. Thus began the First Crusade, though people at the time more often used the word *peregrinatio*, "pilgrimage." Urban promised to free crusaders who had committed sins from their normal penance, or acts of atonement, the usual reward for peaceful pilgrims to Jerusalem.

The First Crusade captured Jerusalem in 1099 and established four crusader principalities, the most important being the Latin Kingdom of Jerusalem. The next two expeditions strove with diminishing success to protect these gains. Muslim forces retook Jerusalem in 1187. By the time of the Fourth Crusade in 1204, the original religious ardor had so diminished that the commanders agreed, at the urging of the Venetians, to sack Constantinople first to defray the cost of transporting the army by ship.

The Impact of the Crusades

Exposure to Muslim culture in Spain, Sicily, and the crusader principalities awakened Europeans to things that were lacking in their own lives. Borrowings from Muslim society occurred gradually and are not always easy to date, but Europeans began to produce pasta, paper, refined sugar, colored glass, and many other formerly exotic items.

Primary Source: Nicetas Choniates: *Annales*
Read a strange tale of heartlessness in battle.

pilgrimage Journey to a sacred shrine by Christians seeking to show their piety, fulfill vows, or gain absolution for sins. Other religions also have pilgrimage traditions, such as the Muslim pilgrimage to Mecca and the pilgrimages made by early Chinese Buddhists to India in search of sacred Buddhist writings.

Greek philosophical and scientific writings and equally important works by Arabs and Iranians were translated into Latin with powerful effect. Some manuscripts came from conquered territory: Sicily, Spain, the Holy Land, and Constantinople. For others, translators worked in parts of Spain still under Muslim rule. Generations passed before all these works were studied and understood, but they eventually transformed the intellectual world of the western Europeans.

Changes in noble lifestyle took place more quickly. Eleanor of Aquitaine (1122–1204), the most influential woman of the crusading era, accompanied her husband, King Louis VII of France, on the Second Crusade (1147–1149). The court life of her uncle Raymond, who ruled the crusader principality of Antioch, particularly appealed to her. Once back in France, a lack of male offspring led to an annulment of her royal marriage, and she married Henry of Anjou instead. Three years later in 1154 he inherited the throne of England as Henry II. Eleanor's sons Richard Lion-Heart, famed as the chivalrous foe of Saladin during the Third Crusade (1189–1192), and John rebelled against their father but eventually succeeded him as kings of England. In Aquitaine, a powerful duchy in southern France, Eleanor maintained her own court for a time. Poet-singers called troubadours enjoyed her favor and made her court a center

for music based on the idea of "courtly love," an idealization of feminine beauty and grace that influenced later European ideas of romance. Surviving troubadour melodies show the influence of poetry styles then current in Muslim Spain. The favorite troubadour instrument, moreover, was the lute, a guitarlike instrument with a bulging shape whose design and name (Arabic *al-ud*) come from Muslim Spain.

Conclusion

The division of the Roman Empire by Constantine into an eastern and a western branch marked Europe from that time on. When the Western Roman Empire collapsed, the Germanic tribes that settled on its territory formed numerous competing kingdoms and principalities. For several centuries, the only unifying factor was the Catholic Church, which provided intellectual and some administrative continuity with the vanished Roman Empire. Secular authorities, however, arose to contest the political authority of the church. Thus, western Europe remained divided among competing states and power centers. After the Viking invasions tapered off in the late tenth century, the economy, culture, and population of western Europe showed a new dynamism that spread to areas of northern Europe that the Romans had never reached. It also carried over into expansionism overseas, against the Muslims of the Levant and against Constantinople itself.

Eastern Europe evolved very differently, under the influence of Constantinople. Though it lost many provinces, the Eastern Roman Empire was not overrun by barbarians as the west had been, but retained its imperial structure for another thousand years. Though Christianity replaced all earlier religions as it did in the west, it was in the form of the Orthodox Church, a subordinate branch of the imperial Byzantine government, rather than an independent and competing organization like the Catholic Church in the west. As northeastern Europe filled in after the Viking raiders settled down to trade and build cities, its peoples adopted the Orthodox form of Christianity and with it the subordination of church to state that prevailed in the Byzantine Empire.

CHAPTER REVIEW

Download the MP3 audio file of the
Chapter Review to listen to on the go.

How did the Byzantine Empire maintain Roman imperial traditions in the east? (page 234)

Divergent ecclesiastical practices paralleled a political separation that dated from the fourth-century division of the Roman Empire into an eastern portion, the Byzantine Empire ruled from Constantinople, and a western portion that became increasingly fragmented as war-like Germanic peoples assumed more and more control. For the east, the collection and analysis of imperial laws symbolized continuing imperial rule. The emperor also assumed control over the Christian church.

How did the culture of early medieval Europe develop in the absence of imperial rule? (page 239)

In the west, the heritage of Rome consisted more in the elite use of Latin and the popular rise of Romance languages. The Roman Empire became more and more a shared memory as great buildings decayed into ruins. This memory, however, could be used as a basis of political power, as the rule of Charlemagne demonstrates. After Charlemagne's death, Viking invasions continued to disrupt European life, but their migrations laid the foundations of powerful states in Russia and Normandy. Although some long-distance trade continued, poor infrastructure and the absence of centralized authority led to the rise of a self-sufficient economy based on the manor. The lords and warriors who protected serfs became a mounted military elite that dominated the system of rights and obligations loosely termed "feudalism."

What role did the Western Church play in the politics and culture of Europe? (p. 246)

Unlike the Eastern Church, where the emperor played a dominating role, the bishops and abbots who spoke for western Christendom sought complete control of both the political and the social realm. They ultimately came into conflict with kings and dukes who resented these claims to power, but the lower ranks of society became increasingly immersed in a Christian culture based on respect for the clergy.

What was the significance of the adoption of Orthodox Christianity by Kievan Russia? (page 249)

The Eastern and Western Churches competed in converting the Slavic peoples. The Poles became Roman Catholics, while the Russians established their own Orthodox Church on the Byzantine pattern. Since the rulers of Kiev were of Scandinavian origin like the Norman rulers of northern France, England, and Sicily, there was potentially a basis for continuing interconnections across northern Europe. The decision to follow the Byzantine form of Christianity eliminated that possibility and raised a barrier between Russia and western Europe that lasted for centuries.

How did Mediterranean trade help revive western Europe? (p. 252)

Byzantium and Russia did not share in the revival of western Europe that began during a period of unprecedented borrowing from the Islamic world. During the twelfth and thirteenth centuries European intellectual life enjoyed the stimulus of scientific and philosophical ideas translated from Arabic into Latin. Shortly thereafter, Muslim manufacturing practices, such as glassmaking and papermaking, and popular pastimes, such as chess and lute playing, began to change European culture. Improved communications provided by Italian seafarers played a crucial role in spreading these new ideas into western Europe.

What were the origins and impact of the Crusades? (page 254)

The Crusades originated as armed pilgrimages aimed at restoring Christian control in the Holy Land. Though the states the crusaders created were short-lived, the experiences of the crusaders living in the Middle East fostered a wider knowledge of the world and a taste for a more refined style of life. Thus the Crusades, in addition to creating a military confrontation with Islam, also contributed to the reinvigoration of culture in western Europe.

Key Terms

Charlemagne *(p. 234)*

medieval *(p. 234)*

Byzantine Empire *(p. 234)*

Kievan Russia *(p. 234)*

schism *(p. 236)*

manor *(p. 242)*

serf *(p. 242)*

fief *(p. 245)*

vassal *(p. 245)*

papacy *(p. 246)*

Holy Roman Empire *(p. 246)*

investiture controversy *(p. 247)*

monasticism *(p. 248)*

horse collar *(p. 252)*

Crusades *(p. 254)*

pilgrimage *(p. 255)*

Web Resources

Pronunciation Guide

Interactive Maps

- MAP 10.1 The Spread of Christianity
- MAP 10.2 Germanic Kingdoms
- MAP 10.3 Kievan Russia and the Byzantine Empire in the Eleventh Century

Primary Sources

- The Life of Charlemagne: The Emperor Himself
- The Rule of Saint Benedict: Work and Pray
- Nicetas Choniates: *Annales*

Answer to the History in Focus Question

See photo on page 236, "Byzantine Church from a Twelfth-Century Manuscript."

CourseMate

Visit the CourseMate website at www.cengagebrain.com for additional study tools and review materials for this chapter.

Inner and East Asia

© Cengage Learning

CHAPTER PREVIEW

The Sui and Tang Empires, 581–755
What was the importance of Inner and Central Asia as a region of interchange during the Tang period?

Rivals for Power in Inner Asia and China, 600–907
What were the effects of the fracturing of power in Central Asia and China?

The Emergence of East Asia, to 1200
How did East Asia develop between the fall of the Tang and 1200?

New Kingdoms in East Asia
To what extent do shared practices justify thinking of East Asia as a unified cultural region in the post-Tang era?

Conclusion

MATERIAL CULTURE: Salt

 Visit the CourseMate website at **www.cengagebrain.com** for additional study tools and review materials for this chapter.

The powerful and expansive Tang Empire (618–907) ended four centuries of rule by short-lived and competing states that had left China in turmoil after the fall of the Han Empire in 220 C.E. (see Chapter 6). Tang rule also encouraged the spread of Buddhism, brought by missionaries from India and by Chinese pilgrims returning with sacred Sanskrit texts. The Tang left an indelible mark on the Chinese imagination long after it too fell. In southern China, it was succeeded by the Song (soong) Empire.

According to surviving memoirs, Song people watched shadow plays and puppet shows, listened to music and scholarly lectures, or took in less edifying spectacles like wrestling and bear baiting in urban entertainment quarters. From the 1170s onward, singer-storytellers spun long romantic narratives that alternated prose passages with sung verse. Master Tung's *Western Chamber Romance* stood out for its literary quality. In 184 prose passages and 5,263 lines of verse the narrator tells of a love affair between Chang, a young Confucian scholar, and Ying-ying, a ravishing damsel. Secondary characters include Ying-ying's shrewd and worldly mother, a general who practices just and efficient administration, and a fighting monk named Fa-ts'ung (fa-soong). The romance is based on *The Story of Ying-ying* by the Tang period author Yuan Chen (you-ahn shen) (779–831).

As the tale begins, the abbot of a Buddhist monastery responds to Chang's request to rent him a study, singing:

> Sir, you're wrong to offer me rent.
> We Buddhists and Confucians are of one family.
> As things stand, I can't give you
> A place in our dormitory,
> But you're welcome to stay
> In one of the guest apartments.

As soon as Chang spies Ying-ying, who lives there with her mother, thoughts of studying flee his mind. Romance takes a detour, however, when bandits attack the monastery, frightening the monks. A prose passage explains:

> During the T'ang dynasty, troops were stationed in the P'u prefecture. The year of our story, the commander of the garrison, Marshal Hun, died.

Because the second-in-command, Ting Wen-ya, did not have firm control of the troops, Flying Tiger Sun, a subordinate general, rebelled with five thousand soldiers. They pillaged and plundered the P'u area. How do I know this to be true? It is corroborated by *The Ballad of the True Story of Ying-ying.*

As the frightened monks dither, one of them lifts his robe to reveal his "three-foot consecrated sword."

> [Prose] Who was this monk? He was none other than Fa-ts'ung. Fa-ts'ung was a descendant of a tribesman from western Shensi. When he was young he took great pleasure in archery, fencing, hunting, and often sneaked into foreign states to steal. He was fierce and courageous. When his parents died, it suddenly became clear to him that the way of the world was frivolous and trivial, so he became a monk in the Temple of Universal Salvation. . . .
>
> [Song] He didn't know how to read sutras; He didn't know how to follow rituals; He was neither pure nor chaste but indomitably courageous . . . [1]

Amidst the love story, the ribaldry, and the derring-do, the author implants historical vignettes that mingle fact and fiction. Sophisticates of the Song era, living a life of ease, enjoyed these romanticized portrayals of Tang society.

The Sui and Tang Empires, 581–755

What was the importance of Inner and Central Asia as a region of interchange during the Tang period?

The reunification of China took place under the Sui (sway) dynasty, father and son rulers who held sway from 581 until Turks from Inner Asia (the part of the Eurasian steppe east of the Pamir Mountains) defeated the son in 615. He was assassinated three years later, and the Tang filled the political vacuum.

The small kingdoms of northern China and Inner Asia that had come and gone during the centuries

---

1. From *Master Tung's Western Chamber Romance*, translated by Li-li Ch'en. Copyright © 1994 Columbia University Press. Reprinted with permission of the publisher.

Chronology

	Inner Asia	China	Northeast Asia	Japan
200	**552** Turks control Tarim Basin	**220–589** China disunited **581–618** Sui unification		
600		**618** Tang Empire founded **626–649** Li Shimin reign **690–705** Wu Zhao reign **755–763** An Lushan rebellion	**668** Silla victory in Korea	**645–655** Taika era **710–784** Nara as capital **752** "Eye-Opening" ceremony
	751 Battle of Talas River			
800	**ca. 850** Buddhist political power secured in Tibet	**840** Suppression of Buddhism **879–881** Huang Chao rebellion **907** End of Tang Empire		**794** Heian era **866–1180** Fujiwara influence
			916 Liao Empire founded **918** Koryo founded	
1000		**960** Song Empire founded		**ca. 1000** The Tale of Genji
			1115 Jin Empire founded	
1200		**1127–1279** Southern Song period		**1185** Kamakura Shogunate founded

following the fall of the Han Empire had structured themselves around a variety of political ideas and institutions. Some favored the Chinese tradition, with an emperor, a bureaucracy using exclusively the Chinese language, and a Confucian state philosophy (see Chapter 6). Others reflected Tibetan, Turkic, or other regional cultures and depended on Buddhism to legitimate their rule. Throughout the period the relationship between northern China and the deserts and steppe of Inner Asia remained a central focus of political life, a key commercial linkage, and a source of new ideas and practices.

The Sui rulers called their new capital Chang'an (chahng-ahn) in honor of the old Han capital nearby in the Wei (way) River Valley (modern Shaanxi province). Though northern China constituted the Sui heartland, population centers along the Yangzi (yahng-zeh) River in the south grew steadily and pointed to what would be the future direction of Chinese expansion. To facilitate communication and trade with the south, the Sui built the 1,100-mile (1,771-kilometer) **Grand Canal** linking the Yellow River with the Yangzi, and they also constructed irrigation systems in the Yangzi Valley. On their northern frontier, the Sui also improved the Great Wall, the barrier against nomadic incursions that had been gradually constructed by several earlier states.

Sui military ambition, which extended to Korea and Vietnam as well as Inner Asia, required high levels of organization and mustering of resources—manpower, livestock, wood, iron, and food supplies. The same was true of their massive public works projects. These burdens proved more than the Sui could sustain. Overextension compounded the political dilemma stemming from the military defeat and subsequent assassination of the second Sui emperor. These circumstances opened the way for another strong leader to establish a new state.

Grand Canal The 1,100-mile (1,771-kilometer) waterway linking the Yellow and the Yangzi Rivers. It was begun in the Han period and completed during the Sui Empire.

University of Pennsylvania Museum, image # 62844

Iron Stirrups This bas-relief from the tomb of Li Shimin depicts the type of horse on which the Tang armies conquered China and Inner Asia. Saddles with high supports in front and back, breastplates, and straps beneath the tail to keep the saddle in place point to the importance of high speeds and quick maneuvering. Iron stirrups, available to Central and East Asian horsemen since the fifth century, could support the weight of shielded and well-armed soldiers rising in the saddle to shoot arrows or use lances.

In 618 the powerful Li family took advantage of Sui disorder to carve out an empire of similar scale and ambition. They adopted the dynastic name Tang (Map 11.1). The brilliant emperor **Li Shimin** (lee shir-meen) (r. 626–649) extended his power primarily westward into Inner Asia. Though he and succeeding rulers of the **Tang Empire** retained many Sui governing practices, they avoided overcentralization by allowing local nobles, gentry, officials, and religious establishments to exercise significant power.

The Tang emperors and nobility descended from the Turkic elites that built small states in northern China after the Han, as well as from Chinese officials and settlers who had moved there. They appreciated the pastoral nomadic culture of Inner Asia (see Chapter 8) as well as Chinese traditions. Some of the most impressive works of Tang art, for example, are large

pottery figurines of the horses and two-humped camels used along the Silk Road, brilliantly colored with glazes devised by Chinese potters. In warfare, the Tang combined Chinese weapons—the crossbow and armored infantrymen—with Inner Asian expertise in horsemanship and the use of iron stirrups. At their peak, from about 650 to 751, the Tang armies were a formidable force.

Li Shimin (599–649) One of the founders of the Tang Empire and its second emperor (r. 626–649). He led the expansion of the empire into Central Asia.

Tang Empire Empire unifying China and part of Central Asia, founded 618 and ended 907. The Tang emperors presided over a magnificent court at their capital, Chang'an.

Buddhism and the Tang Empire

The Tang rulers followed Inner Asian precedents in their political use of Buddhism. State cults based on Buddhism had flourished in Inner Asia and north China since the fall of the Han. Some interpretations of Buddhist doctrine accorded kings and emperors the spiritual function of welding humankind into a harmonious Buddhist society. Protecting spirits were to help the ruler govern and prevent harm from coming to his people.

Mahayana (mah-huh-YAH-nah), or "Great Vehicle," Buddhism predominated. Mahayana fostered faith in enlightened beings—bodhisattvas—who postpone nirvana (see Chapter 5) to help others achieve enlightenment. This permitted the absorption of local gods and goddesses into Mahayana sainthood and thereby made conversion more attractive to the common people. Mahayana also encouraged translating Buddhist scripture into local languages, and it accepted religious practices not based on written texts. The tremendous reach of Mahayana views proved adaptable to different societies and classes of people, invigorating travel, language learning, and cultural exchange.

Early Tang princes competing for political influence enlisted monastic leaders to pray for them, preach on their behalf, counsel aristocrats to support them, and—perhaps most important—contribute monastic wealth to their war chests. In return, the monasteries received tax exemptions, land privileges, and gifts.

To Chang'an by Land and Sea

As the Tang Empire expanded westward, contacts with Central Asia and India increased, and so did the complexity of Buddhist influence throughout

Map 11.1 The Tang Empire in Inner and Eastern Asia, 750 For over a century the Tang Empire controlled China and a very large part of Inner Asia. The defeat of Tang armies in 751 by a force of Arabs, Turks, and Tibetans at the Talas River in present-day Kyrgyzstan ended Tang westward expansion. To the east the Tang dominated Annam. Japan and the Silla kingdom in Korea were leading tributary states of the Tang.   © Cengage Learning

Interactive Map

China. Chang'an, the Tang capital, became the center of a continent-wide system of communication. Central Asians, Tibetans, Vietnamese, Japanese, and Koreans regularly visited the capital and took away with them the most recent ideas and styles. Thus the Mahayana network connecting Inner Asia and China intersected a vigorous commercial world in which material goods and cultural influences mixed. Though Buddhism and Confucianism proved attractive to many different peoples, regional cultures and identities remained strong, just as regional commitments to Tibetan, Uighur, and other languages and writing systems coexisted with the widespread use of written Chinese. Textiles reflected Persian, Korean, and Vietnamese styles, while influences from every part of Asia appeared in sports, music, and painting. Many historians characterize the Tang Empire as "cosmopolitan" because of its breadth and diversity.

Well-maintained roads and water transport connected Chang'an to the coastal towns of south China, most importantly Guangzhou (gwahng-jo) (Canton). Though the Grand Canal did not reach Chang'an, it was the key component of this transportation network. Chang'an became the center of what is often called the **tributary system**, a type of political relationship dating from Han times by which independent countries acknowledged the Chinese emperor's supremacy. Each tributary state sent regular embassies to the capital to pay tribute (see Chapter 6). As symbols of China's political supremacy, these embassies sometimes meant more to the Chinese than to the tribute-payers, who might have seen them primarily as a means of accessing the Chinese trading system.

During the Tang period, Chang'an had something over a million people, only a minority of whom lived in the central city. Most people lived in suburbs that extended beyond the main gates. Many also dwelt in outlying towns that had special responsibilities like maintaining nearby imperial tombs or operating the imperial resort. In Chang'an and other entrepôts, foreigners, whether merchants, students, or ambassadors, resided in special compounds that included living accommodations and general stores. By the end of the Tang period, West Asians in Chang'an probably numbered over 100,000.

In the main parts of the city, restaurants, inns, temples, mosques, and street stalls along the main thoroughfares were busy every evening. At curfew, generally between eight and ten o'clock, commoners returned to their neighborhoods, which were enclosed by brick walls and wooden gates that guards locked until dawn to control crime.

Of the many routes converging on Chang'an, the Grand Canal commanded special importance with its own army patrols, boat design, canal towns, and maintenance budget. It conveyed vital supplies and contributed to the economic and cultural development of eastern China, where later capitals were built within easier reach.

The Tang consolidated Chinese control of the southern coastal region, increasing access to the Indian Ocean and facilitating the spread of Islamic and Jewish influences. A legend credits an uncle of Muhammad with erecting the Red Mosque at Canton in the mid-seventh century. Chinese mariners and shipwrights excelled in compass design and the construction of very large oceangoing vessels. The government took direct responsibility for outfitting grain transport vessels for the Chinese coastal cities and the Grand Canal. Commercial ships, built to sail from south China to the Philippines and Southeast Asia, carried twice as much as contemporary vessels in the Mediterranean Sea or the western parts of the Indian Ocean trading system (see Chapter 8).

Trade and Cultural Exchange

Influences from Central Asia and the Islamic world, largely transmitted by Turkic peoples, introduced lively new motifs to ceramics, painting, and silk designs. At the other end of the Silk Road, Iranian potters imitated the glazes of Tang vessels. Clothing styles changed in north China; working people switched from robes to the pants favored by horse-riding Turks from Central Asia. Inexpensive cotton imported from Central Asia, where cotton production boomed in the early Islamic centuries, gradually

tributary system A system in which, from the time of the Han Empire, countries in East and Southeast Asia not under the direct control of empires based in China nevertheless enrolled as tributary states, acknowledging the superiority of the emperors in China in exchange for trading rights or strategic alliances.

replaced hemp in clothes worn by commoners. The Tang court promoted polo, a pastime from the steppes, and followed the Inner Asian tradition of allowing noblewomen to compete. Various stringed instruments reached China across the Silk Road, along with Turkic folk melodies. Grape wine from West Asia and tea, sugar, and spices from India and Southeast Asia transformed the Chinese diet.

Such changes reflected new economic and trade relationships (see Material Culture: Salt). Silk had dominated the caravan trade across Central Asia in Han times (see Chapter 8). Though China's monopoly on silk disappeared as centers in West Asia learned to compete, China remained the source of superior silks. Tang factories created more and more complex styles, partly to counter foreign competition.

By about the year 1000 the magnitude of exports from Tang territories, facilitated by China's excellent transportation systems, dwarfed Chinese imports from Europe, West Asia, and South Asia. Tang exports tilted the trade balance with both the Central Asia caravan cities and the lands of the Indian Ocean, causing precious metal to flow into China in return

for export goods. As travel along the Silk Road and to the various ports of the Indian Ocean trading system increased, the economies of seaports and entrepôts involved in the trade—even distant ones—became increasingly commercialized, leading to networks of private traders devising new instruments of credit and finance.

SECTION REVIEW

- The Sui reunified China, reestablished Confucianism, and undertook programs of military expansion and public works.

- The Sui fell to the Tang, who built a less centralized empire and adopted Central Asian cultural practices.

- Under Central Asian influence, Mahayana Buddhism was firmly rooted in China and became part of a larger cosmopolitan culture.

- The Tang capital of Chang'an became the center of the tributary system, and transportation technology flourished.

- The Tang presided over an integration of cultures, and Chinese commercial activity shaped the larger international economy.

Xinjiang Uighur Autonomous District Museum

Women of Turfan Grinding Flour Women throughout Inner and East Asia were critical to all facets of economic life. In the Turkic areas of Central and Inner Asia, women commonly headed households, owned property, and managed businesses. These small figurines, made to be placed in tombs, portray women of Turfan—an Inner Asian area crossed by the Silk Road—performing tasks in the preparation of wheat flour.

Material Culture

Salt

Though sodium chloride, or table salt, is one of the world's most abundant chemicals, its abundance in some areas and scarcity in others has frequently given it an important role in economic history. Here are some examples.

Outcroppings of rock salt known as salt licks play a nutritional role in the lives of many wild mammals. Prehistoric human hunters sought game at these natural animal gathering places, and some scholars believe that human provision of salt played an important role in domesticating some species.

Trade in salt from the southern regions of the Sahara Desert is described as early as the ninth century C.E., but it is probably much older because the Saharan deposits formed an important nutritional source for salt-poor sub-Saharan Africa. The legendary exchange of salt for equivalent quantities of gold symbolizes this commercial importance. Bilma, an oasis town in eastern Niger, still produces salt that is distributed by means of camel caravans trekking across the sand dunes of the Ténéré Desert.

In ancient Rome, a strong-smelling sauce known as garum became a cooking staple and an important export item. Garum was made by crushing cut up fish, with their entrails, in a small amount of brine. The salt prevented the sauce from spoiling. For common people, using garum was a way of avoiding the tax on salt.

Early in the fourteenth century C.E. a Flemish fisherman devised a method of preserving herring, a small fish. After the head and certain internal organs were removed, enzymes from the pancreas began to digest the flesh and make it tender. Then the fish were packed with salt in casks. Salted herring and its raw materials, salt and herring, became mainstays of the commerce of Scotland, northern Germany, and in particular the Netherlands. A Dutch proverb maintains that the city of Amsterdam was built on herring casks.

In France, a salt tax known as the gabelle became a permanent part of royal revenues in the late fourteenth century C.E. Everyone over the age of eight was forced to buy a minimum amount of salt every week at a price fixed by the government. Most of the salt was produced by evaporating seawater, but inland provinces in the east exploited salt marshes. Popular resentment against the tax contributed to the French Revolution in 1789. A year later the gabelle was canceled.

In nineteenth-century China, where the salt tax had been a mainstay of government revenues since the Tang dynasty, brine (saltwater) wells around the western city of Zigong became the basis for one of the country's most prosperous industries. The family-based trusts that extracted the salt from as deep as 3,000 feet were

Rivals for Power in Inner Asia and China, 600–907

What were the effects of the fracturing of power in Central Asia and China?

Li Bo, the most renowned Tang poet and one of the greatest ever to write in the Chinese language, wrote in 751 of the seemingly endless succession of wars:

> The beacons are always alight, fighting and
> marching never stop.
> Men die in the field, slashing sword to sword;
> The horses of the conquered neigh piteously to
> Heaven.
> Crows and hawks peck for human guts,

> Carry them in their beaks and hang them on the
> branches of withered trees.
> Captains and soldiers are smeared on the bushes
> and grass;
> The General schemed in vain.
> Know therefore that the sword is a cursed thing
> which the wise man uses only if he must.[2]

Between 600 and 751, when the Tang Empire was at its height, the Turkic-speaking **Uighurs** (WEE-ger) and the Tibetans built large rival states astride the caravan routes of Inner Asia. The Tibetan Empire at its

---

2. From Arthur Waley, *Poetry and Career of Li Po* (London: Unwin Hyman, 1954), 35. © copyright by permission of The Arthur Waley Estate. Reprinted by permission of The Arthur Waley Estate.

comparable in capital accumulation, management skill, and technological innovation to contemporary European corporations.

In 1930 the British monopoly on salt production in India became the center of a peaceful protest led by Mahatma Gandhi. With seventy-eight followers he marched 240 miles to the seacoast, where the protestors picked up a small lump of salt, thereby breaking the law against private harvesting of salt. Though many were imprisoned, the Salt March became an important model of civil disobedience.

Though salt naturally brings a taste to mind, its historic role relates more to its chemical properties. Salt in water passes easily through the membranes that surround the cells of plants and animals. After a period of time, the moisture within the cell acquires the chemical properties of the salty moisture on the outside. Pieces of pork transform into ham, cucumbers and other vegetables become pickles, and sturgeon eggs become caviar. Since high concentrations of salt kill bacteria, salted foods can be transported and stored for long periods without spoiling or becoming dangerous to eat.

Producing salt from seawater and other sources of brine requires evaporation or boiling. But salt is also available in solid form and can be mined. Cities like Salzburg (literally "Salt Town") in Austria may grow up around salt mines. Underground layers of salt, sometimes hundreds of feet thick, are the residue of dried-up prehistoric seas or oceans. In addition to being processed for consumption, rock salt is used on icy roads. Since saltwater freezes at a lower temperature than fresh water, salt deposited on snow or ice causes melting.

Camel Caravan Carrying Salt in West Africa Natural salt deposits, such as those at Bilma in the southern Sahara desert in Niger, have time and again become the bases for extensive regional and international trade. Transporting the salt can be a challenge, however. Camel transport made salt trading an integral part of the trade between the Saharan region and the agricultural countries of west Africa. In northern Europe the salt springs at Lüneburg near Hamburg, Germany fed into a maritime trading network throughout the Baltic and North Sea region. Coastal lands could extract salt from seawater by evaporation, though in colder climates, such as Japan, boiling was needed to supplement the power of natural sunlight and heat.

QUESTIONS FOR ANALYSIS

1. Why did salt become such an important trade product?
2. Why would a tax on salt be easy to administer?
3. How many uses of salt can you think of?

peak stretched well beyond modern Tibet into northeastern India and southwestern China, as well as the Tarim Basin. The contest between these states and the Tang for control of the land routes and nomadic peoples west of China reached a standoff by the end of the period. By the mid-800s all three empires were experiencing political decay and military decline, allowing soldiers, criminals, and freebooters to roam into neighboring territories.

Centralization and integration being most extensively developed in Tang territory, the impact fell most heavily there. By the early 800s, the period reflected in the original romance of Ying-ying described at the start of this chapter, nothing remained of Tang power

but pretense. In the provinces military governors suppressed the rebellion of General An Lushan (ahn loo-shahn), a commander of Central Asian and Turkic origin, which raged from 755 to 763, and then seized power for themselves.

The Uighur and Tibetan Empires

The original homeland of the Turks lay in the northern part of modern Mongolia. After the fall of the Han Empire, Turkic peoples began moving

Uighurs A group of Turkic-speakers who controlled their own centralized empire from 744 to 840 in Mongolia and Central Asia.

south and west, through Mongolia, then west to Central Asia, on the long migration that brought them, after many centuries, to what is today modern Turkey (see Chapter 8). In 552 the Tang established control over the basin of the Tarim River, a largely desert area north of Tibet that formed a vital link on the Silk Road. Yet within a century, a new Turkic group, the Uighurs, had supplanted them.

Under the Uighurs, caravan cities like Kashgar and Khotan (see Map 11.1) enjoyed commercial ties with both the Islamic world and China and showed enthusiasm for Buddhist teachings and religious art derived from northern India. The Uighurs excelled as merchants and as scribes able to transact business in many languages. They adapted the syllabic script of the Sogdians, an Iranian people who lived west of them in Central Asia, to writing Turkic.

Unified Uighur power collapsed after half a century, leaving Tibet as the lone rival to the Tang in Inner Asia. A large, stable empire critically positioned where China, Southeast Asia, South Asia, and Central Asia meet, **Tibet** experienced a variety of cultural influences. In the seventh century Chinese Buddhists on pilgrimage to India advanced contacts between India and Tibet. The Tibetans derived their alphabet from India, as well as a variety of artistic and architectural styles, and India and China both contributed to Tibetan knowledge of mathematics, astronomy, divination, farming, and milling of grain. Islam and the monarchical traditions of Iran and Rome became familiar through Central Asian trading connections. For example, the Tibetan royal family favored Greek medicine transmitted through Iran.

In 634 a Tang princess, called Kongjo by the Tibetans, came to Tibet to marry the Tibetan king and cement an alliance. She brought with her Mahayana Buddhism, which combined with the native religion to create a distinctive form of Buddhism. Tibet also sent ambassadors and students to the Tang imperial capital, and for a time regular contact and Buddhist influences consolidated the Tang-Tibet relationship. The Tibetan kings encouraged Buddhist religious establishments and prided themselves on being cultural intermediaries between India and China.

Horses and armor, techniques borrowed from the Turks, raised Tibetan forces to a level that startled even the Tang. By the late 600s the Tang emperor and the Tibetan king were rivals for religious leadership and political dominance in Inner Asia. War weariness affected both empires after 751, however.

In the 800s a new king in Tibet decided to follow the Tang lead and eliminate the political and social influence of the monasteries (see below). He was assassinated by Buddhist monks, and control of the Tibetan royal family passed into the hands of religious leaders. In the centuries that followed down to modern times, monastic domination isolated Tibet from surrounding regions.

Upheavals and Repression, 750–879

The later years of the Tang Empire saw increasing turmoil. The Confucian elites came to see Buddhism as undermining the idea of the family as the model for the state. In their backlash against "foreigners," they included Buddhists. The Confucian scholar Han Yu (768–824) spoke powerfully for a return to traditional Confucian practices. In "Memorial on the Bone of Buddha" written to the emperor in 819 on the occasion of ceremonies to receive a bone of the Buddha in the imperial palace, he scornfully disparages the Buddha and his followers.

> Now Buddha was a man of the barbarians who did not speak the language of China and wore clothes of a different fashion. His sayings did not concern the ways of our ancient kings, nor did his manner of dress conform to their laws. He understood neither the duties that bind sovereign and subject nor the affections of father and son. If

Primary Source: Memorial on Buddhism Find out what it is about the practice of Buddhism in China that causes Han Yu to report that he is "truly alarmed, truly afraid."

Tibet Country centered on the high, mountain-bounded plateau north of India. Tibetan political power occasionally extended farther to the north and west between the seventh and thirteenth centuries.

he were still alive today and came to our court by order of his ruler, Your Majesty might condescend to receive him, but . . . he would then be escorted to the borders of the state, dismissed, and not allowed to delude the masses. How then, when he has long been dead, could his rotten bones, the foul and unlucky remains of his body, be rightly admitted to the palace? Confucius said, "Respect spiritual beings, while keeping at a distance from them."[3]

Buddhism was also attacked for encouraging women in politics. In 690 Wu Zhao (woo jow), a woman who had married into the imperial family, seized control of the government and declared herself emperor. She based her legitimacy on claiming to be a bodhisattva, an enlightened soul who had chosen to remain on earth to lead others to salvation. She also favored Buddhists and Daoists over Confucianists in her court and government.

Later Confucian writers expressed contempt for Wu Zhao and other powerful women, such as the concubine Yang Guifei (yahng gway-fay). Bo Zhuyi (baw joo-ee), in his poem "Everlasting Remorse," lamented the influence of women at the Tang court, which had caused "the hearts of fathers and mothers everywhere not to value the birth of boys, but the birth of girls."[4] Confucian elites heaped every possible charge on prominent women who offended them, accusing Emperor Wu of grotesque tortures and murders, including tossing the dismembered but still living bodies of enemies into wine vats and cauldrons. They blamed Yang Guifei for the outbreak of the An Lushan rebellion in 755.

Serious historians dismiss the stories about Wu Zhao as stereotypical characterizations of "evil" rulers. Eunuchs (castrated palace servants) charged by historians with controlling Chang'an and the Tang court and publicly executing rival bureaucrats represent a similar stereotype. In fact Wu seems to have ruled effectively and was not deposed until 705, when extreme old age (eighty-plus) incapacitated her. Nevertheless, traditional Chinese historians commonly describe unorthodox rulers and all-powerful women as evil, and the truth about Wu will never be known.

Even Chinese gentry living in safe and prosperous localities associated Buddhism with social ills. People who worried about "barbarians" ruining their society

SECTION REVIEW

- Uighur rule in Central Asia prompted the development of a literate urban culture in which Buddhism flourished.

- Tibet combined a variety of cultural influences and checked Tang imperial designs until it fell under Buddhist religious rule.

- The Tang Empire, along with the rival Uighur and Tibetan states, experienced political problems that steadily weakened it.

- In China, this turmoil resulted in a backlash against foreign cultural influences and especially Buddhism, as Tang elites led a neo-Confucian reaction.

- The Tang fell due to a combination of destabilizing forces.

pointed to Buddhism as evidence of the foreign evil since it had such strong roots in Inner Asia and Tibet. Because Buddhism shunned earthly ties, monks and nuns severed relations with the secular world in search of enlightenment. By the ninth century, hundreds of thousands of people had entered tax-exempt Buddhist institutions. They paid no taxes, served in no army. They deprived their families of advantageous marriage alliances and denied descendants to their ancestors. The Confucian elites saw all this as threatening to the family and to the family estates that underlay the Tang economic and political structure. In 840 the government moved to crush the monasteries whose tax exemption had allowed them to accumulate land, serfs, and precious objects, often as gifts. Within five years 4,600 temples had been destroyed. Now an enormous amount of land and 150,000 workers were returned to the tax rolls.

Buddhist centers like the cave monasteries at Dunhuang were protected by local warlords loyal to Buddhist rulers in Inner Asia. Nevertheless, China's cultural heritage suffered a great loss in the dissolution of the monasteries. Some sculptures and grottoes survived only in defaced form. Wooden temples and façades sheltering great stone carvings burned to the ground. Monasteries became legal again in later times, but Buddhism never recovered the influence of early Tang times.

Buddhist Cave Painting at Dunhuang Hundreds of caves dating to the period when Buddhism enjoyed popularity and government favor in China survive in Gansu province, which was beyond the reach of the Tang rulers when they turned against Buddhism. This cave, dated to the year 538/9, contains elaborate wall decorations narrating the life of the Buddha and depicting scenes from the Western Paradise, where devotees of the Pure Land sect of Buddhism hoped to be reborn.

The End of the Tang Empire, 879–907

The campaigns of expansion in the seventh century had left the empire dependent on local military commanders and a complex tax collection system. Reverses like the Battle of the Talas River in 751, where Arabs halted Chinese expansion into Central Asia, led to military demoralization and underfunding. In 755 An Lushan, a Tang general on the northeast frontier, led about 200,000 soldiers in rebellion. The emperor fled Chang'an and executed his favorite concubine, Yang Guifei, who was rumored to be An Lushan's lover. The rebellion lasted for eight years and resulted in new powers for the provincial military governors who helped suppress it.

A disgruntled member of the gentry, Huang Chao (wang show), led the most devastating uprising between 879 and 881. Despite his ruthless treatment of the villages he controlled, his rebellion attracted poor farmers and tenants who could not protect themselves from local bosses and oppressive landlords, or who simply did not know where else to turn in the deepening chaos. The new hatred of "barbarians" spurred the rebels to murder thousands of foreign residents in Canton and Beijing (bay-jeeng).

Local warlords finally wiped out the rebels, but Tang society did not find peace. Refugees, migrant workers, and homeless people became common sights. Residents of northern China fled to the southern frontiers as groups from Inner Asia moved into localities in the north. Though Tang emperors continued in Chang'an until a warlord terminated their line in 907, they never regained power after Huang Chao's rebellion.

The Emergence of East Asia, to 1200

How did East Asia develop between the fall of the Tang and 1200?

In the aftermath of the Tang, three new states emerged and competed to inherit its legacy. The Liao (lee-OW) Empire of the Khitan (kee-THAN) people, pastoral nomads related to the Mongols living on the northeastern frontier, established their rule in the north. They centered their government on several cities, but their emperors preferred life in nomad encampments. In western China, the Minyak people (cousins of the Tibetans) established a state they called "Tanggut" (TAHNG-gut) to show their connection with the fallen empire. The third state, the Chinese-speaking **Song Empire**, came into being in 960 in central China.

These states embodied the political ambitions of peoples with different religious and philosophical systems—Mahayana Buddhism among the Liao, Tibetan Buddhism among the Tangguts, and Confucianism among the Song. Cut off from Inner Asia, the Song used advanced seafaring and sailing technologies to forge maritime connections with other states in East, West, and Southeast Asia. The Song elite shared the late Tang dislike of "barbaric" or "foreign" influences as they tried to cope with multiple enemies that heavily taxed their military capacities. Meanwhile, Korea, Japan, and some Southeast Asian states strengthened political and cultural ties with China.

Map 11.2 Jin and Southern Song Empires, ca. 1200 After 1127 the Song abandoned its northern territories to Jin. The Southern Song continued the policy of annual payments—to Jin rather than Liao—and maintained high military preparedness to prevent further invasions. © Cengage Learning

 Interactive Map

The Liao and Jin Challenge

The Liao Empire of the Khitan people extended from Siberia to Inner Asia. Variations on the Khitan name became the name for China in these distant regions: "Kitai" for the Mongols, "Khitai" for the Russians, and "Cathay" for Italian merchants like Marco Polo who reported on China in Europe.

The Liao rulers prided themselves on their pastoral traditions as horse and cattle breeders, the continuing source of their military might, and they made no attempt to create a single elite culture. They encouraged Chinese elites to use their own language, study their own classics, and see the emperor through Confucian eyes; and they encouraged other peoples to use their own languages and see the emperor as a champion of Buddhism or as a nomadic chieftain. On balance, Buddhism far outweighed Confucianism in this and other northern states, where rulers depended on their roles as bodhisattvas or as Buddhist kings to legitimate power. Liao rule lasted from 916 to 1121.

Song Empire Empire in central and southern China (960–1126) while the Liao people controlled the north. Empire in southern China (1127–1279; the "Southern Song") while the Jin people controlled the north. Distinguished for its advances in technology, medicine, astronomy, and mathematics.

Su Song's Astronomical Clock This gigantic clock built at Kaifeng between 1088 and 1092 combined mathematics, astronomy, and calendar-making with skillful engineering. The team overseen by Su Song placed an armillary sphere on the observation platform and linked it with chains to the water-driven central mechanism shown in the cutaway view. The water wheel also rotated the Buddha statues in the multistory pagoda the spectators are looking at. Other devices displayed the time of the day, the month, and the year.   From Joseph Needham, ed., *Science and Civilization in China*, after a drawing of Su Song's book of 1090.

Superb horsemen and archers, the Khitans also challenged the Song with siege machines from China and Central Asia. A truce concluded in 1005 required the Song emperor to pay the Liao great quantities of cash and silk annually. A century later, the Song tired of paying tribute and secretly allied with the Jurchens of northeastern Asia, who also resented Liao rule. In 1115 the Jurchens first destroyed the Liao capital in Mongolia and proclaimed their own empire, the Jin (see Map 11.2), and then turned on the Song.

The Jurchens grew rice, millet, and wheat, but they also spent a good deal of time hunting, fishing, and tending livestock. Using Khitan military arts and political organization, they became formidable enemies in an all-out campaign against the Song in 1127. They laid siege to the Song capital, Kaifeng (kie-fuhng), and captured the Song emperor. Within a few years the Song withdrew south of the Yellow River and established a new capital at Hangzhou (hahng-jo), leaving central as well as northern China in Jurchen

control. Annual payments to the Jin Empire staved off further warfare. Historians generally refer to this period as the "Southern Song" (1127–1279).

Song Industries

The Southern Song came closer to initiating an industrial revolution than any other premodern state. Many Song advances in technology, medicine, astronomy, and mathematics had come to China in Tang times, sometimes from very distant places. Song officials, scholars, and businessmen had the motivation and resources to adapt this Tang lore to meet their military, agricultural, and administrative needs.

Song mathematicians introduced the use of fractions, first employing them to describe the phases of the moon. From lunar observations, Song astronomers constructed a very precise calendar and, alone among the world's astronomers, noted the explosion of the Crab Nebula in 1054. Song inventors drew on their knowledge of celestial coordinates, particularly the Pole Star, to refine compass design. The magnetic compass, an earlier Chinese invention, shrank in size and gained a fixed pivot point for the needle. With a protective glass cover, the compass now became suitable for seafaring, a use first attested in 1090.

Development of the seaworthy compass coincided with new techniques in building China's main oceangoing ship, the **junk**. A stern-mounted rudder improved the steering of the large ship in rough seas, and watertight bulkheads helped keep it afloat in emergencies. The shipwrights of the Persian Gulf soon copied these features in their ship designs.

Because they needed iron and steel to make weapons for their army of 1.25 million men, the Song rulers fought their northern rivals for control of mines in north China. Production of coal and iron soared. By the end of the eleventh century cast iron production reached about 125,000 tons (113,700 metric tons) annually, putting it on a par with the output of eighteenth-century Britain. Engineers became skilled at high-temperature metallurgy using enormous bellows, often driven by water wheels, to superheat the molten ore. Military engineers used iron to buttress defensive works because it was impervious to fire or concussion, and armorers mass-produced body armor. Iron construction also appeared in bridges and small buildings. Mass-production techniques for bronze and ceramics in use in China for nearly two thousand years were adapted to iron casting and assembly.

To counter cavalry assaults, the Song experimented with **gunpowder**, which they initially used to propel clusters of flaming arrows. During the wars against the Jurchens in the 1100s the Song introduced a new and terrifying weapon. Shells launched from Song fortifications exploded in the midst of the enemy, blowing out iron shrapnel and dismembering men and horses. However, the short range of these shells limited them to defensive uses.

Economy and Society in Song China

In a warlike era, Song elite culture idealized civil pursuits, and civilians outranked military men socially. Private academies, designed to train young men for the official examinations, became influential in culture and politics. New interpretations of Confucian teachings became so important and influential that the term **neo-Confucianism** is used for Song and later versions of Confucian thought.

Zhu Xi (jew she) (1130–1200), the most important early neo-Confucian thinker, reacted to the many centuries during which Buddhism and Daoism had overshadowed the precepts of Confucius. He and others worked out a systematic approach to cosmology that focused on the central conception that human nature is moral, rational, and essentially good. To combat the Buddhist dismissal of worldly affairs as a transitory distraction, they reemphasized individual moral and social responsibility. Their human ideal was the sage, a person who could preserve mental stability and serenity while dealing conscientiously with troubling social problems. Whereas earlier Confucian thinkers had written about sage kings and political leaders, the neo-Confucians espoused the spiritual idea of universal sagehood, a state that could be achieved through proper study of the new Confucian principles and cosmology.

Popular Buddhist sects also persisted during the Song, as indicated by the song-story line quoted at the beginning of this chapter: "We Buddhists and Confucians are of one family." While historically suitable for the time before the Tang abolition of Buddhist monasteries when the original story of Ying-ying was written, it is unlikely that the line would have pleased a Song audience if anti-Buddhist feelings had remained so ferocious. Some Buddhists elaborated on Tang-era folk practices derived from India and Tibet. The best known, Chan Buddhism (known as **Zen** in Japan and

junk A very large flatbottom sailing ship produced in the Tang, Ming, and Song Empires, specially designed for long-distance commercial travel.

gunpowder A mixture of saltpeter, sulfur, and charcoal, in various proportions. The formula, brought to China in the 400s or 500s, was first used to make fumigators to keep away insect pests and evil spirits. In later centuries it was used to make explosives and grenades and to propel cannonballs, shot, and bullets.

neo-Confucianism Term used to describe new approaches to understanding classic Confucian texts that became the basic ruling philosophy of China from the Song period to the twentieth century.

Zen The Japanese word for a branch of Mahayana Buddhism based on highly disciplined meditation. It is known in Sanskrit as *dhyana*, in Chinese as *chan*, and in Korean as *son*.

as Son in Korea), asserted that mental discipline alone could win salvation.

Meditation, a key Chan practice, was employed by Confucians as well as Buddhists. It afforded prospective officials relief from studying for civil service examinations, which continued into the Song from the Tang period. Unlike the ancient Han policy of hiring and promoting on the basis of recommendations, Song-style examinations involved a large bureaucracy. Test questions, which changed each time the examinations were given, often related to economic management or foreign policy even though they were always based on Confucian classics.

Hereditary class distinctions meant less than they had in Tang times, when noble lineages played a greater role in the structure of power. The new system recruited the most talented men, whatever their origin. Yet men from wealthy families enjoyed an advantage, for preparation for the tests consumed so much time that peasant boys could rarely compete. Success in the examinations brought good marriage prospects, the chance for a high salary, and enormous prestige. Failure could bankrupt a family and ruin a man both socially and psychologically. This put great pressure on candidates, who spent days writing essays in tiny, dim, airless examination cells.

For some, preparation became easier thanks to a technical change from woodblock to an early form of **movable type**, which made printing cheaper. To promote its ideological goals, the Song government authorized the mass production of test preparation books in the years before 1000. Although a man had to be literate to read the preparation books and basic education was still rare, a growing number of candidates without noble, gentry, or elite backgrounds entered the Song bureaucracy.

The availability of printed books changed country life as well, since landlords gained access to expert advice on planting and irrigation techniques, harvesting, tree cultivation, threshing, and weaving. Landlords frequently gathered their tenants and workers to show them illustrated texts on the craft of farming and explain their meaning. New agricultural land was developed south of the Yangzi River, and iron implements such as plows and rakes, first used in the Tang era, were adapted to southern wet-rice cultivation. The growing profitability of agriculture interested ambitious members of the gentry. Still a frontier for Chinese settlers under the Tang, the south saw increasing concentration of land in the hands of a few wealthy families. In the process, the indigenous inhabitants of the region retreated into the mountains or southward toward Vietnam.

During the 1100s the total population of the Chinese territories, spurred by prosperity, rose above 100 million. The leading Song cities were still among the largest cities in the world. Health and crowding posed problems in the Song capitals. Multistory wooden apartment houses fronted on narrow streets—sometimes only 4 or 5 feet (1.2 to 1.5 meters) wide—that were clogged by peddlers or families spending time outdoors. The crush of people called for new techniques in waste management, water supply, and firefighting. In Hangzhou engineers diverted the nearby river to flow through the city, flushing away waste and disease. Arab and European travelers who had firsthand experience with the Song capital and who were sensitive to urban conditions in their own societies expressed amazement at Hangzhou's amenities: restaurants, parks, bookstores, wine shops, tea houses, theaters, and the entertainments mentioned at the start of this chapter.

The idea of credit, originating in the robust long-distance trade of the Tang period, spread widely under the Song. Intercity or interregional credit—what the Song called "flying money"—depended on the acceptance of guarantees that the paper could be redeemed for coinage at another location. The public accepted the practice because credit networks tended to be managed by families, so that brothers and cousins were usually honoring each other's certificates.

Primary Source: Craft of Farming Examine the kind of practical advice that helped farmers prosper during the Song period.

movable type Type in which each individual character is cast on a separate piece of metal. It replaced woodblock printing, allowing for the arrangement of individual letters and other characters on a page, rather than requiring the carving of entire pages at a time. It may have been invented in Korea in the thirteenth century.

The Palace Museum, Beijing

The Players Women, often enslaved, entertained at Chinese courts from early times. Tang art often depicts women with slender figures, but Tang taste also admired more robust physiques. Song women, usually pale with willowy figures, appear as here with bound feet. The practice appeared in Tang times but was not widespread until the Song, when the image of weak, housebound women unable to work became a status symbol and pushed aside the earlier enthusiasm for healthy women who participated in family businesses.

History in Focus *Clothing is a marker of social status, a clue to the values of the day. What do the clothes of these two women emphasize about them and suggest about the priorities of their culture? Find the answer online.*

"Flying money" certificates differed from government-issued paper money, which the Song pioneered. In some years, military expenditures consumed 80 percent of the government budget. The state responded to this financial pressure by distributing paper money. But this made inflation so severe that by the beginning of the 1100s paper money was trading for only 1 percent of its face value. Eventually the government withdrew paper money and instead imposed new taxes, sold monopolies, and offered financial incentives to merchants.

Hard-pressed for the revenue needed to maintain the army, canals, roads, waterworks, and other state functions, the government finally resorted to tax farming, selling the rights to tax collection to private individuals. Tax farmers made their profit by collecting the maximum amount and sending an agreed-upon smaller sum to the government. This meant exorbitant rates for taxable services, such as tolls, and much heavier tax burdens on the common people.

Rapid economic growth undermined the remaining government monopolies and the traditional strict regulation of business. Now merchants and artisans as well as gentry and officials could make fortunes. With land no longer the only source of wealth, the traditional social hierarchy common to an agricultural economy weakened, while cities, commerce, consumption, and the use of money and credit boomed. Urban life reflected the elite's growing taste for fine fabrics, porcelain, exotic foods, large houses, and exquisite paintings and books.

Along with the revival of Confucianism that began under the Tang and intensified under the Song, women were increasingly subordinated, legally disenfranchised, and socially restricted. Merchants spent long periods away from home, and many maintained several wives in different locations. They often depended on wives to manage their homes and even their businesses in their absence. But though women took on responsibility for the management of their husbands' property, their own property rights suffered legal erosion. Under Song law, a woman's property automatically passed to her husband, and she could not remarry if her husband divorced her or died.

As the subordination of women proved compatible with Confucianism, it became fashionable to educate girls just enough to read simplified versions of Confucian philosophy that emphasized the lowly role of women. Literacy made these young women more desirable as companions for the sons of gentry or noble families and as mothers in lower-ranking families aspiring to improve their status. The poet Li Qingzhao (lee CHING-jow) (1083–1141) made fun of her unusual status as a highly celebrated female writer:

> Although I've studied poetry for thirty years
> I try to keep my mouth shut and avoid reputation.
> Now who is this nosy gentleman talking about my
>   poetry
> Like Yang Ching-chih (yahng SHING-she)
> Who spoke of Hsiang Ssu (sang sue) everywhere he
>   went.[5]

(Her reference is to Yang Ching-chih, a hermit poet of the ninth century who was continually and extravagantly praised by a court official.)

Female footbinding first appeared among slave dancers at the Tang court, but it did not become widespread until the Song period. The bindings forced the toes under and toward the heel, so that the bones eventually broke and the woman could not walk on her own. In noble and gentry families, footbinding began between ages five and seven. In less wealthy families, girls worked until they were older, so footbinding began only in a girl's teens.

Many literate men condemned the maiming of innocent girls and the general uselessness of footbinding. Nevertheless, bound feet became a status symbol. By 1200 a woman with unbound feet had become undesirable in elite circles, and mothers of elite status, or aspiring to such status, almost without exception bound their daughters' feet. They knew that girls with unbound feet faced rejection. Working women and the indigenous peoples of the south, where northern practices took a longer time to penetrate, did not practice footbinding. Consequently they enjoyed considerably more mobility and economic independence than did elite Chinese women.

SECTION REVIEW

- Several rival states replaced the fallen Tang Empire, and the close relations between Central Asia and East Asia ended.

- The Liao and Jin Empires encouraged culturally diverse societies and confronted Song China with formidable military threats.

- The Song Empire of central and southern China built upon Tang achievements in technology and science and promoted civil ideals.

- Under the Song, print culture developed, urban populations rose, commercial activity grew through innovation, and women were subordinated to men.

New Kingdoms in East Asia

To what extent do shared practices justify thinking of East Asia as a unified cultural region in the post-Tang era?

The best possibilities for expanding the Confucian world-view of the Song lay with newly emerging kingdoms to the east and south. Korea, Japan, and Vietnam, like Song China, devoted great effort to the cultivation of rice. This fit well with Confucian social ideas. Tending the young rice plants, irrigating the rice paddies, and managing the harvest required coordination among many village and kin groups and rewarded hierarchy, obedience, and self-discipline. Confucianism also justified using agricultural profits to support the education, safety, and comfort of the literate elite. In each of these new kingdoms Song civilization melded with indigenous cultural and historical traditions to create a distinctive synthesis.

Chinese Influences Korea, Japan, and Vietnam had first centralized power under ruling houses in the early Tang period, and their state ideologies continued to resemble that of the early Tang, when Buddhism and Confucianism seemed compatible. Government offices went to noble families and did not depend on passing examinations on Confucian texts. Landowning and agriculture remained the major sources of income, and landowners faced no challenges from a merchant class or urban elite.

Nevertheless, learned men prized literacy in classical Chinese and knowledge of Confucian texts.

Korean Wall Painting This depiction of women dancing before an audience comes from a sixth-century tomb near an early Korean capital north of the Yalu River.

Kim Wonyong, ed., *The Complete Collection of Korean Art*, vol. 4 (Seoul: Tonghwa ch'ulp'an kongsa, 1974), plate 55, p. 76.

Though formal education was available to only a small number of people, the ruling and landholding elites sought to instill Confucian ideals of hierarchy and harmony among the general population.

Korea Our first knowledge of Korea, Japan, and Vietnam comes from early Chinese officials and travelers. When the Qin Empire established its first colony in the Korean peninsula in the third century B.C.E., Chinese bureaucrats began documenting Korean history and customs. Han writers noted the horse breeding, strong hereditary elites, and **shamanism** (belief in the ability of certain individuals to contact ancestors and the invisible spirit world) of Korea's small kingdoms. But Korea quickly absorbed Confucianism and Buddhism.

Mountainous in the east and north, Korea was heavily forested until modern times. The land that can be cultivated (less than 20 percent) lies mostly in the south, where a warm climate and monsoon rains support two crops per year. Population movements from Manchuria, Mongolia, and Siberia to the north and to Japan in the east promoted the spread of languages that were very different from Chinese but distantly related to the Turkic tongues of Inner Asia.

In the early 500s the dominant landholding families made inherited status—the "bone ranks"—permanent in Silla (SILL-ah or SHILL-ah), a kingdom in the southeast of the peninsula. In 668 the northern Koguryo kingdom came to an end after prolonged conflict with the Sui and Tang. Supported by the Tang, Silla took control of much of the Korean peninsula. The Silla rulers imitated Tang government and examined officials on the Confucian classics. The fall of the Tang in the early 900s coincided with Silla's collapse and enabled the ruling house of **Koryo** (KAW-ree-oh), from which the modern name "Korea" derives, to rule a united peninsula for the next three centuries. Threatened constantly by the Liao and then the Jin in northern China, Koryo maintained amicable relations with Song China in the south. The Koryo kings supported Buddhism and made superb printed editions of Buddhist texts.

The oldest surviving woodblock print in Chinese characters comes from Korea in the middle 700s. Commonly used during the Tang period, woodblock printing required great technical skill. A calligrapher would write the text on thin paper, which would then

shamanism The practice of identifying special individuals (shamans) who will interact with spirits for the benefit of the community. Characteristic of the Korean kingdoms of the early medieval period and of early societies of Central Asia.

Koryo Korean kingdom founded in 918 and destroyed by a Mongol invasion in 1259.

be pasted upside down on a block of wood. Once wetted, the characters showed through from the back, and an artisan would carve away the wooden surface surrounding each character. A fresh block had to be carved for each printed page. Korean artisans developed their own advances in printing. By Song times, Korean experiments with movable type reached China, where further improvements led to metal or porcelain type from which texts could be cheaply printed.

Japan

Japan consists of four main islands and many smaller ones stretching in an arc from as far south as Georgia to as far north as Maine. The nearest point of contact with the Asian mainland lies 100 miles away in southern Korea. In early times Japan was even more heavily forested than Korea, with only 11 percent of its land area suitable for cultivation. Mild winters and monsoon rains supported the earliest population centers on the coastlands of the Inland Sea between Honshu and Shikoku Islands. The first rulers to extend their power broadly in the fourth and fifth centuries C.E. were based in the Yamato River Basin on the Kinai Plain at the eastern end of the sea.

The first Chinese description of Japan, dating from the fourth century, tells of an island at the eastern edge of the world, divided into hundreds of small countries and ruled over by a shamaness named Himiko or Pimiko. How Japan became unified remains a question, but horse-riding warriors from Korea may have played a central role in uniting these small countries under the Yamato-based rulers. In the mid-600s these rulers implemented the Taika (TIE-kah) and other reforms, giving the Yamato regime the key features of Tang government, which they knew of from Korean contacts and embassies to Chang'an sent by five different kings. A legal code, an official variety of Confucianism, and an official reverence for Buddhism blended with the local recognition of indigenous and immigrant chieftains as territorial administrators. Within a century a centralized government with a complex system of law had emerged, as attested by a massive history in the Confucian style.

Women from the aristocracy became royal consorts and thereby linked their kinsmen with the royal court. At the death of her husband in 592, Suiko, a woman from the aristocratic family of Soga, became empress. She occupied the throne until 628, enjoying a longer reign than any other ruler down to the nineteenth century. Asuka, her capital, saw a flowering of Buddhist art, and her nephew Shotoku opened relations with Sui China and promulgated in 604 a "Constitution" that had lasting influence on Japan's governing philosophy.

The Japanese mastered Chinese building techniques so well that Nara (NAH-rah) and Kyoto, Japan's early capitals, provide invaluable evidence of the wooden architecture long since vanished from China. During the eighth century Japan in some ways surpassed China in Buddhist studies. In 752 dignitaries from all over Mahayana Buddhist Asia gathered at the enormous Todaiji temple, near Nara, to celebrate the "eye-opening" of the "Great Buddha" statue.

Though the Japanese adopted Chinese building styles and some street plans, Japanese cities were built without walls. Central Japan was not plagued by constant warfare. Also, the Confucian Mandate of Heaven, which justified dynastic changes, played no role in legitimating Japanese government. The tenno—often called "emperor" in English—belonged to a family believed to have ruled Japan since the beginning of history. The dynasty never changed. A prime minister and the leaders of the native religion, in later times called Shinto, or "way of the gods," exercised real control.

By 750 the government in Nara had reached its zenith, employing seven thousand men in its central bureaucracy. The rulers encouraged an extension of Japanese rice-growing culture into the territory of the Hayato people of southern Kyushu and into northeastern Honshu, where the Emishi, a non-Japanese indigenous population, practiced slash-and-burn agriculture.

In 794 the central government moved to Kyoto, usually called by its ancient name, Heian. Though power became decentralized toward the end, legally centralized government lasted there until 1185. During this time members of the **Fujiwara** (foo-jee-WAH-rah) clan—a family of priests, bureaucrats, and warriors who had succeeded the Soga clan in influence—controlled power and protected the emperor. Fujiwara dominance favored men of Confucian learning over the generally illiterate warriors. Noblemen

Scene from the Tale of Genji Written around 1000 by Murasaki Shikibu, a highly educated woman belonging to the aristocratic Fujiwara family, the *Tale of Genji* has supplied subject matter for Japanese painters for centuries. This early scroll painting is in a typical style with the roof of a house removed to reveal the interior and the figures garbed in the elaborate court dress of the time. The story concerns the life and love affairs of Prince Genji, the favorite son of a Japanese emperor.   Tokugawa Reimeikai Foundation, Tokyo, Japan. Photo © AISA/The Bridgeman Art Library International

of the Fujiwara period read the Chinese classics and appreciated painting and poetry.

Pursuit of an aesthetic way of life prompted the Fujiwara nobles to entrust responsibility for local government, policing, and tax collection to their warriors. Though often of humble origins, a small number of warriors had achieved wealth and power by the late 1000s. By the middle 1100s the nobility had lost control, and civil war between rival warrior clans engulfed the capital.

Like other East Asian states influenced by Confucianism, the elite families of Fujiwara Japan did not encourage education for women. However, this did not prevent exceptional women from having a strong cultural impact. The hero of the celebrated Japanese novel about Fujiwara court culture, *The Tale of Genji*, written around the year 1000 by the noblewoman Murasaki Shikibu, remarks: "Women should have a

general knowledge of several subjects, but it gives a bad impression if they show themselves to be attached to a particular branch of learning."[6]

Fujiwara noblewomen lived in near-total isolation, generally spending their time on cultural pursuits and the study of Buddhism. To communicate with their families or among themselves, they depended on writing. The simplified syllabic script that they used represented the Japanese language in its fully inflected form (the Chinese classical script used by Fujiwara men could not do so). Loneliness, free time, and a ready instrument for expression produced an outpouring of poetry, diaries, and storytelling by women of the Fujiwara era. Sei Shonagon (SAY SHON-nah-gohn), a lady attending one of the royal consorts, composed her *Pillow Book* between 996 and 1021. Most likely named for being kept by the author's pillow so she could jot down occasional thoughts, this famous work begins:

> In spring it is the dawn that is most beautiful. As the light creeps over the hills, their outlines are dyed a faint red and wisps of purplish cloud trail over them.
>
> In summer the nights. Not only when the moon shines, but on dark nights too, as the fireflies flit to and fro, and even when it rains, how beautiful it is![7]

Military values acquired increasing importance during the period 1156–1185, and warfare between rival clans culminated in the establishment of the **Kamakura** (kah-mah-KOO-rah) **Shogunate** in eastern Honshu, far from the old religious and political center at Kyoto. The standing of the Fujiwara family fell as nobles and the emperor hurried to accommodate the new warlords. *The Tale of the Heike*, an anonymously composed thirteenth-century epic account of the clan war, reflects a Buddhist appreciation of the impermanence of worldly things, a view that became common among the new warrior class. This class, in later times called samurai, eventually absorbed some of the Fujiwara aristocratic values,

7. From *The Pillow Book of Sei Shonagon*, translated by Ivan Morris. Copyright © 1967 by Ivan Morris, © 1991 Columbia University Press. Reprinted with permission of the publishers, Columbia University Press and Oxford University Press.

Fujiwara Aristocratic family that dominated the Japanese imperial court between the ninth and twelfth centuries.
Kamakura Shogunate The first of Japan's decentralized military governments (1185–1333).

but the ascendancy of the nonmilitary civil elite had come to an end.

Vietnam

Not until Tang times did the relationship between Vietnam and China become close enough for economic and cultural interchange to play an important role. Occupying the coastal regions east of the mountainous spine of mainland Southeast Asia, Vietnam's economic and political life centered on two fertile river valleys, the Red River in the north and the Mekong (may-KONG) in the south. The rice-based agriculture of Vietnam made the region well suited for integration with southern China. In both regions the wet climate and hilly terrain demanded expertise in irrigation.

Early Vietnamese peoples may have preceded the Chinese in using draft animals in farming and working with metal. But in Tang and Song times the elites of "Annam" (ahn-nahm)—as the Chinese called early Vietnam—adopted Confucian bureaucratic training, Mahayana Buddhism, and other aspects of Chinese culture. Annamese elites continued to rule in the Tang style after that dynasty's fall. Annam assumed the name Dai Viet (die vee-yet) in 936 and maintained good relations with Song China as an independent country.

Champa, located in what is now southern Vietnam, rivaled the Dai Viet state. The cultures of India and the Malay Peninsula strongly influenced Champa through maritime networks of trade and communication. During the Tang period, Champa fought with Dai Viet, but both kingdoms cooperated with the less threatening Song. Among the tribute gifts brought to the Song court by Champa emissaries was **Champa rice** (originally from India). Chinese farmers soon made use of this fast-maturing variety to improve their yields of the essential crop.

Vietnam shared the general Confucian interest in hierarchy, but attitudes toward women, like those in Korea and Japan, differed from the Chinese model. None of the societies adopted footbinding. In Korea strong family alliances that functioned like political and economic organizations allowed women a role in negotiating and disposing of property. Before the adoption of Confucianism, Annamese women had enjoyed higher status than women in China, perhaps because both women and men participated in wet-rice cultivation. The Trung sisters of Vietnam, who lived in the

SECTION REVIEW

- Korea, Japan, and Vietnam adapted Chinese cultural and political models, including the Tang blend of Confucianism and Buddhism.
- In all three cultures, landowning and agriculture remained the principal source of wealth.

second century C.E. and led local farmers in resistance against the Han Empire, still serve as national symbols in Vietnam and as local heroes in southern China.

Conclusion

Under the Sui and Tang dynasties, China became a unified state for the first time since the end of the Han in 220 C.E. The Tang rulers were of Turkic origin and expanded the territory under their control to Central Asia, far beyond the lands inhabited by Chinese people. Their empire became cosmopolitan and open to foreign trade and influences, in particular the spread of Buddhism. Meanwhile, people from northern China migrated in ever-larger numbers to the Yangzi Valley and beyond, into tropical southern China. Like the Assyrian, the Roman, and other empires that expanded far from their homeland, maintaining a large army at a great distance eventually weakened the Tang and left them vulnerable to invasion by nomadic herdsmen—whom the Chinese termed *barbarians*—from the northern steppes.

After the fall of the Tang in 907, northern China remained divided for many centuries between competing states and dynasties of Mongolian or Central Asian origin. But southern China, to which the Song dynasty retreated in 1127, attracted immigrants from the north and prospered thanks to a flourishing agriculture and maritime trade with Southeast Asia and the Indian Ocean. As a result of China's great size, ancient culture, and advanced technology, smaller states of East Asia such as Vietnam, Korea, and Japan modeled their political and cultural life on China.

Champa rice Quick-maturing rice that can allow two harvests in one growing season. Originally introduced into Champa from India, it was later sent to China as a tribute gift by the Champa state.

CHAPTER REVIEW

 Download the MP3 audio file of the Chapter Review to listen to on the go.

What was the importance of Inner and Central Asia as a region of interchange during the Tang period? (page 260)

Though the Tang emperors presided over one of the most celebrated periods in Chinese history, they were of Turkic descent and made extensive use of the military and cultural practices of Inner Asian nomads. Silk Road trade flourished under the Tang, and the new popularity of Buddhism entering China from the northwest greatly affected Chinese culture. Nevertheless, most Tang officials came from long-established aristocratic Chinese families.

What were the effects of the fracturing of power in Central Asia and China? (page 266)

After the Tang fell, warlords of different ethnic identities fought for control of northern China. Connections with nomad country remained important, but a simultaneous southward flight of people across the Yangzi River led to the formation of power centers well removed from the northwest frontier. The Song dynasty brought political and economic prominence to southern China for the first time.

How did East Asia develop between the fall of the Tang and 1200? (page 271)

Elsewhere in East Asia, the Tang remained the model of empire. But in Korea and Vietnam, the collapse of the Tang encouraged local independence. Chinese culture continued to be admired and imitated, but the new ruling families rejected Chinese political influence even while recognizing that China provided the greatest market for their trade, particularly under the robust economic conditions of the southern Song.

To what extent do shared practices justify thinking of East Asia as a unified cultural region in the post-Tang era? (page 276)

A reverence for Confucian classics spread from China to all neighboring lands and formed the core of elite education. Buddhism also spread at both the elite and popular levels. However, neither played as strong a political role as Islam did in the Middle East or Christianity in Europe. As a consequence, East Asia emerged during this period as a region with strong cultural links but without a common philosophical or religious tradition of rulership.

Key Terms

Grand Canal (p. 261)	neo-Confucianism (p. 273)
Li Shimin (p. 262)	Zen (p. 273)
Tang Empire (p. 262)	movable type (p. 274)
tributary system (p. 264)	shamanism (p. 277)
Uighurs (p. 266)	Koryo (p. 277)
Tibet (p. 268)	Fujiwara (p. 279)
Song Empire (p. 271)	Kamakura Shogunate (p. 279)
junk (p. 273)	
gunpowder (p. 273)	Champa rice (p. 280)

Web Resources

Pronunciation Guide

Interactive Maps

• MAP 11.1 The Tang Empire in Inner and Eastern Asia, 750

• MAP 11.2 Jin and Southern Song Empires, ca. 1200

Primary Sources

• Memorial on Buddhism

• Craft of Farming

Answer to the History in Focus Question
See photo on page 275, "The Players."

 Visit the CourseMate website at www.cengagebrain.com for additional study tools and review materials for this chapter.

Religious Conversion

Religious conversion has two meanings that often get confused. The term can refer to the inner transformation an individual may feel on joining a new religious community or becoming revitalized in his or her religious belief. Conversions of this sort are often sudden and deeply emotional. In historical terms, they may be important when they transform the lives of prominent individuals.

In its other meaning, religious conversion refers to a change in the religious identity of an entire population, or a large portion of a population. This generally occurs slowly and is hard to trace in historical documents. As a result, historians have sometimes used superficial indicators to trace the spread of a religion. Doing so can result in misleading conclusions, such as considering the spread of the Islamic faith to be the result of forced conversion by Arab conquerors, or taking the routes traveled by Christian or Buddhist missionaries as evidence that the people they encountered adopted their spiritual message, or assuming that a king or chieftain's adherence to a new religion immediately resulted in a religious change among subjects or followers.

In addition to being difficult to document, religious conversion in the broad societal sense has followed different patterns according to changing circumstances of time and place. Historians have devised several models to explain the different conversion patterns. According to one model, religious labels in a society change quickly, through mass baptism, for example, but devotional practices remain largely the same. Evidence for this can be found in the continuation of old religious customs among people who identify themselves as belonging to a new religion. Another model sees religious change as primarily a function of economic benefit or escape from persecution. Taking this approach makes it difficult to explain the endurance of certain religious communities in the face of hardship and discrimination. Nevertheless, most historians pay attention to economic advantage in their assessments of mass conversion. A third model associates a society's religious conversion with its desire to adopt a more sophisticated way of life, by shifting, for example, from a religion that does not use written texts to one that does.

One final conceptual approach to explaining the process of mass religious change draws on the quantitative models of innovation diffusion that were originally developed to analyze the spread of new technologies in the twentieth century. According to this approach, new ideas, whether in the material or religious realm, depend on the spread of information. A few early adopters—missionaries, pilgrims, or conquerors, perhaps—spread word of the new faith to the people they come in contact with, some of whom follow their example and convert. Those converts in turn spread the word to others, and a chain reaction picks up speed in what might be called a bandwagon effect. The period of bandwagon conversion tapers off when the number of people who have not yet been offered an opportunity to convert diminishes. The entire process can be graphed as a logistic or S-shaped curve. Figure 1, the graph of conversion to Islam in Iran based on changes from Persian (non-Islamic) to Arabic (Islamic) names in family genealogies, shows such a curve over a period of almost four centuries.

In societies that were largely illiterate, like those in which Buddhism, Christianity, and Islam slowly achieved spiritual dominance, information spread primarily by word of mouth. The proponents of the new religious views did not always speak the same language as the people they hoped to bring into the faith. Under these circumstances, significant conversion, that is, conversion that involved some understanding of the new religion, as opposed to forced baptism or imposed mouthing of a profession of faith, must surely have started with fairly small numbers.

Language was crucial. Chinese pilgrims undertook lengthy travels to visit early Buddhist sites in India. There they acquired Sanskrit texts, which they translated into Chinese. These translations became the core texts of Chinese Buddhism. In early Christendom, the presence of bilingual (Greek-Aramaic) Jewish communities in the eastern parts of the Roman Empire facilitated the early spread of the religion beyond its Aramaic-speaking homeland. By contrast, Arabic, the language of Islam, was spoken only in the Arabian peninsula and the desert borderlands that extended northwards from Arabia between Syria, Jordan, and Iraq. This initial impediment to the spread of knowledge about Islam dissolved only when intermarriage with non-Muslim, non-Arab women, many of them taken captive and distributed as booty during the conquests, produced bilingual offspring. Bilingual preachers of the Christian faith were similarly needed in the Celtic, Germanic, and Slavic language areas of western and eastern Europe.

This slow process of information diffusion, which varied from region to region, made changing demands on religious leaders and institutions. When a faith was professed primarily by a ruler, his army, and his dependents, religious leaders gave the highest priority to servicing the needs of the ruling minority and perhaps discrediting, denigrating, or exterminating the practices of the majority. Once a few centuries had passed and the new faith had become the religion of the great majority of the population, religious leaders turned to establishing popular institutions and reaching out to the common people. Historical interpretation can benefit from knowing where a society is in a long-term process of conversion.

These various models reinforce the importance of distinguishing between emotional individual conversion experiences and broad changes in a society's religious identity. New converts are commonly thought of as especially zealous in their faith, and that description is often apt in instances of individual conversion experiences. It is less appropriate, however, to broader episodes of conversion. In a conversion wave that starts slowly, builds momentum in the bandwagon phase, and then tapers off, the first individuals to convert are likely to be more spiritually motivated than those who join the movement toward its end. Religious growth depends as much on making the faith attractive to late converts as to ecstatic early converts.

Figure 1 Conversion to Islam in Iran

Source: Richard W. Bullliet, *Conversion to Islam in the Medieval Period*, Cambridge, MA: Harvard University Press, 1979, 23. Copyright © by the President and Fellows of Harvard College.

Part Four

Interregional Patterns of Culture and Contact, 1200–1550

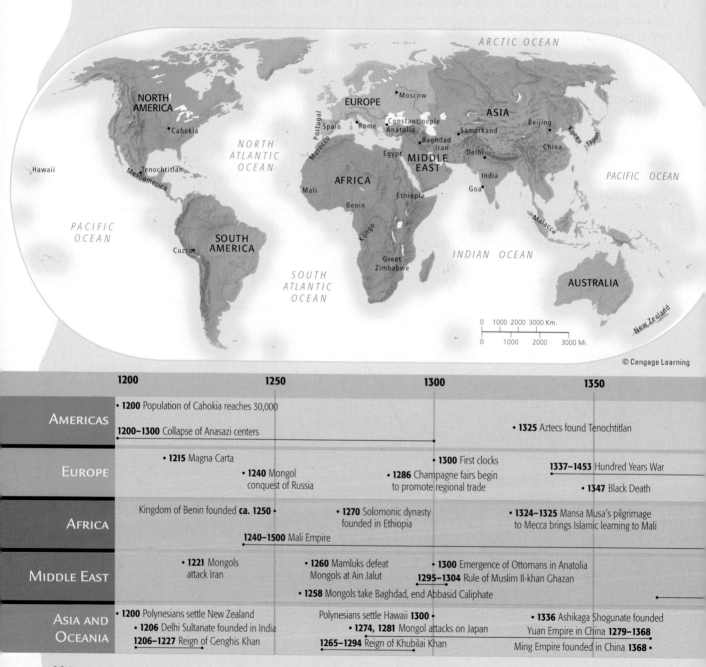

© Cengage Learning

	1200	1250	1300	1350
AMERICAS	• **1200** Population of Cahokia reaches 30,000 **1200–1300** Collapse of Anasazi centers			• **1325** Aztecs found Tenochtitlan
EUROPE	• **1215** Magna Carta	• **1240** Mongol conquest of Russia	• **1300** First clocks • **1286** Champagne fairs begin to promote regional trade	**1337–1453** Hundred Years War • **1347** Black Death
AFRICA	Kingdom of Benin founded **ca. 1250** • **1240–1500** Mali Empire	• **1270** Solomonic dynasty founded in Ethiopia	• **1324–1325** Mansa Musa's pilgrimage to Mecca brings Islamic learning to Mali
MIDDLE EAST	• **1221** Mongols attack Iran	• **1260** Mamluks defeat Mongols at Ain Jalut • **1258** Mongols take Baghdad, end Abbasid Caliphate	• **1300** Emergence of Ottomans in Anatolia **1295–1304** Rule of Muslim Il-khan Ghazan
ASIA AND OCEANIA	• **1200** Polynesians settle New Zealand • **1206** Delhi Sultanate founded in India **1206–1227** Reign of Genghis Khan	Polynesians settle Hawaii **1300** • **1274, 1281** Mongol attacks on Japan **1265–1294** Reign of Khubilai Khan	• **1336** Ashikaga Shogunate founded Yuan Empire in China **1279–1368** Ming Empire founded in China **1368** •

CHAPTER 12
Mongol Eurasia and Its Aftermath, 1200–1500

CHAPTER 13
Tropical Africa and Asia, 1200–1500

CHAPTER 14
The Latin West, 1200–1500

CHAPTER 15
The Maritime Revolution, to 1550

Overland trade along the Silk Road peaked under the Mongols. The empire formed by Genghis Khan's conquests made Mongolia the center of an administrative and trading system linking Europe, the Middle East, Russia, and East Asia. Some lands flourished; others suffered physical devastation or groaned under tax burdens.

Societies that escaped conquest also felt the Mongol impact. Around the eastern Mediterranean coast and in eastern Europe, Southeast Asia, and Japan, fear of Mongol attack stimulated defense planning and accelerated processes of urbanization, technological development, and political centralization.

By 1500, Mongol dominance had waned, and a new Chinese dynasty, the Ming, was expanding its influence in Southeast Asia. The Ottomans had overthrown the Byzantine Empire, and Christian monarchs in Spain and Portugal, victorious over Muslim enemies, were laying the foundations of new overseas empires.

As Eurasia's overland trade faded, merchants, soldiers, and explorers took to the seas. The Chinese state sponsored admiral Zheng He's long-distance voyages, which were spectacular but without long-term results. In the 1300s and 1400s, Africans explored the Atlantic, and Polynesians colonized the central and eastern Pacific. And by 1500 Christopher Columbus had reached the Americas; within twenty-five years a Portuguese ship would sail around the world.

The overland routes of Eurasia had generated massive wealth in East Asia and a growing hunger for commerce in Europe. These factors similarly spurred the development of maritime trade. Exposure to the achievements, wealth, and resources of the Americas, sub-Saharan Africa, and Asia guaranteed the further expansion of European exploration and maritime power.

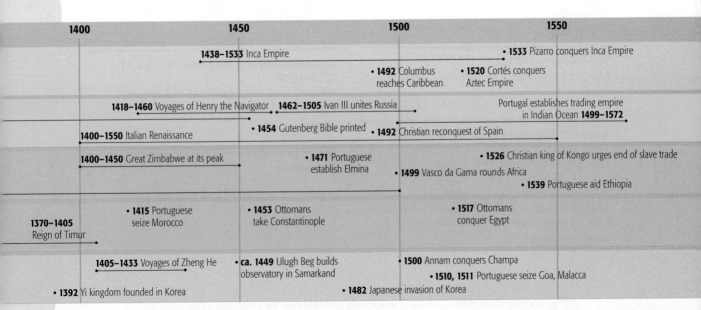

	1400	1450	1500	1550
		1438–1533 Inca Empire		**1533** Pizarro conquers Inca Empire
			1492 Columbus reaches Caribbean	**1520** Cortés conquers Aztec Empire
	1418–1460 Voyages of Henry the Navigator	**1462–1505** Ivan III unites Russia		Portugal establishes trading empire in Indian Ocean **1499–1572**
	1400–1550 Italian Renaissance	**1454** Gutenberg Bible printed	**1492** Christian reconquest of Spain	
	1400–1450 Great Zimbabwe at its peak	**1471** Portuguese establish Elmina	**1499** Vasco da Gama rounds Africa	**1526** Christian king of Kongo urges end of slave trade · **1539** Portuguese aid Ethiopia
1370–1405 Reign of Timur	**1415** Portuguese seize Morocco	**1453** Ottomans take Constantinople	**1517** Ottomans conquer Egypt	
	1405–1433 Voyages of Zheng He	**ca. 1449** Ulugh Beg builds observatory in Samarkand	**1500** Annam conquers Champa · **1510, 1511** Portuguese seize Goa, Malacca	
1392 Yi kingdom founded in Korea		**1482** Japanese invasion of Korea		

Mongol Eurasia and Its Aftermath

© Cengage Learning

CHAPTER PREVIEW

Visit the CourseMate website at **www.cengagebrain.com** for additional study tools and review materials for this chapter.

When the Mongol Temüjin (TEM-uh-jin) was a boy, a rival group murdered his father. Temüjin's mother tried to shelter him, but she could not find a safe haven, so at fifteen Temüjin sought refuge with the leader of the Keraits (keh-rates), a warring confederation whose people spoke Turkic and respected both Christianity and Buddhism. Temüjin learned the importance of religious tolerance, the necessity of dealing harshly with enemies, and the variety of Inner Asia's cultural and economic traditions.

In 1206 the **Mongols** and their allies acknowledged Temüjin as **Genghis Khan** (GENG-iz KAHN), or supreme leader. His advisers spoke many languages and belonged to different religions. His deathbed speech, which cannot be literally true even though a contemporary recorded it, captures the strategy behind Mongol success: "If you want to retain your possessions and conquer your enemies, you must make your subjects submit willingly and unite your diverse energies to a single end."[1] By implementing this strategy, Genghis Khan became the most famous conqueror in history, initiating an expansion of Mongol dominion that by 1250 stretched from Poland to northern China.

European and Asian sources of the time vilified the Mongols as agents of death, suffering, and conflagration, a still-common viewpoint based on reliable accounts of horrible massacres. Scholars today, however, stress the positive developments that transpired under Mongol rule. The tremendous extent of the Mongol Empire promoted the movement of people and ideas from one end of Eurasia to the other. Trade routes improved, markets expanded, and the demand for products grew. Trade on the Silk Road, which had declined with the fall of the Tang Empire (see Chapter 11), revived.

Between 1218 and about 1350 in western Eurasia and down to 1368 in China, the Mongols focused on specific economic and strategic interests, usually permitting local cultures to survive and develop. In some regions, local reactions to Mongol domination sowed seeds of regional and ethnic identity that blossomed in the period of Mongol decline. Regions as widely separated as Russia, Iran, China, Korea, and Japan benefited from the Mongol stimulation of economic and cultural exchange and also found in their opposition to the Mongols new bases for political consolidation and affirmation of cultural difference.

The Rise of the Mongols, 1200–1260

What accounts for the magnitude and speed of the Mongol conquests?

The Mongol Empire owed much of its success to the cultural institutions and political traditions of the Eurasian steppes (prairies) and deserts. The pastoral way of life known as **nomadism** only occasionally gives rise to imperial expansion, and historians disagree about what triggers these episodes. In the case of the Mongols, a precise assessment of the personal contributions of Genghis Khan and his successors remains uncertain.

Nomadism in Central and Inner Asia

The pastoral nomads of the Eurasian steppes played an on-again, off-again role in European, Middle Eastern, and Chinese history for hundreds of years before the rise of the Mongols (see Chapter 8). The Mongol way of life probably did not differ materially from that of those earlier peoples (see Diversity and Dominance: Observations of Mongol Life). Moving regularly and efficiently with flocks and herds required firm decision making, with many voices being heard. A council with representatives from powerful families ratified the decisions of the

Mongols As early as the Tang Empire, Chinese records mention a people of this name living as nomads in northern Eurasia. After 1206, under Genghis Khan, they established an enormous empire linking western and eastern Eurasia.

Genghis Khan (ca. 1167–1227) The title of Temüjin when he ruled the Mongols (1206–1227). It means the "oceanic" or "universal" leader. Genghis Khan was the founder of the Mongol Empire.

nomadism A way of life in which groups of people and their herds of animals continually migrate to find pastures and water.

Mongolian Landscape
The essentials of Inner Asian pastoral life still persist in Mongolia. Here a party of Mongol horsemen carrying their equivalent of lassos ride past a group of yurts. These dwellings made of pieces of felt covering a wooden lattice framework are easily disassembled and moved when the nomads change campsite. Arid plains and bare mountains are typical of Inner Asia.

Claro Cortes IV/Reuters/Corbis

leader, the khan. Yet people who disagreed with a decision could strike off on their own. Even during military campaigns, warriors moved with their families and possessions.

Menial work in camps fell to slaves—people who were either captured during warfare or who sought refuge in slavery to escape starvation. Weak groups secured land rights and protection from strong groups by providing them with slaves, livestock, weapons, silk, or cash. More powerful groups, such as Genghis Khan's extended family and descendants, lived almost entirely off tribute, so they spent less time and fewer resources on herding and more on warfare designed to secure greater tribute.

Leading families combined resources and solidified intergroup alliances through arranged marriages and other acts, a process that helped generate political federations. Marriages were arranged in childhood—in Temujin's case, at the age of eight—and children thus became pawns of diplomacy. Women from prestigious families could wield power in negotiation and management, though they ran the risk of assassination or execution just like men.

The wives and mothers of Mongol rulers traditionally managed state affairs during the interregnum between a ruler's death and the selection of a successor. Princes and heads of ministries treated such regents with great deference and obeyed their commands without question. Since a female regent could not herself succeed to the position of khan, her political machinations usually focused on gaining the succession for a son or other male relative. Families often included believers in two or more religions, most commonly Buddhism, Christianity, or Islam. Virtually all Mongols observed the practices of traditional shamanism, rituals in which special individuals visited and influenced the supernatural world. Whatever their faith, the Mongols believed in world rulership by a khan who, with the aid of his shamans, could speak to and for an ultimate god, represented as Sky or Heaven. This universal ruler transcended particular cultures and dominated them all.

The Mongol Conquests, 1215–1283

Shortly after his acclamation in 1206, Genghis initiated two decades of Mongol aggression. By 1209 he had cowed the Tanggut rulers of northwest China, and in 1215 he captured the Jin capital of Yanjing, today known as Beijing. He turned westward in 1219 with an invasion of Khwarezm, a state east of the Caspian Sea that included much of

Chronology

	Mongolia and China	Central Asia and Middle East	Russia	Korea, Japan, and Southeast Asia
1200	**1206** Temüjin becomes Genghis Khan			
		1219–1221 Invasion of Iran		
	1234 North China seized		**1237–1240** Russia invaded	
		1258 Mongols sack Baghdad		**1258** Mongols conquer Koryo
	1271 Founding of Yuan Empire			
				1274, 1281 Mongols attack Japan
	1279 Southern Song attacked			
1300				
				1333–1338 End of Kamakura Shogunate
			1346 Plague in Kaffa	
		ca. 1350 Plague in Egypt		
	1368 Ming Empire founded			
				1392 Korean Yi kingdom
1400				
		1453 Ottomans capture Constantinople		
			1462–1505 Ivan III tsar	

Iran. After 1221, when most of Iran had fallen, Genghis left the command of most campaigns to subordinate generals.

Ögödei (ERG-uh-day), Genghis's son, became the Great Khan in 1227 after his father's death. He completed the destruction of the Tanggut and the Jin and put their territories under Mongol governors. By 1234 he controlled most of northern China and was threatening the Southern Song (see Chapter 11). Three years later Genghis's grandson Batu (BAH-too) (d. 1255) attacked Russian territories, took control of the towns along the Volga (VOHL-gah) River, and conquered Kievan Russia, Moscow, Poland, and Hungary in a five-year campaign. Only the death of Ögödei in 1241, which caused a suspension of campaigning, saved western Europe from invasion. With Genghis's grandson Güyük (gi-yik) installed as the new Great

Khan, the conquests resumed. In the Middle East a Mongol army sacked Baghdad in 1258 and executed the last Abbasid caliph (see Chapter 9).

Genghis Khan's original objective had probably been collecting tribute, but the success of the Mongol conquests created a new situation. Ögödei unquestionably sought to rule a united empire based at his capital, Karakorum (kah-rah-KOR-um), but after his death family unity began to unravel. The Golden Horde in Russia, the Jagadai domains in Central Asia, and the Il-khans in Iran were subordinate domains (see Map 12.1 on page 292); but when Khubilai (KOO-bih-lie) declared himself Great Khan in 1265, the descendants of Genghis's son Jagadai (d. 1242) and other branches of the family refused to accept him. Since Karakorum was destroyed in the ensuing fighting, Khubilai transferred his court to the old Jin capital now renamed

Diversity & Dominance

Observations of Mongol Life

The Mongols, despite the power, geographical extent, and durability of their empire, are known mainly from the observations made by non-Mongols who either traveled in their territory or worked for them. The following passages come from three such authors.

William of Rubruck, a Franciscan friar, journeyed to the court of the Great Khan Mönke in 1253–1255 after living for some period of time in crusader territory in the Middle East. He carried a letter from the French king, Louis IX (ruled 1226–1270), asking that the friar and a companion be allowed to stay with the Mongols, preach Christianity, and comfort German prisoners. William never made contact with the Germans, but his highly personal observations on Mongol life fascinated European readers.

The dwelling in which they sleep is based on a hoop of interlaced branches, and its supports are made of branches, converging at the top around a smaller hoop, from which projects a neck like a chimney. They cover it with white felt: quite often they also smear the felt with chalk or white clay and ground bones to make it gleam whiter, or sometimes they blacken it. . . . These dwellings are constructed to such a size as to be on occasion thirty feet across: I myself once measured a breadth of twenty feet between the wheeltracks of a wagon, and when the dwelling was on the wagon it protruded beyond the wheels by at least five feet on either side. . . .

The married women make themselves very fine wagons. . . . One rich Mo'al [i.e., Mongol] or Tartar has easily a hundred or two hundred such wagons with chests. Baatu has twenty-six wives, each of whom has a large dwelling, not counting the other, smaller ones placed behind the large one, which are chambers, as it were, where the maids live: to each of these dwellings belong a good two hundred wagons. When they unload the dwellings, the chief wife pitches her residence at the westernmost end, and the others follow according to rank. . . . Hence the court of one wealthy Mo'al will have the appearance of a large town, though there will be very few males in it. . . .

The History of the World-Conqueror by the Iranian historian 'Ata-Malik Juvaini, who worked for the Mongols in Iran, was written in elegant Persian during the 1250s. It combines a glorification of the Mongol rulers with an unflinching picture of the cruelties and devastation inflicted by their conquests.

He [i.e., Chingiz-Khan] paid great attention to the chase and used to say that the hunting of wild beasts was a proper occupation for the commanders of armies; and that instruction and training therein was incumbent on warriors and men-at-arms. . . . Whenever the Khan sets out on the great hunt (which takes place at the beginning of the winter season), he issues orders that the troops stationed around his headquarters and in the neighborhood . . . shall make preparation for the chase. . . .

The right wing, left wing and center of the army are drawn up and entrusted to the great emirs; and they set out together with the Royal Ladies and the concubines, as well as provisions of food and drink. For a month, or two, or three they form a hunting ring and drive the game slowly and gradually before them, taking care lest any escape from the ring. . . . Finally . . . the troops come to a halt all around the ring, standing shoulder to shoulder. The ring is now filled with the cries and commotion of every manner of game and the roaring and tumult of every kind of ferocious beast. . . .

When the ring has been so much contracted that the wild beasts are unable to stir, first the Khan rides in together with some of his retinue; then after he has wearied of the sport, they dismount upon high ground in the center . . . to watch the princes likewise entering the ring, and after them, in due order, the noyons [chiefs], the commanders and the troops. Several days pass in this manner; then, when nothing is left of the game but a few wounded and emaciated stragglers, old men and greybeards humbly approach the Khan, offer up prayers for his well-being and intercede for the lives of the remaining animals asking that they be suffered to depart to someplace nearer to grass and water. . . .

Now war—with its killing, counting of the slain and sparing of the survivors—is after the same fashion, and indeed analogous in every detail, because all that is left in the neighborhood of the battlefield are a few broken-down wretches.

In 1330 Hu Szu-hui, a physician of Chinese-Turkic family background, presented the Yuan emperor with a manual entitled *Proper and Essential Things for the Emperor's Food and Drink*. His work reflects both the meat-heavy diet of the steppes and traditional Chinese concern with good nutrition.

Foods That Cure Various Illnesses [60 entries]

Donkey's Head Gruel

It cures apoplexy-vertigo, debility of hand and foot, annoying pain of extremities, and trouble in speaking:

Black donkey's head (one; remove hair and wash clean), black pepper (two measures), tsaoko cardamom (two measures). Cook ingredients until overcooked. Add the five spices in fermented black bean juice. Flavor with the spices. Flavor evenly. Eat on an empty stomach.

Bear Meat Gruel

It cures the various winds, foot numbness–insensitivity and five flaccidities tendon and muscle spasms:

Bear meat (one measure). [To] ingredient add the five spices in fermented black beans. [Add] onions and sauce. Cook. When done eat on an empty stomach.

Sheep's Stomach Gruel

It cures the various apoplexies:

Sheep's stomach (one; wash clean), non–glutinous rice (two measures), green onions (several), salted fruits, Chinese flower pepper (remove the closed up corns, roast to bring out the juice; 30 corns), sprouting ginger (two measures and a half cut up finely). Combine the six ingredients evenly and put inside the sheep's stomach. Cook until overcooked. When done, flavor with the five spices. Eat on an empty stomach.

Foodstuffs That Mutually Conflict [55 entries]

Horse meat cannot be eaten together with granary rice.

Sheep's liver cannot be eaten together with pepper. It wounds the heart.

Hare meat cannot be eaten together with ginger.

Beef cannot be eaten together with chestnuts.

Mare's milk cannot be eaten together with fish hash. It produces obstruction of the bowels.

Venison cannot be eaten together with catfish.

Beef stomach cannot be eaten together with dog meat. Quail meat cannot be eaten together with pork. The face will turn black.

Pheasant eggs cannot be eaten together with onions. It produces vermin.

Meat of sparrows cannot be eaten together with plums. Eggs cannot be eaten together with turtle meat.

Lettuce cannot be eaten together with cream.

Ground mustard cannot be eaten together with hare meat. It produces sores.

QUESTIONS FOR ANALYSIS

1. Can you determine from the subject matter of these passages the different viewpoints of a European, an Iranian, and a Chinese?

2. Is there anything in these passages to indicate that the Mongols were Muslims, Christians, Buddhists, or Confucians?

3. Do you expect the observations of a traveler to be more or less valuable as historical sources than those of someone who served a Mongol ruler?

Source: From Peter Jackson, tr., *The Mission of Friar William of Rubruck. His Journey to the Court of the Great Khan Mönke 1253–1255*, pp. 73–74. Copyright © 1990. Reprinted by permission of David Higham Associates Limited; From Ata-Malik Juvaini's *The History of the World Conqueror*, vol. 2, translated by Andrew Boyle, pp. 27–29, Collection of Representative works: Persian series, © 1958 by UNESCO. Cambridge, Mass.: Harvard University Press, Copyright © 1958 by Manchester University Press. Reprinted by permission of the publishers, Harvard University Press and UNESCO; Paul D. Buell and Eugene N. Anderson, *A Soup for the Qan* (London: Kegan Paul International, 2000), 428–429, 438–440. Reprinted by permission of Koninklijke BRILL NV.

Interactive Map

Map 12.1 The Mongol Domains in Eurasia in 1300 After the death of Genghis Khan in 1227, his empire was divided among his sons and grandsons. Son Ögödei succeeded Genghis as Great Khan. Grandson Khubilai expanded the domain of the Great Khan into southern China by 1279. Grandson Hülegü was the first Il-khan in the Middle East. Grandson Batu founded the Khanate of the Golden Horde in southern Russia. Son Jagadai ruled the Jagadai Khanate in Central Asia.   © Cengage Learning

Mongol campaigns before 1240
Mongol campaigns after 1240
Route of Marco Polo

Beijing, and in 1271 he declared himself founder of the **Yuan Empire**.

Jagadai's descendants continued to dominate Central Asia and enjoyed close relations with the region's Turkic-speaking nomads. This, plus a continuing hatred of Khubilai, contributed to Central Asia becoming an independent Mongol center and to the spread of Islam there.

After the Yuan destroyed the Southern Song (see Chapter 11) in 1279, Mongol troops attacked Annam—now northern Vietnam. They occupied Hanoi three times and then withdrew after arranging for tribute. In 1283 Khubilai's forces invaded Champa—now southern Vietnam—and made it a tribute nation as well. A plan to invade Java by sea failed, as did two invasions of Japan in 1274 and 1281.

The Mongols seldom outnumbered their enemies, but they were extraordinary riders and utilized superior bows. The Central Asian bow, made by laminating layers of wood, leather, and bone, could shoot one-third farther (and was correspondingly more difficult to pull) than the bows used by sedentary enemies. Rarely did an archer expend all of the five dozen arrows in his quiver. As the battle opened, arrows shot from a distance decimated enemy marksmen. Then the Mongols charged the enemy's infantry to fight with sword, lance, javelin, and mace. The Mongol cavalry met its match only at the Battle of Ain Jalut (ine jah-LOOT) in Palestine, where an under-strength force of Mongols confronted Turkic-speaking mamluks whose war techniques matched their own (see Chapter 9).

The Mongols also fired flaming arrows and hurled enormous projectiles—sometimes flaming—from catapults. The first Mongol catapults, built on Chinese models, transported easily but had short range and poor accuracy. During western campaigns in Central Asia, however, the Mongols encountered a design that was half again as powerful and used it to hammer the cities of Iran and Iraq. Cities that resisted faced siege and annihilation, leaving surrender as the only option. The slaughter the Mongols inflicted on Balkh (bahlk) (in present-day northern Afghanistan) spread terror and caused other cities to surrender. Each conquered area contributed men to the "Mongol" armies; in the Middle East, a few Mongol officers commanded armies of recently recruited Turks and Iranians.

Overland Trade and the Plague

Commercial integration under Mongol rule affected all parts of the empire. Like earlier nomad elites, Mongol nobles had the exclusive right to wear silk, almost all of which came from China. Trade brought new styles and huge quantities of silk westward to feed the luxury trade in the Middle East and Europe, and artistic motifs from Japan and Tibet reached as far as England and Morocco. Porcelain, another eastern luxury, became important in trade and strongly influenced later tastes in the Islamic world.

Merchants encountered ambassadors, scholars, and missionaries over the long routes to the Mongol courts. Some of the resulting travel literature, like the account of the Venetian Marco Polo (1254–1324), freely mixed the fantastic with the factual. Stories of fantastic wealth stimulated a European ambition to find easier routes to Asia.

Exchange also spread disease. In southwestern China **bubonic plague** had festered since the early Tang period. In the mid-thirteenth century, supply trains servicing the Mongol garrison in Yunnan (YOON-nahn) province facilitated the spread of rats carrying infected fleas. Marmots and other rodents along the caravan routes became infected and passed the disease to dogs and people. In 1346 plague incapacitated the Mongol army during their assault on the city of Kaffa (KAH-fah) in Crimea (cry-MEE-ah). They withdrew, but the plague remained. From Kaffa flea-infested rats reached Europe and Egypt by ship (see Chapter 14).

Primary Source: Description of the World
Melons over 6 feet around and big enough to feed twenty or thirty men, dirt from a tomb that can restore a dying person to life, days only six hours long—learn about the strange and interesting countries of the Mongol world.

Yuan Empire (1271–1368) Empire created in China and Siberia by Khubilai Khan.

bubonic plague A bacterial disease that can be transmitted by flea bites to rodents and humans; humans in late stages of the illness can spread the bacteria by coughing. Because of its very high mortality rate and the difficulty of preventing its spread, major outbreaks have created epidemics in many parts of the world.

SECTION REVIEW

- The society of the nomadic Mongols functioned through kinship and tribute ties, in which women often played important roles.

- Genghis Khan began the Mongol conquests to win tribute from Eurasian kingdoms.

- His successors turned to territorial rule, yet internal politics split the empire into smaller ones in China and Central Asia.

- The Mongols won territory through superior battle tactics and integrated it into a vast overland commercial network.

- That network allowed the bubonic plague and other diseases to spread across Asia into Europe.

Typhus, influenza, and smallpox traveled the same route. The combination of these and other diseases created what is called the "great pandemic" of 1347–1352 and spread devastation far in excess of what the Mongol armies inflicted. Peaceful trade, not conquest, ended up taking the greatest toll in lives.

The Mongols and Islam, 1260–1500

How did Mongol expansion and Islam affect each other?

From the perspective of Mongol imperial history, political rivalries determined which branches of the family adopted Islam and which did not. From the standpoint of Islamic history, however, recovery from the devastation that culminated in the destruction of the Abbasid Caliphate in Baghdad in 1258 attests to the vitality of the faith and the ability of Muslims to overcome adversity. Within fifty years of its darkest hour, Islam reemerged as a potent ideological and political force.

Mongol Rivalry By 1260 the **Il-khan** (IL-con) state, established by Genghis's grandson Hülegü, controlled Iran, Azerbaijan, Mesopotamia, and parts of Armenia. North of the Caspian Sea the Mongols who had conquered southern Russia established the capital of their Khanate of the **Golden Horde** (also called the Kipchak [KIP-chahk] Khanate) at Sarai (sah-RYE) on the Volga River. Like the

Passport The Mongol Empire facilitated the movement of products, merchants, and diplomats over long distances. The *paisa* (from a Chinese word for "card" or "sign"), with its inscription in Mongolian, proclaimed that the traveler had the ruler's permission to travel throughout the region. Europeans later adopted the practice, thus making the *paisa* the ancestor of modern passports and visas. Image copyright © The Metropolitan Museum of Art/Art Resource, NY

 History in Focus *Why do governments insist that foreigners traveling through their lands have passports (and often visas as well)? Do you think that the Mongols issuing* paisas *encouraged or discouraged travelers? Find the answer online.*

Il-khans, they ruled an indigenous Muslim population, mostly Turkic-speaking.

Some members of the Mongol imperial family professed Islam before the Mongol assault on the Middle East, and Turkic Muslims served the family

Il-khan A "secondary" or "peripheral" khan based in Persia. The Il-khans' khanate was founded by Hülegü, a grandson of Genghis Khan, and was based at Tabriz in modern Azerbaijan. It controlled much of Iran and Iraq.
Golden Horde Mongol khanate founded by Genghis Khan's grandson Batu. It was based in southern Russia and quickly adopted both the Turkic language and Islam. Also known as the Kipchak Khanate.

in various capacities. Hülegü himself, though a Buddhist, had a trusted Shi'ite adviser and granted privileges to the Shi'ites. However, the Mongols under Hülegü's command came only slowly to Islam.

Islamic doctrines clashed with Mongol ways. Muslims abhorred the Mongols' worship of Buddhist and shamanist idols. Furthermore, Mongol law specified slaughtering animals without spilling blood, which involved opening the chest and stopping the heart. This horrified Muslims, who were forbidden to consume blood and slaughtered animals by slitting their throats and draining the blood.

Islam became a point of inter-Mongol tension when Batu's successor as leader of the Golden Horde declared himself a Muslim. He swore to avenge the murder of the Abbasid caliph and laid claim to the Caucasus—the mountains between the Black and Caspian Seas—which the Il-khans also claimed.

Some European leaders believed that if they helped the non-Muslim Il-khans repel the Golden Horde from the Caucasus, the Il-khans would help them relieve Muslim pressure on the Crusader principalities in Syria, Lebanon, and Palestine (see Chapter 9). This resulted in a brief correspondence between the Il-khan court and Pope Nicholas IV (r. 1288–1292) and a diplomatic mission that sent two Christian Turks to western Europe as Il-khan ambassadors in the late 1200s. The Golden Horde responded by seeking an alliance with the Muslim mamluks in Egypt (see Chapter 9) against both the Crusaders and the Il-khans. Before the Europeans' diplomatic efforts could bear fruit, a new Il-khan ruler, Ghazan (haz-ZAHN) (1271–1304), declared himself a Muslim in 1295. Conflicting indications of Sunni and Shi'ite affiliation, such as coin inscriptions, indicate that Ghazan had a casual attitude toward theological matters. It is similarly unclear whether the Muslim Turkic nomads who served in the army were Shi'ite or Sunni.

Islam and the State

The Il-khans gradually came to appreciate the traditional urban culture of the Muslim territories they ruled. Nevertheless, they used tax farming to extract maximum wealth from their subjects. The government sold tax-collecting contracts to small partnerships, mostly consisting of merchants who might also finance caravans, small industries, or military expeditions. Whoever offered to collect the most revenue for the government won the contracts. They could use whatever methods they chose and could keep anything over the contracted amount.

Contracting tax collection initially lowered administrative costs; but over the long term, the extortions of the tax farmers drove many landowners into debt and servitude. Agricultural productivity declined, making it hard to supply the army. So the government resorted to taking land to grow its own grain. Like land held by religious trusts, this land paid no taxes. Thus the tax base shrank even as the demands of the army and the Mongol nobility continued to grow.

Ghazan faced many economic problems. Citing Islam's humane values, he promised to reduce taxes, but the need for revenue kept the decrease from becoming permanent. The Chinese practice of printing paper money had been tried unsuccessfully by a predecessor. Having no previous exposure to paper money, the Il-khan's subjects pushed the economy into a depression that lasted beyond the end of the Il-khan state in 1349. Mongol nobles competed among themselves for the decreasing revenues, and fighting among Mongol factions destabilized the government.

In the mid-fourteenth century the Golden Horde moved through the Caucasus into the western regions of the Il-khan Empire and then into the Il-khan's central territory, Azerbaijan, briefly occupying its major cities. At the same time a new power was emerging in the Central Asian Khanate of Jagadai (see Map 12.1). The leader **Timur** (TEE-moor), known to Europeans as Tamerlane, maneuvered himself into command of the Jagadai forces and launched campaigns into western Eurasia, apparently seeing himself as a new Genghis Khan. By ethnic background he was a Turk with only an in-law relationship to the family of the Mongol conqueror. This prevented him from assuming the title *khan*, but not from sacking the Muslim sultanate of Delhi in northern India in 1398 or defeating the sultan of the rising Ottoman Empire in Anatolia in 1402. He was reportedly preparing to march on China when he died in 1405. Timur's descendants could not

Timur (1336–1405) Member of a prominent family of the Mongols' Jagadai Khanate, Timur conquered much of Central Asia and Iran. He consolidated the status of Sunni Islam as the orthodox religion, and his descendants, the Timurids, maintained his empire for nearly a century and founded the Mughal Empire in India.

hold the empire together, but they laid the ground-work for the establishment in India of a Muslim regime, the Mughals, in the sixteenth century.

Culture and Science in Islamic Eurasia

The Il-khans and Timurids (descendants of Timur) presided over a brilliant cultural flowering in Iran, Afghanistan, and Central Asia based on blending Iranian and Chinese artistic trends and cultural practices. The dominant cultural tendencies were Muslim, however. Timur died before he could reunite Iran and China, but by transplanting Middle Eastern scholars, artists, and craftsmen to his capital, Samarkand, he fostered the cultural achievements of his descendants.

The historian Juvaini (joo-VINE-nee) (d. 1283), who recorded Genghis Khan's deathbed speech cited at the beginning of this chapter, came from the city of Balkh, which the Mongols had devastated in 1221. His family switched their allegiance to the Mongols, and both Juvaini and his older brother assumed high government posts. The Il-khan Hülegü, seeking to immortalize and justify his conquests, enthusiastically supported Juvaini's writing of the first comprehensive narrative of Genghis Khan's empire.

Juvaini combined a florid style with historical objectivity, often criticizing the Mongols. This approach served as an inspiration to **Rashid al-Din** (ra-SHEED al-DEEN), Ghazan's prime minister, when he attempted the first history of the world. Rashid al-Din's work included the earliest known general history of Europe, derived from conversations with European monks, and a detailed description of China based on information from an important Chinese Muslim official stationed in Iran. The miniature paintings that accompanied some copies of Rashid al-Din's work included depictions of European and Chinese people and events and reflected the artistic traditions of both cultures. Rashid al-Din traveled widely and collaborated with administrators from other parts of the far-flung Mongol dominions. His idea that government should be in accord with the moral principles of the majority of the population buttressed Ghazan's adherence to Islam.

Under the Timurids, the tradition of the Il-khan historians continued. After conquering Damascus, Timur himself met there with the greatest historian of the age, Ibn Khaldun (ee-bin hal-DOON) (1332–1406), a Tunisian. In a scene reminiscent of Ghazan's

Tomb of Timur in Samarkand The turquoise tiles that cover the dome are typical of Timurid architectural decoration. Timur's family ornamented his capital with an enormous mosque, three large religious colleges facing one another on three sides of an open plaza, and a lane of brilliantly tiled family tombs in the midst of a cemetery. Timur brought craftsmen to Samarkand from the lands he conquered to build these magnificent structures.

Sassoon/Robert Harding Picture Library

answering Rashid al-Din's questions on the history of the Mongols, Timur and Ibn Khaldun exchanged historical, philosophical, and geographical viewpoints. Like Genghis, Timur saw himself as a world conqueror. At their capitals of Samarkand and Herat (in western Afghanistan), later Timurid rulers sponsored historical writing in both Persian and Turkish.

A Shi'ite scholar named **Nasir al-Din Tusi** (nah-SEER al-DEEN TOO-si) represents the beginning

Rashid al-Din (d. 1318) Adviser to the Il-khan ruler Ghazan, who converted to Islam on Rashid's advice.
Nasir al-Din Tusi (1201–1274) Persian mathematician and cosmologist whose academy near Tabriz provided the model for the movement of the planets that helped to inspire the Copernican model of the solar system.

of Mongol interest in the scientific traditions of the Muslim lands. Nasir al-Din may have joined the entourage of Hülegü during a campaign in 1256 against the Assassins, a Shi'ite religious sect derived from the Fatimid dynasty in Egypt and at odds with his more mainstream Shi'ite views (see Chapter 9). Nasir al-Din wrote on history, poetry, ethics, and religion, but he made his most outstanding contributions in mathematics and cosmology. Following Omar Khayyam (oh-mar kie-YAM) (1038?–1131), a poet and mathematician of the Seljuk (SEL-jook) period, he laid new foundations for algebra and trigonometry.

Some followers working at an observatory built for Nasir al-Din at Maragheh (mah-RAH-gah), near the Il-khan capital of Tabriz, used the new mathematical techniques to reach a better understanding of celestial orbits. The mathematical tables and geometric models of lunar motion devised by one of his students somehow became known to Nicholas Copernicus (1473–1543), a Polish monk and astronomer. Copernicus adopted this lunar model as his own, virtually without revision, and then proposed the model of lunar movement developed under the Il-khans as the proper model for planetary movement as well—but with the planets circling the sun.

Observational astronomy and calendar-making had engaged the interest of earlier Central Asian rulers, particularly the Uighurs (WEE-ger) and the Seljuks. Under the Il-khans, the astronomers of Maragheh excelled in predicting eclipses, and astrolabes, armillary spheres, three-dimensional quadrants, and other instruments acquired new precision.

The remarkably accurate eclipse predictions and tables prepared by Il-khan and Timurid astronomers reached the mamluk lands in Arabic translation. Byzantine monks took them to Constantinople and translated them into Greek, Christian scholars working in Muslim Spain translated them into Latin, and in India the sultan of Delhi ordered them translated into Sanskrit. The Great Khan Khubilai (see below) summoned a team of Iranians to Beijing to build an observatory for him. Timur's grandson Ulugh Beg (oo-loog bek) (1394–1449), whose avocation was astronomy, constructed a great observatory in Samarkand and actively participated in compiling observational tables that were later translated into Latin and used by European astronomers.

SECTION REVIEW

- For the Mongols of the Il-khan and Golden Horde states, Islam became a matter of political rivalry.
- In the Il-khan state Islamic values struggled with economic needs, and the resulting unrest left it open to invasions by Golden Horde Mongols.
- At the same time, Timur took control of Jagadai and began his own imperial conquests.
- Under the Il-khans and Timurids, Iran and Central Asia experienced a flowering of Islamic culture.
- These rulers fostered great achievements in historical writing, literature, art, mathematics, and science.

A further advance made under Ulugh Beg came from the mathematician Ghiyas al-Din Jamshid al-Kashi (gee-YASS al-DIN jam-SHEED al-KAH-shee), who noted that Chinese astronomers had long used one ten-thousandth of a day as a unit in calculating the occurrence of a new moon. This seems to have inspired him to employ decimal notation, by which quantities less than one could be represented by a marker to show place. Al-Kashi's proposed value for pi (π) was far more precise than any previously calculated. This innovation arrived in Europe by way of Constantinople, where a Greek translation of al-Kashi's work appeared in the fifteenth century.

Regional Responses in Western Eurasia

What benefits resulted from the integration of Eurasia into the Mongol Empire?

Safe, reliable overland trade benefited Mongol ruling centers and commercial cities along the Silk Road. But the countryside, ravaged by conquest, sporadic violence, and heavy taxes, suffered terribly. As Mongol control weakened, regional forces in Russia, eastern Europe, and Anatolia reasserted themselves. Sometimes this meant collaborating with the Mongols; at other times it meant using local ethnic or religious traditions to resist or roll back Mongol influence.

Russia and Rule from Afar The Golden Horde, established after Genghis's grandson Batu defeated a combined Russian and Kipchak (a Turkic people) army in 1223, started as a unified state but gradually lost unity as some districts crystallized into smaller khanates. The White Horde, for instance, ruled much of southeastern Russia in the fifteenth century, and the Crimean khanate on the northern shore of the Black Sea succumbed to Russian power only in 1783.

East-west routes across the steppe and north-south routes along the rivers of Russia and Ukraine (you-CRANE) conferred importance on certain trading entrepôts (places where goods are stored and from which they are distributed), as they had under Kievan Russia (see Chapter 10). The Golden Horde capital was (Old) Sarai, just north of where the Volga flows into the Caspian Sea (see Map 12.1). The Mongols ruled their Russian domains to the north and east from afar. To facilitate control, they granted privileges to the Orthodox Church, a practice that helped reconcile the Russian people to their distant masters.

The politics of language played a role in subsequent history. Old Church Slavonic, an ecclesiastical language, revived; but Russian steadily acquired greater importance and eventually became the dominant written language. Russian scholars shunned Byzantine Greek, previously the main written tongue, even after the Golden Horde permitted renewed contacts with Constantinople. The Golden Horde enlisted Russian princes to act as their agents, primarily as tax collectors and census takers.

The flow of silver and gold into Mongol hands starved the local economy of precious metal. Like the Il-khans, the khans of the Golden Horde attempted to introduce paper money as a response to the currency shortage. The unsuccessful experiment left such a vivid memory that the Russian word for money (*denga* [DENG-ah]) comes from the Mongolian word for the stamp (*tamga* [TAHM-gah]) used to create paper currency. In fact, commerce depended more on barter than on currency transactions.

Alexander Nevskii (nih-EFF-skee) (ca. 1220–1263), the prince of Novgorod, persuaded some fellow princes to submit to the Mongols. In return, the Mongols favored both Novgorod and the emerging town of Moscow, ruled by Alexander's son Daniel. As these towns eclipsed devastated Kiev as political, cultural, and economic centers, they drew people northward to open new agricultural land far from the Mongol steppe lands. Decentralization continued in

Transformation of the Kremlin Like other northern Europeans, the Russians preferred to build in wood, which was easy to handle and comfortable to live in. But they fortified important political centers with stone ramparts. In the 1300s, the city of Moscow emerged as a new capital, and its old wooden palace, the Kremlin, was gradually transformed into a stone structure.

the 1300s, with Moscow only very gradually becoming Russia's dominant political center.

In appraising the Mongol era, some historians stress Mongol destructiveness and brutal tax collection methods. Ukraine, a fertile and well-populated region in the late Kievan period (1000–1230), suffered severe population loss from these sources. Isolated from developments to the west, Russia and parts of eastern Europe are portrayed as suffering under the "Mongol yoke."

Alexander Nevskii (ca. 1220–1263) Prince of Novgorod (r. 1236–1263). He submitted to the invading Mongols in 1240 and received recognition as the leader of the Russian princes under the Golden Horde.

Other historians point out that even before the Mongols struck, Kiev had declined economically and ceased to mint coins. Yet the Russian territories regularly paid the heavy Mongol taxes in silver, indicating both economic surpluses and an ability to convert goods into cash. The burdensome taxes stemmed less from the Mongols than from their tax collectors, Russian princes who often exempted their own lands and shifted the load to the peasants.

As for Russia's cultural isolation, skeptics observe that before the Mongol invasion, the powerful and constructive role played by the Orthodox Church oriented Russia primarily toward Byzantium (see Chapter 10). This situation discouraged but did not eliminate contacts with western Europe, which probably would have become stronger after the fall of Constantinople to the Ottomans in 1453 regardless of Mongol influence.

The traditional structure of local government survived Mongol rule, as did the Russian princely families, who continued to battle among themselves for dominance. The Mongols merely added a new player to those struggles. Ivan (ee-VAHN) III, the prince of Moscow (r. 1462–1505), established himself as an autocratic ruler in the late 1400s. Before Ivan, the title **tsar** (from *caesar*), of Byzantine origin, applied only to foreign rulers, whether the emperors of Byzantium or the Turkic khans of the steppe. Ivan's use of the title probably represents an effort to establish a basis for legitimate rule with the decline of the Golden Horde and the disappearance of the Byzantine Empire.

New States in Eastern Europe and Anatolia

Anatolia and parts of Europe responded dynamically to the Mongol challenges. Raised in Sicily, the Holy Roman Emperor Frederick II (r. 1212–1250) appreciated Muslim culture and did not recoil from negotiating with Muslims. When the pope threatened to excommunicate him unless he waged a crusade, Frederick nominally regained Jerusalem through a flimsy treaty with the mamluk sultan in Egypt. Dissatisfied, the pope continued to quarrel with the emperor, leaving Hungary, Poland, and Lithuania to deal with the Mongol onslaught on their own. Many princes capitulated and went to (Old) Sarai to offer their submission to Batu.

However, the Teutonic (two-TOHN-ik) Knights resisted. These German-speaking warriors were dedicated to Christianizing the Slavic and Kipchak populations of northern Europe and to colonizing their territories with German settlers. To protect Slav territory, Alexander Nevskii joined the Mongols in fighting the Teutonic Knights and their Finnish allies. The latter suffered a catastrophe in 1242, when many broke through an icy northern lake and drowned. This event destroyed the power of the Knights, and the northern Crusades virtually ceased.

The "Mongol" armies encountered by the Europeans consisted mostly of Turks, Chinese, Iranians, a few Europeans, and at least one Englishman, who went to crusade in the Middle East but joined the Mongols and served in Hungary. But most commanders were Mongol.

Initial wild theories describing the Mongols as coming from Hell or from caves where Alexander the Great had confined monsters gradually yielded to a more sophisticated understanding as European embassies to Mongol courts returned with reliable intelligence. In some quarters terror gave way to appreciation. Europeans learned about diplomatic passports, coal mining, movable type, high-temperature metallurgy, higher mathematics, gunpowder, and, in the fourteenth century, the casting and use of bronze cannon. Yet with the outbreak of bubonic plague in the late 1340s (see Chapter 14), the memory of Mongol terror helped ignite religious speculation that God might again be punishing the Christians.

In the fourteenth century several regions, most notably Lithuania, escaped the Mongol grip. When Russia fell to the Mongols, Lithuania had experienced an unprecedented centralization and military strengthening. Like Alexander Nevskii, the Lithuanian leaders maintained their independence by cooperating with the Mongols. In the late 1300s Lithuania capitalized on its privileged position to dominate Poland and ended the Teutonic Knights' hope of regaining power.

In the Balkans independent kingdoms separated themselves from the chaos of the Byzantine Empire

tsar From Latin *caesar*, this Russian title for a monarch was first used in reference to a Russian ruler by Ivan III (r. 1462–1505).

- Mongol conquest devastated Kievan Russia, but the Russian language achieved greater importance, and many Russian traditions survived.

- Mongol conquest prompted decentralization of Russian power away from Kiev, but the Golden Horde's decline set the stage for the rise of Russian autocracy.

- The decline of Mongol power and Byzantine weakness enabled the rise of Lithuania and Serbia in eastern Europe and of the Ottoman Empire in Anatolia.

and thrived amidst the political uncertainties of the Mongol period. The Serbian king Stephen Dushan (ca. 1308–1355) proved the most effective leader. Seizing power from his father in 1331, he took advantage of Byzantine weakness to turn the archbishop of Serbia into an independent patriarch. In 1346 the patriarch crowned him "tsar and autocrat of the Serbs, Greeks, Bulgarians, and Albanians," a title that fairly represents the wide extent of his rule. As in the case of Timur, however, his kingdom declined after his death in 1355 and disappeared entirely after a defeat by the Ottomans at the battle of Kosovo in 1389.

The Turkic nomads whose descendants established the **Ottoman Empire** came to Anatolia in the same wave of Turkic migrations as the Seljuks (see Chapter 9). Though Il-khan influence was strong in eastern Anatolia, a number of small Turkic principalities emerged in the west. The Ottoman principality was situated in the northwest, close to the Sea of Marmara. This not only put them in a position to cross into Europe and take part in the dynastic struggles of the declining Byzantine state, but it also attracted Muslim religious warriors who wished to do battle with Christians on the frontiers. The defeat of the Ottoman sultan by Timur in 1402 was only a temporary setback. In 1453 Sultan Mehmet II captured Constantinople and brought the Byzantine Empire to an end.

The Ottoman sultans, like the rulers of Russia, Lithuania, and Serbia, seized opportunities that arose with the decay of Mongol power. The powerful states they created put strong emphasis on religious and linguistic identity, factors that the Mongols themselves did not stress. As we shall see, Mongol rule stimulated similar reactions in the lands of East and Southeast Asia.

Mongol Domination in China, 1271–1368

How did Mongol rule in China foster cultural and scientific exchange?

After conquering northern China in the 1230s, Great Khan Ögödei told a Confucian adviser that he planned to turn the heavily populated North China Plain into a pasture for livestock. The adviser reacted calmly but argued that taxing the cities and villages would bring greater wealth. The Great Khan agreed, but he imposed an oppressive tax-farming system instead of the fixed-rate method traditional to China.

The Chinese suffered under this system during the early years, but the Yuan Empire, established by Genghis Khan's grandson Khubilai in 1271, also brought benefits: secure trade routes, exchange of experts between eastern and western Eurasia, and transmission of information, ideas, and skills.

The Yuan Empire, 1271–1368

The Yuan sought a fruitful synthesis of the Mongol and Chinese traditions. **Khubilai Khan** gave his oldest son a Chinese name and had Confucianists participate in the boy's education. In public announcements and the crafting of laws, he took Confucian conventions into consideration. Buddhist and Daoist leaders who visited the Great Khan came away believing that they had all but convinced him of their beliefs.

Buddhist priests from Tibet called **lamas** became popular with some Mongol rulers. Their idea of a militant universal ruler bringing the whole world under control of the Buddha and thus pushing it nearer to salvation mirrored an ancient Inner Asian idea of universal rulership.

Ottoman Empire Islamic state founded by Osman in northwestern Anatolia ca. 1300. After the fall of the Byzantine Empire, the Ottoman Empire was based at Istanbul (formerly Constantinople) from 1453 to 1922. It encompassed lands in the Middle East, North Africa, the Caucasus, and eastern Europe.
Khubilai Khan (1215–1294) Last of the Mongol Great Khans (r. 1260–1294) and founder of the Yuan Empire. Original architect of the Forbidden City.
lama In Tibetan Buddhism, a teacher.

Beijing, the Yuan capital, became the center of cultural and economic life. Karakorum had been geographically remote, but Beijing served as the eastern terminus of caravan routes that began near Tabriz, the Il-khan capital, and (Old) Sarai, the Golden Horde capital. A horseback courier system utilizing hundreds of stations maintained communications along routes that were generally safe for travelers. Ambassadors and merchants arriving in Beijing found a city that was much more Chinese in character than Karakorum had been.

Called Great Capital (Dadu) or City of the Khan (khan-balikh [kahn-BAL-ik], Marco Polo's "Cambaluc"), Khubilai's capital included the Forbidden City, a closed imperial complex with wide streets and a network of linked lakes and artificial islands. In summer, Khubilai practiced riding and shooting at a palace and park in Inner Mongolia. This was Shangdu (shahng-DOO), the "Xanadu" (ZAH-nah-doo) with its "stately pleasure dome" celebrated by the English poet Samuel Taylor Coleridge.

Three separate states competed in China before the Mongols reunified the country (see Chapter 11). The Tanggut and Jin Empires controlled the north, the Southern Song most of the area south of the Yellow River. They had different languages, writing systems, forms of government, and elite cultures. The Great Khans destroyed all three and encouraged the restoration or preservation of many features of Chinese government and society.

By law, Mongols ranked highest. Below them came Central Asians and Middle Easterners, then northern Chinese, and finally southern Chinese. This reflected a hierarchy of functions. The Mongols were the empire's warriors, the Central Asians and Middle Easterners its census takers and tax collectors. The northern Chinese outranked the southern Chinese because they came under Mongol control almost two generations earlier.

Though Khubilai included some "Confucians" (under the Yuan, a formal and hereditary status) in government, their position compared poorly with pre-Mongol times. The Confucians disparaged merchants, many of whom were from the Middle East or Central Asia, and physicians. Whereas they regarded doctors as mere technicians or Daoist mystics, the Yuan encouraged doctors and began the process of integrating Chinese medical approaches with those contained in Muslim and Hellenistic sources.

Like the Il-khans, the Yuan rulers stressed census taking and tax collecting. Persian, Arab, and Uighur administrators staffed the offices of taxation and finance, and Muslim scholars worked at calendar-making and astronomy. The Mongols organized all of China into provinces. Central appointment of provincial governors, tax collectors, and garrison commanders marked a radical change by systematizing control in all parts of the country.

Many cities prospered: in north China by being on the caravan routes, in the interior by being on the Grand Canal, and along the coast by participating in maritime grain shipments from south China. The reintegration of East Asia (though not Japan) with the overland Eurasian trade, which had lapsed with the fall of the Tang (see Chapter 11), stimulated the urban economies.

With merchants a privileged group, life in the cities changed. So few government posts were open to the old Chinese elite that families that had previously spent fortunes on educating their sons for government service sought other opportunities. Many gentry families chose commerce. Corporations—investor groups that behaved as single commercial and legal units and shared the risk of doing business—handled most economic activities, starting with financing caravans and expanding into tax farming and lending money to the Mongol aristocracy. Central Asians and Middle Easterners headed most corporations in the early Yuan period; but as Chinese bought shares, many acquired mixed membership, or even complete Chinese ownership.

The agricultural base, damaged by war, overtaxation, and the passage of armies, could not satisfy the financial needs of the Mongol aristocracy. Following earlier precedent, the imperial government made up the shortfall with paper money. But people doubted the value of the notes, which were unsecured. Copper coinage partially offset the failure of the paper currency. During the Song, exports of copper to Japan, where the metal was scarce, had caused a severe shortage in China, leading to a rise in the value of copper in relation to silver. By cutting off trade with Japan, the Mongols stabilized the value of copper coins.

Many gentry families moved from their traditional homes in the countryside to engage in urban

---

Beijing China's northern capital, first used as an imperial capital in 906.

commerce as city life began to cater to the tastes of merchants instead of scholars. Specialized shops selling clothing, grape wine, furniture, and religiously butchered meats became common. Teahouses offered sing-song girls, drum singers, operas, and other entertainments previously considered coarse. Writers published works in the style of everyday speech. And the increasing influence of the northern, Mongolian-influenced Chinese language, often called Mandarin in the West, resulted in lasting linguistic change.

Cottage industries linked to the urban economies dotted the countryside, where 90 percent of the people lived. Some villages cultivated mulberry trees and cotton using dams, water wheels, and irrigation systems patterned in part on Middle Eastern models. Treatises on planting, harvesting, threshing, and butchering were published. One technological innovator, Huang Dao Po (hwahng DOW poh), brought knowledge of cotton growing, spinning, and weaving from her native Hainan Island to the fertile Yangzi Delta.

Yet on the whole, the countryside did poorly during the Yuan period. Initially, the Mongol princes evicted many farmers and subjected the rest to brutal tax collection. By the time the Yuan shifted to lighter taxes and encouragement of farming at the end of the 1200s, it was too late. Servitude or homelessness had overtaken many farmers. Neglect of dams and dikes caused disastrous flooding, particularly on the Yellow River.

According to Song records from before the Mongol conquest and the Ming census taken after their overthrow—each, of course, subject to inaccuracy or exaggeration—China's population may have shrunk by 40 percent during eighty years of Mongol rule, with many localities in northern China losing up to five-sixths of their inhabitants. Scholars have suggested several causes: prolonged warfare, rural distress causing people to resort to female infanticide, bubonic plague, a southward flight of refugees, and flooding of the Yellow River. The last helps explain why losses in the north exceeded those in the south and why the population along the Yangzi River markedly increased.

The Fall of the Yuan Empire

In the 1340s strife broke out among the Mongol princes, and within twenty years farmer rebellions and inter-Mongol feuds engulfed the land. Amidst the chaos, a charismatic Chinese leader, Zhu Yuanzhang (JOO yuwen-JAHNG), mounted a campaign that destroyed the Yuan Empire and brought China under control of his new dynasty, the Ming, in 1368. Many Mongols—as well as the Muslims, Jews, and Christians who had come with them—remained in China. Most of their descendants took Chinese names and became part of the diverse cultural world of China.

Many other Mongols, however, who had never moved out of their home territories in Mongolia, now welcomed back refugees from the Yuan collapse. Though Turkic peoples were becoming predominant in the steppe regions in the west, including territories still ruled by descendants of Genghis Khan, Mongols continued to predominate in Inner Asia, the steppe regions bordering on Mongolia. Some Mongol groups adopted Islam; others favored Tibetan Buddhism. But religious affiliation proved less important than Mongol identity in fostering a renewed sense of unity.

The Ming thus fell short of dominating all the Mongols. The Mongols of Inner Asia paid tribute to the extent that doing so facilitated their trade. Other Mongols, however, remained a continuing threat on the northern Ming frontier.

The Early Ming Empire, 1368–1500

In what ways did the Ming Empire continue or discontinue Mongol practices?

Historians of China, like historians of Russia and Iran, divide over the overall impact of the Mongol

SECTION REVIEW

- The Great Khans reunified China and fostered a synthesis of ideas and cultural traditions.
- Khubilai Khan made Beijing the capital of the Yuan Empire and presided over a social hierarchy with Mongols at the top and southern Chinese at the bottom.
- Mongol rule systematized government, but cities benefited more from Mongol policies than did the countryside.
- China's population shrank as a result of Mongol conquest and rule.
- Mongol-protected trade routes encouraged a steady exchange of scientific and cultural ideas.
- Internal strife weakened the Yuan Empire, which fell to the Ming in 1368, but many Mongols remained in China.

Map 12.2 The Ming Empire and Its Allies, 1368–1500 The Ming Empire controlled China but had a hostile relationship with peoples in Mongolia and Inner Asia who had been under the rule of the Mongol Yuan emperors. Mongol sea campaigns were continued by the Ming mariner Zheng He.　© Cengage Learning

Interactive Map

era. Since the **Ming Empire** reestablished many practices that are seen as purely Chinese, they receive praise from people who ascribe central importance to Chinese traditions. On the other hand, historians who look upon the Mongol era as a pivotal historical moment when communication across the vast interior of Eurasia served to bring east and west together sometimes see the inward-looking Ming as less productive than the Yuan.

Ming China on a Mongol Foundation

Zhu Yuanzhang, a former monk, soldier, and bandit, had watched his parents and other family members die of famine and disease, conditions he blamed on Mongol misrule. During the Yuan Empire's chaotic last decades, he vanquished rival rebels and assumed imperial power under the name Hongwu (r. 1368–1398).

Hongwu moved the capital to Nanjing (nahn-JING) ("southern capital") on the Yangzi River, turning away from the Mongol's Beijing ("northern capital"; see Map 12.2). Though Zhu Yuanzhang the rebel had espoused a radical Buddhist belief in a coming age of salvation, once in power he used Confucianism to depict the emperor as the champion of civilization and virtue.

Hongwu choked off relations with Central Asia and the Middle East and imposed strict limits on

Ming Empire (1368–1644) Empire based in China that Zhu Yuanzhang established after the overthrow of the Yuan Empire. The Ming emperor Yongle sponsored additions to the Forbidden City and the voyages of Zheng He. The later years of the Ming saw a slowdown in technological development and economic decline.

imports and foreign visitors. Silver replaced paper money for tax payments and commerce. These practices, illustrative of an anti-Mongol ideology, proved as economically unhealthy as some of the Yuan economic policies and did not last. Eventually, the Ming government came to resemble the Yuan. Ming rulers retained the provincial structure and continued to observe the hereditary professional categories of the Yuan period. Muslims made calendars and astronomical calculations at a new observatory at Nanjing, a replica of Khubilai's at Beijing. The Mongol calendar continued in use.

Continuities with the Yuan became more evident after an imperial prince seized power through a coup d'état to rule as the emperor **Yongle** (yoong-LAW) (r. 1403–1424). He returned the capital to Beijing, enlarging and improving Khubilai's Forbidden City, which now acquired its present features: moats, orange-red outer walls, golden roofs, and marble bridges. Yongle intended this combination fortress, religious site, bureaucratic center, and imperial residential park to overshadow Nanjing, and it survives today as China's most imposing traditional architectural complex.

Yongle also restored commercial links with the Middle East. Because hostile Mongols still controlled much of the caravan route, Yongle explored maritime connections. In Southeast Asia, Annam became a Ming province as the early emperors continued the Mongol program of aggression. This focus on the southern frontier helped inspire the naval expeditions of the trusted imperial eunuch **Zheng He** (jehng huh) from 1405 to 1433.

A Muslim whose father and grandfather had made the pilgrimage to Mecca, Zheng He had a good knowledge of the Middle East, and his religion eased relations with the states of the Indian subcontinent, to which he directed his first three voyages. Subsequent expeditions reached Hormuz on the Persian Gulf, sailed the southern coast of Arabia and the Horn of Africa (modern Somalia), and possibly reached as far south as the Strait of Madagascar.

On early voyages Zheng He visited long-established Chinese merchant communities in Southeast Asia to cement their allegiance to the Ming Empire and to collect taxes. When a community on the island of Sumatra resisted, he slaughtered the men to set an example. The expeditions added some fifty new tributary states to the Ming imperial universe, but trade did not

increase as dramatically. Sporadic embassies reached Beijing from rulers in India, the Middle East, Africa, and Southeast Asia. During one visit the ruler of Brunei (broo-NIE) died and received a grand burial at the Chinese capital. The expeditions stopped in the 1430s after the deaths of Yongle and Zheng He.

Why did the Chinese not develop seafaring for commercial and military gain? Contemporaries considered the voyages a personal project of Yongle, an upstart ruler who had always sought to prove his worthiness. Building the Forbidden City in Beijing and sponsoring gigantic encyclopedia projects might be taken to reflect a similar character. Yongle may also have been emulating Khubilai Khan's sea expeditions against Japan and Southeast Asia. This would fit with the rumor spread by Yongle's political enemies that he was actually a Mongol.

A less speculative approach starts with the fact that the new commercial opportunities fell short of expectations, despite bringing foreign nations into the Ming orbit. In the meantime, Japanese coastal piracy intensified, and Mongol threats in the north and west grew. The human and financial demands of fortifying the north, redesigning and strengthening Beijing, and outfitting campaigns against the Mongols ultimately took priority over the quest for maritime empire.

Technology and Population

The Ming government limited mining, partly to keep the value of metal coins and partly to tax the industry. As a consequence, metal implements became more expensive for farmers. Techniques for making the high-quality bronze and steel used for weapons also declined. Japan quickly surpassed China in the production of extremely high-quality swords.

After the death of Emperor Yongle in 1424, shipbuilding skills deteriorated, and few advances

Yongle Reign of Zhu Di (1360–1424), the third emperor of the Ming Empire (r. 1403–1424). He sponsored further work on the Forbidden City, the expeditions of Zheng He, and the reopening of China's borders to trade and travel.

Zheng He (1371–1433) An imperial eunuch and Muslim who was entrusted by the Ming emperor Yongle with a series of state voyages that took his ships through the Indian Ocean, from Southeast Asia to Africa.

occurred in printing, timekeeping, and agricultural technology. Agricultural production peaked around the mid-1400s and remained level for more than a century. New weaving techniques did appear, but technological development in this field had peaked by 1500.

Reactivation of the examination system for recruiting government officials (see Chapter 11) drew large numbers of ambitious men into a renewed study of the Confucian classics. This reduced the vitality of commerce, where they had previously been employed, just as population growth was creating a labor surplus. Records indicating a growth from 60 million at the end of the Yuan period in 1368 to nearly 100 million by 1400 may not be entirely reliable, but rapid population growth encouraged the production of staples—wheat, millet, and barley in the north and rice in the south—at the expense of commercial crops such as cotton that had stimulated many technological innovations under the Song. Staple crops yielded lower profits, which further discouraged capital improvements. New foods, such as sweet potatoes, became available but were little adopted. Population growth in southern and central China caused deforestation and raised the price of wood.

Against the Mongol horsemen in the north the Ming used scattershot mortars and explosive canisters. They even used a few cannon, which they knew about from contacts with the Middle East and later with Europeans. Fearing a loss of technological secrets, the government censored the chapters on gunpowder and guns in early Ming encyclopedias. Shipyards and ports shut down to avoid contact with Japanese pirates and to prevent Chinese from migrating to Southeast Asia.

A technology gap with Korea and Japan opened up nevertheless. When superior steel was needed, supplies came from Japan. Korea moved ahead of China in the design and production of firearms and ships, in printing techniques, and in the sciences of weather prediction and calendar-making. The desire to tap the wealthy Ming market spurred some of these advances.

The Ming Achievement

In the late 1300s and the 1400s the wealth and consumerism of the early Ming stimulated high achievement in literature, the decorative arts, and painting. The plain writing of the Yuan period had produced some of the world's earliest novels: *Water Margin*, which

SECTION REVIEW

- The first Ming emperor, Hongwu, based his policies on an anti-Mongol ideology, but the Ming government came to adopt Yuan practices.

- Yongle reestablished international commerce and sent Zheng He to explore maritime connections to the Middle East.

- Technological innovation continued, but with less frequent advances and reduced output, and some techniques became guarded secrets.

- The Ming reestablished the Confucian examination system, reducing the vitality of commerce.

- The greatest Ming achievements were in literature, the arts, and porcelain production.

originated in the raucous drum-song performances loosely related to Chinese opera, and *Romance of the Three Kingdoms*, which describes the attempts of an upright but doomed war leader and his followers to restore the Han Empire of ancient times and resist the power of the cynical but brilliant villain. *Romance of the Three Kingdoms* and *Water Margin* express the militant but joyous pro-China sentiment of the early Ming era and remain among the most appreciated Chinese fictional works.

Probably the best-known product of Ming technological advance was porcelain. The imperial ceramic works at Jingdezhen (JING-deh-JUHN) experimented with new production techniques and new ways of organizing workers. "Ming ware," a blue-on-white style developed in the 1400s from Indian, Central Asian, and Middle Eastern motifs, became especially prized. Other Ming goods in high demand included furniture, lacquered screens, and silk, all of which found ready markets in Southeast Asia and the Pacific, India, the Middle East, and East Africa.

Centralization and Militarism in East Asia, 1200–1500

What are some of the similarities and differences in how Korea and Japan responded to the Mongol threat?

Korea, Japan, and Annam, the other major states of East Asia, were all affected by confrontation with the Mongols, but with differing results. Japan and Annam escaped Mongol conquest but changed in response to the Mongol threat, becoming more effective and expansive regimes with enhanced commitments to independence.

As for Korea, just as the Ming stressed Chinese traditions and identity in the aftermath of Yuan rule, so Mongol domination contributed to revitalized interest in Korea's own language and history. The Mongols conquered Korea after a difficult war, and though Korea suffered socially and economically under Mongol rule, members of the elite associated closely with the Yuan Empire. After the fall of the Yuan, merchants continued the international connections established in the Mongol period, while Korean armies consolidated a new kingdom and fended off pirates.

Korea from the Mongols to the Yi, 1231–1500

Korea was the answer to the Mongols' search for coastal areas from which to launch naval expeditions and choke off the sea trade of their adversaries. When the Mongols attacked in 1231, the leader of a prominent Korean family assumed the role of military commander and protector of the king (not unlike the shoguns of Japan). Twenty years of defensive war left a ravaged countryside, exhausted armies, and burned treasures, including the renowned nine-story pagoda at Hwang-nyong-sa (hwahng-NEEYAHNG-sah) and the wooden printing blocks of the Tripitaka (tri-PIH-tah-kah), a ninth-century masterpiece of printing art. The commander's underlings killed him in 1258. Soon afterward the Koryo (KAW-ree-oh) king surrendered to the Mongols and became a subject monarch by linking his family to the Great Khan by marriage.

By the mid-1300s the Koryo kings were of mostly Mongol descent and favored Mongol dress, customs, and language. The kings, their families, and their entourages often traveled between China and Korea, thus exposing Korea to the philosophical and artistic styles of Yuan China: neo-Confucianism, Chan Buddhism (called Soøn in Korea), and celadon (light green) pottery.

Mongol control broke down centuries of comparative isolation. Cotton was introduced in southern Korea; gunpowder came into use; and the art of calendar-making stimulated astronomical observation and mathematics. Avenues of advancement opened for

Korean scholars willing to learn Mongolian, landowners willing to open their lands to falconry and grazing, and merchants servicing the new royal exchanges with Beijing. These developments contributed to the rise of a new landed and educated class.

When the Yuan Empire fell in 1368, the Koryo ruling family remained loyal to the Mongols and had to be forced to recognize the new Ming Empire. In 1392 the **Yi** (YEE) established a new kingdom with a capital in Seoul and sought to reestablish a distinctive Korean identity. Like Russia and Ming China, the Yi regime publicly rejected the period of Mongol domination. Yet the Yi government continued to employ Mongol-style land surveys, taxation in kind, and military garrison techniques.

Like the Ming emperors, the Yi kings revived the study of the Confucian classics, an activity that required knowledge of Chinese and showed the dedication of the state to learning. This revival may have led to a key technological breakthrough in printing technology. Koreans had begun using Chinese woodblock printing in the 700s. This technology worked well in China, where a large number of buyers wanted copies of a comparatively small number of texts. But in Korea, the comparatively few literate men had interests in a wide range of texts. Movable wooden or ceramic type appeared in Korea in the early thirteenth century and may have been invented there. But the texts were frequently inaccurate and difficult to read. In the 1400s Yi printers, working directly with the king, developed a reliable device to anchor the pieces of type to the printing plate: they replaced the old beeswax adhesive with solid copper frames. This improved the legibility of the printed page, and high-volume, accurate production became possible. Combined with the phonetic han'gul (HAHN-goor) writing system, this printing technology laid the foundation for a high literacy rate in Korea.

Yi publications told readers how to produce and use fertilizer, transplant rice seedlings, and engineer reservoirs. Building on Eurasian knowledge imported by the Mongols and introduced under the Koryo, Yi scholars developed a meteorological science of their own. They invented or redesigned instruments to

Yi (1392–1910) The Yi dynasty ruled Korea after the fall of the Koryo kingdom.

Movable Type The improvement of cast bronze tiles, each showing a single character, eliminated the need to cast or carve whole pages. Individual tiles—the ones shown are Korean—could be moved from page frame to page frame and gave an even and pleasing appearance. All parts of East Asia eventually adopted this form of printing for cheap, popular books. In the mid-1400s Korea also experimented with a fully phonetic form of writing, which in combination with movable type allowed Koreans unprecedented levels of literacy and access to printed works.   Courtesy, Yushin Yoo

measure wind speed and rainfall and perfected a calendar based on minute comparisons of the Chinese and Islamic systems.

In agriculture, farmers expanded the cultivation of cash crops, the reverse of what was happening in Ming China. Cotton, the primary crop, enjoyed such high value that the state accepted it for tax payments. The Yi army used cotton uniforms, and cotton became the favored fabric of the Korean elite. With cotton gins and spinning wheels powered by water, Korea advanced more rapidly than China in mechanization and began to export considerable amounts of cotton to China and Japan.

Although both the Yuan and the Ming withheld the formula for gunpowder from the Korean government, Korean officials acquired the information by subterfuge. By the later 1300s they had mounted cannon on ships that patrolled against pirates and used gunpowder-driven arrow launchers against enemy personnel and the rigging of enemy ships. Combined with skills in armoring ships, these techniques made the small Yi navy a formidable defense force.

Political Transformation in Japan, 1274–1500

Having secured Korea, the Mongols looked toward Japan, a target they could easily reach from Korea. Their first thirty-thousand-man invasion force in 1274 included Mongol cavalry and archers and sailors from Korea and northeastern Asia. Its weaponry included light catapults and incendiary and explosive projectiles of Chinese manufacture. The Mongol forces landed successfully and decimated the Japanese cavalry, but a great storm on Hakata (HAH-kah-tah) Bay on the north side of Kyushu (KYOO-shoo) Island prevented the establishment of a beachhead and forced the Mongols to sail back to Korea.

The invasion hastened social and political changes that were already under way. Under the Kamakura (kah-mah-KOO-rah) Shogunate established in 1185—another powerful family actually exercised control—the shogun, or military leader, distributed land and privileges to his followers. In return they paid him tribute and supplied him with soldiers. This stable, but decentralized, system depended on balancing the power of regional warlords. Lords in the north and east of Japan's main island were remote from those in the south and west. Beyond devotion to the emperor and the shogun, little united them until the terrifying Mongol threat materialized.

After the return of his fleet, Khubilai sent envoys to Japan demanding submission. Japanese leaders executed them and prepared for war. The shogun took steps to centralize his military government. The effect was to increase the influence of warlords from the south and west of Honshu (Japan's main island) and from the island of Kyushu acting under the shogun's orders, because this was where invasion seemed most likely.

Military planners studied Mongol tactics and retrained and outfitted Japanese warriors for defense against advanced weaponry. Farm laborers drafted from all over the country constructed defensive fortifications. This effort demanded, for the first time, a national system to move resources toward western points rather than toward the imperial or shogunal centers to the east.

The Mongols attacked in 1281. They brought 140,000 warriors, including many non-Mongols, as well as thousands of horses, in hundreds of ships. However, the wall the Japanese had built to cut off Hakata Bay from the mainland deprived the Mongol forces of a reliable landing point. Japanese swordsmen

Defending Japan Japanese warriors board Mongol warships with swords to prevent the landing of the invasion force in 1281.

rowed out and boarded the Mongol ships lingering offshore. Their superb steel swords shocked the invaders. After a prolonged standoff, a typhoon struck and sank perhaps half of the Mongol ships. The remainder sailed away, never again to harass Japan. The Japanese gave thanks to the "wind of the Gods"—*kamikaze* (KUM-i-kuh-zee)—for driving away the Mongols.

Nevertheless, the Mongol threat continued to influence Japanese development. Prior to his death in 1294, Khubilai had in mind a third invasion. His successors did not carry through with it, but the shoguns did not know that the Mongols had given up the idea. They rebuilt coastal defenses well into the fourteenth century, helping to consolidate the social position of Japan's warrior elite and stimulating the development of a national infrastructure for trade and communication. But the Kamakura Shogunate, based on regionally collected and regionally dispersed revenues, suffered financial strain in trying to pay for centralized road and defense systems.

Between 1333 and 1338 the emperor Go-Daigo broke the centuries-old tradition of imperial seclusion and aloofness from government and tried to reclaim power from the shoguns. This ignited a civil war that destroyed the Kamakura system. In 1338, with the Mongol threat waning, the **Ashikaga** (ah-shee-KAH-gah) **Shogunate** took control at the imperial center of Kyoto.

Provincial warlords enjoyed renewed independence. Around their imposing castles, they sponsored the development of market towns, religious institutions, and schools. The application of technologies imported in earlier periods, including water wheels, improved plows, and Champa rice, increased agricultural productivity. Growing wealth and relative peace stimulated artistic creativity, mostly reflecting Zen Buddhist beliefs held by the warrior elite. In the simple elegance of architecture and gardens, in the contemplative landscapes of artists, and in the eerie, stylized performances of the Noh theater, the aesthetic code of Zen became established in the Ashikaga era.

Despite the technological advancement, artistic productivity, and rapid urbanization of this period, competition among warlords and their followers led to regional wars. By the later 1400s these conflicts resulted in the near destruction of the warlords. The great Onin War in 1477 left Kyoto devastated and the Ashikaga Shogunate a central government in name

kamikaze The "divine wind" that the Japanese credited with blowing Mongol invaders away from their shores in 1281.

Ashikaga Shogunate (1338–1573) The second of Japan's military governments headed by a shogun (a military ruler). Sometimes called the Muromachi Shogunate.

National Museum of Japanese History/DNP

Noh Drama Performance This slow, rhythmic, chanted form of drama appealed to the military elite with its stories of warriors, women, gods, and demons. The minimal stage is normally bare except for a painting at the rear of a pine tree, symbolizing the means by which deities descend to earth, and a narrow bridge to the left by which major actors enter the stage. The actors wear masks and lavish costumes. Four instrumentalists playing a flute and three types of drum punctuate the chanting.

only. Ambitious but low-ranking warriors, some with links to trade with the continent, began to scramble for control of the provinces.

After the fall of the Yuan in 1368 Japan resumed overseas trade, exporting raw materials and swords, as well as folding fans, invented in Japan during the period of isolation. Japan's primary imports from China were books and porcelain. The volatile political environment in Japan gave rise to partnerships between warlords and local merchants. All worked to strengthen their own towns and treasuries through overseas commerce or, sometimes, through piracy.

The Emergence of Vietnam, 1200–1500

Before the first Mongol attack in 1257, the states of Annam (northern Vietnam) and Champa (southern Vietnam) had clashed frequently. Annam (once called Dai Viet) looked toward China and had once been subject to the Tang. Chinese political ideas, social philosophies, dress, religion, and language heavily influenced its official culture. Champa related more closely to the trading

SECTION REVIEW

- Mongol conquest devastated Korea, but Mongol rule opened it to new ideas and technologies.

- The Yi dynasty succeeded the Koryo and fostered local identity while encouraging economic expansion and technological innovation.

- In Japan, the Mongol threat forced military and organizational innovations, but the expense of these defenses weakened the Kamakura Shogunate.

- Go-Daigo's failed attempt to reassert imperial power resulted in the rise of the Ashikaga Shogunate.

- The warring states of Vietnam avoided Mongol conquest but paid tribute to the Yuan Empire.

- After the Ming withdrawal, Annam conquered Champa, establishing a unified state on both Confucian and local practices.

networks of the Indian Ocean; its official culture was strongly influenced by Indian religion, language, architecture, and dress.

Champa's relationship with China depended in part on how close its enemy Annam was to China at any particular time. During the Song period Annam was neither formally subject to China nor particularly threatening to Champa militarily, so Champa inaugurated a trade and tribute relationship with China that spread fast-ripening Champa rice throughout East Asia.

The Mongols exacted tribute from both Annam and Champa until the fall of the Yuan Empire in 1368. Mongol political and military ambitions were mostly focused elsewhere, however, which minimized their impact on politics and culture. The two Vietnamese kingdoms soon resumed their warfare. When Annam moved its army to reinforce its southern border, Ming troops occupied the capital, Hanoi, and installed a puppet government. Almost thirty years elapsed before Annam regained independence and resumed a tributary status. By then the Ming were turning to meet Mongol challenges to their north. In a series of ruthless campaigns, Annam terminated Champa's independence, and by 1500 the ancestor of the modern state of Vietnam, still called Annam, had been born.

The new state still relied on Confucian bureaucratic government and an examination system, but some practices differed from those in China. The Vietnamese legal code, for example, preserved group landowning and decision making within the villages, as well as women's property rights. Both developments probably had roots in an early rural culture based on the growing of rice in wet paddies; by this time the Annamese considered them distinctive features of their own culture.

Conclusion

The Mongols were the most successful warriors the world had ever seen. In less than a hundred years, they had conquered an empire that covered half of Eurasia and reached from Poland to Vietnam. And yet half a century later, their empire had broken apart and they had lost most of what they had gained. Why were their conquests so short-lived compared with those of the Romans or the Arabs?

The Mongols, though ferocious warriors, were too few in number to manage a huge empire, and so they turned to the peoples they had conquered—Chinese, Persians, Turks, and Arabs—to carry out the tasks of administration. They were famous for tolerating many religions and cultures among the people who accepted their rule, but they had no common religion or ideology upon which to build a lasting political culture. Some Mongols converted to Islam, others to Buddhism, and yet others became Chinese in language and culture. As the Mongol armies were widely scattered, subject peoples whose culture had never been erased by the Mongols reasserted themselves politically and militarily.

Once Mongol rule was in place, travel across the breadth of Eurasia became safer and easier than it had ever been before or was to be for centuries thereafter. Trade flourished, as did the spread of ideas and technologies. Yet with trade came the plague, which decimated all the regions that they occupied. When the subject peoples reasserted themselves, they remembered the Mongols for the violence and brutality of their conquest and for the disease they carried. Unlike the Roman or the Arabs, the Mongols did not leave a legacy of culture, administration, or religion, only memories of death and destruction.

CHAPTER REVIEW

 Download the MP3 audio file of the Chapter Review to listen to on the go.

What accounts for the magnitude and speed of the Mongol conquests? (page 287)

Nomadic mobility and endurance, expertise in military technology, and systematic army organization made the armies of Genghis Khan all but invincible. While the Mongols did not usually outnumber their enemies, they were experts on horseback and used superior bows. Turkic pastoral peoples who suffered defeat often enrolled in the Mongol ranks, thus magnifying the power of the Mongols themselves.

How did Mongol expansion and Islam affect each other? (page 294)

As rivalries mounted between the Il-khan and Golden Horde states, Islam became a point of contention. Rulers who converted to Islam were initially lax in their observance and affiliations. The Il-khans came to value urban Muslim culture, but they taxed farmers mercilessly.

This contributed to a weakness that allowed the Golden Horde to make inroads on Il-khan territory. Meanwhile, Timur rose to power in Jagadai territory and undertook wide-ranging conquests. The Il-khans, Timur, and his successors presided over a flowering of Islamic culture that drew upon Iranian and Chinese cultural elements to contribute notable achievements in historical writing, art, mathematics, and astronomy.

What benefits resulted from the integration of Eurasia into the Mongol Empire? (page 297)

The Great Khans attracted emissaries and traders from all over Eurasia to their court, revitalizing the Silk Road. Cultural contact between east and west had greater long-term impact than the Mongols' political power. Muslim astronomers and calendar makers found a welcome reception in China, and Chinese artistic styles became popular in Iran. Mongol occupation, or the threat of Mongol conquest, also helped non-Mongol political leaders galvanize popular support for local state building.

How did Mongol rule in China foster cultural and scientific exchange? (page 300)

In China, Yuan rule reestablished connections with Inner Asia that had earlier benefited Tang rule (see Chapter 11). The empire rewarded skills more than ethnic or linguistic identity. Beijing, the Yuan capital, developed a dynamic cultural scene, even though the turmoil of the period also produced war casualties, spread of disease, and migration to southern China.

In what ways did the Ming Empire continue or discontinue Mongol practices? (page 302)

The Ming overthrew the Yuan and reaffirmed Chinese ethnicity as a basis for rule. Leaving Beijing, they located their capital in the south and relied on study of the Confucian classics and the examination system for choosing imperial officials. Nevertheless, Mongols still served in the army, and after a time Beijing again became the capital. Though some Yuan administrative practices continued, contact and trade with Inner Asia dwindled because of political disunity in the old Mongol core area.

What are some of the similarities and differences in how Korea and Japan responded to the Mongol threat? (page 305)

The conquered Korean rulers remained loyal to the Yuan and benefited from new technologies and administrative

techniques. When the Yuan fell, however, a Korean dynasty emerged that stressed non-Mongol ethnicity and reviled the earlier Mongol domination, even while retaining many of the innovations of that period.

After twice repelling Mongol invasions, Japan remained highly militarized. Paradoxically, regional warlords embraced cultural innovations, many of Chinese inspiration, that subsequently became central to Japanese identity. Zen Buddhism, Noh drama, and the ritual of the tea ceremony united the Japanese elite even as the warlords, with their samurai armies, seized control from the ineffective imperial government.

Key Terms

Mongols *(p. 287)*	tsar *(p. 299)*
Genghis Khan *(p. 287)*	Ottoman Empire *(p. 300)*
nomadism *(p. 287)*	Khubilai Khan *(p. 300)*
Yuan Empire *(p. 293)*	lama *(p. 300)*
bubonic plague *(p. 293)*	Beijing *(p. 301)*
Il-khan *(p. 294)*	Ming Empire *(p. 303)*
Golden Horde *(p. 294)*	Yongle *(p. 304)*
Timur *(p. 295)*	Zheng He *(p. 304)*
Rashid al-Din *(p. 296)*	Yi *(p. 306)*
Nasir al-Din Tusi *(p. 296)*	kamikaze *(p. 308)*
Alexander Nevskii *(p. 298)*	Ashikaga Shogunate *(p. 308)*

Web Resources

Pronunciation Guide
Interactive Maps
- MAP 12.1 The Mongol Domains in Eurasia in 1300
- MAP 12.2 The Ming Empire and Its Allies, 1368–1500

Primary Source
- Description of the World
Answer to the History in Focus Question
See photo on page 294, "Passport."

 Visit the CourseMate website at www.cengagebrain.com for additional study tools and review materials for this chapter.

Tropical Africa and Asia

© Cengage Learning

Visit the CourseMate website at **www.cengagebrain.com** for additional study tools and review materials for this chapter.

Sultan Abu Bakr (a-BOO BAK-uhr) customarily offered hospitality to distinguished visitors to his city of Mogadishu, an Indian Ocean port on the northeast coast of Africa. In 1331, he provided food and lodging for Muhammad ibn Abdullah **Ibn Battuta** (IB-uhn ba-TOO-tuh) (1304–1369), a young Muslim scholar from Morocco who had set out to explore the Islamic world. Having already made a pilgrimage to Mecca and traveled throughout the Middle East, Ibn Battuta was touring the trading cities of the Red Sea and East Africa. Subsequent travels took him to Central Asia and India, China and Southeast Asia, Muslim Spain, and sub-Saharan West Africa. Recounting some 75,000 miles (120,000 kilometers) of travel over twenty-nine years, Ibn Battuta's journal provides invaluable information on these lands.

Hospitality being considered a noble virtue among Muslims, regardless of physical and cultural differences, his reception at Mogadishu mirrored that at other cities. Ibn Battuta noted that Sultan Abu Bakr had skin darker than his own and spoke a different native language (Somali), but as brothers in faith, they prayed together at Friday services, where the sultan greeted his foreign guest in Arabic, the common language of the Islamic world: "You are heartily welcome, and you have honored our land and given us pleasure." When Sultan Abu Bakr and his jurists heard and decided cases after the mosque service, they used the religious law familiar in all Muslim lands.

In addition to the religion of Islam, the diverse peoples of Africa and southern Asia whom Ibn Battuta visited were also linked by the tropical environment itself. A network of overland and maritime routes joined their lands (see Chapter 8), providing avenues for the spread of beliefs and technologies, as well as goods. Ibn Battuta traveled with merchants who regularly sailed down the coast of East Africa. He joined trading caravans across the Sahara to West Africa. His path to India followed overland trade routes, and a merchant ship carried him on to China. This chapter discusses the lands that Ibn Battuta visited in his long voyages, the natural geographic features they shared, and the commercial, cultural, and religious links that tied them together.

Tropical Lands and Peoples

How did environmental differences shape cultural differences in tropical Africa and Asia?

To obtain food, the people who inhabited the tropical regions of Africa and Asia used methods that generations of experimentation had proved successful, whether at the desert's edge, in grasslands, or in tropical rain forests. Much of their success lay in learning how to blend human activities with the natural order, but they also modified the environment to suit their needs with irrigation works and mining.

The Tropical Environment

Because of the angle of earth's axis, the sun's rays warm the **tropics** year-round. The equator marks the center of the tropical zone, and the Tropic of Cancer and Tropic of Capricorn mark its outer limits. Africa lies almost entirely within the tropics, as do southern Arabia, most of India, and all of the Southeast Asian mainland and islands.

Lacking the hot and cold seasons of temperate lands, the rainy and dry seasons of the Afro-Asian tropics derive from wind patterns across the surrounding oceans. Winds from a permanent high-pressure air mass over the South Atlantic deliver heavy rainfall to the western coast of Africa during much of the year. However, in December and January, large high-pressure zones over northern Africa and Arabia produce a southward movement of dry air that limits the inland penetration of the moist ocean winds.

In the lands around the Indian Ocean, the rainy and dry seasons reflect the influence of alternating

Ibn Battuta (1304–1369) Moroccan Muslim scholar, the most widely traveled individual of his time. He wrote a detailed account of his visits to Islamic lands from China to Spain and the western Sudan.
tropics Equatorial region between the Tropic of Cancer and the Tropic of Capricorn. It is characterized by generally warm or hot temperatures year-round, though much variation exists due to altitude and other factors. Temperate zones north and south of the tropics usually have a winter season.

East African Pastoralists Herding large and small livestock has long been a way of life in the drier parts of the tropics. These herders, perhaps Massai, bring their cattle, goats, and sheep to a river to drink.

© Victor Englebert

History in Focus *What vegetation do you see in the picture? What do you think herds of animals do to the vegetation near watering places? How can herders in dry places balance their animals' need for both water and food? Find the answer online.*

winds known as **monsoons**. Between April and August, as the continent of Asia heats up more than the surrounding seas, it forms a low-pressure zone that creates a northward movement of air from the Indian Ocean (the southwest monsoon) and brings southern Asia the heavy rains of its wet season. From December to March, as the continent cools off, a high pressure zone develops over Tibet and the Himalaya (him-AH-LAY-uh) Mountains that forces air to flow outward toward the ocean: the dry northeast monsoon.

Areas with the heaviest rainfall—the broad belt along the equator in coastal West Africa and West-Central Africa, parts of coastal India, and Southeast Asia—have dense rain forests. Lighter rains produce other forest patterns. The English word *jungle* comes from an Indian word for the tangled undergrowth in the forests that once covered most of India.

Some other parts of the tropics rarely see rain at all. The world's largest desert, the Sahara, stretches across northern Africa and continues eastward across Arabia, southern Iran, Pakistan, and northwest India. Another desert occupies southwestern Africa. Most of tropical India and Africa falls between the deserts and rain forests and experiences moderate rainy seasons. These lands range from fairly wet woodlands to the much drier grasslands characteristic of much of East Africa.

Altitude produces other climatic variations. Thin atmospheres at high altitudes hold less heat than atmospheres at lower elevations. Snow covers some of the volcanic mountains of eastern Africa all or part of the year. The snowcapped Himalayas that form India's northern frontier rise so high that they block cold air from moving south and thus give northern India a more tropical climate than its latitude would suggest. The plateaus of inland Africa and the Deccan (DEK-ahn) Plateau of central India also enjoy cooler temperatures than the coastal plains.

Human Ecosystems

Thinkers in temperate lands once imagined that surviving in the tropics was simply a matter of picking wild fruit off trees. A careful observer touring the tropics in 1200 would have noticed, however, many differences in societies deriving from their particular ecosystems—that is, from how human groups used the

---

monsoons Seasonal winds in the Indian Ocean caused by the differences in temperature between the rapidly heating and cooling landmasses of Africa and Asia and the slowly changing ocean waters. These strong and predictable winds have long been ridden across the open sea by sailors, and the large amounts of rainfall that they deposit on parts of India, Southeast Asia, and China permit the cultivation of several crops a year.

Chronology

	The Arab Lands	Iran and Central Asia
1200		**1206** Delhi Sultanate founded in India
	1230s Mali Empire founded	
	1270 Solomonic dynasty in Ethiopia founded	
1300		**1298** Delhi Sultanate annexes Gujarat
	1324–1325 Mansa Musa's pilgrimage to Mecca	
1400		**1398** Timur sacks Delhi; Delhi Sultanate declines
	1400s Great Zimbabwe at its peak	
	1433 Tuareg retake Timbuktu; Mali declines	
1500		**1500** Port of Malacca at its peak

plants, animals, and other resources of their physical environments.

Domesticated plants and animals had become commonplace long before 1200, but people in some environments continued to rely primarily on hunting, fishing, and gathering. For Pygmy (PIG-mee) hunters in the dense forests of Central Africa, small size permitted pursuit of prey through dense undergrowth. Hunting also prevailed in the upper altitudes of the Himalayas and in some desert environments. A Portuguese expedition led by Vasco da Gama visited the arid coast of southwestern Africa in 1497 and saw there healthy people feeding themselves on "the flesh of seals, whales, and gazelles, and the roots of wild plants." Fishing, which was common along all the major lakes and rivers as well as in the oceans, might be combined with farming. The ocean fishermen of East Africa, Southeast Asia, and coastal India had boating skills that often led to engagement in ocean trade.

Herding provided sustenance in areas too arid for agriculture. Pastoralists consumed milk from their herds and traded hides and meat to farmers in return for grain and vegetables. The world's largest concentration of pastoralists inhabited the arid and semi-arid lands of northeastern Africa and Arabia. Like Ibn Battuta's host at Mogadishu, some Somalis lived in towns, but most grazed goats and camels in the desert hinterland of the Horn of Africa. The western Sahara sustained herds of sheep and camels belonging to the Tuareg (TWAH-reg), whose intimate knowledge of the desert made them invaluable as guides to caravans. Along the Sahara's southern edge the cattle-herding Fulani (foo-LAH-nee) people gradually extended their

range, and by 1500 they had spread throughout the western and central Sudan.

The density of agricultural populations reflected the adequacy of rainfall and soils. South and Southeast Asia were generally wetter than tropical Africa, making intensive cultivation possible. High yields supported dense populations. In 1200, over 100 million people lived in South and Southeast Asia, more than four-fifths of them on the fertile Indian mainland. Though a little less than the population of China, this was triple the number of people living in all of Africa and nearly double the number in Europe.

India's lush vegetation led one Middle Eastern writer to call it "the most agreeable abode on earth. Its delightful plains resemble the garden of Paradise."[1] Rice cultivation dominated in the fertile Ganges plain of northeast India, mainland Southeast Asia, and southern China. In drier areas, farmers grew grains—wheat, sorghum, and millet, and legumes such as peas and beans whose ripening cycles matched the pattern of the rainy and dry seasons. Tubers and tree crops characterized farming in rain-forest clearings.

The spread of farming, including the movement to Africa of Asian crops like yams, cocoyams, and bananas, did not necessarily change the natural environment. In most of sub-Saharan Africa and much of Southeast Asia, extensive rather than intensive cultivation prevailed. Instead of enriching fields with manure and vegetable compost so they could be cultivated year after year, farmers abandoned fields when the natural fertility of the soil fell and cleared new fields—a type of agriculture called swidden. Ashes from the brush, grasses, and tree limbs they cut down and burned boosted the new fields' fertility. Shifting to new land every few years made efficient use of labor in areas with comparatively poor soils.

Water Systems and Irrigation

The inland delta of the Niger River received naturally fertilizing annual floods with which farmers could grow rice for sale to the trading cities along the Niger bend. Elsewhere, tropical farmers had to move the water to their crops. In Vietnam, Java, Malaya, and Burma, farmers had built terraces on hillsides to conserve some of the monsoon rainfall for growing rice during the dry season. North and south India also had water-storage dams and irrigation canals. Villagers in southeast India built stone and earthen dams across rivers to store water for gradual release through elaborate irrigation canals. Extended over many generations, these canals irrigated a wide area.

As had been true since the days of the first river-valley civilizations (see Chapter 1), governments built and controlled the largest irrigation systems. The **Delhi** (DEL-ee) **Sultanate** (1206–1526) in northern India acquired extensive new water-control systems. Ibn Battuta admired a large reservoir constructed in the first quarter of the thirteenth century that supplied the city of Delhi with water. As the water level fell during the dry season, farmers planted sugar cane, cucumbers, and melons along the reservoir's rim. In the fourteenth century, the Delhi sultan built in the Ganges plain a network of irrigation canals that remained unsurpassed until the nineteenth century. Such systems made it possible to grow crops throughout the year.

Since the tenth century, the Indian Ocean island of Ceylon (modern Sri Lanka [shree LAHNG-kuh]) had been home to the world's greatest concentration of irrigation reservoirs and canals. These facilities supported the large population of the Sinhalese (sin-huh-LEEZ) kingdom in arid northern Ceylon. In Southeast Asia, another impressive system of reservoirs and canals served Cambodia's capital city, Angkor (ANG-kor).

Between 1250 and 1400, however, the irrigation complex in Ceylon fell into ruin when invaders from south India disrupted the Sinhalese government. As a result, malaria spread by mosquitoes breeding in the irrigation canals ravaged the population. In the fifteenth century, the great Cambodian system fell into ruin when the government that maintained it collapsed. Neither system was ever rebuilt. The vulnerability of complex irrigation systems built by powerful governments contrasts with village-based irrigation systems. Though invasion and natural calamity might damage the latter, they usually bounced back because they depended on local initiative and simpler technologies.

Mineral Resources

The most productive metal trade in the tropics, ironworking, provided the hoes, axes, and knives farmers used to clear and cultivate their fields. Between 1200 and 1500, the rain forests of coastal West Africa and Southeast Asia opened up for farming. Iron also supplied spear and arrow points, needles, and nails. Indian metalsmiths became known for forging strong and beautiful swords. In Africa, many people attributed magical powers to iron smelters and blacksmiths.

Copper and its alloys had special importance in the Copperbelt of southeastern Africa during the fourteenth and fifteenth centuries. Smelters cast the metal into large X-shaped ingots (metal castings), and local coppersmiths worked these into wire and decorative objects. In the western Sudan, Ibn Battuta described a mining town that produced two sizes of copper bars that served as currency in place of coins. Some coppersmiths in West Africa cast copper and brass (an alloy of copper and zinc) statues and heads that now rank as masterpieces of world art. They utilized the "lost-wax" method, in which molten metal melts a thin layer of wax sandwiched between clay forms, replacing the "lost" wax with hard metal.

African gold moved in quantity across the Sahara and into the Indian Ocean and Red Sea trades. Some came from streambeds along the upper Niger River and farther south in modern Ghana (GAH-nuh). In the hills south of the Zambezi (zam-BEE-zee) River, archaeologists have discovered thousands of mineshafts, dating from 1200, that were sunk up to 100

Delhi Sultanate (1206–1526) Centralized Indian empire, created by Muslim invaders.

feet (30 meters) into the ground to get at gold ores. Although panning for gold remained important in the streams descending from the mountains of northern India, the gold and silver mines in India seem to have been exhausted by this period. Thus, Indians imported from Southeast Asia and Africa considerable quantities of gold for jewelry and temple decoration.

New Islamic Empires

Under what circumstances did the first Islamic empires arise in Africa and India?

The empires of Mali in West Africa and Delhi in northern India, the largest and richest tropical states of the period between 1200 and 1500, both utilized administrative and military systems introduced from the Islamic heartland. Yet **Mali**, an indigenous African dynasty that had earlier adopted Islam through the peaceful influence of Muslim merchants and scholars, differed in many ways from the Delhi Sultanate founded and ruled by invading Turkish and Afghan Muslims. The wealth of Mali depended on trans-Saharan trade, but long-distance trade played only a minor role in Delhi.

Mali in the Western Sudan

Muslim rule beginning in the seventh century (see Chapter 9) greatly stimulated increased trade along the routes that crossed the

Sahara. In the centuries that followed, the faith of Muhammad gradually spread to the lands south of the desert, which the Arabs called the *bilad al-sudan* (bih-LAD uhs-soo-DAN), "land of the blacks."

Muslim Berbers invading out of the desert in 1076 caused the collapse of Ghana, the empire that preceded Mali in the western Sudan (see Chapter 9), but their conquest did little to spread Islam. To the east, the Muslim attacks that destroyed the Christian Nubian kingdoms on the upper Nile in the late thirteenth century opened that area to Muslim influences, but Christian Ethiopia successfully withstood Muslim advances. Instead, Islam's spread south of the Sahara usually followed a pattern of gradual and peaceful conversion. The expansion of commercial contacts in the western Sudan and on the East African coast greatly promoted the conversion process. Most Africans found meaning and benefit in the teachings of Islam. Takrur (TAHK-roor) in the far western Sudan became the first sub-Saharan African state to adopt the new faith around 1030.

Shortly after 1200, Takrur expanded under King Sumanguru (soo-muhn-GOO-roo), only to suffer a major defeat some thirty years later at the hands of Sundiata (soon-JAH-tuh), the upstart leader of the Malinke (muh-LING-kay) people. Though both leaders professed Islam, Malinke legends recall their battles as clashes between powerful magicians, suggesting how much old and new beliefs mingled. Sumanguru could reportedly appear and disappear at will, assume dozens of shapes, and catch arrows in midflight. Sundiata defeated Sumanguru's much larger forces through superior military maneuvers and by successfully wounding his adversary with a special arrow that robbed him of his magical powers. This victory was followed by others that created Sundiata's Mali Empire (see Map 13.1).

Mali, the empire that grew from Sundiata's victories, depended on a well-developed agricultural base and control of the regional and trans-Saharan trade routes, as had Ghana before it. Mali, however, controlled a greater area than Ghana, including not

Mali Empire created by indigenous Muslims in western Sudan of West Africa from the thirteenth to fifteenth century. It was famous for its role in the trans-Saharan gold trade.

Map 13.1 Africa, 1200–1500 Many African states had beneficial links to the trade that crossed the Sahara and the Indian Ocean. Before 1500, sub-Saharan Africa's external ties were primarily with the Islamic world. © Cengage Learning

 Interactive Map

only the core trading area of the upper Niger but also the gold fields of the Niger headwaters to the southwest. Moreover, its rulers fostered the spread of Islam among the empire's political and trading elites. Control of the gold and copper trades and contacts with North African Muslim traders gave Mali unprecedented prosperity.

Under the ruler **Mansa Kankan Musa** (MAHN-suh KAHN-kahn MOO-suh) (r. 1312–1337), the empire's reputation for wealth spread far and wide. Mansa Musa's pilgrimage to Mecca in 1324–1325 fulfilled his personal duty as a Muslim and at the same time put on display his exceptional wealth. He traveled with a large entourage. Besides his senior wife and five hundred of her ladies in waiting and their slaves, one account says there were also sixty thousand porters and a vast caravan of camels carrying supplies and provisions. For purchases and gifts, he

brought along eighty packages of gold, each weighing 122 ounces (3.8 kilograms). In addition, five hundred slaves each carried a golden staff. Mansa Musa dispersed so many gifts when he passed through Cairo that the value of gold was depressed for years.

On his return from this pilgrimage, Mansa Musa built new mosques and opened Quran schools in the cities along the Niger bend. Ibn Battuta, who visited Mali from 1352 to 1354 during the reign of Mansa Musa's successor, Mansa Suleiman (MAHN-suh SOO-lay-mahn) (r. 1341–1360), lauded the Malians for their faithful recitation of prayers and their zeal in teaching

Mansa Kankan Musa Ruler of Mali (r. 1312–1337). His pilgrimage through Egypt to Mecca in 1324–1325 established the empire's reputation for wealth in the Mediterranean world.

King and Queen of Ife This copper-alloy work shows the royal couple of the Yoruba kingdom of Ife, the oldest and most sacred of the Yoruba kingdoms of southwestern Nigeria. The casting dates to the period between 1100 and 1500, except for the reconstruction of the male's face, the original of which shattered in 1957 when the road builder who found it accidentally struck it with his pick.   Andre Held Collection/The Bridgeman Art Library

leatherworking. The central Sudanic state of Kanem-Bornu (KAH-nuhm-BOR-noo) also expanded in the late fifteenth century from the ancient kingdom of Kanem, whose rulers had accepted Islam in about 1085. At its peak around 1250, Kanem had absorbed the state of Bornu south and west of Lake Chad and gained control of routes crossing the central Sahara. As Kanem-Bornu's armies conquered new territories, they also spread the rule of Islam.

The Delhi Sultanate in India

Having long ago lost the defensive unity of the Gupta Empire (see Chapter 5), the divided states of northwest India fell prey to raids by Afghan warlords beginning in the early eleventh century. In the last decades of the twelfth century, a Turkish dynasty armed with powerful crossbows captured the northern Indian cities of Lahore and Delhi. One partisan Muslim chronicler wrote: "The city [Delhi] and its vicinity was freed from idols and idol-worship, and in the sanctuaries of the images of the [Hindu] Gods, mosques were raised by the worshippers of one God."[2] Turkish adventurers from Central Asia flocked to join the invading armies, overwhelming the small Indian states, which were often at war with one another.

Between 1206 and 1236, the Muslim invaders extended their rule over the Hindu princes and chiefs in much of northern India. Sultan Iltutmish (il-TOOT-mish) (r. 1211–1236) consolidated the conquest in a series of military expeditions that made his realm the largest in India (see Map 13.2). He also secured official recognition of the Delhi Sultanate as a Muslim state by the caliph of Baghdad. Although pillaging continued, especially on the frontiers, the incorporation of

children the Quran. He also reported that "complete and general safety" prevailed in the vast territories ruled by Suleiman and that foreign travelers had no reason to fear being robbed or having their goods confiscated if they died. Two centuries after its founding, Mali began to disintegrate. Mansa Suleiman's successors could not prevent rebellions breaking out among the diverse peoples subjected to Malinke rule, while other groups attacked from without. In 1433 the desert Tuareg retook their city of Timbuktu (tim-buk-TOO), and by 1500 the rulers of Mali had dominion over little more than the Malinke heartland.

The cities of the upper Niger survived Mali's collapse, but some trade and intellectual life moved east to the central Sudan. Shortly after 1450, several Hausa city-states officially adopted Islam and took on importance as manufacturing and trading centers, becoming famous for cotton textiles and

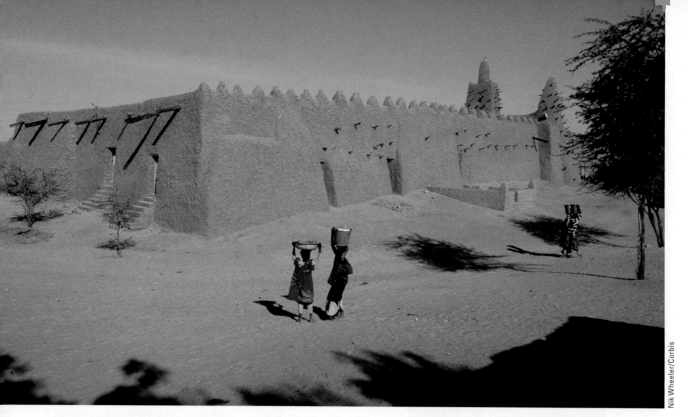

Dijinguere Ber Mosque in Timbuktu Built almost entirely of earth and organic materials, this fourteenth-century mosque can accommodate 2,000 worshippers. Mansa Kankan Musa, the most famous ruler of the Empire of Mali, is said to have paid Abu Ishaq al-Sahili, a native of Granada in Muslim Spain, 200 kilograms of gold for designing this masterful combination of Islamic and African traditions.

north India into the Islamic world marked the beginning of the invaders' transformation from brutal conquerors to somewhat more benign rulers. Muslim commanders extended protection to the conquered, freeing them from persecution in return for payment of a special tax. Yet Hindus never forgot the intolerance and destruction of their first contacts with the invaders.

Iltutmish astonished his ministers by passing over his weak and pleasure-seeking sons and designating as his heir his beloved and talented daughter Raziya (rah-ZEE-uh). When they questioned the unprecedented idea of a woman ruling a Muslim state, he said, "My sons are devoted to the pleasures of youth: no one of them is qualified to be king. . . . There is no one more competent to guide the State than my daughter." Her brother—who delighted in riding his elephant through the bazaar, showering the crowds with coins—ruled ineptly for seven months before the ministers relented and put Raziya on the throne. A chronicler who knew her explained why this able ruler lasted less than four years (r. 1236–1240):

Sultan Raziya was a great monarch. She was wise, just, and generous, a benefactor to her kingdom, a dispenser of justice, the protector of her subjects, and the leader of her armies. She was endowed with all the qualities befitting a king, but she was not born of the right sex, and so in the estimation of men all these virtues were worthless. May God have mercy upon her![3]

Doing her best to prove herself a proper king, Raziya dressed like a man and led her troops atop an elephant. In the end, however, the Turkish chiefs imprisoned her. She escaped, but she was killed by a robber soon after.

After a half-century of stagnation and rebellion, the ruthless but efficient policies of Sultan Ala-ud-din Khalji (uh-LAH-uh-DEEN KAL-jee) (r. 1296–1316) increased control over the empire's outlying provinces. Successful frontier raids and high taxes kept his treasury full, wage and price controls in Delhi kept down the cost of maintaining a large army, and a network of spies stifled intrigue. When a Mongol threat from Central Asia eased, Ala-ud-din's forces extended

Map 13.2 South and Southeast Asia, 1200–1500 The rise of new empires and the expansion of maritime trade reshaped the lives of many tropical Asians. © Cengage Learning

Interactive Map

the sultanate's southern flank, seizing the rich trading state of **Gujarat** (goo-juh-RAHT) in 1298, and then drove southward, briefly seizing the southern tip of the Indian peninsula.

When Ibn Battuta visited Delhi, Sultan Muhammad ibn Tughluq (TOOG-look) (r. 1325–1351) received him in his celebrated Hall of a Thousand Pillars. The world traveler praised the sultan's piety and generosity, but he also recounted his cruelties. The sultan enlarged the sultanate to its greatest extent at the expense of the independent Indian states but balanced his aggressive policy with religious toleration. He even attended Hindu religious festivals. However, his successor, Firuz Shah (fuh-ROOZ shah) (r. 1351–1388), alienated powerful Hindus by taxing the Brahmins, preferring to cultivate good relations with the Muslim elite. Muslim chroniclers praised him for constructing forty mosques, thirty colleges, and a hundred hospitals.

A small minority in a giant land, the Turkish rulers relied on terror to keep their subjects submissive, on harsh military reprisals to put down rebellion, and on pillage and high taxes to sustain the ruling elite in luxury and power. Though little different from most other large states of this time (including Mali) in being more a burden than a benefit to most of its subjects, the sultanate never lost the disadvantage of foreign origins and alien religious identity. Nevertheless, over time, the sultans did incorporate some Hindus into their administrations, and some members of the ruling elite also married women from prominent Hindu families, though the brides had to become Muslim.

Gujarat Region of western India famous for trade and manufacturing; the inhabitants are called Gujaratis.

321

Personal and religious rivalries within the Muslim elite, along with Hindu discontent, threatened the Delhi Sultanate whenever it showed weakness and finally hastened its end. In the mid-fourteenth century, Muslim nobles challenged the sultan's dominion and established the independent Bahmani (bah-MAHN-ee) kingdom (1347–1482) on the Deccan Plateau. Defending against the southward push of Bahmani armies, the Hindu states of south India united to form the Vijayanagar (vee-juh-yah-NAH-gar) Empire (1336–1565), which at its height controlled the rich trading ports on both coasts of south India and held Ceylon as a tributary state.

The elites of Vijayanagar and the Bahmani state turned a blind eye to religious differences when doing so favored their interests. Bahmani rulers sought to balance Muslim domination with the practical policies of incorporating the Hindu leaders into the government, marrying Hindu wives, and appointing Brahmins to high offices. Vijayanagar rulers hired Muslim horsemen and archers to strengthen their military forces and formed an alliance with the Muslim-ruled state of Gujarat.

By 1351, when all of south India had cast off Delhi's rule, much of north India rose in rebellion. In the east, Bengal broke away from the sultanate in 1338, becoming a center of the mystical Sufi tradition of Islam (see Chapter 9). In the west, Gujarat regained its independence by 1390. The weakening of Delhi's central authority tempted fresh Mongol interest in the area. In 1398, the Turko-Mongol leader Timur (see Chapter 12) captured the city of Delhi. When his armies withdrew the next year with vast quantities of loot and tens of thousands of captives, the largest city in southern Asia lay empty and in ruins. The Delhi Sultanate never recovered.

For all its shortcomings, the Delhi Sultanate triggered the development of centralized political authority in India. Prime ministers and provincial governors serving under the sultans established a bureaucracy, improved food production, promoted trade, and put in circulation a common currency. Despite the many conflicts that Muslim conquest and rule provoked, Islam gradually acquired a permanent place in South Asia.

Indian Ocean Trade

How did cultural and ecological differences promote trade, and in turn how did trade and other contacts promote state growth and the spread of Islam?

When the collapse of the Mongol Empire in the fourteenth century disrupted overland routes across Central Asia, the Indian Ocean assumed greater strategic importance in tying together the peoples of Eurasia and Africa. Between 1200 and 1500, the volume of trade in the Indian Ocean increased. The Indian Ocean routes also facilitated the spread of Islam.

Monsoon Mariners The prosperity of Islamic and Mongol empires in Asia, cities in Europe, and new kingdoms in Africa and Southeast Asia stimulated and contributed to the vitality of the Indian Ocean network. The demand for luxuries—precious metals and jewels, rare spices, fine textiles, and other manufactures—rose. Larger ships made shipments of bulk cargoes of ordinary cotton textiles, pepper, food grains (rice, wheat, barley), timber, horses, and other goods profitable.

Some goods were transported from one end of this trading network to the other, but few ships or crews made a complete circuit. Instead, the Indian Ocean trade divided into two legs: from the Middle East across the Arabian Sea to India and from India across the Bay of Bengal to Southeast Asia (see Map 13.2).

Shipyards in ports on the Malabar Coast (southwestern India) built large numbers of dhows (dows), the characteristic cargo and passenger ships of the Arabian Sea. They grew from an average capacity of 100 tons in 1200 to 400 tons in 1500. On a typical expedition, a dhow might sail west from India to Arabia and Africa on the northeast monsoon winds (December to March) and return on the southwest monsoons (April to August). Small dhows kept the coast in sight. Relying on the stars to guide them, skilled pilots steered large vessels by the quicker route straight across the water. A large dhow could sail from the Red Sea to mainland Southeast Asia in two to four months, but few did so. Eastbound cargoes and passengers from dhows reaching India were likely to be transferred to junks, which dominated the eastern half of the Indian Ocean and the South China Sea (see Environment and Technology: The Indian Ocean Dhow).

The largest, most technologically advanced, and most seaworthy vessels of this time, junks first appeared in China and spread with Chinese influence. Enormous nails held together hulls of heavy spruce or fir planks, in contrast with dhows, whose planks were sewn together with palm fiber. Below the deck, watertight compartments minimized flooding in case of damage to the ship's hull. According to Ibn Battuta, the largest junks had twelve sails made of bamboo and carried a crew of a thousand men, including four hundred soldiers. A large junk might accommodate a hundred passenger cabins and a cargo of over 1,000 tons. Junks dominated China's foreign shipping to Southeast Asia and India, but the Chinese did not control all of the junks that plied these waters. During the fifteenth century, similar vessels came out of shipyards in Bengal and Southeast Asia to be sailed by local crews.

Decentralized and cooperative commercial interests, rather than political authorities, connected the several regions that participated in the Indian Ocean trade. The **Swahili** (swah-HEE-lee) **Coast** supplied gold from inland areas of eastern Africa, and ports around the Arabian peninsula supplied horses and goods from the northern parts of the Middle East, the Mediterranean, and eastern Europe. Merchants in the cities of coastal India received goods from east and west, sold some locally, passed others along, and added Indian goods to the trade. The Strait of Malacca (meh-LAK-eh), between the eastern end of the

Indian Ocean and the South China Sea, provided a meeting point for trade from Southeast Asia, China, and the Indian Ocean. In each region, certain ports functioned as giant emporia, consolidating goods from smaller ports and inland areas for transport across the seas.

Africa: The Swahili Coast and Zimbabwe

Trade expanded steadily along the East African coast from about 1250, giving rise to between thirty and forty separate city-states by 1500. After 1200, masonry buildings as much as four stories high replaced mud and thatch dwellings, and archaeological findings include imported glass beads, Chinese porcelain, and other exotic goods. Coastal and island peoples shared a common culture and a language built on African grammar and vocabulary but enriched with many Arabic and Persian terms and written in Arabic script. In time, these people became known as "Swahili," from the Arabic name *sawahil* (suh-WAH-hil) *al-sudan*, meaning "shores of the blacks."

Sometime after Ibn Battuta's visit to Mogadishu in 1331, the more southerly city of Kilwa surpassed it as the Swahili Coast's most important commercial center (see Map 13.1). Ibn Battuta declared Kilwa "one of the most beautiful and well-constructed towns in the world." He noted its inhabitants' dark skins and Muslim piety, and he praised their ruler for the traditional Muslim virtues of humility and generosity.

What attracted the Arab and Iranian merchants whom oral traditions associate with the Swahili Coast's commercial expansion? By the late fifteenth century, Kilwa was annually exporting a ton of gold mined by inland Africans much farther south. Much of it came from or passed through a powerful state on the plateau south of the Zambezi River. At its peak in about 1400, its capital city, now known as **Great Zimbabwe**, occupied 193 acres (78 hectares) and had some 18,000 inhabitants.

Swahili Coast East African shores of the Indian Ocean between the Horn of Africa and the Zambezi River; from the Arabic *sawahil*, meaning "shores."

Great Zimbabwe City, now in ruins (in the modern African country of Zimbabwe), whose many stone structures were built between about 1250 and 1450, when it was a trading center and the capital of a large state.

environment & technology

The Indian Ocean Dhow

The sailing vessels that crossed the Indian Ocean shared the diversity of that trading area. The name by which we know them, dhow, comes from the Swahili language of the East African coast. The planks of teak from which their hulls were constructed were hewn from the tropical forests of south India and Southeast Asia. Their pilots, who navigated by stars at night, used the ancient technique that Arabs had used to find their way across the desert. Some pilots used a magnetic compass, which originated in China.

Dhows came in various sizes and designs, but all shared two distinctive features. The first was hull construction. The hulls of dhows consisted of planks that were sewn together, not nailed. Cord made of fiber from the husk of coconuts or other materials was passed through rows of holes drilled in the planks. Because cord is weaker than nails, outsiders considered this shipbuilding technique strange. Marco Polo fancifully suggested that it indicated sailors' fear that large ocean magnets would pull any nails out of their ships. More probable explanations are that pliant sewn hulls were cheaper to build than rigid nailed hulls and were less likely to be damaged if the ships ran aground on coral reefs.

The second distinctive feature of dhows was their triangular (lateen) sails made of palm leaves or cotton. The sails were suspended from tall masts and could be turned to catch the wind.

The sewn hull and lateen sails were technologies developed centuries earlier, but two innovations were

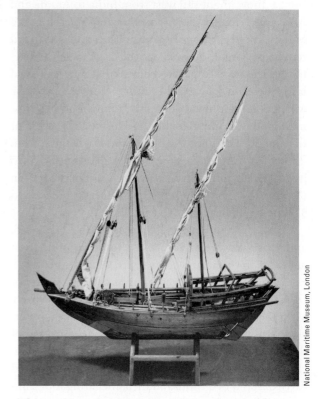

Dhow This model shows the vessel's main features.

National Maritime Museum, London

made between 1200 and 1500. First, a rudder positioned at the stern (rear end) of the ship replaced the large side oar that formerly had controlled steering. Second, shipbuilders increased the size of dhows to accommodate bulkier cargoes.

Between about 1250 and 1450, local African craftsmen built stone structures for Great Zimbabwe's rulers, priests, and wealthy citizens. The largest structure, an enclosure the size and shape of a large football stadium with walls of unmortared stone 17 feet (5 meters) thick and 32 feet (10 meters) high, served as the king's court. A large conical stone tower was among the many buildings inside the walls.

As in Mali, mixed farming and cattle herding provided the economic basis of the Great Zimbabwe state, but long-distance trade brought added wealth. Trade began regionally with copper ingots from the upper Zambezi Valley, salt, and local manufactures. Gold exports to the coast expanded in the fourteenth and fifteenth centuries and brought Zimbabwe to its peak. However, historians suspect that the city's residents

Visual Connection Archive

Royal Enclosure, Great Zimbabwe Inside these oval stone walls the rulers of the trading state of Great Zimbabwe lived. Forced to enter the enclosure through a narrow corridor between two high walls, visitors were meant to be awestruck.

depleted nearby forests for firewood while their cattle overgrazed surrounding grasslands. The resulting ecological crisis hastened the empire's decline in the fifteenth century.

Arabia: Aden and the Red Sea

The city of **Aden** (AY-den) near the southwestern tip of the Arabian peninsula had a double advantage in the Indian Ocean trade. Monsoon winds brought enough rainfall to supply drinking water to a large population and grow grain for export, and its location made it a convenient stopover for trade with India, the Persian Gulf, East Africa, and Egypt. Aden's merchants dealt in cotton cloth and beads from India; spices from Southeast Asia; horses from Arabia and Ethiopia; pearls from the Red Sea; manufactured luxuries from Cairo; slaves, gold, and ivory from Ethiopia; and grain, opium, and dyes from Aden's own hinterland.

After visiting Mecca in 1331, Ibn Battuta sailed down the Red Sea to Aden, probably wedged in among bales of trade goods. His comments on the wealth of Aden's leading merchants include a story about the slave of one merchant who bought a ram for the fabulous sum of 400 dinars in order to keep the slave of another merchant from buying it. Instead of

punishing the slave for extravagance, the master freed him as a reward for outdoing his rival. Ninety years later, a Chinese Muslim visitor, Ma Huan, found "the country . . . rich, and the people numerous," living in stone residences several stories high.

Common commercial interests generally promoted good relations among the different religions and cultures of this region. For example, in the mid-thirteenth century, a wealthy Jew from Aden named Yosef settled in Christian Ethiopia, where he acted as an adviser. South Arabia had been trading with neighboring parts of Africa since before the time of King Solomon of Israel. The dynasty that ruled Ethiopia after 1270 claimed descent from Solomon and from the South Arabian princess Sheba. Solomonic Ethiopia's consolidation accompanied a great increase in trade through the Red Sea port of Zeila (ZEYE-luh), including slaves, amber, and animal pelts, which went to Aden and on to other destinations.

Friction sometimes arose, however. In the fourteenth century, the Sunni Muslim king of Yemen sent

Aden Port city in the south Arabian country of Yemen. It has been a major trading center in the Indian Ocean since ancient times.

materials for building a large mosque in Zeila, but the local Somalis (who were Shi'ite Muslims) threw the stones into the sea. This resulted in a yearlong embargo of Zeila ships in Aden. In the late fifteenth century, Ethiopia's territorial expansion and efforts to increase control over the trade provoked conflicts with Muslims who ruled the coastal states of the Red Sea.

India: Gujarat and the Malabar Coast

The state of Gujarat in western India prospered from the expanding trade of the Arabian Sea and the rise of the Delhi Sultanate. Blessed with a rich agricultural hinterland and a long coastline, Gujarat attracted new trade after the Mongol destruction of Baghdad in 1258 disrupted the northern land routes. After the initial violence of its forced incorporation into the Delhi Sultanate in 1298, Gujarat prospered from increased trade with Delhi's ruling class, despite occasional military crackdowns. Independent again after 1390, the Muslim rulers of Gujarat extended their control over neighboring Hindu states and regained their preeminent position in the Indian Ocean trade.

Gujaratis exported cotton textiles and indigo to the Middle East and Europe, in return for gold and silver. They also shipped cotton cloth, carnelian beads, and foodstuffs to the Swahili Coast in exchange for ebony, slaves, ivory, and gold. During the fifteenth century, traders expanded eastward to the Strait of Malacca. These Gujarati merchants helped spread the Islamic faith among east Indian traders, some of whom even imported specially carved gravestones from Gujarat.

Unlike Kilwa and Aden, Gujarat manufactured goods for trade. According to the thirteenth-century Venetian traveler Marco Polo, Gujarat's leatherworkers dressed enough skins in a year to fill several ships to Arabia and other places. They made sleeping mats for export to the Middle East "in red and blue leather, exquisitely inlaid with figures of birds and beasts, and skillfully embroidered with gold and silver wire," as well as leather cushions embroidered in gold. Later observers compared the Gujarati city of Cambay with cities in Flanders and northern Italy (see Chapter 14) in the scale, artisanry, and diversity of its textile industries. Cotton, linen, and silk cloth, along with carpets and quilts, found a large market in Europe, Africa, the Middle East, and Southeast Asia. Cambay also produced polished gemstones, gold jewelry, carved ivory,

stone beads, and both natural and artificial pearls. At the height of its prosperity in the fifteenth century, its well-laid-out streets and open places boasted fine stone houses with tiled roofs. Although Muslim residents controlled most Gujarati overseas trade, its Hindu merchant caste profited so much from related commercial activities that their wealth and luxurious lives became the envy of other Indians.

More southerly cities on the Malabar Coast duplicated Gujarat's success. Calicut (KAL-ih-cut) and other coastal cities prospered from locally made cotton textiles and locally grown grains and spices, and served as clearing-houses for the long-distance trade of the Indian Ocean. The zamorin (ZAH-much-run) (ruler) of Calicut presided over a loose federation of its Hindu rulers that united the coastal region. As in eastern Africa and Arabia, rulers generally tolerated religious and ethnic groups who contributed to commercial profits. Most trading activity lay in the hands of Muslims, many originally from Iran and Arabia, who intermarried with local Indian Muslims. Jewish merchants also operated from Malabar's trading cities.

Southeast Asia: The Rise of Malacca

At the eastern end of the Indian Ocean, the Strait of Malacca between the Malay Peninsula and the island of Sumatra provided the principal passage into the South China Sea (see Map 13.2). As trade increased in the fourteenth and fifteenth centuries, this commercial choke point became the site of political rivalry. The mainland kingdom of Siam controlled most of the upper Malay Peninsula, while the Java-based kingdom of Majapahit (mah-jah-PAH-hit) extended its dominion over the lower Malay Peninsula and much of Sumatra. Majapahit, however, could not suppress Chinese pirates based at the Sumatran city of Palembang (pah-lem-BONG) who preyed on ships sailing through the strait. In 1407, a fleet sent from China smashed the pirates' power and took their chief back home for trial.

Majapahit, weakened by internal struggles, could not take advantage of China's intervention, making the chief beneficiary the newer port of **Malacca** (or Melaka), which dominated the narrowest part of the strait.

Malacca Port city in the modern Southeast Asian country of Malaysia, founded about 1400 as a trading center on the Strait of Malacca. Also spelled Melaka.

Under a prince from Palembang, Malacca had grown from an obscure fishing village into an important port through a series of astute alliances. Nominally subject to the king of Siam, Malacca also secured an alliance with China that was sealed by the visit of the imperial fleet in 1407. The conversion of an early ruler from Hinduism to Islam helped promote trade with Muslim merchants from Gujarat and elsewhere. Merchants also appreciated Malacca's security and low taxes.

Malacca served not just as a meeting point but also as an emporium for Southeast Asian products: rubies and musk from Burma, tin from Malaya, gold from Sumatra, cloves and nutmeg from the Moluccas (or Spice Islands, as Europeans later dubbed them). Shortly after 1500, when Malacca was at its height, one resident counted eighty-four languages spoken among the merchants gathered there, who came from as far away as Turkey, Ethiopia, and the Swahili Coast. Four officials administered the foreign merchant communities: one for the Gujaratis, one for other Indians and Burmese, one for Southeast Asians, and one for the Chinese and Japanese. Malacca's wealth and its cosmopolitan residents set the standard for luxury in Malaya for centuries to come.

Social and Cultural Change

What social and cultural changes are reflected in the history of peoples living in tropical Africa and Asia during this period?

State growth, commercial expansion, and the spread of Islam between 1200 and 1500 led to many changes in the social and cultural life of tropical peoples. The political and commercial elites grew in size and power, as did the number of slaves they owned. The spread of Muslim practices and beliefs affected social and cultural life—witness words of Arabic origin like *Sahara*, *Sudan*, *Swahili*, and *monsoon*—yet local traditions remained important.

Architecture, Learning, and Religion

Social and cultural changes typically affected cities more than rural areas. As Ibn Battuta and other travelers observed, wealthy merchants and ruling elites spent lavishly on mansions, palaces, and places of worship. Most places of worship surviving from this period blend older traditions and new influences. African Muslims produced Middle Eastern mosque designs in local building materials: sun-baked clay and wood in the western Sudan and coral stone on the Swahili Coast. Hindu temple architecture influenced mosque designs in Gujarat, which sometimes incorporated pieces of older structures. The congregational mosque at Cambay, built in 1325 with the traditional Islamic courtyard, cloisters, and porches, utilized pillars, porches, and arches taken from sacked Hindu and Jain (jine) temples. The mosque erected at the Gujarati capital of Ahmadabad (AH-muhd-ah-bahd) in 1423 had the open courtyard typical of mosques everywhere, but the surrounding verandas incorporated many typical Gujarati details and architectural conventions.

In Africa, King Lalibela (LAH-lee-BEL-uh) of Ethiopia constructed his capital, Lalibela, during the first third of the thirteenth century and ordered eleven churches to be carved out of solid rock, each commemorating a sacred Christian site in Jerusalem. These structures carried on an old Ethiopian tradition of rock sculpture, though on a far grander scale.

Mosques, churches, and temples were centers of education as well as prayer. Muslims promoted literacy among their sons (and sometimes their daughters) so that they could read sacred texts. Ibn Battuta reported seeing several boys in Mali wearing chains until they completed memorizing passages of the Quran. Literacy and Islam spread together in sub-Saharan Africa, where Christian Ethiopia had previously been the only literate society. In time, scholars adapted the Arabic alphabet to write local languages.

Church of Saint George, Ethiopia King Lalibela, who ruled the Christian kingdom of Ethiopia between about 1180 and 1220, had a series of churches carved out of solid volcanic rock to adorn his kingdom's new capital (also named Lalibela). The church of Saint George, excavated to a depth of 40 feet (13 meters) and hollowed out inside, has the shape of a Greek cross.

Islam affected literacy less in India, which had a long literate heritage. Arabic served primarily for religious purposes, while Persian became the language of high culture used at court. Eventually **Urdu** (ER-doo) arose, a Persian-influenced literary form of Hindi written in Arabic characters. Muslims also introduced papermaking in India.

Advanced Muslim scholars studied Islamic law, theology, and administration, as well as works on mathematics, medicine, science, and philosophy, partly derived from ancient Greek writings. In sixteenth-century **Timbuktu** (see Map 13.1) on the Niger River, over 150 schools taught the Quran while leading clerics taught advanced classes in mosques or homes. Books imported from North Africa brought high prices. Al-Hajj Ahmed, a scholar who died in Timbuktu in 1536, possessed some seven hundred volumes, an unusually large library for that time. In Southeast Asia, Malacca became a center of Islamic learning from which scholars spread Islam throughout the region. Other important centers of learning developed in Muslim India, particularly in Delhi, the capital.

Even in lands seized by conquest, Muslim rulers seldom required conversion. Example and persuasion by merchants and Sufis proved more effective. Many Muslims worked hard to persuade others of Islam's superiority. Muslim domination of long-distance trade assisted the adoption of Islam. Commercial transactions could take place across religious boundaries, but the common code of morality and law that Islam provided encouraged trust and drew many local merchants to Islam. From the major trading centers along the Swahili Coast, in the Sudan, in coastal India, and in Southeast Asia, Islam's influence spread along regional trade routes.

Marriage also played a role. Single Muslim men traveling to and settling in tropical Africa and Asia often married local women, and their children grew up in the Islamic faith. Some wealthy men had dozens of children from up to four wives and additional slave concubines. Servants and slaves in such households normally professed Islam.

In India, Muslim invasions eliminated the last strongholds of long-declining Buddhism, including, in 1196, the great Buddhist center of study at Nalanda (nuh-LAN-duh) in Bihar (bee-HAHR). Its manuscripts were burned and thousands of monks killed or driven into exile in Nepal and Tibet. With Buddhism reduced to a minor faith in the land of its birth, Islam emerged as India's second most important religion. Hinduism still prevailed in 1500, but Islam displaced Hinduism in most of maritime Southeast Asia.

Islam also spread among rural peoples, such as the pastoral Fulani of West Africa and Somali of northeastern Africa and various pastoralists in northwest India. In Bengal, Muslim religious figures oversaw the conversion of jungle into farmland and thereby gained many converts.

The spread of Islam did not mean simply the replacement of one set of beliefs by another. Islam adapted to the cultures of the regions it penetrated, developing African, Indian, and Indonesian varieties.

Urdu A Persian-influenced form of Hindi written in Arabic characters and used as a literary language since the 1300s.

Timbuktu City on the Niger River. It was founded by the Tuareg as a seasonal camp sometime after 1000. As part of the Mali empire, Timbuktu became a major terminus of the trans-Saharan trade and a center of Islamic learning.

Social and Gender Distinctions

A growth in slavery accompanied the rising prosperity of the elites. Military campaigns in India, according to Islamic sources, reduced hundreds of thousands of Hindu "infidels" to slavery. Delhi overflowed with slaves. Sultan Ala ud-Din owned 50,000 and Firuz Shah 180,000, including 12,000 skilled artisans. Sultan Tughluq sent 100 male slaves and 100 female slaves as a gift to the emperor of China in return for a similar gift.

Mali and Bornu sent slaves across the Sahara to North Africa, including beautiful maidens and eunuchs (castrated males). The expanding Ethiopian Empire regularly sent captives for sale to Aden traders at Zeila. According to modern estimates, Saharan and Red Sea traders sold about 2.5 million enslaved Africans between 1200 and 1500. African slaves from the Swahili Coast played conspicuous roles in the navies, armies, and administrations of some Indian states, especially in the fifteenth century. A few African slaves even reached China, where a source from about 1225 says that rich families preferred gatekeepers with bodies "black as lacquer."

With "free" labor abundant and cheap, few slaves worked as farmers. In some places, hereditary castes of slaves dominated certain trades and military units. Indeed, the earliest rulers of the Delhi Sultanate rose from military slavery. A slave general in the western Sudan named Askia Muhammad seized control of the Songhai Empire (Mali's successor) in 1493. Less fortunate slaves, like the men and women who mined copper in Mali, did hard menial work.

Wealthy households used many slave servants. Eunuchs guarded the harems of wealthy Muslims, but women predominated as household slaves, serving also as entertainers and concubines. Some rich men aspired to having a concubine from every part of the world. One of Firuz Shah's nobles reportedly had two thousand harem slaves, including women from Turkey and China.

Sultan Ala ud-Din's campaigns against Gujarat at the end of the thirteenth century yielded a booty of twenty thousand maidens in addition to innumerable younger children of both sexes. The supply of captives became so great that the lowest grade of horse sold for five times as much as an ordinary female slave, although beautiful young virgins commanded far higher prices.

Hindu legal digests and commentaries suggest that the position of Hindu women may have improved somewhat compared to earlier periods. The ancient practice of sati (suh-TEE)—that is, of an upper-caste widow throwing herself on her husband's funeral pyre—remained a meritorious act strongly approved by social custom. But Ibn Battuta makes it clear that sati was strictly optional. Since the Hindu commentaries devote considerable attention to the rights of widows without sons to inherit their husbands' estates, one may even conclude that sati was exceptional.

Indian parents still gave their daughters in marriage before the age of puberty, but consummation of the marriage took place only when the young woman was ready. Wives faced far stricter rules of fidelity and chastity than their husbands and could be abandoned for any serious breach. But other offenses against law and custom usually brought lighter penalties than for men. A woman's male master—father, husband, or owner—determined her status. Women seldom played active roles in commerce, administration, or religion.

Besides child rearing, women involved themselves with food preparation and, when not prohibited by religious restrictions, brewing. In many parts of Africa, women commonly made beer from grains or bananas. These mildly alcoholic beverages played an important part in male rituals of hospitality and relaxation.

Throughout tropical Africa and Asia, women did much of the farm work. They also toted home heavy loads of food, firewood, and water balanced on their heads. Other common female activities included making clay pots for cooking and storage and making clothing. In India, the spinning wheel, introduced by the Muslim invaders, greatly reduced the cost of making thread for weaving. Women typically spun at home, leaving weaving to men. In West Africa, women often sold agricultural products, pottery, and other craftwork in the markets.

Adopting Islam did not necessarily mean accepting the social customs of the Arab world. In Mali's capital, Ibn Battuta was appalled that Muslim women both free and slave did not completely cover their bodies and veil their faces when appearing in public. He considered their nakedness an offense to women's (and men's) modesty. In another part of Mali, he berated a Muslim merchant from Morocco for permitting his wife to sit on a couch and chat with her

SECTION REVIEW

- Social and cultural life changed as a result of state formation, commercial expansion, and the spread of Islam.

- These changes mostly affected cities, where elites financed building programs, fostering hybrid styles of religious architecture.

- Islam spread mainly through peaceful adaptation and promoted education and scholarship.

- With rising prosperity came the expansion of slavery, which was endorsed by Islam.

- The position of Indian women seems to have improved, and the spread of Islam did not mean adoption of Arab gender customs.

male friend. The husband replied, "The association of women with men is agreeable to us and part of good manners, to which no suspicion attaches." Ibn Battuta refused to visit the merchant again.

Conclusion

Tropical Africa and Asia encompass a large part of the world, one in which close to half the world's people lived. That vast area possesses many similarities and also great differences. The differences are evident in the climates, from permanent rain forests to barren deserts and from easily accessible seacoasts to the interiors of continents. Yet the social and cultural differences are as important as those of climates and landscapes.

The most striking change in tropical Africa and Asia in the period 1200 to 1500 is the spread of Islam. Once limited to the Arabian peninsula, then to the Middle East and North Africa, after 1200 Islam spread widely into the Indian subcontinent, Southeast Asia, and both West and East Africa. In some areas, it spread slowly but eventually reached all but a few of the inhabitants; this was the case of sub-Saharan Africa and much of Southeast Asia. In India, however, Islam came suddenly but then encountered unexpected resistance. How can we explain the difference?

In both West and East Africa and in Southeast Asia and the Indonesian archipelago, Islam was introduced by merchants who not only traded but also preached the message of the Quran. As contacts with other parts of the world grew, a universal religion like Islam was more convincing than the animist religions and local deities that preceded it. Furthermore, the conduct of the trader-missionaries and the political advantages that local rulers saw in allying themselves with a powerful world-encompassing movement gradually overcame the older religious traditions.

In India, in contrast, Islam came first with conquering Arab armies and then with Afghan and Turkish warriors. In India, they encountered a people who had an ancient and very sophisticated religion—Hinduism—and whose indigenous elites had long benefited from the inequalities enshrined in the caste system. Islam, with its promise of equality among all Muslims, appealed to the poor and lower-caste (or outcaste) Indians but remained a threat to most others. Hence, despite initial successes, Islam did not succeed in converting the majority of Indians as it had in the Middle East and Africa, and India became a region and a civilization permanently divided along religious lines.

CHAPTER REVIEW   Download the MP3 audio file of the Chapter Review to listen to on the go.

How did environmental differences shape cultural differences in tropical Africa and Asia? (page 313)

By 1500 tropical Africa and Asia contained nearly 40 percent of the world's population but just over a quarter of its habitable land. Living in every type of ecosystem, from lush rain forests to arid deserts, tropical peoples had become intimately familiar with their environments, learning not merely to survive but also to prosper in them. African pastoralists tended herds of domestic animals in dry regions, while in Asia the more favorable soil and rainfall enabled farmers to cultivate rice, as well as grains and legumes.

Under what circumstances did the first Islamic empires arise in Africa and India? (page 317)

The period from 1200 to 1500 saw the rise of the first powerful Islamic states outside the Middle East. Chief among these were the Delhi Sultanate, which brought South Asia its greatest political unity since the decline of the Guptas, and the Mali Empire in the western Sudan, which extended the political and trading role pioneered by Ghana. Mali was founded by an indigenous African dynasty that had earlier adopted Islam, while invading Turkish and Afghan Muslims founded the Delhi Sultanate.

How did cultural and ecological differences promote trade, and in turn how did trade and other contacts promote state growth and the spread of Islam? (page 322)

Of greatest importance to the spread of Islam throughout tropical Africa and Asia was the Indian Ocean, which directly connected lands as distant as North and East Africa, Arabia, India, and Southeast Asia. Having mastered the seasonal monsoons, merchant sailors made the Indian Ocean the world's most important and richest trading area. A host of Muslim city-states arose: Kilwa along the Swahili Coast, Aden at the entrance to the Red Sea, Gujarat in India, and Malacca at the entrance to the South China Sea.

What social and cultural changes are reflected in the history of peoples living in tropical Africa and Asia during this period? (page 327)

With the enlargement of Islam's presence in the tropical world came changes that could be brutal as well as beneficial. Slavery, common in many parts of the world at this time, was an integral part of commerce and social life. A woman's status was largely determined by her father, husband, or owner, and women were generally precluded from holding important positions in religious or political life. Muslim culture in this period also brought great benefits, however. The centrality of the Quran in much of social life contributed to a rise in literacy, first in Arabic but later in native languages as well. Centers of higher education arose in which subjects such as mathematics, medicine, and science were significantly advanced.

Key Terms

Ibn Battuta *(p. 313)*	Swahili Coast *(p. 323)*
tropics *(p. 313)*	Great Zimbabwe *(p. 323)*
monsoons *(p. 314)*	Aden *(p. 325)*
Delhi Sultanate *(p. 316)*	Malacca *(p. 326)*
Mali *(p. 317)*	Urdu *(p. 328)*
Mansa Kankan Musa *(p. 318)*	Timbuktu *(p. 328)*
Gujarat *(p. 321)*	

Web Resources

Pronunciation Guide
Interactive Maps
- MAP 13.1 Africa, 1200–1500
- MAP 13.2 South and Southeast Asia, 1200–1500

Answer to the History in Focus Question
See photo on page 314, "East African Pastoralists."

CourseMate Visit the CourseMate website at www.cengagebrain.com for additional study tools and review materials for this chapter.

The Latin West

© Cengage Learning

CHAPTER PREVIEW

Rural Growth and Crisis
How well did inhabitants of the Latin West, rich and poor, urban and rural, deal with their natural environment?

Urban Revival
What social and economic factors led to the growth of cities in late medieval Europe?

Learning, Literature, and the Renaissance
What factors were responsible for the promotion of learning and the arts in the Latin West?

Political and Military Transformations
What social, political, and military developments contributed to the rise of European nations in this period?

Conclusion

DIVERSITY & DOMINANCE: Persecution and Protection of Jews, 1272–1349

Visit the CourseMate website at **www.cengagebrain.com** for additional study tools and review materials for this chapter.

332

In the summer of 1454, a year after the Ottoman Turks captured the Greek Christian city of Constantinople, Aeneas Sylvius Piccolomini (uh-NEE-uhs SIL-vee-uhs pee-kuh-lo-MEE-nee), destined in four years to become pope, expressed doubts as to whether anyone could persuade the rulers of Christian Europe to take up arms together against the Muslims: "Christendom has no head whom all will obey—neither the pope nor the emperor receives his due." The Christian states thought more of fighting each other. French and English armies had been battling for over a century, the German emperor presided over dozens of states but did not really control them, and the numerous kingdoms and principalities of Spain and Italy could not unite. With only slight exaggeration, Aeneas Sylvius moaned, "Every city has its own king, and there are as many princes as there are households." He attributed this lack of unity to European preoccupation with personal welfare and material gain. Both pessimism about human nature and materialism had increased during the previous century, after a devastating plague had carried off half of western Europe's population.

Yet despite all these divisions, disasters, and wars, historians now see the period from 1200 to 1500 (Europe's Late Middle Ages) as a time of unusual progress. Prosperous cities adorned with splendid architecture, institutions of higher learning, and cultural achievements counterbalanced the avarice and greed that Aeneas Sylvius lamented. Frequent wars caused havoc and destruction, but they also promoted the development of military technology and more unified monarchies.

Although their Muslim and Byzantine neighbors commonly called western Europeans "Franks," they ordinarily referred to themselves as "Latins," underscoring their allegiance to Roman Catholicism and the Latin language used in its rituals. Some common elements promoted the **Latin West**'s vigorous revival: competition, the pursuit of success, and the effective use of borrowed technology and learning.

Rural Growth and Crisis

How well did inhabitants of the Latin West, rich and poor, urban and rural, deal with their natural environment?

Between 1200 and 1500, the Latin West brought more land under cultivation using new farming techniques and made greater use of machinery and mechanical forms of energy. Yet for the nine out of ten people who lived in the countryside, hard labor brought meager returns, and famine, epidemics, and war struck often. After the devastation of the Black Death between 1347 and 1351, social changes speeded up by peasant revolts released many persons from serfdom and brought some improvements to rural life.

Peasants, Population, and Plague

In 1200, most western Europeans lived as serfs tilling the soil on large estates owned by the nobility and the church (see Chapter 10). They owed their lord both a share of their harvests and numerous labor services. As a consequence of the inefficiency of farming practices and their obligations to landowners, peasants received meager returns for their hard work. Even with numerous religious holidays, peasants labored some 54 hours a week in their fields, more than half the time in support of the local nobility. Each noble household typically lived from the labor of fifteen to thirty peasant families. The standard of living in the lord's stone castle or manor house contrasted sharply with the peasant's one-room thatched cottage containing little furniture and no luxuries.

Scenes of rural life show both men and women at work in the fields, but equality of labor did not mean equality in decision making at home. In the peasant's hut as elsewhere in medieval Europe, women were subordinate to men. The influential theologian Thomas Aquinas (uh-KWY-nuhs) (1225–1274) spoke for his age

Latin West Historians' name for the territories of Europe that adhered to the Latin rite of Christianity and used the Latin language for intellectual exchange in the period ca. 1000–1500.

when he argued that although both men and women were created in God's image, there was a sense in which "the image of God is found in man, and not in woman: for man is the beginning and end of woman; as God is the beginning and end of every creature."[1]

Rural poverty resulted from rapid population growth as well as inefficient farming methods and social inequality. In 1200, China's population may have exceeded Europe's by two to one; by 1300, the population of each was about 80 million. China's population fell because of the Mongol conquest (see Chapter 12), while Europe's more than doubled between 1100 and 1340. Some historians believe the reviving economy stimulated the increase. Others argue that severe epidemics were few, and warmer-than-usual temperatures reduced mortality from starvation and exposure.

More people required more productive farming and new agricultural settlements. One widespread new technique, the **three-field system**, replaced the custom of leaving half the land fallow (uncultivated) every year to regain its fertility. In the fall, farmers planted wheat or rye on one-third of their fields; in the spring they planted oats, barley, peas, chickpeas, lentils, or beans on a second third; and left the last third fallow. The second and third years, they repeated the process but moved each crop to the next field. The fourth year they returned to the first year's distribution. As a result, each year two-thirds of their fields were productive, instead of half: an increase of 33 percent. Furthermore, this system allowed them to grow oats, the best feed for horses. Finally, peas and beans were not only a source of proteins, but they also enriched the soil with nitrogen from the air, thereby maintaining its fertility. In much of Europe, however, farmers continued to let half of their land lie fallow and used oxen (less efficient but cheaper than horses) to pull their plows.

Population growth also encouraged new agricultural settlements. In the twelfth and thirteenth centuries, large numbers of Germans migrated into the fertile lands east of the Elbe River and into the eastern Baltic states. Knights belonging to Latin Christian religious orders slaughtered or drove away native inhabitants who had not yet adopted Christianity.

Musée Condé, Chantilly, France/Bridgeman-Giraudon/Art Resource, NY

Rural French Peasants Many scenes of peasant life in winter are visible in this small painting by the Flemish Limbourg brothers from the 1410s. Above the snow-covered beehives one man chops firewood, while another drives a donkey loaded with firewood to a little village. At the lower right a woman, blowing on her frozen fingers, heads past the huddled sheep and hungry birds to join other women warming themselves in the cottage (whose outer walls the artists have cut away).

During the thirteenth century, the Order of Teutonic Knights conquered, resettled, and administered a vast area along the Baltic that later became Prussia (see Map 14.1). Other Latin Christians founded new settlements on lands conquered from the Muslims and Byzantines in southern Europe and on Celtic lands in the British Isles.

Draining swamps and clearing forests also brought new land under cultivation. But as population continued to rise, some people had to farm lands that had poor soils or were vulnerable to flooding, frost, or drought. Average crop yields fell after 1250, and more people lived at the edge of starvation. According to one historian, "By 1300, almost every child born in western Europe faced the probability

three-field system A rotational system for agriculture in which one field grows wheat or barley, one grows oats or legumes, and one lies fallow. It gradually replaced the two-field system in medieval Europe.

Chronology

	Technology and Environment	Culture	Politics and Society
1200	**1200s** Widespread use of crossbows and windmills		**1200s** Champagne fairs flourish **1204** Fourth Crusade **1215** Magna Carta issued
		1210s Teutonic Knights, Franciscans, Dominicans **1225–1274** Philosopher-monk Thomas Aquinas	
1300	**1315–1317** Great Famine	**1300–1500** Rise of universities **1313–1375** Giovanni Boccaccio, humanist writer	**1337** Start of Hundred Years War
	1347–1351 Black Death **ca. 1350** Growing deforestation		
		ca. 1390–1441 Jan van Eyck, painter	**1381** Wat Tyler's Rebellion
1400	**1400s** Cannon and hand-held firearms in use		**1415** Portuguese take Ceuta
		1452–1519 Leonardo da Vinci, artist	**1431** Joan of Arc burned **1453** End of Hundred Years War; Ottomans take Constantinople
	1454 Gutenberg Bible	**1492** Expulsion of Jews from Spain	**1492** Fall of Muslim state of Granada

of extreme hunger at least once or twice during his expected 30 to 35 years of life."[2] One unusually cold spell produced the Great Famine of 1315–1317, which affected much of Europe.

The **Black Death** or bubonic plague reversed the population growth. This terrible plague originated in China and spread across Central Asia with the Mongol armies (see Chapter 12). In 1346, the Mongols attacked the city of Kaffa (KAH-fah) on the Black Sea; a year later, Genoese (JEN-oh-eez) traders in Kaffa carried the disease to Italy and southern France. For two years, the Black Death spread across Europe, in some places carrying off two-thirds of the population. Average losses in western Europe amounted to one in two.

Victims developed boils the size of eggs in their groins and armpits, black blotches on their skin, foul body odors, and severe pain. In most cases, death came within a few days. Town officials closed their gates to people from infected areas and burned the victims' possessions. Such measures helped to spare some communities but could not halt the advance of the disease. Bubonic plague, the primary form of the Black Death, spreads from person to person and

through the bites of fleas infesting the fur of black rats. Although medieval doctors did not associate the disease with rats, eliminating the rats that thrived on urban refuse would have been difficult.

The plague left a psychological mark, bringing home to people how sudden and unexpected death could be. Some people became more religious, giving money to the church or hitting themselves with iron-tipped whips to atone for their sins. Others chose reckless enjoyment, spending their money on fancy clothes, feasts, and drinking. Whatever their mood, most people soon resumed their daily routines. Periodic returns of plague made recovery from population losses slow and uneven. Europe's population in 1400 equaled that in 1200. Not until after 1500 did it rise above its preplague level.

Black Death An outbreak of bubonic plague that spread across Asia, North Africa, and Europe in the mid-fourteenth century, carrying off vast numbers of persons.

Map 14.1 Europe in 1453 This year marked the end of the Hundred Years War between France and England and the fall of the Byzantine capital city of Constantinople to the Ottoman Turks. Muslim advances into southeastern Europe were offset by the Latin Christian reconquests of Islamic holdings in southern Italy and the Iberian Peninsula and by the conversion of Lithuania. © Cengage Learning

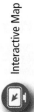 Interactive Map

Spread of Roman Christendom

- In 1000 C.E.
- Added 1000–1200
- Lost 1000–1200 (Regained 1200–1500)
- Added 1200–1500
- Lost 1200–1500
- English holdings, 1360
- Boundary of the Holy Roman Empire

Burying Victims of the Black Death This scene from Tournai, Flanders, captures the magnitude of the plague.   Snark/Art Resource NY

Social Rebellion

In addition to its demographic and psychological effects, the Black Death triggered social changes in western Europe. Laborers who survived demanded higher pay for their services. At first, authorities tried to freeze wages at the old levels. Seeing this as a plot by the rich, peasants rose up against wealthy nobles and churchmen. During a widespread revolt in France in 1358, known as the Jacquerie, peasants looted castles and killed dozens of persons. In a large revolt led by Wat Tyler in 1381, English peasants invaded London, calling for an end to serfdom and obligations to landowners. Demonstrators murdered the archbishop of Canterbury and many royal officials. Authorities put down these rebellions with even greater bloodshed and cruelty, but they could not stave off the higher wages and other social changes the rebels demanded.

Serfdom practically disappeared in western Europe as peasants bought their freedom or ran away. Many free persons earning higher wages saved their money and bought land. Some English landowners who could no longer afford to hire enough fieldworkers began pasturing sheep for their wool. Others grew crops that required less care or made greater use of draft animals and labor-saving tools. Because the plague had not killed animals, survivors had abundant meat and leather for shoes. Thus, the welfare of the rural masses generally improved after the Black Death, though the gap between rich and poor remained wide.

In urban areas, employers raised wages to attract workers. Guilds (see below) shortened the period of apprenticeship. Competition within crafts also became more common. Although the overall economy shrank with the decline in population, per capita production actually rose.

Mills and Mines

Mining, metalworking, and the use of mechanical energy expanded so greatly in the centuries before 1500 that some historians speak of an "industrial revolution" in medieval Europe. That may be too strong a term, but the landscape fairly bristled with mechanical devices. Mills powered by water or wind ground grain, sawed logs, crushed olives, tanned leather, and made paper.

In 1086, 5,600 watermills flanked England's many rivers. After 1200, mills spread rapidly across the western European mainland. By the early fourteenth century, entrepreneurs had crammed sixty-eight watermills into a 1-mile section of the Seine (sen) River in Paris. Less efficient **water wheels** depended on the flow of a river passing beneath them. Greater efficiency came from channeling water to fall over the top of the wheel so that gravity added force to the water's flow. Dams ensured a steady flow of water

water wheel A mechanism that harnesses the energy in flowing water to grind grain or to power machinery. It was used in many parts of the world but was especially common in Europe from 1200 to 1900.

throughout the year. Some watermills in France and England even harnessed the power of ocean tides.

Windmills multiplied in comparatively dry lands like Spain and in northern Europe, where ice made water wheels useless in winter. Designs for watermills dated back to Roman times, and the Islamic world, which inherited Hellenistic technologies, knew both water wheels and windmills. But people in the medieval Latin West used these devices on a much larger scale than did people elsewhere.

Owners invested heavily in building mills, but since nature furnished the energy to run them for free, they returned great profits. While individuals or monasteries constructed some mills, most were built by groups of investors. Rich millers often aroused the jealousy of their neighbors. In his *Canterbury Tales*, the English poet Geoffrey Chaucer (ca. 1340–1400) captured their unsavory reputation by portraying a miller as "a master-hand at stealing grain" by pushing down on the balance scale with his thumb.[3]

Waterpower aided the great expansion of iron making. Water powered the stamping mills that broke up the iron, the trip hammers that pounded it, and the bellows (first documented in the West in 1323) that raised temperatures to the point where the iron was liquid enough to be poured into molds. Blast furnaces producing high-quality iron are documented from 1380. Finished products ranged from armor to nails, from horseshoes to hoes.

Demand stimulated iron mining in many parts of Europe. In addition, new silver, lead, and copper mines in Austria and Hungary supplied metal for coins, church bells, cannon, and statues. Techniques of deep mining developed in central Europe spread west in the latter part of the fifteenth century. A building boom stimulated stone quarrying in France during the eleventh, twelfth, and thirteenth centuries.

Industrial growth changed the landscape. Towns grew outward and new ones were founded, dams and canals changed the flow of rivers, and quarries and mines scarred the hillsides. Human wastes and the runoff from slaughterhouses and from urban tanneries that cured and processed leather polluted streams. England's Parliament enacted the first recorded antipollution law in 1388, but enforcement proved difficult.

Deforestation accelerated. Trees provided timber for buildings and ships, and tanneries stripped bark to make acid for tanning leather. Many forests gave

SECTION REVIEW

- Population growth stimulated improved farming methods and agricultural expansion, but peasant life did not significantly improve.

- Famine and the Black Death reversed the population growth and resulted in social change throughout western Europe.

- Improved mill designs and other technology stimulated further industrial growth, which, in turn, changed the landscape.

way to farmland. The glass and iron industries used great quantities of charcoal, made by controlled burning of oak or other hardwood, to produce the high temperatures required. A single iron furnace could consume all the trees within five-eighths of a mile (1 kilometer) in just forty days. Consequently, the later Middle Ages saw the end of many of western Europe's once-dense forests, except in places where powerful landowners established hunting preserves.

Urban Revival

What social and economic factors led to the growth of cities in late medieval Europe?

In the tenth century, no town in the Latin West could compete in size, wealth, or comfort with the cities of Byzantium and Islam. Yet by the later Middle Ages, the Mediterranean, Baltic, and Atlantic coasts boasted wealthy port cities, as did some major rivers draining into these seas. Some Byzantine and Muslim cities still exceeded those of the West in size, but not in commercial, cultural, and administrative dynamism, as marked by impressive new churches, guild halls, and residences.

Trading Cities   Most urban growth after 1200 resulted from manufacturing and trade, both between cities and their hinterlands and over long distances. Northern Italy particularly benefited from maritime trade with the port cities of the eastern Mediterranean and, through them, the markets of the Indian Ocean and East Asia. In northern Europe, commercial cities in the county of Flanders (roughly today's Belgium) and around the Baltic Sea profited from regional networks and from overland and sea routes to the Mediterranean.

Flemish Weavers, Ypres The spread of textile weaving gave employment to many people in the Netherlands. The city of Ypres in Flanders (now northern Belgium) was an important textile center in the thirteenth century. This drawing from a fourteenth-century manuscript shows a man and a woman weaving cloth on a horizontal loom, while a child makes thread on a spinning wheel.

Stedelijke Openbare Bibliotheek, Ypres

A Venetian-inspired assault in 1204 against the city of Constantinople, misleadingly named the "Fourth Crusade," temporarily eliminated Byzantine control of the passage between the Mediterranean and the Black Sea and thereby allowed Venice to seize Crete and expand its trading colonies around the Black Sea. Another boon to Italian trade came from the westward expansion of the Mongol Empire, which opened trade routes from the Mediterranean to China (see Chapter 12).

In 1271 a young merchant named Marco Polo set out from Venice and reached the Mongol court in China after a long trek across Central Asia. He then served the emperor Khubilai Khan for many years as an ambassador and governor of a Chinese province. It is likely he exaggerated his account of these adventures and of his voyage through the Indian Ocean that brought him back to Venice in 1295 after an absence of twenty-four years. Similar reports of the riches of the East came from other European travelers.

When Mongol decline interrupted the caravan trade in the fourteenth century, Venetian merchants purchased eastern silks and spices brought by other middlemen to Constantinople, Damascus, and Cairo. Three times a year, Venice dispatched convoys of two or three galleys, with sixty oarsmen each, capable of bringing back 2,000 tons of goods. Other merchants explored new overland or sea routes.

The sea trade of Genoa on northern Italy's west coast probably equaled that of Venice. Genoese merchants established colonies in the western and eastern Mediterranean and around the Black Sea. In northern Europe, an association of trading cities known as the **Hanseatic** (han-see-AT-ik) **League** traded extensively in the Baltic, including the coasts of Prussia, newly conquered by German knights. Their merchants ranged eastward to Novgorod in Russia and westward across the North Sea to London.

In the late thirteenth century, Genoese galleys from the Mediterranean and Hanseatic ships from the Baltic were converging on the trading and manufacturing cities in Flanders. Artisans in the Flemish towns of Bruges (broozh), Ghent (gent [hard g as in get]), and Ypres (EE-pruh) transformed raw wool from England into a fine cloth that was softer and smoother than the coarse "homespuns" from simple village looms. Dyed in vivid hues, these Flemish textiles appealed to wealthy Europeans, who also appreciated fine textiles from Asia.

Along the overland route connecting Flanders and northern Italy, important trading fairs developed in the Champagne (sham-PAIN) region of Burgundy. The Champagne fairs began as regional markets, exchanging manufactured goods, livestock, and farm produce once or twice a year. When the king of France gained control of Champagne at the end of the twelfth century, royal guarantees of safe conduct to merchants turned these markets into international fairs

Hanseatic League An economic and defensive alliance of the free towns in northern Germany, founded about 1241 and most powerful in the fourteenth century.

that were important for currency exchange and other financial transactions. A century later, fifteen Italian cities had permanent consulates in Champagne to represent the interests of their citizens. During the fourteenth century, the large volume of trade made it cheaper to ship Flemish woolens to Italy by sea than to pack them overland on animal backs. Champagne's fairs consequently lost some international trade, but they remained important as regional markets.

In the late thirteenth century, the English monarchy raised taxes on exports of raw wool, making cloth manufacture in England more profitable than in Flanders. Flemish specialists crossed the English Channel and introduced the spinning wheel and other devices to England. Annual raw wool exports fell from 35,000 sacks of wool at the beginning of the fourteenth century to 8,000 in the mid-fifteenth century, while English wool cloth production rose from 4,000 pieces just before 1350 to 54,000 a century later.

Florence also replaced Flemish imports with its own woolens industry financed by local banking families. In 1338, Florence manufactured 80,000 pieces of cloth, while importing only 10,000. These changes in the textile industry show how competition promoted the spread of manufacturing and encouraged new specialties.

The growing textile industries used the power of wind and water channeled through gears, pulleys, and belts to drive all sorts of machinery. Flemish mills cleaned and thickened woven cloth by beating it in water, a process known as fulling. Other mills produced paper, starting in southern Europe in the thirteenth century. Unlike the Chinese and Muslim papermakers, who had pursued the craft for centuries, the Europeans introduced machines to do the heavy work.

In the fifteenth century, Venice surpassed its European rivals in the volume of its trade in the Mediterranean as well as across the Alps into central Europe. Its craftspeople manufactured luxury goods once obtainable only from eastern sources, notably silk and cotton textiles, glassware and mirrors, jewelry, and paper. Exports of Italian and northern European woolens to the eastern Mediterranean also rose. In the space of a few centuries, western European cities had used the eastern trade to increase their prosperity and then reduce their dependence on eastern goods.

Civic Life

Most northern Italian and German cities were independent states, much like the port cities of the Indian Ocean Basin (see Chapter 13). Other European cities held royal charters exempting them from the authority of local nobles. Their autonomy enabled them to adapt to changing market conditions more quickly than cities controlled by imperial authorities, as in China and the Islamic world. Since anyone who lived in a chartered city for over a year could claim freedom, urban life promoted social mobility.

Europe's Jews mostly lived in cities. Spain had the largest communities because of the tolerance of earlier Muslim rulers. Commercial cities elsewhere welcomed Jews with manufacturing and business skills. Despite official protection by certain Christian princes and kings, Jews endured violent persecutions or expulsions in times of crisis, such as during the Black Death (see Diversity and Dominance: Persecution and Protection of Jews, 1272–1349). In 1492, the Spanish monarchs expelled all Jews in the name of religious and ethnic purity. Only the papal city of Rome left its Jews undisturbed throughout the centuries before 1500.

Within most towns and cities, powerful associations known as guilds dominated civic life. **Guilds** brought together craft specialists, such as silversmiths, or merchants working in a particular trade to regulate business practices and set prices. They also trained apprentices and promoted members' interests with the city government. By denying membership to outsiders and Jews, guilds protected the interests of families that already belonged to them. They also perpetuated male dominance of most skilled jobs.

Nevertheless, in a few places, women could join guilds either on their own or as the wives, widows, or daughters of male guild members. Large numbers of poor women also toiled in nonguild jobs in urban textile industries and in the food and beverage trades, generally receiving lower wages than men.

Some women advanced socially through marriage to wealthy men. One of Chaucer's *Canterbury Tales*

---

guild In medieval Europe, an association of men (rarely women), such as merchants, artisans, or professors, who worked in a particular trade and banded together to promote their economic and political interests. Guilds were also important in other societies, such as the Ottoman and Safavid Empires.

Diversity & Dominance

Persecution and Protection of Jews, 1272–1349

Because they did not belong to the dominant Latin Christian faith, Jews suffered from periodic discrimination and persecution. For the most part, religious and secular authorities tried to curb such anti-Semitism. Jews, after all, were useful citizens who worshiped the same God as their Christian neighbors. Still, it was hard to know where to draw the line between justifiable and unjustifiable discrimination. The famous reviser of Catholic theology, St. Thomas Aquinas, made one such distinction in his Summa Theologica with regard to attempts at forced conversion.

Now, the practice of the Church never held that the children of Jews should be baptized against the will of their parents. . . . Therefore, it seems dangerous to bring forward this new view, that contrary to the previously established custom of the Church, the children of Jews should be baptized against the will of their parents.

There are two reasons for this position. One stems from danger to faith. For, if children without the use of reason were to receive baptism, then after reaching maturity they could easily be persuaded by their parents to relinquish what they had received in ignorance. This would tend to do harm to the faith.

The second reason is that it is opposed to natural justice . . . it [is] a matter of natural right that a son, before he has the use of reason, is under the care of his father. Hence, it would be against natural justice for the boy, before he has the use of reason, to be removed from the care of his parents, or for anything to be arranged for him against the will of his parents.

The "new view" Aquinas opposed was much in the air, for in 1272 Pope Gregory X issued a decree condemning forced baptism. The pope's decree reviews the history of papal protection given to the Jews, starting with a quotation from Pope Gregory I dating from 598, and decrees two new protections of Jews' legal rights.

Even as it is not allowed to the Jews in their assemblies presumptuously to undertake for themselves more than that which is permitted them by law, even so they ought not to suffer any disadvantage in those [privileges] which have been granted them.

Although they prefer to persist in their stubbornness rather than to recognize the words of their prophets and the mysteries of the Scriptures, and thus to arrive at a knowledge of Christian faith and salvation; nevertheless, inasmuch as they have made an appeal for our protection and help, we therefore admit their petition and offer them the shield of our protection through the clemency of Christian piety. In so doing we follow in the footsteps of our predecessors of happy memory, the popes of Rome—Calixtus, Eugene, Alexander, Clement, Celestine, Innocent, and Honorius.

We decree moreover that no Christian shall compel them or any one of their group to come to baptism unwillingly. But if any one of them shall take refuge of his own accord with Christians, because of conviction, then, after his intention will have been made manifest, he shall be made a Christian without any intrigue. For indeed that person who is known to come to Christian baptism not freely, but unwillingly, is not believed to possess the Christian faith.

Moreover, no Christian shall presume to seize, imprison, wound, torture, mutilate, kill, or inflict violence on them; furthermore no one shall presume, except by judicial action of the authorities of the country, to change the good customs in the land where they live for the purpose of taking their money or goods from them or from others.

In addition, no one shall disturb them in any way during the celebration of their festivals, whether by day or by night, with clubs or stones or anything else. Also no one shall exact any compulsory service of them unless it be that which they have been accustomed to render in previous times.

Inasmuch as the Jews are not able to bear witness against the Christians, we decree furthermore that the testimony of Christians against Jews shall not be valid unless there is among these Christians some Jew who is there for the purpose of offering testimony.

Since it occasionally happens that some Christians lose their Christian children, the Jews are accused by their enemies of secretly carrying off and killing these same Christian children, and of making sacrifices of the heart and blood of these very children. It happens, too, that the parents of these children, or some other Christian enemies of these Jews, secretly hide these very children in order that they may be able to injure these Jews, and in order that they may be able to extort from them a certain amount of money by redeeming them from their straits.

And most falsely do these Christians claim that the Jews have secretly and furtively carried away these children and killed them, and that the Jews offer sacrifice from the heart and the blood of these children, since their law in this matter precisely and expressly forbids Jews to sacrifice, eat, or drink the blood, or eat the flesh of animals having claws. This has been demonstrated many times at our court by Jews converted to the Christian faith: nevertheless very many Jews are often seized and detained unjustly because of this.

We decree, therefore, that Christians need not be obeyed against Jews in such a case or situation of this type, and we order that Jews seized under such a silly pretext be freed from imprisonment, and that they shall not be arrested henceforth on such a miserable pretext, unless—which we do not believe—they be caught in the commission of the crime. We decree that no Christian shall stir up anything against them, but that they should be maintained in that status and position in which they were from the time of our predecessors, from antiquity till now.

We decree, in order to stop the wickedness and avarice of bad men, that no one shall dare to devastate or to destroy a cemetery of the Jews or to dig up human bodies for the sake of getting money [by holding them for ransom]. Moreover, if anyone, after having known the content of this decree, should—which we hope will not happen—attempt audaciously to act contrary to it, then let him suffer punishment in his rank and position, or let him be punished by the penalty of excommunication, unless he makes amends for his boldness by proper recompense. Moreover, we wish that only those Jews who have not attempted to contrive anything toward the destruction of the Christian faith be fortified by the support of such protection. . . .

Despite such decrees, violence against Jews might burst out when fears and emotions were running high. This selection is from the official chronicles of the upper-Rhineland towns.

In the year 1349 there occurred the greatest epidemic that ever happened. Death went from one end of the earth to the other, on that side and this side of the [Mediterranean] sea, and it was greater among the Saracens [Muslims] than among the Christians. In some lands everyone died so that no one was left. Ships were also found on the sea laden with wares; the crew had all died and no one guided the ship. The Bishop of Marseilles and priests and monks and more than half of all the people there died with them. In other kingdoms and cities so many people perished that it would be horrible to describe. The pope at Avignon stopped all sessions of court, locked himself in a room, allowed no one to approach him and had a fire burning before him all the time. And from what this epidemic came, all wise teachers and physicians could only say that it was God's will. And the plague was now here, so it was in other places, and lasted more than a whole year. This epidemic also came to Strasbourg in the summer of the above mentioned year, and it is estimated about sixteen thousand people died.

In the matter of this plague the Jews throughout the world were reviled and accused in all lands of having caused it through the poison which they are said to have put into the water and the wells—that is what they were accused of—and for this reason the Jews were burnt all the way from the Mediterranean into Germany, but not in Avignon, for the pope protected them there.

Nevertheless they tortured a number of Jews in Berne and Zofingen who admitted they had put poison into many wells, and they found the poison in the wells. Thereupon they burnt the Jews in many towns and wrote of this affair to Strasbourg, Freibourg, and Basel in order that they too should burn their Jews. . . . The deputies of the city of Strasbourg were asked what they were going to do with their Jews. They answered and said that they knew no evil of them. Then . . . there was a great indignation and clamor against the deputies from Strasbourg. So finally the Bishop and the lords and the Imperial Cities agreed to do away with the Jews. The result was that they were burnt in many cities, and wherever they were expelled they were caught by the peasants and stabbed to death or drowned. . . .

On Saturday—that was St. Valentine's Day—they burnt the Jews on a wooden platform in their cemetery. There were about two thousand people of them. Those who wanted to baptize themselves were spared. Many small children were taken out of the fire and baptized against the will of their fathers and mothers. And everything that was owed to the Jews was cancelled, and the Jews had to surrender all pledges and notes that they had taken for debts. The council, however, took the cash that the Jews possessed and divided it among the working-men proportionately. The money was indeed the thing that killed the Jews. If they had been poor and if the feudal lords had not been in debt to them, they would not have been burnt.

QUESTIONS FOR ANALYSIS

1. Why do Aquinas and Pope Gregory oppose prejudicial actions against Jews?
2. Why did prejudice increase at the time of the Black Death?
3. What factors account for the differences between the views of Christian leaders and the Christian masses?

Source: First selection reprinted with the permission of Pocket Books, a Division of Simon & Schuster, Inc. and Vernon and Janet Bourke Living Trust from *The Pocket Aquinas*, edited with translations by Vernon G. Bourke. Copyright © 1960 by Washington Square Press. Copyright renewed © 1988 by Simon & Schuster, Inc. Second and third selections from Jacob R. Marcus, ed., *The Jew in the Medieval World: A Source Book, 315–1791* (Cincinnati: Union of American Hebrew Congregations, 1938), 152–154, 45–47. Copyright © 1938. Reprinted with permission of the Hebrew Union College Press, Cincinnati.

concerns a woman from Bath, a city in southern England, who became wealthy by marrying a succession of old men for their money (and then two other husbands for love), "aside from other company in youth." She was also a skilled weaver, Chaucer says: "In making cloth she showed so great a bent, / She bettered those of Ypres and of Ghent." By the fifteenth century, a new class of wealthy merchant-bankers was operating on a vast scale and specializing in money changing and loans and making investments on behalf of other parties. Merchants great and small used their services. They also handled the financial transactions of ecclesiastical and secular officials and arranged for the transmission to the pope of funds known as Peter's pence, a collection taken up annually in every church in the Latin West. Princes and kings supported their wars and lavish courts with credit. Some merchant-bankers even developed their own news services, gathering information on any topic that could affect business.

Florentine financiers invented checking accounts, organized private shareholding companies (the forerunners of modern corporations), and improved bookkeeping techniques. In the fifteenth century, the Medici (MED-ih-chee) family of Florence operated banks in Italy, Flanders, and London. Medicis also controlled the government of Florence and commissioned art works. The Fuggers (FOOG-uhrz) of Augsburg, who had ten times the Medici bank's lending capital, topped Europe's banking fraternity by 1500. Beginning as cloth merchants under Jacob "the Rich" (1459–1525), the family's many activities included the trade in Hungarian copper, essential for casting cannon.

Since Latin Christians generally considered usury (charging interest) sinful, Jews predominated in money lending. Christian bankers devised ways to profit from loans indirectly in order to get around the condemnation of usury. Some borrowers repaid loans in a different currency at a rate of exchange favorable to the lender. Others added to their repayment a "gift" in thanks to the lender. For example, in 1501, church officials agreed to repay a Fugger loan of 6,000 gold ducats in five months along with a "gift" of 400 ducats, amounting to an effective interest rate of 16 percent a year. In fact, the return was less since the church failed to repay the loan on time.

Yet most residents of western European cities lived in poverty and squalor rather than wealth.

SECTION REVIEW

- After 1200, most cities grew through manufacture and trade, particularly those of northern Italy, Flanders, and the Baltic coast.

- Expanding trade and technological innovation ultimately reduced Europe's dependence on eastern goods.

- Cities fostered social mobility, but civic life was dominated by guilds, wealthy merchants, and bankers.

- Most urban residents lived in squalor without the amenities of Islamic Middle Eastern cities.

- Gothic cathedrals became signs of special civic pride and prestige in European cities.

European cities generally lacked the civic amenities, such as public baths and water supply systems, that had existed in the cities of Western antiquity and still survived in cities of the Islamic Middle East.

Gothic Cathedrals

Master builders and associated craftsmen counted among the skilled people in greatest demand. Though cities competed with one another in the magnificence of their guild halls, town halls, and other structures, **Gothic cathedrals**, first appearing about 1140 in France, cost the most and brought the greatest prestige. The pointed, or Gothic, arch, replacing the older round, or Roman, arch, proved a hallmark of the new design. External (flying) buttresses stabilizing the high, thin, stone columns below the arches constituted another distinctive feature. This method of construction enabled master builders to push the Gothic cathedrals to great heights and fill the outside walls with giant windows depicting religious scenes in brilliantly colored stained glass. During the next four centuries, interior heights soared ever higher, towers and spires pierced the heavens, and walls became dazzling curtains of stained glass.

The men who designed and built the cathedrals had little or no formal education and limited understanding of the mathematical principles of modern civil engineering. Master masons sometimes

Gothic cathedrals Large churches originating in twelfth-century France; built in an architectural style featuring pointed arches, tall vaults and spires, flying buttresses, and large stained-glass windows.

miscalculated, causing parts of some overly ambitious cathedrals to collapse. The record-high choir vault of Beauvais Cathedral, for instance—154 feet (47 meters) in height—came tumbling down in 1284. But as builders gained experience and invented novel solutions to their problems, success rose from the rubble of their mistakes. The cathedral spire in Strasbourg reached 466 feet (142 meters) into the air—as high as a forty-story building. Such heights were unsurpassed until the twentieth century.

Learning, Literature, and the Renaissance

What factors were responsible for the promotion of learning and the arts in the Latin West?

Throughout the Middle Ages, people in the Latin West lived amid reminders of the achievements of the Romans. They wrote and worshiped in a version of their language, traveled their roads, and obeyed some of their laws. The vestments and robes of popes, kings, and emperors followed the designs of Roman officials. Yet the learning of Greco-Roman antiquity virtually disappeared with the rise of the biblical world described in the Hebrew and Christian scriptures.

A small revival of learning associated with the court of Charlemagne in the ninth century was followed by a larger renaissance (rebirth) in the twelfth century. Cities became centers of intellectual and artistic life. The universities established across the Latin West after 1200 contributed to this cultural revival. In the mid-fourteenth century, the pace of intellectual and artistic life quickened in what is often called the **Renaissance**, which began in northern Italy and later spread to northern Europe. Some Italian authors saw the Italian Renaissance as a sharp break with an age of darkness. Others see this era as the high noon of a day that had been dawning for several centuries.

Universities and Scholarship

Before 1100, Byzantine and Islamic scholarship generally surpassed scholarship in Latin Europe. When Latin Christians wrested southern Italy from the Byzantines and Sicily and Toledo, Spain, from the Muslims in the eleventh century, they acquired many manuscripts of Greek and Arabic works. These included works by Plato and Aristotle (AR-ih-staht-uhl) and Greek treatises on medicine, mathematics, and geography, as well as scientific and philosophical writings by Muslim writers. Latin translations of the Iranian philosopher Ibn Sina (IB-uhn SEE-nah) (980–1037), known in the West as Avicenna (av-uh-SEN-uh), had great influence because of their sophisticated blend of Aristotelian and Islamic philosophy. Jewish scholars contributed significantly to the translation and explication of Arabic and other manuscripts.

The thirteenth century saw the foundation of two new religious orders, the Dominicans and the Franciscans, some of whose most talented members taught in the independent colleges that arose after 1200. Some scholars believe that the colleges established in Paris and Oxford patterned themselves on similarly endowed places of study then spreading in the Islamic world—*madrasas*, which provided subsidized housing for poor students and paid the salaries of their teachers. The Latin West, however, innovated the idea of **universities**, degree-granting corporations specializing in multidisciplinary research and advanced teaching.

Between 1300 and 1500, sixty universities joined the twenty established before that time. Students banded together to start some of them; guilds of professors founded others. Teaching guilds, like the guilds overseeing manufacturing and commerce, set standards for the profession, trained apprentices and masters, and defended their professional interests.

Universities set the curriculum for each discipline and instituted final examinations for degrees. Students who passed the exams that ended their apprenticeship received a "license" to teach. Students who completed longer training and defended a masterwork of scholarship became "masters" and "doctors." The University of Paris gradually absorbed the city's various colleges,

Renaissance (European) A period of intense artistic and intellectual activity, said to be a "rebirth" of Greco-Roman culture. Usually divided into an Italian Renaissance, from roughly the mid-fourteenth to mid-fifteenth century, and a Northern Renaissance, from roughly the early fifteenth to early seventeenth century.

universities Degree-granting institutions of higher learning. Those that appeared in the Latin West from about 1200 onward became the model of all modern universities.

Dante's Divine Comedy This fifteenth-century painting by Domenico di Michelino shows Dante holding a copy of the *Divine Comedy*. Hell is depicted to the poet's left and the terraces of Purgatory behind him, surmounted by the earthly and heavenly Paradise. The city of Florence, with its recently completed cathedral, appears on the right.

but the colleges of Oxford and Cambridge remained independent, self-governing organizations.

Since all universities used Latin, students and masters could move freely across political and linguistic lines, seeking the courses they wanted and the most interesting professors. Some universities offered specialized training. Legal training centered on Bologna (buh-LOHN-yuh); Montpellier and Salerno focused on medicine; Paris and Oxford excelled in theology.

The prominence of theology stemmed from many students aspiring to ecclesiastical careers, but scholars also saw theology as "queen of the sciences"—the central discipline encompassing all knowledge. Hence, thirteenth-century theologians sought to synthesize the rediscovered philosophical works of Aristotle and the commentaries of Avicenna with the Bible's revealed truth. These efforts to synthesize reason and faith were known as **scholasticism** (skoh-LAS-tih-sizm).

Thomas Aquinas, a brilliant Dominican priest who taught theology at the University of Paris, wrote the most notable scholastic work, the *Summa*

Theologica (SOOM-uh thee-uh-LOH-jih-kuh), between 1267 and 1273. Although his exposition of Christian belief organized on Aristotelian principles came to be accepted as a masterly demonstration of the reasonableness of Christianity, scholasticism upset many traditional thinkers. Some church authorities tried to ban Aristotle from the curriculum. In addition, rivalry between the leading Dominican and Franciscan theological scholars continued over the next two centuries. However, the considerable freedom of medieval universities from both secular and religious authorities enabled the new ideas to prevail over the fears of church administrators.

Humanists and Printers

Dante Alighieri (DAHN-tay ah-lee-GYEH-ree) (1265–1321) completed a long, elegant poem, the *Divine Comedy*, shortly before his death. This supreme expression of medieval preoccupations tells the allegorical story of Dante's journey through the nine circles of Hell and the seven terraces of Purgatory, followed by his entry

 Primary Source: *Summa Theologica*: On Free Will Do humans have free will? Find out what Thomas Aquinas thinks.

scholasticism A philosophical and theological system, associated with Thomas Aquinas, that was devised to reconcile Aristotelian philosophy and Roman Catholic theology in the thirteenth century.

into Paradise. The Roman poet Virgil guides him through Hell and Purgatory; Beatrice, a woman he had loved from afar since childhood and whose death inspired the poem, guides him to Paradise.

The *Divine Comedy* foreshadows the literary fashions of the later Italian Renaissance. Dante wrote in the vernacular spoken in Tuscany (TUS-kuh-nee), the medieval version of Italian. Like Dante, later Italian writers made use of Greco-Roman classical themes and mythology and sometimes courted a broader audience by writing not in Latin but in their local language

The poet Geoffrey Chaucer, many of whose works show the influence of Dante, wrote in vernacular English. The *Canterbury Tales*, a lengthy poem written in the last dozen years of his life, contains often humorous and earthy tales told by fictional pilgrims on their way to the shrine of Thomas à Becket in Canterbury (see Chapter 10). They present a vivid cross-section of medieval people and attitudes.

Dante influenced a literary movement of **humanists** that began in his native Florence in the mid-fourteenth century. The term refers to their interest in grammar, rhetoric, poetry, history, and moral philosophy (ethics)—subjects known collectively as the humanities, an ancient discipline. With the brash exaggeration characteristic of new intellectual fashions, humanist writers like the poet Francesco Petrarch (fran-CHES-koh PAY-trahrk) (1304–1374) and the poet and storyteller Giovanni Boccaccio (jo-VAH-nee boh-KAH-chee-oh) (1313–1375) proclaimed a revival of the classical Greco-Roman tradition they felt had for centuries lain buried under the rubble of the Middle Ages.

This idea of a rebirth of learning dismisses too readily the monastic and university scholars who for centuries had been recovering all sorts of Greco-Roman learning, as well as writers like Dante (whom the humanists revered), who anticipated humanist interests by a generation. Yet the humanists had a great impact as educators, advisers, and reformers. Their greatest influence came in reforming secondary education. They introduced a curriculum centered on the languages and literature of Greco-Roman antiquity, which they felt provided intellectual discipline, moral lessons, and refined tastes. This curriculum dominated European secondary schools well into the twentieth century. The universities felt the humanist influence less, mostly after 1500. Theology, law, medicine, and

branches of philosophy other than ethics remained prominent in university education during this period.

Many humanists tried to duplicate the elegance of classical Latin and (to a lesser extent) Greek, which they revered as the pinnacle of learning, beauty, and wisdom. Boccaccio gained fame with his vernacular writings, which resemble Dante's, and especially for the *Decameron*, an earthy work that has much in common with Chaucer's boisterous tales. Under Petrarch's influence, however, Boccaccio turned to writing in classical Latin.

As humanist scholars mastered Latin and Greek, they turned their language skills to restoring the original texts of Greco-Roman writers and of the Bible. By comparing different manuscripts, they eliminated errors introduced by generations of copyists. To aid in this task, Pope Nicholas V (r. 1447–1455) created the Vatican Library, buying scrolls of Greco-Roman writings and paying to have accurate copies and translations made. Working independently, the Dutch scholar Erasmus (uh-RAZ-muhs) of Rotterdam (ca. 1466–1536) produced a critical edition of the New Testament in Greek. Erasmus corrected many errors and mistranslations in the Latin text that had been in general use throughout the Middle Ages.

The influence of the humanists grew as the new technology of printing made their critical editions of ancient texts, literary works, and moral guides more available. The Chinese and the Arabs used carved woodblocks for printing, and block-printed playing cards circulated in Europe before 1450, but after that date three European improvements revolutionized printing: (1) movable pieces of type consisting of individual letters, (2) new ink suitable for printing on paper, and (3) the **printing press**, a mechanical device that pressed inked type onto sheets of paper.

Johann Gutenberg (yoh-HAHN GOO-ten-burg) (ca. 1394–1468) of Mainz in Germany led the way. The Gutenberg Bible of 1454, the first book in the West

humanists (Renaissance) European scholars, writers, and teachers associated with the study of the humanities (grammar, rhetoric, poetry, history, languages, and moral philosophy), influential in the fifteenth century and later.

printing press A mechanical device for transferring text or graphics from a woodblock or type to paper using ink. Presses using movable type first appeared in Europe in about 1450.

A French Printshop, 1537 A workman operates the "press," quite literally a screw device that presses the paper to the inked type. Other employees examine the printed sheets, each of which holds four pages. When folded, the sheets make a book.

Giraudon/Art Resource, NY

History in Focus *Notice what the figures in this image are doing, how they are dressed, and the features of the space in which they work. What does this image suggest about printing as a kind of work and the position of printers in society? Find the answer online.*

printed from movable type, exhibited a beauty and craftsmanship that bore witness to the printer's years of experimentation. Humanists worked closely with the printers, who spread the new techniques to Italy and France. Erasmus did editing and proofreading for the Italian scholar-printer Aldo Manuzio (1449–1515) in Venice. Manuzio's press published many critical editions of classical Latin and Greek texts.

By 1500, at least 10 million printed volumes flowed from presses in 238 European towns, launching a revolution that affected students, scholars, and a growing literate population. These readers consumed unorthodox political and religious tracts along with ancient texts.

Renaissance Artists

Although the artists of the fourteenth and fifteenth centuries continued to depict biblical subjects, the Greco-Roman revival led some, especially in Italy, to portray ancient deities and myths. Another popular trend involved scenes of daily life.

Neither theme was entirely new, however. Renaissance art, like Renaissance scholarship, owed a debt to earlier generations. Italian painters of the fifteenth century credited the Florentine painter Giotto (JAW-toh) (ca. 1267–1337) with single-handedly reviving the "lost art of painting." In religious scenes, Giotto replaced the stiff, staring figures of the Byzantine style, which were intended to overawe viewers, with more natural and human portraits with whose emotions of grief and love viewers could identify. Rather than floating on backgrounds of gold leaf, his saints inhabit earthly landscapes. North of the Alps, the Flemish painter Jan van Eyck (yahn vahn IKE) (ca. 1390–1441) mixed his pigments with linseed oil in place of the egg yolk of earlier centuries. Oil paints dried more slowly and gave pictures a superior luster. Italian painters quickly copied van Eyck's technique, though his own masterfully realistic paintings on religious and domestic themes remained distinctive.

Leonardo da Vinci (leh-own-AHR-doh dah VIN-chee) (1452–1519) used oil paints for his *Mona Lisa.* Renaissance artists like Leonardo worked in many media, including bronze sculptures and frescos (painting on wet plaster) like *The Last Supper.* Leonardo's notebooks also contain imaginative designs for airplanes, submarines, and tanks. His younger contemporary Michelangelo (my-kuhl-AN-juh-low) (1472–1564) painted frescoes of biblical scenes on the ceiling of the Sistine Chapel in the Vatican, sculpted statues of David and Moses, and designed the dome for a new Saint Peter's Basilica in Rome.

The patronage of wealthy and educated merchants and prelates underlay the artistic blossoming in the cities of northern Italy and Flanders. The Florentine banker Cosimo de' Medici (1389–1464) and his grandson Lorenzo (1449–1492), known as "the Magnificent," spent immense sums on paintings, sculpture, and public buildings. In Rome, the papacy (PAY-puh-see) launched a building program that culminated in the construction of the new Saint Peter's Basilica and a residence for the pope.

These scholarly and artistic achievements exemplify the innovation and striving for excellence of the Late Middle Ages. The new literary themes and artistic styles of this period had lasting influence on Western culture. But the innovations in the organization of universities, in printing, and in oil painting had wider implications, for they were later adopted by cultures all over the world.

Political and Military Transformations

What social, political, and military developments contributed to the rise of European nations in this period?

Stronger and more unified states and armies developed in western Europe in parallel with the economic and cultural revivals (see Map 14.1). Through the prolonged struggle of the Hundred Years War, French and English monarchs forged closer ties with the nobility, the church, and the merchants. Crusades against Muslim states brought consolidation to Spain and Portugal. In Italy and Germany, however, political power remained in the hands of small states and loose alliances.

Monarchs, Nobles, and the Church

Thirteenth-century states continued early medieval state structures (see Chapter 10). Hereditary monarchs topped the political pyramid, but modest treasuries and the rights of nobles and the church limited their powers. Powerful noblemen who controlled vast estates had an important voice in matters of state, and the church guarded closely its traditional rights and independence. Towns, too, had acquired rights and privileges. Towns in Flanders, the Hanseatic League, and Italy approached independence from royal interference. In theory the ruler's noble vassals owed military service in time of war. In practice, vassals sought to limit the monarch's power.

In the year 1200, knights still formed the backbone of western European armies, but changes in weaponry brought this into question. Improved crossbows could shoot metal-tipped arrows with enough force to pierce helmets and light body armor. Professional crossbowmen, hired for wages, became increasingly common and much feared. Indeed, a church council in 1139 outlawed the crossbow—ineffectively—as being too deadly for use against Christians. The arrival in Europe of firearms based on the Chinese invention of gunpowder (see Chapter 12) further transformed the medieval army.

The church also resisted royal control. In 1302, the outraged Pope Boniface VIII (r. 1294–1303) asserted that divine law made the papacy superior to "every human creature," including monarchs. Issuing his own claim of superiority, King Philip "the Fair" of France (r. 1285–1314) sent an army to arrest the pope, a chastisement that hastened Pope Boniface's death. Philip then engineered the election of a French pope, who established a new papal residence at Avignon (ah-vee-NYON) in southern France in 1309.

A succession of French-dominated popes residing in Avignon improved church discipline but at the price of compromising their neutrality in the eyes of other rulers. The **Great Western Schism** between 1378 and 1415 saw rival papal claimants at Avignon and Rome vying for Christian loyalties. The papacy eventually regained its independence and returned to Rome, but the long crisis broke the pope's ability to challenge the rising power of monarchs like Philip, who had used the dispute to persuade his nobles to grant him a new tax.

The English monarchy wielded more centralized power as a result of consolidation that took place after the Norman conquest of 1066. The Anglo-Norman kings also extended their realm by assaults on their Celtic neighbors. Between 1200 and 1400, they incorporated Wales and reasserted control over most of Ireland. Nevertheless, under King John (r. 1199–1216), royal power suffered a severe setback. Forced to acknowledge the pope as his overlord in 1213, he lost his bid to reassert claims to Aquitaine in southern France the following year and then yielded to his nobles by signing the Magna Carta in 1215. This "Great Charter" affirmed that monarchs were subject to established law, confirmed the independence of the church and the city of London, and guaranteed the nobles' hereditary rights.

The Hundred Years War

The conflict between the king of France and his vassals known as the **Hundred Years War** (1337–1453) affords a key example of the transformation in politics and war. These vassals included the kings of England (for lands that belonged to their Norman ancestors), the counts of prosperous and independent-minded Flanders, and the dukes of Brittany and Burgundy. In typical fashion, the conflict grew out of a marriage alliance.

Marriage between Princess Isabella of France and King Edward II of England (r. 1307–1327) should have ensured the king's loyalty, as a vassal, to the French monarchy. However, when the next generation of the French ruling house produced no other sons, Isabella's son, King Edward III of England (r. 1327–1377), laid claim to the French throne in 1337. French courts instead awarded the throne to a more distant (and more French) cousin. Edward decided to fight for his rights.

The new military technology shaped the conflict. Early in the war, hired Italian cross-bowmen reinforced the French cavalry, but the English long-bow proved superior. Adopted from the Welsh, the 6-foot (1.8-meter) longbow could shoot farther and more rapidly than the crossbow. Its arrows could not pierce armor, but concentrated volleys found gaps in the knights' defenses or struck their less-protected horses. Heavier and more encompassing armor provided a defense but limited a knight's movements. Once pulled off his steed by a foot soldier armed with a pike (hooked pole), he could not get up.

Later in the Hundred Years War, firearms gained prominence. The first cannon scared the horses with smoke and noise but did little damage. As they grew larger, however, they proved effective in battering the walls of castles and towns. The first artillery use against the French, at the Battle of Agincourt (1415), gave the English an important victory.

Faced with a young French peasant woman called Joan of Arc, subsequent English gains stalled. Acting, she believed, on God's instructions, she put on armor and rallied the French troops to defeat the English in 1429. Shortly afterward, she fell into English hands; she was tried by English churchmen and burned at the stake as a witch in 1431.

In the final battles, French cannon demolished the walls of once-secure castles held by the English and their allies. The truce that ended the struggle in 1453 left the French monarchy in firm control.

New Monarchies in France and England

The war proved a watershed in the rise of **new monarchies** in France and England, centralized states with fixed national boundaries and stronger representative institutions. English monarchs after 1453 consolidated control over territory within the British Isles, though the Scots defended their independence. The French monarchs

Primary Source: Magna Carta: The Great Charter of Liberties Get a feel for one of history's most important legal documents.

Great Western Schism A division in the Latin (Western) Christian Church between 1378 and 1415, when rival claimants to the papacy existed in Rome and Avignon.

Hundred Years War (1337–1453) Series of campaigns over control of the throne of France, involving English and French royal families and French noble families.

new monarchies Historians' term for the monarchies in France, England, and Spain from 1450 to 1600. The centralization of royal power was increasing within more or less fixed territorial limits.

also turned to consolidating control over powerful noble families, especially those headed by women. Mary of Burgundy (1457–1482) was forced to surrender most of her family's vast holdings to the king. Then in 1491, Anne of Brittany's forced marriage to the king led to the eventual incorporation of her duchy (DUTCH-ee) into France.

Military technology undermined the nobility. Smaller, more mobile cannon developed in the late fifteenth century pounded castle walls. Improvements in hand-held firearms, able by the late fifteenth century to pierce the heaviest armor, ended the domination of the armored knight. Armies now depended less on knights and more on bowmen, pikemen, musketeers, and artillerymen.

The new monarchies needed a way to finance their full-time armies. Some nobles agreed to money payments in place of military service and to additional taxes in time of war. For example, in 1439 and 1445, Charles VII of France (r. 1422–1461) successfully levied a new tax on his vassals' land. This not only paid the costs of the war with England but also provided the monarchy with a financial base for the next 350 years.

Merchants' taxes also provided revenues. Taxes on the English wool trade, begun by King Edward III, paid most of the costs of the Hundred Years War. Some rulers taxed Jewish merchants or extorted large contributions from wealthy towns. Individual merchants sometimes curried royal favor with loans. The fifteenth-century French merchant Jacques Coeur (cur) gained many social and financial benefits for himself and his family by lending money to French courtiers, but his debtors accused him of murder and had his fortune confiscated.

The church provided a third source of revenue through voluntary contributions to support a war. English and French monarchs won the right to appoint important church officials in their realms in the fifteenth century. They subsequently used state power to enforce religious orthodoxy more vigorously than the popes had been able to do. But reformers complained that the church's spiritual mission became subordinate to political and economic concerns.

The shift in power to the monarchs and away from the nobility and the church did not deprive nobles of their social position and roles as government officials and military officers. Moreover, the kings of England and France in 1500 had to deal with representative

SECTION REVIEW

- Between 1200 and 1500, monarchs, nobles, and the church struggled over political power.
- Tensions between the French monarchy and the papacy resulted in the Great Western Schism.
- In England, royal power was checked by the papacy and nobility, the latter imposing the Magna Carta on King John.
- The Hundred Years War between the French monarchy and its vassals introduced new military technologies.
- The war also stimulated the rise of the new centralized monarchies of England and France.
- Spain and Portugal continued the reconquest of Muslim Iberia, a process completed by Ferdinand and Isabella.

institutions that had not existed in 1200. The English Parliament proved a permanent check on royal power: the House of Lords contained the great nobles and church officials, while the House of Commons represented the towns and the leading citizens of the counties. In France, the Estates General, a similar but less effective representative body, represented the church, the nobles, and the towns.

Iberian Unification

Spain and Portugal's **reconquest of Iberia** from Muslim rule expanded the boundaries of Latin Christianity. The knights who pushed the borders of their kingdoms southward furthered both Christianity and their own interests. The spoils of victory included irrigated farmland, rich cities, and ports on the Mediterranean Sea and Atlantic Ocean. Serving God, growing rich, and living off the labor of others became a way of life for the Iberian nobility.

The reconquest proceeded over several centuries. Toledo fell and became a Christian outpost in 1085. English crusaders bound for the Holy Land helped take Lisbon in 1147. It displaced the older city of Oporto (meaning "the port"), from which Portugal took its name, as both capital and the kingdom's leading city. After a Christian victory in 1212 broke the back of

reconquest of Iberia Beginning in the eleventh century, military campaigns by various Iberian Christian states to recapture territory taken by Muslims. In 1492 the last Muslim ruler was defeated, and Spain and Portugal emerged as united kingdoms.

Muslim power, the reconquest accelerated. Within decades, Portuguese and Castilian forces captured the prosperous cities of Cordova (1236) and Seville (1248) and drove the Muslims from the southwestern region known as Algarve (ahl-GAHRV) ("the west" in Arabic). Only the small kingdom of Granada hugging the Mediterranean coast remained in Muslim hands.

By incorporating Algarve in 1249, Portugal attained its modern territorial limits. After a pause to colonize, Christianize, and consolidate this land, Portugal took the crusade to North Africa. In 1415, Portuguese knights seized the port of Ceuta (say-OO-tah) in Morocco, where they learned more about the Saharan caravan trade in gold and slaves. During the next few decades, Portuguese mariners sailed down the Atlantic coast of Africa seeking rumored African Christian allies and access to this trade (see Chapter 15).

Elsewhere in Iberia, the reconquest continued. Spain came into being when the marriage of Princess Isabella of Castile and Prince Ferdinand of Aragon in 1469 led to the union of their kingdoms when they inherited their respective thrones a decade later. Their conquest of Granada in 1492 secured the final piece of Muslim territory for the new kingdom.

Ferdinand and Isabella sponsored the first voyage of Christopher Columbus in 1492 (see Chapter 15). In a third momentous event of that year, the monarchs manifested their crusading mentality by ordering all Jews expelled from their kingdoms. Attempts to convert or expel the remaining Muslims led to a revolt at the end of 1499 that lasted until 1501. The Spanish rulers expelled the last Muslims in 1502. Portugal expelled the Jews in 1496, including 100,000 refugees from Spain.

Conclusion

For seven hundred years after the fall of Rome, western Europe was impoverished economically and culturally compared to the Roman Empire at its height, but also and more importantly, compared to the Byzantine Empire, to the Arab empires, or to China and India during that same period. Though other parts of Eurasia suffered from wars and invasions, western European towns and farmlands were devastated by repeated barbarian invasions until ca. 1100. Despite the efforts of Charlemagne and the Catholic Church to keep Roman traditions alive, life for most people remained dangerous and the towns remained small and poor. Only when the invaders settled down did towns begin to grow, trade picked up, and farmers expanded their fields and increased their harvests.

From then on, life in western Europe was gradually transformed by a series of technological innovations. Farmers increased their yields by planting more of their land and using horses in place of oxen. New wind and water mills substituted inanimate energy for human labor. Intellectual life also picked up as universities were founded and wealthy rulers, first in Italy and later in northern Europe, patronized artists, writers, and musicians and built beautiful new buildings. Though the Black Death decimated the population and set the economy back many decades, western Europe nonetheless rebounded. By the late fifteenth century, it had surpassed the Muslim world economically and was preparing to expand beyond the oceans.

CHAPTER REVIEW

 Download the MP3 audio file of the Chapter Review to listen to on the go.

How well did inhabitants of the Latin West, rich and poor, urban and rural, deal with their natural environment? (page 333)

Ecologically, the peoples of Latin Europe harnessed the power of wind and water and mined and refined their mineral wealth at the cost of localized pollution and deforestation. However, food production and distribution did not keep up with population growth, and the Black Death devastated Europe in the mid-fourteenth century.

What social and economic factors led to the growth of cities in late medieval Europe? (page 338)

Politically, basic features of the modern European state began to emerge. Frequent wars caused kingdoms of moderate size to develop exceptional military strength. The ruling class saw economic strength as the twin of political power and promoted the welfare of cities specializing in trade, manufacturing, and finance, whose profits they taxed.

What factors were responsible for the promotion of learning and the arts in the Latin West? (page 344)

Culturally, autonomous universities and printing supported the advance of knowledge. Art and architecture reached unsurpassed peaks in the Renaissance. Late medieval society also displayed a fundamental fascination with tools and techniques. New inventions and improved versions of old ones underlay the new dynamism in commerce, warfare, industry, and navigation.

What social, political, and military developments contributed to the rise of European nations in this period? (page 348)

Many of the tools that the Latin West would use to challenge Eastern supremacy—printing, firearms, and navigational devices—originally came from the East. However, western European success depended as much on strong motives for expansion. From the eleventh century onward, population pressure, religious zeal, economic enterprise, and intellectual curiosity drove an expansion of territory and resources that took the crusaders to the Holy Land, merchants to the eastern Mediterranean and Black Seas, the English into Wales and Ireland, German settlers across the Elbe River, and Iberian Christians into the Muslim south. The early voyages into the Atlantic, discussed in the next chapter, extended these activities.

Key Terms

Latin West *(p. 333)*

three-field system *(p. 334)*

Black Death *(p. 335)*

water wheel *(p. 337)*

Hanseatic League *(p. 339)*

guild *(p. 340)*

Gothic cathedrals *(p. 343)*

Renaissance (European) *(p. 344)*

universities *(p. 344)*

scholasticism *(p. 345)*

humanists (Renaissance) *(p. 346)*

printing press *(p. 346)*

Great Western Schism *(p. 349)*

Hundred Years War *(p. 349)*

new monarchies *(p. 349)*

reconquest of Iberia *(p. 350)*

Web Resources

Pronunciation Guide

Interactive Maps

• MAP 14.1 Europe in 1453

Primary Sources

• *Summa Theologica*: On Free Will

• Magna Carta: The Great Charter of Liberties

Answer to the History in Focus Question

See photo on page 347, "A French Printshop, 1537."

 Visit the CourseMate website at www.cengagebrain.com for additional study tools and review materials for this chapter.

The Maritime Revolution

© Cengage Learning

CHAPTER PREVIEW

Global Maritime Expansion Before 1450
What were the objectives and major accomplishments of the voyages of exploration undertaken by Chinese, Polynesians, and other non-Western peoples?

Iberian Expansion, 1400–1550
In this era of long-distance exploration, did Europeans have any special advantages over other cultural regions?

Encounters with Europe, 1450–1550
What were the different outcomes of European interactions with Africa, India, and the Americas?

The Columbian Exchange
How did the Columbian Exchange alter the natural environment of the Americas?

Conclusion

DIVERSITY & DOMINANCE:
Kongo's Christian King

 Visit the CourseMate website at **www.cengagebrain.com** for additional study tools and review materials for this chapter.

In 1511, the young Ferdinand Magellan sailed from Europe around the southern tip of Africa and eastward across the Indian Ocean as a member of the first Portuguese expedition to explore the East Indies (maritime Southeast Asia). Eight years later, in the service of Spain, he headed an expedition that sought to reach the East Indies by sailing westward from Europe. By the middle of 1521, Magellan's expedition had sailed across the Atlantic, rounded the southern tip of South America, and crossed the Pacific Ocean—but at a high price.

One of the five ships wrecked on a reef; the captain of another deserted and sailed back to Spain. The passage across the Pacific took much longer than anticipated. Dozens of sailors died of starvation and disease. In the Philippines, Magellan himself was killed on April 27, 1521, while aiding a local king who had promised to become a Christian. Magellan's successor met the same fate a few days later.

The expedition's survivors consolidated their resources by burning the least seaworthy of their remaining three ships and transferring the men and supplies to the smaller *Victoria*, which continued westward across the Indian Ocean, around Africa, and back to Europe. Magellan's flagship, the *Trinidad*, tried unsuccessfully to recross the Pacific to Central America. However, the *Victoria*'s return to Spain on September 8, 1522, confirmed Europe's ability and determination to master the oceans. The Portuguese crown had backed a century of daring and dangerous voyages to open routes to Africa, Brazil, and the Indian Ocean, and since 1492 Spain had opened contacts with the American continents. Now the broad Pacific Ocean had been crossed.

Before 1500, powerful states and the rich trading networks of Asia had led the way in overland and maritime expansion. The Iberians set out on their voyages of exploration to reach Eastern markets, and their success began a new era in which the West gradually became the world's center of power, wealth, and innovation.

Global Maritime Expansion Before 1450

What were the objectives and major accomplishments of the voyages of exploration undertaken by Chinese, Polynesians, and other non-Western peoples?

By 1450, mariners had discovered and settled most of the islands of the Pacific, the Atlantic, and the Indian Oceans, and a great trading system united the peoples

Polynesian Canoes Pacific Ocean mariners sailing canoes such as these, shown in an eighteenth-century painting, made epic voyages of exploration and settlement. A large platform connects two canoes at the left, providing more room for the members of the expedition, and a sail supplements the paddlers. "Tereoboo, King of Owyhee, bringing presents to Captain Cook," D. L Ref. p. xx 2f. 35. Courtesy, The Dixson Library, State Library of New South Wales

Chronology

	Pacific Ocean	Atlantic Ocean	Indian Ocean
Pre-1400	**400–1300** Polynesian settlement of Pacific islands		
1400 to 1500		**700–1200** Viking voyages **1300s** Settlement of Madeira, Azores, Canaries **Early 1300s** Mali voyages	**1405–1433** Voyages of Zheng He
		1418–1460 Voyages of Henry the Navigator **1440s** Slaves from West Africa **1482** Portuguese at Gold Coast and Kongo **1486** Portuguese at Benin **1492** Columbus reaches Caribbean **1493** Columbus returns to Caribbean (second voyage) **1493–1502** Spanish conquer Hispaniola **1498** Columbus reaches mainland of South America (third voyage)	**1498** Vasco da Gama reaches India
1500 to 1550	**1518** Smallpox arrives in Caribbean **1519–1522** Magellan expedition	**1500** Cabral reaches Brazil	**1505** Portuguese bombard Swahili Coast cities **1510** Portuguese take Goa **1511** Portuguese take Malacca
		1513 Ponce de Léon explores Florida	**1515** Portuguese take Hormuz
		1519–1521 Cortés conquers Aztec Empire **1532–1533** Pizarro conquers Inca Empire	
			1535 Portuguese take Diu **1538** Portuguese defeat Ottoman fleet **1539** Portuguese aid Ethiopia

around the Indian Ocean. But we know of no individual crossing the Pacific in either direction. Even the narrower Atlantic formed a barrier that kept the peoples of the Americas, Europe, and Africa in ignorance of each other's existence. The inhabitants of Australia were also completely cut off from contact with the rest of humanity. All this was about to change.

The Pacific Ocean

The vast distances that Polynesian peoples voyaged out of sight of land across the Pacific Ocean are one of the most impressive feats in maritime history before 1450 (see Map 15.1). Though they left no written records, over several thousand years mariners from the Malay (may-LAY) Peninsula of Southeast Asia explored and

Interactive Map

Map 15.1 Exploration and Settlement in the Indian and Pacific Oceans Before 1500 Over many centuries, mariners originating in Southeast Asia gradually colonized the islands of the Pacific and Indian Oceans. The Chinese voyages led by Zheng He in the fifteenth century were lavish official expeditions. © Cengage Learning

settled the island chains of the East Indies and continued on to New Guinea and the smaller islands of Melanesia (mel-uh-NEE-zhuh). Beginning sometime before the Common Era (c.e.), a wave of expansion from the area of Fiji brought the first humans to the islands of the central Pacific known as Polynesia. Their sailing canoes reached the easternmost Marquesas (mar-KAY-suhs) Islands about 400 c.e.; Easter Island, 2,200 miles (3,540 kilometers) off the coast of South America, a century later; and the Hawaiian Islands by 500 c.e. Settlement in New Zealand began about 1200. Between 1100 and 1300, new voyages northward from Tahiti brought more Polynesian settlers to Hawaii.

Historians once puzzled over how the Polynesians reached the eastern Pacific islands without compasses to plot their way, particularly in view of the difficulties Magellan's flagship encountered sailing eastward across the Pacific. However, there is now considerable evidence that Polynesian mariners deliberately set out to settle the islands of the eastern Pacific. The languages of the islanders relate closely to the languages of the western Pacific and ultimately to those

of Malaysia and Indonesia. In addition, accidental voyages could not have brought sufficient numbers of men and women for founding a new colony along with all the plants and domesticated animals common to other Polynesian islands.

In 1976, a Polynesian crew led by anthropologist Ben Finney used traditional navigational methods to sail the *Hokulea*, a 62-foot-long (19-meter-long) double canoe, from Hawaii south to Tahiti. Patterned after old oceangoing canoes, some of which measured 120 feet (35 meters) long, it used inverted triangular sails and was steered by paddles (not by a rudder). The *Hokulea*'s crew navigated using only their observation of the currents, stars, and evidence of land, showing that ancient Polynesians had the means and skills to cross the Pacific Ocean.

The Indian Ocean While Polynesian mariners settled the Pacific islands, other Malayo-Indonesians sailed westward across the Indian Ocean and colonized the large island of Madagascar off the southeastern coast of Africa. These voyages continued through the fifteenth century. To this

Chinese Junk This modern drawing shows how much larger one of Zheng He's ships was than one of Vasco da Gama's vessels. Watertight interior bulkheads made junks one of the most seaworthy large ships of the fifteenth century. Sails made of pleated bamboo matting hung from the junk's masts, and a stern rudder provided steering. European ships of exploration, though smaller, were faster and more maneuverable.

Dugald Stermer

day, the inhabitants of Madagascar speak Malayo-Polynesian languages. However, part of the island's population is descended from Africans who crossed the 600 miles (1,000 kilometers) from the mainland to Madagascar, most likely in the centuries just before 1500.

The rise of Islam gave Indian Ocean trade an important boost. The great Muslim cities of the Middle East provided a demand for valuable commodities, and networks of Muslim traders tied the region together. The Indian Ocean traders operated largely independently of the empires and states that they served, but in East Asia, China's early Ming emperors took an active interest in these wealthy ports of trade, sending Admiral **Zheng He** (jung huh) on a series of expeditions (see Chapter 12).

The first Ming fleet in 1405 consisted of sixty-two specially built "treasure ships," large Chinese junks each about 300 feet long by 150 feet wide (90 by 45 meters). Most of the one hundred smaller accompanying vessels exceeded in size the flagship in which Columbus later sailed across the Atlantic. Each treasure ship had nine masts, twelve sails, many decks, and a carrying capacity of 3,000 tons (six times the capacity of Columbus's entire fleet). One expedition carried over 27,000 individuals, including infantry and cavalry troops. Although the ships carried small cannon, highly accurate crossbows dominated most Chinese sea battles.

One Chinese-Arabic interpreter kept a journal recording the customs, dress, and beliefs of the people visited, along with the trade, towns, and animals of their countries. Among his observations were these: exotic animals such as the black panther of Malaya and the tapir of Sumatra; beliefs in legendary "corpse-headed barbarians" whose heads left their bodies at night and caused infants to die; the division of coastal Indians into five classes, which correspond to the four Hindu varnas and a separate Muslim class; and the fact that traders in the Indian port of Calicut (KAL-ih-kut) could perform error-free calculations by counting on their fingers and toes rather than using the Chinese abacus. After his return, the interpreter went on tour in China, telling of these exotic places and "how far the majestic virtue of [China's] imperial dynasty extended."[1]

Interest in new contacts was not confined to the Chinese side. In 1415–1416, at least three trading cities on the Swahili (swah-HEE-lee) Coast of East Africa sent delegations to China. Although no record of African and Chinese reactions to one another survives,

Zheng He (1371–1433) An imperial eunuch and Muslim, entrusted by the Ming emperor Yongle with a series of state voyages that took his gigantic ships through the Indian Ocean, from Southeast Asia to Africa.

China's lavish gifts to local rulers stimulated the Swahili market for silk and porcelain.

The Atlantic Ocean

For several centuries, the Vikings, northern European raiders and pirates, used their small, open ships to attack coastal European settlements. They also discovered and settled one island after another in the North Atlantic. Like the Polynesians, the Vikings had neither maps nor navigational devices. They found their way using their knowledge of the heavens and the seas.

The Vikings first settled Iceland in 770. From there, some moved on to Greenland in 982, and one group sighted North America in 986. Fifteen years later, Leif Ericsson established a short-lived Viking settlement on the island of Newfoundland, which he called Vinland. When the climate turned colder after 1200, the northern settlements in Greenland went into decline, and Vinland became a mysterious place mentioned in Norse sagas.

Some southern Europeans also explored the Atlantic. In 1291, two Vivaldo brothers from Genoa set out to sail around Africa to India. They were never heard of again. Other Genoese and Portuguese expeditions into the Atlantic in the fourteenth century discovered (and settled) the islands of Madeira (muh-DEER-uh), the Azores (A-zorz), and the Canaries.

Mention also occurs of African voyages of exploration in the Atlantic. The Syrian geographer al-Umari (1301–1349) relates that when Mansa Kankan Musa (MAHN-suh KAHN-kahn MOO-suh), the ruler of the West African empire of Mali, passed through Egypt on his lavish pilgrimage to Mecca in 1324, he told of voyages out into the Atlantic undertaken by his predecessor, Mansa Muhammad. Muhammad had sent out four hundred vessels with men and supplies, telling them, "Do not return until you have reached the other side of the ocean or if you have exhausted your food or water." After a long time, one canoe returned, reporting the others had been swept away by a "violent current in the middle of the sea." Muhammad himself then set out at the head of a second, even larger, expedition, from which no one returned.

On the other side of the Atlantic, Amerindian voyagers from South America colonized the West Indies. By the year 1000, Amerindians known as the **Arawak**

(AR-uh-wahk) had moved from the small islands of the Lesser Antilles (Barbados, Martinique, Guadaloupe) into the Greater Antilles (Cuba, Hispaniola, Jamaica, and Puerto Rico), as well as into the Bahamas. Another people, the Carib, followed their route. By the late fifteenth century, they had overrun most Arawak settlements in the Lesser Antilles and were raiding parts of the Greater Antilles. From the West Indies, Arawak and Carib also undertook voyages to the North American mainland.

Iberian Expansion, 1400–1550

In this era of long-distance exploration, did Europeans have any special advantages over other cultural regions?

The preceding survey shows that maritime exploration occurred in many parts of the world before 1450. The sea voyages sponsored by the Iberian kingdoms of Portugal and Spain attract special interest because they began a maritime revolution that profoundly altered the course of world history, ending the isolation of the Americas and increasing global

Arawak Amerindian peoples who inhabited the Greater Antilles of the Caribbean at the time of Columbus.

interaction. The influence in world affairs of the Iberians and other Europeans who followed them overseas rose steadily after 1500.

Iberian overseas expansion arose from two related phenomena. First, Iberian rulers had strong economic, religious, and political motives to expand their contacts and increase their dominance. Second, improvements in maritime and military technologies gave them the means to master treacherous and unfamiliar ocean environments, seize control of existing maritime trade routes, and conquer new lands.

Background to Iberian Expansion

In many ways, these voyages continued four trends evident in the Latin West from about the year 1000: (1) the revival of urban life and trade, (2) a struggle with Islamic powers for dominance of the Mediterranean that mixed religious motives with the desire for trade with distant lands, (3) growing intellectual curiosity about the outside world, and (4) a peculiarly European alliance between merchants and rulers.

The city-states of northern Italy took the lead in all of these developments. By 1450, they had well-established trade links to northern Europe, the Indian Ocean, and the Black Sea, and their merchant princes had sponsored an intellectual and artistic Renaissance. But the Italian states did not take the lead in exploring the Atlantic, even after the expansion of the Ottoman Empire in the fourteenth and fifteenth centuries disrupted their trade to the East, because Venice and Genoa preferred to continue the lucrative alliances with Muslims that had given their merchants privileged positions and because Mediterranean ships were ill suited to the more violent weather of the Atlantic. However, many individual Italians played leading roles in Atlantic exploration.

By contrast, the Iberian kingdoms had engaged in anti-Muslim warfare since the eighth century, when Muslim forces overran most of the peninsula. By about 1250, the Iberian kingdoms of Portugal, Castile, and Aragon had conquered all the Muslim lands in Iberia except the southern kingdom of Granada. Granada finally fell to the united kingdom of Castile and Aragon in 1492, forming Spain, sixteenth-century Europe's most powerful state.

Christian militancy continued to drive Portugal and Spain in their overseas ventures. But the Iberian rulers and their adventurous subjects also sought material returns. Their small share of the Mediterranean trade made them more willing than the Italians to take risks to find new routes to Africa and Asia through the Atlantic. Moreover, both kingdoms participated in the shipbuilding changes and the gunpowder revolution under way in Atlantic Europe. Though not centers of Renaissance learning, both states had exceptional rulers who appreciated new geographical knowledge.

Portuguese Voyages

When the Muslim government of Morocco in northwestern Africa weakened in the fifteenth century, the Portuguese went on the attack, beginning with the city of Ceuta (say-OO-tuh) in 1415. This assault combined aspects of a religious crusade, a plundering expedition, and a military tournament in which young Portuguese knights displayed their bravery. Despite the capture of several more ports along Morocco's Atlantic coast, the Portuguese could not push inland and gain access to the gold trade they learned about, so they sought more direct contact with the gold producers by sailing down the African coast.

Young Prince Henry (1394–1460), third son of the king of Portugal, led the attack on Ceuta. Because he devoted the rest of his life to promoting exploration, he is known as **Henry the Navigator**. His official biographer emphasized his desire to convert Africans to Christianity, make contact with Christian rulers believed to exist in Africa, and launch joint crusades with them against the Ottomans. Profit also figured in his dreams. His initial explorations focused on Africa. His ships established permanent contact with the islands of Madeira in 1418 and the Azores in 1439. Only later did reaching India become a goal.

Henry himself never ventured farther from home than North Africa. Instead, he founded a sort of research institute at Sagres (SAH-gresh) for studying

Henry the Navigator (1394–1460) Portuguese prince who promoted the study of navigation and directed voyages of exploration down the western coast of Africa.

Map 15.2 European Exploration, 1420–1542 Portuguese and Spanish explorers showed the possibility and practicality of intercontinental maritime trade. Before 1540 European trade with Africa and Asia was much more important than that with the Americas, but after the Spanish conquest of the Aztec and Inca Empires transatlantic trade began to increase. Notice the Tordesillas line, which in theory separated the Spanish and Portuguese spheres of activity. © Cengage Learning

Interactive Map

Os montes claros em affrica.

Serra lioa: Castello damina.

Portuguese Map of Western Africa, 1502 This map shows in great detail a section of African coastline that Portuguese explorers charted and named in the fifteenth century. The cartographer illustrated the African interior, which was almost completely unknown to Europeans, with drawings of birds and views of coastal sights: Sierra Leone (Serra lioa), named for a mountain shaped like a lion, and the Portuguese Castle of the Mine (Castello damina) on the Gold Coast.

akg-images

navigation and collecting information about new lands. His staff drew on the pioneering efforts of Italian merchants, especially the Genoese, who had learned some of the secrets of the trans-Saharan trade, and of fourteenth-century Jewish cartographers who used information from Arab and European sources to produce remarkably accurate sea charts and maps of distant places. They also studied and improved navigational instruments that had come into Europe from China and the Islamic world: the magnetic compass, first developed in China, and the astrolabe, an instrument of Arab or Greek invention that enabled mariners to determine their latitude by measuring the position of the sun or the stars.

The Portuguese developed a new type of long-distance sailing vessel, the **caravel** (KAR-uh-vel). The many-oared galleys of the Mediterranean could not carry enough food and water for long ocean voyages, and the three-masted ships of the North Atlantic, powered by square sails, could not sail against the wind. The caravel, which was only one-fifth the size of the largest European ships and the large Chinese junks, could enter shallow coastal waters and explore upriver, yet it had the strength to weather ocean storms. When equipped with lateen sails, caravels had great maneuverability and could sail deeply into the wind; when sporting square Atlantic sails, they had great speed. The addition of small cannon made them good fighting ships as well. The caravels' economy, speed, agility, and power justified a contemporary's claim that they were "the best ships that sailed the seas."[2]

Pioneering captains had to overcome their crews' fears that the South Atlantic waters were boiling hot or contained ocean currents that would prevent their ever returning home. It took Prince Henry from 1420 to 1434 to coax an expedition to venture beyond southern Morocco (see Map 15.2). The next stretch of coast, 800 miles (1,300 kilometers) of desert, offered little of interest to the explorers. Finally in 1444, the mariners reached the Senegal River and the populous, well-watered lands below the Sahara beginning at

caravel A small, highly maneuverable three-masted ship used by the Portuguese and Spanish in the exploration of the Atlantic.

what they named Cape Verde (Green Cape) because of its vegetation.

In the years that followed, Henry's explorers learned how to return speedily to Portugal. Instead of battling the prevailing northeast trade winds and currents back up the coast, they discovered that by sailing northwest into the Atlantic to the latitude of the Azores, ships could pick up prevailing westerly winds that would blow them back to Portugal. The knowledge that ocean winds tend to form large circular patterns helped explorers discover many other ocean routes.

To pay for the research, ships, and expeditions, Prince Henry drew partly on the income of the Order of Christ, a military religious order of which he was the governor. This order had been founded to inherit the Portuguese properties and the crusading tradition of the Order of Knights Templar, which had disbanded in 1314. The Order of Christ received the exclusive right to promote Christianity in all the lands that were discovered, and the Portuguese emblazoned their ships' sails with the crusaders' red cross.

The first financial returns came from selling into slavery Africans captured in raids on the northwest coast of Africa and the Canary Islands during the 1440s. By the end of the century, the Portuguese had captured or purchased 80,000 Africans. However, gold quickly became more important than slavery. By 1457, enough African gold was coming back to Portugal for the kingdom to issue a new gold coin called the *cruzado* (crusade), another reminder of how deeply the Portuguese entwined religious and secular motives. By the time Prince Henry died in 1460, his explorers had established a base of operations in the uninhabited Cape Verde Islands and explored 600 miles (950 kilometers) of coast beyond Cape Verde, as far as what they named Sierra Leone (see-ER-uh lee-OWN) (Lion Mountain). From there, they knew that the coast of Africa curved sharply toward the east. After spending four decades covering the 1,500 miles (2,400 kilometers) from Lisbon to Sierra Leone, Portuguese explorers traveled the remaining 4,000 miles (6,400 kilometers) to the continent's southern tip in only three decades.

Royal sponsorship continued, but private commercial participation sped the progress. In 1469, a Lisbon merchant named Fernão Gomes purchased from the Crown the privilege of exploring 350 miles (550 kilometers) of new coast a year for five years and a monopoly on any resulting trade. Gomes discovered the uninhabited island of São Tomé (sow toh-MAY) on the equator; in the next century, it became a major source of sugar produced with African slave labor. He also explored what later Europeans called the **Gold Coast**, which became the headquarters of Portugal's West African trade.

The expectation of finding a passage around Africa to the Indian Ocean spurred the final thrust down the African coast. **Bartolomeu Dias** rounded the southern tip of Africa (in 1488) and entered the Indian Ocean. In 1497–1498, **Vasco da Gama** led a Portuguese expedition around Africa to India. In 1500, ships in an expedition under Pedro Alvares Cabral (kah-BRAHL), while swinging wide to the west in the South Atlantic to catch the winds that would sweep them around southern Africa and on to India, came on the eastern coast of South America, laying the basis for Portugal's later claim to Brazil.

Spanish Voyages

Spain's early discoveries owed more to haste and blind luck than to careful planning. Only in the last decade of the fifteenth century did the Spanish monarchs turn their attention from the conquest and organization of previously Muslim territories to overseas exploration. By this time, the Portuguese had already found their route to the Indian Ocean.

The leader of their overseas mission would be **Christopher Columbus** (1451–1506), a Genoese mariner. His three voyages between 1492 and 1498 would reveal the existence of vast and unexpected lands across the Atlantic. But this momentous discovery

Gold Coast (Africa) Region of the Atlantic coast of West Africa occupied by modern Ghana; named for its gold exports to Europe from the 1470s onward.

Bartolomeu Dias (1457–1500) Portuguese explorer who in 1488 led the first expedition to sail around the southern tip of Africa from the Atlantic into the Indian Ocean.

Vasco da Gama (1467–1524) Portuguese explorer. In 1497–1498 he led the first naval expedition from Europe to sail to India, opening an important commercial sea route.

Christopher Columbus (1451–1506) Genoese mariner who in the service of Spain led expeditions across the Atlantic, reestablishing contact between the peoples of the Americas and the Old World and opening the way to Spanish conquest and colonization.

Columbus Prepares to Cross the Atlantic, 1492 This later representation shows Columbus with the ships, soldiers, priests, and seaman that were part of Spain's enterprise.

G. Dagli Orti/The Art Archive

History in Focus *Notice the figures in the foreground aboard the ships and small boat. How do they reflect attitudes and goals that drove Spanish overseas expansion? Now, look at the figures in the background. Who do you think they are? What might they suggest about the attitude of the general Spanish populace to early overseas expansion? Find the answer online.*

fell disappointingly short of Columbus's intention of finding a new route to the Indian Ocean even shorter than that of the Portuguese.

As a younger man, Columbus had gained considerable experience while participating in Portuguese explorations along the African coast, but he dreamed of a shorter way to the riches of the East. By his reckoning (based on a serious misreading of a ninth-century Arab authority), a mere 2,400 nautical miles (4,450 kilometers) separated the Canary Islands from Japan. The actual distance was five times greater.

Portuguese authorities twice rejected his plan to reach the East by sailing west, first in 1485 following a careful study and again in 1488 after Dias had established the feasibility of the African route. Columbus received more sympathy, but initially no support, from Queen Isabel of Castile. A Castilian commission appointed by Isabella studied the proposal for four years and concluded that a westward sea route to the Indies rested on questionable geographical assumptions. Nevertheless, Columbus's persistence finally won over the queen and her husband, King Ferdinand of Aragon. In 1492, elated perhaps by finally expelling the Muslims from Granada, they agreed to fund a modest expedition.

Columbus recorded in his log that the *Santa María*, the *Santa Clara* (nicknamed the *Niña*), and a vessel now known only by its nickname, the *Pinta*, with a mostly Spanish crew of ninety men "departed Friday the third day of August of the year 1492," toward "the regions of India." Their mission, the royal contract stated, was "to discover and acquire certain islands and mainland in the Ocean Sea." Columbus carried letters of introduction from the Spanish sovereigns to Eastern rulers, including one to the "Grand Khan" (meaning the Chinese emperor). An Arabic-speaking Jewish convert to Christianity had the job of communicating with the peoples of eastern Asia.

Unfavorable headwinds had discouraged other attempts to explore the Atlantic west of the Azores. But on earlier voyages along the African coast, Columbus had learned about winds blowing westward at the latitude of the Canaries. After reaching the Canaries,

363

he replaced the *Niña*'s lateen sails with square sails, for he knew that from then on, speed would be more important than maneuverability since his supplies would last for only a fixed number of days.

In October, the expedition encountered the islands of the Caribbean. Columbus called the inhabitants "Indians" because he believed he had reached the East Indies. A second voyage in 1493 did nothing to change his mind. On a third voyage in 1498, two months after Vasco da Gama reached India, Columbus sighted the mainland of South America, which he insisted was part of Asia. But by then, other Europeans had become convinced that his discoveries were of lands previously unknown to the Old World (Europe, Asia, and Africa). Amerigo Vespucci's explorations, first on behalf of Spain and then for Portugal, led mapmakers to name the new continents "America," after him.

To prevent disputes about exploiting these new lands and spreading Christianity among their peoples, Spain and Portugal agreed to split the world between them. Modifying an earlier papal proposal, the Treaty of Tordesillas (tor-duh-SEE-yuhs), negotiated by the pope in 1494, drew an imaginary north-south line down the middle of the Atlantic Ocean. Lands east of the line in Africa and southern Asia could be claimed by Portugal; lands to the west in the Americas belonged to Spain. Cabral's discovery of Brazil, however, gave Portugal a valid claim to the part of South America that bulged east of the line.

But if the Tordesillas line were extended around the earth, where would Spain's and Portugal's spheres of influence divide in the East? Given European ignorance of the earth's true size in 1494, no one knew whether the Moluccas (muh-LOO-kuhz), the source of the valuable spices of the East Indies, belonged to Portugal or Spain. The missing information concerned the size of the Pacific Ocean, which a Spanish adventurer named Vasco Núñez de Balboa (bal-BOH-uh) had spotted in 1513 when he crossed the isthmus (a narrow neck of land) of Panama from the east. The 1519 expedition of **Ferdinand Magellan** (ca.

1480-1521) sought to complete Columbus's interrupted westward voyage by sailing around the Americas and across the Pacific. The Moluccas turned out to lie well within Portugal's sphere, as Spain formally acknowledged in 1529.

Magellan's voyage laid the basis for Spanish colonization of the Philippine Islands after 1564. It also gave Magellan credit, despite his death, for being the first person to encircle the globe, for a decade earlier he had sailed from Europe to the East Indies on an expedition sponsored by his native Portugal.

Columbus and those who followed in his path laid the basis for the colonial empires of Spain and other European nations. In turn, these empires promoted, among the four Atlantic continents, a new trading network whose importance rivaled and eventually surpassed that of the Indian Ocean. Of more immediate importance, Portugal's entry into the Indian Ocean led quickly to a major European presence and profit. Both the eastward and the westward voyages of exploration marked a tremendous expansion of Europe's role in world history.

> **SECTION REVIEW**
>
> - The Portuguese and Spanish expeditions prompted a maritime revolution of global significance.
> - The voyages extended from cultural trends in the Latin West since 1000, but Christian militancy and material gain were especially strong motives.
> - Urged by Henry the Navigator, Portuguese explorers ventured farther into the Atlantic and colonized Madeira, the Azores, and the Canaries.
> - Portuguese explorer-traders and missionaries established bases along the coast of Africa, pushed into the Indian Ocean, and crossed to South America.
> - Spanish overseas expansion began with Columbus's voyages to find a western route to the Indian Ocean.
> - The Treaty of Torsedillas divided the world between Spain and Portugal, a division clarified by Magellan's circumnavigation of the world.

> **Primary Source: Agreement with Columbus of April 17 and April 30, 1492** Find out what sort of material wealth Christopher Columbus stood to gain when he undertook his famous voyage of 1492.

Ferdinand Magellan (1487–1521) Portuguese navigator who led the Spanish expedition of 1519-1522 that was the first to sail around the world.

Library of Congress

Map of the World, ca. 1595 After Ferdinand Magellan, the next explorer to circumnavigate the world was Sir Francis Drake (ca. 1540–1596). Departing with five ships in 1577, Drake completed most of his voyage in a single ship, the *Golden Hind*, returning to England in 1580. This hand-colored engraving by Jadocus Hondius shows his route. On his voyage, Drake raided Spanish ships and ports and returned with great riches. Unlike Magellan, he travelled far northward before crossing the Pacific, harboring for several weeks near San Francisco Bay and making friendly contact with native peoples there.

Encounters with Europe, 1450–1550

What were the different outcomes of European interactions with Africa, India, and the Americas?

The ways in which Africans, Asians, and Amerindians perceived their European visitors and interacted with them influenced their future relations. Some welcomed the Europeans as potential allies; others viewed them as rivals or enemies. In general, Africans and Asians readily recognized the benefits and dangers of European contact. However, the long isolation of the Amerindians added to the strangeness of their

encounter with the Spanish and made them vulnerable to the unfamiliar diseases the Spanish inadvertently introduced.

Western Africa

Many Africans welcomed trade with the Portuguese, which gave them new markets for their exports and access to imports cheaper than those coming by caravan across the Sahara. Miners in the hinterland of the Gold Coast, which the Portuguese first visited in 1471, had long sold their gold to merchants from trading cities along the southern edge of the Sahara for transshipment to North Africa. Recognizing the possibility of more favorable trading terms, coastal Africans negotiated with the royal representative of Portugal, who arrived in 1482 seeking permission to erect a trading fort.

The Portuguese noble in charge and his officers (likely including the young Christopher Columbus, who had entered Portuguese service in 1476) strove to make a proper impression. They dressed in their best clothes, erected a fancy reception platform, celebrated a Catholic Mass, and signaled the start of negotiations with trumpets, tambourines, and drums. The African king, Caramansa, staged his entrance with equal ceremony, arriving with a large retinue of attendants and musicians. Through an African interpreter, the two leaders exchanged flowery speeches pledging goodwill and mutual benefit. Caramansa then gave permission for a small trading fort, assured, he said, by the appearance of these royal delegates that they were honorable persons, unlike the "few, foul, and vile" Portuguese visitors of the previous decade.

Neither side made a show of force, but Caramansa warned that if the Portuguese failed to be peaceful and honest traders, he and his people would move away and deprive their post of food and trade. Trade at the post of Saint George of the Mine (later called Elmina) enriched both sides. The Portuguese crown was soon purchasing gold amounting to one-tenth of the world's production at the time. In return, Africans received shiploads of goods brought by the Portuguese from Asia, Europe, and other parts of Africa.

Early contacts involved a mixture of commercial, military, and religious interests. Some African rulers quickly saw the value of European firearms. Coastal rulers also proved willing to test the value of Christian practices, which the Portuguese eagerly promoted. The rulers of Benin and Kongo, the largest coastal kingdoms, invited Portuguese missionaries and soldiers to accompany them into battle to test the Christians' religion along with their muskets.

The kingdom of Benin in the Niger Delta, near the peak of its power after a century of aggressive expansion, had a large capital city, also known as Benin. Its *oba* (king) responded to a Portuguese visit in 1486 by sending an ambassador to Portugal to learn more about their homeland. Then he established a royal monopoly on Portuguese trade, selling pepper and ivory tusks (to be taken back to Portugal) as well as stone beads, textiles, and prisoners of war (to be resold at Elmina). In return, Portuguese merchants provided

Bronze Figure of Benin Ruler Both this prince and his horse are protected by chainmail introduced in the fifteenth century to Benin by Portuguese merchants. Antenna Gallery Dakar Senegal/G.Dagli Orti/The Art Archive

Benin with copper and brass, fine textiles, glass beads, and a horse for the king's royal procession. In the early sixteenth century, as the demand for slaves for the Portuguese sugar plantations on the nearby island of São Tomé grew, the oba first raised the price of slaves and then imposed restrictions on their sale.

Efforts to spread Catholicism ultimately failed. Early kings showed some interest, but after 1538, the rulers declined to receive further missionaries. They also closed the market in male slaves for the rest of the sixteenth century. Both steps illustrate their power to control how much interaction they wanted.

Farther south, on the lower Congo River, the *manikongo* (mah-NEE-KONG-goh) (king) of Kongo also sent delegates to Portugal, established a royal monopoly on trade, and expressed interest in missionary teachings. But here the royal family made Catholicism the kingdom's official faith. Lacking ivory and pepper, Kongo sold more and more slaves to acquire the goods brought by the Portuguese and to pay missionary expenses.

Soon the royal trade monopoly broke down. In 1526, the Christian manikongo, Afonso I (r. 1506–ca. 1540), wrote to his royal "brother," the king of Portugal, begging for his help in stopping the slave trade because unauthorized Kongolese were kidnapping and selling people, even members of good families. Afonso asked that contacts be limited to "some priests and a few people to teach in the schools, and no other goods except wine and flour for the holy sacrament," but received no reply (see Diversity and Dominance: Kongo's Christian King). After 1540, the major part of the slave trade from this part of Africa moved farther south.

Eastern Africa

As Vasco da Gama sailed up the eastern coast of Africa in 1498, most rulers of the coastal trading states received him coolly. Visitors who painted crusader crosses on their sails raised the suspicions of their Muslim inhabitants. The ruler of Malindi, however, saw in the Portuguese an ally who could help him expand Malindi's trade, and he provided da Gama with a pilot to guide him to India. The suspicions of most rulers came to fruition seven years later when a Portuguese war fleet bombarded and looted most of the coastal cities in the name of Christ and commerce, but spared Malindi.

Christian Ethiopia also saw benefits in allying with the Portuguese. In the fourteenth and fifteenth centuries, Ethiopian conflicts with Muslim states along the Red Sea increased. After the Ottoman Turks conquered Egypt and launched a fleet in the Indian Ocean to counter the Portuguese in 1517, the warlord of the Muslim state of Adal attacked Ethiopia. A decisive victory in 1529 put the Christian kingdom in jeopardy, making Portuguese support a crucial matter.

For decades, delegations from Portugal and Ethiopia had talked of a Christian alliance. Queen Helena of Ethiopia, who acted as regent for her young sons after her husband's death in 1478, sent a letter in 1509 to "our very dear and well-beloved brother," the king of Portugal, along with a gift of two tiny crucifixes said to be made of wood from the cross on which Christ was crucified. She proposed to combine her land army and Portugal's fleet against the Turks. At her death in 1522, no alliance had come into being,

but the worsening situation brought renewed Ethiopian appeals.

Finally, a small Portuguese force commanded by Vasco da Gama's son Christopher reached Ethiopia in 1539. With Portuguese help, another queen rallied the desperate Ethiopians. Muslim foes captured Christopher da Gama and tortured him to death but lost heart when their leader fell in battle. Portuguese aid helped save the Ethiopian kingdom from extinction, but Ethiopia's refusal to transfer its Christian affiliation from the patriarch of Alexandria to the pope prevented a permanent alliance.

As these examples illustrate, African encounters with the Portuguese before 1550 varied considerably. Africans and Portuguese might become royal brothers, bitter opponents, or partners in a mutually profitable trade, but Europeans were still a minor presence in most of Africa in 1550. The Indian Ocean trade by then was occupying most of their attention.

Indian Ocean States

Vasco da Gama's arrival on the Malabar Coast of India in May 1498 did not impress the citizens of Calicut. The Chinese fleets of gigantic junks that had called at Calicut sixty-five years earlier dwarfed his four small ships, which were no larger than many of the dhows (dows) already filling the harbor. The *zamorin* (ruler) of Calicut and his Muslim officials showed mild interest, but the gifts da Gama brought evoked derisive laughter: twelve pieces of striped cloth, four scarlet hoods, six hats, and six wash basins. When da Gama defended his gifts as those of an explorer, not a merchant, the zamorin cut him short, asking whether he had come to discover men or stones: "If he had come to discover men, as he said, why had he brought nothing?"

Coastal rulers soon discovered that the Portuguese had no intention of remaining poor competitors in the Indian Ocean trade. Upon da Gama's return to Portugal in 1499, the jubilant King Manuel styled himself "Lord of the Conquest, Navigation, and Commerce of Ethiopia, Arabia, Persia, and India." Previously, the Indian Ocean had been an open sea, used by merchants (and pirates) of all the surrounding coasts. Now the Portuguese crown intended to make it Portugal's sea, which others might use only on Portuguese terms.

Portugal's hope of controlling the Indian Ocean stemmed from the superiority of its ships and

Diversity & Dominance

Kongo's Christian King

The new overseas voyages brought conquest to some and opportunities for fruitful borrowings and exchanges to others. The decision of the ruler of the kingdom of Kongo to adopt Christianity in 1491 added cultural diversity to Kongolese society and in some ways strengthened the hand of the king. From then on Kongolese rulers sought to introduce Christian beliefs and rituals while at the same time Africanizing Christianity to make it more intelligible to their subjects. In addition, the kings of Kongo sought a variety of more secular aid from Portugal, including schools and medicine. Trade with the Portuguese introduced new social and political tensions, especially in the case of the export trade in slaves for the Portuguese sugar plantations on the island of São Tomé to the north.

Two letters sent to King João (zhwao) III of Portugal in 1526 illustrate how King Afonso of Kongo saw his kingdom's new relationship with Portugal and the problems that resulted from it. (Afonso adopted that name when he was baptized as a young prince.) After the death of his father in 1506, Afonso successfully claimed the throne and ruled until 1542. His son Henrique became the first Catholic bishop of the Kongo in 1521.

These letters were written in Portuguese and penned by the king's secretary João Teixera (tay-SHER-uh), a Kongo Christian who, like Afonso, had been educated by Portuguese missionaries.

6 July 1526

To the very powerful and excellent prince Dom João, our brother:

On the 20th of June just past, we received word that a trading ship from your highness had just come to our port of Sonyo. We were greatly pleased by that arrival for it had been many days since a ship had come to our kingdom, for by it we would get news of your highness, which many times we had desired to know, . . . and likewise as there was a great and dire need for wine and flour for the holy sacrament; and of this we had had no great hope for we have the same need frequently. And that, sir, arises from the great negligence of your highness's officials toward us and toward shipping us those things. . . .

Sir, your highness should know how our kingdom is being lost in so many ways that we will need to provide the needed cure, since this is caused by the excessive license given by your agents and officials to the men and merchants who come to this kingdom to set up shops with goods and many things which have been prohibited by us, and which they spread throughout our kingdoms and domains in such abundance that many of our vassals, whose submission we could once rely on, now act independently so as to get the things in greater abundance than we ourselves; whom we had formerly held content and submissive and under our vassalage and jurisdiction, so it is doing a great harm not only to the service of God, but also to the security and peace of our kingdoms and state.

And we cannot reckon how great the damage is, since every day the mentioned merchants are taking our people, sons of the land and the sons of our noblemen and vassals and our relatives, because the thieves and men of bad conscience grab them so as to have the things and wares of this kingdom that they crave; they grab them and bring them to be sold. In such a manner, sir, has been the corruption and deprivation that our land is becoming completely depopulated, and your highness should not deem this good nor in your service. And to avoid this we need from these kingdoms [of yours] no more than priests and a few people to teach in schools, and no other goods except wine and flour for the holy sacrament, which is why we beg of your highness to help and assist us in this matter. Order your agents to send here neither merchants nor wares, because it is our will that in these kingdoms there should not be any dealing in slaves nor outlet for them, for the reasons stated above. Again we beg your highness's agreement, since otherwise we cannot cure such manifest harm. May Our Lord in His mercy have your highness always under His protection and may you always do the things of His holy service. I kiss your hands many times.

From our city of Kongo. . . .

The King, Dom Afonso

18 October 1526

Very high and very powerful prince King of Portugal, our brother,

Sir, your highness has been so good as to promise us that anything we need we should ask for in our letters, and that everything will be provided. And so that there may be peace and health of our kingdoms, by God's will, in our lifetime. And as there are among us old folks and people who have lived for many days, many and different diseases happen so often that we are pushed to the ultimate extremes. And the same happens to our children, relatives, and people, because this country lacks physicians and surgeons who might know the proper cures for such diseases, as well as pharmacies and drugs to make them better. And for this reason many of those who had been already confirmed and instructed in the things of the holy faith of Our Lord Jesus Christ perish and die. And the rest of the people for the most part cure themselves with herbs and sticks and other ancient methods, so that they live putting all their faith in these herbs and ceremonies, and die believing that they are saved; and this serves God poorly.

And to avoid such a great error, I think, and inconvenience, since it is from God and from your highness that all the good and the drugs and medicines have come to us for our salvation, we ask your merciful highness to send us two physicians and two pharmacists and one surgeon, so that they may come with their pharmacies and necessary things to be in our kingdoms, for we have extreme need of each and every one of them. We will be very good and merciful to them, since sent by your highness, their work and coming should be for good. We ask your highness as a great favor to do this for us, because besides being good in itself it is in the service of God as we have said above.

Moreover, sir, in our kingdoms there is another great inconvenience which is of little service to God, and this is that many of our people, out of great desire for the wares and things of your kingdoms, which are brought here by your people, and in order to satisfy their disordered appetite, seize many of our people, freed and exempt men. And many times noblemen and the sons of noblemen, and our relatives are stolen, and they take them to be sold to the white men who are in our kingdoms and take them hidden or by night, so that they are not recognized. And as soon as they are taken by the white men, they are immediately ironed and branded with fire. And when they are carried off to be embarked, if they are caught by our guards, the whites allege that they have bought them and cannot say from whom, so that it is our duty to do justice and to restore to the free their freedom. And so they went away offended.

And to avoid such a great evil we passed a law so that every white man living in our kingdoms and wanting to purchase slaves by whatever means should first inform three of our noblemen and officials of our court on whom we rely in this matter, namely Dom Pedro Manipunzo and Dom Manuel Manissaba, our head bailiff, and Gonçalo Pires, our chief supplier, who should investigate if the said slaves are captives or free men, and, if cleared with them, there will be no further doubt nor embargo and they can be taken and embarked. And if they reach the opposite conclusion, they will lose the aforementioned slaves. Whatever favor and license we give them [the white men] for the sake of your highness in this case is because we know that it is in your service too that these slaves are taken from our kingdom; otherwise we should not consent to this for the reasons stated above that we make known completely to your highness so that no one could say the contrary, as they said in many other cases to your highness, so that the care and remembrance that we and this kingdom have should not be withdrawn. . . .

We kiss your hands of your highness many times. From our city of Kongo, the 18th day of October,

The King, Dom Afonso

QUESTIONS FOR ANALYSIS

1. What sorts of things does King Afonso desire from the Portuguese?
2. What is he willing and unwilling to do in return?
3. What problem with his own people has the slave trade created, and what has King Afonso done about it?
4. Does King Afonso see himself as an equal to King João or his subordinate? Do you agree with that analysis?

Source: From António Brásio, ed., *Monumenta Missionaria Africana: Africa Ocidental (1471–1531)* (Lisbon: Agência Geral do Ultramar, 1952), I: 468, 470–471, 488–491. Translated by David Northrup.

weapons over the smaller and lightly armed merchant dhows. In 1505, the Portuguese fleet of 81 ships and some 7,000 men bombarded Swahili Coast cities. Goa, on the west coast of India, fell to a well-armed fleet in 1510, becoming the base from which the Portuguese menaced the trading cities of Gujarat (goo-juh-RAHT) to the north and Calicut and other Malabar Coast cities to the south. The port of Hormuz, controlling the entry to the Persian Gulf, fell in 1515. Aden, at the entrance to the Red Sea, preserved its independence, but the capture of the Gujarati port of Diu in 1535 consolidated Portuguese dominance of the western Indian Ocean.

Farther east, the independent city of Malacca (muh-LAH-kuh) on the strait separating the Malay Peninsula and Sumatra became the focus of their attention. During the fifteenth century, Malacca had become the main entrepôt (ON-truh-poh) (a place where goods are stored or deposited and from which they are distributed) for the trade from China, Japan, India, the Southeast Asian mainland, and the Moluccas. The city's 100,000 residents spoke eighty-four different languages, according to a Portuguese source, and included merchants from Cairo, Ethiopia, and the Swahili Coast. Many non-Muslim residents supported letting the Portuguese join this cosmopolitan trading community, perhaps to offset the growing

solidarity of Muslim traders. In 1511, however, the Portuguese seized Malacca with a force of a thousand fighting men, including three hundred recruited in southern India.

On the China coast, local officials and merchants persuaded the imperial government to allow the Portuguese to establish a trading post at Macao (muh-COW) in 1557. Subsequently, Portuguese ships nearly monopolized trade between China and Japan.

Control of the major port cities enabled the Portuguese to enforce their demands that all spices be carried in Portuguese ships, as well as all goods on the major ocean routes such as between Goa and Macao. The Portuguese also tried to control and tax other Indian Ocean trade. Merchant ships entering and leaving their ports had to carry a Portuguese passport and pay customs duties. Portuguese patrols seized vessels that did not comply, confiscated their cargoes, and either killed the captain and crew or sentenced them to forced labor.

Reactions to this power grab varied. Like the emperors of China, the Mughal (MOO-gahl) emperors of India largely ignored Portugal's maritime intrusions. The Ottomans confronted the Christian intruders more aggressively. They supported Egypt's defensive efforts from 1501 to 1509 and then sent their own fleet into the Indian Ocean in 1538. However,

Portuguese in India In the sixteenth century, Portuguese men moved to the Indian Ocean to work as administrators and traders. This Indo-Portuguese drawing from about 1540 shows a Portuguese man speaking to an Indian woman, perhaps to propose marriage.

Ms. 1889, c. 97, Biblioteca Casanateunse Rome. Photo: Humberto Nicoletti Serra

Ottoman galleys proved no match for the faster, better-armed Portuguese vessels in the open ocean. They retained their advantage only in the Red Sea and Persian Gulf, where they controlled many ports.

Smaller trading states also could not challenge the Portuguese because their mutual rivalry kept them from forming a common front. Some cooperated with the Portuguese to safeguard their prosperity and security, while others engaged in evasion and resistance. When the merchants of Calicut put up sustained resistance, the Portuguese embargoed all trade with Aden, Calicut's principal trading partner, and centered their trade on the port of Cochin, which had once been a dependency of Calicut. Some Calicut merchants evaded their patrols, but Calicut's importance shrank as Cochin gradually became the major pepper-exporting port on the Malabar Coast.

Farther north, Gujarat initially resisted Portuguese attempts at monopoly and in 1509 joined Egypt's futile effort to sweep the Portuguese from the Arabian Sea. But in 1535, with his state weakened by Mughal attacks, the ruler allowed the Portuguese to build a fort at Diu in return for their support. Once established, the Portuguese gradually extended their control. By midcentury, they were licensing and taxing all Gujarati ships. Even after the Mughals took control of Gujarat in 1572, the Mughal emperor, Akbar, permitted the Portuguese to continue their maritime monopoly in return for allowing one pilgrim ship a year to sail to Mecca without paying a fee.

The Portuguese never gained complete control of the Indian Ocean trade, but their domination of key ports and trade routes brought them considerable profit in the form of spices and other luxury goods. The Portuguese broke the trading monopoly of Venice and Genoa by selling pepper for less than what they charged for shipments obtained through Egyptian middlemen.

The Americas

In the Americas, the Spanish established a vast territorial empire, in contrast to the trading empire of the Portuguese. The Spanish kingdoms drew on somewhat greater resources, but the Spanish and Portuguese monarchies had similar motives for expansion and used identical ships and weapons. The isolation of the Amerindian peoples provided a key difference. The first European settlers in the Caribbean resorted to conquest and plunder rather than trade. They later extended this practice to the more powerful Amerindian kingdoms on the American mainland. After 1518, deadly epidemics weakened the Amerindians' ability to resist.

The Arawak whom Columbus first encountered on Hispaniola (modern Haiti and the Dominican Republic) in the Greater Antilles and the Bahamas to the north cultivated maize (corn), cassava (a tuber), sweet potatoes, and hot peppers, as well as cotton and tobacco. They mined and worked gold, but they did not trade gold, nor did they have iron. They extended a cautious welcome to Columbus but told him exaggerated stories about gold in other places to persuade him to move on.

Columbus brought with him several hundred settlers from southern Iberia, as well as missionaries, on his second trip to Hispaniola in 1493. The settlers stole gold ornaments, confiscated food, and raped women, provoking the Hispaniola Arawak to war in 1495. With the advantage of horses and body armor, the Spaniards slaughtered tens of thousands of Arawak and forced the survivors to pay a heavy tax in gold, spun cotton, and food. Whoever failed to meet the quotas faced forced labor. Meanwhile, the cattle, pigs, and goats introduced by the settlers devoured the Arawak's food crops, causing deaths from famine and disease. A governor appointed by the Spanish crown in 1502 forced the Arawak on Hispaniola to become laborers under the control of Spanish settlers.

The actions of the Spanish in the Antilles reflected Spanish behavior during the wars against the Muslims in the previous centuries. They sought to serve God by defeating, controlling, and converting nonbelievers and to become rich in the process. Individual **conquistadors** (kon-KEY-stuh-dors) (conquerors) extended that pattern around the Caribbean.

Primary Source: General History of the Things of New Spain Learn the details of the horrible disaster that befell the Aztecs when the Spaniards and the plague descended upon them simultaneously.

conquistadors Early-sixteenth-century Spanish adventurers who conquered Mexico, Central America, and Peru.

Coronation of Emperor Moctezuma This painting by an unnamed Aztec artist depicts the Aztec ruler's coronation. Moctezuma, his nose pierced by a bone, receives the crown from a prince in the palace at Tenochtitlan.

Oronoz

Some raided the Bahamas for gold and labor as both grew scarce on Hispaniola. Arawak from the Bahamas served as slaves on Hispaniola. Juan Ponce de León (1460–1521), a veteran of the conquest of Muslim Spain and the seizure of Hispaniola, conquered the island of Borinquen (Puerto Rico) in 1508 and in 1513 explored southeastern Florida.

An ambitious and ruthless nobleman, **Hernán Cortés** (air-NAHN kor-TEZ) (1485–1547), led the most audacious expedition to the mainland. Cortés left Cuba in 1519 with six hundred fighting men and most of the island's weapons to assault the Mexican mainland in search of slaves and trade. Learning of the rich Aztec Empire in central Mexico, Cortés expanded on the American mainland the exploitation and conquest carried out in the Greater Antilles.

Many of the Amerindians whom the Aztecs had subjugated during the previous century resented the tribute, forced labor, and the large-scale human sacrifices to Aztec gods their rulers imposed on them. Consequently, some gave the Spanish their support as allies against the Aztecs. Like the Caribbean people, the mainland Amerindians had no precedent by which to judge these strangers. Later accounts suggest that some believed Cortés to be the legendary ruler Quetzalcoatl (ket-zahl-COH-ah-tal), whose return to earth had been prophesied, and treated him with great deference.

Another consequence of millennia of isolation proved even more fatal: the lack of acquired resistance to Old World diseases. Smallpox, the most deadly of the early epidemics, appeared for the first time on the island of Hispaniola in late 1518 or early 1519. An infected member of the Cortés expedition then transmitted smallpox to Mexico in 1519, where it spread with deadly efficiency.

The Aztec emperor **Moctezuma II** (mock-teh-ZOO-ma) (r. 1502–1520) sent messengers to greet Cortés and determine whether he was god or man, friend or foe. Cortés advanced steadily toward the capital, Tenochtitlan (teh-noch-TIT-lan), overcoming Aztec opposition with cavalry charges and steel swords and gaining the support of discontented tributary peoples. When the Spaniards drew near, the emperor went out in a great procession, dressed in all his finery, to welcome Cortés with gifts and flower garlands.

Despite Cortés's initial promise of friendship, Moctezuma quickly found himself a prisoner in his own palace. The Spaniards looted his treasury,

Hernán Cortés (1485–1547) Spanish explorer and conquistador who led the conquest of Aztec Mexico in 1519–1521 for Spain.
Moctezuma II (1466–1520) Last Aztec emperor, overthrown by the Spanish conquistador Hernán Cortés.

especially its gold. Soon full-scale battle broke out, during which the Aztecs and their supporters briefly gained the upper hand. They destroyed half the Spanish force and four thousand of their Amerindian allies, sacrificing fifty-three Spanish prisoners and four horses to their gods and displaying their severed heads in rows on pikes. However, reinforcements from Cuba enabled Cortés to regain the advantage. Smallpox, which weakened and killed more of the city's defenders than died in the fighting, also assisted his capture of Tenochtitlan in 1521. One source remembered that the disease "spread over the people as a great destruction."

After the capital fell, the conquistadors took over other parts of Mexico. Once they reached Panama, Spaniards began hearing of another empire in South America. This was the Inca Empire that stretched nearly 3,000 miles (5,000 kilometers) south from the equator and contained half of the population in South America. The Inca had conquered the inhabitants of the Andes Mountains and the Pacific coast of South America during the previous century, but their rule was not fully accepted by the subjugated peoples.

The Inca rulers administered a well-organized empire with highly productive agriculture, exquisite stone cities (such as the capital, Cuzco), and rich gold and silver mines. The power of the Inca emperor rested on the belief that he was descended from the sun-god and on an efficient system of roads and messengers that kept him informed about major events. Yet at the end of the 1520s, before the Spanish had even been heard of, smallpox had claimed countless lives, perhaps including the Inca emperor sometime between 1524 and 1527.

An even more devastating threat loomed: **Francisco Pizarro** (pih-SAHR-oh) (ca. 1478–1541) and his band of 180 men, 37 horses, and 2 cannon. With limited education but some military experience, Pizarro had come to the Americas in 1502 at the age of twenty-five to seek his fortune. He had participated in the conquest of Hispaniola and in Balboa's expedition across the Isthmus of Panama. By 1520 a wealthy landowner and official in Panama, he nevertheless gambled his fortune on exploring the Pacific coast to a point south of the equator, where he learned of the riches of the Inca. With a license from the king of Spain, he set out from Panama in 1531 to conquer them.

In November 1532, Pizarro arranged to meet the new Inca emperor, **Atahualpa** (ah-tuh-WAHL-puh) (r. 1531–1533), near the Andean city of Cajamarca (kah-hah-MAHR-kah). With supreme boldness and brutality, Pizarro's small band grabbed Atahualpa from a rich litter borne by eighty nobles as it passed through an enclosed courtyard. Though surrounded by an Inca army of at least 40,000, the Spaniards used their cannon to create confusion while their swords sliced the emperor's lightly armed retainers and servants to pieces.

Noting the glee with which the Spaniards seized gold, silver, and emeralds, the captive Atahualpa offered them what he thought would satisfy even the greediest among them in exchange for his freedom: a roomful of gold and silver. But after receiving 13,400 pounds (6,000 kilograms) of gold and 26,000 pounds (12,000 kilograms) of silver, the Spaniards gave Atahualpa a choice: being burned at the stake as a heathen or being strangled after a Christian baptism. He chose the latter. His death and the Spanish occupation broke the unity of the Inca Empire.

In 1533, the Spaniards took Cuzco and from there set out to conquer and loot the rest of the empire. After the defeat of a rebellion in 1536, the remaining Inca retreated to a small kingdom in the mountains that lasted until 1572. In 1541, Pizarro himself met a violent death at the hands of Spanish rivals, but the conquest of the mainland continued. Incited by the fabulous wealth of the Aztecs and Inca, conquistadors extended Spanish conquest and exploration in South and North America, dreaming of new treasuries to loot.

Patterns of Dominance

Within fifty years of Columbus's first landing, the Spanish had located and occupied the major population centers of the Americas and penetrated many of the more thinly populated areas. Why did the peoples of the Americas suffer a fate so different from that of peoples

Francisco Pizarro (ca. 1476–1541) Spanish explorer who led the conquest of the Inca Empire of Peru in 1532–1533.
Atahualpa (1497–1533) Last ruling Inca emperor of Peru. He was executed by the Spanish.

in Africa and Asia? Why were the Spanish able to erect a vast land empire in the Americas so quickly?

First, unfamiliar illnesses devastated the Caribbean islands and then the mainland. Contemporaries estimated that between 25 and 50 percent of those infected with smallpox died. Repeated epidemics inhibited the Amerindians' ability to regain control. Estimates of the size of the population before Columbus's arrival, based on sparse evidence, vary widely. Yet historians agree that the Amerindian population fell sharply during the sixteenth century. The Americas became a "widowed land," open to resettlement from across the Atlantic.

A second factor was Spain's superior military technology. Steel swords, protective armor, and horses gave the Spaniards an advantage over their Amerindian opponents. Though few in number, muskets and cannon provided a psychological edge. However, the Spanish conquests also depended heavily on large numbers of Amerindian allies armed with indigenous weapons. The most decisive military advantage may have been the no-holds-barred fighting techniques the Spaniards had developed during their wars at home.

The third factor in Spain's conquest was the precedent established by the reconquest of Granada in 1492: forced labor, forced conversion, and the incorporation of conquered lands into a new empire.

The same three factors help explain the different outcomes elsewhere. Centuries of contacts before 1500 meant that Europeans, Africans, and Asians shared the same Old World diseases and did not suffer a demographic calamity like that of the Americas. The Iberians enjoyed a military advantage at sea, but on land they lacked the advantages against more numerous armies of Africans and Asians that they had in the Americas. Everywhere, Iberian religious zeal went hand in hand with a desire for riches. In Iberia and America, conquest itself brought wealth. But in Africa and Asia, existing trading networks made wealth dependent on commercial domination rather than conquest.

The Columbian Exchange

How did the Columbian Exchange alter the natural environment of the Americas?

The term **Columbian Exchange** refers to the transfer of peoples, animals, plants, diseases, and technology between the New and Old Worlds that European trade in the Atlantic opened up. We have already seen how Old World diseases devastated Amerindian peoples and led to the resettlement of the Americas by Europeans and Africans. In addition, the domesticated livestock and major agricultural crops of the Old World spread over much of the Americas, and Amerindians' staple crops enriched the agricultures of Europe, Asia, and Africa. This vast exchange of plants and animals radically altered diets and lifestyles around the world.

Transfers to the Americas

Within a century of Columbus's first voyage, new settlers in the Americas were growing all the staples of southern European agriculture—wheat,

---

Columbian Exchange The exchange of plants, animals, diseases, and technologies between the Americas and the rest of the world following Columbus's voyages.

E. 79

Oronoz

The Columbian Exchange In this painting an Amerindian woman milks a cow, suggesting how the Columbian Exchange altered native culture and environment. While livestock sometimes destroyed the fields of native peoples, cattle, sheep, pigs, and goats also provided food, leather, and wool.

olives, grapes, and garden vegetables—along with African and Asian crops such as rice, bananas, coconuts, breadfruit, and sugar cane. Native peoples remained loyal to their traditional staples but added many Old World plants to their diet. Citrus fruits, melons, figs, and sugar, as well as onions, radishes, and salad greens, all found a place in Amerindian cuisine.

By the seventeenth century, nearly all of the domesticated animals in the Caribbean were ones that Europeans had introduced. The Spanish brought cattle, pigs, and horses, all of which multiplied rapidly. They also introduced new plants. Of these, bananas and plantain from the Canary Islands were a valuable addition to the food supply,

and sugar and rice formed the basis of plantation agriculture, along with native tobacco. Other food crops arrived with slaves from Africa, including okra, black-eyed peas, yams, grains such as millet and sorghum, and mangoes. Many of these new animals and plants were useful additions to the islands, but they crowded out indigenous species, except maize, which remained a staple.

The introduction of European livestock to the mainland had a dramatic impact. Faced with few natural predators, cattle, pigs, horses, and sheep, as well as pests like rats and rabbits, multiplied rapidly in the open spaces of the Americas. On the vast plains of present-day southern Brazil, Uruguay, and Argentina, herds of wild cattle and horses exceeded 50 million by 1700. Large herds of both animals also appeared in northern Mexico and what became the Southwest of the United States.

Where Old World livestock spread most rapidly, environmental changes were most dramatic. Marauding livestock often had a destructive impact on Amerindian farmers. But on the plains of South America, northern Mexico, and Texas, feral cattle provided indigenous peoples with abundant supplies of meat and hides. In the present-day southwestern United States, the Navajo became sheepherders and expert weavers of woolen cloth. Individual Amerindians became muleteers, cowboys, and sheepherders.

No animal had a more striking effect on the cultures of native peoples than the horse, which increased the efficiency of hunters and the military capacity of warriors on the plains. The horse permitted the Apache, Sioux, Blackfoot, Comanche, Assiniboine, and others to hunt the vast herds of buffalo in North America more efficiently.

The most dramatic change that Europeans wrought in the Americas was the pathogens that accompanied the conquistadors and the devastating epidemics they caused. Because of their long isolation from other continents, the peoples of the New World lacked immunity to diseases introduced from the Old World by explorers and settlers. Diseases that were serious in the Old World, like smallpox, were catastrophic to the Amerindians. Old World childhood diseases like measles and mumps were fatal to adults who had never acquired any resistance to them. In many villages when disease struck, too few healthy people remained to take care of the sick, and many who might have recovered from the diseases instead died of thirst or hunger.

When smallpox arrived in the Caribbean, it killed most of the native peoples there. It was then spread to the mainland by the Spanish conquest of the Aztecs and Incas. Other diseases added to the toll: measles in the 1530s, followed by diphtheria, typhus, influenza, and perhaps pulmonary plague. Epidemic after epidemic swept through the Americas, causing the worst demographic disaster in human history, a holocaust that by 1600 had completely wiped out the indigenous populations of most of the Caribbean island and had reduced the population of Mexico by 90 to 95 percent and other parts of the Americas almost as much. When between 1520 and 1521 influenza and other ailments attacked the Cakchiquel of Guatemala, their chronicler recalled:

> Great was the stench of the dead. After our fathers and grandfathers succumbed, half the people fled to the fields. The dogs and vultures devoured the bodies. . . . So it was that we became orphans, oh my sons! . . . We were born to die![3]

Transfers from the Americas

In return for diseases and domesticated animals, the Americas offered the Old World an abundance of useful plants. The New World staples of maize and potatoes revolutionized agriculture and diet in parts of Europe because they provided more calories per acre than any of the Old World staples except rice. Beans, squash, tomatoes, sweet potatoes, peanuts, chilis, and chocolate also gained widespread acceptance in Europe and other parts of the Old World. The New World also provided the Old with plants that provided dyes, medicines, and tobacco.

Maize and cassava (a Brazilian plant cultivated for its edible roots) moved across the Atlantic to Africa. Cassava became the most important New World food in Africa. It had the highest yield of calories per acre of any staple food and thrived even in poor soils and during droughts. Both the leaves and the root could be eaten.

Cassava and maize were probably introduced accidentally into Africa by Portuguese ships from Brazil that discarded leftover supplies after reaching Angola. It did not take long for local Africans to recognize the food value of these new crops, especially in drought-prone areas. By the eighteenth century, Central African rulers hundreds of miles from the Angolan coast were actively promoting the cultivation of maize and cassava on their royal estates in order to provide a more secure food supply. Some historians believe that in the inland areas these Amerindian food crops provided the nutritional base for a population increase that partially offset losses due to the Atlantic slave trade.

Only one disease may have originated in the Americas and spread to the Eastern Hemisphere. Syphilis appeared in Spain soon after Columbus returned from the Caribbean, bringing with him an Indian who may have carried the disease; however, it is also possible that syphilis may have been a mutated form of yaws, a skin disease prevalent in Africa. Whatever its origin, a virulent form of syphilis soon spread throughout Europe. While many individuals died, it

- The Columbian Exchange brought to the Americas southern European, African, and Asian crops.
- Old World plants and livestock altered New World environments and cultures.
- New World crops revolutionized agriculture and diet in Europe and Africa.
- Old World diseases decimated the population of the New World, but only syphilis may have crossed the Atlantic from west to east.

did not have the demographic impact that Old World diseases had on the New World, or that the bubonic plague had had on Europe in the fourteenth century.

Conclusion

The rapid expansion of European empires and the projection of European military power around the world, one of the most important events in world history, would have seemed unlikely in 1492. No European power matched the military and economic strength of China, and few could rival the Ottomans. Spain lacked strong national institutions and Portugal had a small population; both had limited economic resources. Because of these limitations, the monarchs of Spain and Portugal allowed their subjects greater

initiative. While royal sponsorship was often crucial in the Portuguese contacts with Africa and the first voyages to Asia, many of the commercial and military expeditions were effectively organized and financed as private companies. Very often the kings of Spain and Portugal struggled to catch up with their restless and ambitious subjects, sometimes taking decades to establish royal control in new colonies.

The pace and character of European expansion were different in Africa and Asia than in the Americas. In Africa local rulers were generally able to limit European military power to coastal outposts and to control European trade. Only in the Kongo were the Portuguese able to project their power inland. When Europeans arrived in the Indian Ocean, mature markets and specialized production for distant consumers already existed. Although Portuguese naval power allowed Europeans to harvest large profits and influence local commercial patterns, most native populations continued to enjoy autonomy for centuries.

In the Americas the terrible effects of epidemic disease and the destructiveness of the conquest led to the rapid creation of European settlements and the subordination of the surviving indigenous population. As we shall see in Chapter 16, the gold, silver, and sugar that eventually produced great wealth resulted from the introduction of new technologies, the imposition of forced labor, and the development of new roads and ports.

CHAPTER REVIEW

Download the MP3 audio file of the Chapter Review to listen to on the go.

What were the objectives and major accomplishments of the voyages of exploration undertaken by Chinese, Polynesians, and other non-Western peoples? (page 354)

The voyages of exploration undertaken by the Chinese and Polynesians pursued diverse objectives. In the Chinese case, the great voyages of the early fifteenth century

were made out of interest in trade, curiosity, and the projection of imperial power. The Polynesians' explorations demonstrated their seafaring expertise and opened the opportunity to settle satellite populations that would relieve population pressures on limited resources. In both cases new connections were made and societies were invigorated. The Vikings had similarly explored new lands in the North Atlantic, using their knowledge of the heavens and seas to establish settlements. There is also evidence of African voyages in the Atlantic during this same period, although their purpose is less clear.

In this era of long-distance exploration, did Europeans have any special advantages over other cultural regions? (page 358)

The projection of European influence between 1450 and 1550 was in some ways similar to that of other cultural regions in that it expanded commercial linkages, increased cross-cultural contacts, and served the ambitions of political leaders. But the result was a major turning point in world history. During those years European explorers opened new long-distance trade routes across the world's three major oceans, for the first time establishing regular contact among all the continents. As a result, a new balance of power arose in parts of Atlantic Africa, the Indian Ocean, and the Americas.

What were the different outcomes of European interactions with Africa, India, and the Americas? (page 365)

Europeans created colonial empires in the Americas quite rapidly, while their progress in Africa and Asia was much slower. Many Amerindians welcomed the Spanish settlers at first, only to have them tax their labors, steal their food, introduce disease and warfare, and eventually subjugate them. In contrast, Portuguese visitors to Africa remained a minor presence in 1550. In some regions, the Portuguese were welcomed as trading partners; in others they were regarded as potential political and military allies. The real focus of the Portuguese was to capture the rich trade of the Indian Ocean. While they never gained complete control, they used their superior military strength to dominate key ports and major trade routes.

As dramatic and momentous as these events were, they were not completely unprecedented. The riches of the Indian Ocean trade that brought a gleam to the eye of many Europeans had been developed over many centuries by the trading peoples who inhabited the surrounding lands. While rapid, the European conquest of the Americas was no more rapid or brutal than the earlier Mongol conquests of Eurasia. Even the crossing of the Pacific had been done before, though in stages, by Polynesians.

What gave this maritime revolution unprecedented importance had more to do with what happened after 1550 than with what happened earlier. The overseas empires of the Europeans would endure longer than the Mongols' and would continue to expand for three centuries after 1600. Unlike the Chinese, the Europeans did not turn their backs on the world after an initial burst of exploration. Not content with dominance in the Indian Ocean trade, Europeans opened an Atlantic maritime network that grew to rival the Indian Ocean network in the wealth of its trade; they also pioneered trade across the Pacific. The maritime expansion begun in the period from 1450 to 1550 marked the beginning of a new age of growing global interaction.

How did the Columbian Exchange alter the natural environment of the Americas? (page 374)

The arrival of Europeans dramatically changed the natural environments and peoples of the Americas. Animals brought deliberately or inadvertently from the Old World spread rapidly through the Americas, often damaging the native flora and replacing many native animals. Though Europeans brought their familiar crops, they soon found that the Americas offered many more useful plants that provided food for a growing population in the Old World. Most dramatic was the effect of the Old World diseases that accompanied the Europeans (and their African slaves) and killed nine-tenths of the Amerindian population, leaving empty lands that were taken over by herds of Old World animals or by Europeans and Africans.

Key Terms

Zheng He (p. 357)	Ferdinand Magellan (p. 364)
Arawak (p. 358)	
Henry the Navigator (p. 359)	conquistadors (p. 371)
caravel (p. 361)	Hernán Cortés (p. 372)
Gold Coast (Africa) (p. 362)	Moctezuma II (p. 372)
Bartolomeu Dias (p. 362)	Francisco Pizarro (p. 373)
Vasco da Gama (p. 362)	Atahualpa (p. 373)
Christopher Columbus (p. 362)	Columbian Exchange (p. 374)

Web Resources

Pronunciation Guide

Interactive Maps

- MAP 15.1 Exploration and Settlement in the Indian and Pacific Oceans Before 1500
- MAP 15.2 European Exploration, 1420–1542

 Visit the CourseMate website at www.cengagebrain.com for additional study tools and review materials for this chapter.

Primary Sources

- Agreement with Columbus of April 17 and April 30, 1492
- General History of the Things of New Spain

Answer to the History in Focus Question

See photo on page 363, "Columbus Prepares to Cross the Atlantic, 1492."

Periodization

Dividing history into time periods is second nature to historians. Major events like Columbus's voyages to the Western Hemisphere or the American Civil War make memorable turning points, as do the lives of well-known figures like Muhammad or Julius Caesar and the advent of major new technologies, such as printing, steam power, electrical generation, atomic energy, and the computer.

Just as common are period labels that fit the historian's interpretive scheme. European history, for example, is commonly divided into prehistoric, ancient, late ancient, early medieval, late medieval, early modern, modern, and contemporary periods. Historians of Europe do not agree precisely on the dates of these periods, but there is sufficient agreement to make them useful. Nevertheless, a historian following a Marxist interpretive framework is likely to prefer labels like *primitive communist, feudal, bourgeois,* and *socialist.*

When the study of non-European history was less common than it is today, historians specializing on other world regions adopted and adapted terms that were originally used for Europe. Terms like *medieval China, medieval Japan, medieval India,* and *medieval Islam* became commonplace even though historical writings in the native languages of those societies did not provide such labels.

Chinese writings labeled historical and cultural developments in terms of the time periods of different dynasties: Han, Tang, Song, Yuan, Ming, etc. Japanese sources named periods for capital cities—Nara, Kyoto, Edo—or dominant families—Fujiwara, Ashikaga, Tokugawa. Indian writings mention kingdoms that ruled only parts of the subcontinent, often overlapping with one another in time, and offer no time scheme for the region as a whole. Islamic histories focus on stages in the evolution of the caliphate, from Rashidun, to Umayyad, to Abbasid, and then on empires like the Ottomans and Safavids after the invading Mongols brought the Abbasid Caliphate to an end.

The study of world history poses a problem of periodization that neither indigenous historical sources nor writers in the European historical tradition had to address. Does the history of the globe as a whole fall into periods? Archaeologists answer this question positively, but they recognize that the sequence of periods, and the dates of transition from one period to the next, vary from region to region. *Paleolithic, Neolithic, Bronze Age,* and *Iron Age* are useful labels for describing the material remains of past societies, but bronze-smelting in South America, to take one example, first appeared as much as three thousand years later than the parallel craft in Mesopotamia or China.

When faced with the simplest traditional division of history, that into ancient, medieval, and modern, world historians have reached no consensus on chronological turning points. Moreover, they are reluctant to say that region X entered the modern era before or after region Y when this determination might be interpreted as a sign that region X was "more advanced" or its societies "more developed." Periodization does not necessarily imply improvement or "progress" toward some end, and most historians are careful to avoid this implication.

Some historians have sought at least a partial solution to the problem by emphasizing moments in time when different parts of the world first came to know of one another or entered into substantially closer contact. The conquests of Alexander the Great, the Arab armies inspired by the teachings of Islam, and the Mongols of Genghis Khan afford such turning points. So do the voyages of exploration that brought Europeans to the New World and the establishment of European colonial empires. Yet few of these turning points affect world history as a whole.

This does not mean that there have been no turning points affecting all or most of the planet. Some episodes of deadly disease might qualify, such as the Black Death that ravaged Europe and Asia (but not the Western Hemisphere) in the fourteenth century or the influenza epidemic of 1918, just after the end of World War I, that killed 50 million people worldwide, three times the number killed in the war. In the future, studies of climate may also suggest a sequence of periods based on hemisphere-wide or global changes in weather patterns.

Yet historians are reluctant to see history hinging on events like plagues or changes in climate over which humans have no control. They prefer to think of the watersheds that separate one period of history from another as the consequences of deliberate human action.

To put yourself in the place of a historian trying to identify historical turning points, think about the fall of the Soviet Union in 1991, the 9/11 terrorist attacks of 2001, and the global financial crisis of 2008. Do any of these qualify as turning points in history? Or as markers of the beginnings or ends of historical eras?

Part Five

The Globe Encompassed, 1500–1800

© Cengage Learning

	1500	**1550**	**1600**	**1650**
AMERICAS	• **1500** Portuguese discover Brazil	• **1540** Viceroyalty of Peru • **1535** Viceroyalty of Mexico • **1545** Silver discovered at Potosí, Bolivia	Brazil is world's main source of sugar **1600** •	Dutch bring sugar and slavery to West Indies **1640s** • **1607–1640** England and France found colonies
EUROPE	**1500–1600** Spain's golden century • **1519** Protestant Reformation begins	• **1545** Catholic Reformation begins • **1550** Scientific Revolution begins	• **1588** English defeat Spanish Armada **1600–1700** Netherlands' golden century	**1618–1648** Thirty Years War
AFRICA	• **1505** Portuguese begin assault on Swahili cities		• **1591** Morocco conquers Songhai Empire Expansion of transatlantic slave trade **1640's** •	
MIDDLE EAST		**1520–1566** Reign of Ottoman sultan Suleiman the Magnificent	• **1571** Ottoman defeat at Lepanto **1588–1629** Reign of Safavid shah Abbas the Great	• **1622** Iranians expel Portuguese from Hormuz
ASIA AND OCEANIA		• **1526** Mughal Empire founded in India **1556–1605** Reign of Mughal emperor Akbar	• **1582** Russia conquers Sibir Khanate	• **1603** Tokugawa Shogunate founded in Japan "Closing" of Japan **1639** • Qing Empire begins in China **1644** •

The decades between 1500 and 1800 witnessed a tremendous expansion of commercial, cultural, and biological exchanges around the world. New long-distance sea routes linked Europe with sub-Saharan Africa and the existing maritime networks of the Indian Ocean and East Asia, and Spanish and Portuguese voyages ended the isolation of the Americas and created new webs of exchange in the Atlantic and Pacific. Overland expansion of Muslim, Russian, and Chinese empires also increased global interaction.

These expanding contacts had major demographic and cultural consequences. As we saw in Chapter 15, domesticated animals and crops from the Old World transformed agriculture in the Americas, while Amerindian foods such as the potato became staples of the diet of the Old World. European diseases, meanwhile, devastated the Amerindian population, facilitating the establishment of large Spanish, Portuguese, French, and British empires. As Europeans introduced enslaved Africans to relieve the labor shortage, immigrant Africans and Europeans brought new languages, religious practices, music, and forms of personal adornment.

In Asia and Africa, by contrast, the most important changes owed more to internal forces than to European actions. Although the Portuguese seized control of some important trading ports and networks in the Indian Ocean and pioneered new contacts with China and Japan, and although the Dutch, French, and English later expanded these profitable connections, in 1750 Europeans were still primarily a maritime force. Asians and Africans generally retained control of their lands and participated freely in overseas trade.

In the Islamic world, the Ottoman Empire dramatically expanded in the Middle East, the Safavid Empire became established in Iran, and the Mughal Empire formed in South Asia. In northern Eurasia, Russia and China acquired vast new territories and populations, while a new national government in Japan promoted economic development and stemmed foreign influence

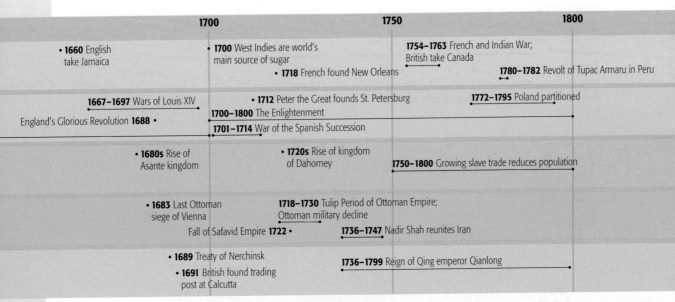

	1700	1750	1800
• **1660** English take Jamaica	• **1700** West Indies are world's main source of sugar	**1754–1763** French and Indian War; British take Canada	
		• **1718** French found New Orleans	**1780–1782** Revolt of Tupac Armaru in Peru
1667–1697 Wars of Louis XIV	• **1712** Peter the Great founds St. Petersburg	**1772–1795** Poland partitioned	
England's Glorious Revolution **1688** •	**1700–1800** The Enlightenment		
	1701–1714 War of the Spanish Succession		
• **1680s** Rise of Asante kingdom	• **1720s** Rise of kingdom of Dahomey	**1750–1800** Growing slave trade reduces population	
• **1683** Last Ottoman siege of Vienna	**1718–1730** Tulip Period of Ottoman Empire; Ottoman military decline		
Fall of Safavid Empire **1722** •	**1736–1747** Nadir Shah reunites Iran		
• **1689** Treaty of Nerchinsk	**1736–1799** Reign of Qing emperor Qianlong		
• **1691** British found trading post at Calcutta			

Transformations in Europe

© Cengage Learning

Visit the CourseMate website at **www.cengagebrain.com** for additional study tools and review materials for this chapter.

s he neared the end of his life in 1575, the French scholar and humanist Loys Le Roy (lwa-EES le RWAH) reflected on the times in which he lived. It was, he believed, a golden age for Europe, and he ticked off the names of more than 130 scholars and translators, writers and poets, artists and sculptors, and explorers and philosophers whose work over the preceding two centuries had restored the standards of ancient learning. Later ages would call this scholarly and artistic revival the European **Renaissance**.

In addition, Le Roy enumerated a series of technological innovations that he believed had also transformed his age: printing, the marine compass, and cannonry. He put printing first because its rapid spread across Europe had done so much to communicate the literary and scholarly revival. The marine compass had made possible the sea voyages that now connected Europe directly to Africa and Asia and had led to the discovery and conquest of the Americas.

Le Roy gave third place to firearms because they had transformed warfare. Cannon and more recently devised hand-held weapons had swept before them all older military instruments. His enthusiasm for this transformation was dampened by the demonstrated capacity of firearms to cause devastation and ruin. Among the other evils of his age Le Roy enumerated syphilis and the spread of religious heresies and sects.

Reading Loys Le Roy's analysis more than four centuries later, one is struck not only by the acuity of his judgment and the beauty and clarity of his prose, but also by the astonishing geographical and historical range of his understanding. He credits both ancient and modern Greeks and Italians for their cultural contributions, the Germans for their role in perfecting printing and cannonry, and the Spanish for their overseas voyages. But his frame of reference is not confined to Europe. He cites the mathematical skills of ancient Egyptians; the military conquests of Mongols, Turks, and Persians (Iranians); Arabs' contributions to science and medicine; and China's contributions to the development of printing.

The global framework of Le Roy's analysis led him to conclude that he was living at a turning point in world history. For long centuries, he argued, the military might of the Mongols and Turks had threatened the peoples of Europe, and Safavid Iran and mamluk Egypt had surpassed any European land in riches. Now the West was in the ascendancy. Europeans' military might equaled that of their Middle Eastern neighbors. They were amassing new wealth from Asian trade and American silver. Most of all, the explosion of learning and knowledge had given Europe intellectual equality and perhaps superiority. Le Roy noted perceptively that while printing presses were in use all across Europe, the Islamic world had closed itself off from the benefits of this new technology, refusing to allow presses to be set up and even forbidding the printing of Arabic works about their lands in Europe.

Culture and Ideas

How was the cultural history of early modern Europe determined by the interplay of traditional beliefs and revolutionary ideas?

The period from 1500 to 1750 saw both conflict and continuity in the world of ideas. Theological controversies broke the religious unity of the Latin Church and contributed to violent wars, and a huge witch scare showed the power of Christian and folk beliefs about the Devil. Although classical ideas from Greco-Roman antiquity impressed many better-educated people, some thinkers challenged the authority of the ancients. Their new models of planetary motion encouraged others to challenge traditional social and political systems, with important implications for the period after 1750. The technology of the printing press enhanced the impact of all of these developments.

Renaissance (European) A period of intense artistic and intellectual activity, said to be a "rebirth" of Greco-Roman culture. Usually divided into an Italian Renaissance, from roughly the mid-fourteenth to mid-fifteenth century, and a Northern Renaissance, from roughly the early fifteenth to early seventeenth century.

Religious Reformation

In 1500 the **papacy**, the central government of Latin Christianity, was simultaneously gaining stature and suffering from corruption and dissent. During the sixteenth century, as larger donations and tax receipts let popes fund ambitious construction projects, Rome, their capital city, gained fifty-four new churches and other buildings that showcased the artistic Renaissance then under way. However, such wealth and power also attracted ambitious men, including some who led scandalous personal lives.

The jewel of the building projects was the new Saint Peter's Basilica in Rome. The unprecedented size and splendor of this church were intended to glorify God and enhance the standing of the papacy. Such a project required refined tastes and vast sums of money. Pope Leo X (r. 1513–1521), a member of the wealthy Medici (MED-ih-chee) family of Florence, oversaw the design and financing of the new basilica. Pope Leo's artistic taste was superb and his personal life free from scandal, but he was more a man of action than a spiritual leader. One way he raised building funds was by authorizing **indulgences**—absolutions for past sins granted to reward a pious act such as making a pilgrimage, saying a particular prayer, or making a financial donation.

A young professor of sacred scripture, Martin Luther (1483–1546), objected to the way the new indulgences were preached. Having forsaken money and marriage for a monastic life of prayer, self-denial, and study, Luther found personal consolation in a passage in Saint Paul's Epistle to the Romans stating that salvation came not from "doing certain things" but from religious faith. That passage led Luther to object to the indulgence preachers' emphasis on giving money more than on the faith behind the donation. He complained about this abuse to Pope Leo and challenged the preachers to debate the theology of indulgences.

Largely ignoring Luther's theological objections, Pope Leo regarded his letter as a challenge to papal power and moved to silence him. During a debate

Scala/Art Resource, NY

St. Peter's Basilica in Rome Extravagant spending on church buildings and ornamentation helped spark Martin Luther's break with the papacy. The luxurious St. Peter's Basilica, with room for 60,000 worshipers, provided the most outstanding example. Work on the basilica began in 1506 and continued for more than a century. Shown here is the spectacular *baldacchino*, a sculptured bronze canopy above the main altar. It is 98 feet (30 meters) high and was executed by Gian Lorenzo Bernini between 1623 and 1633.

in 1519, a papal representative led Luther into open disagreement with church doctrines, for which the papacy condemned him. Unable to reform the church from within, Luther burned the papal bull (document) of condemnation, rejecting the pope's authority and beginning the movement known as the **Protestant Reformation**.

papacy The central administration of the Roman Catholic Church, of which the pope is the head.
indulgence The forgiveness of the punishment due for past sins, granted by the Catholic Church authorities as a reward for a pious act. Martin Luther's protest against the sale of indulgences is often seen as touching off the Protestant Reformation.
Protestant Reformation Religious reform movement within the Latin Christian Church beginning in 1519. It resulted in the "protesters" forming several new Christian denominations, including the Lutheran and Reformed Churches and the Church of England.

 Primary Source: Table Talk Find out what word "creates more alarm at Rome than thunderbolts from heaven or the day of judgment."

Chronology

	Politics and Culture	Environment and Technology	Warfare
1500	**1500s** Spain's golden century	**Mid-1500s** Increasing land drainage in Holland	
	1519 Protestant Reformation begins		
			1526–1571 Ottoman wars
	1540s Scientific Revolution begins **1545** Catholic Reformation begins		
			1546–1555 German Wars of Religion **1562–1598** French Wars of Religion **1566–1648** Netherlands Revolt
		1590s Dutch develop flyboats; Little Ice Age begins	
1600	**Late 1500s** Witch-hunts increase **1600s** Holland's golden century	**1600s** Depletion of forests growing **1609** Galileo's astronomical telescope	
			1618–1648 Thirty Years War **1642–1648** English Civil War **1652–1678** Anglo-Dutch Wars **1667–1697** Wars of Louis XIV
		1682 Canal du Midi completed	
1700	**1700s** The Enlightenment begins		**1683–1697** Ottoman wars **1700–1721** Great Northern War **1701–1714** War of the Spanish Succession
		1750 English mine nearly 5 million tons of coal a year **1755** Lisbon earthquake	

Accusing those whom he called "Romanists" (Roman Catholics) of relying on "good works," Luther insisted that the only way to salvation was through faith in Jesus Christ. He further declared that Christian belief must be based on the word of God in the Bible and on Christian tradition, not on the authority of the pope. Eventually his conclusions led him to abandon his monastic prayers and penances and to marry a former nun.

Today Roman Catholics and Lutherans have resolved many of their theological differences, but in the sixteenth century stubbornness on both sides made reconciliation impossible. Moreover, Luther's use of the printing press to promote his ideas won him the support of powerful Germans, who responded to his portrayal of the dispute as an effort by an Italian pope to beautify his city with German funds.

Inspired by Luther's denunciation of corruption, leaders elsewhere called for a return to authentic Christian practices and beliefs. John Calvin (1509–1564), a Frenchman who turned from the study of law to theology after experiencing a religious conversion, became a highly influential Protestant leader. Calvin's *The Institutes of the Christian Religion* (1535) set forth his synthesis of Christian teachings, which differed from that of Roman Catholics and Lutherans in two respects. First, while exalting faith over works, Calvin nevertheless denied that faith alone could ensure salvation. Heaven, said Calvin, was a gift God gave to those he "predestined" for salvation.

Map 16.1 Religious Reformation in Europe The Reformation brought greater religious freedom but also led to religious conflict and persecution. In many places the Reformation accelerated the trend toward state control of religion and added religious differences to the motives for wars among Europeans.   © Cengage Learning

Interactive Map

Predominant religion in 1555

- Lutheran
- Calvinist (Reformed)
- Church of England
- Roman Catholic
- Orthodox
- Muslim
- ▲ Spread of Calvinism
- ▲ Huguenot center
- ◯ Ottoman Empire, 1566

ATLANTIC OCEAN

North Sea

Baltic Sea

Black Sea

Mediterranean Sea

Adriatic Sea

IRELAND
Dublin

SCOTLAND 1560
Edinburgh
John Knox,
1505–1572

ENGLAND 1536
London
Oxford
John Wyclif,
1320–1384
Plymouth
Penetration of Calvinism to England after 1558

NORWAY 1536/1607
Bergen

SWEDEN
Stockholm
Helsinki

Riga

LITHUANIA
Warsaw

PRUSSIA

POLAND

DENMARK
Copenhagen
Hamburg

SAXONY
Wittenberg
Martin Luther
Eisleben
Birthplace of Martin Luther,
1483–1546
Erfurt
Leipzig

BRANDENBURG

NETHERLANDS
Amsterdam
Antwerp
Brussels
Münster
Marburg

HOLY ROMAN EMPIRE
Worms
Edict of Worms,
1521
Speyer
Nuremberg
Stuttgart
Augsburg
Munich

BOHEMIA
Prague
Jan Hus,
1369–1415

MORAVIA

AUSTRIA
Vienna
Council of Trent,
1545–1563
Trent

Noyon
Birthplace of John Calvin,
1509–1564
Paris
Rennes
Orléans

FRANCE
Nantes
Edict of Nantes,
1598
La Rochelle
Bordeaux
Toulouse
Avignon
Marseilles

Basel
Strasbourg
Zürich
Ulrich Zwingli,
1484–1531
Geneva
John Calvin
Milan
Pavia
Genoa
Venice

ITALY
Pisa
Florence
Rome
Roman Inquisition established, 1542
Naples
Bari

Corsica
Sardinia
Sicily

Loyola
Birthplace of Ignatius Loyola,
1491–1556

SPAIN
Madrid
Toledo
Barcelona
Valencia
Granada
Seville

PORTUGAL
Lisbon

Balearic Is.

MOROCCO

ALGIERS

TUNIS

OTTOMAN EMPIRE

OTTOMAN EMPIRE

BULGARIA
SERBIA
Belgrade

HUNGARY
Buda
Pest

TRANSYLVANIA

WALLACHIA
Danube R.

MOLDAVIA

BESSARABIA

GREECE

50°N
60°N
50°N
0°
10°E
20°E
30°E

N

0   200   400 Km.
0   200   400 Mi.

Second, Calvin went beyond Luther in curtailing the power of the clergy and simplifying religious rituals. Calvinist congregations elected their governing committees and in time created regional and national synods (councils) to regulate doctrinal issues. Calvinists also emphasized simplicity in dress, life, and worship. In an age of ornate garments, they wore simple black clothes, avoided ostentatious living, and worshiped in churches devoid of statues, most musical instruments, stained-glass windows, incense, and vestments.

The Reformers appealed to genuine religious sentiments, but their successes and failures were also due to political circumstances (discussed below) and the social agendas of their followers. Lutheranism appealed strongly to German speakers and linguistically related Scandinavians. Peasants and urban laborers sometimes defied their masters by adopting a different faith. Protestants were no more inclined than Roman Catholics to question male dominance in the church and the family, but most Protestants rejected the tradition of celibate priests and nuns and advocated Christian marriage for all adults.

Shaken by the Protestant Reformers' popularity, the Catholic Church undertook its own reforms. A council that met at the city of Trent, in northern Italy, in three sessions between 1545 and 1563 painstakingly distinguished proper Catholic doctrines from Protestant "errors." It also reaffirmed the supremacy of the pope and called for a number of reforms, including requiring each bishop to reside in his diocese and each diocese to have a theological seminary to train priests. Also important to this **Catholic Reformation** were the activities of a new religious order—the Society of Jesus, or "Jesuits," that Ignatius of Loyola (1491–1556), a Spanish nobleman, founded in 1540. Well-educated Jesuits helped win back some adherents by their teaching and preaching (see Map 16.1). Other Jesuits became missionaries overseas.

Given the intensity of the emotions that the Protestant Reformation stirred, it is not surprising that violence often flared up. Both sides persecuted and even executed those of differing views. Bitter "wars of religion," fought over a mixture of religious and secular issues, continued in parts of Europe until 1648.

Traditional Thinking and Witch-Hunts

Religious differences continued to generate animosity long after the first generation of reformers, but from a global perspective European Christians still had much in common both in their theology and in the local folk customs and pre-Christian beliefs that remained powerful everywhere in Europe. The widespread **witch-hunts** pursued by both Protestants and Catholics arose from those common beliefs.

Two distinct traditions marked European ideas about the natural world: folklore about magic and forest spirits passed down orally from pre-Christian times, and biblical teachings heard in church and read by growing numbers in vernacular translations. Christian teachings about miracles, saints, and devils mingled with folklore in the minds of many. Like people elsewhere, most Europeans believed that natural events could have supernatural causes. When crops failed or domestic animals died unexpectedly, many people blamed unseen spirits. People also attributed human triumphs and tragedies to supernatural causes. When an earthquake destroyed much of Lisbon, Portugal's capital city, in November 1755, for example, both educated and uneducated people saw the event as a divine punishment. A Jesuit charged it "scandalous to pretend that the earthquake was just a natural event." An English Protestant leader agreed, comparing Lisbon's fate with that of Sodom, the sinful biblical city that God destroyed.

The fear of witches that swept across northern Europe in the late sixteenth and seventeenth centuries grew out of these beliefs. Secular and church authorities tried over a hundred thousand people—some three-fourths of them women—for practicing witchcraft. Some were acquitted; some recanted; but more than half were executed—mostly in Protestant lands. Torture and harsh interrogation persuaded many accused witches to confess to casting spells and

Catholic Reformation Religious reform movement within the Latin Christian Church, begun in response to the Protestant Reformation. It clarified Catholic theology and reformed clerical training and discipline.
witch-hunt The pursuit of people suspected of witchcraft, especially in northern Europe in the late sixteenth and seventeenth centuries.

Death to Witches This woodcut from 1574 depicts three women convicted of witchcraft being burned alive in Baden, Switzerland. The well-dressed townsmen look on stolidly.

to describe in vivid detail their encounters with the Devil and their attendance at nighttime assemblies of witches.

Trial records make it clear that both the accusers and the accused believed that it was possible for angry and jealous individuals to use evil magic and the power of the Devil to attack people and domestic animals or to cause crops to wither in the fields. Though researchers think that at least some of those accused may really have tried using witchcraft to harm their enemies, it was the Reformation's focus on the Devil that made such malevolence a serious crime and helped revive pre-Christian fears of witchcraft.

Modern historians also argue that accusations against widows and independent-minded women arose from a widespread distrust of women not directly controlled by fathers or husbands. Such women played important roles in tending animals and the sick and in childbirth, which also made them suspects if death occurred.

No single reason can explain the witchcraft hysteria in early modern Europe, but, for both the accusers and the accused, there are plausible connections between the witch-hunts and rising social tensions, rural poverty, and environmental strains. Far from being a bizarre aberration, witch-hunts reflected the larger social climate.

The Scientific Revolution

Educated people ignored folklore and looked to the Bible and the writings of antiquity, many of them newly discovered by Renaissance scholars, for guides to the natural world. Their authority on physics was Aristotle, who taught that everything on earth was reducible to four elements: earth and water on the surface and air and fire floating above the ground. Higher still were the sun, moon, planets, and stars, light, pure bodies embedded in crystalline spheres. This theory accorded perfectly with the commonsense perception that all heavenly bodies revolved around the earth.

The ideas of the ancient Greek mathematician Pythagoras supported this view. Pythagoreans attached special significance to the simplest (to them

Tycho Brahe at Work Between 1576 and 1597, on the island of Ven between Denmark and Sweden, Tycho built the best observatory in Europe and set a new standard for accurate celestial observations before the invention of the telescope. The contemporary hand-colored engraving shows the Danish astronomer at work.

History in Focus *In the image, Tycho Brahe is shown twice, both times surrounded by clocks, globes, and other instruments, but no telescope. How much information about the heavens could he obtain without a telescope? How much more could Galileo and other astronomers get with the simple telescope of the sixteenth century? Find the answer online.*

perfect) geometrical shapes: the circle (a point rotated around another point) and the sphere (a circle rotated on its axis). They believed that celestial objects were perfect spheres orbiting the earth in perfectly circular orbits.

In the sixteenth century, however, careful observations and mathematical calculations, many of them made by Muslims and translated into Latin, led some

imaginative European investigators to challenge these views. These pioneers of the **Scientific Revolution** rejected the accumulation of ingenious theories used to explain some seemingly irregular celestial movements. A Polish monk and mathematician named Nicholas Copernicus (1473–1543), possibly building on the theories of Muslim astronomers, came up with a mathematically simpler solution: switching the center of the different orbits from the earth to the sun.

Copernicus did not challenge the idea that the sun, moon, and planets were light, perfect spheres or that they moved in circular orbits. But his placement of the sun, not the earth, at the center of things began a revolution in understanding the structure of the heavens and the place of humans in the universe. To escape the anticipated controversies, Copernicus delayed the publication of his heliocentric (sun-centered) theory until the end of his life.

Other astronomers, including the Dane Tycho Brahe (1546–1601) and his German assistant Johannes Kepler (1571–1630), improved on the Copernican model by showing that planets actually move in elliptical, not circular, orbits. The most brilliant of the Copernicans was the Italian Galileo Galilei (gal-uh-LAY-oh gal-uh-LAY-ee) (1564–1642). In 1609 Galileo built a telescope through which he took a closer look at the heavens. Viewing distant objects at a magnification thirty times that of the naked eye, Galileo perceived that heavenly bodies were not the perfectly smooth spheres of the Aristotelians. The moon, he reported in *The Starry Messenger* (1610), had mountains and valleys; the sun had spots; other planets had their own moons. In other words, the earth was not alone in being heavy and changeable.

At first, the Copernicans endured much criticism because their views so directly challenged not just popular ideas but also classical and biblical authority. How, demanded Aristotle's defenders, could the heavy earth rotate around the sun without shaking to pieces? Does the Bible lie, asked the theologians, when the Book of Joshua says that, by God's command, "the

Primary Source: Letter to the Grand Duchess Christina Hear what the quick-witted Galileo Galilei has to say to his detractors.

Scientific Revolution The intellectual movement in Europe, initially associated with planetary motion and other aspects of physics, that by the seventeenth century had laid the groundwork for modern science.

sun [not the earth] stood still . . . for about a whole day" to give the ancient Israelites victory in their conquest of Palestine? If Aristotle's physics was wrong, worried other traditionalists, would not the theological synthesis built on other parts of his philosophy be open to question?

Most Protestant leaders, following the lead of Martin Luther, condemned the heliocentric universe as contrary to the Bible. Catholic authorities waited longer to act. After all, both Copernicus and Galileo were Roman Catholics. Copernicus had dedicated his book to the pope, and in 1582 another pope, Gregory XIII, had used the latest astronomical findings to issue the new and more accurate Gregorian calendar still used today. Galileo ingeniously argued that the conflict between scripture and science was only apparent: the word of God revealed in the Bible was expressed in the imperfect language of ordinary people, but in nature God's truth was revealed in a language that could be learned by careful observation and scientific reasoning.

Unfortunately, Galileo ridiculed those who were slow to accept his findings, charging that Copernican ideas were "mocked and hooted at by an infinite multitude . . . of fools." Stung by such sarcasm, some Jesuits and other critics got his ideas condemned by the Roman Inquisition in 1616. *The Starry Messenger* went onto the Index of Forbidden Books, and Galileo was barred from publishing further on the subject. (In 1992 the Catholic Church officially retracted its condemnation of Galileo.)

Index or no Index, printed books spread the new scientific ideas among scholars across Europe. In England, Robert Boyle (1627–1691) used experimental methods and a trial-and-error approach to examine the inner workings of chemistry. Through the Royal Society, chartered in London in 1662 to promote knowledge of the natural world, Boyle and others became enthusiastic missionaries of mechanical science and fierce opponents of the Aristotelians.

Meanwhile, English mathematician Isaac Newton (1642–1727) was carrying to its logical conclusion Galileo's demonstration that the heavens and earth share a common physics. Newton formulated a set of mathematical laws that all physical objects obeyed. It was the force of gravity—not angels—that governed the elliptical orbits of heavenly bodies. It was gravitation that caused cannonballs to fall back to earth. From 1703 until his death Newton served as president of the Royal Society and as an icon of the new science.

Galileo's condemnation demonstrates that in 1700 most religious and intellectual leaders viewed the new science with suspicion or outright hostility. Yet the principal pioneers of the Scientific Revolution were convinced that scientific discoveries and revealed religion were not in conflict. At the peak of his fame Newton promoted a series of lectures devoted to proving the validity of Christianity. However, by showing that Aristotelian and biblical ideas about the natural world were naive and not based on facts, these pioneers opened the door for others who used reason to challenge a broader range of traditions and superstitions.

The Early Enlightenment

The advances in scientific thought inspired a few brave souls to question the reasonableness of everything from agricultural methods to laws, religion, and social hierarchies. The belief that human reason could discover scientific laws governing social behavior, parallel to those governing physical properties, energized a movement known as the **Enlightenment**. Like the Scientific Revolution, this movement was the work of a few "enlightened" individuals, who often faced bitter opposition. Leading Enlightenment thinkers became accustomed to having their books banned and spending long periods in exile to escape imprisonment.

The partisan bickering and bloodshed of the Reformation had led some people to doubt the superiority of any theological position and to recommend toleration of all religions. The killing of suspected witches also shocked many thoughtful people. The

Primary Source: Treatise on Tolerance Discover Voltaire's eloquent argument for tolerance and learn why be calls human beings "atoms of the moment."

Enlightenment A philosophical movement in eighteenth-century Europe that fostered the belief that one could reform society by discovering rational laws that governed social behavior and were just as scientific as the laws of physics.

SECTION REVIEW

- Conflicts among ideas, enhanced by print technology, profoundly affected the culture of early modern Europe.

- Outraged by corrupt church practices, reformers like Luther and Calvin challenged papal authority and traditional Catholic theology.

- In response to the Protestant reformers, the Church launched a Catholic Reformation.

- At the same time, both Protestants and Catholics, driven by traditional ideas, undertook widespread witch-hunts.

- The thinkers of the Scientific Revolution challenged traditional biblical and Greco-Roman conceptions of the cosmos.

- The advances in science prompted Enlightenment thinkers to question many conventional ideas and practices.

leading French thinker Voltaire (1694–1778) declared: "No opinion is worth burning your neighbor for."

Explorers' accounts of cultures in other parts of the world raised questions about Europe's superiority. Romantic reports of Amerindian life, for example, led some to conclude that so-called "savages" were in many ways nobler than European Christians. Matteo Ricci, a Jesuit missionary to China whose journals were widely read, contrasted the lack of territorial ambition of the Chinese with the constant warfare in the West and attributed the difference to China's being ruled by educated men whom he called "Philosophers."

Although many circumstances shaped "enlightened" thinking, the new scientific methods and discoveries provided the clearest model for changing European society. Voltaire posed the issues in these terms: "it would be very peculiar that all nature, all the planets, should obey eternal laws" but a human being, "in contempt of these laws, could act as he pleased solely according to his caprice." The English poet Alexander Pope (1688–1774) made a similar point in verse: "Nature and Nature's laws lay hidden in night; / God said, 'Let Newton be' and all was light."

The Enlightenment was more a frame of mind than a coherent movement. By 1750 its proponents were clearer about what they disliked than about what new institutions should be created. Nearly all

were optimistic that—at least in the long run—human beliefs and institutions could be improved. This belief in progress would help foster political and social revolutions after 1750, as Chapter 20 recounts.

Despite the enthusiasm the Enlightenment aroused in some circles, it was decidedly unpopular with many absolutist rulers and with most clergymen. Europe in 1750 was neither enlightened nor scientific.

Social and Economic Life

What factors contributed to the wealth of some Europeans and the great poverty of others?

From a distance European society seemed quite rigid. At the top of the social pyramid a small number of noble families monopolized church, government, and military offices and enjoyed many privileges, including exemption from taxation. Merchants and professionals, who had acquired wealth but no legal privileges, ranked well below them. At the base of the pyramid were the masses, mostly rural peasants and landless laborers. The subordination of women to men seemed equally rigid.

Nevertheless, some social mobility did occur, particularly in the middle. The principal engine of social change was the economy, and the places where social change occurred most readily were the cities. A secondary means of change was education—for those who could get it.

The Bourgeoisie

Europe's growing cities were the products of a changing economy. In 1500 Paris was the only northern European city with over 100,000 inhabitants. By 1700 both Paris and London had populations over 500,000, and twenty other European cities contained over 60,000 people.

The wealth of the cities came from manufacturing, finance, and especially trade, both within Europe and overseas. The French called the economically dynamic urban class the **bourgeoisie**

---

bourgeoisie In early modern Europe, the class of well-off town dwellers whose wealth came from manufacturing, finance, commerce, and allied professions.

Port of Amsterdam Ships, barges, and boats of all types are visible in this busy seventeenth-century scene. The large building in the center is the Admiralty House, the headquarters of the Dutch East India Company. Mansell/TimeLife Pictures/ Getty Images

(boor-zhwah-ZEE) (burghers, town dwellers). Members of the bourgeoisie poured much of their profit back into their businesses or into new ventures. Even so, they had enough money to live comfortably in large houses with many servants. In the seventeenth and eighteenth centuries they could buy exotic luxuries imported from the far corners of the earth—Caribbean and Brazilian sugar and rum, Mexican chocolate, Virginia tobacco, North American furs, East Indian cottons and spices, and Chinese tea.

In the seventeenth century the Netherlands flourished with a wide variety of goods flowing from factories and workshops. The highly successful textile industry concentrated on weaving and printing cloth, leaving the spinning of thread to low-paid workers elsewhere. Along with fine woolens and linens the Dutch made cheaper textiles for mass markets. Other factories in Holland refined West Indian sugar, brewed beer from Baltic grain, processed Virginia tobacco, and made imitations of Chinese ceramics. Free from the censorship imposed in neighboring countries, Holland's printers published books in many languages, including manuals with the latest advances in machinery, metallurgy, and agriculture. For a small province barely above sea level,

lacking timber and other natural resources, this was a remarkable achievement.

Burgeoning from a fishing village to a metropolis of some 200,000 by 1700, Amsterdam was Holland's largest city and Europe's major port. The bourgeoisie there and in other cities developed huge commercial fleets that dominated sea trade in Europe and overseas. Eighty percent of the trade between Spain and northern Europe sailed on Dutch ships, even while Spain and the Netherlands were at war. Amsterdam also served as Europe's financial center. Seventeenth-century Dutch banks had such a reputation for security that wealthy individuals and governments from all over western Europe entrusted them with their money. The banks in turn invested these funds in real estate, loaned money to factory owners and governments, and provided capital for business operations overseas.

Maritime expansion led to new ship designs. In this, too, the Dutch played a dominant role, using timber imported from northern Europe to build their own fleets as well as ships for export. Especially successful was the fluit, or "flyboat," a large-capacity cargo ship developed in the 1590s. It was inexpensive to build and required only a small crew. Another successful type was the heavily armed "East Indiaman," which helped the Dutch establish their supremacy in the Indian Ocean. The Dutch also excelled at map-making (see Environment and Technology: Mapping the World).

Like merchants elsewhere, Europeans relied on family and ethnic networks. Many northern cities contained merchant colonies from Venice, Florence, Genoa, and other Italian cities. Amsterdam and Hamburg sheltered Jewish merchants who had fled religious persecution in Iberia. Other Jewish communities expanded out of eastern Europe into the German states, especially after the Thirty Years War. Armenian merchants from Iran were moving into the Mediterranean and became important in Russia in the seventeenth century.

Leading merchants sought alliances with European monarchs who believed that economic growth would increase state revenues. These alliances led to the formation of **joint-stock companies**. The first such companies were the Dutch East India Company, which received a monopoly over trade to the East Indies, and the Dutch West India Company, which received the same for the New World. France and England also chartered joint-stock companies. The companies sold shares to individuals to spread the risks (and profits) among many investors (see Chapter 17). Investors bought and sold shares in specialized markets called **stock exchanges**, an Italian innovation transferred to the cities of northwestern Europe in the sixteenth century. The greatest stock market in the seventeenth and eighteenth centuries was the Amsterdam Exchange, founded in 1530. Large insurance companies also emerged in this period, and insuring long voyages against loss became a standard practice after 1700.

Governments also undertook large projects to improve water transport. The Dutch built canals for transport and to drain the lowlands for agriculture. Other governments also financed canals. One of the most important was the 150-mile (240-kilometer) Canal du Midi in France, built by the French government between 1661 and 1682 to link the Atlantic and the Mediterranean. By the seventeenth century rulers sought the talents of successful businessmen as administrators. Jean Baptiste Colbert (kohl-BEAR) (1619–1683), Louis XIV's able minister of finance, was a notable example.

Successful bourgeoisie in England and France traded wealth for social status. By retiring from their businesses and buying country estates, they could become members of the **gentry** and follow the lifestyle of the old aristocracy. The gentry loaned money to impoverished peasants and to members of the nobility and in time increased their ownership of land. Some families sought aristocratic husbands for their daughters. The old nobility found such alliances attractive because of the large dowries that the bourgeoisie provided. In France a family could gain the exemption from taxation by living in gentility for three generations or, more quickly, by purchasing a title from the king.

Peasants and Laborers

At the other end of society things were bad, but they had been worse. Though serfdom expanded in eastern Europe, in the west it faded away after the Black Death of the mid-fourteenth century. Slavery, which had briefly expanded in southern Europe around 1500 as the result of the Atlantic slave trade from sub-Saharan Africa, declined. After 1600, Europeans shipped nearly all African slaves to the Americas. Thus western Europe continued to depend on unfree labor, though at a distance rather than at home.

Legal freedom did not make a peasant's life more secure. Agricultural efficiency had improved little since 1300. As a result, bad years brought famine, and good ones provided only small surpluses. Indeed, prolonged warfare, environmental problems, and varying economic conditions may have lowered the conditions of life for the average person between 1500 and 1750. In addition, Europeans felt the effects of a century of relatively cool weather that began in the 1590s. During this **Little Ice Age** an average temperature decline of only a few degrees had startling results.

joint-stock company A business, often backed by a government charter, that sold shares to individuals to raise money for its trading enterprises and to spread the risks (and profits) among many investors.

stock exchange A place where shares in a company or business enterprise are bought and sold.

gentry The class of landholding families in England and France below the aristocracy.

Little Ice Age A century-long period of cool climate that began in the 1590s. Its ill effects on agriculture in northern Europe were notable.

Mapping the World

In 1602 in China the Jesuit missionary Matteo Ricci printed an elaborate map of the world. Working from maps produced in Europe and incorporating the latest knowledge gathered by European maritime explorers, Ricci introduced two changes to make the map more appealing to his Chinese hosts. He labeled it in Chinese characters, and he split his map down the middle of the Atlantic so that China lay in the center. This version pleased the Chinese elite, who considered China the "Middle Kingdom" surrounded by lesser states. A copy of Ricci's map in six large panels adorned the emperor's Beijing palace.

The stunningly beautiful maps and globes of sixteenth-century Europe were the most complete, detailed, and useful representations of the earth that any society had ever produced. The best mapmaker of the century was Gerhard Kremer, who is remembered as Mercator (the merchant) because his maps were so useful to European ocean traders. By incorporating the latest discoveries and scientific measurements, Mercator could depict the outlines of the major continents in painstaking detail, even if their interiors were still largely unknown to outsiders.

To represent the spherical globe on a flat map, Mercator drew the lines of longitude as parallel lines. Because such lines actually meet at the poles, Mercator's projection greatly exaggerated the size of every landmass and body of water distant from the equator. However, Mercator's rendering offered a very practical advantage: sailors could plot their course by drawing a straight line between their point of departure and their destination. Because of this useful feature, the Mercator projection of the world remained in common use until quite recently. To some extent, its popularity came from the exaggerated size this projection gave to Europe. Like the Chinese, Europeans liked to think of themselves as at the center of things. Europeans also understood their true geographical position better than people in any other part of the world.

Dutch World Map, 1641 It is easy to see why the Chinese would not have liked to see their empire at the far right edge of this widely printed map. Besides the distortions caused by the Mercator projection, geographical ignorance exaggerates the size of North America and Antarctica.

Hunters in the Snow, 1565
This January scene by the Flemish artist Pieter Bruegel, the Elder, shows many everyday activities.

Kunsthistorisches Museum, Vienna/The Bridgeman Art Library

By 1700, however, high-yielding new crops from the Americas were helping the rural poor avoid starvation. Potatoes sustained life in northeastern and central Europe and in Ireland, and poor peasants in Italy subsisted on maize. Ironically, all of these lands were major exporters of wheat, which the agricultural laborers could not afford to eat. Instead, the grain was shipped to the cities of western Europe. Other fleets brought wine from southern to northern Europe. Parisians downed 100,000 barrels of wine a year at the end of the seventeenth century. Some of the grain was made into beer, which the poor drank because it was cheaper than wine. In 1750 Parisian breweries brewed 23 million quarts (22 million liters) of beer for local consumption.

The expanding iron industry in England provided work for woodcutters and charcoal makers, but the high consumption of wood fuel for this and other purposes caused serious **deforestation**. One early-seventeenth-century observer lamented: "within man's memory, it was held impossible to have any want of wood in England. But . . . at present, through the great consuming of wood . . . and the neglect of planting of woods, there is a great scarcity of wood throughout the whole kingdom."[1] Ironworks managers in England met the shortages by importing timber and charcoal from heavily forested Scandinavian

countries and Russia. Eventually, the high price of wood and charcoal encouraged smelters to use coal as an alternative fuel. England's coal mining increased twelvefold, from 210,000 tons in 1550 to 2,500,000 tons in 1700. Starting in 1709, coke—coal baked to remove impurities—gradually replaced charcoal in the smelting of iron. These new demands drove English coal production to nearly 5 million tons a year by 1750.

France was more forested than England, but deforestation there prompted Colbert to predict that "France will perish for lack of wood." By the late eighteenth century, local iron production made deforestation an issue even in Sweden and Russia. Fear of running out of the high-quality timbers of exceptional size and curvature needed for naval vessels spurred new laws to protect forests in France and England. Although wood consumption remained high, rising prices encouraged some individuals to plant trees for future harvest. Everywhere in Europe the rural poor felt the depletion of the forests most strongly, since for centuries they had depended on woodlands for wild nuts and berries, free firewood and building materials, and wild game.

deforestation The removal of trees faster than forests can replace themselves.

The Fishwife, 1572
Women were essential partners in most Dutch family businesses. This scene by the Dutch artist Adriaen van Ostade shows a woman preparing fish for retail sale.

Improvements in food production were sometimes overwhelmed by population growth. Rural women had long supplemented household incomes by spinning yarn. From the mid-1600s rising wages in towns led textile manufacturers to farm more and more weaving out to rural areas with high underemployment. This provided men and women with enough to survive on, but the piecework paid very little for long hours of tedious labor.

Many rural poor migrated to the towns and cities in hopes of better jobs, but few met success. Even in the prosperous Dutch towns, half the population lived in acute poverty. Authorities estimated that those permanent city residents who were too poor to tax, the "deserving poor," made up 10 to 20 percent of the population. This left out the large numbers of "unworthy poor"—recent migrants, peddlers traveling from place to place, and beggars (many with horrible deformities and sores) who tried to survive on charity. Desperation forced many young women into prostitution and many men into crime, while organized gangs practiced everything from picking pockets to highway robbery.

The pervasive poverty shocked those who were not hardened to it. Around 1580 the mayor of the French city of Bordeaux (bor-DOH) asked a group of visiting Amerindian chiefs what impressed them most about European cities. The chiefs are said to have expressed astonishment at the disparity between the fat, well-fed people and the poor, half-starved men and women in rags. Why, the visitors wondered, did the poor not grab the rich by the throat or set fire to their homes?[2]

In fact, misery provoked many rebellions. For example, in 1525 peasant rebels in the Alps attacked both nobles and clergy as representatives of the privileged and landowning classes. They had no love for merchants either, whom they denounced for lending at interest and charging high prices. In southwestern France alone some 450 uprisings occurred between 1590 and 1715, many of them set off by food shortages and tax increases. The exemption of the wealthy from taxation was a frequent source of complaint. A rebellion in southern France in 1670 began when a mob of townswomen attacked the tax collector. It quickly spread to the country, where peasant leaders cried, "Death to the people's oppressors!" Authorities dealt severely with such revolts and executed or maimed their leaders.

Women and Family

Women's status and work were closely tied to those of their husbands and families. In rare instances, a woman in a royal family might inherit a throne in the absence of a male heir (see Table 16.1 for examples), but such exceptions do not negate the rule that women everywhere ranked below men. Nevertheless, class and wealth defined a woman's position in life more than gender. A wife or daughter in a rich family, for example, had a much better life than any poor man. Occasionally, a single woman might be secure and respected, as in the case of women from good families heading convents of nuns in Catholic countries. But unmarried women and widows fared poorly compared to their married sisters.

Men and women most often chose their own spouses. Privileged families controlled marriage plans more often than poor ones. Royal and noble families carefully plotted their children's marriages to further the family's status. Bourgeois parents were less likely to force their children into arranged marriages. Nevertheless, nearly all found spouses within their social class, sometimes to buttress business connections.

Europeans also married late. The children of craftspeople and the poor had to delay marriage until they could afford to live on their own. Young men served long apprenticeships to learn trades. Young women worked helping their parents, or as domestic servants, or in some other capacity to save money for their dowry: the money and household goods—the amount varied by social class—that enabled a young couple to begin marriage independent of their parents. The typical groom in western and central Europe could not hope to marry before his late twenties. His bride would be a few years younger. Marriage also came late in bourgeois families, in part to allow young men to complete their education.

The late age of marriage held down the birthrate and thus limited family size. Even so, about one in ten urban babies was born to an unmarried woman, often a servant. Such newborns were generally left on the doorsteps of churches, convents, or rich homes. Many perished. Public brothels also went with delayed marriage. They provided a place for young men to satisfy their desires at the expense of unfortunate young women, often newly arrived from impoverished villages. Nevertheless, rape was a common occurrence, especially assaults by gangs of young men. Some historians believe these crimes reflect the envy poor young men had of older men's easier access to women.

SECTION REVIEW

- Early modern European society was less rigid than it appeared, with the economy and education the primary means of social change.
- The urban bourgeoisie, especially in the Netherlands, created much of Europe's wealth through trade, manufacture, finance, and technological innovation.
- Governments sought lucrative alliances with the bourgeoisie, whose wealth afforded them political and social advancement.
- Oppressed by economic and environmental trends, peasants and laborers generally lived in poverty, and their misery often provoked rebellion.
- Although women remained subordinate to men, class and wealth were the main determinants of their positions in life.

Bourgeois parents focused on giving their children the education and training necessary for success. They promoted the establishment of municipal schools where they could learn Latin and perhaps Greek. Then they sent their sons abroad to learn modern languages or to a university to earn a law degree. Legal training helped them conduct business and was necessary for obtaining a judgeship or treasury position. Daughters were less likely to be groomed for business careers, but wives often helped their husbands as bookkeepers and sometimes inherited businesses.

The fact that most schools, like most guilds and professions, barred females explains why women were not prominent in the cultural movements of the period. Yet from a global perspective, women in early modern Europe were more prominent in the creation of high culture than were women in most other parts of the world. Recent research has identified successful women who were painters, musicians, and writers. Indeed, the spread of learning, the stress on religious reading, and the growth of business may have made Europe the leading area of the world in female literacy. Nevertheless, illiteracy was widespread for both sexes, and only women in wealthier families might have a good education. From the late 1600s some wealthy French women ran intellectual gatherings in their homes. Others were prominent letter writers. Galileo's daughter, Maria Celeste Galilei, carried on a detailed correspondence with her father from behind the walls of her convent, which she had vowed never to leave.

Political Innovations

How did differing policies on religion, foreign relations, and economics influence the history of early modern European states?

The monarchs of early modern Europe occupied the apex of the social order, arbitrated intellectual and religious conflicts, and influenced economic life. In addition, royal political agendas introduced new elements of conflict and change.

Though no unified European empire emerged, political centralization increased in separate kingdoms. The frequent civil and international conflicts of this era sometimes promoted cooperation and often encouraged innovation. Leadership and success passed from Spain to the Netherlands and then to England and France.

State Development

Political diversity characterized Europe. City-states and principalities abounded, either independently or bound into loose federations, of which the **Holy Roman Empire** of the German heartland was the foremost example. In western Europe the strong monarchies that had emerged earlier were acquiring national identities, but some rulers dreamed of a European empire comparable to that of Rome.

In 1519 electors of the Holy Roman Empire chose Charles V (r. 1519–1556) as emperor. Like his predecessors for three generations, Charles belonged to the powerful **Habsburg** (HABZ-berg) family of Austria, but he had recently inherited the Spanish thrones of Castile and Aragon. With the vast resources of these lands behind him, Charles hoped to centralize his imperial power and lead a Christian coalition to halt the advance into southeastern Europe of the Ottoman Empire, which had recently conquered Egypt and Syria.

Stout defense and bad weather prevented the Ottomans from taking Vienna in 1529, but Ottoman attacks continued on and off until 1697. King Francis I of France, who had lost to Charles in the imperial election, openly supported the Ottomans, whom the Europeans usually called Turks, to weaken his rival. In addition, some imperial states used Luther's religious Reformation to frustrate Charles's efforts to control them. Luther's appeals to German national

sentiment encouraged many German princes to oppose Charles's defense of Catholic doctrine in the imperial Diet (assembly).

After decades of bitter squabbles turned to open warfare in 1546 (the German Wars of Religion), Charles V finally gave up on unification, handed his various possessions over to different heirs, and retired to a monastery. By the Peace of Augsburg (1555), he recognized the princes' right to choose either Catholicism or Lutheranism as their state religion, and he allowed them to keep any church lands they had seized before 1552. The triumph of religious diversity postponed German political unification for three centuries.

Meanwhile, the rulers of Spain, France, and England met greater success in political centralization and religious unity. Getting control of the church in the sixteenth century was a stormy process, but the outcome was clear. Bringing the nobles and other powerful interests into a centralized political system took longer and led to more diverse outcomes.

Religious Policies

The rulers of Spain and France successfully defended the Catholic tradition against Protestant challenges. Learning from his predecessors how to suppress Jews and Muslims, King Philip II of Spain used an ecclesiastical court, the Spanish Inquisition, to bring into line those who resisted his authority. Suspected Protestants, as well as critics of the king, were accused of heresy, an offense punishable by death. Those who were acquitted learned not to oppose the king again.

In France the Calvinist opponents of the Valois rulers gained the military advantage in the French Wars of Religion (1562–1598), but in the interest of forging lasting unity, their leader Prince Henry of Navarre then embraced the Catholic faith of the majority of his subjects. The Bourbon king who followed him, Henry IV, his son King Louis XIII, and

Holy Roman Empire Loose federation of mostly German states and principalities, headed by an emperor elected by the princes. It lasted from 962 to 1806.
Habsburg A powerful European family that provided many Holy Roman Emperors, founded the Austrian (later Austro-Hungarian) Empire, and ruled sixteenth- and seventeenth-century Spain.

TABLE 16.1 Rulers in Early Modern Western Europe

Spain	France	England/Great Britain
Habsburg Dynasty	**Valois Dynasty**	**Tudor Dynasty**
Charles 1 (1516–1556) (Holy Roman Emperor Charles V)	Francis I (1515–1547)	Henry VIII (1509–1547)
	Henry II (1547–1559)	Edward VI (1547–1553)
Philip II (1556–1598)	Francis II (1559–1560)	Mary I (1553–1558)
	Charles IX (1560–1574)	Elizabeth I (1558–1603)
	Henry III (1574–1589)	
	Bourbon Dynasty	**Stuart Dynasty**
Philip III (1598–1621)	Henry IV (1589–1610)[a]	James I (1603–1625)
Philip IV(1621–1665)	Louis XIII (1610–1643)	Charles I (1625–1649)[a,b]
Charles II (1665–1700)	Louis XIV (1643–1715)	(Puritan Republic, 1649–1660)
		Charles II (1660–1685)
		James II (1685–1688)[b]
		William III (1689–1702) and Mary II (1689–1694)
		Anne (1702–1714)
Bourbon Dynasty		**Hanoverian Dynasty**
Philip V (1700–1746)		
Ferdinand VI (1746–1759)		George I (1714–1727)
	Louis XV (1715–1774)	George II (1727–1760)

[a] Died a violent death. [b] Was overthrown.

his grandson King Louis XIV supported the Catholic Church as ardently as the Spanish kings did. In 1685 Louis XIV even revoked the Edict of Nantes (nahnt), by which his grandfather had granted the Protestants religious freedom in 1598.

In England King Henry VIII initially defended the papacy against Lutheran criticism. But when the pope refused to annul his marriage to Catherine of Aragon, who had not produced a male heir, Henry ordered the English archbishop of Canterbury to annul the marriage in 1533. The breach with Rome was sealed the next year when Parliament made the English monarch head of the Church of England.

Like many Protestant rulers, Henry disbanded monasteries and convents and seized their lands. He gave some lands to his powerful allies and sold others to pay for his new navy. Yet the ritual and theology of the new Anglican Church resembled their Catholic counterparts too closely to satisfy English Puritans (Calvinists who wanted to "purify" the Anglican Church of Catholic practices and beliefs). In 1603 the first Stuart king, James I, dismissed a Puritan petition to eliminate bishops with the statement "No bishops, no king"—a reminder of the essential role of the church in supporting royal power.

Monarchies in England and France

Over the course of the seventeenth century, the rulers of England and France contested with their leading subjects over the limits of royal authority. Religion was never absent in these struggles, but the different constitutional outcomes were more significant in the long run.

To evade any check on his power, King Charles I of England (see Table 16.1) ruled for eleven years without summoning Parliament, his kingdom's representative body. Lacking Parliament's consent to new taxes, he raised funds by coercing "loans" from wealthy subjects and applying existing tax laws more broadly. Then in 1640 a rebellion in Scotland forced

The Palace of Versailles
The Palace of Versailles, seen here from its immense gardens and reflecting pool, was the pet project of King Louis XIV of France. He designed it to be the largest and most elaborate palace in the world. Built in stages from 1664 to 1710, it was the seat of the royal court during most of Louis' reign and the symbol of royal absolutism.

him to summon a Parliament to approve new taxes to pay for an army. Noblemen and churchmen sat in the House of Lords, while representatives from the towns and counties sat in the House of Commons. Before it would authorize new taxes, Parliament insisted on strict guarantees that the king would never again ignore the body's traditional rights. Charles refused. When he ordered the arrest of his leading critics in the House of Commons in 1642, he plunged the kingdom into the **English Civil War**.

Even after defeat on the battlefield, Charles refused to compromise. In 1649 a "Rump" Parliament (one purged of his supporters) ordered him executed and replaced the monarchy with a republic under Oliver Cromwell, a Puritan general. Cromwell expanded England's presence overseas and imposed firm control over Ireland and Scotland, but he was as unwilling as the Stuart kings to share power with Parliament. After his death Parliament restored the Stuart line, making it unclear, for a time, which side had won the war.

King James II clarified matters when he refused to respect Parliament's rights and had his heir baptized a Roman Catholic. Parliament responded by forcing James into exile in the bloodless coup known as "the Glorious Revolution of 1688." The Bill of Rights of 1689 specified that Parliament had to be called frequently and had to consent to changes in laws and to the raising of an army in peacetime. Another law reaffirmed the official status of the Church of England but extended religious toleration to the Puritans. A similar struggle in France produced a different outcome.

There the Estates General represented the traditional rights of the clergy, the nobility, and the towns (that is, the bourgeoisie). The Estates General had asserted its rights during the sixteenth-century French Wars of Religion, when the monarchy was weak. But thereafter the Bourbon monarchs generally ruled without calling it into session. They avoided financial crises by more efficient tax collection and by selling appointments to high government offices. In justification they claimed that the monarch had absolute authority to rule in God's name.

Louis XIV's gigantic new palace at **Versailles** (vuhr-SIGH) symbolized the monarch's triumph over the nobility, clergy, and towns. Capable of housing ten thousand people and surrounded by elaborately landscaped grounds and parks, the palace was a sort of theme park of royal absolutism. Elaborate ceremonies and banquets centered on the king deterred the nobles who lived at Versailles from plotting rebellion.

English Civil War (1642–1648) A conflict over royal versus parliamentary rights, caused by King Charles I's arrest of his parliamentary critics and ending with his execution. Its outcome checked the growth of royal absolutism and, with the Glorious Revolution of 1688 and the English Bill of Rights of 1689, ensured that England would be a constitutional monarchy.
Versailles The huge palace built for French King Louis XIV west of Paris. The palace symbolized the preeminence of French power and architecture in Europe and the triumph of royal authority over the French nobility.

According to one of them, the duke of Saint-Simon (san-see-MOHN), "no one was so clever in devising petty distractions" as the king.

Most European rulers admired and imitated the centralized powers and absolutist claims of the French until well after 1750, and some built imitations of Versailles. The English model of balanced powers gained influence more slowly. In his *Second Treatise of Civil Government* (1690), the English political philosopher John Locke (1632–1704) disputed monarchial claims to absolute authority by divine right. Rather, he argued, rulers derived their authority from the consent of the governed and, like everyone else, were subject to the law. If monarchs overstepped the law, citizens had not only the right but also the duty to rebel.

Warfare and Diplomacy

In addition to their bitter civil wars, European monarchies engaged in numerous international conflicts. Warfare was almost constant (see the Chronology at the beginning of the chapter). The worst of the international conflicts, the Thirty Years War (1618–1648), caused long-lasting depopulation and economic decline in much of the Holy Roman Empire.

Not surprisingly, weaponry and war-making skills improved dramatically, making European armed forces the most powerful in the world. The numbers of men in arms increased steadily. French forces, for example, grew from about 150,000 in 1630 to 400,000 by the early eighteenth century. Sweden, with under a million people, had one of the best-armed military forces in seventeenth-century Europe. Prussia, a country with fewer than 2 million inhabitants in 1700, had an army that made it a major power.

Larger armies required better command structures. As a modern historian remarked, European armies "evolved . . . the equivalent of a central nervous system, capable of activating technologically differentiated claws and teeth."[3] New signaling techniques improved battlefield maneuvers. Frequent marching drills trained troops to obey orders instantly and gave them a close sense of comradeship. Since battles between evenly matched armies often ended in prolonged stalemates, victory increasingly depended on naval superiority.

England alone did without a peacetime standing army, but England's rise as a sea power had begun under King Henry VIII, who spent heavily on ships and promoted a domestic iron-smelting industry to supply cannon. The Royal Navy also copied innovative ship designs from the Dutch. By the early eighteenth century the Royal Navy surpassed the rival French fleet in numbers. By then, England had merged with Scotland to become Great Britain, annexed Ireland, and built a North American empire.

Although France was Europe's most powerful state, Louis XIV's efforts to expand were increasingly frustrated by coalitions of other powers. In a series of eighteenth-century wars beginning with the War of the Spanish Succession (1701–1714), the combination of Britain's naval strength and the land armies of its Austrian and Prussian allies blocked French ambitions and prevented the Bourbons from uniting the thrones of France and Spain.

France's defeat illustrates the principle of **balance of power** in international relations: the major European states formed temporary alliances to prevent any one state from becoming too powerful. Russia emerged as a major power after its modernized armies defeated Sweden in the Great Northern War (1700–1721). During the next two centuries, though adhering to four different branches of Christianity, the great powers of Europe—Catholic France, Anglican Britain, Catholic Austria, Lutheran Prussia, and Orthodox Russia (see Map 16.2)—maintained an effective balance of power by shifting their alliances for geopolitical rather than religious reasons. These pragmatic alliances were the first successful efforts at international peacekeeping.

Paying the Piper

European rulers needed revenue to pay for their wars. The most successful of them after 1600 allied with the rising commercial elite. Both sides understood that trade thrived where government taxation and regulation were not excessive, where courts enforced contracts

---

balance of power The policy in international relations by which, beginning in the eighteenth century, the major European states acted together to prevent any one of them from becoming too powerful.

Map 16.2 Europe in 1740 By the middle of the eighteenth century the great powers of Europe were France, the Austrian Empire, Great Britain, Prussia, and Russia. Spain, the Holy Roman Empire, and the Ottoman Empire were far weaker in 1740 than they had been two centuries earlier. © Cengage Learning

 Interactive Map

and collected debts, and where military power protected overseas expansion.

Spain, sixteenth-century Europe's mightiest state, illustrates how the financial drains of an aggressive military policy and the failure to promote economic development could lead to decline. Expensive wars against the Ottomans, northern European Protestants, and rebellious Dutch subjects caused the treasury to default on its debts four times during the reign of King Philip II. Insistence on religious uniformity and aristocratic privilege further undermined the economy. In the name of religious uniformity the rulers expelled Jewish merchants, persecuted Protestant dissenters, and forced tens of thousands of farmers and artisans into exile because of their Muslim ancestry. In the name of aristocratic privilege the 3 percent of the population that controlled 97 percent of the land in 1600 was exempt from taxation. Yet high sales taxes discouraged manufacturing.

Vast imports of silver and gold bullion from Spain's American colonies filled the government treasury, but they also triggered severe inflation in Spain and throughout the rest of Europe. As a Spanish saying put it: American silver was like rain on the roof—it poured down and washed away. Huge debts for foreign wars drained bullion from Spain to its creditors. More wealth flowed out to purchase manufactured goods and even food in the seventeenth century. Opposite policies supported the rise of the Netherlands as an economic power. The Spanish crown had acquired the Netherlands as part of Charles V's inheritance. But King Philip II's decision to impose Spain's ruinously heavy sales tax and enforce Catholic orthodoxy drove the Dutch to revolt in 1566 and again in 1572. If successful, those measures would have discouraged business and driven away the Calvinists, Jews, and other key contributors to Dutch prosperity. However, the Dutch raised and trained an army and a navy that were among the most effective in Europe, and in 1609 Spain agreed to a truce that recognized the autonomy of the northern part of the Netherlands. In 1648, after eight decades of warfare, the independence of these seven United Provinces of the Free Netherlands (their full name) became final.

Rather than being ruined by the long war, the United Netherlands emerged as the dominant commercial power in Europe and the world's greatest trading nation. This economic success owed much to a decentralized government. During the struggle against Spain, the provinces united around the prince of Orange, their sovereign and commander-in-chief. But in economic matters each province pursued its own interests. The maritime province of Holland grew rich by favoring commercial interests.

After 1650 the Dutch faced growing competition from England, where business was also allied with government. In a series of wars (1652–1678) England's naval might broke Dutch dominance in overseas trade. With government support, the English merchant fleet doubled between 1660 and 1700, and foreign trade rose by 50 percent. State revenue from customs duties tripled. During the eighteenth century Britain's trading position strengthened still more.

The debts run up by the Anglo-Dutch Wars persuaded the English monarchy to enlarge the government's role in managing the economy. The outcome has been called a "financial revolution." The government increased revenues by taxing the formerly exempt landed estates of the aristocrats and by collecting taxes directly. Previously, private individuals known as tax farmers had advanced the government

SECTION REVIEW

- Greater political centralization enabled early modern monarchs to exert considerable influence on economic, religious, and social life.

- While the Holy Roman Empire fragmented along religious and political lines, Spain, France, and England achieved greater centralization and religious unity.

- Spain enforced Catholic unity through the Inquisition and France through Bourbon policy, while in England the church became an arm of royal power.

- In both England and France, monarchs struggled with other powers over the limits of royal authority.

- Armies grew larger and more sophisticated, and through diplomacy and nearly constant warfare, the European powers strove to maintain the balance of power.

- High military costs drove the European powers to attempt a variety of tax and financial policies, the most successful being those of England and the Netherlands.

a fixed sum of money; in return they could keep whatever money they were able to collect from taxpayers. England also followed the Dutch lead in creating a central bank, from which the government was able to obtain long-term loans at low rates.

Under the leadership of Colbert, the French too experienced economic development. He streamlined tax collection, promoted French manufacturing and shipping by imposing taxes on foreign goods, and improved inland transportation. Yet the power of the wealthy aristocrats kept the French government from following England's lead in taxing wealthy landowners, collecting taxes directly, and securing low-cost loans. Nor did France succeed in managing its debt as efficiently as England.

Conclusion

European historians have used the word *revolution* to describe many different changes taking place in Europe between 1500 and 1750. The expansion of trade has been called a commercial revolution, the reform of state spending a financial revolution, and the changes in weapons and warfare a military revolution. We have also encountered a scientific revolution and the religious revolution of the Reformation.

Yet the years from 1500 to 1750 were not simply—perhaps not even primarily—an age of progress for Europe. For many, the ferocious competition of European armies, merchants, and ideas was a wrenching experience. The growth of powerful states exacted a terrible price in death, destruction, and misery. The Reformation brought greater individual choice in religion but widespread persecution as well. The expanding economy benefited the emerging merchant elite and their political allies, but most Europeans became worse off as prices rose faster than wages. New scientific and enlightened ideas ignited controversies long before they yielded any tangible benefits.

The historical significance of this period of European history is clearer when viewed in a global context. What stands out are the powerful and efficient European armies, economies, and governments. From a global perspective, the balance of political and economic power was shifting slowly, but inexorably, in the Europeans' favor. In 1500 the Ottomans threatened Europe. By 1750, Europeans had brought the world's seas and a growing portion of its lands and peoples under their control. No single group of Europeans accomplished this. The Dutch eclipsed the pioneering Portuguese and Spanish; then the English and French bested the Dutch. Competition, too, was a factor in European success.

CHAPTER REVIEW

Download the MP3 audio file of the Chapter Review to listen to on the go.

How was the cultural history of early modern Europe determined by the interplay of traditional beliefs and revolutionary ideas? (page 385)

Early modern Europe underwent the Scientific Revolution as well as the fragmentation of the Catholic Church. Traditional antifeminist beliefs and pagan folklore about witchcraft fed a witch-hunting craze that took thousands of lives. Supporting the belief in witchcraft was a more fundamental idea that human misfortune could be blamed on supernatural forces, but this idea was powerfully challenged by pioneers of the Scientific Revolution such as Copernicus and Newton, who showed that the

workings of the physical universe could be explained in natural terms. These scientists did not see any conflict between science and religion, and they paved the way for influential figures of the Enlightenment, who believed that human reason was capable of discovering the laws that govern social behavior.

What factors contributed to the wealth of some Europeans and the great poverty of others? (page 393)

Thanks to foreign and domestic trade, European cities experienced rapid growth and the rise of a wealthy commercial class. The Netherlands in particular prospered from expanded manufacturing and trade. For peasants and laborers, however, life did not improve much: serfdom ended in western Europe but rose in eastern Europe. Agricultural techniques had not improved since medieval times, and deforestation caused great difficulties for the poor. Rural poverty, coupled with aristocratic exemption from taxation, sparked numerous armed rebellions.

How did differing policies on religion, foreign relations, and economics influence the history of early modern European states? (page 400)

Monarchs like Charles V of the Holy Roman Empire and Louis XIV of France impressed contemporaries with their military might and aggressive ambitions. In the long run, however, tolerance of religious diversity and cooperation between rulers and the rising class of merchants brought a country greater success. The Netherlands, a group of provinces marked by their religious tolerance, won independence from their intolerant Spanish overlord and went on to become Europe's most prosperous trading nation. England endured a civil war based on religious

disagreement and conflict between kings and Parliament but eventually rose to contest the maritime supremacy of the Dutch. Here too religious tolerance and collaboration between merchants and the Crown proved a winning combination.

Key Terms

Renaissance (European) (p.385)	joint-stock company (p. 395)
papacy (p. 386)	stock exchange (p. 395)
indulgence (p. 386)	gentry (p. 395)
Protestant Reformation (p. 386)	Little Ice Age (p. 395)
Catholic Reformation (p. 389)	deforestation (p. 397)
witch-hunt (p. 389)	Holy Roman Empire (p. 400)
Scientific Revolution (p. 391)	Habsburg (p. 400)
Enlightenment (p. 392)	English Civil War (p. 402)
bourgeoisie (p. 393)	Versailles (p. 402)
	balance of power (p. 403)

Web Resources

Pronunciation Guide

Interactive Maps

- MAP 16.1 Religious Reformation in Europe
- MAP 16.2 Europe in 1740

 Visit the CourseMate website at www.cengagebrain.com for additional study tools and review materials for this chapter.

Primary Sources

- Table Talk
- Letter to the Grand Duchess Christina
- Treatise on Tolerance

Answer to the History in Focus Question

See photo on page 391, "Tycho Brahe at Work."

The Americas, the Atlantic, and Africa

© Cengage Learning

Visit the CourseMate website at **www.cengagebrain.com** for additional study tools and review materials for this chapter.

408

After 1600, Spain became increasingly impoverished and had difficulty protecting its American empire from pirates, privateers, and the rising powers of Europe: the Netherlands, France, and Britain. These nations, like Spain before them, benefited from the advantage that diseases gave to their people in their encounters with Native Americans. As with the Spanish colonies before them, the development of English and French colonies in North America in the seventeenth century led to similar patterns of contagion and mortality. In 1616 and 1617, epidemics nearly exterminated many of New England's indigenous groups. French fur traders transmitted measles, smallpox, and other diseases as far as Hudson Bay and the Great Lakes.

Although there is very little evidence that Europeans consciously used disease as a tool of empire, yet by making native peoples live in denser concentrations, they inadvertently increased the rate of contagion. The deadly results of contact with Europeans undermined the ability of native peoples to resist European settlement, and Europeans and their African slaves occupied these depopulated lands. Transformed biologically and culturally, the Americas were subjected to Europeans' political and economic demands.

The colonies of the Americas were crucial pieces of a new **Atlantic system**, a network of trading links that moved people and cultures as well as goods and wealth around the Atlantic. The Atlantic system also affected Africa, but less severely than the Americas. Despite the loss of millions of people to the slave trade, Africa did not suffer population loss due to epidemics as the Americas. On the contrary, the diseases prevalent in Africa—especially malaria and yellow fever—killed most of the Europeans who visited that continent. As a result, Africans remained in control of their lands, except for small enclaves on the coast.

Amerindians, Europeans, and Africans all contributed to the creation of new cultures in the Americas. The societies that arose reflected each colony's mix of native peoples, its connections to the slave trade, and the policies of its European rulers.

Spanish America and Brazil

What role did forced labor play in the main industries in Spanish America and Brazil?

Within one hundred years of Columbus's first voyage to the Western Hemisphere, the Spanish Empire in America included most of the islands of the Caribbean, Mexico, Central America, the Caribbean and Pacific coasts of South America, the Andean highlands, and parts of the American Southwest and the Rio de la Plata region (a region that includes the modern nations of Argentina, Uruguay, and Paraguay). Although Portuguese settlement in the New World developed more slowly, before the end of the sixteenth century Portugal occupied most of the Brazilian coast.

Early settlers from Spain and Portugal sought to create colonial societies based on the institutions and customs of their homelands. They viewed society as a vertical arrangement of social classes, as uniformly Catholic, and as an arrangement of patriarchal extended-family networks. But despite the imposition of foreign institutions and the massive loss of life caused by epidemics, indigenous peoples still exercised a powerful influence on the development of colonial societies. Aztec and Inca elite families sought to protect their traditional privileges and rights through marriage or less formal alliances with the Spanish settlers, and they often used colonial courts to defend their claims to land. Nearly everywhere, Amerindian religious beliefs and practices survived beneath the surface of an imposed Christianity. Amerindian languages, cuisine, medical practices, and agricultural techniques also survived the conquest and influenced the development of Latin American culture.

The African slave trade added a third cultural stream to colonial Latin American society. By the end of the colonial era, Africans and their descendants were living throughout Latin America, enriching colonial societies with their traditional agricultural practices, music, religious beliefs, cuisine, and social customs.

Atlantic System   The network of trading links after 1500 that moved goods, wealth, people, and cultures around the Atlantic Ocean Basin.

State and Church

The Spanish crown moved quickly to curb the independent power of the conquistadors and establish royal authority over both the defeated native populations and the rising tide of European settlers. Created in 1524, the **Council of the Indies** in Spain supervised all government, ecclesiastical, and commercial activity in the Spanish colonies. Political and economic power was concentrated in Mexico City, capital of the Viceroyalty of New Spain (created in 1535), and in Lima, capital of the Viceroyalty of Peru (created in the 1540s). Each viceroyalty was divided into a number of judicial and administrative districts. Until the seventeenth century, almost all of the officials appointed to high positions in Spain's colonial bureaucracy were born in Spain. Later, local-born members of the colonial elite gained many offices.

In the sixteenth century, Portugal concentrated its resources and energies on Asia and Africa, because early settlers found neither mineral wealth nor rich native empires in Brazil. Finally, the king appointed a governor-general in 1549 and designated Salvador, in the northern province of Bahia, Brazil's capital. The first viceroy of Brazil was named in 1720 (see Map 17.1).

Just as these colonial bureaucracies imposed Iberian economic and political institutions, the Catholic Church became the primary agent for the introduction and transmission of Christian belief and European culture in South America. Spain and Portugal justified their American conquests by assuming an obligation to convert native populations to Christianity. In Mexico alone, hundreds of thousands of conversions and baptisms were achieved within a few years of the conquest.

The Catholic clergy sought to win over the Amerindians by converting native elites. But these efforts were abandoned when church authorities discovered that many converts were secretly observing old beliefs and rituals. As Amerindian populations declined from the effects of epidemics, priests in both Spanish America and Brazil forced native populations to relocate, often worsening the disease mortality. At times priests used forced conversions, such as in the 1560s among the Maya. Repelled by these excesses, the church ended both the violent repression of native religious practice and ambitious efforts to recruit Amerindians for the clergy.

With all its failures, the Catholic clergy did provide native peoples with some protections against the abuse and exploitation of settlers. For example, the priest **Bartolomé de Las Casas** (1474–1566) was an important advocate for native peoples. His most important achievement was the enactment of the New Laws of 1542, which outlawed the enslavement of Amerindians and limited other forms of forced labor in the Spanish colonies.

Despite European disapproval, Amerindians blended Catholic Christian beliefs with important elements of traditional native cosmology and ritual. Most commonly, indigenous beliefs and rituals came to be embedded in the celebration of saints' days or Catholic rituals associated with the Virgin Mary. This cultural borrowing and innovation contributed to a distinct and original Latin American culture.

After 1600, the Catholic Church redirected most of its resources from the countryside to growing colonial cities and towns with large European populations. This altered mission included the founding of universities and secondary schools, which stimulated urban intellectual life.

Colonial Economies

The silver mines of Peru and Mexico and the sugar plantations of Brazil dominated the colonial economy and fueled the early development of European capitalism. Profits produced in these economic centers also

---

Primary Source: A Dominican Voice in the Wilderness: Preaching Against Tyranny in Hispaniola Listen to the story of one friar who bravely speaks out against the brutality of the Spanish toward the native people of Hispaniola.

Council of the Indies The institution responsible for supervising Spain's colonies in the Americas from 1524 to the early eighteenth century, when it lost all but judicial responsibilities.

Bartolomé de Las Casas (1474–1566) First bishop of Chiapas, in southern Mexico. He devoted most of his life to protecting Amerindian peoples from exploitation. His major achievement was the New Laws of 1542, which limited the ability of Spanish settlers to compel Amerindians to labor for them.

Chronology

	Latin America	North America	West Indies	Atlantic
1500			**ca. 1500** Spanish settlers introduce sugar-cane cultivation	
	1535 Creation of Viceroyalty of New Spain **1540s** Creation of Viceroyalty of Peru **1542** New Laws outlaw Amerindian enslavement **1545** Silver discovered at Potosi, Bolivia			
1600		**1607** Jamestown founded **1608** Quebec founded **1620** Plymouth founded		
	By 1620 African slaves the majority of Brazilian plantation workers		**1620s and 1630s** English and French colonies in Caribbean	
				1621 Dutch West India Company chartered
			1640s Dutch bring sugar plantation system from Brazil **1655** English take Jamaica	
		1660 Slavery in Virginia begins to grow rapidly **1664** English take New York from Dutch		**1660s** English Navigation Acts
			1670s French occupy western half of Hispaniola	
				1672 Royal African Company chartered **1698** French *Exclusif*
		1699 Louisiana founded		
1700	**1713** Beginning of Bourbon dynasty in Spain **1700–1790** Reforms in Brazil and Spanish America	**1756–1763** French and Indian War	**1700** West Indies surpass Brazil in sugar production	

promoted the growth of colonial cities, concentrated scarce investment capital and labor resources, and stimulated the development of livestock raising and agriculture in neighboring rural areas. Dependence on mineral and agricultural exports was an enduring theme in Latin America. Although millions of pesos of gold were mined in Latin America, silver mines generated more wealth and exercised greater economic influence. In 1545, the single richest silver deposit in

the Americas was discovered at **Potosí** (poh-toh-SEE), in what is now Bolivia, and until 1680 the silver production of Bolivia and Peru dominated the Spanish colonial economy.

Potosí Located in Bolivia, one of the richest silver mining centers and most populous cities in colonial Spanish America.

Map 17.1 Colonial Latin America in the Eighteenth Century Spain and Portugal controlled most of the Western Hemisphere in the eighteenth century. In the sixteenth century they had created new administrative jurisdictions—viceroyalties—to defend their respective colonies against European rivals. Taxes assessed on colonial products helped pay for this extension of governmental authority.

© Cengage Learning

Interactive Map

NEW FRANCE
(Conquered by England, 1760)

ENGLISH COLONIES
(Independence declared, 1776)

ATLANTIC OCEAN

Effective frontier of Spanish settlement

Silver
Silver
COAHUILA
Guadalajara
BAJÍO LEÓN (1535)
✗ Zacatecas
✗ Guanajuato
Mexico City •
Silver
• Veracruz

VICEROYALTY OF NEW SPAIN

Gulf of Mexico

FLORIDA
(Ceded to England, 1763–1783)

Sugar cane
Beef
Tobacco
• Havana

HAITI [SAINT-DOMINGUE]
(Ceded to France, 1697)

PUERTO RICO
Sugar cane
Beef
Sugar cane

Sugar cane
Indigo
Cacao

BRITISH HONDURAS
Sugar cane
Cochineal
Cochineal
Cacao
Indigo
• Guatemala
Silver

Sugar cane

JAMAICA
(Conquered by England, 1655)

SANTO DOMINGO

Sugar cane

Caribbean Sea

Pearls
Caracas •
Cacao
Gold

GUIANA

VICEROYALTY OF NEW GRANADA
(Separated from Viceroyalty of Peru, 1717, 1739)

• Bogotá

Quito •

Equator   0°

Amazon R.

Forest products

VICEROYALTY OF PERU
(1590s)
Lima •

Sugar cane

• Cuzco

VICEROYALTY OF BRAZIL
(1720)

Sugar cane
• Pernambuco

Sugar cane
• Salvador

PACIFIC OCEAN

Sugar cane
La Paz •

Chuquisaca
(La Plata; Sucre)
✗ Potosí

Cacao

Diamonds
Gold

Rio de Janeiro
(Capital, 1763)

São Paulo •

20°S

Yerba
Tobacco

VICEROYALTY OF LA PLATA
(Separated from Viceroyalty of Peru, 1776)

Wheat

AUDIENCIA OF CHILE
(Retained by Viceroyalty of Peru, 1776)

Santiago •

Beef and hides
Buenos Aires •
Beef and hides
• Montevideo

Claimed but not settled by Spain

Islas Malvinas
(Falkland Islands)

Cape Horn

80°W   60°W

40°W

40°N

20°N

ANDES

Orinoco R.
Magdalena R.
Paraná R.
Rio Grande
Colorado R.
Mississippi R.

N

0   500   1,000 Km.
0   500   1,000 Mi.

Territories claimed by Spain
Viceroyalty of New Spain
Viceroyalty of New Granada
Viceroyalty of Peru and Audiencia of Chile
Viceroyalty of Rio de la Plata

Territories claimed by Portugal
Viceroyalty of Brazil

✗ Silver mine

Silver Mines at Potosí This town in Bolivia was founded in 1546 below a mountain with such rich deposits of silver ore that over 45,000 tons of the precious metal were refined and exported over the following two centuries. This drawing shows a water wheel operating the trip-hammers that crushed the ore and the rectangular ponds where the crushed ore was mixed with mercury, which bonded with the silver. Drying the amalgam, as the mixture was called, gave off poisonous mercury fumes that contributed to a high death rate among the workers.   Courtesy, the Hispanic Society of America

Silver mining also greatly altered the environment. Within a short time, wasteful use of forest resources for fuel destroyed forests near the mining centers. Faced with rising fuel costs, miners developed an efficient method of chemical extraction that relied on mixing mercury with the silver ore. But mercury is a poison, and its use contaminated the environment and sickened the Amerindian work force.

From the time of Columbus, indigenous populations had been compelled to provide labor for European settlers in the Americas. Until the 1540s in Spanish colonies, Amerindian peoples were divided among the settlers and were forced to provide them with labor or with textiles, food, or other goods. This form of forced labor was called the ***encomienda*** (en-co-mee-EN-dah). The discovery of silver in Peru led to a new form of compulsory labor called the *mita* (MEE-tah). Under this system, one-seventh of the adult male Amerindians were compelled to work for six months each year in mines or on farms or in textile factories. The most dangerous working conditions existed in the silver mines. Because few Amerindian workers in the Spanish mita could survive on their wages, wives and children were commonly forced to join the work force to help meet expenses. Even those who remained behind in the village were forced to send food and cash to support mita workers.

The Portuguese, who had developed sugar plantations that depended on slave labor on the Atlantic islands of Madeira, the Azores, the Cape Verdes, and São Tomé, transferred this profitable form of agriculture to Brazil. By the seventeenth century, sugar dominated the Brazilian economy. At first, the Portuguese enslaved Amerindians as field hands, but sugar planters eventually came to rely more on African slaves as epidemics decimated the Amerindian population. Imports of African slaves rose from an average of 2,000 per year in the late sixteenth century to approximately 7,000 per year a century later, far outstripping the immigration of free Portuguese settlers.

The mining centers of Latin America exercised global economic influence. American silver increased

encomienda A grant of authority over a population of Amerindians in the Spanish colonies. It provided the grant holder with a supply of cheap labor and periodic payments of goods by the Amerindians and obligated the grant holder to Christianize the Amerindians.

Market in Rio de Janeiro In many of the cities of colonial Latin America, female slaves and black free women dominated retail markets. In this scene from late colonial Brazil, Afro-Brazilian women sell a variety of foods and crafts. Sir Henry Chamberlain, *Views and Costumes of the City and Neighborhoods of Rio de Janeiro*, London, 1822

History in Focus *Examine this image, paying special attention to what the figures are wearing and appear to be doing. What does the image suggest about the nature of the economy that black women dominated? Who were their most likely customers, and what kind of living was it possible for them to make? Find the answer online.*

the European money supply, promoting commercial expansion. Large amounts of silver also flowed across the Pacific, where it was exchanged for Asian spices, silks, and porcelain. The sugar plantations of Brazil played a similar role in integrating the economy of the South Atlantic region. At the end of the seventeenth century, the discovery of gold in Brazil helped overcome this large region's currency shortage and promoted further economic integration.

Both Spain and Portugal attempted to control the trade of their American colonies, but the combination of monopoly commerce and convoy shipping slowed the flow of European goods to the colonies and kept prices high. Frustrated by these restraints, colonial populations established illegal commercial relations with the English, French, and Dutch. By the middle of the seventeenth century, a majority of European imports were arriving in Latin America illegally.

Society in Colonial Latin America

With the exception of a few early viceroys, few members of Spain's great noble families came to the New World. *Hidalgos* (ee-DAHL-goes)—lesser nobles—were well represented, as were Spanish merchants, artisans, miners, priests, and lawyers. Small numbers of criminals, beggars, and prostitutes also found their way to the colonies. Spanish settlers, however, were always a tiny minority in a colonial society numerically dominated by Amerindians and rapidly growing populations of Africans, **creoles** (whites born in America to European parents), and people of mixed ancestry.

Conquistadors and early settlers who received from the Crown grants of labor and tribute goods (encomienda) from Amerindian communities as rewards for service to Spain sought to create a hereditary social and political class comparable to the nobles of Europe. But the position of these *encomenderos* was undermined by their abuse of Amerindian communities, the catastrophic epidemics of the sixteenth century, and the growing power of colonial viceroys, judges, and bishops appointed by the king.

By the end of the sixteenth century, the elite of Spanish America included both European immigrants and creoles. Europeans dominated the highest levels of the church and government, as well as commerce, while creoles commonly controlled colonial

creole In colonial Spanish America, the term used to describe someone of European descent born in the New World. Elsewhere in the Americas, it is used to describe all nonnative peoples.

agriculture and mining. Although tensions between Spaniards and creoles were inevitable, most elite families had members from both groups.

Before the Europeans arrived in the Americas, the native peoples were members of a large number of distinct cultural and linguistic groups. Cultural diversity and class distinctions were present even in the highly centralized Aztec and Inca Empires. The loss of life provoked by the European conquest undermined this rich social and cultural complexity, and the imposition of Catholic Christianity further eroded ethnic boundaries among native peoples. Colonial administrators and settlers broadly applied the racial label *Indian,* which facilitated the imposition of special taxes and labor obligations while erasing longstanding class and ethnic differences.

Indigenous Amerindian elites survived only briefly. Some of the conquistadors and early settlers married or established less formal relations with elite Amerindian women, but these alliances diminished after European women began to arrive. Some descendants of the powerful Amerindian families prospered as ranchers, muleteers, and merchants, but many others lived in the same materially deprived conditions as Amerindian commoners.

Thousands of blacks participated in the conquest and settlement of Spanish America, and the opening of a direct slave trade with Africa added millions more. Settlers' views of African slaves' cultural differences as signs of inferiority ultimately served as a justification for slavery. By 1600, anyone with black ancestry was barred from positions in church, government, and many skilled crafts. Even so, African languages, religious beliefs, and marriage customs mixed with European (and in some cases Amerindian) languages and beliefs to forge distinct local cultures. The rapid growth of an American-born slave population accelerated cultural change.

The colonial development of Brazil took place in the absence of rich and powerful indigenous civilizations such as those of the Aztecs and Inca. Fewer Europeans immigrated to Brazil than to the Spanish colonies, but those who did exercised the same sort of domination. The growth of cities and the creation of imperial institutions eventually duplicated in outline the social structures found in Spanish America, but with an important difference. By the early seventeenth

SECTION REVIEW

- European, Amerindian, and African elements combined to form the hybrid culture of colonial Latin America.

- Spain and Portugal imposed Iberian political and economic institutions on their colonies and tried to promote Catholic uniformity, with mixed success.

- Silver and sugar dominated the economy of colonial Latin America and integrated it with the global economy.

- A social order developed that was stratified along lines of ethnicity and birthplace, but Amerindian and African languages and cultural practices survived and blended with European ways.

century, Africans and their American-born descendants were by far the largest racial group in Brazil. As a result, Brazilian colonial society (unlike Spanish Mexico and Peru) was influenced more by African culture than by Amerindian culture.

African slaves became skilled artisans, musicians, servants, artists, cowboys, and even soldiers in Brazil and Spanish America. However, the vast majority worked in agriculture. To escape harsh discipline, brutal punishments, and backbreaking labor, many slaves rebelled or ran away. Communities of runaways, called *quilombos* (key-LOM-bos) in Brazil and *palenques* (pal-EN-kays) in Spanish colonies, were common. The largest quilombo was Palmares, where thousands of slaves defended themselves against Brazilian authorities for sixty years until they were finally overrun in 1694.

English and French Colonies in North America

What were the differences between the English and French colonies of North America?

The North American colonial empires of England and France and the colonies of Spain and Portugal had many characteristics in common. The governments of England and France hoped to find precious metals or great indigenous empires like those of the Aztecs or Inca. Like the Spanish and Portuguese, English

Tobacco Factory Machinery in Colonial Mexico This tobacco factory in eighteenth-century Mexico City used a horse-driven mechanical shredder to produce snuff and cigarette tobacco.

Vista de una Máquina, para cernír Tabáco enla R.¹ Fabrica de Sigarrᵒˢ

VIVA EL REY.

© Archivo General de Indias, Seville, Spain

and French settlers responded to native peoples with a mixture of diplomacy and violence. African slaves proved crucial to the development of all four colonial economies.

There were also important differences. The English and French colonies were founded nearly a century after Cortés's conquest of Mexico and initial Portuguese settlement in Brazil. Distracted by ventures elsewhere, neither England nor France imitated the large and expensive colonial bureaucracies that Spain and Portugal established. Instead, private companies and individual proprietors pioneered development. This practice led to greater regional variety in economic activity, political institutions and culture, and social structure than was evident in Latin American colonies.

The South

London investors, organized as the privately funded Virginia Company, got off to a rocky start. Nearly 80 percent of the settlers at Jamestown in 1607 and 1608 soon died of disease or Amerindian attacks. After the English crown dissolved the Virginia Company in 1624 because of its mismanagement, colonists pushed deeper into the interior, developing a sustainable economy based on furs, timber, and, increasingly, tobacco. The profits from tobacco soon attracted new immigrants and new

capital. Along the shoreline of Chesapeake Bay and the rivers that fed it, settlers spread out, developing plantations and farms.

Indentured servants eventually accounted for approximately 80 percent of all English immigrants to the Chesapeake Bay region. Young men and women unable to pay for their transportation to the New World accepted indentures (contracts) that bound them to a term ranging from four to seven years of labor in return for passage, a small parcel of land, and some tools and clothes. During the seventeenth century, approximately fifteen hundred indentured servants, mostly male, arrived each year. As life expectancy improved, planters began to purchase more slaves. They calculated that greater profits could be secured by paying the higher initial cost of slaves owned for life than by purchasing the contracts of indentured servants bound for short periods of time. As a result, Virginia's slave population grew rapidly, from 950 in 1660 to 120,000 by 1756.

Ironically, this increase in the colony's slave population occurred along with the expansion in colonial

indentured servant A migrant to British colonies in the Americas who paid for passage by agreeing to work for a set term ranging from four to seven years.

Choctaw Village in Louisiana at Time of French Colonial Rule In this scene of village life we see strong indications of integration in the colonial economy. While natives are shown pursuing traditional tasks, a black slave and European trade goods obtained in exchange for deerskins are arrayed along the riverbank.

liberties and political rights. At first, colonial government had been administered by a Crown-appointed governor and his council, as well as by representatives of towns meeting together as the **House of Burgesses**. When these representatives began to meet alone as a deliberative body, they initiated a form of democratic representation that distinguished the English colonies of North America from the colonies of other European powers. The intertwined evolution of freedom and slavery gave England's southern colonies a unique and conflicted political character.

Colonial South Carolina was the most hierarchical society in British North America. Planters controlled the economy and political life. The richest maintained households in both the countryside and Charleston, the largest city in the southern colonies. Small farmers, cattlemen, artisans, merchants, and fur traders held an intermediate but clearly subordinate social position. At the bottom were slaves, on which South Carolina depended. African slaves were present from the founding of Charleston and were instrumental in introducing irrigated rice agriculture and in developing indigo (a plant that produced a blue dye) plantations. Although native peoples remained influential participants in colonial society through commercial contacts and alliances, they were increasingly marginalized.

New England

New England was colonized by two separate groups of Protestant dissenters. The **Pilgrims** established the coastal colony of Plymouth in present-day Massachusetts in 1620. Although nearly half of the settlers died during the first winter, the colony survived. In 1691, Plymouth was absorbed into the larger Massachusetts Bay Colony of the **Puritans**. By 1643, more than 20,000 Puritans had settled in the Bay Colony.

House of Burgesses Elected assembly in colonial Virginia, created in 1618.
Pilgrims Group of English Protestant dissenters who established Plymouth Colony in Massachusetts in 1620 to seek religious freedom after having lived briefly in the Netherlands.
Puritans English Protestant dissenters who believed that God predestined souls to Heaven or Hell before birth. They founded Massachusetts Bay Colony in 1629.

Unlike in the southern colonies, most newcomers to Massachusetts arrived with their families. A normal gender balance and a healthy climate resulted in a rapid increase in population. Massachusetts also was more homogeneous and less hierarchical than the southern colonies.

Political institutions evolved out of the terms of the Puritans' royal charter. A governor was elected, along with a council of magistrates drawn from the board of directors of the Massachusetts Bay Company. Disagreements between this council and elected representatives of the towns led, by 1650, to the creation of a lower legislative house that selected its own speaker and began to develop procedures and rules similar to those of the House of Commons in England.

Economically, agriculture met basic needs, but the poor soils and harsh climate did not favor cash crops like tobacco or rice. To pay for imported tools, textiles, and other essentials, the colonists provided commercial and shipping services to the southern colonies, the smaller Caribbean islands, Africa, and Europe. In contrast to Latin America's heavily capitalized monopolies, New England merchants depended on market intelligence, flexibility, and streamlined organization. By 1740, Boston, with 16,000 inhabitants, was the largest city in British North America.

Middle Atlantic Region

The rapid economic development and cultural diversity of the Middle Atlantic colonies added to the success of English-speaking North America. The **Iroquois Confederacy**, an alliance of several native peoples, established treaties and trading relationships with the Dutch. When confronted by an English military expedition in 1664, the Dutch surrendered their colony of New Netherland without a fight. Renamed New York, the colony's success depended on the development of New York City as a commercial and shipping center. Located at the mouth of the Hudson River, the city connected the region's grain farmers to the booming markets of the Caribbean and southern Europe. By the early eighteenth century, New York Colony had a diverse population that included (in addition to English colonists) Dutch, German, and Swedish settlers, as well as a large slave community.

Pennsylvania began as a proprietary colony in 1682 and as a refuge for Quakers, a persecuted religious minority. The founder, William Penn, quickly lost control of the colony's political life, but the colony enjoyed remarkable success. By 1700, Pennsylvania had a population of more than 21,000, and Philadelphia, its capital, soon passed Boston to become the largest city in the British colonies. Healthy climate, excellent land, and relatively peaceful relations with native peoples attracted free workers, including many German families. As a result, Pennsylvania's economic expansion in the late seventeenth century occurred without reproducing South Carolina's hierarchical and repressive social order based on slavery. By the early eighteenth century, however, the prosperous city of Philadelphia included a large population of black slaves, servants, and skilled tradesmen.

French North America

French settlement patterns more closely resembled those of Spain and Portugal than of England. The French were committed to missionary activity among Amerindian peoples and emphasized extracting resources—in this case, furs.

Coming to Canada after spending years in the West Indies, Samuel de Champlain founded the colony of **New France** at Quebec (kwuh-BEC), on the banks of the St. Lawrence River, in 1608. The European market for fur, especially beaver, fueled French settlement. Young Frenchmen were sent to live among native peoples to master their languages and customs, and these men and their children by native women organized the fur trade and led French expansion to the west and south. Amerindians actively participated in this trade because they came to depend on the goods they received in exchange for furs: firearms, metal tools and utensils, textiles, and alcohol.

Iroquois Confederacy An alliance of five northeastern Amerindian peoples (six after 1722) that made decisions on military and diplomatic issues through a council of representatives. Allied first with the Dutch and later with the English, the Confederacy dominated the area from western New England to the Great Lakes.

New France French colony in North America, with a capital in Quebec, founded in 1608. New France fell to the British in 1763.

Canadian Fur Traders The fur trade provided the economic foundation of early Canadian settlement. Serving as cultural intermediaries, fur traders brought European technologies and products like firearms and machine-made textiles to native peoples and native technologies and products like canoes and furs to European settlers. This canoe with sixteen paddlers was adapted from the native craft by fur traders to transport large cargoes. Frances Anne Hopkins, "Shooting the Rapids," Library and Archives Canada, Ref. #C-2774

The Iroquois Confederacy responded to the increased military strength of France's Algonquin allies by forging commercial and military links with Dutch and later English settlements in the Hudson River Valley. Well armed by the Dutch and English, the Iroquois Confederacy nearly eradicated the Huron in 1649 and inflicted a series of humiliating defeats on the French. At the high point of their power in the early 1680s, Iroquois hunters and military forces gained control of much of the Great Lakes region and the Ohio River Valley. A large French military expedition and a relentless attack focused on Iroquois villages and agriculture finally checked Iroquois power in 1701.

Use of firearms in hunting and warfare moved west and south, reaching indigenous plains cultures that previously had adopted the horse introduced by the Spanish. This intersection of horse and gun frontiers in the early eighteenth century multiplied the military power and hunting efficiency of the Sioux, Comanche, Cheyenne, and other indigenous peoples and slowed the pace of European settlement.

In French Canada, the Jesuits led the effort to convert native peoples to Christianity. Building on earlier evangelical efforts in Brazil and Paraguay, French Catholic missionaries mastered native languages, created boarding schools for young boys and girls, and set up model agricultural communities for converts. Their greatest successes coincided with a wave of epidemics and renewed warfare among native peoples in the 1630s. Nevertheless, local cultures persisted.

Although the fur trade flourished, settlers in Canada were few. Founded at about the same time, Virginia had twenty times as many European residents as Canada by 1627. The small settler population and the fur trade's dependence on Amerindians allowed indigenous peoples to retain greater independence and more control over their encounters with new religious, technological, and market realities. Nevertheless, the French aggressively expanded and in 1699 founded Louisiana, which also depended on the fur trade with Amerindians.

France's North American colonies were ultimately threatened by a series of wars with England and the neighboring English colonies. The "French and Indian War" (also known as the Seven Years War, 1756–1763) proved to be the final contest for the North American empire. England committed a larger military force to the struggle and, despite early defeats, took the French capital of Quebec in 1759. The peace agreement forced France to yield Canada to the English and cede Louisiana to Spain.

Plantations in the West Indies

What factors contributed to the development of plantations in the West Indies?

The West Indies was the first place in the Americas that Columbus reached and the first part of the Americas where native populations collapsed. It took a long time to repopulate these islands from abroad and forge new economic links between them and other parts of the Atlantic. But after 1650, sugar plantations, African slaves, and European capital made these islands a major center of the Atlantic economy.

Spanish settlers had introduced sugar-cane cultivation into the West Indies shortly after 1500, but these colonies soon fell into neglect as attention shifted to colonizing the American mainland. In the 1620s and 1630s, the West Indies revived as a focus of colonization, this time by English and French settlers interested in growing tobacco and other crops. The islands' value mushroomed after the Dutch reintroduced sugar cultivation from Brazil in the 1640s and supplied the African slaves and European capital necessary to create a new economy.

Sugar and Slaves

The English colony of Barbados illustrates the dramatic transformation that sugar brought to the seventeenth-century Caribbean. In 1640, Barbados's economy depended largely on tobacco, mostly grown by European settlers, both free and indentured. By the 1680s, sugar had become the colony's principal crop, and enslaved Africans were three times as numerous as Europeans. Exporting up to 15,000 tons of sugar a year, Barbados had become the wealthiest and most populous of England's American colonies. By 1700, the West Indies had surpassed Brazil as the world's principal source of sugar.

The expansion of sugar plantations in the West Indies required a sharp increase in the volume of the slave trade from Africa. During the first half of the seventeenth century, about 10,000 slaves a year had arrived from Africa, most destined for Brazil and the mainland Spanish colonies. In the second half of the century, the trade averaged 20,000 slaves a year. More than half were intended for the English, French, and Dutch West Indies and most of the rest for Brazil. A century later, the volume of the Atlantic slave trade was three times larger.

What produced this shift in favor of African slaves? Recent scholarship has cast doubt on the once-common assertion that Africans were more suited than Europeans to field labor; in fact, both died in large numbers in the American tropics. The West Indian historian Eric Williams has also refuted the idea that the rise of African slave labor was primarily motivated by prejudice. Citing the West Indian colonies' prior use of enslaved Amerindians and indentured Europeans, along with European convicts and prisoners of war, he argued, "Slavery was not born of racism: rather, racism was the consequence of slavery."[1] Williams suggested that the shift was due to the lower cost of African labor.

Yet slaves were far from cheap. Cash-short tobacco planters in the seventeenth century preferred indentured Europeans because they cost half as much as African slaves. Poor European men and women were willing to work for little to get to the Americas, where they could acquire their own land cheaply at the end of their term of service. However, as the cultivation of sugar spread after 1750, rich speculators drove the price of land in the West Indies up so high that end-of-term indentured servants could not afford to buy it. As a result, poor Europeans chose to indenture themselves in the mainland North American colonies, where cheap land was still available. Rather than raise wages to attract European laborers, Caribbean sugar planters switched to slaves.

Rising sugar prices helped the West Indian sugar planters afford the higher cost of African slaves. The planters could rely on the Dutch and other traders to supply them with enough new slaves to meet the demands of the expanding plantations. Rising demand drove slave prices up steadily during the eighteenth century. These high labor costs were one more factor favoring large plantations over smaller operations.

To find more land for sugar plantations, France and England founded new Caribbean colonies. In 1655, the English had wrested the island of Jamaica from the Spanish (see Map 17.1), and in the 1670s the French seized the western half of the large Spanish island of Hispaniola. During the eighteenth century, this new French colony of Saint Domingue (san doh-MANGH) (present-day Haiti) became the greatest producer of sugar in the Atlantic world, while Jamaica surpassed Barbados as England's most important sugar colony. Later, Spanish Cuba became a major sugar producer.

Technology and Environment

What made the sugar plantation a complex investment was that it had to be a factory as well as a farm. Freshly cut canes needed to be crushed within a few hours to extract the sugary sap. Thus, for maximum efficiency, each plantation needed its own expensive crushing and processing equipment.

At the heart of the sugar works was the mill where canes were crushed between sets of heavy rollers. From the mill, lead-lined wooden troughs carried the cane juice to a series of large copper kettles in the boiling shed, where the excess water boiled off, leaving a thick syrup. Workers poured the syrup into conical molds in the drying shed. The sugar crystals that formed in the molds were packed in wooden barrels for shipment to Europe.

To make their operation more efficient and profitable, investors gradually increased the size of the typical West Indian plantation from around 100 acres (40 hectares) in the seventeenth century to at least twice that size in the eighteenth century. A plantation became a huge investment. One source estimated that a planter had to invest nearly £20,000 ($100,000) to acquire a Jamaican plantation of 600 acres (240 hectares) in 1774: a third for land, a quarter for equipment, and £8,000 for 200 slaves. Jamaica specialized so heavily in sugar production that the island had to

Caribbean Sugar Mill
The windmill crushes sugar cane, whose juice is boiled down in the smoking building next door. From William Clark, *Ten Views in the Islands of Antigua*, 1823. British Library

import most of its food. Saint Domingue was more diverse in its economy.

In some ways, the mature sugar plantation was environmentally responsible. The crushing mill was powered by water, wind, or animal power, not fossil fuels. The boilers were largely fueled by burning the crushed canes, and the fields were fertilized by cattle manure. In two respects, however, the plantation was very damaging to the environment: soil exhaustion and deforestation. Instead of rotating sugar with other crops to restore the nutrients naturally, planters found it more profitable to clear new lands when yields declined too much in the old fields. When land close to the sea was exhausted, planters moved on to new islands. Many of the English who first settled Jamaica were from Barbados, and the pioneer planters on Saint Domingue came from older French sugar colonies. In the second half of the eighteenth century, Jamaican sugar production began to fall behind that of Saint Domingue, which still had access to virgin land. Thus, the plantations of this period were not a stable form of agriculture but one that gradually laid waste to the landscape.

Deforestation, the second form of environmental damage, continued a trend begun in the sixteenth century. By the end of the eighteenth century, only land in the interior of the islands retained dense forests.

The most tragic and dramatic transformation in the West Indies occurred in the human population. During the eighteenth century, West Indian plantation colonies were the world's most polarized societies. On most islands, 90 percent or more of the inhabitants were slaves. A small number of very rich men owned most of the slaves and most of the land as well. Between the slaves and the masters might be found only a few others: a few estate managers and government officials and, in the French islands, some small farmers, both white and black.

The profitability of a Caribbean plantation depended on extracting as much work as possible from the slaves through the use and threat of force. On a typical Jamaican plantation, about 80 percent of the slaves actively engaged in productive tasks; the only exceptions were infants, the seriously ill, and the very old. Slave labor was organized by age, sex, and ability. About 70 percent of the able-bodied slaves worked in the fields, generally in one of three labor

gangs. Women formed the majority of the field laborers, even in the great gang. A little over half of the adult males were employed in nongang work, tending the livestock or serving as blacksmiths and carpenters. The most important artisan slave was the head boiler, who oversaw the delicate process of reducing the cane sap to crystallized sugar and molasses.

Skilled slaves received rewards of food and clothing or time off for good work, but the most common reason for working hard was to escape punishment. A slave gang was headed by a privileged male slave, appropriately called the **driver**, whose job was to ensure that the gang completed its work. Production quotas were high, and slaves toiled in the fields from sunup to sunset, except for meal breaks. Those who fell behind because of fatigue or illness soon felt the sting of the whip. Openly rebellious slaves who refused to work, disobeyed orders, or tried to escape were punished with flogging, confinement in irons, or mutilation.

The harsh conditions of plantation life played a major role in shortening slaves' lives, but the greatest killer was disease. The very young were carried off by dysentery caused by contaminated food and water. Slaves newly arrived from Africa went through a period of adjustment to the new environment known as **seasoning**, during which one-third on average died of unfamiliar diseases. Slaves also suffered from diseases they brought with them, including malaria. On one plantation, for example, more than half of the slaves incapacitated by illness had yaws, a painful and debilitating skin disease common in Africa.

Such high mortality greatly added to the volume of the Atlantic slave trade, since plantations had to purchase new slaves every year or two to replace those who had died. The additional imports of slaves to permit the expansion of the sugar plantations meant that the majority of slaves on most West Indian plantations were African-born. As a result, African

---

driver A privileged male slave whose job was to ensure that a slave gang did its work on a plantation.
seasoning An often difficult period of adjustment to new climates, disease environments, and work routines, such as that experienced by slaves newly arrived in the Americas.

- During the seventeenth and eighteenth centuries, sugar planting and African slavery expanded rapidly in the West Indies.
- The preference for African slaves grew from the effects of rising sugar prices and land speculation.
- As demand for land grew, England and France established more island colonies.
- The need for efficiency made plantations into large, self-sufficient, and expensive units.
- The plantation system caused environmental damage and exacted huge human costs.
- Harsh conditions provoked rebellions and flight, and fugitives created maroon communities.

religious beliefs, patterns of speech, styles of dress and adornment, and music were prominent parts of West Indian life.

Given the harsh conditions of their lives, it is not surprising that slaves in the West Indies often sought to regain the freedom into which most had been born. Individual slaves often ran away, hoping to elude the men and dogs that would track them. Sometimes large groups of plantation slaves rose in rebellion against their bondage and abuse. For example, a large rebellion in Jamaica in 1760 was led by a slave named Tacky, who had been a chief on the Gold Coast of Africa. One night, his followers broke into a fort and armed themselves. Joined by slaves from nearby plantations, they stormed several plantations, setting them on fire and killing the planter families. Tacky died in the fighting that followed, and three other rebel leaders stoically endured cruel deaths by torture that were meant to deter others from rebellion.

Because they believed rebellions were usually led by slaves with the strongest African heritage, European planters tried to curtail African cultural traditions. They required slaves to learn the colonial language and discouraged the use of African languages by deliberately mixing slaves from different parts of Africa. In French and Portuguese colonies, slaves were encouraged to adopt Catholic religious practices, though African deities and beliefs also survived. In the British West Indies, where only Quaker slave owners encouraged Christianity among their slaves before 1800, African herbal medicine remained strong, as did African beliefs concerning nature spirits and witchcraft.

As in Latin America, slavery also provoked flight. In the Caribbean, runaways were known as **maroons**. Maroon communities were especially numerous in the mountainous interiors of Jamaica and Hispaniola, as well as in the island parts of the Guianas (guy-AHN-uhs). The Jamaican maroons, after withstanding several attacks by the colony's militia, signed a treaty in 1739 that recognized their independence in return for their cooperation in stopping new runaways and suppressing slave revolts. Similar treaties with the large maroon population in the Dutch colony of Surinam (Dutch Guiana) recognized their possession of large inland regions.

Creating the Atlantic Economy

What conditions created the Atlantic economy?

The West Indian plantation colonies were at once archaic in their cruel system of slavery and oddly modern in their specialization in a single product. Yet they played a crucial role in the emerging Atlantic economy. The plantation system profitably dominated a broad region from the Chesapeake to the Caribbean and then to northern South America and Brazil. African slaves made the plantation economies possible, and profits from the exports of plantation products helped finance commercial and manufacturing expansion. Three other elements went into the creation of the new Atlantic economy: new economic institutions, new partnerships between private investors and governments in Europe, and new working relationships between European and African merchants. The new trading system is a prime example of how European capitalist relationships were reshaping the world.

maroon A slave who ran away from his or her master. Often a member of a community of runaway slaves in the West Indies and South America.

Capitalism and Mercantilism

The Spanish and Portuguese voyages of exploration in the fifteenth and sixteenth centuries were government ventures, and both countries tried to keep their overseas trade and colonies royal monopolies. Monopoly control, however, proved both expensive and inefficient. The success of the Atlantic economy in the seventeenth and eighteenth centuries owed much to private enterprise, which made trading venues more efficient and profitable.

Two European innovations, capitalism and mercantilism, enabled private investors to fund the rapid growth of the Atlantic economy. **Capitalism** was a system of large financial institutions—banks, stock exchanges, and chartered trading companies—that enabled wealthy investors to reduce risks and increase profits. Early capitalism was buttressed by **mercantilism**, policies adopted by European states to promote their citizens' overseas trade and defend it, by armed force when necessary.

Chartered companies were one of the first examples of mercantilist capitalism. A charter issued by the government of the Netherlands in 1602 gave the Dutch East India Company a legal monopoly over all Dutch trade in the Indian Ocean. This privilege encouraged private investors to buy shares in the company. They were amply rewarded when the Dutch East India Company captured control of the long-distance trade routes in the Indian Ocean from the Portuguese (see Chapter 18). A sister firm, the **Dutch West India Company**, was chartered in 1621 to engage in the Atlantic trade and to seize sugar-producing areas in Brazil and African slaving ports from the Portuguese.

Such successes inspired other governments to set up their own chartered companies. In 1672, a royal charter placed all English trade with West Africa in the hands of the new **Royal African Company**, which established its headquarters at Cape Coast Castle, just east of Elmina on the Gold Coast. The French government chartered East India and West India companies to reduce French colonies' dependence on Dutch and English traders. The Spanish and Portuguese governments imitated this model.

French and English governments also used military force in pursuit of commercial dominance, especially to break the trading advantage of the Dutch in the Americas. Restrictions on Dutch access to French and English colonies provoked a series of wars with the Netherlands between 1652 and 1678, during which the larger English and French navies defeated the Dutch and drove the Dutch West India Company into bankruptcy.

With Dutch competition in the Atlantic reduced, the French and English governments moved to revoke the monopoly privileges of their chartered companies. England opened trade in Africa to any English subject in 1698 on the grounds that ending monopolies would be "highly beneficial and advantageous to this kingdom." It was hoped that such competition would also cut the cost of slaves to West Indian planters, though the demand for slaves soon drove the prices up again.

Such new mercantilist policies fostered competition among a nation's own citizens, while using high tariffs and restrictions to exclude foreigners. In the 1660s, England had passed a series of Navigation Acts that confined trade with its colonies to English ships and cargoes. The French called their mercantilist legislation, first codified in 1698, the *Exclusif* (ek-skloo-SEEF), highlighting its exclusionary intentions. Other mercantilist laws defended manufacturing and processing interests in Europe against competition from colonies, imposing prohibitively high taxes on

capitalism The economic system of large financial institutions—banks, stock exchanges, investment companies—that first developed in early modern Europe. *Commercial capitalism,* the trading system of the early modern economy, is often distinguished from *industrial capitalism,* the system based on machine production.

mercantilism European government policies of the sixteenth, seventeenth, and eighteenth centuries designed to promote overseas trade between a country and its colonies and to accumulate precious metals by requiring colonies to trade only with their motherland country. The British system was defined by the Navigation Acts, the French system by laws known as the *Exclusif.*

chartered companies Groups of private investors who paid an annual fee to France and England in exchange for a monopoly over trade to the West Indies colonies.

Dutch West India Company (1621–1794) Trading company chartered by the Dutch government to conduct its merchants' trade in the Americas and Africa.

Royal African Company Trading company chartered by the English government to conduct its merchants' trade in the Americas and Africa.

- Capitalism and mercantilism encouraged private funding of the Atlantic economy.
- These systems often worked through chartered companies and military force.
- Mercantilism promoted competition among a country's citizens while blocking foreign competition.

any manufactured goods and refined sugar imported from the colonies.

As a result of such mercantilist measures, the Atlantic became Britain, France, and Portugal's most important overseas trading area in the eighteenth century. Britain's imports from its West Indian colonies in this period accounted for over one-fifth of the value of total British imports. The French West Indian colonies played an even larger role in France's overseas trade. Only the Dutch, closed out of much of the American trade, found Asian trade of greater value. Profits from the Atlantic economy, in turn, promoted further economic expansion and increased the revenues of European governments.

Colonial Expansion and Conflict

What were the effects of the colonial reforms and wars among imperial powers that dominated the Americas during the eighteenth century?

In the last decades of the seventeenth century, all of the European colonies in the Americas began to experience a long period of economic and demographic expansion. In the next century, the imperial powers responded by strengthening their administrative and economic controls in the colonies. They also sought to force colonial populations to pay a larger share of the costs of administration and defense. These efforts at reform and restructuring coincided with a series of imperial wars fought along Atlantic trade routes and in the Americas. France's loss of its North American colonies in 1763 was one of the most important results of these struggles. Equally significant, colonial populations throughout the Americas became more aware of separate national identities and more aggressive in asserting local interests against the will of distant monarchs.

Imperial Reform in Spanish America and Brazil

Spain's Habsburg dynasty ended when the Spanish king Charles II died without an heir in 1700. After thirteen years of conflict involving the major European powers and factions within Spain, Philip of Bourbon, grandson of Louis XIV of France, gained the Spanish throne. Under Philip V and his Bourbon heirs, Spain's colonial administration and tax collection were reorganized. For most of the Spanish Empire, the eighteenth century was a period of remarkable economic expansion associated with population growth and enhanced commerce. Mining, the heart of the Spanish colonial economy, increased as silver production in Mexico and Peru rose steadily into the 1780s. Agricultural exports also expanded: tobacco, dyes, hides, chocolate, cotton, and sugar joined the flow of goods to Europe.

Brazil experienced a similar period of expansion and reform after 1700, as Portugal created new administrative positions and gave monopoly companies exclusive rights to little-developed regions. As in Spanish America, this led to rebellions and plots. The discovery of gold in the 1690s and diamonds after 1720 in Brazil financed an aggressive period of reform. This economic expansion led to an increase in the slave trade: nearly 2 million African slaves were imported in the eighteenth century.

The Spanish and Portuguese kings also sought to reduce the power of the Catholic Church in their colonies while at the same time transferring some church wealth to their treasuries. These efforts led to a succession of confrontations between colonial officials and the church hierarchy. In both the Spanish and Portuguese empires, these disputes began to undermine the clergy's previously reliable support for the colonial state. Many colonists saw the reforms as an abuse of power. In Spanish America tax rebellions, urban riots, and Amerindian uprisings tied to these reforms began in the 1770s. In Brazil, as in Spanish America, a more intrusive colonial government that imposed new taxes led to rebellions and plots, including open warfare in 1707 between "sons of the soil" and "outsiders" in São Paulo.

Reform and Reorganization in British America

After the period of Cromwell's Puritan Republic (see Chapter 16), the restored Stuart king, Charles II, undertook an ambitious campaign to establish greater Crown control over the colonies. Between 1651 and 1673 a series of Navigation Acts sought to severely limit colonial trade and production that competed directly with English manufacturers. Because the New England colonies were viewed as centers of smuggling, the king temporarily suspended their elected assemblies. At the same time, he appointed colonial governors and granted them new fiscal and legislative powers.

During the eighteenth century the English colonies experienced renewed economic growth and attracted a new wave of European immigration, but social divisions were increasingly evident. The colonial population in 1770 was more urban, more clearly divided by class and race, and more vulnerable to economic downturns. Crises were provoked when imperial wars with France and Spain disrupted trade in the Atlantic, increased tax burdens, forced military mobilizations, and provoked frontier conflicts with the Amerindians.

Africa and the Atlantic

How did the Atlantic system affect Africa?

The Atlantic system took a terrible toll in African lives both during the Middle Passage (the journey from Africa to America) and under the harsh conditions of plantation slavery. Many other Africans died while being marched to African coastal ports for sale overseas. The overall effects on Africa of these losses and of other aspects of the slave trade have been the subject of considerable historical debate. It is clear that the trade's impact depended on the intensity and terms of different African regions' involvement.

Any assessment of the Atlantic system's effects in Africa must also take into consideration the fact that some Africans profited from the trade by capturing and selling slaves (see Diversity and Dominance: Slavery in West Africa and the Americas). They chained the slaves together or bound them to forked sticks for the march to the coast, then bartered them to the European slavers for trade goods. The effects on the enslaver were different from the effects on the enslaved.

The Gold Coast and the Slave Coast

The transition to slave trading was not sudden. Even as slaves were becoming Atlantic Africa's most valuable export, nonslave goods remained a significant part of the total trade. For example, during its eight decades of operation from 1672 to 1752, the English Royal African Company made 40 percent of its profits from dealings in gold, ivory, and forest products. In some parts of West Africa, such nonslave exports remained predominant even at the peak of the trade.

African merchants were very discriminating about what merchandise they received in return for slaves or other goods. A European ship that arrived with goods of low quality or unsuited to local tastes found it hard to purchase a cargo at a profitable price. Africans' greatest demands were for textiles, hardware, and guns. Of the goods the Royal African Company traded in West Africa in the 1680s, over 60 percent were Indian and European textiles and 30 percent hardware and weaponry. Beads and other jewelry formed 3 percent. The rest consisted of cowrie shells, which were used as money. In the eighteenth century,

Primary Source: A Voyage to New Calabar River in the Year 1699 Learn the details of a transaction in which men and women are traded for bars of iron.

Diversity & Dominance

Slavery in West Africa and the Americas

Social diversity was common in Africa, and the domination of masters over slaves was a feature of many societies. Ahmad Baba (1556–1627) was an outstanding Islamic scholar from an old Muslim family in the city of Timbuktu. In about 1615 he replied to some questions that had been sent to him. His answers reveal a great deal about the official and unofficial condition of slavery in the Sudan of West Africa, especially in the Hausa states of Kano and Katsina.

You asked: What have you to say concerning the slaves imported from the lands of the Sudan whose people are acknowledged to be Muslims, such as Bornu, . . . Kano, Goa, Songhay, Katsina and others among whom Islam is widespread? Is it permissible to possess them [as slaves] or not?

Know—may God grant us and you success—that these lands, as you have stated are Muslim. . . . But close to each of them are lands in which are unbelievers whom the Muslim inhabitants of these lands raid. Some of these unbelievers are under the Muslims' protection and pay them [taxes]. . . . Sometimes there is war between the Muslim sultans of some of these lands and one attacks the other, taking as many prisoners as he can and selling the captive though he is a free-born Muslim. . . . This is a common practice among them in Hausaland; Katsina raids Kano, as do others, though their language is one and their situations parallel; the only difference they recognize among themselves is that so-and-so is a born Muslim and so-and-so is a born unbeliever. . . .

Whoever is taken prisoner in a state of unbelief may become someone's property, whoever he is, as opposed to those who have become Muslims of their own free will . . . and may not be possessed at all.

A little over a century later another African provided information about enslavement practices in the Western Sudan. Ayuba Suleiman Diallo (ah-YOO-bah SOO-lay-mahn JAH-loh) (1701–?) of the state of Bondu some 200 miles from the Gambia River was enslaved and transported to Maryland, where he was a slave from 1731 to 1733. When an Englishman learned of Ayuba's literacy in Arabic, he recorded his life story, anglicizing his

Ayuba Suleiman Diallo (1701–?)

British Library

name to Job Solomon. According to the account, slaves in Bondu did much of the hard work, while men of Ayuba's class were free to devote themselves to the study of Islamic texts.

In February, 1730, Job's father hearing of an English ship at Gambia River, sent him, with two servants to attend him, to sell two Negroes, and to buy paper, and some other necessaries; but desired him not to venture over the river, because the country of the Mandingoes, who are enemies to the people of Futa, lies on the other side. Job not agreeing with Captain Pike (who commanded the ship, lying then at Gambia, in the service of Captain Henry Hunt, brother to Mr. William Hunt, merchant, in Little Tower-street, London) sent back the two servants to acquaint his father with it, and to let him know that he intended to go no farther. Accordingly . . . he crossed the River Gambia, and disposed of his Negroes for some cows. As he was returning home, he stopped for some refreshment at the house of an old acquaintance; and the weather being hot, he hung up his arms in the house, while he refreshed himself. . . . It happened that a company of the Mandingoes, . . . passing by at that time, and observing him unarmed, rushed in, to the number of seven or eight at once, at a back door, and pinioned Job, before he could get his arms, together with his interpreter, who is a slave in Maryland still. They then shaved their heads and beards, which Job and his man resented as the highest indignity; tho' the Mandingoes meant no more by it, than to make them appear like slaves taken in war. On the 27th of February, 1730, they carried them to Captain Pike at Gambia, who purchased them; and on the first of March they were put on board. Soon after Job found means to acquaint Captain Pike that he was the same person that came to trade with him a few days before, and after what manner he had been taken. Upon this Captain Pike gave him free leave to redeem himself and his man; and Job sent to an acquaintance of his father's, near Gambia, who promised to send to Job's father, to inform him of what had happened, that he might take some course to have him set at liberty. But it being a fortnight's [two weeks'] journey between that friend's house and his father's, and the ship sailing in about a week after, Job was brought with the rest of the slaves to Annapolis in Maryland, and delivered to Mr. Vachell Denton. . . .

Mr. Vachell Denton sold Job to one Mr. Tolsey in Kent Island in Maryland, who put him to work in making tobacco; but he was soon convinced that Job had never been used to such labour. He every day showed more and more uneasiness under this exercise, and at last grew sick, being no way able to bear it; so his master was obliged to find easier work for him, and therefore put him to tend the cattle. Job would often leave the cattle, and withdraw into the woods to pray; but a white boy frequently watched him, and whilst he was at his devotion would mock him and throw dirt in his face. This very much disturbed Job, and added considerably to his other misfortunes; all which were increased by his ignorance of the English language, which prevented his complaining, or telling his case to any person about him. Grown in some measure desperate, by reason of his present hardships, he resolved to travel at a venture; thinking he might possibly be taken up by some master, who would use him better, or otherwise meet with some lucky accident, to divert or abate his grief. Accordingly, he travelled thro' the woods, till he came to the County of Kent, upon Delaware Bay. . . . There is a law in force, throughout the [mid-Atlantic] colonies . . . as far as Boston in New England, viz. that any Negroe, or white servant who is not known in the county, or has no pass, may be secured by any person, and kept in the common [jail], till the master of such servant shall fetch him. Therefore Job being able to give no account of himself, was put in prison there.

This happened about the beginning of June 1731, when I, who was attending the courts there, and heard of Job, went with several gentlemen to the [jailer's] house, being a tavern, and desired to see him. He was brought into the tavern to us, but could not speak one word of English. Upon our talking and making signs to him, he wrote a line to two before us, and when he read it, pronounced the words Allah and Mahommed; by which, and his refusing a glass of wine we offered him, we perceived he was a Mahometan [Muslim], but could not imagine of what country he was, or how he got thither; for by his affable carriage, and the easy composure of his countenance, we could perceive he was no common slave.

When Job had been some time confined, an old Negroe man, who lived in that neighborhood, and could speak the Jalloff [Wolof] language, which Job also understood, went to him, and conversed with him. By this Negroe the keeper was informed to whom Job belonged, and what was the cause of his leaving his master. The keeper thereupon wrote to his master, who soon after fetched him home, and was much kinder to him than before; allowing him place to pray in, and in some other conveniences, in order to make his slavery as easy as possible. Yet slavery and confinement was by no means agreeable to Job, who had never been used to it; he therefore wrote a letter in Arabick to his father, acquainting him with his misfortunes, hoping he might yet find means to redeem him. . . . It happened that this letter was seen by James Oglethorpe, Esq. [founder of the colony of Georgia and director of the Royal African Company]; who, according to his usual goodness and generosity, took compassion on Job, and [bought him from his master]; his master being very willing to part with him, as finding him no ways fit for his business.

In spring 1733 Job's benefactors took him to England, teaching him passable English during the voyage, and introduced him to the English gentry. Job attracted such attention that local men took up a collection to buy his freedom and pay his debts, and they also introduced him at the royal court. In 1735 Job returned to Gambia in a Royal African Company ship, richly clothed and accompanied by many gifts.

QUESTIONS FOR ANALYSIS

1. Since Ahmad Baba points out that Islamic law permitted a Muslim to raid and enslave non-Muslims, do you think that the non-Muslim Mandinka (Mandingos) would have considered it justifiable to enslave Ayuba, since he was a Muslim?
2. Which aspects of Ayuba Suleiman's experiences of enslavement were normal, and which unusual?
3. How different might Ayuba's experiences of slavery have been had he been sold in Jamaica rather than Maryland?
4. How strictly was the ban against enslaving Muslims observed in Hausaland?

Source: Thomas Hodgkin, ed., *Nigerian Perspectives: An Historical Anthology*, 2nd ed. (London: Oxford University Press, 1975), 154–156, copyright © 1975. By permission of Oxford University Press; Thomas Bluett, *Some Memoirs of the Life of Job, the Son of Solomon the High Priest of Boonda in Africa* (London: Richard Ford, 1734), 16–24.

tobacco and rum from the Americas became welcome imports.

Both Europeans and Africans naturally attempted to drive the best bargain for themselves and sometimes engaged in deceitful practices. The strength of the African bargaining position, however, may be inferred from the fact that as the demand for slaves rose, so too did their price in Africa. In the course of the eighteenth century, the goods needed to purchase a slave on the Gold Coast doubled and in some places tripled or quadrupled.

African governments on the Gold Coast and the Slave Coast just east of it made Europeans observe African trading customs and prevented them from taking control of African territory. Rivalry among European nations, each of which established its own trading "castles" along the Gold Coast, also reduced Europeans' bargaining strength.

How did African kings and merchants obtain slaves for sale? Most accounts agree that prisoners taken in war were the greatest source of slaves for the Atlantic trade, but it is difficult to say how often capturing slaves for export was the main cause of warfare. An early-nineteenth-century king of Asante stated, "I cannot make war to catch slaves in the bush, like a thief. My ancestors never did so. But if I fight a king, and kill him when he is insolent, then certainly I must have his gold, and his slaves, and his people are mine too. Do not the white kings act like this?"[2] English rulers had indeed sentenced seventeenth-century Scottish and Irish prisoners to forced labor in the West Indies.

The Bight of Biafra and Angola

In the eighteenth century, the slave trade expanded eastward to the Bight (bay) of Biafra. In contrast to the Gold and Slave Coasts, where strong kingdoms predominated, the densely populated interior of the Bight of Biafra contained no large states. Even so, the powerful merchant princes of the coastal ports made European traders give them rich presents. Because of the absence of sizeable states, there were no large-scale wars and consequently few prisoners of war. Instead, kidnapping was the major means of getting slaves.

As the volume of the Atlantic trade along the Bight of Biafra expanded in the late eighteenth century, some inland markets evolved into giant fairs, with different sections specializing in slaves and imported goods. An English ship's doctor reported that in the 1780s slaves were "bought by the black traders at fairs, which are held for that purpose, at a distance of upwards of two hundred miles from the sea coast." He reported seeing from twelve hundred to fifteen hundred enslaved men and women arriving at the coast from a single fair.[4]

Angola, south of the Congo estuary, was the greatest source of slaves for the Atlantic trade. This was also the one place along the Atlantic coast where a single European nation, Portugal, controlled a significant amount of territory. Portuguese residents of the main coastal ports served as middlemen between caravans that arrived from the far interior and ships from Brazil. Many of the slaves sold at Angolan markets were prisoners of war captured by expanding African states. As elsewhere in Africa, such prisoners seem to have been a byproduct of African wars rather than the purpose for which the wars were fought.

Recent research has linked other enslavement with environmental crises in the hinterland of Angola. During the eighteenth century, these southern grasslands periodically suffered severe droughts, which drove famished refugees to areas with more plentiful water. In return for food and water, powerful African leaders gained control of many refugees and sold into the Atlantic trade the men, who were more likely than the women and children to escape or challenge the ruler's authority. The most successful of these inland Angolan leaders became heads of powerful new states that stabilized areas devastated by war and drought and repopulated them with the refugees and prisoners they retained. The slave frontier then moved farther inland. This cruel system worked to the benefit of a few African rulers and merchants at the expense of the many thousands of Africans who were sent to death or perpetual bondage in the Americas.

It is impossible to assess with precision the complex effects of the goods received in sub-Saharan Africa from these trades. Africans were very particular about what they received, so it is unlikely that they could have been consistently cheated. Some researchers have suggested that imports of textiles and metals undermined African weavers and metalworkers, but most economic historians calculate that, on a per capita basis, the volume of these imports was too small to have idled many African artisans. Imports supplemented rather than replaced local production.

The goods received in sub-Saharan Africa were intended for consumption and thus did not develop the economy. Likewise, the sugar, tea, and chocolate Europeans consumed did little to promote economic development in Europe. However, both African and European merchants profited from trading these consumer goods. Because they directed the whole Atlantic system, Europeans gained far more wealth than Africans did.

Historians disagree in their assessment of how deeply European capitalism dominated Africa before 1800, but Europeans clearly had much less political and economic impact in Africa than in the West Indies or in other parts of the Americas. Still, it is significant that Western capitalism was expanding rapidly in the seventeenth century, while the Ottoman Empire, the dominant state of the Middle East, was entering a period of economic and political decline (see Chapter 18). The tide of influence in Africa was thus running in the Europeans' direction.

Conclusion

The New World colonial empires of Spain, Portugal, France, and England had many characteristics in common. All subjugated Amerindian peoples, introduced large numbers of enslaved Africans, and transformed the American environment by introducing Old World animals, plants, and technologies. Each of the New World empires also reflected the distinctive cultural and institutional heritages of its colonizing power.

Spain's discovery of mineral wealth allowed it to develop the largest and most centralized colonial government. Portugal and France pursued similar objectives, but neither Brazil's agricultural economy, based on sugar, nor France's Canadian fur trade permitted the level of political control achieved by Spain. There was greater cultural and religious diversity in British North America, and the British colonial government was less centralized and in some cases more responsive to local interests.

From the seventeenth century onward European powers expanded and created new colonies in the Caribbean. Spain's early control of the region was lost as settlers moved to the mainland once gold and silver were discovered. The British, French, and Dutch also established colonies. While tobacco initially dominated these economies, sugar eventually made these once-isolated islands part of a dynamic trading system controlled from Europe and dependent on slave labor. Spain's most important Caribbean colony, Cuba, joined the sugar revolution late and became the major producer of sugar by 1820.

Historians have seen the Atlantic system that tied European colonies in the Americas to Africa and Europe as a model of the kind of highly interactive economy that became global in later centuries. For that reason the Atlantic system was a milestone in a much larger historical process. Its transformations were destructive as well as creative, producing victims of Amerindians and African slaves while benefiting European commercial and manufacturing interests. Africa played an essential role by importing trade goods and exporting slaves to the Americas. However, it was less dominated by the Atlantic system than were Europe's American colonies. Africans remained in control of their continent and interacted culturally and politically with the Islamic world more than with the Atlantic (see Chapter 13).

CHAPTER REVIEW

Download the MP3 audio file of the
Chapter Review to listen to on the go.

What role did forced labor play in the main industries in Spanish America and Brazil? (page 409)

The development of Spanish colonies was promoted by the discovery of rich gold and silver mines and by the encomienda and mita, which forced tens of thousands of indigenous laborers to work in mines, farms, and factories. The sugar industry was crucial to Brazil. At first the enslavement of Amerindians provided labor for the sugar plantations, but eventually Brazil depended on the African slave trade, importing nearly 2 million slaves in the eighteenth century.

What were the differences between the English and French colonies of North America? (page 415)

While French Canada was founded with the hope that mineral wealth would be discovered, it survived because of the modest profits of the fur trade. Population grew slowly, and France relied on alliances with native peoples to exploit the fur trade and protect its North American colony. The English colonies of North America followed a different path. Settlements were first created by groups of private investors or by religious minorities, and England never established centralized political institutions to control all its colonies as did the Spanish and later Portuguese. As a result, settlers exercised greater political power. The economies of Britain's North American colonies were more diverse and much less profitable than were the colonies of Spain and Portugal. The northern English-speaking colonies relied on diverse economic activities such as commercial services and shipbuilding and attracted large numbers of free immigrants, while England's southern colonies depended on agricultural exports like rice and tobacco and on slave labor.

What factors contributed to the development of plantations in the West Indies? (page 420)

The islands of the West Indies were divided among a number of European powers. After devastating epidemics eliminated the indigenous populations, settlers relied heavily on slavery to produce a range of export crops.

When settlers and European investors realized sugar's profitability, they were willing to finance the forced transfer of hundreds of thousands of Africans to work the Caribbean plantations. Since Africans and their American-born descendants outnumbered Europeans across the area, African culture took root and served as an important basis for these new American societies.

What conditions created the Atlantic economy? (page 423)

European merchants and investors played a central role in the creation of the Atlantic system. In the century before Columbus they traded over longer distances and introduced new credit mechanisms. By the seventeenth century a more confident and adventurous European investor class was ready to promote colonial production and long-distance trade in a much more aggressive way. The development of banks, stock exchanges, and chartered companies supported these new ambitions.

What were the effects of the colonial reforms and wars among imperial powers that dominated the Americas during the eighteenth century? (page 425)

In the eighteenth century the European colonies in the Americas experienced economic and population growth. The century also witnessed a series of destructive and costly wars among the European colonial powers. In an effort to force the colonies to pay a greater share of the costs of imperial defense, Spain, Portugal, England, and France all introduced new taxes and created more intrusive colonial governments. With these reforms came increased resentment among colonial populations as well as tax rebellions and riots.

How did the Atlantic system affect Africa? (page 426)

The Atlantic slave trade that began in the late fifteenth century grew spectacularly after the introduction of sugar to the Caribbean islands. The slave trade provided kingdoms on the coast of west and equatorial Africa with weapons with which they waged war against the peoples of the interior, selling their captives to European traders. The production of sugar in the Americas and the volume of the African slave trade crested together in the eighteenth century.

Key Terms

Atlantic system *(p. 409)*

Council of the Indies *(p. 410)*

Bartolomé de Las Casas *(p. 410)*

Potosí *(p. 411)*

encomienda *(p. 413)*

creole *(p. 414)*

indentured servant *(p. 416)*

House of Burgesses *(p. 417)*

Pilgrims *(p. 417)*

Puritans *(p. 417)*

Iroquois Confederacy *(p. 418)*

New France *(p. 418)*

driver *(p. 422)*

seasoning *(p. 422)*

maroon *(p. 423)*

capitalism *(p. 424)*

mercantilism *(p. 424)*

chartered companies *(p. 424)*

Dutch West India Company *(p. 424)*

Royal African Company *(p. 424)*

Web Resources

Pronunciation Guide

Interactive Map

- MAP 17.1 Colonial Latin America in the Eighteenth Century

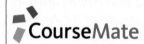

Visit the CourseMate website at www.cengagebrain.com for additional study tools and review materials for this chapter.

Primary Sources

- A Dominican Voice in the Wilderness: Preaching Against Tyranny in Hispaniola
- A Voyage to New Calabar River in the Year 1699

Answer to the History in Focus Question

See photo on page 414, "Market in Rio de Janeiro."

Southwest Asia and the Indian Ocean

© Cengage Learning

Visit the CourseMate website at **www.cengagebrain.com** for additional study tools and review materials for this chapter.

In 1541 a woman named Sabah appeared before an Ottoman judge in the town of Aintab in southern Turkey to answer several charges: that she had brought men and women together illegally and that she had fostered heresy. In her court testimony, she stated the following:

> I gather girls and brides and women in my home. I negotiated with Ibrahim b. Nazih and the two youths who are his apprentices, and in exchange for paying them a month's fee, I had them come every day to the girls and brides in my house and I had them preach and give instruction. There are no males at those sessions besides the said Ibrahim and his apprentices; there are only women and girls and young brides. This kind of thing is what I have always done for a living.[1]

Two male neighbors testified differently:

> She holds gatherings of girls and brides and women in her home.... While she says that she has [Ibrahim] preach, she actually has him speak evil things. She has him conduct spiritual conversations with these girls and brides.... [I]n the ceremonies, the girls and brides and women spin around waving their hands, and they bring themselves into a trancelike state by swaying and dancing. They perform the ceremonies according to Kizilbash teachings. We too have wives and families, and we are opposed to illegal activities like this.[2]

The judge made no finding on the charge of heresy, but he ordered Sabah to be publicly humiliated and banished from town for unlawfully mixing the sexes. Ibrahim was also banished.

This uncommon story taken from Ottoman religious court records sheds light on several aspects of daily life in a provincial town. It provides an example of a woman making her living by arranging religious instruction for other women. It also demonstrates the willingness of neighbors, in this case males, to complain in court about activities they considered immoral. And its suggestion that Sabah was promoting the qizilbash heresy, which at that time was considered a state threat because it was the ideology of the enemy Safavid Empire next door, shows that townspeople thought it plausible that women could act to promote religious doctrines.

Studies of everyday life through court records and other state and nonstate documents are a recent development in Ottoman and Safavid history. They produce an image of these societies that differs greatly from the pomp and formality conveyed by European travelers and official histories. As a consequence, accounts of capricious and despotic actions taken by shahs and sultans are increasingly being balanced by stories of common people, who were much more concerned with the maintenance of a sound legal and moral order than were some of the denizens of the imperial palaces. The doings of rulers remain an important historical focus, of course, but stories about ordinary folk perhaps give a better picture of the habits and mores of the majority of the population.

The Ottoman Empire

How did the Ottoman Empire rise to power, and what factors contributed to its transformation?

The most long-lived of the post-Mongol Muslim empires was the **Ottoman Empire**, founded around 1300 (see Map 18.1). By extending Islamic conquests into eastern Europe, starting in the late fourteenth century, and by taking Syria and Egypt from the mamluk rulers in the early sixteenth, the Ottomans seemed to recreate the might of the original Islamic caliphate, the empire established by the Muslim Arab conquests in the seventh century. However, the empire was actually more like the new centralized monarchies of France and Spain (see Chapter 16) than any medieval model.

Ottoman Empire Islamic state founded by Osman in northwestern Anatolia ca. 1300. After the fall of the Byzantine Empire, the Ottoman Empire was based at Istanbul (formerly Constantinople) from 1453 to 1922. It encompassed lands in the Middle East, North Africa, the Caucasus, and eastern Europe.

Chronology

	Ottoman Empire	Safavid Empire	Mughal Empire
1500		**1502–1524** Shah Ismail establishes Safavid rule in Iran	
	1516–1517 Selim I conquers Egypt and Syria		
	1520–1566 Reign of Suleiman the Magnificent; peak of Ottoman Empire		
			1526 Babur defeats last sultan of Delhi
	1529 First Ottoman siege of Vienna		**1556–1605** Akbar rules in Agra; peak of Mughal Empire
	1571 Ottoman naval defeat at Lepanto	**1587–1629** Reign of Shah Abbas the Great; peak of Safavid Empire	
1600	**1610** End of Anatolian revolts		**1658–1707** Aurangzeb imposes conservative Islamic regime
1700		**1722** Afghan invaders topple last Safavid shah	
	1730 Janissary revolt begins period of Ottoman conservatism	**1736–1747** Nadir Shah temporarily reunites Iran; invades India (1739)	
			1739 Iranians under Nadir Shah sack Delhi

Enduring more than five centuries until 1922, the Ottoman Empire survived several periods of wrenching change, some caused by internal problems, others by the growing power of European adversaries. These periods of change reveal the problems faced by huge land-based empires around the world.

Expansion and Frontiers

Established around 1300, the Ottoman Empire grew from a tiny state in northwestern Anatolia because of three factors: (1) the shrewdness of its founder, Osman (from which the name *Ottoman* comes), and his descendants, (2) control of a strategic link between Europe and Asia on the Dardanelles strait, and (3) the creation of an army that took advantage of the traditional skills of the Turkish cavalryman and the new military possibilities presented by gunpowder. At first, Ottoman armies concentrated on Christian enemies in Greece and the Balkans, in 1389 conquering a strong Serbian kingdom at the Battle of Kosovo (KO-so-vo). Much of southeastern Europe and Anatolia was under the control of the sultans by 1402. In 1453, Sultan Mehmed II, "the Conqueror," laid siege to Constantinople. His forces used enormous cannon to bash in the city's walls, dragged warships over a high hill from the Bosporus strait to the city's inner harbor to get around its sea defenses, and finally penetrated the city's land walls through a series of direct

Map 18.1 Muslim Empires in the Sixteenth and Seventeenth Centuries Iran, a Shi'ite state flanked by Sunni Ottomans on the west and Sunni Mughals on the east, had the least exposure to European influences. Ottoman expansion across the southern Mediterranean Sea intensified European fears of Islam. The areas of strongest Mughal control dictated that Islam's spread into Southeast Asia would be heavily influenced by merchants and religious figures from Gujarat instead of from eastern India. © Cengage Learning

infantry assaults. The fall of Constantinople—henceforth commonly known as Istanbul—brought to an end over eleven hundred years of Byzantine rule and made the Ottomans seem invincible.

Selim (seh-LEEM) I, "the Grim," conquered Egypt and Syria in 1516 and 1517, making the Red Sea the Ottomans' southern frontier. His son, **Suleiman (SOO-lay-mahn) the Magnificent** (r. 1520–1566), presided over the greatest Ottoman assault on Christian Europe. Suleiman seemed unstoppable: he conquered

Belgrade in 1521, expelled the Knights of the Hospital of St. John from the island of Rhodes the following year, and laid siege to Vienna in 1529. Vienna was saved by the need to retreat before the onset of winter

Suleiman the Magnificent (1494–1566) The most illustrious sultan of the Ottoman Empire (r. 1520–1566); also known as Suleiman Kanuni, "The Lawgiver." He significantly expanded the empire in the Balkans and eastern Mediterranean.

more than by military action. In later centuries, Ottoman historians looked back on the reign of Suleiman as the period when the imperial system worked to perfection, and they spoke of it as the golden age of Ottoman greatness.

While Ottoman armies pressed deeper and deeper into eastern Europe, the sultans also sought to control the Mediterranean. Between 1453 and 1502, the Ottomans fought the opening rounds of a two-century war with Venice, the most powerful of Italy's commercial city-states. The initial fighting left Venice in control of its lucrative islands for another century. But it also left Venice a reduced military power compelled to pay tribute to the Ottomans.

In the early sixteenth century, merchants from southern India and Sumatra sent emissaries to Istanbul requesting naval support against the Portuguese. The Ottomans responded vigorously to Portuguese threats close to their territories, such as at Aden at the southern entrance to the Red Sea, but their efforts farther afield were insufficient to stifle growing Portuguese domination. There were several reasons for this failure. For one thing, Eastern luxury products still flowed to Ottoman markets. Moreover, Portuguese power was territorially limited to fortified coastal points, such as Hormuz at the entrance to the Persian Gulf, Goa in western India, and Malacca in Malaya. It never occurred to the Ottomans that a sea empire held together by flimsy ships could truly rival a great land empire fielding an army of a hundred thousand men. Why commit major resources to subduing an enemy whose main threat was a demand that merchant vessels, mostly belonging to non-Ottoman Muslims, buy protection from Portuguese attack? The Ottomans did send a small naval force to Indonesia, but they never formulated a consistent or aggressive policy with regard to political and economic developments in the Indian Ocean.

Central Institutions

By the 1520s, the Ottoman Empire was the most powerful and best-organized state in either Europe or the Islamic world. Its military was balanced between cavalry archers, primarily Turks, and Christian prisoners of war induced to serve as military slaves.

Slave soldiery had a long history in Islamic lands, but the conquest of Christian territories in the

An Ottoman Janissary Soldier The Venetian artist Gentile Bellini (d. 1507) was sent by his government to Constantinople in 1478, only twenty-four years after its capture by the Ottomans. Among the images he produced was this one of a soldier wearing the distinctive headgear of the Janissary corps. Though the Janissaries were noted for their training in gunpowder weapons, this soldier is equipped with the more traditional bow and sword.

Balkans in the late fourteenth century gave the Ottomans access to a new military resource. Converted to Islam, these "new troops," called *yeni cheri* in Turkish and *Janissaries* (JAN-nih-seh-rees) in English, gave the Ottomans unusual military flexibility. Since horseback riding and bowmanship were not part of their cultural backgrounds, they readily accepted the idea of fighting on foot and learning to use guns, which at that time were still too heavy and awkward for a cavalryman to load and fire. The Janissaries lived in barracks and trained all year round.

Janissaries Infantry, originally of slave origin, armed with firearms and constituting the elite of the Ottoman army from the fifteenth century until the corps was abolished in 1826.

The process of selection for Janissary training changed early in the fifteenth century. The new system imposed a regular levy of male children on Christian villages in the Balkans and occasionally elsewhere. Recruited children were placed with Turkish families to learn their language and then were sent to the sultan's palace in Istanbul for an education that included instruction in Islam, military training, and, for the most talented, what we might call liberal arts. This regime, sophisticated for its time, produced not only the Janissary soldiers but also, from among the chosen few who received special training, senior military commanders and heads of government departments up to the rank of grand vizier.

The cavalrymen were supported by land grants and administered most rural areas in Anatolia and the Balkans. They maintained order, collected taxes, and reported for each summer's campaign with their horses, retainers, and supplies, all paid for from the taxes they collected. When not campaigning, they stayed at home.

A galley-equipped navy was manned by Greek, Turkish, Algerian, and Tunisian sailors, usually under the command of an admiral from one of the North African ports. The balance of the Ottoman land forces brought success to Ottoman arms in recurrent wars with the Safavids, who were much slower to adopt firearms, and in the inexorable conquest of the Balkans. Expansion by sea was less dramatic. A major expedition against Malta in the western Mediterranean failed in 1565. Combined Christian forces also achieved a massive naval victory at the Battle of Lepanto, off Greece, in 1571. But the Ottomans' resources were so extensive that in a year's time they had replaced all of the galleys sunk in that battle.

The Ottoman Empire became cosmopolitan in character. The sophisticated court language, Osmanli (os-MAHN-lee) (the Turkish form of *Ottoman*), shared basic grammar and vocabulary with Turkish, but Arabic and Persian elements made it distinct from the language spoken by Anatolia's nomads and villagers. Everyone who served in the military or the bureaucracy and conversed in Osmanli was considered to belong to the *askeri* (AS-keh-ree), or "military," class. Members of this class were exempt from taxes and owed their well-being to the sultan.

The Ottomans saw the sultan as providing justice for his "flock of sheep" (*raya* RAH-yah]) and the military protecting them. In return, the raya paid the taxes that supported both the sultan and the military. In reality, the sultan's government remained comparatively isolated from the lives of most subjects. As Islam gradually became the majority religion in Balkan regions, Islamic law (the Shari'a [sha-REE-ah]) conditioned urban institutions and social life. Local customs prevailed among non-Muslims and in many rural areas, while non-Muslims looked to their own religious leaders for guidance in family and spiritual matters.

Crisis of the Military State, 1585–1650

As military technology evolved, cannon and lighter-weight firearms played an ever-larger role on the battlefield. Accordingly, the size of the Janissary corps—and its cost to the government—grew steadily, and the role of the Turkish cavalry diminished. To pay the Janissaries, the sultan started reducing the number of landholding cavalrymen. Revenues previously spent on their living expenses and military equipment went directly into the imperial treasury. Inflation caused by a flood of cheap silver from the New World bankrupted many of the remaining landholders, who were restricted by law to collecting a fixed amount of taxes. When their land was returned to the state, displaced cavalrymen, armed and unhappy, became a restive element in rural Anatolia.

This complicated situation resulted in revolts that devastated Anatolia between 1590 and 1610. Former landholding cavalrymen, short-term soldiers released at the end of the campaign season, peasants overburdened by emergency taxes, and even impoverished students of religion formed bands of marauders. Anatolia experienced the worst of the rebellions and suffered greatly from emigration and the loss of agricultural production. But an increase in banditry, made worse by the government's inability to stem the spread of muskets among the general public, beset other parts of the empire as well.

In the meantime, the Janissaries took advantage of their growing influence to gain relief from prohibitions on their marrying and engaging in business. Janissaries who involved themselves in commerce lessened the burden on the state budget, and married Janissaries who enrolled sons or relatives in the corps made it possible in the seventeenth century for the government to save state funds by abolishing forced recruitment. These savings, however, were more than offset by the increase in the total number of Janissaries and in their steady deterioration as a military force, which necessitated the hiring of more and more supplemental troops.

Economic Change and Growing Weakness

A very different Ottoman Empire emerged from this crisis. The sultan once had led armies. Now he mostly resided in his palace and had little experience of the real world, and the affairs of government were overseen more and more by the chief administrators—the grand viziers.

The Janissaries took advantage of their increased power to make membership in their corps hereditary. Their involvement in crafts and trading took a toll on their military skills, but they continued to be a powerful faction in urban politics. Land grants in return for military service also disappeared, and tax farming arose in their place. Tax farmers paid specific taxes, such as customs duties, in advance in return for the privilege of collecting a greater amount from the actual taxpayers.

Rural administration, already disrupted by the rebellions, suffered from the transition to tax farms. Whereas the former military landholders had kept order on their lands to maintain their incomes, tax farmers were less likely to live on the land. The imperial government therefore faced greater administrative burdens and came to rely heavily on powerful provincial governors or on wealthy men who purchased lifelong tax collection rights and behaved more or less like private landowners.

Rural disorder and decline in administrative control sometimes opened the way for new economic opportunities. The port of Izmir (IZ-meer), known to Europeans by the ancient name "Smyrna," had a population in 1580 of around 2,000, many of them Greek-speaking Christians. By 1650 the population had increased to between 30,000 and 40,000. Along with refugees from the Anatolian uprisings and from European pirate attacks along the coast came European

merchants and large colonies of Armenians and Jews. A French traveler in 1621 wrote: "At present, Izmir has a great traffic in wool, beeswax, cotton, and silk, which the Armenians bring there instead of going to Aleppo . . . because they do not pay as many dues."[3]

Izmir transformed itself between 1580 and 1650 from a small town into a multiethnic, multireligious, multilinguistic entrepôt because of the Ottoman government's inability to control trade and the slowly growing dominance of European traders in the Indian Ocean. Spices from the East, though still traded in Aleppo and other long-established Ottoman centers, were not to be found in Izmir. Aside from Iranian silk brought in by caravan, European traders at Izmir purchased local agricultural products—dried fruits, sesame seeds, nuts, and olive oil. As a consequence, local farmers who previously had grown grain for subsistence shifted their plantings more and more to cotton and other cash crops, including, after its introduction in the 1590s, tobacco, which quickly became popular in the Ottoman Empire despite government prohibitions (see Environment and Technology: Tobacco and Waterpipes). In this way, the agricultural economy of western Anatolia, the Balkans, and the Mediterranean coast—the Ottoman lands most accessible to Europe (see Map 18.1)—became enmeshed in a growing European commercial network.

At the same time, military power slowly ebbed. The ill-trained Janissaries sometimes resorted to hiring substitutes to go on campaign, and the sultans relied on partially trained seasonal recruits and on armies raised by the governors of frontier provinces. A second mighty siege on Vienna failed in 1683, and by the middle of the eighteenth century it was obvious to the Austrians and Russians that the Ottoman Empire was weakening. On the eastern front, however, Ottoman exhaustion after many wars was matched by the demise in 1722 of their perennial adversary, the Safavid state of Iran.

The Ottoman Empire lacked both the wealth and the inclination to match European economic advances. Overland trade from the East dwindled as political disorder in Safavid Iran cut deeply into Iranian silk production. Coffee, an Arabian product that rose from obscurity in the fifteenth century to become the rage first in the Ottoman Empire and

Tobacco and Waterpipes

Tobacco, a plant native to the Western Hemisphere, may have been introduced into Ottoman Syria as early as 1570 and was certainly known in Istanbul by 1600. In Iran, one historian noted that when an Uzbek ruler entered the northeast province of Khurasan in 1612 and called for tobacco, it was quickly provided for him, while a Spanish diplomat remarked just a few years later that Shah Abbas, who had banned smoking as a sinful practice, nevertheless permitted an envoy from the Mughal sultan to indulge. European traders initially brought tobacco by sea, but it quickly became a cultivated crop in Mughal India, whence it was exported to Iran. By the middle of the seventeenth century, however, it had also become a significant crop in Ottoman and Safavid territories.

The waterpipe became a distinctive means of smoking in the Islamic world, but when the device came into use is disputed. Iranian historians assert that it was invented in Iran, where one reference in poetry goes back to before 1550. This early date suggests that waterpipes may have been used for smoking some other substance before tobacco became known. Straight pipes of clay or wood were also used, especially in Turkish areas and among poorer people.

The Persian word for a waterpipe, qalyan, comes from an Arabic verb meaning "to boil, or bubble." Arabic has two common words: nargila, which derives ultimately from the Sanskrit word for "coconut," and shisha, which means "glass" in Persian. In India, where coconuts were often used to contain the water, the usual term was hookah, meaning "jar." The absence of a clear linguistic indication of the country of origin enhances the possibility that waterpipes evolved and spread before the introduction of tobacco.

All levels of society took to smoking, with women enjoying it as much as men. The leisurely ceremony of preparing and lighting the waterpipe made it an ideal pastime in coffeehouses, which became popular in both the Ottoman and Safavid Empires. In other settings, the size and fragility of the waterpipe could cause inconvenience. When traveling, wealthy Iranian men

Iranian Waterpipe Moistened tobacco is placed in cup A, and a glowing coal is put on top of it to make it smolder. When the smoker draws on the stem sticking out to the side, the smoke bubbles up from beneath the water, which cools and filters it. The sophisticated manufacture shown in this drawing, which was rendered in 1622, supports the theory that the waterpipe went through a lengthy period of development before the seventeenth century. From Rudi Matthee, *The Pursuit of Pleasure: Drugs and Stimulants in Iranian History, 1500–1900* [Princeton: Princeton University Press] p. 125

sometimes had a pipe carrier in their entourage who carried the qalyan in his hand and had a small pot containing hot coals dangling from his saddle in case his master should wish to light up on the road.

then in Europe, was grown in the highlands of Yemen and exported by way of Egypt. By 1770, however, Muslim merchants trading in the Yemeni port of Mocha (MOH-kuh) (literally "the coffee place") were charged 15 percent in duties and fees. But European traders, benefiting from long-standing trade agreements with the Ottoman Empire, paid little more than 3 percent.

Such trade agreements, called capitulations, were first granted as favors by powerful sultans, but they eventually led to European domination of Ottoman seaborne trade. Nevertheless, the Europeans did not control strategic ports in the Mediterranean comparable to Malacca in the Indian Ocean and Hormuz on the Persian Gulf, so their economic power stopped short of colonial settlement or direct control in Ottoman territories.

A few astute Ottoman statesmen observed the growing disarray of the empire and advised the sultans to reestablish the land-grant system and the recruitment of Christian boys for the Janissary corps practiced in Suleiman's reign. Most people, however, could not perceive the downward course of imperial power, much less the reasons behind it. Ottoman historians named the period between 1718 and 1730 the **"Tulip Period"** because of the craze for high-priced tulip bulbs that swept Ottoman ruling circles. The craze echoed a Dutch tulip mania that had begun in the mid-sixteenth century, when the flower was introduced into Holland from Istanbul, and had peaked in 1636 with particularly rare bulbs going for 2,500 florins apiece—the value of twenty-two oxen. Far from seeing Europe as the enemy that would eventually dismantle the empire, the Istanbul elite experimented with European clothing and furniture styles and purchased printed books from the empire's first (and short-lived) press.

In 1730, however, gala soirees at which guests watched turtles with candles on their backs wander in the dark through massive tulip beds gave way to a conservative Janissary revolt with strong religious overtones. Sultan Ahmed III abdicated, and the leader of the revolt, Patrona Halil (pa-TROH-nuh ha-LEEL), an Albanian former seaman and stoker of the public baths, swaggered around the capital for several months dictating government policies before he was seized and executed.

SECTION REVIEW

- The Ottoman Empire grew through the skill of its founding rulers, control of strategic territory, and military power.

- The empire expanded into southern and eastern Europe, the Middle East, and Africa, reaching its height under Suleiman the Magnificent.

- Unwilling to build a strong navy, the Ottomans never adapted to developments in the Indian Ocean.

- The empire rested on the military led by the sultan, and changes in military structure ultimately weakened the state.

- As the imperial economy reoriented toward Europe, the central government weakened, permitting the rise of local powers.

The Patrona Halil rebellion confirmed the perceptions of a few that the Ottoman Empire was facing severe difficulties. Yet decay at the center brought benefits elsewhere. In the provinces, ambitious and competent governors, wealthy landholders, urban notables, and nomad chieftains took advantage of the central government's weakness. By the middle of the eighteenth century groups of mamluks had regained a dominant position in Egypt. Though Selim I had defeated the mamluk sultanate in the early sixteenth century, the practice of buying slaves in the Caucasus and training them as soldiers reappeared by the end of the century in several Arab cities. In Baghdad, Janissary commanders and Georgian mamluks competed for power, with the latter emerging triumphant by the mid-eighteenth century. In Aleppo and Damascus, however, the Janissaries came out on top. Meanwhile, in central Arabia, a puritanical Sunni movement inspired by Muhammad ibn Abd al-Wahhab began a remarkable rise beyond the reach of Ottoman power. Although no region declared full independence, the sultan's power was slipping away to the advantage of a broad array of lower officials and upstart chieftains in all parts of the empire while the Ottoman economy was reorienting itself toward Europe.

Tulip Period (1718–1730) Last years of the reign of Ottoman sultan Ahmed III, during which European styles and attitudes became briefly popular in Istanbul.

The Safavid Empire, 1502–1722

How did the Safavid Empire both resemble and differ from its neighbors?

The **Safavid Empire** of Iran (see Map 18.1) resembled its long-time Ottoman foe in many ways: it initially relied militarily on cavalry paid through land grants; its population spoke several different languages; and it was oriented inward away from the sea. It also had distinct qualities that to this day set Iran off from its neighbors: it derived part of its legitimacy from the pre-Islamic dynasties of ancient Iran, and it adopted the Shi'ite form of Islam.

Safavid Society and Religion

The ultimate victor in a complicated struggle for power among Turkish chieftains west of the Ottoman Empire was Ismail (IS-ma-eel), a boy of Kurdish, Iranian, and Greek ancestry. In 1502, at the age of sixteen, Ismail proclaimed himself shah of Iran and declared that from that time forward his realm would be devoted to **Shi'ite** Islam, which revered the family of Muhammad's son-in-law Ali. Although Ismail's reasons for compelling Iran's conversion to Shi'ism are unknown, the effect of this radical act was to create a deep chasm between Iran and its neighbors, all of which were Sunni. Iran became a truly separate country for the first time since its incorporation into the Islamic caliphate in the seventh century.

The imposition of Shi'ite belief made the split permanent, but differences between Iran and its neighbors had long been in the making. Persian, written in the Arabic script from the tenth century onward, had emerged as the second language of Islam. Iranian scholars and writers normally read Arabic as well as Persian and sprinkled their writings with Arabic phrases, but their Arab counterparts were much less inclined to learn Persian. After the Mongols destroyed Baghdad, the capital of the Islamic caliphate, in 1258, Iran developed largely on its own, having more extensive contacts with India—where Muslim rulers favored the Persian language—than with the Arabs.

 Primary Source: Letter to Shah Ismail of Persia Discover why Sultan Selim I, animated by the spirit of a fatwa, launches an attack on Shah Ismail of Persia.

In the post-Mongol period, artistic styles in Iran, Afghanistan, and Central Asia also went their own way. Painted and molded tiles and tile mosaics, often in vivid turquoise blue, became the standard exterior decoration of mosques in Iran but were never used in Syria and Egypt. Persian poets raised verse to peaks of perfection that had no reflection in Arabic poetry, generally considered to be in a state of decline.

To be sure, Islam itself provided a tradition of belief, learning, and law that crossed ethnic and linguistic borders, but Shah Ismail's imposition of Shi'ism set Iran significantly apart. Shi'ite doctrine says that all temporal rulers, regardless of title, are temporary stand-ins for the **"Hidden Imam"**: the twelfth descendant of Ali, the prophet Muhammad's cousin and son-in-law who disappeared as a child in the ninth century. Some Shi'ite scholars concluded that the faithful should calmly accept the world as it was and wait quietly for the Hidden Imam's return. Others maintained that they themselves should play a stronger role in political affairs because they were best qualified to know the Hidden Imam's wishes. These two positions, which still play a role in Iranian Shi'ism, tended to enhance the self-image of religious scholars as independent of imperial authority and stood in the way of their becoming subordinate government functionaries, as happened in the Ottoman Empire.

Shi'ism also affected the psychological life of the people. Annual commemoration of the martyrdom of Imam Husayn (d. 680), Ali's son and the third Imam, regularized an emotional outpouring with no parallel in Sunni lands. Day after day for two weeks, preachers recite the woeful tale to crowds of weeping believers, and elaborate street processions, often organized by craft guilds, paraded chanting and self-flagellating

Safavid Empire Iranian kingdom (1502–1722) established by Ismail Safavi, who declared Iran a Shi'ite state.

Shi'ites Muslims belonging to the branch of Islam that believes that God vests leadership of the community in a descendant of Muhammad's son-in-law Ali. Shi'ism is the state religion of Iran.

Hidden Imam Last in a series of twelve descendants of Muhammad's son-in-law Ali, whom Shi'ites consider divinely appointed leaders of the Muslim community. In occlusion since ca. 873, he is expected to return as a messiah at the end of time.

Aya Sofya Mosque in Istanbul Originally a Byzantine cathedral, Aya Sofya (in Greek, Hagia Sophia) was transformed into a mosque after 1453, and four minarets were added. It then became a model for subsequent Ottoman mosques. To the right behind it is the Bosporus strait dividing Europe and Asia, to the left the Golden Horn inlet separating the old city of Istanbul from the newer parts. The gate to the Ottoman sultan's palace is to the right of the mosque. The pointed tower to the left of the dome is part of the palace.

men past crowds of reverent onlookers. Of course, Shi'ites elsewhere observed rites of mourning for Imam Husayn, but the impact of these rites was especially great in Iran, where 90 percent of the population was Shi'ite. Over time, the subjects of the Safavid shahs came to feel more than ever a people apart.

A Tale of Two Cities: Isfahan and Istanbul

Outwardly, the Ottoman capital of Istanbul looked quite different from Isfahan (is-fah-HAHN), which became Iran's capital in 1598 by decree of **Shah Abbas I** (r. 1587–1629). Built on seven hills on the south side of the narrow Golden Horn inlet, Istanbul boasted a skyline punctuated by the gray stone domes and thin, pointed minarets of the great imperial mosques. The mosques surrounding the royal plaza in Isfahan, in contrast, had unobtrusive minarets and brightly tiled domes that rose to gentle peaks. Whereas high walls surrounded the sultan's palace in Istanbul, Shah Abbas in Isfahan focused his capital on the giant royal plaza, which was large enough for his army to play polo, and he used an airy palace overlooking the plaza to receive dignitaries and review his troops.

The harbor of Istanbul, the primary Ottoman seaport, teemed with sailing ships and smaller craft, many of them belonging to a colony of European merchants perched on a hilltop on the north side of the Golden Horn. Isfahan, far from the sea, was only occasionally visited by Europeans. Most of its trade was in the hands of Jews, Hindus, and especially a colony of Armenian Christians brought in by Shah Abbas.

Beneath these superficial differences, the two capitals had much in common. Wheeled vehicles were scarce in hilly Istanbul and nonexistent in Isfahan. Both cities were built for walking and, aside from the royal plaza in Isfahan, lacked the open spaces common in contemporary European cities. Streets were narrow and irregular, and houses crowded against each other in dead-end lanes. Residents enjoyed their privacy in interior courtyards. Artisans and merchants organized themselves into guilds that had

Shah Abbas I (r. 1587–1629) The fifth and most renowned ruler of the Safavid dynasty in Iran. Abbas moved the royal capital to Isfahan in 1598.

Austrian National Library, Vienna, picture archives

Istanbul Family on the Way to a Bath House Public baths, an important feature of Islamic cities, set different hours for men and women. Young boys, such as the lad in the turban shown here, went with their mothers and sisters. Notice that the children wear the same styles as the adults.

 History in Focus *During the period described in this chapter, bath houses were common in the Ottoman Empire and other parts of the Islamic world, but rare in Christian Europe, even in royal palaces like Versailles. What role did religion play in personal cleanliness? Find the answer online.*

strong social and religious as well as economic bonds and whose shops adjoined each other in the markets.

Women were seldom seen in public, even in Istanbul's mazelike covered market or in Isfahan's long, serpentine bazaar. At home, the women's quarters—called *anderun* (an-deh-ROON), or "interior," in Iran and *harem*, or "forbidden area," in Istanbul—were separate from the public rooms where the men of the family received visitors. In both areas, low cushions, charcoal braziers for warmth, carpets, and small tables constituted most of the furnishings.

The private side of family life has left few traces, but it is apparent that women's society—consisting of wives, children, female servants, and sometimes one or more eunuchs—was not entirely cut off from the outside world. Ottoman court records reveal that women, using male agents, were very active in the urban real estate market. Often they were selling inherited shares of their father's estate, but some both bought and sold

real estate on a regular basis and even established religious endowments for pious purposes. The fact that Islamic law, unlike some European codes, permitted a wife to retain her property after marriage gave some women a stake in the general economy and a degree of independence from their spouses. Women also appeared in other types of court cases, where they often testified for themselves, for Islamic courts did not recognize the role of attorney. Although comparable Safavid court records do not survive, historians assume that a parallel situation prevailed in Iran.

European travelers commented on the veiling of women outside the home, but the norm for both sexes was complete coverage of arms, legs, and hair. Miniature paintings indicate that ordinary female garb consisted of a long, ample dress with a scarf or long shawl pulled tight over the forehead to conceal the hair. Lightweight trousers, either close-fitting or baggy, were often worn under the dress. This mode of dress was not far different from that of men. Poor men wore light trousers, a long shirt, a jacket, and a hat or turban. Wealthier men wore over their trousers ankle-length caftans, often closely fitted around the chest.

Public life was almost entirely the domain of men. Poetry and art, both somewhat more elegantly developed in Isfahan than in Istanbul, were as likely to extol the charms of beardless boys as pretty women. Despite religious disapproval of homosexuality, attachments to adolescent boys were neither unusual nor hidden. Women who appeared in public—aside from non-Muslims, the aged, and the very poor—were likely to be slaves. Miniature paintings frequently depict female dancers, musicians, and even acrobats in attitudes and costumes that range from decorous to decidedly erotic.

Despite social similarities, the overall flavors of Isfahan and Istanbul were not the same. Isfahan had its prosperous Armenian quarter across the river from the city's center, but it was not a truly cosmopolitan capital, just as the peoples of the Safavid realm were not remarkably diverse. Like other rulers of extensive land empires, Shah Abbas located his capital toward the center of his domain within comparatively easy reach of any threatened frontier. Istanbul, in contrast, was a great seaport and a crossroads located on the straits separating the sultan's European and Asian possessions. People of all sorts lived or spent time in Istanbul: Venetians, Genoese, Arabs, Turks, Greeks, Armenians, Albanians, Serbs, Jews, Bulgarians, and more. In this respect, Istanbul conveyed the cosmopolitan character of major seaports from London to Canton (Guangzhou) and belied the fact that its prosperity rested on the vast reach of the sultan's territories rather than on the voyages of its merchants.

Economic Crisis and Political Collapse

The silk fabrics of northern Iran were the mainstay of the Safavid Empire's foreign trade. However, the manufacture that eventually became most powerfully associated with Iran was the deep-pile carpet made by knotting colored yarns around stretched warp threads, work that was often done by women and girls. Different cities produced distinctive carpet designs.

Overall, Iran's manufacturing sector was neither large nor notably productive. Most of the shah's subjects, whether Iranians, Turks, Kurds, or Arabs, lived by subsistence farming or herding. Neither area of activity recorded significant technological advances during the Safavid period.

The Safavids, like the Ottomans, had difficulty finding the money to pay troops armed with firearms. This crisis occurred somewhat later in Iran because of its greater distance from Europe. By the end of the sixteenth century, it was evident that a more systematic adoption of cannon and firearms in the Safavid Empire would be needed to hold off the Ottomans and the Uzbeks (UHZ-bex), Turkish rulers who had succeeded the Timurids on Iran's Central Asian frontier (see Map 18.1). Like the Ottoman cavalry a century earlier, the warriors furnished by the nomad leaders were not inclined to trade in their bows for firearms. Shah Abbas responded by establishing a slave corps of year-round soldiers and arming them with guns. The Christian converts to Islam who initially provided the manpower for the new corps were mostly captives taken in raids on Georgia in the Caucasus (CAW-kuh-suhs).

In the late sixteenth century, the inflation caused by cheap silver spread into Iran; then overland trade through Safavid territory declined because of mismanagement of the silk monopoly after Shah Abbas's death in 1629. As a result, the country faced the

SECTION REVIEW

- The rise of the Shi'ite Safavid Empire completed the long-growing split between Iran and its neighbors.
- Despite significant differences, Istanbul and Isfahan showed some cultural similarities between the Ottoman and Safavid Empires.
- Silks and carpets were important manufactures, but most Safavid subjects made a living by farming or herding.
- High military costs, inflation, and decline of overland trade weakened the state, which fell to Afghan invaders in 1722.

unsolvable problem of finding money to pay the army and bureaucracy. Trying to unseat the nomads from their lands to regain control of taxes was more difficult and more disruptive militarily than the piecemeal dismantlement of the land-grant system in the Ottoman Empire. The nomads were still a cohesive military force, and pressure from the center simply caused them to withdraw to their mountain pastures until the pressure subsided. By 1722, the government had become so weak and commanded so little support from the nomadic groups that an army of marauding Afghans was able to capture Isfahan and effectively end Safavid rule.

The Mughal Empire

How did the Mughal Empire combine Muslim and Hindu elements into an effective state?

What distinguished the Indian empire of the Mughal (MOH-guhl) sultans from the empires of the Ottomans and Safavids was the fact that India was a land of Hindus ruled by a Muslim minority. Muslim dominion in India was the result of repeated military campaigns from the early eleventh century onward, and the Mughals had to contend with the Hindus' long-standing resentment of the destruction of their culture by Muslims. Thus, the challenge facing the Mughals was not just conquering and organizing a large territorial state but also finding a formula for Hindu-Muslim coexistence.

Freer Gallery of Art, Smithsonian Institution, Washington, D.C. Purchase, F1945.9A

Mughal Emperor Jahangir Embracing the Safavid Shah Abbas Painted by the Mughal artist Abu al-Hasan around 1620, this miniature shows the artist's patron, Jahangir, standing on a lion, dominating the diminutive Abbas, standing on a sheep. Though this reflected Jahangir's view of their relationship, in fact Shah Abbas was a powerful rival for control of Afghanistan, the gateway to India. The globe the monarchs stand on shows the spread of accurate geographical information to the Muslim world.

Political Foundations

Babur (BAH-bur) (1483–1530), the founder of the **Mughal Empire**, was a Muslim descendant of both Timur and Genghis Khan (*Mughal* is Persian for "Mongol"). Invading from Central Asia, Babur defeated the last Muslim sultan of Delhi (DEL-ee) in 1526. Babur's grandson **Akbar** (r. 1556–1605), established the central

 Primary Source: Akbarnama Learn about life in the court of Akbar, where arts and customs from conquered lands were routinely presented for the sultan's review.

administration of the expanding state. Under him and his three successors—the last of whom died in 1707—all but the southern tip of India fell under Mughal rule, administered first from Agra and then from Delhi.

Akbar, a brilliant but mercurial man, granted land revenues to military officers and government officials in return for their service. Ranks, called ***mansabs*** (MAN-sabz), some high and some low, entitled their holders to revenue assignments. As in the other Islamic empires, revenue grants were not considered hereditary, and the central government kept careful track of their issuance.

With a population of a 100 million, a thriving trading economy based on cotton cloth, and a generally efficient administration, India under Akbar was probably the most prosperous empire of the sixteenth century. He and his successors faced few external threats and experienced generally peaceful conditions in their northern Indian heartland.

Foreign trade boomed at the port of Surat in the northwest, which also served as an embarkation point for pilgrims on their way to Mecca. Like the Safavids, the Mughals had no navy or merchant ships. The government saw the Europeans—after Akbar's time, primarily Dutch and English, the Portuguese having lost most of their Indian ports—less as enemies than as shipmasters whose naval support could be procured as needed in return for trading privileges.

Hindus and Muslims

The Mughal state inherited traditions of unified imperial rule from both the Islamic caliphate and the more recent examples of Genghis Khan and Timur. Those traditions did not necessarily mean religious intolerance. Seventy percent of the *mansabdars* (man-sab-DAHRZ) (officials holding land revenues) appointed under Akbar were Muslim soldiers born outside India, but 15 percent were Hindus. Most of the Hindu appointees were

Mughal Empire Muslim state (1526–1857) exercising dominion over most of India in the sixteenth and seventeenth centuries.
Akbar (1542–1605) Most illustrious sultan of the Mughal Empire in India (r. 1556–1605). He expanded the empire and pursued a policy of conciliation with Hindus.
mansabs In India, grants of land given in return for service by rulers of the Mughal Empire.

Victoria and Albert Museum, London/The Bridgeman Art Library

Elephants Breaking Bridge of Boats This illustration of an incident in the life of Akbar shows the ability of Mughal miniature painters to depict unconventional action scenes. Because the flow of rivers in India varied greatly from dry to wet season, boat bridges were much more common than permanent constructions.

warriors from the north called **Rajputs** (RAHJ-putz), one of whom rose to be a powerful revenue minister.

Akbar, the most illustrious ruler of his dynasty, differed from his Ottoman and Safavid counterparts—Suleiman the Magnificent and Shah Abbas the Great—in his striving for social harmony and not just for more territory and revenue. His marriage to a Rajput princess signaled his desire for reconciliation and even intermarriage between Muslims and Hindus. The birth of a son in 1569 ensured that future rulers would have both Muslim and Hindu ancestry.

Akbar ruled that in legal disputes between two Hindus, decisions would be made according to village custom or Hindu law as interpreted by local Hindu scholars. Shari'a law was in force for Muslims. Akbar

made himself the legal court of last resort, creating an appeals process not usually present in Islamic jurisprudence.

Akbar also made himself the center of a new "Divine Faith" incorporating Muslim, Hindu, Zoroastrian, Sikh (seek), and Christian beliefs. He was strongly attracted by Sufi ideas, which permeated the religious rituals he instituted at his court. To promote serious consideration of his religious principles, he oversaw, from a catwalk high above the audience, debates among scholars of all religions assembled in his octagonal private audience chamber. When courtiers uttered the Muslim exclamation "Allahu Akbar"—"God is great"—they also understood it in its second grammatical meaning: "God is Akbar."

Akbar's religious views did not survive him, but the court culture he fostered, reflecting a mixture of Muslim and Hindu traditions, flourished until his zealous great-grandson Aurangzeb (ow-rang-ZEB) (r. 1658–1707) reinstituted many restrictions on Hindus. Mughal and Rajput miniature paintings reveled in precise portraits of political figures and depictions of scantily clad women, even though they brought frowns to the faces of pious Muslims, who deplored the representation of human beings. Most of the leading painters were Hindus. In addition to the florid style of Persian verse favored at court, a new taste developed for poetry and prose in the popular language of the Delhi region. The modern descendant of this language is called *Urdu* in Pakistan and *Hindi* in India.

Central Decay and Regional Challenges

Mughal power did not long survive Aurangzeb's death in 1707. Some historians consider the land-grant system a central element in the rapid decline of imperial authority, but other factors were at play as well. Aurangzeb's additions to Mughal territory in southern India were not all well integrated into the imperial structure, and strong regional powers arose to challenge Mughal military supremacy. A climax came in 1739 when Nadir Shah, a warlord who had seized power in Iran after the fall of the Safavids,

Rajputs Members of a mainly Hindu warrior caste from northwest India. The Mughal emperors drew most of their Hindu officials from this caste, and Akbar married a Rajput princess.

- Founded by Babur, the Mughal Empire grew under Akbar and his successors to encompass most of India.

- The empire prospered through trade and granted trade privileges to Europeans in exchange for naval support.

- Akbar included both Muslims and Hindus in his government, respected Hindu customs, and strove for religious harmony.

- A hybrid culture flourished, but Aurangzeb practiced Muslim intolerance.

- After Aurangzeb's death, the empire declined through foreign invasion, the rise of regional powers, and European encroachment.

invaded the Mughal capital and carried off to Iran the "peacock throne," the priceless jewel-encrusted symbol of Mughal grandeur. Another throne was found for the later Mughals to sit on; but their empire, which survived in name to 1857, was finished.

In 1723, Nizam al-Mulk (nee-ZAHM al-MULK), the powerful vizier of the Mughal sultan, gave up on the central government and established his own nearly independent state at Hyderabad in the eastern Deccan. Other officials bearing the title *nawab* (NAH-wab) became similarly independent in Bengal and Oudh (OW-ad) in the northeast, as did the Marathas in the center. In the northwest, simultaneous Iranian and Mughal weakness allowed the Afghans to establish an independent kingdom.

Some of these regional powers, and the smaller princely states that arose on former Mughal territory, were prosperous and benefited from the removal of the sultan's heavy hand. Linguistic and religious communities, freed from the religious intolerance instituted during the reign of Aurangzeb, similarly enjoyed greater opportunity for political expression. However, this disintegration of central power favored the intrusion of European adventurers.

In 1741 Joseph François Dupleix (doo-PLAY) took over the presidency of the French stronghold of Pondicherry (pon-dih-CHER-ree), thus beginning a new phase of European involvement in India. He captured the English trading center of Madras and used his small contingent of European and European-trained Indian troops to become a power broker in southern India. Though offered the title *nawab*, Dupleix preferred to operate behind the scenes,

using Indian princes as puppets. His career ended in 1754 when he was called home. Deeply involved in wars in Europe, the French government was unwilling to pursue further adventures in India. Dupleix's departure opened the way for the British, whose ventures in India are described in Chapter 23.

The Maritime Worlds of Islam, 1500–1750

What role does maritime history play in the political and economic life of this period?

As land powers, the Mughal, Safavid, and Ottoman Empires faced similar problems in the seventeenth and eighteenth centuries. Complex changes in military technology and in the world economy, along with the increasing difficulty of basing an extensive land empire on military forces paid through land grants, affected them all adversely. These difficulties contributed to the often-dynamic development of power centers away from the imperial capital.

The new pressures faced by land powers were less important to seafaring countries intent on turning trade networks into maritime empires. Improvements in ship design, navigation accuracy, and the use of cannon gave an ever-increasing edge to European powers competing with local seafaring peoples. Moreover, the development of joint-stock companies, in which many merchants pooled their capital, provided a flexible and efficient financial instrument for exploiting new possibilities. The English East India Company was founded in 1600; the Dutch East India Company in 1602.

Although the Ottomans, Safavids, and Mughals did not effectively contest the growth of Portuguese and then Dutch, English, and French maritime power, the majority of non-European shipbuilders, captains, sailors, and traders were Muslim. Groups of Armenian, Jewish, and Hindu traders were also active, but they remained almost as aloof from the Europeans as the Muslims did. The presence in every port of Muslims following the same legal traditions and practicing their faith in similar ways cemented the Muslims' trading network. Islam, from its very outset in the life and preaching of Muhammad (570–632), had favored trade and traders. Unlike Hinduism, it was a proselytizing religion, a factor that encouraged the growth of coastal Muslim communities as local non-Muslims associated with Muslim commercial activities converted and intermarried with Muslims from abroad.

Although European missionaries, particularly the Jesuits, tried to extend Christianity into Asia and Africa (see Chapters 15 and 19), most Europeans, the Portuguese excepted, did not treat local converts or the offspring of mixed marriages as full members of their communities. Islam was generally more welcoming. As a consequence, Islam spread extensively into East Africa and Southeast Asia during precisely the same time as rapid European commercial expansion. Even without the support of the Muslim land empires, Islam became a source of resistance to growing European domination.

Muslims in Southeast Asia

Historians disagree about the chronology and manner of Islam's spread in Southeast Asia. Arab traders appeared in southern China as early as the eighth century, so Muslims probably reached the East Indies (the island portions of Southeast Asia) at a similarly early date. Nevertheless, the dominance of Indian cultural influences in the area for several centuries thereafter indicates that early Muslim visitors had little impact on local beliefs. Clearer indications of conversion and the formation of Muslim communities date from roughly the fourteenth century, with the strongest overseas linkage being to the port of Cambay in India (see Map 18.2) rather than to the Arab world. Islam first took root in port cities and in some royal courts and spread inland only slowly, possibly transmitted by itinerant Sufis.

Although appeals to the Ottoman sultan for support against the Europeans ultimately proved futile, Islam strengthened resistance to Portuguese, Spanish, and Dutch intruders. When the Spaniards conquered the Philippines during the decades following the establishment of their first fort in 1565, they encountered Muslims on the southern island of Mindanao (min-duh-NOW) and the nearby Sulu archipelago. They called them "Moros," the Spanish term for their old enemies, the Muslims of North Africa. In the ensuing Moro wars, the Spaniards portrayed the Moros as greedy pirates who raided non-Muslim territories for slaves. In fact, they were political, religious, and commercial competitors whose perseverance enabled them to establish the Sulu Empire based in the southern Philippines, one of the strongest states in Southeast Asia from 1768 to 1848.

Other local kingdoms that looked on Islam as a force to counter the aggressive Christianity of the Europeans included the actively proselytizing Brunei (BROO-nie) Sultanate in northern Borneo and the **Acheh** (AH-cheh) **Sultanate** in northern Sumatra. At its peak in the early seventeenth century, Acheh succeeded Malacca as the main center of Islamic expansion in Southeast Asia. It prospered by trading pepper for cotton cloth from Gujarat in India. Acheh declined after the Dutch seized Malacca from Portugal in 1641.

How well Islam was understood in these Muslim kingdoms is open to question. In Acheh, for example, a series of women ruled between 1641 and 1699. This practice ended when local Muslim scholars obtained a ruling from scholars in Mecca and Medina that Islam did not approve of female rulers. After this ruling, scholarly understandings of Islam gained greater prominence in the East Indies.

Historians have looked at merchants, Sufi preachers, or both as the first propagators of Islam in Southeast Asia. The scholarly vision of Islam, however, took root in the sixteenth century by way of pilgrims returning from years of study in Mecca and Medina. Islam promoted the dissemination of writing in the region. Some of the returning pilgrims wrote in Arabic, others in Malay or Javanese. As Islam continued to spread, *adat* ("custom"), a form of Islam rooted in pre-Muslim religious and social practices, retained its preeminence in rural areas over practices centered on the Shari'a, the religious law. But the royal courts in the port cities began to heed the views of the pilgrim teachers. Though different in many ways, both varieties of Islam provided believers with a firm basis of identification in the face of the growing European presence. Christian missionaries gained most of their converts in regions that had not yet converted to Islam, such as the northern Philippines.

Muslims in Coastal Africa

Muslim rulers also governed the East African ports that the Portuguese began to visit in the fifteenth century, though they were not allied politically (see Map 18.2). People living in the millet and rice

Acheh Sultanate Muslim kingdom in northern Sumatra. Main center of Islamic expansion in Southeast Asia in the early seventeenth century, it declined after the Dutch seized Malacca from Portugal in 1641.

Map 18.2 European Colonization in the Indian Ocean, to 1750 Since Portuguese explorers were the first Europeans to reach India by rounding Africa, Portugal gained a strong foothold in both areas. Rival Spain was barred from colonizing the region by the Treaty of Tordesillas in 1494, which limited Spanish efforts to lands west of a line drawn through the mid-Atlantic Ocean. The line carried around the globe provided justification of Spanish colonization in the Philippines. French, British, and Dutch colonies date from after 1600, when joint-stock companies provided a new stimulus for overseas commerce. © Cengage Learning

 Interactive Map

lands of the Swahili Coast—from the Arabic *sawahil* (suh-WAH-hil) meaning "coasts"—had little contact with those in the dry hinterlands. Throughout this period, the East African lakes region and the highlands of Kenya witnessed unprecedented migration and relocation of peoples because of drought conditions that persisted from the late sixteenth through most of the seventeenth century.

Cooperation among the trading ports of Kilwa, Mombasa, and Malindi was hindered by the thick bush country that separated the cultivated tracts of coastal land and by the fact that the ports competed with one another in the export of ivory, ambergris (AM-ber-grees) (a whale byproduct used in perfumes), and forest products such as beeswax, copal tree resin, and wood. Kilwa also exported gold. In the eighteenth

Portuguese Fort Guarding Musqat Harbor Musqat in Oman and Aden in Yemen, the best harbors in southern Arabia, were targets for imperial navies trying to establish dominance in the Indian Ocean. Musqat's harbor is small and circular, with one narrow entrance overlooked by this fortress. The palace of the sultan of Oman is still located at the opposite end of the harbor.

century slave trading, primarily to Arabian ports but also to India, increased in importance. Because Europeans—the only peoples who kept consistent records of slave-trading activities—played a minor role in this slave trade, few records have survived to indicate its extent. Perhaps the best estimate is that 2.1 million slaves were exported between 1500 and 1890, a little over 12.5 percent of the total traffic in African slaves during that period (see Chapter 17).

The Portuguese conquered all the coastal ports from Mozambique northward except Malindi, with whose ruler Portugal cooperated. A Portuguese description of the ruler names some of the cloth and metal goods that Malindi imported, as well as some local manufactures:

> The King wore a robe of damask trimmed with green satin and a rich [cap]. He was seated on two cushioned chairs of bronze, beneath a rough sunshade of crimson satin attached to a pole. An old man, who attended him as a page, carried a short sword in a silver sheath. There were many players on [horns], and two trumpets of ivory richly carved and of the size of a man, which were blown through a hole in the side, and made sweet harmony with the [horns].[4]

Initially, the Portuguese favored the port of Malindi, which caused the decline of Kilwa and Mombasa.

Repeatedly plagued by local rebellion, Portuguese power suffered severe blows when the Arabs of **Oman** in southeastern Arabia captured their south Arabian stronghold at Musqat (1650) and then went on to seize Mombasa (1698), which had become the Portuguese capital in East Africa. The Portuguese briefly retook Mombasa but lost control permanently in 1729. From then on, the Portuguese had to content themselves with Mozambique in East Africa and a few remaining ports in India (Goa) and farther east (Macao and Timor).

The Omanis created a maritime empire of their own, one that worked in greater cooperation with the African populations. The Bantu language of the coast, broadened by the absorption of Arabic, Persian, and Portuguese loanwords, developed into **Swahili** (swah-HEE-lee), which was spoken throughout the region. Arabs and other Muslims who settled in the region intermarried with local families, giving rise to

Oman Arab state based in Musqat, the main port in the southeastern region of the Arabian Peninsula. Oman succeeded Portugal as a power in the western Indian Ocean in the eighteenth century.
Swahili Bantu language with Arabic loanwords spoken in coastal regions of East Africa.

451

a mixed population that played an important role in developing a distinctive Swahili culture.

Islam also spread in the southern Sudan in this period, particularly in the dry areas away from the Nile River. This growth coincided with a waning of Ethiopian power as a result of Portugal's stifling of trade in the Red Sea. Yet no significant contact developed between the emerging Muslim Swahili culture and that of the Muslims in the Sudan to the north.

In northwest Africa the seizure by Portugal and Spain of coastal strongholds in Morocco provoked a militant response. The Sa'adi family, which claimed descent from the Prophet Muhammad, led a resistance to Portuguese aggression that climaxed in victory at the battle of al-Qasr al-Kabir (Ksar el Kebir) in 1578. The triumphant Moroccan sultan, Ahmad al-Mansur, restored his country's strength and independence. By the early seventeenth century naval expeditions from the port of Salé, referred to in British records as "the Sally Rovers," raided European shipping as far as Britain itself.

Corsairs, or sea raiders, working out of Algerian, Tunisian, and Libyan ports brought the same sort of warfare to the Mediterranean. European governments called these Muslim raiders pirates and slave-takers, and they leveled the same charges against other Muslim mariners in the Persian Gulf and the Sulu Sea. But there was little distinction between the actions of the Muslims and of their European adversaries.

European Powers in Southern Seas

The Dutch played a major role in driving the Portuguese from their possessions in the East Indies. They were better organized than the Portuguese through the Dutch East India Company. Just as the Portuguese had tried to dominate the trade in spices, so the Dutch concentrated at first on the spice-producing islands of Southeast Asia. The Portuguese had seized Malacca, a strategic town on the narrow strait at the end of the Malay Peninsula, from a local Malay ruler in 1511 (see Chapter 15). The Dutch took it away from them in 1641, leaving Portugal little foothold in the East Indies except the islands of Ambon (am-BOHN) and Timor (see Map 18.2).

Although the United Netherlands was one of the least autocratic countries of Europe, the

SECTION REVIEW

- From its inception in the time of Muhammad, Islam flowered in places of trade, and beginning around 1500, the majority of non-European shipbuilders, captains, sailors, and traders were Muslim.

- A number of local kingdoms in Southeast Asia took on Islam as a force to resist the aggressive Christianity of the Europeans.

- Many Muslims in coastal Africa intermarried with locals, creating a mixed population that played a key part in the development of a distinctive Swahili culture.

- Over time the successes of European trading companies changed the balance of power in the southern seas, but local merchants never completely disappeared from the commercial scene.

governors-general appointed by the Dutch East India Company deployed almost unlimited powers in their efforts to maintain their trade monopoly. They could even order the execution of their own employees for "smuggling"—that is, trading on their own. Under strong governors-general, the Dutch fought a series of wars against Acheh and other local kingdoms on Sumatra and Java. In 1628 and 1629 their new capital at **Batavia**, now the city of Jakarta on Java, was besieged by a fleet of fifty ships belonging to the sultan of Mataram (MAH-tah-ram), a Javanese kingdom. The Dutch held out with difficulty and eventually prevailed when the sultan was unable to get effective help from the English.

Suppressing local rulers, however, was not enough to control the spice trade once other European countries adopted Dutch methods, learned more about where goods might be acquired, and started to send more ships to Southeast Asia. In the course of the eighteenth century, therefore, the Dutch gradually turned from being middlemen between Southeast Asian producers and European buyers to producing crops in areas they controlled, notably in Java.

Batavia Fort established ca. 1619 as headquarters of Dutch East India Company operations in Indonesia; today the city of Jakarta.

Javanese teak forests yielded high-quality lumber, and coffee, transplanted from Yemen, grew well in the western hilly regions. In this new phase of colonial export production, Batavia developed from being the headquarters town of a far-flung enterprise to being the administrative capital of a conquered land.

Beyond the East Indies, the Dutch utilized their discovery of a band of powerful eastward-blowing winds (called the "Roaring Forties" because they blow throughout the year between 40 and 50 degrees south latitude) to reach Australia in 1606. In 1642 and 1643 Abel Tasman became the first European to set foot on Tasmania and New Zealand and to sail around Australia, signaling European involvement in that region (see Chapter 23).

Conclusion

The period 1500 to 1750 saw a remarkable shift in the relative positions of Europe and the three great Islamic empires. In the 1500s, the Ottoman, Safavid, and Mughal Empires were powerful and prosperous, with seemingly invincible military forces. The Ottomans in particular seemed on the verge of conquering most of the Middle East and large parts of Europe. Outside of the Americas, Europeans at the time were successful only at sea. What few land areas they acquired—ports where they built warehouses and forts—were tolerated by the regional powers because of the trade they brought.

By 1750, the three Islamic empires were growing weaker as the Europeans grew stronger. How can we account for this shift? Partly, the answer lies in the internal weaknesses of the Muslim empires. Their tax base shrank even as their military expenses mounted. Their armed forces, based on foreigners or independent-minded tribesmen, grew more assertive and less trustworthy. Rebellions weakened the power of the state. And finally, a series of incompetent rulers prevented reforms.

But another reason is the competitive nature of European societies. Frequent conflicts between the European kingdoms hastened military innovations; as France, Britain, and the Netherlands grew stronger at the expense of Spain and Portugal, their rivalries spilled over into competition for overseas colonies. Private enterprises such as the East and West India Companies obtained state support for ventures in distant waters. Increased shipping and naval warfare caused the technologies of shipbuilding, navigation, and naval gunnery to advance rapidly. And finally, the wealth of the Americas, especially silver, benefited the more commercial-minded states of Europe at the expense of traditional land-based states.

These changes did not result in an immediate shift in the balance of power between Europe and the Muslim empires, however. People living in 1750 would not have been able to predict whether advancing Arabs or Mongols or Ottomans would again threaten Europe as in the past, or whether the maritime powers of Europe would overtake the land-based empires of Asia.

CHAPTER REVIEW

 Download the MP3 audio file of the Chapter Review to listen to on the go.

How did the Ottoman Empire rise to power, and what factors contributed to its transformation? (page 434)

Strategic location and a centralized army well balanced between mounted bowmen and an infantry armed with gunpowder weapons were keys to Ottoman success during the empire's first two centuries. With territorial growth, however, the borders became too distant from the capital for the efficient deployment of a centralized army, and economic pressures, notably those associated with a flood of cheap silver from the New World, forced modifications in the ruling system. Military, and increasingly political, power devolved to commanders and governors in provincial capitals and border districts, while new fiscal arrangements captured more tax revenue for the central government and the Istanbul elite.

How did the Safavid Empire both resemble and differ from its neighbors? (page 442)

The Safavid Empire embodied some of the same Turkish tribal traditions and Islamic governing institutions that were found among the Ottomans, but the formal adoption of Shi'ism as the state religion at the beginning of the sixteenth century created such a gulf between them that these similarities were seldom recognized. In some respects, such as their practice of using Christian prisoners of war as infantry, the Safavids followed the Ottoman lead. By contrast, the Mughals drew military forces from Central Asia and Afghanistan and adopted Persian as the language of government but never enjoyed the religious and cultural homogeneity that was a hallmark of Safavid Iran.

How did the Mughal Empire combine Muslim and Hindu elements into an effective state? (page 445)

Dealing with the Hindu majority in their domain was a continuing problem for the Mughal rulers. Akbar took the path of accommodation by appointing Hindu officials and trying to harmonize religious differences. Aurangzeb, his great-grandson, took the opposite path of persecuting Hindus and exalting Islam. Both rulers enjoyed military success against various Indian adversaries, but neither hit on a formula that would permanently bridge the gap between the Muslim ruling minority and the non-Muslim majority. Nevertheless, by comparison with most earlier Indian states, and measured by the problems and successes of the contemporary Ottoman and Safavid realms, Mughal rule must be deemed effective.

What role does maritime history play in the political and economic life of this period? (page 448)

Muslim rulers who saw greater opportunities and dangers along imperial land frontiers than at sea saw nothing threatening in the vigorous commercial activity of the non-Muslim merchants in their realms—Jews, Christians, and Hindus—or even the European trading companies. To be sure, the Ottoman navy was a formidable military force in the Mediterranean, and Muslim rulers in Morocco, Oman, and Southeast Asia sometimes reacted effectively to European maritime pressure. But the greatest battles were fought on land, and acquisition or loss of territory was taken by Muslims and non-Muslims alike as a more important sign of an empire's strength than its command of maritime trade routes. Over time, the economic gains made by the European trading companies changed the balance of power in the region, but local merchants never disappeared from the commercial scene, either as maritime traders or as manufacturers producing goods like Indian cotton cloth for export.

Key Terms

Ottoman Empire (p. 434)	Mughal Empire (p. 446)
Suleiman the Magnificent (p. 436)	Akbar (p. 446)
	mansabs (p. 446)
Janissaries (p. 437)	Rajputs (p. 447)
Tulip Period (p. 441)	Acheh Sultanate (p. 449)
Safavid Empire (p. 442)	Oman (p. 451)
Shi'ites (p. 442)	Swahili (p. 451)
Hidden Imam (p. 442)	Batavia (p. 452)
Shah Abbas I (p. 443)	

Web Resources

Pronunciation Guide

Interactive Maps

- MAP 18.1 Muslim Empires in the Sixteenth and Seventeenth Centuries
- MAP 18.2 European Colonization in the Indian Ocean, to 1750

Primary Sources

- Letter to Shah Ismail of Persia
- Akbarnama

Answer to the History in Focus Question

See photo on page 444, "Istanbul Family on the Way to a Bath House."

Visit the CourseMate website at www.cengagebrain.com for additional study tools and review materials for this chapter.

Northern Eurasia

© Cengage Learning

CHAPTER PREVIEW

Japanese Reunification
How did Japan respond to domestic social changes and the challenges posed by contact with foreign cultures?

The Later Ming and Early Qing Empires
How did China deal with military and political challenges both inside and outside its borders?

The Russian Empire
To what extent was Russia's expanding empire influenced by relations with western Europe in this period?

Conclusion

MATERIAL CULTURE: Four-Wheeled Vehicles

Visit the CourseMate website at **www.cengagebrain.com** for additional study tools and review materials for this chapter.

In the seventeenth century, the Ming dynasty in China was threatened by Manchu armies from Manchuria in the northeast. To pay the army defending Beijing (bay-JING), the emperor slashed the government payroll. Among those thrown out of his job as an apprentice ironworker was one Li Zicheng (lee ZUH-cheng). By 1630 Li Zicheng had found work as a soldier, but he and his fellow soldiers mutinied when the government failed to provide needed supplies. A natural leader, Li soon headed several thousand Chinese rebels. In 1635 he and other rebel leaders gained control over much of north central China.

Wedged between the Manchu armies to the north and the rebels to the southwest, the Ming government tottered. Li Zicheng's forces began to move toward Beijing, along the way conscripting young men from captured towns into their army. The rebels promised to end the abuses of the Ming and restore peace and prosperity. In April 1644 Li's forces took over Beijing without a fight. The last Ming emperor hanged himself in the palace garden, bringing to an end the dynasty that had ruled China since 1368.

Victory was short-lived, however. Fearful of uneducated, violent men like Li ruling the land, the Ming general Wu Sangui joined forces with the **Manchus**. Li had incidentally captured one of the general's favorite concubines and taken her for himself. Together Wu and the Manchus retook Beijing in June. Li's forces scattered, and a year later he was dead, either a suicide or beaten to death by peasants whose food he tried to steal.[1]

Meanwhile, the Manchus made it clear that they were the new masters of China. They installed their young sovereign as emperor and over the next two decades hunted down the last of the Ming loyalists and heirs to the throne.

China was not the only state in northern Eurasia facing foreign threats and uprisings from within. In the period from 1500 to 1800 Japan and Russia experienced similar turbulence as they underwent massive political change and economic growth. Besides challenges from nearby neighbors, the three also faced new contacts and challenges from the growing commercial and military power of European states.

Japanese Reunification

How did Japan respond to domestic social changes and the challenges posed by contact with foreign cultures?

Like China and Russia in the centuries between 1500 and 1800, Japan experienced three major changes: internal and external military conflicts, political growth and strengthening, and expanded commercial and cultural contacts. Japan's culturally homogenous population, natural boundaries, and smaller size made the process of political unification shorter than in the great empires of China and Russia. Japan also differed in its responses to new contacts with western Europeans.

Civil War and the Invasion of Korea, 1500–1603

In the twelfth century different parts of Japan had fallen under the rule of warlords known as *daimyo* (DIE mee-oh) (see Chapter 12). Each daimyo had a castle town, a small bureaucracy, and a band of warriors, the *samurai* (SAH-moo-rye). The daimyo pledged a loose allegiance to the Japanese emperor residing in the capital city of Kyoto (KYOH-toh) and to the shogun, the hereditary chief of the emperor's government and armies. But neither figure held significant political power.

Warfare among the different daimyo was common, and in the late 1500s it culminated in a prolonged civil war. The warlord to emerge was Hideyoshi (HEE-duh-YOH-shee). In 1592, buoyed with his success in Japan, the supremely confident Hideyoshi invaded the Asian mainland with 160,000 men. His apparent intention was not just to conquer the Korean peninsula but also to make himself emperor of China.

Manchu Federation of Northeast Asian peoples who founded the Qing Empire.

daimyo Literally, "great name(s)." Japanese warlords and great landowners, whose armed samurai gave them control of the Japanese islands from the eighth to the later nineteenth century. Under the Tokugawa Shogunate they were subordinated to the imperial government.

samurai Literally, "those who serve"; the hereditary military elite of the Tokugawa Shogunate.

Chronology

	Korea and Japan	China and Central Asia	Russia
1500	**1543** First Portuguese contacts	**1517** Portuguese embassy to China	**1547** Ivan IV adopts title of tsar **1582** Russians conquer Khanate of Sibir
1600	**1592** Japanese invasion of Korea **1603** Tokugawa Shogunate formed **1633–1639** Edicts close down trade with Europe	**1601** Matteo Ricci allowed to reside in Beijing **1644** Qing conquest of Beijing	**1613–1645** Rule of Mikhail, the first Romanov tsar **1649** Subordination of serfs complete
		1662–1722 Rule of Emperor Kangxi **1689** Treaty of Nerchinsk with Russia **1691** Qing control of Inner Mongolia	**1689–1725** Rule of Peter the Great
1700	**1702** Trial of the Forty-Seven Ronin		**1712** St. Petersburg becomes Russia's capital
		1736–1796 Rule of Emperor Qianlong	**1762–1796** Rule of Catherine the Great
	1792 Russian ships first spotted off the coast of Japan		**1799** Alaska becomes a Russian colony

The Korean and Japanese languages are closely related, but the dominant influence on Korean culture had long been China, to which Korean rulers generally paid tribute. In many ways the Yi dynasty that ruled Korea from 1392 to 1910 was a model Confucian state. Although Korea had developed its own system of writing in 1443 and made extensive use of printing with movable type from the fifteenth century on, most printing continued to use Chinese characters.

Against Hideyoshi's invaders the Koreans employed all the technological and military skill for which the Yi period was renowned. Ingenious covered warships, or "turtle boats," intercepted a portion of the Japanese fleet. The mentally unstable Hideyoshi countered with brutal punitive measures as his armies advanced through the Korean peninsula and into the Chinese province of Manchuria. However, after Hideyoshi's death in 1598, the other Japanese military leaders withdrew their forces, and the Japanese government made peace in 1606.

The invasion devastated Korea. In the turmoil after the Japanese withdrawal, the Korean *yangban* (nobility) were able to lay claim to so much taxpaying land that royal revenues may have fallen by two-thirds. China, however, suffered even more dire consequences. The battles in Manchuria weakened Chinese garrisons there, permitting Manchu opposition to consolidate. Manchu forces invaded Korea in the 1620s and eventually compelled the Yi to become a tributary state. As already related, the Manchus were in possession of Beijing, China's capital, by 1644.

The Tokugawa Shogunate, to 1800

After Hideyoshi's demise, Tokugawa Ieyasu (TOH-koo-GAH-wah ee-ay-YAH-soo) (1543–1616) asserted his domination over other daimyo and in 1603 established a new military government known as the **Tokugawa Shogunate**. The shoguns created a new administrative capital at Edo (ED-oh) (now Tokyo). Trade along the well-maintained road between Edo and the imperial capital of Kyoto promoted the development of the Japanese economy and the formation of other trading centers (see Map 19.1).

The Tokugawa Shogunate gave Japan more political unity than the islands had seen in centuries, but the regionally based daimyo still had a great deal of power and autonomy. Although Ieyasu and his successors worked hard to keep the political system from disintegrating, economic integration was more a feature of Tokugawa Japan than political centralization. Because shoguns required the daimyo to visit Edo frequently, good roads and maritime transport linked the city to the castle towns on three of Japan's four main islands. Commercial traffic developed along these routes. The shogun paid the lords in rice, and the lords in turn used rice to pay their followers. Recipients converted much of this rice into cash, a practice that led to the development of rice exchanges at Edo and at Osaka (OH-sah-kah), where merchants speculated in rice prices. By the late seventeenth century Edo was one of the largest cities in the world, with nearly a million inhabitants.

The domestic peace of the Tokugawa era forced the warrior class to adapt itself to the growing bureaucratic needs of the state. As the samurai became better educated and more attuned to the tastes of the civil elite, they became important customers for merchants dealing in silks, *sake* (SAH-kay) (rice wine), fans, porcelain, lacquer ware, books, and moneylending. The state attempted—unsuccessfully—to curb the independence of the merchants when the economic well-being of the samurai was threatened by low rice prices or high interest rates.

The 1600s and 1700s were centuries of high achievement in artisanship, and Japanese skills in steel making, pottery, and lacquer ware were joined by excellence in the production and decoration of porcelain, thanks in no small part to Korean experts brought back to Japan after the invasion of 1592. In the early 1600s manufacturers and merchants amassed enormous family fortunes. Several of the most important industrial and financial enterprises—for instance, the Mitsui (MIT-soo-ee) companies—had their origins in sake breweries of the early Tokugawa period and then branched out into manufacturing, finance, and transport.

Wealthy merchants weakened the Tokugawa policy of controlling commerce by cultivating close alliances with their regional daimyo and, if possible, with the shogun himself. By the end of the 1700s the merchant families of Tokugawa Japan held the key to future modernization and the development of heavy industry.

Japan and the Europeans

Direct contacts with Europeans presented Japan with new opportunities and problems. Within thirty years of the arrival of the first Portuguese in 1543, the daimyo were fighting with Western-style firearms, copied and improved upon by Japanese armorers.

The Japanese welcomed but closely regulated traders from Portugal, Spain, the Netherlands, and England. Aside from the brief boom in porcelain exports in the seventeenth century, few Japanese goods went to Europe, and not much from Europe found a market in Japan. The Japanese sold the Dutch copper and silver, which the Dutch exchanged in

Primary Source: Some Observations on Merchants Discover what happens to merchants who try to trick samurai.

Tokugawa Shogunate (1603–1868) The last of the three shogunates of Japan.

China for silks that they then resold in Japan. The Japanese, of course, had their own trade with China.

Portuguese and Spanish merchant ships also brought Catholic missionaries. One of the first, Francis Xavier, had spent time in India in the mid-sixteenth century looking for converts and later traveled throughout Southeast and East Asia. He spent two years in Japan and died in 1552, hoping to gain entry to China. Japanese responses to Xavier and other Jesuits were decidedly mixed. Many ordinary Japanese found the new faith deeply meaningful, but the Japanese elite more often opposed it as disruptive and foreign. By 1580 more than 100,000 Japanese had become Christians, and one daimyo gave Jesuit missionaries the port city of Nagasaki (NAH-guh-SAHK-kee). In 1613 Date Masamune (DAH-tay mah-suh-MOO-nay), the fierce and independent daimyo of northern Honshu (HOHN-shoo), sent his own embassy to the Vatican by way of the Philippines (where there were significant communities of Japanese merchants and pirates) and Mexico City. Some daimyo converts ordered their subjects to become Christians as well.

By the early seventeenth century there were some 300,000 Japanese Christians and even some Japanese priests. However, suspicions about the intentions of the Europeans and their well-armed ships turned the new shogunate in Edo into a center of hostility toward Christianity. A decree issued in 1614 banned Christianity and charged its adherents with seeking to overthrow true doctrine, change the government, and seize the country. Some missionaries left Japan; others worked underground. The government began persecutions in earnest in 1617, and the beheadings, crucifixions, and forced recantations over the next several decades destroyed almost the entire Christian community.

To keep Christianity from resurfacing, a series of decrees issued between 1633 and 1639 sharply curtailed trade with Europe. Europeans who entered illegally faced the death penalty. Japanese subjects were required to produce certificates from Buddhist temples attesting to their religious orthodoxy and loyalty to the regime. However, the exclusion of Europe was not total. A few Dutch were permitted to reside on a small artificial island in Nagasaki's harbor, and a few Japanese were licensed to supply their needs. What these intermediaries learned about European weapons technology, shipbuilding, mathematics and astronomy, anatomy and medicine, and geography was termed "Dutch studies."

Tokugawa restrictions on the number of Chinese ships that could trade in Japan were harder to enforce. Regional lords in northern and southern Japan not only pursued overseas trade and piracy but also claimed dominion over islands between Japan and Korea and southward toward Taiwan, including present-day Okinawa. Despite such evasions, the new shogunate unquestionably achieved substantial success in exercising its authority.

Elite Decline and Social Crisis

During the 1700s population growth put a great strain on the well-developed lands of central Japan. In more remote provinces, where the lords promoted new settlements and agricultural expansion, the rate of economic growth was significantly greater.

Also troubling the Tokugawa government in the 1700s was its inability to stabilize rice prices and halt the economic decline of the samurai. The Tokugawa government realized that the rice brokers could manipulate rice prices and interest rates to enrich themselves at the expense of the samurai, who had to convert their rice allotments into cash. Early Tokugawa laws designed to regulate interest and prices were later supplemented by laws requiring moneylenders to forgive samurai debts. But these laws were not always enforced. By the early 1700s many lords and samurai were dependent on the willingness of merchants to provide credit.

The legitimacy of the Tokugawa shoguns rested on their ability to reward and protect the interests of the lords and samurai who had supported their rise to power. Moreover, the Tokugawa government, like the governments of China, Korea, and Vietnam, accepted the Confucian idea that agriculture should be the basis of state wealth and that merchants, who were considered morally weak, should occupy lowly positions in society. Tokugawa decentralization, however, not only failed to hinder but actually stimulated the growth of commercial activities. From the founding of the Tokugawa Shogunate in 1603 until 1800, the economy grew faster than the population. Household amenities and cultural resources that in China appeared only in the cities were common in the

Woodblock Print of the "Forty-Seven Ronin"
Story The saga of the forty-seven ronin and the avenging of their fallen leader has fascinated the Japanese public since the event occurred in 1702. This watercolor from the Tokugawa period shows the leaders of the group pausing on the snowy banks of the Sumida River in Edo (Tokyo) before storming their enemy's residence.

SECTION REVIEW

- From the civil war among the daimyo emerged Hideyoshi, who, as supreme warlord, invaded Korea and China.

- After Hideyoshi's death, Tokugawa Ieyasu established the Tokugawa Shogunate, with its capital at Edo.

- The Tokugawa shoguns provided political unity and fostered economic expansion but failed to control commerce.

- The Japanese engaged in regulated trade with Europeans, but rising suspicions caused the Tokugawa shoguns to persecute Christians and restrict foreign contacts.

- Economic growth nourished a new merchant-class culture, but the position of the samurai deteriorated under economic and social pressures.

Japanese countryside. Despite official disapproval, merchants enjoyed relative freedom and influence in eighteenth-century Japan. They produced a vivid culture of their own, fostering the development of *kabuki* theater, colorful woodblock prints and silk-screened fabrics, and restaurants.

The "Forty-Seven Ronin" (ROH-neen) incident of 1701–1703 exemplified the ideological and social crisis of Japan's transformation from a military into a civil society. A senior minister provoked a young daimyo into drawing his sword at the shogun's court. For this offense the young lord was sentenced to commit *seppuku* (SEP-poo-koo), the ritual suicide of the samurai. His own followers then became *ronin*, "masterless samurai," obliged by the traditional code of the warrior to avenge their deceased master. They broke into the house of the senior minister and killed him and others in his household. Then they withdrew to a temple in Edo and notified the shogun of what they had done out of loyalty to their lord and to avenge his death.

A legal debate ensued. To deny the righteousness of the ronin would be to deny samurai values. But to approve their actions would create social chaos,

undermine laws against murder, and deny the shogunal government the right to try cases of samurai violence. The shogun ruled that the ronin had to die but would be permitted to die honorably by committing seppuku. Traditional samurai values had to surrender to the supremacy of law. The purity of purpose of the ronin is still celebrated in Japan, but since then Japanese writers, historians, and teachers have recognized that the self-sacrifice of the ronin for the sake of upholding civil law was necessary.

The Later Ming and Early Qing Empires

How did China deal with military and political challenges both inside and outside its borders?

Like Japan, China after 1500 experienced civil and foreign wars, an important change in government, and new trading and cultural relations with Europe and its neighbors. The internal and external forces at work in China were different and operated on a much larger scale, but they led in similar directions. By 1800 China had a greatly enhanced empire, an expanding economy, and growing doubts about the benefits of European trade and Christianity.

The Ming Empire, 1500–1644

The economic and cultural achievements of the early **Ming Empire** (see Chapter 12) continued during the 1500s. But this productive period was followed by many decades of political weakness, warfare, and rural woes until a new dynasty, the Qing (ching) from Manchuria, guided China back to peace and prosperity.

The Europeans whose ships began to seek out new contacts with China in the early sixteenth century left many accounts of their impressions. They were astonished at Ming China's imperial power, exquisite manufactures, and vast population. European merchants bought such large quantities of the high-grade blue-on-white porcelain commonly used by China's upper classes that in English all fine dishes became known simply as "china."

The growing integration of China into the world economy stimulated rapid growth in the silk, cotton, and porcelain industries. Agricultural regions that supplied raw materials to these industries and food for the expanding urban populations also prospered. In exchange for Chinese exports, tens of thousands of tons of silver from Japan and Latin America flooded into China in the century before 1640. The influx of silver led many Chinese to substitute payments in silver for land taxes, labor obligations, and other kinds of dues.

Ming cities had long been culturally and commercially vibrant. Many large landowners and absentee landlords lived in town, as did officials, artists, and rich merchants who had purchased ranks or prepared their sons for the examinations. The elite classes had created a brilliant culture in which novels, operas, poetry, porcelain, and painting were all closely interwoven. Small businesses catering to the urban elites prospered through printing, tailoring, running restaurants, or selling paper, ink, ink-stones, and writing brushes. Enormous government factory complexes at Jingdezhen and elsewhere invented assembly-line techniques and produced large quantities of silk and high-quality ceramics for sale in China and abroad.

Chinese Export Ware Though Europe developed its own porcelain industry, dishes from China continued to command a large market. Some, like the one depicted here, featured Chinese interpretations of European landscapes and patterns.   © Christie's Images Ltd.

Despite these achievements, serious problems developed that left the Ming Empire economically and politically exhausted. There is evidence that the climate changes known as the Little Ice Age in seventeenth-century Europe affected the climate in China as well. Annual temperatures dropped, reached a low point about 1645, and remained low until the early 1700s. The resulting agricultural distress and famine fueled large uprisings that speeded the end of the Ming Empire.

The rapid urban growth and business speculation that were part of the burgeoning of the trading economy also produced problems. Some provinces suffered from price inflation caused by the flood of silver. In contrast to the growing involvement of European governments in promoting economic growth, the Ming government pursued some policies that hindered growth. Despite the fact that earlier experiments with

Ming Empire Empire based in China that Zhu Yuan-zhang established in 1368 after the overthrow of the Yuan Empire. The Ming emperor Yongle sponsored additions to the Forbidden City and the voyages of Zheng He. The later years of the Ming saw a slowdown in technological development and economic decline. The empire was overthrown in 1644.

paper currency had failed, Ming governments persisted in issuing new paper money and copper coinage, even after abundant supplies of silver had won the approval of the markets. Corruption was also a serious government problem. By the end of the Ming period disorder and inefficiency plagued the imperial factories, touching off strikes in the late sixteenth and seventeenth centuries. During a labor protest at Jingdezhen in 1601, workers threw themselves into the kilns to protest working conditions.

Yet the urban and industrial sectors of later Ming society fared much better than the agricultural sector, which failed to maintain the strong growth of early Ming times. Despite knowledge of new African and American crops gained from European traders, farmers were slow to change their ways. Neither the rice-growing regions in southern China nor the wheat-growing regions in northern China experienced a meaningful increase in productivity under the later Ming. After 1500 economic depression in the countryside, combined with recurring epidemics in central and southern China, kept rural population growth in check.

Ming Collapse and the Rise of the Qing

Although these environmental, economic, and administrative problems existed, the primary reasons for the fall of the Ming Empire were internal rebellion and rising Manchu power. Insecure boundaries had been a recurrent peril.

Map 19.1 The Qing Empire, 1644–1783 The Qing Empire began in Manchuria and captured north China in 1644. Between 1644 and 1783 the Qing conquered all the former Ming territories and added Taiwan, the lower Amur River Basin, Inner Mongolia, eastern Turkestan, and Tibet. The resulting state was more than twice the size of the Ming Empire.   © Cengage Learning

Interactive Map

The Ming had long been under pressure from the powerful Mongol federations of the north and west. In the late 1500s large numbers of Mongols were unified by their devotion to the Dalai Lama (DAH-lie LAH-mah), or universal teacher of Tibetan Buddhism. Building on this spiritual unity, a brilliant leader named Galdan restored Mongolia as a regional military power around 1600. The Manchus, an agricultural people who controlled the region north of Korea, grew stronger in the northeast.

In the southwest, native peoples repeatedly resisted the immigration of Chinese farmers. Pirates based in Okinawa and Taiwan, many of them Japanese, frequently looted the southeast coast. Ming military resources, concentrated against the Mongols and the Manchus in the north, could not be deployed to defend the coasts. As a result, many southern Chinese migrated to Southeast Asia to profit from the sea-trading networks of the Indian Ocean.

The Japanese invasion of 1592 to 1598 described earlier prompted the Ming to seek the assistance of Manchu troops that they were then unable to restrain. With the rebel leader Li Zicheng in possession of Beijing and the emperor dead by his own hand, a Ming general joined forces with the Manchu leaders in the summer of 1644. Instead of restoring the Ming, however, the Manchus claimed China for their own and began a forty-year conquest of the rest of the Ming territories, as well as Taiwan and parts of Mongolia and Central Asia (see Map 19.1).

A Manchu family headed the new **Qing Empire**, and Manchu generals commanded the military forces. But Manchus made up a very small portion of the population. The overwhelming majority of Qing officials, soldiers, merchants, and farmers were ethnic Chinese. Like other successful invaders of China, the Qing soon adopted Chinese institutions and policies.

Trading Companies and Missionaries

For European merchants, the China trade was second in importance only to the spice trade of southern Asia. China's vast population and manufacturing skills drew a steady stream of ships from western Europe, but enthusiasm for the trade developed only slowly at the imperial court of China.

A Portuguese ship reached China at the end of 1513 but was not permitted to trade. Four years later a formal Portuguese embassy got bogged down in Chinese protocol and procrastination, and in 1522 China expelled the Portuguese. Finally, in 1557 the Portuguese gained the right to trade from a base in Macao (muh-KOW) on the southern coast. Spain's Asian trade was conducted from Manila in the Philippines, which also linked with South America across the Pacific. For a time, the Spanish and the Dutch both maintained trading outposts on the island of Taiwan, but in 1662 they were forced to concede control to the Qing, who for the first time incorporated Taiwan into China. By then, the Dutch East India Company (*Vereenigde Oost-Indische Compagnie* or VOC) had displaced the Portuguese as the major European trader in the Indian Ocean and was establishing itself as the main European trader in East Asia. VOC representatives courted official favor in China by acknowledging the moral superiority of the emperor. They performed the ritual kowtow (in which the visitor knocked his head on the floor while crawling toward the throne) to the Ming emperor.

Catholic missionaries accompanied the Portuguese and Spanish merchants to China, just as they did to Japan. While the Franciscans and Dominicans pursued the conversion efforts at the bottom of society that had worked so well in Japan, the Jesuits focused on China's intellectual and political elite. In this they were far more successful than they had been in Japan—at least until the eighteenth century.

The outstanding Jesuit of late Ming China, Matteo Ricci (mah-TAY-oh REE-chee) (1552–1610), became expert in the Chinese language and an accomplished scholar of the Confucian classics. Under Ricci's leadership, the Jesuits adapted Catholicism to Chinese cultural traditions while introducing the Chinese to the latest science and technology from Europe. From 1601 Ricci resided in Beijing on an imperial stipend as a Western scholar. Later Jesuits headed the office of astronomy that issued the official calendar.

Qing Empire Empire established in China by Manchus who overthrew the Ming Empire in 1644. At various times the Qing also controlled Manchuria, Mongolia, Turkestan, and Tibet. The last Qing emperor was overthrown in 1911.

From the Jesuit Library at Beijing Jesuits such as Matteo Ricci were willing to share books on technology and science with Chinese scholars. But without firsthand experience it was impossible for Chinese translators to convey how the devices actually worked. Here, a man walking in a wheel drives a shaft that changes the pressure inside two pumps. In the Chinese translation of the drawing, the mechanisms were all lost.

TROMBE DA ROTA PER CAVAR AQVA

Left: From Zonca, *Trombe da Rota per Cavar Aqua* (1607). Right: "Diagram Number Eight" from *Qitushuo (Illustrations on Energy)* (1627).

Emperor Kangxi

The seventeenth and eighteenth centuries—particularly the reigns of the **Kangxi** (KAHNG-shee) (r. 1662–1722) and Qianlong (chee-YEN-loong) (r. 1736–1796) emperors—were a period of economic, military, and cultural achievement in China. The early Qing emperors repaired the roads and waterworks, lowered transit taxes, cut rents and interest rates, and established incentives for resettling areas devastated by peasant rebellions. Foreign trade was encouraged. Vietnam, Burma, and Nepal sent embassies to the Qing tribute court and carried the latest Chinese fashions back home. At the same time, overland routes from Korea to Central Asia revived.

The Manchu aristocrats who led the conquest of Beijing and north China dominated the first Qing emperor and served as regents for his young son, who was declared emperor in 1662. This child-emperor, Kangxi, sparred politically with the regents until

1669, when at age sixteen he executed the chief regent and thereby gained real control of the government. An intellectual prodigy who had mastered classical Chinese, Manchu, and Mongolian and memorized the Chinese classics, Kangxi guided imperial expansion and maintained stability until his death in 1722.

In the north, the Qing rulers feared an alliance between Galdan's Mongol state and the expanding Russian presence along the **Amur** (AH-moor) **River**. In the 1680s Qing forces attacked the wooden forts built by hardy Russian scouts on the river's northern bank. Neither empire sent large forces into the Amur territories, so the contest was partly a struggle for the goodwill of the local peoples. The Qing emperor emphasized the importance of treading lightly in the struggle:

> Upon reaching the lands of the Evenks and the Dagurs you will send to announce that you have come to hunt deer. Meanwhile, keep a careful record of the distance and go, while hunting,

Primary Source: Journals Find out what happens when a contingent of Chinese locals accuse certain Jesuit priests of treason against the throne and call for them to be either sentenced to death or "banished from the realm, to some deserted island in the sea."

Kangxi (1654–1722) Qing emperor (r. 1662–1722) who oversaw the greatest expansion of the Qing Empire.

Amur River This river valley was a contested frontier between northern China and eastern Russia until the settlement arranged in the Treaty of Nerchinsk (1689).

Emperor Kangxi In a portrait from about 1690, the young Manchu ruler is portrayed as a refined scholar in the Confucian tradition. He was a scholar and had great intellectual curiosity, but this portrait would not suggest that he was also a capable battlefield leader.

History in Focus *The caption for this image calls your attention to the emperor's representation as a refined Confucian scholar. Look carefully at his dress, the furnishings of the space he occupies, and the paper on the desk. What do you notice about those features, and what more do they suggest about how Kangxi wished to be seen? Find the answer online.*

along the northern bank of the Amur until you come by the shortest route to the town of Russian settlement at Albazin. Thoroughly reconnoiter its location and situation. I don't think the Russians will take a chance on attacking you. If they offer you food, accept it and show your gratitude. If they do attack you, don't fight back. In that case, lead your people and withdraw into our own territories.[2]

Qing forces twice attacked Albazin. The Qing were worried about Russian alliances with other frontier peoples, while Russia wished to protect its access to the furs, timber, and metals concentrated in

Siberia, Manchuria, and Yakutsk. The Qing and Russians were also rivals for control of northern Asia's Pacific coast. Seeing little benefit in continued conflict, in 1689 the two empires negotiated the Treaty of Nerchinsk, using Jesuit missionaries as interpreters. The treaty fixed the border along the Amur River and regulated trade across it. Although this was a thinly settled area, the treaty proved important, and the frontier it demarcated has long endured.

The next step was to settle the Mongolian frontier. Kangxi personally led troops in the great campaigns that defeated Galdan and brought Inner Mongolia under Qing control by 1691. Unlike the rulers of Japan, who drove Christian missionaries out, Kangxi welcomed Jesuit advisers, discussed scientific and philosophical issues with them, and put them in important offices. Jesuits helped create maps in the European style as practical guides to newly conquered regions and as symbols of Qing dominance. Kangxi considered introducing the European calendar, but protests from the Confucian elite caused him to drop the plan. When he fell ill with malaria in the 1690s, Jesuit medical treatment (in this case, South American quinine) aided his recovery. Kangxi also ordered the creation of illustrated books in Manchu detailing European anatomical and pharmaceutical knowledge.

To gain converts, the Jesuits made important compromises in their religious teaching. Most importantly, they tolerated Confucian ancestor worship. This aroused controversy between the Jesuits and their Catholic rivals in China, the Franciscans and Dominicans, and also between the Jesuits and the pope. In 1690 the disagreement reached a high pitch. Kangxi wrote to Rome supporting the Jesuit position and after further dispute ordered the expulsion of all missionaries who refused to sign a certificate accepting his position. The Jesuit presence in China declined in the eighteenth century, and later Qing emperors persecuted Christians rather than naming them to high offices.

Chinese Influences on Europe

The exchange of information that Kangxi had fostered was never one-way. While the Jesuits brought forward new knowledge of anatomy, for example, the Qing demonstrated an early form of inoculation, called "variolation," that had helped curtail smallpox after the conquest of Beijing. The technique inspired Europeans to develop other vaccines.

Similarly, Jesuit writings about China excited admiration in Europe. The wealthy and the aspiring middle classes demanded Chinese things—or things that looked to Europeans as if they could be Chinese. Silk, porcelain, and tea were avidly sought, along with cloisonné jewelry, jade, lacquered and jeweled room dividers, painted fans, and carved ivory (which originated in Africa and was finished in China). Wallpaper began as an adaptation of the Chinese practice of covering walls with enormous loose-hanging watercolors or calligraphy scrolls. By the mid-1700s special workshops throughout China were producing wallpaper and other consumer items according to the specifications of European merchants. The items were exported to Europe via Canton.

Qing political philosophy impressed Europeans, too. In the late 1770s poems supposedly written by Emperor Qianlong were translated into French and disseminated in intellectual circles. In them the Qing emperors rule as benevolent despots campaigning against superstition and ignorance, curbing aristocratic excesses, and patronizing science and the arts. This image of a practical, secular, compassionate ruler impressed the French thinker Voltaire, who proclaimed that Qing emperors were model philosopher-kings and advocated such rulership as a protection against the growth of aristocratic privilege.

Tea and Diplomacy

To maintain control over trade, facilitate tax collection, and suppress piracy, the Qing permitted only one market point for each foreign sector. Thus Europeans could trade only at Canton.

This system worked well enough until the late 1700s, when Britain became worried about its massive trade deficit with China. From bases in India and Singapore, British traders moved eastward and by the early 1700s dominated European trading in Canton, displacing the Dutch. The directors of the East India Company (EIC) anticipated limitless profits from China's gigantic markets and advanced technologies.

In medieval times tea from China, carried overland to Russia, Central Asia, and the Middle East, had become a prized import. Consumers knew it by its northern Chinese name, *cha*—as did the Portuguese. Other western Europeans acquired tea brought by sea and with it the name used in the Fujian province of coastal China and Taiwan: *te*. In much of Europe, by

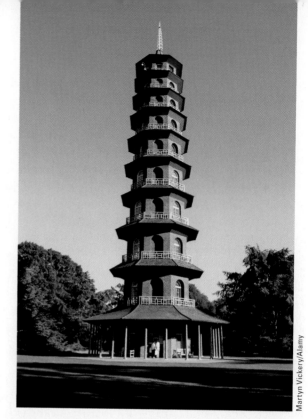

Great Pagoda at Kew Gardens A testament to Europeans' fascination with Chinese culture is the towering pagoda at the Royal Botanic Gardens near London. Completed in 1762, it was designed by Sir William Chambers as the principal ornament in the pleasure grounds of the White House at Kew, residence of August, mother of King George III.

Martyn Vickery/Alamy

the mid-1600s tea competed with chocolate and coffee as a fashionable drink.

British tea importers accumulated great fortunes. However, the Qing Empire took payment in silver and rarely bought anything from Britain. With domestic revenues declining in the later 1700s, the Qing government needed the silver and was disinclined to loosen import restrictions. To make matters worse, the East India Company had managed its worldwide holdings badly. As it teetered on bankruptcy, its attempts to manipulate Parliament became increasingly intrusive. In 1792 the British government dispatched Lord George Macartney, a well-connected peer with practical experience in Russia and India, to China. Staffed by scientists, artists, and translators as well as guards and diplomats, the **Macartney mission** showed

Macartney mission The unsuccessful attempt in 1792–1793 by the British Empire to establish diplomatic relations with the Qing Empire.

Britain's great interest in the Qing Empire as well as the EIC's desire to revise the trade system.

To fit Chinese traditions, Macartney portrayed himself as a "tribute emissary" come to salute the Qianlong emperor's eightieth birthday. However, he steadfastly refused to perform the kowtow, though he did agree to bow on one knee as he would to King George III. The Qianlong emperor received Macartney courteously in September 1793 but refused to alter the Canton trading system, open new ports of trade, or allow the British to establish a permanent mission in Beijing. The emperor sent a letter to King George explaining that China had no need to increase its foreign trade, had no use for Britain's ingenious devices and manufacturers, and set no value on closer diplomatic ties.

Dutch, French, and Russian missions to achieve what Macartney could not do also failed. European frustration mounted while admiration for China faded. The Qing court would not communicate with foreign envoys or observe the simplest rules of the European diplomatic system. In Macartney's view, China was like a venerable old warship, well maintained and splendid to look at, but obsolete and no longer up to the task.

Population and Social Stress

The Chinese who escorted Macartney and his entourage in 1792–1793 took them through China's prosperous cities and productive farmland. They did not see the economic and environmental decline that had set in during the last decades of the 1700s.

Population growth—a tripling in size since 1500—had intensified demand for food and for more intensive agriculture. With an estimated 350 million people in the late 1700s, China had twice the population of all of Europe. Despite efficient farming and the gradual adoption of New World crops like corn and sweet potatoes, population pressure touched off social and environmental problems. Increased demand for building materials and firewood reduced woodlands.

 Primary Source: Edict on Trade with Great Britain Find out why Emperor Qianlong accuses England of making impossible requests and setting a bad example for barbarian tribes the world over.

SECTION REVIEW

- Ming economic and cultural achievement continued, but after the year 1500, financial, environmental, and administrative problems weakened the empire, and it fell to the Manchus.

- European merchants pursued trade contacts with China despite official resistance, and missionaries worked successfully until the eighteenth century.

- Kangxi expanded the Qing Empire's borders, subdued or contained rival powers, and presided over a flourishing economy and culture.

- The Qing and Europeans engaged in productive exchanges of ideas, and Chinese producers supplied growing European consumer markets.

- The one-sided Qing trade system prompted the Macartney mission and other European embassies to the Qing court, but the Qing refused all requests for more equitable trading conditions.

- By the late eighteenth century, population growth had created social and environmental problems that the Qing could not control.

Deforestation, in turn, accelerated wind and water erosion and increased flooding. Dams and dikes were not maintained, and silted-up river channels were not dredged. By the end of the eighteenth century parts of the thousand-year-old Grand Canal linking the rivers of north and south China were nearly unusable, and the towns that bordered it were starved for commerce.

Some interior districts responded to this misery by increasing their output of export goods like tea, cotton, and silk. Some peasants sought seasonal jobs in better-off agricultural areas or worked in low-status jobs as barge pullers, charcoal burners, or human waste carriers. Begging, prostitution, and theft increased in the cities. Rebellions broke out in flood-ravaged central and southwestern China. Indigenous peoples concentrated in the less fertile lands in the south and in the northern and western borderlands of the empire often joined in revolts.

The Qing government was not up to controlling its vast empire. Though it was twice the size of the Ming, it employed about the same number of officials. The government's dependence on working alliances with local elites had led to widespread corruption and shrinking government revenues. The Qing's spectacular rise had ended, and decline had set in.

The Russian Empire

To what extent was Russia's expanding empire influenced by relations with western Europe in this period?

From modest beginnings in 1500, Russia expanded rapidly during the next three centuries to create an empire that stretched from eastern Europe across northern Asia and into North America. By 1750, Russia had become one of the major powers of Europe.

The Drive Across Northern Asia

During the centuries just before 1500, the history of the Russians had been dominated by steppe nomads (see Chapter 12). From the 1240s until 1480, the Mongol Khanate of the Golden Horde ruled the Russians and their neighbors. Under the Golden Horde Moscow became the most important Russian city and the center of political power. Moscow lay in the forest zone that stretched across Eurasia north of the treeless steppe (grasslands) favored by Mongol horsemen. The princes of **Muscovy** (MUSS-koe-vee), the territory surrounding the city of Moscow, led the movement against the Golden Horde and ruthlessly annexed the territories of the neighboring Russian state of Novgorod in 1478.

Once free from Mongol domination, the princes of Moscovy set out on conquests that in time made them masters of all the Golden Horde territories and then of a far greater empire. Prince Ivan IV (r. 1533–1584) pushed the conquests south and east at the expense of the Khanates of Kazan and Astrakhan (see Map 19.2). By the end of the sixteenth century, Russians ruled the largest state in Europe and large territories on the Asian side of the **Ural Mountains** as well. Since 1547 the Russian ruler used the title **tsar** (zahr) (from the Roman imperial title *caesar*), the term Russians had used for the rulers of the Mongol Empire. The Russian church promoted the idea of Moscow as the "third Rome," successor to the Roman Empire's second capital, Constantinople, which had fallen to the Ottoman Turks in 1453.

Yet Russian claims to greatness were also exaggerated: in 1600 the empire was poor, backward, and landlocked. Only one seaport—often frozen Arkhangelsk in the north—connected to the world's oceans. The Crimean Turks to the south were powerful enough to sack Moscow in 1571. Beyond them, the Ottoman Empire controlled access to the Black Sea, while the Safavid rulers of Iran dominated the trade of southern Central Asia. The powerful kingdoms of Sweden and Poland-Lithuania to the west similarly blocked Russian access to the Baltic Sea.

The one route open to expansion, **Siberia**, had much to recommend it. Many Russians preferred the forested north to the open steppes; and the thinly inhabited region abounded in valuable resources, most notably the soft, dense fur that forest animals grew to survive the long winters. Russian pioneers in Siberia made a living from animal pelts. The foreign merchants who came to buy these furs in Moscow provided the tsars with revenue and European contacts.

The Strogonovs, a wealthy Russian trading family, led the early Russian exploration of Siberia. The small indigenous bands of foragers had no way of resisting the armed adventurers the Strogonovs hired. Using rifles, their troops attacked and destroyed the only political power in the region, the Khanate of Sibir, in 1582. Moving through the dense forests by river, Russian fur trappers were able to reach the Pacific during the seventeenth century and soon crossed over into Alaska. Russian political control followed more slowly into what was more a frontier zone with widely scattered forts than a province under full control. Beginning in the early seventeenth century the tsar also used Siberia as a penal colony for criminals and political prisoners.

In the 1640s Russian settlers began to grow grain in the Amur River Valley east of Mongolia. As seen

Muscovy The Russian principality that emerged gradually during the era of Mongol domination. The Muscovite dynasty ruled without interruption from 1276 to 1598.

Ural Mountains This north-south range separates Siberia from the rest of Russia. It is commonly considered the boundary between the continents of Europe and Asia.

tsar (czar) From Latin *caesar*, this Russian title for a monarch was first used in reference to a Russian ruler by Ivan III (r. 1462–1505).

Siberia The extreme northeastern sector of Asia, including the Kamchatka Peninsula and the present Russian coast of the Arctic Ocean, the Bering Strait, and the Sea of Okhotsk.

Interactive Map

Map 19.2 The Expansion of Russia, 1500–1800 Sweden and Poland initially blocked Russian expansion in Europe, while the Ottoman Empire blocked the southwest. In the sixteenth century, Russia began to expand east, toward Siberia and the Pacific Ocean. By the end of the rule of Catherine the Great in 1796, Russia encompassed all of northern and northeastern Eurasia. © Cengage Learning

Russian Ambassadors to Holland Display Their Furs, 1576 Representatives from Muscovy impressed the court of King Maximilian II of Bohemia with their sable coats and caps. Ria-Novositi

already, by the time the Qing reacted to the Russian presence, the worrisome threat of Galdan's Mongol military power had arisen. Equally concerned about the Mongols, the Russians were pleased to work out a frontier agreement. The 1689 Treaty of Nerchinsk recognized Russian claims west of Mongolia but required the Russians to withdraw their settlements farther east.

Russian Society and Politics, to 1725

Russian expansion involved demographic changes as well as new relations between the tsar and the elite classes. A third transformation affected the freedom and mobility of the Russian peasantry.

As the empire expanded, it incorporated people with different languages, religious beliefs, and ethnic identities. Orthodox missionaries made great efforts to Christianize the peoples of Siberia in much the same way that Catholic missionaries did in Canada. But among the relatively more populous steppe peoples, Islam prevailed over Christianity as the dominant religion. Differences in how people made their living were equally fundamental. Russians tended to live as farmers, hunters, builders, scribes, or merchants, while those newly incorporated into the empire were mostly herders, caravan workers, and soldiers.

As people mixed, individual and group identities became complex. There was diversity even among Russian speakers who were Russian Orthodox in faith. The name **Cossack**, which applied to bands of people living on the steppes between Moscovy and the Caspian and Black Seas, probably comes from a Turkic word for a warrior or mercenary soldier. Actually, Cossacks had diverse origins and beliefs, but they all belonged to close-knit bands, fought superbly from the saddle, and terrified both villagers and legal authorities. Because loyalty to the chiefs of their bands was paramount, the Cossacks made only temporary allegiances with rulers.

Cossacks provided most of the soldiers and settlers employed by the Strogonovs, and they founded every major town in Russian Siberia. They also manned the Russian camps on the Amur River. West of the Urals the Cossacks defended Russia against Swedish and Ottoman incursions, but they also preserved their political autonomy. Those in the rich and populous lands of the Ukraine, for example, rebelled when the tsar agreed to a division of their lands with Poland-Lithuania in 1667.

Cossacks Peoples of the Russian Empire who lived outside the farming villages, often as herders, mercenaries, or outlaws. Cossacks led the conquest of Siberia in the sixteenth and seventeenth centuries.

In the early seventeenth century Swedish and Polish forces briefly occupied Moscow on separate occasions. This "Time of Troubles" marked the end of the old line of Muscovite rulers. The Russian aristocracy—the boyars (BOY-ars)—allowed one of their own, Mikhail Romanov (ROH-man-off) (r. 1613–1645), to inaugurate a dynasty that would soon consolidate its own authority while successfully competing with neighboring powers. The Romanovs often represented conflicts between Slavic Russians and Turkic steppe peoples as being between Christians and "infidels" or between the civilized and the "barbaric." Despite this rhetoric, it is important to understand that these cultural groups were defined less by blood ties than by the ways in which they lived.

As centralized tsarist power rose, the freedom of the peasants who tilled the land in European Russia fell. The Moscovy rulers and early tsars rewarded their loyal nobles with grants of land that obliged the local peasants to work for the lords. Law and custom permitted peasants to change masters during a two-week period each year, which encouraged lords to treat their peasants well; but the rising commercialization of agriculture also raised the value of these labor obligations.

Long periods of warfare in the late sixteenth and early seventeenth centuries disrupted peasant life and caused many to flee to the Cossacks or across the Urals. Some who couldn't flee sold themselves into slavery to keep from starving. When peace returned, landlords sought to recover the runaways and bind them more tightly to their land. A law change in 1649 finally transformed the peasants into **serfs** by eliminating the period when they could change masters and ordering runaways to return to their masters.

Like slavery, serfdom was hereditary. In theory the serf was tied to a piece of land, not owned by a master. In practice, strict laws narrowed the difference between serf and slave. In the Russian census of 1795, serfs made up over half the population. Landowners made up only 2 percent, or roughly the same as they did in the Caribbean.

Peter the Great

The greatest of the Romanovs, Tsar **Peter the Great** (r. 1689–1725), reduced Russia's isolation and increased the empire's size and power. He turned Russia away from its Asian cultural connections and toward what he deemed the advanced civilization of the West. In fact, he accelerated trends under way for some time. When he ascended the throne, there were already hundreds of foreign merchants in Moscow. Military officers from western Europe had already trained a major part of the army in new weapons and techniques, and Italian builders were already influencing church and palace architecture. Peter accelerated these tendencies.

Peter matured quickly both physically and mentally. In his youth the government was in the hands of his half-sister Sophia, who was regent for him and her sickly brother Ivan. Living on an estate near the foreigners' quarter outside Moscow, Peter learned what he could of life outside Russia and busied himself gaining practical skills in blacksmithing, carpentry, shipbuilding, and the arts of war. He organized his own military drill unit among other young men. When Princess Sophia tried to take complete control of the government in 1689, Peter rallied enough support to send her to a monastery, secure the abdication of Ivan, and take charge of Russia. He was still in his teens.

Peter concerned himself with Russia's expansion and modernization. To secure a port on the Black Sea, he constructed a small but formidable navy. Describing his wars with the Ottoman Empire as a new crusade to liberate Constantinople from the Muslim sultans, Peter fancied himself the legal protector of Orthodox Christians living under Ottoman rule. His

---

Primary Source: Edicts and Decrees Learn about Peter the Great's feelings on such things as freedom of religion, proper dress, shaving, and military advancement.

---

serf In medieval Europe, an agricultural laborer legally bound to a lord's property and obligated to perform set services for the lord. In Russia some serfs worked as artisans and in factories; serfdom was not abolished there until 1861.

Peter the Great (1672–1725) Russian tsar (r. 1689–1725). He enthusiastically introduced Western languages and technologies to the Russian elite and moved the capital from Moscow to the new city of St. Petersburg.

Collection, Countess Bobrinskoy/Michael Holford

Peter the Great This portrait from his time as a student in Holland in 1697 shows Peter as ruggedly masculine and practical, quite unlike most royal portraits of the day that posed rulers in foppish elegance and haughty majesty. Peter was a popular military leader as well as an autocratic ruler.

forces seized the port of Azov in 1696 but lost it again in 1713, thus calling a halt to southward expansion.

In the winter of 1697–1698, after his Black Sea campaign, Peter traveled in disguise across Europe to discover how western European societies were becoming so powerful and wealthy. He paid special attention to ships and weapons, even working for a time as a ship's carpenter in the Netherlands. With great insight, he perceived that western European success owed as much to trade and toleration as to technology. Trade generated the money to spend on weapons, while toleration attracted talented persons fleeing persecution. Upon his return to Russia, Peter resolved to expand and reform his vast and backward empire.

In the long and costly Great Northern War (1700–1721), Peter's modernized armies broke Swedish control of the Baltic Sea, making possible more direct contacts between Russia and Europe. This victory forced the European powers to recognize Russia as a major power for the first time. On land captured from Sweden at the eastern end of the Baltic, Peter built St. Petersburg, his window on the West. In 1712 the city became Russia's capital. To demonstrate Russia's new sophistication, Peter ordered architects to build St. Petersburg's houses and public buildings in the baroque style then fashionable in France.

Peter also pushed the Russian elite to imitate European fashions. He personally shaved off his noblemen's long beards to conform to Western styles. To end the traditional seclusion of upper-class Russian women, Peter required officials, military officers, and merchants to bring their wives to the social gatherings he organized in the capital. (For what they probably came in, see Material Culture: Four-Wheeled Carriages.) He also directed the nobles to educate their children.

Another strategy was to reorganize Russian government along the lines of the powerful German state of Prussia. He sharply reduced the traditional roles of the boyars in government and the army, replacing the old boyar council with a group of appointed advisers in St. Petersburg. Members of the traditional nobility continued to serve as generals and admirals, but officers in Peter's modern, professional army and navy were promoted according to merit, not birth.

A decree of 1716 proclaimed that the tsar "is not obliged to answer to anyone in the world for his doings, but possesses power and authority over his kingdom and land, to rule them at his will and pleasure as a Christian ruler." Under this expansive definition of his role, Peter brought the Russian Orthodox Church more firmly under state control, built factories and iron and copper foundries to provide munitions and supplies for the military, and increased the burdens of taxes and forced labor on the serfs. Peter was an absolutist ruler of the sort then common in western Europe, and he had no more intention of improving the conditions of the serfs than did the European slave owners of the Americas.

Consolidation of the Empire

Russia's eastward expansion continued under Peter the Great and his successors. The frontier settlement with China and Qianlong's quashing of Inner Mongolia in 1689 freed Russians to concentrate on the

Material Culture

Four-Wheeled Vehicles

Most modern motor transport is based on the principle of the four-wheeled vehicle. Yet prior to the spread of European technologies and tastes in the age of imperialism, four-wheeled vehicles were rarely seen outside of Europe. The wheeled transport of India, East Asia, and Southeast Asia was almost exclusively of the two-wheeled cart variety.

Economically, the two-wheeled cart was generally superior to the four-wheeled wagon throughout the era of animal-drawn transport. The power a team of oxen or horses could exert did not change with the number of wheels. But each added axle, that is, each additional pair of wheels, increased the friction the animals had to overcome in pulling and also added

Nineteenth-Century Children's Carriage This nineteenth-century children's carriage shows the essential changes that defined the coach. The small front wheels turn under the body of the carriage when the front axle pivots in the center. The back wheels are much larger. And the passenger compartment is suspended on springs that run from the front to the back of the vehicle.

Erich Lessing/Art Resource, NY

weight to the vehicle. So even though a wagon might have more space than a cart, the weight that could be loaded was invariably smaller.

Four-wheeled vehicles had the additional disadvantage of being difficult to steer. Paved roads were rare, and rutted dirt tracks made for a bumpy ride unless the wheels were of great diameter. Three feet (1 meter) was a common size. However, such large wheels could not turn very far when the front axle pivoted because they hit the frame of the wagon. Raising the wagon-bed more than 3 feet above the ground made the vehicle unstable. Limited to a turning radius of only a few degrees, or more often being constrained by a nonpivoting axle, four-wheeled vehicles could not readily operate in towns and other places where sharp turns were required. Yet making the front wheels smaller so they could turn underneath the wagon-bed made the vehicle difficult to use on rough roads.

Despite these limitations, archaeological evidence shows that both four-wheeled and two-wheeled vehicles were used in Europe, Central Asia, and the Middle East from the fourth millennium B.C.E. onward. Eventually wagons disappeared in the latter two regions, but they continued to be used in Europe. The reasons for European persistence in an inefficient mode of transport are not clear. However, ancient and medieval images suggest that four-wheeled wagons were used primarily for passengers from the upper classes. More specifically, many images show groups of female passengers.

Wagons had advantages as conveyances for elite women. They could easily be enclosed for privacy, and they could hold a noblewoman and her female attendants, thus eliminating the dangers of traveling with only a male driver. By the later days of the Roman Empire, the two-wheeled chariot, formerly the vehicle of warriors, had disappeared, and noblemen had taken to riding horseback.

Increased comfort probably played a role in a series of technological improvements that began around the fifteenth century. The word coach, of Hungarian origin, signaled the new designs. Pivoting front axles became common. Better paving, particularly in towns, accommodated the required smaller wheels. The passenger cabin was first suspended on chains or leather straps, and later on springs, to reduce jolting. Efficient harnessing techniques that had first appeared centuries earlier made possible larger teams of animals, heavier vehicles, and faster speeds. And brakes were developed to help manage the heavier loads.

Coach and carriage designs, particularly associated with the upper classes, became more sophisticated over the following centuries. Charles Darwin's grandfather, Erasmus Darwin, was the first to design a steering system of the type used today on automobiles in which each front wheel turns separately while the axle remains fixed. The four-wheeled coach became the basis for steam locomotives and railway carriages, and eventually for the automobile. Other parts of the world adopted European transport designs as symbols of modernity.

However, the question remains: Why did the Europeans stick with inefficient four-wheeled wagons for over four thousand years when other parts of the world opted exclusively for the two-wheeled alternative? It is unlikely that providing a private traveling compartment for groups of elite women was the sole reason. But the fact that such traveling accommodations became available may offer a technological clue as to why upper-class women in the Middle East, China, India, and other non-European lands were so often prohibited from leaving the house whereas European women enjoyed relatively greater freedom of movement.

QUESTIONS FOR ANALYSIS

1. Why did most societies prefer two-wheeled transportation?
2. How do different societies solve the problem of providing privacy and safety to women who are traveling?
3. Which is more important in the technological development of transport vehicles, social status or gender?

---

northern Pacific. The Pacific northeast was colonized, and in 1741 an expedition led by Captain Vitus Bering crossed the strait (later named for him) into North America. In 1799 a Russian company of merchants received a monopoly over the Alaskan fur trade, and its agents were soon active along the entire northwestern coast of North America.

Far more important than these immense territories in the cold and thinly populated north were the populous agricultural lands to the west acquired during the reign of Catherine the Great (r. 1762–1796). A successful war with the Ottoman Empire gave Russia control of the north shore of the Black Sea by 1783, though not of the straits leading to the Mediterranean. Three successive partitions of the once powerful kingdom of Poland between 1772 and 1795 advanced Russia's frontiers 600 miles (nearly 1,000 kilometers) to the west (see Map 19.2). When Catherine died, the Russian Empire extended from Poland in the west to Alaska in the east, from the Barents Sea in the north to the Black Sea in the south.

Catherine also made important additions to Peter's policies of promoting industry and building a canal

SECTION REVIEW

- Muscovy became the center of Russian political power and led the movement against Mongol domination.
- Ivan IV expanded Muscovy, and the Strogonovs sponsored exploration of fur-rich Siberia.
- Russian society blended diverse ethnicities, religions, and cultural practices, a mixture embodied in the Cossacks.
- Emerging from the Time of Troubles, the Romanov tsars worked to centralize royal authority and to institutionalize serfdom.
- Peter the Great accelerated Russia's westernization, fought wars of expansion, and enlarged the power of the tsar.
- Expansion continued eastward and westward, and Catherine the Great continued Peter's westernizing policies.

system to improve trade. Besides furs, the Russians had also become major exporters of gold, iron, and timber. Catherine implemented administrative reforms and showed a special talent for diplomacy. Through her promotion of Western ideas, she expanded Peter's policies of westernizing the Russian elite.

Conclusion

China and Russia are examples of the phenomenal flourishing of empires in Eurasia between 1500 and 1800. Already a vast empire under the Ming, China doubled in size under the Qing, mostly through westward expansion into less densely populated areas. In expanding from a modestly sized principality into the world's largest land empire, Russia added rich and well-populated lands to the west and south and far larger but less populous lands to the east. Russia and China were land based, just like the Ottoman and Mughal Empires, with the strengths and problems of administrative control and tax collection that size entailed.

Japan was different. Though nominally headed by an emperor, Japan's size and ethnic homogeneity do not support calling it an empire like China and Russia. Tokugawa Japan was similar in size and population to France, the most powerful state of western Europe, but its political system was much more decentralized. Japan's efforts to add colonies on the East Asian mainland had failed.

China had once led the world in military innovation (including the first uses of gunpowder), but the modern "gunpowder revolution" of the fifteenth and sixteenth centuries was centered in the Ottoman Empire and western European states. Although the centuries after 1500 were full of successful military operations, Chinese armies continued to depend on superior numbers and tactics for their success, rather than on new technology. As in the past, infantrymen armed with guns served alongside others armed with bows and arrows, swords, and spears.

The military forces of Japan and Russia underwent more innovative changes than those of China, in part through Western contacts. In the course of its sixteenth-century wars of unification, Japan produced its own gunpowder revolution but thereafter lacked the motivation and the means to stay abreast of the world's most advanced military technology. By the eighteenth century Russia had made greater progress in catching up with its European neighbors, but its armies still relied more on their size than on the sophistication of their weapons.

Naval power provides the greatest military contrast among China, Russia, and Japan. Eighteenth-century Russia constructed modern fleets of warships in the Baltic and Black Seas, but neither China nor Japan developed navies commensurate with their size and coastlines. China's defenses against pirates and other sea invaders were left to its maritime provinces, whose small war junks were armed with only a half-dozen cannon. Japan's naval capacity was similarly decentralized. In 1792, when Russian ships exploring the North Pacific turned toward the Japanese coast, the local daimyo used his own forces to chase them away. All Japanese daimyo understood that they would be on their own if foreign incursions increased.

The expansion of China and Russia incorporated not just new lands but also diverse new peoples. Chinese society had long been diverse, and its geographical, occupational, linguistic, and religious differences grew as the Qing expanded (see Map 19.1). China had also long used Confucian models, imperial customs, and a common system of writing to transcend such differences and to assimilate elites. Russia likewise approached its new peoples with a mixture of pragmatic tolerance and a propensity for seeing Russian ways and beliefs as superior. The Russian language was strongly promoted. Religion was a particular sore point, as Russian Orthodox missionaries, with the support of the tsars, encouraged conversion of Siberian peoples. Russia absorbed new ideas and styles from western Europe, although even among the elite these influences often overlay Russian traditions in a very superficial way. In contrast, Japan remained more culturally homogeneous, and the government reacted with great intolerance to the growing influence of converts to western Christianity.

Forced labor remained common in the Russian and Chinese Empires. Serfdom grew more brutal and widespread in Russia in the seventeenth and eighteenth centuries, although the expansion of the frontier eastward across Siberia also opened an escape route for many peasants and serfs. Some Chinese peasants also improved their lot by moving to new territories, but population growth increased overall misery in the eighteenth century. China was also notable for the size of its popular insurrections, especially the one that toppled the Ming.

CHAPTER REVIEW

 Download the MP3 audio file of the
Chapter Review to listen to on the go.

How did Japan respond to domestic social changes and the challenges posed by contact with foreign cultures?
(page 456)

The formation of the Tokugawa Shogunate in Japan is a clear example of a society changing from within. The decisions of the government to suppress Christianity and sharply curtail commercial and intellectual contacts with distant Europe illustrate how easily even the most decentralized state could control its dealings with outsiders.

How did China deal with military and political challenges both inside and outside its borders?
(page 460)

China's history illustrates a complex interplay of internal and external forces. During the final days of the Ming dynasty, China suffered from internal rebellions caused by deteriorating economic conditions, to which the Ming responded ineffectively. When Japan invaded, the Ming sought help from the Manchus, who then turned on them and established the Qing Empire. The Qing's settlement of the Amur frontier with Russia illustrates how diplomacy and compromise could serve mutual interests. Finally, the Chinese added new European customers to already extensive internal and external markets and developed both positive and problematic cultural relations with the Jesuits and some other Europeans. From a Chinese perspective, European contacts could be useful but were neither essential nor of great importance.

To what extent was Russia's expanding empire influenced by relations with western Europe in this period?
(page 468)

During this period Russia increased its trade with the West and through its conquests and territorial expansion emerged as a great power. Moreover, both Peter the Great and Catherine the Great labored to westernize their people. Though Western influences were very important, their importance can easily be exaggerated. The impetus for Muscovy's expansion came out of its own history and domination by the Mongols, and trade with western Europe was not the center of the Russian economy. Tsar Peter was more interested in Western technology than in the full range of Western culture.

Key Terms

Manchu *(p. 456)*

daimyo (p. 456)

samurai (p. 456)

Tokugawa Shogunate
(p. 458)

Ming Empire *(p. 461)*

Qing Empire *(p. 463)*

Kangxi *(p. 464)*

Amur River *(p. 464)*

Macartney mission *(p. 466)*

Muscovy *(p. 468)*

Ural Mountains *(p. 468)*

tsar (czar) *(p. 468)*

Siberia *(p. 468)*

Cossacks *(p. 470)*

serf *(p. 471)*

Peter the Great *(p. 471)*

Web Resources

Pronunciation Guide

Interactive Maps

- MAP 19.1 The Qing Empire, 1644–1783
- MAP 19.2 The Expansion of Russia, 1500–1800

Primary Sources

- Some Observations on Merchants
- Journals
- Edict on Trade with Great Britain
- Edicts and Decrees

Answer to the History in Focus Question

See photo on page 465, "Emperor Kangxi."

 Visit the CourseMate website at www.cengagebrain.com for additional study tools and review materials for this chapter.

The Little Ice Age

In 1600 a giant volcano, Mount Huanyaputina (hoo-AHN-yah-poo-TEE-nuh), erupted in the Peruvian Andes. When volcanic ash from the eruption shot into the upper atmosphere and spread around the world, it screened out sunlight and affected the weather in many parts of the world for several years. As a result, the summer of 1601 was the coldest in two hundred years in the Northern Hemisphere.

Archaeologist Brian Fagan has pointed out that Mount Huanyaputina's chilling effects were a spectacular event in a much longer pattern of climate change that has been called the Little Ice Age.[1] Although global climate had been cooling since the late 1200s, in the northern temperate regions the 1590s had been exceptionally cold. Temperatures remained cooler than normal throughout the seventeenth century.

The most detailed information on the Little Ice Age comes from Europe. Glaciers in the Alps grew much larger. Trade became difficult when rivers and canals that had once been navigable in winter froze solid from bank to bank. In the coldest years, the growing season in some places was as much as two months shorter than normal. Unexpectedly late frosts withered the tender shoots of newly planted crops in spring, and wheat and barley ripened more slowly during cooler summers and were often damaged by early fall frosts.

People could survive a smaller-than-average harvest in one year by drawing on food reserves, but when cold weather damaged crops in two or more successive years, the consequences were devastating. Deaths due to malnutrition and cold increased sharply when summer temperatures in northern Europe registered 2.7°F (1.5°C) lower than average in 1674 and 1675 and again in 1694 and 1695. The cold spell of 1694 and 1695 caused a famine in Finland that carried off a quarter to a third of the population.

At the time people had no idea what was causing the unusual cold of the Little Ice Age. Advances in climate history make it clear that the cause was not a single terrestrial event such as the eruption of Mount Huanyaputina. Nor was the Little Ice Age the product of human actions, unlike some climate changes such as today's global warming.

Ultimately, the earth's weather is governed by the sun. In the seventeenth century astronomers in Europe reported seeing fewer sunspots, dark spots on the sun's surface that are indicative of solar activity and thus the sun's warming power. Diminished activity in the sun was primarily responsible for the Little Ice Age.

If the sun was the root cause, the effects of global cooling should not have been confined to northern Europe. Although contemporary accounts are much scarcer in other parts of the world, there is evidence of climate changes around the world in this period. Observations of sunspots in China, Korea, and Japan drop to zero between 1639 and 1700. China experienced unusually cool weather in the seventeenth century, but the warfare and disruption accompanying the fall of the Ming and the rise of the Qing probably were much more to blame for the famines and rural distress of that period.

By itself, a relatively slight decrease in average annual temperature would not have a significant effect on human life outside the northern temperate areas. However, evidence suggests that there was also a significant rise in humidity in other parts of the world. Ice cores drilled into ancient glaciers in the Arctic and Antarctic show increased snowfall. Information compiled by historian James L. A. Webb, Jr., shows that lands south of the Sahara received more rainfall between 1550 and 1750 than they had during the previous era.[2] Increased rainfall would have been favorable for pastoral people, whose herds found new pasture in what had once been desert, and for the farmers farther south, whose crops got more rain.

In the eighteenth century the sun's activity began to return to normal. Rising temperatures led to milder winters and better harvests in northern Eurasia, while falling rainfall allowed the Sahara to advance southward, forcing the agricultural frontier to retreat.

Part Six

Revolutions Reshape the World, 1750–1870

© Cengage Learning

		1750		1775		1800	
AMERICAS		**1754–1763** French and Indian War	• **1776** U.S. Declaration of Independence		• **1791** Slaves revolt in Haiti	• **1803** Louisiana Purchase	**1809–1825** Wars for independence in Spanish America
				• **1789** U.S. Constitution ratified			
EUROPE		• **ca. 1750** Industrial Revolution begins in Britain			**1789–1799** French Revolution		**1814–1815** Congress of Vienna
		1756–1763 Seven Years War				**1799–1815** Rule of Napoleon in France	
AFRICA		**1750–1800** Growing slave trade reduces population			• **1795** Britain takes Cape Colony	• **1809** Sokoto Caliphate founded	
						Shaka founds Zulu kingdom **1818** •	
MIDDLE EAST			**1769–1772** High point of restored Mamluk influence in Egypt		**1789–1807** Reign of Ottoman sultan Selim III		
					• **1798** Napoleon invades Egypt		
				Muhammad Ali founds dynasty in Egypt **1805** •			
ASIA AND OCEANIA		• **1755** Qing conquest of Turkestan	**1769–1778** Captain Cook's exploration of Australia, New Zealand			**1796–1804** White Lotus Rebellion in China	East India Company creates Bombay presidency **1818** •
			• **1765** East India Company rule of Bengal begins				

Between 1750 and 1870, nearly every part of the world experienced dramatic political, economic, and social change. The beginnings of industrialization, the American and French Revolutions, and the revolutions for independence in Latin America transformed political and economic life. European nations expanded into Africa, Asia, and the Middle East while Russia and the United States acquired vast new territories.

The Industrial Revolution introduced new technologies and patterns of work that made these societies wealthier and militarily more powerful. Western intellectual life became more secular. The Atlantic slave trade and later slavery itself were abolished, and efforts to improve the status of women were initiated.

The Industrial Revolution led to a new wave of imperialism. France conquered Algeria and Great Britain expanded its colonial rule in India and established colonies in Australia and New Zealand. European political and economic influence also expanded in Africa and Asia. The Ottoman Empire and the Qing Empire met this challenge by implementing reform programs that preserved traditional structures while adopting elements of Western technology and organization. Though lagging behind western Europe in transforming its economy and political institutions, Russia attempted modernization efforts, including the abolition of serfdom.

The economic, political, and social revolutions that began in the mid-eighteenth century shook the foundations of European culture and led to the expansion of Western power around the globe. Some of the nations of Asia, Africa, and Latin America reformed and strengthened their own institutions and economies, while others pushed for more radical change. After 1870 Western imperialism became more aggressive, and few parts of the world were able to resist it.

1825	1850	1875
• **1822** Independence of Brazil	• **1848** Women's Rights Convention in Seneca Falls, New York	**1862–1867** French invasion of Mexico **1861–1865** U.S. Civil War • **1867** Creation of Dominion of Canada
• **1830** Revolutions of 1830 • **1834** Abolition of slavery in British Empire	**1852–1870** Rule of Napoleon III in France • **1848** Revolutions of 1848 • **1861** Russia abolishes serfdom **1853–1856** Crimean War	
• **1821** Republic of Liberia founded	**1836–1839** Afrikaners' Great Trek	• **1869** Jaja founds Opobo
• **1826** Ottoman ruler Mahmud II dissolves Janissary corps	• **1839** Ottoman ruler Abdul Mejid launches Tanzimat reforms	• **1860s** Beginning of Young Turk movement • **1869** Suez Canal opens
• **1826** East India Company annexes Assam, northern Burma **1839–1842** Opium War **1829–1864** Russia completes conquest of Central Asia	**1850–1864** Taiping Rebellion in China **1857–1858** Sepoy Rebellion in India	

Revolutionary Changes in the Atlantic World

© Cengage Learning

 Visit the CourseMate website at **www.cengagebrain.com** for additional study tools and review materials for this chapter.

On the evening of August 14, 1791, more than two hundred slaves and black freedmen met in secret in the plantation district of northern Saint Domingue (san doe-MANG) (present-day Haiti) to set the date for an armed uprising against local slave owners. Although the delegates agreed to delay the attack for a week, violence began almost immediately. During the following decade, the Haitian rebels abolished slavery, defeated military forces from Britain and France, and gained independence.

News and rumors about revolutionary events in France that had spread through the island incited the slave community and divided the island's white population between royalists (supporters of France's King Louis XVI) and republicans (supporters of democracy). The free mixed-race population initially gained some political rights from the French Assembly but was then forced to rebel when the slave-owning elite reacted violently.

Among those planning the insurrection was Toussaint L'Ouverture (too-SAN loo-ver-TYURE), a black freedman. This remarkable revolutionary organized the rebels into a potent military force, negotiated with the island's royalist and republican factions, and, with representatives of Great Britain and France, wrote his nation's first constitution. Throughout the Western Hemisphere, Toussaint became a towering symbol of resistance to oppression for slaves and a fiend in the eyes of slave owners.

The Haitian slave rebellion was an important episode in the long and painful political and cultural transformation of the modern Western world. While economic expansion and the growth of trade were creating unprecedented wealth, intellectuals were questioning the traditional place of monarchy and slavery in society. An emerging class of merchants, professionals, and manufacturers began to press for a larger political role, and economies were increasingly opened to competition.

Imperial powers resisted the loss of colonies, and monarchs and nobles struggled to retain their ancient privileges. As revolutionary steps forward were often matched by reactionary steps backward, the liberal and nationalist ideals of the eighteenth-century revolutionary movements were only imperfectly realized in Europe and the Americas in the nineteenth century.

Prelude to Revolution: War and the Enlightenment

How did the costs of imperial wars and the Enlightenment challenge the established authority of monarchs in Europe and the American colonies?

The cost of wars fought among Europe's major powers over colonies and trade helped precipitate the revolutionary era that began in 1775 with the American Revolution. The struggle of Britain, France, and Spain for political preeminence in western Europe and overseas produced many violent conflicts during the eighteenth century. In the Seven Years War (1756–1763)—known as the French and Indian War in America—Britain gained dominance in North America and in India. All parties suffered from the enormous costs of these conflicts.

However, new Western ideas and political environments now made people much more critical of any effort to extend the power of a monarch or impose new taxes, and they also raised questions about the rights of individuals. As Chapter 16 recounted, the **Enlightenment** applied the methods and questions of the Scientific Revolution to the study of human society. Some thinkers challenged long-established religious and political institutions. They argued that if scientists could understand the laws of nature, then surely similar forms of disciplined investigation might reveal laws of human nature. Others wondered whether society and government might be better regulated and more productive if guided by reason rather than by hereditary rulers and the church.

These new perspectives and the intellectual optimism that fed them helped guide the English political

Enlightenment A philosophical movement in eighteenth-century Europe that fostered the belief that one could reform society by discovering rational laws that governed social behavior and were just as scientific as the laws of physics.

***Beer Street* (1751)** This engraving by William Hogarth shows an idealized London street scene where beer drinking is associated with manly strength, good humor, and prosperity. The self-satisfied corpulent figure in the left foreground has been reading a copy of the king's speech to Parliament. We can imagine him offering a running commentary to his drinking companions as he reads.

Courtesy, Dover Publications

SECTION REVIEW

- The costs of the imperial wars among England, France, and Spain helped to spark the era of revolutions.

- Also important were the ideas and critical spirit of the Enlightenment, particularly the political ideas of Locke and Rousseau.

- These new ideas received support of reformist nobility and monarchs.

- Progressive intellectual debate spread to the colonial societies of the Western Hemisphere.

philosopher John Locke (1632–1704). Locke argued in 1690 that governments were created to protect life, liberty, and property and that the people had a right to rebel when a monarch violated these natural rights. In *The Social Contract*, published in 1762, the French-Swiss intellectual Jean-Jacques Rousseau (zhahn-zhock roo-SOE) (1712–1778) asserted that the will of the people was sacred and that the legitimacy of the monarch depended on the consent of the people. Although both men believed that government rested on the will of the people rather than divine will, Locke emphasized the importance of individual rights, and Rousseau envisioned the people acting collectively because of their shared historical experience.

The Enlightenment is commonly associated with hostility toward monarchy, but Voltaire, one of the Enlightenment's most critical intellects, believed that Europe's monarchs were likely agents of political and economic reform, and he wrote favorably of China's Qing (ching) emperors. Indeed, some sympathetic members of the nobility and reforming monarchs in Spain, Russia, Austria, and Prussia actively sponsored and promoted the dissemination of new ideas, providing patronage for many intellectuals. They recognized that elements of the Enlightenment critique of the *ancien régime* (ahn-see-EN ray-ZHEEM) buttressed their own efforts to expand royal authority at the expense of religious institutions, the nobility, and regional autonomy. Monarchs also understood that the era's passion for science and technology held the potential of fattening national treasuries and improving economic performance.

The Western Hemisphere shared in the debates of Europe. In colonial societies where political rights were even more limited than in Europe, the idea that government authority ultimately rested on the consent of the governed was potentially explosive. The efforts of ordinary men and women to resist the growth of government power and the imposition of new cultural forms provide an important political undercurrent to much of the revolutionary agitation and conflict from 1750 to 1850. But spontaneous popular uprisings gained revolutionary potential only when they coincided with ideological divisions and conflicts within the governing class itself.

Primary Source: Rousseau Espouses Popular Sovereignty and the General Will What is "the government"? Find out what Jean-Jacques Rousseau believes, and consider how his ideas helped shape the revolutionary movements of his time.

Chronology

	The Americas		Europe
1750	**1756–1763** French and Indian War **1770** Boston Massacre **1776** American Declaration of Independence **1783** Treaty of Paris ends American Revolution **1791** Slaves revolt in Saint Domingue (Haiti)		**1756–1763** Seven Years War **1789** Storming of Bastille begins French Revolution **1793–1794** Reign of Terror in France **1795–1799** The Directory rules France
1800	**1798** Toussaint L'Ouverture defeats British in Haiti **1804** Haitians defeat French invasion and declare independence **1808** Portuguese royal family arrives in Brazil **1808–1809** Revolutions for independence begin in Spanish South America **1822** Brazil gains independence		**1799** Napoleon overthrows the Directory **1804** Napoleon crowns himself emperor **1804–1814** Napoleon occupies most of Europe **1812** Napoleon fails to conquer Russia **1814** Napoleon abdicates; Congress of Vienna opens
1825			**1830** Greece gains independence; revolution in France
	1848 Women's Rights Convention in Seneca Falls, New York		**1848** Revolutions in France, Austria, Germany, Hungary, and Italy
1850	**1861–1865** American Civil War **1865** End of slavery in United States		
1875	**1886** End of slavery in Cuba **1888** End of slavery in Brazil		

The American Revolution

What were the direct causes of the American Revolution?

After defeating France in the French and Indian War, the British government faced two related problems in its North American colonies. One was the likelihood of armed conflict with Amerindian peoples as settlers quickly pushed west of the Appalachian Mountains and across the Ohio River. Already burdened with war debts, Britain desperately wanted to avoid additional expenditures for frontier defense. The other problem was how to get the colonists to shoulder more of the costs of imperial defense and colonial administration. Every effort to impose new taxes or prevent the settlement of the trans-Appalachian frontier provoked angry protests in the colonies. The confrontational and impolitic way in which a succession of weak

British governments responded made the situation politically explosive.

Frontiers and Taxes The British Proclamation of 1763, which sought to establish an effective western limit for settlement, threw into question the claims of thousands of already established farmers without effectively protecting Amerindian land. The Quebec Act of 1774 annexed disputed lands to the province of Quebec, thus denying eastern colonies the authority to distribute lands claimed as a result of original charters. Colonists saw the Quebec Act as punitive and tyrannical, and Amerindian peoples received no relief from the continuous assault on their land.

Britain's attempt to draw money from the colonies also created friction. New commercial regulations that increased the cost of foreign molasses and

The Tarring and Feathering of a British Official, 1774 This illustration from a British periodical shows the unfortunate John Malcomb, commissioner of customs at Boston, being tarred and feathered. By the mid-1770s British periodicals were focusing public opinion on mob violence and the breakdown of public order in the colonies. British critics of colonial political protests viewed the demand for liberty as little more than an excuse for mob violence.

LIBERTY TREE

THE BOSTONIANS PAYING THE EXCISE-MAN OR TARRING & FEATHERING

The Granger Collection, New York

endangered New England's profitable trade with Spanish and French Caribbean sugar colonies provoked widespread boycotts of British goods. The Stamp Act of 1765, which imposed a tax on all legal documents, newspapers, pamphlets, and other types of printed material, led to violent protest and more effective boycotts. But the British Parliament imposed new taxes and duties soon after repealing the Stamp Act in 1766, even sending British troops to quell urban riots. Unable to control the streets of Boston, British authorities reacted by threatening traditional liberties, dissolving the colonial legislature of Massachusetts, and dispatching a warship and two regiments of soldiers to reestablish control. Support for a complete break with Britain grew when a British force fired on an angry Boston crowd on March 5, 1770, killing five civilians. This "Boston Massacre," which seemed to expose the naked force on which colonial rule rested, radicalized public opinion throughout the colonies.

Parliament attempted to calm public opinion by repealing some of the taxes and duties, then stumbled into another crisis by granting the British East India Company a monopoly for importing tea to the colonies, which raised anew the constitutional issue of Parliament's right to tax the colonies. It also offended wealthy colonial merchants, who were excluded from this profitable commerce. The crisis came to a head in the already politically overheated port of Boston when tea worth £10,000 was dumped into the harbor by protesters disguised as Amerindians.

The Course of the Revolution

As the crisis mounted, patriots created new governing bodies, effectively deposed many British governors and other officials, passed laws, appointed judges, and even took control of colonial militias.

 History in Focus *In addition to what the caption tells, what do the figures and their surroundings, particularly the Liberty Tree, tell you about how some in Britain viewed the American colonists and their cause? If this picture had appeared in an American magazine, how might it have been different? Find the answer online.*

Simultaneously, radical leaders organized crowds to intimidate loyalists—people who were pro-British—and to enforce the boycott of British goods. Events were propelling the colonies toward revolution. Elected representatives, meeting in Philadelphia as the Continental Congress in 1775, assumed the powers of government, creating a currency and organizing an army. **George Washington** (1732–1799), a Virginia planter who had served in the French and Indian War,

George Washington (1732–1799) Military commander of the American Revolution. He was the first elected president of the United States (1789–1799).

was named commander. On July 4, 1776, Congress approved the Declaration of Independence, the document that proved to be the most enduring statement of the revolutionary era's ideology:

> We hold these truths to be self evident: That all men are created equal; that they are endowed by their creator with certain unalienable rights; that among these are life, liberty and the pursuit of happiness; that, to secure these rights, governments are instituted among men, deriving their just powers from the consent of the governed.

This affirmation of popular sovereignty and individual rights influenced the language of revolution and popular protest around the world.

To shore up British authority, Great Britain sent more than 400 ships, 50,000 soldiers, and 30,000 German mercenaries. But this military commitment proved futile. Although British forces won most of the battles, Washington slowly built a competent Continental army and civilian support networks that provided supplies and financial resources. In the final decisive battle, fought at Yorktown, Virginia, an American army, supported by French soldiers, besieged a British army led by General Charles Cornwallis. With escape cut off by a French fleet, Cornwallis surrendered to Washington as the British military band played "The World Turned Upside-Down."

New Republican Institutions

Ignoring the British example of an unwritten constitution, representatives in each of the newly independent states drafted formal charters and submitted the results to voters for ratification. Europeans were fascinated by these written constitutions and by their formal ratification by the people. Here was the social contract of Locke and Rousseau made manifest. The state constitutions also placed severe limits on executive authority but granted legislatures greater powers than in colonial times. Many states also inserted in their constitutions a bill of rights to provide further protection against government tyranny.

 Primary Source: The United States Declaration of Independence Consider Thomas Jefferson's famous words, and find out how he and his cohorts justified their separation from Great Britain.

An effective constitution for the new national government was developed more slowly and hesitantly. The Articles of Confederation—the first constitution of the United States—were not accepted by all the states until 1781. With the coming of peace in 1783, there was an effort to fashion a new constitution. Debate at the **Constitutional Convention**, which began meeting in May 1787, focused on several issues: representation, electoral procedures, executive powers, and the relationship between the federal government and the states. The final compromise provided for a two-house legislature: the lower house (the House of Representatives) to be elected directly by voters and the upper house (the Senate) to be elected by state legislatures. The chief executive—the president—was to be elected indirectly by "electors" selected by ballot in the states (each state had a number of electors equal to the number of its representatives and senators).

Although the U.S. Constitution created the most democratic government of the era, only a minority of the adult population was given full rights. Southern leaders were able to protect the institution of slavery by counting three-fifths of the slave population in the calculations that determined their states' congressional representatives. Although women had led prewar boycotts and had organized relief and charitable

Constitutional Convention Meeting in 1787 of the elected representatives of the thirteen original states to write the Constitution of the United States.

organizations during the war, they also were denied political rights in the new republic.

The French Revolution

What were the origins and accomplishments of the French Revolution?

The French Revolution confronted the entrenched privileges of an established church, monarchy, and aristocracy more directly than the American Revolution did. It also expanded mass participation in political life and radicalized the democratic tradition. But in the end, the passions unleashed in France by revolutionary events could not be sustained.

French Society and Fiscal Crisis

French society was divided into three groups, called Estates. The clergy, the First Estate, numbered about 130,000 in a nation of 28 million. The Catholic Church owned about 10 percent of the nation's land and extracted substantial amounts of wealth from the economy in the form of tithes and ecclesiastical fees. Despite its substantial wealth, the church was exempted from nearly all taxes.

The 300,000 members of the nobility, the Second Estate, controlled about 30 percent of the land and retained ancient rights on much of the rest. Nobles held the vast majority of high administrative, judicial, military, and church positions. Though traditionally barred from some types of commercial activity, nobles were also important participants in wholesale trade, banking, manufacturing, and mining.

The Third Estate included everyone else. There were three times as many members of the bourgeoisie (boor-zhwah-ZEE) in 1774, when Louis XVI took the throne, as there had been in 1715, at the end of Louis XIV's reign. Peasants accounted for 80 percent of the French population. They owned some property and lived decently when crops were good and prices stable. By 1780, however, poor harvests had decreased their incomes.

The nation's poor were a large, growing, and troublesome sector. Urban streets swarmed with beggars and prostitutes. Unable to afford decent housing, obtain steady employment, or protect their children, the poor periodically erupted in violent protest and

Parisian Stocking Mender The poor lived very difficult lives. This woman uses a discarded wine barrel as a shop where she mends stockings.

Private Collection

rage. In the countryside, violence was often the reaction to increased dues and fees. In towns and cities, an increase in the price of bread often provided the spark.

These explosive episodes, however, were not revolutionary in character. The remedies sought were conventional and immediate rather than structural and long term. That was to change when the Crown tried to solve its fiscal crisis by imposing new taxes on the nobility and on other groups that in the past had enjoyed exemptions. But this effort failed in the face of widespread protest and the refusal of the Parlement of Paris, a court of appeal that heard appeals from local courts throughout France, to register the new tax. In 1768, frustrated authorities exiled the members of that Parlement and pushed through a series of unpopular fiscal measures.

Despite the worsening fiscal crisis, the French government took on the heavy burden of supporting the American Revolution, delaying collapse by borrowing enormous sums. By the end of the war with Britain, more than half of France's national budget was required to service the debt alone. In 1787, the desperate

Parisians Storm Bastille An eye-witness to the storming of the Bastille on July 14, 1789, painted this representation of this epochal event, still celebrated by the French as their national holiday.

Photos12.com–AJR

king called an Assembly of Notables to approve a radical and comprehensive reform of the economy and fiscal policy. Although the members of this assembly were selected by the king's advisers from the high nobility, the judiciary, and the clergy, they proved unwilling to act as a rubber stamp for the proposed reforms or new taxes. Instead, these representatives of France's most privileged classes sought to protect their interests by questioning the competence of the king and his ministers to supervise the nation's affairs, thus creating the conditions for political revolution.

Protest Turns to Revolution

Unable to extract needed tax concessions from the notables, King Louis XVI was forced to call the **Estates General**, the French national legislature, which had not met since 1614. Traditionally, the three estates met separately, and a positive vote by two of the three was required for action. Tradition, however, was quickly overturned when the Third Estate refused to conduct business until the king ordered the other two estates to sit with it in a single body. During a six-week period of stalemate, many parish priests deserted the First Estate to meet with the Third Estate.

When this expanded Third Estate declared itself the **National Assembly**, the king and his advisers recognized that the reformers intended to force them to accept a constitutional monarchy. Louis's agenda for fiscal reform was being displaced by the central ideas of the era: the people were sovereign, and the legitimacy of political institutions and individual

rulers ultimately depended on their carrying out the people's will. Louis prepared for a confrontation with the National Assembly by moving military forces to Versailles. But before he could act, the people of Paris intervened.

A succession of bad harvests beginning in 1785 had propelled bread prices upward throughout France and provoked an economic depression. By the time the Estates General met, nearly a third of the Parisian work force was unemployed. Hunger and anger marched hand in hand through working-class neighborhoods. When the people of Paris heard that the king was massing troops to arrest their representatives, crowds of common people began to seize arms and mobilize. On July 14, 1789, a crowd searching for military supplies attacked the Bastille (bass-TEEL), a medieval fortress used as a prison. The futile defense of the Bastille cost ninety-eight lives before its garrison surrendered. Enraged, the attackers hacked the commander to death and then paraded through the

Estates General France's traditional national assembly with representatives of the three estates, or classes, in French society: the clergy, nobility, and commoners. The calling of the Estates General in 1789 led to the French Revolution.

National Assembly French Revolutionary assembly (1789–1791). Called first as the Estates General, the three estates came together and demanded radical change. It passed the Declaration of the Rights of Man and of the Citizen in 1789.

Playing Cards from the French Revolution Even playing cards could be used to attack the aristocracy and Catholic Church. In this pack of cards, "Equality" and "Liberty" replaced kings and queens.

city with his head and that of Paris's chief magistrate stuck on pikes.

These events coincided with uprisings in the country. Peasants sacked manor houses, destroyed documents that recorded their traditional obligations, refused to pay taxes and dues to landowners, and seized common lands. Forced to recognize the fury raging through rural areas, the National Assembly voted to end traditional obligations and to reform the tax system. Having forced acceptance of their narrow agenda, the peasants ceased their revolt.

These popular uprisings strengthened the hand of the National Assembly in its dealings with the king. One manifestation of this altered relationship was passage of the **Declaration of the Rights of Man and of the Citizen**, which was more sweeping in its language than the American Declaration of Independence. Among the enumerated natural rights were "liberty, property, security, and resistance to oppression." The Declaration of the Rights of Man and of the Citizen also guaranteed free expression of ideas, equality before the law, and representative government.

While delegates debated political issues in Versailles, the economic crisis worsened in Paris. Because the working women of Paris faced high food prices every day as they struggled to feed their families, their anger had a hard edge. On October 5, market women organized a crowd of thousands to march the 12 miles (19 kilometers) to Versailles (vuhr-SIGH). Once there, they forced their way into the National Assembly to demand action from the frightened representatives: "The point is that we want bread." The crowd then entered the royal apartments, killed some of the king's guards, and searched for Queen Marie Antoinette (ann-twah-NET), whom they loathed as a symbol of extravagance. Eventually, the crowd demanded that the royal family return to Paris. Preceded by the heads of two aristocrats carried on pikes and hauling away the palace's supply of flour, the triumphant crowd escorted the royal family to Paris.

In the next two years the National Assembly achieved a radically restructured French society. It passed a new constitution that dramatically limited monarchical power and abolished the nobility as a hereditary class. Economic reforms swept away monopolies and trade barriers within France. The Legislative Assembly created by the new constitution seized church lands to use as collateral for a new paper currency, and priests, who were to be elected, were put on the state payroll. When the government tried to force priests to take a loyalty oath, however, many Catholics joined a growing counterrevolutionary movement.

Primary Source: The Declaration of the Rights of Man and of the Citizen Learn about the assertions of the French National Assembly and see how its views compare to those expressed in the American Declaration of Independence.

Declaration of the Rights of Man and of the Citizen (1789) Statement of fundamental political rights adopted by the French National Assembly at the beginning of the French Revolution.

At first, many European monarchs had welcomed the weakening of the French king, but by 1791 Austria and Prussia threatened to intervene in support of the monarchy. The Legislative Assembly responded by declaring war. Although the war went badly at first for French forces, people across France responded patriotically to foreign invasions, forming huge new volunteer armies and mobilizing national resources to meet the challenge. By the end of 1792, French armies had gained the upper hand everywhere.

In this period of national crisis and foreign threat, the French Revolution entered its most radical phase. A failed effort by the king and queen to escape from Paris and find foreign allies cost the king any remaining popular support. As foreign armies crossed into France, his behavior was increasingly viewed as treasonous. In August 1792, the Legislative Assembly suspended the king, ordered his imprisonment, and called for the formation of a new National Convention to be elected by the vote of all men. Swept along by popular passion, the newly elected National Convention convicted Louis XVI of treason, sentenced him to death, and proclaimed France a republic.

The guillotine ended the king's life in January 1793. Invented in the spirit of the era as a more humane way to execute the condemned, this machine was to become the bloody symbol of the Revolution. During the period of repression called the Reign of Terror (1793–1794), approximately 40,000 people were executed or died in prison. This radical phase ended in July 1794 when the Terror's leaders were themselves executed by guillotine.

Reaction and Dictatorship

Purged of the radicals, the National Convention—the new legislative assembly of the French republic— began to undo the radical reforms. It removed many of the emergency economic controls that had been holding down prices and protecting the working class. When the Paris working class rose in protest in 1795, the Convention approved the use of overwhelming military force. It also permitted the Catholic Church to regain much of its former influence, but it would not return the church's confiscated wealth. Finally, it ratified a more conservative constitution, which protected property, established a voting process that reduced the power of the masses, and created a new executive authority, the Directory. Once installed in power, however, the Directory proved unable to end the foreign wars or solve domestic economic problems.

After losing the election of 1797, the Directory suspended the results. The republican phase of the Revolution was clearly dead. Legitimacy was now based on coercive power rather than on elections. Two years later, **Napoleon Bonaparte** (1769–1821), a brilliant young general in the French army, seized power. Just as the American and French Revolutions had been the start of the modern democratic tradition, the military intervention that brought Napoleon to power in 1799 marked the advent of another modern form of government: popular authoritarianism.

In contrast to the National Convention, Napoleon proved capable of realizing France's dream of dominating Europe and providing effective protection for persons and property at home. Negotiations with the Catholic Church led to the Concordat of 1801, which gave French Catholics the right to practice their religion freely. Napoleon's Civil Code of 1804 asserted two basic principles inherited from the moderate first stage of the French Revolution: equality in law and protection of property. Even some members of the nobility became supporters after Napoleon declared himself emperor and France an empire in 1804.

While providing personal security, however, the Napoleonic system restricted many individual rights. Women were denied basic political rights, and free speech and free expression were limited. Criticism of the government, viewed as subversive, was proscribed, and most opposition newspapers disappeared.

Ultimately, the Napoleonic system depended on the success of French arms and French diplomacy (see Map 20.1). From Napoleon's assumption of power until his fall, no single European state could defeat the French military. Austria and Prussia were forced to become allies of France. Only Britain, protected

Napoleon Bonaparte (Napoleon I) (1769–1821) The general who overthrew the French Directory in 1799 and became emperor of the French in 1804. He failed to defeat Great Britain and abdicated in 1814, then returned to power briefly in 1815 but was defeated and died in exile.

Map 20.1 Napoleon's Europe, 1810 By 1810 Great Britain was the only remaining European power at war with Napoleon. Because of the loss of the French fleet at the Battle of Trafalgar in 1805, Napoleon was unable to threaten Britain with invasion, and Britain was able to actively assist the resistance movements in Spain and Portugal, thereby helping weaken French power. © Cengage Learning

  Interactive Map

French empire
Dependent states
Allied with Napoleon
At war with Napoleon
★ Major battle

by its powerful navy, remained able to thwart Napoleon's plans to dominate Europe. In June 1812, Napoleon made the fateful decision to invade Russia with 600,000 men, the largest army ever assembled in Europe. Five weeks after occupying Moscow, he was forced to retreat, his army destroyed by the brutal Russian winter and attacks by Russian forces. A broken and battered fragment of 30,000 men returned home to France.

After the debacle in Russia, Austria and Prussia deserted Napoleon and allied themselves with Britain and Russia. Unable to defend Paris, Napoleon was forced to abdicate the French throne in April 1814. The allies then exiled him to the island of Elba off the coast of Italy and restored the French monarchy.

Retrenchment, Reform, and Revolution

The French Revolution and Napoleon's imperial ambitions had threatened the survival of the old European order by overturning ancient monarchies and tossing aside long-established political institutions. The very existence of the nobility and church had been put at risk. Under the leadership of the Austrian foreign minister, Prince Klemens von Metternich (MET-uhr-nik) (1773–1859), Britain, Russia, Austria, and Prussia, along with representatives of other nations, worked together in Vienna to create a comprehensive peace settlement that they hoped would safeguard the conservative order. Because the participants in the **Congress of Vienna** believed that a strong and stable France was the best guarantee of future peace, the French monarchy was reestablished, and Metternich sought to offset French strength with a balance of power.

Despite the power of the conservative monarchs, popular support for national self-determination and democratic reform grew throughout Europe. In 1821, Greek patriots launched a movement for independence from Ottoman control, and in 1830 Russia, France, and Great Britain forced the Ottoman Empire to recognize Greek independence. That same year, the people of Paris rose up and forced King Charles X to abdicate. His successor, Louis Philippe (loo-EE fee-LEEP) (r. 1830–1848), reestablished the constitution and extended voting privileges.

Despite limited political reform, conservatives continued to hold the upper hand in Europe. Finally,

SECTION REVIEW

- The French Revolution grew from mounting social and financial crises after 1765.

- The crisis within the Estates General sparked the Revolution when the Third Estate declared itself the National Assembly.

- Popular uprisings thwarted military intervention and enabled the National Assembly to press its reforms on the monarchy.

- Economic crisis and foreign intervention radicalized the Revolution, resulting in the execution of Louis XVI and the Reign of Terror.

- Reaction against the Terror resulted in the conservative Directory and the dictatorship of Napoleon.

- Despite conservative retrenchment after Napoleon's fall, liberal reform and revolution continued through the failed 1848 revolutions.

in 1848, the desire for democratic reform and national self-determination and the frustrations of urban workers led to upheavals across Europe. The **Revolutions of 1848** began in Paris, where members of the middle class and workers united to overthrow the regime of Louis Philippe and create the Second French Republic. Adult men were given voting rights, slavery was abolished in French colonies, the death penalty was ended, and a ten-hour workday was legislated for Paris. But Parisian workers' demand for programs to reduce unemployment and lower prices provoked conflicts with the middle class, which wanted to protect property rights. Desiring the reestablishment of order, the French elected Louis Napoleon, nephew of the former emperor, as president in December 1848. Three years later, he overturned the constitution as a result of popular plebiscite and, after ruling briefly as dictator, became Emperor Napoleon III. He remained in power until 1871. Despite their heroism on the barricades of Vienna, Rome, and Berlin, the revolutionaries

Congress of Vienna (1814–1815) Meeting of representatives of European monarchs called to reestablish the old order after the defeat of Napoleon I.
Revolutions of 1848 Democratic and nationalist revolutions that swept across Europe. In France the monarchy was overthrown. In Germany, Austria, Italy, and Hungary the revolutions failed.

of 1848 failed to gain either their nationalist or their republican objectives. Metternich, the symbol of reaction, fled Vienna in disguise, but little lasting change occurred. Monarchs retained the support not only of aristocrats but also of professional militaries, largely recruited from among peasants who had little sympathy for urban workers.

Revolution in Haiti and Latin America

How did revolution in one country help incite revolution elsewhere?

In the Americas, the revolutionary ideology of the American and French Revolutions was spreading and taking hold. On the island of Hispaniola, a revolution ended slavery and French rule in Saint Domingue. The same economic and political forces that had undermined British rule in the colonies that became the United States were present in Spanish America and Brazil.

The Haitian Revolution

The French colony of Saint Domingue produced two-thirds of France's tropical imports and generated nearly one-third of all French foreign trade. This impressive wealth depended on a brutal slave regime. The harsh punishments and high mortality inflicted on the slaves of Saint Domingue were notorious throughout the Caribbean.

In 1789, when news of the calling of France's Estates General arrived on the island, wealthy white planters sent a delegation to Paris charged with seeking more home rule and greater economic freedom. The *gens de couleur* (zhahn duh koo-LUHR) also sent representatives. Mostly small planters or urban merchants, these free mixed-race delegates focused on ending race discrimination and political inequality. They did not seek freedom for slaves, because the most prosperous were slave owners themselves.

The political turmoil in France weakened colonial authority, permitting rich planters, poor whites, *gens de couleur*, and slaves to pursue their narrow interests, in an increasingly bitter and confrontational struggle. By 1791, whites and *gens de couleur* were engaged in open warfare. This breach between the two groups of slave owners gave the slaves an

opening. Their rebellion began on the plantations of the north and spread throughout the colony. Slaves destroyed plantations, killed masters and overseers, and burned crops.

The rebellious slaves eventually gained the upper hand under the military leadership of **Toussaint L'Ouverture**, a former domestic slave. Politically strengthened in 1794 when the radical National Convention in Paris abolished slavery in all French possessions, Toussaint overcame his rivals in Saint Domingue, defeated a British expeditionary force in 1798, and then led an invasion of the neighboring Spanish colony of Santo Domingo, freeing the slaves there. Toussaint continued to assert his loyalty to France but gave the French government no effective role in local affairs.

In 1802, Napoleon sent a large military force to Saint Domingue to reestablish both French authority and slavery. At first, the French forces were successful. Toussaint was captured and sent to France, where he died in prison. Eventually, however, French losses to yellow fever and the resistance of the revolutionaries turned the tide. Whereas few slave women had taken up arms during the early stages of the Haitian Revolution, they now joined the armed resistance. In 1804, the free republic of Haiti joined the United States as the second independent nation in the Western Hemisphere. But independence and emancipation were achieved at a terrible price. Tens of thousands had died, and the economy was destroyed.

Latin American Revolutions

The great works of the Enlightenment as well as revolutionary documents like the Declaration of Independence and the Declaration of the Rights of Man and of the Citizen circulated widely in Latin America. But it was Napoleon's decision to invade Portugal (1807) and Spain (1808), not revolutionary ideas, that ignited Latin America's struggle for independence.

In 1808, the royal family of Portugal fled to Brazil and maintained court there for over a decade. In

gens de couleur Free mixed-race men and women in Haiti. They sought greater political rights and later supported the Haitian Revolution.

Toussaint L'Ouverture (1743–1803) Leader of the Haitian Revolution. He freed the slaves and gained effective independence for Haiti despite military interventions by the British and French.

Burning of Cap Français, Saint Domingue, in 1793 In 1791, the slaves of Saint Domingue, France's richest colony, began a rebellion that, after years of struggle, ended slavery and created the Western Hemisphere's second independent nation, Haiti.

Spain, in contrast, Napoleon forced King Ferdinand VII to abdicate and placed his own brother, Joseph Bonaparte, on the throne. When Spanish patriots fighting against the French created a new political body, the *Junta Central* (HUN-tah cen-TRAHL), and claimed the right to exercise the king's powers over Spain's colonies, a vocal minority of powerful colonists objected. In late 1808 and 1809, popular movements overthrew Spanish colonial officials in Venezuela, Mexico, and Bolivia and created local *juntas* or councils. In each case, Spanish officials' harsh repression gave rise to a greater sense of a separate American nationality. By 1810, Spanish colonial authorities were facing a new round of revolutions more clearly focused on the achievement of independence.

In Caracas (the capital city of modern Venezuela), a revolutionary junta led by creoles (colonial-born whites) declared independence in 1811. Its leaders were large landowners who espoused popular sovereignty and representative democracy, defended slavery, and opposed full citizenship for the black and mixed-race majority. The junta's narrow agenda spurred loyalists in the colonial administration and church hierarchy

to rally thousands of free blacks and slaves to defend the Spanish Empire. In response, the revolutionaries made **Simón Bolívar** (see-MOAN bow-LEE-varh) (1783–1830) the preeminent leader of the independence movement in Spanish South America.

Between 1813 and 1817, military advantage shifted back and forth between the patriots and loyalists, but by 1820, momentum swung irreversibly to the patriots. After liberating present-day Venezuela, Colombia, Ecuador, Peru, and Bolivia, Bolívar's army defeated the last Spanish armies in Peru in 1824. But Bolívar's attempt to draw the former Spanish colonies into a formal confederation failed (see Map 20.2).

Buenos Aires (the capital city of modern Argentina) was the second important center of revolutionary activity in Spanish South America. In the south, a coalition of militia commanders, merchants, and ranchers declared independence as the United Provinces of Río

Simón Bolívar (1783–1830) The most important military leader in the struggle for independence in South America. Born in Venezuela, he led military forces there and in Colombia, Ecuador, Peru, and Bolivia.

OREGON COUNTRY
(Joint U.S.-British occupation)

BRITISH NORTH AMERICA
(CANADA)
(Gr. Br.)

Mississippi R.

Colorado R.

UNITED STATES

New York
Philadelphia
Washington, D.C.

MEXICO
1821

Rio Grande

San Antonio
New Orleans
Charleston

Gulf of Mexico

ATLANTIC
OCEAN

N

Mexico City
Veracruz

BAHAMA IS.
(Gr. Br.)

Havana
CUBA
(Spain)

HAITI 1804

40°W

40°N

20°N

BRITISH HONDURAS (Gr. Br.)

JAMAICA
(Gr. Br.)

PUERTO RICO (Spain)

GUATEMALA
Guatemala City

Caribbean Sea

UNITED PROVINCES OF
CENTRAL AMERICA
1823–1839

Panama

TRINIDAD (Gr. Br.)

Caracas

BR. GUIANA (Gr. Br.)

DUTCH GUIANA (Neth.)

VENEZUELA

Magdalena R.

Orinoco R.

FRENCH GUIANA (France)

Socorro
Bogotá

GRAN COLOMBIA
1819–1830

Quito
ECUADOR

*Galápagos
Islands*

Amazon R.

Equator 0°

EMPIRE OF BRAZIL
1822

PACIFIC
OCEAN

Lima

PERU
1824

BOLIVIA
1825
La Paz

Sucre

Salvador

PARAGUAY
1811

São Paulo

Rio de Janeiro

20°S

Paraná R.

**Map 20.2 Latin America by
1830** By 1830 patriot forces had
overturned the Spanish and Portuguese Empires of the Western Hemisphere. Regional conflicts, local wars,
and foreign interventions challenged
the survival of many of these new
nations following independence.

© Cengage Learning

CHILE
1817

Valparaíso
Santiago

UNITED
PROVINCES OF
THE RIO DE
LA PLATA
1816

ARGENTINA

Buenos Aires

URUGUAY
1828

Montevideo

Bahía
Blanca

Interactive Map

PATAGONIA
(Disputed between
Argentina and Chile)

*Islas Malvinas
(Falkland Islands)*

80°W

60°W

0   500   1000 Km.

0   500   1000 Mi.

1811 Year independence gained

Colony

Schaalkwijk/Art Resource, NY

Padre Hidalgo   Padre Manuel Hidalgo y Costilla led the first stage of Mexico's revolution for independence by rallying the rural masses. His defeat, trial, and execution made him one of Mexico's most important political martyrs.

SECTION REVIEW

- Revolutionary events in France prompted Saint Domingue's whites and *gens de couleur* to demand reforms.

- As the revolution radicalized, these groups fought in open warfare, enabling slaves under Toussaint L'Ouverture to defeat both and establish the republic of Haiti.

- Napoleon invaded Portugal and Spain, Portugal's royal family fled to Brazil, and popular uprisings broke out in Venezuela, Mexico, and Bolivia.

- Throughout Latin America, loyalists battled separatists, while Spanish-born colonists, creoles, Amerindians, and mixed-race people struggled for control.

- Bolívar and San Martín won the independence of the Spanish South American nations, while Brazil broke from Portugal as a constitutional monarchy.

- Mexico's revolution unfolded as both an independence and class struggle with conservative elements retaining considerable power.

de la Plata in 1816. Patriot leaders in Buenos Aires at first sought to retain control over the old Viceroyalty of Río de la Plata, but a separatist movement defeated these ambitions, and Argentina descended into chaos. However, a mixed force of Chileans and Argentines, led by José de San Martín (hoe-SAY deh san mar-TEEN) (1778–1850), liberated Chile in 1820.

The arrival of the Portuguese royal family in Brazil in 1808 had helped to maintain the loyalty of the colonial elite and to stimulate the local economy. But when King John VI returned to Portugal in 1821, Brazilians began to reevaluate Brazil's relationship with Portugal and to talk openly of independence.

Unwilling to return to Portugal and committed to maintaining his family's hold on Brazil, King John's son Pedro aligned himself with the rising tide of independence sentiment. In 1822, he declared Brazilian independence. Unlike its neighbors, which became constitutional republics, Brazil gained independence

as a constitutional monarchy with Pedro I, heir to the throne of Portugal, as emperor. The monarchy lasted until 1889, when it was overthrown by republicans.

Mexico   In 1810, Mexico was Spain's richest and most populous colony. But the sharp distinctions among its creole, native, and Spanish populations made it ripe for revolution. The first stage of the revolution against Spain occurred in central Mexico, where wealthy ranchers and farmers had aggressively expelled many Amerindian communities from their traditional agricultural lands. By the time news of Napoleon's invasion of Spain reached the region, crop failures and epidemics had further afflicted the poor.

On September 16, 1810, **Miguel Hidalgo y Costilla** (mee-GEHL ee-DAHL-go ee cos-TEA-ah), parish priest of the small town of Dolores, rang the church bells, attracting thousands (see Material Culture: Bells, Gongs, and Drums). In a fiery speech, he urged

Primary Source: The Jamaica Letter   Read from this famous political manifesto and see what grand hopes Simón Bolívar was able to sustain for South America even at the lowest of times.

Miguel Hidalgo y Costilla (1753–1811)   Mexican priest who led the first stage of the Mexican independence war in 1810. He was captured and executed in 1811.

Material Culture

Bells, Gongs, and Drums

Thunder, the roar of surf, the gusting of wind—these were the loudest sounds normally heard in prehistoric communities. Other natural sounds were quieter: birdsong, insect whines, the occasional animal bark, grunt, or snuffle. The loudest sounds humans made for themselves were probably shouts, cries, and the pounding of wood and stone. Some loud sounds, such as thunderclaps or the braying of donkeys and the crowing of roosters, gave rise to strong feelings. Thunder seemed to be of supernatural origin, the cockcrow was associated with dawn, and the braying of donkeys, at least in the imaginations of ancient peoples in Egypt and western Asia, was a token of death and the underworld.

When humans devised their own ways of producing loud sounds, they often used them in religious rituals or as symbols of high social rank. Drums were undoubtedly the first manmade devices for making loud sounds. Though the date of 6000 B.C.E. is often given for the first drums, the generally poor preservation of wood and skin in archaeological sites makes it likely that they were in use much earlier but left no identifiable remains. Drumming retained its great ceremonial and political importance in sub-Saharan Africa and pre-Columbian America down to the modern era.

Bells and gongs, the latter either flat metal disks or upward-opening bowls, come much later. Bronze made from copper and tin, the preferred metal for these instruments, does not appear in western Asian archaeological sites before 3000 B.C.E. Bronze in China is almost as early, and it shows up somewhat later in tin-rich Southeast Asia.

Magnificent bronze drums were made and exported from Vietnam after 1000 B.C.E. But bells were more important than drums in early Chinese culture. By the late first millennium B.C.E., court ceremonies and musical performers utilized sets of tuned bells covering five octaves. Some could produce two separate notes depending on where they were struck. Gongs appeared in China around 500 C.E. and spread from there to Southeast Asia, where they play a central role in Indonesian percussion orchestras. Centuries later, when Buddhism spread in East Asia, bells became an essential part of Buddhist worship.

Though tin bronze may have originated in western Asia, large bells were not greatly used in ancient Egypt and Mesopotamia or in Greco-Roman antiquity. Following Jewish precedent, early Christian communities in Egypt and Syria summoned their congregations with trumpets. Around the sixth century C.E., rhythmic pounding with a mallet on a long piece of wood or metal called a "semantron" superseded trumpet calls in Eastern Orthodox churches. This device is still used in some Russian Orthodox monasteries.

Christian churches may have used bells as early as 500 C.E., but evidence of bell use becomes strong

---

the crowd to rise up against the oppression of Spanish officials. The tens of thousands of the rural and urban poor who joined his movement lacked military discipline and adequate weapons but knew who their oppressors were. At first sympathetic to Hidalgo's objectives, wealthy Mexicans eventually turned against Hidalgo, who was captured, tried, and executed in 1811.

Although insurgents continued to wage war against Spanish forces, colonial rule seemed secure in 1820. However, news of the military revolt in Spain unsettled the conservative groups and church officials who had defended Spanish rule against Hidalgo and José Morelos, who continued the revolution after Hidalgo's execution. In 1821, Colonel Agustín de Iturbide (ah-goos-TEEN deh ee-tur-BEE-deh) and other loyalist commanders forged an alliance with remaining insurgents and declared Mexico's independence. The conservative origins of Mexico's transition to independence were highlighted by the decision to create a monarchial form of government and crown Iturbide as emperor. In early 1823, however, the army overthrew Iturbide and Mexico became a republic.

only a century later, mostly in connection with Irish churches. The Latin word *clocca*, from which English *clock* derives, comes from the Irish word *clog*, meaning "bell." More than sixty early Irish bells still survive, the earliest made of iron, with bronze becoming the preferred metal by 900 C.E.

Early Protestant claims that Catholic ceremonies for blessing bells were superstitious may reflect the fact that many rural communities did attribute supernatural powers to bells. As late as the eighteenth century many French villagers believed that they could ward off crop-damaging hail by ringing their church bell. At the end of the century, such beliefs contributed to villages defying the demand of the secular French Republic that all bells be melted down and the metal recast as cannon. Well into the nineteenth century France witnessed many struggles between secular and religious officials—mayors and priests—for control of the village bell.

Some bells have gained symbolic importance more recently. In 1871 the New York Stock Exchange adopted a Chinese gong to signal its daily opening and closing in place of the traditional gavel. In 1903 a bell replaced the gong, but the "opening bell" became a media event only in 1995 when guests ranging from corporate executives and foreign dignitaries to basketball star LeBron James, actress Sarah Jessica Parker, and scourge of the universe Darth Vader were invited to mount the podium and perform the ceremony.

Vanni/Art Resource, NY

Bell Pavilion in Nara, Japan The Bell Pavilion at the Todai-ji Temple in Nara houses the biggest bell in Japan, cast in 752. Like all wooden buildings in Japan, the pavilion itself has been rebuilt several times, most recently in 1966–1967.

QUESTIONS FOR ANALYSIS

1. What comparison can you make between the sound environment of a modern city and that of the preindustrial countryside?
2. What makes the sound of a bell, gong, or drum more impressive than an equally loud automobile alarm or steam whistle?
3. Do drums have a greater or smaller emotional impact than bells and gongs?

Economic and Social Liberation Movements

What economic and social liberation movements rose during the nineteenth century?

During the nineteenth century, the newly independent nations of the Western Hemisphere struggled to realize the Enlightenment ideals of freedom and individual liberty. The persistence of slavery and women's inequality raised troubling questions about these ideals. By century's end, reform movements in many of the hemisphere's nations had made significant progress, but much remained to be done.

The Abolition of Slavery In both the United States and Latin America, strong antislavery sentiments were expressed during the struggles for independence. In nearly all the new nations of the Western Hemisphere, revolutionary leaders asserted universal ideals of freedom and citizenship that contrasted sharply with the reality of slavery. Men and women who wanted to outlaw slavery were called **abolitionists**. Despite their efforts, slavery survived in much of the hemisphere until the 1850s. In regions where the export of plantation products was most important—such as the United States, Brazil, and Cuba—the abolition of slavery was achieved with great difficulty.

In the United States, some northern states had abolished slavery after the Revolution, and Congress banned the importation of new slaves in 1808. But this progress was stalled by the profitable expansion of cotton agriculture after the War of 1812 between Britain and the United States. In Spanish America, tens of thousands of slaves gained freedom by joining revolutionary armies during the wars for independence. After independence, most Spanish American republics prohibited the slave trade. Counteracting that trend was the growing international demand for sugar and coffee, products traditionally produced on plantations by slaves. As prices rose for plantation products in the first half of the nineteenth century, Brazil and Cuba (a Spanish colony until 1899) increased their imports of slaves.

During the long struggle to end slavery in the United States, American abolitionists argued that slavery offended both morality and the universal rights asserted in the Declaration of Independence. Two groups denied full rights of citizenship under the Constitution, women and free African Americans, played important roles in the abolition of slavery. Women served on the executive committee of the American Anti-Slavery Society and produced some of the most effective propaganda against slavery. Many women abolitionists advocated female suffrage as well. Frederick Douglass, a former slave, became one of the most effective abolitionist speakers and writers. More radical black leaders saw civil war or slave insurrection as necessary for ending slavery.

In 1860, after Abraham Lincoln was elected president, the southern states where slavery was legal seceded from the United States to form a new nation, the Confederate States of America. During the Civil War that broke out between the northern states of the Union and the Confederacy, pressure for emancipation rose as tens of thousands of black freemen and escaped slaves joined the Union army. Hundreds of thousands of other slaves fled their masters' plantations and farms for the protection of advancing northern armies. In 1863, in the midst of the Civil War, President Lincoln began the abolition of slavery by issuing the Emancipation Proclamation, which ended slavery in rebel states not occupied by the Union army. Final abolition was accomplished in 1865 by the Thirteenth Amendment to the Constitution.

After Britain ended its participation in the slave trade in 1807, it negotiated treaties with Spain, Brazil, and other importers of slaves to eliminate the slave trade to the Americas. But enforcement proved difficult. For example, Brazil, despite its treaty of 1830, illegally imported over a half-million more African slaves before the British navy finally forced compliance in the 1850s. The Brazilian parliament abolished slavery in 1888.

Slavery lasted longest in Cuba. Despite strong British pressure, the Spanish colony continued to import large numbers of African slaves until the 1860s. More important, however, was the growth of support for abolition in these colonies. Both Cuba and Puerto Rico had larger white and free colored populations than did the Caribbean colonies of Britain and France. As a result, there was less fear in Cuba and Puerto Rico that abolition would lead to the political ascendancy of former slaves as had occurred in Haiti. In Puerto Rico, where slaves numbered approximately thirty thousand, local reformers sought and gained the abolition of slavery in 1873. Eventually, during a decade-long war to defeat forces seeking the independence of Cuba, the Spanish government moved toward gradual abolition. Finally, in 1886, slavery was abolished.

Equal Rights for Women and Blacks

The abolition of slavery in the Western Hemisphere did not end racial discrimination or provide full political rights for every citizen. Not only blacks but also women suffered political and economic discrimination during the nineteenth century.

abolitionists Men and women who agitated for a complete end to slavery. Abolitionist pressure ended the British transatlantic slave trade in 1808 and slavery in British colonies in 1834. In the United States the activities of abolitionists were one factor leading to the Civil War (1861–1865).

In 1848, a group of women angered by their exclusion from an international antislavery meeting issued a call for a meeting to discuss women's rights. The **Women's Rights Convention** at Seneca Falls, New York, issued a statement that said in part, "We hold these truths to be self-evident: that all men and women are equal." While moderates focused on the issues of greater economic independence and full legal rights, increasing numbers of women demanded the right to vote. Others lobbied to provide better conditions for women working outside the home, especially in textile factories.

Progress toward equality between men and women was equally slow in Canada and Latin America. Canada's first women doctors received their training in the United States because no woman could receive a medical degree in Canada until 1895. Argentina and Uruguay were among the first Latin American nations to provide public education for women, and both nations introduced coeducation in the 1870s. Chilean women gained access to some careers in medicine and law in the 1870s. In Brazil, where many women were active in the abolitionist movement, four women graduated in medicine by 1882. Throughout the hemisphere, more rapid progress was achieved in lower-status careers that threatened male economic power less directly, and by the end of the century, women dominated elementary school teaching throughout the Western Hemisphere.

From Canada to Argentina and Chile, the majority of working-class women had no direct involvement in these reform movements, but in their daily lives, they succeeded in transforming gender relations. By the end of the nineteenth century, large numbers of poor women worked outside the home on farms, in markets, and, increasingly, in factories.

Throughout the hemisphere, there was little progress toward eliminating racial discrimination. Blacks were denied the vote throughout the southern United States and subjected to the indignity of segregation. Racial discrimination against men and women of African descent was also common in Latin America, though seldom spelled out in legal codes. Latin Americans tended to view racial identity across a continuum of physical characteristics rather than in the narrow terms of black and white that defined race relations in the United States.

Conclusion

The last decades of the eighteenth century began a long period of revolutionary upheaval in the Atlantic world. Costly wars in Europe and along Europe's colonial frontiers in the Americas and Asia helped to provoke change, forcing European monarchs to impose new and unpopular taxes. The American Revolution initiated these transformations. Having defeated Britain, the citizens of this new American republic created the most democratic government of the time. While full rights were limited and slavery persisted, many Europeans saw this experiment as demonstrating the efficacy of the Enlightenment's most revolutionary political ideas. In the end, however, the compromises over slavery that had made the Constitution possible in 1787 failed, and the new nation nearly disintegrated after 1860.

The French Revolution led temporarily to a more radical formulation of representative democracy, but it also led to the Terror, which cost thousands of lives, the militarization of western Europe, and a destructive cycle of wars. Yet, despite these terrible costs, the

Women's Rights Convention An 1848 gathering of women angered by their exclusion from an international antislavery meeting. They met at Seneca Falls, New York, to discuss women's rights.

French Revolution propelled the idea of democracy and the ideal of equality far beyond the boundaries established earlier by the American Revolution. The Haitian Revolution, set in motion by events in France, not only created the second independent nation of the Western Hemisphere but also delivered a powerful blow to the institution of slavery. In Europe the excesses of the French Revolution and the wars that followed in its wake promoted the political ascent of Napoleon Bonaparte and democracy's modern nemesis, popular authoritarianism.

Each revolution had its own character. The revolutions in France and Haiti proved to be more violent and destructive than the American Revolution. First, there was no slave rebellion in North America. Although slavery was crucial to the most profitable exports such as tobacco, cotton, and rice, slaves in British North America remained a minority except along the South Carolina coast. In addition, revolutionaries in France and Haiti faced more strongly entrenched and more powerful oppositions as well as greater social inequalities than did the revolutionaries in North America. The resistance of entrenched and privileged elites led inexorably to greater violence. Both French and Haitian revolutionaries also faced powerful foreign interventions that intensified the bloodshed and destructiveness of these revolutions.

The conservative retrenchment that followed the defeat of Napoleon succeeded in the short term.

Monarchy, multinational empires, and the established church retained their hold on the loyalty of millions of Europeans and could count on the support of many of Europe's wealthiest and most powerful individuals. But liberalism and nationalism continued to stir revolutionary sentiment. The contest between adherents of the old order and partisans of change was to continue well into the nineteenth century. In the end, the nation-state, the Enlightenment legacy of rational inquiry, broadened political participation, and secular intellectual culture prevailed. This outcome was determined in large measure by the old order's inability to satisfy the new social classes that appeared with the emerging industrial economy. The material transformation produced by industrial capitalism could not be contained in the narrow confines of a hereditary social system, nor could the rapid expansion of scientific learning be contained within the doctrines of traditional religion.

The revolutions of the late eighteenth century began the transformation of Western society, but they did not complete it. Only a minority gained full political rights. Women did not achieve full political rights until the twentieth century. Democratic institutions, as in revolutionary France, often failed. Moreover, slavery endured in the Americas past the mid-1800s, despite the revolutionary era's enthusiasm for individual liberty.

CHAPTER REVIEW

 Download the MP3 audio file of the Chapter Review to listen to on the go.

How did the costs of imperial wars and the Enlightenment challenge the established authority of monarchs in Europe and the American colonies? (page 483)

This era of revolution was, in large measure, the product of a long period of costly warfare among the imperial nations of Europe. Britain and France in particular faced fiscal crises as a result of colonial wars. Using taxes and institutions inherited from the past, they found it increasingly difficult to fund distant wars in the Americas or in Asia. In the British case, the costs of the French and Indian War led the government to attempt to impose unpopular taxes on its colonies. France faced an even more dire fiscal emergency as a result of this war and later aid to the American revolutionaries. The refusal of powerful French interests to accept new taxes forced the king to call the Estates General and ultimately led to the French Revolution.

Meanwhile, the spread of literacy and the greater availability of books helped create an Enlightenment culture more open to reform and to the revolutionary change of existing institutions in Europe and in the Americas. But there were many distinct, even contradictory, currents in the Enlightenment. If the ideas of Locke and Rousseau guided critics of monarchy toward a new political culture of elections and representative institutions, these ideas were difficult to reconcile. Nevertheless, the intellectual ferment of the era gave educated men and women the tools to criticize existing political institutions and the confidence to design new ones. The language of liberty and equality, even if poorly realized in the actions of revolutionary governments, proved a powerful solvent when applied to hierarchy and privilege.

What were the direct causes of the American Revolution? (page 485)

The American Revolution grew from British colonial policy after the French and Indian War. To avoid new military costs, Britain tried unsuccessfully through the Quebec Act to restrict western settlement and thus reduce conflict with the Amerindians. To pay its war debt, Britain imposed new taxes, duties, and commercial regulations on the colonies, including the Stamp Act. These acts led to violent unrest that culminated with the "Boston Massacre." Parliament repealed some of these acts but then gave the British East India Company a tea monopoly, thus provoking more violence. Colonial patriots met in the Continental Congress, assumed government powers, raised an army, and issued the Declaration of Independence.

What were the origins and accomplishments of the French Revolution? (page 488)

The French Revolution erupted from the crises provoked by France's archaic social and tax system, financial collapse, urban unrest, and division between the monarchy and aristocracy. The immediate cause was the crisis within the Estates General, during which the Third Estate broke away and declared itself the National Assembly. Uprisings in Paris and the countryside strengthened the Assembly's position, enabling it to press reforms embodied in the Declaration of the Rights

of Man and of the Citizen. Further reforms restructured France's society and economy. However, foreign intervention pushed the Legislative Assembly to radical extremes that culminated with the execution of Louis XVI and the Reign of Terror.

Reaction against the Terror resulted in the conservative Directory and the even more repressive dictatorship of Napoleon Bonaparte. Napoleon's military adventures ultimately led to his fall, and the Congress of Vienna sought to establish a conservative balance of power. Despite this retrenchment, revolutionary struggles continued, especially in France, where the 1830 uprising replaced Charles X with Louis-Philippe. In 1848 nationalist and republican revolutions flared throughout Europe. These won few lasting gains, however, and in France they resulted in the imperial rule of Napoleon III.

How did revolution in one country help incite revolution elsewhere? (page 494)

Each new revolutionary development served as example and provocation for dissatisfied women and men elsewhere. French officers who took part in the American Revolution helped ignite the French Revolution. The constitutions of new American states and the new national constitution were published across Europe and read by thousands. Free black militiamen from Saint Domingue served along French units in support of the American Revolution. With the first stage of the French Revolution black freemen from Haiti traveled to France to seek their rights and returned to spread revolutionary passions. With the success of the Haitian Revolution, slaves throughout the Western Hemisphere took heart, and some rose in rebellion.

What economic and social liberation movements rose during the nineteenth century? (page 499)

In the newly independent nations of the Americas, the persistence of slavery and gender inequality clashed with the Enlightenment ideals that had fostered their revolutions. Rising demand for export crops after 1800 strengthened slavery in the southern United States and parts of Latin America. U.S. abolitionists, many of whom were women and free blacks, produced powerful antislavery propaganda. Although Lincoln issued the Emancipation Proclamation during the Civil War, final abolition did not come until the Thirteenth Amendment passed in 1865. Britain ceased to participate in the slave trade in 1807 and worked to end the Atlantic trade through treaties with slave importers. Although Britain's navy forced compliance on Latin American importers, slavery continued in Brazil, Cuba, and Puerto Rico until late in the nineteenth century. The movement for women's rights in the United States began with the Seneca Falls Women's Rights Convention, but progress on gender equality was slow throughout the Western Hemisphere. Equally slow was the elimination of racial discrimination. Legalized in the southern United States, it also persisted in Latin America without formal codification.

Key Terms

Enlightenment *(p. 483)*

George Washington *(p. 486)*

Constitutional Convention *(p. 487)*

Estates General *(p. 489)*

National Assembly *(p. 489)*

Declaration of the Rights of Man and of the Citizen *(p. 490)*

Napoleon Bonaparte *(p. 491)*

Congress of Vienna *(p. 493)*

Revolutions of 1848 *(p. 493)*

gens de couleur (p. 494)

Toussaint L'Ouverture *(p. 494)*

Simón Bolívar *(p. 495)*

Miguel Hidalgo y Costilla *(p. 497)*

abolitionists *(p. 500)*

Women's Rights Convention *(p. 501)*

Web Resources

Pronunciation Guide

Interactive Maps

- MAP 20.1 Napoleon's Europe, 1810
- MAP 20.2 Latin America by 1830

Primary Sources

- Rousseau Espouses Popular Sovereignty and the General Will
- The United States Declaration of Independence
- The Declaration of the Rights of Man and of the Citizen
- The Jamaica Letter

Answer to the History in Focus Question

See photo on page 486, "The Tarring and Feathering of a British Official, 1774."

Visit the CourseMate website at www.cengagebrain.com for additional study tools and review materials for this chapter.

The Early Industrial Revolution

© Cengage Learning

CHAPTER PREVIEW

Causes of the Industrial Revolution
What caused the Industrial Revolution?

The Technological Revolution
What were the key innovations that increased productivity and drove industrialization?

The Impact of the Industrial Revolution
What was the impact of these changes on the society and environment of the industrializing countries?

New Economic and Political Ideas
How did the Industrial Revolution influence the rise of new economic and political ideas?

The Limits of Industrialization Outside the West
How did the Industrial Revolution affect the relations between the industrialized and the nonindustrialized parts of the world?

Conclusion

DIVERSITY & DOMINANCE: Adam Smith and the Division of Labor

 Visit the CourseMate website at **www.cengagebrain.com** for additional study tools and review materials for this chapter.

Manchester was a small town in northern England in the early eighteenth century. A hundred years later, it had become the fastest-growing city in history. To contemporary visitors, it was both a marvel and a horror. In the inner city, cotton mills and other factories were interspersed with workers' housing, built as cheaply as possible. Here is how the economist Nassau Senior described these workers' quarters:

> But when I went through their habitations . . . my only wonder was that tolerable health could be maintained by the inmates of such houses. These towns . . . have been erected by small speculators with an utter disregard to everything except immediate profit. . . . Not a house in this street escaped cholera. And, generally speaking, . . . the streets are unpaved, with a dunghill or a pond in the middle; the houses built back to back, without ventilation or drainage, and whole families occupy each a corner of a cellar or of a garret.[1]

Not everyone deplored the living conditions in the new industrial city. Friedrich Engels, one of the foremost critics of industrial capitalism, recounts a meeting with a well-to-do citizen:

One day I walked with one of these middle-class gentlemen into Manchester. I spoke to him about the disgraceful unhealthy slums and drew his attention to the disgusting condition of that part of the town in which the factory workers lived. I declared that I had never seen so badly built a town in my life. He listened patiently and at the corner of the street at which we parted company, he remarked: "And yet there is a great deal of money made here. Good morning, Sir!"[2]

Manchester's rise was a result of what historians call the **Industrial Revolution**, the most profound and wrenching transformation in human life since the development of agriculture 10,000 years earlier. The Industrial Revolution brought misery to many, but in the long run made it possible for increasing numbers of people (including those in Manchester) to lead longer, healthier, richer, and more productive lives than could have been possible before.

This revolution involved dramatic innovations in manufacturing, mining, transportation, and communications and equally rapid changes in society and commerce. New relationships between social groups created an environment that was conducive to technical innovation and economic growth. New technologies and new social and economic arrangements allowed the industrializing countries—first

Manchester, the First Industrial City The first cotton mills, built on the banks of the River Irwell in northern England, transformed Manchester from a country town into a booming industrial city. The use of chemicals to bleach and dye the cloth and the introduction of steam engines in the early nineteenth century to power the spinning and weaving machines made Manchester, for a time, the most polluted city on earth.

IAM/akg-images

Chronology

Technology	Economy, Society, and Politics
1750	
1759 Josiah Wedgwood opens pottery factory	
1764 Spinning jenny	
1769 Richard Arkwright's water frame; James Watt patents steam engine	
	1776 Adam Smith's *Wealth of Nations*
	1776–1783 American Revolution
1779 First iron bridge	
1785 Boulton and Watt sell steam engines; Samuel Crompton's mule	
	1789–1799 French Revolution
1793 Eli Whitney's cotton gin	
1800	**1800** Alessandro Volta's battery
	1804–1815 Napoleonic Wars
1807 Robert Fulton's *North River*	
1820s Construction of Erie Canal	**1820s** U.S. cotton industry begins
	1833 Factory Act in Britain
	1834 Robert Owen's Grand National Consolidated Trade Union
1837 Wheatstone and Cooke's telegraph	
1838 First ships steam across the Atlantic	
1840 *Nemesis* sails to China	
1843 Samuel Morse's Baltimore-to-Washington telegraph	
	1847–1848 Irish famine
	1848 Collapse of Chartist movement; revolutions in Europe
1850	
1851 Crystal Palace opens in London	

Britain, then western Europe and the United States—to unleash massive increases in production and productivity, exploit the world's natural resources as never before, and transform the environment and human life in unprecedented ways.

The distribution of power and wealth generated by the Industrial Revolution was very uneven, for industrialization widened the gap between rich and poor. Those who owned and controlled the innovations amassed power over other people and lived lives of spectacular luxury, while workers, including children, worked long hours in dangerous factories and lived crowded together in unsanitary tenements.

The effect of the Industrial Revolution around the world was also very uneven. The first countries to industrialize grew rich and powerful. In Egypt and India, the economic and military power of the European countries stifled the tentative beginnings of industrialization. Regions that had little or no industry were easily taken advantage of. The disparity between the industrial and the developing countries that exists today has its origins in the early nineteenth century.

Industrial Revolution The transformation of the economy, the environment, and living conditions, occurring first in England in the eighteenth century, that resulted from the use of steam engines, the mechanization of manufacturing in factories, and innovations in transportation and communication.

Causes of the Industrial Revolution

What caused the Industrial Revolution?

What caused the Industrial Revolution, and why did it begin in England in the late eighteenth century? The basic preconditions of this momentous event seem to have been population growth, an agricultural revolution, the expansion of trade, and an openness to innovation.

Preconditions for Industrialization

The population of Europe rose in the eighteenth century—slowly at first, faster after 1780, then even faster in the early nineteenth century. The population of England and Wales rose unusually fast—from 5.5 million in 1688 to 18 million by 1851. Industrialization and the population boom reinforced each other. A high birthrate meant a large percentage of children, which explains both the vitality of the British people in that period and the widespread use of child labor.

This population explosion and urbanization depended upon an **agricultural revolution** that provided food for city dwellers and forced poorer peasants off the land. Long before the eighteenth century, the acceptance of the potato and maize from the Americas had increased food supplies in Europe. In the cool and humid regions of Europe, from Ireland to Russia, potatoes yielded two or three times more food per acre than grain. Maize (American corn) was grown across Europe from southwestern France to the Balkans.

During the seventeenth century, rich English landowners began draining marshes, improving the soil, and introducing crop rotation using turnips, legumes, and clover that did not deplete the soil and could be fed to cattle. Additional manure from improved breeds of livestock fertilized the soil for other crops. Some also "enclosed" land—that is, consolidated their holdings, including commons that in the past had been open to all. This "enclosure movement" also turned tenants and sharecroppers into landless farm laborers. Many moved to the cities to seek work; others became homeless migrants and vagrants; still others emigrated.

Trade expansion accompanied the growth in population and food supply. Most of it was local, but a growing share involved imports, like tea and sugar, and simple goods that even middle-class people could afford, such as cotton textiles, iron hardware, and pottery. Trade also stimulated a growing interest in technology and innovation among educated people throughout Europe and eastern North America. They read descriptions of new techniques and inventions in many publications, and some experimented on their own.

Britain's Advantages

These changes were widespread, but Britain in the eighteenth century had the fastest-growing population, food supply, and overseas trade. The British also put inventions into practice more quickly than other people, thus making Britain the world's leading exporter of tools, guns, hardware, and other craft goods. Its mining and metal industries employed engineers willing to experiment with new ideas. It also had the largest merchant marine and produced more ships, naval supplies, and navigation instruments than other countries.

Moreover, Britain had a fluid society. Political power was not as centralized as on the European continent, and the government employed fewer bureaucrats and officials. Class lines eased as members of the gentry, and even some aristocrats, married into merchant families. Intermarriage among the families of petty merchants, yeoman farmers, and town craftsmen was common.

With land transportation as costly as ever, Great Britain had good water transportation, thanks to its indented coastline, navigable rivers, and growing network of canals (see Map 21.1). Its unified internal market, with none of the duties and tolls that goods had to pay every few miles in France, encouraged

agricultural revolution (eighteenth century) The transformation of farming that resulted in the eighteenth century from the spread of new crops, improvements in cultivation techniques and livestock breeding, and the consolidation of small holdings into large farms from which tenants and sharecroppers were forcibly expelled.

Map 21.1 The Industrial Revolution in Britain, ca. 1850 The first industries arose in northern and western England. These regions had abundant coal and iron-ore deposits for the iron industry and moist climate and fast-flowing rivers for the cotton textile industry. © Cengage Learning

Interactive Map

Towns with over 20,000 people are shown

50   400   2.4
Thousand   Million
Cities with over 100,000 people are labeled

Exposed coalfields

Industrial areas

Centers of woolen cloth production, 18th century

Principal railroads

0   50 Km.
0   50 Mi.

SCOTLAND

Durham

Cotton and woolen textiles
Machinery, Iron

Bradford

Leeds

Manchester

Liverpool

Sheffield

Iron
Hardware

Norwich

WALES

Birmingham

Iron
Machinery
Pottery

Iron

Bristol
Bath

London

Machinery
Consumer goods 2°E

Exeter

Tin and copper
mining

Irish Sea

North Sea

English Channel

N

specialization and trade. More people there were involved in production for export and in trade and finance than in any other major country. Finally, Britain's financial and insurance institutions supported growing business enterprises, and its patent system protected inventors' profits.

By 1830, western Europe had as favorable a climate for business as Britain had had a half-century earlier. Industrialization first took hold in Belgium and northern France, as their businessmen visited

Britain to observe the changes and to spy out industrial secrets. In spite of British laws forbidding the emigration of skilled workers and the export of textile machinery, many slipped through, setting up machines, training workers in the new methods, and even starting their own businesses. European governments founded technical schools, eliminated internal tariff barriers, tolls, and other hindrances to trade, and encouraged the formation of joint-stock companies and banks to channel private savings into industrial

SECTION REVIEW

- The Industrial Revolution began in Britain because of rapid population growth, an agricultural revolution, expansion of trade, and technological innovation.

- Britain's advantages included a large merchant marine, its position as an exporter, and the ability of its people to put inventions to practical use.

- Britain also had a relatively fluid society, good water transportation, and a unified internal market.

- By 1830, conditions elsewhere in Europe had caught up with those in Britain.

Mary Evans Picture Library

investments. On the European continent, as in Britain, cotton was the first industry to industrialize.

The Technological Revolution

What were the key innovations that increased productivity and drove industrialization?

Five revolutionary innovations spurred industrialization: (1) mass production through the division of labor, (2) new machines and mechanization, (3) a great increase in the supply of iron, (4) the steam engine and the changes it made possible in industry and transportation, and (5) the electric telegraph.

Wedgwood's Potteries In Staffordshire, England, Josiah Wedgwood established a factory to mass-produce beautiful and inexpensive china. The bottle-shaped buildings are kilns in which thousands of pieces of china could be fired at one time. Kilns, factories, and housing were all mixed together in pottery towns, and smoke from burning coal filled the air.

Mass Production and Mechanization

The pottery industry offers a good example of **mass production**, the making of many identical items by breaking the manufacturing process into simple repetitive tasks. **Josiah Wedgwood** opened a pottery business in 1759 that was able to produce porcelain cheaply, by means of the **division of labor**. He subdivided the work into highly specialized and repetitive tasks, such as unloading the clay, mixing it, pressing flat pieces, dipping the pieces in glaze, putting handles on cups, packing kilns, and carrying things from one part of his plant to another. He also used molds instead of the potter's wheel wherever possible, a change that both saved labor and created identical plates and bowls that could be stacked. These innovations allowed Wedgwood to lower the cost of his products while improving their quality. Accordingly, his factory grew far larger than his com-

petitors' factories, and his salesmen traveled throughout England touting his goods.

New technologies intrigued Wedgwood. He invested in toll roads and canals so that clay could be shipped economically from southwestern England

mass production The manufacture of many identical products by the division of labor into many small repetitive tasks. This method was introduced into the manufacture of pottery and into the spinning of cotton thread.

Josiah Wedgwood (1730–1795) English industrialist whose pottery works were the first to produce fine-quality pottery by industrial methods.

division of labor A manufacturing technique that breaks down a craft into many simple and repetitive tasks that can be performed by unskilled workers. Pioneered in the pottery works of Josiah Wedgwood and in other eighteenth-century factories, it greatly increased the productivity of labor and lowered the cost of manufactured goods.

to his factories in the Midlands. In 1782, to mix clay and grind flint, he purchased one of the first steam engines to be used in industry. Wedgwood's interest in applying technology to manufacturing was reflected in his membership in the Birmingham Lunar Society, a group of manufacturers, scientists, and inventors who met to exchange ideas and discoveries. Similar societies throughout Britain were creating a vogue for science and giving the word *progress* a new meaning: "change for the better."

The cotton industry, the largest of the period, illustrates the role of **mechanization**, the use of machines to do work previously done by hand. The cotton plant did not grow in Europe, but the cloth was so much cooler, softer, and cleaner than wool that wealthy Europeans developed a liking for this costly import. When the powerful English woolen industry persuaded Parliament to forbid the import of cotton cloth into England, it stimulated attempts to import cotton fiber and make the cloth locally. Here was an opportunity for enterprising inventors to reduce costs with laborsaving machinery.

Beginning in the 1760s, a series of inventions—the spinning jenny, the water frame, and the mule—revolutionized the spinning of cotton thread and allowed British industry to undersell high-quality handmade cotton cloth from India. British cotton output increased tenfold between 1770 and 1790.

When the boom in thread production and the soaring demand for cloth created bottlenecks in weaving, inventors rose to the challenge with power looms, carding machines, chlorine bleach, and cylindrical printing presses. By the 1830s, large English textile mills powered by steam engines were turning raw cotton into printed cloth. This was a far cry from the cottage industries of the previous century.

Mechanization offered two advantages: (1) productivity for the manufacturer and (2) economy for the consumer. In India it took 500 hours to spin a pound of cotton; the improved mule of 1830 required only 80 minutes. Cotton mills needed few skilled workers, and managers often hired children to tend the spinning machines. Mechanization and cheap labor allowed the price of cloth to fall by 90 percent from 1782 to 1812, and it kept on dropping.

Britain's industrialization made cotton America's most valuable crop. In 1793, the American Eli Whitney patented his cotton gin, a simple device that separated the seeds from the fiber and made it economical to grow short-staple cotton. This permitted the spread of cotton farming into Georgia, then into Alabama, Mississippi, and Louisiana, and finally as far west as Texas. By the late 1850s, the southern states were producing a million tons of cotton a year, five-sixths of the world's total.

With the help of British craftsmen who introduced jennies, mules, and power looms, Americans also developed a cotton industry in the 1820s. By 1840, the United States had 1,200 cotton mills, two-thirds of them in New England, powered by water rather than steam.

The Iron Industry

For over two thousand years iron had been used for tools, weapons, and household items such as knives, pots, hinges, and locks. Wherever it was produced, however, deforestation eventually drove up the cost of charcoal (used for smelting) and restricted output. Furthermore, iron had to be repeatedly heated and hammered to drive out impurities, a difficult and costly process. Then in 1709, Abraham Darby discovered that coke (coal from which the impurities have been removed by baking) could be used in place of charcoal. The resulting metal was of lower quality than charcoal iron but much cheaper to produce, for coal was plentiful. Just as importantly, in 1784 Henry Cort found a way to remove some of the impurities in coke-iron by puddling—stirring the molten iron with long rods. Cort's process made it possible to turn high-sulfur English coal into coke to produce wrought iron (a soft and malleable form of iron) very cheaply.

By 1790 four-fifths of Britain's iron was made with coke, while other countries were still using charcoal. Coke-iron allowed a great expansion in the size of individual blast furnaces, substantially reducing its cost. There seemed almost no limit to the quantity of iron that could be produced with coke. Britain's iron production began rising fast, from 17,000 tons in

mechanization The application of machinery to manufacturing and other activities. Among the first processes to be mechanized were the spinning of cotton thread and the weaving of cloth in late-eighteenth- and early-nineteenth-century England.

Pit Head of a Coal Mine This is a small coal mine. In the center of this picture stands a Newcomen engine used to pump water. The work of hauling coal out of the mine was still done by horses and mules. The smoke coming out of the smokestack is a trademark of the early industrial era.

History In Focus *What do you think the artist's attitude toward the new industrial technology is? Why? Find the answer online.*

1740 to 3 million tons in 1844, as much as in the rest of the world put together.

In turn, there seemed no limit to the amount of iron that an industrializing society would purchase or to the novel applications for this cheap and useful material. In 1779 the iron manufacturer Abraham Darby III (grandson of the first Abraham Darby) built a bridge of iron across the Severn River. In 1851 Londoners marveled at the **Crystal Palace**, a huge greenhouse made entirely of iron and glass and large enough to enclose the tallest trees.

The availability of cheap iron made it worthwhile to mass-produce objects such as guns, hardware, and tools. However, fitting together the parts of these products required a great deal of labor. To reduce labor costs, manufacturers turned to the idea of interchangeable parts. This idea originated in the eighteenth century when French army officers attempted, without success, to persuade gun makers to produce precisely identical parts. Craftsmen continued to use traditional methods to make parts that had to be filed to fit together with other parts. By the mid-nineteenth century, however, interchangeable-parts procedures had been adopted in the manufacture of firearms, farm equipment, and sewing machines. At the Crystal Palace exhibition

of 1851, Europeans called it the "American system of manufactures" because American arms manufacturers were the first to adopt it in order to save labor costs. In the next hundred years the use of machinery to mass-produce consumer items was to become the hallmark of American industry.

The Steam Engine

The first machine to transform fossil fuel into mechanical energy was the **steam engine**. Although the mechanization of manufacturing was very important, the steam engine was what set the Industrial Revolution apart from all previous periods of growth and innovation.

Crystal Palace A gigantic greenhouse erected in Hyde Park, London, for the Great Exhibition of 1851. Made of iron and glass, it was a symbol of the industrial age.
steam engine A machine that turns the energy released by burning fuel into motion. Thomas Newcomen built the first crude but workable steam engine in 1712. James Watt vastly improved his device in the 1760s and 1770s. Steam power was later applied to moving machinery in factories and to powering ships and locomotives.

Before the eighteenth century, lack of energy had limited many activities. For example, deep mines filled with water faster than horses could pump it out. Scientists understood the concept of atmospheric pressure and had created experimental devices to turn heat into motion, but they had not found a way to put those devices to practical use. Then, between 1702 and 1712 Thomas Newcomen developed the first practical steam engine, a crude but effective device. One engine could pump water out of a mine as fast as four horses and could run day and night without getting tired.

The Newcomen engine's voracious appetite for fuel mattered little in coal mines, where fuel was cheap, but it made the engine too costly for other uses. In 1764 **James Watt**, an instrument maker at Glasgow University in Scotland, was asked to repair the university's model Newcomen engine. Watt realized that the engine wasted fuel because the cylinder had to be alternately heated and cooled. He developed a separate condenser—a vessel into which the steam was allowed to escape after it had done work, leaving the cylinder always hot and the condenser always cold. Watt patented his idea in 1769 and enlisted the help of the iron manufacturer Matthew Boulton to turn his invention into a commercial product. Their first engines were used to pump water out of copper and tin mines, where fuel was too costly for Newcomen engines. In 1781 Watt invented the sun-and-planet gear, which turned the back-and-forth action of the piston into rotary motion. This allowed steam engines to power machinery in flour and cotton mills, pottery factories, and other industries.

Watt's steam engine was the most celebrated invention of the eighteenth century. Because coal supplies seemed unlimited, steam-generated energy seemed an inexhaustible source of power that could be used where animal, wind, and water power were lacking. Inspired by Watt's engine, inventors in France, the United States, and England in the 1780s put steam engines on boats. The first commercially successful steamboat was Robert Fulton's *North River*, which steamed between New York City and Albany in 1807. Soon steamboats were launched on other American rivers. In the 1820s the Erie Canal linked the Atlantic seaboard with the Great Lakes and opened Ohio, Indiana, and Illinois to European settlement. Steamboats also proliferated west of the Appalachian Mountains; by 1830 some three hundred plied the Mississippi and its tributaries. To counter the competition from New York State, Pennsylvania built a thousand miles of canals by 1840. The United States was fast becoming a nation that moved by water.

Oceangoing steam-powered ships were much more difficult to build than riverboats, for the first steam engines used so much coal that no ship could carry more than a few days' supply. The *Savannah*, which crossed the Atlantic in 1819, was a sailing ship with an auxiliary steam engine that was used for only ninety hours of its twenty-nine-day trip. However, engineers soon developed more efficient engines, and in 1838 two steamers, the *Great Western* and the *Sirius*, crossed the Atlantic on steam power alone.

Railroads

Steam engines were initially too heavy and weak to pull any weight. After Watt's patent expired in 1800, however, inventors experimented with lighter, more powerful high-pressure engines. In the early 1800s they built several steam-powered vehicles able to travel on roads or rails. Between 1830 and 1850, a railroad-building mania swept Britain. The first lines linked towns and mines with the nearest harbor or waterway. As passenger traffic soared, entrepreneurs built lines between the major cities and then to small towns as well. Railroads were far cheaper, faster, and more comfortable than stagecoaches.

In the United States, entrepreneurs built railroads as fast and cheaply as possible. By the 1840s, 6,000 miles (10,000 kilometers) of track radiated westward from Boston, New York, Philadelphia, and Baltimore. The boom of the 1840s was dwarfed by the mania of the 1850s, when 21,000 miles (34,000 kilometers) of new track were laid, much of it westward across the Appalachians to Memphis, St. Louis, and Chicago.

James Watt (1736–1819) Scot who invented the condenser and other improvements that made the steam engine a practical source of power for industry and transportation. The watt, an electrical measurement, is named after him.

The *De Witt Clinton* Locomotive, 1835–1840 The *De Witt Clinton* was the first steam locomotive built in the United States. The high smokestack let the hot cinders cool so they would not set fire to nearby trees, an important consideration at a time when eastern North America was still covered with forests. The three passenger cars are clearly horse carriages fitted with railroad wheels.

Bettmann/Corbis

The trip from New York to Chicago, which once took three weeks by boat and on horseback, could now be made in forty-eight hours. The railroads opened up the Midwest, turning the vast prairie into wheat fields and pasture for cattle to feed the industrial cities of the eastern United States.

Railways triggered the industrialization of Europe. Belgium, independent since 1830, quickly copied the British. State-planned and -supervised railroad construction in the mid-1840s in France and Prussia not only satisfied the long-standing need for transportation but also stimulated the iron, machinery, and construction industries. In the 1850s and 1860s, the states of Germany also experienced an industrial boom.

Communication over Wires

The advent of railroads coincided with the development of the **electric telegraph**. After the Italian scientist Alessandro Volta invented the battery in 1800, making it possible to produce an electric current, many inventors tried to apply electricity to communication. The first practical telegraphy systems were developed almost simultaneously in England and America. In England, Wheatstone and Cooke introduced a five-needle telegraph in 1837; it remained in use until the early twentieth century. That same year, the American Samuel Morse introduced a code of dots and dashes that could be transmitted with a single wire; in 1843, he erected a line between Washington and Baltimore.

By the late 1840s, telegraph wires were being strung throughout the eastern United States and western Europe. In 1851, the first submarine telegraph cable was laid across the English Channel from England to France. Thus began a network that eventually enclosed the entire globe. The world was rapidly shrinking, to the applause of Europeans and Americans, for whom speed was a clear measure of progress. No longer were communications limited to the speed by which a ship could sail or a horse could gallop.

electric telegraph A device for rapid, long-distance transmission of information over an electric wire. It was introduced in England and North America in the 1830s and 1840s.

- The technological revolution involved the development of cost-saving machines and processes, such as mass production through the division of labor.

- Beginning in the 1760s a series of inventions mechanized the British cotton industry and encouraged cotton farming and industry in the United States.

- Innovations in processing transformed the British iron industry, making cheap iron widely available for various applications.

- With the perfection of the steam engine, steamboats and railroads proliferated, the latter spurring the industrialization of Europe.

- Practical electric telegraphs appeared in England and America and quickly spread.

The Impact of the Industrial Revolution

What was the impact of these changes on the society and environment of the industrializing countries?

The Industrial Revolution brought many changes in society, politics, and the economy. Early changes—smoky cities, slum neighborhoods, polluted water, child labor in mines and textile mills—were being alleviated by the mid-nineteenth century. But by then national or even international problems were replacing these local ones: business cycles, labor conflicts, and the transformation of entire regions into industrial landscapes.

New Industrial Cities

The most dramatic environmental changes occurred in the towns. Never before had towns grown so fast. London, one of the largest cities in Europe in 1700 with 500,000 inhabitants, grew to 959,000 by 1800 and to 2,363,000 by 1850, making it the largest city in the world. Smaller towns grew even faster. Manchester's population increased eightfold in a century, and Liverpool grew sixfold in the first sixty years of the nineteenth century. New York City, already 100,000 strong in 1815, reached 600,000 (including Brooklyn) in 1850. In some areas, towns merged and formed megalopolises, such as Greater London, the English Midlands, central Belgium, and the Ruhr district of Germany.

An Industrial Canal In the late eighteenth and early nineteenth centuries, before railroads were introduced, many canals were constructed in England so that barges could transport heavy materials cheaply, such as coal for industrial works and steam engines, stone and bricks for buildings, clay for pottery works, and ores for metal foundries. Canals such as this one, which ran alongside a copper foundry, contributed greatly to Britain's industrial development.

Industrialization generated wealth that manifested itself in fine new homes, churches, museums, and theaters. Yet by all accounts, the industrial cities grew much too fast. As poor migrants streamed in from the countryside, developers built cheap, shoddy row houses for them to rent. These tenements were dangerously overcrowded, with several families often living in one small room. Moreover, town dwellers recently arrived from the country brought country ways with them. People threw their sewage and trash out the windows to be washed down the gutters in the streets. The poor kept pigs and chickens, the rich kept horses, and pedestrians stepped into the street at their own risk. Air pollution from burning coal got steadily worse, and people drank water drawn from wells and rivers contaminated by sewage and industrial runoff. The River Irwell, which ran through Manchester, was, in the words of one visitor, "considerably less a river than a flood of liquid manure."[3]

To the long list of preindustrial urban diseases such as smallpox, dysentery, and tuberculosis, industrialization added new ailments. Rickets, a bone disease caused by lack of sunshine, became endemic in dark and smoky industrial cities. Steamships brought cholera from India, causing great epidemics that struck poor neighborhoods especially hard. In the 1850s, when the average life expectancy in England was forty years, it was only twenty-four years in Manchester, and around seventeen years in Manchester's poorest neighborhoods, because of the high infant mortality. However, shocking reports of slum life eventually led to municipal reforms, such as garbage removal, water and sewage systems, and parks and schools. After midcentury these measures began to alleviate the ills of urban life.

Rural Environments

Long before the Industrial Revolution, wilderness areas had largely disappeared in Britain and much of western Europe, as human activity had turned almost every exploitable piece of land into fields, pastures, or towns. The most serious problem was deforestation. People cut timber to build ships and houses, to heat homes and cook food, and to manufacture bricks, iron, glass, beer, bread, and many other items.

Americans transformed their environment even faster than Europeans did. Settlers viewed forests not as a valuable resource but as a hindrance to development. In their haste to "open up the West," pioneers felled trees and burned them, built houses and abandoned them when they moved on. The cultivation of cotton was especially harmful. Planters cut down forests, grew cotton for a few years until it depleted the soil, and then moved west, abandoning the land to scrub pines. The American idea of nature as an obstacle to be overcome and dominated persisted long after the entire continent was occupied.

To contemporaries, the new transportation systems brought the most obvious changes in rural life. Governments and private trusts built numerous roads. Canal building boomed in Britain, France, and the Low Countries in the late eighteenth century. Canals were marvels of construction, with deep cuts, tunnels, and even aqueducts that carried barges over rivers. They also were a sort of school where engineers learned skills they were able to apply to the next great transportation system: the railroads. They laid track across rolling country by cutting deeply into hillsides and erecting daringly long bridges of stone and iron across valleys. Soon, clanking trains pulled by puffing, smoke-belching locomotives invaded long-isolated districts.

Thus, in the century after industrialization began, the landscape of industrializing countries was transformed more rapidly than ever before. But the ecological changes, like the technological and economic changes that caused them, were only beginning.

Working Conditions

Most industrial jobs were unskilled, repetitive, and boring. Factory work did not vary with the seasons or the time of day but began and ended by the clock. Factories used the invention of gas lighting to expand the working day past sunset. Workdays were long, there were few breaks, and foremen watched the workers constantly. Workers who performed one simple task over and over had little sense of achievement or pride in the finished product. Industrial accidents were common and could ruin a family. Unlike even the poorest preindustrial farmer or artisan, factory workers had no control over their tools, jobs, or working hours.

Women workers were concentrated in textile mills, partly because of ancient traditions, and partly because textile work required less strength than metalworking, construction, or hauling. On average, women earned one-third to one-half as much as men. Young unmarried women worked to support themselves or to save for marriage, while married women took factory jobs when their husbands were unable to support the family. Mothers of infants faced a hard choice: whether to leave their babies with wet nurses at great expense and danger or to bring them to the factory and keep them quiet with opiates. Rather than working together as family units, husbands and wives increasingly worked in different places.

However, factory work was never the main occupation of working women. Most young women who sought paid employment in the early years of industrialization became domestic servants in spite of the low pay, drudgery, and risk of sexual abuse. Other women with small children tried hard to find work they could do at home, such as laundry, sewing, embroidery, millinery, or taking in lodgers.

Even with both parents working, poor families found it hard to make ends meet. As in preindustrial societies, parents thought children should contribute to their upkeep as soon as they were able to. The first generation of workers brought their children with them to the factories and mines as early as age five or six; they had little choice, since there were no public schools or day-care centers. Employers encouraged the practice and even hired orphans. They preferred children because they were cheaper and more docile than adults and were better able to tie broken threads or crawl under machines to sweep the dust. Mine operators also used children to pull coal carts along the low passageways from the coal face to the mine shaft. In the mid-nineteenth century, when the British government began restricting child labor, mill owners increasingly recruited Irish immigrants.

American industry began on a somewhat different note than the British. When Francis Cabot Lowell built a cotton mill in Massachusetts, he deliberately hired the unmarried daughters of New England farmers, promising decent wages and housing in dormitories under careful moral supervision. Other manufacturers eager to combine profits with morality followed his example. But soon the profit motive won out, and manufacturers imposed longer hours, harsher working conditions, and lower wages. When the young women went on strike, the factory owners replaced them with Irish immigrant women willing to accept lower pay and worse conditions.

The rising demand for cotton and the abolition of the African slave trade in the United States in 1808 (see Chapter 20) caused an increase in the price of slaves. As the "Cotton Kingdom" expanded, the number of slaves rose through natural increase, from 700,000 in the 1790s to 3,200,000 by 1850. Similarly, Europe and North America's surging demand for tea and coffee prolonged slavery on sugar plantations in the West Indies and caused it to spread to the coffee-growing regions of southern Brazil. Slavery was part and parcel of the Industrial Revolution, just as much as child labor in Britain, the clothes that people wore, and the beverages they drank.

Changes in Society

Industrialization accentuated the polarization of society and disparities of income. In Britain, the worst-off were those who clung to an obsolete skill or craft. Even by working more hours, handloom weavers could not compete with power looms and were reduced to destitution. Whereas their wages declined steadily, the wages and standard of living of factory workers fluctuated wildly with the cycles of economic growth and contraction. During the war years 1792 to 1815, the poor suffered hardship when the price of food rose faster than wages. Then, in the 1820s, real wages and public health began to improve, as industrial production grew at over 3 percent a year, pulling the rest of the economy along. Prices fell so that even the poor could afford comfortable, washable cotton clothes.

Overall, the benefits of industrialization—cheaper food, clothing, and utensils—did not improve workers' standard of living until the 1850s. The real beneficiaries of the early Industrial Revolution were the entrepreneurs whose money came from manufacturing. Most were the sons of middling shopkeepers, craftsmen, or farmers who had a little capital to start a cotton-spinning or machine-building business. Many tried and some succeeded, largely by plowing their profits back into the business. A generation later, in the nineteenth century, some newly rich industrialists bought their way into high society. With industrialization also came a "cult of domesticity" that removed middle-class women from contact with the business world and left

SECTION REVIEW

- The Industrial Revolution spurred rapid urbanization, causing severe pollution, overcrowding, and myriad health and hygiene problems.

- Industrialization hastened deforestation and brought pollution to rural environments.

- Industrial working conditions were harsh and dangerous, especially for children, until Britain passed child-labor laws.

- Women often faced difficult choices between factory work and family obligations, and slavery persisted because of industrialization.

- Industrialization benefited owners more quickly than workers, the former often being able to rise in society, while the cult of domesticity shaped women's lives.

them responsible for the home, the servants, the education of children, and the family's social life.

New Economic and Political Ideas

How did the Industrial Revolution influence the rise of new economic and political ideas?

Changes as profound as the Industrial Revolution could not occur without political ferment and ideological conflict. So many other momentous events took place during those years—the American Revolution (1776–1783), the French Revolution (1789–1799), the Napoleonic Wars (1804–1815), and the reactions and revolts that periodically swept over Europe after 1815 (see Chapter 20)—that we cannot neatly separate out the consequences of industrialization from the rest. But it is clear that the Industrial Revolution strengthened the ideas of laissez faire and socialism and sparked workers' protests.

Laissez Faire

The most celebrated exponent of **laissez faire** (lay-say fair) ("let them do") was Adam Smith (1723–1790), a Scottish economist. In *The Wealth of Nations* (1776), Smith argued that if individuals were allowed to seek their personal gain, the effect, as though guided by an "invisible hand," would be to increase the general welfare (see Diversity and Dominance: Adam Smith and the Division of

Labor). Except to protect private property, the government should refrain from interfering in business; it should even allow duty-free trade with foreign countries.

Although it was true that governments at the time were incompetent at regulating their national economies, it was becoming obvious that industrialization was not improving the general welfare but was for some causing great misery. Some thinkers blamed the workers' plight on the population boom, which outstripped the food supply and led to falling wages. The workers' poverty, they claimed, was as much a result of "natural law" as the wealth of successful businessmen, and the only way the working class could avoid mass famine was to delay marriage and practice self-restraint and sexual abstinence.

Laissez faire provided an ideological justification for a special kind of capitalism: banks, stock markets, and chartered companies allowed investors to obtain profits with reasonable risks but with much less government control and interference than in the past. But not everyone accepted the grim conclusions of the "dismal science," as economics was then known. Jeremy Bentham (1748–1832) believed that it was possible to maximize "the greatest happiness of the greatest number," if only a Parliament of enlightened reformers would study the social problems of the day and pass appropriate legislation; his philosophy became known as utilitarianism.

Positivism and Utopian Socialism

Some French social thinkers, moved by sincere concern for the poor, offered a more radically new vision of a just civilization. Espousing a philosophy called **positivism**, the count of Saint-Simon (1760–1825) argued that the scientific method could

laissez faire The idea that government should refrain from interfering in economic affairs. The classic exposition of laissez-faire principles is Adam Smith's *Wealth of Nations* (1776).

positivism A philosophy developed by the French count of Saint-Simon. Positivists believed that social and economic problems could be solved by the application of the scientific method, leading to continuous progress. Their ideas became popular in France and Latin America in the nineteenth century.

Adam Smith and the Division of Labor

Adam Smith (1723–1790), a Scottish philosopher, is famous for his book An Inquiry into the Nature and Causes of the Wealth of Nations, first published in 1776. It was the first work to explain the economy of a nation as a system. Smith criticized the notion, common in the eighteenth century, that a nation's wealth was synonymous with the amount of gold and silver in the government's coffers. Instead, he defined wealth as the amount of goods and services produced by a nation's people. By this definition, labor and its products are an essential element in a nation's prosperity.

In the passage that follows, Smith contrasts two methods of making pins. In one a team of workers divided up the job of making pins and produced a great many every day; in the other pin workers "wrought separately and independently" and produced very few pins per day. It is clear that the division of labor produces more pins per worker per day. But who benefits? Left unsaid is that a pin factory had to be owned and operated by a manufacturer who hired workers and assigned a task to each one.

The illustration shows a pin-maker's workshop in late-eighteenth-century France. Each worker is performing a specific task on a few pins at once, and all the energy comes from human muscles. These are the characteristics of a proto-industrial workshop.

To take an example, therefore, from a very trifling manufacture—but one in which the division of labour has been very often taken notice of—the trade of the pin-maker: a workman not educated to this business (which the division of labour has rendered a distinct trade), nor acquainted with the use of machinery employed in it (to the invention of which the same division of labour has probably given occasion), could scarce, perhaps, with his utmost industry, make one pin in a day, and certainly could not make twenty. But in the way in which this business is now carried on, not only the whole work is a peculiar trade, but it is divided into a number of branches, of which the greater part are likewise peculiar trades. One man draws out the wire, another straights it, a third cuts it, a fourth points it, a fifth grinds it at the top for receiving the head; to make the head requires two or three distinct operations, to put it on, is a peculiar business, to whiten the pins is another; it is even a trade by itself to put them into the paper; and the important business of making a pin is, in this manner, divided into about eighteen distinct operations, which, in some manufactories, are all

A Pin-Maker's Workshop The man in the middle (Fig. 2) is pulling wire off a spindle (G) and through a series of posts. This ensures that the wire will be perfectly straight. The worker seated on the lower right (Fig. 3) takes the long pieces of straightened wire and cuts them into shorter lengths. The man in the lower left-hand corner (Fig. 5) sharpens twelve to fifteen wires at a time by holding them against a grindstone turned by the worker in Fig. 6. The men in Figs. 4 and 7 put the finishing touches on the points. Other operations—such as forming the wire to the proper thickness, cleaning and coating it with tin, and attaching the heads—are depicted in other engravings in the same encyclopedia.

performed by distinct hands, though in others the same man will sometimes perform two or three of them. I have seen a small manufactory of this kind where ten men only were employed, and where some of them, consequently, performed two or three distinct operations. But though they were very poor, and therefore but indifferently accommodated with the necessary machinery, they could, when they exerted themselves, make among them about twelve pounds of pins in a day.

There are in a pound upwards of four thousand pins of a middling size. Those ten persons, therefore, could make among them upwards of forty-eight thousand pins in a day. Each person, therefore, making a tenth part of forty-eight thousand pins, might be considered as making four thousand eight hundred pins a day. But if they had all wrought separately and independently, and without any of them having been educated to this peculiar business, they certainly could not each of them have made twenty, perhaps not one pin in a day; that is, certainly, not the two hundred and fortieth, perhaps not the four thousand eight hundredth part of what they are at present capable of performing, in consequence of a proper division and combination of their different operations.

QUESTIONS FOR ANALYSIS

1. Why does dividing the job of pin-making into ten or more operations result in the production of more pins per worker? How much more productive are these workers than if each one made complete pins from start to finish?
2. How closely does the picture of a pin-maker's workshop illustrate Smith's verbal description?
3. What disadvantage would there be to working in a pin factory where the job was divided as in Smith's example, compared to making entire pins from start to finish?
4. What other examples can you think of, from Adam Smith's day or from more recent times, of the advantages of the division of labor?

Source: Adam Smith, *An Inquiry into the Nature and Causes of the Wealth of Nations*, ed. Edward Gibbon Wakefield (London: Charles Knight and Co., 1843), 7–9.

solve social as well as technical problems. He recommended that the poor, guided by scientists and artists, form workers' communities under the protection of benevolent business leaders. These ideas found no following among workers, but they attracted the enthusiastic support of bankers and entrepreneurs who were inspired by visions of railroads, canals, and other symbols of progress and invested their money accordingly.

Meanwhile, the **utopian** (you-TOE-pee-uhn) **socialism** of Charles Fourier (1768–1837), who loathed capitalists, imagined an ideal society in which groups of sixteen hundred workers would live in dormitories and work together on the land and in workshops where music, wine, and pastries would soften the hardships of labor. For this idea, critics called him a "utopian"—a dreamer.

The person who came closest to creating a utopian community was the Englishman Robert Owen (1771–1858), a successful cotton manufacturer who believed that industry could provide prosperity for all. Conscience-stricken by the appalling plight of the workers, Owen took over the management of New Lanark, a mill town south of Glasgow. He improved the housing and added schools, a church, and other amenities. He also testified before Parliament against child labor and for government inspection of working conditions, thereby angering his fellow industrialists.

Protests and Reforms

Workers benefited little from the ideas of these middle-class philosophers. Instead, they resisted the harsh working conditions in their own ways. They changed jobs frequently and were often absent, especially on Mondays. Periodically, workers rioted or went on strike. Such acts of resistance did nothing, however, to change the nature of industrial work. Not until workers learned to act together could they hope to have much influence.

Gradually, workers formed benevolent societies and organizations to demand universal male

utopian socialism A philosophy introduced by the Frenchman Charles Fourier in the early nineteenth century. Utopian socialists hoped to create humane alternatives to industrial capitalism by building self-sustaining communities whose inhabitants would work cooperatively.

suffrage and shorter workdays. In 1834, Robert Owen organized the Grand National Consolidated Trade Union to lobby for an eight-hour workday; it gained half a million members but failed a few months later in the face of government prosecution of trade union activities. The Chartist movement had more success, gathering petitions by the thousands to present to Parliament. Although Chartism collapsed in 1848, it left a legacy of labor organizing.

Eventually, mass movements persuaded political leaders to look into the abuses of industrial life, despite the prevailing laissez-faire philosophy. In the 1820s and 1830s, the British Parliament began investigating conditions in the factories and mines. The Factory Act of 1833 prohibited the employment of children under age nine in textile mills and limited the working hours of children between the ages of nine and eighteen. The Mines Act of 1842 prohibited the employment of all women and of boys under age ten underground. However, several decades passed before the government appointed enough inspectors to enforce the new laws. Meanwhile, on the European continent, the revolutions of 1848 (see Chapter 20) revealed widespread discontent with repressive governments but failed to soften the hardships of industrialization.

Emigration

Another response to growing population, rural crises, and business cycles was emigration. Many poor Irish emigrated to England in search of work in construction and factories. When the potato crop failed in Ireland in 1847–1848, one-quarter of the Irish population died in the resulting famine and another quarter emigrated to England and America. On the European continent, the negative effects of economic downturns were tempered by the existence of small family farms to which urban workers could return when they were laid off, but vast numbers still left Europe in search of better opportunities in the Western Hemisphere.

The United States received approximately 600,000 European immigrants in the 1830s, 1.5 million in the 1840s, and then 2.5 million per decade until 1880. In the 1890s, an astonishing total of 5.2 million immigrants arrived. European immigration to Latin America also increased dramatically after 1880. Immigrants from Europe faced prejudice and discrimination from those who believed that they

SECTION REVIEW

- Industrialization reinforced Adam Smith's theories even in the face of conditions that prompted competing ideas such as utilitarianism.

- French social thinkers responded to industrialization with positivism and utopian socialism, but Robert Owen came closest to realizing such visions.

- Britain led the way in both labor organization and government reform, while on the continent the 1848 revolutions did little to ease workers' conditions.

- The broad economic effects of industrialization prompted emigration from Europe and Asia to the Western Hemisphere.

threatened the well-being of native-born workers by accepting low wages and threatened national culture by resisting assimilation.

Asian immigration to the Western Hemisphere also increased after 1850. Between 1849 and 1875, approximately 570,000 Chinese immigrants arrived in the Americas, half in the United States. India also contributed more than a half-million immigrants to the Caribbean region. Asians faced more obstacles to immigration than did Europeans and were often victims of violence and more extreme forms of discrimination in the New World.

Despite discrimination, most immigrants were eager to assimilate. Many intellectuals and political leaders wondered if the evolving mix of culturally diverse populations could sustain a common citizenship. As a result, efforts were directed toward compelling immigrants to assimilate. They learned the language spoken in their adopted countries as fast as possible in order to improve their earning capacity.

Union movements and electoral politics in the hemisphere also felt the influence of new arrivals who aggressively sought to influence government and improve working conditions. Immigrants introduced new languages, foods, and customs. Mutual benevolent societies and less formal ethnic associations pooled resources to help immigrants open businesses, aid the immigration of their relatives, or bury their family members, sometimes worsening the fears of the native-born that immigration posed a threat to national culture. They also established links with political movements, sometimes exchanging votes for favors.

A Railroad Bridge Across the Nile In the second half of the nineteenth century, industrialized nations, especially Great Britain, sent engineers and equipment to build railroads in less-industrialized parts of the world, such as India, South Africa, Latin America, and the Middle East. One such railway connected Cairo and Alexandria in Egypt. Here a railroad bridge crosses the Nile at Benha near the Pyramids. Corbis

The Limits of Industrialization Outside the West

How did the Industrial Revolution affect the relations between the industrialized and the nonindustrialized parts of the world?

The spread of the Industrial Revolution in the early nineteenth century transformed the relations of western Europe and North America with the rest of the world. In Egypt and India cheap industrial imports, backed by the power of Great Britain, delayed industrialization for a century or more, and China was defeated and humiliated by the products of industrial manufacture. In these three cases, we can discern the outlines of the Western domination that has characterized the history of the world since the late nineteenth century.

Egypt, strongly influenced by European ideas since the French invasion of 1798, began to industrialize in the early nineteenth century. The driving force was its ruler, Muhammad Ali (1769–1849), a man who was to play a major role not only in the history of Egypt but also in the Middle East and East Africa (see Chapters 22 and 23). He wanted to build up the Egyptian economy and military in order to become less dependent on the Ottoman sultan, his nominal overlord. To do so, he imported advisers and technicians from Europe and built cotton mills, foundries, shipyards, weapons factories, and other industrial enterprises. To pay for

all this, he made the peasants grow wheat and cotton, which the government bought at a low price and exported at a profit. He also imposed high tariffs on imported goods to force the pace of industrialization.

Muhammad Ali's efforts fell afoul of the British, who did not want a powerful country threatening to interrupt the flow of travelers and mail across Egypt, the shortest route between Europe and India. When Egypt went to war against the Ottoman Empire in 1839, Britain intervened and forced Muhammad Ali to eliminate all import duties in the name of free trade. Unprotected, Egypt's fledgling industries could not compete with the flood of cheap British products. Thereafter, Egypt exported raw cotton, imported manufactured goods, and became, in effect, an economic dependency of Britain.

Until the late eighteenth century, India had been the world's largest producer and exporter of cotton textiles, handmade by skilled spinners and weavers. The British East India Company took over large parts of India just as the Industrial Revolution was beginning in Britain (see Chapter 23 and Map 23.2). It allowed cheap British factory-made yarn and cloth to flood the Indian market duty-free, putting spinners and later handloom weavers out of work. Unlike Britain, India had no factories to which displaced handicraft workers could turn for work. Most of them became landless peasants, eking out a precarious living.

Like other tropical regions, India became an exporter of raw materials and an importer of British industrial goods. To hasten the process, British entrepreneurs and colonial officials introduced railroads into the subcontinent. The construction of India's railroad network began in the mid-1850s, along with coal mining to fuel the locomotives and the installation of telegraph lines to connect the major cities.

Some Indian entrepreneurs saw opportunities in the atmosphere of change that the British created. In 1854 the Bombay merchant Cowasjee Nanabhoy Davar imported an engineer, four skilled workers, and several textile machines from Britain and started India's first textile mill. This was the beginning of India's mechanized cotton industry. Despite many gifted entrepreneurs, however, India's industrialization proceeded at a snail's pace, for the government was in British hands and the British did nothing to encourage Indian industry.

China's stagnation in the late eighteenth and early nineteenth centuries, at the very time when first Britain and then western Europe and North America were becoming industrialized, has long puzzled historians. China had the resources, both human and natural, to advance technologically and economically, but a conservative elite and a growing population of poor peasants stood in the way of change (see Chapter 19). As a result, when faced with Western industrial technology, China became weaker rather than stronger.

In January 1840 a shipyard in Britain launched a radically new ship. The *Nemesis* had an iron hull, a flat bottom that allowed it to navigate in shallow waters, and a steam engine to power it upriver and against the wind. In November it arrived off the coast of China, heavily armed. Though ships from Europe had been sailing to China for three hundred years, the *Nemesis* was the first steam-powered iron gunboat seen in Chinese waters. A Chinese observer noted: "Iron is employed to make it strong. The hull is painted black, weaver's shuttle fashion. On each side is a wheel, which by the use of coal fire is made to revolve as fast as a running horse.... At the vessel's head is a Marine God, and at the head, stern, and sides are cannon, which give it a terrific appearance. Steam vessels are a wonderful invention of foreigners, and are calculated to offer delight to many."[4]

Instead of offering delight, the *Nemesis* and other steam-powered warships that soon joined it steamed up the Chinese rivers, bombarded forts and cities, and transported troops and supplies from place to place along the coast and up rivers far more quickly than Chinese soldiers could move on foot. With this new weapon, Britain, a small island nation half a world away, was able to defeat the largest and most populated country in the world (see Chapter 22).

Conclusion

The Industrial Revolution and the political revolutions that accompanied it represent a key turning point in the history of the world. The surge in production that mechanization fostered, the mastery of inanimate energy from fossil fuels, and the renewal of society and politics brought about by the revolutions unleashed a rapid increase in the power of industrialized societies over the natural world. But this new power was far from evenly distributed. Within the industrializing nations—first Great Britain, then western Europe and the northern United States—the benefits went to those who had introduced industrialization, and only a generation or two later did the advantages of mass production and rapid transportation improve the lives of ordinary citizens. Even more striking is the shift in the balance of power between the peoples and civilizations of the world. Before the Industrial Revolution, Europe and North America were but two out of several independent cultural areas, neither more nor less important than sub-Saharan Africa, the Middle East, India, or China. Industrialization gave Europeans and North Americans an advantage over other peoples that first prevented others from industrializing and finally culminated in a century-long Western domination of the world, as you will read in the following chapters.

CHAPTER REVIEW

 Download the MP3 audio file of the Chapter Review to listen to on the go.

What caused the Industrial Revolution? (page 508)

The Industrial Revolution arose from a combination of factors in European society in the eighteenth and early nineteenth centuries. The population grew, but so did the food supply, thanks to improvements in agriculture. Among upper- and middle-class Europeans, practical subjects like business, science, and technology became fashionable. Great Britain had a particularly fluid society open to talents and enterprise. On the European continent, the revolutions of 1789–1815 swept away the restrictions of the old aristocratic regimes (see Chapter 20).

What were the key innovations that increased productivity and drove industrialization? (page 510)

A series of technological and organizational innovations transformed the manufacture of many products, reducing their costs and increasing their productivity. New machines, assembled in mills, mass-produced cotton yarn and cloth. Work formerly done by skilled craftsmen was divided into many simple tasks assigned to workers in factories. New techniques also made iron cheap and abundant. Steam engines provided power to factories, ships, and railroads, while electricity found its first practical application in telegraphy.

What was the impact of these changes on the society and environment of the industrializing countries? (page 515)

The Industrial Revolution changed people's lives and the environments in which they lived. Cities grew huge and, for most of their inhabitants, unsightly and unhealthy. While middle-class women were consigned to caring for the home and children, working-class women and children as well as men were obliged to earn their living in mines and factories. In the industrial cities, social problems such as unemployment, alcoholism, and the abandonment of children became acute. Rural environments were also transformed as roads, canals, and railroads crisscrossed open land.

How did the Industrial Revolution influence the rise of new economic and political ideas? (page 518)

Some thinkers defended the growing disparities between rich and poor in the name of laissez faire. Governments and businesspeople eagerly adopted many of the free-market capitalist views of Adam Smith. Others, such as positivists and utopian socialists, criticized the injustices caused by industrialization and offered a new vision of just communities. Workers created labor unions, leading political leaders to reexamine the working conditions of factories and mines, especially as they concerned women and children. However, not until the mid-nineteenth century did industrialization begin to raise living standards in the industrialized countries.

How did the Industrial Revolution affect the relations between the industrialized and the nonindustrialized parts of the world? (page 522)

The Industrial Revolution changed life around the world because it gave the newly industrial nations of the West new powers to coerce non-Western societies. In particular, Britain snuffed out the incipient industrialization of Egypt and India and turned those countries into producers of raw materials, and British steam-powered gunboats forced China to open its doors to unequal trade.

Key Terms

Industrial Revolution (p. 506)

agricultural revolution (eighteenth century) (p. 508)

mass production (p. 510)

Josiah Wedgwood (p. 510)

division of labor (p. 510)

mechanization (p. 511)

Crystal Palace (p. 512)

steam engine (p. 512)

James Watt (p. 513)

electric telegraph (p. 514)

laissez faire (p. 518)

positivism (p. 518)

utopian socialism (p. 520)

Web Resources

Pronunciation Guide

Interactive Map

- MAP 21.1 The Industrial Revolution in Britain, ca. 1850

Answer to the History in Focus Question

See photo on page 512, "Pit Head of a Coal Mine."

 Visit the CourseMate website at www.cengagebrain.com for additional study tools and review materials for this chapter.

Land Empires in the Age of Imperialism

© Cengage Learning

CHAPTER PREVIEW

The Ottoman Empire
What were the benefits and the drawbacks to the Ottoman Empire of the reforms adopted during the Tanzimat period?

The Russian Empire
How did the Russian Empire maintain its status as both a European power and a great Asian land empire?

The Qing Empire
How did the impact of European imperialism on China differ from its impact on Russia and the Ottoman Empire?

Conclusion

ENVIRONMENT & TECHNOLOGY:
The Web of War

Visit the CourseMate website at **www.cengagebrain.com** for additional study tools and review materials for this chapter.

When the Qianlong emperor of the Qing (ching) dynasty died in 1796, the imperial court received a shock. For decades officials had known that the emperor was indulging his handsome young favorite, Heshen (huh-shun), allowing him extraordinary privileges and power. Senior bureaucrats hated Heshen, suspecting him of overseeing a widespread network of corruption. They believed he had been scheming to prolong the inconclusive wars against the native Miao (mee-ow) peoples of southwest China in the late 1700s. Glowing reports of successes against the rebels had poured into the capital, and enormous sums of government money had flowed to the battlefields. But there was no adequate accounting for the funds, and the war persisted.

After the emperor's death, Heshen's enemies ordered his arrest. When they searched his mansion, they discovered a magnificent hoard of silk, furs, porcelain, furniture, and gold and silver. His personal cash alone exceeded what remained in the imperial treasury. The new emperor ordered Heshen to commit suicide with a rope of gold silk. The government seized Heshen's fortune, but the financial damage could not be undone. The declining agricultural base could not replenish the state coffers, and much of the income that did flow in was squandered by an increasingly corrupt bureaucracy. In the 1800s the Qing Empire faced increasing challenges from Europe and the United States with an empty treasury, a stagnant economy, and a troubled society.

The Qing Empire's problems were not unique. They were common to all the land-based empires of Eurasia, where old and inefficient ways of governing put states at risk. Meanwhile, the international climate was increasingly dominated by industrializing European economies drawing on the wealth of their overseas colonies. During the early 1800s rapid population growth and slow agricultural growth affected much of Eurasia. Earlier military expansion had stretched the resources of imperial treasuries (see Chapter 19), leaving the land-based empires vulnerable to European military pressure. Responses to this pressure varied, with reform and adaptation gaining headway in some lands and tradition being reasserted

in others. In the long run, attempts to meet western Europe's economic and political demands produced financial indebtedness to France, Britain, and other Western powers.

This chapter contrasts the experiences of the Qing Empire with those of the Russian and Ottoman Empires. Whereas the Qing opted for resistance, the others made varying attempts to adapt and reform. Russia eventually became part of Europe and shared in many aspects of European culture, while the Ottomans and the Qing became subject to ever-greater imperialist pressure. These different responses raise the question of the role of culture in shaping western Europe's relations with the rest of the world in the nineteenth century.

The Ottoman Empire

What were the benefits and the drawbacks to the Ottoman Empire of the reforms adopted during the Tanzimat period?

During the eighteenth century the central government of the Ottoman Empire lost much of its power to provincial governors, military commanders, ethnic leaders, and bandit chiefs. In several parts of the empire local officials and large landholders tried to increase their independence and divert imperial funds into their own coffers.

A kingdom in Arabia led by the Saud (sa-OOD) family, following the puritanical and fundamentalist religious views of an eighteenth-century leader named Muhammad ibn Abd al-Wahhab (moo-HAH-muhd ib-uhn ab-dahl-wa-HAHB), took control of the holy cities of Mecca and Medina and deprived the Ottoman sultan of the honor of organizing the annual pilgrimage. In Egypt factions of mamluk slave-soldiers, purchased as boys in the Caucasus and educated for war, reasserted their influence. Such soldiers had ruled Egypt between 1260 and 1517, when they were defeated by the Ottomans. Now Ottoman weakness

Primary Source: The History and Doctrine of the Wahhabis Find out what happens when the *Wahhabis* enter the holy city of Mecca.

Interior of the Ottoman Financial Bureau This engraving from the eighteenth century depicts the governing style of the Ottoman Empire before the era of westernizing reforms. By the end of the Tanzimat period in 1876, government offices and the costumes of officials looked much more like those in contemporary European capitals. From Ignatius Mouradgea d'Ohsson, *Tableau General de l'Empire Ottoman*, large folio edition, Paris, 1787–1820, pi. 178, following p. 340

allowed mamluk factions based on a revival of the slave-soldier tradition to reemerge as local military forces.

For the sultans, the outlook was bleak. At the end of the eighteenth century, the inefficient Janissary corps used the political power it enjoyed in Istanbul to force Sultan Selim III to abandon efforts to train a modern, European-style army. This situation unexpectedly changed when France invaded Egypt.

Egypt and the Napoleonic Example

Napoleon Bonaparte and an invasion force of 36,000 men and four hundred ships invaded Egypt in May 1798. The French quickly defeated the mamluk forces that for several decades had dominated the country under the loose jurisdiction of the Ottoman sultan in Istanbul. Fifteen months later, after being stopped by Ottoman land and British naval forces from invading Syria, Napoleon secretly left Cairo and returned to France. In three months he had seized power and made himself emperor.

Left in Egypt, Napoleon's generals tried to administer a country that they only poorly understood. Cut off from France by British ships in the Mediterranean, they had little hope of remaining in power and agreed to withdraw in 1801. For the second time in three years, a collapse of military power produced a power vacuum in Egypt. The winner of the ensuing contest was **Muhammad Ali** (moo-HAM-mad AH-lee), the commander of a contingent of Albanian soldiers sent by the sultan to restore imperial control. By 1805 he had taken the place of the official Ottoman governor,

and by 1811 he had dispossessed the mamluks of their lands and privileges.

Muhammad Ali's rise to power coincided with the meteoric career of Emperor Napoleon I. It is not surprising, therefore, that he adopted many French practices in rebuilding the Egyptian state. Militarily, he established special schools for training artillery and cavalry officers, army surgeons, military bandmasters, and others. The curricula of these schools featured European skills and sciences, and Muhammad Ali began to send promising officer trainees to France for education. In 1824 he started a gazette devoted to official affairs, the first newspaper in the Islamic world. As discussed in Chapter 21, Muhammad Ali also built all sorts of factories to outfit his new army. These did not prove efficient enough to survive, but they showed a determination to achieve independence and parity with the European powers.

In the 1830s Muhammad Ali's son Ibrahim invaded Syria and instituted some of the changes already under way in Egypt. The improved quality of the new Egyptian army had been proven during the Greek war of independence (see below), when Ibrahim had commanded an expeditionary force to help the sultan. In response, the sultan embarked on building his own new army in 1826. The two armies met when

Muhammad Ali (1769–1849) Leader of Egyptian modernization in the early nineteenth century. He ruled Egypt as an Ottoman governor but also had imperial ambitions. His descendants ruled Egypt until overthrown in 1952.

528

Chronology

	Ottoman Empire	Russian Empire	Qing Empire
			1794–1804 White Lotus Rebellion
1800		**1801–1825** Reign of Alexander I	
	1805–1849 Muhammad Ali governs Egypt		
	1808–1839 Rule of Mahmud II		
		1812 Napoleon's retreat from Moscow	
		1825 Decembrist revolt	
		1825–1855 Reign of Nicholas I	
	1826 Janissary corps dissolved		
	1829 Greek independence		
	1839 Abdul Mejid begins Tanzimat reforms		**1839–1842** Opium War
1850			**1850–1864** Taiping Rebellion
	1853–1856 Crimean War	**1853–1856** Crimean War	
		1855–1881 Reign of Alexander II	
			1856–1860 Arrow War
		1861 Emancipation of the serfs	
	1876 First constitution by an Islamic government		

Ibrahim invaded Anatolia in 1839 and defeated the army of his suzerain, the Ottoman sultan. Just as the road to Istanbul seemed open, however, the European powers intervened and forced Ibrahim to withdraw to Egypt.

Muhammad Ali remained Egypt's ruler, under the suzerainty of the sultan, until his death in 1849, and his family continued to rule the country until 1952. But his dream of making Egypt a mighty country capable of standing up to Europe faded. What survived was the example he had set for the sultans in Istanbul.

Ottoman Reform and the European Model, 1807–1853

At the end of the eighteenth century Sultan Selim (seh-LEEM) III (r. 1789–1807), a forward-looking ruler who stayed abreast of events in Europe, introduced reforms to create European-style military units, bring provincial governors under central government control, and standardize taxation. The rise in government expenditures to implement the reforms was supposed to be offset by taxes on selected items, primarily tobacco and coffee.

The reforms failed for political more than economic reasons. The most violent and persistent opposition came from the **Janissary** (JAN-nih-say-ree) military corps (see Chapter 18). The Janissaries had originally been Christian boys taken from their homes in the Balkans, converted to Islam, and required to serve for life in the Ottoman army. But in the eighteenth century they became a significant political force in Istanbul and in provincial capitals like Damascus and Aleppo. Their interest in preserving special economic privileges for themselves and their sons made them resist the creation of new military units.

At times, Janissary power caused military uprisings. In the Ottoman territory of **Serbia**, local residents intensely resented the control exercised by Janissary governors. The Orthodox Christians

Janissaries Infantry, originally of slave origin, who were armed with firearms and constituted the elite of the Ottoman army from the fifteenth century until the corps was abolished in 1826.

Serbia The Ottoman province in the Balkans that rose up against Janissary control in the early 1800s.

Map 22.1 The Ottoman and Russian Empires, 1829–1914 At its height the Ottoman Empire had controlled most of the perimeter of the Mediterranean Sea. But in the 1800s Ottoman territory shrank as many of its provinces gained their independence. The Black Sea, where the Turkish coast was vulnerable to assault, became a weak spot as Russian naval power grew. Russian challenges to the Ottomans at the eastern end of the Black Sea and to the Persians east and west of the Caspian aroused fears in Europe that Russia was trying to reach the Indian Ocean. © Cengage Learning

 Interactive Map

claimed that the Janissaries abused them. In response, Selim threatened to reassign the Janissaries to Istanbul. Suspecting that the sultan wanted to curb their political power, in 1805 the Janissaries revolted and massacred Christians in Serbia. Unable to reestablish central Ottoman rule over Serbia, the sultan had to rely on the ruler of Bosnia, another Balkan province, who joined his troops with the peasants of Serbia to suppress the Janissary uprising. When the threat of Russian intervention prevented the Ottomans from disarming the victorious Serbians, Serbia became effectively independent.

Other opponents of reform included ulama, or Muslim religious scholars, who distrusted the secularization of law and taxation that Selim proposed. In the face of widespread rejection of his reforms, Selim suspended his program in 1806. Nevertheless, a massive military uprising occurred at Istanbul, and the sultan was deposed and imprisoned. Reform forces recaptured the capital, but not before Selim had been executed. Selim's cousin, Sultan Mahmud (MAH-mood) II (r. 1808–1839), cautiously revived Selim's program, but he realized that reforms needed to be more systematic and imposed more forcefully. The effectiveness of radical reform in Muhammad Ali's Egypt drove this lesson home.

So did the insurrection in Greece, during which the Egyptian military performed much better than the main Ottoman army. The Greek independence movement, started in 1821 by a combination of Greek nationalist organizations and interlopers from Albania, had dramatic international significance. Europe's interest in the classical age of Greece and Rome led many Europeans to interpret the Greeks' struggle for independence as a campaign to recapture their classical glory from Muslim oppression. Some—including the English poet Lord Byron, who lost his life in the war—went to Greece to fight as volunteers. When the combined squadrons of the British, French, and Russian fleets, under orders to observe but not intervene in the war, made an unauthorized attack that sank the Ottoman fleet at the Battle of Navarino, Greek victory was assured (see Map 22.1).

Mahmud II concurred with the pro-Greek Europeans in viewing Ottoman military reversals in Greece as a sign of profound weakness. With popular outrage over the military setbacks strong, the sultan made his move in 1826. First he announced the creation of a new artillery unit, which he had secretly been training. When the Janissaries rose in revolt, he ordered the new unit to bombard the Janissary barracks. The Janissary corps was officially dissolved.

Like Muhammad Ali, Mahmud felt he could not implement major changes without reducing the political power of the religious elite. He visualized restructuring the bureaucracy and the educational and legal systems, where ulama power was strongest. Before such strong measures could be undertaken, however, Ibrahim attacked from Syria in 1839. Battlefield defeat, the decision of the rebuilt Ottoman navy to switch sides and support Egypt, and the death of Mahmud, all in the same year, left the empire completely dependent on the European powers for survival.

Mahmud's reforming ideas received their widest expression in the **Tanzimat** (TAHNZ-ee-MAT) ("reorganization"), a series of reforms announced by his sixteen-year-old son and successor, Abdul Mejid (abdul meh-JEED), in 1839 and strongly endorsed by the European ambassadors. One proclamation called for public trials and equal protection under the law for all, whether Muslim, Christian, or Jew. It also guaranteed some rights of privacy, equalized the eligibility of men for conscription into the army (a practice copied from Egypt), and provided for a new, formalized method of tax collection that legally ended tax farming in the Ottoman Empire. It took many years and strenuous efforts by reforming bureaucrats, known as the "men of the Tanzimat," to give substance to these reforms. European observers praised the reforms for their noble principles and rejection of religious influence. Ottoman citizens were more divided; the Christians and Jews, for whom the Europeans showed the greatest concern, were generally more enthusiastic than the Muslims. Many historians see the Tanzimat as the dawn of modern thought and enlightened government in the Middle East. Others point out that removing the religious elite from influence in government also removed the one remaining check on authoritarian rule.

Over time, one legal code after another—commercial, criminal, civil procedure—was introduced to take the place of the corresponding areas of religious legal jurisdiction. All the codes were modeled closely on those of Europe. The Shari'a, or Islamic law, gradually became restricted to matters of family law such as marriage and inheritance. As the Shari'a was displaced, job opportunities for the ulama shrank.

Like Muhammad Ali, Sultan Mahmud had sent military cadets to France and the German states for training. In the 1830s an Ottoman imperial school of military sciences, later to become Istanbul University, was established, where instructors from western Europe taught chemistry, engineering, mathematics, and physics in addition to military history. Military education became the model for more general educational reforms. In 1838 the first medical school was established to train army doctors and surgeons. Later, a national system of preparatory schools was created to feed graduates into the military schools. The subjects that were taught and many of the teachers were foreign, raising the issue of whether Turkish should

Primary Source: Imperial Rescript Learn about the rights and freedoms granted to the Ottoman citizens during the first half of the nineteenth century.

Tanzimat "Restructuring" reforms by the nineteenth-century Ottoman rulers intended to move civil law away from the control of religious elites and make the military and the bureaucracy more efficient.

be a language of instruction. Because it was easier to import and use foreign textbooks than to write new ones in Turkish, French became the preferred language in all advanced professional and scientific training. However, the great majority of students still learned to read and write in Quran schools down to the twentieth century.

In the capital city Istanbul, the reforms stimulated the growth of a small but cosmopolitan milieu embracing European language and culture. The first Turkish newspaper, a government gazette modeled on that of Muhammad Ali, appeared in 1831. Other newspapers followed, many written in French. Travel to Europe—particularly to England and France—became popular among wealthy Turks. Interest in importing European military, industrial, and communications technology remained strong through the 1800s.

Changes in military practice had unforeseen cultural and social effects. Accepting the European notion that modern weapons and drill required modern military dress, beards were deemed unhygienic and, in artillery units, a fire hazard. Military headgear also became controversial. European military caps, which had leather bills on the front to protect against the glare of the sun, were not acceptable because they interfered with Muslim soldiers' touching their foreheads to the ground in prayer. The compromise was the brimless cap now called the *fez*, which was adopted by the military and then by Ottoman civil officials in the early years of Mahmud II's reign.

The empire's new orientation spread beyond the military. Government ministries that normally recruited from traditional bureaucratic families and relied on on-the-job training were gradually transformed into formal civil services hiring men educated in the new schools. Among self-consciously progressive men, particularly those in government service, European dress became the fashion in the Ottoman cities of the later 1800s. Traditional dress became a symbol of the religious, the rural, and the parochial.

Secularization of the legal code particularly affected non-Muslim Ottoman subjects. Islamic law had required non-Muslims to pay a special head tax that was sometimes explained as a substitute for military service. Under the Tanzimat, the tax was abolished and non-Muslims became liable for military service—unless they bought their way out by paying a new military exemption tax. The new law codes gave all male subjects equal access to the civil courts, while the operations of the Islamic law courts shrank. What enhanced the status of non-Muslims most, however, was the strong concern for their welfare consistently expressed by the European powers. The Ottoman Empire became a rich field of operation for Christian missionaries and European supporters of Jewish community life in the Muslim world.

The public rights and political participation granted during the Tanzimat applied specifically to men. Private life, including everything connected to marriage and divorce, remained within the sphere of religious law, and at no time was there a question of political participation or reformed education for women. Indeed, the reforms may have decreased the influence of women. The political changes ran parallel to economic changes that also narrowed women's opportunities.

After silver from the Americas began to flood the empire in the 1600s, workers were increasingly paid in cash rather than in goods, and businesses associated with banking and finance developed. But women were barred from the early industrial labor and the professions, while traditional "woman's work" such as weaving was increasingly mechanized and done by men.

Nevertheless, in the early 1800s women retained considerable power in the management and disposal of their own property, gained mostly through fixed shares of inheritance. After marriage a woman was often pressured to convert her landholdings to cash in order to transfer her personal wealth to her husband's family, with whom she and her husband would reside. However, this was not a requirement, since men were legally obligated to support their families single-handedly. Until the 1820s many wealthy women retained their say in the distribution of property through the creation of charitable trusts

Primary Source: An Ottoman Government Decree Defines the Official Notion of the "Modern" Citizen, June 19, 1870 Find out how progress and modernization among the Ottomans affected the area's nomadic tribespeople.

for their sons. Because these trusts were set up in the religious courts, they could be designed to conform to the wishes of family members. Then, in the 1820s and 1830s the secularizing reforms of Mahmud II transferred jurisdiction over the charitable trusts from religious courts to the state and ended women's control over this form of property.

The Crimean War and Its Aftermath

Since the reign of Peter the Great (r. 1689–1725) the Russian Empire had attempted to expand southward at the Ottomans' expense. By 1815 Russia had pried the Georgian region of the Caucasus away from the Ottomans, and the threat of Russian intervention had prevented the Ottomans from crushing Serbian independence. When Muhammad Ali's Egyptian army invaded Syria in 1833, Russia signed a treaty in support of the Ottomans. In return, the sultan recognized Russia's claim to being the protector of all of the empire's Orthodox subjects. This set the stage for an obscure dispute that resulted in war.

Bowing to British and French pressure, the sultan named France Protector of the Holy Sepulchre in Jerusalem in 1852. Russia protested, but the sultan held firm. So Russia invaded Ottoman territories in what is today Romania, and Britain and France went to war as allies of the sultan. The real causes of the war went beyond church quarrels in Jerusalem and involved diplomatic maneuvering among European powers over whether the Ottoman Empire should continue to exist and, if not, who should take over its territory. The *Eastern Question* was the simple name given to this complex issue. Though the powers, including Russia, had agreed to save the empire in 1839, Britain subsequently became suspicious of Russian ambitions. Prominent anti-Russian politicians in Britain feared that Russia would threaten the British hold on India.

Between 1853 and 1856 the **Crimean** (cry-ME-uhn) **War** raged in Romania, on the Black Sea, and on the Crimean peninsula. Britain, France, and the Italian kingdom of Sardinia-Piedmont sided with the Ottomans. Austria mediated the outcome. Britain and France trapped the Russian fleet in the Black Sea, where its commanders decided to sink the ships to protect the approaches to Sevastopol, their main base in Crimea. An army largely made up of British and French troops landed and laid siege to the city.

Official corruption and lack of railways hampered the Russians' attempts to supply their forces. On the Romanian front, the Ottomans resisted effectively. At Sevastopol, the Russians were outmatched militarily and suffered badly from disease. Tsar Nicholas died as defeat loomed, leaving his successor, Alexander II (r. 1855–1881), to sue for peace when Sevastopol finally fell three months later.

The Crimean War brought significant changes to all the combatants. The tsar and his government, already beset by demands for the reform of serfdom, education, and the military, were further discredited. In Britain and France, the conflict was accompanied by massive propaganda campaigns. For the first time newspapers effectively mobilized public support for a war. British press accounts so glamorized British participation that the false impression has lingered that Ottoman troops played a negligible role in the conflict. At the time, however, British and French commanders noted the massive losses among Turkish troops in particular. The French press, dominant in Istanbul, promoted a sense of unity between Turkish and French society that continued to influence many aspects of Turkish urban culture.

The larger significance of the Crimean War was that it marked the transition from traditional to modern warfare (see Environment and Technology: The Web of War). All the combatants had previously prided themselves on the use of highly trained cavalry to smash through the front lines of infantry. Cavalry coexisted with firearms until the early 1800s, primarily because early rifles were awkward to load and not very accurate. Cavalry could attack during the intervals between volleys. Then in the 1830s and 1840s percussion caps that did away with pouring gunpowder into the barrel of a musket came into use. In Crimean War battles many cavalry units were destroyed by the rapid fire of rifles that loaded at the breech rather than down the barrel. That was the fate of the famed British Light Brigade, which was sent to relieve an Ottoman unit surrounded by Russian troops.

Crimean War (1853–1856) Conflict between the Russian and Ottoman Empires fought primarily in the Crimean peninsula. To prevent Russian expansion, Britain and France sent troops to support the Ottomans.

The Web of War

The lethal military technologies of the mid-nineteenth century that were used on battlefields in the United States, Russia, India, and China were rapidly transmitted from one conflict to the next. This dissemination was due not only to the rapid development of communications but also to the existence of a new international network of soldiers who moved from one trouble spot to another, bringing expertise in the use of new techniques.

General Charles Gordon (1833–1885), for instance, was commissioned in the British army in 1852, then served in the Crimean War after Britain entered on the side of the Ottomans. In 1860 he was dispatched to China, where he served with British forces during the Arrow War and took part in the sack of Beijing. Afterward, he stayed in China and was seconded to the Qing imperial government until the suppression of the Taipings in 1864, earning himself the nickname "Chinese" Gordon. Gordon later served the Ottoman rulers of Egypt as governor of territory along the Nile. He was killed in Egypt in 1885 while leading his Egyptian troops in defense of the city of Khartoum against an uprising by the Sudanese religious leader, the Mahdi.

Journalism played an important part in the developing web of telegraph communications that sped orders to and from the battlefields. Readers in London could learn details of the drama occurring in the Crimea or in China within a week—or in some cases days—after they occurred. Print and, later, photographic journalism created new "stars" from these war experiences. Charles Gordon was one. Florence Nightingale was another.

In the great wars of the 1800s, the vast majority of deaths resulted from infection or excessive bleeding, not from the wounds themselves. Florence Nightingale (1820–1910), while still a young woman, became interested in hospital management and nursing and went to Prussia and France to study advanced techniques. Before the outbreak of the Crimean War she was credited with bringing about marked improvement in British health care. When the public reacted to news reports of the suffering in the Crimea, the British government sent Nightingale to the region. Within a year of her arrival the death rate in the military hospitals there dropped from 45 percent to under 5 percent. Her techniques for preventing septicemia and dysentery, essentially sanitary measures like washing bed linens after a death and emptying toilet buckets outside, were quickly adopted by those working for and with her. On her return to London, Nightingale established institutes for nursing that soon were recognized as leaders around the world. She herself was lionized by the British public and received the Order of Merit in 1907, three years before her death.

The importance of Nightingale's innovations in public hygiene is underscored by the life of her contemporary, Mary Seacole (1805–1881). A Jamaican woman who volunteered to nurse British troops in the Crimean War, Seacole was repeatedly excluded from nursing service by British authorities. She eventually went to the Crimea and used her own funds to run a hospital there, bankrupting herself in the process. The drama of the Crimean War moved the British public to support Seacole after her sacrifices were publicized. She was awarded medals by the British, French, and Turkish governments and today is recognized with her contemporary Florence Nightingale as an innovative field nurse and a champion of public hygiene in peacetime.

Florence Nightingale During Crimean War This 1856 lithograph shows Florence Nightingale supervising nursing care in a hospital in Scutari (Uskudar) across the Bosphorus strait from Istanbul. Though the artist may have exaggerated the neatness and cleanliness of the ward, sanitary measures proved the key to Nightingale's success in raising the survival rate of sick and wounded soldiers.

From Edward William Lane, *The Manners and Customs of the Modern Egyptians* (London: J. M. D. & Co. 1860)

Street Scene in Cairo This engraving from Edward William Lane's influential travel book *Account of the Manners and Customs of the Modern Egyptians written in Egypt during the Years 1833–1835* conveys the image of narrow lanes and small stores that became stock features of European thinking about Middle Eastern cities.

After the Crimean War, the Ottoman Empire increased its involvement with European commerce. The Ottoman imperial bank was founded in 1840, and a few years later currency reform pegged the value of Ottoman gold coins to the British pound. Sweeping changes in the 1850s expedited the creation of banks, insurance companies, and legal firms throughout the empire. Bustling trade also encouraged a migration from country to city between about 1850 and 1880. Many of the major cities of the empire—Istanbul, Damascus, Beirut, Alexandria, Cairo—expanded. A small but influential urban professional class emerged, as did a considerable class of wage laborers.

However, commercial vigor and urbanization could not make up for declining revenues and the chronic insolvency and corruption of the imperial government. From the conclusion of the Crimean War

in 1856 on, the Ottoman government became heavily dependent on foreign loans. In return it lowered tariffs to favor European imports and allowed European banks to open in Ottoman cities. Europeans living in Istanbul and other commercial centers enjoyed **extraterritoriality**, the right to be subject to their own laws and exempt from Ottoman jurisdiction.

As the result of these measures, imported goods multiplied, but—apart from tobacco and the Turkish opium that American traders took to China to compete with British opium from India—Anatolia produced few exports. As foreign debt grew, so did inflationary trends that left urban populations in a precarious position. By contrast, Egyptian cotton exports soared during the American Civil War, when American cotton exports plummeted; but the profits benefited Muhammad Ali's descendants, who had become the hereditary governors of Egypt, rather than the Ottoman government. The Suez Canal, which was partly financed by cotton profits, opened in 1869, and Cairo was redesigned and beautified. Eventually overexpenditure on such projects plunged Egypt into the same debt crisis that plagued the empire as a whole.

The decline of Ottoman power and prosperity had a strong impact on a group of well-educated young urban men who aspired to wealth and influence. They doubted that the empire's rulers and the Tanzimat officials who worked for them would ever stand up to European domination. Though lacking a sophisticated organization, these **Young Ottomans** (sometimes called Young Turks, though that term properly applies to a later movement) promoted a mixture of liberal ideas derived from Europe, national pride in Ottoman independence, and modernist views of Islam. Prominent Young Ottomans helped draft a constitution that was promulgated in 1876 by a new and as yet untried sultan, Abdul Hamid II. This

extraterritoriality The right of foreign residents in a country to live under the laws of their native country and disregard the laws of the host country. In the nineteenth and early twentieth centuries, European and American nationals living in certain areas of Chinese and Ottoman cities were granted this right.

Young Ottomans Movement of young intellectuals to institute liberal reforms and build a feeling of national identity in the Ottoman Empire in the second half of the nineteenth century.

apparent triumph of liberal reform was short-lived. With war against Russia again threatening in the Balkans in 1877, Abdul Hamid suspended the constitution and the parliament that had been elected that year. Though he ruthlessly opposed further political reforms, the Tanzimat programs of extending modern schooling, utilizing European military practices and advisers, and making the government bureaucracy more orderly continued during his reign.

The Russian Empire

How did the Russian Empire maintain its status as both a European power and a great Asian land empire?

In 1812, when Napoleon's march on Moscow ended in a disastrous retreat, the European image of Russia changed. Just as Napoleon's withdrawal from Egypt led to Muhammad Ali briefly becoming a political power, so his withdrawal from Russia conferred status on Tsar Alexander I (r. 1801–1825). Conservative Europeans still saw Russia as alien, backward, and oppressive, but they acknowledged its immensity and potential and included the tsar in efforts to suppress revolutionary tendencies throughout Europe.

In several important respects Russia resembled the Ottoman Empire more than the conservative kingdoms of Europe whose autocratic practices it so staunchly supported. Socially dominated by nobles whose country estates were worked by unfree serfs, Russia had almost no middle class. Industry was still at the threshold of development by the standards of the rapidly industrializing European powers, though it was somewhat more dynamic than Ottoman industry. Like Egypt and the Ottoman Empire, Russia engaged in reforms from the top down under Alexander I, but when his conservative brother Nicholas I (r. 1825–1855) succeeded to the throne, iron discipline and suspicion of modern ideas took priority over reform.

Russia and Europe   In 1700 only three Russians out of a hundred lived in cities, two-thirds of them in Moscow alone. By the mid-1800s the town population had grown tenfold, though it still accounted for only 6 percent of the total because the territories of the tsars had grown greatly through wars and colonization (see Chapter 19). These figures demonstrate that, like the Ottoman Empire, Russia was an overwhelmingly agricultural land. However, it had poorer transportation than the Ottoman Empire, since many Ottoman cities were seaports. Both empires encompassed peoples speaking many different languages.

Well-engineered roads did not begin to appear until 1817, and steam navigation commenced on the Volga in 1843. Tsar Nicholas I built the first railroad from St. Petersburg, the Russian capital, to his summer palace in 1837. A few years later his commitment to strict discipline led him to insist that the trunk line from St. Petersburg to Moscow run in a perfectly straight line. Industrialization projects depended heavily on foreign expertise. While American engineers oversaw the laying of track and built locomotive workshops, British engineers set up the textile mills that gave woolens and cottons a prominent place among Russia's industries.

Until the late nineteenth century the Russian government's interest in industry was limited. An industrial revolution required educated and independent-minded artisans and entrepreneurs, but Nicholas feared the spread of literacy and modern education—especially anything smacking of liberalism, socialism, or revolution—beyond the minimum

Visual Connection Library

Raising of the Alexander Monument in St. Petersburg The death of Alexander I in 1825 brought to power his conservative brother Nicholas I. Yet Alexander remained a heroic figure for his resistance to Napoleon. This monument in Winter Palace Square was erected in 1829.

needed to train the officer corps and the bureaucracy. He preferred serfs to factory workers, and he paid for imported industrial goods with exports of grain and timber.

Like Egypt and the Ottoman Empire, Russia aspired to Western-style economic development. But when France and Britain entered the Crimean War, they faced a Russian army equipped with obsolete weapons and bogged down by lack of transportation. At a time when European engineers were making major breakthroughs in loading cannon through an opening at the breech end, muzzle-loading artillery remained the Russian standard.

Yet in some ways Russia bore a closer resemblance to other European countries than the Ottoman Empire did. From the point of view of the French and the British, the Cyrillic alphabet and the Russian Orthodox form of Christianity seemed foreign, but they were not nearly as foreign as the Arabic alphabet and the Muslim faith. Britain and France feared Russia as a rival for power in the east, but they increasingly accepted Tsar Nicholas's view of the Ottoman Empire as "the sick man of Europe," capable of surviving only so long as the European powers permitted.

From the Russian point of view, kinship with western Europe was of questionable value. Westernizers, like the men of the Tanzimat in the Ottoman

Empire, put their trust in technical advances and governmental reform. Opposing them were intellectuals known as **Slavophiles**, who considered the Orthodox faith, the solidity of peasant life, and the tsar's absolute rule to be the proper bases of Russian civilization. After Russia's humiliation in the Crimea, the Slavophile tendency gave rise to **Pan-Slavism**, a militant political doctrine advocating unity of all the Slavic peoples, including those living under Austrian and Ottoman rule.

On the diplomatic front, the tsar's inclusion as a major European ruler contrasted sharply with the sultan's exclusion. However, this did not prevent a powerful sense of Russophobia from developing in the West. Britain in particular saw Russia as a threat to India and despised the subjection of the serfs, who gained their freedom only in 1861, twenty-seven years after the British had abolished slavery. The

Slavophiles Russian intellectuals in the early nineteenth century who favored resisting western European influences and taking pride in the traditional peasant values and institutions of the Slavic people.
Pan-Slavism Movement among Russian intellectuals in the second half of the nineteenth century to identify culturally and politically with the Slavic peoples of eastern Europe.

passions generated by the Crimean War and its outcome affected the relations of Russia, Europe, and the Ottoman Empire for the remainder of the nineteenth century.

Russia and Asia

The Russian drive to the east in the eighteenth century brought the tsar's empire to the Pacific Ocean and the frontiers of China (see Map 19.2) by century's end. In the nineteenth century Russian expansionism focused on the south. There the backwardness of the Russian military did not matter since the peoples they faced were even less technologically advanced. In 1860 Russia established a military outpost on the Pacific coast that would eventually grow into the great naval port of Vladivostok. In Central Asia the steppe lands of the Kazakh nomads came under Russian control early in the century, setting the stage for a confrontation with three Uzbek states farther south. They succumbed one by one, beginning in 1865, giving rise to the new province of Turkestan, with its capital at Tashkent in present-day Uzbekistan. In the Caucasus Mountains, the third area of southward expansion, Russia first took over Christian Georgia (1786), Muslim Azerbaijan (ah-zer-by-JAHN) (1801), and Christian Armenia (1813) before gobbling up the many small principalities in the heart of the mountains. Between 1829 and 1864 Dagestan, Chechnya (CHECH-nee-yah), and Abkhazia (ab-KAH-zee-yah) became parts of the Russian Empire.

The drive to the south intensified political friction with Russia's new neighbors: Qing China and Japan in the east, Iran on the Central Asian and Caucasus frontiers, and the Ottoman Empire at the eastern end of the Black Sea. In the latter two instances, Muslim refugees from the territories newly absorbed by Russia spread anti-Russian feelings, though some of them brought with them modern skills and ideas gained from exposure to Russian administration and education.

 Primary Source: The Treaty of Peace and Commerce (Treaty of Turkmanchai) Between Iran and Russia, February 10–22, 1828 Learn details of the agreement through which Russia and Iran resolve to live in peace.

The Russian drive to the south added a new element to the Eastern Question. Many British statesmen and strategists reckoned that a warlike Russia would press on until it had conquered all the lands separating it from British India, a prospect that made them shudder, given India's enormous contribution to Britain's prosperity. The competition that ensued over which power would control southern Central Asia resulted in a standoff in Afghanistan, which became a buffer zone under the control of neither. In Iran, the standoff between the powers helped preserve the weak Qajar dynasty of shahs.

Cultural Trends

Unlike Egypt and the Ottoman Empire, which began to send students to Europe for training only in the nineteenth century, Russia had been in cultural contact with western Europe since the time of Peter the Great (r. 1689–1725). Members of the Russian court knew Western languages, and the tsars employed officials and advisers from Western countries. Peter had also enlisted the well-educated Ukrainian clerics who headed the Russian Orthodox Church to help spread a Western spirit of education. As a result, Alexander I's reforms met a more positive reception than those of Muhammad Ali and Mahmud II. However, his reforms promised more on paper than they brought about in practice. It took many years to develop a sufficient pool of trained bureaucrats to make the reforms effective.

Ironically, much of the opposition to Alexander's reforms came from well-established families that were not at all unfriendly to Western ideas. Their fear was that the new government bureaucrats, who often came from humbler social origins, would act as agents of imperial tyranny. Individuals favoring more liberal reforms, including military officers who had served in western Europe, intellectuals who read Western political tracts, and members of Masonic lodges who exchanged views with Freemasons in the West, formed secret societies of opposition. Some placed their highest priority on freeing the serfs; others advocated a constitution and a republican form of government. When Alexander I died in December 1825, confusion over who was to succeed him encouraged a group of reform-minded army officers to try to take over the government and provoke an uprising.

The so-called **Decembrist revolt** failed, and many of the participants were severely punished. These events ensured that the new tsar, Nicholas I, would pay little heed to calls for reform over the next thirty years. His conservative reign realized the liberals' worst fears in the same way that the Tanzimat-inspired bureaucracy of the Ottoman Empire served the despotic purposes of Sultan Abdul Hamid II after 1877.

The great powers meeting in Paris to settle the Crimean War in 1856 forced Russia to return land to the Ottomans in both Europe and Asia. This humiliation spurred Nicholas's son and successor, Alexander II (r. 1855–1881), to institute major new reforms to reinvigorate the country. The greatest of his reforms was the emancipation of the serfs in 1861. He also authorized new joint-stock companies, projected a railroad network to tie the country together, and modernized the legal and administrative arms of government.

Earlier intellectual and cultural trends flourished under Alexander II, with more and more people becoming involved in intellectual, artistic, and professional life. Most prominent intellectuals received some amount of instruction at Moscow University or some German university. Universities also appeared in provincial cities like Kharkov in Ukraine and Kazan on the Volga River. Student clubs, along with Masonic lodges, became places for discussing new ideas. As Russian scholars and scientists began to achieve recognition for their contributions to European thought, scholarly careers attracted young men from clerical families, who in turn helped stimulate reforms in religious education.

Just as the Tanzimat reforms of the Ottoman Empire preceded the emergence of the Young Ottomans as a new and assertive political and intellectual force in the second half of the nineteenth century, so the initially ineffective reforms of Alexander I set in motion cultural currents that would make Russia a dynamic center of intellectual, artistic, and political life under his nephew Alexander II. Thus Russia belonged to two different spheres of development. It entered the nineteenth century a recognized force in European politics, but in other ways it resembled the Ottoman Empire. Rulers in both empires instituted reforms, overcame opposition, and increased the power of their governments. These activities stimulated intellectual and political trends that would ultimately work against the absolute rule of tsar and

SECTION REVIEW

- Russian society resembled Ottoman society, but Alexander I undertook top-down westernizing reforms.

- Nicholas I's suspicion of Western ideas stalled reform and slowed industrial development.

- Slavophiles opposed westernizers and, after the Crimean War, embraced Pan-Slavism, contributing to Russophobia in the West.

- Russian expansion southward and eastward added vast territories to the empire and caused friction with China, Japan, Iran, and the Ottoman Empire.

- Resistance to Alexander I's bureaucratic reforms sparked the Decembrist revolt, which stiffened Nicholas I's hostility to Western ideas.

- The humiliation of the Crimean War drove Alexander II's reforms, including emancipation of the serfs.

sultan. Yet Russia would eventually develop much closer relations with western Europe and become an arena for every sort of European intellectual, artistic, and political tendency, while the Ottoman Empire would ultimately succumb to European imperialism.

The Qing Empire

How did the impact of European imperialism on China differ from its impact on Russia and the Ottoman Empire?

In 1800 the Qing Empire faced many problems, but no reform movement of the kind initiated by Sultan Selim III emerged in China. The reasons are not difficult to understand. The Qing emperors had skillfully countered Russian strategic and diplomatic moves in the 1600s. Instead of having a Napoleon threatening them with invasion, they enjoyed the admiration of Jesuit priests, who likened them to enlightened philosopher-kings. In 1793, however, a British attempt to establish diplomatic and trade relations—the Macartney mission—turned European opinion against China (see Chapter 19).

China's most serious crises were domestic, not foreign: rebellions by displaced indigenous peoples and

Decembrist revolt Abortive attempt by army officers to take control of the Russian government upon the death of Tsar Alexander I in 1825.

the poor, and protests against the injustice of the local magistrates. The Qing dealt with these problems in the usual way, by suppressing rebels and dismissing incompetent or untrustworthy officials. They paid little attention to the far-off Europeans and brushed aside the complaints from European merchants who chafed against the restrictions of the "Canton system" by which the Qing limited and controlled foreign trade.

Economic and Social Disorder

Early Qing successes and territorial expansion sowed the seeds of later domestic and political chaos. The early emperors encouraged the recovery of farmland, the opening of previously uncultivated areas, and the restoration and expansion of the road and canal systems. These measures expanded the agricultural base and supported a doubling of the population between about 1650 and 1800. Enormous numbers of farmers, merchants, and day laborers migrated in search of less crowded conditions, and a permanent floating population of the unemployed and homeless emerged. By 1800 population strain had caused serious environmental damage in some parts of central and western China.

While farmers tried to cope with agricultural deterioration, other groups vented grievances against the government: minority peoples in central and southwestern China complained about being driven off their lands during the boom of the 1700s, while Mongols resented appropriation of their grazing lands and the displacement of their traditional elites. In some regions, village vigilante organizations took over policing and governing functions from Qing officials who had lost control. Growing numbers of people mistrusted the government, suspecting that all officials were corrupt. The increasing presence of foreign merchants and missionaries in Canton and in the Portuguese colony of Macao aggravated discontent in neighboring districts.

In some parts of China the Qing were hated as foreign conquerors and were suspected of sympathy with the Europeans. In 1794 the White Lotus

Primary Source: Letter to Queen Victoria, 1839 Read Lin Zexu's stern warning to England about the consequences of continuing to bring opium into China.

Rebellion—partly inspired by a messianic ideology that predicted the restoration of the Chinese Ming dynasty and the coming of the Buddha—raged across central China and was not suppressed until 1804. It initiated a series of internal conflicts that continued through the 1800s. Ignited by deepening social instabilities, these movements were sometimes intensified by local ethnic conflicts and by unapproved religions. The ability of some village militias to defend themselves and attack others intensified the conflicts, though the same techniques proved useful to southern coastal populations attempting to fend off British invasion.

The Opium War and Its Aftermath, 1839–1850

Unlike the Ottomans, the Qing knew little about the enormous fortunes being made in the early 1800s by European and American merchants smuggling opium into China. They did not know that silver gained in this illegal trade was helping finance the industrial transformation of England and the United States. Only slowly did Qing officials become aware of British colonies in India that grew and exported opium, and of the major naval base at Singapore through which British opium reached East Asia.

The first Qing law banning opium imports was promulgated in 1729. By 1800, however, opium smuggling had swelled to as many as 4,000 chests per year. Though British merchants had pioneered this profitable trade, Chinese merchants likewise profited from distributing the drugs. A price war in the early 1820s stemming from competition between British and American importers raised demand so sharply that as many as 30,000 chests were being imported by the 1830s. Addiction spread to people at all levels of Qing society, including high-ranking officials. The Qing emperor and his officials debated whether to

Opium War (1839–1842) War between Britain and the Qing Empire that was, in the British view, occasioned by the Qing government's refusal to permit the importation of opium into its territories. The victorious British imposed the one-sided Treaty of Nanking on China.

Bannermen Hereditary military servants of the Qing Empire, mostly descendants of various peoples who had fought for the founders of the empire.

legalize and tax opium or to enforce the existing ban more strictly. Having decided to root out the use and importation of opium, in 1839 they sent a high official to Canton to deal with the matter.

Britain considered the ban on opium importation an intolerable limitation on trade, a direct threat to Britain's economic health, and a cause for war. British naval and marine forces arrived on the south China coast in late 1839. The **Opium War** (1839–1842) broke

out when negotiations between the Qing official and British representatives reached a stalemate. The war exposed the fact that the traditional, hereditary soldiers of the Qing Empire—the **Bannermen**—were, like the Janissaries of the Ottoman Empire, hopelessly obsolete. As in the Crimean War, the British excelled at sea, where they deployed superior technology. British ships landed marines who pillaged coastal cities and then sailed to new destinations (see Map 22.2).

Map 22.2 Conflicts in the Qing Empire, 1839–1870 In both the Opium War of 1839–1842 and the Arrow War of 1856–1860, the seacoasts saw most of the action. Since the Qing had no imperial navy, the well-armed British ships encountered little resistance as they shelled the southern coasts. In inland conflicts, such as the Taiping Rebellion, the opposing armies were massive and slow moving. Battles on land were often prolonged attempts by one side to starve out the other side before making a major assault. © Cengage Learning

Interactive Map

Military Modernization in China The Opium War revealed a serious technology gap between the Manchu Bannermen and the British troops. Many Bannermen still fought with swords and spears as they had in the eighteenth century. After the war China adopted a variety of Western weapons. This later photograph from the Nanjing arsenal shows a Gatling gun. Invented during the American Civil War (1860–1865) by Dr. Richard J. Gatling, each barrel discharged a single shot as the operator turned a crank to make the firing continuous.

The Qing had no imperial navy. Thus until they were able to engage the British in prolonged fighting on land, they were unable to defend themselves against British attacks. Even in the land engagements, Qing resources proved woefully inadequate. The British could quickly transport their forces by sea along the coast, while Qing troops moved primarily on foot. Moving Qing reinforcements from central to eastern China took more than three months; and when the defense forces arrived, they were exhausted and basically without weapons.

The Bannermen used the few muskets the Qing had imported during the 1700s. The weapons were matchlocks, which required the soldiers to ignite the gunpowder by hand. Firing the weapons was dangerous, and the canisters of gunpowder that each musketeer carried on his belt were likely to explode if a fire broke out nearby—a frequent occurrence in encounters with British artillery. Most of the Bannermen, however, had no guns at all and fought with swords, knives, spears, and clubs. Soldiers under British command—many of them Indians—carried percussion-cap rifles, which were far quicker, safer, and more accurate than the matchlocks. In addition, the long-range British artillery could be moved from place to place and proved deadly in the cities and villages of eastern China.

Assuming that British gunboats rode so low in the water that they could not sail up the Chinese rivers, Qing commanders evacuated the coastal areas to counter the British threat. But the British deployed new gunboats for shallow waters and moved without difficulty up the Yangzi River (see Chapter 21).

When the invaders approached Nanjing, the former Ming capital, the Qing decided to negotiate. The **Treaty of Nanking** (the British name for Nanjing) of 1842 dismantled the old Canton system. The number of **treaty ports**—cities opened to foreign residents—increased from one (Canton) to five (Canton, Xiamen, Fuzhou, Ningbo, and Shanghai [shahng-hie]). The island of Hong Kong became a British colony, and British residents in China gained extraterritorial rights. The Qing government agreed to set a low tariff of 5 percent on imports and to pay Britain an

Treaty of Nanking (1842) The treaty that concluded the Opium War. It awarded Britain a large indemnity from the Qing Empire, denied the Qing government tariff control over some of its own borders, opened additional ports of residence to Britons, and ceded the island of Hong Kong to Britain.

treaty ports Cities opened to foreign residents as a result of the forced treaties between the Qing Empire and foreign signatories. In the treaty ports, foreigners enjoyed extraterritoriality.

indemnity of 21 million ounces of silver as a penalty for having started the war. A supplementary treaty the following year guaranteed **most-favored-nation status** to Britain: any privileges that China granted to any other country would be automatically extended to Britain as well. This provision effectively prevented the colonization of China, because giving land to one country would have necessitated giving it to all. With each round of treaties came a new round of privileges for foreigners. In 1860 a new treaty legalized their right to import opium. Later, French treaties established the rights of foreign missionaries to travel in the Chinese countryside and preach their religion. The number of treaty ports grew, too; by 1900 they numbered more than ninety. The treaty system and the principle of extraterritoriality resulted in the colonization of small pockets of Qing territory, where foreign merchants lived at ease.

Greater territorial losses resulted when outlying regions gained independence or were ceded to neighboring countries. Districts north and south of the Amur River in the northeast fell to Russia by treaty in 1858 and 1860; parts of modern Kazakhstan and Kirgizstan in the northwest met the same fate in 1864. From 1865 onward the British gradually gained control of territories on China's Indian frontier. In the late 1800s France forced the court of Vietnam to end its tribute relationship to the Qing, while Britain encouraged Tibetan independence.

In Canton, Shanghai, and other coastal cities, Europeans and Americans maintained offices and factories that employed local Chinese as menial laborers. The foreigners built comfortable housing in zones where Chinese were not permitted to live, and they entertained themselves in exclusive restaurants and bars. Around the foreign establishments, gambling and prostitution offered employment to part of the local urban population.

Whether in town or in the countryside, Christian missionaries whose congregations sponsored hospitals, shelters, and soup kitchens or gave stipends to Chinese who attended church enjoyed a good reputation. But just as often the missionaries themselves were regarded as another evil. They seemed to subvert Confucian beliefs by condemning ancestor worship, pressuring poor families to put their children into orphanages, or fulminating against footbinding. The growing numbers of foreigners, and their growing privileges, became targets of resentment for a deeply dissatisfied, daily more impoverished, and increasingly militarized society.

The Taiping Rebellion, 1850–1864

The inflammatory mixture of social unhappiness and foreign intrusion exploded in the great civil war usually called the **Taiping** (tie-PING) **Rebellion**. In Guangxi, where the Taiping movement originated, entrenched social problems had been generating disorders for half a century. Agriculture in the region was unstable, and many people made their living from arduous and despised trades such as disposing of human waste, making charcoal, and mining. Ethnic divisions complicated economic distress. The lowliest trades frequently involved a minority group, the Hakkas, and tensions between them and the majority were rising. Problems may have been intensified by sharp fluctuations in the opium trade and reactions to the cultural and economic impact of the Europeans and Americans in Canton.

Hong Xiuquan (hoong shee-OH-chew-an), the founder of the Taiping movement, experienced all of these influences. Hong came from a humble Hakka background. After years of study, he competed in the provincial Confucian examinations, hoping for a post in government. He failed the examinations repeatedly, and it appears that he suffered a nervous breakdown in his late thirties. Afterward he spent some time in Canton, where he met both Chinese and American Protestant missionaries, who inspired him with their teachings. Hong had his own interpretation of the Christian message. He saw himself as the younger brother of Jesus, commissioned by God to found a new kingdom on earth and drive the Manchu conquerors, the Qing, out of China. The result would be universal peace. Hong called his new religious movement the "Heavenly Kingdom of Great Peace."

most-favored-nation status A clause in a commercial treaty that automatically awards to the signatory all the privileges granted to the most favored of other signatories.
Taiping Rebellion (1850–1864) A Christian-inspired rural rebellion that threatened to topple the Qing Empire. It was the most destructive civil war before the twentieth century.

Nanjing Encircled The Taipings held the city of Nanjing as their capital for a decade, and for years Qing and international troops attempted to break their hold. By the summer of 1864, Qing forces had built tunnels leading to the foundations of Nanjing's city walls and had planted explosives. The detonation of the explosives signaled the final Qing assault on the rebel capital. As shown here, the common people of the city, along with their starving livestock, were caught in the crossfire. Many of the Taiping leaders escaped the debacle at Nanjing, but nearly all were hunted down and executed. Roger-Viollet/Getty Images

History in Focus *Examine the image "Nanjing Encircled," paying particular attention to how it depicts warfare in nineteenth-century China. What does it tell you about the disadvantages of the Qing Empire in the face of Western imperialism? Find the answer online.*

Hong quickly attracted a community of believers, primarily Hakkas like himself. They believed in the prophecy of dreams and claimed they could walk on air. Hong and his rivals for leadership in the movement went in and out of ecstatic trances and denounced the Manchus as creatures of Satan. After news of the sect reached the government, Qing troops arrived to arrest the Taiping leaders but were soundly repelled. Local loyalty to the Taipings spread quickly, their numbers multiplied, and they began to enlarge their domain.

The Taipings relied at first on Hakka sympathy and the charismatic appeal of their religious doctrine to attract followers. But as their numbers and power grew, they altered their methods of preaching and governing, replacing the anti-Chinese appeals used to enlist Hakkas with anti-Manchu rhetoric designed to enlist Chinese. They also forced captured villages to join their movement. Once people were absorbed, the Taipings strictly monitored their activities, segregating men and women and organizing them into work and military teams. Women were forbidden to bind their feet (the Hakkas had never practiced footbinding) and participated fully in farming and labor. Brigades of women soldiers took to the field against Qing forces.

As the movement grew, it began to move toward eastern and northern China (see Map 22.2). Panic preceded the Taipings. Villagers feared being forced into

Taiping units, and Confucian elites recoiled in horror from the bizarre ideology of foreign gods, totalitarian rule, and walking, working, warring women. But the huge numbers the Taipings were able to muster overwhelmed attempts at local defense. The tremendous growth in the number of Taiping followers required the movement to establish a permanent base. When the rebel army conquered Nanjing in 1853, the Taiping leaders decided to settle there and make it the capital of the new "Heavenly Kingdom of Great Peace."

Qing forces attempting to defend north China became more successful as problems of organization and growing numbers slowed Taiping momentum. Increasing Qing military success resulted mainly from the flexibility of the imperial military commanders in the face of an unprecedented challenge. In addition, the military commanders received strong backing from a group of civilian provincial governors who had studied the techniques developed by local militia forces for self-defense. Certain provincial governors combined their knowledge of civilian self-defense and local terrain with more efficient organization and the use of modern weaponry. The result was the formation of new military units, in which many of the Bannermen voluntarily served under civilian governors. The Qing court agreed to special taxes to fund the new armies and acknowledged the new combined leadership.

When the Taipings settled into Nanjing, the new Qing armies surrounded the city, hoping to starve out the rebels. The Taipings, however, had provisioned and fortified themselves well. They also had the services of several brilliant young military commanders, who mobilized enormous campaigns in nearby parts of eastern China, scavenging supplies and attempting to break the encirclement of Nanjing. For more than a decade the Taiping leadership remained ensconced at Nanjing, and the "Heavenly Kingdom" endured.

In 1856 Britain and France, freed from their preoccupation with the Crimean War, turned their attention to China. European and American missionaries had visited Nanjing, curious to see what their fellow Christians were up to. Their reports were discouraging. Hong Xiuquan and the other leaders appeared to lead lives of indulgence and abandon, and more than one missionary accused them of homosexual practices. Relieved of the possible accusation of quashing

a pious Christian movement, the British and French surveyed the situation. Though the Taipings were not going to topple the Qing, rebellious Nian ("Bands") in northern China added a new threat in the 1850s. A series of simultaneous large insurrections might indeed destroy the empire. Moreover, since the Qing had not observed all the provisions of the treaties signed after the Opium War, Britain and France were now considering renewing war on the Qing themselves.

In 1856 the British and French launched a series of swift, brutal coastal attacks—a second opium war, called the Arrow War (1856–1860)—that culminated in a British and French invasion of Beijing and the sacking of the Summer Palace in 1860. A new round of treaties punished the Qing for not enacting all the provisions of the Treaty of Nanking. Having secured their principal objective, the British and French forces then joined the Qing campaign against the Taipings. Attempts to coordinate the international forces were sometimes riotous and sometimes tragic, but the injection of European weaponry and money helped quell both the Taiping and the Nian rebellions during the 1860s.

The Taiping Rebellion ranks as the world's bloodiest civil war and the greatest armed conflict before the twentieth century. Estimates of deaths range from 20 million to 30 million. The loss of life came primarily from starvation and disease, for most engagements consisted of surrounding fortified cities and waiting until the enemy forces died, surrendered, or were so weakened that they could be easily defeated. Many sieges continued for months. Reports of people eating grass, leather, hemp, and human flesh were widespread. The dead were rarely buried properly, and epidemic disease was common.

The area of early Taiping fighting was close to the regions of southwest China in which bubonic plague had been lingering for centuries. When the rebellion was suppressed, many Taiping followers sought safety in the highlands of Laos and Vietnam, which soon showed infestation by plague. Within a few years the disease reached Hong Kong, and from there it spread to Singapore, San Francisco, Calcutta, and London. In the late 1800s there was intense apprehension over the possibility of a worldwide outbreak, and Chinese immigrants were regarded as likely carriers. This fear became a contributing factor in the passage of

Trade Warehouse in Guangzhou A European merchant enters in the background while Chinese workers pack tea and porcelain.

discriminatory immigration bans on Chinese in the United States in 1882.

The Taiping Rebellion devastated the agricultural centers of China. Many of the most intensely cultivated regions of central and eastern China were depopulated. Some were still uninhabited decades later, and major portions of the country did not recover until the twentieth century.

Cities, too, were hard hit. Shanghai, a treaty port of modest size before the rebellion, saw its population multiplied many times by the arrival of refugees from war-blasted neighboring provinces. The city then endured months of siege by the Taipings. Major cultural centers in eastern China lost masterpieces of art and architecture; imperial libraries were burned or their collections exposed to the weather; and the printing blocks used to make books were destroyed. Finally, while the empire faced the enormous challenge of dealing with the material and cultural destruction of the war, it also was burdened by a major ecological disaster in the north. The Yellow River changed course in 1855, destroying the southern part of impoverished Shandong province with flood and initiating decades of drought along the former riverbed in northern Shandong.

Decentralization at the End of the Qing Empire, 1864–1875

The Qing government emerged from the 1850s with no hope of achieving solvency. The corruption of the 1700s, attempts in the very early 1800s to restore waterworks and roads, and declining yields from land taxes had bankrupted the treasury. By 1850, before the Taiping Rebellion, Qing government expenditures were ten times revenues. The indemnities demanded by Europeans after the Opium and Arrow Wars compounded the problem. Vast stretches of formerly productive rice land were devastated and the population was dispersed. Refugees pleaded for relief, and the imperial, volunteer, foreign, and mercenary troops that had suppressed the Taipings demanded unpaid wages.

Britain and France became active participants in the period of recovery that followed the rebellion. To ensure repayment of the debt to Britain, Robert Hart was installed as inspector-general of a newly created Imperial Maritime Customs Service. Britain and the Qing split the revenues he collected. Britons and Americans worked for the Qing government as advisers and ambassadors, attempting to smooth communications between the Qing, Europe, and the United States.

The real work of the recovery, however, was managed by provincial governors who had come to the forefront in the struggle against the Taipings. To prosecute the war, they had won the right to levy their own taxes, raise their own troops, and run their own bureaucracies. These special powers were not entirely canceled when the war ended. Chief among these governors was Zeng Guofan (zung gwoh-FAN), who oversaw programs to restore agriculture, communications, education, and publishing, as well as efforts

Cixi's Allies In the 1860s and 1870s, Cixi was a supporter of reform (see page 547). In later years she was widely regarded as corrupt and self-centered and as an obstacle to reform. Her greatest allies were the court eunuchs. Introduced to palace life in early China as managers of the imperial harems, eunuchs became powerful at court. The first Qing emperors refused to allow the eunuchs any political influence, but by Cixi's time, eunuchs were again a political factor. Freer Gallery of Art and Arthur M. Sackler Gallery Archives, Smithsonian Institution, Washington, D.C., Purchase, 1963-1964. Neg # SC-GR 261

to reform the military and industrialize armaments manufacture.

Like many provincial governors, Zeng preferred to look to the United States rather than to Britain for models and aid, hiring American advisers to run his weapons factories, shipyards, and military academies. He also sponsored a daring program in which promising Chinese boys were sent to Hartford, Connecticut, a center of missionary activity, to learn English, science, mathematics, engineering, and history. They returned to China to assume some of the positions previously held by foreign advisers. Though Zeng was never an advocate of participation in public life by women, his Confucian convictions taught him that educated mothers were more than ever a necessity. He not only encouraged but also partly oversaw the advanced classical education of his own daughters. Zeng's death in 1872 deprived the empire of a major force for reform.

The period of recovery marked a fundamental structural change in the Qing Empire. Although the emperors after 1850 were ineffective rulers, a coalition of aristocrats supported the reform and recovery programs. Without their legitimization of the new powers of provincial governors like Zeng Guofan, the empire might have evaporated within a generation. A crucial member of this alliance was Cixi (TSUH-shee), who was known as the "Empress Dowager" after the 1880s. Later observers, both Chinese and foreign, reviled her as a monster of corruption and arrogance. But in the 1860s and 1870s Cixi supported the provincial governors, some of whom became so powerful that they were managing Qing foreign policy as well as domestic affairs.

No longer a conquest regime dominated by a Manchu military caste and its Chinese civilian appointees, the empire came under the control of a group of reformist aristocrats and military men, independently powerful civilian governors, and a small number of foreign advisers. The Qing lacked strong, central, unified leadership and could not recover their powers of taxation, legislation, and military command once these had been granted to the provincial governors. From the 1860s forward, the Qing Empire disintegrated into a number of large power zones in which provincial governors handed over leadership to their protégés in a pattern that the Qing court eventually could only ritually legitimate.

SECTION REVIEW

- Social unrest grew in Qing China through a combination of discontent among the poor and displaced indigenous peoples and resentment of growing European influence.

- Qing attempts to ban opium imports provoked the Opium War with Britain, which exposed Qing military inferiority.

- The Treaty of Nanking gave extraterritoriality and other privileges to Britain and led to further losses to other Western powers.

- Social resentment and foreign intrusion ignited the Taiping Rebellion, which, after the Arrow War, the Qing quelled with British and French aid.

- The rebellion encouraged epidemics, devastated agriculture, produced overcrowded cities filled with refugees, and coincided with environmental disasters.

- The rebellion and China's recovery afterward resulted in a process of decentralization led by reformist aristocrats.

Conclusion

Most of the subjects of the Ottoman, Russian, and Qing rulers did not think of European pressure or competition as determining factors in their lives during the first half of the nineteenth century. They continued to live according to the social and economic institutions they inherited from previous generations. By the 1870s, however, the challenge of Europe had become widely realized. The Crimean War, where European allies achieved a hollow victory for the Ottomans and then pressured the sultan for more reforms, confirmed both Ottoman and Russian military weakness. The Opium War did the same for China. But China, unlike the other empires, was also stricken by rampaging civil war and regional uprisings.

Though all three empires faced similar problems of reform, military rebuilding, and financial disarray, China was geographically remote from Europe and thus removed from the geostrategic tug-of-war between Britain and Russia. Despite British fears about Russian threats to India, the tsars enjoyed the advantage of being included in high-level deliberations among European powers. The Ottoman Empire, which had once dominated eastern Europe, was largely excluded from these deliberations. To many European diplomats and overseas investors, its final demise seemed only a matter of time, leaving up in the air the question of who would reap the benefits.

In analyzing the crises of the three empires, historians today stress European economic pressures and observe that all three empires ultimately became insolvent and saw the overthrow of their ruling dynasties. However, at the time what most impressed the Ottomans, Russians, and Chinese was European military superiority, as demonstrated in the Greek war of independence, the Crimean War, and the Opium War. Thus for all three empires, dealing with military emergency took priority over deeper reforms throughout most of the time period of this chapter.

CHAPTER REVIEW

 Download the MP3 audio file of the Chapter Review to listen to on the go.

What were the benefits and the drawbacks to the Ottoman Empire of the reforms adopted during the Tanzimat period? (page 527)

Although the Tanzimat period began with the sultan declaring in 1839 a measure of equality for all Ottoman citizens, improving military performance was at the center of the reforming effort. This reform enhanced the role of the military while other administrative changes reduced the social role and governmental influence of the religious elite. The result was an unbalanced reform effort that eventually led to a military takeover of the country.

How did the Russian Empire maintain its status as both a European power and a great Asian land empire? (page 536)

For Russians, defeat in the Crimean War and the revelation that Russian arms were no match for modern European weaponry were counterbalanced by the comparative weakness of the peoples to the east and south into whose territories they aggressively expanded. Thus, while lagging far behind in industrialization and having an inefficient government, Russia, like the other European states, engaged in imperialist expansion.

How did the impact of European imperialism on China differ from its impact on Russia and the Ottoman Empire? (page 539)

The course of Russian expansion into Asia made it a neighbor of Qing China, but other European powers were seen as greater threats. Britain, France, and the United States used every means available to gain the freedom to exploit China economically. With respect to the empires nearer to home, however, European imperialists—the United States had minimal involvement—considered financial investment to be somewhat less important than limiting Russian expansion or weakening the Ottoman state and improving the lives of its Christian and Jewish populations.

Key Terms

Muhammad Ali *(p. 528)*
Janissaries *(p. 529)*
Serbia *(p. 529)*
Tanzimat *(p. 531)*
Crimean War *(p. 533)*
extraterritoriality *(p. 535)*
Young Ottomans *(p. 535)*
Slavophiles *(p. 537)*
Pan-Slavism *(p. 537)*
Decembrist revolt *(p. 539)*
Opium War *(p. 541)*
Bannermen *(p. 541)*
Treaty of Nanking *(p. 542)*
treaty ports *(p. 542)*
most-favored-nation status *(p. 543)*
Taiping Rebellion *(p. 543)*

Web Resources

Pronunciation Guide

Interactive Maps
- MAP 22.1 The Ottoman and Russian Empires, 1829–1914
- MAP 22.2 Conflicts in the Qing Empire, 1839–1870

Primary Sources
- The History and Doctrine of the Wahhabis
- Imperial Rescript
- An Ottoman Government Decree Defines the Official Notion of the "Modern" Citizen, June 19, 1870
- The Treaty of Peace and Commerce (Treaty of Turkmanchai) Between Iran and Russia, February 10–22, 1828
- Letter to Queen Victoria, 1839

Answer to the History in Focus Question
See photo on page 544, "Nanjing Encircled."

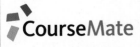 **CourseMate** Visit the CourseMate website at www.cengagebrain.com for additional study tools and review materials for this chapter.

Africa, India, and the New British Empire

© Cengage Learning

 Visit the CourseMate website at **www.cengagebrain.com** for additional study tools and review materials for this chapter.

In 1782, Tipu Sultan inherited the throne of Mysore (MY-sore), which his father had made the most powerful state in south India. The talented new ruler also inherited a healthy distrust of the British East India Company's territorial ambitions. Before the company could invade Mysore, Tipu Sultan launched his own attack in 1785. He then sent an embassy to France in 1788 seeking an alliance against Britain.

Neither of these ventures was immediately successful, but a decade later the French did agree to a loose alliance to challenge Britain's supremacy in the Indian Ocean. When General Napoleon Bonaparte invaded Egypt in 1798, he hoped to use the alliance with Tipu Sultan to threaten the British in India. Tipu's alliance with France did not protect him from the East India Company, whose military victory in 1792 deprived him of most of his seacoast. Tipu lost his life in 1799 while defending his capital against another British assault. Mysore was divided between the British and their Indian allies.

As these events illustrate, talented local leaders and European powers vied to expand their influence in South Asia and Africa between 1750 and 1870. Midway through that period, it was by no means clear who would gain the upper hand. By 1870, however, Britain had gained a decisive advantage over France, had established commercial dominance in Africa, the Indian Ocean, and East Asia, and had created a new colonial empire in the East.

Changes and Exchanges in Africa

How did different African leaders react to modern times, and how did European nations' relationship to African peoples change during this period?

During the century before 1870, Africa underwent dynamic political changes and a great expansion of foreign trade. Indigenous African leaders as well as Middle Eastern and European imperialists built powerful new states or expanded old ones. As the continent's external slave trades to the Americas and to Islamic lands died slowly under British pressure, trade in goods such as palm oil, ivory, timber, and gold grew sharply. In return, Africans imported large quantities of machine-made textiles and firearms.

New African States

Internal forces produced clusters of new states in two parts of sub-Saharan Africa (see Map 23.1). In the fertile coastlands of southeastern Africa (in modern South Africa), a serious drought at the beginning of the nineteenth century led to conflict for grazing and farming lands among the small, independent chiefdoms of the region. An upstart named Shaka emerged in 1818 as head of a new **Zulu** kingdom, and the Zulu's military discipline and courage soon made them the most feared fighters in southern Africa. Shaka's regiments raided his African neighbors, seized their cattle, and captured their women and children. To protect themselves from the Zulu, some neighboring Africans created their own states.

Although Shaka ruled for little more than a decade, he successfully instilled a new national identity into his newly conquered subjects. He grouped all the young people into regiments that lived together and were taught Zulu customs and fighting methods. At public festivals, regiments of young men and women paraded, danced, and pledged their loyalty to Shaka.

Meanwhile, Islamic reform movements were creating another powerful state in the savannas of West Africa. The reformers followed a classic Muslim pattern: a *jihad* (holy war) added new lands, spreading Islamic beliefs and laws among conquered people. The largest reform movement was led by Usuman dan Fodio (OO-soo-mahn dahn FOH-dee-oh) (1745–1817), whose armed supporters conquered and combined the older Hausa states into a new empire ruled by a caliph in the city of Sokoto. The **Sokoto Caliphate** (1809–1906) was the largest state in West Africa since the fall of Songhai in the sixteenth century (see Chapter 13).

Zulu A people of modern South Africa whom King Shaka united in 1818.
Sokoto Caliphate A large Muslim state founded in 1809 in what is now northern Nigeria.

Map 23.1 **Africa in the Nineteenth Century** Expanding internal and overseas trade drew much of Africa into global networks, but foreign colonies in 1870 were largely confined to Algeria and southern Africa. Growing trade, Islamic reform movements, and other internal forces created important new states throughout the continent. © Cengage Learning

 Interactive Map

In addition to being a center of Islamic learning and reform, the Sokoto Caliphate became a center of slavery. Many soldiers captured in the wars were enslaved and put to work in the empire or sold away across the Sahara or the Atlantic.

Modernization in Egypt and Ethiopia

In northeastern Africa, the African states of Egypt and Ethiopia were undergoing a period of growth and **modernization**. Napoleon's invasion of Egypt ended in 1801, but the shock of this

Chronology

	Africa	India	Empire
1750		**1756** Black Hole of Calcutta	**1763** End of Seven Years War
		1765 East India Company (EIC) rule of Bengal begins	**1769–1778** Captain James Cook explores New Zealand and eastern Australia
	1795 Britain seizes Cape Colony from Dutch	**1795** Britain seizes Ceylon from the Dutch	**1795** End of Dutch East India Company
	1798 Napoleon invades Egypt	**1799** EIC defeats Mysore	
1800	**1805** Muhammad Ali seizes Egypt		
	1807–1808 Britain outlaws slave trade and takes over Sierra Leone		**1808** Britain outlaws slave trade
	1809 Sokoto Caliphate founded		
	1818 Shaka founds Zulu kingdom	**1818** EIC creates Bombay Presidency	
	1821 Foundation of Republic of Liberia; Egypt takes control of Sudan		
		1826 EIC annexes Assam and northern Burma	
		1828 Brahmo Samaj founded	
	1830–1847 Algerians resist French takeover		
	1834 Britain abolishes slavery		**1834** Britain abolishes slavery
	1840 Omani sultan moves capital to Zanzibar		
1850		**1857–1858** Sepoy Rebellion leads to end of EIC rule and Mughal rule	
	1867 End of Atlantic slave trade		**1867** End of Atlantic slave trade
		1885 First Indian National Congress	
	1889 Menelik unites modern Ethiopia		

display of European strength and Egyptian weakness prompted **Muhammad Ali**, who eliminated his rivals and ruled Egypt from 1805 to 1848, to begin military and economic reforms.

As we saw in the last chapter, Muhammad Ali's central aim was to strengthen Egypt militarily by making use of European experts and technology. Despite the shattering of his imperial dreams by the British

modernization The process of reforming political, military, economic, social, and cultural traditions in imitation of the early success of Western societies, often with regard for accommodating local traditions in non-Western societies.

Muhammad Ali Leader of Egyptian modernization in the early nineteenth century. He ruled Egypt as an Ottoman governor, but had imperial ambitions. His descendants ruled Egypt until 1952.

Téwodros's Mighty Cannon In 1861 Emperor Téwodros of Ethiopia forced resident European missionaries and craftsmen to build guns and cannon, including this 7-ton behemoth nicknamed "Sebastapol" after the Black Sea port that had been the center of the Crimean War. It took five hundred men to haul the cannon across Ethiopia's hilly terrain.

From Hormuzd Rassam, *Narrative of the British Mission to Theodore, King of Abyssinia, II*, London 1869, John Murray

after 1839, by the end of Muhammad Ali's reign in 1848, modernization was well rooted in Egypt. Trade with Europe had expanded by almost 600 percent.

Muhammad Ali's grandson Ismail (is-MAH-eel) (r. 1863–1879) placed even more emphasis on westernizing Egypt. "My country is no longer in Africa," Ismail declared. "It is in Europe."[1] Massive cotton exports during the American Civil War helped finance a network of new irrigation canals, 800 miles (1,300 kilometers) of railroads, a modern postal service, and dazzling changes in the capital city of Cairo.

State building and reform also were under way in the ancient Christian kingdom of Ethiopia. Beginning in the 1840s, Ethiopian rulers purchased modern weapons from European sources and created strong armies loyal to the ruler. Emperor Téwodros (tay-WOH-druhs) II (r. 1833–1868) and his successor, Yohannes (yoh-HAHN-nehs) IV (r. 1872–1889), brought back under imperial rule large areas of ancient Ethiopia. When King Menelik of Shoa succeeded Yohannes as emperor in 1889, the merger of their separate realms created the modern boundaries of Ethiopia.

European Penetration

France's long and difficult war to conquer the North African country of Algeria from 1830 to 1847 was a rare example of European use of force in Africa before 1870. More typical was the peaceful penetration of European explorers, missionaries, and traders. Small expeditions of adventurous explorers, using their own funds or financed by private geographical societies, sought knowledge of inner Africa and of the course of Africa's great rivers: the Niger, the Nile, and the Congo.

In contrast to these heavily financed expeditions with hundreds of African porters, the Scottish missionary David Livingstone (1813–1873) organized modest treks through southern and Central Africa to scout out locations for Christian missions. His several expeditions in southern and equatorial Africa made him a celebrity. In 1871, he was met by the Welsh-American journalist Henry Morton Stanley (1841–1904) on a publicity-motivated search for the "lost" missionary doctor. On an expedition from 1874 to 1877, Stanley descended the Congo River to its mouth.

Commerce governed most European enterprises. No sooner was the mouth of the Niger River discovered in 1830 than eager adventurers moved up the river to discover its potential for trade. Trade between Africa and the other Atlantic continents more than doubled between the 1730s and the 1780s, then doubled again by 1870.[2] Before about 1825, the slave trade accounted for most of that increase, but thereafter African exports of vegetable oils, gold, ivory, and other goods drove overseas trade to new heights.

As Chapter 20 recounted, Western criticism of slavery was rising. Once the world's greatest slave traders, the British became the most aggressive abolitionists. During the half-century after 1815, Britain spent some $60 million (£12 million) in its efforts to end the slave trade through naval patrols. This equaled the profits British slave traders had made in the fifty years before the trade was banned in 1807. Although British patrols captured 1,635 slave ships and liberated over 160,000 enslaved Africans, continued demand for slaves in Cuba and Brazil kept the trade going until 1867.

To satisfy their desires for cloth, metals, and other imported goods after slavery was outlawed, Africans expanded their **"legitimate" trade** (exports other than slaves). The most successful new export from West Africa was palm oil, a substance used by British manufacturers for soap, candles, and lubricants. From the mid-1830s, the trading states of the Niger Delta emerged as the premier exporters of palm oil. Coastal Africans grew rich and purchased large numbers of male slaves to paddle the giant dugout canoes that transported palm oil from inland markets along the narrow delta creeks to the trading ports.

Suppressing the slave trade helped spread Western cultural influences in West Africa. In 1808 the British had taken over the small colony of Sierra Leone (see-ER-ah lee-OWN) as a base for their anti-slave trade naval squadron. In the following years, 130,000 men, women, and children taken from "captured" vessels were liberated in Sierra Leone. Christian missionaries helped settle these impoverished and dispirited **recaptives** in and around Freetown, the capital. In time, the mission churches and schools made many willing converts among such unfortunates.

Sierra Leone's schools produced a number of distinguished graduates. For example, Samuel Adjai Crowther (1808–1891), freed as a youth from a slave ship in 1821, became the first Anglican bishop in West Africa in 1864, administering a pioneering diocese along the lower Niger River. James Africanus Horton (1835–1882), the son of a slave liberated in Sierra Leone, became a doctor and the author of many studies of West Africa.

Other Western cultural influences came from people of African birth or descent returning to their ancestral homeland. In 1821, to the south of Sierra Leone, free black Americans began a settlement that grew into the Republic of Liberia, a place of liberty at a time when slavery was legal and flourishing in the United States. Free blacks from Brazil and Cuba chartered ships to return to their West African homelands, bringing with them Roman Catholicism, architectural motifs, and clothing fashions from the New World. Although the number of Africans exposed to Western culture in 1870 was still small, this influence grew rapidly.

Secondary Empires in Eastern Africa

With the British patrolling West Africa, slavers moved southward and then around the tip of the continent to eastern Africa, where an existing trade in slaves to the Muslim world was still expanding. Two-thirds of the 1.2 million slaves exported from eastern Africa in the nineteenth century went to markets in North Africa and the Middle East; the other third went to European plantations in the Americas and the Indian Ocean.

Between 1800 and 1873 local Arab and Swahili owners purchased some 700,000 slaves from inland eastern Africa to do the labor-intensive work of harvesting cloves on plantations on Zanzibar Island and the neighboring coast. These territories belonged to the sultan of Oman, a realm in southeastern Arabia. The sultan moved his court to Zanzibar in 1840. Zanzibar also exported ivory, mostly to India, where much of it was carved into decorative objects for middle-class Europeans.

Caravans led by African and Arab merchants also brought ivory from hundreds of miles inland. Some of these merchants created large personal empires by using capital they had borrowed from Indian bankers and modern firearms they had bought from Europeans and Americans. These modern rifles felled countless elephants for their ivory tusks and inflicted widespread devastation and misery on the inland people.

Since Europeans supplied the weapons used by the invaders and were major consumers of ivory and

Primary Source: The Interesting Narrative of Olaudah Equiano as Written by Himself Read a boy's personal account of being kidnapped and forced into slavery.

"legitimate" trade Exports from Africa in the nineteenth century that did not include the newly outlawed slave trade.

recaptives Africans rescued by Britain's Royal Navy from the illegal slave trade of the nineteenth century and restored to free status.

SECTION REVIEW

- Vital new states rose in Africa: the Zulu kingdom in southeastern Africa and the Sokoto Caliphate in West Africa.

- Egypt under Muhammad Ali and Ismail and Ethiopia under Téwodros and his successors undertook European-influenced modernization programs.

- Before 1870, European penetration of Africa was largely peaceful, small in scale, and concerned mainly with trade, missionary work, and exploration.

- The most important European influence was the suppression of the Atlantic slave trade and its resulting commercial and cultural shifts.

- Secondary slave- and ivory-trading empires grew along the coast of East Africa.

cloves, historians refer to the states carved out of eastern Africa as "secondary empires," in contrast to the empire that Britain was establishing directly. At the same time, Britain was working to bring the slave trade to an end in eastern Africa. British officials pressured the sultan of Oman into halting the Indian Ocean slave trade from Zanzibar in 1857 and ending the import of slaves into Zanzibar in 1873.

India Under British Rule

How did Britain secure its hold on India, and what colonial policies led to the beginnings of Indian nationalism?

The people of South Asia felt the impact of European commercial, cultural, and colonial expansion more immediately and profoundly than did the Africans. Europeans laid claim to only small parts of Africa between 1750 and 1870, but nearly all of India (with three times the population of Africa) came under Britain's direct or indirect rule. After the founding of the East India Company in 1600, it took British interests 250 years to commandeer the colonies and trade of the Dutch, fight off French and Indian challenges, and pick up the pieces of the decaying Mughal (MOO-guhl) Empire. By 1763 the French were stymied, in 1795 the Dutch company was dissolved, and in 1858 the last Mughal emperor was dethroned, leaving the vast subcontinent in British hands.

Company Men As Mughal power weakened in the eighteenth century, British, Dutch, and French companies expanded into India (see Map 23.2). The success of these far-flung European enterprises depended on hard-drinking and ambitious young "Company Men," who used hard bargaining, and hard fighting when necessary, to persuade Indian rulers to allow them to establish trading posts at strategic points along the coast. To protect their fortified warehouses from attack by other Europeans or by native states, the companies hired and trained Indian troops known as **sepoys** (SEE-poys). In fragmented India, these private armies came to hold the balance of power.

In 1691, the East India Company (EIC) had convinced the **nawab** (NAH-wab) (the term used for Mughal governors) of Bengal in northeast India to let the company establish a fortified outpost at the fishing port of Calcutta. A new nawab seeking additional tribute from the prospering port overran the fort in 1756 and imprisoned a group of EIC men in a cell so small that many died of suffocation. To avenge their deaths in this "Black Hole of Calcutta," a large EIC force from Madras overthrew the nawab. The weak Mughal emperor was persuaded to acknowledge the EIC's right to rule Bengal in 1765. By 1788 Calcutta had grown into a city of 250,000.

In southern India, EIC forces secured victory for the British Indian candidate for nawab of Arcot during the Seven Years War, thereby gaining an advantage over French traders who had supported the loser. The defeat of Tipu Sultan of Mysore at the end of the century (described earlier) secured south India for the company and prevented a French resurgence.

Along with Calcutta and Madras, the third major center of British power in India was Bombay, on the western coast. There, after a long conflict with Indian rulers, the EIC gained a decisive advantage in 1818, annexing large territories to form the core of what was called the "Bombay Presidency." Some states were taken over completely, as Bengal had been, but many

sepoy A soldier in South Asia, especially in the service of the British.
nawab A Muslim prince allied to British India; technically, a semi-autonomous deputy of the Mughal emperor.

Map 23.2 India, 1707–1805 As Mughal power weakened during the eighteenth century, other Indian states and the British East India Company expanded their territories. © Cengage Learning

  Interactive Map

others remained in the hands of local princes who accepted the political control of the company.

Raj and Rebellion, 1818–1857

In 1818, the EIC controlled an empire with fifty times the population of the colonies the British had lost in North America. One thrust of the **British raj** (regime) was to remake India through administrative measures, economic development, and modern technology. But the Company Men—like the Mughals before them—had to temper their interference with Indian social and religious customs lest they provoke rebellion or lose the support of their Indian princely allies. This immense and complex task led to many inconsistencies in Britain's policies toward India.

The main policy was to create a powerful and efficient system of government. British rule before 1850 relied heavily on military power—170 sepoy regiments and 16 European regiments. Another policy was to disarm approximately 2 million warriors who had served India's many states and turn them to civilian tasks, mostly cultivation. A third policy gave freer rein to Christian missionaries eager to convert and uplift India's masses. Few converts were made, but the missionaries kept up steady pressure for social reforms.

British raj The rule over much of South Asia between 1765 and 1947 by the East India Company and then by a British government.

Delhi Durbar, January 1, 1903 The parade of Indian princes on ornately decorated elephants and accompanied by retainers fostered their sense of belonging to the vast empire of India that British rule had created. The durbar was meant to evoke the glories of India's earlier empires, but many of the details and ceremonies were nineteenth-century creations.

 History in Focus *As the caption for this image suggests, the purpose of these parades was to showcase Indian princes. What evidence of British colonial power can you detect in this photo? In this context, does the date of the parade strike you as significant? Find the answer online.*

Another key British policy was to turn India's complex and overlapping patterns of landholding into private property. In Bengal, this reform worked to the advantage of large landowners, but in Mysore, the peasantry gained. Private ownership made it easier for the state to collect the taxes that were needed to pay for the costs of administration, the army, and economic reform.

Such policies of "westernization, Anglicization, and modernization," as they have been called, were only one side of British rule. The other side was the bolstering of "traditions"—both real and newly invented. In the name of tradition, the Indian princes who ruled nearly half of British India were permitted to expand their power and splendor. The British rulers themselves invented many "traditions"—including elaborate parades and displays—half borrowed from European royal pomp, half freely improvised from Mughal ceremonies.

The British and Indian elites danced sometimes in close partnership, sometimes in apparent opposition. But the ordinary people of India—women of every status, members of subordinate Hindu castes, the "untouchables" and "tribals" outside the caste system, and the poor generally—found less benefit in the British reforms and much new oppression in the new taxes and "traditions."

The transformation of British India's economy was doubled-edged. On the one hand, the growth in internal and external trade created many new jobs, as did the expansion of farming: opium in Bengal (largely for export to China), coffee in Ceylon (an island off the tip of India), and tea in Assam (in northeastern India). On the other hand, competition from cheap cotton goods produced in Britain's industrial mills ruined the handicraft textile industry. In the eighteenth century, India had been the world's greatest exporter of cotton textiles; in the nineteenth century, India increasingly shipped raw cotton fiber to Britain.

Economic changes, including beneficial ones, caused disruption. Thus, local rebellions by displaced ruling elites, disgruntled religious traditionalists, and the economically dispossessed were almost constant during the first half of the nineteenth century. The greatest concern was over the loyalty of Indian sepoys in the EIC's army.

In the early decades of EIC rule, most sepoys came from Bengal, one of the first states the company had annexed. The Bengali sepoys resented the recruitment of other ethnic groups into the army after 1848, such as Sikhs (seeks) from Punjab and Gurkhas from Nepal. Many high-caste Hindus also objected to a new law in 1856 permitting service assignment overseas, for their religion prohibited ocean travel. Then in 1857 the replacement of the standard musket by the more accurate Enfield rifle sparked outrage because the soldiers were ordered to use their teeth to tear open the ammunition cartridges, which were greased with animal fat. Fat from cattle offended Hindus; fat from pigs offended Muslims.

A quick change of the cartridge-opening procedure could not forestall a rebellion by Hindu sepoys in May 1857. As Muslim sepoys, peasants, and discontented elites joined in, the rebels asserted old traditions: sepoy officers in Delhi proclaimed their loyalty to the Mughal emperor; others rallied behind the Maratha leader Nana Sahib. The rebellion was put down by March 1858, but it shook British India to its core.

Historians have attached different names and meanings to the events of 1857 and 1858. Seeing only an unlawful action by soldiers, nineteenth-century British historians labeled it the **"Sepoy Rebellion"** or the "Mutiny," names that are still commonly used. Seeing these events as the beginnings of the later movement for independence, some modern Indian historians have termed it the "Revolution of 1857."

Political Reform and Industrial Impact

Whatever its label, the rebellion of 1857–1858 was a historical turning point. In its wake, Indians gained a new centralized government, entered a period of rapid economic growth, and began to develop a new national consciousness.

The changes in government were immediate. In 1858, Britain eliminated the last traces of Mughal and EIC rule. In their place, a new secretary of state for India in London oversaw Indian policy, and a new governor-general in Delhi acted as the British monarch's viceroy on the spot. A proclamation by Queen Victoria in November 1858 guaranteed all Indians

equal protection of the law and the freedom to practice their religions and social customs; it also assured Indian princes that so long as they were loyal to the queen, British India would respect their control of territories and "their rights, dignity and honour."[3]

A powerful and efficient bureaucracy controlled India. Members of the elite **Indian Civil Service** (ICS), mostly graduates of Oxford and Cambridge Universities, held the senior administrative and judicial posts. Numbering only a thousand men at the end of the nineteenth century, they visited the villages in their districts, heard lawsuits and complaints, and passed judgments. A far greater number of Indian officials and employees served beneath them. Recruitment into the ICS was by open examination given only in England and thus inaccessible to most Indians. In 1870, only one Indian was a member of the ICS. Subsequent reforms led to fifty-seven Indian appointments by 1887, but there the process stalled.

British industry spurred a second transformation. The government invested millions of pounds sterling in harbors, buildings, irrigation canals, telegraph lines, and other public works. British interests felled forests to make way for tea plantations, persuaded Indian farmers to grow cotton and jute for export, and created great irrigation systems to boost agricultural production and alleviate famines. As a result, India's trade expanded rapidly.

Most of the exports were agricultural commodities: cotton fiber, opium, tea, silk, and sugar. In return, India imported manufactured goods, including the flood of machine-made cotton textiles that undercut handloom weavers. Individual experiences varied enormously. Some women found jobs at very low pay on plantations or in the growing cities, where prostitution flourished. Others struggled to hold families together or ran away from abusive husbands. Everywhere in India, poverty remained the norm.

New technologies were introduced in India soon after their appearance in Britain. Beginning in the

Sepoy Rebellion The revolt of Indian soldiers in 1857 against certain practices that violated religious customs; also known as the Sepoy Mutiny.

Indian Civil Service The elite professional class of officials who administered the government of British India. Originally composed exclusively of well-educated British men, it gradually added qualified Indians.

Indian Railroad Station, 1866 British India built the largest network of railroads in Asia. People of every social class traveled by train.

1850s, after an earlier enthusiasm for canals and river steamers, a railroad boom (subsidized by tax revenues) gave India a national transportation network. Indeed, in 1870, India had the greatest rail network in Asia and the fourth largest in the world.

Easier movement and urbanization promoted the spread of cholera (KAHL-uhr-uh), a disease transmitted through water contaminated by human feces. In 1867, officials demonstrated the close connection between cholera and pilgrims who bathed in and drank from sacred pools and rivers. The installation of a new sewerage system (1865) and a filtered water supply (1869) in Calcutta dramatically reduced cholera deaths there. Similar measures in Bombay and Madras also led to great reductions, but most Indians lived in small villages, where famine and lack of sanitation kept cholera deaths high.

Rising Indian Nationalism

Both the successes and the failures of British rule stimulated the development of Indian nationalism. The failure of the rebellion of 1857 led some thoughtful Indians to argue that the only way to regain control of their destiny was to reduce their country's social and ethnic divisions.

Individuals such as Rammohun Roy (1772–1833) had promoted pan-Indian nationalism a generation earlier. A Western-educated Bengali from a Brahmin family, Roy was a successful administrator for the EIC and a thoughtful student of comparative religion. His Brahmo Samaj (BRAH-moh suh-MAHJ) (Divine Society), founded in 1828, attracted Indians who sought to reconcile the values they found in the West with the ancient religious traditions of India. They backed the British outlawing of *sati* (suh-TEE) (widow burning) in 1829 and of slavery in 1834 and sought to correct other abuses of women and female infanticide. Roy and his followers advocated reforming the caste system and urged a return to the founding principles set out in the Upanishads, ancient sacred writings of Hinduism.

Although Brahmo Samaj remained an influential movement, a growing number of Indian intellectuals based their nationalism on secular values learned in Western schools, often with the help of European and American missionaries. In 1870, there were 790,000 Indians in over 24,000 elementary and secondary schools, and India's three universities (established in 1857) awarded 345 degrees. Many new nationalists arose from the Indian middle class, and in 1885

- British, Dutch, and French "Company Men" advanced European trade interests in India, with the British EIC winning major concessions in Bengal.

- The EIC fought French rivals and native rulers to establish bases at Madras and Bombay.

- EIC rulers undertook westernization, Anglicization, and modernization but also supported "traditions," all with mixed results

- Discontent among the EIC's Indian soldiers erupted into the Sepoy Rebellion/Revolution.

- Direct British rule led to the creation of the Indian Civil Service and involvement with Britain's industrialization.

- British rule spurred the rise of Indian nationalism, from which emerged the secular, middle-class Indian National Congress.

nationalists convened the first **Indian National Congress**, which called for a larger Indian role in the civil service and for greater efforts to reduce poverty.

Britain's Eastern Empire

What role did the abolition of slavery and the continued growth of British overseas trade play in the immigration of peoples from Africa, India, and Asia?

Military victories over rival trading nations, policies favoring free trade over mercantilism, and shipbuilding improvements that increased the speed and volume of shipping transformed Britain into a colossus that straddled the world. Linked to these changes were new European settlements in southern Africa, Australia, and New Zealand and the growth of a new long-distance trade in indentured labor.

Colonies and Commerce

France was still a serious rival for dominion in the Indian Ocean at the end of the eighteenth century. However, Napoleon's dream of restoring French dominance overseas did not outlive his empire. Napoleon's wars also gutted the Dutch overseas empire. When French armies occupied the Netherlands, the Dutch ruler, who had fled to Britain in January 1795, authorized the British to take over his overseas possessions to keep them out of French hands. During 1795 and 1796 British forces occupied the Cape Colony at the tip of southern Africa, the strategic Dutch port of Malacca on the strait between the Indian Ocean and the South China Sea, and the island of Ceylon (modern Sri Lanka).

Then the British occupied Dutch Guiana and Trinidad in the southern Caribbean. In 1811 they seized the island of Java, the center of the Netherlands' East Indian empire. British forces also seized control of the French islands of Mauritius and Réunion in the southwestern Indian Ocean. At the end of the Napoleonic Wars in 1814, Britain returned Java to the Dutch and Réunion to the French but kept the Cape Colony, British Guiana (once part of Dutch Guiana), Trinidad, Ceylon, Malacca, and Mauritius.

The Cape Colony was valuable because of Cape Town's strategic importance as a supply station for ships making the long voyages between Britain and India. With the port city came some twenty thousand descendants of earlier Dutch and French settlers who occupied far-flung farms and ranches in its hinterland. Despite their European origins, these people thought of themselves as permanent residents of Africa and were beginning to refer to themselves as "Afrikaners" ("Africans" in their dialect of Dutch). British governors prohibited any expansion of the white settler frontier because such expansion invariably led to wars with indigenous Africans. This decision, along with the imposition of laws protecting African rights within Cape Colony (including the emancipation of slaves in 1834), alienated many Afrikaners.

Between 1836 and 1839 parties of Afrikaners embarked on a "Great Trek," leaving British-ruled Cape Colony for the fertile high *veld* (plateau) to the north that two decades of Zulu wars had depopulated. The Great Trek led to the foundation of three new settler colonies by 1850: the Afrikaners' Orange Free State and Transvaal on the high veld and the British colony of Natal on the Indian Ocean coast. Although firearms enabled the settlers to win some important battles against the Zulu and other Africans, they were

Indian National Congress A movement and political party founded in 1885 to demand greater Indian participation in government. Its membership was middle class, and its demands at first were modest.

Great Trek Aided by African servants, the ox-drawn wagons of the Afrikaners struggled over the Drakensberg Mountains to the high plains in an effort to escape British control.

still a tiny minority surrounded by populous and powerful African kingdoms that had grown up at the beginning of the century.

Britain established another strategic outpost in Southeast Asia. In 1824 Thomas Stamford Raffles, who had governed Java during the period of British occupation from 1811 to 1814, helped the British East India Company establish a new free port at Singapore, a small Malay fishing village with a superb harbor. British merchants and Chinese businessmen and laborers quickly made Singapore the center of trade and shipping between the Indian Ocean and China. Along with Malacca and other possessions on the strait, Singapore formed the "Straits Settlements," which British India administered until 1867.

Further British expansion in Malaya (now Malaysia) did not occur until after 1874, but it came more quickly in neighboring Burma. By 1750 Burma had emerged as a powerful kingdom, and in 1785 it tried to annex neighboring territories of Siam (now Thailand) to the east. Thwarted by a coalition of Thai leaders in 1802, Burma next attacked Assam to the west. This led to war with British India, which also bordered Assam. The result was that India annexed Assam in 1826 and occupied two coastal provinces of northern Burma. As rice and timber trade from these provinces grew, the occupation became permanent, and in 1852 British India annexed the port of Rangoon and the rest of coastal Burma.

Imperial Policies and Shipping

By 1870 Britain had added several dozen colonies to the twenty-six it had in 1792, after the loss of the thirteen in North America. Nevertheless, Britain appears in many histories as a reluctant empire builder, its leaders unwilling to acquire new outposts that could prove difficult and expensive to administer. This is not a contradiction. The underlying goal of most British imperial expansion was not territory but trade. Most of the new colonies served as ports for a shipping network that encircled the globe, or as production and distribution centers for that network.

Whether colonized or not, more and more African, Asian, and Pacific lands became connected with the commercial networks created by British expansion and industrialization. From uncolonized parts of West Africa, Britain bought vegetable oils for industrial and domestic use and forest products for dyes and construction, while uncolonized eastern Africa exported ivory for piano keys and household decorations. From the far corners of the world came coffee, cocoa, and tea (along with sugar to sweeten them) for the tables of the new industrial classes in Britain and other parts of Europe.

In return, the industrialized nations sold manufactured goods at attractive prices. Sales of cotton cloth to Africa increased 950 percent from the 1820s to the 1860s (see Material Culture: Cotton Clothing on page 564). British trade to India grew 350 percent between 1841 and 1870, while India's exports increased 400 percent. In most cases such trade benefited both sides, but there is no question that the industrial nations were the dominant partners.

A second impetus to global commercial expansion was the technological revolution in the construction of oceangoing ships. The middle decades of the

562

Hulton Archive/Getty Images

century were a golden age for sailing ships. Using iron to fasten timbers together enabled shipbuilders to construct much larger vessels. Eighteenth-century merchant ships rarely exceeded 300 tons, but after 1850 swift American-built **clipper ships** of 2,000 tons set the standard. Ships from the East Indies or India had taken six months to reach Europe in the seventeenth century; ships built after 1850 could complete the voyage in three.

This increase in size and speed lowered shipping costs. The growth in size and numbers of ships increased the tonnage of British merchant shipping by 400 percent between 1778 and 1860. To extend the life of such ships in tropical lands, clippers intended for Eastern service generally were built of teak and other tropical hardwoods from new British colonies in South and Southeast Asia. Although tropical forests began to be cleared for rice and sugar plantations as well as for timbers, the effects on the environment and people of Southeast Asia came primarily after 1870.

Colonization of Australia and New Zealand

Rather than rule indigenous populations, as they did in India, or set up commercial outposts, as they did in Singapore and Cape Town, British settlers displaced indigenous populations in the new colonies of Australia and New Zealand, just as they had done in North America.

Portuguese mariners had sighted Australia in the early seventeenth century, but it was too remote to be of interest. However, after the English adventurer Captain James Cook systematically explored New Zealand and the fertile eastern coast of Australia between 1769 and 1778, expanding shipping networks brought in growing numbers of visitors and settlers.

The Australia Cook visited was home for about 650,000 hunting-and-gathering people, whose Melanesian (mel-uh-NEE-zhuhn) ancestors had arrived some forty thousand years earlier. About 250,000 Maori (MOW-ree [ow as in cow]) inhabited the two islands of New Zealand, lying 1,000 miles (1,600 kilometers) southeast of Australia. They practiced hunting, fishing, and simple forms of agriculture, which their Polynesian ancestors had introduced around 1200. These two populations were as vulnerable as the Amerindians had been to unfamiliar diseases introduced by overseas contacts. By the 1890s only 93,000

aboriginal Australians and 42,000 Maori had survived, and British settler populations both outnumbered and dominated them.

The first permanent British settlers in Australia were 736 convicts, of whom 188 were women, sent into exile from British prisons in 1788. Australian penal colonies grew slowly and had only slight contact with the indigenous population, whom the British called "Aborigines." However, the discovery of gold in 1851 brought a flood of free European settlers (and some Chinese) and hastened the end of the penal colonies. When the gold rush subsided, government subsidies enabled tens of thousands of British settlers to settle "down under." Although, even with improved sailing ships, it still took more than three months to reach Australia from Britain, by 1860 Australia had a million immigrants, and the settler population doubled during the next fifteen years.

British settlement in New Zealand proceeded more slowly. Initially a few temporary residents along the coast slaughtered seals and exported pelts to Western countries to be made into men's felt hats. A single ship in 1806 took away sixty thousand sealskins, and by the early 1820s overhunting had nearly exterminated the seal population. Sperm whales were also targeted; whalers hunted them near New Zealand for their oil, used for lubrication, soap, and lamps; ambergris (AM-ber-grees), an ingredient in perfume; and bone, used in women's corsets. Military suppression of Maori resistance, a brief gold rush, and the availability of faster ships and subsidized passages attracted more British immigrants after 1860. The colony especially courted women immigrants to offset the preponderance of single men. By the early 1880s the fertile agricultural lands of this most distant frontier of the British Empire had a settler population of 500,000.

Britain encouraged the settlers in Australia and New Zealand to become self-governing, following the 1867 model that had formed the Dominion of Canada out of the very diverse and thinly settled colonies

clipper ship Large, fast, streamlined sailing vessel, often American built, of the mid-to-late nineteenth century rigged with vast canvas sails hung from tall masts.

Material Culture

Cotton Clothing

Of all the things that bring us comfort, nothing compares to cotton. For clothes, sheets, and towels, it is the world's favorite textile. And no wonder: cotton is cool next to the skin, can be dyed in bright colors, absorbs moisture, and, unlike other fabrics such as wool, can be washed easily.

The use of cotton for clothing has a long history dating back to 3000 B.C.E., when it was grown in the Indus River Valley. Originally, the cotton plant was grown and the cloth woven only in India, Mexico, Peru, and a few other places in the tropics. The Maya wove fine textiles from cotton and traded them with other parts of Mesoamerica. Indian cottons were particularly fine and exported as luxury items to China and Rome. In China, cotton replaced hemp clothing and was used extensively by the Mongols for turbans, pants, and other items of clothing. Many of our names for particular kinds of cotton fabric come from cities in India or the Middle East, like *calico* (from Calicut), *madras*, *damask* (from Damascus), or *muslin* (from Mosul in Iraq).

The Arabs spread cotton growing and weaving to the Middle East and Spain, and by the tenth century, it was a major crop in Iran and elsewhere in the region. Around 800 C.E., Arab merchants brought cotton cloth to Europe, where it became as precious as silk. With the invention of machines like the spinning jenny and the water frame in the eighteenth century (see Chapter 21), cotton became less precious and more available. Cotton yarn and cloth were the first items to be mass-produced in the Industrial Revolution, with important consequences for India, the American South, and other countries.

Mass production means mass consumption. In the nineteenth century, for the first time, the poor could afford to wear bright, colorful clothes and—even more important—to wash them. These clothes were made almost exclusively by women. Wealthy European families hired seamstresses who came to the house, took measurements, and returned a few days later with finished clothes. Other women sewed clothes for themselves and their families.

Sewing by hand was very time-consuming and increasingly costly compared to the declining price of cloth. By the mid-nineteenth century, prosperity and a faster pace of life in Europe and America provided an incentive for inventors to devise a machine that could sew. In 1850, Isaac Singer manufactured the first practical machine for commercial use, and a few years later, he designed the "Singer Family Sewing Machine" with an iron stand and a foot-treadle for home use. By 1891 Singer alone had manufactured 10 million machines

---

of British North America. In 1901 a unified Australia emerged from the federation of six separate colonies. New Zealand became a self-governing dominion in 1907.

By gradually turning over governing power to the colonies' inhabitants, Britain accomplished three things. It satisfied the settlers' desire for greater local control; it muted demands for independence; and it made the colonial governments responsible for most of their own expenses. Indigenous peoples were outvoted by the settlers or even excluded from voting.

North American patterns also shaped the indigenous peoples' fate. An 1897 Australian law segregated the remaining Aborigines onto reservations, where they lacked the rights of Australian citizenship. The requirement that voters had to be able to read and write English kept Maori from voting in early New Zealand elections, but four seats in the lower house of the legislature were reserved for Maori from 1867 on.

In other ways the new settler colonies were more progressive. Australia developed very powerful trade unions, which improved the welfare of skilled and semiskilled urban white male workers, promoted democratic values, and exercised considerable political clout. In New Zealand, where sheep raising was the main occupation, populist and progressive sentiments promoted the availability of land for the common in the United States and Europe. Some were industrial machines sold to makers of ready-to-wear clothes in the new garment districts. Others were home models, some inexpensive enough for the working class. There were even portable models that seamstresses could take with them to their clients' homes.

The combination of cotton cloth and sewing machines revolutionized clothing. A shirt that took fourteen and a half hours to sew by hand could be made in an hour and a quarter on a machine; an apron could be made in nine minutes instead of an hour and a half. Now the poor could afford to own several shirts, skirts, or pants, even underwear. Better-off homemakers subscribed to fashion magazines, bought patterns, and made blouses and dresses, even complicated items like crinolines and hoopskirts, which would once have been too tedious to sew by hand.

Today, the world uses more cotton than any other fiber. China is the largest producer (and consumer) of cotton, followed by the United States, India, and Pakistan. Almost all of the cotton clothing sold is produced on powerful computerized machines in the developing countries of Asia and Latin America.

Private Collection

The Sewing Machine The Japanese imported many innovations from the West after the Meiji Restoration of 1868. Among the most popular were Western-style clothing and sewing machines. Sewing was a gendered activity in Japan as in the West, with the woman sewing and the man looking on.

QUESTIONS FOR ANALYSIS

1. What advantages does cotton offer over other fibers?
2. As a plant requiring a long, hot growing season, how did cotton affect world trade?
3. How did the mechanization of cotton weaving and sewing shape patterns of labor use?

person. Australia and New Zealand were also among the first states in the world to grant women the right to vote, beginning in 1894.

New Labor Migrations

Between 1834 and 1870 many thousands of Indians, Chinese, and Africans responded to labor recruiters, especially to work overseas on sugar plantations. In the half-century after 1870 tens of thousands of Asians and Pacific islanders made similar voyages.

In part these migrations were linked to the end of slavery. After their emancipation in British colonies in 1834, freed slaves were no longer willing to put in the long hours they had been forced to work. Given freedom of movement, many left the plantations. To compete with slave-manned sugar plantations in Cuba, Brazil, and the French Caribbean, British colonies had to recruit new laborers.

India's poor provided one alternative. After planters on Mauritius, an Indian Ocean island, successfully introduced Indian laborers, the Indian labor trade moved to the British Caribbean in 1838. Three years later the British government allowed Caribbean planters to recruit Africans rescued from slave ships and liberated. By 1870 nearly 40,000 Africans had settled in British colonies, along with over 500,000 Indians and over 18,000 Chinese. After the French and Dutch abolished slavery in 1848, their colonies

Indentured Labor Register This page comes from the passenger roster of the ship *Fatal Razack*, which brought the first Indian indentured laborers to Trinidad in 1845, five years after the final abolition of slavery there. The trip took 90 days. Over 140,000 more Indians followed these new arrivals, who are identified by name, father's name, sex, and age.

recruited over 150,000 new laborers from Asia and Africa.

Slavery continued in Cuba until 1886, but the rising cost of slaves led the sugar planters to recruit 138,000 new laborers from China between 1847 and 1873. Indentured labor recruits became the mainstay of new sugar plantations in places that had never known slave labor. After 1850 American planters in Hawaii recruited labor from China and Japan; British planters in Natal recruited from India; and those in Queensland (in northeastern Australia) relied on laborers from South Pacific islands.

Larger, faster ships made transporting such laborers affordable. Nevertheless, despite close regulation of shipboard conditions, crowded accommodations

encouraged the spread of cholera and other contagious diseases. All of these laborers served under **contracts of indenture**, which bound them to work for a specified period (usually from five to seven years) in return for free passage to their overseas destination. They were paid a small salary and provided with housing, clothing, and medical care. Indian indentured laborers also received free passage home if they worked a second five-year contract. To promote family life, British Caribbean colonies required forty women to be recruited for every hundred men. So many Indians chose to stay in Mauritius, Trinidad, British Guiana, and Fiji that they constituted a third or more of the total population by the early twentieth century.

Although many early recruits from China and the Pacific islands were kidnapped or otherwise coerced into leaving home, in most cases the new indentured migrants had much in common with contemporary immigrants from Europe. Both groups hoped to improve their economic and social conditions, and both earned modest salaries. Many brought money back when they returned home, or used their earnings to buy land or to start a business in their new countries. One major difference was that people recruited as indentured laborers were generally so much poorer than emigrants from Europe that they had to accept lower-paying jobs in less desirable areas because they could not pay their own way. Many European immigrants into distant places like Australia and New Zealand also had their passages subsidized but did not have to sign a contract of indenture. This shows that racial and cultural preferences, not just economics, shaped the flow of labor into European colonies.

A person's decision to accept an indentured labor contract could also be shaped by political circumstances. In India disruption brought by British colonial policies and the suppression of the 1857 rebellion contributed significantly to people's desire to emigrate. Poverty, famine, and warfare had not been strangers in precolonial India. Nor were these causes of emigration absent in China and Japan.

contract of indenture A voluntary agreement binding a person to work for a specified period of years in return for free passage to an overseas destination. Before 1800 most indentured servants were Europeans; after 1800 most were Asians.

SECTION REVIEW

- By the end of the Napoleonic Wars, Britain controlled most Dutch and French possessions in the Indian Ocean and the Caribbean.

- The Afrikaners' Great Trek resulted in three new colonies in southern Africa, and British expansion in Malaya added Singapore and Burma to the empire.

- Driven by free trade and technological innovation, Britain's overseas expansion drew more and more of the world into its commercial networks.

- New ships and shipping encouraged the colonization of Australia and New Zealand, where settlers displaced native peoples.

- To avoid the conflicts that led to the American Revolution, Britain encouraged self-government in Australia and New Zealand.

- The decline of slavery prompted migrations of indentured workers from Africa and Asia, mainly to agricultural colonies.

Conclusion

One perspective on the changes described in this chapter stresses the exploitation of the weak by the strong, of African, Asian, and Pacific peoples by aggressive Europeans. In this view, Britain's emergence as a dominant power in the Indian Ocean Basin and South Pacific continued the European expansion dating back to the Portuguese and the Spanish voyages of exploration and the subsequent conquest and colonization of the Americas.

From another perspective what was most important about this period was not the political and military strength of the Europeans but their growing commercial domination. In this view, the British, like other Europeans, were drawn to Africa and southern Asia by a desire to obtain new materials.

However, Britain's commercial expansion in the nineteenth century was also the product of non-European demand for industrial manufactures. The growing exchanges could be mutually beneficial. African and Asian consumers found industrial goods far cheaper and sometimes better than the handicrafts they replaced or supplemented. Industrialization also created new markets for African and Asian agricultural commodities. There were also negative impacts, as in the case of the displaced weavers of India.

Africa, Asia, and the Pacific did not become mere appendages of Europe. While the balance of military and economic power shifted in the Europeans' favor between 1750 and 1870, other cultures were still vibrant and local initiatives often dominant. Islamic reform movements and the rise of the Zulu nation had greater significance for their respective regions of Africa than did Western forces. Despite European inroads, Southeast Asians were still largely in control of their own destinies. Even in India, most people's lives and beliefs showed overwhelming continuity with the past.

Finally, it must not be imagined that Asians and Africans were powerless in dealing with European expansion. The Indian princes who extracted concessions from the British in return for their cooperation and the Indians who rebelled against the raj both forced the system to accommodate their needs. Moreover, some Asians and Africans were beginning to use European education, technology, and methods to transform their own societies. Leaders in Egypt, India, and other lands, like those in Russia, the Ottoman Empire, and China (see Chapter 22), were learning to challenge the power of the West on its own terms.

CHAPTER REVIEW

 Download the MP3 audio file of the Chapter Review to listen to on the go.

How did different African leaders react to modern times, and how did European nations' relationship to African peoples change during this period? (page 551)

New African states arose in this period, among them the Sokoto Caliphate in the west. Some old states were also reinvigorated. In Egypt and Ethiopia enterprising rulers modernized their armies to consolidate power.

Commerce between Europe and Africa grew enormously, owing first to the slave trade and then to trade in vegetable oils, gold, and ivory. No country enforced the abolition of slavery more effectively than Britain. British antislavery naval operations freed more than 100,000 captives, settling them in Freetown, the capital of Sierra Leone.

How did Britain secure its hold on India, and what colonial policies led to the beginnings of Indian nationalism? (page 556)

The British East India Company, using negotiation or force in dealing with local princes, was able to secure control of the cities of Calcutta, Madras, and Bombay. The British instituted a powerful colonial government and skillfully exploited native traditions and local rulers. In 1857–1858 the Sepoy Rebellion prompted a wave of reforms: Queen Victoria promised all Indians freedom of religion and equal protection under the law, and great sums of money were invested in harbors, canals, railroads, and telegraph lines. However, the profits from such enterprises remained in colonial hands, and the loss of manufacturing jobs and an increasingly educated middle class sparked the rise of Indian nationalism.

What role did the abolition of slavery and the continued growth of British overseas trade play in the immigration of peoples from Africa, India, and Asia? (page 561)

After Britain, France, and the Netherlands had abolished slavery, thousands of Indians, Chinese, Africans, and Pacific islanders immigrated to British colonies, above all to the Caribbean, under contracts of indenture. By 1778, when James Cook had explored New Zealand and eastern Australia, expanding shipping networks brought growing numbers of white settlers there, displacing the native Maori and Australian peoples. Europeans brought new and devastating diseases, as they had done to Amerindian peoples two centuries before: over 80 percent of native New Zealanders and Australians perished in just over a century.

Key Terms

Zulu (p. 551)	British raj (p. 557)
Sokoto Caliphate (p. 551)	Sepoy Rebellion (p. 559)
modernization (p. 552)	Indian Civil Service (p. 559)
Muhammad Ali (p. 553)	Indian National Congress (p. 561)
"legitimate" trade (p. 555)	clipper ship (p. 563)
recaptives (p. 555)	contract of indenture (p. 566)
sepoy (p. 556)	
nawab (p. 556)	

Web Resources

Pronunciation Guide

Interactive Maps
- MAP 23.1 Africa in the Nineteenth Century
- MAP 23.2 India, 1707–1805

Primary Source
- The Interesting Narrative of Olaudah Equiano as Written by Himself

Answer to the History in Focus Question
  See photo on page 558, "Delhi Durbar, January 1, 1903."

CourseMate — Visit the CourseMate website at www.cengagebrain.com for additional study tools and review materials for this chapter.

Issues in World History

State Power, the Census, and the Question of Identity

Between the American Revolution and the last decades of the nineteenth century, Europe and the Americas were transformed. The ancient power of kings and the authority of religion were eclipsed by muscular new ways of organizing political, economic, and intellectual life. The Western world was vastly different in 1870 than it had been a century earlier. One of the less heralded but enduringly significant changes was the huge expansion of government statistical services.

The rise of the nation-state was associated with the development of modern bureaucratic departments that depended on reliable statistics to measure the nation's achievements and discover its failures. The nation-state, whether democratic or not, mobilized resources on a previously unimaginable scale. Modern states were more powerful and wealthier, and they were also more ambitious and more intrusive. The growth of their power can be seen in the modernization of militaries, the commitment to internal improvements such as railroads, and the growth in state revenues. In recent years historians have begun to examine a less visible but equally important manifestation of growing state power: census taking.

Governments and religious authorities have counted people since early times. Our best estimates of the Amerindian population of the Western Hemisphere in 1500 rest almost entirely on what were little more than missionaries' guesses about the numbers of people they baptized. Spanish and Portuguese kings were eager to count native populations, since "indios" (adult male Amerindians) were subject to special labor obligations and tribute payments. So, from the mid-sixteenth century onward, imperial officials conducted regular censuses of Amerindians, adapting practices already in place in Europe.

The effort to measure and categorize populations was transformed in the last decades of the eighteenth century when the nature of European governments began to change. The Enlightenment belief that the scientific method could be applied to human society proved to be attractive both to political radicals, like the French Revolutionaries, and to reforming monarchs like Maria Theresa of Austria. Enlightenment philosophers had argued that a science of government could remove the inefficiencies and irrationalities that had long subverted the human potential for prosperity and happiness. The French intellectual Condorcet wrote in 1782:

> Those sciences, created almost in our own days, the object of which is man himself, the direct goal of which is the happiness of man, will enjoy a progress no less sure than that of the physical sciences. . . . In meditating on the nature of the moral sciences [what we now call the social sciences], one cannot help seeing that, as they are based like the physical sciences on the observation of fact, they must follow the method, acquire a language equally exact and precise, attaining the same degree of certainty.[1]

As confidence in this new "science" grew, the term previously used to describe the collection of numbers about society, *political arithmetic*, was abandoned by governments and practitioners in favor of *statistics*, a term that clearly suggests its close ties to the "state." In the nineteenth century the new objectives set out by Condorcet and others led to both the formal university training of statisticians and the creation of government statistical services.

The ambitions of governments in this new era were great. Nation-states self-consciously sought to transform society, sponsoring economic development, education, and improvements in health and welfare. They depended on statistics to measure the effectiveness of their policies and, as a result, were interested in nearly everything. They counted taverns, urban buildings, births and deaths, and arrests and convictions. They also counted their populations with a thoroughness never before seen. As statistical reporting became more uniform across Europe and the Americas, governments could measure not only their own progress but also that of their neighbors and rivals.

The revolutionary governments of France modernized the census practices of the overthrown monarchy. They spent much more money, hired many more census takers, and devoted much more energy to training the staff that designed censuses and analyzed results. Great Britain set up an official census in 1801 but established a special administrative structure only in the 1830s. In the Western Hemisphere nearly every independent nation provided for "scientific" censuses. In the United States the federal constitution required that a census be taken every ten years. Latin American nations, often torn by civil war in the nineteenth century, took censuses less regularly, but even the poorest nations took censuses when they could. It was as if the census itself confirmed the existence of the government, demonstrating its modernity and seriousness.

Until recently, historians who relied on these documents in their research on economic performance, issues of race and ethnicity, family life, and fertility and mortality asked few questions about the politics of census design. What could be more objective than rows of numbers? But the advocates of statistics who managed census taking were uninhibited in advertising the usefulness of reliable numbers to the governments that employed them. At the 1860 International Statistical Congress held in London one speaker said, "I think the true meaning to be attached to 'statistics' is not every collection of figures, but figures collected with the sole purpose of applying the principles deduced from them to questions of importance to the state."[2] The desire to be useful meant that statistics could not be fully objective.

Subjectivity was an unavoidable problem with censuses. Censuses identified citizens and foreign residents by place of residence, sex, age, and family relationships within households as well as profession and literacy. These determinations were sometimes subjective. Modern scholars have demonstrated that census takers also often undercounted the poor and those living in rural areas.

Because census takers, as agents of nation-states, were determined to be useful, they were necessarily concerned with issues of nationality and, in the Americas, with race because these characteristics commonly determined political rights and citizenship. The assessment and recording of nationality and race would prove to be among the most politically problematic objectives of the new social sciences.

Nationality had not been a central question for traditional monarchies, but for the emerging nation-state, nationality was central. A nation's strength was assumed to depend in large measure on the growth of its population, a standard that, once articulated, suggested that the growth of minority populations was dangerous. Who was French? Who was Austrian or Hungarian? European statisticians relied on both language of use and mother tongue as proxies for nationality, the first term being flexible enough to recognize the assimilation of minorities, the second suggesting a more permanent identity based on a person's original language. Both terms forced bilingual populations to simplify their more complex identities. Ethnic minorities, once identified, were sometimes subject to discrimination such as exclusion from military careers or from universities. In parts of Spanish America language was used as a proxy for race. Those who spoke Spanish were citizens in the full sense, even if they were indistinguishable from Amerindians in appearance. Those who spoke indigenous languages were "indios" and therefore subject to special taxes and labor obligations and effectively denied the right to vote.

Beyond providing a justification for continuing discrimination, census categories compressed and distorted the complexity and variety of human society to fit the preconceptions of bureaucrats and politicians. Large percentages of the residents of Mexico, Peru, and Bolivia, among other parts of the Americas, were descended from both Europeans and Amerindians and, in the Caribbean region, from Europeans and Africans. Census categories never adequately captured the complexities of these biological and cultural mixtures. We now know that the poor were often identified as "indios" or "blacks" and the better-off were often called something else, "Americanos," "criollos" (créoles), or even whites. Since this process flattened and streamlined the complexities of identity, censuses on their own are not reliable guides to the distribution of ethnicity and race in a population.

In Europe the issue of nationality proved similarly perplexing for census takers and similarly dangerous to those identified as minorities. Linguistic and ethnic minorities had always lived among the politically dominant majorities: Jewish and Polish minorities in areas controlled by German speakers, German speakers among the French, and Serbo-Croatian speakers among Hungarians, for example. The frontiers between these minority populations and their neighbors were always porous. Sexual unions and marriages were common, and two or more generations of a family often lived together in the same household, with the elder members speaking one language and the younger members another. Who was what? In a very real sense, nationality, like race in the Americas, was ultimately fixed by the census process, where the nation-state forced a limited array of politically utilitarian categories onto the rich diversity of ethnicity and culture.

Part Seven

Global Diversity and Dominance, 1850–1949

© Cengage Learning

	1850	1870	1890
AMERICAS		• **1861–1865** U.S. Civil War · **1867** Creation of Dominion of Canada	• **1880s** British build railroads in Brazil and Argentina • **1880–1914** Immigration from southern and eastern Europe surges	• **1898** Spanish-American War
EUROPE	• **1851** Majority of British population living in cities · **1856** Transformation of steel and chemical industries begins	**1870–1914** Era of the New Imperialism • **1871** Unification of Germany, Italy	**1894–1906** Dreyfus affair in France
AFRICA	End of transatlantic slave trade **1867** •	West Africa conquered by France and Britain **1880s** • · **1884–1885** Berlin Africa Conference · Nigeria becomes British protectorate **1899** •	• **1896** Ethiopians defeat Italian army at Adowa
MIDDLE EAST	**1863–1879** Ismail westernizes Egypt · • **1869** Suez Canal opens	• **1882** British occupy Egypt · • **1878** Ottoman Empire loses most of its European territories	
ASIA AND OCEANIA	• **1858** Direct British rule in India · • **1862** French conquer Indochina	• **1868** Meiji Restoration in Japan · First Indian National Congress **1885** •	• **1894** Sino-Japanese War · Boxer Rebellion in China **1900** • · **1884–1887** Russia conquers Central Asia

In 1850, the world still embraced a huge diversity of societies, cultures, and states. During the century that followed, European nations, the United States, and Japan dominated much of the world in a wave of conquest we call the New Imperialism and tried to convert their new subjects to their own cultures and ways of life.

In Europe, mounting tensions and the awesome power of modern armaments led to the devastating Great War of 1914–1918. Russia and China erupted in revolution. Soon after, the heartland of the Ottoman Empire became modern Turkey, while its Arab provinces were taken over by France and Britain.

The political and economic system the Western powers and Japan crafted after the war fell apart in the 1930s. While the capitalist nations fell into a deep economic depression, the Soviet Union industrialized at breakneck speed. In Germany and Japan, extremists sought to solve their countries' grievances by military conquest. In World War II nationalism and industrial warfare led to the massacre of millions of people and the destruction of countless cities. The war also weakened the great powers' control of their overseas empires, as nationalists in Asia, Latin America, and Africa became inspired by Western ideas and by the desire to acquire the benefits of industrialization. India gained its independence in 1947, and two years later, Mao Zedong led the Chinese communists to victory. Latin American leaders embraced nationalist economic and social policies. Of all the once great powers, only the United States and the Soviet Union remained to compete for global dominance.

1910   **1930**   **1950**

1906–1914 U.S. builds Panama Canal
1917 U.S. enters World War I
1911–1920 Mexican Revolution
1929 U.S. stock market crash leads to Great Depression
1938 Mexico nationalizes oil industry
1946 Juan Perón becomes president of Argentina

1905 Revolution of 1905 in Russia
1922–1945 Fascism in Italy
1917 Russian Revolutions
1933 Hitler takes power in Germany
1914–1918 World War I
1939–1945 World War II

1908 Congo annexed by Belgium
1909 African National Congress founded
1939–1945 A million Africans serve in World War II

Balfour Declaration **1917**
1922–1938 Atatürk secularizes Turkey
1948 State of Israel founded
1904 Young Turk reforms in Ottoman Empire
1918 Breakup of Ottoman Empire
1915–1918 Arab Revolt against Ottomans

1904–1905 Russo-Japanese War
1910 Korea annexed by Japan
1911 Overthrow of Qing dynasty in China
1931 Japanese invasion of Manchuria
1941 Japan attacks U.S.
1945 U.S. atomic bombs force Japanese surrender
1947 India and Pakistan win independence
1949 Communists take power in China

The New Power Balance

© Cengage Learning

 Visit the CourseMate website at **www.cengagebrain.com** for additional study tools and review materials for this chapter.

O n July 8, 1853, four American warships, two of them steam-powered, appeared in Edo Bay, close to Edo (now Tokyo), the capital of Japan. The commander of the fleet, **Commodore Matthew Perry**, delivered a letter from President Millard Fillmore, demanding that Japan open its ports to foreign trade. Although foreign ships had occasionally appeared in Japanese waters, Perry's "black ships," as the Japanese called them, broke through the barriers that had kept Japan isolated from the rest of the world for two and a half centuries.

A year later, Perry returned with a fleet of seven ships to receive the answer from the Japanese government. A piece of track and a little steam locomotive, a short telegraph line, and other marvels of Western technology that the Americans set up made a big impression on the Japanese who saw them. For the next twenty years, Japanese society was torn between those who wanted to retreat into isolation and those who wished to embrace the foreign ways and acquire their machines and the industries that made them. For it soon became clear that industrialization gave power and that only by industrializing could Japan join the ranks of the powerful nations and escape the fate of weaker ones that were then being overwhelmed by imperialism.

New Technologies and the World Economy

What new technologies and industries appeared between 1850 and 1900, and how did they affect the world economy?

After 1850, industrialization took off in new directions. Germany and the United States surpassed Great Britain as the world's leading industrial powers by 1890. Small companies were overshadowed by large corporations owned by wealthy capitalists or (especially in Russia and Japan) by governments. New technologies based on advances in physics and chemistry revolutionized everyday life and transformed the world economy.

Railroads

By the mid-nineteenth century, steam engines had become the prime mover of industry and commerce. Nowhere was this more evident than in the spread of **railroads**. By 1850 the first railroads had proved so successful that every industrializing country, and many that aspired to become industrial, began to build lines. The next fifty years saw a tremendous expansion of the world's rail networks. After a rapid spurt of building new lines, British railroad mileage leveled off at around 20,000 miles (over 32,000 kilometers) in the 1870s. France and Germany built networks longer than Britain's, as did Canada and Russia. By the early twentieth century, rail lines reached every city and province in Japan (see Map 24.2 on page 590).

The American rail network was the largest by far. At the end of its Civil War in 1865 the United States already had 35,000 miles (over 56,000 kilometers) of track, three times as much as Britain. By 1915 the American network reached 390,000 miles (around 628,000 kilometers), more than the next seven longest networks combined.

Railroads were not confined to the industrialized nations; they could be constructed almost anywhere they would be of value to business or government. That included regions with abundant raw materials or agricultural products, like South Africa, Mexico, and Argentina, and densely populated countries like Egypt. The British built the fourth largest rail network in the world in India to reinforce their presence and develop trade with their largest colony. Until the opening of the Panama Canal in 1915, a railroad across the isthmus carried freight between the Atlantic and Pacific Oceans.

Commodore Matthew Perry A navy commander who, on July 8, 1853, became the first foreigner to break through the barriers that had kept Japan isolated from the rest of the world for 250 years.

railroads Networks of iron (later steel) rails on which steam (later electric or diesel) locomotives pulled long trains at high speeds. The first railroads were built in England in the 1830s. Their success caused a railroad-building boom throughout the world that lasted well into the twentieth century.

Arrivals from the East In 1853, Commodore Matthew Perry's fleet sailed into Edo (now Tokyo) Bay. The first steam-powered warships to appear in Japanese waters caused a sensation among the Japanese. In this print done after the Meiji Restoration, the traditionally dressed local samurai go out to confront the mysterious "black ships."

With one exception, European or American engineers built these railroads with equipment imported from the West. In 1855, barely a year after Commodore Perry's visit, the Japanese instrument maker Tanaka Hisashige built a model steam train that he demonstrated to an admiring audience. In the 1870s the Japanese government hired British engineers to build the first line from Tokyo to Yokohama and sent them home again as soon as they had trained Japanese engineers. Within a few years, Japan began manufacturing its own equipment.

Railroads consumed huge amounts of land. Many old cities doubled in size to accommodate railroad stations, sidings, tracks, warehouses, and repair shops. In the countryside, railroads required bridges, tunnels, and embankments. They also consumed vast quantities of timber for ties to hold the rails and for bridges, often using up whole forests for miles on either side of the tracks. Throughout the world, they opened new land to agriculture, mining, and other human exploitation of natural resources, whether for the benefit of the local inhabitants, as in Europe and North America, or for a distant power, as in the colonial empires.

Steamships and Telegraph Cables

Steam-powered ships dated back to the 1830s but were initially too costly for anything but first-class passenger traffic. Then, by mid-century, a series of developments radically transformed ocean shipping. First iron, then steel, replaced the wood that had been used for hulls since shipbuilding began. Propellers replaced paddle wheels, and engineers built more powerful and fuel-efficient engines. By the turn of the century a marine engine could convert the heat produced by burning a single sheet of paper into the power to move one ton over half a mile. The average size of freighters increased from 200 tons in 1850 to 7,500 tons in 1900. Coaling stations and ports able to handle large ships were built around the world. Most of all, the Suez Canal, constructed in 1869, shortened the distance between Europe and Asia and triggered a massive switch from sail power to steam (see Chapter 25).

The steamers of the turn of the century were so costly they had to be used as efficiently as possible. As the world's fleet of merchant ships grew from 9 million tons in 1850 to 35 million tons in 1910, new organizations developed to make the best use of them. Shipping lines, companies that offered fast and reliable service on a fixed schedule, transported passengers, mail, and perishable freight. Most ships, however, were tramp freighters that voyaged from one port to another under orders from their company headquarters in Europe or North America.

To control their ships around the globe, shipping companies used a new medium of communications: **submarine telegraph cables** laid on the ocean floor. Cables were stretched across the Atlantic in 1866, to

Chronology

	Europe	United States	East Asia
1850	**1851** Majority of British population living in cities	**1850–1914** Surge of immigration from southern and eastern Europe	
			1853 Commodore Perry "opens" Japan
	1859 Charles Darwin, *On the Origin of Species* **1861** Emancipation of serfs (Russia)		
		1865 Civil War ends; economic expansion begins	
	1866 Alfred Nobel develops dynamite **1867** Karl Marx, *Das Kapital*		
			1868 Meiji Restoration begins modernization drive in Japan
	1870 Unification of Italy **1871** Unification of Germany		
1875			
		1879 Thomas Edison develops incandescent lamp	
			1894 Sino-Japanese War
1900			
			1900 Boxer Uprising ends **1904–1905** Russo-Japanese War
	1905 Revolution of 1905 (Russia)		**1910** Japan annexes Korea

India in 1870, to China, Japan, and Australia in 1871 and 1872, to Latin America in 1872 and 1873, to East and South Africa in 1879, and to West Africa in 1886. By the turn of the century cables connected every country and almost every inhabited island. As cables became the indispensable tools of modern shipping and business, the public and the press extolled the "annihilation of time and space."

The Steel and Chemical Industries

Steel is a special form of iron, both hard and elastic. A series of inventions in the 1850s made steel the cheapest and most versatile metal ever known. As a result, world steel production rose from a half-million tons in 1870 to 28 million in 1900, of which the United States produced 10 million,

Germany 8, and Britain 4.9. Steel became cheap and abundant enough to make rails, bridges, ships, and even "tin" cans meant to be used once and thrown away.

The new steel mills were hungry consumers of coal, iron ore, limestone, and other raw materials. They took up as much space as whole towns, belched

submarine telegraph cables Insulated copper cables laid along the bottom of a sea or ocean for telegraphic communication. The first short cable was laid across the English Channel in 1851; the first successful transatlantic cable was laid in 1866.

steel A form of iron that is both durable and flexible. It was first mass-produced in the 1860s and quickly became the most widely used metal in construction, machinery, and railroad equipment.

smoke and particulates night and day, and left behind huge hills of slag and other waste products. Environmental degradation affected steel-producing regions such as the English Midlands, the German Ruhr, parts of Pennsylvania, and the regions around Tokyo and Osaka in Japan.

The chemical industry followed a similar pattern. In the early nineteenth century, only soda, sulfuric acid, and chlorine bleach (used in the cotton industry) were manufactured on a large scale, especially in Britain. Then in 1856, the development of aniline purple, a synthetic dye made from coal tar, launched the mass production of organic chemicals—compounds containing carbon atoms. These bright, long-lasting synthetic dyes delighted consumers but hurt tropical countries, such as India, that produced indigo, a blue vegetable dye.

Chemistry also advanced the manufacture of explosives. In 1866, the Swedish scientist Alfred Nobel found a way to turn nitroglycerin into a stable solid—dynamite. This and other new explosives were useful in mining and the construction of railroads and canals. They also enabled armies and navies to arm themselves with increasingly accurate and powerful rifles and cannon.

The growing complexity of industrial chemistry made it one of the first fields where science and technology interacted on a daily basis. This development gave a great advantage to Germany, which then had the most advanced engineering schools and scientific institutes. By the end of the nineteenth century, Germany was the world's leading producer of dyes, drugs, synthetic fertilizers, ammonia, and nitrates used in making explosives.

Electricity

No innovation of the late nineteenth century changed people's lives as radically as **electricity**. In the early nineteenth century, electric current from batteries cost so much that it was used only for electroplating and telegraphy. In 1831 the Englishman Michael Faraday showed that the motion of a copper wire through a magnetic field induced an electric current in the wire. Based on his discovery, inventors in the 1870s devised efficient generators that turned mechanical energy into electric current. Electricity was more flexible and much easier to use than waterpower or the stationary steam engine, which had powered industrialization until then.

Electricity opened the way to a host of new applications. Arc lamps lit up public squares, theaters, and stores. For a while, homes continued to rely on gas lamps, which produced a softer light. Then in 1879 in the United States **Thomas Edison** developed an incandescent lamp well suited to lighting small rooms. In 1882 Edison created the world's first electrical distribution network in New York City. By the turn of the century electric lighting was rapidly replacing dim and smelly gas lamps in the cities of Europe and North America.

Other uses of electricity quickly appeared. Electric streetcars and, later, subways helped reduce the traffic jams that clogged the large cities of Europe and North America. Electric motors replaced steam engines and power belts, increasing productivity and improving workers' safety. As demand for electricity grew, engineers built hydroelectric plants to produce electricity from waterpower. The plant at Niagara Falls, on the border between Ontario, Canada, and New York State, produced an incredible 11,000 horsepower when it opened in 1895. At the newly created Imperial College of Engineering in Japan, an Englishman, William Ayrton, became the first professor of electrical engineering anywhere in the world; his students later went on to found major corporations and government research institutes.

World Trade and Finance

Thanks to the growing speed and falling cost of transportation between 1850 and 1913, world trade expanded tenfold, transforming the economies of different parts of the world in different ways. The capitalist economies of western Europe and North America grew more prosperous and diversified, despite periodic depressions in which workers lost their jobs and investors their fortunes.

---

electricity A form of energy used in telegraphy from the 1840s on and for lighting, industrial motors, and railroads beginning in the 1880s.

Thomas Edison (1847–1931) American inventor best known for inventing the electric light bulb, acoustic recording on wax cylinders, and motion pictures.

Long after German and American industries surpassed the British, Britain continued to dominate the flow of trade, finance, and information. In 1900, two-thirds of the world's submarine cables were British or passed through Britain, and over half of the world's shipping was British owned. Britain invested one-fourth of its national wealth overseas, much of it in the United States and Argentina.

Nonindustrial areas were more vulnerable to changes in price and demand than were the industrialized nations, for many of them produced raw materials that could be replaced by synthetic substitutes or alternative sources of supply. Nevertheless, until World War I, the value of exports from the tropical countries generally remained high.

Social Changes

How did the societies of the industrial countries change during this period? How did industrialization contribute to socialist and labor movements?

The technological and economic changes of the late nineteenth century sparked profound social changes in the industrial nations. A fast-growing population swelled cities to unprecedented size, and millions of Europeans immigrated to the Americas. Workers spawned labor movements and new forms of radical policies, and women's lives were dramatically altered.

Population and Migrations

The population of Europe grew faster from 1850 to 1914 than ever before or since, almost doubling from 265 million to 468 million, despite mass migrations of Europeans to the United States, Canada, Australia, New Zealand, and Argentina. Between 1850 and 1900, on average, 400,000 Europeans migrated overseas every year; between 1900 and 1914, the flood rose to over 1 million a year. People of European ancestry rose from one-fifth to one-third in the world's population.

Much of the increase came from a drop in the death rate, as epidemics and starvation became less common. The Irish famine of 1847–1848 was the last peacetime famine in European history. North American wheat supplemented Europe's food, and year-round supplies of meat, fruit, vegetables, and oils improved the diet of European and North American city dwellers.

Urbanization and Urban Environments

In 1851, Britain became the first nation to have a majority of its population living in towns and cities. By 1914, 80 percent of its population was urban, as were 60 percent of the German and 45 percent of the French populations. London grew from 2.7 million in 1850 to 6.6 million in 1900. New York reached 3.4 million by 1900, a fiftyfold increase in the century. In the English Midlands, in the German Ruhr, and around Tokyo Bay, towns fused into one another, filling in the fields and woods that once had separated them.

In early industrial cities, the poor crowded together in unsanitary tenements. However, new urban technologies transformed city life for most residents. Pipes brought in clean water and carried away sewage. First gas and then electric lighting made cities safer and more pleasant at night. By the end of the century, municipal governments provided police and fire departments, schools, parks, and other amenities unheard of a century earlier.

As sanitation improved, urban death rates fell below birthrates for the first time. Confident that their children would survive infancy, couples began to limit the number of children they had. To accommodate the growing population, planners laid out new cities on a rectangular grid, and middle-class families

Civiche Raccolte delle Stampe Achille Bertarelli, Milano

Paris Lit Up by Electricity, 1900 The electric light bulb was invented in the United States and Britain, but Paris made such extensive use of the new technology that it was nicknamed "City of Lights." To mark the Paris Exposition of 1900, the Eiffel Tower and all the surrounding buildings were illuminated with strings of light bulbs while powerful spotlights swept the sky.

moved to new developments on the edges of cities. In Paris, older neighborhoods with narrow, crooked streets and rickety tenements were replaced with broad boulevards and modern apartment buildings. Brilliantly lit by gas and electricity, Paris became the "City of Lights," a model for city planners from New Delhi to Buenos Aires. By 1900, electric streetcars and subways allowed working-class people to live miles from their workplaces.

In fast-growing cities such as London, New York, and Chicago, newcomers arrived so quickly that housing construction and municipal services could not keep up. Immigrants who saved their money to reunite their families could not afford costly municipal services. As a result, the poorest neighborhoods remained as overcrowded, unhealthy, and dangerous as they had been since the early decades of industrialization.

While urban environments improved in many ways, air quality worsened. Coal, burned to power

steam engines and heat buildings, polluted the air, coating everything with a film of grimy dust. And the thousands of horses that pulled the carts and carriages covered the streets with their wastes, causing a terrible stench.

Middle-Class Women's "Separate Sphere"

In English-speaking countries the period from about 1850 to 1901 is known as the **Victorian Age**. The expression refers not only to the reign of Queen Victoria of England (r. 1837–1901) but also to rules of behavior

Victorian Age The reign of Queen Victoria of Great Britain (r. 1837–1901). The term is also used to describe late-nineteenth-century society, with its rigid moral standards and sharply differentiated roles for men and women and for middle-class and working-class people.

Mary Evans Picture Library

Visual Connection

Separate Spheres in Great Britain In the Victorian Age, men and women of the middle and upper classes led largely separate lives. In *Aunt Emily's Visit* (1845), we see women and children at home, tended by a servant. *The Royal Exchange,* meanwhile, was a place for men to transact business.

and to an ideology surrounding the family and the relations between men and women. The Victorians contrasted the masculine ideals of strength and courage with the feminine virtues of beauty and kindness, and they idealized the home as a peaceful and loving refuge from the dog-eat-dog world of competitive capitalism.

Victorian morality claimed to be universal, yet it best fit upper- and middle-class European families. Men and women were thought to belong in **"separate spheres."** While successful businessmen spent their time at work or relaxing in men's clubs, they put their wives in charge of rearing the children, running the household, and spending the family money to enhance the family's social status.

Before electric appliances, maintaining a middle-class home involved enormous amounts of work. Families were larger, and middle-class couples entertained often and lavishly. Carrying out these tasks required servants. A family's status and the activities and lifestyle of the "mistress of the house" depended on the availability of servants to help with household tasks.

Toward the turn of the century modern technology began to transform middle-class homes. Plumbing eliminated the pump and the outhouse, while central heating replaced fireplaces, stoves, and endless dusting. Gas and electricity lit houses and cooked food without soot, smoke, and ashes. Vacuum cleaners and washing machines came in the early twentieth century. These technological advances did not mean less housework for middle-class women, however. As middle-class families acquired new household technologies, they raised their standards of cleanliness. Meanwhile, young working-class women increasingly preferred factory or office work to domestic service, and the burden of housework fell increasingly on the mistress of the house.

Unlike the rich of previous eras who handed their children over to wet nurses and tutors, Victorian mothers nursed their own babies and showered their children with love and attention. Even those who could afford nannies and governesses remained personally involved in their children's education. Girls received an education very different from that of boys. While boys were being prepared for the business world or the professions, girls were taught embroidery,

"separate spheres" Nineteenth-century idea in Western societies that men and women, especially of the middle class, should have clearly differentiated roles in society: women as wives, mothers, and homemakers; men as breadwinners and participants in business and politics.

drawing, and music, activities that offered no monetary reward or professional preparation but enhanced their social graces and marriage prospects.

Victorian morality frowned on middle-class women working. Young women could work until they got married, but only in genteel places like stores and offices, never in factories. When the typewriter and telephone entered the business world in the 1880s, businessmen found that they could get better work at lower wages from educated young women than from men. Operating these machines became typecast as women's work.

Most professional careers were closed to women. Until late in the century few universities granted degrees to women. In the United States higher education was available to women only at elite colleges in the East and teachers' colleges in the Midwest. European women had fewer opportunities. Before 1914 very few women became doctors, lawyers, or professional musicians.

The first profession open to women was teaching, due to laws calling for universal compulsory education. By 1911, for instance, 73 percent of all teachers in England were women. They were considered well suited to teaching young children and girls—an extension of the duties of Victorian mothers. Teaching, however, was judged suitable only for single women. When a woman married, she was expected to get pregnant right away and to stay home taking care of her own children rather than the children of other people.

A home life, no matter how busy, did not satisfy all middle-class women. Some became volunteer nurses or social workers, for little or no pay. Others organized to fight prostitution, alcohol, and child labor. By the turn of the century a few were challenging male domination of politics and the law. Women suffragists, led in Britain by Emmeline Pankhurst and in the United States by Elizabeth Cady Stanton and Susan B. Anthony, demanded the right to vote. By 1914 U.S. women had won the right to vote in twelve states. British women did not vote until 1918.

Working-Class Women

In the new industrial cities, men and women no longer worked together at home or in the fields. The separation of work and home affected women's lives even more than men's lives. Women formed a majority of the workers in the textile industries and in domestic service. Yet working-class women needed to keep homes and raise children as well as earn their living. As a result, they led lives of toil and pain, considerably harder than the lives of their menfolk. In Japan, as in Ireland and New England, tenant farmers, squeezed by rising taxes and rents, were forced to send their daughters to work in textile mills. Others became domestic servants, commonly working sixteen hours a day, six and a half days a week, for little more than room and board. Their living quarters, usually in attics or basements, contrasted with the luxurious quarters of their masters. Without appliances, much of their work was physically hard: hauling coal and water up stairs, washing laundry by hand.

Female servants were vulnerable to sexual abuse by their masters or their masters' sons. A well-known case is that of Helene Demuth, who worked for Karl and Jenny Marx all her life. At age thirty-one she bore a son by Karl Marx and placed him with foster parents rather than leave the family. She was more fortunate than most; the majority of families fired servants who got pregnant, rather than embarrass the master of the house.

Young women often preferred factory work to domestic service. Here, too, Victorian society practiced a strict division of labor by gender. Men worked in construction, iron and steel, heavy machinery, or on railroads; women worked in textiles and the clothing trades, extensions of traditional women's household work. Appalled by the abuses of women and children in the early years of industrialization, most industrial countries passed protective legislation limiting the hours or forbidding the employment of women in the hardest and most dangerous occupations, such as mining and foundry work. Such legislation limited abuses but also reinforced gender divisions in industry, keeping women in low-paid, subordinate positions. Denied access to the better-paid jobs of foremen or machine repairmen, female factory workers earned between one-third and two-thirds of men's wages.

Married women with children were expected to stay home, even if their husbands did not make enough to support the family. Most working-class married women had double responsibilities within the home: not only the work of child rearing and housework but also that of contributing to the family's income. Families who had room to spare, even a bed or a corner in the kitchen, took in boarders. Many women did piecework such as sewing dresses, making hats or gloves, or weaving baskets. The hardest and worst-paid work was washing other people's clothes. Many women worked at home ten to twelve hours a day and enlisted the help of their small children, perpetuating practices long outlawed in factories.

Socialism and Labor Movements

Industrialization combined with the revolutionary ideas of the late eighteenth century to produce two kinds of movements—socialism and labor movements—calling for further changes. **Socialism** was an ideology developed by radical thinkers who questioned the sanctity of private property and argued in support of industrial workers against their employers. **Labor unions** were organizations formed by industrial workers to defend their interests in negotiations with employers. The socialist and labor movements were never identical. Most of the time they were allies; occasionally they were rivals.

Socialism began as an intellectual movement. By far the best-known socialist was **Karl Marx** (1818–1883), a German journalist and writer who spent most of his life in England and collaborated with another socialist, Friedrich Engels (1820–1895), author of *The Condition of the Working Class in England in 1844* (1845). Together, they combined German philosophy, French revolutionary ideas, and knowledge of British industrial conditions.

Marx expressed his ideas succinctly in the *Communist Manifesto* (1848) and in great detail in *Das Kapital* (DUSS cop-ee-TAHL) (1867). He saw history as a series of conflicts between social classes, the latest being between property owners (the bourgeoisie) and workers (the proletariat). He argued that the capitalist system allowed the bourgeoisie to extract the "surplus value" of workers' labor—that is, the difference between their wages and the value of the goods they manufactured. He saw business enterprises becoming larger and more monopolistic and workers growing more numerous and impoverished. He concluded that this conflict would inevitably lead to a revolutionary overthrow of the bourgeoisie,

after which the workers would establish a communist society without classes (see Diversity and Dominance: Marx and Engels on Global Trade and the Bourgeoisie).

What Marx called "scientific socialism" provided an intellectual framework for the growing dissatisfaction with raw industrial capitalism. In the late nineteenth century business tycoons spent money lavishly on mansions, yachts, private railroad cars, and other displays of wealth that contrasted sharply with the poverty of the workers. Even though industrial workers were not becoming poorer as Marx believed, the class struggle between workers and employers was brutally real. What Marx did was to offer a persuasive explanation of the causes of this contrast and the antagonisms it bred.

Marx was not just a philosopher; he also had a direct impact on politics. In 1864 he helped found the International Working Man's Association (later known as the First International), a movement he hoped would bring about the overthrow of the bourgeoisie. However, it attracted more intellectuals than workers. Workers found other means of redressing their grievances, such as the vote and labor unions.

Since the beginning of the nineteenth century, workers had united to create "friendly societies" for mutual assistance in times of difficulty. Anti-combination laws, however, forbade workers to strike. These laws were abolished in Britain in the 1850s and in the rest of Europe in subsequent decades. Labor unions sought better wages as well as improved working conditions and insurance against illness,

socialism A political ideology that originated in Europe in the 1830s. Socialists advocated government protection of workers from exploitation by property owners and government ownership of industries. This ideology led to the founding of socialist or labor parties throughout Europe in the second half of the nineteenth century.

labor union An organization of workers in a particular industry or trade, created to defend the interests of members through strikes or negotiations with employers.

Karl Marx (1818–1883) German journalist and philosopher, founder of the Marxist branch of socialism. He is known for two books: *The Communist Manifesto* (1848) and *Das Kapital* (1867–1894).

Diversity & Dominance

Marx and Engels on Global Trade and the Bourgeoisie

*I*n 1848 Karl Marx (1818–1883) and Friedrich Engels (1820–1895) published the Manifesto of the Communist Party. In it, they tried to explain why business owners—the "bourgeoisie"—had become the wealthiest and most powerful class of people in industrializing countries like Britain, and why industrial workers—the "proletariat"—lived in poverty. In their view, the dominance of the bourgeoisie was destroying the diversity of human cultures, reducing all classes in Europe and all cultures to the status of proletarians selling their labor.

In the Manifesto, Marx and Engels called for a revolution in which the workers would overthrow the bourgeoisie and establish a new society without private property or government. Their Manifesto was soon translated into many languages and became the best-known expression of radical communist ideology.

Marx and Engels's ideas are especially interesting from the perspective of global history because of the way in which they connect the rise of the bourgeoisie with world trade and industrial technology. The following paragraphs explain these connections.

The history of all hitherto existing society is the history of class struggles. . . .

In the earlier epochs of history, we find almost everywhere a complicated arrangement of society into various orders, a manifold gradation of social rank. In ancient Rome we have patricians, knights, plebeians, slaves; in the middle ages, feudal lords, vassals, guild-masters, journeymen, apprentices, serfs; in almost all of these classes, again, subordinate gradations.

The modern bourgeois society that has sprouted from the ruins of feudal society, has not done away with class antagonisms. It has but established new classes, new conditions of oppression, new forms of struggle in place of the old ones.

Our epoch, the epoch of the bourgeoisie, possesses, however, this distinctive feature; it has simplified the class antagonisms. Society as a whole is more and more splitting up into two great hostile camps, into two great classes directly facing each other: Bourgeoisie and Proletariat. . . .

The discovery of America, the rounding of the Cape, opened up fresh ground for the rising bourgeoisie. The East-Indian and Chinese markets, the colonization of America, trade with the colonies, the increase in the means of exchange and in commodities generally, gave to commerce, to navigation, to industry, an impulse never before known, and thereby, to the revolutionary element in the tottering feudal society, a rapid development. . . .

Modern industry has established the world-market, for which the discovery of America paved the way. This market has given an immense importance to commerce, to navigation, to communication by land. This development has, in its turn, reacted on the extension of industry; and in proportion as industry, commerce, navigation, railways extended, in the same proportion the bourgeoisie developed, increased its capital, and pushed into the background every class handed down from the Middle Ages. . . .

The bourgeoisie, historically, has played a most revolutionary part. . . .

It has been the first to show what man's activity can bring about. It has accomplished wonders far surpassing Egyptian pyramids, Roman aqueducts, and Gothic cathedrals; it has conducted expeditions that put in the shade all former Exoduses of nations and crusades. . . .

disability, and old age. They grew slowly because they required a permanent staff and a great deal of money to sustain their members during strikes. By the end of the century British labor unions counted 2 million members, and German and American unions had 1 million members each.

The nineteenth century saw a gradual extension of the right to vote throughout Europe and North America. Universal male suffrage became law in the United States in 1870, in France and Germany in 1871, in Britain in 1885, and in the rest of Europe soon thereafter. Because there were so many

The need of a constantly expanding market for its products chases the bourgeoisie over the whole surface of the globe. It must nestle everywhere, settle everywhere, establish connexions everywhere.

The bourgeoisie has through its exploitation of the world-market given a cosmopolitan character to production and consumption in every country. To the great chagrin of Reactionists, it has drawn from under the feet of industry the national ground on which it stood. All old-fashioned national industries have been destroyed or are daily being destroyed. They are dislodged by new industries, whose introduction becomes a life or death question for all civilised nations, by industries that no longer work up indigenous raw material, but raw material drawn from the remotest zones; industries whose products are consumed, not only at home, but in every quarter of the globe. In place of the old wants, satisfied by the productions of the country, we find new wants, requiring for their satisfaction the products of distant lands and climes. In place of the old local and national seclusion and self-sufficiency, we have intercourse in every direction, universal inter-dependence of nations. And as in material, so also in intellectual production. The intellectual creations of individual nations become common property. National one-sidedness and narrow-mindedness become more and more impossible, and from the numerous national and local literatures there arises a world-literature.

The bourgeoisie, by the rapid improvement of all instruments of production, by the immensely facilitated means of communication, draws all, even the most barbarian, nations into civilisation. The cheap prices of its commodities are the heavy artillery with which it batters down all Chinese walls, with which it forces the barbarians' intensely obstinate hatred of foreigners to capitulate. It compels all nations, on pain of extinction, to adopt the bourgeois mode of production; it compels them to introduce what it calls civilisation into their midst, i.e., to become bourgeois themselves. In a word, it creates a world after its own image.

The bourgeoisie has subjected the country to the rule of the towns. It has created enormous cities, has greatly increased the urban population as compared with the rural, and has thus rescued a considerable part of the population from the idiocy of rural life. Just as it has made the country dependent on the towns, so it has made barbarian and semi-barbarian countries dependent on the civilised ones, nations of peasants on nations of bourgeois, the East on the West. . . .

The bourgeoisie, during its rule of scarce one hundred years, has created more massive and more colossal productive forces than have all preceding generations together. Subjection of Nature's forces to man, machinery, application of chemistry to industry and agriculture, steam-navigation, railways, electric telegraphs, clearing of whole continents for cultivation, canalization of rivers, whole populations conjured out of the ground—what earlier century had even a presentiment that such productive forces slumbered in the lap of social labour?

QUESTIONS FOR ANALYSIS

1. How did the growth of world trade since the European discovery of America affect relations between social classes in Europe?

2. Compare Marx and Engels's views on industrial production with those of Adam Smith that you read in Chapter 21. Do they contradict each other? Or does Smith's description of pin-making explain the rise of what Marx and Engels call "the giant, Modern Industry"?

3. What effect did the growth of trade and industry have on products, intellectual creations, and consumer tastes around the world?

Source: Karl Marx and Frederick Engels, *Manifesto of the Communist Party*, Authorized English Translation: Edited and Annotated by Frederick Engels (Chicago: Charles H. Kerr & Company, 1906), 12–20.

newly enfranchised workers, universal male suffrage meant that socialist politicians could expect to capture many seats in their nations' parliaments. Unlike Marx, who predicted that workers would seize power through revolution, the socialists expected workers to use their voting power to obtain concessions from government and eventually even to form a government.

The Social Democratic Party of Germany was founded in 1875 with a revolutionary socialist program. Within two years it won a half-million votes and several seats in the Reichstag (RIKES-tog) (the lower

SECTION REVIEW

- Between 1850 and 1914, Europe's population nearly doubled, and millions migrated to North America, Argentina, Australia, and New Zealand.

- Urbanization accelerated in the industrial world, but new technologies, plans, and policies helped to reduce earlier urban problems.

- Victorian values idealized the home and divided upper- and middle-class men and women into separate spheres.

- Gender divisions widened between working-class men and women; women often worked in domestic service or in their homes or were forced into prostitution.

- Industrialization and revolutionary ideologies prompted the rise of the labor and socialist movements, including Marxism.

- Expanding suffrage after 1870 enabled socialists to participate in electoral politics.

house of the German parliament). Through superb organizing efforts and important concessions wrung from the government, the party grew fast, garnering 4.2 million votes in 1912 and winning more seats in the Reichstag than any other party. In pursuit of electoral success, the Social Democrats became more reformist and less radical. By joining the electoral process, they abandoned the idea of violent revolution.

Working-class women were not welcome in the male-dominated trade unions or radical political parties. A few radical women, such as the German socialist Rosa Luxemburg and Emma Goldman in the United States, an **anarchist** who believed in abolishing all governments, became famous but did not have large followings. It was never easy to reconcile the demands of workers and those of women. In 1889 the German socialist Clara Zetkin wrote: "Just as the male worker is subjected by the capitalist, so is the woman by the man, and she will always remain in subjugation until she is economically independent. Work is the indispensable condition for economic independence." Six years later, she recognized that the liberation of women would have to await a change in the position of the working class as a whole: "The proletarian woman cannot attain her highest ideal through a movement for the equality of the female sex, she attains salvation only through the fight for the emancipation of labor."[1]

Nationalism and the Rise of Italy, Germany, and Japan

What was nationalism, and how did it contribute to the formation of new states?

The most influential idea of the nineteenth century was **nationalism**. The French revolutionaries had defined people, previously considered the subjects of a sovereign, as the citizens of a *nation*—a concept identified with a territory, the state that ruled it, and the culture of its people. While Italians and Germans looked inward to create unified nations, the Japanese would eventually look outward, embracing Western ideas and institutions as a way to protect and strengthen their country.

Language and National Identity in Europe Before 1871

Language was usually the crucial element in creating a feeling of national unity. It was important both as a way to unite the people of a nation and as the means of persuasion by which political leaders inspired their followers. Yet language and citizenship seldom coincided.

The fit between France and the French language was closer than in most large countries, though some French-speakers lived outside of France and some French people spoke other languages. Italian- and German-speaking people, however, were divided among many small states. Living in the Austrian Empire were peoples who spoke German, Czech, Slovak, Hungarian, Polish, and other languages. Even where people spoke a common language, they could be divided by religion or institutions. The Irish, though

anarchists Revolutionaries who wanted to abolish all private property and governments, usually by violence, and replace them with free associations of groups.
nationalism A political ideology that stresses people's membership in a nation—a community defined by a common culture and history as well as by territory. In the late eighteenth and early nineteenth centuries, nationalism was a force for unity in western Europe. In the late nineteenth century it hastened the disintegration of the Austro-Hungarian and Ottoman Empires. In the twentieth century it provided the ideological foundation for scores of independent countries emerging from colonialism.

English-speaking, were mostly Catholic, whereas the English were primarily Protestant.

The idea of redrawing the boundaries of states to accommodate linguistic, religious, or cultural differences was revolutionary. In Italy and Germany it led to the forging of large new states out of many small ones in 1871. In central and eastern Europe, nationalism threatened to break up large states into smaller ones.

Until the 1860s nationalism was associated with **liberalism**, the revolutionary middle-class ideology that asserted the sovereignty of the people and demanded constitutional government, a national parliament, and freedom of expression. The most famous nationalist of the early nineteenth century was the Italian liberal Giuseppe Mazzini (jew-SEP-pay mots-EE-nee) (1805–1872), the leader of the failed revolution of 1848 in Italy. Mazzini not only sought to unify the Italian peninsula into one nation but also associated with like-minded revolutionaries elsewhere to bring nationhood and liberty to peoples oppressed by tyrants and foreigners. These new ideas could not be quashed. Even conservative regimes like Russia, Prussia, and Austria required educated personnel to staff the bureaucracies and police forces they needed to maintain control, and education meant universities, the seedbeds of new ideas transmitted by a national language.

The Unification of Italy, 1860–1870

The Austrian statesman Prince Metternich once described Italy as "a geographical expression." By midcentury, however, popular sentiment was building throughout Italy for unification. Opposing it were Pope Pius IX, who abhorred everything modern, and Austria, which controlled two Italian provinces, Lombardy and Venetia. The prime minister of the Kingdom of Piedmont-Sardinia, Count Camillo Benso di Cavour, saw the rivalry between France and Austria as an opportunity to unify Italy. He secretly formed an alliance with France and then instigated a war with Austria in 1858. The war triggered uprisings throughout northern and central Italy in favor of joining Piedmont-Sardinia, a moderate constitutional monarchy under King Victor Emmanuel.

If the conservative, top-down approach to unification prevailed in the north, a more radical approach arose in the south. In 1860 the fiery revolutionary **Giuseppe Garibaldi** (jew-SEP-pay gar-y-BAHL-dee) and a small band of followers landed in Sicily and then in southern Italy, overthrew the Kingdom of the Two Sicilies, and prepared to found a democratic republic. The royalist Cavour, however, took advantage of the unsettled situation to sideline Garibaldi and expand Piedmont-Sardinia into a new Kingdom of Italy. Unification was completed with the addition of Venetia in 1866 and the Papal States in 1870.

The process of unification illustrates the shift of nationalism from a radical democratic idea to a conservative method of building popular support for a strong centralized government, even an aristocratic and monarchical one.

The Unification of Germany

Some German nationalists wanted to unite all Germans under the Catholic Austrian throne. Others wanted to exclude Austria with its many non-Germanic peoples and unite all other German-speaking areas under Lutheran Prussia. The Prussian state had two advantages: (1) the newly developed industries of the Rhineland and (2) the first European army to make use of railroads, telegraphs, breechloading rifles, steel artillery, and other products of modern industry. The king of Prussia, Wilhelm I (r. 1861–1888), had entrusted the running of his

Primary Source: Extracts from History of Germany in the Nineteenth Century and Historical and Political Writings Learn why the image of the "hypocritical Englishman, with the Bible in one hand and a pipe of opium in the other," rang true for some Germans.

liberalism A political ideology that emphasizes the civil rights of citizens, representative government, and the protection of private property. This ideology, derived from the Enlightenment, was especially popular among the property-owning middle classes of Europe and North America.

Giuseppe Garibaldi (1807–1882) Italian nationalist and revolutionary who conquered Sicily and Naples and added them to a unified Italy in 1860.

Map 24.1 The Unification of Germany, 1866–1871 Germany was united after a series of short, successful wars by the kingdom of Prussia against Austria in 1866 and against France in 1871. © Cengage Learning

Interactive Map

government to his chancellor, the brilliant and authoritarian aristocrat **Otto von Bismarck** (1815–1898), who was determined to use the Prussian military and German nationalism to advance the interests of the Prussian state.

In 1864, after a quick victory against Denmark, Bismarck set his sights on Austria, which surrendered in 1866. To everyone's surprise, Prussia took no Austrian territory. Instead, Prussia and some smaller states formed the North German Confederation, the nucleus of a future Germany. Then in 1870, Bismarck

Otto von Bismarck (1815–1898) Chancellor (prime minister) of Prussia from 1862 until 1871, when he became chancellor of Germany. A conservative nationalist, he led Prussia to victory against Austria (1866) and France (1870) and was responsible for the creation of the German Empire in 1871.

provoked a war with France. In this "Franco-Prussian War," German armies used their superior firepower and tactics to achieve a quick victory.

The spoils of victory included a large indemnity and two provinces of Alsace and Lorraine (see Map 24.1). To the Germans, this region was German because a majority of its inhabitants spoke German. To the French, it was French because it had been so when the nation of France was forged in the Revolution and because most of its inhabitants considered themselves French. These two conflicting definitions of nationalism kept enmity between France and Germany smoldering for decades.

The West Challenges Japan

In Japan a completely different political organization was in place. The emperor was revered but had no power. Instead, Japan was governed by the Tokugawa Shogunate—a secular government under a military leader, or *shogun*, who had come to power in 1600 (see Chapter 19). Local lords, called *daimyo*, were permitted to control their lands and populations with very little interference from the shogunate.

Because this system did not permit the coordination of resources necessary to resist foreign invasion, the shoguns attempted to minimize exposure to foreigners. In the early 1600s they prohibited foreigners from entering Japan and Japanese from going abroad. The most flagrant violators of these rules were powerful daimyo in southern Japan who ran large pirate or black-market operations. These lords benefited from the decentralization of the shogunal political system. But when a genuine foreign threat was suggested—as when, in 1792, Russian and British ships were spotted off the Japanese coast—the local lords realized that Japan was perilously weak and decentralized.

Some regional lords began to develop their own reformed armies, arsenals, and shipyards. By the 1800s Satsuma (SAT-soo-mah) and Choshu (CHOE-shoo), two large domains in southern Japan, had become wealthy and ambitious, enjoying high rates of revenue and population growth. Their remoteness from the capital Edo and their economic vigor fostered a strong sense of local self-reliance.

In 1853, as mentioned earlier, the American commodore Matthew C. Perry arrived off the coast of Japan and demanded that Japan open its ports to trade and allow American ships to refuel and take on supplies. Perry's demands sparked a crisis in the shogunate. After consultation with the provincial daimyo, the shogun's advisers advocated capitulation to Perry. They pointed to China's humiliating defeats in the Opium and Arrow Wars (see Chapter 22). In 1854, when Perry returned, representatives of the shogun indicated their willingness to sign the Treaty of Kanagawa (KAH-nah-GAH-wah), modeled on the unequal treaties between China and the Western powers. Angry and disappointed, some provincial governors encouraged an underground movement calling for the destruction of the Tokugawa regime and the banning of foreigners from Japan.

Tensions between the shogunate and some provincial leaders, particularly in Choshu and Satsuma, increased in the early 1860s. When British and French ships shelled the southwestern coasts in 1864 to protest the treatment of foreigners, the action enraged the provincial samurai, who rejected the Treaty of Kanagawa. Young, ambitious, educated men who faced mediocre prospects under the rigid Tokugawa class system emerged as provincial leaders. In 1867 the Choshu leaders Yamagata Aritomo and Ito Hirobumi finally realized that they should stop warring with their rival province, Satsuma, and jointly rebel against the shogunate.

The Meiji Restoration and the Modernization of Japan, 1868–1894

The civil war was intense but brief. In 1868 provincial rebels overthrew the Tokugawa Shogunate and declared young emperor Mutsuhito (moo-tsoo-HE-toe) (r. 1868–1912) "restored." The new leaders called their regime the **Meiji** (MAY-gee) **Restoration** after Mutsuhito's reign name (*Meiji* means "enlightened rule"). The "Meiji oligarchs," as the new rulers were known, were extraordinarily talented and farsighted. Though imposed from above, the Meiji

Meiji Restoration The political program that followed the destruction of the Tokugawa Shogunate in 1868, in which a collection of young leaders set Japan on the path of centralization, industrialization, and imperialism.

Map 24.2 Expansion and Modernization of Japan, 1868–1918 As Japan acquired modern industry, it followed the example of the European powers in seeking overseas colonies. Its colonial empire grew at the expense of its neighbors: Taiwan was taken from China in 1895; Karafutu (Sakhalin) acquired from Russia in 1905; and all of Korea became a colony in 1910. © Cengage Learning

Interactive Map

Restoration marked as profound a change as the French Revolution (see Map 24.2).

The oligarchs knew they would have to transform their institutions and their society. In the Charter Oath issued in 1868, the young emperor included a prophetic phrase: "Knowledge shall be sought throughout the world and thus shall be strengthened the foundation of the imperial polity." It was to be the motto of a new Japan, which embraced all foreign ideas, institutions, and techniques that could strengthen the nation. The literacy rate in Japan was the highest in Asia at the time, and the oligarchs shrewdly exploited it in their introduction of new educational systems, a conscript army, and new

SECTION REVIEW

- The most influential nineteenth-century idea was nationalism, which was associated with revolutionary liberalism before the 1860s.

- After the 1848 revolutions, conservative governments adopted nationalism to preserve the status quo.

- Bismarck exploited German nationalism to unify Germany under militarist Prussia.

- In Japan power was in the hands of the Tokugawa Shogunate until, forced to open to foreign trade and influence, the shogunate fell to a rebellion of provincial leaders.

- The Meiji Restoration later brought to power reformers who modernized Japan's government, economy, education system, and military.

- Social Darwinism offered "scientific" support for policies of racial, political, and economic dominance.

Tsuneo Tamba Collection/Laurie Platt Winfrey, Inc.

Japan's New Army After the Meiji Restoration in 1868, the leaders of the new government set out to make Japan "a rich country with a strong army." They modeled the new army on the European armies of the time, with Western-style uniforms, rifles, cannon, and musical instruments.

communications. The government was able to establish heavy industry through the use of judicious deficit financing without extensive foreign debt, thanks to decades of experimentation with industrial development and financing in the provinces in the earlier 1800s.

The Meiji leaders copied the government structure of imperial Germany. They modeled the new Japanese navy on the British and the army on the Prussian. They introduced Western-style postal and telegraph services, railroads and harbors, banking, clocks, and calendars. To learn the secrets of Western strength, they sent hundreds of students to Britain, Germany, and the United States. Western-style hairstyles and clothing, including military and police uniforms, became popular. Even pastimes were affected, with garden parties and formal dances becoming common.

Especially interested in Western technology, the government opened vocational, technical, and agricultural schools and founded four imperial universities. It also brought in foreign experts to advise on medicine, science, and engineering. To encourage industrialization, the government set up state-owned enterprises to manufacture cloth and inexpensive consumer goods for sale abroad. The first Japanese industries, some of which had been founded in the early nineteenth century, exploited their workers ruthlessly, just as the first industries in Europe and America had done. In 1881, to pay off its debts, the government sold these enterprises to private investors, mainly large *zaibatsu* (zye-BOT-soo), or conglomerates. Individual technological innovation was encouraged. Thus the carpenter Toyoda Sakichi founded the Toyoda Loom Works (now Toyota Motor Company) in 1906; ten years later he patented the world's most advanced automatic loom.

The Metropolitan Museum of Art gift of Lincoln Kirstein, 1959 [JP 3346]. Photograph by Otto E Nelson. Photograph, 1986 The Metropolitan Museum of Art

Silk Factory in Japan Silk manufacture Japan's best-known industry, began to be mechanized in the 1870s. In this factory, as in most textile mills, the workers were women.

History in Focus *Examine the image "Silk Factory in Japan," and then look back at the image "The Pit Head of a Coal Mine" in Chapter 21. Compare the two images. How do these representations of machines and workers resemble and differ from each other? What does the Japanese image suggest about the process of modernization in Japan? Find the answer online.*

Nationalism and Social Darwinism

In many countries, the dominant group used nationalism to justify imposing its language, religion, or customs on minority populations. The Russian Empire attempted to "Russify" its diverse ethnic populations. The Spanish government made the Spanish language compulsory in the schools, newspapers, and courts of its Basque- and Catalan-speaking provinces.

Some people looked to science for support of political dominance. One of the most influential scientists of the century, and the one whose ideas were most widely cited and misinterpreted, was the English biologist **Charles Darwin** (1809–1882), who based his theory of evolution on the observations he made during a research voyage in South America and while observing English livestock breeders. His famous book, *On the Origin of Species by Means of Natural Selection* (1859), argued that, over hundreds of thousands of years, living beings had either evolved in the struggle for survival or become extinct. The philosopher Herbert Spencer (1820–1903) and others took up Darwin's ideas of "natural selection" and "survival of the fittest" and applied them to human society. Extreme Social Darwinists developed elaborate pseudo-scientific theories of racial differences, claiming that they were the result not of history but of biology.

Primary Source: Letter to Mitsubishi Employees The responsibilities of the Mitsubishi Company are "even greater than the full weight of Mt. Fuji thrust upon" its shoulders. Find out why.

Charles Darwin (1809–1882) He developed the theory of evolution through natural selection. Author of *On the Origin of Species* (1859).

The Great Powers of Europe, 1871–1900

How did the forces of nationalism affect the major powers of Europe?

After 1871, politicians and journalists discovered how easily they could whip up popular frenzy against neighboring countries. Rivalries over colonial territories, ideological differences between liberal and conservative governments, and even minor border incidents or trade disagreements contributed to a growing atmosphere of international tension.

Germany at the Center of Europe

International relations revolved around a united Germany, because Germany was located in the center of Europe and had the most powerful army on the European continent. After creating a unified Germany in 1871, Bismarck worked to maintain peace in Europe. To isolate France, he forged a loose coalition with Austria-Hungary and Russia, which he was able to keep together for twenty years.

Bismarck proved equally adept at manipulating mass politics at home. To weaken the influence of middle-class liberals, he extended the vote to all adult men. By imposing high tariffs on manufactured goods and wheat, he gained the support of both the wealthy industrialists of the Rhineland and the great landowners of eastern Germany. He stole the thunder of the socialists by introducing social legislation—medical, unemployment, and disability insurance and old-age pensions—long before other industrial countries did. Under his leadership, the German people developed a strong sense of national unity and pride in their industrial and military power.

In 1888, Wilhelm I was succeeded by his grandson Wilhelm II (r. 1888–1918), who dismissed Chancellor Bismarck. Wilhelm II talked about his "global policy" and demanded that Germany, with the mightiest army and the largest industrial economy in Europe, have a colonial empire, "a place in the sun."

The Liberal Powers: France and Great Britain

France had difficulty reconciling itself to being second to Germany. Its population and its army lagged far behind Germany's, and its industry was growing more slowly, because it had lost the iron and coal mines of Lorraine in 1871. The French people were deeply divided politically: some were monarchists and Catholics; a growing number were republican and anticlerical. Despite these problems, a long tradition of popular participation in politics and a strong sense of nationhood, reinforced by a fine system of universal public education, gave the French people a deeper cohesion than appeared on the surface.

Great Britain was the only other country in Europe with a democratic tradition. The British government alternated smoothly between the Liberal and Conservative Parties, and the income gap between rich and poor gradually narrowed. Nevertheless, Britain had problems. One was Irish resentment of English rule as a foreign occupying force. Another was the British economy. Great Britain lagged behind the United States and Germany in iron and steel, chemicals, electricity, and textiles. Germany was even catching up in shipbuilding. Finally, Britain's far-flung empire was a constant drain on government finances.

SECTION REVIEW

- Powerful unified Germany became the center of European politics, as Bismarck sought to maintain peace, isolate France, and strengthen authoritarian rule at home.

- Under Wilhelm II, Germany became more aggressive and pursued colonial expansion.

- Despite military defeat and social and political division, France maintained a strong sense of democratic national unity.

- In democratic Britain, the division between rich and poor narrowed, but ethnic and economic problems became increasingly apparent.

- Nationalism weakened ethnically diverse Austria-Hungary but drove it to continue trying to dominate Slavic minorities.

- Nationalism also undermined Russia, where traditional social divisions persisted and economic and military development lagged.

The Doss House Late nineteenth-century cities showed more physical than social improvements. This painting by Makovsky of a street in St. Petersburg contrasts the broad avenue and impressive new buildings with the poverty of the crowd.

The Conservative Powers: Russia and Austria-Hungary

The forces of nationalism weakened rather than strengthened Russia and Austria-Hungary. The reason for this effect was that their populations were far more divided, socially and ethnically, than were the German, French, or British peoples.

Nationalism was most divisive in the Austrian Empire. The decision to rename itself the Austro-Hungarian Empire in 1867 appeased its Hungarian critics but alienated its Slavic-speaking minorities. The Austro-Hungarian Empire still considered itself a great power and attempted to dominate the Balkans. This strategy irritated Russia, which thought of itself as the protector of Slavic peoples everywhere, and it eventually led to war.

Russia was the most misunderstood country in Europe. Its enormous size and population led many Europeans to exaggerate its military potential, but it was weakened by national and social divisions. All in all, only 45 percent of the peoples of the tsarist empire

spoke Russian. To strengthen the bonds between the monarchy and the Russian people and promote industrialization by enlarging the labor pool, the moderate conservative Tsar Alexander II (r. 1855–1881) emancipated the peasants from serfdom in 1861. That measure, however, did not create a modern society but only turned serfs into communal farmers with few skills and little capital. Though technically "emancipated," the great majority of Russians had little education, few legal rights, and no say in their government.

After Alexander's assassination in 1881, his successors Alexander III (r. 1881–1894) and Nicholas II (r. 1894–1917) opposed all forms of social change. Industrialization consisted largely of state-sponsored projects, such as railroads, iron foundries, and armament factories, and led to social unrest among urban workers. Wealthy landowning aristocrats continued to dominate the Russian court and administration and succeeded in blocking most reforms.

The weaknesses in Russia's society and government became glaringly obvious after Russia's defeat in the Russo-Japanese War of 1904–1905 (see below). The shock of defeat caused a popular uprising, the Revolution of 1905, that forced Tsar Nicholas II to grant a constitution and an elected Duma (parliament). But as soon as he was able to rebuild the army and the police, he reverted to the traditional despotism of his forefathers. Small groups of radical intellectuals, angered by the contrast between the wealth of the elite and the poverty of the common people, began plotting the violent overthrow of the tsarist autocracy.

China, Japan, and the Western Powers

How did Western pressures affect East Asia?

After 1850 China and Japan—the two largest countries in East Asia—felt the influence of the Western powers as never before, but their responses were completely opposite. China resisted Western influence and became weaker, while Japan transformed itself into a major industrial and military power. One reason for this difference was the Western powers' heavy involvement in China. More important was the difference between the Chinese and Japanese elites' attitudes toward foreign cultures.

China in Turmoil

China had been devastated by the Taiping (tie-PING) Rebellion that raged from 1850 to 1864 (see Chapter 22). Taking advantage of this weakness, the French and British demanded treaty ports where they could trade at will, and the British took over China's customs and allowed the free import of opium until 1917.

China's attempts to resist these changes were ultimately self-defeating. A Chinese "self-strengthening movement" tried in vain to bring about significant reforms by reducing government expenditures and eliminating corruption. The **Empress Dowager Cixi** (TSUH-shee) (r. 1862–1908), who had once encouraged the construction of shipyards, arsenals, and telegraph lines, opposed railways and other foreign technologies that could carry foreign influences to the interior. Government officials, who did not dare resist the Westerners outright, secretly encouraged crowds to attack and destroy the intrusive devices. They were able to slow the foreign intrusion, but in

SECTION REVIEW

- The French and British became heavily involved in trade in China despite Chinese attempts to sabotage foreign enterprises.
- Chinese resistance to the new technologies of the West contributed to its decline in power and status.
- While the European powers were caught up in a rush to secure the world's remaining unclaimed territory, Japan was in the process of becoming a great power.
- After 1894, Japan began a program of imperial expansion, winning new territories through successful wars with China and Russia.

doing so, they denied themselves the best means of defense against foreign pressure.

Japan Confronts China

The motive for the transformation of Japan was defensive—to protect the nation from the Western powers—but the methods that strengthened Japan against the imperial ambitions of others could also be used offensively. Japan's path to imperialism was laid out by **Yamagata Aritomo**, a leader of the Meiji oligarchs. He believed that an independent Japan required a "sphere of influence" that included Korea, Manchuria, and part of China. If other countries controlled this sphere, Japan would be at risk. To protect this sphere of influence, Yamagata insisted, Japan must accelerate its military industrialization, culminating in the building of battleships.

As Japan grew stronger, China grew weaker. In 1894 the two nations went to war over Japanese encroachments in Korea. The Sino-Japanese War lasted less than six months, and it forced China to evacuate Korea, cede Taiwan and the Liaodong (li-AH-oh-dong) Peninsula, and pay a heavy indemnity.

Empress Dowager Cixi (1835–1908) Empress of China and mother of Emperor Guangxi. She put her son under house arrest, supported antiforeign movements, and resisted reforms of the Chinese government and armed forces.

Yamagata Aritomo (1838–1922) One of the leaders of the Meiji Restoration.

France, Germany, Britain, Russia, and the United States, upset at seeing a newcomer join the ranks of the imperialists, made Japan give up Liaodong in the name of the "territorial integrity" of China. In exchange for their "protection," the Western powers then made China grant them territorial and trade concessions, including ninety treaty ports.

In 1900 Chinese officials around the Empress Dowager Cixi encouraged a series of antiforeign riots known as the Boxer Uprising. Military forces from the European powers, Japan, and the United States put down the riots and occupied Beijing. Emboldened by China's obvious weakness, Japan and Russia competed for possession of the mineral-rich Chinese province of Manchuria.

Japan's participation in the suppression of the Boxer Uprising demonstrated its military power in East Asia. In 1905 Japan surprised the world by defeating Russia in the Russo-Japanese War. By the Treaty of Portsmouth that ended the war, Japan established a protectorate over Korea. In spite of Western attempts to restrict it to the role of junior partner, Japan continued to increase its influence. It gained control of southern Manchuria, with its industries and railroads, and in 1910 it finally annexed Korea, joining the ranks of the world's colonial powers.

Primary Source: Two Proclamations of the Boxer Uprising Find out how the supporters of the Boxer Uprising planned to deal with Christian converts.

Conclusion

The late nineteenth century witnessed the most rapid changes in technology, society, and politics that had ever taken place until that time. The changes were concentrated in a few regions of the world—Europe, the United States, and Japan—but would have repercussions everywhere.

Two primary causes—industrialization and nationalism—were responsible for the changes. Industrialization provided an abundance of goods as well as new and much better means of transportation and communication. After 1850, some of the worst abuses of industrialization that had characterized the previous age were attenuated, and new technologies promised to improve the lives of workers, city dwellers, and women.

Industrialization and the new politics of national identity increased the power of certain states but threatened others. States founded on a strong sense of national identity, such as France and Japan, found that the politics of nationalism benefited them and their citizens. But nationalism could also threaten the cohesion of multinational states like Russia and Austria-Hungary or weaken traditional states like China. The two great revolutions of the eighteenth and early nineteenth centuries—the industrial and the political—were about to destabilize the world, first in the nonindustrial regions, as we will see in Chapter 25, and then, in Chapter 26, in the very heartland of the industrial world.

CHAPTER REVIEW

 Download the MP3 audio file of the Chapter Review to listen to on the go.

What new technologies and industries appeared between 1850 and 1900, and how did they affect the world economy? (page 575)

After World War I broke out in 1914, many people, especially in Europe, looked back on the period from 1850 to 1914 as a golden age. For some, and in certain ways,

it was. Industrialization was a powerful torrent changing Europe, North America, and East Asia. While other technologies like shipping and railroads increased their global reach, new ones—electricity, the steel and chemical industries, and the global telegraph network—contributed to the enrichment and empowerment of the industrial nations. World trade increased tenfold during this period, and many countries' economies were transformed.

How did the societies of the industrial countries change during this period? How did industrialization contribute to socialist and labor movements? (page 579)

With these new technologies, memories of the great scourges—famines, wars, and epidemics—faded. Clean water, electric lights, and railways began to improve the lives of city dwellers, even the poor. Municipal services made city life less dangerous and chaotic. Goods from distant lands, even travel to other continents, came within the reach of millions. While middle-class women continued to focus on domestic pursuits and lived in a "separate sphere" from men, many working-class women took jobs in the textile industry. Yet their work outside the home did not lessen their domestic and child-rearing responsibilities.

Industrialization created a large class of factory and railroad workers. Karl Marx predicted a class struggle between workers and employers, but socialism became more of an intellectual movement. Through labor unions, workers achieved some measure of recognition and security. By the turn of the century, liberal political reforms had taken hold in western Europe and seemed about to triumph in Russia as well. Universal male suffrage became law in the United States in 1870 and in various parts of Europe by the 1880s. Morality and legislation aimed at providing security for women and families, though equality between the sexes was still beyond reach.

What was nationalism, and how did it contribute to the formation of new states? (page 586)

The framework for all these changes was the nation-state. Until the 1860s nationalism was associated with liberalism, but later generations of conservatives used public education, military service, and colonial conquests to build a sense of national unity. By 1871 both Italy and Germany had become unified states. In Japan, the Meiji Restoration gave power to reformers in the name of the emperor and ushered in a period of Western influences.

How did the forces of nationalism affect the major powers of Europe? (page 593)

The world economy, international politics, and even cultural and social issues revolved around a handful of countries—the great powers—that believed they controlled the destiny of the world. These included the most powerful European nations of the previous century, as well as three newcomers—Germany, the United States, and Japan—that were to play important roles in the future. Under the leadership of Bismarck, the German people developed a strong sense of national pride. Religious differences proved to be a hindrance to nationalism in France. Great Britain's problems were due to economic issues and Irish resentment of English rule.

How did Western pressures affect East Asia? (page 595)

China was weakened by the Taiping Rebellion, a reactionary government under Empress Dowager Cixi, and the demands of the West. Japan, in contrast, built up its military and industrial strength and became another imperial power, taking advantage of China's weakness to seize Korea, Taiwan, and southern Manchuria.

Key Terms

Commodore Matthew Perry (p. 575)

railroads (p. 575)

submarine telegraph cables (p. 576)

steel (p. 577)

electricity (p. 578)

Thomas Edison (p. 578)

Victorian Age (p. 580)

"separate spheres" (p. 581)

socialism (p. 583)

labor union (p. 583)

Karl Marx (p. 583)

anarchists (p. 586)

nationalism (p. 586)

liberalism (p. 587)

Giuseppe Garibaldi (p. 587)

Otto von Bismarck (p. 588)

Meiji Restoration (p. 589)

Charles Darwin (p. 592)

Empress Dowager Cixi (p. 595)

Yamagata Aritomo (p. 595)

Web Resources

Pronunciation Guide

Interactive Maps

- MAP 24.1 The Unification of Germany, 1866–1871
- MAP 24.2 Expansion and Modernization of Japan, 1868–1918

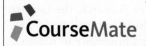 Visit the CourseMate website at www.cengagebrain.com for additional study tools and review materials for this chapter.

Primary Sources

- Extracts from History of Germany in the Nineteenth Century and Historical and Political Writings
- Letter to Mitsubishi Employees
- Two Proclamations of the Boxer Uprising

Answer to the History in Focus Question

See photo on page 591, "Silk Factory in Japan."

The New Imperialism

© Cengage Learning

 Visit the CourseMate website at **www.cengagebrain.com** for additional study tools and review materials for this chapter.

In 1869 Ismail (is-mah-EEL), the khedive (kuh-DEEV) (ruler) of Egypt, invited all the Christian princes of Europe and all the Muslim princes of Asia and Africa—except the Ottoman sultan, his nominal overlord—to celebrate the inauguration of the greatest construction project of the century: the **Suez Canal**. Among the sixteen hundred dignitaries from the Middle East and Europe who assembled at Port Said (port sah-EED) were Emperor Francis Joseph of Austria-Hungary and Empress Eugénie of France. A French journalist wrote:

> This multitude, coming from all parts of the world, presented the most varied and singular spectacle. All races were represented. . . . We saw, coming to attend this festival of civilization, men of the Orient wearing clothes of dazzling colors, chiefs of African tribes wrapped in their great coats, Circassians in war costumes, officers of the British army of India with their shakos [hats] wrapped in muslin, Hungarian magnates wearing their national costumes.[1]

Ismail used the occasion to emphasize the harmony and cooperation between the peoples of Africa, Asia, and Europe and to show that Egypt was independent and an equal of the great powers. To bless the inauguration, Ismail had invited clergy of the Muslim, Orthodox, and Catholic faiths. A reporter noted: "The Khedive . . . wished to symbolize thereby the unity of men and their brotherhood before God, without distinction of religion; it was the first time that the Orient had seen such a meeting of faiths to celebrate and bless together a great event and a great work."[2]

The canal was a great success, but not in the way Ismail intended. Ships using it could travel between Europe and India in less than two weeks—much less time than the month or longer consumed by sailing around Africa and across the Indian Ocean. By lowering freight costs, the canal stimulated shipping and the construction of steamships, giving an advantage to nations that had heavy industry and a large maritime trade over land-based empires and countries with few merchant ships. Great Britain, which long opposed construction of the canal for fear that it might fall into enemy hands, benefited more than any other nation. France, which provided half the capital and most of the engineers, came in a distant second, for it had less trade with Asia than Britain did. Egypt, which contributed the other half of the money and most of the labor, was the loser. Instead of making it powerful and independent, the Suez Canal provided the excuse for a British invasion and occupation of Egypt.

Far from inaugurating an era of harmony among the peoples of three continents and three faiths, the canal triggered a wave of European domination over Africa and Asia. Between 1869 and 1914 Germany, France, Britain, Russia, Japan, and the United States used industrial technology to impose their will on the nonindustrial parts of the world. Historians use the expression **New Imperialism** to describe this exercise of power.

The New Imperialism: Motives and Methods

What motivated the industrial nations to conquer new territories, and what means did they use?

The New Imperialism was characterized by an explosion of territorial conquests even more rapid than the Spanish conquests of the sixteenth century. Between 1869 and 1914, in a land grab of unprecedented speed, Europeans seized territories in Africa and Central Asia, and both Europeans and Americans took territories in Southeast Asia and the Pacific. Approximately 10 million square miles (26 million square

Suez Canal Ship canal dug across the Isthmus of Suez in Egypt, designed by Ferdinand de Lesseps. It opened to shipping in 1869 and shortened the sea voyage between Europe and Asia. Its strategic importance led to the British conquest of Egypt in 1882.

New Imperialism Historians' term for the late-nineteenth- and early-twentieth-century wave of conquests by European powers, the United States, and Japan, which were followed by the development and exploitation of the newly conquered territories for the benefit of the colonial powers.

Chronology

	The Scramble for Africa	Asia and Western Dominance	Imperialism in Latin America
		1862–1895 French conquer Indochina **1865–1876** Russian forces advance into Central Asia	
1870	**1869** Opening of the Suez Canal		**1870–1910** Railroad building boom; British companies in Argentina and Brazil
	1874 Warfare between the British and the Asante (Gold Coast) **1877–1879** Warfare between the British and the Xhosa and between the British and the Zulu (South Africa)		
		1878 United States obtains Pago Pago Harbor (Samoa)	
	1882 British forces occupy Egypt **1884–1885** Berlin Conference; Leopold II obtains Congo Free State	**1885** Britain completes conquest of Burma	
1890		**1887** United States obtains Pearl Harbor (Hawaii) **1894–1895** China defeated in Sino-Japanese War **1895** France completes conquest of Indochina	**1895–1898** Cubans revolt against Spanish rule
	1896 Ethiopians defeat Italian army at Adowa; warfare between the British and the Asante **1898** Battle of Omdurman	**1898** United States annexes Hawaii and purchases Philippines from Spain	**1898** Spanish-American War; United States annexes Puerto Rico and Guam
	1899–1902 South African War between Afrikaners and the British **1902** First Aswan Dam completed (Egypt)	**1899–1902** U.S. forces conquer and occupy Philippines	**1901** United States imposes Platt Amendment on Cuba
		1903 Russia completes Trans-Siberian Railway **1904–1905** Russia defeated in Russo Japanese War	**1903** United States backs secession of Panama from Colombia **1904–1907,1916** U.S. troops occupy Dominican Republic **1904–1914** United States builds Panama Canal
	1908 Belgium annexes Congo		**1912** U.S. troops occupy Nicaragua and Honduras

Opening the Suez Canal
When the canal opened in 1869, thousands of dignitaries and ordinary people gathered to watch the ships go by.

Bildarchiv Preussischer Kulturbesitz//Art Resource, NY

kilometers) and 150 million people fell under the rule of Europe and the United States in this period.

The New Imperialism was more than a land grab. The imperial powers used economic and technological means to reorganize dependent regions and bring them into the world economy as suppliers of foodstuffs and raw materials and as consumers of industrial products. In Africa and other parts of the world, this was done by conquest and colonial administration. In the Latin American republics the same result was achieved indirectly. Even though they remained politically independent, they became economic dependencies of the United States and Europe.

What inspired Europeans and Americans to venture overseas and impose their will on other societies? There is no simple answer to this question. Economic, cultural, and political motives were involved in all cases.

Political Motives

The great powers of the late nineteenth century, as well as less powerful countries like Italy, Portugal, and Belgium, were competitive and hypersensitive about their status. France, humiliated by its defeat by Prussia in 1871 (see Chapter 24), sought to reestablish its prestige through territorial acquisitions overseas. Great Britain, already in possession of the world's largest and richest empire,

felt the need to protect India, its "jewel in the crown," by acquiring colonies in East Africa and Southeast Asia. German chancellor Otto von Bismarck had little interest in acquiring colonies, but many Germans believed that a country as important as theirs deserved an overseas empire.

Political motives were not limited to statesmen in the capital cities. Colonial governors and political officers practiced their own diplomacy, often making a claim to a territory just to forestall some rival. Armies fighting frontier wars found it easier to defeat their neighbors than to make peace with them. In response to border skirmishes with neighboring states, colonial agents were likely to send in troops, take over their neighbors' territories, and then inform their home governments. Governments felt obligated to back up their men-on-the-spot in order not to lose face. The great powers of Europe acquired much of West Africa, Southeast Asia, and the Pacific islands in this manner.

Cultural Motives

The late nineteenth century saw a Christian revival in Europe and North America, as both Catholics and Protestants founded new missionary societies. Their purpose was not only religious—to convert nonbelievers, whom they regarded as "heathen"—but also cultural in a broader sense. They sought to export their own norms of "civilized" behavior: they were determined to abolish slavery in Africa and bring Western education, medicine, hygiene, monogamous marriage, and modest dress to all the world's peoples.

Many women joined missionary societies to become teachers and nurses, sometimes attaining positions of greater authority than they could hope to find at home. Their influence often helped soften the harshness of colonial rule—for example, by calling attention to issues of maternity and women's health. Mary Slessor, a British missionary who lived for forty years among the people of southeastern Nigeria, campaigned against slavery, human sacrifice, and the killing of twins and, generally, for women's rights. In India missionaries denounced the customs of child marriages and *sati* (the burning of widows on their husbands' funeral pyres). Such views often clashed with the customs of the people among whom they settled.

The sense of moral duty and cultural superiority was not limited to missionaries. Many Europeans and Americans equated technological innovations with "progress" and believed that Western technology proved the superiority of Western ideas, customs, and culture. While some concluded that non-Western peoples could achieve, through education, the same cultural level as Europeans and Americans, many others espoused racist ideas that relegated non-Europeans to a status of permanent inferiority. Racists assigned different stages of biological development to the world's various peoples based on physical appearance and ranked these races in a hierarchy that ranged from "civilized" at the highest level down through "semi-barbarous," "barbarian," and finally, at the bottom, "savage." Caucasians—whites—were always at the top of this ranking. Such ideas were often presented as an excuse for permanent rule over Africans and Asians.

Imperialism first interested small groups of explorers, clergy, and businessmen but soon attracted people from other walks of life. Young men, finding few opportunities for adventure and glory at home in an era of peace, sought them overseas as the Spanish conquistadors had done over three centuries earlier. At first, European people and parliaments were indifferent or hostile to overseas adventures, but a few easy victories in the 1880s helped to overcome their reluctance. The United States was fully preoccupied with its westward expansion until the 1880s,

but in the 1890s popular attention shifted to lands outside North America. Newspapers, which achieved wide readership in the second half of the nineteenth century, discovered that they could boost circulation with reports of wars and conquests. By the 1890s imperialism was a popular cause, the overseas extension of the nationalism propelling the power politics of the time.

Economic Motives

The industrialization of Europe and North America stimulated the demand for minerals—copper for electrical wiring, tin for canning, chrome and manganese for the steel industry, coal for steam engines, and, most of all, gold and diamonds. The demand for such industrial crops as cotton and rubber and for stimulants such as sugar, coffee, tea, and tobacco also grew. These products were found in the tropics, but never in sufficient quantities.

An economic depression lasting from the mid-1870s to the mid-1890s caused European merchants, manufacturers, and shippers to seek protection against foreign competition. They argued that their respective countries needed secure sources of tropical raw materials and protected markets for their industries. Declining business opportunities at home prompted entrepreneurs and investors to look for profits from mines, plantations, and railroads in Asia, Africa, and Latin America. Since these investments were often extremely risky, businessmen sought the backing of their governments, preferably with soldiers.

The sudden increase in the power that industrial peoples could wield over nonindustrial peoples and over the forces of nature underlay the new imperialism as much as did cultural and political factors. Indeed, technological advances explain both the motives and the outcome of the New Imperialism.

The Tools of the Imperialists

To succeed, empire builders needed the means to achieve their objectives at a reasonable cost. The Industrial Revolution (see Chapter 21) provided these means. In the early part of the nineteenth century technological innovations began to tip the balance of power in favor of Europe.

Dominant at sea since about 1500, the Europeans increased their naval power still more with the introduction of steamships. The first steamer reached India in 1825; regular mail service followed in the 1830s. The long voyage around Africa was at first too costly for cargo steamers, for coal had to be shipped from England. The building of the Suez Canal and the development of increasingly efficient engines solved this problem and led to a boom in shipping to the Indian Ocean and East Asia. Whenever fighting broke out, passenger liners were requisitioned as troopships. This advantage in mobility was enhanced by the development of a global network of submarine telegraph cables connecting Europe with North America in the 1860s, with Latin America and Asia in the 1870s, with Africa in the 1880s, and finally across the Pacific in 1904.

Until the middle of the nineteenth century, western Europeans were much weaker on land than at sea. Thereafter, Europeans used steam-powered gunboats with considerable success in China, Burma, Indochina, and the Congo Basin. Although gunboats opened the major river basins to European penetration, the invaders often found themselves hampered by other natural obstacles. *Falciparum* malaria, found only in Africa, was so deadly to Europeans that few explorers survived before the 1850s. In 1854 a British doctor discovered that the drug quinine, taken regularly during one's stay in Africa, could prevent the disease. This and a few sanitary precautions reduced the annual death rate among whites in West Africa from between 250 and 750 per 1,000 in the early nineteenth century to between 50 and 100 per 1,000 after 1850. This reduction was sufficient to open the continent to merchants, officials, and missionaries.

Muzzle-loading smoothbore muskets had been used in Europe, Asia, and the Americas since the late seventeenth century, and by the early nineteenth century they were also common in much of Africa. The development of new and much deadlier firearms in the 1860s and 1870s shifted the balance of power on land between Westerners and other peoples. One of these was the breechloading rifle: ten times faster to load and five or six times longer in range than a musket. By the 1870s all European and American armies had switched to these new rifles. The 1880s saw two more innovations: smokeless powder, which did not foul the gun or reveal the soldier's position, and repeating rifles, which could shoot fifteen rounds

in fifteen seconds. Machine guns, which could fire eleven bullets per second, appeared a decade later.

In the course of the century Asians and Africans also acquired better firearms, mostly old weapons that European armies had discarded. As European firearms improved, however, the firepower gap widened, making colonial conquests easier than ever. By the 1880s and 1890s European-led forces of a few hundred could defeat non-European armies of thousands. Against the latest weapons, African and Asian soldiers armed with muskets or, in some cases, with spears did not stand a chance, no matter how numerous and courageous they were.

At the **Battle of Omdurman** in Sudan, on September 2, 1898, forty thousand Sudanese attacked an Anglo-Egyptian expedition that had come up the Nile on six steamers and four other boats. General Horatio Kitchener's troops had twenty machine guns and four artillery pieces; the Sudanese were equipped with muskets and spears. Within a few hours eleven thousand Sudanese and forty-eight British lay dead. Winston Churchill, the future British prime minister, witnessed the battle and called it

> the most signal triumph ever gained by the arms of science over barbarians. Within the space of five hours the strongest and best-armed savage army yet arrayed against a modern European Power had been destroyed and dispersed, with hardly any difficulty, comparatively small risk, and insignificant loss to the victors.[3]

Colonial Agents and Administration

Once colonial agents took over a territory, their home government expected them to cover their own costs and, if possible, return some profit to the home country. The system of administering and exploiting territories for the benefit of the home country is known as **colonialism**. In some places, such as along the West African coast or in

---

Battle of Omdurman British victory over the Mahdi in the Sudan in 1898. General Kitchener led a mixed force of British and Egyptian troops armed with rapid-firing rifles and machine guns.

colonialism Policy by which a nation administers a foreign territory and develops its resources for the benefit of the colonial power.

The Art Archive

The Battle of Omdurman In the late nineteenth century, most battles between European (or European-led) troops and African forces were one-sided encounters because of the disparity in the opponents' firearms and tactics. The Battle of Omdurman in Sudan in 1898 is a dramatic example. The forces of the Mahdi, some on horseback, were armed with spears and single-shot muskets. The British troops and their Egyptian allies, lined up in the foreground, used repeating rifles and machine guns able to shoot much farther than the Sudanese weapons. As a result, there were many Sudanese casualties but very few British or Egyptian casualties.

 History in Focus *Review the opening section, "The New Imperialism: Motives and Methods," paying special attention to Winston Churchill's words quoted at the end of the section. Now examine the image "The Battle of Omdurman." Does the painting illustrate Churchill's pronouncement? Does it depict the battle from a European point of view? Why or why not? If so, how do you think the depiction would be different if an African Mahdi sympathizer had painted it? Find the answer online.*

Indochina, there was already a considerable trade that could be taxed. In other places profits could come only from investments and by reorganizing the indigenous societies. In applying modern scientific and industrial methods to their colonies, colonialists started the transformation of Asian and African societies and landscapes that has continued to our day.

Legal experts and academics emphasized the differences between various systems of colonial government and debated whether colonies eventually should be assimilated into the ruling nation, associated in a federation, or allowed to rule themselves. Colonies that were protectorates retained their traditional governments, even their monarchs, but had a European "resident" or "consul-general" to "advise" them. Other

colonies were directly administered by a European governor. In fact, the impact of colonial rule depended much more on economic and social conditions than on narrow legal distinctions.

One important factor was the presence or absence of European settlers. In Canada, Australia, and New Zealand, whites were already in the majority by 1869, and their colonial "mother-country," Britain, encouraged them to elect parliaments and rule themselves. Where European settlers were numerous but still a minority of the population, as in Algeria and South Africa, settlers and the home country contested for control over the indigenous population. In colonies with few white settlers, the European governors ruled autocratically.

SECTION REVIEW

- The political motives of the New Imperialism included European nationalism and the initiatives of colonial officials.

- Cultural motives included a Christian revival in the West, a sense of superiority born of technological advancement, and adventurism among young men.

- The economic motives were the demands of industrialization, the effects of a long depression, and a general sense of power bred by industrial might.

- Imperialists made good use of sea power, new drugs and sanitary methods, and advanced military technology.

- Colonies were expected to pay their own expenses and were administered in a variety of ways, depending on the number of European settlers.

In the early years of the New Imperialism, colonial administrations consisted of a governor and his staff, a few troops to keep order, and a small number of tax collectors and magistrates. The cooperation of indigenous elites was essential to the maintenance of order. In most cases the colonial governors exercised power through traditional rulers willing to cooperate. Areas governed indirectly in this fashion were called "princely states." In addition, colonial governments educated a few local youths for "modern" jobs as clerks, policemen, customs inspectors, and the like.

These individuals came in time to rival the traditional rulers.

Western women seldom took part in the early stages of colonial expansion. Once peace was achieved and steamships and railroads made travel less difficult, however, colonial officials and settlers began bringing their wives to the colonies. By the 1880s the British Women's Emigration Association was recruiting single women to go out to the colonies to marry British settlers. As one of its founders, Ellen Joyce, explained, "The possibility of the settler marrying his own countrywoman is of imperial as well as family importance."[4]

The arrival of white women in Asia and Africa increased racial segregation. Sylvia Leith-Ross, wife of a colonial officer in Nigeria, explained: "When you are alone, among thousands of unknown, unpredictable people, dazed by unaccustomed sights and sounds, bemused by strange ways of life and thought, you need to remember who you are, where you come from, what your standards are."[5] Many colonial wives found themselves in command of numerous servants and expected to follow the complex etiquette of colonial entertainment in support of their husbands' official positions. Occasionally they found opportunities to exercise personal initiatives, usually charitable work involving indigenous women and children. However well meaning, their efforts were always subordinate to the work of men.

A Colonial Lady In many tropical colonies in the nineteenth century, there were few good roads, but labor was abundant. European colonial officials and their wives often traveled in a tonjon, or sedan chair carried by porters. This image of a lady in India dates from 1828.

A Tonjon, or Ladies Carriage.

Eileen Tweedy/The Art Archive

The Scramble for Africa

Why were imperialists interested in conquering Africa, and how did their presence on that continent change the environment?

Until the 1870s African history was largely shaped by internal forces and local initiatives (see Chapter 23). Outside of Algeria and southern Africa, only a handful of Europeans had ever visited the interior of Africa, and European countries possessed only small enclaves on the coasts. As late as 1879 Africans ruled more than 90 percent of the continent. Then, within a decade, Africa was invaded and divided among the European powers in a movement often referred to as the **"scramble" for Africa** (see Map 25.1). This invasion affected all regions of the continent.

Egypt

Ironically, European involvement in Egypt resulted from Egypt's attempt to free itself from Ottoman Turkish rule. The khedives of Egypt, hereditary governors descended from Muhammad Ali (see Chapter 22), used profits from exporting cotton during the American Civil War to modernize their armed forces and build canals, harbors, railroads, and other public works. Their support for the Suez Canal project was part of this policy. Khedive Ismail even tried to make Egypt the center of an empire reaching south into Sudan and Ethiopia.

Once cotton prices returned to normal after 1865, the khedives supported their ambitions by borrowing from European creditors at high interest rates. By 1876 Egypt's foreign debt had risen to £100 million sterling. Interest payments alone consumed one-third of its foreign export earnings. To avoid bankruptcy the Egyptian government sold its shares in the Suez Canal to Great Britain and accepted four foreign "commissioners of the debt" to oversee its finances. French and British bankers, still not satisfied, lobbied their governments to secure the loans

by stronger measures. In 1878 the two governments obliged Ismail to appoint a Frenchman as minister of public works and a Briton as minister of finance. When high taxes caused hardship and popular discontent, the French and British persuaded the Ottoman sultan to depose Ismail. This foreign intervention provoked a military uprising under Egyptian army colonel Arabi Pasha, which threatened the Suez Canal.

Fearing for their investments, the British sent an army into Egypt in 1882. They intended to occupy Egypt for only a year or two. But because theirs was a seaborne empire that depended on secure communications between Britain and India, the Suez Canal was so important to their maritime supremacy that they stayed for seventy years. During those years the British ruled Egypt "indirectly"—that is, they maintained the Egyptian government and the fiction of Egyptian sovereignty but retained real power in their own hands.

Eager to develop Egyptian agriculture, especially cotton production, the British brought in engineers and contractors to build the first dam across the Nile, at Aswan in upper Egypt. When completed in 1902, it was one of the largest dams in the world. It captured the annual Nile flood and released its waters throughout the year, allowing farmers to grow two, sometimes three, crops a year. This doubled the effective acreage compared with the basin system of irrigation practiced since the time of the pharaohs, in which the annual floodwaters of the Nile were retained by low dikes around the fields.

The economic development of Egypt by the British enriched a small elite of landowners and merchants, many of them foreigners. Egyptian peasants got little relief from the heavy taxes collected to pay for their country's crushing foreign debt and the expenses of the British army of occupation. Western ways that conflicted with the teachings of Islam—such as the drinking of alcohol and the relative

 Primary Source: Convention on Free Navigation of the Suez Canal Between the European Powers and the Ottoman Empire, October 29, 1888 Learn about the ways in which nations work together to ensure free travel along a key waterway.

"scramble" for Africa Sudden wave of conquests in Africa by European powers in the 1880s and 1890s. Britain obtained most of eastern Africa, France most of northwestern Africa. Other countries (Germany, Belgium, Portugal, Italy, and Spain) acquired lesser amounts.

Map 25.1 Africa in 1878 and 1914 In 1878 the European colonial presence was limited to a few coastal enclaves, plus portions of Algeria and South Africa. By 1914, Europeans had taken over all of Africa except Ethiopia and Liberia. © Cengage Learning

 Interactive Map

freedom of women—offended Muslim religious leaders. Most Egyptians found British rule more onerous than that of the Ottomans. By the 1890s Egyptian politicians and intellectuals were demanding that the British leave, to no avail.

Western and Equatorial Africa

While the British were taking over Egypt, the French were planning to extend their empire into the interior of West Africa. Starting from the coast of Senegal, which had been in French hands

A Steamboat for the Congo River Soon after the Congo Basin was occupied by Europeans, the new colonial rulers realized they needed to improve transportation. Since access from the sea was blocked by rapids on the lower Congo River, steamboats had to be brought in sections, hauled from the coast by thousands of Congolese over very difficult terrain. This picture shows the pieces arriving at Stanley Pool, ready to be reassembled.

for centuries, they hoped to build a railroad from the upper Senegal River to the upper Niger to open the interior to French merchants. This in turn led the French military to undertake the conquest of western Sudan.

Meanwhile, the actions of three individuals, rather than a government, brought about the occupation of the Congo Basin, an enormous forested region in the heart of equatorial Africa (see Map 25.1). In 1879 the American journalist **Henry Morton Stanley**, who had explored the area, persuaded King **Leopold II** of Belgium to invest his personal fortune in "opening up" equatorial Africa. With Leopold's money, Stanley returned to Africa from 1879 to 1884 to establish trading posts along the southern bank of the Congo River. At the same time, **Savorgnan de Brazza**, an Italian officer serving in the French army, obtained from an African ruler living on the opposite bank a treaty that placed the area under the "protection" of France.

These events sparked a flurry of diplomatic activity. German chancellor Bismarck called the **Berlin Conference** on Africa of 1884 and 1885. There the major powers agreed that henceforth "effective occupation" would replace the former trading relations between Africans and Europeans. This meant that every country with colonial ambitions had to send

troops into Africa and participate in the division of the spoils. As a reward for triggering the "scramble" for Africa, Leopold II acquired a personal domain under the name "Congo Free State," while France and Portugal took most of the rest of equatorial Africa. In this manner, the European powers and King Leopold managed to divide Africa among themselves, at least on paper.

"Effective occupation" required many years of effort. In the interior of West Africa, Muslim rulers resisted the French invasion for up to thirty years. The French advance encouraged the Germans to stake claims to parts of the region and the British to move

Henry Morton Stanley (1841–1904) British-American explorer of Africa, famous for his expeditions in search of Dr. David Livingstone. Stanley helped King Leopold II establish the Congo Free State.

Leopold II (1835–1909) King of Belgium (r. 1865–1909). He was active in encouraging the exploration of Central Africa and became the ruler of the Congo Free State (to 1908).

Savorgnan de Brazza (1852–1905) Franco-Italian explorer sent by the French government to claim part of equatorial Africa for France. Founded Brazzaville, capital of the French Congo, in 1880.

Berlin Conference (1884–1885) Conference that German chancellor Otto von Bismarck called to set rules for the partition of Africa. It led to the creation of the Congo Free State under King Leopold II of Belgium.

north from their coastal enclaves, until the entire region was occupied by Britain, France, and Germany.

Because West Africa had long had a flourishing trade, the new rulers took advantage of existing trade networks, taxing merchants and farmers, investing the profits in railroads and harbors, and paying dividends to European stockholders. In the Gold Coast (now Ghana) British trading companies bought the cocoa grown by African farmers at low prices and resold it for large profits. The interior of French West Africa lagged behind. Although the region could produce cotton, peanuts, and other crops, the difficulties of transportation limited its development before 1914.

Compared to West Africa, equatorial Africa had few inhabitants and little trade. Rather than try to govern these vast territories directly, authorities in the Congo Free State, the French Congo, and the Portuguese colonies of Angola and Mozambique granted huge pieces of land as concessions to private companies that thereby gained monopolies on natural resources and trade and the right to employ soldiers and impose taxes.

Freed from outside supervision, the companies forced the African inhabitants at gunpoint to produce cash crops and carry them, on their heads or backs, to the nearest railroad or navigable river. The worst abuses took place in the Congo Free State, where a rubber boom lasting from 1895 to 1905 made it profitable for private companies to coerce Africans to collect latex from vines that grew in the forests. One Congolese refugee told the British consul Roger Casement who investigated the atrocities:

> We begged the white men to leave us alone, saying we could get no more rubber, but the white men and their soldiers said: "Go. You are only beasts yourselves, you are only *nyama* (meat)." We tried, always going further into the forest, and when we failed and our rubber was short, the soldiers came to our towns and killed us. Many were shot, some had their ears cut off; others were tied up with ropes around their necks and bodies and taken away.[6]

After 1906 the British press began publicizing the horrors. The public outcry that followed, coinciding with the end of the rubber boom, convinced the Belgian government to take over Leopold's private empire in 1908.

Southern Africa

The history of white settlers in southern Africa between 1869 and 1914 differs from that of the rest of the continent. **Afrikaners**, descendants of Dutch settlers on the Cape of Good Hope, moved inland throughout the nineteenth century; British prospectors and settlers arrived later in the century; and, finally, Indians were brought over by the British and stayed.

Southern Africa attracted European settlers because of its good pastures and farmland and its phenomenal deposits of diamonds, gold, and copper, as well as coal and iron ore. This was the new El Dorado that imperialists had dreamed of since the heyday of the Spanish Empire in Peru and Mexico in the sixteenth century. The discovery of diamonds at Kimberley in 1868 lured thousands of European prospectors as well as Africans looking for work. It also attracted the interest of Great Britain, colonial ruler of the Cape Colony, which annexed the diamond area in 1871, thereby angering the Afrikaners. Once in the interior, the British defeated the Xhosa (KOH-sah) people in 1877 and 1878. Then in 1879 they confronted the Zulu, militarily the most powerful of the African peoples in the region.

The Zulu, led by their king Cetshwayo (set-SHWAH-yo), resented their encirclement by Afrikaners and British. A growing sense of nationalism and their proud military tradition led them into a war with the British in 1879. At first they held their own, defeating the British at Isandhlwana (ee-sawn-dull-WAH-nuh), but a few months later they were defeated. Cetshwayo was captured and sent into exile, and the Zulu lands were given to white ranchers. Yet throughout those bitter times, the Zulu's sense of nationhood remained strong.

Relations between the British and the Afrikaners, already tense as a result of British encroachment, took a turn for the worse when gold was discovered in the Afrikaner republic of Transvaal (trans-VAHL) in

Afrikaners South Africans descended from Dutch and French settlers of the seventeenth century. Their Great Trek founded new settler colonies in the nineteenth century. Though a minority among South Africans, they held political power after 1910, imposing a system of racial segregation called apartheid after 1949.

1886. In the gold rush that ensued, the British soon outnumbered the Afrikaners.

Britain's invasion of southern Africa was driven in part by the ambition of **Cecil Rhodes** (1853–1902), who once declared that he would "annex the stars" if he could. Rhodes made his fortune in the Kimberley diamond fields, founding De Beers Consolidated, a company that has dominated the world's diamond trade ever since. He then turned to politics. He encouraged a concession company, the British South Africa Company, to push north into Central Africa, where he named two new colonies after himself: Southern Rhodesia (now Zimbabwe) and Northern Rhodesia (now Zambia). The Ndebele (en-duh-BELL-ay) and Shona peoples, who inhabited the region, resisted this invasion, but the machine guns of the British finally defeated them.

British attempts to annex the two Afrikaner republics, Transvaal and Orange Free State, and the inflow of English-speaking whites into the gold- and diamond-mining areas led to the South African War (also called the Boer War), which lasted from 1899 to 1902. At first the Afrikaners had the upper hand, for they were highly motivated, possessed modern rifles, and knew the land. In 1901, however, Great Britain brought in 450,000 troops and crushed the Afrikaner armies. Ironically, the Afrikaners' defeat in 1902 led to their ultimate victory. Wary of costly commitments overseas, the British government expected European settlers in Africa to manage their own affairs, as they were doing in Canada, Australia, and New Zealand. Thus, in 1910 the European settlers created the Union of South Africa, in which the Afrikaners eventually emerged as the ruling element.

Unlike Canada, Australia, and New Zealand, South Africa had a majority of indigenous inhabitants and substantial numbers of Indians and "Cape Coloureds" (people of mixed ancestry). Yet the Europeans were both numerous enough to demand self-rule and powerful enough to deny the vote and other civil rights to the majority. In 1913 the South African parliament passed the Natives Land Act, assigning Africans to reservations and forbidding them to own land elsewhere. This and other racial policies turned South Africa into a land of segregation, oppression, and bitter divisions.

Political and Social Consequences

Africa was home to a wide variety of indigenous societies, some of them long-established kingdoms with aristocracies or commercial towns dominated by a merchant class, others centered on agricultural villages without any outside government, and still others consisting of pastoral nomads organized along military lines. Not surprisingly, these societies responded in very different ways to the European invasion (see Diversity and Dominance: Two Africans Recall the Arrival of the Europeans).

Some peoples welcomed the invaders as allies against local enemies. Once colonial rule was established, they sought work in government service or in European firms and sent their children to mission schools. In exchange, they were often the first to receive benefits such as clinics and roads. Others, especially peoples with a pastoral or a warrior tradition, fought tenaciously. Examples abound, from the Zulu and Ndebele of southern Africa to the pastoral Herero (hair-AIR-oh) people of Southwest Africa (now Namibia), who rose up against German invaders in 1904; in repressing their uprising, the Germans

Primary Source: His Story Examine a first-person account of the arrival of the "white men" in southern Africa.

Primary Source: Memorandum to Lord Selborne, High Commissioner of Transvaal, October 1905 See how a British Indian in Potchefstroom attempts to speak up for himself and his fellow tradespeople before the British High Commissioner of Transvaal.

Cecil Rhodes (1853–1902) British entrepreneur and politician involved in the expansion of the British Empire from South Africa into Central Africa. The colonies of Southern Rhodesia (now Zimbabwe) and Northern Rhodesia (now Zambia) were named after him.

Diversity & Dominance

Two Africans Recall the Arrival of the Europeans

We know a great deal about the arrival of the Europeans into the interior of Africa from the perspective of the conquerors, but very little about how the events were experienced by Africans. Here are two accounts by African women, one from northern Nigeria whose land was occupied by the British, the other from the Congo Free State, a colony of King Leopold II of Belgium. They show not only how Africans experienced European colonial dominance, but also the great diversity of their experiences.

Baba of Karo, a Nigerian Woman, Remembers Her Childhood

When I was a maiden the Europeans first arrived. Ever since we were quite small the malams had been saying that the Europeans would come with a thing called a train, they would come with a thing called a motorcar, in them you would go and come back in a trice. They would stop wars, they would repair the world, they would stop oppression and lawlessness, we should live at peace with them. We used to go and sit quietly and listen to the prophecies.

I remember when a European came to Karo on a horse, and some of his foot soldiers went into the town. Everyone came out to look at them, but in Zerewa they didn't see the European. Everyone at Karo ran away—"There's a European, there's a European!"

At that time Yusufu was the king of Kano. He did not like the Europeans, he did not wish them, he would not sign their treaty. Then he say that perforce he would have to agree, so he did. We Habe wanted them to come, it was the Fulani who did not like it. When the Europeans came the Habe saw that if you worked for them they paid you for it, they didn't say, like the Fulani, "Commoner, give me this! Commoner, bring me that!" Yes, the Habe wanted them; they saw no harm in them.

The Europeans said that there were to be no more slaves; if someone said "Slave!" you could complain to the alkali who would punish the master who said it, the judge said, "That is what the Europeans have decreed."

The first order said that any slave, if he was younger than you, was your younger brother, if he was older than you was your elder brother—they were all brothers of their master's family. No one used the word "slave" any more. When slavery was stopped, nothing much happened at our rinji except that some slaves whom we had bought in the market ran away. Our own father went to his farm and worked, he and his son took up their large hoes; they loaned out their spare farms. Tsoho our father and Kadiri my brother with whom I live now and Babambo worked, they farmed guineacorn and millet and groundnuts and everything; before this they had supervised the slaves' work—now they did their own.

In the old days if the chief liked the look of your daughter he would take her and put her in his house; you could do nothing about it. Now they don't do that.

Ilanga, a Congolese Woman, Recounts Her Capture by Agents of the Congo Free State

. . . we were all busy in the fields hoeing our plantations, for it was the rainy season, and the weeds sprang quickly up, when a runner came to the village saying that a large band of men was coming, that they all wore red caps and blue cloth, and carried guns and long knives, and that many white men were with them, the chief of whom was Kibalanga (Michaux). Niendo at once called all the chief men to his house, while the drums were beaten to summon the people to the village. A long consultation was held, and finally we were all told to go quietly to the fields and bring in ground-nuts, plantains, and cassava for the warriors who were coming, and goats and fowl for the white men. The women all went with baskets and filled them, and put them in the road, which was blocked up, so many were there. Niendo then commanded everyone to go and sit quietly in the houses until he gave other orders. This we did, everyone remaining quietly seated while Niendo went up the road with the head men to meet the white chief. We did not know what to think, for most of us feared that so many armed men coming boded evil; but Niendo thought that, by giving presents of much food, he would induce the strangers to pass on without harming us. And so it proved, for the soldiers took the baskets, and were then ordered by the white men to move off through the village. Many of the soldiers looked into the houses and shouted at us words we did not understand. We were glad when they were all gone, for we were much in fear of the white men and the strange warriors, who are known to all the people as being great fighters, bringing war wherever they go. . . .

When the white men and their warriors had gone, we went again to our work, and were hoping that they would not return; but this they did in a very short time. As before, we brought in great heaps of food; but this time Kibalanga did not move away directly, but camped near our village, and his soldiers came and stole all our fowl and goats and tore up our cassava; but we did not mind as long as they did not harm us. The next morning it was reported that the white men were going away; but soon after the sun rose over the hill, a large band of soldiers came into the village, and we all went into the houses and sat down. We were not long seated when the soldiers came rushing in shouting, and threatening Niendo with their guns. They rushed into the houses and dragged the people out. Three or four came to our house and caught hold of me, also my husband Oleka and my sister Katinga. We were dragged into the road, and were tied together with cords about our necks, so that we could not escape. We were all crying, for now we knew that we were to be taken away to be slaves. The soldiers beat us with the iron sticks from their guns, and compelled us to march to the camp of Kibalanga, who ordered the women to be tied up separately, ten to each cord, and the men in the same way. When we were all collected—and there were many from other villages whom we now saw, and many from Waniendo—the soldiers brought baskets of food for us to carry, in some of which was smoked human flesh (niama na nitu).

We then set off marching very quickly. My sister Katinga had her baby in her arms, and was not compelled to carry a basket; but my husband Oleka was made to carry a goat. We marched until the afternoon, when we camped near a stream, where we were glad to drink, for we were much athirst. We had nothing to eat, for

the soldiers would give us nothing, so we lay upon the ground, and at night went to sleep. The next day we continued the march, and when we camped at noon were given some maize and plantains, which were gathered near a village from which the people had run away. So it continued each day until the fifth day, when the soldiers took my sister's baby and threw it in the grass, leaving it to die, and made her carry some cooking pots which they found in the deserted village. On the sixth day we became very weak from lack of food and from constant marching and sleeping in the damp grass, and my husband, who marched behind us with the goat, could not stand up longer, and so he sat down beside the path and refused to walk more. The soldiers beat him, but still he refused to move. Then one of them struck him on the head with the end of his gun, and he fell upon the ground. One of the soldiers caught the goat, while two or three others stuck the long knives they put on the ends of their guns into my husband. I saw the blood spurt out, and then saw him no more, for we passed over the brow of a hill and he was out of sight. Many of the young men were killed the same way, and many babies thrown into the grass to die. A few escaped; but we were so well guarded that it was almost impossible.

QUESTIONS FOR ANALYSIS

1. How do Baba and Ilanga recall their existence before the Europeans came?
2. What did they expect when they first heard of the arrival of Europeans? Instead, what happened to them, their relatives, and their towns?
3. How do you explain the difference between these two accounts?

Source: First selection: From M. F. Smith, ed., *Baba of Karo: A Woman of the Muslim Hausa* (New York: Philosophical Library, 1955), 66–68. Reprinted by permission of the Philosophical Library. Second selection: From Edgar Canisius, *A Campaign Amongst Cannibals* (London: R. A. Everett & Co., 1903), 250–256. Used by permission of the Philosophical Library.

exterminated two-thirds of them. In the Sahel, a belt of grasslands south of the Sahara, charismatic leaders rose up in the name of a purified Islam, gathered a following of warriors, and led them on partly religious, partly empire-building campaigns called *jihads*. These leaders included Samori Toure in

western Sudan (now Mali), Rabih in the Chad basin, and the Mahdi (MAH-dee) in eastern Sudan. All of them eventually came into conflict with European-led military expeditions and were defeated.

Some commercial states with long histories of contact with Europeans also fought back. The kingdom of **Asante** (uh-SAWN-tay) in Gold Coast rose up in 1874, 1896, and 1900 before it was finally overwhelmed. In the Niger Delta, the ancient city of Benin, rich with artistic treasures, resisted colonial control until 1897, when a British "punitive expedition" set it on fire and carted its works of art off to Europe.

One resistance movement succeeded, to the astonishment of Europeans and Africans alike. When **Menelik II** became emperor of Ethiopia in 1889 (see Chapter 23), his country was threatened by Sudanese Muslims to the west and by France and Italy, which controlled the Red Sea coast to the east. For many years, Ethiopia had been purchasing weapons, and by the Treaty of Wichelle (1889), it secured more weapons from Italy. Six years later, when Italians attempted to establish a protectorate over Ethiopia, they found the Ethiopians armed with thousands of rifles and even a few machine guns and artillery pieces. Although Italy sent twenty thousand troops to attack Ethiopia, in 1896 they were defeated at Adowa (AH-do-ah) by a larger and better-trained Ethiopian army.

Most Africans neither joined nor fought the European invaders but tried to continue living as before. They found this increasingly difficult because colonial rule disrupted every traditional society. The presence of colonial officials meant that rights to land, commercial transactions, and legal disputes were handled very differently and that traditional rulers lost all authority, except where Europeans used them as local administrators.

Changes in landholding were especially disruptive, for most Africans were farmers or herders for whom access to land was a necessity. In areas with a high population density, such as Egypt and West Africa, colonial rulers left peasants in place, encouraged them to grow cash crops, and collected taxes on the harvest. Elsewhere, the new rulers declared any land that was not farmed to be "waste" or "vacant" and gave it to private companies or to European planters and ranchers. In Kenya, Northern Rhodesia, and South Africa, Europeans found the land and climate to their liking, in contrast to other parts of Africa, where soldiers, officials, missionaries, or traders stayed only a few years. White settlers forced Africans to become squatters, sharecroppers, or ranch hands on land they had farmed for generations. In South

Africa they forced many Africans off their lands and onto "reserves," much like the nomadic peoples of North America, Russia, and Australia.

The colonial rulers were even more interested in African labor than in the land. To get workers to take low-paid jobs on plantations, railroads, or other European enterprises, they imposed various taxes, such as the hut tax and the head tax. To pay the tax, Africans had little choice but to accept whatever work the Europeans offered. In the South African mines Africans were paid, on average, one-tenth as much as Europeans.

Some Africans migrated great distances to the cities and mining camps in search of a better life. Most migrant workers were men who left their wives and children behind in villages and on reserves, sometimes for years. Only occasionally did the authorities allow them to bring their families and settle permanently. This caused great hardship for African women, who had to grow food for their families during the men's absences and care for sick and aged workers. Long separations between spouses also led to prostitution and the spread of sexually transmitted diseases.

Some African women welcomed colonial rule, for it brought an end to fighting and slave raiding, but others were led into captivity. A few succeeded in becoming wealthy traders or owners of livestock. On the whole, however, African women benefited even less than men from the economic changes that colonialism introduced. Whenever colonial rulers replaced communal property (traditional in most of Africa) with private property, property rights were assigned to the head of the household—that is, to the man. Almost all the jobs open to Africans, even those considered "women's work" in Europe, such as nursing and domestic service, were reserved for men.

Asante African kingdom on the Gold Coast that expanded rapidly after 1680. Asante participated in the Atlantic economy, trading gold, slaves, and ivory. It resisted British imperial ambitions for a quarter century before being absorbed into Britain's Gold Coast colony in 1902.

Menelik II (1844–1911) Emperor of Ethiopia (r. 1889–1911). He enlarged Ethiopia to its present dimensions and defeated an Italian invasion at Adowa (1896).

Cultural Responses

Africans came into contact with missionaries more than with any other Europeans. Mission schools taught reading, writing, and arithmetic to village children. Boys learned crafts like carpentry and blacksmithing, while girls were taught domestic skills.

The first generation of Africans educated in mission schools also acquired Western ideas of justice and progress. Samuel Ajayi Crowther, a Yoruba rescued from slavery as a boy and educated in mission schools in Sierra Leone, went on to become an Anglican minister and, in 1864, the first African bishop. Crowther thought that Africa needed European assistance in achieving both spiritual and economic development:

> Africa has neither knowledge nor skill ... to bring out her vast resources for her own improvement.... Therefore to claim Africa for the Africans alone, is to claim for her the right of a continued ignorance.... For it is certain, unless help [comes] from without, a nation can never rise above its present state.[7]

After the first generation, many mission teachers were themselves African, the products of a mission education. They discovered that Christian ideals clashed with the reality of colonial exploitation. One convert wrote in 1911:

> There is too much failure among all Europeans in Nyasaland. The three combined bodies— Missionaries, Government and Companies or gainers of money—do form the same rule to look upon the native with mockery eyes.... If we had enough power to communicate ourselves to Europe, we would advise them not to call themselves Christendom, but Europeandom. Therefore the life of the three combined bodies is altogether too cheaty, too thefty, too mockery. Instead of "Give," they say "Take away from." There is too much breakage of God's pure law.[8]

Missionaries were not the only ones to bring religious change to Africa. In southern and Central Africa indigenous preachers adapted Christianity to African values and customs and founded new denominations known as "Ethiopian" churches.

Christianity proved successful in converting followers of traditional religions but made no inroads among Muslims. Instead, Islam, long predominant in northern and eastern Africa, spread southward as Muslim teachers established Quranic schools and

founded Muslim brotherhoods. European colonialism unwittingly helped the diffusion of Islam. By building cities and increasing trade, colonial rule permitted Muslims to settle in new areas. As Islam—a universal religion untainted by colonialism—became increasingly relevant to Africans, the number of Muslims in sub-Saharan Africa probably doubled between 1869 and 1914.

Imperialism in Asia and the Pacific

What were the social and cultural effects of imperialism in Asia?

From 1869 to 1914 the pressure of the industrial powers was felt throughout Asia, the East Indies, and the Pacific islands (see Map 25.2). As trade with these regions grew in the late nineteenth century, so did their attractiveness to imperialists eager for economic benefits and national prestige. By 1869 Britain already controlled most of India and Burma; Spain occupied the Philippines; and the Netherlands held large parts of the East Indies (now Indonesia). Between 1862 and 1895 France conquered Indochina (now Vietnam, Kampuchea, and Laos).

Map 25.2 Asia in 1914 By 1914, much of Asia was claimed by colonial powers. The southern rim, from the Pacific Gulf to the Pacific, was occupied by Great Britain, France, the Netherlands, and the United States. Central Asia had been incorporated into the Russian Empire. Japan, now industrialized, had joined the Western imperialist powers in expanding its territory and influence at the expense of China. © Cengage Learning

Interactive Map

Central Asia

Farther north, Russia continued its colonial expansion, aided by the acquisition of modern rifles and artillery. Between 1865 and 1876 Russian forces advanced into Central Asia. Nomads like the Kazakhs, who lived east of the Caspian Sea, resisted; but soon Kazakhstan became home to 200,000 Russian settlers. Although the governments of Tsar Alexander II (r. 1855–1881) and Tsar Alexander III (r. 1881–1894) claimed not to interfere in indigenous customs, they declared communally owned grazing lands "waste" or "vacant" and turned them over to farmers from Russia. By the end of the century the nomads were fenced out and reduced to starvation. An eminent Russian jurist declared: "International rights cannot be taken into account when dealing with semibarbarous peoples."

South of the Kazakh steppe the fabled cities of Tashkent, Bukhara, and Samarkand served the caravan trade between China and the Middle East. By the 1860s and 1870s the Qing Empire was losing control over Central Asia, so it was fairly easy for Russian expeditions to conquer the indigenous peoples. Russia thereby acquired land suitable for cotton, along with a large Muslim population.

The Russians abolished slavery, built railroads to link the region with Europe, and planted hundreds of thousands of acres of cotton. Unlike the British in India, however, they did not attempt to change the customs, languages, or religious beliefs of their subjects.

Southeast Asia and Indonesia

Until the mid-nineteenth century, independent kingdoms ruled most of the Southeast Asian peninsula and the Indonesian archipelago. As in Africa, colonialism varied considerably from region to region. Burma (now Myanmar), nearest India, was gradually taken over by the British, the last piece being annexed in 1885. Indochina fell under French control bit by bit until it was finally subdued in 1895. Similarly, Malaya (now Malaysia) came under British rule in stages during the 1870s and 1880s. By the early 1900s the Dutch had subdued northern Sumatra, the last part of the Dutch East Indies to be conquered. Only Siam (now Thailand) remained independent, although it lost several border provinces.

Despite their varied political histories, all these regions had features in common: fertile soil, constant warmth, and heavy rains along with a long tradition of intensive gardening, irrigation, and terracing. Where the population was sparse, Europeans imported landless laborers from China and India. The climate favored the transfer of commercially valuable plants from other parts of the world. Tobacco, cinchona (sin-CHO-nah) (an antimalarial drug), manioc (an edible root crop), maize (corn), and natural rubber came from the Americas; sugar from India; tea from China; and coffee and oil palms from Africa. By 1914 much of the world's supply of these valuable products—in the case of rubber, almost all—came from Southeast Asia and Indonesia.

A Rubber Plantation As bicycles and automobiles proliferated in the early twentieth century, the demand for rubber outstripped the supply available from wild rubber trees in the Amazon forest. Rubber grown on plantations in Southeast Asia came on the market from 1910 on. The rubber trees had to be tapped very carefully and on a regular schedule to obtain the latex or sap from which rubber was extracted. In this picture a woman and a boy perform this operation on a plantation in British Malaya.

Mary Evans Picture Library/The Image Works

Europe and North America formed the export market for most of these products. In exchange, the inhabitants of the region benefited from peace and a reliable food supply. As a result, their numbers increased at an unprecedented rate. For instance, the population of Java (an island the size of Pennsylvania) doubled from 16 million in 1870 to over 30 million in 1914.

Colonialism and population growth spurred many social changes. Agricultural and commercial peoples gradually moved into mountainous and forested areas, displacing groups that practiced hunting and gathering or shifting agriculture and had not experienced as much population growth. Javanese migrating to Borneo and Sumatra are but one example. Immigrants from China and India changed the ethnic composition and culture of every country in the region. Thus the population of the Malay Peninsula became one-third Malay, one-third Chinese, and one-third Indian.

As in Africa, European missionaries spread Christianity under the colonial umbrella. Islam, however, was much more successful in gaining new converts, for it had been established in the region for centuries and people did not consider it a religion imposed on them by foreigners.

Education and European ideas had an impact on the political perceptions in Southeast Asia and Indonesia, as did events in neighboring Asian countries: in India, where a nationalist movement arose in the 1880s; in China, where modernizers were undermining the authority of the Qing; and especially in Japan, whose rapid industrialization culminated in its brilliant victory over Russia in the Russo-Japanese War (1904–1905). A young Vietnamese writing soon after the Russo-Japanese War expressed the spirit of a rising generation:

> I, . . . an obscure student, having had occasion to study new books and new doctrines, have discovered in a recent history of Japan how they have been able to conquer the impotent Europeans. This is the reason why we have formed an orga-

 Primary Source: Letter to the French Chamber of Deputies Learn how a Vietnamese citizen defends his attempts to rid his country of the French Indochinese government.

nization. . . . We have selected from young Annamites [Vietnamese] the most energetic, with great capacities for courage, and are sending them to Japan for study. . . . Several years have passed without the French being aware of the movement. . . . Our only aim is to prepare the population for the future.[9]

Hawaii and the Philippines, 1878–1902

By the 1890s the United States had a fast-growing population and industries that produced more manufactured goods than they could sell at home. Merchants and bankers began to look for export markets. The political mood was also expansionist, and many echoed the feelings of the naval strategist Alfred T. Mahan (mah-HAHN): "Whether they will or no, Americans must now begin to look outward. The growing production of the country requires it."

Some Americans had been looking outward for quite some time, especially across the Pacific to China and Japan. In 1878 the United States obtained the harbor of Pago Pago in Samoa as a coaling and naval station, and in 1887 it secured the use of Pearl Harbor in Hawaii for the same purpose. Six years later American settlers in Hawaii deposed Queen Liliuokalani (1838–1917) and offered the Hawaiian Islands to the United States. At the time President Grover Cleveland (1893–1897) was opposed to annexation, and the settlers had to content themselves with an informal protectorate. By 1898, however, the United States under President William McKinley (1897–1901) had become openly imperialistic, and it annexed Hawaii as a steppingstone to Asia. As the United States became ever more involved in Asian affairs, Hawaii's strategic location brought an inflow of U.S. military personnel, and its fertile land caused planters to import farm laborers from Japan, China, and the Philippines. These immigrants soon outnumbered the native Hawaiians.

While large parts of Asia were falling under colonial domination, the people of the Philippines were chafing under their Spanish rulers. The movement for independence began among young Filipinos studying in Europe. José Rizal, a young doctor working in Spain, was arrested and executed in 1896 for writing anti-Spanish and anticlerical novels. Thereafter, the center of resistance shifted to the Philippines, where

Emilio Aguinaldo In 1896, a revolt led by Emilio Aguinaldo attempted to expel Spaniards from the Philippines. When the United States purchased the Philippines from Spain two years later, the Filipino people were not consulted. Aguinaldo continued his campaign, this time against the American occupation forces, until his capture in 1901. In this picture, he appears on horseback, surrounded by some of his troops.

Emilio Aguinaldo, leader of a secret society, rose in revolt and proclaimed a republic in 1899. The revolutionaries had a good chance of winning independence, for Spain had its hands full with a revolution in Cuba (see below).

Unfortunately for Aguinaldo and his followers, the United States went to war against Spain in April 1898 and quickly overcame Spanish forces in the Philippines and Cuba. President McKinley had not originally intended to acquire the Philippines; but after the Spanish defeat, he realized that a weakened Spain might lose the islands to another imperialist power. Japan, having recently defeated China in the Sino-Japanese War (1894–1895) and annexed Taiwan, was eager to expand. So was Germany, which had taken over parts of New Guinea and Samoa and several Pacific archipelagoes during the 1880s. To forestall them, McKinley purchased the Philippines from Spain for $20 million.

The Filipinos were not eager to trade one master for another. For a while, Aguinaldo cooperated with the Americans in the hope of achieving full independence. When his plan was rejected, he rose up again in 1899 and proclaimed the independence of his country. In spite of protests by anti-imperialists in the United States, the U.S. government decided that its global interests outweighed the interests of the Filipino people. In rebel areas, a U.S. army of occupation tortured prisoners, burned villages and crops, and forced the inhabitants into "reconcentration camps." Many American soldiers tended to look on Filipinos with the same racial contempt with which Europeans viewed their colonial subjects. By the end of the insurrection in 1902, the war had cost the lives of 5,000 Americans and 200,000 Filipinos.

After the insurrection ended, the United States attempted to soften its rule with public works and economic development projects. New buildings went up in the city of Manila; roads, harbors, and railroads were built; and the Philippine economy was tied ever more closely to that of the United States. In 1907 Filipinos were allowed to elect representatives to a legislative assembly, but ultimate authority remained in the hands of a governor appointed by the president of the United States. An American promise of independence made in 1916 was not fulfilled until thirty years later.

Emilio Aguinaldo (1869–1964) Leader of the Filipino independence movement against Spain (1895–1898). He proclaimed the independence of the Philippines in 1899, but his movement was crushed and he was captured by the United States Army in 1901.

619

Imperialism in Latin America

What were the economic motives behind imperialism in Latin America?

Nations in the Americas followed two divergent paths. In Canada and the United States manufacturing industries, powerful corporations, and wealthy financial institutions arose. By contrast, Latin America and the Caribbean exported raw materials and imported manufactured goods. The poverty of their people, the preferences of their elites, and the pressures of the world economy made them increasingly dependent on the industrialized countries. Instead of suffering outright annexation by the colonial empires, they experienced manipulation by the industrial powers, including the United States, in a form of economic dependence called **free-trade imperialism**.

In the Western Hemisphere, therefore, the New Imperialism manifested itself not by a "scramble" for territories but in two other ways. In the larger republics of South America, the pressure was mostly financial and economic. In Central America and the Caribbean, it also included military intervention by the United States.

Railroads and the Imperialism of Free Trade

Latin America's economic potential was huge, for the region could produce many agricultural and mineral products in demand in the industrial countries. What was needed was a means of opening the interior to development. Railroads seemed the perfect answer.

Foreign merchants and bankers as well as Latin American landowners and politicians embraced the new technology. Starting in the 1870s almost every country in Latin America acquired railroads, usually connecting mines or agricultural regions with the nearest port rather than linking up the different parts of the interior. Since Latin America did not have any steel or mechanical industries, railroad equipment and building materials came from Britain or the United States. So did the money to build the networks, the engineers who designed and maintained them, and the managers who ran them.

Argentina, a rich source of wheat, beef, and hides, gained the longest and best-developed rail network south of the United States. By 1914, British firms owned 86 percent of the railroads in Argentina; 40 percent of the employees were British; and the official railroad language was English, not Spanish. Similar situations arose elsewhere throughout Latin America. The Argentine nationalist Juan Justo saw a parallel with Ireland:

> English capital has done what English armies could not do. Today our country is tributary to England . . . the gold that the English capitalists take out of Argentina or carry off in the form of products does us no more good than the Irish get from the revenues that the English lords take out of Ireland.[10]

The Irish, however, had little say in the matter because they were under British rule. But in Latin America the political elites encouraged foreign companies with generous concessions as the most rapid way to modernize their countries and enrich the property owners. In countries where the majority of the poor were Indians (as in Mexico and Peru) or of African origin (as in Brazil), they were neither consulted nor allowed to benefit from the railroad boom.

free-trade imperialism Economic dominance of a weaker country by a more powerful one, while maintaining the legal independence of the weaker state. In the late nineteenth century, free-trade imperialism characterized the relations between the Latin American republics, on the one hand, and Great Britain and the United States, on the other.

American Expansionism and the Spanish-American War, 1898

After 1865 Europeans used their financial power to penetrate Latin America. But they avoided territorial acquisitions for four reasons: (1) they were overextended in Africa and Asia; (2) there was no need, because the Latin American governments provided the political backing for their economic penetration; (3) Mexico's resistance to the French in the 1860s had shown that invasion would not be easy; and (4) the United States claimed to defend the entire Western Hemisphere against all outside intervention. This claim, made in the Monroe Doctrine (1823), did not prevent the United States itself from intervening in Latin American affairs.

The United States had long had interests in Cuba, the closest and richest of the Caribbean islands and a Spanish colony. American businesses had invested great sums of money in Cuba's sugar and tobacco industries, and tens of thousands of Cubans had migrated to the United States. In 1895 the Cuban nationalist José Martí started a revolution against Spanish rule. American newspapers thrilled readers with lurid stories of Spanish atrocities; businessmen worried about their investments; and politicians demanded that the U.S. government help liberate Cuba.

On February 15, 1898, the U.S. battleship *Maine* accidentally blew up in Havana harbor, killing 266 American sailors. The U.S. government immediately blamed Spain and issued an ultimatum that the Spanish evacuate Cuba. Spain accepted the ultimatum, but the American press and Congress were eager for war, and President McKinley did not restrain them.

The Spanish-American War was over quickly. On May 1, 1898, U.S. warships destroyed the Spanish fleet at Manila in the Philippines. Two months later the United States Navy sank the Spanish Atlantic fleet off Santiago, Cuba. By mid-August Spain was suing for peace. U.S. secretary of state John Hay called it "a splendid little war." The United States purchased the Philippines from Spain but took over Puerto Rico and Guam as war booty; the two islands remain American possessions to this day. Cuba became an independent republic, subject, however, to intense interference by the United States.

SECTION REVIEW

- In Latin America, industrial powers pursued free-trade imperialism to control agricultural and mineral resources.

- To tap these resources, foreign interests, with the support of Latin American elites, financed, built, and maintained railroads.

- Avoiding territorial expansion, Europeans relied instead on financial power.

- Through the Spanish-American War, the United States gained territories from Spain and guarded commercial interests in Cuba.

- The United States repeatedly intervened in Central America and the Caribbean, supporting Panamanian rebels to gain rights to build the Panama Canal.

American Intervention in the Caribbean and Central America, 1901–1914

The nations of the Caribbean and Central America were small and poor, and their governments were corrupt, unstable, and often bankrupt. They seemed to offer an open invitation to foreign interference. A government would borrow money to pay for railroads, harbors, electric power, and other symbols of modernity. When it could not repay the loan, the lending banks in Europe or the United States would ask for assistance from their home governments. To ward off European intervention, the United States sent in the marines on more than one occasion.

Presidents Theodore Roosevelt (1901–1909), William Taft (1909–1913), and Woodrow Wilson (1913–1921) felt impelled to intervene in the region, though they differed sharply on the proper policy the United States should follow toward the small nations to the south. Roosevelt encouraged regimes friendly to the United States, like Mexico; Taft sought to influence them through loans from American banks; and the moralist Wilson tried to impose clean governments through military means.

Having "liberated" Cuba from Spain, the United States forced the Cuban government to accept the Platt Amendment in 1901. This gave the United States the "right to intervene" to maintain order on the island. The United States used this excuse to occupy

Building the Panama Canal When it opened in 1914, after ten years of construction, the canal shortened the sailing distance between San Francisco and New York from 14,000 miles (22,500 kilometers) to 6,000 miles (9,500 kilometers). With two sets of locks and numerous artificial lakes and channels, the canal is 47.9 miles (77.1 kilometers) long and today takes about nine hours to sail through. This picture shows dredges working to deepen a channel through the mountains.

Cuba militarily from 1906 to 1909, in 1912, and again from 1917 to 1922. In all but name Cuba became an American protectorate. U.S. troops also occupied the Dominican Republic from 1904 to 1907 and again in 1916, Nicaragua and Honduras in 1912, and Haiti in 1915. They brought sanitation and material progress but no political improvements.

The United States was especially forceful in Panama, which was a province of Colombia. Here the issue was not corruption or debts but the construction of a canal to speed shipping between the east and west coasts of the United States. In 1878 the Frenchman Ferdinand de Lesseps, builder of the Suez Canal, had obtained a concession from Colombia to construct a canal across the Isthmus of Panama, which lay in Colombian territory. Financial scandals and yellow fever, however, doomed his project.

When the United States acquired Hawaii and the Philippines, it recognized the strategic value of a canal

that would allow warships to move quickly between the Atlantic and Pacific Oceans. The main obstacle was Colombia, whose senate refused to give the United States a piece of its territory. In 1903 the U.S. government supported a Panamanian rebellion against Colombia and quickly recognized the independence of Panama. In exchange, it obtained the right to build a canal and to occupy a zone 5 miles (8 kilometers) wide on either side of it. Work began in 1904, and the **Panama Canal** opened on August 15, 1914.

Panama Canal Ship canal cut across the Isthmus of Panama by U.S. Army engineers; it opened in 1914. It greatly shortened the sea voyage between the east and west coasts of North America. The United States turned the canal over to Panama on January 1, 2000.

The World Economy and the Global Environment

How did imperialism contribute to the growth and globalization of the world economy?

The New Imperialists were not traditional conquerors or empire builders like the Spanish conquistadors. Their aim was not only to extend their power over new territories and peoples, but also to control both natural resources and indigenous societies and put them efficiently to work. Both their goals and their methods were industrial. A railroad, for example, was an act of faith as well as a means of transportation. The imperialists expressed their belief in progress and their good intentions in the clichés of the time: "the conquest of nature," "the annihilation of time and space," "the taming of the wilderness," and "our civilizing mission."

Expansion of the World Economy

The Industrial Revolution vastly expanded the traditional demand for tropical products. Imports of foods and stimulants such as tea, coffee, and cocoa increased substantially during the nineteenth century. The trade in industrial raw materials, whether agricultural (cotton, jute for bags, and palm oil for soap and lubricants) or mineral (diamonds, gold, and copper), grew even faster. The industrial nations also imported wild forest products that were later cultivated: timber for buildings and railroad ties, cinchona bark, rubber for rainwear and tires, and gutta-percha (gut-tah-PER-cha) to insulate electric cables.

The growing needs of the industrial world could not be met by the traditional methods of production and transportation of the nonindustrial world. When the U.S. Civil War interrupted the export of cotton to England in the 1860s, the British turned to India, only to find that Indian cotton was ruined by exposure to rain and dust while being carted from interior regions to the harbors. To prevent such technological backwardness in the colonies from stifling the expansion of industry, the imperialists made every effort to bring those territories into the mainstream of the world market.

Transportation was key. The Suez and Panama Canals cut travel time and lowered freight costs dramatically. Steamships became more numerous, and as their size increased, deeper harbors were needed. As for railroads, India alone had 37,000 miles (nearly 60,000 kilometers) of track by 1915, almost as much as Germany or Russia. Railroads reached into the interior of Latin America, Canada, China, and Australia. In 1903 the Russians completed the Trans-Siberian Railway from Moscow to Vladivostok on the Pacific. Visionaries even made plans for railroads from Europe to India and from Egypt to South Africa.

Transformation of the Global Environment

The economic changes brought by Europeans and Americans altered environments around the world. The British, whose craving for tea could not be satisfied with the limited exports available from China, introduced tea into the warm, rainy hill country of Ceylon and northeastern India. In those areas and in Java, thousands of square miles of tropical rain forests were felled to make way for tea plantations.

Economic botany and agricultural science were applied to every promising plant species. European botanists had long collected and classified exotic plants from around the world. In the nineteenth century they founded botanical gardens in Java, India, Mauritius (maw-REE-shuss), Ceylon, Jamaica, and other tropical colonies. These gardens not only collected local plants but also exchanged plants with other gardens. They were especially active in systematically transferring commercially valuable plant species from one tropical region to another. Cinchona, tobacco, sugar, and other crops were introduced, improved, and vastly expanded in the colonies of Southeast Asia and Indonesia. Cocoa and coffee growing spread over large areas of Brazil and Africa, and oil-palm plantations were established in Nigeria and the Congo Basin. Rubber originally came from the latex of *Hevea* trees growing wild in the Brazilian rain forest. Then, in the 1870s, British agents smuggled seedlings from Brazil to the Royal Botanic Gardens at Kew near London, and from there to the Botanic Garden of Singapore. These plants formed the nucleus of the enormous rubber economy of Southeast Asia.

Throughout the tropics forests and lands devoted to shifting slash-and-burn agriculture gave way to

SECTION REVIEW

- To feed their industries, the industrial nations strove for efficient control of the natural resources and peoples of their colonies.

- The Industrial Revolution increased the demand for tropical products and raw materials, a demand that could not be met by traditional means in nonindustrial countries.

- Economic changes in colonized territories led to the transformation of environments.

- Economic botany and agricultural science improved crops and thus expanded their cultivation.

- Railroad building and mineral extraction scarred the land even as they moved, employed, and enriched people.

permanent farms and plantations. Even in areas not developed to export crops, growing populations put pressure on the land. In Java and India farmers felled trees to obtain arable land and firewood, terraced hillsides, drained swamps, and dug wells.

Irrigation and water control transformed the dry parts of the tropics as well. In the 1830s British engineers in India had restored ancient canals that had fallen into disrepair. Their success led them to build new irrigation canals, turning thousands of previously barren acres into well-watered, densely populated farmland. The migration of European experts spread the newest techniques of irrigation engineering around the world. By the turn of the century irrigation projects were under way wherever rivers flowed through dry lands. In Egypt and Central Asia irrigation brought more acres under cultivation in one forty-year span than in all previous history.

Railroads had voracious appetites for land and resources. They cut into mountains, spanned rivers and canyons with trestles, and covered as much land with their freight yards as whole cities had needed in previous centuries. They also consumed vast quantities of iron, timber for ties, and coal or wood for fuel. Most important of all, railroads brought people and their cities, farms, and industries to areas previously occupied by small, scattered populations.

Prospectors looking for valuable minerals opened the earth to reveal its riches: gold in South Africa, Australia, and Canada; tin in Nigeria, Malaya, and Bolivia; copper in Chile and Central Africa; iron ore

in northern India; and much else. Where mines were dug deep inside the earth, the dirt and rocks brought up with the ores formed huge mounds near mine entrances. Open mines dug to obtain ores lying close to the surface created a landscape of lunar craters, and runoff from the minerals poisoned the water for miles around. Refineries that processed the ores fouled the environment with slag heaps and more toxic runoff.

The transformation of the land by human beings, a constant throughout history, accelerated sharply. Only the changes occurring since 1914 can compare with the transformation of the global environment that took place between 1869 and 1914.

Conclusion

The last third of the nineteenth century and the first decade of the twentieth witnessed the most rapid conquests in the history of the world. During the era of the New Imperialism the newly industrializing powers of Europe, the United States, and Japan used modern weapons, means of transportation, and other industrial technologies to impose their will on the nonindustrial parts of the world. To produce the agricultural products and minerals that their consumers and industries demanded, they transformed the economies, societies, and environments of the less developed parts of the world.

Yet there were substantial differences among the experiences of different parts of the world, depending on how valuable the local resources were and how tightly the imperialists exercised control over the local population. In Latin America, local elites cooperated with British and American business interests, and imperialism was limited to economic pressures and occasional military interventions. In Egypt, Tunisia, and Morocco, as in parts of India and Nigeria, the Europeans kept the local governments in office but manipulated them from behind the scenes. In South Africa, with its substantial European minority, power was handed over to the white settlers in exchange for economic cooperation. And in the rest of the colonial world, European, American, and Japanese administrators ruled directly. Colonialism was thus a flexible means of assuring maximum benefit to the colonial power at a minimum of expense.

CHAPTER REVIEW

 Download the MP3 audio file of the Chapter Review to listen to on the go.

What motivated the industrial nations to conquer new territories, and what means did they use? (page 600)

European and American imperial expansion was driven by economic, cultural, and political motives. Many governments used overseas colonies as a way to help reestablish their nations' prestige and power. Catholic and Protestant missionaries sought not only to convert the native peoples to their religious beliefs but also to "civilize" their behavior. This sense of moral and cultural superiority was common among the colonizing nations. Finally, colonizing nations were led by the demand for minerals and natural resources. The imperialists used tools provided by the Industrial Revolution, such as steamships, gunboats, and improved firearms, to build their empires.

Why were imperialists interested in conquering Africa, and how did their presence on that continent change the environment? (page 607)

Africans ruled over 90 percent of the continent until the European "scramble" for Africa began after the 1870s. Europeans took control of African resources to further their own military and economic power. After the British secured the Suez Canal, they constructed a dam across the Nile to help develop agriculture. In other parts of the continent, European companies invested in rubber and palm-oil plantations, gold and diamond mines, and other resources. Local reaction to colonial rule varied greatly, traditional land use patterns were disrupted, and all Africans were affected by changes in social and cultural customs.

What were the social and cultural effects of imperialism in Asia? (page 615)

The effects of colonialism varied throughout Asia, although in all regions the economic profits benefited the Europeans rather than the indigenous peoples. Southeast Asia's fertile soil and heavy rains made farming of various crops, most importantly rubber, quite profitable. As laborers were brought in from overseas, they gradually displaced the earlier inhabitants. A similar situation occurred in Hawaii, where U.S. military personnel and foreign farm laborers eventually outnumbered the native Hawaiians. Europeans differed in their approach to indigenous cultures and religions. In Central Asia, the Russians did not attempt to impose their customs, language, or religious beliefs on their subjects. Christian missionaries in Southeast Asia, meanwhile, worked to spread their beliefs. Their efforts gained only limited success in a land where Islam had been dominant for centuries.

What were the economic motives behind imperialism in Latin America? (page 620)

Latin America had great economic potential because of its wealth of agricultural and mineral products. The construction of railroads, using equipment, engineers, and funding from Britain and the United States, helped to connect the interior regions with the coastal ports. Americans also saw economic potential in Cuba and invested heavily in the sugar and tobacco industries there. After the Spanish-American War, they issued the Platt Amendment to maintain their influence in Cuba. The United States also supported the Panamanian secession from Colombia in 1903 in order to build the Panama Canal.

How did imperialism contribute to the growth and globalization of the world economy? (page 623)

Imperialism, both formal and informal, opened up the world to increased trade and communication. Shipping, canals, and railroads were the most visible means of globalization. Other activities—farming, mining, labor migrations, and urbanization—were profoundly affected as well. In the process, natural environments were transformed as never before. Forests were replaced by plantations. Irrigation schemes opened dry lands to agriculture. And railroads and mines cut into the landscape, leaving scars and pollution.

Key Terms

Suez Canal *(p. 600)*

New Imperialism *(p. 600)*

Battle of Omdurman *(p. 604)*

colonialism *(p. 604)*

"scramble" for Africa *(p. 607)*

Henry Morton Stanley *(p. 609)*

Leopold II *(p. 609)*

Savorgnan de Brazza *(p. 609)*

Berlin Conference *(p. 609)*

Afrikaners *(p. 610)*

Cecil Rhodes *(p. 611)*

Asante *(p. 614)*

Menelik II *(p. 614)*

Emilio Aguinaldo *(p. 619)*

free-trade imperialism *(p. 620)*

Panama Canal *(p. 622)*

Web Resources

Pronunciation Guide

Interactive Maps

- MAP 25.1 Africa in 1878 and 1914
- Map 25.2 Asia in 1914

Primary Sources

- Convention on Free Navigation of the Suez Canal Between the European Powers and the Ottoman Empire, October 29, 1888
- His Story
- Memorandum to Lord Selborne, High Commissioner of Transvaal, October 1905
- Letter to the French Chamber of Deputies

Answer to the History in Focus Question

See photo on page 605, "The Battle of Omdurman."

Visit the CourseMate website at www.cengagebrain.com for additional study tools and review materials for this chapter.

CHAPTER 26

1900–1929

The Crisis of the Imperial Order

© Cengage Learning

 Visit the CourseMate website at **www.cengagebrain.com** for additional study
tools and review materials for this chapter.

On June 28, 1914, Archduke Franz Ferdinand, heir to the throne of Austria-Hungary, was riding in an open carriage through Sarajevo, capital of the province of Bosnia-Herzegovina, which Austria had annexed six years before. When the carriage stopped momentarily, Gavrilo Princip, a member of a pro-Serbian conspiracy, fired his pistol twice, killing the archduke and his wife.

Those shots ignited a European war that pitted France, Britain, and Russia against Germany and Austria-Hungary, and then turned into a global war as the Ottoman Empire fought against Britain in the Middle East and Japan attacked German positions in China. France and Britain involved their empires in the war and brought Africans, Indians, Australians, and Canadians to Europe to fight and labor on the front lines. Finally, in 1917, the United States entered the fray.

This chapter looks at the causes of war between the great powers, the consequences of that conflict in Europe, the Middle East, and Russia, and the upheavals in China and Japan. It also reviews the accelerating rate of technological change that made the first half of the twentieth century so violent and so hopeful. Entirely new technologies made war more dangerous yet allowed far more people to live healthier, more comfortable, and more interesting lives than ever before.

Origins of the Crisis in Europe and the Middle East

What led to the outbreak of the First World War?

When the twentieth century opened, the world seemed firmly under the control of the great powers. Its first decade saw peace, economic growth, and the spread of new technologies: airplanes, automobiles, radio, and cinema. The only international war of the period, the Russo-Japanese War (1904–1905), ended quickly with a decisive Japanese victory.

However, two major changes were undermining the apparent stability of the world. In Europe, Germany challenged Britain at sea and France in

Morocco. And in the Ottoman Empire, government weakness in the face of chaos in the Balkans gradually drew the European powers into a whirlpool.

The Ottoman Empire and the Balkans

By 1900, the once-great Ottoman Empire had become the "sick man of Europe" and was losing its outlying provinces. Between 1902 and 1913, Macedonia rebelled, Austria-Hungary annexed Bosnia, Crete merged with Greece, Italy conquered Libya, and Albania became independent. In 1912–1913, Serbia, Bulgaria, Romania, and Greece chased the Turks out of the Balkans, except for a small enclave around Constantinople. Russia and Austria-Hungary competed to become the protector of the Slavic peoples of the Balkans. France and Britain, the empire's creditors, controlled Ottoman finances, taxes, railroads, mines, and public utilities.

In reaction, Turks began to assert themselves against rebellious minorities and meddling foreigners. In 1908–1909, a revolutionary group known as the Young Turks overthrew the sultan and replaced him with his brother. The new regime began to reform the police, the bureaucracy, and the education system and hired a German general to modernize Turkey's armed forces. At the same time, it cracked down on Greek and Armenian minorities.

Nationalism, Alliances, and Military Strategy

Nationalism united the citizens of France, Britain, Italy, and Germany behind their respective governments and gave them tremendous cohesion and strength of purpose. But nationalism could divide as well as unify. In the large but fragile multinational empires—Russia, Austria-Hungary, and the Ottoman Empire—ethnic and religious minorities were stirring. The easy victories in the wars of the New Imperialism (see Chapter 25) led some in power to believe that only war could heal the divisions in their societies.

What turned assassination of the Archduke Franz Ferdinand into a conflict involving all the great powers was the system of alliances that had accumulated over the previous decades. Germany stood at Europe's center as the most heavily industrialized country in Europe. Its army was the best trained and equipped, and its battleships were challenging Great Britain's

Chronology

	Europe and North America	Middle East	East Asia
1900			**1900** Boxer Uprising in China **1904–1905** Russo-Japanese War
	1907 British-French-Russian Entente		
		1909 Young Turks overthrow Sultan Abdul Hamid	
1910			**1911** Chinese revolutionaries led by Sun Yat-sen overthrow Qing dynasty
	1912–1913 Balkan Wars **1914** Assassination of Archduke Franz Ferdinand sparks World War I		**1915** Japan presents Twenty-One Demands to China
	1916 Battles of Verdun and the Somme **1917** Russian Revolutions; United States enters the war **1918** Armistice ends World War I **1919** Treaty of Versailles	**1916** Arab Revolt in Arabia **1917** Balfour Declaration	**1919** May Fourth Movement in China
1920	**1920** First commercial radio broadcast (United States) **1921** New Economic Policy in Russia		
		1922 Egypt nominally independent **1923** Mustafa Kemal proclaims Turkey a republic	
	1927 Charles Lindbergh flies alone across the Atlantic		**1927** Guomindang forces occupy Shanghai and expel communists

naval supremacy. Germany joined Austria-Hungary and Italy in the Triple Alliance in 1882. When in 1907 Britain, France, and Russia formed an Entente (on-TONT) ("understanding"), Europe was divided into two blocs of roughly equal power (see Map 26.1).

The alliance system was cursed by inflexible military planning. Anticipating possible war, military planners in France and Germany had worked out elaborate railroad timetables to mobilize their respective armies in a few days. Other countries were less well prepared. Russia with its underdeveloped rail system needed several weeks to mobilize. Britain, with only a tiny volunteer army, had no mobilization plans.

German generals, believing that the British would stay out of a European war, made plans to defeat France in a matter of days and then transport their entire army by train across Germany to the Russian border before Russia could fully mobilize.

On July 28, 1914, emboldened by the backing of Germany, Austria-Hungary declared war on Serbia, triggering mobilization plans in Russia, France, and Germany. The next day, Russia ordered general mobilization to force Austria to back down. On August 1, France honored its treaty obligation to Russia and ordered general mobilization. Minutes later, Germany did the same. War was now unavoidable.

Map 26.1 The First World War in Europe Most of the fighting in World War I took place on two fronts. After an initial surge through Belgium into northern France, the German offensive bogged down for four years along the Western Front. To the east, the German armies conquered a large part of Russia during 1917 and early 1918. Despite spectacular victories in the east, Germany lost the war because its armies collapsed along the strategically important Western Front. © Cengage Learning

 Interactive Map

SECTION REVIEW

- Ottoman decline and German self-assertion undermined European stability.
- The weakening Ottoman Empire lost outlying provinces, and newly independent Balkan states pushed it to the edge of Europe.
- European powers meddled in Ottoman affairs, provoking the coup led by the Young Turks.
- Nationalism, the alliance system, and inflexible military plans drove the European powers into war after the assassination of Archduke Franz Ferdinand.

The German General Staff expected France to capitulate before the British could get involved. But on August 3, when German troops entered Belgium, Britain demanded their withdrawal. When Germany refused, Britain declared war on Germany.

The "Great War" and the Russian Revolutions, 1914–1918

How did the war lead to revolution in Russia?

Throughout Europe, people greeted the outbreak of war with parades and hopes for a quick victory. The German sociologist Max Weber wrote: "This war, with all its ghastliness, is nevertheless grand and wonderful. It is worth experiencing." Very few imagined that their side might not win. No one foresaw that everyone would lose.

Stalemate, 1914–1917 The generals' carefully drawn-up plans went awry from the start. Believing that a spirited attack would always prevail, French generals hurled their troops against the well-defended German border and suffered a crushing defeat. By early September, the German armies held Belgium and northern France and were fast approaching Paris. German victory seemed assured. But when Russia attacked, German troops needed for the final push into France were shifted to the eastern front. A gap opened between two German armies along the Marne River, into which France's last reserves moved. At the Battle of the Marne, the Germans were thrown back several miles.

During the next month, both sides spread out until they formed an unbroken battlefront extending over 300 miles (some 500 kilometers) from the North Sea to the border of Switzerland. All along this **Western Front**, machine guns provided an almost impenetrable defense against advancing infantry but were useless for the offensive because they were too heavy for one man to carry and took too much time to set up. To escape the deadly streams of bullets, soldiers dug holes for themselves in the ground, connected the holes to form shallow trenches, and then dug communications trenches to the rear. Within weeks, the battlefields were scarred with lines of trenches several feet deep, their tops protected by sandbags and their floors covered with planks.

For four years, generals on each side again and again ordered thousands of young men to climb out of their trenches, race across the open fields, and be mowed down by enemy machine-gun fire. Poison gas added to the horror of battle.

The year 1916 saw the bloodiest and most futile battles of the war. The Germans attacked French forts at Verdun, losing 281,000 men and causing 315,000 French casualties. In retaliation, the British attacked the Germans at the Somme River and suffered 420,000 casualties—60,000 on the first day alone—while the Germans lost 450,000 and the French 200,000.

This was not warfare as it had ever been waged before; it was mass slaughter. Neither side could win, for the armies were stalemated by trenches and machine guns. During four years of the bloodiest fighting the world had ever seen, the Western Front moved no more than a few miles one way or another.

At sea, the war was just as inconclusive. As soon as the war broke out, the British cut the German overseas telegraph cables, blockaded the coasts of Germany and Austria-Hungary, and set out to capture or sink all enemy ships still at sea. The German High Seas Fleet, built at enormous cost, seldom left port. Only

Western Front A line of trenches and fortifications in World War I that stretched without a break from Switzerland to the North Sea. Scene of most of the fighting between Germany, on the one hand, and France and Britain, on the other.

Trench Warfare in World War I German and Allied soldiers on the Western Front faced each other from elaborate networks of trenches. Attacking meant jumping out of the trenches and racing across a no man's land of mud and barbed wire. Here we see Princess Patricia's Canadian Light Infantry repelling a German attack near Ypres, in northern France, in March 1915, using machine guns, rifles, and hand grenades.

The Second Battle of Ypres, 1917 (oil on canvas), Jack, Richard (1866–1952)/Canadian War Museum, Ottawa, Canada/The Bridgeman Art Library

once, in May 1916, did it confront the British Grand Fleet. At the Battle of Jutland, off the coast of Denmark, the two fleets lost roughly equal numbers of ships, and the Germans escaped back to their harbors.

In early 1915, in retaliation for the British naval blockade, Germany announced a blockade of Britain by submarines. German submarines attacked every vessel they could. One attack sank the British ocean liner *Lusitania*, killing 1,198 people, 139 of them Americans. When the United States protested, Germany ceased its submarine campaign, hoping to keep America neutral.

The Home Front and the War Economy

The war economy transformed civilian life. In France and Britain, food rations were allocated according to need, improving nutrition among the poor. Unemployment vanished, and thousands of Africans, Indians, and Chinese were recruited for heavy labor in Europe. Employers also hired women to fill jobs in steel mills, mines, and munitions plants. Women became streetcar drivers, mail carriers, and police officers or found work in government bureaucracies. Many joined auxiliary military services as doctors, nurses, mechanics, and ambulance drivers. These positions gave thousands of women a sense of participation and a taste of independence.

The British naval blockade punished Germany's civilians. German chemists developed synthetic explosives and fuel, but not synthetic food. Wheat flour disappeared, replaced first by rye, then by potatoes and turnips, then by acorns and chestnuts, and finally by sawdust. After the failure of the potato crop in 1916 came the "turnip winter," when people had to survive on 1,000 calories per day, half of the normal adult amount. Women, children, and the elderly were especially hard hit. Even soldiers went hungry.

Abroad the British and French overran all of Germany's African colonies except German East Africa, which remained undefeated until the end of the war (see Map 25.1). In many African colonies, war policies imposed heavy taxes, low prices for requisitioned supplies, and military recruitment. Many Europeans stationed in Africa left to join the war, leaving large areas with little or no European presence. Over a million Africans served in the various armies, and perhaps three times that number were drafted as porters to carry army equipment. In some places, these impositions provoked African uprisings that lasted for years.

One country grew rich during the war: the United States, which for two and a half years stayed

ON HER THEIR LIVES DEPEND

WOMEN MUNITION WORKERS

Enrol at once

Imperial War Museum/The Art Archive

Women in World War I Women played a more important role in World War I than in previous wars. As the armies drafted millions of men, employers hired women for essential war work. This poster extols the importance of women in supplying munitions.

technically neutral while its companies did a roaring business supplying France and Britain with food and war materiel. After the United States entered the war in 1917, civilians were exhorted to help the war effort by investing their savings in war bonds and growing food in backyard "victory gardens." Employment created by the war opened up jobs for women and African Americans.

Primary Source: Letter from Turkey, Summer 1915 Read a detailed account of one Armenian woman's ghastly experiences on the forced march away from her homeland.

The Ottoman Empire at War

On August 2, 1914, the Turks signed a secret alliance with Germany. In November, they joined the fighting, hoping to gain land at Russia's expense. But the campaign in the Caucasus proved disastrous for both sides. Suspecting the local Armenian population of being pro-Russian, the Turks forced them to march from their homelands across the mountains in the winter, a trek during which hundreds of thousands of Armenians died of hunger and exposure. Famine stalked the empire.

The Turks also closed the Dardanelles, the strait between the Mediterranean and Black Seas (see Map 26.1). When a British attack on the Dardanelles failed disastrously, they tried to subvert the Ottoman Empire from within by promising the emir (governor) of Mecca, Hussein ibn Ali, a kingdom of his own. In 1916, Hussein started an Arab revolt against the Turks. His son **Faisal I** (fie-SAHL) led an Arab army into Palestine and Syria in support of the British advance from Egypt, thereby contributing to the Ottoman defeat.

The British made promises to Chaim Weizmann (hi-um VITES-mun), leader of the British Zionists, that a Jewish homeland in Palestine would be carved out of the Ottoman Empire and placed under British protection. In November 1917, as British armies were advancing on Jerusalem, Foreign Secretary Sir Arthur Balfour wrote that "His Majesty's Government view with favor the establishment in Palestine of a national home for the Jewish people and will use their best endeavours to facilitate the achievement of that object, it being clearly understood that nothing shall be done which may prejudice the civil and religious rights of existing non-Jewish communities in Palestine." The British did not foresee that this statement, known as the **Balfour Declaration**, would lead to conflicts between Palestinians and Jewish settlers.

Faisal I (1885–1933) Arab prince, leader of the Arab Revolt in World War I. The British made him king of Iraq in 1921, and he reigned under British protection until 1933.
Balfour Declaration Statement issued by Britain's Foreign Secretary Arthur Balfour in 1917 favoring the establishment of a Jewish national homeland in Palestine.

Double Revolution in Russia, 1917

Russia began the war with the largest army in the world, but its generals were incompetent, supplies were lacking, and soldiers were poorly trained and equipped. In August 1914, two Russian armies were thrown back in eastern Germany. Russia did better against the Austro-Hungarian army but again was defeated by the Germans. In 1916, after a string of defeats, the Russian army ran out of ammunition and other essential supplies. Soldiers were ordered into battle unarmed and told to pick up the rifles of fallen comrades.

With so many men in the army, railroads broke down for lack of fuel and parts, and crops rotted in the fields. Civilians faced shortages and widespread hunger. In the cities, food and fuel became scarce. During the bitterly cold winter of 1916–1917, factory workers and housewives had to line up in front of grocery stores before dawn to get something to eat. The court of Tsar (zahr) Nicholas II, however, remained as extravagant and corrupt as ever.

When food ran out in Petrograd, the capital, in early March 1917, housewives and women factory workers staged mass demonstrations. Soldiers mutinied and joined striking workers to form *soviets* (councils) to take over factories and barracks. A few days later, the tsar abdicated, and leaders of the parliamentary parties formed a Provisional Government. Thus began what Russians called the "February Revolution" because their calendar was two weeks behind the one in use elsewhere.

Revolutionary groups came out of hiding. Most numerous were the Social Revolutionaries, who advocated redistributing land to the peasants. The Social Democrats, a Marxist party, were divided. The Mensheviks, who advocated electoral politics and reform in the tradition of European Socialists, had a large following among intellectuals and factory workers. The rival **Bolsheviks** were a small but tightly disciplined group dedicated to revolution. **Vladimir Lenin** (1870–1924), the Bolshevik leader, became a revolutionary in his teens when his older brother was executed for plotting to kill the tsar. His goal was to create a party that would lead the revolution rather than wait for it.

In early April 1917, the German government, hoping to destabilize Russia, allowed Lenin to travel from exile in Switzerland to Russia in a sealed railway car. As soon as he arrived in Petrograd, he announced his program: immediate peace, all power to the soviets, and transfers of land to the peasants and factories to the workers. This plan proved immensely popular among the soldiers and workers exhausted by the war.

SECTION REVIEW

- During the stalemate of trench warfare, indecisive battles were fought at Verdun and the Somme, while German submarine warfare prompted American protests.

- The war economy brought both greater employment and privation, drew upon far-flung colonial resources, and enriched the United States.

- Allied with Germany, the Ottoman Empire massacred Armenians and repulsed a British invasion.

- Britain sought to undermine the Ottomans by supporting the Arab Revolt and backing the Balfour Declaration, which promised a Jewish homeland.

- In Russia, the February Revolution replaced the tsar with a Provisional Government, which later fell to the Bolshevik-led October Revolution.

- In 1917–1918, U.S. troops reinvigorated the Allies and the German offensives failed, forcing Germany to sign an armistice.

Bolsheviks Radical Marxist political party founded by Vladimir Lenin in 1903. Under Lenin's leadership, the Bolsheviks seized power in November 1917 during the Russian Revolution.

Vladimir Lenin (1870–1924) Leader of the Bolshevik (later Communist) Party. He lived in exile in Switzerland until 1917, then returned to Russia to lead the Bolsheviks to victory during the Russian Revolution and the civil war that followed.

Lenin the Orator The leader of the Bolshevik revolutionaries was a spellbinding orator. Here Lenin is addressing Red Army soldiers in Sverdlov Square, Moscow, in 1920. (Trotsky, who originally appeared in this picture, was airbrushed out.) At the time, the Bolsheviks were mopping up the last anti-Bolshevik forces and were fully engaged in a war with Poland. The fate of the Revolution depended on the fighting spirit of the Red Army soldiers and on their loyalty to Lenin.

When the Provisional Government ordered another offensive against the Germans a few months later, Russian soldiers deserted by the hundreds of thousands, throwing away their rifles and walking back to their villages. The Bolsheviks, meanwhile, were gaining support among the workers of Petrograd and the soldiers and sailors stationed there. On November 6, 1917 (October 24 in the Russian calendar), they rose up and took over the city. This "October Revolution" overthrew the Provisional Government and arrested Mensheviks, Social Revolutionaries, and other rivals.

The Bolsheviks nationalized all private land and ordered the peasants to hand over their crops without compensation. The peasants, having seized their landlords' estates, resisted. In the cities, the Bolsheviks took over the factories and drafted the workers into compulsory labor brigades. To enforce his rule, Lenin created the Cheka, a secret police force with powers to arrest and execute opponents. The Bolsheviks also sued for peace with Germany and Austria-Hungary. By the Treaty of Brest-Litovsk, signed on March 3, 1918, Russia forfeited territories containing a third of its population and wealth.

The End of the War in Western Europe, 1917–1918

Like many Americans, President **Woodrow Wilson** wanted to stay out of the European conflict. For nearly three years, he kept the United States neutral and tried to persuade the belligerents to compromise. But in late 1916, Germany's decision to starve the British by using submarines to sink food ships risked bringing the United States into the war. German leaders were willing to gamble that Britain and France

Woodrow Wilson (1856–1924) President of the United States (1913–1921) and the leading figure at the Paris Peace Conference of 1919. He was unable to persuade the U.S. Congress to ratify the Treaty of Versailles or join the League of Nations.

would collapse before the United States could send a decisive number of troops.

The German gamble failed. The British organized their merchant ships into convoys protected by destroyers, and on April 6, 1917, President Wilson asked the United States Congress to declare war on Germany.

On the Western Front, the two sides were so evenly matched in 1917 that the war seemed unlikely to end until one side or the other ran out of young men. Losing hope of winning, soldiers began to mutiny. In May 1917, before the arrival of U.S. forces, fifty-four of one hundred French divisions along the Western Front refused to attack. At Caporetto, Italian troops were so demoralized that 275,000 were taken prisoner.

Between March and August 1918, German general Erich von Ludendorff launched a series of surprise attacks that broke through the front at several places and pushed to within 40 miles (64 kilometers) of Paris. But victory eluded him. Meanwhile, every month was bringing another 250,000 American troops to the front. In August, the Allies counterattacked, and the Germans began a retreat that could not be halted, for German soldiers, many of them sick with the flu, had lost the will to fight.

In late October, Ludendorff resigned, and sailors in the German fleet mutinied. Two weeks later, Kaiser Wilhelm fled to Holland as a new German government signed an armistice. On November 11 at 11 A.M., the guns on the Western Front went silent.

Peace and Dislocation in Europe, 1919–1929

What role did the war play in eroding European dominance in the world?

The Great War lasted four years. It took almost twice as long for Europe to recover. Millions of people had died or been disabled, political tensions lingered, and national economies remained depressed until the

Primary Source: Mud and Khaki, Memoirs of an Incomplete Soldier Follow a day in the life of a soldier fighting in the trenches during World War I.

mid-1920s. The return of peace and prosperity in the late 1920s soon proved illusory.

The Impact of the War

It is estimated that between 8 million and 10 million people died, almost all of them young men. Perhaps twice that many returned home wounded, gassed, or shell-shocked, many of them disabled for life. In addition, the war created millions of refugees.

France welcomed 1.5 million refugees, but the preferred destination was the United States. About 800,000 immigrants succeeded in reaching it before U.S. immigration laws passed in 1921 and 1924 closed the door to eastern and southern Europeans. Canada, Australia, and New Zealand adopted similar restrictions on immigration. The Latin American republics welcomed European refugees, but their poverty discouraged potential immigrants.

One unexpected disaster was the great influenza epidemic of 1918–1919, which started among soldiers heading for the Western Front. This was no ordinary flu but a virulent strain that infected almost everyone on earth and killed one person in every forty. Half a million Americans perished in the epidemic—five times as many as died in the war. Worldwide, some 30 million people died, 20 million in India alone.

The war also seriously damaged the environment. No place on earth was ever so completely devastated as the scar across France and Belgium known as the Western Front. The fighting ravaged forests and demolished towns. The earth was gouged by trenches, pitted with craters, and littered with ammunition, broken weapons, chunks of concrete, and the bones of countless soldiers. After the war, it took a decade to clear away the debris and create military cemeteries with neat rows of crosses stretching for miles.

The Peace Treaties

In early 1919, delegates of the victorious Allies met in Paris. The defeated powers were kept out until the treaties were ready for signing. Russia, in the throes of civil war, was not invited.

From the start, three men dominated the Paris Peace Conference: President Wilson, British prime minister David Lloyd George, and French premier Georges Clemenceau (zhorzh cluh-mon-SO). They ignored the Italians, who had joined the Allies in 1915, and paid even less attention to the smaller European nations. They rejected the Japanese proposal that all races be treated equally and ignored the call of the Pan-African Congress for attention to the concerns of Africans. They also ignored delegates who did not represent sovereign states and who came to Paris to lobby for their causes—the Arab leader Faisal, the Zionist Chaim Weizmann, and several Armenian delegations.

Each man had his own agenda. Wilson wanted to apply the principle of self-determination, by which he meant creating nations that reflected European ethnic or linguistic divisions. He proposed a **League of Nations**, a world organization to safeguard the peace and foster international cooperation. His idealism clashed with the more hardheaded and self-serving nationalism of the Europeans. Lloyd George insisted that Germany pay a heavy indemnity. Clemenceau wanted Germany to give back Alsace and Lorraine, cede the industrial Saar region to France, and make the Rhineland a buffer state.

The result was a series of compromises that satisfied no one. The European powers formed a League of Nations, but the United States Congress, reflecting the isolationist feelings of the American people, refused to join. France recovered Alsace and Lorraine but was unable to detach the Rhineland and had to content itself with vague promises of British and American protection if Germany ever rebuilt its army. Britain acquired new territories in Africa and the Middle East but was greatly weakened by human losses and the disruption of its trade.

On June 28, 1919, the German delegates reluctantly signed the **Treaty of Versailles** (vuhr-SIGH). Germany was forbidden to have an air force and was permitted only a token army and navy. It also gave up large parts of its eastern territory to a newly reconstituted Poland. The Allies made Germany promise to pay reparations, but they did not set a figure or a period of time for payment. A "guilt clause," which was to rankle for years to come, obliged the Germans to accept "responsibility for causing all the loss and damage" of the war. The Treaty of Versailles left Germany humiliated but largely intact and potentially the most powerful nation in Europe. Establishing a peace neither of punishment nor of reconciliation, the treaty was one of the great failures in history.

In eastern Europe, the Allies created new national states in the lands lost by the old Russian, German, and Austro-Hungarian Empires. Austria and Hungary became separate states; Poland was resurrected after over a century; Czechoslovakia and Yugoslavia were created from parts of Austria-Hungary. These small nations all contained disaffected minorities and were safe only so long as Germany and Russia remained weak.

Russian Civil War and the New Economic Policy

Fighting continued in Russia for another three years after the end of the Great War. The Bolshevik Revolution had provoked Allied intervention, and, in December 1918, civil war broke out in Russia. The communists, as the Bolsheviks now called themselves, held central Russia, but all the surrounding provinces rose up against

Primary Source: The Zionist Organization's Memorandum . . . State in Palestine Read how the Zionist Organization presented its case in 1919 for the establishment of a Jewish state in Palestine.

Primary Source: Comments of the German Delegation . . . October 1919 Read about the innate rights and responsibilities of nations in times of war and peace, from the perspective of the German Delegation after World War I.

Primary Source: An Economist Analyzes the Versailles Treaty and Finds It Lacking Find out what a noted economist thinks of the Treaty of Versailles and the situation of the world in 1919.

League of Nations International organization founded in 1919 to promote world peace and cooperation but greatly weakened by the refusal of the United States to join. It proved ineffectual in stopping aggression by Italy, Japan, and Germany in the 1930s, and it was superseded by the United Nations in 1945.

Treaty of Versailles (1919) The treaty imposed on Germany by France, Great Britain, the United States, and other Allied Powers after World War I. It demanded that Germany dismantle its military and give up some lands to Poland. It was resented by many Germans.

them. Counterrevolutionary armies led by former tsarist officers obtained weapons and supplies from the Allies. However, by 1921, the superior discipline of the Red Army, led by Leon Trotsky, gave the communists victory.

Gradually, the communists reunited the old Russian Empire. In 1920, Ukrainian communists declared the independence of a Soviet republic of Ukraine; then, in 1922, this merged with Russia to create the Union of Soviet Socialist Republics (USSR), or Soviet Union. In 1920–1921, the Red Army reconquered the oil-rich Caucasus and established Soviet control over Central Asia. In 1922, the new Soviet republics of Georgia, Armenia, and Azerbaijan joined the USSR.

By then, the Russian economy was in a state of ruin. Factories and railroads had shut down, and farmland had been devastated and livestock killed. Lenin decided to release the economy from party and government control. In March 1921, he announced the **New Economic Policy** (NEP), which allowed peasants to own land and sell their crops, private merchants to trade, and private workshops to produce goods and sell them on the free market. Only the biggest businesses, such as banks, railroads, and factories, remained under government ownership.

The relaxation of controls had an immediate effect. Production began to climb, and food and other goods became available. In the cities, food remained scarce because farmers used their crops to feed their livestock rather than sell them. But the NEP reflected no change in the communist goal of creating a modern industrial economy without private property. It merely provided breathing space—what Lenin called "one step back to advance two steps forward." This meant investing in heavy industry and electrification, moving farmers to the new industries, and providing food for the urban workers. In other words, it meant making the peasants, the great majority of the Soviet people, pay for the industrialization of Russia.

When Lenin died in January 1924, his associates jockeyed for power. Leon Trotsky, commander of the Red Army, had the support of many "Old Bolsheviks" who had joined the party before the Revolution, but Joseph Stalin, general secretary of the Communist Party, got the support of the majority and filled the party bureaucracy with individuals loyal to himself. In January 1929, he forced Trotsky to flee the country.

Then, as absolute master of the party, he prepared to industrialize the Soviet Union at breakneck speed.

An Ephemeral Peace

After the war came five years of painful recovery and readjustment (1919–1923), followed by six years of growing peace and prosperity (1924–1929). One of the big adjustments in many Western societies was granting political rights to women (see "Class and Gender" below). Changes in international politics and economics were more upsetting. In the first period, the German government had printed money recklessly to fund reparations payments, causing a devastating inflation. As Germany teetered on the brink of civil war, radical nationalists called for revenge and tried to overthrow the government. Finally, the German government issued a new currency and promised to resume reparations payments, and the French agreed to withdraw their troops from the Ruhr.

Then in 1924, the vexed issue of reparations vanished as Germany borrowed money from New York banks to make its payments to France and Britain, which used the money to repay their wartime loans from the United States. This triangular flow of money stimulated the rapid recovery of the European economies. France began rebuilding its war-torn northern zone, Germany recovered from its hyperinflation and joined the League of Nations, and in the United States a boom began that was to last over five years.

While their economies flourished, governments grew more cautious and businesslike. Yet Germany and the Soviet Union did not accept their borders with the small nations that had arisen between them. In 1922, they signed a secret pact allowing the German army to conduct maneuvers in Russia (in violation of the Versailles treaty) in exchange for German help in building up Russian industry.

For a time, the League of Nations proved adept at resolving issues pertaining to health, labor relations, and postal and telegraph communications. But without U.S. participation, sanctions against states that violated League rules carried little weight.

New Economic Policy Policy proclaimed by Vladimir Lenin in 1921 to encourage the revival of the Soviet economy by allowing small private enterprises.

China and Japan: Contrasting Destinies

Why did China and Japan follow such divergent paths in this period?

China and Japan took different directions in the early twentieth century. Still in need of deep internal reform, giant China went through a revolution but soon collapsed into chaos. Japan's reforms before 1900 had gained it industry and a powerful military, which it used to take advantage of China's weakness.

Revolution in China

China's population—about 400 million in 1900—was the largest in the world and growing fast. Most Chinese worked incessantly, survived on a diet of grain and vegetables, and spent their lives in fear of floods, bandits, and tax collectors. Peasant plots averaged half what they had been two generations earlier. Meanwhile, landowners lived off the rents of their tenants, and officials, chosen through an elaborate examination system, enriched themselves from taxes and the government's monopolies on salt, iron, and other products. Wealthy merchants handled China's growing import-export trade in collaboration with foreign companies. The contrast between the squalor in which most urban residents lived and the luxury of the foreigners' enclaves in the treaty ports sharpened the resentment of educated Chinese.

When China's **Empress Dowager Cixi** (TSUH-shee) died in 1908, eight years after the Boxer Uprising that she had encouraged (see Chapter 24), the Revolutionary Alliance led by **Sun Yat-sen** (soon yot-SEN) (Sun Zhongshan, 1867–1925) prepared to take over. Sun had spent much of his life in Japan, England, and the United States, plotting the overthrow of the Qing dynasty. His tenacious spirit and his ideas, a mixture of nationalism, socialism, and Confucian philosophy, attracted a large following. A revolutionary assembly elected Sun president of China in December 1911, and the last Qing ruler, the boy-emperor Puyi, abdicated the throne. But Sun had no military forces at his command. To avoid a clash with the army, he resigned after a few weeks, and a new national assembly elected **Yuan Shikai** (you-AHN she-KIE), the most powerful of the regional generals, president of the new Chinese republic.

Yuan was an able military leader, but he had no political program. When Sun reorganized his followers into a political party called the **Guomindang** (gwo-min-dong) (National People's Party), Yuan quashed every attempt at creating a Western-style government and harassed Sun's followers.

Japan and World War I

Japan's population reached 60 million in 1925 and was increasing by a million a year. The crash program of industrialization begun in 1868 by the Meiji oligarchs (see Chapter 24) accelerated during the First World War when the Japanese suddenly found their textiles, consumer goods, and munitions in great demand.

Empress Dowager Cixi (1835–1908) Empress of China and mother of Emperor Guangxi. She put her son under house arrest, supported antiforeign movements, and resisted reforms of the Chinese government and armed forces.

Sun Yat-sen (1867–1925) Chinese nationalist revolutionary, founder and leader of the Guomindang until his death. He attempted to create a liberal democratic political movement in China but was thwarted by military leaders.

Yuan Shikai (1859–1916) Chinese general and first president of the Chinese Republic (1912–1916). He stood in the way of the democratic movement led by Sun Yat-sen.

Guomindang Nationalist political party founded on democratic principles by Sun Yat-sen in 1912. After 1925, the party was headed by Chiang Kai-shek, who turned it into an increasingly authoritarian movement.

The Bund in Shanghai On the Bund, the most important street in Shanghai, banks, corporate headquarters, and luxury hotels faced the waterfront where ships from around the world docked. Although Shanghai was China's commercial and industrial center, many of its workers loaded and unloaded ships by hand or pulled wealthy customers in rickshaws.

The Japanese economy grew four times faster than western Europe's and eight times faster than China's. Blessed with a rainy climate and many fast-flowing rivers, Japan expanded its hydroelectric capacity. By the mid-1930s, 89 percent of Japanese households had electric lights, compared with 44 percent of British households.

The *zaibatsu* (zie-BOT-soo), four giant corporations—Mitsubishi, Sumitomo, Yasuda, and Mitsui—that controlled most of Japan's industry and commerce profited the most. Farmers, who constituted half the population, remained poor; some, in desperation, sold their daughters to textile mills or into domestic service, where young women formed the bulk of the labor force. Labor unions were weak and repressed by the police.

Japan was quick to join the Allied side in World War I. Japanese forces soon conquered the German colonies in the northern Pacific and on the coast of China, and then turned their attention to the rest of China. In 1915, Japan presented China with Twenty-One Demands, which would have turned it into a virtual protectorate. Britain and the United States persuaded Japan to soften the demands but could not prevent it from keeping the German coastal enclaves and extracting railroad and mining concessions at China's expense. Thus began a bitter struggle that was to last for thirty years.

China in the 1920s

To many educated Chinese, the Western powers' decision at the Paris Peace Conference to agree to Japan's seizure of the German enclaves in China was a cruel insult. On May 4, 1919, students demonstrated in front of the Forbidden City of Beijing. Despite a government ban, the May Fourth Movement spread to other parts of China.

China's regional generals—the warlords—still supported their armies through plunder and arbitrary taxation, frightening off trade and investment. While neglecting the dikes and canals on which Chinese farmers depended, they fought one another and protected the gangsters who ran the opium trade. During the warlord era, China grew poorer. Only the treaty ports prospered.

Sun Yat-sen tried to make a comeback in Canton (Guangzhou) in the early 1920s. Though not a

Primary Source: The Three People's Principles and the Future of the Chinese People Discover the motivation behind Chinese revolutionary Sun Yat-sen's efforts to end taxation in China and to adopt a constitution.

- By 1900, the Qing presided over corruption and economic stagnation.
- Sun Yat-sen's Revolutionary Alliance overthrew the Qing, but the military thwarted Guomindang attempts to set up a Western-style government.
- During World War I and after, when Japanese industry boomed, the *zaibatsu* corporations benefited most from the growing prosperity.
- Japan joined the Allies, captured German colonies, and tried to impose the Twenty-One Demands on China.
- In 1919, the May Fourth Movement rose to protest treatment by Western powers, but the warlords controlled China throughout the 1920s.
- To subdue the warlords, Chiang Kai-shek allied with the communists, and his government then crushed the communists and attempted top-down modernization.

communist, he was impressed with the efficiency of Lenin's revolutionary tactics and let a Soviet adviser reorganize the Guomindang along Leninist lines. He also welcomed members of the newly created Chinese Communist Party into the Guomindang.

When Sun died in 1925, the leadership of his party passed to Chiang Kai-shek (chang kie-shek) (1886–1975). An officer and director of the military academy, Chiang trained several hundred young officers, who remained loyal to him thereafter. In 1927, he determined to crush the regional warlords. Moving north from his base in Canton, he briefly formed an alliance with the communists. Once Shanghai was occupied, however, he allied himself with local gangsters to crush the labor unions and decimate the communists, whom he considered a threat. He then defeated or co-opted most of the other warlords and established a dictatorship.

Chiang's government issued ambitious plans to revitalize the economy, but his followers were neither competent administrators like the Japanese officials of the Meiji Restoration nor ruthless modernizers like the Russian Bolsheviks. Instead, the government attracted thousands of opportunists whose goal was to "become an official and get rich" by taxing and plundering businesses. In the countryside, tax collectors and landowners squeezed the peasants ever harder.

The New Middle East

How did the Middle East change as a result of the war?

At the Paris Peace Conference, France, Britain, Italy, and Japan proposed to divide the territories of the Ottoman Empire among themselves, but their ambitions clashed with President Wilson's ideal of national self-determination. While Turkish nationalists fought for and achieved independence, the Arab-speaking territories of the old Ottoman Empire became part of the League of Nations' new **mandate system**, run by French and British administrations charged with promoting "the material and moral well-being and the social progress of the inhabitants." In Palestine, Zionists accelerated Jewish immigration (see Map 26.2).

The Rise of Modern Turkey

At war's end, Allied forces occupied the Ottoman Empire and made the sultan give up most of his lands. But they had to reckon with Mustafa Kemal, a war hero who formed a nationalist government in central Anatolia with the backing of fellow army officers. His armies defeated a Greek army of occupation in western Anatolia in 1922. An ensuing population exchange moved hundreds of thousands of Greeks to Greece and brought Muslims from that country to Turkey.

As a war hero proclaimed savior of his country, Kemal was able to impose wrenching changes on his people. An outspoken modernizer, he was eager to bring Turkey closer to Europe as quickly as possible. He abolished the sultanate, declared Turkey a secular republic in 1923, and introduced European laws. In a radical break with Islamic tradition, he suppressed Muslim courts, schools, and religious orders and replaced the Arabic alphabet with the Latin alphabet.

Women received civil equality, including the right to vote and to be elected to the national assembly. Kemal forbade polygamy and instituted civil marriage and divorce. He even changed people's clothing, strongly discouraging women from veiling their faces

mandate system Allocation of former German colonies and Ottoman possessions to the victorious powers after World War I, to be administered under League of Nations supervision.

Interactive Map

Map 26.2 **Territorial Changes in the Middle East After World War I** The defeat and dismemberment of the Ottoman Empire at the end of World War I resulted in an entirely new political map of the region. The Turkish Republic inherited Anatolia and a small piece of Europe, while the Ottoman Empire's Arab provinces were divided between France and Great Britain as "Class A Mandates." The French acquired Syria and Lebanon, and the British got Iraq and Palestine (now Israel, Jordan, and the Palestinian Territories). © Cengage Learning and ordering Turkish men to wear European brimmed hats instead of the fez. He ordered everyone to take a family name, choosing the name Atatürk ("father of the Turks") for himself.

Arab Lands and the Question of Palestine

Among the Arab people, the thinly disguised colonialism of the mandate system set off protests and rebellions. Arabs viewed the European presence not as "liberation" from Ottoman "oppression" but as foreign occupation.

The British attempted to control the Middle East with a mixture of bribery and intimidation. They helped Faisal, leader of the Arab Revolt, become king of Syria. When the French ousted him, the British made him king of Iraq and used aerial bombing to quell the resulting rural insurrections. In 1931, Britain granted Iraq official independence in exchange for a military alliance, the right to keep two air bases, and an assured flow of petroleum. France, meanwhile, sent thousands of troops to Syria and Lebanon to crush nationalist uprisings.

In Egypt as in Iraq, the British substituted a phony independence for official colonialism. They declared Egypt independent in 1922 but reserved the right to station troops along the Suez Canal to secure their link with India. Despite nationalist opposition, Britain was successful in keeping Egypt in limbo—neither independent nor a colony—thanks to an alliance with King Fuad (sultan 1917-1922; king 1922-1936) and conservative Egyptian politicians who feared both secular and religious radicalism.

As soon as Palestine became a British mandate in 1920, Jewish immigrants, encouraged by the Balfour Declaration of 1917, arrived to join the small community that had immigrated in the nineteenth century. Most settled in the cities, but some purchased land to establish *kibbutzim*, communal farms. The purchases of land by Jewish agencies angered the indigenous Palestinians, especially tenant farmers who had been evicted to make room for settlers. In 1920-1921, riots erupted between Jews and Arabs. When far more Jewish immigrants arrived than they had anticipated, the British tried to limit immigration, thereby alienating the Jews without mollifying the Arabs. Increasingly, Jews arrived without papers, smuggled in by militant Zionist organizations. In the 1930s, the country was torn by strikes and guerrilla warfare that the British could not control. In the process, Britain earned the hatred of both sides.

The Jewish Settlement of Palestine The Jewish population of Israel originated with the immigration to Palestine of thousands of Jews fleeing persecution and discrimination in Europe. Many settled on the land and founded *kibbutzim*, or collective farms. In this picture taken 1912, an eighty-four-year-old immigrant from Russia learns to plow the land.

Hulton Archive/Getty Images

- Wilson's self-determination principle clashed with British, French, Italian, and Greek attempts to partition the Ottoman Empire.

- After World War I, Mustafa Kemal led Turkish nationalists against European occupiers and expelled the Greeks from Turkey.

- Kemal declared Turkey a secular republic and, under the name Atatürk, westernized Turkey's economy and society.

- In Arab lands under the mandate system, Britain and France used military force to crush nationalist uprisings.

- In Egypt, Britain substituted phony independence for colonialism.

- Jewish immigration to Palestine created tension, often erupting into violence, between Jews and Palestinian Arabs.

Society, Culture, and Technology in the Industrialized World

How did European and North American society and technology change in the aftermath of the war?

Advances in science offered astonishing new insights into the mysteries of nature and the universe. New technologies, many of them pioneered in the United States, promised to change the daily lives of millions of people. At the same time, new cultural trends developed that had profound effects.

Class and Gender

After the war, class distinctions began to fade. Many European aristocrats had died on the battlefields, and with them went their class's long domination of the army, the diplomatic corps, and other elite sectors of society. On both sides of the Atlantic, engineers, businessmen, lawyers, and other professionals rose to prominence, increasing the relative importance of the middle class.

The activities of governments had expanded during the war and continued to grow. Governments provided housing, highways, schools, public health facilities, broadcasting, and other services. This growth of government influence created a need for thousands more bureaucrats. Department stores, banks, insurance companies, and other businesses also increased the white-collar work force.

In contrast with the middle class, the working class did not expand. The introduction of new machines and new ways of organizing work, such as the automobile assembly line that Henry Ford devised, increased workers' productivity so that greater outputs could be achieved without a larger labor force.

Women's lives changed more rapidly in the 1920s than in any previous decade. Although the end of the war marked a retreat from wartime job opportunities, some women remained in the work force as wage earners and salaried professionals. The young and wealthy enjoyed new personal freedoms; they drove cars, played sports, traveled alone, and smoked in public. For others the upheavals of war brought more suffering than liberation. Millions of women had lost their fathers, brothers, sons, husbands, and fiancés in the war or in the great influenza epidemic. The shortage of young men caused many single women to lead lives of loneliness and destitution.

In Europe and North America advocates of women's rights had been demanding the vote for women since the 1890s. Before the twentieth century, only New Zealand granted women the vote. Norway followed in 1915, Russia in 1917, and Canada and Germany in 1918. Britain gave the vote to women over thirty in 1918 and later extended it to younger women. The Nineteenth Amendment to the U.S. Constitution granted suffrage to American women in 1920. Women in Turkey began voting in 1934. Most other countries withheld suffrage until after 1945.

In dictatorships voting rights for women made no difference, and in democratic countries women tended to vote like their male relatives. In the British elections of 1918—the first to include women—they overwhelmingly voted for the Conservative Party. Everywhere, their influence on politics was less radical than feminists had hoped and conservatives had feared.

On both sides of the Atlantic women participated in social reform movements to prevent the mistreatment of women, children, and industrial workers. In the United States such reforms were championed by Progressives such as Jane Addams (1860–1935), who founded a settlement house in a poor neighborhood and received the Nobel Peace Prize in 1931. In Europe reformers were generally aligned with Socialist or Labour Parties.

Since 1874 the Women's Christian Temperance Union had campaigned against alcohol and taverns. In the early twentieth century the American Carrie Nation (1846–1911) became famous for destroying saloons and lecturing in the United States and Europe against the evils of liquor. As a result of this campaign, the Eighteenth Amendment imposed prohibition in the United States from 1919 until it was revoked by the Twenty-First Amendment fourteen years later.

Among the most controversial, and eventually most effective, of the reformers were those who advocated contraception, such as the American **Margaret Sanger** (1883–1966). Her campaign brought her into conflict with the authorities, who equated birth control with pornography. Finally, in 1923 she was able to found a birth control clinic in New York. In France, however, the government prohibited contraception and abortion in 1920 in an effort to increase the birthrate and make up for the loss of so many young men in the war. Only the Russian communists allowed abortion, for ideological reasons.

Revolution in the Sciences

At the end of the nineteenth century, a revolution in physics undermined all the old certainties about nature. Physicists discovered that atoms, the building blocks of matter, are not indivisible but consist of far smaller subatomic particles. In 1900, the German physicist **Max Planck** (1858–1947) found that light and energy do not flow in a continuous stream but travel in small units, which he called *quanta*. These findings seemed strange enough, but what really undermined Newtonian physics was the theory of relativity developed by **Albert Einstein** (1879–1955), another German physicist. In 1916, Einstein announced that not only is matter made of insubstantial particles, but also that time, space, and mass are not fixed but are relative to one another.

Primary Source: Women and the Vote in Syria . . . in the Proposed State Follow along as members of the Syrian parliament debate whether or not to grant Syrian women the right to vote.

To nonscientists, it seemed as though theories expressed in arcane mathematical formulas were replacing truth and common sense. Far from being mere speculation, however, the new physics promised to unlock the secrets of matter and provide humans with plentiful—and potentially dangerous—new sources of energy.

The new social sciences were even more unsettling than the new physics, for they challenged Victorian morality, middle-class values, and notions of Western superiority. Sigmund Freud (1856–1939), a Viennese physician, developed a technique—psychoanalysis—to probe the minds of his patients. He found not only rationality but also hidden layers of emotion and desire repressed by social restraints. "The primitive, savage and evil impulses have not vanished from any individual, but continue their existence, although in a repressed state," he warned. Meanwhile, sociologists and anthropologists had begun the empirical study of societies, both Western and non-Western. Before the war, the French sociologist Emile Durkheim (1858–1917) had come to the then-shocking conclusion that "there are no religions that are false. All are true in their own fashion."

If the words *primitive* and *savage* applied to Europeans as well as to other peoples, and if religions were all equally "true," then what remained of the superiority of Western civilization? Cultural relativism, as the new approach to human societies was called, was as unnerving as relativity in physics.

The New Technologies of Modernity

In North America, even working-class people could afford some of the new products of scientific research, inventors' ingenuity, and industrial production. Mass consumption lagged in

Margaret Sanger (1883–1966) American nurse and author; pioneer in the movement for family planning; organized conferences and established birth control clinics.

Max Planck (1858–1947) German physicist who developed quantum theory and was awarded the Nobel Prize for physics in 1918.

Albert Einstein (1879–1955) German physicist who developed the theory of relativity, which states that time, space, and mass are relative to each other and not fixed.

Europe, but science and technology were just as advanced, and public fascination with the latest inventions—the cult of the modern—was just as strong.

No innovation attracted more public interest than the airplane. In 1903, two young American mechanics, Wilbur and Orville Wright, built the first aircraft that was heavier than air and could be maneuvered in flight. From that moment on, wherever they appeared, airplanes fascinated people. During the war, the exploits of air aces relieved the tedium of news from the front. In the 1920s, aviation became a sport and a form of entertainment. Among the most celebrated pilots were three Americans: Amelia Earhart, the first woman to fly across the Atlantic Ocean; Richard Byrd, the first to fly over the North Pole, in 1926; and Charles Lindbergh, the first person to fly alone across the Atlantic, in 1927. The heroic age of flight lasted until the late 1930s, when aviation became a means of transportation (see Environment and Technology: The Birth of Civil Aviation).

Electricity's impact on home life was more sweeping. The first home use of electricity was for lighting, thanks to the economical and long-lasting incandescent bulb. Then electrical utilities joined manufacturers in advertising electric irons, fans, washing machines, hot plates, radios, and other electric appliances. After the war, radio moved from the battlefield into the home. The first commercial station began broadcasting in Pittsburgh in 1920. By 1930, hundreds of stations were broadcasting news, sports, soap operas, and advertising to 12 million homes in North America. In Europe, radio spread more slowly because governments reserved the airwaves for cultural and official programs and taxed radio owners to pay for the service.

Another medium that spread explosively in the 1920s was film. Motion pictures had begun in France in 1895 and flourished in Europe. In the United States, filmmaking started at almost the same time, but American filmmakers saw the medium's

> **Primary Source: U.S. Senate Speech, June 29, 1922** Read one of the earliest arguments for censorship in the motion picture industry.

potential to entertain audiences rather than preserve outstanding theatrical performances. After World War I, filmmaking took root and flourished in Japan, India, Turkey, Egypt, and a suburb of Los Angeles, California, called Hollywood. American and European movie studios were both successful in exporting films, since silent movies presented no language problems. Then in 1927 the United States introduced the first "talking" motion picture, *The Jazz Singer*, which changed all the rules. Hollywood studios began the diffusion of American culture that has continued to this day.

Advances in medicine—some learned in the war—were another important technology. Wounds were regularly disinfected and x-ray machines diagnosed fractures. After the war, cities built costly water supply and sewage treatment systems. By the 1920s, indoor plumbing and flush toilets penetrated even working-class neighborhoods. Interest in cleanliness altered private life. Soap and appliance manufacturers filled women's magazines with advertisements for products to help housewives keep their family's homes and clothing spotless and their meals fresh and wholesome. The decline in infant mortality and the improvements in general health and life expectancy in this period owe as much to the cult of cleanliness as to advances in medicine.

Technology and the Environment

Two new technologies—the skyscraper and the automobile—transformed the urban environment. At the end of the nineteenth century, architects had begun to design ever-higher buildings using load-bearing steel frames and passenger elevators. Major corporations in Chicago and New York competed to build the most daring buildings in the world, such as New York's 55-story Woolworth Building (1912) and Chicago's 34-story Tribune Tower (1923). A building boom in the late 1920s produced dozens of skyscrapers, culminating with the 86-story, 1,239-foot (377-meter) Empire State Building in New York City, completed in 1932.

European cities restricted the height of buildings to protect their architectural heritage; Paris forbade buildings over 56 feet (17 meters) high. In innovative designs, however, European architects led the way. In the 1920s, the Swiss architect known as Le Corbusier

environment & technology

The Birth of Civil Aviation

Antoine de Saint-Exupéry, best known for his children's book The Little Prince, was a pilot for Aéropostale, a French airline that served South America. In his book *Vol de Nuit* (Night Flight), he tells a harrowing tale of a pilot blown out to sea in a storm over Argentina:

> One of the radio operators at the Comodoro Rivadavia station in Patagonia made a sudden gesture and all those who were keeping a helpless vigil there crowded around him. . . .
>
> "Storm?"
>
> He nodded yes; static prevented him from hearing the message. Then he scrawled some illegible signs, then words. Then the text came out:
>
> "Cut off at 12,000 feet above the storm. Proceeding due west toward interior; we were carried out to sea. No visibility below. Do not know if still flying over sea. Report if storm extends interior." . . .

Buenos Aires transmitted a reply.

> "Storm covers all interior. How much gasoline left?"
>
> "Half an hour."

These words sped from post to post back to Buenos Aires. The plane was doomed to plunge in less than half an hour into a hurricane that would smash it to earth. . . .

Today, airplanes are safer than cars, but in the 1920s, when regular airline service began, air travel was dangerous. Airplanes, many of them converted World War I bombers, were made of wood and cloth, with open cockpits for the pilot and navigator and wicker chairs for passengers. Pilots located their position by looking for towns and railroad tracks. At night and in cloudy weather, they often got lost. And yet, with these machines they conquered the skies.

Source: Antoine de Saint-Exupéry, *Vol de nuit* (Paris: Gallimard, 1939), 147–149.

An Early Passenger Plane After World War I, aviators and aircraft manufacturers turned their attention to civil aviation, such as airmail service, crop dusting, and carrying passengers. This British-made De Havilland-34 bi-plane, photographed before 1924, was designed to carry up to ten passengers.

Mary Evans Picture Library/The Image Works

The Archetypal Automobile City As Los Angeles grew from a modest town into a sprawling metropolis, broad avenues, parking lots, and garages were built to accommodate automobiles. By 1929, most families owned a car, and streetcar lines had closed for lack of passengers. This photograph shows a street in the downtown business district.

History in Focus *The skyscraper and the automobile transformed the twentieth-century urban environment. The photo "The Archetypal Automobile City" clearly illustrates the effect of the automobile on Los Angeles. Does the skyscraper appear to have had the same effect? Why or why not? Find the answer online.*

(luh cor-booz-YEH) outlined a new approach to architecture that featured simplicity of form, absence of surface ornamentation, easy manufacture, and inexpensive materials. Other architects—including the Finn Eero Saarinen, the Germans Ludwig Mies van der Rohe (LOOD-vig MEES fahn der ROW-uh) and Walter Gropius, and the American Frank Lloyd Wright—advanced his lines of thought and added their own to create what became known as the International Style.

While central business districts were reaching for the sky, outlying areas were spreading into the countryside, thanks to the automobile. The assembly line pioneered by Henry Ford mass-produced vehicles in ever-greater volume and at falling prices. By 1929, the United States had one car for every five people, five-sixths of the world's automobiles. Far from being blamed for their exhaust emissions, automobiles were praised as the solution to urban pollution. As cars replaced carts and carriages, horses disappeared from city streets, as did tons of manure.

The most important environmental effect of automobiles was suburban sprawl. Middle-class families could now live in single-family homes that were too far apart to be served by public transportation. As middle- and working-class families bought cars, cities acquired rings of automobile suburbs. Los Angeles, the first true automobile city, consisted of suburbs spread over hundreds of square miles and linked together by broad avenues. In those sections of the city where streetcar lines went out of business, the automobile became a necessity for commuters. Many Americans saw Los Angeles as the portent of a glorious future when everyone would have a car; only a few foresaw the congestion and pollution that would ensue.

- After the war, class distinctions loosened and governments and businesses grew, encouraging the expansion of the middle class.

- Women's lives changed as many gained the right to vote, remained in the work force, and participated in social reform movements.

- Modern physicists challenged Newtonian physics, while social scientists undermined Victorian values and ideas of Western superiority.

- New technologies, such as aircraft, motion pictures, and advances in medicine, transformed daily life in the industrialized world.

- Skyscrapers transformed urban environments, and modern architects developed the International Style.

- Mass-produced automobiles offered low-cost transportation and encouraged suburban sprawl and the expansion of road systems.

Conclusion

The Great War caused a major realignment among the nations of the world. France and Britain, the two leading colonial powers, emerged economically weakened despite their victory. The war brought defeat and humiliation to Germany but did not reduce its military or industrial potential. It destroyed the old regime of Russia, leading to civil war and revolution from which the victorious powers sought to isolate themselves. Two other old empires—the Austro-Hungarian and the Ottoman—were divided into many smaller and weaker nations.

Only two countries benefited from the war. Japan took advantage of the European conflict to develop its industries and press its demands on a China weakened by domestic turmoil. The United States emerged as the most prosperous and potentially most powerful nation, restrained only by strong isolationist sentiments.

In the Middle East, the fall of the Ottoman Empire awakened aspirations for nationhood among various ethnic groups. These aspirations were thwarted when France and Great Britain tried to impose their rule upon the former Ottoman lands, causing conflicts and bitter enmities.

CHAPTER REVIEW

Download the MP3 audio file of the Chapter Review to listen to on the go.

What led to the outbreak of the First World War? (page 628)

In 1914 the great powers of Europe had not had a major conflict in decades and believed a war would be quick and victorious. Each of the two alliances they formed—the Central Powers and the Entente—was locked into a rigid timetable of mobilizations and railroad schedules. When competing nationalisms in the Balkans triggered a conflict between Serbia and Austria-Hungary, the alliances quickly drew Russia, Germany, France, and Britain into the conflict.

How did the war lead to revolution in Russia? (page 631)

Russia was the least prepared for war. Chaotic mobilization and a string of defeats disrupted the economy, causing severe shortages. As the war progressed, soldiers began to desert, and the government lost control of the army and the population. The moderate government that replaced the tsar in March 1917 could neither satisfy the people nor pursue the war. Its failure allowed the Bolsheviks to overthrow it in a second revolution.

What role did the war play in eroding European dominance in the world? (page 636)

France, Great Britain, and Italy expected to reap the benefits of victory and expand their empires at the expense of the defeated powers. However, with the exception of the United States, which withdrew to the Western Hemisphere, the victors were exhausted and impoverished by the war and had lost the will to fight in colonial wars. Meanwhile, the idea of self-determination had spread to the Middle East and Asia, where nationalist politicians and their followers were determined to resist European dominance.

Why did China and Japan follow such divergent paths in this period? (page 639)

After 1868, Japan established a strong government and built an industrial economy comparable to those of Europe. Meanwhile China, long ruled by the Qing dynasty, erupted after 1911 in civil wars in which warlords and political factions vied for power. The Japanese military and major industries seized the opportunity of Europe's involvement in the Great War to build up Japan's economy at China's expense.

How did the Middle East change as a result of the war? (page 641)

In Anatolia, the heartland of the Ottoman Empire, a movement for national unity led by Kemal Atatürk fought for and achieved Turkish independence. In the predominantly Arab lands, nationalist leaders decried European domination. Jewish immigration into Palestine provoked a violent reaction from the Palestinians, which their British overlords found hard to control.

How did European and North American society and technology change in the aftermath of the war? (page 644)

Many women who had participated in the war effort remained in the work force and demanded voting and other rights. Governments took on new responsibilities for education, public health, and social welfare. Automobiles, movies, and radio broadcasts were eagerly adopted. Advances in the sciences, especially in physics and psychology, undermined the old cultural certainties, while birth control and family planning provoked considerable opposition from traditionalists.

Key Terms

Western Front (p. 631)	Empress Dowager Cixi (p. 639)
Faisal I (p. 633)	
Balfour Declaration (p. 633)	Sun Yat-sen (p. 639)
Bolsheviks (p. 634)	Yuan Shikai (p. 639)
Vladimir Lenin (p. 634)	Guomindang (p. 639)
Woodrow Wilson (p. 635)	mandate system (p. 641)
League of Nations (p. 637)	Margaret Sanger (p. 645)
Treaty of Versailles (p. 637)	Max Planck (p. 645)
New Economic Policy (p. 638)	Albert Einstein (p. 645)

Web Resources

Pronunciation Guide

Interactive Maps
- MAP 26.1 The First World War in Europe
- MAP 26.2 Territorial Changes in the Middle East After World War I

Primary Sources
- Letter from Turkey, Summer 1915
- The Balfour Declaration
- Mud and Khaki, Memoirs of an Incomplete Soldier

- The Zionist Organization's Memorandum . . . State in Palestine
- Comments of the German Delegation . . . October 1919
- An Economist Analyzes the Versailles Treaty and Finds It Lacking
- The Three People's Principles and the Future of the Chinese People
- Women and the Vote in Syria . . . in the Proposed State
- U.S. Senate Speech, June 29, 1922

Answer to the History in Focus Question
See photo on page 648, "The Archetypal Automobile City."

Visit the CourseMate website at www.cengagebrain.com for additional study tools and review materials for this chapter.

The Collapse of the Old Order

© Cengage Learning

Visit the CourseMate website at **www.cengagebrain.com** for additional study tools and review materials for this chapter.

efore the First World War, the Italian futurist poets exalted violence as a noble and manly idea. Filippo Marinetti defined their creed in these words: "We want to glorify war, the world's only hygiene—militarism, deed, destroyer of anarchisms, the beautiful ideas that are death-bringing, and the subordination of women." His friend Gabriele d'Annunzio said: "If it is a crime to incite citizens to violence, I shall boast of this crime."[1]

The war taught most survivors to abhor violence. During the 1920s, the world seemed to return to what United States president Warren Harding called "normalcy": prosperity in Europe and America, European colonialism in Asia and Africa, paternalistic U.S. domination of Latin America, and peace almost everywhere. But for a few, war and domination became a creed and a goal.

In 1929, the artificial normalcy of the 1920s began to come apart. The Great Depression caused governments to turn against one another in a desperate attempt to protect their people's livelihood. As the economic crisis spread around the world, businesses went bankrupt, prices fell, factories closed, and workers were laid off. Even wholly agricultural nations and colonies suffered as markets for their exports shriveled.

Some countries chose to solve their problems by violent means. When nations shut their doors to Japan's products, the Japanese military tried to save their country by conquering China. In Germany, the Depression reawakened resentments against the victors of the Great War; people who feared communism or blamed Jews for their troubles turned to Hitler and the Nazis, who promised to save their society by dominating others. In the Soviet Union, Stalin used energetic and murderous means to force his country into a communist version of the Industrial Revolution.

The result was war. The Second World War engulfed more lands and peoples and caused far more death and destruction than any previous conflict. At the end of it, much of Europe and East Asia lay in ruins, and millions of destitute refugees sought safety in other lands. The European colonial powers were either defeated or so weakened that they could no longer hold on to their empires when Asian and African peoples asserted their desire for independence.

The Stalin Revolution

How did the Soviet Union change under Stalin, and at what cost?

After **Joseph Stalin** (1879–1953) achieved total mastery over the USSR in early 1929 (see Chapter 26), he led it through another revolution: an economic and social transformation that turned it into a great industrial and military power and intensified both admiration for and fear of communism throughout the world.

Five-Year Plans

Stalin's ambition to turn the USSR into an industrial nation was not intended initially to produce consumer goods for a mass market, much less enrich individuals as in Britain and the United States. Instead, his aim was to increase the power of the Communist Party domestically and the power of the Soviet Union in relation to other countries. By building up Russia's industry, Stalin was determined to prevent a repetition of the humiliating defeat Russia had suffered at the hands of Germany in 1917.

Stalin encouraged rapid industrialization through a series of **Five-Year Plans**, a system of centralized control copied from the German experience of World War I. The goal of the first Five-Year Plan was to quintuple the output of electricity and double that of heavy industry: iron, steel, coal, and machinery. Beginning in October 1928, the communist government created whole industries and cities from scratch, then recruited millions of

Joseph Stalin (1879–1953) Bolshevik revolutionary, head of the Soviet Communist Party after 1924, and dictator of the Soviet Union from 1929 to 1953. He led the Soviet Union with an iron fist, using Five-Year Plans to increase industrial production and terror to crush all opposition.

Five-Year Plans Plans that Joseph Stalin introduced to industrialize the Soviet Union rapidly, beginning in 1928. They set goals for the output of steel, electricity, machinery, and most other products and were enforced by the police powers of the state. They succeeded in making the Soviet Union a major industrial power before World War II.

Chronology

	Europe and North Africa	Asia and the Pacific
1930		
	1931 Great Depression reaches Europe **1933** Hitler comes to power in Germany	**1931** Japanese forces occupy Manchuria
1935		
	1936 Hitler invades the Rhineland	
		1937 Japanese troops invade China, conquer coastal provinces; Chiang Kai-shek flees to Sichuan **1937–1938** Japanese troops take Nanjing
	1939 (Sept. 1) German forces invade Poland	
1940	**1940** (March–April) German forces conquer Denmark, Norway, the Netherlands, and Belgium **1940** (May–June) German forces conquer France **1940** (June–Sept.) Battle of Britain	
	1941 (June 21) German forces invade USSR **1942–1943** Allies and Germany battle for control of North Africa; Soviet victory in Battle of Stalingrad (1943)	**1941** (Dec. 7) Japanese aircraft bomb Pearl Harbor **1942** (Jan.–March) Japanese conquer Thailand, Philippines, Malaya **1942** (June) United States Navy defeats Japan at Battle of Midway
	1943–1944 Red Army slowly pushes Wehrmacht back to Germany **1944** (June 6) D-day: U.S., British, and Canadian troops land in Normandy	
1945	**1945** (May 7) Germany surrenders	**1945** (Aug. 6) United States drops atomic bomb on Hiroshima **1945** (Aug. 14) Japan surrenders **1945–1949** Civil war in China **1949** Communists defeat Guomindang; Mao proclaims People's Republic (Oct. 1)

peasants and trained them to work in the new factories and mines and offices. In every way except actual fighting, Stalin's Russia resembled a nation at war.

Rapid industrialization hastened environmental changes. Hydroelectric dams turned rivers into strings of reservoirs. Roads, canals, and railroad tracks cut the landscape. Forests and grassland were turned into farmland. From an environmental perspective, the outcome of the Five-Year Plans resembled the transformation that had occurred in the United States and Canada a few decades earlier.

Collectivization of Agriculture

Since the Soviet Union was still a predominantly agrarian country, the only way to pay for these massive investments, provide the labor, and feed the millions of new industrial workers was to squeeze the peasantry. Stalin therefore proceeded with the most radical social experiment conceived up to that time: the collectivization of agriculture.

Collectivization meant consolidating small private farms into vast collectives and making the farmers work together in commonly owned fields. Each collective was expected to supply the government with a fixed amount of food and distribute what was left among its members. Collectives were to become outdoor factories through the use of machinery and techniques of mass production. Collectivization was expected to bring the peasants once and for all under government control so they never again could withhold food supplies as they had done during the period of Lenin's New Economic Policy (see Chapter 26).

The government mounted a massive propaganda campaign to enlist the farmers' support. At first, all seemed to go well, but soon *kulaks* (COO-lox) ("fists"), the better-off peasants, began to resist giving up all their property. When soldiers came to force them into collectives at gunpoint, the kulaks burned their own crops, smashed their own equipment, and slaughtered their own livestock. Within a few months, they slaughtered half of the Soviet Union's horses and cattle and two-thirds of its sheep and goats. In retaliation, Stalin ruthlessly ordered the "liquidation of kulaks as a class" and incited the poor peasants to attack their wealthier neighbors. Over 8 million kulaks were arrested. Many were executed, and the rest were sent to slave labor camps, where most starved to death.

The peasants who were left had been the least successful before collectivization and proved to be the least competent after. Many were sent to work in factories. The rest were forbidden to leave their farms. With half of their draft animals gone, they could not plant or harvest enough to meet the swelling demands of the cities. Yet government agents took whatever they could find, leaving little or nothing for the farmers themselves. After bad harvests in 1933 and 1934, a famine swept through the countryside, killing some 5 million people, about one in every twenty farmers.

Stalin's second Five-Year Plan, designed to run from 1933 to 1937, was originally intended to increase the output of consumer goods. But when the Nazis took over Germany in 1933 (see below), Stalin changed the plan to emphasize heavy industries that could produce armaments. Between 1927 and 1937, the Soviet output of metals and machines increased fourteen-fold while consumer goods became scarce and food was rationed. After a decade of Stalinism, the Soviet people were more poorly clothed, fed, and housed than they had been during the years of the New Economic Policy.

Terror and Opportunities

The 1930s brought both terror and new opportunities to the Soviet people. The forced pace of industrialization, the collectivization of agriculture, and the uprooting of millions of people could be accomplished only under duress. To prevent any possible resistance or rebellion, the NKVD, Stalin's secret police force, created a climate of suspicion and fear. The terror that pervaded the country was a reflection of Stalin's own paranoia, for he distrusted everyone and feared for his life.

First "Old Bolsheviks" and high officials were put on trial; then the terror spread steadily downward. The government regularly made demands on people that they could not meet, so everyone was guilty of breaking some regulation. People from all walks of life were arrested—sometimes on a mere suspicion or because of a false accusation by a jealous coworker or neighbor, sometimes for expressing a doubt or

The Collectivization of Soviet Agriculture One of the goals of collectivization was to introduce modern farm machinery. This poster shows delighted farmers operating new tractors and threshers.

David King Collection

working too hard or not hard enough, sometimes for being related to someone previously arrested, sometimes for no reason at all. Millions of people were sentenced without a trial. At the height of the terror, some 8 million were sent to *gulags* (GOO-logs) (labor camps), where perhaps a million died each year of exposure or malnutrition. To its victims, the terror seemed capricious and random.

Yet Stalin's regime received the support of many Soviet citizens. Suddenly, with so many people gone and new industries and cities being built everywhere, there were opportunities for those who remained, especially the poor and the young. Women entered careers and jobs previously closed to them, becoming steelworkers, physicians, and office managers; but they retained their household and child-rearing duties, receiving little help from men (see Diversity and Dominance: Women, Family Values, and the Russian Revolution). People who moved to the cities, worked enthusiastically, and asked no questions could hope to rise into the upper ranks of the Communist Party, the military, the government, or the professions, where the privileges and rewards were many.

Stalin's brutal methods helped the Soviet Union industrialize faster than any country had ever done. By the late 1930s, the USSR was the world's third largest industrial power, after the United States and Germany. To foreign observers, it seemed to be booming with construction projects, production increases, and labor shortages. Even anticommunist observers admitted that only a planned economy subject to strict government control could avoid the Depression. To millions of Soviet citizens who took pride in the

new strength of their country, and to many foreigners who contrasted conditions in the Soviet Union with the unemployment and despair in the West, Stalin's achievement seemed worth any price.

The Depression

What caused the Depression, and what effects did it have on the world?

On October 24, 1929—"Black Thursday"—the New York stock market went into a dive. Within days, stocks lost half their value, and their value continued to fall for three years. Thousands of banks and businesses collapsed. Millions of workers lost their jobs. The stock market crash started the deepest and most widespread depression in history.

Economic Crisis

As consumers reduced their purchases, businesses cut production. General Motors, for example, saw its sales drop by half between 1929 and 1931. Companies laid off thousands of workers, throwing them onto public charity. Business and government agencies replaced their women workers with men, arguing that men had to support their families, whereas women worked only for "pin money." Jobless men deserted their families. As farm prices fell, small farmers went bankrupt and lost their land. By mid-1932, the American economy had fallen by half, and 25 percent of the work force was unemployed. Government spending on welfare and public works was unable to restore prosperity. Many observers thought the free-enterprise system would be replaced by bread lines, soup kitchens, men selling apples on street corners, and hoboes riding freight trains.

Frightened by the stock market collapse, the New York banks called in their loans to Germany and Austria. Without American money, Germany and Austria stopped paying reparations to France and Britain, which then could not repay their war loans to America. By 1931, the Depression had spread to Europe. Governments canceled both reparations payments and war loans, but it was too late to save the world economy.

In 1930, the U.S. government, hoping to protect domestic industries from foreign competition,

Diversity & Dominance

Women, Family Values, and the Russian Revolution

The Bolsheviks were of two minds on the subject of women. They were opposed to bourgeois morality and to the oppression of women, especially working-class women, under capitalism. But what to put in its place?

Alexandra Kollontai was the most outspoken of the Bolsheviks on the subject of women's rights. She advocated the liberation of women, the replacement of housework by communal kitchens and laundries, and divorce on demand. Under socialism, love, sex, and marriage would be entirely equal, reciprocal, and free of economic obligations. Childbearing would be encouraged, but children would be raised communally: "The worker mother . . . must remember that there are henceforth only our children, those of the communist state, the common possession of all workers."

In a lecture she gave at Sverdlov University in 1921, Kollontai declared:

. . . it is important to preserve not only the interests of the woman but also the life of the child, and this is to be done by giving the woman the opportunity to combine labour and maternity. Soviet power tries to create a situation where a woman does not have to cling to a man she has learned to loathe only because she has nowhere else to go with her children, and where a woman alone does not have to fear for her life and the life of her child. In the labour republic it is not the philanthropists with their humiliating charity but the workers and peasants, fellow-creators of the new society, who hasten to help the working woman and strive to lighten the burden of motherhood. . . . I would like to say a few words about a question which is closely connected with the problem of maternity— the question of abortion, and Soviet Russia's attitude toward it. On 20 November 1920 the labour republic issued a law abolishing the penalties that had been attached to abortion. What is the reason behind this new attitude? Russia after all suffers not from an over-production of living labour but rather from a lack of it.

Russia is thinly, not densely populated. Every unit of labour power is precious. Why then have we declared abortion to be no longer a criminal offence? . . .

Abortion exists and flourishes everywhere, and no laws or punitive measures have succeeded in rooting it out. A way round the law is always found. But "secret help" only cripples women; they become a burden on the labour government, and the size of the labour force is reduced. Abortion, when carried out under proper medical conditions, is less harmful and dangerous, and the woman can get back to work quicker. Soviet power realizes that the need for abortion will only disappear on the one hand when Russia has a broad and developed network of institutions protecting motherhood and providing social education, and on the other hand when women understand that childbirth is a social obligation; Soviet power has therefore allowed abortion to be performed openly and in clinical conditions.

Besides the large-scale development of motherhood protection, the task of labour Russia is to strengthen in women the healthy instinct of motherhood, to make motherhood and labour for the collective compatible and thus do away with the need for abortion. This is the approach of the labour republic to the question of abortion, which still faces women in the bourgeois countries in all its magnitude. In these countries women are exhausted by the dual burden of hired labour for capital and motherhood. In Soviet Russia the working woman and peasant woman are helping the Communist Party to build a new society and to undermine the old way of life that has enslaved women. As soon as woman is viewed as being essentially a labour unit, the key to the solution of the complex question of maternity can be found. . . . The emancipation of women can only be completed when a fundamental transformation of living is effected; and life-styles will change only with the fundamental transformation of all production and the establishment of a communist economy. The revolution in everyday life is unfolding before our very eyes, and in this process the liberation of women is being introduced in practice.

Fifteen years later Joseph Stalin reversed the Soviet policy on abortion.

The published draft of the law prohibiting abortion and providing material assistance to mothers has provoked a lively reaction throughout the country. It is being heatedly discussed by tens of millions of people and there is no doubt that it will serve as a further strengthening of the Soviet family. . . .

When we speak of strengthening the Soviet family, we are speaking precisely of the struggle against the survivals of a bourgeois attitude towards marriage, women, and children. So-called "free love" and all disorderly sex life are bourgeois through and through, and have nothing to do with either socialist principles or the ethics and standards of conduct of the Soviet citizens. Socialist doctrine shows this, and it is proved by life itself.

The elite of our country, the best of the Soviet youth, are as a rule also excellent family men who dearly love their children. And vice versa: the man who does not take marriage seriously, and abandons his children to the whims of fate, is usually also a bad worker and a poor member of society. . . .

It is impossible even to compare the present state of the family with that which obtained before the Soviet regime—so great has been the improvement towards greater stability and, above all, greater humanity and goodness. The single fact that millions of women have become economically independent and are no longer at the mercy of men's whims, speaks volumes. Compare, for instance, the modern woman collective farmer who sometimes earns more than her husband, with the pre-revolutionary peasant woman who completely depended on her husband and was a slave in the household. Has not this fundamentally changed family relations, has it not rationalized and strengthened the family? The very motives for setting up a family, for getting married, have changed for the better, have been cleansed of atavistic and barbaric elements. Marriage has ceased to be a matter of sell-and-buy. Nowadays a girl from a collective farm is not given away (or should we say "sold away"?) by her father, for now she is her own mistress, and no one can give her away. She will marry the man she loves. . . .

We alone have all the conditions under which a working woman can fulfill her duties as a citizen and as a mother responsible for the birth and early upbringing of her children.

A woman without children merits our pity, for she does not know the full joy of life. Our Soviet women, full-blooded citizens of the freest country in the world, have been given the bliss of motherhood. We must safeguard the family and raise and rear healthy Soviet heroes!

QUESTIONS FOR ANALYSIS

1. How does Kollontai expect women to be both workers and mothers without depending on a man? How would Soviet society make this possible?

2. Why does Alexandra Kollontai advocate the legalization of abortion in Soviet Russia? Does she view abortion as a permanent right or as a temporary necessity?

3. Why does Stalin characterize "all disorderly sex life" as "bourgeois through and through"?

4. How does Stalin's image of the Soviet family differ from Kollontai's? Are his views a variation of her views, or the opposite?

Source: First selection from Alexandra Kollontai, "The Labour of Women in the Revolution of the Economy," in *Selected Writings of Alexandra Kollontai*, translated by Alix Holt (Lawrence Hill Books, 1977), 148–149. Used with permission of Lawrence Hill Books. Second selection from Joseph Stalin, *Law on the Abolition of Legal Abortion* (1936).

Two Views of the American Way In this classic photograph, *Life* magazine photographer Margaret Bourke-White captured the contrast between advertisers' view of the ideal American family and the reality of bread lines for the poor.

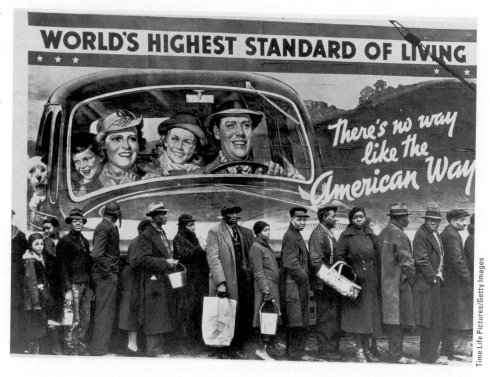

Time Life Pictures/Getty Images

imposed the highest import duty in American history. In retaliation, other countries also raised their tariffs. As a result, global industrial production declined by 36 percent between 1929 and 1932, while world trade dropped by a breathtaking 62 percent.

Depression in Industrial Nations

This massive economic upheaval had profound political repercussions. In the United States, Franklin D. Roosevelt was elected president in 1932 on a "New Deal" platform of government programs to stimulate and revitalize the economy. British and French governments also intervened in their economies and escaped the worst of the Depression by making their colonial empires purchase their products. In the Soviet Union, the Five-Year Plans continued to provide jobs and economic growth.

Nations that relied on exports to pay for imported food and fuel, in particular Japan and Germany, suffered much more. In Germany, unemployment reached 6 million by 1932, twice as high as in Britain. Half the German population lived in poverty. In Japan, the burden of the Depression fell on the farmers and fishermen, who saw their incomes drop sharply. Some, in desperation, revived the ancient

practice of selling their daughters. As economic grievances worsened, radical politicians took over the governments in Germany and Japan, manipulated the economies, and turned their nations' military might to acquiring empires large enough to support a self-sufficient economy.

Depression in Nonindustrial Regions

The Depression affected Asia, Africa, and Latin America in different ways. Because a wall of new import duties protected India's infant industries from foreign competition, living standards stagnated but did not drop. The Depression added little to China's problems, except in coastal regions.

However, countries that depended on exports were hard hit by the Depression. When automobile production dropped by half in the United States and Europe, so did imports of rubber, devastating the economies of Southeast Asia. In Cuba, American tourists vanished from beaches and bars, and with them went Cuba's prosperity. The industrialization of Argentina and Brazil was set back a decade or more by the loss of their export markets. In response, military officers seized power in several Latin American countries, consciously imitating dictatorships emerging in Europe.

Southern and Central Africa recovered from the Depression quickly because falling prices made their gold and other minerals more valuable. But this mining boom benefited only a small number of mine owners and investors. For Africans, it was at best a mixed blessing, for mining offered jobs and cash wages to men, while women had to manage without them in the villages.

The Rise of Fascism

How did fascism in Italy and Germany lead to the Second World War?

The Depression sharpened the polarization of European society that had been under way for decades. Many underpaid or unemployed workers saw in the seeming collapse of the capitalist economy an opportunity as well as temporary suffering. They urged the establishment of a socialist society through the ballot box and strikes instead of the violent revolution that had torn Russia apart.

Frightened investors and factory owners, along with conservative elements in society such as the church and the military, feared the consequences of this political shift to the left. In the democracies of western Europe and North America, middle-income voters kept politics in balance. But in some societies, the war and the Depression left people vulnerable to the propaganda of ultranationalist politicians who

became adept at appealing to people's fears. They promised to bring back full employment, stop the spread of communism, and achieve the territorial conquests that World War I had denied them.

Mussolini's Italy

The first country to seek radical answers was Italy. World War I, which had never been popular, left thousands of veterans who found neither pride in their victory nor jobs in the postwar economy. Unemployed veterans and violent youths banded together into *fasci di combattimento* (fighting units) to demand action and intimidate politicians. When socialist unions threatened to strike, factory and property owners hired gangs of these *fascisti* to defend them.

Benito Mussolini (1883–1945), a spellbinding orator, quickly became the leader of the **Fascist Party**, which glorified warfare and the Italian nation. By 1921, the party had 300,000 members, many of whom used violent tactics to repress strikes, intimidate voters, and seize municipal governments. A year later, when the fascists failed to win an election, Mussolini threatened to march on Rome if he was not appointed prime minister. The government gave in.

Mussolini then proceeded to install Fascist Party members in all government jobs, crush all opposition parties, and jail anyone who criticized him. The party took over the press, public education, and youth activities and gave employers control over their workers. The fascist regime lowered living standards but reduced unemployment and provided social security and public services. On the whole, they proved to be neither ruthless radicals nor competent administrators.

What Mussolini and the fascist movement really excelled at was publicity: bombastic speeches, spectacular parades, news bulletins full of praise for *Il Duce* (eel DOO-chay) ("the leader"), and signs everywhere

Benito Mussolini (1883–1945) Fascist dictator of Italy (1922–1943). He led Italy to conquer Ethiopia (1935), joined Germany in the Axis pact (1936), and allied Italy with Germany in World War II. He was overthrown in 1943 when the Allies invaded Italy.

Fascist Party Italian political party created by Benito Mussolini during World War I. It emphasized aggressive nationalism and was Mussolini's instrument for the creation of a dictatorship in Italy from 1922 to 1943.

A Nazi Rally In the years leading up to World War II, Hitler organized mass rallies at Nuremberg to whip up popular support for his regime and to indoctrinate young Germans with martial spirit. Thousands of men in uniform marched in torch-lit parades before Hitler and his top officials.

AP Images/Wide World Photos

proclaiming "Il Duce is always right!" Mussolini's genius was to apply the techniques of modern mass communications and advertisement to political life. Billboards, movie footage, and radio news bulletins galvanized the masses in ways never before seen in peacetime. Although his rhetoric was filled with words like *war, violence,* and *struggle,* his foreign policy was cautious. But his techniques of whipping up public enthusiasm were not lost on other radicals. By the 1930s, fascist movements had appeared in most European countries, as well as in Latin America, China, and Japan.

Hitler's Germany

Like Mussolini, **Adolf Hitler** (1889–1945) had served in World War I and looked back fondly on the clear lines of authority and the camaraderie he had experienced in battle. After the war, he too recreated that experience in a paramilitary group, the National Socialist German Workers' Party—**Nazis** for short. Hitler used his gifts as an orator to appeal to Germans disappointed at their country's humiliation after the war and the hyperinflation of 1923. In 1924, he too led an uprising,

but the attempted seizure of Munich was a failure. Germany was not yet ready to follow Italy's path.

The Depression changed that. While serving a jail sentence for the coup attempt, Hitler wrote *Mein Kampf* (mine compf) (*My Struggle*), but when it was published in 1925, no one took the book or its author's extreme nationalist, racist, and anti-Jewish ideas seriously. Hitler believed that Germany should incorporate all German-speaking people, even those who lived in neighboring countries. He distinguished between a "master race" of Aryans (he meant Germans, Scandinavians, and Britons), a degenerate "Alpine" race of French and Italians, and an inferior race of Russian and eastern European Slavs, who, he believed, were fit only to be slaves of the master race. He reserved his most intense hatred for Jews, on whom he blamed every disaster that had befallen Germany, especially the defeat of 1918.

 Primary Source: The Centerpiece of Nazi Racial Legislation: The Nuremberg Laws Find out how the Nazis defined what it was to be a Jew.

Adolf Hitler (1889–1945) Born in Austria, Hitler became a radical German nationalist during World War I. He led the National Socialist German Workers' Party—the Nazis—in the 1920s and became dictator of Germany in 1933. He led Europe into World War II.

Nazis German political party joined by Adolf Hitler, emphasizing nationalism, racism, and war. When Hitler became chancellor of Germany in 1933, the Nazis became the only legal party and an instrument of Hitler's absolute rule. The party's formal name was National Socialist German Workers' Party.

He glorified violence, which would enable the "master race" to defeat and subjugate all others.

When the Depression hit, the Nazis gained supporters among the unemployed who believed Nazi promises of jobs for all and among property owners frightened by the growing popularity of communists. In March 1933, as leader of the largest party in Germany, Hitler became chancellor.

Once in office, he quickly assumed dictatorial power, just as Mussolini had done. He expelled the Communist Party from the Reichstag (RIKES-tog) (parliament), intimidated it to give him dictatorial powers, and then put Nazis in charge of all government agencies, educational institutions, and professional organizations. He banned all other political parties and threw their leaders into concentration camps. The Nazis deprived Jews of their citizenship and civil rights, prohibited them from marrying "Aryans," ousted them from the professions, and confiscated their property. In August 1934, Hitler proclaimed himself *Führer* (FEW-rer) ("leader") and called Germany the "Third Reich" (empire)—the third after the Holy Roman Empire and the German Empire of 1871 to 1918.

The Nazis' economic and social policies were spectacularly effective. The government undertook massive public works projects and gave contracts to businesses to manufacture weapons for the armed forces. Women, who had entered the work force during and after World War I, were urged to return to *"Kinder, Kirche, Küche"* (children, church, kitchen), releasing jobs for men. By 1936, business was booming, unemployment was at its lowest level since the 1920s, and living standards were rising. Hitler's popularity soared because most Germans believed their economic well-being outweighed the loss of liberty.

The Road to War, 1933–1939

What Hitler really wanted was not prosperity or popularity, but conquest. As soon as he came to office, he began to build up the armed forces with conquest in mind. Meanwhile, he tested the reactions of the other powers through a series of surprise moves followed by protestations of peaceful intent.

In 1933, when Hitler withdrew Germany from the League of Nations, France and Britain hesitated to retaliate by blockading or invading Germany. Two years later, he announced that Germany was going to introduce conscription, build up its army, and create an air force—in violation of the Versailles treaty. Instead of protesting, Britain signed a naval agreement with Germany. The message was clear: neither Britain nor France was willing to risk war by standing up to Germany. The United States, absorbed in its own domestic economic problems, had reverted to isolationism.

Emboldened by the weakness of the democracies, Italy in 1935 invaded Ethiopia, one of only two independent states in Africa and a member of the League of Nations. The League and the democracies protested but refused to close the Suez Canal to Italian ships or impose an oil embargo. The following year, when Hitler sent troops into the Rhineland on the borders of France and Belgium, the other powers merely protested.

By 1938, Hitler decided his rearmament plans were far enough advanced that he could escalate his demands. In March, Germany invaded and soon annexed Austria, with little protest from its German-speaking citizens. Then came the turn of Czechoslovakia. Hitler first demanded autonomy for its German-speaking borderlands, then their annexation to Germany. At the Munich Conference of September 1938, the leaders of France, Britain, and Italy gave Hitler everything he wanted to keep him from starting a war. Once again, Hitler learned that aggression paid off and that the democracies always gave in.

The democracies' policy of "appeasement" ran counter to the European balance-of-power tradition for three reasons. The first was the deep-seated fear of war among all people who had lived through World War I. The second was fear of communism. The conservative politicians who ruled France and Britain were more afraid of Stalin than of Hitler, for Hitler claimed to respect Christianity and private property. Rather than revive the pre–World War I alliance of Britain, France, and Russia, they sold out the Czechs. The third cause was the very novelty of fascist tactics. Britain's prime minister, Neville Chamberlain, assumed that political leaders (other than the

Primary Source: Speech to the National Socialist Women's Association Learn about efforts to inspire German women to stand alongside German men in supporting the Nazi cause.

SECTION REVIEW

- In Italy, Mussolini exploited postwar frustrations and fears of communism to lead his Fascist Party to power.

- Although authoritarian rulers, the fascists were poor administrators who were only adept at political theater.

- In Germany, Hitler also played upon postwar fears and resentments, promoting extreme nationalism and vicious anti-Semitism.

- The Depression enabled the Nazis to seize power, after which they initiated new economic and social policies, including the systematic persecution of Jews.

- Italian and German aggression and the democracies' appeasement policy pushed Europe toward war.

- War broke out when Germany invaded Poland on September 1, 1939.

Bolsheviks) were honorable men and that an agreement was as valid as a business contract. Thus, when Hitler said he had "no further territorial demands," Chamberlain believed him.

After Munich, it was too late to stop Hitler, short of war. Germany and Italy were now united in an alliance called the Axis. In March 1939, Germany invaded what was left of Czechoslovakia. Belatedly realizing that Hitler could not be trusted, France and Britain sought Soviet help. Stalin, however, distrusted the "capitalists" as much as they distrusted him. Hitler, meanwhile, offered to divide Poland between Germany and the Soviet Union. On August 23, Stalin accepted. The Nazi-Soviet Pact freed Hitler from the fear of a two-front war and gave Stalin two more years of peace to build up his armies. One week later, on September 1, 1939, German forces swept into Poland across the Eastern Front. The war was on.

East Asia, 1931–1945

Why did Japan invade Manchuria?

When the Depression ruined Japan's export trade, ultranationalists, including young army officers, resented their country's dependence on foreign trade. If only Japan had a colonial empire, they thought, it would not be beholden to the rest of the world. But Europeans and Americans had already taken most potential colonies in Asia. Japan had only Korea,

Taiwan, and a railroad in Manchuria. Japanese nationalists saw China, with its vast population and resources, as the solution to their country's problems.

The Manchurian Incident of 1931

Meanwhile, the Guomindang (gwo-min-dong) was becoming stronger in China and preparing to challenge the Japanese presence in Manchuria, a province rich in coal and iron ore. Junior officers in the Japanese army guarding the South Manchurian Railway, frustrated by the caution of their superiors, determined to take action. In September 1931, an explosion on a railroad track, probably staged, gave them an excuse to conquer the entire province. In Tokyo, weak civilian ministers acquiesced to the attack to avoid losing face and shortly recognized the "independence" of Manchuria under the name *Manchukuo* (man-CHEW-coo-oh).

The U.S. government condemned the Japanese conquest. The League of Nations refused to recognize Manchukuo and urged the Japanese to remove their troops from China. Persuaded that the Western powers would not fight, Japan resigned from the League.

During the next few years, the Japanese built railways and heavy industries in Manchuria and northeastern China and sped up their rearmament. The government grew more authoritarian, jailing thousands of dissidents. On several occasions, superpatriotic junior officers who mutinied or assassinated leading political figures received mild punishments, and generals and admirals sympathetic to their views replaced more moderate civilian politicians.

The Chinese Communists and the Long March

Until the Japanese seized Manchuria, the Chinese government seemed to be consolidating its power and creating the conditions for a national recovery. The main challenge to the government of **Chiang Kai-shek** (chang kie-shek) came

Chiang Kai-shek (1886–1975) Chinese military and political leader. He succeeded Sun Yat-sen as head of the Guomindang in 1925; headed the Chinese government from 1928 to 1948; and fought against the Chinese communists and Japanese invaders. After 1949 he headed the Chinese Nationalist government in Taiwan.

from the Chinese communists, who were organizing industrial workers and who worked in alliance with the Nationalists until 1927, when Chiang Kai-shek arrested and executed communists and labor leaders alike.

The few communists who escaped the mass arrests fled to the remote mountains of Jiangxi (jang-she), in southeastern China. Among them was **Mao Zedong** (ma-oh zay-dong) (1893–1976), a farmer's son who had left home to study philosophy.

In the early 1920s, Mao discovered the works of Karl Marx, joined the Communist Party, and soon became one of its leaders. In Jiangxi, Mao began studying conditions among the peasants, in whom communists had previously shown no interest. He planned to redistribute land from the wealthier to the poorer peasants, thereby gaining adherents for the coming struggle with the Guomindang army.

Mao's reliance on the peasantry was a radical departure from Marxist-Leninist ideology, which stressed the backwardness of the peasants and pinned its hopes on industrial workers. Mao was also an advocate of women's equality. Before 1927, the communists had organized the women who worked in Shanghai's textile mills, the most exploited of all Chinese workers. Later, in their mountain stronghold in Jiangxi, they organized women farmers, allowed divorce, and banned arranged marriages and footbinding.

The Guomindang army pursued the communists into the mountains, building small forts throughout the countryside. Rather than risk direct confrontations, Mao responded with guerrilla warfare. Whereas government troops often mistreated civilians, Mao insisted that his soldiers help the peasants, pay a fair price for food and supplies, and treat women with respect. But in spite of their good relations with the peasants of Jiangxi, the communists decided to break out of the southern mountains and trek to Shaanxi (SHAWN-she), an even more remote province in northwestern China. The so-called **Long March** took them 6,000 miles (nearly 9,700 kilometers) in one year, 17 miles (27 kilometers) a day over desolate mountains and through swamps and deserts, pursued by the army and bombed by Chiang's aircraft. Of the 100,000 communists who left Jiangxi in October 1934, only 4,000 reached Shaanxi a year later.

The Sino-Japanese War, 1937–1945

On July 7, 1937, Japanese troops attacked Chinese forces near Beijing. As in 1931, the junior officers who ordered the attack quickly obtained the support of their commanders and then, reluctantly, of the government. By November, Japanese troops had seized Beijing, Tianjin, Shanghai, and other coastal cities, and the Japanese navy had blockaded the entire coast of China.

Once again, the United States and the League of Nations denounced the Japanese atrocities. Yet the Western powers were too preoccupied with events in Europe and with their own economic problems to risk a military confrontation in Asia. When the Japanese sank a U.S. gunboat and shelled a British ship on the Yangzi River, the U.S. and British governments responded only with righteous indignation and pious resolutions.

The large Chinese armies were poorly led and armed and lost every battle. Within a year, Japan controlled the coastal provinces of China and the lower Yangzi and Yellow River Valleys, China's richest and most populated regions, but the Chinese people continued to resist, either in the army or, increasingly, with the communist guerrilla forces. Japan's periodic attempts to turn the tide by conquering one more piece of China only pushed Japan deeper into the quagmire.

Warfare between the Chinese and Japanese was incredibly violent. In the winter of 1937–1938, Japanese troops took Nanjing, raped 20,000 women, killed 200,000 prisoners and civilians, and looted and burned the city. To slow them down, Chiang ordered the Yellow River dikes blasted open, causing a flood

Mao Zedong (1893–1976) Leader of the Chinese Communist Party (1927–1976). He led the communists on the Long March (1934–1935) and rebuilt the Communist Party and Red Army during the Japanese occupation of China (1937–1945). After World War II, he led the communists to victory over the Guomindang.

Long March (1934–1935) The 6,000-mile (9,700-kilometer) flight of Chinese communists from southeastern to northwestern China. The communists, led by Mao Zedong, were pursued by the Chinese army under orders from Chiang Kai-shek. The four thousand survivors of the march formed the nucleus of a revived communist movement that defeated the Guomindang after World War II.

that destroyed 4,000 villages, killed 890,000 people, and made 12.5 million homeless. Two years later, when the communists ordered a massive offensive, the Japanese retaliated with a "kill all, burn all, loot all" campaign, destroying hundreds of villages down to the last person, building, and farm animal.

The Chinese government, led by Chiang Kai-shek, escaped to the mountains of Sichuan in the center of the country. There he built up a huge army, both to fight Japan and to prepare for a future confrontation with the communists. The army drafted over 3 million men, even though it had only a million rifles and could not provide food or clothing for all its soldiers. The Guomindang raised farmers' taxes, even when famine forced farmers to eat the bark of trees. Such taxes were not enough to support both a large army and the thousands of government officials and hangers-on who had fled to Sichuan. To avoid taxing its wealthy supporters, the government printed money, causing inflation, hoarding, and corruption.

From his capital of Yan'an in Shaanxi province, Mao also built up his army and formed a government. Unlike the Guomindang, the communists listened to the grievances of the peasants, especially the poor, to whom they distributed land confiscated from wealthy landowners. Because they could present themselves as the only group in China that was serious about fighting the Japanese, the communists obtained support and intelligence from farmers in Japanese-occupied territory.

The Second World War

How was the war fought, and why did Japan and Germany lose?

The Second World War was much bigger and deadlier than the first in every way. It was fought around the world, from Norway to New Guinea, from Hawaii to Egypt, and on every ocean. It was a total war that showed how effectively industry, science, and nationalism could be channeled into mass destruction.

The War of Movement

Defensive maneuvers had dominated in World War I. In World War II, motorized weapons gave back the advantage to the offensive. Opposing forces moved fast, their victories hinging as much on the aggressive spirit of their commanders and the military intelligence they obtained as on numbers of troops or firepower.

The Wehrmacht (VAIR-mokt), or German armed forces, was the first to learn this lesson. It not only had tanks, trucks, and fighter planes, but also had perfected their combined use in a tactic called *blitzkrieg* (BLITS-creeg) (lightning war): fighter planes scattered enemy troops and disrupted communications, and tanks punctured the enemy's defenses and then, with the help of the infantry, encircled and captured enemy troops. At sea, the navies of both Japan and the United States had developed aircraft carriers that could launch planes against targets hundreds of miles away.

The very size and mobility of the opposing forces made the fighting far different from any the world had ever seen. Countries were conquered in a matter of days or weeks. The belligerents mobilized the economies of entire continents, squeezing them for every possible resource. They tried not only to defeat their enemies' armed forces but—by means of blockades, submarine attacks on shipping, and bombing raids on industrial areas—to damage the economies that supported those armed forces. They thought of enemy civilians not as innocent bystanders but as legitimate targets and, later, as vermin to be exterminated.

War in Europe and North Africa

It took less than a month for the Wehrmacht to conquer Poland. Britain and France declared war on Germany but took no military action. Meanwhile, the Soviet Union invaded eastern

German Dive-Bomber over Eastern Europe In this painting, a German ME-110 fighter plane attacks a Soviet troop convoy on the Eastern Front.

akg-images

 History in Focus *What does this image tell you about the effect—material and psychological—of the German blitzkrieg tactics? Find the answer online.*

Poland and the Baltic republics of Lithuania, Latvia, and Estonia. Although the Poles fought bravely, the Polish infantry and cavalry were no match for German or Russian tanks. During the winter of 1939–1940, Germany and the Western democracies faced each other in what soldiers called a "phony war" and watched as the Soviet Union attacked Finland, which resisted for many months.

In April 1940, Hitler went on the offensive again, conquering Denmark, Norway, the Netherlands, and Belgium in less than two months. In May, he attacked France. Although the French army had as many soldiers, tanks, and aircraft as the Wehrmacht, its morale was low, and it quickly collapsed. By the end of June, Hitler was master of all of Europe between Russia and Spain.

Germany still had to face one enemy: Britain. The British had no army to speak of, but they had other assets: the English Channel, the Royal Navy and Air Force, and a tough new prime minister, Winston Churchill. The Germans knew they could invade Britain only by gaining control of the airspace over the Channel, so they launched a massive air attack—the

Battle of Britain—lasting from June through September 1940. They failed, however, because the Royal Air Force had better fighters and used radar and code breaking to detect approaching German planes.

Frustrated, Hitler turned his attention eastward. In June 1941, the Wehrmacht invaded the Soviet Union. In five months, it conquered the Baltic states, Ukraine, and half of European Russia; captured a million prisoners of war; and stood at the very gates of Moscow and Leningrad (now St. Petersburg). The USSR seemed on the verge of collapse when suddenly the weather turned cold, machines froze, and the fighting came to a halt. Like Napoleon, Hitler had ignored the environment of Russia at his peril.

The next spring, the Wehrmacht renewed its offensive and surrounded Leningrad in a siege that cost a million lives. Leaving Moscow aside, it turned toward the Caucasus and its oil wells. In August 1942, the Germans attacked **Stalingrad** (now Volgograd),

Stalingrad City in Russia, site of a Red Army victory over the German army in 1942–1943. The Battle of Stalingrad was the turning point in the war between Germany and the Soviet Union. Today it is known as Volgograd.

the key to the Volga River and the supply of oil. For months, German and Soviet soldiers fought over every street and every house. When winter came, the Red Army counterattacked and encircled the city, and in February 1943, the remnants of the German army in Stalingrad surrendered. Hitler had lost his greatest gamble (see Map 27.1).

From Europe, the war spread to Africa. During 1941, British forces conquered Italian East Africa and invaded Libya as well. The Italian rout in North

Map 27.1 World War II in Europe and North Africa In a series of quick and decisive campaigns from September 1939 to December 1941, German forces overran much of Europe and North Africa. There followed three years of bitter fighting as the Allies slowly pushed the Germans back. This map shows the maximum extent of Germany's conquests and alliances, as well as the key battles and the front lines at various times.   © Cengage Learning

 Interactive Map

Soviet Tanks at Stalingrad In the winter of 1942–1943, the Red Army encircled a German army at Stalingrad, a strategic city in southern Russia that marked the furthest eastward advance of the Wehrmacht. The Soviets deployed their new T-34s, the best tanks in the world at the time. Unlike the Germans, Soviet soldiers were equipped with warm winter uniforms with a white outer layer for camouflage in the snow.

TASS-Sovfoto

Africa brought the Germans to their rescue. During 1942, the German army and the forces of the British Empire seesawed back and forth across the deserts of Libya and Egypt. Because the British could decode German messages and had more weapons and supplies, they were finally able to expel the Germans from Africa in May 1943.

War in Asia and the Pacific

The war presented Japan with the opportunity to take over European colonies in Southeast Asia, with their abundant oil, rubber, and other strategic materials. After Japanese forces occupied French Indochina in September 1940, the United States and Britain cut off shipments of steel, scrap iron, oil, and other products that Japan desperately needed. This left Japan with three alternatives: accept the shame and humiliation of giving up its conquests, as the Americans insisted; face economic ruin; or widen the war. Japan chose war. On December 7, 1941, Japanese planes bombed the U.S. naval base at **Pearl Harbor**, Hawaii, sinking or damaging scores of warships. Then, between December 1941 and March 1942, the Japanese bombed Singapore and occupied Thailand, the Philippines, and Malaya. Within a few months,

they occupied all of Southeast Asia and the Dutch East Indies. The Japanese claimed to be liberating the inhabitants of these lands from European colonialism. But they soon began to confiscate food and raw materials and demand heavy labor from the inhabitants, whom they treated with contempt. Those who protested were brutally punished.

The Pearl Harbor attack had finally mobilized the United States, and its entry into the war challenged Japan's dream of an East Asian empire. In April 1942, American planes bombed Tokyo, and in May, the United States Navy defeated a Japanese fleet in the Coral Sea, ending Japanese plans to conquer Australia. A month later, at the **Battle of Midway**, Japan lost four of its six largest aircraft carriers. Japan did not have enough industry to replace them, for its war

Pearl Harbor Naval base in Hawaii attacked by Japanese aircraft on December 7, 1941. The sinking of much of the U.S. Pacific Fleet brought the United States into World War II.
Battle of Midway U.S. naval victory over the Japanese fleet in June 1942, in which the Japanese lost four of their best aircraft carriers. It marked a turning point in World War II.

Map 27.2   World War II in Asia and the Pacific After having conquered much of China between 1937 and 1941, Japanese forces launched a sudden attack on Southeast Asia, Indonesia, and the Pacific in late 1941 and early 1942. American forces slowly reconquered the Pacific islands and the Philippines until August 1945, when the atomic bombing of Hiroshima and Nagasaki forced Japan's surrender.   © Cengage Learning

Interactive Map

production was only one-tenth that of the United States. In the vastness of the Pacific Ocean, aircraft carriers held the key to victory, and without them, Japan faced a long and hopeless war (see Map 27.2).

The End of the War

America's entry into the war also helped the Soviet Union capitalize on the advantage it had won in the Battle of Stalingrad. Aided by a growing stream of supplies

from factories in the United States, the Red Army began pushing the Wehrmacht back toward Germany. The Western powers, meanwhile, staged two invasions of Europe. Beginning in July 1943, they captured Sicily and invaded Italy. Mussolini resigned, and Italy signed an armistice, but German troops held off the Allied advance for two years. Then on D-day (June 6, 1944), 156,000 British, American, and Canadian troops landed on the coast of Normandy in western France.

Hiroshima After the Atomic Bomb On August 6, 1945, an atomic bomb destroyed the city, killing over fifty thousand people. This photo shows the devastation of the city center, where only a few concrete buildings remained standing.

Within a week, the Allies had more troops in France than Germany did. To meet this growing force, Hitler had to transfer part of the Wehrmacht from the Eastern Front. Despite advancing armies on three sides, Germany held out for almost a year. Finally, on May 7, 1945, a week after Hitler committed suicide, German military leaders surrendered.

By June 1944, U.S. bombers were also attacking Japan from newly captured island bases in the Pacific, and U.S. submarines were sinking large numbers of Japanese merchant ships, gradually cutting off Japan's oil and other raw materials. After May 1945, with the Japanese air force grounded for lack of fuel, U.S. planes began destroying Japanese shipping, industries, and cities at will.

On August 6, 1945, the United States dropped an atomic bomb on **Hiroshima**, killing some 80,000 people in a flash and leaving about 120,000 more to die agonizing deaths from burns and radiation. Three days later, another atomic bomb destroyed Nagasaki. On August 14, Japan offered to surrender, and Emperor Hirohito gave the order to lay down arms. Two weeks later, Japanese leaders signed the terms of surrender. The war was officially over.

Chinese Civil War and Communist Victory

The Japanese surrender also meant the end of Japanese occupation of much of China. Instead of bringing peace, however, it marked an intensification of the contest between the Guomindang and the communists. Guomindang forces started with many advantages: more troops and weapons, U.S. support, and control of China's cities. But their behavior eroded whatever

 Primary Source: The Decision to Use the Atomic Bomb Learn about some of the considerations that went into the U.S. decision to use the atomic bomb and reflections on that decision after the fact.

Hiroshima City in Japan, the first to be destroyed by an atomic bomb, on August 6, 1945. The bombing hastened the end of World War II.

popular support they had. They taxed the people they "liberated" more heavily than the Japanese had, looted businesses, confiscated supplies, and enriched themselves at the expense of the population. To pay its bills, Chiang's government printed money so fast that it soon lost all its value, ruining merchants and causing hoarding and shortages. In the countryside, the Guomindang's brutality alienated the peasants.

In contrast, the communists' land reform programs had won them popular support, which was even more important than the heavy equipment brought over by Guomindang soldiers, who began deserting by the thousands, and the Japanese equipment seized by the Soviets in the last weeks of the war. By 1949, the Guomindang armies were collapsing everywhere, defeated more by their own greed and ineptness than by the communists. As the communists advanced, high-ranking members of the Guomindang fled to Taiwan, protected from the mainland by the United States Navy. On October 1, 1949, Mao Zedong announced the founding of the People's Republic of China.

The Character of Warfare

How did science and technology change the nature of warfare?

The war left an enormous death toll. Recent estimates place the figure at close to 60 million deaths, six to eight times more than in World War I. Over half of the dead were civilian victims of massacres, famines, or bombs. The Soviet Union lost between 20 and 25 million people, more than any other country. China suffered 15 million deaths; Poland lost some 6 million, of whom half were Jewish; the Jewish people lost another 3 million outside Poland. Over 4 million Germans and over 2 million Japanese died. In much of the world, almost every family mourned one or more of its members. In contrast, Great Britain lost 400,000 people, the United States 300,000.

One reason for the terrible toll in human lives and suffering was a change in moral values, as belligerents identified not just soldiers but entire peoples as enemies. Another reason for the devastation was the appearance of new technologies that carried destruction deep into enemy territory far beyond the traditional battlefields.

The War of Science

Scientists made many contributions to the technology of warfare. Chemists found ways to make synthetic rubber from coal or oil. Physicists perfected radar, which warned of approaching enemy aircraft and submarines. Others broke enemy codes and developed antibiotics that saved the lives of countless wounded soldiers.

Aircraft development was especially striking. As war approached, German, British, and Japanese aircraft manufacturers developed fast, maneuverable fighter planes. U.S. industry produced aircraft of every sort but was especially noted for its heavy bombers designed to fly in huge formations and drop tons of bombs on enemy cities. The Japanese developed the Mitsubishi "Zero" fighter plane—light, fast, and agile. Unable to produce heavy planes in large numbers, Germany responded with radically new designs, including the first jet fighters, low-flying buzz bombs, and fearful V-2 missiles.

In October 1939, President Roosevelt received a letter from physicist Albert Einstein, a Jewish refugee from Nazism, warning of the dangers of nuclear power. Fearing that Germany might develop a nuclear bomb first, Roosevelt placed the vast resources of the U.S. government at the disposal of physicists and engineers, both Americans and refugees from Europe. By 1945, they had built two atomic bombs, each one powerful enough to annihilate an entire city.

Bombing Raids

The Germans began the war from the air, but it was the British and Americans who excelled at large-scale urban bombardment. Since it was very hard to pinpoint individual buildings, especially at night, such raids were aimed at weakening the morale of the civilian population.

In May 1942, 1,000 British planes dropped incendiary bombs on Cologne, setting fire to most of the old city. Between July 24 and August 2, 1943, 3,330 British and Americans bombers set fire to Hamburg, killing 50,000 people. Later raids destroyed Berlin, Dresden, and other German cities. All in all, the bombing raids against Germany killed 600,000 people—more than half of them women and children—and injured 800,000. If the air strategists had hoped thereby to break the morale of the German people, they failed. The only effective bombing raids were those directed against oil depots and synthetic fuel plants; by early 1945, they had almost brought the German war effort to a standstill.

American bombing raids on Japanese cities were even more devastating than the fire-bombing of German cities, for Japanese cities were built of wood. In March 1945, a large raid set Tokyo ablaze, killing 80,000 people and leaving a million homeless. Five months later, each atomic bomb did as much damage as a thousand-plane raid.

The Holocaust

The Nazis killed defenseless civilians on an even larger scale. Their murders were not the byproducts of some military goal but a calculated policy of extermination.

Their first targets were Jews. Soon after Hitler came to power, he deprived German Jews of their citizenship and legal rights. When eastern Europe fell under Nazi rule, the Nazis herded its large Jewish population into ghettos in the major cities, where many died of starvation and disease. Then, in early 1942, the Nazis decided to carry out Hitler's "final solution to the Jewish problem" by applying modern industrial methods to the slaughter of human beings. German companies built huge extermination camps in eastern Europe. Every day, trainloads of cattle cars arrived at the camps and disgorged thousands of captives and the corpses of those who had died of starvation or asphyxiation along the way. The strongest survivors were put to work and fed almost nothing until they died. Women, children, the elderly, and the sick were shoved into gas chambers and asphyxiated with poison gas. **Auschwitz**, the biggest camp, was a giant industrial complex designed to kill up to twelve thousand people a day. Most horrifying of all were the tortures inflicted on prisoners selected by Nazi doctors for "medical experiments." This mass extermination, now called the **Holocaust** ("burning"), claimed some 6 million Jewish lives.

Besides the Jews, the Nazis also killed 3 million Polish Catholics—especially professionals, army officers, and the educated—in an effort to reduce the Polish people to slavery. They also exterminated homosexuals, Jehovah's Witnesses, Gypsies, the disabled, and the mentally ill—all in the interests of "racial purity." Whenever a German was killed in an occupied country, the Nazis retaliated by burning a village with all its inhabitants. After the invasion of Russia, the Wehrmacht was given orders to execute all captured communists, government employees, and officers. They also worked millions of prisoners of war to death or let them die of starvation.

The Home Front

Rapid military movements and air power carried the war to people's homes in China, Japan, Southeast Asia, and Europe. Armies swept through the land, confiscating food, fuel, and anything else of value. Bombers and heavy artillery pounded cities into rubble, leaving only the skeletons of buildings, while survivors cowered in

Primary Source: Memoirs Read the words of Rudolph Hoss, commandant at Auschwitz, as he describes his initial reaction to the order to "annihilate all the Jews" and his feelings as the process commenced, progressed, and finally came to an end.

Auschwitz Nazi extermination camp in Poland, the largest center of mass murder during the Holocaust. Close to a million Jews, Gypsies, communists, and others were killed there.

Holocaust Nazis program during World War II to kill people they considered undesirable. Some 6 million Jews perished during the Holocaust, along with millions of Poles, Gypsies, communists, socialists, and others.

German Citizens Made to View Corpses At the end of World War II, German citizens from towns located near extermination camps were ordered to view the corpses of the victims of Nazi atrocities.

cellars. Air-raid sirens awakened people throughout the night. Millions fled their homes in terror. Of all the major belligerents, only Americans escaped such nightmares, and war production ended the deprivations of the Depression years.

The war demanded an enormous production effort from civilians. In the face of advancing Germans in 1941, the Soviets dismantled over fifteen hundred factories and rebuilt them in the Ural Mountains and Siberia, where workers soon turned out more tanks and artillery than the Axis. American factories produced an unending supply of ships, aircraft, trucks, tanks, and other materiel for the Allied effort. The Axis powers could not compete with this vast outpouring.

With so many men mobilized for war, women were responsible for much of this production. Six million American women entered the labor force during the war, 2.5 million of them in manufacturing jobs previously considered "men's work." Soviet women took over half of all industrial and three-quarters of all agricultural jobs. In the other belligerent countries, women also played a major role in the war effort, replacing men in fields, factories, and offices. The Nazis, in contrast, believed that German women should stay home and bear children, and imported 7 million "guest workers"—a euphemism for war prisoners and captured foreigners—to man their factories.

War and the Environment

As in World War I, battles scarred the landscape, leaving behind spent ammunition and damaged equipment. Retreating armies flooded large areas of China and the Netherlands. The bombing of cities left ruins that remained visible for a generation or more. The main cause of environmental stress, however, was not the fighting but the economic development that sustained it.

- New technologies and shifts in moral values were responsible for the war's huge death toll.
- Scientists pioneered many military technologies, including new aircraft and nuclear weapons.
- Britain and the United States perfected the large-scale bombing raid, devastating German and Japanese cities.
- The Nazis carried out programs of systematic extermination, killing mainly Jews but also members of other groups deemed inferior.
- Civilian populations, particularly women, endured both the horrors of warfare and the demands of wartime production.
- Battles and growing war industries scarred the environment; the demand for raw materials reached into Africa and Latin America.

As war industries boomed—the United States increased its industrial production fourfold during the war—so did the demand for raw materials. Mining companies opened new mines and towns in Central Africa to supply strategic minerals. Brazil, Argentina, and other Latin American countries deprived of manufactured imports began building their own steel mills, factories, and shipyards. In India, China, and Europe, timber felling accelerated far beyond forest regrowth. Yet the environmental impact of the war was quite modest compared to the damage inflicted on the earth by the long consumer boom that began after World War II.

Conclusion

During the two decades from 1929 to 1949, industrialization and nationalism led the industrialized nations into depression, political violence, and war. In the Soviet Union, the need to industrialize quickly to catch up with western Europe and prepare for a future war with Germany could only be accomplished by the use of terror. In the United States and western Europe, a shaky economy based on credit and speculation collapsed, causing misery and unemployment. And in Italy, Germany, and Japan, the economic tumoil, the disillusionment with liberal parliamentary politics, and nationalist resentments played into the hands of extremists who believed that war and genocide offered solutions to their nations' problems.

The Second World War was not just another war between states and armed forces, but a war against peoples. Modern industrial technologies like aviation that had been developed for peaceful purposes, as well as new scientific breakthroughs like nuclear physics, were turned into engines of destruction. The war that resulted was by far the most violent and deadly in the history of humanity.

CHAPTER REVIEW

How did the Soviet Union change under Stalin, and at what cost? (page 652)

After the Great War ended, the world seemed to return to its prewar state, but it was an illusion. In the Soviet Union, Joseph Stalin was determined to turn his country into a modern industrial state at breakneck speed, regardless of the human cost. Several million people—most of them peasants—died and millions more were enslaved during the Five-Year Plans and the collectivization of agriculture.

By 1941 Soviet industry was much better prepared for a war with Germany than it had been in 1914–1917.

What caused the Depression, and what effects did it have on the world? (page 655)

In 1929, after a few years of prosperity, excessive speculation based on shaky loans caused the New York stock market to collapse; within a few months, the world economy fell into the Great Depression, which threw millions out of work, not only in the industrial nations but also throughout the world. Countries such as France and Britain survived the Depression by making their colonial empires purchase their products. Countries that were dependent on exports, such as Germany and Japan, suffered more. Only the USSR and southern Africa, where gold became more valuable, boomed during the 1930s.

How did fascism in Italy and Germany lead to the Second World War? (page 659)

In Italy, the government that was already fascist became more tyrannical. Mussolini installed Fascist Party members in all government jobs and jailed anyone who criticized him. In Germany, economic collapse led people to entrust their government to Adolf Hitler and his Nazi followers, who quickly set to work establishing a totalitarian government. Nazi Germany's rebuilding of its military and its invasion of Austria and Czechoslovakia were greeted with a policy of appeasement by Western democracies, until finally they could no longer overlook Germany's intentions.

Why did Japan invade Manchuria? (page 662)

The Depression hit Japan hard because the worldwide demand for silk and rice collapsed. Japan saw China as a potential new colony with a vast population and resources to help solve its economic problems. In 1931, Japan conquered Manchuria and proceeded to build railways and heavy industries there. The United States and the League of Nations protested but did little else. The Sino-Japanese War, which began with the Japanese invasion of Beijing in 1937, was a long and brutal war that became a drain on the Japanese economy and resources. Meanwhile, the communists, led by Mao Zedong, were slowly gaining support in the Chinese countryside.

How was the war fought, and why did Japan and Germany lose? (page 664)

Italy conquered Ethiopia in 1935, and Japan attacked China in 1937, while the Western democracies disapproved but took no action. The war spread to Europe in 1939 when Germany conquered Poland, then Denmark, Norway, the Low Countries, and, in 1940, France. The war turned global when Germany invaded the Soviet Union and Japan attacked the United States in 1941. The Allies won because of Russia's hard fighting and its victory at Stalingrad; the Allies' overwhelming materiel resources, especially those of the United States; the invasion of D-day, which put enough men on the European continent to finally drive back Germany; and U.S. naval victories in the Pacific and its use of atomic weapons against Japan.

How did science and technology change the nature of warfare? (page 670)

The Second World War was by far the deadliest and most horrific in history. Modern mechanized forces swept across entire nations and oceans. Their targets were not only each other's armed forces, but their civilian populations as well. Though Germany had considerable scientific and technical talent, the war favored the nations with the most heavy industries, namely, the United States and the Soviet Union. The Allies destroyed German and Japanese cities with fire-bombs, and the United States dropped atomic bombs on Hiroshima and Nagasaki. Of the roughly 60 million people who died in the war, most were civilians.

Key Terms

Joseph Stalin (p. 652)	Long March (p. 663)
Five-Year Plans (p. 652)	Stalingrad (p. 665)
Benito Mussolini (p. 659)	Pearl Harbor (p. 667)
Fascist Party (p. 659)	Battle of Midway (p. 667)
Adolf Hitler (p. 660)	Hiroshima (p. 669)
Nazis (p. 660)	Auschwitz (p. 671)
Chiang Kai-shek (p. 662)	Holocaust (p. 671)
Mao Zedong (p. 663)	

Web Resources

Pronunciation Guide

Interactive Maps

- MAP 27.1 World War II in Europe and North Africa
- MAP 27.2 World War II in Asia and the Pacific

Primary Sources

- The Centerpiece of Nazi Racial Legislation: The Nuremberg Laws
- Speech to the National Socialist Women's Association
- The Decision to Use the Atomic Bomb
- Memoirs

Visit the CourseMate website at www.cengagebrain.com for additional study tools and review materials for this chapter.

Answer to the History in Focus Question

See photo on page 665, "German Dive-Bomber over Eastern Europe."

Striving for Independence: India, Africa, and Latin America

© Cengage Learning

Visit the CourseMate website at **www.cengagebrain.com** for additional study tools and review materials for this chapter.

Modern technologies, such as mass transit, airlines, and radio systems, first appeared in the wealthier countries of Europe and North America. When they were transferred to Asia, Africa, and Latin America, they reinforced the dependence of these less developed parts of the world on the industrialized countries and widened the gap between their social classes. The tensions of modernization contributed to popular movements for independence and social justice.

The previous two chapters focused on a world convulsed by war and revolution. The world wars involved Europe, East Asia, the Middle East, and the United States, and they sparked violent revolutions in Russia and China. They accelerated the development of aviation, electronics, nuclear power, and other technologies. Although these momentous events dominate the history of the first half of the twentieth century, parts of the world that were little touched by war also underwent profound changes in this period, partly for internal reasons and partly because of the warfare and revolution in other parts of the world.

In this chapter we examine the changes that took place in India, in sub-Saharan Africa, and in three major countries of Latin America—Mexico, Brazil, and Argentina. These three regions represent three very distinct cultures, yet they had much in common. India and Africa were colonies of Europe, both politically and economically. Though politically independent, the Latin American republics were dependent on Europe and the United States for the sale of raw materials and commodities and for imports of manufactured goods, technology, and capital. In all three regions independence movements tried to wrest control from distant foreigners and improve the livelihood of their peoples. Their success was partial at best.

The Indian Independence Movement, 1905–1947

Why did the educated elites of India want independence? What were ordinary Indians hoping for?

Under British rule the Indian subcontinent acquired many of the trappings of Western-style economic development, such as railroads, harbors, modern cities, and cotton and steel mills, as well as an active and worldly middle class. The economic transformation of the region awakened in this educated middle class a sense of national dignity that demanded political fulfillment. In response, the British gradually granted India limited political autonomy while maintaining overall control. Religious and communal tensions among the Indian peoples were carefully papered over under British rule. After the British finally withdrew in 1947, these tensions erupted in violent conflicts that tore India apart.

The Land and the People

Despite periodic famines, notably between 1896 and 1900, when 2 million people died of starvation, the Indian population grew from 250 million in 1900 to 319 million in 1921 and 389 million in 1941. This growth caused landless young men to converge on the cities, exceeding the number of jobs available in the slowly expanding industries. To produce timber for construction and railroad ties, and to clear land for tea and rubber plantations, government foresters cut down most of the tropical hardwood forests that had covered the subcontinent in the nineteenth century. In spite of deforestation and extensive irrigation, the amount of land available per peasant family shrank with each successive generation.

Economic development—what the British called the "moral and material progress of India"—hardly benefited the average Indian. After paying rent to the landowner, interest to the village moneylender, and taxes to the government, peasants—always the great majority—had little left to improve their land or raise their standard of living. The government protected property owners, from village moneylenders all the way up to the maharajahs (mah-huh-RAH-juh), or ruling princes who owned huge tracts of land. The cities were crowded with craftsmen, traders, and workers of all sorts, most very poor. Although the British had banned the burning of widows on their husbands' funeral pyres, in other respects women's lives changed little under British rule.

The peoples of India spoke many different languages: Hindi in the north, Tamil in the south, Bengali in the east, Gujerati around Bombay, Urdu in the northwest, and dozens of others. As a result of British rule and increasing trade and travel, English became, like Latin in medieval Europe, the common medium of communication of the Western-educated middle class. This new class of English-speaking government bureaucrats, professionals, and merchants was to play a leading role in the independence movement.

The majority of Indians practiced Hinduism and were subdivided into hundreds of castes, each affiliated with a particular occupation. Hinduism discouraged intermarriage and other social interactions among the castes and with people who were not Hindus. Muslims constituted one-quarter of the people of India but formed a majority in the northwest and in eastern Bengal. Muslim rulers had dominated northern and central India until they were displaced by the British in the eighteenth century. More reluctant than Hindus to learn English, Muslims felt discriminated against by both British and Hindus.

British Rule and Nationalism

Colonial India was ruled by a viceroy appointed by the British government and administered by a few thousand members of the Indian Civil Service. Drawn mostly from the English gentry, they liked to think of India as a land of lords and peasants. They believed it was their duty to protect the Indian people from the dangers of industrialization, while defending their own positions from Indian nationalists.

The British administrators admired modern technology but tried to control its introduction into India so as to maximize the benefits to Britain and to themselves. For example, they encouraged railroads, harbors, telegraphs, and other communications technologies, as well as irrigation and plantations, because

these increased India's foreign trade and strengthened British control. At the same time, they discouraged the cotton and steel industries and limited the training of Indian engineers, ostensibly to spare India the social upheavals that had accompanied the Industrial Revolution in Europe, while actually protecting British industry from Indian competition.

At the turn of the century the majority of Indians accepted British rule. But the Europeans' racist attitude toward dark-skinned people increasingly offended a limited number of Indians who had learned English and absorbed English ideas of freedom and representative government, only to discover that thinly disguised racial quotas excluded them from the Indian Civil Service, the officer corps, and prestigious country clubs.

In 1885 a small group of English-speaking Hindu professionals founded a political organization called the **Indian National Congress**. For twenty years its members respectfully petitioned the government for access to the higher administrative positions and for a voice in official decisions, but they had little influence outside intellectual circles. Then, in 1905, Viceroy Lord Curzon divided the province of **Bengal** in two to improve the efficiency of its administration. This decision, made without consulting anyone, angered not only educated Indians, who saw it as a way to lessen their influence, but also millions of uneducated Hindu Bengalis, who suddenly found themselves outnumbered by Muslims in East Bengal. Soon Bengal was the scene of demonstrations, boycotts of British goods, and incidents of anti-British violence.

Indian National Congress A movement and political party founded in 1885 to demand greater Indian participation in government. Its membership was middle class, and its demands were modest until World War I. Led after 1920 by Mohandas K. Gandhi, it appealed increasingly to the poor, and it organized mass protests demanding self-government and independence.

Bengal Region of northeastern India. It was the first part of India to be conquered by the British in the eighteenth century and remained the political and economic center of British India throughout the nineteenth century. The 1905 split of the province into predominantly Hindu West Bengal and predominantly Muslim East Bengal (now Bangladesh) sparked anti-British riots.

Chronology

India	Africa	Latin America
		1876–1910 Porfirio Díaz, dictator of Mexico
1900	**1900s** Railroads connect ports to the interior	
1905 Viceroy Curzon splits Bengal; mass demonstrations		
1906 Muslims found All-India Muslim League		
1911 British transfer capital from Calcutta to Delhi		**1911–1919** Mexican Revolution; Emiliano Zapata and Pancho Villa against the Constitutionalists
	1912 African National Congress founded	
		1917 New constitution proclaimed in Mexico
1919 Amritsar Massacre	**1920s** J. E. Casely Hayford organizes political movement in British West Africa	
1920		
		1928 Plutarco Elías Calles founds Mexico's National Revolutionary Party
1929 Gandhi leads Walk to the Sea		
1930s Gandhi calls for independence; he is repeatedly arrested		**1930–1945** Getulio Vargas, dictator of Brazil
		1934–1940 Lázaro Cárdenas, president of Mexico
		1938 Cárdenas nationalizes Mexican oil industry; Vargas proclaims Estado Novo in Brazil
1939 British bring India into World War II	**1939–1945** A million Africans serve in World War II	
1940 **1940** Muhammad Ali Jinnah demands a separate nation for Muslims		
		1943 Juan Perón leads military coup in Argentina
		1946 Perón elected president of Argentina
1947 Partition and independence of India and Pakistan		

Muslims, fearful of Hindu dominance elsewhere in India, founded the **All-India Muslim League** in 1906. The government responded to the political agitation by granting Indians a limited franchise based on wealth. Muslims, however, were on average poorer than Hindus, for many poor and low-caste Hindus

All-India Muslim League Political organization founded in India in 1906 to defend the interests of India's Muslim minority. Led by Muhammad Ali Jinnah, it attempted to negotiate with the Indian National Congress. In 1940, the League began demanding a separate state for Muslims, to be called Pakistan.

had converted to Islam to escape caste discrimination. Accordingly, the British instituted separate representation and different voting qualifications for Hindus and Muslims. Then, in 1911, the British transferred the capital of India from Calcutta to Delhi (DEL-ee), the former Mughal (MOO-guhl) capital. These changes raised the political consciousness of Indians of all classes and religions, giving rise to two mass movements: one by Hindus and one by Muslims.

Fearful of social upheavals, the British resisted the idea that India could, or should, industrialize. Their geologists looked for minerals, such as coal or manganese, that British industry required. However, when the only Indian member of the Indian Geological Service, Pramatha Nath Bose, wanted to prospect for iron ore, he had to resign because the government wanted no part of an Indian steel industry that could compete with that of Britain. Bose joined forces with Jamsetji Tata, a Bombay textile magnate who decided to produce steel anyway. With the help of German and American engineers and equipment, Tata's son Dorabji opened the first steel mill in India in 1911, in a town called Jamshedpur in honor of his father. Although it produced only a fraction of the steel that India required, Jamshedpur became a powerful symbol of Indian national pride.

During World War I Indians supported Britain enthusiastically; 1.2 million men volunteered for the army, and millions more voluntarily contributed money to the government. Many expected the British to reward their loyalty with political concessions. Others organized to demand a voice in the government. Responding to the agitation, the British announced in 1917 "the gradual development of self-governing institutions with a view to the progressive realization of responsible government in India as an integral part of the British Empire." This sounded like a promise of self-government, but the timetable was so vague that nationalists denounced it as a devious trick to postpone India's independence.

In late 1918 and early 1919 the great influenza pandemic began in the war zone of northern France (see Chapter 26). Of the 30 million people who died around the world, two-thirds were Indian. This dreadful toll increased the mounting political tensions. Leaders of the Indian National Congress declared that the British reform proposals were too little, too late.

On April 13, 1919, in the city of Amritsar in Punjab, General Reginald Dyer ordered his troops to fire into a peaceful crowd of some 10,000 demonstrators, killing at least 379 and wounding 1,200. Although waves of angry demonstrations swept over India, the government waited six months to appoint a committee to investigate the massacre. After General Dyer retired, the British House of Lords voted to approve his actions, and a fund was raised in appreciation of his services. Indians interpreted these gestures as showing British contempt for their colonial subjects, effectively bringing to a close the period of gradual accommodation between the British and the Indians.

Mahatma Gandhi and Militant Nonviolence

For the next twenty years violent uprisings and harsh repression, possibly even war, seemed imminent. That the worst did not come to pass was due to **Mohandas K. Gandhi** (GAHN-dee) (1869–1948), a man known to his followers as "Mahatma," the "great soul."

Gandhi began life with every advantage. His wealthy family sent him to England for his education. After his studies he lived in South Africa and practiced law for the small Indian community there. During World War I he returned to India and was one of many Western-educated Hindu intellectuals who joined the Indian National Congress.

Gandhi had some unusual political ideas. Unlike many radical political thinkers of his time, he denounced the popular ideals of power, struggle, and combat. Instead, inspired by both Hindu and Christian concepts, he preached the virtues of *ahimsa* (uh-HIM-sah) (nonviolence) and *satyagraha* (suh-TYAH-gruh-huh) (the search for truth). He refused to countenance violence among his followers, and he called off several demonstrations when they turned violent.

Mohandas K. (Mahatma) Gandhi (1869–1948) Leader of the Indian independence movement and advocate of nonviolent resistance. After being educated as a lawyer in England, he returned to India and became leader of the Indian National Congress in 1920. He appealed to the poor, led nonviolent demonstrations against British colonial rule, and was jailed many times. Soon after independence he was assassinated for attempting to stop Hindu-Muslim rioting.

Gandhi had an affinity for the poor that was unusual even among socialist politicians. In 1921 he gave up both Western-style suits and the finery of wealthy Indians and henceforth wore simple peasant garb: a length of homespun cloth below his waist and a shawl to cover his torso. He spoke for the farmers and the outcasts, whom he called *harijan* (HAH-ree-jahn), "children of God." He attracted ever-larger numbers of followers among the poor and the illiterate, who soon began to revere him; and he transformed the cause of Indian independence from an elite movement of the educated into a mass movement with a quasi-religious aura.

Gandhi was a brilliant political tactician and a master of public relations gestures. In 1929, in a well-publicized act of civil disregard for the government's monopoly on salt, he led a few followers on an 80-mile (129-kilometer) walk, camped on a beach, and gathered salt from the sea. But he discovered that unleashing the power of popular participation was one thing and controlling its direction was quite another. Within days of his "Walk to the Sea," demonstrations of support broke out all over India, in which the police killed a hundred demonstrators and arrested over sixty thousand.

Many times during the 1930s Gandhi threatened to fast "unto death," and several times he did come close to death, to protest the violence of both the police and his followers and to demand independence. He was repeatedly arrested and spent a total of six years in jail. But arrest only made him more popular. He became an iconic figure not only in his own country but also in the Western media. In the words of historian Percival Spear, he made the British "uncomfortable in their cherished field of moral rectitude," and he gave Indians the feeling that theirs was the ethically superior cause.

India Moves Toward Independence

In the 1920s, the British slowly began to give in to the pressure of the Indian National Congress and the Muslim League. They handed over control of "national" areas such as education, the economy, and public works, and they also admitted more Indians into the Civil Service and the officer corps. Economically, Indian politicians obtained the right to erect high tariff barriers against imports to protect India's infant industries. Behind these barriers, Indian entrepreneurs built plants to manufacture iron and steel, cement, paper, cotton and jute textiles, and sugar. While these manufactures did not improve the lives of the peasants or urban poor, they helped create a class of wealthy Indian businessmen who supported the Indian National Congress and its demands for independence. Though paying homage to Gandhi, they preferred his designated successor as leader of the Indian National Congress, **Jawaharlal Nehru** (NAY-roo) (1889–1964). A highly educated nationalist and subtle thinker, Nehru, unlike Gandhi, looked forward to creating a modern industrial India (see Environment and Technology: Gandhi and Technology).

Congress politicians won regional elections but continued to be excluded from the viceroy's cabinet, the true center of power. When World War II began in September 1939, Viceroy Lord Linlithgow declared war without consulting a single Indian. The Congress-dominated provincial governments resigned in protest and found that boycotting government office increased their popular support. When the British offered to give India its independence once the war ended, Gandhi called the offer a "postdated cheque on a failing bank" and demanded full independence immediately. His "Quit India" campaign aroused popular demonstrations against the British and provoked a wave of arrests. Nehru declared: "I would fight Japan sword in hand, but I can only do so as a free man."

Most Indian soldiers felt they were fighting to defend their country rather than to support the British Empire. As in World War I, Indians contributed heavily to the Allied war effort, supplying 2 million soldiers and enormous amounts of resources. A small number of Indians, however, were so anti-British that they joined the Japanese side.

India's subordination to British interests was vividly demonstrated in the famine of 1943 in Bengal. Unlike previous famines, this one was caused not by drought but by the Japanese conquest of Burma, which cut off imports of Burmese rice. Food was

Jawaharlal Nehru (1889–1964) Indian statesman who succeeded Mohandas K. Gandhi as leader of the Indian National Congress. He negotiated the end of British colonial rule in India and became India's first prime minister (1947–1964).

Gandhi and Technology

In the twentieth century all political leaders but one embraced modern industrial technology. That one exception is Gandhi.

After deciding to wear only handmade cloth, Gandhi made a bonfire of imported factory-made cloth and began spending half an hour every day spinning yarn on a simple spinning wheel, a task he called a "sacrament." The spinning wheel became the symbol of his movement and was later incorporated into the Indian flag. Any Indian who wished to come before him had to dress in handwoven cloth.

Gandhi had several reasons for reviving this ancient craft. One was his revulsion against "the incessant search for material comforts," an evil to which Europeans were "becoming slaves." He blamed the impoverishment of the Indian people on the cotton industries of England and Japan, which had ruined the traditional cotton manufacturing by which India had once supplied all her own needs. Gandhi looked back to a time before India became a colony of Britain, when "our women spun fine yarns in their own cottages, and supplemented the earnings of their husbands." The spinning wheel, he believed, was "presented to the nation for giving occupation to the millions who had, at least four months of the year, nothing to do." A return to the spinning wheel would provide employment to millions of Indians and would also become a symbol of "national consciousness and a contribution by every individual to a definite constructive national work."

Nevertheless, Gandhi was a shrewd politician who understood the usefulness of modern devices for mobilizing the masses and organizing his followers. He wore a watch and used the telephone and the printing press to keep in touch with his followers. When he traveled by train, he rode third class—but in a third-class railroad car of his own. His goal was the independence of his country, and he pursued it with every nonviolent means he could find.

Gandhi's ideas challenge us to rethink the purpose of technology. Was he opposed on principle to all modern devices? Was he an opportunist who used those devices that served his political ends and rejected those that did not? Or did he have a higher principle that accounts for his willingness to use the telephone and the railroad but not factory-made cloth?

Gandhi at the Spinning Wheel Mahatma Gandhi chose the spinning wheel as his symbol because it represented the traditional activity of millions of rural Indians whose livelihoods were threatened by industrialization.

Margaret Bourke-White, Time Life Pictures/Getty Images LIFE Magazine. © Time Warner Inc.

available elsewhere in India, but the British army had requisitioned the railroads to transport troops and equipment in preparation for a Japanese invasion. As a result, supplies ran short in Bengal and surrounding areas, while speculators hoarded whatever they could find. Some 2 million people starved to death before the army was ordered to supply food.

Partition and Independence

When the war ended, Britain's new Labour Party government prepared for Indian independence, but deep suspicions between Hindus and Muslims complicated the process. The break between the two communities had started in 1937, when the Indian National Congress won provincial elections and

The Partition of India When India became independent, Muslims fled from Hindu regions, and Hindus fled from Muslim regions. Margaret Bourke-White photographed a long line of refugees, with their cows, carts, and belongings, trudging down a country road toward safety.

Time Life Pictures/Getty Images

 History in Focus *Why did independence lead to the flight of millions of people from their homes? If tensions existed between Hindus and Muslims, why did they not erupt in violence before independence? Find the answer online.*

refused to share power with the Muslim League. In 1940 the leader of the League, **Muhammad Ali Jinnah** (jee-NAH) (1876–1948), demanded what many Muslims had long dreamt of: a country of their own, to be called Pakistan (from "Punjab-Afghans-Kashmir-Sind" plus the Persian suffix *-stan* meaning "home of").

As independence approached, talks between Jinnah and Nehru broke down, and violent rioting between Hindus and Muslims broke out in Bengal and Bihar. Gandhi's appeals for tolerance and cooperation fell on deaf ears. In despair, he retreated to his home near Ahmedabad. The British made frantic proposals to keep India united, but their authority was waning fast.

By early 1947 the Indian National Congress had accepted the idea of a partition of India into two states, one secular but dominated by Hindus, the other Muslim. In June Lord Mountbatten, the last viceroy, decided that independence must come immediately. On August 15, British India gave way to a new India and Pakistan. The Indian National Congress, led by Nehru, formed the first government of India. Jinnah and the Muslim League established a government for the provinces that made up Pakistan.

Violent clashes between Muslims and Hindus marred any celebration of independence. Throughout the land, Muslim and Hindu neighbors turned on one another, and armed members of one faith hunted down people of the other faith. For centuries Hindus and Muslims had intermingled throughout most of India. Now, leaving most of their possessions behind, Hindus fled from predominantly Muslim areas, and Muslims fled from Hindu areas. Trainloads of desperate refugees were attacked and massacred by members of the opposite faith. Within a few months some 12 million people had abandoned their ancestral homes and a half-million lay dead. In January 1948 Gandhi died too, gunned down by an angry Hindu refugee.

When the dust cleared, few Hindus remained in Pakistan, and Muslims were a minority in all but one state of India. That state was Kashmir, a strategically important region in the foothills of the Himalayas. India annexed Kashmir because the local maharajah was Hindu and because the state held the headwaters of the rivers that irrigated millions of acres of Indian farmland. The majority of the inhabitants of Kashmir

Muhammad Ali Jinnah (1876–1948) Indian Muslim politician who founded the state of Pakistan. A lawyer by training, he joined the All-India Muslim League in 1913. As leader of the League from the 1920s on, he negotiated with the British and the Indian National Congress for Muslim participation in Indian politics. From 1940 on, he led the movement for the independence of India's Muslims in a separate state of Pakistan, founded in 1947.

SECTION REVIEW

- The inequities of British rule caused the rising class of English-speaking Indian professionals to create an independence movement.

- Changes in colonial administration and voting rights played upon religious divisions and created parallel Hindu and Muslim political movements.

- World War I and its aftermath stimulated nationalist agitation, which turned violent after the Amritsar Massacre.

- Employing militant nonviolence, Gandhi built a morally charged mass independence movement.

- Under Nehru's leadership, Indians pushed for greater independence, but World War II subordinated India to British interests.

- After gaining independence, India split into two states, and violence erupted between Hindus and Muslims.

were Muslims, however, and would probably have joined Pakistan if they had been allowed to choose. Partition and the Kashmir question turned India and Pakistan into bitter enemies that have fought several wars in the past half-century.

Sub-Saharan Africa, 1900–1945

What changes did foreign rule bring to Africa, and how did Africans respond?

The first half of the twentieth century, the time when nationalist movements threatened European rule in Asia, was Africa's period of classic colonialism. After World War I Britain, France, Belgium, and South Africa divided Germany's African colonies among themselves. In the 1930s Italy invaded Ethiopia. The colonial empires reached their peak shortly before World War II.

Colonial Africa: Economic and Social Changes

Outside of Algeria, Kenya, and South Africa, few Europeans lived in Africa. In 1930 Nigeria, with a population of 20 million, was ruled by 386 British officials and by 8,000 policemen and military, of whom 150 were European. Yet even such a small presence stimulated deep social and economic changes.

Since the turn of the century the colonial powers had built railroads from coastal cities to mines and plantations in the interior to access raw materials. But the economic boom of the interwar years benefited few Africans. Colonial governments took lands that Africans owned communally and sold or leased them to European companies or, in eastern and southern Africa, to white settlers. Large European companies dominated wholesale commerce, while immigrants from various countries—Indians in East Africa, Greeks and Syrians in West Africa—handled much of the retail trade.

Where land was divided into small farms, some Africans benefited from the boom. Farmers in the Gold Coast (now Ghana [GAH-nah]) profited from the high price of cocoa, as did palm-oil producers in Nigeria and coffee growers in East Africa. In most of Africa women played a major role in the retail trades, selling pots and pans, cloth, food, and other items in the markets. Many maintained their economic independence and kept their household finances separate from those of their husbands, following a custom that predated the colonial period.

For many Africans, however, economic development meant working in European-owned mines and plantations, often under compulsion. Colonial governments were eager to develop the resources of their territories but could not afford to pay high enough wages to attract workers. Instead, they used police power to force Africans to work under harsh conditions for little or no pay. In the 1920s, when the government of French Equatorial Africa decided to build a railroad from Brazzaville to the Atlantic coast, a distance of 312 miles (502 kilometers), it drafted 127,000 men to carve a roadbed across mountains and through rain forests. Lacking adequate food, clothing, and medical care, 20,000 of them died, an average of 64 deaths per mile of track.

Europeans prided themselves on bringing modern health care to Africa; yet before the 1930s there was too little of it to help the majority of Africans, and other aspects of colonialism actually worsened public health. Migrants to cities, mines, and plantations and soldiers moving from post to post spread syphilis, gonorrhea, tuberculosis, and malaria. Sleeping sickness and smallpox epidemics raged throughout Central Africa. In recruiting men to work, colonial governments depleted

African Farmers in the Gold Coast African farmers in the Gold Coast (now Ghana) sold their cocoa beans to government agents. The government kept the prices artificially low in order to profit on the transactions.

Popperfoto/Getty Images

rural areas of farmers needed to plant and harvest crops. Forced requisitions of food to feed the workers left the remaining populations undernourished and vulnerable to diseases. Not until the 1930s did colonial governments realize the negative consequences of their labor policies and begin to invest in agricultural development and health care for Africans.

In 1900 Ibadan (ee-BAH-dahn) in Nigeria was the only city in sub-Saharan Africa with more than 100,000 inhabitants; fifty years later, dozens of cities had reached that size, including Nairobi (nie-ROE-bee) in Kenya, Johannesburg in South Africa, Lagos in Nigeria, Accra in Gold Coast, and Dakar in Senegal. Africans migrated to cities for jobs, excitement, and, for a few, the chance to become wealthy.

However, migrations damaged family life, for almost all the migrants were men leaving women in the countryside to farm and raise children. Cities built during the colonial period had racially segregated housing, clubs, restaurants, hospitals, and other institutions. Racial discrimination was most rigid in the white-settler colonies of eastern and southern Africa.

Religious and Political Changes

Traditional religious belief could not explain the dislocations that foreign rule, migrations, and sudden economic changes brought to the lives of Africans. Many therefore turned to one of the two universal religions, Christianity and Islam, for guidance.

Christianity, introduced by Western missionaries (except in Ethiopia, where it was indigenous) met its greatest success in the coastal regions of West and South Africa, where European influence was strongest. Mission schools, which taught both craft skills and basic literacy, provided access to employment as minor functionaries, teachers, and shopkeepers. These schools also imparted Western political ideas to a new educated elite. Many Africans read the suffering of their own peoples into the biblical stories of Moses and the parables of Jesus. The churches trained some of the brighter pupils to become catechists, teachers, and clergymen. A few rose to high positions, such as James Johnson, a Yoruba who became the Anglican bishop of the Niger Delta Pastorate. Independent Christian churches—known as "Ethiopian" churches—associated Christian beliefs with radical ideas of racial equality and political participation.

Through the influence and example of Arab and African merchants, Islam spread inland from the East African coast and southward from the Sahel (SAH-hel) toward the West African coast. Islam also emphasized literacy—in Arabic through Quranic schools rather than in a European language—and was less disruptive of traditional African customs such as polygamy.

In a few places, such as Dakar in Senegal and Cape Town in South Africa, small numbers of Africans could obtain secondary education. Even smaller numbers went on to college in Europe or America. Though few in number, they became the leaders of political movements. The contrast between the liberal ideas imparted by Western education and the realities of racial discrimination under colonial rule contributed to the rise of nationalism among educated Africans. In Senegal **Blaise Diagne** (dee-AHN-yuh) agitated for African participation in politics and fair treatment in the French army. In the 1920s J. E. Casely Hayford began organizing a movement for greater autonomy in British West Africa. In South Africa Western-educated lawyers and journalists founded the **African National Congress** in 1912 to defend the interests of Africans. These nationalist movements were partly inspired by the ideas of Pan-Africanists from America such as W. E. B. Du Bois and Marcus Garvey, who advocated the unity of African peoples around the world. Before World War II, however, they were small and had little influence.

During the Second World War increased forced labor, inflation, and requisitions of raw materials had a profound effect even on Africans who were far removed from the theaters of war. Yet the war also brought hope. During the campaign to oust the Italians from Ethiopia, Emperor **Haile Selassie** (HI-lee

SECTION REVIEW

- Colonial empires in Africa reached their peak just before World War II.
- In general, interwar economic development benefited European residents and farm owners.
- Urbanization damaged traditional family life, and colonial labor policies caused severe health problems.
- Many Africans turned to Christianity and Islam for solace and education, and educated Africans joined nationalist movements.
- Urbanization, economic development, and involvement in World War II all contributed to the postwar independence movements.

seh-LASS-ee) (r. 1930–1974) led his own troops into Addis Ababa, his capital, and reclaimed his title. A million Africans served as soldiers and porters in Burma, North Africa, and Europe. They listened to Allied propaganda in favor of European liberation movements and against Nazi racism, and they returned to their countries with new and radical ideas.

After the Second World War the building of cities, railroads, and other enterprises brought Africa into the global economy, often at great human cost. Colonialism also brought changes to African culture and religion, hastening the spread of Christianity and Islam. And the foreign occupation awakened political ideas that inspired the next generation of Africans to demand independence (see Chapter 29).

 Primary Source: Education, Civilization, and "Foreignization" in Buganda Find out how one man views his country's wholesale acquisition of Western education and customs.

Primary Source: London Manifesto Hear an argument for Pan-Africanism as expressed by the Pan-African Congress of 1921.

 Primary Source: Parable of the Eagle, Limbo, Prayer for Peace, Vultures Find out why an eagle will always remain an eagle even when it has been trained to be a chicken.

Blaise Diagne (1872–1934) Senegalese political leader, the first African elected to the French National Assembly. During World War I, in exchange for promises to give French citizenship to Senegalese, he helped recruit Africans to serve in the French army. After the war, he led a movement to abolish forced labor in Africa.

African National Congress An organization dedicated to obtaining equal voting and civil rights for black inhabitants of South Africa. Founded in 1912 as the South African Native National Congress, it changed its name in 1923. Though it was banned and its leaders were jailed for many years, it eventually helped bring majority rule to South Africa.

Haile Selassie (1892–1975) Emperor of Ethiopia (r. 1930–1974) and symbol of African independence. He fought the Italian invasion of his country in 1935 and regained his throne during World War II, when British forces expelled the Italians. He ruled Ethiopia as a traditional autocracy until he was overthrown in 1974.

Mexico, Argentina, and Brazil, 1900–1949

What could Latin Americans do to achieve social justice and economic development? Were these two goals compatible?

In the nineteenth century Latin America achieved independence from Spain and Portugal but did not industrialize. Most of the new states suffered from ideological divisions, unstable governments, and violent upheavals. Foreign investment and the exchange of raw materials and agricultural products for foreign manufactured goods made them economically dependent on the wealthier countries to the north, especially the United States and Great Britain. Their societies remained deeply split between wealthy landowners and desperately poor peasants.

Mexico, Brazil, and Argentina contained well over half of Latin America's land, population, and wealth, and their relations with other countries and their economies were similar. Mexico, however, underwent a traumatic social revolution, while Argentina and Brazil evolved more peaceably.

Background to Revolution: Mexico in 1910

A Mexican saying observed wryly: "Poor Mexico: so far from God, so close to the United States." In Mexico the chasm between rich and poor was so deep that only a revolution could move the country toward prosperity and democracy. Mexico was the Latin American country most influenced by the Spanish during three centuries of colonial rule, and after independence in 1821 it suffered from a half-century of political turmoil. At the beginning of the twentieth century Mexican society was divided into rich and poor and into persons of Spanish, Indian, and mixed ancestry. A few very wealthy families of Spanish origin, less than 1 percent of the population, owned 85 percent of Mexico's land, mostly in huge *haciendas* (estates). A handful of American and British companies closely tied to this elite controlled most of Mexico's railroads, silver mines, and plantations. At the other end of the social scale were Indians, many of whom did not speak Spanish. *Mestizos* (mess-TEE-zohs), people of mixed Indian and European ancestry, were only slightly better off;

most of them were peasants who worked on the haciendas or farmed small communal plots near their ancestral villages.

The urban middle class was small and had little political influence. Few professional and government positions were open to them, and foreigners owned most businesses. Industrial workers also were few in number; the only significant groups were textile workers in the port of Veracruz on the Gulf of Mexico and railroad workers spread throughout the country.

During the colonial period, the Spanish government had made halfhearted efforts to defend Indians and mestizos from the land-grabbing tactics of the haciendas. After independence in 1821, wealthy Mexican families and American companies used bribery and force to acquire millions of acres of good agricultural land from villages in southern Mexico. Peasants lost not only their fields but also access to firewood and pasture for their animals. Sugar, cotton, and other commercial crops replaced corn and beans. To survive, the peasants had to buy food and other necessities on credit from the hacienda owners' stores. Eventually, they fell permanently into debt.

In the 1880s American investors purchased from the Mexican government dubious claims to more than 2.5 million acres (1 million hectares) traditionally held by the Yaqui people of Sonora, in northern Mexico. When the Yaqui resisted the expropriation of their lands, they were brutally repressed by the Mexican army.

Northern Mexicans had no peasant tradition of communal ownership, for the northern half of the country was too dry for farming, unlike the tropical and densely populated south. The north was a region of silver mines and cattle ranches, some of them enormous, and was thinly populated by cowboys and miners. The harshness of their lives and the vast inequities in the distribution of income made northern Mexicans as resentful as people in the south.

Despite many upheavals in Mexico in the nineteenth century, in 1910 the government seemed in control. For thirty-four years General Porfirio Díaz (DEE-as) (1830–1915) had ruled Mexico under the motto "Liberty, Order, Progress." To Díaz "liberty" meant freedom for rich hacienda owners and foreign investors to acquire more land. The government imposed "order" through rigged elections and a policy of *pan o palo* (bread or the stick)—that is, bribes for Díaz's supporters and summary justice for those who opposed him. "Progress" meant mainly the importing of foreign capital, machinery, and technicians to take advantage of Mexico's labor, soil, and natural resources.

During the Díaz regime (1876–1910) Mexico City—with paved streets, streetcar lines, electric street lighting, and public parks—became a showplace, and new telegraph and railroad lines connected cities and towns throughout Mexico. But this material progress benefited only a handful of well-connected businessmen. The boom in railroads, agriculture, and mining at the turn of the century actually caused a decline in the average Mexican's standard of living.

Though a mestizo himself, Díaz discriminated against the nonwhite majority of Mexicans, and he and his supporters tried to eradicate what they saw as Mexico's embarrassingly rustic traditions. On many middle- and upper-class tables French cuisine replaced traditional Mexican dishes, while the wealthy replaced sombreros and ponchos with European garments. Though bullfighting and cock-fighting remained popular, the well-to-do preferred horse racing and soccer. To the educated middle class—the only group with a strong sense of Mexican nationhood—this devaluation of Mexican culture became a symbol of the Díaz regime's failure to defend national interests against foreign influences.

Brown Brothers

Emiliano Zapata Zapata, the leader of a peasant rebellion in southern Mexico during the Mexican Revolution, stands in full revolutionary regalia: sword, rifles, bandoleers, boots, and sombrero.

Revolution and Civil War in Mexico

Unlike the independence movement in India, the Mexican Revolution was a social revolution and was not the work of one party with a well-defined ideology. Instead, it developed haphazardly, led by a series of ambitious but limited leaders, each representing a different segment of Mexican society.

The first was Francisco I. Madero (1873–1913), the son of a wealthy landowning and mining family, educated in the United States. When minor uprisings broke out in 1911, the government collapsed and

Díaz fled into exile. The new Madero presidency was welcomed by some, but it aroused opposition from peasant leaders like **Emiliano Zapata** (sah-PAH-tah) (1879–1919). In 1913, after two years as president, Madero was overthrown and murdered by one of his former supporters, General Victoriano Huerta. Woodrow Wilson (1856–1924), president of the United

Primary Source: The Plan of Ayala Examine the Mexican revolutionaries' call for the overthrow of the established government and the return of Mexico to her people.

Emiliano Zapata (1879–1919) Revolutionary and leader of peasants in the Mexican Revolution. He mobilized landless peasants in south-central Mexico in an attempt to seize and divide the lands of the wealthy landowners. Though successful for a time, he was ultimately defeated and assassinated.

Francisco "Pancho" Villa Francisco "Pancho" Villa led an army of cowboys and ranch hands in northern Mexico during the revolution. He became very popular by confiscating large haciendas and dividing them among the poor. In March 1916 he entered the United States with 500 soldiers and attacked the town of Columbus, New Mexico, provoking an American invasion of Mexico. He was assassinated in 1923.

States, showed his displeasure by sending the United States Marines to occupy Veracruz.

The inequities of Mexican society and foreign intervention in Mexico's affairs angered Mexico's middle class and industrial workers. They found leaders in Venustiano Carranza, a landowner, and in Alvaro Obregón (oh-bray-GAWN), a schoolteacher. Calling themselves Constitutionalists, Carranza and Obregón organized private armies and succeeded in overthrowing Huerta in 1914. By then, the revolution had spread to the countryside.

As early as 1911 Zapata, an Indian farmer, had led a revolt against the haciendas in the mountains of Morelos, south of Mexico City (see Map 28.1). His soldiers were peasants, some of them women, mounted on horseback and armed with pistols and rifles. For several years they periodically came down from the mountains, burned hacienda buildings, and returned land to the Indian villages to which it had once belonged.

Another leader appeared in Chihuahua, a northern state where seventeen individuals owned two-fifths of the land and 95 percent of the people had no land at all. Starting in 1913, **Francisco "Pancho" Villa** (1877–1923), a former ranch hand, mule driver, and bandit, organized an army of three thousand men, most of them cowboys. They too seized land from the large haciendas, not to rebuild traditional communities as in southern Mexico but to create family ranches.

Zapata and Villa were part agrarian rebels, part social revolutionaries. They enjoyed tremendous popular support but could never rise above their origins and lead a national revolution. The Constitutionalists had fewer soldiers than Zapata and Villa, but they held the major cities, controlled the country's oil exports, and used the proceeds to buy modern weapons. Gradually the Constitutionalists took over most of Mexico. In 1919 they defeated and killed Zapata; Villa was assassinated four years later. An estimated 2 million people lost their lives in the civil war, and much of Mexico lay in ruins.

The Constitutionalists adopted many of their rivals' agrarian reforms, such as restoring communal lands to the Indians of Morelos. They also proposed social programs aimed at workers and the middle class. The Constitution of 1917 promised universal suffrage and a one-term presidency, state-run education, the end of debt peonage, restrictions on foreign ownership of property, and laws specifying minimum wages and maximum hours to protect laborers. Though not immediately implemented, these reforms carried symbolic meaning. They enshrined the dignity of Mexicans and the equality of Indians, mestizos, and whites, as well as of peasants and city people.

In the early 1920s, after years of violence that exhausted all classes, the Mexican Revolution lost momentum. Only in Morelos did peasants receive land, and President Obregón and his closest associates made all the important decisions. In 1928 Obregón was assassinated. His successor, Plutarco Elías Calles (KAH-yace), founded the National Revolutionary

---

Francisco "Pancho" Villa (1877–1923) A popular leader during the Mexican Revolution. An outlaw in his youth, when the revolution started he formed a cavalry army in the north of Mexico and fought for the rights of the landless in collaboration with Emiliano Zapata. He was assassinated in 1923.

Party, or PNR (the abbreviation of its name in Spanish). The PNR was a forum where all the pressure groups and vested interests—labor, peasants, businessmen, landowners, the military—worked out compromises. The establishment of the PNR gave the Mexican Revolution a second wind.

Lázaro Cárdenas (LAH-sah-roe KAHR-deh-nahs), chosen by Calles to be president in 1934, brought peasants' and workers' organizations into the party, renamed it the Mexican Revolutionary Party (PRM), and removed the generals from government positions. Then he set to work implementing the reforms promised in the Constitution. Cárdenas redistributed 44 million acres (17.6 million hectares) to peasant communes, replaced church-run schools with government schools, and nationalized the railroads and other businesses.

Most dramatic was the expropriation of foreign-owned oil companies. In the early 1920s Mexico was the world's leading producer of oil, but a handful of American and British companies exported almost all of it. In 1938 Cárdenas seized the foreign-owned oil industry, more as a matter of national pride than of economics. The oil companies expected the governments of the United States and Great Britain to come to their rescue, perhaps with military force. But Mexico and the United States chose to resolve the issue through negotiation, and Mexico retained control of its oil industry.

When Cárdenas's term ended in 1940, Mexico, like India, was still a land of poor farmers with a small industrial base. Yet the political system was free of both chaos and dictatorships, and land and other resources were no longer monopolized by a small

Map 28.1   The Mexican Revolution The Mexican Revolution began in two distinct regions of the country. One was the mountainous and densely populated area south of Mexico City, particularly Morelos, homeland of Emiliano Zapata. The other was the dry and thinly populated ranch country of the north, such as Chihuahua, home of Pancho Villa. The fighting that ensued crisscrossed the country along the main railroad lines, shown on the map.   © Cengage Learning

 Interactive Map

group of people. The military was tamed; the Catholic Church no longer controlled education; and the nationalization of oil had demonstrated Mexico's independence.

In the arts the Mexican Revolution sparked a surge of creativity. The political murals of José Clemente Orozco and Diego Rivera and the paintings of Frida Kahlo focused on social themes, showing peasants, workers, and soldiers in scenes from the Revolution. These works of art gave Mexicans a sense of national unity and pride in the achievements of the Revolution that lasted long after the revolutionary fervor had dissipated.

What did the Mexican Revolution accomplish? It did not fulfill the democratic promise of Madero's campaign, for it brought to power a party that monopolized the government for eighty years. However, it allowed far wider participation in politics and promised far-reaching social reforms. These long-delayed reforms began to be implemented during the Cárdenas administration. They fell short of the ideals expressed by the revolutionaries, but they laid the foundation for Mexico's later industrialization.

The Transformation of Argentina

Most of Argentina consists of *pampas* (POM-pus), flat, fertile land that is easy to till, much like the prairies of the Midwestern United States and Canada. Throughout the nineteenth century Argentina's economy was based on two exports: the hides of longhorn creole cattle and the wool of merino sheep, which roamed the pampas in huge herds.

At the end of the nineteenth century railroads and refrigerator ships that transported meat safely changed not only the composition of Argentina's exports but also the way they were produced. European consumers preferred the soft flesh of Lincoln sheep and Hereford cattle to the tough, sinewy meat of creole cattle and merino sheep. The valuable Lincolns and Herefords, however, had to be carefully bred and receive a diet of alfalfa and oats. To safeguard them, the pampas had to be divided, plowed, cultivated, and fenced with barbed wire. Once fenced, the land could be used to produce wheat as well as beef and mutton. Within a few years grasslands that had stretched to the horizon were transformed into farmland. Like the North American Midwest, the pampas became one of the world's great producers of wheat and meat.

Argentina's government represented the interests of the *oligarquía* (oh-lee-gar-KEE-ah), a very small group of wealthy hacienda owners. They also owned fine homes in Buenos Aires (BWAY-nus EYE-ress), a city that was built to look like Paris. They traveled frequently to Europe and spent so lavishly that the French coined the superlative "rich as an Argentine." Focused on producing wheat and meat, they were content to let foreign—mainly British—companies build Argentina's railroads, processing plants, and public utilities. In exchange for its agricultural exports Argentina imported almost all its manufactured goods from Europe and the United States. So important were British interests in the Argentinean economy that English, not Spanish, was used on the railroads, and the biggest department store in Buenos Aires was a branch of Harrods of London.

Brazil and Argentina, to 1929

Before the First World War Brazil produced most of the world's coffee and cacao, grown on vast estates, and natural rubber, gathered by Indians from rubber trees growing wild in the Amazon rain forest. Planters and rubber exporters made up Brazil's elite. Like their Argentinean counterparts, they spent their money lavishly, building palaces in Rio de Janeiro (REE-oh day-zhuh-NAIR-oh) and one of the world's most beautiful opera houses in Manaus (meh-NOWSE), deep in the Amazon. As in Argentina, British companies built railroads, harbors, and other infrastructure and imported most manufactured goods.

Primary Source: Speech to the Nation Hear Mexican president Lázaro Cárdenas explain to his country and the world that be intends to take control of the foreign-owned oil industry in Mexico.

Lázaro Cárdenas (1895–1970) President of Mexico (1934–1940). He brought major changes to Mexican life by distributing millions of acres of land to the peasants, bringing representatives of workers and farmers into the inner circles of politics, and nationalizing the oil industry.

Both Argentina and Brazil had small but outspoken middle classes that demanded a share in government and looked to Europe as a model. Beneath each middle class were the poor. In Argentina these were mainly Spanish and Italian immigrants who had ended up as landless farm laborers or workers in urban packing plants. In Brazil there was a large class of sharecroppers and plantation workers, many of them descendants of slaves.

Rubber exports collapsed after 1912, replaced by cheaper plantation rubber from Southeast Asia. The outbreak of war in 1914 put an end to imports from Europe as Britain and France focused all their industries on war production and Germany was cut off entirely. These disruptions weakened the landowning class. In Argentina the urban middle class obtained the secret ballot and universal male suffrage in 1916 and elected a liberal politician, **Hipólito Irigoyen** (ee-POH-lee-toe ee-ree-GO-yen), as president. To a certain extent, the United States replaced the European countries as suppliers of machinery and consumers of coffee. European immigrants built factories to manufacture textiles and household goods. Desperate for money to pay for the war, Great Britain sold many of its railroad, streetcar, and other companies to the governments of Argentina and Brazil.

South America prospered during the postwar years. Trade with Europe resumed; export prices remained high; and both Argentina and Brazil used accumulated profits to industrialize and improve their transportation systems and public utilities. Nevertheless, workers and middle-class professionals demanded social reforms and a larger voice in politics. In Argentina, students' and workers' demonstrations were brutally crushed. In Brazil, junior officers rebelled several times, calling for universal suffrage, social reforms, and freedom for labor unions. Though they accomplished little, they laid the groundwork for later reformist movements. In neither country did the urban middle class take power away from the wealthy landowners. Instead, the two classes shared power at the expense of both the landless peasants and the urban workers.

Though Argentina and Brazil moved forward, new technologies again left them dependent on the advanced industrial countries. Brazilians are justly proud that the first person to fly an airplane outside

the United States was Alberto Santos-Dumont, a Brazilian. But he did so in 1906 in France, where he lived most of his life and had access to engine manufacturers and technical assistance. Aviation reached Latin America after World War I, when European and American companies such as Aéropostale and Pan American Airways introduced airmail service between cities and linked Latin America with the United States and Europe.

Before and during World War I, radio—then called "wireless telegraphy"—was used not for broadcasting but for point-to-point communications. Transmitters powerful enough to send messages across oceans or continents were extraordinarily complex and expensive. Their antennas covered many acres; they used as much electricity as a small town; and they cost tens of thousands of pounds sterling (millions of dollars in today's money).

Right after the war, the major powers scrambled to build powerful transmitters on every continent to compete with the telegraph cable companies and take advantage of the boom in international business and news reporting. However, no Latin American country possessed the knowledge or funds to build its own transmitters. In 1919, therefore, President Irigoyen of Argentina granted a radio concession to a German firm. France and Britain protested this decision, and eventually four powerful radio companies—one British, one French, one German, and one American—formed a cartel to control all radio communications in Latin America. This cartel set up a national radio company in each republic, installing a prominent local politician as its president. But the cartel held all the stock and therefore received all the profits.

The Depression and the Vargas Regime in Brazil

The Depression hit Latin America as hard as Europe and the United States; in many ways, it marks a more important turning point for the region than either of the world wars. As long-term customers cut back their orders, the

---

Hipólito Irigoyen (1850–1933) Argentine politician, president of Argentina from 1916 to 1922 and 1928 to 1930. The first president elected by universal male suffrage, he began his presidency as a reformer but later became conservative.

value of agricultural and mineral exports fell by two-thirds between 1929 and 1932. Argentina and Brazil could no longer afford to import manufactured goods. An imploding economy also undermined their shaky political systems. Like European countries, Argentina and Brazil veered toward authoritarianism.

In 1930 **Getulio Vargas** (jay-TOO-lee-oh VAR-gus) (1883–1954), a state governor, staged a coup and proclaimed himself president of Brazil. He proved to be a masterful politician. He wrote a new constitution that broadened the franchise and limited the president to one term. He also raised import duties and promoted national firms and state-owned enterprises, culminating in the construction of the Volta Redonda steel mill in the 1930s. By 1936 industrial production had doubled, especially in textiles and small manufactures. Brazil was on its way to becoming an industrial country. Vargas's policy, called **import-substitution industrialization**, became a model for other Latin American countries as they attempted to break away from neocolonial dependency.

The industrialization of Brazil brought all the familiar environmental consequences. Powerful new machines allowed the reopening of old mines and the digging of new ones. Cities grew as poor peasants looking for work arrived from the countryside. Around the older neighborhoods of Rio de Janeiro and São Paulo (sow POW-loh), the poor turned steep hillsides and vacant lands into immense *favelas* (feh-VEL-luhs) (slums) of makeshift shacks.

The countryside also was transformed. Scrubland was turned into pasture, and new acreage was planted in wheat, corn, and sugar cane. Even the Amazon rain forest—half the land area of Brazil—was affected. In 1930 American industrialist Henry Ford invested $8 million to clear land along the Tapajós River and prepare it to become the site of the world's largest rubber plantation. Ford encountered opposition from Brazilian workers and politicians; the rubber trees proved vulnerable to diseases; and he had to abandon the project—but not before leaving 3 million acres (1.2 million hectares) denuded of trees. The ecological changes of the Vargas era were but a tiny forerunner of the degradation of the Brazilian environment that was to take place later in the century.

Vargas's reforms brought labor unions, pension plans, and disability insurance to urban workers, but

Genevieve Naylor, photographer/Reznikoff Artistic Partnership, NY

Rush Hour in Brazil In Latin American countries, modern conveniences, when first introduced, were often insufficient to meet the demand from eager customers. Here the Sao Januario streetcar in Rio de Janeiro carries twice as many passengers as it was designed for.

he refused to take measures to help the millions of landless peasants or harm the interests of the great landowners. Although the Brazilian economy recovered from the Depression, the benefits of recovery were

Getulio Vargas (1883–1954) Dictator of Brazil from 1930 to 1945 and from 1951 to 1954. Defeated in the presidential election of 1930, he overthrew the government and created a dictatorship that emphasized industrialization and helped the urban poor but did little to alleviate the problems of the peasants.

import-substitution industrialization An economic system aimed at building a country's industry by restricting foreign trade. It was especially popular in Latin American countries such as Mexico, Argentina, and Brazil in the mid-twentieth century. It proved successful for a time but could not keep up with technological advances in Europe and North America.

so unequally distributed that communist and fascist movements demanded even more radical changes.

Prohibited by his own constitution from being reelected in 1938, Vargas staged another coup, abolished the constitution, and instituted the Estado Novo (esh-TAH-doe NO-vo), or "New State," with himself as supreme leader. He banned political parties, jailed opposition leaders, and turned Brazil into a fascist state. When the Second World War broke out, however, Vargas aligned Brazil with the United States and contributed troops and ships to the Allied war effort.

Despite his economic achievements, Vargas harmed Brazil. By running roughshod over laws, constitutions, and rights, he infected not only Brazil but all of South America with the temptations of political violence. It is ironic, but not surprising, that Vargas was overthrown in 1945 by a military coup.

Argentina After 1930

Economically, the Depression hurt Argentina badly. Politically, however, the consequences were delayed. In 1930 General José Uriburu (hoe-SAY oo-ree-BOO-roo) overthrew the popularly elected President Irigoyen. The Uriburu government represented the large landowners and big business interests. For thirteen years the generals and the oligarquía ruled, doing nothing to lessen the poverty of the workers or the frustrations of the middle class. When World War II broke out, Argentina sympathized with the Axis but remained officially neutral.

In 1943 another military revolt flared, this one among junior officers angry at conservative politicians. It was led by Colonel **Juan Perón** (hoo-OWN) (1895–1974). The intentions of the rebels were clear: "Civilians will never understand the greatness of our ideal; we shall therefore have to eliminate them from the government and give them the only mission which corresponds to them: work and obedience."[1] Once in power the officers took over the highest positions in government and business and began to lavish money on military equipment and their own salaries. Their goal, inspired by Nazi victories, was nothing less than the conquest of South America.

As the war turned against the Nazis, the officers saw their popularity collapse. Perón, however, had other plans. Inspired by his charismatic wife **Eva**

SECTION REVIEW

- By 1910, Mexico was sharply divided along ethnic and class lines, with most of its wealth controlled by elites and foreign businesses.

- Elites and foreigners enjoyed the support of Díaz's government, which also tried to impose European cultural values.

- After Díaz's fall, local revolutionary leaders emerged, including the Constitutionalists, Zapata, and Villa. They initiated reforms and fought among themselves, but some changes occurred.

- Cárdenas and the PRM expanded party representation, implemented reforms, and nationalized foreign-owned oil companies.

- Both Argentina and Brazil developed agricultural economies dependent on European technology, consumer demand, and manufactured goods.

- In both countries, wealthy elites dominated small middle classes and large working classes composed mainly of agricultural laborers.

- World War I prompted economic and political changes, especially in Argentina.

- During the interwar years, both countries enjoyed prosperity but remained dependent on industrialized nations for new technologies.

- The hardships of the Depression caused political instability, from which emerged authoritarian regimes devoted to rapid industrialization.

Duarte Perón (AY-va doo-AR-tay pair-OWN) (1919–1952), he appealed to the urban workers. Eva became the champion of the *descamisados* (des-cah-mee-SAH-dohs), or "shirtless ones," and campaigned tirelessly for social benefits and for the cause of women and children. With his wife's help, Perón won the presi-

Juan Perón (1895–1974) President of Argentina (1946–1955, 1973–1974). As a military officer, he championed the rights of labor. Aided by his wife Eva Duarte Perón, he was elected president in 1946. He built up Argentinean industry, became very popular among the urban poor, but harmed the economy.
Eva Duarte Perón (1919–1952) Wife of Juan Perón and champion of the poor in Argentina. She was a gifted speaker and popular political leader who campaigned to improve the life of the urban poor by founding schools and hospitals and providing other social benefits.

Bettmann/Corbis

Juan and Eva Perón Juan Perón's presidency of Argentina (1946–1955) relied on his, and especially on his wife Eva's, popularity with the working class. To sustain their popularity, they often organized parades and demonstrations in imitation of the fascist dictators of Europe. This picture shows them riding in a procession in Buenos Aires in 1952.

dency in 1946 and created a populist dictatorship in imitation of the Vargas regime in Brazil.

Like Brazil, Argentina industrialized rapidly under state sponsorship. Perón spent lavishly on social welfare projects as well as on the military, depleting the capital that Argentina had earned during the war. Though a skillful demagogue who played off the army against the navy and both against the labor unions, Perón could not create a stable government out of the chaos of coups and conspiracies. He had to back down from a plan to make Eva his vice president. When she died in 1952, he lost his political skills (or perhaps they were hers), and soon thereafter he was overthrown in yet another military coup.

Conclusion

The wars and revolutions that engulfed the Northern Hemisphere between 1900 and 1949 affected India, sub-Saharan Africa, and Latin America by placing heavy demands on their peoples and raising their hopes for a better life. Sub-Saharan Africa and India were still under colonial rule. Political life revolved around the desire of their elites for political independence while ordinary people yearned for social justice. Mexico, Argentina, and Brazil were politically independent, but their economies, like those of Africa and India, were closely tied to the economies of the industrial nations. When the Depression hit, all three turned to state intervention and import-substitution industrialization. Like all industrializing countries, they did so by mining, farming, ranching, cutting down forests, and irrigating land, all at the expense of the natural environment.

In Mexico social stresses brought about a long and violent revolution, out of which Mexicans forged a lasting sense of national identity. Argentina and Brazil moved toward greater economic independence, but the price was social unrest, militarism, and dictatorship. They languished under conservative regimes devoted to the interests of wealthy landowners, sporadically interrupted by military coups and populist demagogues. In India, growing expectations conflicted with the reality of colonial rule. A movement for independence and an ethnic split tore the nation apart. In sub-Saharan Africa, demands for national self-determination and economic development were only beginning to be voiced by 1949 and did not come to fruition until the second half of the century.

Nationalism and the yearning for social justice were the two most powerful forces for change in the early twentieth century. These ideas originated in the industrialized countries but resonated in the independent countries of Latin America as well as in colonial regions such as the Indian subcontinent and sub-Saharan Africa. However, they did not always unite people against their colonial rulers or foreign oppressors; instead, they often divided them along social, ethnic, or religious lines. Western-educated elites looked to industrialization as a means of modernizing their country and ensuring their position in it, while peasants and urban workers supported nationalist and revolutionary movements in the hope of improving their lives. Often these goals were not compatible.

CHAPTER REVIEW

Download the MP3 audio file of the Chapter Review to listen to on the go.

Why did the educated elites of India want independence? What were ordinary Indians hoping for? (page 677)

In the late nineteenth century, educated Indians began to resent the racist condescension with which they were treated by their colonial masters. They believed that they could govern India and develop its economy better than the British could. Poorer Indians were persuaded by Mahatma Gandhi, the Indian National Congress, and the Muslim League that national independence would alleviate their poverty.

What changes did foreign rule bring to Africa, and how did Africans respond? (page 684)

Sub-Saharan Africa was radically transformed by its colonial rulers, who built cities, railroads, harbors, mines, and plantations. Africans were forced to provide the labor for these projects and received few benefits from them. Many turned to Christianity or Islam for spiritual guidance during these upheavals.

What could Latin Americans do to achieve social justice and economic development? Were these two goals compatible? (page 687)

Decades of modernization had left most Mexicans poorer than before. The revolution that broke out in 1911 promised to repair the injustices of the past, but it fell short of the ideals for which it was fought. Brazil and Argentina avoided a revolution but remained dependent on Britain and the United States. In both countries, as in Mexico, economic growth was difficult to achieve, democracy was fragile and often repressed by dictators, and social justice proved just as elusive as in earlier centuries.

Key Terms

Indian National Congress (p. 678)

Bengal (p. 678)

All-India Muslim League (p. 679)

Mohandas K. Gandhi (p. 680)

Jawaharlal Nehru (p. 681)

Muhammad Ali Jinnah (p. 683)

Blaise Diagne (p. 686)

African National Congress (p. 686)

Haile Selassie (p. 686)

Emiliano Zapata (p. 688)

Francisco "Pancho" Villa (p. 689)

Lázaro Cárdenas (p. 691)

Hipólito Irigoyen (p. 692)

Getulio Vargas (p. 693)

import-substitution industrialization (p. 693)

Juan Perón (p. 694)

Eva Duarte Perón (p. 694)

Web Resources

Pronunciation Guide

Interactive Map

• MAP 28.1 The Mexican Revolution

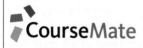

Visit the CourseMate website at www.cengagebrain.com for additional study tools and review materials for this chapter.

Primary Sources

• Education, Civilization, and "Foreignization" in Buganda

• London Manifesto

• Parable of the Eagle, Limbo, Prayer for Peace, Vultures

• The Plan of Ayala

• Speech to the Nation

Answer to History in Focus Question

See photo on page 683, "The Partition of India."

Famines and Politics

Nature is never reliable, and all living things periodically suffer from a catastrophic drop in food supplies. Human history is filled with tales of famines—times when crops failed, food supplies ran out, and people starved.

Natural Famines

India, dependent on the monsoon rains, has been particularly prone to such calamities, with famines striking two to four times a century, whenever the rains failed for several years in succession. Three times in the eighteenth century (1702–1704, 1769–1770, and 1790–1792) famines killed several million people in different parts of the subcontinent. The nineteenth century was worse, with famines in 1803–1804, 1837–1838, 1868–1870, and 1876–1878. The last famine also afflicted northern China, causing between 9 and 13 million deaths from hunger and from the diseases of malnutrition. There were even incidents of cannibalism, as starving adults killed and ate starving children.

When a drought hit a region, it decimated not only the human population but also the animals they relied on to transport goods and plow the land. Likewise, droughts lowered the water levels in rivers and canals, so food could not be moved from one place to another.

Commercial Famines

That all changed in the nineteenth century. Railroads and steamships could transport food-stuffs across great distances in a matter of days or weeks, regardless of drought or heavy rains. Great Britain became dependent on imports of wheat from Russia and the American Midwest, and later of beef from Argentina. Yet famines were worse than ever, and the global death toll from starvation has been far higher since the mid-nineteenth century than it ever was in earlier times. Why?

Consider the Irish famine of 1845–1848. By the early nineteenth century the potato had become the main source of nutrition for the Irish people. Potatoes grew abundantly in the cool, moist climate of Ireland and produced more calories per acre than any other crop. Most of the Irish were poor tenant farmers, and potatoes had allowed their population to increase far more than wheat or rye could have. In fall 1845 the blight turned the potatoes in the fields black, mushy, and inedible. The harvest was ruined the following year as well. It recovered slightly in 1847, but was bad again in 1848. Tens of thousands died of starvation, while hundreds of thousands died from the diseases that strike malnourished people, especially dysentery, typhus, and cholera. Travelers saw corpses rotting in their hovels or on the sides of roads. Altogether, a million or more people died, while another million managed to emigrate, reducing the population of Ireland by half.

Throughout those years, wheat grew in Ireland, but much of it was exported to England, where customers had money to pay for it. Like any other commodity, food cost money. The Irish farmers, poor even before the famines, were destitute and could not afford to buy the wheat. The British government, wedded to the ideology of laissez faire, was convinced that interfering with the free market would only make things worse. Relief efforts were half-hearted at best; the official responsible for Irish affairs preferred to leave the situation to "the operation of natural causes."

The same held true in India, like Ireland a colony of Great Britain. The drought of 1876–1878 killed over 5 million Indians in the Deccan region, while British officials were helpless or indifferent. Part of the problem was transportation. In the 1870s only a few railway lines connected major cities. Most goods were still transported in bullock carts, but the bullocks also starved during the drought. Another obstacle was political. The idea that a government should be responsible for feeding the population was unthinkable at the time. And so, while millions were starving in the Deccan, the Punjab region was exporting wheat to Britain.

Over the next twenty years so-called famine railways were built in the regions historically most affected by the failures of the monsoon. When drought struck again at the end of the century, the railways were ready to transport food to areas that had previously been accessible only by bullock carts. However, the inhabitants of the affected regions had no money with which to buy what little food there was, and the government was still reluctant to interfere with free enterprise. Grain merchants bought all the stocks, hoarded them until the price rose, then used the railways to transport them out of the famine regions to regions where the harvests were better and people had more money.

In the twentieth century commercial famines became rare, as governments have come to realize that they have a responsibility for food supplies not only for their own people, but for people in other countries as well. Yet commercial famines have not entirely disappeared. In 1974, when a catastrophic flood covered half of Bangladesh, the government was too disorganized to distribute its stocks of rice, while merchants bought what they could and exported it to India. Thousands died, and thousands more survived only because of belated shipments of food from donor countries.

Political Famines

To say that governments are responsible for food supplies does not mean that they exercise that responsibility for the good of the people. Some do, but in many instances food is used as a weapon. In the twentieth century global food supplies were always adequate for the population of the world, and transportation was seldom a problem. Yet the century witnessed the most murderous famines ever recorded.

War-induced famines were not new. In 1812, as the Russian army retreated, it practiced a "scorched-earth" policy of burning food stocks to prevent them from falling into the hands of Napoleon's army. In doing so, it also caused a famine among Russian peasants. Similar famines resulted from the destruction or requisitioning of crops in the Russian civil war of

1921–1922, the Japanese occupation of Indochina in 1942–1945, and the Biafran war in Nigeria in 1967–1969.

The Bengal famine of 1943 was also war-related. In 1942 the Japanese army had conquered Burma, a rich rice-producing colony. Food supplies in Bengal, which imported rice from Burma, dropped by 5 percent. As prices began to rise, merchants bought stocks of rice and held them in the hope that prices would continue to increase. Sharecroppers sold their stocks to pay off their debts to landlords and village moneylenders. Meanwhile, the railroads that in peacetime would have carried food from other parts of India were fully occupied with military traffic. In October 1943, when a new viceroy, Lord Wavell, arrived in India and ordered the army to transport food to Bengal, food prices dropped to a level that the poor could afford. By then, however, between 1.5 and 2 million Bengalis had starved to death.

Worst of all were the famines that happened in peacetime as a result of the deliberate decisions of governments. The most famous of these political famines was caused by Stalin's collectivization of agriculture in 1932–1934. The Communist Party tried to force the peasants to give up their land and livestock and join collectives, where they could be made to work harder and provide food for the growing cities and industries. When they resisted, their crops were seized. Millions were sent to prison camps, and millions of others died of starvation. Stalin chided the overly enthusiastic party members who had caused the famine for being "dizzy with success."

An even worse famine took place in China from 1958 to 1961 during the "Great Leap Forward" (see Chapter 29). Communist Party chairman Mao Zedong decided to hasten the transformation of China into a communist state and industrial power by relying not on the expertise of economists and technocrats but on the enthusiasm of the masses. All farms were consolidated into huge communes. Peasants were mobilized to work on giant construction projects or to make steel out of household utensils and tools in backyard furnaces. The harvest of 1959 was poor, and later ones were even worse. The amount of grain per person declined from 452 pounds (205 kilograms) in 1957 to 340 pounds (154 kilograms) in 1961. Since the Central Statistical Bureau had been shut down, the central government was unaware of the shortages and demanded ever-higher requisitions of food to feed the army and urban and industrial workers and to export to the Soviet Union to pay off China's debts. The amount of food left to the farmers was between one-fifth and one-half of their usual subsistence diet. From 1958 to 1961 between 20 and 30 million Chinese are estimated to have starved or died of the diseases of malnutrition in the most catastrophic famine in the history of the world. The leaders of the Communist Party either were unaware of its extent or, if they knew, did not dare mention it for fear of displeasing Mao, who denied its existence.

Nothing quite as horrible has happened since the Great Leap Forward. During the droughts in Africa in the 1970s and 1980s, most people in the affected regions received international food aid, but the governments of Ethiopia and Sudan either denied that their people were hungry or prevented food shipments from reaching drought victims in order to crush rebellions.

In the world today, natural disasters are as frequent as ever, and many countries are vulnerable to food shortages. No one now claims, as many did in the nineteenth century, that governments have no business providing free food to the starving. Though food is not equitably distributed, there is enough for all human beings now, and there will be enough for the foreseeable future. However, humanitarian feelings compete with other political agendas, and the specter of politically motivated famines still stalks the world.

Part Eight

Perils and Promises of a Global Community, 1945 to the Present

© Cengage Learning

	1950	1960	1970
AMERICAS	•1945 United Nations charter signed in San Francisco •1946 International Monetary Fund and World Bank founded •1952 U.S. tests first hydrogen bomb	Military takes power in Brazil 1964• Cuban Revolution 1959• •1962 Cuban missile crisis Neil Armstrong walks on moon 1969•	Military coup overthrows Allende in Chile 1973•
EUROPE	1948–1952 Marshall Plan helps rebuild western Europe •1949 NATO founded •1955 Warsaw Pact formed Soviet troops crush revolt in Hungary 1956• •1957 Common Market founded	•1961 Berlin Wall built	•1968 Student uprising in France
AFRICA	Apartheid becomes official in South Africa 1948•	Guinea wins independence from France 1958• Ghana first British colony in West Africa to win independence 1957•	•1960 Nigeria, Congo, Somalia, Togo win independence •1963 Kenya independent	1970–1980 White domination of Rhodesia yields to international pressure
MIDDLE EAST	•1948 State of Israel founded; first Arab-Israeli War	•1956 Suez crisis 1954–1962 Algerian war for Independence	•1960 Organization of Petroleum Exporting Countries founded	•1967 Six Day Arab- Israeli War October Arab-Israeli War leads to oil embargo, price hikes 1973•
ASIA AND OCEANIA	Communist Revolution in China 1949•	•1949 Indonesia wins independence from Netherlands 1951–1953 Korean War 1954–1975 Vietnam War	Japan becomes world economic power 1970s•	1966–1969 Cultural Revolution in China •1971 Independence of Bangladesh

An increasingly interconnected world faced new hopes and fears after World War II. The United Nations promoted peace, international cooperation, and human rights, but Cold War rhetoric and nuclear stalemate dispelled dreams of world peace. Wars in Korea and Vietnam, as well as proxy conflicts from Nicaragua to Afghanistan, pitted the United States against communist regimes.

The industrialized nations, including Germany and Japan, recovered well from World War II. Elsewhere economic development came slowly, except in a handful of countries: South Korea, Taiwan, Brazil, Argentina, and, after 2000, China and India. In Africa and other poor regions, population growth usually offset economic gains.

Although the Green Revolution of the 1960s and genetic engineering thirty years later alleviated much world hunger, industrial growth and automobile use increased pollution and competition for petroleum supplies. Global warming became an international concern, along with overfishing, deforestation, and endangerment of wild species.

Globalization affected culture as well. Transnational corporations threatened local economic enterprises. Western popular culture, the Internet, and the emergence of English as the global language improved international communication but also stimulated fears that cultural diversity would be lost.

Following the end of the Cold War, nuclear proliferation and terrorism became top concerns. The 9/11 attacks by Muslim zealots on the World Trade Center and the Pentagon triggered an American "global war on terrorism." The ensuing invasions of Afghanistan and Iraq made the Middle East a top danger spot.

1980	1990	2000

- **1976** Military takes power in Argentina
- **1983–1989** Democracy restored in Brazil, Argentina, Chile
- **1994** NAFTA agreement among Canada, U.S., Mexico
- **1994** Maya uprising in southern Mexico
- **2001** Terrorists attack New York, Washington, D.C.

- **1975** Helsinki Accords
- **1980** Solidarity union founded in Poland
- Fall of communist regimes in eastern Europe **1989** •
- End of USSR **1991** •
- **1990** Reunification of Germany
- Introduction of euro **1999** •
- **1992–2000** Disintegration of Yugoslavia
- European Union admits ten new members **2004** •
- **2005** Terrorists bomb London buses

- **1975** Angola and Mozambique win independence from Portugal
- **1985** Africa equals Europe in population
- **1994–1999** Nelson Mandela president of South Africa
- **1999** Democracy restored in Nigeria

- **1979** Islamic Revolution overthrows shah of Iran
- **1980–1988** Iran-Iraq War
- **1991** Persian Gulf War
- **2003** U.S., Britain invade, occupy Iraq
- **2006** Israel and Hezbollah war in Lebanon

- **1979** USSR enters war in Afghanistan
- **1980s** Taiwan, South Korea, Singapore industrialize
- **1989** Chinese troops suppress Tiananmen Square protest
- **1997** Asian financial crisis starts in Thailand
- **1999** East Timor wins independence from Indonesia

The Cold War and Decolonization

© Cengage Learning

CHAPTER PREVIEW

The Cold War
What were the major threats to world peace during the Cold War?

Decolonization and Nation Building
What problems did less developed nations face?

Revolution, Reform, and Repression in Latin America
How did U.S. policies during the Cold War affect Latin America?

Japan, China, and the Four Tigers
Why were developments in China so different from those in other parts of East Asia?

National and Religious Conflicts in the Middle East
What roles did nationalism and religious fundamentalism play in Middle Eastern politics?

The End of the Bipolar World
What led to the collapse of the Soviet bloc?

Conclusion

DIVERSITY & DOMINANCE: Race and the Struggle for Justice in South Africa

Visit the CourseMate website at **www.cengagebrain.com** for additional study tools and review materials for this chapter.

The Cold War

What were the major threats to world peace during the Cold War?

In 1946, Great Britain's wartime leader Winston Churchill declared that "an Iron Curtain has descended across the Continent [of Europe], . . . I am convinced there is nothing they [the communists] so much admire as strength, and there is nothing for which they have less respect than weakness, especially military weakness." The phrase **"Iron Curtain"** became a watchword of the **Cold War**, the state of political tension and military rivalry that was then beginning between the United States and its allies and the Soviet Union and its allies.

In the early years of World War II, Churchill and President Franklin Roosevelt had looked forward to a postwar world of economic cooperation and restoration of sovereignty to peoples suffering Axis occupation and, above all, to a world where war and territorial conquest would not be tolerated. By the time Churchill delivered his "Iron Curtain" speech, however, American troops, armed with atomic bombs, occupied Japan and western Germany, while the Soviet Union dominated eastern Europe and supported communist movements in China, Iran, Turkey, Greece, and Korea. Confrontation rather than cooperation was the hallmark of relations between East and West.

Meanwhile, an even more important phenomenon occupied the world stage. Western domination of Asia, Africa, and Latin America was ending, and the colonial empires of the New Imperialism were gradually dismantled. Some new nations sided openly with the United States and some with the Soviet Union. Others proclaimed their nonalignment and spoke about their need for economic and technical assistance and the obligation of the wealthy nations to satisfy those needs. A new generation of national leaders faced the difficult task of nation building as they struggled to educate their citizens, nurture industry, and escape the economic constraints imposed by their former colonial masters.

The wartime alliance between the United States, Great Britain, and the Soviet Union had been an uneasy one. Political and economic leaders committed to free markets and untrammeled capital investment loathed communism. After World War II, the Iron Curtain in Europe and communist insurgencies in China and elsewhere seemed to confirm the threat of worldwide revolution.

To defend themselves against the Soviet Union, which they perceived as threatening to start a new war, the United States and the countries of western Europe established the **North Atlantic Treaty Organization (NATO)**, a military alliance, in 1949. Soviet leaders, in turn, felt themselves surrounded by hostile nations just when they were trying to recover from the terrible losses sustained in the war. The distrust and suspicion between the two sides played out in the United Nations.

The United Nations

Founded on October 24, 1945, the **United Nations** had two main bodies: the General Assembly, with representatives from all fifty-one member states; and the Security Council, with five permanent members—China, France, Great Britain, the United States, and

Iron Curtain Winston Churchill's term for the Cold War division between the Soviet-dominated East and the U.S.-dominated West.

Cold War (1945–1991) The ideological struggle between communism (Soviet Union) and capitalism (United States) for world influence. The Soviet Union and the United States came to the brink of actual war during the Cuban Missile Crisis but never attacked one another. The Cold War came to an end when the Soviet Union dissolved in 1991.

North Atlantic Treaty Organization (NATO) Organization formed in 1949 as a military alliance of western European and North American states against the Soviet Union and its east European allies.

United Nations International organization founded in 1945 to promote world peace and cooperation. It replaced the League of Nations.

the Soviet Union—and seven rotating members. The United Nations operated by majority vote, except that the five permanent members of the Security Council had veto power in that chamber. All signatories to the United Nations Charter renounced war and territorial conquest. Yet the permanent members often exercised their veto to protect their friends and interests, though from time to time they authorized the United Nations to send observers or peacekeeping forces to monitor truces or agreements.

The decolonization of Africa and Asia greatly swelled the size of the General Assembly. As many of the new nations looked to the United Nations for material assistance and access to a wider political world, the General Assembly became an arena for expressing opinions on many issues involving decolonization, a movement that the Soviet Union strongly encouraged but the European colonial powers resisted.

In the early years of the United Nations, General Assembly resolutions carried great weight; an example is a 1947 resolution that sought to divide Palestine into sovereign Jewish and Arab states. Gradually, though, the flood of new members produced a voting majority concerned more with poverty, racial discrimination, and the struggle against imperialism than with the Cold War. As a result, the Western powers increasingly disregarded the General Assembly, allowing the new nations of the world to have their say but not to act collectively.

Capitalism and Communism

In July 1944, economic specialists representing over forty countries met at Bretton Woods, a New Hampshire resort, to devise a new international monetary system. The signatories agreed to fix exchange rates. They also created the International Monetary Fund (IMF) to finance temporary trade deficits and the **World Bank** to provide funds for reconstructing Europe and helping needy countries.

The Soviet Union attended the Bretton Woods Conference and signed the agreements, but by 1946 suspicion between the Soviet Union and the West had deepened. While most countries moved to a monetary system that relied for stability on holding reserves of dollars and on the United States holding reserves of gold, the Soviet Union established a closed monetary system for itself and the new communist regimes in

eastern Europe. In the West, supply and demand determined prices; in the Soviet command economy, government agencies allocated goods and set prices, irrespective of market forces.

Many leaders from the newly independent states preferred the Soviet Union's socialist example to the capitalism of their former colonizers. Thus, the relative success of economies patterned on Eastern or Western models became an element in the Cold War rivalry. Each side trumpeted economic successes measured by such things as industrial output, changes in per capita income, and productivity gains as evidence of its superiority.

After World War II, the United States enjoyed prosperity and an international competitive advantage, while European economies were still heavily damaged from the war. To support European reconstruction, the American **Marshall Plan** provided $12.5 billion to friendly countries between 1948 and 1952. In 1948, European governments also promoted economic cooperation and integration with the creation of the Organization of European Economic Cooperation (OEEC). After cooperative policies on coal and steel proved successful, some OEEC countries were ready to begin lowering tariffs to encourage the movement of goods and capital. In 1957, France, West Germany, Italy, the Netherlands, Belgium, and Luxembourg signed a treaty creating the European Economic Community, also known as the Common Market. The word *economic* was dropped from the group's title in 1967, making it simply the **European Community (EC)**. By 1963, a resurgent European economy had doubled 1940 output, and by the 1970s the EC nations had nearly overtaken the United

World Bank A specialized agency of the United Nations that makes loans to countries for economic development, trade promotion, and debt consolidation. Its formal name is the International Bank for Reconstruction and Development.

Marshall Plan U.S. program to support the reconstruction of western Europe after World War II. By 1961 more than $20 billion in economic aid had been disbursed.

European Community (EC) An organization promoting economic unity in Europe, formed in 1967 by consolidation of earlier, more limited, agreements. It was replaced by the European Union (EU) in 1993.

Chronology

	Europe	Americas	Middle East and Africa	Asia
1940s	**1948–1949** Berlin Airlift **1949** NATO founded			**1947** Partition of India **1949** Dutch withdraw from Indonesia
1950s	**1955** Warsaw Pact founded **1956** Soviet Union represses Hungarian uprising **1957** USSR launches first artificial satellite into orbit	**1952** U.S. detonates first hydrogen bomb **1954** CIA intervenes in Guatemala **1959** Fidel Castro leads revolution in Cuba	**1957** Ghana becomes first British colony in Africa to gain independence	**1950–1953** Korean War **1954** Defeat at Dienbienphu ends French hold on Vietnam **1955** Bandung Conference
1960s	**1961** East Germany builds Berlin Wall	**1962** Cuban Missile Crisis **1964** Military takeover in Brazil	**1960** Shootings in Sharpeville intensify South African struggle against apartheid; Nigeria becomes independent **1962** Algeria wins independence	
1970s		**1970** Salvador Allende elected president of Chile **1973** Allende overthrown **1976** Military takeover in Argentina **1979** Sandinistas overthrow Somoza in Nicaragua	**1979** Islamic Revolution overthrows shah of Iran **1979** USSR sends troops to Afghanistan	**1971** Bangladesh secedes from Pakistan
1980s	**1985** Mikhail Gorbachev becomes Soviet head of state **1989–1991** End of communism in eastern Europe		**1980–1988** Iran-Iraq War **1989** USSR withdraws from Afghanistan	
1990s	**1990** Reunification of Germany	**1990** Sandinistas defeated in Nicaraguan election	**1990** Iraq invades Kuwait **1991** Persian Gulf War	

States in industrial production. The economic alliance expanded after 1970, as Great Britain, Denmark, Greece, Ireland, Spain, Portugal, Finland, Sweden, and Austria joined.

Prosperity brought dramatic changes to European society. Average wages increased, unemployment fell, and social welfare benefits were expanded. Governments increased spending on health care, unemployment benefits, old-age pensions, public housing, and grants to poor families with children.

The combination of economic growth and income redistribution raised living standards and fueled demand for consumer goods.

The Soviet experience provided a dramatic contrast. The economy of the Soviet Union was even more devastated at the end of the Second World War than those of western Europe. However, with enormous natural resources, a large population, and abundant energy at its disposal, Soviet recovery was rapid at first. Moreover, Soviet planners had made large investments in technical and scientific education, and the Soviet state had developed heavy industry in the 1930s and during the war years. But as the postwar period progressed, bureaucratic control of the economy grew less efficient. In the 1970s, the gap with the West widened as the Soviet economy failed to meet domestic demand for clothing, housing, food, automobiles, and consumer electronics. In addition, agricultural inefficiency forced the Soviet Union to rely on food imports. The communist nations of eastern Europe were compelled to follow the Soviet economic model. Though their economies grew, the inefficiencies and failures that plagued the Soviet economy troubled them as well.

West Versus East in Europe and Korea

For Germany, Austria, and Japan, peace brought foreign military occupation and new governments that were initially controlled by the occupiers. The Soviet Union seemed willing to accept governments in neighboring states that included a mix of parties as long as they were not hostile to local communist groups or to the Soviets. Many were willing to embrace the communists as a hedge against those who had supported fascism or cooperated with the Germans. As relations between the Soviets and the West worsened in the late 1940s, local communists, supported by Soviet military occupation forces, gained victories across eastern Europe. Western leaders saw the rapid emergence of communist regimes in Poland, Czechoslovakia, Hungary, Bulgaria, Romania, Yugoslavia, and Albania as a threat.

In the waning days of World War II, the United States had seemed amenable to the Soviet desire for freer access to the Mediterranean through the Turkish straits. But in July 1947, the **Truman Doctrine** offered military aid to help Turkey and Greece resist Soviet military pressure and subversion. In 1951, Greece and Turkey were admitted to NATO, and in 1955 the Soviet Union founded the **Warsaw Pact** in response to the Western powers' decision to allow West Germany to rearm.

The Soviet Union tested Western resolve in 1948–1949 by blockading the British, French, and American zones of Berlin, which were surrounded by Soviet-controlled East Germany. Airlifts of food and

fuel defeated the blockade. Then in 1961, the East German government built the Berlin Wall to prevent its citizens from fleeing to the noncommunist western part of that city. Soviet power set clear limits on how far any eastern European country might stray from Soviet domination. In 1956, Soviet troops crushed an anti-Soviet revolt in Hungary. Czechoslovakia suffered Hungary's fate in 1968. The West had to acknowledge that the Soviet Union had the right to intervene in the domestic affairs of any Soviet-bloc nation whenever it wished.

A more explosive crisis erupted in Korea, where the Second World War had left Soviet troops in control north of the thirty-eighth parallel and American troops in control to the south. When no agreement could be reached on holding countrywide elections, communist North Korea and noncommunist South Korea became independent states in 1948. Two years later, North Korea invaded South Korea. In the absence of the Soviet delegation, the U.N. Security Council condemned the invasion and called on members of the United Nations to come to the defense of South Korea. The United States was the primary ally of South Korea, while the People's Republic of China supported North Korea. The **Korean War** lasted until 1953, when the two sides eventually agreed to a truce along the thirty-eighth parallel, but no peace treaty was concluded.

The Nuclear Arms Race

Fear of nuclear war affected strategic decisions in the Korean and Vietnam Wars, as well as all other aspects of Cold War confrontation. The devastation of Hiroshima and Nagasaki by atomic weapons (see Chapter 27) had ushered in a new era. The Soviet Union exploded its first nuclear device in 1949. The United

---

Truman Doctrine Foreign policy initiated by U.S. president Harry Truman in 1947. It offered military aid to help Turkey and Greece resist Soviet military pressure and subversion.

Warsaw Pact The 1955 treaty binding the Soviet Union and countries of eastern Europe in an alliance against the North Atlantic Treaty Organization.

Korean War (1950–1953) Conflict that began with North Korea's invasion of South Korea and came to involve the United Nations (primarily the United States) allying with South Korea against North Korea and the People's Republic of China.

- At the outset of the Cold War, the Soviet Union occupied eastern Europe and the United States and western European countries established NATO, thus fueling mutual fear and suspicion.

- The goals of the United Nations were limited by the conflicting aims of member nations.

- The United States, the USSR, and their respective allies and supporters formed competing economic systems.

- While western Europe prospered through economic integration, the Soviet-bloc economies steadily fell behind.

- Superpower rivalry divided Europe and fueled the Korean War.

- The superpower nuclear rivalry culminated with the Cuban Missile Crisis, after which the superpowers practiced restraint and engaged in arms limitation negotiations.

States exploded a far more powerful weapon, the hydrogen bomb, in 1952 and the Soviet Union followed suit less than a year later. The conviction that the superpowers were willing to use their nuclear weapons if their vital interests were threatened spread fear around the world.

Everyone's worst fears seemed about to be realized in the **Cuban Missile Crisis** of 1962. When the Soviet Union deployed nuclear-tipped missiles in Cuba in response to the U.S. missiles in Turkey, the world held its breath. Confronted by unyielding diplomatic pressure and military threats from President Kennedy, Khrushchev backed down and pulled the missiles from Cuba. Subsequently, the United States removed its missiles from Turkey.

Arms limitation also saw progress. In 1963, Great Britain, the United States, and the Soviet Union agreed to ban the testing of nuclear weapons in the atmosphere, in space, and under water, thus reducing the danger of radioactive fallout. In 1968, the United States and the Soviet Union together proposed a world treaty against further proliferation of nuclear weapons. It was signed by 137 countries.

Space exploration was another offshoot of the nuclear arms race. The contest to build larger and more accurate missiles for delivery of warheads prompted the superpowers to prove their skills in rocketry by launching space satellites. In October 1957 the Soviet Union placed a small *Sputnik* satellite into orbit around the earth, thereby administering a deep shock to American pride and confidence. The United States responded with its own satellite three months later. In 1969, two Americans, Neil A. Armstrong and Edwin E. "Buzz" Aldrin, became the first humans to walk on the moon.

Despite rhetorical Cold War saber-rattling by Soviet and American leaders, the threat of nuclear war forced a measure of restraint on the superpower adversaries. Because fighting each other directly would have risked escalation to the level of nuclear exchange, they carefully avoided crises that might provoke such confrontations.

Decolonization and Nation Building

What problems did less developed nations face?

Whereas the losing countries in World War I were stripped of colonies, it was primarily countries on the winning side in World War II that ended up losing their colonies (see Map 29.1). Circumstances differed profoundly from place to place. In some Asian countries, where colonial rule was of long standing, newly independent states found themselves in possession of viable industries, communications networks, and education systems. In other countries, notably in Africa, decolonization gave birth to nations facing dire economic problems and internal disunity.

Challenges of Nation Building

Decolonization occurred on a vast scale. Fifty-one nations signed the United Nations Charter in the closing months of 1945. During the United Nations' first decade, twenty-five new members joined, a third of them upon gaining independence. During the

Cuban Missile Crisis (1962) Brink-of-war confrontation between the United States and the Soviet Union over the latter's placement of nuclear-armed missiles in Cuba.

Map 29.1 Decolonization, 1947–1999 Notice that independence came a decade or so earlier in South and Southeast Asia than in Africa. Numerous countries that gained independence after World War II in the Caribbean, in South and Central America, and in the Pacific are not shown.   © Cengage Learning

Interactive Map

1960 Year independence achieved

Former ruler

Great Britain	Belgium
France	Portugal
Netherlands	United States
Italy	Other

next decade forty-six more new members were admitted, nearly all of them former colonial territories.

Each of these nations had to organize and institute some form of government. Comparatively few were able to do so without experiencing coups, rewritten constitutions, or regional rebellions. Leaders did not always agree on the form independence should take. In the absence of established constitutional traditions, they frequently tried to impose their own visions by force. Most of the new nations, while trying to establish political stability, also faced severe economic challenges, including foreign ownership and operation of key resources and the need to build infrastructure. Overdependence on world demand for raw materials and on imported manufactured goods persisted in many places long after independence.

Because the achievement of political and economic goals called for educated and skilled personnel, education was another common concern in newly emerging nations. Addressing that concern required more than building and staffing schools. In some countries, leaders had to decide which language to teach and how to inculcate a sense of national unity in students from different—and sometimes historically antagonistic—ethnic, religious, and linguistic groups. Another problem was how to provide satisfying jobs for new graduates, many of whom had high expectations because of their education. Only rarely were the new nations able to surmount these hurdles. Even the most economically and educationally successful, such as South Korea, suffered from tendencies toward authoritarian rule.

The Superpowers and the Nonaligned Movement

Although the East-West superpower rivalry dominated world affairs, newly independent states had concerns that were primarily domestic and regional. The challenge they faced was to find a way to pursue their ends within the bipolar structure of the Cold War—and possibly to take advantage of the East-West rivalry. In short, the superpowers dominated the world but did not control it. And as time progressed, they dominated it less and less.

As one of the most successful leaders of the decolonization movement, Indonesia's President Sukarno was an appropriate figure to host a meeting in 1955 of twenty-nine African and Asian countries at Bandung, Indonesia. The conferees proclaimed solidarity among all peoples fighting against colonial rule. The Bandung Conference marked the beginning of an effort by the many new, poor, mostly non-European nations emerging from colonialism to gain more weight in world affairs by banding together. The terms **nonaligned nations** and **Third World**, which became commonplace in the following years, signaled these countries' collective stance toward the rival sides in the Cold War. If the West, led by the United States, and the East, led by the Soviet Union, represented two worlds locked in mortal struggle, the Third World consisted of everyone else.

Leaders of the so-called Third World countries preferred the label *nonaligned*, which signified freedom from membership on either side. However, because the Soviet Union supported national liberation movements and the nonaligned movement included communist countries such as China and Yugoslavia, many Western leaders did not take the term *nonaligned* seriously. They saw Sukarno, Nehru, Nkrumah, and Egypt's Gamal Abd al-Nasir (gah-MAHL AHB-d al-NAH-suhr) as stalking horses for a communist takeover of the world. This may also have been the hope of some Soviet leaders, who were quick to offer some of these countries military and financial aid.

For the movement's leaders, however, nonalignment was a means to extract money and support from one or both superpowers. By flirting with the Soviet Union, the United States, or the People's Republic of China, some skillful nonaligned leaders were able to gain from both sides. Nasir, who ruled Egypt from 1952 to 1970, and his successor, Anwar Sadat (sah-DAT), played the game well. The United States offered to build a dam at Aswan (AS-wahn), on the Nile River, to increase Egypt's electrical generating and irrigation capacity. When Egypt turned to the Soviet Union for arms, the United States reneged on the dam project in 1956. The Soviet Union then picked it up and in the 1960s brought it to conclusion.

nonaligned nations Developing countries that announced their neutrality in the Cold War.
Third World Term applied to developing countries who professed nonalignment during the Cold War.

Bandung Conference, 1955 India's Jawaharlal Nehru (in white hat) was a central figure at the conference held in Indonesia to promote solidarity among nonaligned developing nations.

AP Images

Another situation occurred after 1956, when Israel, Great Britain, and France conspired to invade Egypt. Their objective was to overthrow Nasir, regain the Suez Canal that he had recently nationalized, and secure Israel from any Egyptian threat. The invasion succeeded militarily, but both the United States and the Soviet Union pressured the invaders to withdraw, thus saving Nasir's government. In 1972, Sadat evicted his Soviet military advisers but a year later used his Soviet weapons to attack Israel. After he lost that war, he announced his faith in the power of the United States to solve Egypt's political and economic problems.

Numerous other countries adopted similar balancing strategies. In each case, local leaders were trying to develop their nation's economy and assert or preserve their nation's interests. Manipulating the superpowers was simply a means toward those ends and implied very little about true ideological orientation.

New Nations in Southern Asia

The independence of the Indian subcontinent from Great Britain in 1947 resulted in two new nations (see Chapter 28). Newly independent India and Pakistan were strikingly dissimilar.

Muslim Pakistan defined itself according to religion and quickly fell under the control of military leaders. Though 90 percent Hindu, the much larger republic of India was secular. It inherited most of the considerable industrial and educational resources the British had developed, along with the larger share of trained civil servants and military officers.

The decision of the Hindu ruler of the northwestern state of Jammu and Kashmir to join India without consulting his overwhelmingly Muslim subjects led to a war between India and Pakistan in 1947 that ended with an uneasy truce. Pakistan and India have since fought two wars: a brief one in 1965 over Kashmir, and another in 1971 over the secession of East Bengal from Pakistan, with India's help, to form the new nation of Bangladesh. Despite the truce between the two nations, Kashmir remains a flash point of patriotic feeling on both sides.

Elsewhere in the region, nationalist movements won independence as well. Britain granted independence to Burma (now Myanmar [myahn-MAHR]) in 1948 and established the Malay Federation that same year. Singapore, once a member of the federation, became an independent city-state itself in 1965. In

Dana Stone/stockphoto.com

The Vietnamese People at War American and South Vietnamese troops burned many villages to deprive the enemy of civilian refuges. This policy undermined support for the South Vietnamese government in the countryside.

 History in Focus *To what extent do you think communist ideology motivated many South Vietnamese to support the northern side? Find the answer online.*

1946, the United States kept its promise of postwar independence for the Philippine Islands but retained close economic ties and leases on military bases. In the Dutch East Indies, Sukarno (1901–1970) had cooperated with the Japanese occupation in hopes that the Dutch would never return. After a military confrontation, Dutch withdrawal was finally negotiated in 1949, and Sukarno went on to become the dictator of his resource-rich but underdeveloped nation of Indonesia.

The Long War for Indochina

Throughout Asia, communist insurgents plagued the departing colonial powers and the newly formed governments. The most important postwar communist movement arose in French Indochina. There, Ho Chi Minh (hoe chee min) (1890–1969), who had spent several years in France during World War I, played the pivotal role. After training in Moscow, he returned to Vietnam to found the Indochina Communist Party in 1930. Ho Chi Minh's nationalist coalition, then called the Viet Minh, fought the French with help from the People's Republic of China. In 1954, United States president Dwight D. Eisenhower (1953–1961) and his foreign policy advisers decided not to aid France in its effort to sustain colonial rule in Vietnam, perceiving that the days of the European colonial empires were numbered. In 1954, Viet Minh overran the French stronghold of Dienbienphu (dyen-byen-foo), ending France's colonial rule. Ho's Viet Minh government took over in the north, and a noncommunist nationalist government ruled in the south.

After winning independence, communist North Vietnam supported a guerrilla movement—the Viet Cong—against the noncommunist government of South Vietnam. When John F. Kennedy became president in 1961, he and his advisers decided to support the South Vietnamese government of President Ngo Dinh Diem (dee-EM), even though they realized it was corrupt and unpopular, because they feared that a communist victory would encourage communist movements throughout Southeast Asia and alter the Cold War balance of power. Kennedy steadily increased the number of American military advisers from 685 to almost 16,000 while secretly encouraging the overthrow and execution of Diem in hopes of seeing a more popular and honest government come to power.

Lyndon Johnson, who became president (1963–1969) after Kennedy was assassinated, gained support from Congress for unlimited expansion of U.S. military deployment. By the end of 1966, 365,000 U.S. troops were engaged in the **Vietnam War**. Nothing the Americans tried, however, succeeded in stopping the Viet Cong guerrillas and their North Vietnamese allies. Diem's successors turned out to be just as corrupt and unpopular as he was, and the heroic nationalist image of North Vietnam's leader, Ho Chi Minh, evoked strong sympathies among many South Vietnamese.

Vietnam War (1954–1975) Conflict pitting North Vietnam and South Vietnamese communist guerrillas against the South Vietnamese government, aided after 1961 by the United States.

In 1973, a treaty between North Vietnam and the United States ended U.S. involvement in the war and promised future elections. Two years later, in violation of the treaty, Viet Cong and North Vietnamese troops overran the South Vietnamese army and captured the southern capital of Saigon, renaming it Ho Chi Minh City. The two parts of Vietnam were reunited in a single state ruled from the north. The Vietnam War had been bloody and traumatic. The Vietnamese had over a million casualties, and the deaths of 58,000 Americans overseas and the vigorous antiwar movement at home ensured that the United States would not easily be drawn into another shooting war.

The Struggle for Independence in Africa

In the quarter-century between 1955 and 1980, African nationalists succeeded in ending European colonial rule. Mostly they gained their independence peacefully, but where European settlers were numerous, violence became the norm.

In 1954, the Muslim people of Algeria rebelled against France. Having lost Indochina, France was determined to hold on to Algeria because 10 percent of the Algerian population was European and Algeria's economy was strongly oriented toward France. Both sides fought with great brutality. When the Algerians finally won independence in 1962, the departure of the settlers to France undermined the Algerian economy because very few Muslims had received technical training or acquired management experience.

None of the independence movements in sub-Saharan Africa matched the Algerian struggle in scale or brutality. Some of the politicians who led the nationalist movements had devoted their lives to ridding their homelands of foreign occupation. An example is Kwame Nkrumah (KWAH-mee nn-KROO-muh) (1909–1972), who in 1957 became prime minister of Ghana (formerly the Gold Coast), the first British colony in Africa to achieve independence. Only a few hundred Ghanaian children of Nkrumah's generation had graduated each year from the seven-year elementary schools, and he was one of only a handful who

made it through teacher training college. After graduation, he spent a decade reading philosophy and theology in the United States and absorbing ideas about black pride and independence then being propounded by black leaders W. E. B. Du Bois and Marcus Garvey.

After a brief stay in Britain, Nkrumah returned in 1947 to the Gold Coast to work for independence. Great Britain had already freed its Asian colonies, and Nkrumah quickly united the people of Ghana behind him. Independence thus came without bloodshed. However, Nkrumah turned out to be more effective internationally as a spokesman for colonized peoples than he was at home as an administrator. In 1966, a group of army officers ousted him.

Jomo Kenyatta (ca. 1894–1978) traveled a more difficult road in Kenya, where a substantial number of European coffee planters strengthened Britain's desire to retain control. A movement the settlers called Mau Mau, formed mostly by the Kikuyu (kih-KOO-you) people, became active in 1952. As violence between settlers and movement fighters escalated, British troops hunted down the leaders and resettled the Kikuyu. The British charged Kenyatta with being a Mau Mau leader and held him in prison and then in internal exile for eight years during a declared state of emergency. They released him in 1961, and negotiations with the British to write a constitution for an independent Kenya followed. In 1964, Kenyatta was elected the first president of the Republic of Kenya. He proved to be an effective, though autocratic, ruler.

In contrast, African leaders in the French colonies of sub-Saharan Africa were slow to call for independence. They believed in the promises of greater political and civil rights made in 1944 by General Charles de Gaulle at a conference in Brazzaville. This Brazzaville Conference had also promised to expand French education at the village level, to improve health services, and to open more lower-level administrative positions to Africans, but the word *independence* was never mentioned.

African politicians also realized that some French colonies—such as Ivory Coast with its coffee and cacao exports, fishing, and hardwood forests—had good economic prospects while others, such as land-locked desert Niger, did not. As the Malagasy politician Philibert Tsiranana said in 1958, "When I let my heart talk, I am a partisan of total and immediate independence [for

Primary Source: Comments on Algeria Find out why Charles de Gaulle believes Algeria is more trouble to France than it is worth.

Jomo Kenyatta Jomo Kenyatta, newly elected premier, is cheered by crowds in Nairobi in 1963. Kenyatta (waving ceremonial "whisk") had led the struggle to end British colonial rule in Kenya.

Madagascar]; when I make my reason speak, I realize that it is impossible."[1] Ultimately, however, the heart prevailed everywhere. Guinea, under the dynamic leadership of Sékou Touré (SAY-koo too-RAY), led the way in 1958. By the time Nigeria, the most populous West African state, achieved independence from Great Britain in 1960, the leaders of many former French colonies in West Africa attended the celebrations as independent heads of state.

European settlers fought hard to hold on in southern Africa. The African struggle against Portuguese rule in Angola and Mozambique dragged on until frustrated Portuguese military commanders overthrew the government of Portugal in 1974 and granted the African colonies independence the following year. After a ten-year fight, European settlers in the British colony of Southern Rhodesia ceded power in 1980 to the African majority, who renamed the country Zimbabwe. The change had been swift; a century after the "scramble" for Africa began, European colonial rule in Africa had ended.

Only South Africa and neighboring Southwest Africa remained in the hands of European minorities. After World War II, the white minority government had reconstructed South Africa according to extreme racial separation, or apartheid (uh-PART-hate). The cities, the best jobs, and most of the land were reserved for Europeans. Africans and others classified as "non-whites" were subjected to strict limitations on place of residence, right to travel, and access to jobs and public facilities.

The African National Congress (ANC), formed in 1912, led the fight against apartheid and in favor of a nonracial society. After police fired on demonstrators in the African town of Sharpeville in 1960, an African lawyer named Nelson Mandela (b. 1918) organized guerrilla resistance by the ANC. Mandela was sentenced to life in prison in 1964, and the government outlawed the ANC and other opposition organizations. For a time, things were quiet, but in 1976 young students reignited the bloody and prolonged struggle

> **Primary Source: The Rivonia Trial Speech to the Court** Find out why Nelson Mandela decided that violence was the only way out for Africans.

that would force an end to apartheid (see Diversity and Dominance: Race and the Struggle for Justice in South Africa).

Revolution, Reform, and Repression in Latin America

How did U.S. policies during the Cold War affect Latin America?

In Latin America, the postwar decades saw continuing struggles over foreign ownership and social inequality. American and European companies dominated Chile's copper, Cuba's sugar and resort hotels, Colombia's coffee, Guatemala's bananas, and the communications networks of several countries. Even in a country like Mexico, where the ruling Institutional Revolutionary Party, or PRI, was officially committed to revolutionary independence and economic development, a yawning gulf between rich and poor, urban and rural, persisted. According to one estimate from the mid-1960s, some three hundred foreign and eight hundred Mexican companies dominated the country, and some two thousand families made up the industrial-financial elite. At the other end of the economic scale were peasants and the 14 percent of the population classified as Indian.

U.S. Intervention in Guatemala

Jacobo Arbenz Guzman, elected president of Guatemala in 1951, was typical of Latin American leaders who tried to confront the power of foreign interests. His expropriation of large estates angered the United Fruit Company, a U.S. corporation that dominated banana exports and held vast tracts of land in reserve. Reacting to reports that Arbenz was becoming friendly toward communism, the United States Central Intelligence Agency (CIA) prompted a takeover by the Guatemalan military in 1954. CIA intervention removed Arbenz from the scene; it also condemned Guatemala to decades of governmental instability and growing violence between leftist and rightist elements in society.

Castro and the Cuban Revolution

In Cuba, U.S. companies owned 40 percent of raw sugar production, 23 percent of nonsugar industry, 90 percent of telephone and electrical services, and 50 percent of public service railways. The needs of the U.S. economy largely determined Cuban foreign trade and held back development. Profits went north to the United States or to a small class of wealthy Cubans, many of foreign origin. Cuba's ruler during that period, Fulgencio Batista, became a symbol of corruption, repression, and foreign economic domination.

In 1959, a popular rebellion forced Batista to flee the country. Fidel Castro, the leader of the rebels, his brother Raul Castro, and Ernesto "Che" Guevara (chay geh-VAHR-ah), the main theorist of communist revolution in Latin America, created a new regime. Within a year, Fidel Castro's government had redistributed land, lowered urban rents, and raised wages, effectively transferring 15 percent of the national income from rich to poor. Within twenty-two months, the Castro government seized almost all U.S. property in Cuba and most Cuban corporations. This action resulted in a blockade by the United States, the flight of middle-class and technically trained Cubans, a drop in foreign investment, and the beginning of chronic food shortages.

Little evidence supports the view that Castro undertook his revolution to install a communist government. But at that time, the East-West rivalry of the Cold War was increasingly influencing international politics, and Castro soon turned to the Soviet Union for economic aid. In doing so, he unwittingly committed his nation to economic stagnation and dependence on a foreign power as damaging as the previous relationship with the United States had been.

Race and the Struggle for Justice in South Africa

One of South Africa's martyrs in the struggle against apartheid was Steve Biko (1946–1977), a thinker and activist. Biko was one of the founders of the Black Consciousness Movement, which focused on the ways in which white settlers had stripped Africans of their freedom. Between 1975 and 1977 police arrested and interrogated him four times. After his arrest in August 1977 the police severely beat him and denied him medical care. His death in police custody caused worldwide outrage.

[T]hese are not the people we are concerned with [those who support apartheid]. We are concerned with that curious bunch of nonconformists who explain their participation in negative terms: that bunch of do-gooders that goes under all sorts of names—liberals, leftists etc. These are the people who argue that they are not responsible for white racism and the country's "inhumanity to the black man." These are the people who claim that they too feel the oppression just as acutely as the blacks and therefore should be jointly involved in the black man's struggle for a place under the sun. In short, these are the people who say that they have black souls wrapped up in white skins.

The role of the white liberal in the black man's history in South Africa is a curious one. Very few black organisations were not under white direction. True to their image, the white liberals always knew what was good for the blacks and told them so. The wonder of it all is that the black people have believed in them for so long. It was only at the end of the 50s that the blacks started demanding to be their own guardians.

Nowhere is the arrogance of the liberal ideology demonstrated so well as in their insistence that the problems of the country can only be solved by a bilateral approach involving both black and white. This has, by and large, come to be taken in all seriousness as the modus operandi in South Africa by all those who claim they would like a change in the status quo. Hence the multiracial political organisations and parties and the "nonracial" student organisations, all of which insist on integration not only as an end goal but also as a means.

The integration they talk about is first of all artificial in that it is a response to conscious manoeuvre rather than to the dictates of the inner soul. In other words the people forming the integrated complex have been extracted from various segregated societies with their in built [sic] complexes of superiority and inferiority and these continue to manifest themselves even in the "nonracial" setup of the integrated complex. As a result the integration so achieved is a one-way course, with the whites doing all the talking and the blacks the listening. Let me hasten to say that I am not claiming that segregation is necessarily the natural order; however, given the facts of the situation where a group experiences privilege at the expense of others, then it becomes obvious that a hastily arranged integration cannot be the solution to the problem. It is rather like expecting the slave to work together with the slave-master's son to remove all the conditions leading to [his] enslavement.

. . .

It will not sound anachronistic to anybody genuinely interested in real integration to learn that blacks are asserting themselves in a society where they are being treated as perpetual under-16s. One does not need to plan for or actively encourage real integration. Once the various groups within a given community have asserted themselves to the point that mutual respect has to be shown then you have the ingredients for a true and meaningful integration. At the heart of true integration is the provision for each man, each group to rise and attain the envisioned self. Each group must be able to attain its style of existence without encroaching on or being thwarted by another. Out of this mutual respect for each other and complete freedom of self-determination there will obviously arise a genuine fusion of the life-styles of the various groups. This is true integration.

From this it becomes clear that as long as blacks are suffering from [an] inferiority complex—a result of 300 years of deliberate oppression, denigration and derision—they will be useless as co-architects of a normal society where man is nothing else but man for his own sake. Hence what is necessary as a prelude to anything else that may come is a very strong grass-roots build-up of black consciousness such that blacks can learn to assert themselves and stake their rightful claim.

Thus in adopting the line of a nonracial approach, the liberals are playing their old game. They are claiming a "monopoly on intelligence and moral judgement" and setting the pattern and pace for the realisation of the black man's aspirations. They want to remain in good books with both the black and white worlds. They want to shy away from all forms of "extremisms," condemning "white supremacy" as being just as bad as "Black Power"! They vacillate between the two worlds, verbalising all the complaints of the blacks beautifully while skilfully extracting what suits them from the exclusive pool of white privileges. But ask them for a moment to give a concrete meaningful programme that they intend adopting, then you will see on whose side they really are. Their protests are directed at and appeal to white conscience, everything they do is directed at finally convincing the white electorate that the black man is also a man and that at some future date he should be given a place at the white man's table.

In the following selection Anglican bishop Desmond Tutu (b. 1931) expressed his personal anguish at the death of Steve Biko, summarizing Biko's contributions to the struggle for justice in South Africa. Tutu won the Noble Peace Prize in 1984 and was named archbishop in 1988. From 1995 to 1998 he chaired the Truth and Reconciliation Commission, which investigated atrocities in South Africa during the years of apartheid. He stated that his objective was to create "a democratic and just society without racial divisions."

When we heard the news "Steve Biko is dead" we were struck numb with disbelief. No, it can't be true! No, it must be a horrible nightmare, and we will awake and find that really it is different—that Steve is alive even if it be in detention. But no, dear friends, he is dead and we are still numb with grief, and groan with anguish "Oh God, where are you? Oh God, do you really care—how can you let this happen to us?"

It all seems such a senseless waste of a wonderfully gifted person, struck down in the bloom of youth, a youthful bloom that some wanted to see blighted. What can be the purpose of such wanton destruction? God, do you really love us? What must we do which we have not done, what must we say which we have not said a thousand times over, oh, for so many years—that all we want is what belongs to all God's children, what belongs as an inalienable right—a place in the sun in our own beloved mother country. Oh God, how long can we go on? How long can we go on appealing for a more just ordering of society where we all, black and white together, count not because of some accident of birth or a biological irrelevance—where all of us black and white count because we are human persons, human persons created in your own image.

God called Steve Biko to be his servant in South Africa—to speak up on behalf of God, declaring what the will of this God must be in a situation such as ours, a situation of evil, injustice, oppression and exploitation. God called him to be the founder father of the Black Consciousness Movement against which we have had tirades and fulminations. It is a movement by which God, through Steve, sought to awaken in the Black person a sense of his intrinsic value and worth as a child of God, not needing to apologise for his existential condition as a black person, calling on blacks to glorify and praise God that he had created them black. Steve, with his brilliant mind that always saw to the heart of things, realised that until blacks asserted their humanity and their personhood, there was not the remotest chance for reconciliation in South Africa. For true reconciliation is a deeply personal matter. It can happen only between persons who assert their own personhood, and who acknowledge and respect that of others. You don't get reconciled to your dog, do you? Steve knew and believed fervently that being pro-black was not the same thing as being anti-white. The Black Consciousness Movement is not a "hate white movement," despite all you may have heard to the contrary. He had a far too profound respect for persons as persons, to want to deal with them under readymade, shopsoiled [sic] categories.

All who met him had this tremendous sense of a warm-hearted man, and as a notable acquaintance of his told me, a man who was utterly indestructible, of massive intellect and yet reticent; quite unshakeable in his commitment to principle and to radical change in South Africa by peaceful means; a man of real reconciliation, truly an instrument of God's peace, unshakeable in his commitment to the liberation of all South Africans, black and white, striving for a more just and more open South Africa.

1. What are Steve Biko's charges against white liberals in South Africa?

2. What was the proper role for whites in the anti-apartheid movement according to Biko?

3. How does Bishop Tutu's eulogy differ from the political spirit and point of view expressed in Biko's 1970 essay?

4. According to Bishop Tutu, what were Biko's strongest characteristics? Were these characteristics demonstrated in Biko's essay?

Source: First selection from Steve Biko, *I Write What I Like*, ed. by Aelred Stubbs (Harper & Row, 1972). Reprinted by permission of Robert Dudley Agency; second selection from *Crying in the Wilderness: The Struggle for Justice in South Africa*, ed. John Webster (William B. Eerdmans Publishing Co., 1982) pp. 61–63. Reprinted by permission of the Continuum International Publishing Group.

In April 1961, some fifteen hundred Cuban exiles, whom the CIA had trained for a year in Guatemala, landed at the Bay of Pigs in an effort to overthrow Castro. The Cuban army defeated the attempted invasion in a matter of days, partly because the new U.S. president, John F. Kennedy, decided not to provide all the air support that the plan originally called for. The failure of the Bay of Pigs invasion tarnished the reputation of the United States and the CIA and provoked Castro into declaring that he and his revolution were and always had been Marxist-Leninist.

The Era of Violence and Repression

In the 1970s Latin America entered a dark era of political violence. Revolutionary movements challenged the established order in many nations, and democratic governments were overturned by military revolts. A region of weak democracy in 1960 became a region of military dictatorships fifteen years later. The new authoritarian leaders had little patience with civil liberties and human rights.

The ongoing confrontation between Fidel Castro and the government of the United States helped propel the region toward crisis. The fact that Cuba's communist government survived opposition from the United States energized the revolutionary left throughout Latin America. In response, the United States increased support for its political and military allies. Many of the military leaders who came to power in this period were trained by the United States.

Brazil was the first nation to experience fully the conservative reaction to the Cuban Revolution. Claiming that Brazil's civilian political leaders could not protect it against communist subversion, the army overthrew the government of President João Goulart (ju-wow go-LARHT) in 1964. The military

Fidel Castro Arrives in Havana
Castro and his supporters overthrew a brutal dictatorship and began the revolutionary transformation of Cuba that led to a confrontation with the United States.

Bettmann/Corbis

717

suspended the constitution, outlawed political parties, and exiled former presidents and opposition leaders. Death squads—illegal paramilitary organizations sanctioned by the government—detained, tortured, and executed thousands of citizens. The dictatorship also undertook an ambitious economic program that promoted industrialization through import substitution, using tax and tariff policies to compel foreign-owned companies to increase investment in manufacturing.

This combination of dictatorship, violent repression, and government promotion of industrialization was called the "Brazilian Solution." Elements of this "solution" spread across much of the region in the 1970s and early 1980s. In 1970 Chile's new president, **Salvador Allende** (sal-vah-DOR ah-YEHN-day), undertook ambitious socialist reforms. He nationalized most of Chile's heavy industry and mines, including the American-owned copper companies that dominated the Chilean economy. From the beginning of Allende's presidency the administration of President Richard Nixon (1969–1973) opposed his reforms. Amidst inflation, mass consumer protests, and declining foreign trade, a military uprising led by General Augusto Pinochet (ah-GOOS-toh pin-oh-SHAY) and supported by the United States overthrew Allende in 1973. President Allende and thousands of Chileans died in the uprising. Thousands more were illegally seized, tortured, and imprisoned. Pinochet rolled back Allende's social reforms, reduced state participation in the economy, and encouraged foreign investment.

In 1976 Argentina followed Brazil and Chile into dictatorship. Isabel Martínez de Perón (EES-ah-bell mar-TEEN-ehz deh pair-OWN) became president after the death of her husband Juan Perón in 1974. Argentina was wracked by inflation, terrorism, and labor protests. Losing trust in the president, the military seized power and suspended the constitution. During the next seven years the military fought what it called the Dirty War against terrorism. More than nine thousand Argentines lost their lives; thousands of others endured arrest, torture, and the loss of property.

Yet some revolutionary movements persisted, reaching a peak in 1979 in Nicaragua with the overthrow of the corrupt dictatorship of Anastasio Somoza. The broad alliance of revolutionaries and

SECTION REVIEW

- Latin American struggles for economic independence often flared into violence and revolution and provoked U.S. intervention.
- In Guatemala, the United States intervened to stop a reform movement.
- In Cuba, revolutionaries led by Fidel Castro were able to end American domination, but only by creating a communist dictatorship with Soviet help.
- In Brazil, Argenina, Chile, and elsewhere, military dictatorship crushed revolutionary and reform movements.

reformers that took power called themselves **Sandinistas** (sahn-din-EES-tahs), from Augusto César Sandino, who had led Nicaraguan opposition to U.S. military intervention between 1927 and 1932. The Sandinistas sought to imitate the command economies of Cuba and the Soviet Union, nationalizing properties owned by members of the Nicaraguan elite and U.S. citizens.

Japan, China, and the Four Tigers

Why were developments in China so different from those in other parts of East Asia?

East Asia had suffered as much as Europe from the Second World War. Eastern China had been invaded and occupied by Japanese forces from 1937 to 1945, and the rest of China had been the scene of a long and bitter civil war (1934–1949) between the Nationalist (or Guomindang) army supported by the United States and the communist People's Liberation Army (see Chapter 27). War continued on the Korean Peninsula until 1953. After that, it took many decades before prosperity came to East Asia.

Salvador Allende Socialist president of Chile elected in 1970 and overthrown and killed by the military in 1973.

Sandinistas Members of a leftist coalition that overthrew the Nicaraguan dictator Anastasio Somoza in 1979 and attempted to install a socialist economy. The United States financed an armed uprising against the Sandinista government. In 1990 the Sandinistas lost power after a national election.

The Nicaraguan Revolution Overturns Somoza A revolutionary coalition that included Marxists drove the dictator Anastasio Somoza from power in 1979. The Somoza family had ruled Nicaragua since the 1930s and maintained a close relationship with the United States.

Susan Meiselas/Magnum Photos, Inc.

The Japanese Economic Miracle

Japan signed a peace treaty with most of its former enemies in 1951 and regained independence from American occupation the following year. Renouncing militarism and its imperialist past, Japan remained on the sidelines throughout the Korean War. Its new constitution, written under American supervision in 1946, allowed only a limited self-defense force, banned the deployment of Japanese troops abroad, and gave the vote to women.

Japan benefited from the Korean War in an unexpected way. Massive purchases of supplies by the United States and spending by American servicemen on leave provided a financial stimulus to the Japanese economy similar to the stimulus that Europe received from the Marshall Plan. The Japanese turned their talents and energies to rebuilding their industries and engaging in world commerce. By isolating Japan from most world political issues, the Cold War provided an exceptionally favorable environment for Japan to develop its economic strength.

Three industries that took advantage of government aid and the newest technologies paved the way for Japan's emergence as an economic superpower after 1975. Projects producing 60 million kilowatts of electricity were completed between 1951 and 1970, almost a third through dams on Japan's many rivers. Between 1960 and 1970, steel production more than quadrupled, reaching 15.7 percent of the total capacity of countries outside the Soviet bloc. The shipbuilding industry produced six times as much tonnage in 1970 as in 1960, almost half of the new tonnage produced outside the Soviet bloc.

Although Japan has few mineral resources and is dependent on oil imports, the Japanese economy weathered the recession of the 1970s better than did the economies of Europe and the United States. In fact, Japan's economy grew at the stupendous rate of about 10 percent a year during the 1970s and 1980s. Average income also increased rapidly, overtaking that of the United States in 1986.

The Japanese industrial model differed from the American and European models. During the American occupation, Japanese industrial conglomerates, *zaibatsu*, were broken up. Although ownership of major industries became less concentrated, new industrial alliances appeared. There are now six major **keiretsu** (kay-RET-soo) that each include firms in industry, commerce, and construction tied together with a major bank in an interlocking ownership structure. Minor keiretsu may form around a major corporation, like Toyota, and its major suppliers. These industrial combinations have close relationships with government, which imposes tariffs and import regulations to inhibit foreign competition. Such support was crucial

---

keiretsu Alliances of corporations and banks that dominate the Japanese economy.

in fostering the development of Japan's automobile and semiconductor industries.

Through the 1970s and 1980s, the Japanese superiority in manufactured goods produced huge trade surpluses. Attempts by the United States and the European Community to pry open the Japanese market through negotiation had only limited success. In 1990, Japan's trade surplus was double that of 1985. Many experts assumed that the competitive advantages that Japan enjoyed in the 1980s would propel Japan past the United States as the world's preeminent industrial economy. But the Japanese economy began to stall at the end of the decade.

Mao Zedong's Many Revolutions

While Japan benefited from being outside the Cold War, China was deeply involved in Cold War politics. When Mao Zedong (maow dzuh-dong) and the communists defeated the Nationalists in 1949 and established the People's Republic of China (PRC), their main ally and source of arms was the Soviet Union. By 1956, however, the PRC and the Soviet Union were beginning to diverge politically, partly in reaction to the Soviet rejection of Stalinism and partly because of China's reluctance to be cast forever in the role of student. Mao had his own notions of communism, focusing strongly on the peasantry, whom the Soviets ignored in favor of the industrial working class.

In 1958, Mao started a Great Leap Forward in the hopes of vaulting China into the ranks of world industrial powers by maximizing the use of labor in small-scale, village-level industries. The policy failed but demonstrated Mao's willingness to carry out massive economic and social projects of his own devising.

In 1966, in another radical nationwide program called the **Cultural Revolution**, Mao ordered the mass mobilization of Chinese youth into Red Guard units. His goal was to kindle revolutionary fervor in a new generation and to ward off the stagnation and bureaucratization he saw in the Soviet Union. To this end, Red Guard units criticized and purged teachers, party officials, and intellectuals for "bourgeois values." Internal party conflict continued until 1971, when Mao admitted that attacks on individuals had gotten out of hand. Meanwhile, small-scale industrialization resulted in record levels of agricultural and industrial production. The last years of the Cultural Revolution were dominated by radicals led by Mao's wife, Jiang Qing (jyahn ching), who restricted artistic and intellectual activity.

In the meantime, the rift between the PRC and the Soviet Union had opened so wide that United States President Richard Nixon (1969–1974), by reputation a staunch anticommunist, dropped objections to the PRC's joining the United Nations. In 1971, the PRC occupied China's permanent seat on the Security Council, displacing the Chinese Nationalist government on Taiwan. The following year, Nixon visited Beijing, making dramatically clear the new cooperation between the People's Republic of China and the United States.

The Four Tigers

A few other Asian states imitated the Japanese model of close cooperation between government and industry. South Korea overcame the devastation of the Korean War in little more than a decade through a combination of inexpensive labor, strong technical education, and substantial domestic capital reserves. It developed heavy industries like steel and shipbuilding, as well as consumer industries like automobiles and consumer electronics. Japanese investment and technology transfers accelerated this process.

Taiwan, Hong Kong, and Singapore moved so rapidly in the same direction that these three nations and South Korea were often called the **Asian Tigers**. Taiwan suffered a number of political reverses, including the loss of its United Nations seat to the People's Republic of China in 1971 and the withdrawal of diplomatic recognition by the United States. Nevertheless, it achieved remarkable economic progress, based on smaller, more specialized companies and investment in the People's Republic of China.

Cultural Revolution (China) (1966–1969) Campaign in China ordered by Mao Zedong to purge the Communist Party of his opponents and instill revolutionary values in the younger generation.
Asian Tigers South Korea, Taiwan, Hong Kong, and Singapore, so-called because their economies expanded so fast.

- Under the American strategic umbrella, Japan renounced military force and became an economic powerhouse.
- China, led by Mao Zedong, underwent a series of economic and social upheavals.
- South Korea, Taiwan, Hong Kong, and Singapore (the "Asian Tigers") followed Japan's example and developed their economies.

Hong Kong and Singapore were former British colonies with limited resources. Singapore's economy rested on its busy port and on banking and commercial services. After separating from Malaysia in 1965, this society of around 4 million people diversified by building textile and electronics industries. Hong Kong's economic prosperity, based on its port as well as its banking and commercial services, was increasingly tied to China's growing economy. Worried about Hong Kong's reintegration into the People's Republic of China in 1997, local capitalists moved significant amounts of capital to safe havens like the United States and Canada, but in recent years Hong Kong has regained its dynamism and is now even more closely tied to the rapidly expanding Chinese economy.

These **newly industrialized economies (NIEs)** all had disciplined and hardworking labor forces and invested heavily in education. As early as 1980 Korea had as many engineering graduates as Germany, Britain, and Sweden combined. These countries also emphasized outward-looking export strategies and had high rates of personal saving—about 35 percent of GDP—that allowed them to fund investment in new technology. Like Japan, they practiced government sponsorship and protection.

 Primary Source: One Hundred Items for Destroying the Old and Establishing the New Would you be willing to give up your blue jeans for the Cultural Revolution? Find out what following Mao Zedong required.

National and Religious Conflicts in the Middle East

What roles did nationalism and religious fundamentalism play in Middle Eastern politics?

Independence had come gradually to the Arab countries of the Middle East. Britain granted Syria and Lebanon independence after World War II. Other Arab countries—Iraq, Egypt, Jordan—enjoyed nominal independence during the interwar period but remained under indirect British control until the 1950s.

The Arab-Israeli Conflicts

Overshadowing all Arab politics, however, was the struggle with the new state of Israel. British policy on Palestine between the wars oscillated between favoring Zionist Jewish immigrants and the indigenous Palestinian Arabs. After the war, under intense pressure to resettle European Jewish refugees, Britain handed the Palestine problem over to the United Nations. In November 1947, the General Assembly voted in favor of partitioning Palestine into two states, one Jewish and one Arab. The Jewish community made plans to declare independence, while the Palestinians, who felt the proposed land division was unfair, reacted in horror and took up arms. When Israel declared its independence in May 1948, neighboring Arab countries sent armies to help the Palestinians crush the newborn state.

Israel, however, prevailed on all fronts. Some 700,000 Palestinians refugees found shelter in United Nations refugee camps in Jordan, Syria, Lebanon, and the Gaza Strip (a bit of coastal land on the Egyptian-Israeli border). The right of these refugees to return home remains a focal point of Arab politics. In 1967, Israel responded to threatening military moves by Egypt's Nasir by preemptively attacking Egyptian and Syrian air bases. In six days, Israel won a smashing victory. It also won control of Jerusalem (previously split with Jordan), the West Bank, the Gaza Strip, the

newly industrialized economies (NIEs) Rapidly growing new industrializing nations of the late twentieth century, including the Asian Tigers.

Map 29.2 Middle East Oil and the Arab-Israeli Conflict, 1947–1973 Oil resources were long controlled by private European and American companies. In the 1960s most countries, guided by OPEC, negotiated agreements for sharing control, eventually leading to national ownership. This set the stage for the use of oil as a weapon in the 1973 Arab-Israeli war and for subsequent price increases. © Cengage Learning

Interactive Map

The following labels appear on the map:

Soviet occupation, 1979–1989
U.S. aid to rebels, 1980s
International and Northern Alliance forces defeat Taliban, 2001

U.S. troops, 1958, 1983–1984

U.S. arms sales, 1955–1978:
$20.8 billion
Shah overthrown, 1979
American hostages taken, 1979–1981

Principal center of al activity, 2004–

U.S. and allies launch First U.S.-Iraq War, 1991

U.S. arms sales, 1980s, during Iran-Iraq War
Iraq invades Kuwait, 1990
Second U.S.-Iraq War, 2003

Oil embargo, 1973
Source of 17% of U.S. oil imports in 1975
Largest buyer of U.S. arms, 1978

Al-Qaeda headquarters, 1992–1996

Bombing of USS Cole by al-Qaeda, 2000

U.S. troops assist in relief of famine, 1992–1993.
U.S. troops withdrawn, 1994.
U.S.-backed Ethiopian invasion removes Islamist government, 2006

Members of the Organization of Petroleum Exporting Countries (OPEC)

Oil fields

Legend (inset — ARAB-ISRAELI CONFLICT):
Jewish state after UN partition of Palestine, 1947
Israel after War of 1948–1949
Area controlled by Israel after Six-Day War, 1967
Israeli-occupied area after Yom Kippur War, 1973

By Egyptian-Israeli agreements of 1975 and 1979, Israel withdrew from the Sinai in 1982. In 1981 Israel annexed the Golan Heights. Through negotiations between Israel and the PLO, Jericho and the Gaza Strip were placed under Palestinian self-rule, and Israeli troops were withdrawn in 1994. In 1994 Israel and Jordan signed an agreement opening their borders and normalizing their relations.

Shortage at the Pumps
As prices rose in the late 1970s, consumers tried to hoard supplies by filling gas cans at neighborhood stations. For the first time gas prices exceeded $1 a gallon.

James Pozarik/Getty Images

strategic Golan Heights in southern Syria, and the entire Sinai Peninsula (see Map 29.2). Acquiring all of Jerusalem satisfied the Jews' deep longing to return to their holiest city, but Palestinians continued to regard Jerusalem as their destined capital, and Muslims in many countries protested Israeli control of the Dome of the Rock, a revered Islamic shrine located in the city. These acquisitions resulted in a new wave of Palestinian refugees.

The rival claims to Palestine continued to plague Middle Eastern politics. The Palestine Liberation Organization (PLO), headed by Yasir Arafat (AR-ah-fat), waged guerrilla war against Israel, frequently engaging in acts of terrorism. The militarized Israelis were able to blunt or absorb these attacks and launch counterstrikes that involved assassinations and bombings. Though the United States proved a firm friend of Israel and the Soviet Union armed the Arab states, neither superpower saw the struggle between Zionism and Palestinian nationalism as a vital concern—until oil became a political issue.

The Oil Crisis of 1973

The phenomenal concentration of oil wealth in the Persian Gulf states—Iran, Iraq, Kuwait, Saudi Arabia, Qatar, Bahrain, and the United Arab Emirates—was not fully realized until after World War II, when demand for

oil rose sharply as civilian economies recovered. As a world oversupply diminished in the face of rising demand, oil-producing states in 1960 formed the **Organization of Petroleum Exporting Countries (OPEC)** to promote their collective interest in higher revenues.

Oil politics and the Arab-Israeli conflict intersected in October 1973. A surprise Egyptian attack across the Suez Canal threw the Israelis into temporary disarray, but within days the war turned in Israel's favor, and an Egyptian army was trapped at the canal's southern end. The United States then arranged a cease-fire and the disengagement of forces. But before that could happen, the Arab oil-producing countries voted to embargo oil shipments to the United States and the Netherlands as punishment for their support of Israel.

The implications of oil as an economic weapon profoundly disturbed the worldwide oil industry. Prices rose—along with feelings of insecurity. In 1974, OPEC responded to the turmoil in the oil market

Organization of Petroleum Exporting Countries (OPEC) Organization formed in 1960 by oil-producing states to promote their collective interest in generating revenue from oil.

by quadrupling prices, setting the stage for massive transfers of wealth to the producing countries and provoking a feeling of crisis throughout the consuming countries.

Islamic Revolutions in Iran and Afghanistan

Although the Arab-Israeli conflict and the oil crisis concerned both superpowers, the prospect of direct military involvement remained remote. When unexpected crises developed in Iran and Afghanistan, however, significant strategic issues came to the foreground. Both countries adjoined Soviet territory. Exercising post–Vietnam War caution, the United States reacted with restraint. The Soviet Union chose a bolder and ultimately disastrous course.

Muhammad Reza Pahlavi (REH-zah PAH-lah-vee) succeeded his father as shah of Iran in 1941. In 1953, covert intervention by the United States Central Intelligence Agency (CIA) helped the shah retain his throne in the face of a movement to usurp royal power. Even after nationalizing the foreign-owned oil industry, the shah continued to enjoy American support. When oil income mushroomed following the price increases of 1973–1974, the United States encouraged the shah to spend his nation's growing wealth on advanced American weaponry. By the mid-1970s, popular resentment against the shah's dependence on the United States, the ballooning wealth of the elite families that supported him, and the brutality, inefficiency, malfeasance, and corruption of his government grew into mass opposition.

Ayatollah Ruhollah Khomeini (eye-uh-TOLL-uh ROOH-ol-LAH ko-MAY-nee), a Shi'ite (SHE-ite) philosopher-cleric who had spent most of his eighty-plus years in religious and academic pursuits, became the voice and symbolic leader of the opposition. Massive street demonstrations and crippling strikes forced the shah to flee Iran and ended the monarchy in 1979. In the Islamic Republic of Iran, which replaced the monarchy, Ayatollah Khomeini was supreme arbiter of disputes and guarantor of religious legitimacy. Elections were held, but monarchists, communists, and other groups opposed to the idea of an Islamic Republic were barred from office. Shi'ite clerics with little training for government service emerged in many of the highest posts, and stringent measures were taken to replace Western styles and culture with Islamic

norms. Universities temporarily closed as their faculties were purged of secularists and monarchists. Women were compelled to wear modest Islamic garments outside the house while semi-official vigilante committees policed public morals and cast a pall over entertainment and social life.

The United States under President Carter had criticized the shah's repression, but the overthrow of a long-standing ally and the creation of the Islamic Republic were blows to American prestige. Khomeini saw the United States as a "Great Satan" and encouraged Islamic revolutionary movements elsewhere, to the distress of both the United States and Israel. In November 1979, Iranian radicals seized the U.S. embassy in Tehran and then held fifty-two diplomats hostage for 444 days. Americans felt humiliated by their inability to do anything, particularly after the failure of a military rescue attempt.

In the fall of 1980, shortly after negotiations for release of the hostages began, **Saddam Husayn** (sah-DAHM who-SANE), the ruler of neighboring Iraq, invaded Iran to topple the Islamic Republic. His own dictatorial rule rested on a secular Arab nationalist philosophy and long-standing friendship with the Soviet Union, which supplied his army. He feared that Iran's revolutionary fervor would infect his own country's Shi'ite majority and threaten his power. While the war pitted American weapons in Iranian hands against Soviet weapons in Iraqi hands, the superpowers avoided overt involvement. Covertly, however, the Reagan administration sent arms via Israel to Iran, hoping to gain the release of other American hostages held by Muslim radicals in Lebanon and to secretly finance the Contra war against the Sandinista government of Nicaragua. When this deal came to light in 1986, the resulting political scandal intensified American hostility toward Iran. Openly tilting toward Iraq, President Reagan sent the United States Navy to the Persian Gulf, ostensibly to protect nonbelligerent shipping. This threatening move helped persuade Iran to accept a cease-fire in 1988.

Ayatollah Ruhollah Khomeini Shi'ite philosopher and cleric who led the overthrow of the Shah of Iran in 1979 and created an Islamic republic.

Saddam Husayn President of Iraq from 1979 until overthrown by the American invasion in 2003. Waged war on Iran from 1980 to 1988. His invasion of Kuwait was repulsed in the Persian Gulf War of 1991.

While the United States experienced anguish and frustration in Iran, the Soviet Union found itself facing even more serious problems in neighboring Afghanistan. In 1978 a Marxist party with a secular reform agenda seized power in Afghanistan. Offended by these efforts to reform education and grant rights to women, traditional ethnic and religious leaders led a successful rebellion. In 1979, the Soviet Union responded by sending its army to Afghanistan to bolster communist rule.

With the United States, Saudi Arabia, and Pakistan paying, equipping, and training the Afghan rebels, the Soviet Union found itself in the same kind of unwinnable war the United States had stumbled into in Vietnam. Unable to justify the continuing drain on manpower, morale, and economic resources and facing widespread domestic discontent, Soviet leaders finally withdrew their troops in 1989. The Afghan communists held on for another three years, and then rebel groups took control of the entire country and began to fight among themselves over who should rule.

The End of the Bipolar World

What led to the collapse of the Soviet bloc?

Few in 1980 predicted the startling collapse of the Soviet Union and the socialist nations of the Warsaw Pact. The once-independent nations and ethnic groups that had been brought within the Soviet Union and the eastern European nations seemed securely transformed by the experiences and institutions of communism. By 1990, however, nationalism was resurgent, and communism was nearly finished.

Crisis in the Soviet Union

Under United States president Ronald Reagan and the Soviet Union's general secretary, Leonid Brezhnev (leh-oh-NEED BREZH-nef), the rhetoric of the Cold War remained intense. Massive new U.S. investments in armaments placed heavy burdens on a Soviet economy unable to absorb the cost of developing similar weapons. Soviet economic problems were systemic; shortages had become a part of Soviet life. Obsolete industrial plants and centralized planning that stifled initiative led to a declining standard of living relative to the West, while the arbitrariness of the bureaucracy, the cynical manipulation of information, and deprivations created a generalized crisis in morale.

Despite the growing discontent, Brezhnev refused to modify his rigid and unsuccessful policies. But he was unable to contain an underground current of protest. In a series of powerful books, the writer Alexander Solzhenitsyn (sol-zhi-NEET-sin) castigated the Soviet system and particularly the Stalinist prison camps. He won a Nobel Prize in literature but was charged with treason and expelled from the country in 1974. *Samizdat* [sah-meez-DAHT]), self-published underground writings by critics of the regime, circulated widely despite government efforts to suppress them.

By the time **Mikhail Gorbachev** (MEE-hile GORE-beh-CHOF) took up the reins of the Soviet government in 1985, war weariness, economic decay, and vocal protest had reached critical levels. Casting aside Brezhnev's hard line, Gorbachev authorized major reforms in an attempt to stave off total collapse. His policy of political openness (*glasnost*) permitted criticism of the government and the Communist Party. His policy of *perestroika* (per-i-STROY-kuh) ("restructuring") was an attempt to address long-suppressed economic problems by moving away from central state planning and toward a more open economic system. In 1989 he ended the unpopular war in Afghanistan.

Mikhail Gorbachev (b. 1931) Head of the Soviet Union from 1985 to 1991. His liberalization effort improved relations with the West, but he lost power after his reforms led to the collapse of communist governments in eastern Europe.

perestroika Policy of "restructuring" that was the centerpiece of Mikhail Gorbachev's efforts to liberalize communism in the Soviet Union.

Map labels and callouts:

- Communist regimes overthrown since 1989
- Soviet Union, dissolved in 1991
- Yugoslavia, dissolved in civil war, 1991–1992

- Elections, 1989
- Berlin Wall opened, Nov. 1989 German reunification, 1990
- Czechoslovakia broke into Czech Republic and Slovakia in 1993
- Largest and most influential of the former Soviet republics after 1991
- Gorbachev in power, 1985–1991 Moscow coup fails; Boris Yeltsin declared president of Russia, 1990
- Chechnya declares independence 1991; Russia attacks, 1994
- NATO airwar against Serbia to protect Kosovo, 1994
- U.S. troops join NATO peacekeeping forces, Dec. 1995

Map 29.3 The End of Soviet Domination in Eastern Europe The creation of new countries out of Yugoslavia and Czechoslovakia and the reunification of Germany marked the most complicated changes of national borders since World War I. The Czech Republic and Slovakia separated peacefully, but Slovenia, Croatia, Macedonia, and Bosnia and Herzegovina achieved independence only after bitter fighting. © Cengage Learning

 Interactive Map

The Collapse of the Socialist Bloc

Events in eastern Europe were very important in forcing change on the Soviet Union. In 1980, protests by Polish shipyard workers in the city of Gdansk led to the formation of **Solidarity**, a labor union that soon enrolled 9 million members. The Roman Catholic Church in Poland, strengthened by the elevation of a Pole, Karol Wojtyla (KAH-rol voy-TIL-ah), to the papacy as John Paul II in 1978, gave strong moral support to the protest movement. As Gorbachev loosened political controls in the Soviet Union after 1985, communist leaders elsewhere lost confidence in Soviet resolve, and critics and reformers in Poland and throughout the rest of eastern Europe were emboldened (see Map 29.3).

Beleaguered Warsaw Pact governments vacillated between relaxation of control and the suppression of dissent. As the Catholic clergy in Poland had supported Solidarity, Protestant and Orthodox religious leaders aided the rise of opposition groups elsewhere. This combination of nationalism and religion provided a powerful base for opponents of the communist regimes. Threatened by these forces, communist governments sought to quiet the opposition by seeking solutions to their severe economic problems. They turned to the West for trade and financial assistance and opened their nations to travelers, ideas, styles,

Solidarity Polish trade union created in 1980 to protest working conditions and political repression. It began the nationalist opposition to communist rule that led in 1989 to the fall of communism in eastern Europe.

and money from Western countries, all of which accelerated the demand for change.

By the end of 1989, communist governments across eastern Europe had fallen. The dismantling of the Berlin Wall, the symbol of a divided Europe and the bipolar world, vividly represented this transformation. In Poland, Hungary, Czechoslovakia, and Bulgaria, communist leaders decided that change was inevitable and initiated political reforms. When Romanian dictator Nicolae Ceausescu (neh-koh-LIE chow-CHES-koo) refused to surrender power, he provoked a rebellion that ended with his arrest and execution. The comprehensiveness of these changes became clear in 1990, when Solidarity leader Lech Walesa (leck wah-LEN-suh) was elected president of Poland and dissident playwright Vaclav Havel (vahc-SLAV hah-VEL) was elected president of Czechoslovakia. That same year, East and West Germany were reunited, and the eastern Baltic states of Lithuania, Estonia, and Latvia declared their independence from the Soviet Union.

The end of the Soviet Union came suddenly in 1991. Gorbachev's efforts to transform the Soviet system could not keep up with the tide of change sweeping through the region. After communist hardliners botched a poorly conceived coup against Gorbachev, disgust with communism boiled over. Boris Yeltsin, the president of the Russian Republic and long-time member of the Communist Party, led popular resistance to the coup in Moscow and emerged as the most powerful leader in the country. Russia, the largest republic in the Soviet Union, was effectively taking the place of the disintegrating USSR. In September 1991, as the smaller republics of the Soviet Union declared their independence, the Congress of People's Deputies voted to dissolve the union. Mikhail Gorbachev went into retirement.

Conclusion

Shortly after World War II, the Soviet Union and the Western democracies led by the United States began to prepare for a new round of hostilities, establishing competing military alliances and attempting to influence the new governments of nations formerly occupied by the Axis. Each side portrayed this tension as a struggle between irreconcilably different social and

The Fall of the Berlin Wall The Berlin Wall was the most important symbol of the Cold War. Constructed to keep residents of East Germany from fleeing to the West and defended by armed guards and barbed wire, it was the public face of communism. As the Soviet system fell apart, the residents of East and West Berlin broke down sections of the wall.

Bossu Regis/Corbis Sygma

economic systems. The boundary that separated the United States and its allies and the Soviet Union and its allies and that Churchill had called an "Iron Curtain" was soon defended by massive armies and powerful nuclear weapons.

This Cold War quickly became global in character as distant civil wars, regional conflicts, and nationalist revolutions were transformed by support provided by these contestants for global ascendancy. Many of the flash points in this war were provided by the desire of colonized peoples to establish independent nations. The most powerful force in the postwar era was nationalism, the desire of peoples to control their own destinies. This reality was obscured by the global contest of the Cold War.

In Africa, the Middle East, South Asia, and East Asia this desire to throw off foreign controls would lead to the creation of scores of new nations by the 1970s. Each nation's struggle had its own character. While in India and Pakistan these passions led to independence, similar sentiments led in China to the overthrow of a weak pro-Western government and to

the creation of a communist dictatorship. In much of Africa, the Middle East, and the Caribbean, nationalism was manifested as traditional anticolonial struggles. In the Middle East the desire for self-government was complicated by the creation of the state of Israel. In Latin America, where most nations had long been independent, the era's nationalist sentiment manifested itself as a desire for economic independence and an end to foreign interventions. For this reason Castro found it easy to connect his revolutionary ambitions to anticolonial movements elsewhere.

The end of Japanese control in Korea and Vietnam led to territorial partitions that separated Soviet-leaning and Western-allied states. Civil war and foreign interventions soon followed. In both cases the Soviet Union and China supported communist forces. The United States committed large military forces to protect the anticommunist governments, gaining a stalemate in Korea and eventually losing in Vietnam. While the outcomes were mixed for the superpowers, the wars were contained and managed so as to prevent direct engagement and nuclear conflict.

CHAPTER REVIEW

Download the MP3 audio file of the Chapter Review to listen to on the go.

What were the major threats to world peace during the Cold War? (page 703)

The arms race associated with the rivalry between the West and the Soviets produced the largest peacetime militaries in world history. The reliance of both sides on nuclear weapons meant that any direct conflict had the potential to escalate into a global holocaust. For more than fifty years massed armies faced each other across Europe. This confrontation was projected into space, as each side sought to advertise its technological capacity through satellite launches and finally a moon landing. During the Cold War leaders of the opposing alliances viewed their struggle as a global conflict between irreconcilable systems. This meant that every popular movement, revolution, or civil war was strategically important and could involve the superpowers or their allies.

What problems did less developed nations face? (page 707)

In the postwar period, the end of colonial rule in Africa and South Asia left behind territorial conflicts that led to wars between India and Pakistan and between Israel and its Arab neighbors. In China frustration with the weak and corrupt government helped propel Mao Zedong's communist revolutionaries to power. Faced with exploding populations and intractable poverty, many newly installed nationalist governments adopted Soviet-style economic institutions and policies to foster economic development and political self-determination.

How did U.S. policies during the Cold War affect Latin America? (page 714)

Latin American nationalists aimed for economic independence and an end to foreign intervention. Fidel Castro identified these goals with those of countries struggling for independence in Asia and Africa. Fear of communist revolution led the United States to support counter-revolutionary uprisings, coups, and military dictatorships in several Latin American countries.

Why were developments in China so different from those in other parts of East Asia? (page 718)

Protected by the American strategic umbrella, Japan turned its energies to building the world's second-largest capitalist economy, and was quickly followed by the four Asian Tigers. In China, in contrast, victory against the Nationalists and war against the United States and its allies allowed Mao Zedong to instigate social revolutions along communist lines.

What roles did nationalism and religious fundamentalism play in Middle Eastern politics? (page 721)

In the Middle East, nationalist movements were directed not just at former colonial powers, but also at Israel and its allies in the West. In Iran and Afghanistan, nationalism rejected both Western-style secular nationalism and Soviet-style communism and found expression in a revival of Islamic fundamentalism.

What led to the collapse of the Soviet bloc? (page 725)

The decline of the Soviet economy and its defeat in Afghanistan weakened the hold of the Communist Party on the Soviet people and of the USSR on the nations of eastern Europe. As communists lost control, first the eastern European nations and then the smaller republics of the Soviet Union declared their independence.

Key Terms

Iron Curtain *(p. 703)*

Cold War *(p. 703)*

North Atlantic Treaty Organization (NATO) *(p. 703)*

United Nations *(p. 703)*

World Bank *(p. 704)*

Marshall Plan *(p. 704)*

European Community (EC) *(p. 704)*

Truman Doctrine *(p. 706)*

Warsaw Pact *(p. 706)*

Korean War *(p. 706)*

Cuban Missile Crisis *(p. 707)*

nonaligned nations *(p. 709)*

Third World *(p. 709)*

Vietnam War *(p. 711)*

Salvador Allende *(p. 718)*

Sandinistas *(p. 718)*

keiretsu (p. 719)

Cultural Revolution (China) *(p. 720)*

Asian Tigers *(p. 720)*

newly industrialized economies (NIEs) *(p. 721)*

Organization of Petroleum Exporting Countries (OPEC) *(p. 723)*

Ayatollah Ruhollah Khomeini *(p. 724)*

Saddam Husayn *(p. 724)*

Mikhail Gorbachev *(p. 725)*

perestroika (p. 725)

Solidarity *(p. 726)*

Web Resources

Pronunciation Guide

Interactive Maps

- MAP 29.1 Decolonization, 1947–1999
- MAP 29.2 Middle East Oil and the Arab-Israeli Conflict, 1947–1973
- MAP 29.3 The End of Soviet Domination in Eastern Europe

Primary Sources

- Comments on Algeria
- The Rivonia Trial Speech to the Court
- One Hundred Items for Destroying the Old and Establishing the New

Answer to the History in Focus Question

See photo on page 711, "The Vietnamese People at War."

 CourseMate Visit the CourseMate website at www.cengagebrain.com for additional study tools and review materials for this chapter.

Challenges of the New Century

© Cengage Learning

CHAPTER PREVIEW

Technological Change and the World Economy
How have recent technological changes impacted the world economy?

The Population Boom
What explains differences in the rate of population growth among the world's regions?

Unequal Development and the Movement of Peoples
How have differences in wealth between nations influenced global migration patterns?

The Global Environment
What is causing changes in the global environment, and how are people responding to it?

Global Culture and Traditions
What has caused the rise of a global culture, and what reactions has it provoked?

Trends and Visions
What roles do religious beliefs and secular ideologies play in the contemporary world?

Conclusion

DIVERSITY & DOMINANCE:
Conflict and Civilization

Visit the CourseMate website at **www.cengagebrain.com** for additional study tools and review materials for this chapter.

On October 12, 1999, the population of the earth reached 6 billion: there were now over three times as many people as there had been a hundred years earlier. A decade later, on February 16, 2010, there were 803 million more humans in the world than there were in 1999.

The pace of technology has been equally fast. In 1999, there were approximately 600 million cars and light trucks; ten years later, there were 200 million more. At the beginning of the twentieth century, as we saw in Chapter 24, people in the industrialized nations had just experienced the most rapid changes in technology the world had ever seen. Yet at the time there were only a few hundred cars in the world, all of them hand-made; there were also no airplanes, televisions or radios, cell phones, computers or the Internet, rockets, or satellites. Genetic engineering and nuclear power were unknown.

Population growth and technological change are the engines that have changed the world and promise to change it even more in the future. They, in turn, have caused long-range changes in the environment and in world culture. These trends will continue to transform the world. As the first twenty-nine chapters in this book have shown, however, history is also a narrative of sudden shocks: wars, revolutions, assassinations, economic crashes, and other unexpected events. In 1988 no one would have predicted that the Soviet Union would be dissolved three years later.

The fact that so much of history is unexpected means we cannot know what surprises the new century holds for the world. Yet major trends can be predicted with a fair degree of probability. This chapter discusses the underlying trends of the current world.

Technological Change and the World Economy

How have recent technological changes impacted the world economy?

The technological innovations that powered the economic expansion after World War II did so by increasing productivity and disseminating human creativity.

Because most of the economic benefits were concentrated in the advanced industrialized nations, technology increased the power of those nations relative to the developing world. Even within developed nations, postwar technological innovations did not benefit all classes, industries, and regions equally.

The multiplication of farms, factories, and cars intensified environmental threats. Loss of rain forest, soil erosion, global warming, pollution of air and water, and extinction of species imperiled the future. Environmental regulations progressed furthest in the wealthiest societies but did not stem the tide of environmental change.

Improvements in existing technologies accounted for much of the developed world's productivity increases during the 1950s and 1960s. Larger and faster trucks, trains, and airplanes cut transportation costs. Both capitalist and socialist governments expanded highway systems, improved railroads, and constructed airports and nuclear power plants.

Yet no technology had a greater impact than the computer. By the mid-1980s, desktop computers had replaced typewriters in most of the developed world's offices, and technological advances continued. By the beginning of the twenty-first century, personal computers were in every home, and even cars, cell phones, and other devices contained computer chips. Each new generation of computers was faster and more powerful than the one before.

Computers also altered manufacturing. Small dedicated computers were used to control and monitor machinery in some industries. European and Japanese companies were the first to introduce such robots into the factory. The transnational corporation became the primary agent of these technological changes. In the post–World War II years, many companies with multinational ownership and management invested in and marketed products throughout the world. International trade agreements and open markets furthered the process.

As transnational manufacturers, agricultural conglomerates, and financial giants became wealthier and more powerful, they increasingly escaped the controls imposed by national governments. If labor costs were too high in Japan, antipollution measures too intrusive in the United States, or taxes too high in Great Britain, transnational companies relocated—or threatened to do so. Governments in the developing world were often hard-pressed to control the actions of these powerful enterprises. As a result, the worst abuses of labor or of the environment usually occurred in poor nations.

Globalization of the World Economy

The turn of the millennium saw the intensification of **globalization** trends that had been building since the 1970s. Growing trade and travel and new technologies were bringing all parts of the world into closer economic, political, and cultural integration. The collapse of the Soviet Union had completed the dissolution of territorial empires that had been under way throughout the twentieth century. In their place were some two hundred independent nations, a growing number of which embraced democratic institutions. The rapid integration of world trade and markets convinced world leaders of the need to balance national autonomy with international agreements and associations.

The expansion of global trade and communications and the privatization of government enterprises fueled an economic boom in the 1990s and again from 2002 to 2008. The United States was crucial to the world economic system. The gigantic U.S. economy, larger than the economies of the next five countries combined—Japan, Germany, Great Britain, China (including Hong Kong), and France—also consumed by far the largest portion of the world's natural resources, including over a quarter of annual global oil production.

The economies of China and India grew quickly after 2001, and the very large populations of these two countries marked them as future world economic powers. Their growth put particular pressure on world energy supplies. OPEC's manipulation of world oil prices, combined with political events like the Iranian Revolution of 1979, had caused crude oil prices to soar between 1973 and 1985. But aside from those years, the average price of oil remained consistently below $20 per barrel (adjusted for inflation) throughout the second half of the twentieth century. In the year 2000, however, oil prices began a new period of increase caused by rising demand, especially in the United States and Asia, and by political turmoil in the Middle East. By the middle of 2006, the price of

a barrel of crude had crept past $70. A year and a half later it hit $100. This increase not only boosted the national incomes of major producing countries such as Russia, Iran, and Saudi Arabia but also caused energy security to overtake the formation of international trade associations as a matter of global economic concern.

Among the regional trade associations that had come into being to promote growth, reduce the economic vulnerability of member states, and, less explicitly, balance American economic dominance, the European Union (EU) was the most successful (see Map 30.1). Twelve member states adopted a new common currency, the euro, in 2002, making the Euro-bloc a formidable competitor with the United States for investment and banking. Ten new members from eastern Europe were admitted to the EU in May 2004. Despite the EU's expansion, the North American Free Trade Agreement (NAFTA), which eliminated tariffs among the United States, Canada, and Mexico in 1994, governed the world's largest free-trade zone. However, a heated debate in the United States over illegal immigration across the Mexican border limited popular enthusiasm for the agreement. The third largest free-trade zone, Mercosur, created by Argentina, Brazil, Paraguay, and Uruguay in 1991, decided in 2002 to allow the free movement of people within its area and gave equal employment rights to the citizens of all member states. Other free-trade associations operated in West Africa, southern Africa, Southeast Asia, Central America, the Pacific Basin, and the Caribbean.

The Shanghai Cooperation Organization (SCO), which formed in 2001 with China, Russia, and four former parts of the USSR—Kazakhstan (KAH-zahk-stahn), Kyrgyzstan (KER-gihz-stahn), Tajikistan (tah-JEHK-ih-stahn), and Uzbekistan (ooz-BEHK-ih-stahn)—as members, originally pursued common security interests, such as combating separatist movements and terrorism. But its announced twenty-year plan for reducing barriers to trade and population movements took a step forward in 2006 when Iran,

globalization The economic, political, and cultural integration and interaction of all parts of the world brought about by increasing trade, travel, and technology.

Chronology

	Politics	Economics and Society
2000	**2000** Al-Qaeda attacks American destroyer USS Cole in Yemen	
2001	**2001** Terrorists destroy the World Trade Center and damage the Pentagon on September 11	**2001** Shanghai Cooperation Organization formed **2001** U.S. withdraws from Kyoto Protocol on global warming **2001** Al-Jazeera television in Qatar begins broadcasting statements by Usama bin Laden
2002		**2002** Euro currency adopted in twelve European countries
2003	**2003** United States and Britain invade and occupy Iraq	
2004	**2004** Terrorists bomb Spanish trains	**2004** Ten new members admitted to European Union
2005	**2005** Terrorists bomb London transit system	
2008	**2008** Barack Obama elected president of the United States	

a country with observer status, signaled its desire to expand relations with the SCO. Bringing Iran's oil-rich economy into alignment with a rapidly developing China and a similarly oil-rich Russia, then recovering from the period of post-Soviet economic turmoil, promised to complicate the world economic and political picture.

Because of the inequalities and downturns that are intrinsic to free economic markets, the global bodies that tried to manage world trade and finance found it hard to convince poorer nations that they were not concerned only with the welfare of richer countries. In 1995 the world's major trading powers established the **World Trade Organization (WTO)** to encourage reduced trading barriers and enforce international trade agreements. Despite a membership of 150 nations by 2007, the WTO had many critics and regularly encountered street protests during its ministerial meetings. Some protesters feared that low-cost foreign manufacturers would shrink the job opportunities in richer states; others demanded continuing tariff protection for local farmers.

Countries in economic trouble had little choice but to turn to the international financial agencies for funds to keep things from getting worse. The International Monetary Fund (IMF) and World Bank (see Chapter 29) made their assistance conditional on

internal economic reforms that were often politically unpopular, such as terminating government subsidies for basic foodstuffs, cutting social programs, and liberalizing investment. The bitter pill of economic reform sometimes paid off in long-term improvement, but it also fueled popular criticism of the international economic system.

The emphasis on free trade led to changes in government-to-government aid programs. During the Cold War, countries had often gained funds for economic development by allying themselves with one of the superpowers. When the Cold War ended, foreign economic aid to poor nations fell by a third. On an African tour in 2000 President Bill Clinton told African countries that the days of large handouts were over and that they would have to rely on their own efforts to expand their economies.

In the face of rising criticism at home and protests at international meetings, however, world leaders rethought their positions and pledged to increase attention to the problem of economic despair, especially in Africa. At a Millennium Summit in September 2000 the states of the United Nations agreed to

World Trade Organization (WTO) An international body established in 1995 to foster and bring order to international trade.

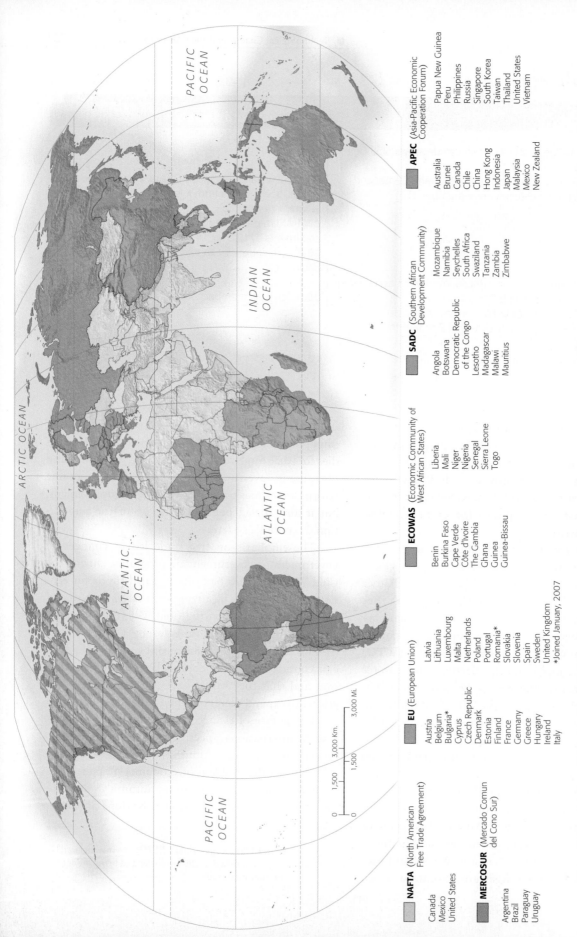

NAFTA (North American Free Trade Agreement)

Canada
Mexico
United States

MERCOSUR (Mercado Comun del Cono Sur)

Argentina
Brazil
Paraguay
Uruguay

EU (European Union)

Austria
Belgium*
Bulgaria*
Cyprus
Czech Republic
Denmark
Estonia
Finland
France
Germany
Greece
Hungary
Ireland
Italy

Latvia
Lithuania
Luxembourg
Malta
Netherlands
Poland
Portugal
Romania*
Slovakia
Slovenia
Spain
Sweden
United Kingdom

*Joined January, 2007

ECOWAS (Economic Community of West African States)

Benin
Burkina Faso
Cape Verde
Côte d'Ivoire
The Gambia
Ghana
Guinea
Guinea-Bissau

Liberia
Mali
Niger
Nigeria
Senegal
Sierra Leone
Togo

SADC (Southern African Development Community)

Angola
Botswana
Democratic Republic of the Congo
Lesotho
Madagascar
Malawi
Mauritius

Mozambique
Namibia
Seychelles
South Africa
Swaziland
Tanzania
Zambia
Zimbabwe

APEC (Asia-Pacific Economic Cooperation Forum)

Australia
Brunei
Canada
Chile
China
Hong Kong
Indonesia
Japan
Malaysia
Mexico
New Zealand

Papua New Guinea
Peru
Philippines
Russia
Singapore
South Korea
Taiwan
Thailand
United States
Vietnam

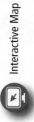 Interactive Map

Map 30.1 Regional Trade Associations, 2004 International trade and development are major concerns of governments in developed and developing countries. NAFTA, Mercosur, and the EU are free-trade areas. The other associations promote trade and development. © Cengage Learning

make sustainable development and the elimination of world poverty their highest priorities. A 2002 United Nations meeting in Monterrey, Mexico, called for special commitments to Africa. In practice, however, special consideration of Africa's economic plight seldom resulted in major increases in support.

China Rejoins the World Economy

After Mao Zedong's death in 1976 the Chinese communist leadership began economic reforms that relaxed state control, allowing more initiative and permitting individuals to accumulate wealth. Under China's leader **Deng Xiaoping** (dung shee-yao-peng) China permitted foreign investment for the first time since the communists came to power in 1949. Between 1979 and 2005 foreign direct investment in China grew to $618 billion as McDonald's, General Motors, Coca-Cola, Airbus, and many other foreign companies began doing business. But state-owned enterprises still employed more than 100 million workers, and most foreign-owned companies were limited to special economic zones. The result was a dual industrial sector—one modern, efficient, and connected to international markets, the other directed by political decisions. The combination of economic reforms, massive investments, and technology transfers from developed nations made China one of the world's major industrial powers in the early twenty-first century. By 2009 it had the world's third largest economy, after the United States and Japan.

Despite great improvements, the Chinese people remained poor on average. Per capita GDP in China reached $2,360 in 2009, one-third that of Mexico.

 History in Focus *Why, in an age of motor vehicles and skyscrapers, does the woman in the picture carry her goods in baskets? What does this tell you about the pace and unevenness of modernization in China? Find the answer online.*

Shanghai—Old Meets New The city of Shanghai is one of the great success stories in a rapidly growing Chinese economy, but its prosperity has left many behind. In this photo a poor woman walks past Shanghai's modern skyline carrying goods to market in baskets and a neck yoke, a technology thousands of years old.

Dennis Cox/China Stock

Further progress depended on the ability of an ever more globalized market to consume China's growing production. When a worldwide crisis began in 2008, Chinese exports fell, yet the Chinese economy continued to grow to fulfill domestic demand.

The Population Boom

What explains differences in the rate of population growth among the world's regions?

For most of human history, population growth was viewed as beneficial, and human beings were seen as a source of wealth. Since the late eighteenth century, however, population growth has been viewed with increasing alarm. Some feared that food supplies could not keep up with population growth. Others foresaw class and ethnic struggle as numbers overwhelmed resources. By the second half of the twentieth century, population growth was increasingly seen as a threat to the environment.

The Industrialized Nations

In the late eighteenth and early twentieth centuries, educated Europeans were ambivalent about the rapid increase in human population. Some saw it as a blessing that would promote economic well-being. Others warned that the seemingly relentless increase would bring disaster. The best-known pessimist was the English cleric **Thomas Malthus**, who in 1798 argued that unchecked population growth would outstrip food production. To terrify his European readers, he claimed that a visitor to China "will not be surprised that mothers destroy or expose many of their children; that parents sell their daughters for a trifle; . . . and that there should be such a number of robbers. The surprise is that nothing still more dreadful should happen."[1]

The population of Europe almost doubled between 1850 and 1914, putting enormous pressure on rural land and urban housing and overwhelming fragile public institutions. This dramatic growth forced a large wave of immigration across the Atlantic, helping to develop the Western Hemisphere and invigorating the Atlantic economy. Population growth also contributed to Europe's Industrial Revolution by lowering labor costs and increasing consumer demand.

In the generation that came of age after World War II, the views of Malthus were casually dismissed as industrial and agricultural productivity multiplied supplies of food and other necessities, while expanded female employment, older age at marriage, and more effective family planning combined to slow the rate of population increase. By the late 1960s Europe and other industrial societies had made what was called the **demographic transition** to lower fertility rates (average number of births per woman) and reduced mortality. The number of births in the developed nations was just adequate for the maintenance of current population levels.

In much of Europe and Japan at the beginning of the twenty-first century, fertility levels are so low that population will fall unless immigration increases. In Japan, women have an average of 1.39 children; in Italy, the number is 1.2. Sweden provides cash payments, tax incentives, and job leaves to families with children, but the average number of births there fell to 1.4 in recent years. The low fertility found in mature industrial nations is tied to higher levels of female education and employment, the material values of consumer culture, and access to contraception and abortion. Educated women now defer marriage and child rearing until they are established in careers.

As fertility has declined in the industrialized nations of western Europe, life expectancy has improved because of more abundant food, improved hygiene, and better medical care. Italy, for example, soon will have more than twenty adults fifty years

Deng Xiaoping (1904–1997) Communist Party leader who forced Chinese economic reforms after the death of Mao Zedong.

Thomas Malthus (1766–1834) Eighteenth-century English intellectual who warned that population growth threatened future generations because, in his view, population growth would always outstrip increases in agricultural production.

demographic transition A change in the rates of population growth. Before the transition, both birthrates and death rates are high, resulting in a slowly growing population; then the death rate drops but the birthrate remains high, causing a population explosion; finally the birthrate drops and the population growth slows down. This transition took place in Europe in the late nineteenth and early twentieth centuries, in North America and East Asia in the mid-twentieth century, and, most recently, in Latin America and South Asia.

TABLE 30.1　**Population for World and Major Areas, 1750–2050**

Population Size (Millions) (estimated)

Major Area	1750	1800	1850	1900	1950	1995	2050
World	791	978	1,262	1,650	2,521	5,666	8,909
Africa	106	107	111	133	221	697	1,766
Asia	502	635	809	947	1,402	3437	5,268
Europe	163	203	276	408	547	728	628
Latin America and the Caribbean	16	24	38	74	167	480	809
North America	2	7	26	82	172	297	392
Oceania	2	2	2	6	13	28	46

Percentage Distribution (estimated)

Major Area	1750	1800	1850	1900	1950	1995	2050
World	100.0	100.0	100.0	100.0	100.0	100.0	100.0
Africa	13.4	10.9	8.8	8.1	8.8	12.0	19.8
Asia	63.5	64.9	64.1	574	55.6	61.0	59.1
Europe	20.6	20.8	21.9	24.7	21.7	13.0	7.0
Latin America and the Caribbean	2.0	2.5	3.0	4.5	6.6	8.0	9.1
North America	0.3	0.7	2.1	5.0	6.8	5.0	4.4
Oceania	0.3	0.2	0.2	0.4	0.5	1.0	0.5

Source: J. D. Durand, "Historical Estimates of World Population: An Evaluation" (Philadelphia: University of Pennsylvania, Population Studies Center, 1974, mimeographed); United Nations, *The Determinants and Consequences of Population Trends*, vol. 1 (New York: United Nations, 1973); United Nations, *World Population Prospects as Assessed in 1963* (New York: United Nations, 1966); United Nations, *World Population Prospects: The 1998 Revision* (New York: United Nations, forthcoming); United Nations Population Division, Department of Economic and Social Affairs, http://www.census.gov/ipc/prod/wp98/wp98 .pdf, page A-3.

old or over for each five-year-old child. Japan faces an even more drastic aging of its population. This demographic transformation presents a challenge very different from the one foreseen by Malthus. These nations generally offer a broad array of social services, including retirement income, medical services, and housing supplements for the elderly. As the number of retirees increases relative to the number of people who are employed, the costs of these services may become unsustainable.

In contrast, in Russia and some former communist nations, life expectancy and birthrates have both fallen. Life expectancy for Russian men is now only fifty-seven years, down almost ten years since 1980. In the Czech Republic, Hungary, and Poland, life expectancy is improving in response to improved economic conditions, but most of the rest of eastern Europe follows the Russian pattern of declining life expectancy. High unemployment, low incomes, food shortages, and the dismantling of the social welfare system of the communist era have all contributed to this decline.

The Developing Nations

Unlike population growth in the eighteenth and nineteenth centuries, when much of the increase occurred in the wealthiest nations, population growth at the end of the twentieth century was overwhelmingly in the poorest nations. Although fertility rates dropped in most developing nations, they remained much higher than rates in the industrialized nations. At the same time, improvements in hygiene and nutrition caused mortality rates to fall. The result has been rapid population growth.

At current rates, 95 percent of all future population growth will be in developing nations (see Table 30.1). A comparison between Europe and Africa illustrates these changes. In 1950, Europe had twice the population of Africa. By 1985, Africa had drawn even. According to projections, by 2025 Africa's population will be three times larger than Europe's.

By the late 1970s, the demographic transition had not occurred in the poorer countries and the issue of population growth became politicized. The leaders of some developing nations argued that larger populations would increase national power. Industrialized, mostly white, nations raised concerns about rapid population growth in Asia, Africa, and Latin America. Populist political leaders in those regions asked whether these concerns were not fundamentally racist. The question temporarily disarmed Western advocates of birth control.

However, once the economic shocks of the 1970s and 1980s revealed the vulnerability of developing economies, governments in the developing world jettisoned policies that promoted population growth. In the 1970s the government of Mexico had encouraged high fertility, and population growth rose to 3 percent per year. In the 1980s, after the Mexican government began to promote birth control, its annual population growth fell in the 1990s to 1.7 percent.

Mortality rates have also increased in some areas as improved transportation facilitates the transmission of disease. The rapid spread of HIV/AIDS is an example of this phenomenon. Less-developed regions with poorly funded public health institutions and with few resources to invest in prevention and treatment experience the highest rates of infection and the greatest mortality. In Russia, for example, new HIV infections rose from under five thousand in 1997 to over ninety thousand in 2001. AIDS has spread at a similar pace in China. But the disease has developed most quickly and with the most devastating results in Africa, the home of 28 million of the world's 40 million infected people.

SECTION REVIEW

- In the twentieth century, populations exploded in the world's poorest nations.
- The demographic transition of the industrialized nations failed to occur in the Third World, politicizing the population issue.
- Economic hardships of the 1970s and 1980s forced developing nations to discourage population growth.
- Populations continue to expand in the developing world.
- In Japan and much of industrialized Europe, low fertility rates and higher life expectancy have effected a demographic transformation.

As the 1990s ended, the populations of India and China continued to grow despite government efforts to reduce family size. In China, efforts to enforce a limit of one child per family led to large-scale female infanticide as rural families sought to produce male heirs. India's policies of forced sterilization created widespread outrage and led to the electoral defeat of the ruling Congress Party. Yet both countries achieved some successes. Between 1960 and 1982, India's birthrate fell from 48 to 34 per 1,000, while China's rate declined even more sharply—from 39 to 19. Still, by 2025, China and India will each have some 1.5 billion people.

Chinese Family-Planning Campaign Hoping to slow population growth, the Chinese government has sought to limit parents to a single child. Billboards and other forms of mass advertising have been an essential part of the campaign to gain compliance with national family-planning directives.

Picard/Sipa Press

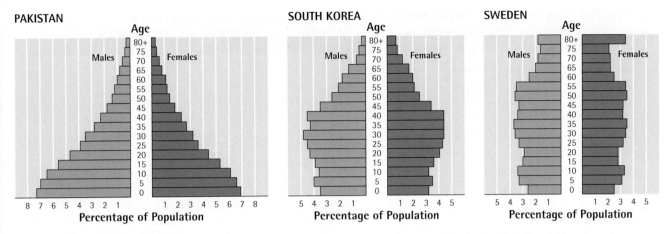

Figure 30.1 Age Structure Comparison Islamic Nation (Pakistan), Non-Islamic Developing Nation (South Korea), and Developed Nation (Sweden), 2001. *Source*: U.S. Bureau of the Census, *International Database*, 2001.

Old and Young Populations

Population pyramids generated by demographers clearly illustrate the profound transformation in human reproductive patterns and life expectancy in the years since World War II. Figure 30.1 shows the 2001 age distributions in Pakistan, South Korea, and Sweden—nations at three different stages of economic development. Sweden is a mature industrial nation. South Korea is rapidly industrializing and has surpassed many European nations in both industrial output and per capita wealth. Pakistan is a poor, traditional Muslim nation with rudimentary industrialization, low educational levels, and little effective family planning.

In 2001 nearly 50 percent of Pakistan's population was under age sixteen. The resulting pressures on the economy have been extraordinary. Every year approximately 150,000 men reach age sixty-five—and another 1.2 million turn sixteen. Pakistan, therefore, has to create more than a million new jobs a year or face steadily growing unemployment and steadily declining wages. Sweden confronts a different problem. Sweden's aging population, growing demand for social welfare benefits, and declining labor pool means that its industries may become less competitive and living standards may decline. In South Korea, a decline in fertility dramatically altered the ratio of children to adults, creating an age distribution similar to that of western Europe earlier in the twentieth century. South Korea does not face Pakistan's impossible task of creating new jobs or Sweden's growing demands for welfare benefits for the aged.

The demographic problem and potential technological adjustments are most clearly visible in Japan. Japan has the oldest population in the world, with a current median age of forty-one. Whereas large numbers of young immigrants from poorer nations are entering the work forces of Canada, Germany, the United States, and most other industrialized nations, slowing the aging of these populations, Japan has resisted immigration, instead investing heavily in technological solutions to the problems created by its aging labor force. As of 1994 Japan had 75 percent of the world's industrial robots. Although Japanese industries are able to produce more goods with fewer workers, Japan will still face long-term increases in social welfare payments.

Unequal Development and the Movement of Peoples

How have differences in wealth between nations influenced global migration patterns?

Two characteristics of the postwar world should now be clear. First, despite decades of experimentation with state-directed economic development, most nations that were poor in 1960 were as poor or poorer at the end of the 1990s. The only exceptions were a few rapidly developing Asian industrial nations and an equally small number of oil-exporting nations. Second, world population increased to startlingly high levels, and most of the increase was in the poorest nations.

| TABLE 30.2 | The World's Largest Metropolitan Areas (population of 10 million or more) |

City	1950	City	1975	City	2000	City	2015
1 New York	12.3	1 Tokyo	19.8	1 Tokyo	26.4	1 Tokyo	26.4
		2 New York	15.9	2 Mexico City	18.1	2 Bombay	26.1
		3 Shanghai	11.4	3 Bombay	18.1	3 Lagos	23.2
		4 Mexico City	11.2	4 Sao Paulo	17.8	4 Dhaka	21.1
		5 São Paulo	10.0	5 New York	16.6	5 Sao Paulo	20.4
				6 Lagos	13.4	6 Karachi	19.2
				7 Los Angeles	13.1	7 Mexico City	19.2
				8 Calcutta	12.9	8 New York	17.4
				9 Shanghai	12.9	9 Jakarta	17.3
				10 Buenos Aires	12.6	10 Calcutta	17.3
				11 Dhaka	12.3	11 Delhi	16.8
				12 Karachi	11.8	12 Metro Manila	14.8
				13 Delhi	11.7	13 Shanghai	14.6
				14 Jakarta	11.0	14 Los Angeles	14.1
				15 Osaka	11.0	15 Buenos Aires	14.1
				16 Metro Manila	10.9	16 Cairo	13.8
				17 Beijing	10.8	17 Istanbul	12.5
				18 Rio de Janeiro	10.6	18 Beijing	12.3
				19 Cairo	10.6	19 Rio de Janeiro	11.9
						20 Osaka	11.0
						21 Tianjin	10.7
						22 Hyderabad	10.5
						23 Bangkok	10.1

Source: International Migration Report 2002, United Nations, Department of Economic and Social Affairs, Population Division, "World Urbanization Prospects: The 1999 Revision," p. 6. The United Nations is the author of the original material. Reprinted by permission of United Nations Publications.

The combination of intractable poverty and growing population generated a surge in international migration, both legal and illegal. Few other issues stirred more controversy. Even moderate voices sometimes framed the discussion of immigration as a competition among peoples. One commentator summarized his analysis this way: "As the better-off families of the northern hemisphere individually decide that having only one or at the most two children is sufficient, they may not recognize that they are in a small way vacating future space (that is, jobs, parts of inner cities, shares of population, shares of market preferences) to faster-growing ethnic groups both inside and outside their boundaries. But that, in fact, is what they are doing."[2]

The Problem of Growing Inequality

Since 1945, global economic productivity has expanded more rapidly than at any other time in the past. Faster, cheaper communications and transportation have combined with improvements in industrial and agricultural technologies to create levels of material abundance that would have amazed those who experienced the first Industrial Revolution (see Chapter 21). Despite this remarkable economic expansion and growing market integration, the majority of the world's population remains in poverty. The industrialized nations of the Northern Hemisphere now enjoy a larger share of the world's wealth than they did a century ago. As a result, the gap between rich and poor nations has grown much wider. The thousands of homeless street children who live among the gleaming glass and steel towers of Rio's banking district can be seen as a metaphor for the social consequences of postwar economic development.

Inequalities of wealth between regions within nations also grew, especially in developing nations. Capital cities such as Buenos Aires, in Argentina, and Lagos, in Nigeria, attracted large numbers of migrants from rural areas because they offer more opportunities, even if those opportunities could not compare to the ones available in developed nations.

Garbage Dump in Manila, Philippines In Third World nations thousands of poor families live by sorting and selling bottles, aluminum cans, plastic, and newspapers in urban landfills.

Even in the industrialized world, people were divided into haves and have-nots. During the presidency of Ronald Reagan (1981–1989), wealth inequality in the United States reached its highest level since the 1929 stock market crash. Some scholars estimated that the wealthiest 1 percent of households in the United States controlled more than 30 percent of the nation's total wealth. Even in Europe, where tax and inheritance laws redistributed wealth, unemployment, homelessness, and substandard housing were increasingly common.

Internal Migration: The Growth of Cities

Migration from rural areas to urban centers in developing nations increased threefold from 1925 to 1950. After that, the pace accelerated (see Table 30.2). Shantytowns sprawling around major cities in developing nations are commonly seen as signs of social breakdown and economic failure. Nevertheless, even in the shantytowns city life was generally better than life in the countryside. A World Bank study esti-

mated that three out of four migrants to cities made economic gains. Residents of cities in sub-Saharan Africa, for example, were six times more likely than rural residents to have safe water. An unskilled migrant from the depressed northeast of Brazil could triple his or her income by moving to Rio de Janeiro.

As the scale of rural-to-urban migration grew, these benefits proved more elusive, however. In many West African cities, basic services crumbled under the pressure of rapid population growth. In 1990 in Mexico City, one of the world's largest cities, more than thirty thousand people lived in garbage dumps, where they scavenged for food and clothing.

Worsening conditions and the threat of crime and political instability led many governments to try to slow migration to cities and, in some cases, to return people to the countryside. Indonesia, for example, has relocated more than half a million urban residents since 1969. Despite some successes with slowing the rate of internal migration, nearly every poor nation still faces the challenge of rapidly growing cities.

SECTION REVIEW

- Despite rapid postwar economic growth, most of the world remains impoverished.
- Wealth inequality within nations and between industrialized and developing nations continues to grow.
- Internal migration from rural to urban areas has rapidly increased the size of cities in developing nations since World War II.
- Migrants initially made economic gains, but their numbers are overwhelming limited urban resources.
- Migration from developing to industrialized nations has created growing social and cultural tensions in host countries.

Global Migration

Each year, hundreds of thousands of men and women leave the developing world to emigrate to industrialized nations. After 1960, this movement increased in scale, and ethnic and racial tensions in the host nations worsened. By the 1990s, levels of immigration posed daunting social and cultural challenges for both host nations and immigrants.

When an expanding European economy first confronted labor shortages in the 1960s, many European nations actively promoted guest worker programs and other inducements to immigration. However, attitudes toward immigrants changed as the size of the immigrant population grew and as European economies slowed in the 1980s. Facing higher levels of unemployment, native-born workers saw immigrants as competitors willing to work for lower wages and less likely to support unions.

Because immigrants generally are young adults and retain the positive attitudes toward early marriage and large families common in their native lands, immigrant communities in Europe and the United States tended to have higher fertility rates than the host populations. In Germany in 1975, for example, immigrants made up about 7 percent of the population but accounted for nearly 15 percent of all births. Although the fertility of the Hispanic population in the United States is lower than in Mexico and other Latin American nations, Hispanics will contribute well over 20 percent of all population growth in the United States during the next twenty-five years.

As the Muslim population in Europe and the Asian and Latin American populations in the United States expand in the twenty-first century, cultural conflicts will test definitions of citizenship and nationality. The United States will have some advantages in meeting these challenges because of long experience with immigration and relatively open access to citizenship. Yet in the 1990s, the United States was moving slowly in the direction of European efforts to restrict immigration and defend a culturally conservative definition of nationality.

The Global Environment

What is causing changes in the global environment, and how are people responding to it?

In the 1960s, environmental activists and political leaders began warning about the devastating environmental consequences of population growth, industrialization, and the expansion of agriculture onto marginal lands. Assaults on rain forests and redwoods, the disappearance of species, and the poisoning of streams and rivers raised public consciousness. Environmental damage occurred in the advanced industrial economies and in the poorest of the developing nations. Perhaps the worst environmental record was achieved in the former Soviet Union, where industrial and nuclear wastes were often dumped with little concern for environmental consequences. The accumulated effect of scientific studies and public debate led to national and international efforts to slow, if not undo, damage to the environment.

The expanding global population required increasing quantities of food, housing, energy, and other resources as the twentieth century ended (see Map 30.2). In the developed world, the consumer-driven economic expansion of the post–World War II years became an obstacle to addressing environmental problems. How could the United States, Germany, or Japan change consumption patterns to protect the environment without endangering corporate profits, wages, and employment levels?

Many developing countries saw exploitation of their environmental resources and industrialization as the solution to their rapidly growing populations. The results were predictable: erosion and pollution.

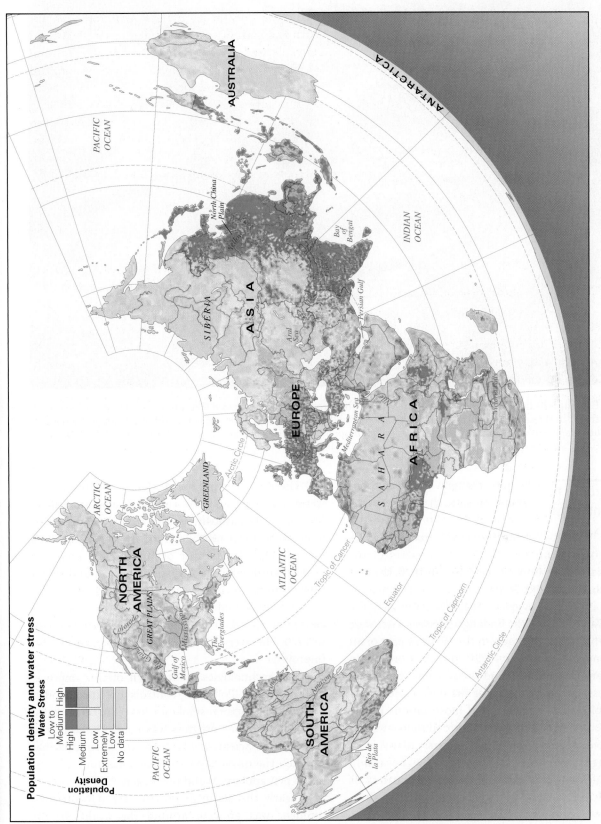

Map 30.2 Fresh Water Resources This map links population density and the availability of water. Red areas are highly stressed environments where populations use at least 40 percent or more of available water. Less stressed environments are blue. The deeper the shade of red or blue the greater the environmental stress. *Source:* From "Global Water Stress," *National Geographic,* September 2002, pp. 14–16. NGS/National Geographic Image Collection. Reprinted by permission of the National Geographic Society.

Loss of Brazilian Rain Forest The destruction of large portions of Brazil's virgin rain forest has come to symbolize the growing threat to the environment caused by population growth and economic development. In this photograph we see a tragic moonscape of tree stumps and fragile topsoil ripped open by settlers. The name given to this place is "Bom Futuro" ("Good Future" in English).

Responding to Environmental Threats

Despite the gravity of environmental threats, there were many successful efforts to preserve and protect the environment. In 1968, a wave of student unrest swept many parts of the world. Earth Day was first celebrated in 1970, the year in which the United States established its Environmental Protection Agency. The Clean Air Act, the Clean Water Act, and the Endangered Species Act were passed in the United States in the 1970s as part of an environmental effort that included the nations of the European Community and Japan. Environmental awareness spread by means of the media and grassroots political movements, and most nations in the developed world enforced strict antipollution laws and sponsored massive recycling efforts. Many also encouraged resource conservation by rewarding energy-efficient factories and the manufacturers of fuel-efficient cars and by promoting the use of alternative energy sources such as solar and wind power.

These efforts produced significant results. In western Europe and the United States, air quality improved dramatically. In the United States, smog levels were down nearly a third from 1970 to 2000 even though the number of automobiles increased more than 80 percent. Emissions of lead and sulfur dioxide were down as well. The Great Lakes, Long Island Sound, and Chesapeake Bay were all much cleaner at the end of the century than they had been in 1970. The rivers of North America and Europe also improved.

New technologies made much of this improvement possible. Pollution controls on automobiles, planes, and factory smokestacks reduced harmful emissions. Similar progress was made in the chemical industry. Scientists identified the chemicals that threaten the ozone layer, and the phase-out of their use in new appliances and cars began.

Clearly the desire to preserve the natural environment was growing around the world. In the

Flooding in Bangladesh Typhoon-driven floods submerge the low-lying farmlands of Bangladesh with tragic regularity. Any significant rise in the sea level will make parts of the country nearly uninhabitable.

Dominique Auberl/Corbis Sygma

developed nations, continued political organization and enhanced awareness of environmental issues seemed likely to lead to step-by-step improvements in environmental policy. In the developing world and most of the former Soviet bloc, however, population pressures and weak governments were major obstacles to effective environmental policies. In China, for example, respiratory disease caused by pollution was the leading cause of death. Thus, it was likely that the industrialized nations would have to fund global improvements, and the cost was likely to be high.

Global Warming

Until the 1980s environmental alarms focused mainly on localized episodes of air and water pollution, exposure to toxic substances, waste management, and the disappearance of wilderness. The development of increasingly powerful computers and complex models of ecological interactions in the 1990s, however, made people aware of the global scope of certain environmental problems.

Many scientists and policymakers came to perceive global warming, the slow increase in the temperature of the earth's lower atmosphere, as an environmental threat requiring preventive action on an international scale. The warming is caused by a layer of atmospheric gases (carbon dioxide, methane, nitrous oxide, and ozone) that allow solar radiation to reach earth and warm it but that keep infrared energy (heat) from radiating from earth's surface into space. Called the greenhouse effect, this process normally keeps the earth's temperature at a level suitable for life. However, increases in greenhouse-gas emissions—particularly from the burning of fossil fuels in industry and transportation—have added to this insulating atmospheric layer.

Recent events have confirmed predictions of global temperature increases and melting glaciers and icecaps. Record heat hit northern Europe in the summer of 2003. Greenland glaciers and Arctic Ocean sea ice melted at record rates during 2002, and a huge section of the Antarctic ice shelf broke up and floated away. Andean glaciers are shrinking so fast they could disappear in a decade, imperiling water supplies for drinking, irrigation, and hydroelectric production. Drought has affected much of the United States in recent years, and in 2002 Australia experienced the "Big Dry," its worst drought in a century.

Despite this evidence, governments of the industrialized countries that produce the most greenhouse gases have been slow to adopt measures stringent enough to reduce emissions because of the negative effects they believe this could have on their economies. There is also fear that it may be already too late to reverse global warming. The pledges that representatives from 178 countries made at the first Earth Summit in Rio de Janeiro in 1992 to limit their *increase* in greenhouse-gas production have so far been ineffective. Fearing limits on gas emissions could cripple their plans for industrial and economic expansion, many nations hesitated to sign the 1997 Kyoto Protocol, the first international agreement to impose penalties on countries that failed to cut greenhouse-gas emissions. It was a major environmental victory when Japan added its signature in March 2001, but to the consternation of many world leaders President George W. Bush rejected the agreement. Ostensibly, he acted because he was unconvinced by the scientific evidence for global warming and reluctant to impose burdens on American businesses, but global security concerns also made the environment a lower American priority. Until the destructive effects of global warming, such as the inundation of coastal regions and large cities by rising sea levels, match the destruction of terrorists, the political focus is unlikely to shift.

Global Culture and Traditions

What has caused the rise of a global culture, and what reactions has it provoked?

Along with trade and migrations, cultural globalization was also proceeding rapidly at the turn of the millennium. A global language, a global educational system, and global forms of artistic expression have all come into being. Rapid and inexpensive electronic communications have enabled global cultural influences to move deeper into many societies, and a sort of global popular culture has also emerged. These changes have angered some and delighted others.

The Media and the Message

Although cultural influences from every continent travel around the world, the fact that the most pervasive elements of global culture have their origins in the West raises concerns in many quarters about **cultural imperialism**. Critics complain that entertainment conglomerates are flooding the world's movie theaters and television screens with Western tastes and styles and that manufacturers are flooding world markets with Western-style goods—both relying on sophisticated advertising techniques that promote consumption and cultural conformity. In this view, global marketing is an especially insidious effort to overwhelm the world with a Western outlook shaped by capitalist ideology and to suppress or devalue traditional cultures and alternative ideologies. As the leader of the capitalist world, the United States is viewed as the primary culprit.

But in truth, technology plays a more central role than ideology in spreading Western culture. Even though imperialist forces old and new shape choices, democratic forces are also at work as people around the world make their selections in the cultural marketplace. Thus, a diversity of voices is more characteristic of cultural globalization than the cultural imperialism thesis maintains.

Technological Innovations

The pace of cultural globalization began to quicken during the economic recovery after World War II. The Hollywood films and American jazz recordings that had become popular in Europe continued to spread. The birth of electronic technology opened

---

cultural imperialism Domination of one culture over another by a deliberate policy or by economic or technological superiority.

contacts with large numbers of people who could never have afforded to go to a movie or buy a record.

The first step was the development of cheap transistor radios that could run for months on a couple of small batteries. Perfected by American scientists in 1948, transistors replaced power-hungry tubes in radios and other devices. Small portable transistor radios, most made in Asia, spread rapidly in parts of the world where homes lacked electricity. The transistor radios sold in Asia and Africa brought people in remote villages the news, views, and music that American, European, Soviet, and Chinese transmitters beamed to the world. For the first time in history, the whole world could learn of major political and cultural events simultaneously. Although such broadcasts came in local and regional languages, many were in English. Audiotape and CD players added to the diversity of music available everywhere.

Television, which became widely available to Western consumers in the 1950s, spread to poorer parts of the world in the 1980s and 1990s after mass production and cheap transistors made sets more affordable and reliable. Outside the United States, television broadcasting was usually a government monopoly at first, following the pattern of telegraph and postal service and radio broadcasting. Governments expected news reports and other programming to disseminate a unified national viewpoint.

Government monopolies eroded as the high cost of television production opened up global markets for American soap operas, adventure series, and situation comedies. By the 1990s a global network of satellites brought television broadcasting to even remote areas of the world, and the VCR (videocassette recorder) brought an even greater variety of programs to people everywhere.

As a result of wider circulation of programming, people often became familiar with different dialects and languages. People in Portugal have become avid fans of Brazilian soap operas, and immigrants from Albania and North Africa often arrive in Italy with a command of Italian learned from Italian stations whose signals they could pick up at home. Specializing in rock music videos aimed at a youth audience, MTV (Music Television) became an international enterprise offering special editions in different parts of the world. Music videos shown in Uzbekistan, for example, often featured Russian bands, and Chinese groups appeared in MTV programs shown in Singapore. CNN (Cable News Network) expanded its international market after becoming the most-viewed and informative news source during the 1991 Persian Gulf War, when it broadcast live from Baghdad. CNN's fundamentally American view of the news stimulated broadcasters in other countries to develop their own round-the-clock coverage. Al-Jazeera, based in the Persian Gulf emirate of Qatar, offered video footage and interpretation that differed greatly from American news coverage after the war in Iraq began in 2003.

The Internet, a linkage of academic, government, and business computer networks, began to transform world culture in the early years of the twenty-first century. Personal computers proliferated in the 1980s, and with the establishment of the easy-to-use World Wide Web in 1994, the number of Internet users skyrocketed. Myriad new companies formed to exploit "e-commerce," the commercial dimension of the Internet, and college students were soon spending less time studying books and scholarly resources than they were exploring the Web for information and entertainment. Blogs offered a vehicle for anyone in the world to place his or her opinions, experiences, and creative efforts before anyone with access to a computer.

As so often happens, technological developments had unanticipated consequences. Although the new telecommunications and entertainment technologies derived disproportionately from American inventions, Japan and other East Asian nations came to dominate the manufacture and refinement of computer devices. In the 1990s Japan introduced digital television broadcasting at about the time that digital video disks (DVDs) containing movies and video games became available. High-definition television (HDTV), mostly in digital format, debuted in the first decade of the century and seemed destined to become the global standard. At the miniaturized end of the visual scale, cell phones became increasingly used for taking and transmitting pictures and connecting to the Internet.

The Spread of Pop Culture

New technologies changed perceptions of culture as well as its distribution around the world and among different social classes. For most of history, popular culture was folk culture, highly localized ways of dress, food, music, and expression. Only the educated and urban few had access to the riches of a broader "great tradition," such as Confucianism in East Asia or Western culture in Europe and the Americas. The schools of modern nation-states promoted national values and beliefs, as well as tastes in painting, literature, and art. Governments also promoted a common language and frequently suppressed local traditions and languages. The new electronic media helped break down barriers and create a global popular culture that transcended regional great traditions and national cultures.

Initially, the content of **global pop culture** was heavily American. Singer Michael Jackson was almost as well known to the youth of Tanzania and Thailand as to American fans. Basketball star Michael Jordan became a worldwide celebrity, heavily promoted by Nike, McDonald's, and television. American television programs such as *Wheel of Fortune* and *Friends* acquired immense followings and inspired local imitations. American movies, which had long had great popular appeal, steadily increased their share of world markets.

But the United States did not have a lock on global pop culture. Latin American soap operas, *telenovelas*, had a vast following in the Americas, eastern Europe, and elsewhere. Bombay, India, long the largest producer of films in the world, began to make films for an international audience, rather than just for the home market. And the highly successful martial arts filmmakers of Hong Kong saw their style flourish in high-budget international spectaculars like director Ang Lee's Academy Award–winning *Crouching Tiger, Hidden Dragon* (2000) and the *Matrix* trilogy (1999–2003), which relied heavily on the skills of Hong Kong fight choreographers.

Emerging Global Culture

While the globalization of popular culture has been criticized, cultural links across national and ethnic boundaries at a more elite level have generated little controversy. The end of the Cold War reopened intellectual and cultural contacts between former adversaries, making possible such things as Russian-American collaboration on space missions and extensive business contacts among former rivals. The English language, modern science, and higher education became the key elements of this **global elite culture**.

The emergence of English as the first global language depended on developments that had been building for centuries. Britain introduced the language to its far-flung colonies. When the parts of the British Empire gained independence after World War II, most former colonies continued to use English as their official language because it provided national unity and a link to the outside world that the dozens or hundreds of local languages could not. Newly independent countries that made a local language official for nationalist reasons often found the decision counterproductive. Indian nationalists who had pushed for Hindi to be India's official language found that students taught in Hindi were unable to compete internationally because of poor knowledge of English. Sri Lanka, which had made Sinhala its official language in 1956, reversed itself in 1989 after reports that prominent officials were sending their children to private English-language schools.

The use of English as a second language was greatly stimulated by the importance of the United States in world affairs. Individuals recognized the importance of mastering English for successful business, diplomatic, and military careers. After the collapse of Soviet domination, students in eastern Europe flocked to study English instead of Russian. Ninety percent of students in Cambodia, a former French colony, chose to study English instead of French. In the 1990s China made the study of English as a second language nearly universal from junior high school onwards.

English has become the language of choice for most international academic conferences, business meetings, and diplomatic gatherings. International organizations that provide equal status to many languages, such as the United Nations and the European

global pop culture Popular cultural practices and institutions that have been adopted internationally, such as music, the Internet, television, food, and fashion.

global elite culture At the beginning of the twenty-first century, the attitudes and outlook of well-educated, prosperous, Western-oriented people around the world, largely expressed in European languages, especially English.

Union, tend to conduct all informal committee meetings in English. English has even replaced Latin as the working language in the Catholic Church. In cities throughout the world, signs and notices are now posted in the local language and English.

The rise of English as a global language is also evident in the emergence of an international literature in English. The trend has been evident for decades in former British colonies in Africa, where most writers use English to reach both national and international audiences. Wole Soyinka, the first sub-Saharan African to win the Nobel Prize in literature for 1986, wrote in English, the national language of Nigeria, rather than his native Yoruba. When Arundhati Roy won the prestigious Booker Prize in 1997 for *The God of Small Things*, a novel set in her native state of Kerala in southwest India, she was part of an English-language literary tradition that has been growing in India for a century. V. S. Naipaul, winner of the Nobel Prize in literature for 2001, whose ancestors had emigrated from India to Trinidad in the nineteenth century, is a good example of the way global migration has fostered the use of English.

World literature remains highly diverse in form and language, but science and technology have become standardized components of global culture. Though imperialism helped spread the Western disciplines of biology, chemistry, and physics around the world, their popularity continued to expand even after imperial systems ended because they worked so much better than other approaches to the natural world. Global manufacturing could not function without a common system of applied science. Because of their scientific basis, Western medicine and drugs are increasingly accepted as the best treatments, even though many cultures also use traditional remedies.

The third pillar of global elite culture is the university. The structure and curricula of modern universities are nearly indistinguishable around the world, permitting students today to cross national boundaries as freely as students in the Latin West or the Muslim world did in medieval times. Instruction in the pure sciences varies little from place to place, and standardization is nearly as common in the social sciences and applied sciences such as engineering and medicine.

While university subjects are taught in many languages, instruction in English is spreading rapidly.

Because discoveries are often first published in English, advanced students in science, business, and international relations need to know that language to keep up with the latest developments. The global mobility of professors and students also promotes classroom instruction in the most global language. Many courses in the Netherlands and in Scandinavian countries have long been offered in English, and elsewhere in Europe offering more courses in English was the obvious way to facilitate the European Union's efforts to encourage students to study outside their countries of origin. When South Africa ended the apartheid educational systems that had required people to study in their own languages, most students chose to study in English.

Enduring Cultural Diversity

Although protesters regularly denounce the "Americanization" of the world, a closer look suggests that cultural globalization is more complex and multifaceted. Just as English has largely spread as a second language, so global culture is primarily a second culture that dominates some contexts but does not displace other traditions. From this perspective, American music, fast food, and fashions are more likely to add to a society's options than to displace local culture.

Japan first demonstrated that a country with a non-Western culture could perform at a high industrial level. Individuality was less valued in Japan than the ability of each person to fit into a group, whether as an employee, a member of an athletic team, or a student in a class. Moreover, the Japanese considered it unmannerly to directly contradict, correct, or refuse the request of another person. From a Western point of view, these Japanese customs seemed to discourage individual initiative and personality development and to preserve traditional hierarchies. Even though Japanese women often worked outside the home, they responded slowly to the Western feminists' advocacy of gender equality. However, the Japanese approach to social relations was well suited to an industrial economy. The efficiency, pride in workmanship, and group solidarity of Japanese workers, supported by closely coordinated government and corporate policies, played a major role in transforming Japan into an economic power by the 1980s.

Japan's success in the modern industrial world called into question the older assumption that successful industrialization required the adoption of Western culture. As awareness of the economic impact of Japanese culture and society began to spread, it became apparent that Taiwan, South Korea, Singapore, and Hong Kong were developing dynamic industrial economies of their own. The prospect of India and China following the same path led many observers to predict that by the end of the twenty-first century the United States and Europe would no longer dominate the globe in industrial creativity and might.

This does not mean that the world's cultural diversity is secure. Every decade a number of minority languages cease to be spoken. Televised national ceremonies or performances for tourists may prevent folk customs and costumes from dying out, but they also tend to devitalize rituals that once had many local variations. While a century ago it was possible to recognize the nationality of people from their clothing and grooming, today most urban men dress the same the world over, although women's clothing shows greater variety. As much as one may regret the disappearance or commercialization of some folkways, most anthropologists would agree that change is characteristic of all healthy cultures. What doesn't change risks extinction.

Trends and Visions

What roles do religious beliefs and secular ideologies play in the contemporary world?

As people around the world faced the opportunities and problems of globalization, they tried to make sense of these changes in terms of their own cultures and beliefs. With 6 billion people, the world was big enough to include many different approaches, whether religious or secular, local or international, traditional or visionary. In some cases, however, conflicting visions fed violence.

Faith and Politics

Religious beliefs increasingly inspired political actions during the second half of the twentieth century, and the trend intensified as the new century began. Though for Americans this change reversed two centuries of growing secularism, Western analysts did not agree on the cause of the religious revival.

Evangelical Protestants have become a powerful conservative political force in the United States. Catholic conservatives led by Pope John Paul II, who died in 2005, and his successor Pope Benedict XVI forcefully reiterated politically sensitive teachings, such as opposition to abortion, homosexuality, marriage of priests, and admission of women to the priesthood. In Israel, ultra-orthodox Jews played a leading role in settling the West Bank and Gaza, the Palestinian territories captured by Israel in 1967. And in India, Hindu zealots made the BJP party a powerful political force.

Yet Islam became the focus of most discussions of faith and politics. The birth of the Islamic Republic of Iran in 1979 made the current of Muslim political assertiveness, which had been building in several Muslim countries for twenty years, visible to all. But by the year 2000 acts of **terrorism** perpetrated by Muslim groups claiming to be acting for religious reasons were capturing the headlines.

Terrorism is a political tactic by which comparatively weak militants use violent acts against civilians to convince a frightened public that danger is everywhere and the government is incapable of protecting them. Though terrorism has a long history, instantaneous communications and the tradition in the news

terrorism Political belief that extreme and seemingly random violence will destabilize a government and permit the terrorists to gain political advantage. Though an old technique, terrorism gained prominence in the late twentieth century with the growth of worldwide mass media that, through their news coverage, amplified public fears of terrorist acts.

David Allocca/Timepix/Time Life Pictures/Getty Images

Terrorists Attack New York On September 11, 2001, two airplanes commandeered by Al Qaeda terrorists crashed into the twin towers of the World Trade Center in New York City, destroying them and killing over three thousand people. In this photograph, an airplane has just crashed into the building on the left while the one on the right, having been hit a few minutes earlier, is already collapsing.

business of publicizing violence increased its effectiveness from the 1980s onward.

Bombings, kidnappings, and assassinations made political sense to all sorts of political groups: Palestinians confronting Israel; national separatists like the Tamils in Sri Lanka, Basques in Spain, and Chechens in Russia; Catholic and Protestant extremists in Northern Ireland; and racialist militias in Rwanda and Darfur, to name a few. But al-Qaeda gained the lion's share of attention because it targeted the United States and Europe, concentrated on spectacular attacks, drew from Muslims all over the world, and made effective use of video and audio communications from its charismatic leader, **Usama bin Laden**.

Born into a wealthy Saudi family and educated as an engineer, bin Laden fought against the Soviet Union in Afghanistan and there recruited and trained a core group of fighters called al-Qaeda. Though his family disowned him and Saudi Arabia stripped him of his citizenship, his calls for a holy war (*jihad*) and his portrayal of the United States as an evil puppet-master manipulating both non-Muslim and Muslim governments to murder and oppress innocent Muslims made sense to millions of Muslims, even if only a very few committed themselves to follow him into battle.

Al-Qaeda blew up the American embassies in Kenya and Tanzania in 1998, crippled the U.S. Navy destroyer *Cole* while it was making a port call in Yemen in 2000, and then capped everything by crashing hijacked jetliners into the World Trade Center and the Pentagon on September 11, 2001. Though the "global war on terrorism" declared in response by President George W. Bush successfully destroyed the Afghan government that had given bin Laden safe haven, bin Laden and his primary deputy, the Egyptian Ayman Zawahiri, could not be found. Further terrorist attacks—by Indonesians on tourists on the island of Bali in 2002, by North Africans on commuter trains servicing Madrid in 2004, and by English-born Muslims on the London transit system in 2005—made it clear that the violence unleashed by al-Qaeda had become decentralized and that recruits and cells might no longer be taking orders from bin Laden.

In trying to explain a current of violence that seemed to be centered on Muslims, some people argued that Islam encouraged violence against non-Muslims and that rigidly conservative Muslims like Usama bin Laden were opposed to freedom and modernity. The counterargument pointed out that the vast majority of Muslims saw their religion as one of peace, that al-Qaeda used modern military and propaganda techniques, and that many of its operatives, like bin Laden himself, graduated from modern technical programs. To those who argued that the United States had instigated al-Qaeda's wrath by supporting

Usama bin Laden Saudi-born Muslim extremist who founded the al-Qaeda organization that was responsible for several terrorist attacks, including those on the World Trade Center and the Pentagon in 2001.

Diversity & Dominance

Conflict and Civilization

In 1993 Samuel P. Huntington, a professor of government at Harvard University, published "The Clash of Civilizations?" in the journal Foreign Affairs. *This article provoked extraordinary debate, particularly after the 9/11 attacks on the World Trade Center and the Pentagon. Some readers deemed it an accurate description of a post–Cold War world in which Islamic countries were destined to conflict violently with the countries of Europe and North America. Others saw it as imprecise in its failure to clarify what a "civilization" is, imperialistic in its unquestioning assumption of Western superiority, and encouraging of anti-Muslim prejudice.*

The interactions between civilizations vary greatly in the extent to which they are likely to be characterized by violence. Economic competition clearly predominates between the American and European subcivilizations of the West and between both of them and Japan. . . . In Eurasia the great historic fault lines between civilizations are once more aflame. This is particularly true along the boundaries of the crescent-shaped Islamic bloc of nations from the bulge of Africa to central Asia. Violence also occurs between Muslims, on the one hand, and Orthodox Serbs in the Balkans, Jews in Israel, Hindus in India, Buddhists in Burma and Catholics in the Philippines. Islam has bloody borders.

Huntington drew his inspiration and his key phrase from "The Roots of Muslim Rage," a 1990 article in The Atlantic Monthly *by Bernard Lewis, an influential historian of the Middle East who was frequently and favorably cited by key members of the Bush administration.*

At first the Muslim response to Western civilization was one of admiration and emulation—an immense respect for the achievements of the West, and a desire to imitate and adopt them. This desire arose from a keen and growing awareness of the weakness, poverty, and backwardness of the Islamic world as compared with the advancing West. . . .

In our time this mood of admiration and emulation has, among many Muslims, given way to one of hostility and rejection. In part this mood is surely due to a feeling of humiliation—growing awareness, among the heirs of an old, proud, and long dominant civilization, of having been overtaken, overborne, and overwhelmed by those whom they regarded as their inferiors. . . .

Ultimately, the struggle of the fundamentalists is against two enemies, secularism and modernism. The war against secularism is conscious and explicit, and there is by now a whole literature denouncing secularism as an evil neo-pagan force in the modern world and attributing it variously to the Jews, the West, and the United States. The war against modernity is for the most part neither conscious nor explicit, and is directed against the whole process of change that has taken place in the Islamic world in the past century or more and has transformed the political, economic, social, and even cultural structures of Muslim countries. Islamic fundamentalism has given an aim and a form to the otherwise aimless and formless resentment and anger of the Muslim masses at the forces that have devalued their traditional values and loyalties and, in the final analysis, robbed them of their beliefs, their aspirations, their dignity, and to an increasing extent even their livelihood.

There is something in the religious culture of Islam which inspired, in even the humblest peasant or peddler, a dignity and a courtesy toward others never exceeded and rarely equaled in other civilizations. And yet, in moments of upheaval and disruption, when the deeper passions are stirred, this dignity and courtesy toward others can give way to an explosive mixture of rage and hatred which impels even the government of an ancient and civilized country—even the spokesman of a great spiritual and ethical religion—to espouse kidnapping and assassination, and try to find, in the life of their Prophet, approval and indeed precedent for such actions. . . .

It should be now be clear that we are facing a mood and a movement far transcending the level of issues and policies and the governments that pursue them. This is no less than a clash of civilizations—the perhaps irrational but surely historic reaction of an ancient rival against our Judeo-Christian heritage, our secular present, and the worldwide expansion of both. It is crucially important that we on our side should not be provoked into an equally historic but also equally irrational reaction against that rival.

Rejoinders to Huntington's thesis saw it as a cornerstone of the aggressive policies adopted by the Bush administration after 9/11. As an alternative, they stressed the common values held by peaceful societies and the need for intercultural understanding. Mohammed Khatami, the president of the Islamic Republic of Iran, found support for a more positive framing of the matter when the United Nations, following his proposal, declared 2001 the year of "Dialogue Among Civilizations." Almost simultaneously, the Organization of the Islamic Conference, a fifty-seven-member international body headquartered in Saudi Arabia and composed of states with large Muslim populations, elaborated upon this concept in the "Tehran Declaration on Dialogue Among Civilizations."

Tehran Declaration on Dialogue Among Civilizations

Praise be to Allah and peace and blessing be upon His prophet and kin and companion.

The representatives of Heads of State and Government of OIC member states ... [recognizing] the United Nations General Assembly resolution 53/22, designating the year 2001 as the United Nations year of Dialogue among Civilizations;

Guided by the noble Islamic teachings and values [each of the following principles is accompanied by reference to a verse in the Quran] on human dignity and equality, tolerance, peace and justice for humankind, and promotion of virtues and proscription of vice and evil;

Drawing upon the Islamic principles of celebration of human diversity, recognition of diversified sources of knowledge, promotion of dialogue and mutual understanding, genuine mutual respect in human interchanges, and encouragement of courteous and civilized discourse based on reason and logic;

Reaffirming the commitment of their Governments to promote dialogue and understanding among various cultures and civilizations, aimed at reaching a global consensus to build a new order for the next millennium founded in faith as well as common moral and ethical values of contemporary civilizations;

Requests the Secretary-General of the OIC to submit this declaration for endorsement to the Chairman of the Eighth Islamic Summit and the 26th Islamic Conference of Foreign Ministers for appropriate action:

A) General principles of dialogue among civilizations
1. Respect for the dignity and equality of all human beings without distinctions of any kind and of nations large and small;
2. Genuine acceptance of cultural diversity as a permanent of human society and a cherished asset for the advancement and welfare of humanity at large;
3. Mutual respect and tolerance for the views and values of various cultures and civilizations, as well as the right of members of all civilizations to preserve their cultural heritage and values, and rejection of desecration of moral, religious or cultural values, sanctities and sanctuaries;
4. Recognition of diversified sources of knowledge throughout time and space, and the imperative of drawing upon the areas of strengths, richness and wisdom of each civilization in a genuine process of mutual enrichment;
5. Rejection of attempts for cultural domination and imposition as well as doctrines and practices promoting confrontation and clash between civilizations;
6. Search for common grounds between and within various civilizations in order to face common global challenges;

Acceptance of cooperation and search for understanding as the appropriate mechanism for the promotion of common universal values as well as for the suppression of global threats;
7. Commitment to participation of all peoples and nations, without any discrimination, in their own domestic as well as global decision-making and value distribution processes;
8. Compliance with principles of justice, equity, peace and solidarity as well as fundamental principles of international law and the United Nations Charter. . . .

A few years later, a joint proposal by the governments of Spain and Turkey received a similar endorsement by the United Nations. This led to the creation of the Alliance of Civilizations. The underlying principles of this organization were expressed in the 2006 report of its "High-level Group," a body of eminent political, intellectual, and spiritual figures from around the world.

Alliance of Civilizations Report of the High-Level Group

I. Bridging the World's Divides

1.1 Our world is alarmingly out of balance. For many, the last century brought unprecedented progress, prosperity, and freedom. For others, it marked an era of subjugation, humiliation and dispossession. Ours is a world of great inequalities and paradoxes: a world where the income of the planet's three richest people is greater than the combined income of the world's least developed countries; where modern medicine performs daily miracles and yet 3 million people die every year of preventable diseases; where we know more about distant universes than ever before, yet 130 million children have no access to education; where despite the existence of multilateral covenants and institutions, the international community often seems helpless in the face of conflict and genocide. For most of humanity, freedom from want and freedom from fear appear as elusive as ever.

1.2 We also live in an increasingly complex world, where polarized perceptions, fueled by injustice and inequality, often lead to violence and conflict, threatening international stability. Over the past few years, wars, occupation and acts of terror have exacerbated mutual suspicion and fear within and among societies. Some political leaders and sectors of the media, as well as radical groups have exploited this environment, painting mirror images of a world made up of mutually exclusive cultures, religions, or civilizations, historically distinct and destined for confrontation.

1.3 The anxiety and confusion caused by the "clash of civilizations" theory regrettably has distorted the terms of the discourse on the real nature of the predicament the world is facing. The history of relations between cultures is not only one of wars and confrontation. It is also based on centuries of constructive exchanges, cross-fertilization, and peaceful co-existence. Moreover, classifying internally fluid and diverse societies along hard-and-fast lines of civilizations interferes with more illuminating ways of understanding questions of identity, motivation and behavior. Rifts between the powerful and the powerless or the rich and the poor or between different political groups, classes, occupations and nationalities have greater explanatory power than such cultural categories. Indeed, the latter stereotypes only serve to entrench already polarized opinions. Worse, by promoting the misguided view that cultures are set on an unavoidable collision course, they help turn negotiable disputes into seemingly intractable identity-based conflicts that take hold of the popular imagination. It is essential, therefore, to counter the stereotypes and misconceptions that deepen patterns of hostility and mistrust among societies.

QUESTIONS FOR ANALYSIS

1. How important are culture and religion, as opposed to governing ideology or economic inequality, in explaining current world conflicts?

2. Do statements like these reflect the realities of international and intercommunal relations? Or do they merely serve the political interests of the authors?

3. Should general statements about culture play a role at the level of personal relations in the neighborhood, the workplace, or the classroom?

Sources: First selection: Samuel P. Huntington, "The Clash of Civilizations?," *Foreign Affairs* 72, no. 3 (Summer 1993); Second selection: Excerpts from Bernard Lewis, "The Roots of Muslim Rage," *The Atlantic Monthly*, September 1990, pp. 47–60. Reprinted by permission of the author. Third selection: "The Tehran Declaration on Dialogue Among Civilizations," Organization of the Islamic Conference, available online at www.isesco.org.ma/english/publications/dlg/CH11.php; Fourth selection: "High-Level Group Report," Alliance of Civilizations, from www.unaoc.org/content/view/6494/lang.english/, a publication of the UN Alliance of Civilizations. Reprinted by permission of the United Nations Alliance of Civilizations.

Israel and stationing troops in Saudi Arabia, others pointed out that the United States had championed the Muslim cause in Bosnia.

Whether Islam and the West were destined to fight one another in a "clash of civilizations," as political scientist Samuel Huntington predicted, or whether their differences would eventually be resolved within a common "Islamo-Christian civilization," as Richard W. Bulliet maintained in response to Huntington, fear of terrorism became pervasive throughout the world, and many peaceful Muslims found themselves suspect because of their beliefs (see Diversity and Dominance: Conflict and Civilization).

Universal Rights and Values

Alongside the growing influence of religion on politics, efforts to promote adherence to universal standards of human rights also expanded. The modern human rights movement grew out of the French Declaration of the Rights of Man (1789) and the U.S. Constitution (1788) and Bill of Rights (1791). Over the next century, the logic of universal rights moved Westerners to undertake international campaigns to end slave trading and slavery throughout the world and to secure equal rights for women.

International organizations in the twentieth century secured agreement on labor standards, the

President Barack Obama at Cairo's Sultan Hassan Mosque Tensions between the United States and the Muslim world diminished somewhat after President Obama gave a speech in Cairo directed at Muslims. Speaking less than five months after taking office, he praised the positive elements of Islam and recognized the negative impact of American policies related to the Iraq War and the stringent anti-terrorist measures taken by the Bush administration. Iman Abdel Fateh, standing between the president and Secretary of State Hillary Rodham Clinton, served as a guide.

rules of war, and the rights of refugees. The pinnacle of these efforts was the **Universal Declaration of Human Rights**, passed by the United Nations General Assembly in 1948, which proclaimed itself "a common standard of achievement for all peoples and nations." Its thirty articles condemned slavery, torture, cruel and inhuman punishment, and arbitrary arrest, detention, and exile. The Declaration called for freedom of movement, assembly, and thought. It asserted rights to life, liberty, and security of person; to impartial public trials; and to education, employment, and leisure. The principle of equality was most fully articulated in Article 2:

> Everyone is entitled to all the rights and freedoms set forth in this Declaration, without distinction of any kind, such as race, color, sex, language, religion, or political or other opinion, national or social origin, property, birth or other status.[3]

This passage reflected an international consensus against racism and imperialism and a growing acceptance of the importance of social and economic equality. Most newly independent countries joining the United Nations willingly signed the Declaration because it implicitly condemned European colonial regimes.

The idea of universal human rights has not gone unchallenged. Some have asked whether a set of principles whose origins are so clearly Western can be called universal. Others have been uneasy with the idea of subordinating the traditional values of their culture or religion to a broader philosophical standard. Despite these objections, important gains have been made in implementing these standards.

Besides the official actions of the United Nations and various national governments, **nongovernmental organizations (NGOs)** have been important forces

---

Universal Declaration of Human Rights A 1948 United Nations covenant binding signatory nations to the observance of specified rights.

nongovernmental organizations (NGOs) Nonprofit international organizations devoted to investigating human rights abuses and providing humanitarian relief. Two NGOs won the Nobel Peace Prize in the 1990s: International Campaign to Ban Landmines (1997) and Doctors Without Borders (1999).

for promoting human rights. Amnesty International, founded in 1961 and numbering 1.8 million members in 162 countries by the 1990s, concentrates on gaining the freedom of people who have been tortured or imprisoned without trial and on campaigns against summary execution by government death squads and other gross violations of rights. Other NGOs have devoted themselves to famine relief, refugee assistance, and health care around the world. Médecins Sans Frontières (Doctors Without Borders), founded in 1971, was awarded the Nobel Peace Prize for 1999 for the medical assistance it offered in scores of crisis situations.

While NGOs often worked on individual situations in specific countries, other universal goals became enshrined in international agreements. Such agreements have made genocide a crime and have promoted environmental protection of the seas, of Antarctica, and of the atmosphere. However, the United States and a few other nations were greatly concerned that such treaties would unduly limit their sovereignty or threaten their national interests. For this reason the U.S. Congress delayed ratifying the 1949 convention on genocide until 1986. More recently the United States demanded exemption for Americans from the jurisdiction of the International Criminal Court, created in 2002 to try international criminals, and declared that "enemy combatants" taken prisoner during the "global war on terrorism" should not be treated in accordance with the Third Geneva Convention (1950) on humane treatment of prisoners of war. While these two actions grew out of America's acknowledged role as the one superpower capable of intervening in military crises anywhere in the world, the American withdrawal in 2001 from the 1997 Kyoto Protocol requiring industrial nations to reduce pollutants that damage the atmosphere reflected the economic interests of power companies, vehicle makers, and manufacturers.

Women's Rights

The women's rights movement, which began on both sides of the North Atlantic in the nineteenth century, became an important human rights issue in the twentieth century. Rights for women became accepted in Western countries and were enshrined in the constitutions of many nations newly freed from colonial rule. In 1979

the United Nations General Assembly adopted the Convention on the Elimination of All Forms of Discrimination Against Women, and in 1985 the first international conference on the status of women, sponsored by the United Nations Division for the Advancement of Women, was held in Nairobi, Kenya. A second conference in Beijing ten years later added momentum to the women's rights movement. By 2007, 183 countries had endorsed the 1979 convention.

Besides highlighting the similarity of the problems women face around the world, international conferences have also revealed great variety in the views and concerns of women. Feminists from the West, who had been accustomed to dictating the agenda and who had pushed for the liberation of women in other parts of the world, were sometimes accused of having narrow concerns and condescending attitudes. Some non-Western women complained about Western feminists' endorsement of sexual liberation and about the deterioration of family life in the West. They also found Western feminists' concern with matters such as comfortable clothing misplaced and trivial compared to the issues of poverty and disease.

Other cultures came in for their share of criticism. Western women and many secular leaders in Muslim countries protested Islam's requirement that a woman cover her head and wear loose-fitting garments to conceal the shape of her body, practices enforced by law in countries such as Iran and Saudi Arabia. Nevertheless, many outspoken Muslim women voluntarily donned concealing garments as expressions of personal belief, statements of resistance to secular dictatorship, or defense against coarse male behavior. Much Western criticism focused on the African custom of female circumcision, a form of genital mutilation that can cause chronic infections or permanently impair sexual enjoyment. While not denying the problems this practice can lead to, many African women saw deteriorating economic conditions, rape, and AIDS as more important issues.

The conferences were more important for the attention they focused on women's issues than for the solutions they generated. The search for a universally accepted women's rights agenda proved elusive because of local concerns and strong disagreement on abortion and other issues. Nevertheless, increases in women's education, access to employment, political participation, and control of fertility augured well for the eventual achievement of gender equality.

Such efforts raised the prominence of human rights as a global concern and put pressure on governments to consider human rights when making foreign policy decisions. Skeptics observed, however, that a Western country could successfully prod a non-Western country to improve its human rights performance—for example, by granting women more equal access to education and careers—but that reverse criticism of a Western country often fell on deaf ears—for example, condemnation of the death penalty in the United States. For such critics the human rights movement was seen not as an effort to make the world more humane but as another form of Western cultural imperialism, a club with which to beat former colonial societies. Still, support for universal rights has grown, especially because increasing globalization has made common standards of behavior more important.

Conclusion

Unlike the conclusion of previous chapters, the conclusion of this chapter, which describes the current situation of the world, looks toward a future that is only partially clear. For, as the introduction to this chapter pointed out, the future consists of both trends, which we can predict, and events, which we cannot.

Many of the trends outlined in this chapter will continue for a generation or more. Technology will continue to advance, especially in areas such as the media and telecommunications, new sources of energy, and breakthroughs in biotechnology. The populations of the richer countries will stabilize or shrink, while those of the poorer countries will continue to rise, causing economic hardships and increased migrations to the wealthier countries. The global environment will become warmer and more polluted, contributing to the economic difficulties of both rich and poor countries, especially low-lying parts of the world like Bangladesh and Florida. Global cultures will continue to merge and integrate, increasing economic opportunities but also threatening the world's diversity of languages and cultural traditions. Religious differences will continue to cause political conflicts. While English will remain the world's dominant language, the rise of China as an economic power will challenge the dominance of the United States. International meetings and organizations will continue to emphasize human rights, women's rights, the mitigation of environmental problems, and the peaceful resolution of conflicts, but their resolutions will not be matched by actions that conflict with the economic advantages that nations derive from current practices.

In contrast to trends, events are by nature unpredictable. Since 1945 the world has avoided a global war, even while nuclear arms proliferate. We cannot predict that this will continue, nor that it will end. Although the rise of China has so far been an economic success story, nations seldom change their relative economic positions without political repercussions. Terrorism, which operates in the shadows, remains a concern. Although we can make many intelligent guesses about what will happen in these conditions, we cannot know for sure.

Reflecting this dual nature of history, this text has described long-term trends as well as surprising and world-changing events. People have always stood "at the crossroads." Today's crossroads, which involve high technology and global integration, are different from those of a medieval knight on horseback, but they have the same dual quality of certainty and uncertainty. Like the generations of peoples who came before, the peoples of the world today can say they live in interesting times.

CHAPTER REVIEW

Download the MP3 audio file of the
Chapter Review to listen to on the go.

How have recent technological changes impacted the world economy? (page 731)

Dramatic changes in technology—especially in computers, communications networks, and the media—have helped integrate national and regional economies into a global economy that has benefited from improved efficiencies and a growing demand. The spectacular growth in the economy of China, fueled by the world's insatiable demand for its products, has been the most impressive change in the global economy.

What explains differences in the rate of population growth among the world's regions? (page 736)

The population growth of the richer nations of the world and of the former Soviet-bloc nations has slowed, and their populations have aged. The populations of Latin America and Asia have also slowed, but not as fast as they did in the mid-twentieth century. Meanwhile, despite severe health problems such as HIV/AIDS, the population of the poorest regions, especially sub-Saharan Africa, is still growing fast and therefore consists predominantly of young people.

How have differences in wealth between nations influenced global migration patterns? (page 739)

The poor, especially those living in rural areas, are leaving their homes in search of better opportunities. Most migrate to cities in their home countries, in numbers that far outstrip the ability of cities to provide jobs, housing, education, water, and sanitation. Many others cross continents and seas at great expense and risk to reach the richer countries of Europe and North America. Though they are willing to work hard for little pay, their presence is often resented by the native inhabitants, who fear the changes in culture and customs that immigrants bring.

What is causing changes in the global environment, and how are people responding to it? (page 742)

A growing economy has had profound effects on the global environment. The burning of fossil fuels and the release of other chemical emissions have caused the earth's climate to warm considerably since the mid-twentieth century. More warming is yet to come, which will cause changes in the weather and a rise in sea levels. International efforts to alleviate these problems have begun, but so far they have been insufficient to curb pollution and to slow down global warming.

What has caused the rise of a global culture, and what reactions has it provoked? (page 746)

Global communications have encouraged the rise of two common global cultures. Popular culture, especially in dress, food, and entertainment, was initially formed from Western values but now also includes many elements from other cultures. The parallel growth of a global elite culture has resulted from the spread of the English language, modern science, and increasingly uniform university curricula.

What roles do religious beliefs and secular ideologies play in the contemporary world? (page 750)

In much of the world, religious movements are gaining adherents. The growing influence of Islam has been particularly important, in part as a reaction to Western values and the secular ideologies of earlier generations of rulers. Extremists have used religion as an excuse to commit acts of terrorism. Meanwhile, certain universal values are also gaining ground. Among the most important are human rights and the rights of women.

Key Terms

globalization *(p. 732)*

World Trade Organization *(p. 733)*

Deng Xiaoping *(p. 735)*

Thomas Malthus *(p. 736)*

demographic transition *(p. 736)*

cultural imperialism *(p. 746)*

global pop culture *(p. 748)*

global elite culture *(p. 748)*

terrorism *(p. 750)*

Usama bin Laden *(p. 751)*

Universal Declaration of Human Rights *(p. 755)*

nongovernmental organizations (NGOs) *(p. 755)*

Web Resources

Pronunciation Guide

Interactive Map
• MAP 30.1 Regional Trade Associations, 2004

 Visit the CourseMate website at www.cengagebrain.com for additional study tools and review materials for this chapter.

Answer to the History in Focus Question
See photo on page 735, "Shanghai–Old Meets New."

Abbasid Caliphate Descendants of the Prophet Muhammad's uncle, al-Abbas, the Abbasids overthrew the Umayyad Caliphate and ruled an Islamic empire from their capital in Baghdad (founded 762) from 750 to 1258. (p. 219)

abolitionists Men and women who agitated for a complete end to slavery. Abolitionist pressure ended the British transatlantic slave trade in 1808 and slavery in British colonies in 1834. In the United States the activities of abolitionists were one factor leading to the Civil War (1861–1865). (p. 500)

Acheh Sultanate Muslim kingdom in northern Sumatra. Main center of Islamic expansion in Southeast Asia in the early seventeenth century, it declined after the Dutch seized Malacca from Portugal in 1641. (p. 449)

Aden Port city in the south Arabian country of Yemen. It has been a major trading center in the Indian Ocean since ancient times. (p. 325)

Adolf Hitler (1889–1945) Born in Austria, Hitler became a radical German nationalist during World War I. He led the National Socialist German Workers' Party—the Nazis—in the 1920s and became dictator of Germany in 1933. He led Europe into World War II. (p. 660)

African National Congress An organization dedicated to obtaining equal voting and civil rights for black inhabitants of South Africa. Founded in 1912 as the South African Native National Congress, it changed its name in 1923. Though it was banned and its leaders were jailed for many years, it eventually helped bring majority rule to South Africa. (p. 686)

Afrikaners South Africans descended from Dutch and French settlers of the seventeenth century. Their Great Trek founded new settler colonies in the nineteenth century. Though a minority among South Africans, they held political power after 1910, imposing a system of racial segregation called apartheid after 1949. (p. 610)

agricultural revolution (eighteenth century) The transformation of farming that resulted in the eighteenth century from the spread of new crops, improvements in cultivation techniques and livestock breeding, and the consolidation of small holdings into large farms from which tenants and sharecroppers were forcibly expelled. (p. 508)

Agricultural Revolutions (ancient) The change from food gathering to food production that occurred between ca. 8000 and 2000 B.C.E. Also known as the Neolithic Revolution. (p. 8)

Akbar (1542–1605) Most illustrious sultan of the Mughal Empire in India (r. 1556–1605). He expanded the empire and pursued a policy of conciliation with Hindus. (p. 446)

Akhenaten Egyptian pharaoh (r. 1353–1335 B.C.E.). He built a new capital at Amarna, fostered a new style of naturalistic art, and created a religious revolution by imposing worship of the sun-disk. The Amarna letters, largely from his reign, preserve official correspondence with subjects and neighbors. (p. 59)

Albert Einstein (1879–1955) German physicist who developed the theory of relativity, which states that time, space, and mass are relative to each other and not fixed. (p. 645)

Alexander (356–323 B.C.E.) King of Macedonia in northern Greece. Between 334 and 323 B.C.E. he conquered the Persian Empire, reached the Indus Valley, founded many Greek-style cities, and spread Greek culture across the Middle East. Later known as Alexander the Great. (p. 105)

Alexander Nevskii (ca. 1220–1263) Prince of Novgorod (r. 1236–1263). He submitted to the invading Mongols in 1240 and received recognition as the leader of the Russian princes under the Golden Horde. (p. 298)

Alexandria City on the Mediterranean coast of Egypt founded by Alexander. It became the capital of the Hellenistic kingdom of the Ptolemies. It contained the famous Library and the Museum—a center for leading scientific and literary figures. Its merchants engaged in trade with areas bordering the Mediterranean and the Indian Ocean. (p. 107)

All-India Muslim League Political organization founded in India in 1906 to defend the interests of India's Muslim minority. Led by Muhammad Ali Jinnah, it attempted to negotiate with the Indian National Congress. In 1940, the League began demanding a separate state for Muslims, to be called Pakistan. (p. 679)

altepetl An ethnic state in ancient Mesoamerica, the common political building block of that region. (p. 173)

amulet Small charm meant to protect the bearer from evil. Found frequently in archaeological excavations in Mesopotamia and Egypt, amulets reflect the religious practices of the common people. (p. 20)

Amur River This river valley was a contested frontier between northern China and eastern Russia until the settlement arranged in the Treaty of Nerchinsk (1689). (p. 464)

anarchists Revolutionaries who wanted to abolish all private property and governments, usually by violence, and replace them with free associations of groups. (p. 586)

Anasazi Important culture of what is now the southwest United States (700–1200). Centered on Chaco Canyon in New Mexico and Mesa Verde in Colorado, the Anasazi culture built multi-story residences and worshiped in subterranean buildings called kivas. (p. 176)

aqueduct A conduit, either elevated or underground, that used gravity to carry water from a source to a location—usually a city—that needed it. The Romans built many aqueducts in a period of substantial urbanization. (p. 147)

Arawak Amerindian peoples who inhabited the Greater Antilles of the Caribbean at the time of Columbus. (p. 358)

Armenia One of the earliest Christian kingdoms, situated in eastern Anatolia and the western Caucasus and occupied by speakers of the Armenian language. (p. 205)

Asante African kingdom on the Gold Coast that expanded rapidly after 1680. Asante participated in the Atlantic economy, trading gold, slaves, and ivory. It resisted British imperial ambitions for a quarter century before being absorbed into Britain's Gold Coast colony in 1902. (p. 614)

Ashikaga Shogunate (1338–1573) The second of Japan's military governments headed by a shogun (a military ruler). Sometimes called the Muromachi Shogunate. (p. 308)

Ashoka Third ruler of the Mauryan Empire in India (r. 269–232 B.C.E.). He converted to Buddhism and broadcast his precepts on inscribed stones and pillars, the earliest surviving Indian writing. (p. 123)

Ashurbanipal The seventh century B.C.E. Assyrian ruler who assembled a large collection of writings drawn from the ancient literary, religious, and scientific traditions of Mesopotamia. The many tablets unearthed by archaeologists constitute one of the most important sources of present-day knowledge of the long literary tradition of Mesopotamia.   (p. 68)

Asian Tigers   South Korea, Taiwan, Hong Kong, and Singapore, so-called because their economies expanded so fast.   (p. 720)

Atahualpa (1497–1533)   Last ruling Inca emperor of Peru. He was executed by the Spanish.   (p. 373)

Atlantic System   The network of trading links after 1500 that moved goods, wealth, people, and cultures around the Atlantic Ocean Basin.   (p. 409)

Augustus (63 B.C.E.–14 C.E.)   Honorific name of Octavian, founder of the Roman Principate, the military dictatorship that replaced the failing rule of the Roman Senate. After defeating all rivals, between 31 B.C.E. and 14 C.E. he laid the groundwork for several centuries of stability and prosperity in the Roman Empire.   (p. 142)

Auschwitz   Nazi extermination camp in Poland, the largest center of mass murder during the Holocaust. Close to a million Jews, Gypsies, communists, and others were killed there.   (p. 671)

Ayatollah Ruhollah Khomeini   Shi'ite philosopher and cleric who led the overthrow of the Shah of Iran in 1979 and created an Islamic republic.   (p. 724)

ayllu   Andean lineage group or kin-based community.   (p. 179)

Aztecs   Also known as Mexica, the Aztecs created a powerful empire in central Mexico (1325–1521). They forced defeated peoples to provide goods and labor.   (p. 173)

Babylon   The largest and most important city in Mesopotamia. It achieved particular eminence as the capital of the Amorite king Hammurabi in the eighteenth century B.C.E. and the Neo-Babylonian king Nebuchadnezzar in the sixth century B.C.E.   (p. 13)

balance of power   The policy in international relations by which, beginning in the eighteenth century, the major European states acted together to prevent any one of them from becoming too powerful.   (p. 403)

Balfour Declaration   Statement issued by Britain's Foreign Secretary Arthur Balfour in 1917 favoring the establishment of a Jewish national homeland in Palestine.   (p. 633)

Bannermen   Hereditary military servants of the Qing Empire, mostly descendants of various peoples who had fought for the founders of the empire.   (p. 540)

Bantu   Collective name of a large group of sub-Saharan African languages and of the peoples speaking these languages.   (p. 203)

Bartolomé de Las Casas (1474–1566)   First bishop of Chiapas, in southern Mexico. He devoted most of his life to protecting Amerindian peoples from exploitation. His major achievement was the New Laws of 1542, which limited the ability of Spanish settlers to compel Amerindians to labor for them.   (p. 410)

Bartolomeu Dias (1457–1500)   Portuguese explorer who in 1488 led the first expedition to sail around the southern tip of Africa from the Atlantic into the Indian Ocean.   (p. 362)

Batavia   Fort established ca. 1619 as headquarters of Dutch East India Company operations in Indonesia; today the city of Jakarta.   (p. 452)

Battle of Midway   U.S. naval victory over the Japanese fleet in June 1942, in which the Japanese lost four of their best aircraft carriers. It marked a turning point in World War II.   (p. 667)

Battle of Omdurman   British victory over the Mahdi in the Sudan in 1898. General Kitchener led a mixed force of British and Egyptian troops armed with rapid-firing rifles and machine guns.   (p. 604)

Beijing   China's northern capital, first used as an imperial capital in 906.   (p. 301)

Bengal   Region of northeastern India. It was the first part of India to be conquered by the British in the eighteenth century and remained the political and economic center of British India throughout the nineteenth century. The 1905 split of the province into predominantly Hindu West Bengal and predominantly Muslim East Bengal (now Bangladesh) sparked anti-British riots.   (p. 678)

Benito Mussolini (1883–1945)   Fascist dictator of Italy (1922–1943). He led Italy to conquer Ethiopia (1935), joined Germany in the Axis pact (1936), and allied Italy with Germany in World War II. He was overthrown in 1943 when the Allies invaded Italy.   (p. 659)

Berlin Conference (1884–1885)   Conference that German chancellor Otto von Bismarck called to set rules for the partition of Africa. It led to the creation of the Congo Free State under King Leopold II of Belgium.   (p. 609)

Bhagavad-Gita   The most important work of Indian sacred literature, a dialogue between the great warrior Arjuna and the god Krishna on duty and the fate of the spirit.   (p. 124)

Black Death   An outbreak of bubonic plague that spread across Asia, North Africa, and Europe in the mid-fourteenth century, carrying off vast numbers of persons.   (p. 335)

Blaise Diagne (1872–1934)   Senegalese political leader, the first African elected to the French National Assembly. During World War I, in exchange for promises to give French citizenship to Senegalese, he helped recruit Africans to serve in the French army. After the war, he led a movement to abolish forced labor in Africa.   (p. 686)

Bolsheviks   Radical Marxist political party founded by Vladimir Lenin in 1903. Under Lenin's leadership, the Bolsheviks seized power in November 1917 during the Russian Revolution.   (p. 634)

Borobodur   A massive stone monument on the Indonesian island of Java, erected by the Sailendra kings around 800 C.E. The winding ascent through ten levels, decorated with rich relief carving, is a Buddhist allegory for the progressive stages of enlightenment.   (p. 131)

bourgeoisie   In early modern Europe, the class of well-off town dwellers whose wealth came from manufacturing, finance, commerce, and allied professions.   (p. 393)

British raj   The rule over much of South Asia between 1765 and 1947 by the East India Company and then by a British government.   (p. 557)

bubonic plague   A bacterial disease that can be transmitted by flea bites to rodents and humans; humans in late stages of the illness can spread the bacteria by coughing. Because of its very high mortality rate and the difficulty of preventing its spread, major outbreaks have created epidemics in many parts of the world.   (p. 293)

Buddha (563–483 B.C.E.)   An Indian prince named Siddhartha Gautama, who renounced his wealth and social position. After becoming "enlightened" (the meaning of *Buddha*) he enunciated the principles of Buddhism. This doctrine evolved and spread throughout India and to Southeast, East, and Central Asia.   (p. 119)

Byzantine Empire   Historians' name for the eastern portion of the Roman Empire from the fourth century onward, taken from "Byzantion," an early name for Constantinople, the Byzantine capital city.   (p. 234)

caliphate   Office established in succession to the Prophet Muhammad, to rule the Islamic empire; also the name of that empire.   (p. 217)

calpolli   A group of up to a hundred families that served as a social building block of an altepetl in ancient Mesoamerica.   (p. 173)

capitalism The economic system of large financial institutions—banks, stock exchanges, investment companies—that first developed in early modern Europe. *Commercial capitalism,* the trading system of the early modern economy, is often distinguished from *industrial capitalism,* the system based on machine production. (p. 424)

caravel A small, highly maneuverable three-masted ship used by the Portuguese and Spanish in the exploration of the Atlantic. (p. 361)

Carthage City located in present-day Tunisia, founded by Phoenicians ca. 800 B.C.E. It became a major commercial center and naval power in the western Mediterranean until defeated by Rome in the third century B.C.E. (p. 76)

Catholic Reformation Religious reform movement within the Latin Christian Church, begun in response to the Protestant Reformation. It clarified Catholic theology and reformed clerical training and discipline. (p. 389)

Cecil Rhodes (1853–1902) British entrepreneur and politician involved in the expansion of the British Empire from South Africa into Central Africa. The colonies of Southern Rhodesia (now Zimbabwe) and Northern Rhodesia (now Zambia) were named after him. (p. 611)

Celts Peoples sharing a common language and culture that originated in central Europe in the first half of the first millennium B.C.E. After 500 B.C.E., they spread as far as Anatolia in the east and Spain and the British Isles in the west. They were later overtaken by Roman conquest and Germanic invasions. Their descendants survive on the western fringe of Europe (Brittany, Wales, Scotland, and Ireland). (p. 49)

Champa rice Quick-maturing rice that can allow two harvests in one growing season. Originally introduced into Champa from India, it was later sent to China as a tribute gift by the Champa state. (p. 280)

Chang'an City in the Wei Valley in eastern China. It became the capital of the Qin and early Han Empires. Its main features were imitated in the cities and towns that sprang up throughout the Han Empire. (p. 153)

Charlemagne (742–814) King of the Franks (r. 768–814); emperor (r. 800–814). Through a series of military conquests he established the Carolingian Empire, which encompassed all of Gaul and parts of Germany and Italy. Though illiterate himself, he sponsored a brief intellectual revival. (p. 234)

Charles Darwin (1809–1882) He developed the theory of evolution through natural selection. Author of *On the Origin of Species* (1859). (p. 592)

chartered companies Groups of private investors who paid an annual fee to France and England in exchange for a monopoly over trade to the West Indies colonies. (p. 424)

Chavín The first major urban civilization in South America (900–250 B.C.E.). Its capital, Chavín de Huántar, was located high in the Andes Mountains of Peru. Chavín became politically and economically dominant in a densely populated region that included two distinct ecological zones, the Peruvian coastal plain and the Andean foothills. (p. 165)

Chiang Kai-shek (1886–1975) Chinese military and political leader. He succeeded Sun Yat-sen as head of the Guomindang in 1925; headed the Chinese government from 1928 to 1948; and fought against the Chinese communists and Japanese invaders. After 1949 he headed the Chinese Nationalist government in Taiwan. (p. 662)

chiefdom Form of political organization with rule by a hereditary leader who held power over a collection of villages and towns. Less powerful than kingdoms and empires, chiefdoms were based on gift giving and commercial links. (p. 177)

Chimú Powerful Peruvian civilization based on conquest. Located in the region earlier dominated by Moche. Conquered by Inca in 1465. (p. 180)

chinampas Raised fields constructed along lakeshores in Mesoamerica to increase agricultural yields. (p. 169)

Christopher Columbus (1451–1506) Genoese mariner who in the service of Spain led expeditions across the Atlantic, reestablishing contact between the peoples of the Americas and the Old World and opening the way to Spanish conquest and colonization. (p. 362)

city-state A small independent state consisting of an urban center and the surrounding agricultural territory. A characteristic political form in early Mesopotamia, archaic and classical Greece, Phoenicia, and early Italy. (p. 15)

civilization An ambiguous term often used to denote more complex societies but sometimes used by anthropologists to describe any group of people sharing a set of cultural traits. (p. 5)

clipper ship Large, fast, streamlined sailing vessel, often American built, of the mid-to-late nineteenth century rigged with vast canvas sails hung from tall masts. (p. 563)

Cold War (1945–1991) The ideological struggle between communism (Soviet Union) and capitalism (United States) for world influence. The Soviet Union and the United States came to the brink of actual war during the Cuban Missile Crisis but never attacked one another. The Cold War came to an end when the Soviet Union dissolved in 1991. (p. 703)

colonialism Policy by which a nation administers a foreign territory and develops its resources for the benefit of the colonial power. (p. 604)

Columbian Exchange The exchange of plants, animals, diseases, and technologies between the Americas and the rest of the world following Columbus's voyages. (p. 374)

Commodore Matthew Perry A navy commander who, on July 8, 1853, became the first foreigner to break through the barriers that had kept Japan isolated from the rest of the world for 250 years. (p. 575)

Confucius Western name for the Chinese philosopher Kongzi (551–479 B.C.E.). His doctrine of duty and public service had a great influence on subsequent Chinese thought and served as a code of conduct for government officials. (p. 41)

Congress of Vienna (1814–1815) Meeting of representatives of European monarchs called to reestablish the old order after the defeat of Napoleon I. (p. 493)

conquistadors Early-sixteenth-century Spanish adventurers who conquered Mexico, Central America, and Peru. (p. 371)

Constantine (285–337 C.E.) Roman emperor (r. 306–337). After reuniting the Roman Empire, he moved the capital to Constantinople and made Christianity a favored religion. (p. 148)

Constitutional Convention Meeting in 1787 of the elected representatives of the thirteen original states to write the Constitution of the United States. (p. 487)

contract of indenture A voluntary agreement binding a person to work for a specified period of years in return for free passage to an overseas destination. Before 1800 most indentured servants were Europeans; after 1800 most were Asians. (p. 566)

Cossacks Peoples of the Russian Empire who lived outside the farming villages, often as herders, mercenaries, or outlaws. Cossacks led the conquest of Siberia in the sixteenth and seventeenth centuries. (p. 470)

Council of the Indies The institution responsible for supervising Spain's colonies in the Americas from 1524 to the early eighteenth century, when it lost all but judicial responsibilities. (p. 410)

creole In colonial Spanish America, the term used to describe someone of European descent born in the New World. Elsewhere in the Americas, it is used to describe all nonnative peoples. (p. 414)

Crimean War (1853–1856) Conflict between the Russian and Ottoman Empires fought primarily in the Crimean peninsula. To prevent Russian expansion, Britain and France sent troops to support the Ottomans. (p. 533)

Crusades (1095–1204) Armed pilgrimages to the Holy Land by Christians determined to recover Jerusalem from Muslim rule. The Crusades brought an end to western Europe's centuries of intellectual and cultural isolation. (p. 254)

Crystal Palace A gigantic greenhouse erected in Hyde Park, London, for the Great Exhibition of 1851. Made of iron and glass, it was a symbol of the industrial age. (p. 512)

Cuban Missile Crisis (1962) Brink-of-war confrontation between the United States and the Soviet Union over the latter's placement of nuclear-armed missiles in Cuba. (p. 707)

cultural imperialism Domination of one culture over another by a deliberate policy or by economic or technological superiority. (p. 746)

Cultural Revolution (China) (1966–1969) Campaign in China ordered by Mao Zedong to purge the Communist Party of his opponents and instill revolutionary values in the younger generation. (p. 720)

culture Socially transmitted patterns of action and expression. *Material culture* refers to physical objects, such as dwellings, clothing, tools, and crafts. Culture also includes arts, beliefs, knowledge, and technology. (p. 6)

cuneiform a system of writing in which wedge-shaped symbols represented words or syllables. It originated in Mesopotamia and was used initially for Sumerian and Akkadian but later was adapted to represent other languages of western Asia. Because so many symbols had to be learned, literacy was confined to a relatively small group of administrators and scribes. (p. 20)

Cyrus (600–530 B.C.E.) Founder of the Achaemenid Persian Empire. Between 550 and 530 B.C.E. he conquered Media, Lydia, and Babylon. Revered in the traditions of both Iran and the subject peoples, he employed Persians and Medes in his administration and respected the institutions and beliefs of subject peoples. (p. 88)

daimyo Literally, "great name(s)." Japanese warlords and great landowners, whose armed samurai gave them control of the Japanese islands from the eighth to the later nineteenth century. Under the Tokugawa Shogunate they were subordinated to the imperial government. (p. 456)

Daoism Chinese school of thought, originating in the Warring States Period with Laozi (604–531 B.C.E.). Daoism offered an alternative to the Confucian emphasis on hierarchy and duty. Daoists believe that the world is always changing and is devoid of absolute morality or meaning. They accept the world as they find it, avoid futile struggles, and deviate as little as possible from the Dao, or "path" of nature. (p. 41)

Darius I (ca. 558–486 B.C.E.) Third ruler of the Persian Empire (r. 522–486 B.C.E.). He crushed the widespread initial resistance to his rule and gave all major government posts to Persians rather than to Medes. He established a system of provinces and tribute, began construction of Persepolis, and expanded Persian control in the east (Pakistan) and west (northern Greece). (p. 89)

Decembrist revolt Abortive attempt by army officers to take control of the Russian government upon the death of Tsar Alexander I in 1825. (p. 539)

Declaration of the Rights of Man and of the Citizen (1789) Statement of fundamental political rights adopted by the French National Assembly at the beginning of the French Revolution. (p. 490)

deforestation The removal of trees faster than forests can replace themselves. (p. 397)

Delhi Sultanate (1206–1526) Centralized Indian empire, created by Muslim invaders. (p. 316)

democracy A system of government in which all "citizens" (however defined) have equal political and legal rights, privileges, and protections, as in the Greek city-state of Athens in the fifth and fourth centuries B.C.E. (p. 94)

demographic transition A change in the rates of population growth. Before the transition, both birthrates and death rates are high, resulting in a slowly growing population; then the death rate drops but the birthrate remains high, causing a population explosion; finally the birthrate drops and the population growth slows down. This transition took place in Europe in the late nineteenth and early twentieth centuries, in North America and East Asia in the mid-twentieth century, and, most recently, in Latin America and South Asia. (p. 736)

Deng Xiaoping (1904–1997) Communist Party leader who forced Chinese economic reforms after the death of Mao Zedong. (p. 736)

Diaspora A Greek word meaning "dispersal," used to describe the communities of a given ethnic group living outside their homeland. Jews, for example, spread from Israel to western Asia and Mediterranean lands in antiquity and today can be found throughout the world. (p. 72)

division of labor A manufacturing technique that breaks down a craft into many simple and repetitive tasks that can be performed by unskilled workers. Pioneered in the pottery works of Josiah Wedgwood and in other eighteenth-century factories, it greatly increased the productivity of labor and lowered the cost of manufactured goods. (p. 510)

driver A privileged male slave whose job was to ensure that a slave gang did its work on a plantation. (p. 422)

Druids The class of religious experts who conducted rituals and preserved sacred lore among some ancient Celtic peoples. They provided education and mediated disputes between kinship groups. (p. 50)

Dutch West India Company (1621–1794) Trading company chartered by the Dutch government to conduct its merchants' trade in the Americas and Africa. (p. 424)

electricity A form of energy used in telegraphy from the 1840s on and for lighting, industrial motors, and railroads beginning in the 1880s. (p. 578)

electric telegraph A device for rapid, long-distance transmission of information over an electric wire. It was introduced in England and North America in the 1830s and 1840s. (p. 514)

Emiliano Zapata (1879–1919) Revolutionary and leader of peasants in the Mexican Revolution. He mobilized landless peasants in south-central Mexico in an attempt to seize and divide the lands of the wealthy landowners. Though successful for a time, he was ultimately defeated and assassinated. (p. 688)

Emilio Aguinaldo (1869–1964) Leader of the Filipino independence movement against Spain (1895–1898). He proclaimed the independence of the Philippines in 1899, but his movement was crushed and he was captured by the United States Army in 1901. (p. 619)

Empress Dowager Cixi (1835–1908) Empress of China and mother of Emperor Guangxi. She put her son under house arrest, supported antiforeign movements, and resisted reforms of the Chinese government and armed forces. (pp. 595, 639)

encomienda A grant of authority over a population of Amerindians in the Spanish colonies. It provided the grant holder with a supply of cheap labor and periodic payments of goods by the Amerindians and obligated the grant holder to Christianize the Amerindians. (p. 413)

English Civil War (1642–1648) A conflict over royal versus parliamentary rights, caused by King Charles I's arrest of his parliamentary critics and ending with his execution. Its outcome checked the growth of royal absolutism and, with the Glorious Revolution of 1688 and the English Bill of Rights of 1689, ensured that England would be a constitutional monarchy. (p. 402)

Enlightenment A philosophical movement in eighteenth-century Europe that fostered the belief that one could reform society by discovering rational laws that governed social behavior and were just as scientific as the laws of physics. (pp. 392, 483)

equites In ancient Italy, prosperous landowners second in wealth and status to the senatorial aristocracy. The Roman emperors allied with this group to counterbalance the influence of the old aristocracy and used the *equites* to staff the imperial civil service. (p. 143)

Estates General France's traditional national assembly with representatives of the three estates, or classes, in French society: the clergy, nobility, and commoners. The calling of the Estates General in 1789 led to the French Revolution. (p. 489)

Ethiopia East African highland nation lying east of the Nile River. (p. 205)

European Community (EC) An organization promoting economic unity in Europe, formed in 1967 by consolidation of earlier, more limited, agreements. It was replaced by the European Union (EU) in 1993. (p. 704)

Eva Duarte Perón (1919–1952) Wife of Juan Perón and champion of the poor in Argentina. She was a gifted speaker and popular political leader who campaigned to improve the life of the urban poor by founding schools and hospitals and providing other social benefits. (p. 694)

extraterritoriality The right of foreign residents in a country to live under the laws of their native country and disregard the laws of the host country. In the nineteenth and early twentieth centuries, European and American nationals living in certain areas of Chinese and Ottoman cities were granted this right. (p. 535)

Faisal I (1885–1933) Arab prince, leader of the Arab Revolt in World War I. The British made him king of Iraq in 1921, and he reigned under British protection until 1933. (p. 633)

Fascist Party Italian political party created by Benito Mussolini during World War I. It emphasized aggressive nationalism and was Mussolini's instrument for the creation of a dictatorship in Italy from 1922 to 1943. (p. 659)

Ferdinand Magellan (1487–1521) Portuguese navigator who led the Spanish expedition of 1519–1522 that was the first to sail around the world. (p. 364)

fief In medieval Europe, land granted in return for a sworn oath to provide specified military service. (p. 245)

First Temple A monumental sanctuary built in Jerusalem by King Solomon in the tenth century B.C.E. to be the religious center for the Israelite god Yahweh. The Temple priesthood conducted sacrifices, received a tithe or percentage of agricultural revenues, and became economically and politically powerful. The First Temple was destroyed by the Babylonians in 587 B.C.E. and was rebuilt on a modest scale in the late sixth century B.C.E. It was replaced by King Herod's Second Temple in the late first century B.C.E. and destroyed by the Romans in 70 C.E. (p. 71)

Five-Year Plans Plans that Joseph Stalin introduced to industrialize the Soviet Union rapidly, beginning in 1928. They set goals for the output of steel, electricity, machinery, and most other products and were enforced by the police powers of the state. They succeeded in making the Soviet Union a major industrial power before World War II. (p. 652)

foragers People who support themselves by hunting wild animals and gathering wild edible plants and insects. (p. 6)

Francisco "Pancho" Villa (1877–1923) A popular leader during the Mexican Revolution. An outlaw in his youth, when the revolution started he formed a cavalry army in the north of Mexico and fought for the rights of the landless in collaboration with Emiliano Zapata. He was assassinated in 1923. (p. 689)

Francisco Pizarro (ca. 1476–1541) Spanish explorer who led the conquest of the Inca Empire of Peru in 1532–1533. (p. 373)

free-trade imperialism Economic dominance of a weaker country by a more powerful one, while maintaining the legal independence of the weaker state. In the late nineteenth century, free-trade imperialism characterized the relations between the Latin American republics, on the one hand, and Great Britain and the United States, on the other. (p. 620)

Fujiwara Aristocratic family that dominated the Japanese imperial court between the ninth and twelfth centuries. (p. 279)

Funan An early complex society in Southeast Asia between the first and sixth centuries C.E. It was centered in the rich rice-growing region of southern Vietnam, and it controlled the passage of trade across the Malaysian isthmus. (p. 129)

Genghis Khan (ca. 1167–1227) The title of Temüjin when he ruled the Mongols (1206–1227). It means the "oceanic" or "universal" leader. Genghis Khan was the founder of the Mongol Empire. (p. 287)

gens de couleur Free mixed-race men and women in Haiti. They sought greater political rights and later supported the Haitian Revolution. (p. 494)

gentry In China, the class of prosperous families, next in wealth below the rural aristocrats, from which the emperors drew their administrative personnel. Respected for their education and expertise, these officials became a privileged group and made the government more efficient and responsive than in the past. In England and France, the class of landholding families below the aristocracy. (pp. 154, 395)

George Washington (1732–1799) Military commander of the American Revolution. He was the first elected president of the United States (1789–1799). (p. 486)

Getulio Vargas (1883–1954) Dictator of Brazil from 1930 to 1945 and from 1951 to 1954. Defeated in the presidential election of 1930, he overthrew the government and created a dictatorship that emphasized industrialization and helped the urban poor but did little to alleviate the problems of the peasants. (p. 693)

Ghana First known kingdom in sub-Saharan West Africa between the sixth and thirteenth centuries C.E. Also the modern West African country once known as the Gold Coast. (p. 222)

Giuseppe Garibaldi (1807–1882) Italian nationalist and revolutionary who conquered Sicily and Naples and added them to a unified Italy in 1860. (p. 587)

global elite culture At the beginning of the twenty-first century, the attitudes and outlook of well-educated, prosperous, Western-oriented people around the world, largely expressed in European languages, especially English. (p. 748)

globalization The economic, political, and cultural integration and interaction of all parts of the world brought about by increasing trade, travel, and technology. (p. 732)

global pop culture Popular cultural practices and institutions that have been adopted internationally, such as music, the Internet, television, food, and fashion. (p. 748)

Gold Coast (Africa) Region of the Atlantic coast of West Africa occupied by modern Ghana; named for its gold exports to Europe from the 1470s onward. (p. 362)

Golden Horde Mongol khanate founded by Genghis Khan's grandson Batu. It was based in southern Russia and quickly adopted both the Turkic language and Islam. Also known as the Kipchak Khanate. (p. 294)

Gothic cathedrals Large churches originating in twelfth-century France; built in an architectural style featuring pointed arches, tall vaults and spires, flying buttresses, and large stained-glass windows. (p. 343)

Grand Canal The 1,100-mile (1,771-kilometer) waterway linking the Yellow and the Yangzi Rivers. It was begun in the Han period and completed during the Sui Empire. (p. 261)

"great traditions" Anthropologists' term for a literate, well-institutionalized complex of religious and social beliefs and practices adhered to by diverse societies over a broad geographical area. (p. 201)

Great Western Schism A division in the Latin (Western) Christian Church between 1378 and 1415, when rival claimants to the papacy existed in Rome and Avignon. (p. 349)

Great Zimbabwe City, now in ruins (in the modern African country of Zimbabwe), whose many stone structures were built between about 1250 and 1450, when it was a trading center and the capital of a large state. (p. 323)

guild In medieval Europe, an association of men (rarely women), such as merchants, artisans, or professors, who worked in a particular trade and banded together to promote their economic and political interests. Guilds were also important in other societies, such as the Ottoman and Safavid Empires. (p. 340)

Gujarat Region of western India famous for trade and manufacturing; the inhabitants are called Gujaratis. (p. 321)

gunpowder A mixture of saltpeter, sulfur, and charcoal, in various proportions. The formula, brought to China in the 400s or 500s, was first used to make fumigators to keep away insect pests and evil spirits. In later centuries it was used to make explosives and grenades and to propel cannonballs, shot, and bullets. (p. 273)

Guomindang Nationalist political party founded on democratic principles by Sun Yat-sen in 1912. After 1925, the party was headed by Chiang Kai-shek, who turned it into an increasingly authoritarian movement. (p. 639)

Gupta Empire A powerful Indian state based, like its Mauryan predecessor, on a capital at Pataliputra in the Ganges Valley. It controlled most of the Indian subcontinent through a combination of military force and its prestige as a center of sophisticated culture. (p. 126)

Habsburg A powerful European family that provided many Holy Roman Emperors, founded the Austrian (later Austro-Hungarian) Empire, and ruled sixteenth- and seventeenth-century Spain. (p. 400)

hadith A tradition relating the words or deeds of the Prophet Muhammad; next to the Quran, the most important basis for Islamic law. (p. 226)

Haile Selassie (1892–1975) Emperor of Ethiopia (r. 1930–1974) and symbol of African independence. He fought the Italian invasion of his country in 1935 and regained his throne during World War II, when British forces expelled the Italians. He ruled Ethiopia as a traditional autocracy until he was overthrown in 1974. (p. 686)

Hammurabi Amorite ruler of Babylon (r. 1792–1750 B.C.E.). He conquered many city-states in southern and northern Mesopotamia and is best known for a code of laws, inscribed on a black stone pillar, illustrating the principles to be used in legal cases. (p. 17)

Han A term used to designate the ethnic Chinese people who originated in the Yellow River Valley and spread throughout regions of China suitable for agriculture, as well as the dynasty of emperors who ruled from 206 B.C.E. to 220 C.E. (p. 153)

Hanseatic League An economic and defensive alliance of the free towns in northern Germany, founded about 1241 and most powerful in the fourteenth century. (p. 339)

Harappa Site of one of the great cities of the Indus Valley civilization of the third millennium B.C.E. It was located on the northwest frontier of the zone of cultivation (in modern Pakistan) and may have been a center for the acquisition of raw materials, such as metals and precious stones, from Afghanistan and Iran. (p. 113)

Hatshepsut Queen of Egypt (r. 1473–1458 B.C.E.). She dispatched a naval expedition down the Red Sea to Punt (possibly northeast Sudan or Eritria), the faraway source of myrrh. There is evidence of opposition to a woman as ruler, and after her death her name and image were frequently defaced. (p. 59)

Hebrew Bible A collection of sacred books containing diverse materials concerning the origins, experiences, beliefs, and practices of the Israelites. Most of the extant text was compiled by members of the priestly class in the fifth century B.C.E. and reflects the concerns and views of this group. (p. 69)

Hellenistic Age Historians' term for the era, usually dated 323–30 B.C.E., in which Greek culture spread across western Asia and northeastern Africa after the conquests of Alexander the Great. The period ended with the fall of the last major Hellenistic kingdom to Rome, but Greek cultural influence persisted until the seventh century C.E. (p. 105)

Henry Morton Stanley (1841–1904) British-American explorer of Africa, famous for his expeditions in search of Dr. David Livingstone. Stanley helped King Leopold II establish the Congo Free State. (p. 609)

Henry the Navigator (1394–1460) Portuguese prince who promoted the study of navigation and directed voyages of exploration down the western coast of Africa. (p. 359)

Hernán Cortés (1485–1547) Spanish explorer and conquistador who led the conquest of Aztec Mexico in 1519–1521 for Spain. (p. 372)

Herodotus (ca. 485–425 B.C.E.) Heir to the technique of historia—"investigation"—developed by Greeks in the late Archaic period. He came from a Greek community in Anatolia and traveled extensively collecting information in western Asia and the Mediterranean lands. He traced the antecedents of and chronicled the Persian Wars between the Greek city-states and the Persian Empire, thus originating the Western tradition of historical writing. (p. 96)

Hidden Imam Last in a series of twelve descendants of Muhammad's son-in-law Ali, whom Shi'ites consider divinely appointed leaders of the Muslim community. In occlusion since ca. 873, he is expected to return as a messiah at the end of time. (p. 442)

hieroglyphics A system of writing in which pictorial symbols represented sounds, syllables, or concepts. It was used for official and monumental inscriptions in ancient Egypt. Because of the long period of study required to master this system, literacy in hieroglyphics was confined to a relatively small group of scribes and administrators. Cursive symbol-forms were developed for rapid composition on other media, such as papyrus. (p. 27)

Hinduism A general term for a wide variety of beliefs and ritual practices that have developed in the Indian subcontinent since antiquity. Hinduism has roots in ancient Vedic, Buddhist, and south Indian religious concepts and practices. It spread along the trade routes to Southeast Asia. (p. 121)

Hipólito Irigoyen (1850–1933) Argentine politician, president of Argentina from 1916 to 1922 and 1928 to 1930. The first president elected by universal male suffrage, he began his presidency as a reformer but later became conservative. (p. 692)

Hiroshima City in Japan, the first to be destroyed by an atomic bomb, on August 6, 1945. The bombing hastened the end of World War II. (p. 669)

history The study of past events and changes in the development, transmission, and transformation of cultural practices. (p. 6)

Hittites A people from central Anatolia who established an empire in Anatolia and Syria in the Late Bronze Age. With wealth from the trade in metals and military power based on chariot forces, the Hittites vied with New Kingdom Egypt for control of Syria-Palestine before falling to unidentified attackers ca. 1200 B.C.E. (p. 57)

Holocaust Nazis' program during World War II to kill people they considered undesirable. Some 6 million Jews perished during the Holocaust, along with millions of Poles, Gypsies, communists, socialists, and others. (p. 671)

Holocene The geological era since the end of the Great Ice Age about 13,000 years ago. (p. 10)

Holy Roman Empire Loose federation of mostly German states and principalities, headed by an emperor elected by the princes. It lasted from 962 to 1806. (pp. 246, 400)

hoplite A heavily armored Greek infantryman of the Archaic and Classical periods who fought in the close-packed phalanx formation. Hoplite armies—militias composed of middle- and upper-class citizens supplying their own equipment—were for centuries superior to all other military forces. (p. 93)

horse collar Harnessing method that increased the efficiency of horses by shifting the point of traction from the animal's neck to the shoulders; its adoption favors the spread of horse-drawn plows and vehicles. (p. 252)

House of Burgesses Elected assembly in colonial Virginia, created in 1618. (p. 417)

humanists (Renaissance) European scholars, writers, and teachers associated with the study of the humanities (grammar, rhetoric, poetry, history, languages, and moral philosophy), influential in the fifteenth century and later. (p. 346)

Hundred Years War (1337–1453) Series of campaigns over control of the throne of France, involving English and French royal families and French noble families. (p. 349)

Ibn Battuta (1304–1369) Moroccan Muslim scholar, the most widely traveled individual of his time. He wrote a detailed account of his visits to Islamic lands from China to Spain and the western Sudan. (p. 313)

Il-khan A "secondary" or "peripheral" khan based in Persia. The Il-khans' khanate was founded by Hülegü, a grandson of Genghis Khan, and was based at Tabriz in modern Azerbaijan. It controlled much of Iran and Iraq. (p. 294)

import-substitution industrialization An economic system aimed at building a country's industry by restricting foreign trade. It was especially popular in Latin American countries such as Mexico, Argentina, and Brazil in the mid-twentieth century. It proved successful for a time but could not keep up with technological advances in Europe and North America. (p. 693)

Inca Largest and most powerful Andean empire. Controlled the Pacific coast of South America from Ecuador to Chile from its capital of Cuzco. (p. 182)

indentured servant A migrant to British colonies in the Americas who paid for passage by agreeing to work for a set term ranging from four to seven years. (p. 416)

Indian Civil Service The elite professional class of officials who administered the government of British India. Originally composed exclusively of well-educated British men, it gradually added qualified Indians. (p. 559)

Indian National Congress A movement and political party founded in 1885 to demand greater Indian participation in government. Its membership was middle class, and its demands were modest until World War I. Led after 1920 by Mohandas K. Gandhi, it appealed increasingly to the poor, and it organized mass protests demanding self-government and independence. (pp. 561, 678)

Indian Ocean Maritime System In premodern times, a network of seaports, trade routes, and maritime culture linking countries on the rim of the Indian Ocean from Africa to Indonesia. (p. 193)

indulgence The forgiveness of the punishment due for past sins, granted by the Catholic Church authorities as a reward for a pious act. Martin Luther's protest against the sale of indulgences is often seen as touching off the Protestant Reformation. (p. 386)

Industrial Revolution The transformation of the economy, the environment, and living conditions, occurring first in England in the eighteenth century, that resulted from the use of steam engines, the mechanization of manufacturing in factories, and innovations in transportation and communication. (p. 507)

investiture controversy Dispute between the popes and the Holy Roman Emperors over who held ultimate authority over bishops in imperial lands. (p. 247)

Iron Age Historians' term for the period during which iron was the primary metal for tools and weapons. The advent of iron technology began at different times in different parts of the world. (p. 55)

Iron Curtain Winston Churchill's term for the Cold War division between the Soviet-dominated East and the U.S.-dominated West. (p. 703)

Iroquois Confederacy An alliance of five northeastern Amerindian peoples (six after 1722) that made decisions on military and diplomatic issues through a council of representatives. Allied first with the Dutch and later with the English, the Confederacy dominated the area from western New England to the Great Lakes. (p. 418)

Islam Religion expounded by the Prophet Muhammad (570–632 C.E.) on the basis of his reception of divine revelations, which were collected after his death into the Quran. In the tradition of Judaism and Christianity, and sharing much of their lore, Islam calls on all people to recognize one creator god—Allah—who rewards or punishes believers after death according to how they led their lives. (p. 216)

Israel In antiquity, the land between the eastern shore of the Mediterranean and the Jordan River, occupied by the Israelites from the early second millennium B.C.E. (p. 68)

James Watt (1736–1819) Scot who invented the condenser and other improvements that made the steam engine a practical source of power for industry and transportation. The watt, an electrical measurement, is named after him. (p. 513)

Janissaries Infantry, originally of slave origin, armed with firearms and constituting the elite of the Ottoman army from the fifteenth century until the corps was abolished in 1826. (pp. 437, 529)

Jawaharlal Nehru (1889–1964) Indian statesman who succeeded Mohandas K. Gandhi as leader of the Indian National Congress. He negotiated the end of British colonial rule in India and became India's first prime minister (1947–1964). (p. 681)

Jesus (ca. 5 B.C.E.–34 C.E.) A Jew from Galilee in northern Israel who sought to reform Jewish beliefs and practices. He was executed as a revolutionary by the Romans. Hailed as the Messiah and son of God by his followers, he became the central figure in Christianity, a belief system that developed in the centuries after his death. (p. 145)

joint-stock company A business, often backed by a government charter, that sold shares to individuals to raise money for its trading enterprises and to spread the risks (and profits) among many investors. (p. 395)

Joseph Stalin (1879–1953) Bolshevik revolutionary, head of the Soviet Communist Party after 1924, and dictator of the Soviet Union from 1929 to 1953. He led the Soviet Union with an iron fist, using Five-Year Plans to increase industrial production and terror to crush all opposition. (p. 652)

Josiah Wedgwood (1730–1795) English industrialist whose pottery works were the first to produce fine-quality pottery by industrial methods. (p. 510)

Juan Perón (1895–1974) President of Argentina (1946–1955, 1973–1974). As a military officer, he championed the rights of labor. Aided by his wife Eva Duarte Perón, he was elected president in 1946. He built up Argentinean industry, became very popular among the urban poor, but harmed the economy. (p. 694)

junk A very large flatbottom sailing ship produced in the Tang, Ming, and Song Empires, specially designed for long-distance commercial travel. (p. 273)

Kamakura Shogunate The first of Japan's decentralized military governments (1185–1333). (p. 279)

kamikaze The "divine wind" that the Japanese credited with blowing Mongol invaders away from their shores in 1281. (p. 308)

Kangxi (1654–1722) Qing emperor (r. 1662–1722) who oversaw the greatest expansion of the Qing Empire. (p. 464)

Karl Marx (1818–1883) German journalist and philosopher, founder of the Marxist branch of socialism. He is known for two books: *The Communist Manifesto* (1848) and *Das Kapital* (1867–1894). (p. 583)

karma In Indian tradition, the residue of deeds performed in past and present lives that adheres to a "spirit" and determines what form it will assume in its next life cycle. The doctrines of karma and reincarnation were used by the elite in ancient India to encourage people to accept their social position and do their duty. (p. 118)

keiretsu Alliances of corporations and banks that dominate the Japanese economy. (p. 719)

khipus System of knotted colored cords used by preliterate Andean peoples to transmit information. (p. 178)

Khubilai Khan (1215–1294) Last of the Mongol Great Khans (r. 1260–1294) and founder of the Yuan Empire. Original architect of the Forbidden City. (p. 300)

Kievan Russia State established at Kiev in Ukraine ca. 879 by Scandinavian adventurers asserting authority over a mostly Slavic farming population. (p. 234)

Korean War (1950–1953) Conflict that began with North Korea's invasion of South Korea and came to involve the United Nations (primarily the United States) allying with South Korea against North Korea and the People's Republic of China. (p. 706)

Koryo Korean kingdom founded in 918 and destroyed by a Mongol invasion in 1259. (p. 277)

Kush An Egyptian name for Nubia, the region alongside the Nile River south of Egypt, where an indigenous kingdom with its own distinctive institutions and cultural traditions arose in the early second millennium B.C.E. It was deeply influenced by Egyptian culture and at times under the control of Egypt, which coveted its rich deposits of gold and luxury products from sub-Saharan Africa carried up the Nile corridor. (p. 45)

labor union An organization of workers in a particular industry or trade, created to defend the interests of members through strikes or negotiations with employers. (p. 583)

laissez faire The idea that government should refrain from interfering in economic affairs. The classic exposition of laissez-faire principles is Adam Smith's *Wealth of Nations* (1776). (p. 518)

lama In Tibetan Buddhism, a teacher. (p. 300)

Latin West Historians' name for the territories of Europe that adhered to the Latin rite of Christianity and used the Latin language for intellectual exchange in the period ca. 1000–1500. (p. 333)

Lázaro Cárdenas (1895–1970) President of Mexico (1934–1940). He brought major changes to Mexican life by distributing millions of acres of land to the peasants, bringing representatives of workers and farmers into the inner circles of politics, and nationalizing the oil industry. (p. 691)

League of Nations International organization founded in 1919 to promote world peace and cooperation but greatly weakened by the refusal of the United States to join. It proved ineffectual in stopping aggression by Italy, Japan, and Germany in the 1930s, and it was superseded by the United Nations in 1945. (p. 637)

Legalism In China, a political philosophy that emphasized the unruliness of human nature and justified state coercion and control. The ruling class invoked it to validate the authoritarian nature of the regime and its profligate expenditure of subjects' lives and labor. It was later superseded by a more benevolent Confucian doctrine of governmental moderation. (p. 41)

"legitimate" trade Exports from Africa in the nineteenth century that did not include the newly outlawed slave trade. (p. 555)

Leopold II (1835–1909) King of Belgium (r. 1865–1909). He was active in encouraging the exploration of Central Africa and became the ruler of the Congo Free State (to 1908). (p. 609)

liberalism A political ideology that emphasizes the civil rights of citizens, representative government, and the protection of private property. This ideology, derived from the Enlightenment, was especially popular among the property-owning middle classes of Europe and North America. (p. 587)

Linear B A set of syllabic symbols, derived from the writing system of Minoan Crete, used in the Mycenaean palaces of the Late Bronze Age to write an early form of Greek. It was used primarily for palace records, and the surviving Linear B tablets provide substantial information about the economic organization of Mycenaean society and tantalizing clues about political, social, and religious institutions. (p. 63)

Li Shimin (599–649) One of the founders of the Tang Empire and its second emperor (r. 626–649). He led the expansion of the empire into Central Asia. (p. 262)

Little Ice Age A century-long period of cool climate that began in the 1590s. Its ill effects on agriculture in northern Europe were notable. (p. 395)

llama A hoofed animal indigenous to the Andes Mountains. It was the only domesticated beast of burden in the Americas before the arrival of Europeans. The use of llamas to transport goods made possible specialized production and trade among people living in different ecological zones and fostered the integration of these zones by Chavín and later Andean states. (p. 166)

loess A fine, light silt deposited by wind and water. It constitutes the fertile soil of the Yellow River Valley in northern China. Because loess soil is not compacted, it can be worked with a simple digging stick, but it leaves the region vulnerable to devastating floods. (p. 37)

Long March (1934–1935) The 6,000-mile (9,700-kilometer) flight of Chinese communists from southeastern to northwestern China. The communists, led by Mao Zedong, were pursued by the Chinese army under orders from Chiang Kai-shek. The four thousand survivors of the march formed the nucleus of a revived communist movement that defeated the Guomindang after World War II. (p. 663)

ma'at Egyptian term for the concept of divinely created and maintained order in the universe. Reflecting the ancient Egyptians' belief in an essentially beneficent world, the divine ruler was the earthly guarantor of this order. (p. 25)

Macartney mission The unsuccessful attempt in 1792–1793 by the British Empire to establish diplomatic relations with the Qing Empire. (p. 466)

Mahabharata A vast epic chronicling the events leading up to a cataclysmic battle between related kinship groups in early India. It includes the Bhagavad-Gita, the most important work of Indian sacred literature. (p. 124)

Mahayana Buddhism "Great Vehicle" branch of Buddhism followed in China, Japan, and Central Asia. The focus is on reverence for Buddha and for bodhisattvas, enlightened persons who have postponed nirvana to help others attain enlightenment. (p. 120)

Malacca Port city in the modern Southeast Asian country of Malaysia, founded about 1400 as a trading center on the Strait of Malacca. Also spelled Melaka. (p. 326)

Mali Empire created by indigenous Muslims in western Sudan of West Africa from the thirteenth to fifteenth century. It was famous for its role in the trans-Saharan gold trade. (p. 317)

mamluks Under the Islamic system of military slavery, Turkic military slaves who formed an important part of the armed forces of the Abbasid Caliphate of the ninth and tenth centuries. Mamluks eventually founded their own state, ruling Egypt and Syria (1250–1517). (p. 220)

Manchu Federation of Northeast Asian peoples who founded the Qing Empire. (p. 456)

Mandate of Heaven Chinese religious and political ideology developed by the Zhou, according to which it was the prerogative of Heaven, the chief deity, to grant power to the ruler of China and to take away that power if the ruler failed to conduct himself justly and in the best interests of his subjects. (p. 40)

mandate system Allocation of former German colonies and Ottoman possessions to the victorious powers after World War I, to be administered under League of Nations supervision. (p. 641)

manor In medieval Europe, a large, self-sufficient landholding consisting of the lord's residence (manor house), outbuildings, peasant village, and surrounding land. (p. 242)

mansabs In India, grants of land given in return for service by rulers of the Mughal Empire. (p. 446)

Mansa Kankan Musa Ruler of Mali (r. 1312–1337). His pilgrimage through Egypt to Mecca in 1324–1325 established the empire's reputation for wealth in the Mediterranean world. (p. 318)

Mao Zedong (1893–1976) Leader of the Chinese Communist Party (1927–1976). He led the communists on the Long March (1934–1935) and rebuilt the Communist Party and Red Army during the Japanese occupation of China (1937–1945). After World War II, he led the communists to victory over the Guomindang. (p. 663)

Margaret Sanger (1883–1966) American nurse and author; pioneer in the movement for family planning; organized conferences and established birth control clinics. (p. 645)

maroon A slave who ran away from his or her master. Often a member of a community of runaway slaves in the West Indies and South America. (p. 423)

Marshall Plan U.S. program to support the reconstruction of western Europe after World War II. By 1961 more than $20 billion in economic aid had been disbursed. (p. 704)

mass deportation The forcible removal and relocation of large numbers of people or entire populations. The mass deportations practiced by the Assyrian and Persian Empires were meant as a terrifying warning of the consequences of rebellion. They also brought labor to the imperial center. (p. 67)

mass production The manufacture of many identical products by the division of labor into many small repetitive tasks. This method was introduced into the manufacture of pottery and into the spinning of cotton thread. (p. 510)

Mauryan Empire The first state to unify most of the Indian subcontinent. It was founded by Chandragupta Maurya in 324 B.C.E. and survived until 184 B.C.E. From its capital at Pataliputra in the Ganges Valley it grew wealthy from taxes on agriculture, iron mining, and control of trade routes. (p. 123)

Max Planck (1858–1947) German physicist who developed quantum theory and was awarded the Nobel Prize for physics in 1918. (p. 645)

Maya Mesoamerican civilization concentrated in Mexico's Yucatán Peninsula and in Guatemala and Honduras but never unified into a single empire. Major contributions were in mathematics, astronomy, and development of the calendar. (p. 170)

Mecca City in Arabia; birthplace of Muhammad; location of the Ka'ba, the holiest shrine in Islam. (p. 214)

mechanization The application of machinery to manufacturing and other activities. Among the first processes to be mechanized were the spinning of cotton thread and the weaving of cloth in late-eighteenth- and early-nineteenth-century England. (p. 511)

medieval Literally "middle age," a term that historians of Europe use for the period ca. 500 to ca. 1500, signifying its intermediate point between Greco-Roman antiquity and the Renaissance. (p. 234)

Medina City in western Arabia to which the Prophet Muhammad and his followers emigrated in 622 to escape persecution in Mecca. (p. 216)

megaliths Structures and complexes of very large stones constructed for ceremonial and religious purposes in Neolithic times. (p. 11)

Meiji Restoration The political program that followed the destruction of the Tokugawa Shogunate in 1868, in which a collection of young leaders set Japan on the path of centralization, industrialization, and imperialism. (p. 589)

Memphis The capital of Old Kingdom Egypt, near the head of the Nile Delta. Early rulers were interred in the nearby pyramids. (p. 26)

Menelik II (1844–1911) Emperor of Ethiopia (r. 1889–1911). He enlarged Ethiopia to its present dimensions and defeated an Italian invasion at Adowa (1896). (p. 614)

mercantilism European government policies of the sixteenth, seventeenth, and eighteenth centuries designed to promote overseas trade between a country and its colonies and to accumulate precious metals by requiring colonies to trade only with their motherland country. The British system was defined by the Navigation Acts, the French system by laws known as the *Exclusif.* (p. 424)

Meroë Capital of a flourishing kingdom in southern Nubia from the fourth century B.C.E. to the fourth century C.E. In this period Nubian culture shows more independence from Egypt and the influence of sub-Saharan Africa. (p. 47)

Miguel Hidalgo y Costilla (1753–1811) Mexican priest who led the first stage of the Mexican independence war in 1810. He was captured and executed in 1811. (p. 497)

Mikhail Gorbachev (b. 1931) Head of the Soviet Union from 1985 to 1991. His liberalization effort improved relations with the West, but he lost power after his reforms led to the collapse of communist governments in eastern Europe. (p. 725)

Ming Empire (1368–1644) Empire based in China that Zhu Yuanzhang established after the overthrow of the Yuan Empire. The Ming emperor Yongle sponsored additions to the Forbidden City and the voyages of Zheng He. The later years of the Ming saw a slowdown in technological development and economic decline. (pp. 303, 461)

Minoan Prosperous civilization on the Aegean island of Crete in the second millennium B.C.E. The Minoans engaged in far-flung commerce around the Mediterranean and exerted powerful cultural influences on the early Greeks. (p. 61)

mit'a Andean labor system based on shared obligations to help kinsmen and work on behalf of the ruler and religious organizations. (p. 179)

Moche Civilization of north coast of Peru (200–700 C.E.). An important Andean civilization that built extensive irrigation networks as well as impressive urban centers dominated by brick temples. (p. 179)

Moctezuma II (1466–1520) Last Aztec emperor, overthrown by the Spanish conquistador Hernán Cortés. (p. 372)

modernization The process of reforming political, military, economic, social, and cultural traditions in imitation of the early success of Western societies, often with regard for accommodating local traditions in non-Western societies. (p. 553)

Mohandas K. (Mahatma) Gandhi (1869–1948) Leader of the Indian independence movement and advocate of nonviolent resistance. After being educated as a lawyer in England, he returned to India and became leader of the Indian National Congress in 1920. He appealed to the poor, led nonviolent demonstrations against British colonial rule, and was jailed many times. Soon after independence he was assassinated for attempting to stop Hindu-Muslim rioting. (p. 680)

Mohenjo-Daro Largest of the cities of the Indus Valley civilization. It was centrally located in the extensive floodplain of the Indus River in contemporary Pakistan. Little is known about the political institutions of Indus Valley communities, but the large scale of construction at Mohenjo-Daro, the orderly grid of streets, and the standardization of building materials are evidence of central planning. (p. 113)

moksha The Hindu concept of the spirit's "liberation" from the endless cycle of rebirths. There are various avenues—such as physical discipline, meditation, and acts of devotion to the gods—by which the spirit can distance itself from desire for the things of this world and be merged with the divine force that animates the universe. (p. 119)

monasticism Living in a religious community apart from secular society and adhering to a rule stipulating chastity, obedience, and poverty. It was a prominent element of medieval Christianity and Buddhism. Monasteries were the primary centers of learning and literacy in early medieval Europe. (p. 248)

Mongols As early as the Tang Empire, Chinese records mention a people of this name living as nomads in northern Eurasia. After 1206, under Genghis Khan, they established an enormous empire linking western and eastern Eurasia. (p. 287)

monotheism Belief in the existence of a single divine entity. Some scholars cite the devotion of the Egyptian pharaoh Akhenaten to Aten (sun-disk) and his suppression of traditional gods as the earliest instance. The Israelite worship of Yahweh developed into an exclusive belief in one god, and this concept passed into Christianity and Islam. (p. 72)

monsoon Seasonal winds in the Indian Ocean caused by the differences in temperature between the rapidly heating and cooling landmasses of Africa and Asia and the slowly changing ocean waters. These strong and predictable winds have long been ridden across the open sea by sailors, and the large amounts of rainfall that they deposit on parts of India, Southeast Asia, and China allow for the cultivation of several crops a year. (pp. 116, 314)

most-favored-nation status A clause in a commercial treaty that automatically awards to the signatory all the privileges granted to the most favored of other signatories. (p. 543)

movable type Type in which each individual character is cast on a separate piece of metal. It replaced woodblock printing, allowing for the arrangement of individual letters and other characters on a page, rather than requiring the carving of entire pages at a time. It may have been invented in Korea in the thirteenth century. (p. 274)

Mughal Empire Muslim state (1526–1857) exercising dominion over most of India in the sixteenth and seventeenth centuries. (p. 446)

Muhammad (570–632 C.E.) Arab prophet; founder of religion of Islam. (p. 215)

Muhammad Ali (1769–1849) Leader of Egyptian modernization in the early nineteenth century. He ruled Egypt as an Ottoman governor but also had imperial ambitions. His descendants ruled Egypt until overthrown in 1952. (pp. 528, 553)

Muhammad Ali Jinnah (1876–1948) Indian Muslim politician who founded the state of Pakistan. A lawyer by training, he joined the All-India Muslim League in 1913. As leader of the League from the 1920s on, he negotiated with the British and the Indian National Congress for Muslim participation in Indian politics. From 1940 on, he led the movement for the independence of India's Muslims in a separate state of Pakistan, founded in 1947. (p. 683)

mummy A body preserved by chemical processes or special natural circumstances, often in the belief that the deceased will need it again in the afterlife. In ancient Egypt the bodies of people who could afford mummification underwent a complex process of removing organs, filling body cavities, dehydrating the corpse, and then wrapping the body with linen bandages and enclosing it in a wooden sarcophagus. (p. 30)

Muscovy The Russian principality that emerged gradually during the era of Mongol domination. The Muscovite dynasty ruled without interruption from 1276 to 1598. (p. 468)

Muslim An adherent of the Islamic religion; a person who "submits" (in Arabic, *Islam* means "submission") to the will of God. (p. 216)

Mycenae Site of a fortified palace complex in southern Greece that controlled a Late Bronze Age kingdom. In Homer's epic poems, Mycenae was the base of King Agamemnon, who commanded the Greeks besieging Troy. Contemporary archaeologists call the complex Greek society of the second millennium B.C.E. "Mycenaean." (p. 62)

Napoleon Bonaparte (Napoleon I) (1769–1821) The general who overthrew the French Directory in 1799 and became emperor of the French in 1804. He failed to defeat Great Britain and abdicated in 1814, then returned to power briefly in 1815 but was defeated and died in exile.   (p. 491)

Nasir al-Din Tusi (1201–1274) Persian mathematician and cosmologist whose academy near Tabriz provided the model for the movement of the planets that helped to inspire the Copernican model of the solar system.   (p. 296)

National Assembly French Revolutionary assembly (1789–1791). Called first as the Estates General, the three estates came together and demanded radical change. It passed the Declaration of the Rights of Man and of the Citizen in 1789.   (p. 489)

nationalism A political ideology that stresses people's membership in a nation—a community defined by a common culture and history as well as by territory. In the late eighteenth and early nineteenth centuries, nationalism was a force for unity in western Europe. In the late nineteenth century it hastened the disintegration of the Austro-Hungarian and Ottoman Empires. In the twentieth century it provided the ideological foundation for scores of independent countries emerging from colonialism.   (p. 586)

nawab A Muslim prince allied to British India; technically, a semi-autonomous deputy of the Mughal emperor.   (p. 556)

Nazis German political party joined by Adolf Hitler, emphasizing nationalism, racism, and war. When Hitler became chancellor of Germany in 1933, the Nazis became the only legal party and an instrument of Hitler's absolute rule. The party's formal name was National Socialist German Workers' Party.   (p. 660)

Neo-Assyrian Empire An empire extending from western Iran to Syria-Palestine, conquered by the Assyrians of northern Mesopotamia between the tenth and seventh centuries B.C.E. They used force and terror and exploited the wealth and labor of their subjects. They also preserved and continued the cultural and scientific developments of Mesopotamian civilization.   (p. 65)

neo-Confucianism Term used to describe new approaches to understanding classic Confucian texts that became the basic ruling philosophy of China from the Song period to the twentieth century.   (p. 273)

Neolithic The period of the Stone Age associated with the ancient Agricultural Revolutions. It follows the Paleolithic period.   (p. 6)

New Economic Policy Policy proclaimed by Vladimir Lenin in 1921 to encourage the revival of the Soviet economy by allowing small private enterprises.   (p. 638)

New France French colony in North America, with a capital in Quebec, founded in 1608. New France fell to the British in 1763.   (p. 418)

New Imperialism Historians' term for the late-nineteenth- and early-twentieth-century wave of conquests by European powers, the United States, and Japan, which were followed by the development and exploitation of the newly conquered territories for the benefit of the colonial powers.   (p. 600)

newly industrialized economies (NIEs) Rapidly growing new industrializing nations of the late twentieth century, including the Asian Tigers.   (p. 721)

new monarchies Historians' term for the monarchies in France, England, and Spain from 1450 to 1600. The centralization of royal power was increasing within more or less fixed territorial limits.   (p. 349)

nomadism A way of life in which groups of people and their herds of animals continually migrate to find pastures and water.   (p. 287)

nonaligned nations Developing countries that announced their neutrality in the Cold War.   (p. 709)

nongovernmental organizations (NGOs) Nonprofit international organizations devoted to investigating human rights abuses and providing humanitarian relief. Two NGOs won the Nobel Peace Prize in the 1990s: International Campaign to Ban Landmines (1997) and Doctors Without Borders (1999).   (p. 755)

North Atlantic Treaty Organization (NATO) Organization formed in 1949 as a military alliance of western European and North American states against the Soviet Union and its east European allies.   (p. 703)

Olmec The first Mesoamerican civilization. Between ca. 1200 and 400 B.C.E., the Olmec people of central Mexico created a vibrant civilization that included intensive agriculture, wide-ranging trade, ceremonial centers, and monumental construction. The Olmec had great cultural influence on later Mesoamerican societies.   (p. 162)

Oman Arab state based in Musqat, the main port in the southeastern region of the Arabian Peninsula. Oman succeeded Portugal as a power in the western Indian Ocean in the eighteenth century.   (p. 451)

Opium War (1839–1842) War between Britain and the Qing Empire that was, in the British view, occasioned by the Qing government's refusal to permit the importation of opium into its territories. The victorious British imposed the one-sided Treaty of Nanking on China.   (p. 540)

Organization of Petroleum Exporting Countries (OPEC) Organization formed in 1960 by oil-producing states to promote their collective interest in generating revenue from oil.   (p. 723)

Ottoman Empire Islamic state founded by Osman in northwestern Anatolia ca. 1300. After the fall of the Byzantine Empire, the Ottoman Empire was based at Istanbul (formerly Constantinople) from 1453 to 1922. It encompassed lands in the Middle East, North Africa, the Caucasus, and eastern Europe.   (pp. 300, 434)

Otto von Bismarck (1815–1898) Chancellor (prime minister) of Prussia from 1862 until 1871, when he became chancellor of Germany. A conservative nationalist, he led Prussia to victory against Austria (1866) and France (1870) and was responsible for the creation of the German Empire in 1871.   (p. 588)

Paleolithic The period of the Stone Age associated with the evolution of humans. It predates the Neolithic period.   (p. 6)

Panama Canal Ship canal cut across the Isthmus of Panama by U.S. Army engineers; it opened in 1914. It greatly shortened the sea voyage between the east and west coasts of North America. The United States turned the canal over to Panama on January 1, 2000.   (p. 622)

Pan-Slavism Movement among Russian intellectuals in the second half of the nineteenth century to identify culturally and politically with the Slavic peoples of eastern Europe.   (p. 537)

papacy The central administration of the Roman Catholic Church, of which the pope is the head.   (pp. 246, 386)

papyrus A reed that grows along the banks of the Nile River in Egypt. From it was produced a paper-like writing medium used by the Egyptians and many other peoples in the ancient Mediterranean and Middle East.   (p. 27)

Parthians Iranian ruling dynasty between ca. 247 B.C.E. and 224 C.E.   (p. 189)

patron/client relationship In ancient Rome, a fundamental social relationship in which the patron—a wealthy and powerful individual—provided legal and economic protection and assistance to clients, men of lesser status and means, and in return the clients supported the political careers and economic interests of their patron.   (p. 137)

Paul (ca. 5–65 c.e.) A Jew from the Greek city of Tarsus in Anatolia, he initially persecuted the followers of Jesus but became a Christian after receiving a revelation on the road to Syrian Damascus. Taking advantage of his Hellenized background and Roman citizenship, he traveled throughout Syria-Palestine, Anatolia, and Greece, preaching the new religion and establishing churches. Finding his greatest success among pagans ("gentiles"), he began the process by which Christianity separated from Judaism.   (p. 146)

pax romana Literally, "Roman peace," it connoted the stability and prosperity that Roman rule brought to the lands of the Roman Empire in the first two centuries c.e. The movement of people and trade goods along Roman roads and safe seas allowed for the spread of cultural practices, technologies, and religious ideas.   (p. 144)

Pearl Harbor Naval base in Hawaii attacked by Japanese aircraft on December 7, 1941. The sinking of much of the U.S. Pacific Fleet brought the United States into World War II.   (p. 667)

Peloponnesian War A protracted (431–404 b.c.e.) and costly conflict between the Athenian and Spartan alliance systems that convulsed most of the Greek world. The war was largely a consequence of Athenian imperialism. Possession of a naval empire allowed Athens to fight a war of attrition. Ultimately Sparta prevailed because of Athenian errors and Persian financial support.   (p. 102)

perestroika Policy of "restructuring" that was the centerpiece of Mikhail Gorbachev's efforts to liberalize communism in the Soviet Union.   (p. 725)

Pericles (ca. 495–429 b.c.e.) Aristocratic leader who guided the Athenian state through the transformation to full participatory democracy for all male citizens, supervised construction of the Acropolis, and pursued a policy of imperial expansion that led to the Peloponnesian War. He formulated a strategy of attrition but died from the plague early in the war.   (p. 98)

Persepolis A complex of palaces, reception halls, and treasury buildings erected by the Persian kings Darius I and Xerxes in the Persian homeland. It is believed that the New Year's festival was celebrated here, as well as the coronations, weddings, and funerals of the Persian kings, who were buried in cliff-tombs nearby.   (p. 90)

Persian Wars Conflicts between Greek city-states and the Persian Empire, ranging from the Ionian Revolt (499–494 b.c.e.) through Darius's punitive expedition that failed at Marathon (490 b.c.e.) and the defeat of Xerxes' massive invasion of Greece by the Spartan-led Hellenic League (480–479 b.c.e.). This first major setback for Persian arms launched the Greeks into their period of greatest cultural productivity. Herodotus chronicled these events in the first "history" in the Western tradition.   (p. 99)

Peter the Great (1672–1725) Russian tsar (r. 1689–1725). He enthusiastically introduced Western languages and technologies to the Russian elite and moved the capital from Moscow to the new city of St. Petersburg.   (p. 471)

pharaoh The central figure in the ancient Egyptian state. Believed to be an earthly manifestation of the gods, he used his absolute power to maintain the safety and prosperity of Egypt.   (p. 25)

Phoenicians Semitic-speaking Canaanites living on the coast of Lebanon and Syria in the first millennium b.c.e. From major cities such as Tyre and Sidon, Phoenician merchants and sailors explored the Mediterranean, engaged in widespread commerce, and founded Carthage and other colonies in the western Mediterranean.   (p. 73)

pilgrimage Journey to a sacred shrine by Christians seeking to show their piety, fulfill vows, or gain absolution for sins. Other religions also have pilgrimage traditions, such as the Muslim pilgrimage to Mecca and the pilgrimages made by early Chinese Buddhists to India in search of sacred Buddhist writings.   (p. 255)

Pilgrims Group of English Protestant dissenters who established Plymouth Colony in Massachusetts in 1620 to seek religious freedom after having lived briefly in the Netherlands.   (p. 417)

polis The Greek term for a city-state, an urban center and the agricultural territory under its control. It was the characteristic form of political organization in southern and central Greece in the Archaic and Classical periods. Of the hundreds of city-states in the Mediterranean and Black Sea regions settled by Greeks, some were oligarchic, others democratic, depending on the powers delegated to the Council and the Assembly.   (p. 93)

positivism A philosophy developed by the French count of Saint-Simon. Positivists believed that social and economic problems could be solved by the application of the scientific method, leading to continuous progress. Their ideas became popular in France and Latin America in the nineteenth century.   (p. 518)

Potosí Located in Bolivia, one of the richest silver mining centers and most populous cities in colonial Spanish America.   (p. 411)

printing press A mechanical device for transferring text or graphics from a woodblock or type to paper using ink. Presses using movable type first appeared in Europe in about 1450.   (p. 346)

Protestant Reformation Religious reform movement within the Latin Christian Church beginning in 1519. It resulted in the "protesters" forming several new Christian denominations, including the Lutheran and Reformed Churches and the Church of England.   (p. 386)

Ptolemies The Macedonian dynasty descended from one of Alexander the Great's officers that ruled Egypt for three centuries (323–30 b.c.e.). From their magnificent capital at Alexandria on the Mediterranean coast, the Ptolemies largely took over the system created by Egyptian pharaohs to extract the wealth of the land, rewarding Greeks and Hellenized non-Greeks serving in the military and administration.   (p. 107)

Puritans English Protestant dissenters who believed that God predestined souls to Heaven or Hell before birth. They founded Massachusetts Bay Colony in 1629.   (p. 417)

pyramid A large, triangular stone monument, used in Egypt and Nubia as a burial place for the king. The largest pyramids, erected during the Old Kingdom near Memphis with stone tools and compulsory labor, reflect the Egyptian belief that the proper and spectacular burial of the divine ruler would guarantee the continued prosperity of the land.   (p. 25)

Qin A people and state in the Wei Valley of eastern China that conquered rival states and created the first Chinese empire (221–206 b.c.e.). The Qin ruler, Shi Huangdi, standardized many features of Chinese society and ruthlessly marshaled subjects for military and construction projects, engendering hostility that led to the fall of his dynasty shortly after his death. The Qin framework was largely taken over by the succeeding Han Empire.   (p. 151)

Qing Empire Empire established in China by Manchus who overthrew the Ming Empire in 1644. At various times the Qing also controlled Manchuria, Mongolia, Turkestan, and Tibet. The last Qing emperor was overthrown in 1911.   (p. 463)

Quran Book composed of divine revelations made to the Prophet Muhammad between ca. 610 and his death in 632; the sacred text of the religion of Islam.   (p. 217)

railroads Networks of iron (later steel) rails on which steam (later electric or diesel) locomotives pulled long trains at high speeds. The first railroads were built in England in the 1830s. Their success caused a railroad-building boom throughout the world that lasted well into the twentieth century. (p. 575)

Rajputs Members of a mainly Hindu warrior caste from north-west India. The Mughal emperors drew most of their Hindu officials from this caste, and Akbar married a Rajput princess. (p. 447)

Ramesses II A long-lived ruler of New Kingdom Egypt (r. 1290–1224 B.C.E.). He reached an accommodation with the Hittites of Anatolia after a standoff in battle at Kadesh in Syria. He built on a grand scale throughout Egypt. (p. 60)

Rashid al-Din (d. 1318) Adviser to the Il-khan ruler Ghazan, who converted to Islam on Rashid's advice. (p. 296)

recaptives Africans rescued by Britain's Royal Navy from the illegal slave trade of the nineteenth century and restored to free status. (p. 555)

reconquest of Iberia Beginning in the eleventh century, military campaigns by various Iberian Christian states to recapture territory taken by Muslims. In 1492 the last Muslim ruler was defeated, and Spain and Portugal emerged as united kingdoms. (p. 350)

Renaissance (European) A period of intense artistic and intellectual activity, said to be a "rebirth" of Greco-Roman culture. Usually divided into an Italian Renaissance, from roughly the mid-fourteenth to mid-fifteenth century, and a Northern Renaissance, from roughly the early fifteenth to early seventeenth century. (pp. 344, 385)

Revolutions of 1848 Democratic and nationalist revolutions that swept across Europe. In France the monarchy was overthrown. In Germany, Austria, Italy, and Hungary the revolutions failed. (p. 493)

Romanization The process by which the Latin language and Roman culture became dominant in the western provinces of the Roman Empire. The Roman government did not actively seek to Romanize the subject peoples, but indigenous peoples in the provinces often chose to Romanize because of the political and economic advantages that it brought, as well as the allure of Roman success. (p. 145)

Roman Principate A term used to characterize Roman government in the first three centuries C.E., based on the ambiguous title *princeps* ("first citizen") adopted by Augustus to conceal his military dictatorship. (p. 142)

Roman Republic The period from 507 to 31 B.C.E., during which Rome was largely governed by the aristocratic Roman Senate. (p. 137)

Roman Senate A council whose members were the heads of wealthy, landowning families. Originally an advisory body to the early kings, in the era of the Roman Republic the Senate effectively governed the Roman state and the growing empire. Under Senate leadership, Rome conquered an empire of unprecedented extent in the lands surrounding the Mediterranean Sea. In the first century B.C.E. quarrels among powerful and ambitious senators and failure to address social and economic problems led to civil wars and the emergence of the rule of the emperors. (p. 137)

Royal African Company Trading company chartered by the English government to conduct its merchants' trade in the Americas and Africa. (p. 424)

sacrifice A gift given to a deity, often with the aim of creating a relationship, gaining favor, and obligating the god to provide some benefit to the sacrificer, sometimes in order to sustain the deity and thereby guarantee the continuing vitality of the natural world. The object devoted to the deity could be as simple as a cup of wine poured on the ground, a live animal slain on the altar, or, in the most extreme case, the ritual killing of a human being. (p. 95)

Saddam Husayn President of Iraq from 1979 until overthrown by the American invasion in 2003. Waged war on Iran from 1980 to 1988. His invasion of Kuwait was repulsed in the Persian Gulf War of 1991. (p. 724)

Safavid Empire Iranian kingdom (1502–1722) established by Ismail Safavi, who declared Iran a Shi'ite state. (p. 442)

Sahel Belt south of the Sahara; literally "the coast" in Arabic. (p. 200)

Salvador Allende Socialist president of Chile elected in 1970 and overthrown and killed by the military in 1973. (p. 718)

samurai Literally, "those who serve"; the hereditary military elite of the Tokugawa Shogunate. (p. 456)

Sandinistas Members of a leftist coalition that overthrew the Nicaraguan dictator Anastasio Somoza in 1979 and attempted to install a socialist economy. The United States financed an armed uprising against the Sandinista government. In 1990 the Sandinistas lost power after a national election. (p. 718)

Sasanid Empire Iranian empire, established ca. 224, with a capital in Ctesiphon, Mesopotamia. The Sasanid emperors established Zoroastrianism as the state religion. Islamic Arab armies overthrew the empire ca. 640. (p. 191)

satrap The governor of a province in the Achaemenid Persian Empire, often a relative of the king. He was responsible for protection of the province and for forwarding tribute to the central administration. Satraps in outlying provinces enjoyed considerable autonomy. (p. 89)

savanna Tropical or subtropical grassland, either treeless or with occasional clumps of trees. Most extensive in sub-Saharan Africa but also present in South America. (p. 201)

Savorgnan de Brazza (1852–1905) Franco-Italian explorer sent by the French government to claim part of equatorial Africa for France. Founded Brazzaville, capital of the French Congo, in 1880. (p. 609)

schism A formal split within a religious community. (p. 236)

scholasticism A philosophical and theological system, associated with Thomas Aquinas, that was devised to reconcile Aristotelian philosophy and Roman Catholic theology in the thirteenth century. (p. 345)

Scientific Revolution The intellectual movement in Europe, initially associated with planetary motion and other aspects of physics, that by the seventeenth century had laid the groundwork for modern science. (p. 391)

"scramble" for Africa Sudden wave of conquests in Africa by European powers in the 1880s and 1890s. Britain obtained most of eastern Africa, France most of northwestern Africa. Other countries (Germany, Belgium, Portugal, Italy, and Spain) acquired lesser amounts. (p. 607)

scribe In the governments of many ancient societies, a professional position reserved for men who had undergone the lengthy training required to be able to read and write using cuneiforms, hieroglyphics, or other early, cumbersome writing systems. (p. 18)

seasoning An often difficult period of adjustment to new climates, disease environments, and work routines, such as that experienced by slaves newly arrived in the Americas. (p. 422)

Semitic Family of related languages long spoken across parts of western Asia and northern Africa. In antiquity these languages included Hebrew, Aramaic, and Phoenician. The most widespread modern members of the Semitic family are Arabic and Hebrew. (p. 14)

"separate spheres" Nineteenth-century idea in Western societies that men and women, especially of the middle class, should have clearly differentiated roles in society: women as wives, mothers, and homemakers; men as breadwinners and participants in business and politics.   (p. 581)

sepoy A soldier in South Asia, especially in the service of the British.   (p. 556)

Sepoy Rebellion The revolt of Indian soldiers in 1857 against certain practices that violated religious customs; also known as the Sepoy Mutiny.   (p. 559)

Serbia The Ottoman province in the Balkans that rose up against Janissary control in the early 1800s.   (p. 529)

serf In medieval Europe, an agricultural laborer legally bound to a lord's property and obligated to perform set services for the lord. In Russia some serfs worked as artisans and in factories; serfdom was not abolished there until 1861.   (pp. 242, 471)

shaft graves A term used for the burial sites of elite members of Mycenaean Greek society in the mid-second millennium B.C.E. At the bottom of deep shafts lined with stone slabs, the bodies were laid out along with gold and bronze jewelry, implements, weapons, and masks.   (p. 62)

Shah Abbas I (r. 1587–1629) The fifth and most renowned ruler of the Safavid dynasty in Iran. Abbas moved the royal capital to Isfahan in 1598.   (p. 443)

shamanism The practice of identifying special individuals (shamans) who will interact with spirits for the benefit of the community. Characteristic of the Korean kingdoms of the early medieval period and of early societies of Central Asia.   (p. 277)

Shang The dominant people in the earliest Chinese dynasty for which we have written records (ca. 1750–1027 B.C.E.). Ancestor worship, divination by means of oracle bones, and the use of bronze vessels for ritual purposes were major elements of Shang culture.   (p. 38)

Shi Huangdi Founder of the short-lived Qin dynasty and creator of the first Chinese Empire (r. 221–210 B.C.E.). He is remembered for his ruthless conquests of rival states, standardization of practices, and forcible organization of labor for military and engineering tasks. His tomb, with its army of life-size terracotta soldiers, has been partially excavated.   (p. 151)

Shi'ites Muslims belonging to the branch of Islam that believes that God vests leadership of the community in a descendant of Muhammad's son-in-law Ali. Shi'ism is the state religion of Iran.   (pp. 217, 442)

Siberia The extreme northeastern sector of Asia, including the Kamchatka Peninsula and the present Russian coast of the Arctic Ocean, the Bering Strait, and the Sea of Okhotsk.   (p. 468)

Silk Road Caravan routes connecting China and the Middle East across Central Asia and Iran.   (p. 187)

Simón Bolivar (1783–1830) The most important military leader in the struggle for independence in South America. Born in Venezuela, he led military forces there and in Colombia, Ecuador, Peru, and Bolivia.   (p. 495)

Slavophiles Russian intellectuals in the early nineteenth century who favored resisting western European influences and taking pride in the traditional peasant values and institutions of the Slavic people.   (p. 537)

"small traditions" Anthropologists' term for a localized, usually nonliterate, set of customs and beliefs adhered to by a single society, often in conjunction with a "great tradition."   (p. 201)

socialism A political ideology that originated in Europe in the 1830s. Socialists advocated government protection of workers from exploitation by property owners and government ownership of industries. This ideology led to the founding of socialist or labor parties throughout Europe in the second half of the nineteenth century.   (p. 583)

Socrates Athenian philosopher (ca. 470–399 B.C.E.) who shifted the emphasis of philosophical investigation from questions of natural science to ethics and human behavior. He attracted young disciples from elite families but made enemies by revealing the ignorance and pretensions of others, culminating in his trial and execution by the Athenian state.   (p. 101)

Sokoto Caliphate A large Muslim state founded in 1809 in what is now northern Nigeria.   (p. 551)

Solidarity Polish trade union created in 1980 to protest working conditions and political repression. It began the nationalist opposition to communist rule that led in 1989 to the fall of communism in eastern Europe.   (p. 726)

Song Empire Empire in central and southern China (960–1126) while the Liao people controlled the north. Empire in southern China (1127–1279; the "Southern Song") while the Jin people controlled the north. Distinguished for its advances in technology, medicine, astronomy, and mathematics.   (p. 271)

Srivijaya A state based on the Indonesian island of Sumatra, between the seventh and eleventh centuries C.E. It amassed wealth and power by a combination of selective adaptation of Indian technologies and concepts, control of the lucrative trade routes between India and China, and skillful showmanship and diplomacy in holding together a disparate realm of inland and coastal territories.   (p. 130)

Stalingrad City in Russia, site of a Red Army victory over the German army in 1942–1943. The Battle of Stalingrad was the turning point in the war between Germany and the Soviet Union. Today it is known as Volgograd.   (p. 665)

steam engine A machine that turns the energy released by burning fuel into motion. Thomas Newcomen built the first crude but workable steam engine in 1712. James Watt vastly improved his device in the 1760s and 1770s. Steam power was later applied to moving machinery in factories and to powering ships and locomotives.   (p. 512)

steel A form of iron that is both durable and flexible. It was first mass-produced in the 1860s and quickly became the most widely used metal in construction, machinery, and railroad equipment.   (p. 577)

stirrup Device for securing a horseman's feet, enabling him to wield weapons more effectively. First evidence of the use of stirrups was among the Kushan people of northern Afghanistan in approximately the first century C.E.   (p. 192)

stock exchange A place where shares in a company or business enterprise are bought and sold.   (p. 395)

Stone Age The historical period characterized by the production of tools from stone and other nonmetallic substances. It was followed in some places by the Bronze Age and more generally by the Iron Age.   (p. 6)

submarine telegraph cables Insulated copper cables laid along the bottom of a sea or ocean for telegraphic communication. The first short cable was laid across the English Channel in 1851; the first successful transatlantic cable was laid in 1866.   (p. 577)

sub-Saharan Africa Portion of the African continent lying south of the Sahara.   (p. 200)

Suez Canal Ship canal dug across the Isthmus of Suez in Egypt, designed by Ferdinand de Lesseps. It opened to shipping in 1869 and shortened the sea voyage between Europe and Asia. Its strategic importance led to the British conquest of Egypt in 1882.   (p. 600)

Suleiman the Magnificent (1494–1566) The most illustrious sultan of the Ottoman Empire (r. 1520–1566); also known as Suleiman Kanuni, "The Lawgiver." He significantly expanded the empire in the Balkans and eastern Mediterranean.   (p. 436)

Sumerians The people who dominated southern Mesopotamia through the end of the third millennium B.C.E. They were responsible for the creation of many fundamental elements of Mesopotamian culture—such as irrigation technology, cuneiform writing, and religious conceptions—later adopted by their Semitic successors.   (p. 14)

Sunnis Muslims belonging to the branch of Islam that believes that the community should select its own leadership. The majority religion in most Islamic countries.   (p. 218)

Sun Yat-sen (1867–1925) Chinese nationalist revolutionary, founder and leader of the Guomindang until his death. He attempted to create a liberal democratic political movement in China but was thwarted by military leaders.   (p. 639)

Swahili Bantu language with Arabic loanwords spoken in coastal regions of East Africa.   (p. 451)

Swahili Coast East African shores of the Indian Ocean between the Horn of Africa and the Zambezi River; from the Arabic *sawahil*, meaning "shores."   (p. 323)

Taiping Rebellion (1850–1864) A Christian-inspired rural rebellion that threatened to topple the Qing Empire. It was the most destructive civil war before the twentieth century.   (p. 543)

Tamil kingdoms The kingdoms of southern India, inhabited primarily by speakers of Dravidian languages, which developed in partial isolation, and somewhat differently, from the Aryan north. They produced epics, poetry, and performance arts. Elements of Tamil religious beliefs were merged into the Hindu synthesis.   (p. 124)

Tang Empire Empire unifying China and part of Central Asia, founded 618 and ended 907. The Tang emperors presided over a magnificent court at their capital, Chang'an.   (p. 262)

Tanzimat "Restructuring" reforms by the nineteenth-century Ottoman rulers intended to move civil law away from the control of religious elites and make the military and the bureaucracy more efficient.   (p. 531)

Tenochtitlan Capital of the Aztec Empire, located on an island in Lake Texcoco. Its population was about 150,000 on the eve of Spanish conquest. Mexico City was constructed on its ruins.   (p. 174)

Teotihuacan A powerful city-state in central Mexico (100 B.C.E.–750 C.E.). Its population was about 150,000 at its peak in 600.   (p. 168)

terrorism Political belief that extreme and seemingly random violence will destabilize a government and permit the terrorists to gain political advantage. Though an old technique, terrorism gained prominence in the late twentieth century with the growth of worldwide mass media that, through their news coverage, amplified public fears of terrorist acts.   (p. 750)

theater-state Historians' term for a state that acquires prestige and power by developing attractive cultural forms and staging elaborate public ceremonies (as well as redistributing valuable resources) to attract and bind subjects to the center. The Gupta Empire is an example of such a state.   (p. 126)

Thebes Capital city of Egypt and home of the ruling dynasties during the Middle and New Kingdoms. Amon, patron deity of Thebes, became one of the chief gods of Egypt. Monarchs were buried across the river in the Valley of the Kings.   (p. 26)

Theravada Buddhism "Way of the Elders" branch of Buddhism followed in Sri Lanka and much of Southeast Asia. Theravada remains close to the original principles set forth by the Buddha; it downplays the importance of gods and emphasizes austerity and the individual's search for enlightenment.   (p. 120)

third-century crisis Historians' term for the political, military, and economic turmoil that beset the Roman Empire during much of the third century C.E.: frequent changes of ruler, civil wars, barbarian invasions, decline of urban centers, and near-destruction of long-distance commerce and the monetary economy. After 284 C.E. Diocletian restored order by making fundamental changes.   (p. 147)

Third World Term applied to developing countries who professed nonalignment during the Cold War.   (p. 709)

Thomas Edison (1847–1931) American inventor best known for inventing the electric light bulb, acoustic recording on wax cylinders, and motion pictures.   (p. 578)

Thomas Malthus (1766–1834) Eighteenth-century English intellectual who warned that population growth threatened future generations because, in his view, population growth would always outstrip increases in agricultural production.   (p. 736)

three-field system A rotational system for agriculture in which one field grows wheat or barley, one grows oats or legumes, and one lies fallow. It gradually replaced the two-field system in medieval Europe.   (p. 334)

Tibet Country centered on the high, mountain-bounded plateau north of India. Tibetan political power occasionally extended farther to the north and west between the seventh and thirteenth centuries.   (p. 268)

Timbuktu City on the Niger River. It was founded by the Tuareg as a seasonal camp sometime after 1000. As part of the Mali empire, Timbuktu became a major terminus of the trans-Saharan trade and a center of Islamic learning.   (p. 328)

Timur (1336–1405) Member of a prominent family of the Mongols' Jagadai Khanate, Timur conquered much of Central Asia and Iran. He consolidated the status of Sunni Islam as the orthodox religion, and his descendants, the Timurids, maintained his empire for nearly a century and founded the Mughal Empire in India.   (p. 295)

Tiwanaku Name of capital city and empire centered on the region near Lake Titicaca in modern Bolivia (500–1000 C.E.).   (p. 180)

Tokugawa Shogunate (1603–1868) The last of the three shogunates of Japan.   (p. 458)

Toltecs Powerful postclassic empire in central Mexico (900–1156) that influenced much of Mesoamerica. Aztecs claimed ties to this earlier civilization.   (p. 173)

Toussaint L'Ouverture (1743–1803) Leader of the Haitian Revolution. He freed the slaves and gained effective independence for Haiti despite military interventions by the British and French.   (p. 494)

trans-Saharan caravan routes Trading network linking North Africa with sub-Saharan Africa across the Sahara.   (p. 197)

Treaty of Nanking (1842) The treaty that concluded the Opium War. It awarded Britain a large indemnity from the Qing Empire, denied the Qing government tariff control over some of its own borders, opened additional ports of residence to Britons, and ceded the island of Hong Kong to Britain.   (p. 542)

Treaty of Versailles (1919) The treaty imposed on Germany by France, Great Britain, the United States, and other Allied Powers after World War I. It demanded that Germany dismantle its military and give up some lands to Poland. It was resented by many Germans.   (p. 637)

treaty ports Cities opened to foreign residents as a result of the forced treaties between the Qing Empire and foreign signatories. In the treaty ports, foreigners enjoyed extraterritoriality.   (p. 542)

tributary system A system in which, from the time of the Han Empire, countries in East and Southeast Asia not under the direct control of empires based in China nevertheless enrolled as tributary states, acknowledging the superiority of the emperors in China in exchange for trading rights or strategic alliances.   (p. 264)

tribute system A system in which defeated peoples were forced to pay a tax in the form of goods and labor. This forced transfer of food, cloth, and other goods subsidized the development of large cities. An important component of the Aztec and Inca economies.   (p. 174)

trireme Greek and Phoenician warship of the fifth and fourth centuries B.C.E. It was sleek and light, powered by 170 oars arranged in three vertical tiers. Manned by skilled sailors, it was capable of short bursts of speed and complex maneuvers.   (p. 100)

tropical rain forest High-precipitation forest zones of the Americas, Africa, and Asia lying between the Tropic of Cancer and the Tropic of Capricorn.   (p. 201)

tropics Equatorial region between the Tropic of Cancer and the Tropic of Capricorn. It is characterized by generally warm or hot temperatures year-round, though much variation exists due to altitude and other factors. Temperate zones north and south of the tropics usually have a winter season.   (p. 313)

Truman Doctrine Foreign policy initiated by U.S. president Harry Truman in 1947. It offered military aid to help Turkey and Greece resist Soviet military pressure and subversion.   (p. 706)

tsar (czar) From Latin *caesar*, this Russian title for a monarch was first used in reference to a Russian ruler by Ivan III (r. 1462–1505). (pp. 299, 468)

Tulip Period (1718–1730) Last years of the reign of Ottoman sultan Ahmed III, during which European styles and attitudes became briefly popular in Istanbul.   (p. 441)

tyrant The term the Greeks used to describe someone who seized and held power in violation of the normal procedures and traditions of the community. Tyrants appeared in many Greek city-states in the seventh and sixth centuries B.C.E., often taking advantage of the disaffection of the emerging middle class and, by weakening the old elite, unwittingly contributing to the evolution of democracy.   (p. 94)

Uighurs A group of Turkic-speakers who controlled their own centralized empire from 744 to 840 in Mongolia and Central Asia.   (p. 267)

ulama Muslim religious scholars. From the ninth century onward, the primary interpreters of Islamic law and the social core of Muslim urban societies.   (p. 224)

Umayyad Caliphate First hereditary dynasty of Muslim caliphs (661 to 750). From their capital at Damascus, the Umayyads ruled an empire that extended from Spain to India. Overthrown by the Abbasid Caliphate.   (p. 218)

umma The community of all Muslims. A major innovation against the background of seventh-century Arabia, where traditionally kinship rather than faith had determined membership in a community.   (p. 216)

United Nations International organization founded in 1945 to promote world peace and cooperation. It replaced the League of Nations.   (p. 703)

Universal Declaration of Human Rights A 1948 United Nations covenant binding signatory nations to the observance of specified rights.   (p. 755)

universities Degree-granting institutions of higher learning. Those that appeared in the Latin West from about 1200 onward became the model of all modern universities.   (p. 344)

Ural Mountains This north-south range separates Siberia from the rest of Russia. It is commonly considered the boundary between the continents of Europe and Asia.   (p. 468)

Urdu A Persian-influenced form of Hindi written in Arabic characters and used as a literary language since the 1300s.   (p. 328)

Usama bin Laden Saudi-born Muslim extremist who founded the al-Qaeda organization that was responsible for several terrorist attacks, including those on the World Trade Center and the Pentagon in 2001.   (p. 751)

utopian socialism A philosophy introduced by the Frenchman Charles Fourier in the early nineteenth century. Utopian socialists hoped to create humane alternatives to industrial capitalism by building self-sustaining communities whose inhabitants would work cooperatively.   (p. 520)

varna/jati Two categories of social identity of great importance in Indian history. *Varna* are the four major social divisions: the *Brahmin* priest class, the *Kshatriya* warrior/administrator class, the *Vaishya* merchant/farmer class, and the *Shudra* laborer class. Within the system *varna* are many jati, regional groups of people who have a common occupational sphere, and who marry, eat, and generally interact with other members of their group.   (p. 118)

Vasco da Gama (1467–1524) Portuguese explorer. In 1497–1498 he led the first naval expedition from Europe to sail to India, opening an important commercial sea route.   (p. 362)

vassal In medieval Europe, a sworn supporter of a king or lord committed to rendering specified military service to that king or lord.   (p. 245)

Vedas Early Indian sacred "knowledge"—the literal meaning of the term—long preserved and communicated orally by Brahmin priests and eventually written down. These religious texts, including the thousand poetic hymns to various deities contained in the Rig Veda, are our main source of information about the Vedic period (ca. 1500–500 B.C.E.).   (p. 116)

Versailles The huge palace built for French King Louis XIV west of Paris. The palace symbolized the preeminence of French power and architecture in Europe and the triumph of royal authority over the French nobility.   (p. 402)

Victorian Age The reign of Queen Victoria of Great Britain (r. 1837–1901). The term is also used to describe late-nineteenth-century society, with its rigid moral standards and sharply differentiated roles for men and women and for middle-class and working-class people.   (p. 580)

Vietnam War (1954–1975) Conflict pitting North Vietnam and South Vietnamese communist guerrillas against the South Vietnamese government, aided after 1961 by the United States.   (p. 711)

Vladimir Lenin (1870–1924) Leader of the Bolshevik (later Communist) Party. He lived in exile in Switzerland until 1917, then returned to Russia to lead the Bolsheviks to victory during the Russian Revolution and the civil war that followed.   (p. 634)

Wari Andean civilization culturally linked to Tiwanaku, perhaps beginning as a colony of Tiwanaku.   (p. 180)

Warsaw Pact The 1955 treaty binding the Soviet Union and countries of eastern Europe in an alliance against the North Atlantic Treaty Organization.   (p. 706)

water wheel A mechanism that harnesses the energy in flowing water to grind grain or to power machinery. It was used in many parts of the world but was especially common in Europe from 1200 to 1900.   (p. 337)

Western Front A line of trenches and fortifications in World War I that stretched without a break from Switzerland to the North Sea. Scene of most of the fighting between Germany, on the one hand, and France and Britain, on the other.   (p. 631)

witch-hunt The pursuit of people suspected of witchcraft, especially in northern Europe in the late sixteenth and seventeenth centuries. (p. 389)

Women's Rights Convention An 1848 gathering of women angered by their exclusion from an international antislavery meeting. They met at Seneca Falls, New York, to discuss women's rights. (p. 501)

Woodrow Wilson (1856–1924) President of the United States (1913–1921) and the leading figure at the Paris Peace Conference of 1919. He was unable to persuade the U.S. Congress to ratify the Treaty of Versailles or join the League of Nations. (p. 635)

World Bank A specialized agency of the United Nations that makes loans to countries for economic development, trade promotion, and debt consolidation. Its formal name is the International Bank for Reconstruction and Development. (p. 704)

World Trade Organization (WTO) An international body established in 1995 to foster and bring order to international trade. (p. 733)

Xiongnu A confederation of nomadic peoples living beyond the northwest frontier of ancient China. Chinese rulers tried a variety of defenses and stratagems to ward off these "barbarians," as they called them, and finally succeeded in dispersing the Xiongnu in the first century C.E. (p. 156)

Yamagata Aritomo (1838–1922) One of the leaders of the Meiji Restoration. (p. 595)

Yi (1392–1910) The Yi dynasty ruled Korea after the fall of the Koryo kingdom. (p. 306)

yin/yang In Chinese belief, complementary factors that help to maintain the equilibrium of the world. Yin is associated with feminine, dark, and passive qualities; yang with masculine, light, and active qualities. (p. 44)

Yongle Reign of Zhu Di (1360–1424), the third emperor of the Ming Empire (r. 1403–1424). He sponsored further work on the Forbidden City, the expeditions of Zheng He, and the reopening of China's borders to trade and travel. (p. 304)

Young Ottomans Movement of young intellectuals to institute liberal reforms and build a feeling of national identity in the Ottoman Empire in the second half of the nineteenth century. (p. 535)

Yuan Empire (1271–1368) Empire created in China and Siberia by Khubilai Khan. (p. 293)

Yuan Shikai (1859–1916) Chinese general and first president of the Chinese Republic (1912–1916). He stood in the way of the democratic movement led by Sun Yat-sen. (p. 639)

Zen The Japanese word for a branch of Mahayana Buddhism based on highly disciplined meditation. It is known in Sanskrit as *dhyana*, in Chinese as *chan*, and in Korean as *son*. (p. 273)

Zheng He (1371–1433) An imperial eunuch and Muslim who was entrusted by the Ming emperor Yongle with a series of state voyages that took his ships through the Indian Ocean, from Southeast Asia to Africa. (pp. 304, 357)

Zhou The people and dynasty that took over the dominant position in north China from the Shang and created the concept of the Mandate of Heaven to justify their rule. The Zhou era, particularly the vigorous early period (1027–771 B.C.E.), was remembered in Chinese tradition as a time of prosperity and benevolent rule. In the later Zhou period (771–221 B.C.E.), centralized control broke down, and warfare among many small states became frequent. (p. 39)

ziggurat A massive pyramidal stepped tower made of mud bricks. It is associated with religious complexes in ancient Mesopotamian cities, but its function is unknown. (p. 20)

Zoroastrianism A religion originating in ancient Iran with the prophet Zoroaster. It centered on a single benevolent deity—Ahuramazda—who engaged in a twelve-thousand-year struggle with demonic forces before prevailing and restoring a pristine world. Emphasizing truth-telling, purity, and reverence for nature, the religion demanded that humans choose sides in the struggle between good and evil. Those whose good conduct indicated their support for Ahuramazda would be rewarded in the afterlife. Others would be punished. The religion of the Achaemenid Persians, Zoroastrianism may have spread within their realms and influenced Judaism, Christianity, and other faiths. (p. 91)

Zulu A people of modern South Africa whom King Shaka united in 1818. (p. 551)

Chapter 1

1. N. K. Sandars, *The Epic of Gilgamesh* (Baltimore: Penguin Books, 1960), 61–63.

2. Colin McEvedy and Richard Jones, *Atlas of World Population History* (New York: Penguin Books, 1978), 13–15.

3. Colin Renfrew, *Archaeology and Language: The Puzzle of Indo-European Origins* (Cambridge: Cambridge University Press, 1988), 125, 150.

4. Luigi Cavalli-Sforza, L. Luca, Paolo Menozzi, and Alberto Piazza, *The History and Geography of Human Genes* (Princeton, NJ: Princeton University Press, 1994).

5. James Mellaart, *Çatal Hüyük: A Neolithic Town in Anatolia* (New York: McGraw-Hill, 1967), 202.

Chapter 2

1. Quoted in Miriam Lichtheim, ed., *Ancient Egyptian Literature: A Book of Readings* (Berkeley: University of California Press, 1978).

Chapter 3

1. Plutarch, *Moralia,* 799 D, trans. B. H. Warmington, *Carthage* (Harmondsworth, England: Penguin 1960), 163.

Chapter 4

1. Quoted in Roland G. Kent, *Old Persian: Grammar, Texts, Lexicon,* 2nd ed. (New Haven, CT: American Oriental Society, 1953), 138, 140.

2. Richmond Lattimore, *Greek Lyrics,* 2nd ed. (Chicago: University of Chicago Press, 1960), 2.

3. G. S. Kirk and J. E. Raven, *The Presocratic Philosophers: A Critical History with a Selection of Texts* (Cambridge, England: Cambridge University Press, 1957), 169.

4. Herodotus, *The History,* trans. David Grene (Chicago: University of Chicago Press, 1988), 33 (Herodotus 1.1).

5. Plutarch, *Pericles* 12, trans. Ian Scott-Kilvert, *The Rise and Fall of Athens: Nine Greek Lives by Plutarch* (Harmondsworth: Penguin Books, 1960), 178.

Chapter 5

1. Barbara Stoler Miller, *The Bhagavad-Gita: Krishna's Counsel in Time of War* (New York: Bantam, 1986), 98–99.

2. B. G. Gokhale, *Asoka Maurya* (New York: Twayne, 1966), 152–153, 156–157, 160.

3. James Legge, *The Travels of Fa-hien: Fa-hien's Record of Buddhistic Kingdoms* (Delhi: Oriental Publishers, 1971), 77–79.

Chapter 6

1. Patricia Buckley Ebrey, ed., *Chinese Civilization and Society: A Sourcebook* (New York: Free Press, 1981), 33–34.

Chapter 7

1. Before 1492, the inhabitants of the Western Hemisphere had no single name for themselves, no sense that physical similarities created a shared identity. Identity derived from kin groups, language, cultural practices, and political structures. Conquest and the occupation by Europeans after 1492 imposed on America's original inhabitants a racial consciousness and racial identity. All collective terms for these first American peoples reflect this history. *Indians, Native Americans, Amerindians, First Peoples,* and *Indigenous Peoples* find common usage. This book uses the names of individual cultures and states wherever possible. It tries to reserve *Amerindian* and other terms that suggest transcultural identity and experience for the period after 1492.

2. From the Florentine Codex, quoted in Inga Clendinnen, *Aztecs* (Cambridge: Cambridge University Press, 1991), 213.

3. Quoted in Nigel Davies, *The Toltec Heritage: From the Fall of Tula to the Rise of Tenochtitlan* (Norman: University of Oklahoma Press, 1980), 3.

4. Bernal Díaz del Castillo, *The Conquest of New Spain,* trans. J. M. Cohen (London: Penguin Books, 1963), 217.

5. Hernando Cortés, *Five Letters, 1519–1526,* trans. J. Bayard Morris (New York: Norton, 1991), 87

6. Quoted in Irene Silverblatt, *Moon, Sun, and Witches: Gender Ideologies and Class in Inca and Colonial Peru* (Princeton, NJ: Princeton University Press, 1987), 10.

Chapter 8

1. Victor H. Mair, ed., *The Columbia Anthology of Traditional Chinese Literature* (New York: Columbia University Press, 1994), 485; translated by Victor H. Mair.

Issues in World History: Oral Societies and the Consequences of Literacy

1. D. T. Niane, *Sundiata: An Epic of Old Mali* (Harlow, U.K.: Longman, 1986), 41.

Chapter 9

1. Quran. Sura 96, verses 1–5.

2. Quran. Sura 92, verses 1–10.

3. Richard W. Bulliet, *Islam: The View from the Edge* (New York: Columbia University Press, 1994), 87.

4. Abu Najib al-Suhrawardi, *A Sufi Rule for Novices,* trans. Menahem Milson (Cambridge, MA: Harvard University Press, 1975), 45–58.

5. Ibid., 73–82.

Chapter 10

1. A. A. Vasiliev, *History of the Byzantine Empire, 324–1453,* vol. 1 (Madison: University of Wisconsin Press, 1978), 79–80.

2. Ibid., 71.

3. A. P. Kazhdan and Ann Wharton Epstein, *Change in Byzantine Culture in the Eleventh and Twelfth Centuries* (Berkeley: University of California Press, 1985), 71.

4. Ibid., 248.

5. Ibid., 255.

6. R. W. Southern, *Western Society and the Church in the Middle Ages* (Harmondsworth, England: Penguin, 1970), 102.

7. S. A. Zenkovsky, ed., *Medieval Russia's Epics, Chronicles, and Tales* (New York: New American Library, 1974), 67.

Chapter 11

1. *Master Tung's Western Chamber Romance,* trans. Li-li Ch'en (New York: Columbia University Press, 1994), 22, 42–43, 45–46.

2. Arthur Waley, *Poetry and Career of Li Po* (London: Unwin Hyman, 1954), 35.

3. Theodore de Bary, ed., *Sources of Chinese Tradition,* vol. 1, 2nd ed. (New York: Columbia University Press, 1999), 584.

4. Quoted in David Lattimore, "Allusion in T'ang Poetry," in *Perspectives on the T'ang,* ed. Arthur F. Wright and David Twitchett (New Haven, CT: Yale University Press, 1973), 436.

5. Quoted at "Women's Early Music, Art, Poetry," http://music.acu.edu/www/iawm/pages/reference/tzusongs.html.

6. Quoted in Ivan Morris, *The World of the Shining Prince: Court Life in Ancient Japan* (New York: Penguin Books, 1979), 221–222.

7. Quoted in Ivan Morris, trans., *The Pillow Book of Sei Shonagon* (New York: Columbia University Press, 1967), 1.

Chapter 12

1. Quotation adapted from Desmond Martin, *Chingis Khan and His Conquest of North China* (Baltimore: Johns Hopkins Press, 1950), 303.

Chapter 13

1. Tarikh-i-Wassaf, in Henry M. Elliot, *The History of India as Told by Its Own Historians,* ed. John Dowson (London: Trübner and Co., 1869–1871), 2:28.

2. Hasan Nizami, Taju-l Ma-asir, in ibid., 2:219.

3. Minhaju-s Siraj, Tabakat-i Nasiri, in ibid., 2:332–333.

Chapter 14

1. Quoted in Marina Warner, *Alone of All Her Sex: The Myth and Cult of the Virgin Mary* (New York: Random House, 1983), 179.

2. Harry Miskimin, *The Economy of the Early Renaissance, 1300–1460* (Englewood Cliffs, NJ: Prentice Hall, 1969), 26–27.

3. Quotations here and later in the chapter are from Geoffrey Chaucer, *The Canterbury Tales,* trans. Nevill Coghill (New York: Penguin Books, 1952), 25, 29, 32.

Chapter 15

1. Ma Huan, *Ying-yai Sheng-lan: "The Overall Survey of the Ocean's Shores,"* ed. Feng Ch'eng-Chün, trans. J. V. G. Mills (Cambridge, England: Cambridge University Press, 1970), 180.

2. Alvise da Cadamosto in *The Voyages of Cadamosto and Other Documents,* ed. and trans. G. R. Crone (London: Hakluyt Society, 1937), 2.

3. Quoted in Alfred W. Crosby, Jr., *The Columbian Exchange: Biological and Cultural Consequences of 1492* (Westport, CT: Greenwood, 1972), 58.

Chapter 16

1. Quoted by Carlo M. Cipolla, "Introduction," *The Fontana Economic History of Europe,* vol. 2, *The Sixteenth and Seventeenth Centuries* (Glasgow: Collins/Fontana Books, 1974), 11–12.

2. Michel de Montaigne, *Essais* (1588), ch. 31, "Des Cannibales."

3. William H. McNeill, *The Pursuit of Power: Technology, Armed Force, and Society Since A.D. 1000* (Chicago: University of Chicago Press, 1982), 124.

Chapter 17

1. Eric Williams, *Capitalism and Slavery* (Charlotte: University of North Carolina Press, 1944), 7.

2. King Osei Bonsu, quoted in David Northrup, ed., *The Atlantic Slave Trade,* 2nd ed. (Boston: Houghton Mifflin, 2001), 176.

3. Alexander Falconbridge, *Account of the Slave Trade on the Coast of Africa* (London: J. Phillips, 1788), 12.

Chapter 18

1. Leslie Peirce, *Morality Tales: Law and Gender in the Ottoman Court of Aintab* (Berkeley: University of California Press, 2003), 258.

2. Ibid., 262.

3. Daniel Goffman, *Izmir and the Levantine World, 1550–1650* (Seattle: University of Washington Press, 1990), 52.

4. Edmund Bradley Martin and Chryssee Perry Martin, *Cargoes of the East: The Ports, Trade and Culture of the Arabian Seas and Western Indian Ocean* (1978), 17.

Chapter 19

1. Adapted from Jonathan D. Spence, *The Search for Modern China* (New York: W. W. Norton, 1990), 21–25.

2. Adapted from G. V. Melikhov, "Manzhou Penetration into the Basin of the Upper Amur in the 1680s," in S. L. Tikhvinshii, ed., *Manzhou Rule in China* (Moscow: Progress Publishers, 1983).

Issues in World History: The Little Ice Age

1. Brian Fagan, *The Littlest Ice Age: How Climate Made History, 1300–1850* (New York: Basic Books, 2000).

2. James L. A. Webb, Jr., *Desert Frontier: Ecological Change Along the Western Sahel, 1600–1850* (Madison: University of Wisconsin Press, 1995).

Chapter 21

1. Nassau W Senior, *Letters on the Factory Act, as it affects the cotton manufacture, addressed to the Right Honourable, the President of the Board of Trade,* 2nd ed. (London: Fellows, 1844), 20.

2. Friedrich Engels, *Condition of the Working Class in England,* trans. and ed. by W O. Henderson and W H. Chaloner (Oxford: Blackwell, 1958), 312.

3. Quoted in Lewis Mumford, *The City in History* (New York: Harcourt Brace, 1961), 460.

4. *Nautical Magazine* 12 (1843): 346.

Chapter 23

1. Quoted in P. J. Vatikiotis, *The History of Modern Egypt: From Muhammad Ali to Mubarak,* 4th ed. (Baltimore: Johns Hopkins University Press, 1991), 74.

2. David Eltis, "Precolonial Western Africa and the Atlantic Economy," in *Slavery and the Rise of the Atlantic Economy,* ed. Barbara Solow (New York: Cambridge University Press, 1991), table 1.

3. Quoted by Bernard S. Cohn, "Representing Authority in Victorian England," in *The Invention of Tradition,* ed. Eric Hobsbawm and Terence Ranger (Cambridge: Cambridge University Press, 1983), 165.

Issues in World History: State Power, the Census, and the Question of Identity

1. Quoted in James C. Scott, *Seeing like a State: How Certain Schemes to Improve the Human Condition Have Failed* (New Haven: Yale University Press, 1998), 91.

2. This discussion relies heavily on Eliza Johnson (now Ablovatski), "Counting and Categorizing: The Hungarian Gypsy Census of 1893" (M.A. Thesis, Columbia University, 1996), especially Chapter III. *She quotes from the Proceedings of the Sixth International Statistical Congress Held in London, 1860,* 379.

Chapter 24

1. Quoted in Bonnie S. Anderson and Judith P. Zinsser, *A History of Their Own: Women in Europe from Prehistory to the Present,* vol. 2 (New York: Harper & Row, 1988), 372, 387.

Chapter 25

1. *Journal Officiel* (November 29, 1869), quoted in Georges Douin, *Histoire du Règne du Khédive Ismail* (Rome: Reale Society di Geografia d'Egitto, 1933), 453.

2. E. Desplaces in *Journal de l'Union des Deux Mers* (December 15, 1869), quoted in ibid., 453.

3. Winston Churchill, *The River War: An Account of the Reconquest of the Soudan* (New York: Charles Scribner's Sons, 1933), 300.

4. Margaret Strobel, *European Women and the Second British Empire* (Bloomington: University of Indiana Press, 1991), 26.

5. Michael Adas, *Islamic and European Expansion* (Philadelphia: Temple University Press, 1993), 365.

6. "Correspondence and Report from His Majesty's Consul at Boma Respecting the Administration of the Independent State of the Congo," *British Parliamentary Papers, Accounts and Papers,* 1904 (Cd. 1933), lxii, 357.

7. Robert W. July, *A History of the African People,* 3rd ed. (New York: Charles Scribner's Sons, 1980), 323.

8. George Shepperson and Thomas Price, *Independent African: John Chilembwe and the Origins, Setting, and Significance of the Nyasaland Native Rising of 1915* (Edinburgh: University Press, 1958), 163–164, quoted in Roland Oliver and Anthony Atmore, *Africa Since 1800,* 4th ed. (Cambridge: Cambridge University Press, 1994), 150.

9. Thomas Edson Ennis, *French Policy and Development in Indochina* (Chicago: University of Chicago Press, 1936), 178, quoted in K. M. Panikkar, *Asia and Western Dominance* (New York: Collier, 1969), 167.

10. Quoted in Stanley J. Stein and Barbara H. Stein, *The Colonial Heritage of Latin America* (New York: Oxford University Press, 1970), 151.

Chapter 27

1. Umbro Apollonio, ed. *Documents of 20th Century Art: Futurist Manifestos,* translated by Robert Brain, R. W. Flint, J. C. Higgitt, and Caroline Tisdall (New York: Viking Press, 1973), pp. 20-21.

Chapter 28

1. George Blankstein, *Perón's Argentina* (Chicago: University of Chicago Press, 1953), 37.

Chapter 29

1. Michael Crowder, "Independence as a Goal in French West African Politics," in *French-Speaking Africa: The Search for Identity,* ed. William H. Lewis (New York: Walker, 1965), p. 32.

Chapter 30

1. Quoted in Antony Flew, "Introduction," in Thomas Robert Malthus, *An Essay on the Principle of Population and a Summary View of the Principle of Population* (New York: Penguin Books, 1970), 30.

2. Paul Kennedy, *Preparing for the Twenty-first Century* (New York: Random House, 1993), 45.

3. "Universal Declaration of Human Rights," in *Twenty-five Human Rights Documents* (New York: Center for the Study of Human Rights, Columbia University, 1994), 6.